Encyclopedia of
Women and Religion
in North America

Editorial Board

Encyclopedia of
Women and Religion
in North America

Edited by
Rosemary Skinner Keller
and
Rosemary Radford Ruether

Associate Editor
Marie Cantlon

VOLUME 1

Introduction: Integrating the Worlds of Women's Religious Experience
in North America

Part I. Approaches to the History of Women and Religion

Part II. Women in Indigenous and African Traditions

Part III. Catholicism

Part IV. Protestantism

INDIANA UNIVERSITY PRESS
Bloomington and Indianapolis

This book is a publication of

Indiana University Press
601 North Morton Street
Bloomington, Indiana 47404-3797 USA

http://iupress.indiana.edu

Telephone orders   800-842-6796
Fax orders   812-855-7931
Orders by e-mail   iuporder@indiana.edu

The paper used in this publication meets the minimum requirements of American
National Standard for Information Sciences—Permanence of Paper for Printed Library
Materials, ANSI Z39.48-1984.

Manufactured in the United States of America

Library of Congress Cataloging-in-Publication Data

The encyclopedia of women and religion in North America / Rosemary Skinner Keller
and Rosemary Radford Ruether, editors ; Marie Cantlon, associate editor.
  p. cm.
 Includes bibliographical references and index.
 ISBN 0-253-34685-1 (cloth, set) — ISBN 0-253-34686-X (v. 1) — ISBN 0-253-34687-8
(v. 2) — ISBN 0-253-34688-6 (v. 3) 1. Women and religion—North America—
Encyclopedias. 2. Women—Religious life—North America—Encyclopedias. 3. Women—
Religious aspects—North America—Encyclopedias. I. Keller, Rosemary Skinner. II.
Ruether, Rosemary Radford. III. Cantlon, Marie.
 BL458.E52   2006
 200.82'0973—dc22   2005032429

1 2 3 4 5 11 10 09 08 07 06

Contents

Contributors

Phyllis D. Airhart teaches at Emmanuel College, University of Toronto. She is author of *Serving the Present Age: Revivalism, Progressivism, and the Methodist Tradition in Canada,* and co-editor of *Faith Traditions and the Family* and *Doing Ethics in a Pluralistic World: Essays in Honour of Roger C. Hutchinson.*

William Michael Ashcraft teaches in the social science division at Truman State University, Kirksville, Mo.

Dianne Ashton is Professor of Religion and Director of American Studies at Rowan University. She is author of *Rebecca Gratz: Women and Judaism in Antebellum America; Jewish Life in Pennsylvania;* and co-editor of *Four Centuries of Jewish Women's Spirituality.* She writes widely on American Jewish history.

Jocelyn M. Eclarin Azada is a graduate of Garrett-Evangelical Theological Seminary, Chicago, Ill. She contributed the chapter on the economic influences on immigration and the implications for gender roles in the Filipino family in *Gender, Ethnicity, and Religion: Views from the Other Side,* edited by Rosemary Radford Ruether.

Dori Grinenko Baker is Adjunct Assistant Professor of Christian education at Garrett-Evangelical Theological Seminary and author of *Doing Girlfriend Theology: God-Talk with Young Women.*

Mary Farrell Bednarowski is Professor Emerita of Religious Studies at United Theological Seminary of the Twin Cities. Her research focuses on religion in American culture and the reciprocal dynamic between theological innovation and conservation. She is author of *The Religious Imagination of American Women* and *New Religions and the Theological Imagination in America.*

Margaret L. Bendroth is author of *Fundamentalism and Gender, 1875 to the Present; Fundamentalists in the City: Conflict and Division in Boston's Churches, 1885–1950;*

and *Growing Up Protestant: Parents, Children, and Mainline Churches* and editor (with Phyllis D. Airhart) of *Faith Traditions and the Family.*

Carolyn D. Blevins, Associate Professor of Religion, Carson-Newman College, Jefferson City, Tenn., teaches church history and women's studies. She is author of *A Bibliography of Women in Church History; Women's Place in Baptist Life;* and several articles on women in Baptist history.

Barbara J. Blodgett is Director of Supervised Ministries at Yale Divinity School. Ordained to the ministry of the United Church of Christ, she served as associate pastor of a congregation in Amherst, Mass.; coordinated Working at Teaching, a teacher-training program of the Yale University Graduate School; and was a member of the faculty of Oberlin College before joining the Divinity School administration. Her research interests include feminist, sexual, and professional ethics. She is author of *Constructing the Erotic: Sexual Ethics and Adolescent Girls.*

Edith Blumhofer is Professor of History at Wheaton College, Wheaton, Ill., and Director of the Institute for the Study of American Evangelicals. Her books include biographies of evangelist Aimee Semple McPherson and the hymn writer Fanny J. Crosby.

Sandy Boucher is author of a number of books on the subject of women in Buddhism, including *Dancing in the Dharma: The Life and Teaching of Ruth Denison; Hidden Spring: A Buddhist Woman Confronts Cancer; Discovering Kwan Yin;* and *Turning the Wheel: American Women Creating the New Buddhism.*

Lois A. Boyd retired from Trinity University, San Antonio, Tex., and now resides in Denver, Colo. She holds an undergraduate degree from the University of Texas, Austin, and a master of arts degree from Trinity University. She is co-author, with R. Douglas Brackenridge, of *Presbyterian Women in America: Two Centuries of a Quest for Status.*

Mary C. Boys, S.N.J., is the Skinner and McAlpin Professor of Practical Theology at Union Theological Seminary, N.Y. She is author of *Biblical Interpretation in Religious Education; Educating in Faith: Maps and Visions; Jewish-Christian Dialogue: One Woman's Experience;* and *Has God Only One Blessing? Judaism as a Source of Christian Self-Understanding.* Her edited books include *Seeing Judaism Anew: A Sacred Obligation of Christians.*

Ann Braude is Director of the Women's Studies in Religion Program and Senior Lecturer on the History of Christianity at the Harvard Divinity School. She is co-editor of *Root of Bitterness: Documents of the Social History of American Women* and author of *Women and American Religion* and *Radical Spirits: Spiritualism and Women's Rights in Nineteenth-Century America.*

Catherine A. Brekus is Associate Professor of the History of Christianity at the University of Chicago Divinity School. She is author of *Strangers and Pilgrims: Female Preaching in America, 1740–1845.*

Virginia Lieson Brereton (1944–2004) was Lecturer in English at Tufts University and author of *Training God's Army: The American Bible School, 1880–1940* and *From Sin to Salvation: Stories of Women's Conversions, 1800 to the Present,* and co-editor (with Margaret Bendroth) of *Women and 20th-Century Protestantism.*

Rita Nakashima Brock is a research associate at the Harvard Divinity School Initiatives on Religion in Public Life and author of *Journeys by Heart: A Christology of Erotic Power,* which won the 1988 Crossroad Press Award for most outstanding manuscript in women's studies. She is co-author of *Proverbs of Ashes: Violence, Redemptive Suffering, and the Search for What Saves Us* and *Casting Stones: Prostitution and Liberation in Asia and the United States,* which won the 1996 Catholic Press Award for gender studies.

Claudia L. Bushman teaches history and American studies at Columbia University. She is author of *"A Good Poor Man's Wife": Being a Chronicle of Harriet Hanson Robinson and Her Family in Nineteenth Century New England; In Old Virginia: Slavery, Farming, and Society in the Journal of John Walker;* and *Contemporary Mormonism: Latter-day Saints in Modern America* and co-author (with Richard Lyman Bushman) of *Building the Kingdom: A History of Mormons in America.*

Anthea D. Butler is Assistant Professor of Religion, University of Rochester. Her recent works include the essay "Religion in the South: Protestants and Others in History and Culture." Her book *Making a Sanctified World: Women in the Church of God in Christ* is forthcoming.

Her research focuses on the Women's Department of the Church of God in Christ, the largest African American Pentecostal denomination.

Debra Campbell is Professor of Religious Studies at Colby College, Waterville, Maine. She co-authored *Transforming Parish Ministries* with Jay P. Dolan, R. Scott Appleby, and Patricia Byrne. Her most recent work is *Graceful Exits: Catholic Women and the Art of Departure.*

Diane Capitani is Associate Professor of English and Literature at Kendall College in Chicago, Ill. She received her Ph.D. in theology and history from the Garrett-Evangelical Theological Seminary. Diane has been an instructor at Kendall College since 1995.

Carlos F. Cardoza-Orlandi is Associate Professor of World Christianity, Columbia Theological Seminary, Atlanta, and an ordained minister of the Christian Church (Disciples of Christ) in Puerto Rico, the United States, and Canada. He is author of *Mission: An Essential Guide.*

James C. Carper is Professor of Foundations of Education and coordinator of programs in educational psychology, research, and foundations of education at the University of South Carolina. His research interests include history of education in the United States, education and religion, and private schools. His work has been published in *History of Education Quarterly; Educational Forum; Journal of Church and State;* and *Educational Policy.*

Carol P. Christ is author of *She Who Changes; Rebirth of the Goddess; Odyssey with the Goddess; Laughter of Aphrodite; Diving Deep and Surfacing; Womanspirit Rising;* and *Weaving the Visions,* books that have changed women's lives and helped them transform the teaching and study of religion. Christ is the director of Ariadne Institute (www.goddessariadne.org) and leads Goddess journeys in Greece.

J. Shannon Clarkson is Adjunct Professor at San Francisco Theological Seminary and co-Coordinator of the International Feminist Doctor of Ministry program at SFTS. She is co-editor of *Dictionary of Feminist Theologies* and editor of *Conflict and Community in the Corinthian Church.*

Elizabeth Conde-Frazier is Associate Professor of Religious Education at Claremont School of Theology and co-author (with S. Steven Kang and Gary A. Parrett) of *A Many Colored Kingdom: Multicultural Dynamics for Spiritual Formation.*

Sharon Anne Cook is Professor of Women's History at the University of Ottawa. Her research focuses on women and educational pressure groups, women and evangelical religion, gender issues in education, and the history of health education, including anti-alcohol and anti-tobacco. She is author of *"Through sunshine and shadow": The Woman's Christian Temperance Union, evangelicalism and reform in Ontario 1874–1930* and co-editor (with Kate O'Rourke and Lorna McLean) of *Framing Our Past: Canadian Women's History in the Twentieth Century.*

Sarah Gardner Cunningham teaches in the history department at the Marymount School of New York. A graduate of Princeton, she holds M.Div. and Ph.D. degrees from Union Theological Seminary in New York. Her work focuses on women and the exercise of power in the development of religious institutions in the United States.

Dell deChant is instructor in religious studies and undergraduate director at the University of South Florida. His primary areas of interest and specialization are religion and modernization, contemporary religious movements, history of Christianity, and religion and ethics. He contributed a chapter to *Women's Leadership in Marginal Religions* (Catherine Wessinger, ed.) and is co-author of *Tampa Bay's Marginal Religions.*

Janine M. Denomme is grants manager for the Center on Halsted in Chicago, Ill., a community center for lesbian, gay, bisexual, and transgender (LGBT) persons.

Hasia R. Diner is the Paul S. and Sylvia Steinberg Professor of American Jewish History at New York University. Her most recent book is *The Jews of the United States.* With Jeffrey Shandler and Beth S. Wegner, she edited *Remembering the Lower East Side: American Jewish Reflections.*

Kelly Brown Douglas is Professor of Religion and Chair of the Department of Philosophy of Religion at Goucher College, Baltimore, Md. Douglas has written numerous journal articles and book chapters and is author of *Sexuality and the Black Church; The Black Christ;* and *What's Faith Got to Do with It?*

Angelyn Dries is the Danforth Chair in the Department of Theological Studies at Saint Louis University. Her pioneering work, *The Missionary Movement in American Catholic History,* charted the field for the first time. She has published many articles and book chapters bringing to light the historical experience of U.S. Catholic women missionaries overseas.

Heather Eaton has taught at the University of Ottawa and St. Michael's College at the University of Toronto in eco-theology and women and ecology. She received an interdisciplinary doctorate in theology and ecology from the University of Toronto. Her areas of concentration are religious responses to the ecological crisis, eco-

feminism, cosmology, religion and science, feminist theology, and social-ecological justice.

Cynthia Eller is Associate Professor of Women's Studies and Religious Studies at Montclair State University, N.J. She is author of *Am I a Woman? A Skeptic's Guide to Gender; The Myth of the Matriarchal Prehistory: Why an Invented Past Will Not Give Women a Future;* and *Living in the Lap of the Goddess: The Feminist Spirituality Movement in America.*

Marlene Epp is Associate Professor of History and of Peace and Conflict Studies at Conrad Grebel University at the University of Waterloo, Ontario. Her research focuses on women and gender in Mennonite history and she is author of *Women without Men: Mennonite Refugees of the Second World War.*

Kathleen M. Erndl is Associate Professor of Religion at Florida State University. Her publications include *Victory to the Mother: The Hindu Goddess of Northwest India in Myth, Ritual and Symbol* and articles on Sakta traditions, women's religious expressions, methodology, and gender issues in Hinduism. She is co-editor (with Alf Hiltebeitel) of *Is the Goddess a Feminist? The Politics of South Asian Goddesses* and is currently writing a book on Kangra Hinduism.

Gastón Espinosa is Assistant Professor in Philosophy and Religious Studies at Claremont McKenna College and has been a visiting scholar at the University of California, Santa Barbara and Northwestern University. He is author of *Latino Religions and Civic Activism in the United States* and is currently working on studies of Latino religions and American public life and a biography of Francisco Olazábal.

Maureen Fiedler, SL, is the host of *Interfaith Voices,* a public radio show broadcast in the U.S. and in Canada and has been active in the movement to ordain women in the Roman Catholic Church since 1976. She holds a Ph.D. in government from Georgetown University.

Reta Halteman Finger is Assistant Professor of New Testament at Messiah College, Grantham, Pa., and former editor of the *Daughters of Sarah* magazine. Her research interests are the Pauline letters, Acts, and feminist biblical interpretation.

Holly Folk is a doctoral candidate in religious studies at Indiana University. She is preparing a dissertation tentatively titled "American Popular Vitalism: The Origins of Alternative Medicine and Chiropractic."

Selena Fox is a psychotherapist, teacher, writer, photographer, ritual performance artist, and priestess. She is founder and co-executive director of Circle Sanctuary, an international Nature Spirituality resource center headquartered on a 200-acre nature preserve in southwestern Wisconsin. Selena has been a Wiccan priestess and Pagan artist since 1973. She is author of *Goddess Communion Rituals and Meditations* and *When Goddess Is God.*

Reena Sigman Friedman is Associate Professor of Modern Jewish History at the Reconstructionist Rabbinical College. She is author of *These Are Our Children: Jewish Orphanages in the United States, 1880–1925;* chapters in *Freedom and Responsibility: Exploring the Challenges of Jewish Continuity* (Geffen and Edelman, eds.) and *Jewish American Voluntary Organizations* (Dobkowski, ed.); entries in *Jewish Women in America: A Historical Encyclopedia* (Hyman and Moore, eds.); and numerous articles.

Mary Van Vleck Garman was educated at Kalamazoo College, Earlham School of Religion, and the joint program between Garrett-Evangelical Theological Seminary. She is a recorded Friends minister, a pastor in Indianapolis and Richmond, Ind., and is currently active in Clear Creek Meeting. Professor of Religion at Earlham College, she is co-editor of *Hidden in Plain Sight.* Her current research includes ethics of friendship in spiritual/political engagement.

Carolyn DeSwarte Gifford is a historian of American women's religious experience and social reform activity. She edited *"Writing Out My Heart": Selections from the Journal of Frances E. Willard, 1855–1896;* co-edited *Gender and the Social Gospel;* and is currently co-editing a collection of speeches and writings of Frances E. Willard.

Cheryl Townsend Gilkes is the John D. and Catherine T. MacArthur Professor of Sociology and African-American Studies at Colby College in Waterville, Maine. She is author of *If It Wasn't for the Women: Black Women's Experience and Womanist Culture in Church and Community.* An ordained Baptist minister, she serves as the assistant pastor for special projects at the Union Baptist Church in Cambridge, Mass.

Karla Goldman is Historian in Residence at the Jewish Women's Archive. Her interests focus on nineteenth-century American Judaism, black-Jewish relations, and women in American Jewish history. She is author of *Beyond the Synagogue Gallery: Finding a Place for Women in American Judaism.* She was the first woman faculty member on the Cincinnati campus of Hebrew Union College-Institute for Religion, where she taught from 1991 to 2000.

Blu Greenberg is an author and lecturer who has published widely on issues of feminism, Orthodoxy, and the Jewish family, as well as on other subjects of scholarly interest. Greenberg is author of *On Women and Judaism: A View from Tradition; How to Run a Traditional Jewish Household; Black Bread: Poems after the Holocaust;* and *King Solomon and the Queen of Sheba,* a children's book

co-authored with Rev. Linda Tarry. Since 1973, she has been active in the movement to bridge feminism and Orthodox Judaism.

R. Marie Griffith is Associate Professor of Religion at Princeton University. She is author of *God's Daughters: Evangelical Women and the Power of Submission* and *Born Again Bodies: Flesh and Spirit in American Christianity.* She is also co-editor of the forthcoming *Women and Religion in the African Diaspora.*

Rita M. Gross is Professor Emerita of Philosophy and Religious Studies at the University of Wisconsin, Eau Claire and author of *Buddhism after Patriarchy: A Feminist History, Analysis, and Reconstruction of Buddhism.* Much of her current work is in the area of inter-religious exchange. She is also a senior teacher of Buddhism in a Tibetan Buddhist lineage led by Venerable Khandro Rinpoche, one of the few women lineage holders of Tibetan Buddhism.

Cathy Gutierrez, Assistant Professor of Religion at Sweet Briar College, holds a Ph.D. in religion from Syracuse University. She has published on American millennialism, spiritualism, and women's spirituality.

Yvonne Yazbeck Haddad is Professor of the History of Islam and Christian-Muslim Relations at the Center for Muslim-Christian Understanding, Georgetown University. She received her Ph.D. from Harford Seminary. Author and editor of many books, her most recent publications are *A Vanishing Minority: Christians in the Middle East (An Annotated Bibliography); Islam and the West Post-9/11;* and *Not Quite American?: The Shaping of Arab and Muslim Identity in the United States.*

Nancy A. Hardesty, a coordinator emerita of EEWC (Evangelical and Ecumenical Women's Caucus), is Professor of Religion at Clemson University in Clemson, S.C. She is author of *Faith Cure: Divine Healing in the Early Holiness and Pentecostal Movements; Inclusive Language in the Church; Women Called to Witness;* and (with Letha Dawson Scanzoni) *All We're Meant to Be: Biblical Feminism for Today.*

Jane Harris is Associate Professor of Religion and Area Chair for Hendrix College, Conway, Ark. She teaches American religion and focuses her research on women and American religious life and religion in the American South. Her article "Holiness and Pentecostal Traditions: Making the Spirit Count" appeared in the Religion by Region series, *Religion and Public Life in the Southern Crossroads: Showdown States.*

Susan M. Hartmann is Professor of U.S. History and Women's Studies at Ohio State University and has published extensively on women in the twentieth century, feminism, and women's rights movements. Among her books are *The Home Front and Beyond: American Women in the 1940s; From Margin to Mainstream: American Women and Politics since the 1960s;* a textbook, *The American Promise;* and *The Other Feminists,* a study of women's rights activism in the 1960s and 1970s.

Katharine R. Henderson is the executive vice president of Auburn Theological Seminary in New York City and co-founder of Face to Face/Faith to Faith. She is preparing a book, *Breakthrough Leadership for Women of Faith.* Her interests include multi-faith education, women and philanthropy, and women's public leadership.

Alison Duncan Hirsch is editor of the *Journal of the Lycoming County Historical Society* and has been Visiting Assistant Professor of American Studies and History at Dickinson College.

Richard Hollinger is editor of *Community Histories: Studies in the Babi and Baha'i Faiths* and co-editor of *'Abdu'l-Baha in America: Anges Parsons Diary, April 11, 1912–November 11, 1912, Supplemented with Episodes from Mamud's Diary.*

S. Sue Horner is an independent scholar and writer, most recently Associate Professor of Women's Studies at North Park University, Chicago. Her research area is religion and American culture, particularly the intersection of feminism and evangelicalism. She is currently working on a memoir reflecting her journey of faith and feminism.

Mary E. Hunt, Ph.D., is a feminist theologian who is co-founder and co-director of the Women's Alliance for Theology, Ethics and Ritual (WATER) in Silver Spring, Md. A Roman Catholic active in the women-church movement, she lectures and writes on theology and ethics with particular attention to liberation issues.

Kathleen S. Hurty is a graduate of Bethany College, Lindsborg, Ks., and earned a Ph.D. from the University of California, Berkeley. Her dissertation focused on leadership and power perspectives of women principals. A researcher and writer, she has served as a public school teacher and principal, and as a national ecumenical administrator.

Sandra Hutchinson contributed the foreword to *'Abdu'l-Baha in America: Agnes Parsons Diary, April 11, 1912–November 11, 1912, Supplemented with Episodes from Mamud's Diary,* edited by Richard Hollinger.

Ada María Isasi-Díaz is Professor of Theology and Ethics at the Theological School of Drew University. She received her Ph.D. at Union Theological Seminary in New York. She is author of *La Lucha Continues: Mujerista Theology; En La Lucha: Elaborating a Mujerista The-* ology; and *Mujerista Theology: A Theology for the 21st Century.*

Demetra Velisarios Jaquet, M.Div., D.Min., BCC, AAPC Fellow, is a pastoral psychotherapist and spiritual director at pastoral counseling for Denver, and adjunct faculty in religious studies at Regis University, School for Professional Studies, Denver. She is founder and chair of the Women's Orthodox Ministries and Education Network (WOMEN), on the Web at www.OrthodoxWomensNetwork.org, and is president of the Orthodox Christian Association of Medicine, Psychology and Religion (OCAMPR).

Norma Baumel Joseph is Associate Professor and Chair of Religion at Concordia University, and director of the women and religion specialization. Her teaching and research areas include women and Judaism, Jewish law and ethics, and women and religion. She appeared in and was consultant to the films *Half the Kingdom* and *Untying the Bond . . . Jewish Divorce.* Her doctoral dissertation focused on the legal decisions of Rabbi Moses Feinstein as they describe and delineate separate spheres for women in the Jewish community. Her current research focuses on Jewish law and gender, and food, identity, and gender.

Cynthia A. Jurisson is Associate Professor of American Church History at Lutheran School of Theology in Chicago. She earned her Ph.D. at Princeton Theological Seminary. Her dissertation is entitled "Federalist, Feminist, Revivalist: Harriet Livermore (1788–1868) and the Limits of Democratization in the Early Republic."

Valerie A. Karras, theologian, has been Research Associate at the Thesaurus Linguae Graecae, University of California, Irvine and taught Greek Patristics in the department of Theological Studies at Saint Louis University, St. Louis, Mo.

David E. Kaufman is Associate Professor of Contemporary American Jewish Studies at Hebrew Union College-Jewish Institute of Religion. Previously, he served as an adjunct professor of American Jewish history at the Jewish Theological Seminary of America, York College/City University of New York, The New School, Queens College and Baruch College. He is author of *Shul with a Pool: The "Synagogue-Center" in American Jewish History.*

Rosemary Skinner Keller is academic dean emerita and Professor of Church History Emerita at Union Theological Seminary in New York. She held similar positions previously at Garrett-Evangelical Theological Seminary. Co-editor with Rosemary Radford Ruether of the three-volume *Women and Religion in America* and *In Our Voices: Four Centuries of American Women's Religious Writing,* she has authored two biographies, *Georgia*

Harkness: For Such a Time as This and *Patriotism and the Female Sex: Abigail Adams and the American Revolution.* At present she is a senior scholar at Garrett-Evangelical Theological Seminary.

Nami Kim earned her doctoral degree from Harvard Divinity School. Currently she is Assistant Professor of Religion in the Department of Philosophy and Religious Studies at Spelman College, Atlanta, Ga.

Cheryl A. Kirk-Duggan is Professor of Religion and Women's Studies at Shaw University. The former director of Graduate Theological Union's Center for Women and Religion, she is author of *Misbegotten Anguish: A Theology and Ethics of Violence; Refiner's Fire: A Religious Engagement with Violence;* and *The Undivided Soul: Helping Congregations Connect Body and Spirit* and editor of *Pregnant Passion: Gender, Sex, and Violence in the Bible.*

Frances Kissling, president of Catholics for a Free Choice since 1982, is a highly regarded speaker on issues of religion, reproductive health, women's rights, and population policy. She serves on the boards of the Religious Coalition for Reproductive Choice, the Alan Guttmacher Institute, and Ibis Reproductive Health, and is a founder of the Global Fund for Women.

Rebecca Larson received her M.A. in history and a Ph.D. in the history of American civilization from Harvard University. She is author of *Daughters of Light: Quaker Women Preaching and Prophesying in the Colonies and Abroad, 1700–1775* and is a contributor to journals on women and religion.

Amy Lavine has a doctorate in history of religions from the University of Chicago. Her work with the Tibetan refugee community in New York City culminated in her dissertation, entitled "The Politics of Nostalgia: Social Memory and National Identity among Diaspora Tibetans in New York City." She currently works at the Lesbian, Gay, Bisexual & Transgender Community Center in New York City where she created the "Out & Faithful: LGBT People, Religion and Spirituality Series." Lavine is working on a book about how people find meaning in their lives.

Marilyn J. Legge is Associate Professor of Christian Ethics at Emmanuel College of Victoria University in the University of Toronto. Her teaching and research interests are in social ethics and critical social and cultural theories and practices, including post-colonial and social postmodernism in global and Canadian contexts. She is author of *The Grace of Difference: A Canadian Feminist Theological Ethic,* and co-editor of several volumes, including *Liberation Theology: An Introductory Reader.* She has been president of the Canadian Theological Society

and coordinating editor of *Studies in Women and Religion.*

Rita M. Lester is Assistant Professor of Religion at Nebraska Wesleyan University in Lincoln, Nebr., where she teaches courses on religious diversity in the United States, Christian history, contemporary theology, and world religions. Awarded a Harvard Pluralism Project research grant and a Methodist Exemplary Teaching Award, she also facilitates adult education in local synagogues and churches.

Miriam Levering is Professor of Religious Studies at the University of Tennessee and is completing a book entitled *The Zen of Women: Women Masters in Zen through the Sung Dynasty* and is author of many articles on Buddhism and women.

Susan Hill Lindley is Professor of Religion at Saint Olaf College in Northfield, Minn. She is author of *"You Have Stept out of Your Place": A History of Women and Religion in America* and editor of the forthcoming *Westminster Dictionary of Women in American Religious History.*

Loretta M. Long received her Ph.D. from Georgetown University and is author of *The Life of Selina Campbell: A Fellow Soldier in the Cause of Restoration.* She currently teaches at Pepperdine University in Malibu, Calif.

Cynthia Lynn Lyerly is author of *Methodism and the Southern Mind* and numerous articles on southern women and religion. She received her Ph.D. from Rice University and is an associate professor of history at Boston College.

Daisy L. Machado is Dean at Lexington Theological Seminary and Professor of the History of Christianity. She is author of *Of Borders and Margins: Hispanic Disciples in the Southwest, 1888–1942* and co-editor (with María Pilar Aquino and Jeanette Rodríguez) of *A Reader in Latina Feminist Theology: Religion and Justice.* Her research focuses on gender and globalization, the role of religion in the borderlands, and the history of U.S. missionary enterprises in the Spanish-speaking Caribbean and Latin America.

Debra Mubashir Majeed is Associate Professor of Philosophy and Religious Studies at Beloit College and is completing a book entitled *Close Encounters of Intimate Sisterhood: Polygyny in the World of African American Muslims.*

Sandy Dwayne Martin is Professor of Religion and department head at the University of Georgia and teaches in the areas of American and African American religious history and the history of Christianity. He is author of *Black Baptists and African Missions: The Origins of a Movement, 1880–1915* and *For God and Race: The Reli-*

gious and Political Leadership of AMEZ Bishop James Walker Hood.

Ingrid Mattson is Professor of Islamic Studies and Director of Islamic Chaplaincy at Hartford Seminary in Hartford, Conn. She earned her Ph.D. in Islamic Studies from the University of Chicago. Mattson has served as vice president of the Islamic Society of North America (ASNA).

Aminah Beverly McCloud is Professor of Religious Studies at DePaul University in Chicago and author of *African American Islam.*

Jeanne P. McLean is Dean of the School of Divinity and Associate Professor of Philosophy at the University of St. Thomas, Minn., and is author of a book on academic leadership, *Leading from the Center: Chief Academic Officers in Theological Schools.* McLean has a Ph.D. in philosophy from Loyola University of Chicago and has held both faculty and administrative appointments in higher education.

Lara Medina is Associate Professor in the Department of Chicano and Chicana Studies, California State University, Northridge, and author of *Las Hermanas: Chicana/Latina Religious-Political Activism in the U.S. Catholic Church.*

Barbara J. Merguerian is affiliated with the Armenian International Women's Association and has co-edited (with Doris D. Jafferian) *Armenian Women in a Changing World* and (with Joy Renjilian-Burgy) *Voices of Armenian Women.* She was formerly with the Armenian studies program at California State University, Fresno.

Patrick Neal Minges received his Ph.D. in American religious history from Union Theological Seminary in New York. He is author of *Slavery in the Cherokee Nation: The Keetoowah Society and the Defining of a People, 1855–1867.*

Cecilia A. Moore is Assistant Professor of Religious Studies at the University of Dayton and the Institute of Black Catholic Studies at Xavier University of Louisiana. She is a graduate of Sweet Briar College and holds a Ph.D. in American religious history from the University of Virginia. Her primary research focus is the history of African American Catholics in the twentieth century.

Kathleen Ann Myers is Professor of Literatures in Spanish at Indiana University, Bloomington, and author of *Word from New Spain: The Spiritual Autobiography of María de San José (1656–1719); "A Wild Country out in the Garden": The Spiritual Journals of a Colonial Mexican Nun* (with Amanda Powell); *Neither Saints nor Sinners: Writing the Lives of Spanish American Women;* and *New World, New History: Fernández de Oviedo's Historia General y Natural de las Indias* (forthcoming).

Sara J. Myers is Professor of Theological Bibliography and Director of the Burke Library at Union Theological Seminary in New York. Her research interests include women in American society, religious biography and autobiography, and the impact of technology on theological research.

Pamela S. Nadell is Professor of History and Director of the Jewish Studies Program at American University. She is author or editor of four books, including *Women Who Would Be Rabbis: A History of Women's Ordination, 1889–1985,* a finalist for the National Jewish Book Award, and *American Jewish Women's History: A Reader.*

Vasudha Narayanan is Professor of Religion at the University of Florida and a past president of the American Academy of Religion. Educated at the Universities of Madras and Bombay in India, and at Harvard University, she is author of *Hinduism; The Vernacular Veda: Revelation, Recitation, and Ritual; The Way and the Goal: Expressions of Devotion in the Early Srivaisnava Tradition;* and *The Tamil Veda: Pillan's Interpretation of the Tiruvaymoli* (co-authored with John Carman). Her current research is on Hindu temples and Vaishnava traditions in Cambodia.

Vivian-Lee Nyitray is Professor of Religious Studies and also teaches in the Asian languages and cultures program at the University of California, Riverside. She is author of *Mirrors of Virtue,* a study of four Han dynasty biographies, and co-editor of *The Life of Chinese Religion.* She has published articles on the Buddhist-Taoist sea goddess Mazu and on the function of memory in early Chinese historical biographies, and her current research focuses on the confrontation between Confucianism and feminist discourse in Chinese cultural contexts.

Laura R. Olson is Associate Professor of Political Science at Clemson University and author of (with Sue E. S. Crawford) *Women with a Mission: Religion, Gender, and the Politics of Women Clergy; Religion and Politics in America: Faith, Culture, and Strategic Choices* (with Robert Booth Fowler, Allen D. Hertzke, and Kevin R. den Dulk); *Christian Clergy in American Politics* (with Sue E. S. Crawford); and *Filled with Spirit and Power.*

Loida I. Martell Otero is a veterinary medical doctor and an ordained minister in the American Baptist Churches (USA). She is Associate Professor of Constructive Theology at Palmer Theological Seminary in Wynnewood, Pa. She is co-editor (with José D. Rodríguez) of *Teología en Conjunto: A Collaborative Hispanic Protestant Theology* and has published articles on Latina *evangélica* theology and is author of "Satos and Saints: Salvation from the Periphery."

Susan J. Palmer is Professor of Religious Studies at Dawson College, Quebec, and an adjunct professor at

Concordia University. She has written or edited six books on new religions, including *Alien Apocalypse; Moon Sisters, Krisha Mothers, Rajneesh Sisters;* and *Millennium, Messiahs, and Mayhem* (edited with Tom Robbins).

Lori Pierce holds a Master's of Theological Studies from Harvard Divinity School and a Ph.D. from the University of Hawaii. She currently teaches race and ethnic studies in the American Studies Program at DePaul University in Chicago.

Nancy Pineda-Madrid is Assistant Professor of Theology and Latino/a Ministry at the Institute of Religious Education and Pastoral Ministry, Boston College. She received her Ph.D. from the Graduate Theological Union. Her research focuses on feminist theologies, U.S. Latino theologies, and Latina feminist theologies.

Judith Plaskow is Professor of Religious Studies at Manhattan College and a Jewish feminist theologian. She is author of many articles and books on feminist theology, among them *Standing Again at Sinai: Judaism from a Feminist Perspective.*

Lisa J. M. Poirier is Assistant Professor of Comparative Religion at Miami University of Ohio. She received her Ph.D. from Syracuse University with the dissertation "Translators and Converts: Religion, Exchange, and Orientation in Colonial New France, 1608–1680."

Dolly Pomerleau co-founded the Quixote Center, a Catholic-based social justice organization, in 1976, which she continues to co-direct. She also co-founded the Women's Ordination Conference, Potters for Peace, and the Nicaraguan Cultural Alliance. She serves on the Board of the Women's Ordination Conference.

Priscilla Pope-Levison is Professor of Theology and Assistant Director of Women's Studies at Seattle Pacific University. Her most recent book is titled *Turn the Pulpit Loose: Two Centuries of American Women Evangelists.*

Riv-Ellen Prell, an anthropologist, is Professor of American Studies at the University of Minnesota. She is author of *Fighting to Become Americans: Jews, Gender and the Anxiety of Assimilation* and *Prayer and Community: The Havurah in American Judaism,* and co-editor of *Interpreting Women's Lives: Personal Narratives and Feminist Theory.*

Rebecca Button Prichard is pastor of Tustin Presbyterian Church in Tustin, Calif. She also serves as adjunct professor of preaching and worship at San Francisco Theological Seminary, Southern California. She is author of *Sensing the Spirit: The Holy Spirit in Feminist Perspective.*

Mary L. Putrow, OP, is Assistant Professor of Religious Education at Sacred Heart Major Seminary. Her primary work is in the field of catechetics, the preparation of candidates for priestly and diaconal ministry and men and women for lay ecclesial ministry. Her research interest is women and their contributions to the faith life of children and adults.

Brian D. Ray is a researcher, writer, and speaker, a former professor of education and science, a former middle school and high school classroom teacher, and is the president of the National Home Education Research Institute in Salem, Ore. He holds a Ph.D. in science education from Oregon State University.

Marcia Y. Riggs is J. Erskine Love Professor of Christian Ethics at Columbia Theological Seminary in Decatur, Ga. Her research focuses on the relationship between social oppression and socio-religious ethical praxis, ethical discourse that bridges the gap between womanist religious scholarship and the Church's practice of ministry, the moral foundations of public policy, and the Church's role in social justice ministry.

Dana L. Robert is Truman Collins Professor of World Mission at the Boston University School of Theology. Her books include *Gospel Bearers; Gender Barriers: Missionary Women in the Twentieth Century;* and *"Occupy Until I Come": A. T. Pierson and the Evangelization of the World.* She edits the book series "African Initiatives in Christian Mission."

Jeanette Rodriguez is Professor of Theology and Religious Studies at Seattle University and former president of the Academy of Catholic Hispanic Theologians in the United States. Her scholarly focus includes theologies of liberation, cultural memory, and religion and social conflict. She received her Ph.D. in religion and the personality sciences at the Graduate Theological Union in Berkeley and is author of *Our Lady of Guadelupe: Faith and Empowerment among Mexican American Women* and *Stories We Live,* as well as numerous articles on U.S. Latino/a theology and women's spirituality. She is also co-editor of *A Reader in U.S. Latina Feminist Theology* (with Maria Pilar Aquino and Daisy Machado).

Rosetta E. Ross is a womanist scholar and Christian social ethicist. She is Associate Professor of Religion at Spelman College in Atlanta, Ga., and author of *Witnessing and Testifying: Black Women, Religion, and the Civil Rights Movement.*

Rosemary Radford Ruether is a Catholic feminist theologian. She is Carpenter Professor of Feminist Theology, emeritus, Graduate Theological Union, Berkeley and visiting scholar in feminist theology, Claremont Graduate University and Claremont School of Theology. She taught for many years at Garrett-Evangelical Theological Seminary and was a member of the Graduate

Faculty of Northwestern University in Evanston, Ill. She is editor of 12 collections and author of 28 books, including *Goddesses and the Divine Feminine: A Western Religious History*; *Sexism and God-talk: Toward a Feminist Theology*; *Woman-Church: Theology and Practice of Feminist Liturgical Communities*; *Christianity and the Making of the Modern Family*; and *Gaia and God: An Ecofeminist Theology of Earth Healing*.

Letty M. Russell is Professor Emerita of Theology at Yale Divinity School and co-Coordinator of the International Feminist Doctor of Ministry Program at San Francisco Theological Seminary. She is co-editor of *Dictionary of Feminist Theologies* and editor of *Feminist Interpretation of the Bible*.

Teresa Chávez Sauceda is Executive Director of Manos Unidas Community and Development Center in San Francisco. She holds a Ph.D. in religion and society from the Graduate Theological Union in Berkeley, Calif.

Tracy Schier is co-founder of the Boston College Institute for Administrators in Catholic Higher Education and, since 1986, a consultant to Lilly Endowment. She directed a project at Yale that resulted in the volume *Catholic Women's Colleges in America* and is advisor to numerous national and regional boards.

Grace Jill Schireson is an ordained Zen priest in the Suzuki-roshi lineage and a trained clinical psychologist. She is the founder of Empty Nest Zendo (North Fork, Calif.) and the guiding teacher for the Fresno River Zen Group and the Valley Heartland Zen Group (www.emptynestzendo.org). She has taught Zen throughout the United States and in Japan.

Jean Miller Schmidt is Gerald L. Schlessman Professor of Methodist Studies and Professor of Modern Church History at Iliff School of Theology in Denver, Colo. She is author of *Souls or the Social Order: The Two-Party System in American Protestantism* and *Grace Sufficient: A History of Women in American Methodism*. With Russell E. Richey and Kenneth E. Rowe, she is currently working on a new history of American Methodism.

Shuly Rubin Schwartz is the Irving Lehrman Research Assistant Professor of American Jewish History and Dean of the Albert A. List College of Jewish Studies at the Jewish Theological Seminary, New York. Author of *The Emergence of Jewish Scholarship in America: The Publication of the Jewish Encyclopedia*, she has just completed *The Rabbi's Wife: The Rebbetzin in American Jewish Life*.

Susan M. Setta is Associate Professor of Philosophy and Religion at Northeastern University, where she is also coordinator of undergraduate research at the Center for Experiential Education and director of the women's studies program. She is author of *The Secularizing Impulse and Theological Education: A History of Hartford Seminary* and *Woman of the Apocalypse: Images of Ann Christ in the Shaker Tradition*. She is preparing a book on women, religion, and healing in American religion.

Carolyn Sharp is Assistant Professor of Theology at St. Paul University in Ottawa. Her main research interest is feminist liberation theologies. She has published a number of articles on theology in Quebec, the work of Luce Irigaray, and feminist theology and Christology.

Rita DasGupta Sherma is the chair for the Council for Hindu Studies, Claremont Graduate University and a senior research associate, Berghoffer Institute, New York. Her book on constructive Hindu theology, titled *Eros, Ecology and Enlightenment: Towards a New Vision of Hindu Theology*, is forthcoming. She is the past president of the Himalayan Arts and Religion Council and holds a Ph.D. in Theology and Ethics from Claremont Graduate University, Claremont, Calif.

Judith Simmer-Brown is Professor of Religious Studies at Naropa University. Her research interests are in the areas of Indo-Tibetan Buddhism, gender symbolism, American Buddhism, and inter-religious dialogue. She is author of *Dakini's Warm Breath: The Feminine Principle in Tibetan Buddhism* and *Benedict's Dharma: Buddhists Comment on the Rule of St. Benedict* (Br. David Steindl-Rast, Joseph Goldstein, Norm Fischer, Ven. Yifa, and Sr. Mary Margaret Funk).

Nikky-Guninder Kaur Singh is Crawford Family Professor of Religious Studies at Colby College, Maine, where her research focuses on poetics and feminist issues. She is author of *The Birth of the Khalsa: A Feminist Re-Memory of Sikh Identity*; *The Feminine Principle in the Sikh Vision of the Transcendent*; *The Name of My Beloved: Verses of the Sikh Gurus*; and *Metaphysics and Physics of the Guru Granth Sahib*.

Andrea Smith (Cherokee) is Assistant Professor of American Studies and Women's Studies at the University of Michigan. She is author of *Conquest, Sexual Violence and American Indian Genocide*. She is also a co-founder of Incite! Women of Color against Violence.

Jane I. Smith is Professor of Islamic Studies and Co-director, The Duncan Black Macdonald Center for the Study of Islam and Christian-Muslim Relations at Hartford Theological Seminary. She is currently co-editor of *The Muslim World*, a journal dedicated to the study of Islam and Christian-Muslim relations. Her recent publications include *Islam in America*; "Islam and Christendom" in *The Oxford Dictionary of Islam*; *Muslim Communities in America*; and *Mission to America: Five Islamic Communities in the United States*.

Anna M. Speicher is the director and editor of a curriculum project for the Church of the Brethren, Mennonite Church USA and Mennonite Church Canada. Her scholarship is in the area of women, religion, and antislavery, and she is author of *The Religious World of Antislavery Women: Spirituality in the Lives of Five Abolitionist Lecturers.*

Eleanor J. Stebner is J. S. Woodsworth Chair and Associate Professor of Religion and social change at Simon Fraser University. She is author of *The Women of Hull House; GEM: The Life of Sister Mac;* and numerous articles related to women, Christianity, and social change.

Dianne M. Stewart is Associate Professor of Religion and African American Studies at Emory University. Her publications include *Three Eyes for the Journey: African Dimensions of the Jamaican Religious Experience* and various articles on theologies and religious practices of the African diaspora. She earned her M.Div. from Harvard Divinity School and her Ph.D. in Theology from Union Theological Seminary.

Kim Stone (Shawnee-Eastern Cherokee) is a student of Political Science at University of Michigan, Ann Arbor. Her area of interest is Native American women's politics, and organizing among minority women. She is also the former treasurer and cultural advocate of the Genesee Valley Indian Association in Michigan and founder of the Kwewag Intertribal Society, a Native women's social group.

Ruth M. Tabrah (1921–2004) was author of many books on Buddhism and Hawaii, including *Living Shin Buddhism: An Account of a Visit with Hanada-Sensei; The Monk's Wife* (a novel); *Ni'ihau: The Last Hawaiian Island;* and *The Monk Who Dared: A Novel about Shinran.*

Lucy Tatman is author of *Knowledge That Matters: A Feminist Theological Paradigm and Epistemology.* An itinerant teacher and writer, her thoughts have traveled from feminist theological paradigms to myths and figures of the sacred, and she is currently pondering incarnate temporalities, or the matter of time.

Susan Thistlewaite is Professor of Theology and President of Chicago Theological Seminary. She received her Ph.D. from Duke University and her Master of Divinity (summa cum laude) from Duke Divinity School. She is author of *Casting Stones: Prostitution and Liberation in Asia and the United States* (with Rita Nakashima Brock) and *The New Testament and Psalms: An Inclusive Translation,* and is editor (with Mary Potter Engel) of *Lift Every Voice: Constructing Christian Theologies from the Underside.* She works in the area of contextual theologies of liberation, specializing in issues of violence and violation.

Fredrica Harris Thompsett is the Mary Wolfe Professor of Historical Theology at the Episcopal Divinity School in Cambridge, Mass., and author of books and articles on church history and Episcopal women's history. Her recent publications include *Deeper Joy: Laywomen's Vocations in the 20th Century Episcopal Church* and *Living with History.*

Mary Todd has taught history at Concordia College in Forest Park, Ill., and is author of *Authority Vested: A Story of Identity and Change in the Lutheran Church Missouri Synod.* She received her Ph.D. from the University of Illinois, Chicago. Her dissertation was entitled "Not in God's Lifetime: The Question of the Ordination of Women in the Lutheran Church-Missouri Synod."

Emilie M. Townes is Professor of African American Studies in Religion at Yale Divinity School and was formerly on the faculties of Union Theological Seminary in New York and St. Paul School of Theology. She is author of *Womanist Justice, Womanist Hope; A Troubling in My Soul;* and *Breaking the Fine Rain of Death: African American Health Care and a Womanist Ethic of Care.*

Tracy J. Trothen is Assistant Professor of Systematic Theology and Ethics, and a director of field education at Queen's Theological College, Queen's University, Canada. She is author of *Linking Sexuality and Gender: Naming Violence against Women in The United Church of Canada.* She was ordained in The United Church of Canada.

Cynthia Grant Tucker's writings on Unitarian women include *Healer in Harm's Way: Mary Collson, A Clergywoman in Christian Science; Prophetic Sisterhood: Liberal Women of the Frontier, 1880–1930;* and forthcoming, *No Silent Witness: The Eliot Family and Women's Voices in Liberal Religious Life.*

Ann Belford Ulanov is Christiane Brooks Johnson Memorial Professor of Psychiatry and Religion at Union Theological Seminary in New York. She received her M.Div. and Ph.D. from Union Theological Seminary and has an honorary doctorate degree (L.H.D.) from Virginia Theological Seminary and from Loyola in Maryland. Her teaching and research are in psychiatry and religion with a special interest in issues of prayer and the spiritual life, aggression, anxiety, fantasy and dream, identity, and the feminine.

Anne Vallely is Assistant Professor of Religious Studies at the University of Ottawa and author of *Guardians of the Transcendent: An Ethnography of a Jain Ascetic Community.* Her research focuses on Jainism, religious orders and women in India, and the Jain diaspora in Canada.

Janet Walton is Professor of Worship at Union Theological Seminary in New York. Her research and teaching are in worship as its traditions and practices are experienced in religious communities, with particular interest in aesthetic dimensions of worship as well as feminist perspectives of worship. She is author of *Art and Worship: A Vital Connection* and *Feminist Liturgy: A Matter of Justice.*

Laura Adams Weaver is an instructor of English and Native American studies at the University of Georgia. Completing a Ph.D. in English at the University of California, Santa Barbara, she specializes in Native American and African American literatures and Narrative Theory. She is currently at work on a dissertation entitled "Keeping Time: Temporality in American Indian Storytelling."

Mary Jo Weaver, Professor of Religious Studies, Indiana University, has published books in three broad areas: Catholic modernism, American Catholic feminism (*New Catholic Women: A Contemporary Challenge to Traditional Religious Authority*), and late-twentieth-century American Catholic discord (*Being Right: Conservative Catholics in America* [with R. Scott Appleby] and *What's Left? Liberal American Catholics*). Her latest book is *Cloister and Community: Life within a Carmelite Monastery.*

Judith Weisenfeld is Associate Professor of Religion at Vassar College, author of *African American Women and Christian Activism: New York's YWCA, 1905–1945,* and co-editor, with Richard Newman, of *This Far By Faith: Readings in African American Women's Religious Biography.* She is currently at work on a book on African American religion in American film from 1929 to 1950.

Catherine Wessinger is Professor of the History of Religions and Women's Studies at Loyola University, New Orleans. She is author of *Annie Besant and Progressive Messianism,* editor of *Women's Leadership in Marginal Religions: Explorations outside the Mainstream,* and editor of *Religious Institutions and Women's Leadership: New Roles inside the Mainstream.* She has also written and edited books on millennialism. She is co–general editor of *Nova Religio: The Journal of Alternative and Emergent Religions.*

Marilyn Färdig Whiteley is an independent scholar. She is author of *Canadian Methodist Women, 1766–1925: Marys, Marthas, Mothers in Israel* and editor of *The Life and Letters of Annie Leake Tuttle* and (with Elizabeth Gillan Muir) of *Changing Roles of Women within the Christian Church in Canada.*

Lois M. Wilson is an ordained minister of the United Church of Canada and its first female moderator. She is past president of the Canadian Council of Churches and the World Council of Churches, as well as a Canadian senator.

Diane Winston is Professor of Journalism and Knight Chair in Media and Religion at the Annenberg School of Communication, University of Southern California. She has worked as a reporter for several of the nation's leading newspapers, including the Baltimore *Sun,* Dallas *Morning News,* Dallas *Times Herald,* and *The News and Observer* in Raleigh, N.C., and is author of *Red-Hot and Righteous: The Urban Religion of the Salvation Army* and co-editor (with John Michael Giggie) of *Faith in the Market: Religion and the Rise of Urban Commercial Culture.*

Valarie Ziegler is Professor of Religious Studies at DePauw University. She received her Ph.D. in historical theology from Emory University and her Master of Divinity degree, cum laude, from Yale University. She is author of *Diva Julia: The Public Romance and Private Agony of Julia Ward Howe; The Advocates of Peace in Antebellum America;* and co-editor (with Kristen E. Kvam and Linda S. Schearing) of *Eve and Adam: Jewish, Christian, and Muslim Readings on Genesis and Gender.*

Barbara Brown Zikmund holds a Ph.D. from Duke University in American religious history. She has taught at several liberal arts colleges, Chicago Theological Seminary, Pacific School of Religion, Hartford Seminary, and Doshisha University in Kyoto, Japan. She is a visiting research professor at the Life Cycle Institute at Catholic University of America.

Acknowledgments

THIS AMBITIOUS PROJECT was made possible by a collaborative grant from the Lilly Endowment, Inc. and the Henry W. Luce Foundation. We never would have been able to complete this work without their generous contributions. We are grateful, also, to Union Theological Seminary for providing the financial management of the funds.

Our thanks to Indiana University Press for recognizing the importance of this work and especially to Robert J. Sloan, the project director at the Press for his persistence and patience throughout the publication process. And to Ralph Carlson who, as Editor-at-Large, initiated and expertly shepherded the project through its first stages of development. Without the generous sharing of knowledge, time, and support by the distinguished members of our Editorial Board, the encyclopedia could not have come to fruition.

Our great appreciation also goes to Marie Cantlon, the Associate Editor, for her expert and careful editing of the manuscripts of all the articles. The outstanding management of Marie Cantlon and Elizabeth Howe, the Project Coordinator, brought the detailed work of the encyclopedia together. Similar thanks to Rebecca Davison who was in charge of photographs and rights and permissions for them. Our appreciation, too, to Jane Hicks, who worked on the initial coordination of the project, and to Miki Bird and her staff at Indiana University Press for proofreading the entire work.

Finally, we thank the 147 authors who wrote essays for this *Encyclopedia of Women and Religion in North America.* This is the first comprehensive scholarly work on this subject. It came together because so many people contributed their expertise on the countless areas of the subject.

Rosemary Skinner Keller
Rosemary Radford Ruether

Introduction

Integrating the Worlds of Women's Religious Experience in North America

THIS ENCYCLOPEDIA IS non-traditional in every way. Typically, an encyclopedia contains brief descriptive statements that define institutions, movements, and individuals. A large number of the entries may be biographical sketches. The articles are organized alphabetically and only accidentally do related subjects happen to follow one another. While meant to cover a comprehensive list of topics, an encyclopedia gives only succinct introductions to a field of inquiry. If readers seek further information, the reference work provides a foundation from which to explore other sources.

We as editors had a very different vision when we conceived this encyclopedia in 1996. Our purpose was to cover in depth the relationship of women to religion. We wanted to portray women's history through the lens of religious history, a viewpoint that has been widely overlooked. The writing of women's history from a secular viewpoint began in the 1960s. Major studies that capture the centrality of religion to women's experience in North America have been written since then. Even so, a secular perspective remains the primary focus of women's history today. Further, in religious history, the work of white men is still the primary theme, with gender, like race, usually remaining a specific, peripheral topic within the field.

The vast amount of knowledge that has been gained over the past four decades about women and religion in North America cannot be presented in the traditional encyclopedic form of short definitive entries. Instead this volume has almost 150 longer essays that enable major themes to be developed in their deeper dimensions. The articles focus on institutions, movements, and ideas. We intentionally sought to have authors weave biographical sketches into their articles to give them a more personal and humanizing quality, and to recognize the women responsible for the gains made over the centuries. The essays demonstrate that neither the story of women nor of religion in North America can be accu-

rately told unless the religious experience of women is integrated into the center of women's and religious history.

Our vision was that a volume that developed the history of women and religion in depth had to be an *interpretive* encyclopedia. It needed to analyze, rather than simply describe subjects, as entries in traditional encyclopedias are meant to do. Because of the work that has been done on women and religion in North America over recent decades, there is now an explicitly feminist reflection that transverses all the world's religions in North America that can be discussed and compared. A feminist perspective, the view that society should be transformed to include full participation of women, is the interpretive frame through which this encyclopedia is written. Most of the contributors speak from that viewpoint.

Finally, we envisioned that an interpretive encyclopedia also had to *integrate* the wide worlds of women and religion in North America. This work is the first comprehensive history of the interaction of women and religion on this continent over four centuries. Only now, at the beginning of the twenty-first century is it possible to create this encyclopedia. In the 1960s and 1970s this historical work was just beginning in the more liberal branches of Protestantism. Catholics, Jews, and other Protestant Christians soon followed, with work on women in Islam, Asian religions, and new religious movements being done more recently. Obviously, there are notable differences in the lives of women and their relationships to their many religious, as well as racial, traditions. However, when we as editors read the nearly 150 essays that were written for this volume, we were struck with the major similarities in women's religious lives in North America. Those patterns were formed first historically by women in the Protestant Christian tradition. The striking fact demonstrated in these articles is that those patterns are replicated throughout the institutions and movements of women across both religious and racial divides. This work seeks to integrate the wide worlds of women's religious experience in North America to enable readers to explore the likenesses and differences in the lives of women of diverse faiths and races, not just read about individual sub-topics in a fragmented way.

This encyclopedia is also non-traditional in the audiences for whom it is written. Of course, it is addressed to libraries, where it will be the primary reference work in the history of women and religion in North America. Beyond this natural repository of encyclopedias, we intend these volumes to reach the shelves of highly diverse readers. Our hope is that non-academics will use it for their personal exploration of individual topics, as well as for discussion in church and social study groups. Too, college and seminary students will use these articles in writing papers for a variety of courses in the history and culture of North America, women, and religion. We believe that teachers and scholars at every level will find this work to be a basic resource in their classroom presentations and assignments and in delving more deeply into researching topics that build upon individual subjects and comparative topics in this field of inquiry. Finally, may these essays open doors and inspire authors to write dissertations and monographs that explore even further worlds of women's religious experience in North America.

For us as editors, this work has been in process for many years, though we had no plans for an encyclopedia until recently. Twenty-three years ago, in 1981, we co-edited the first of a three-volume *Women and Religion in America: The Nineteenth Century—A Documentary History*, an initial effort to bring together primary sources and essays on women in the Christian, Jewish, and alternative religious movements in the United States. Marie Cantlon, associate editor of this encyclopedia, was then senior religion editor for HarperSan Francisco and conceived this series with us. Since then, countless books and articles have been published, dissertations written, and sources on the history of women and religion in North America collected. Larger numbers of historians and other scholars now realize the significance of religion at the heart of women's and religious life, though its integration into broader fields of history still lags behind.

Nineteen hundred and eighty-one marked another important beginning point in writing the history of women and religion in North America. In that year, Abingdon Press published volume 1 of *Women in New Worlds*, co-edited by Hilah Thomas and Rosemary Keller, papers from the first conference on the history of women in a Protestant denomination, the United Methodist Church, held in Cincinnati, Ohio, in February 1980. Kathryn Sklar, a plenary speaker and now Distinguished Professor of History at the State University of

New York, Binghamton, pointed to that time as a benchmark in the writing of the history of women and religion. Her periodization of historical writing in this field provides a launching point to analyze where the study of women and religion in North America is today, twenty-six years later.

She characterized four stages that had taken place by 1980 in historical scholarship on women and religion in North America. The first stage extended from the 1880s to the mid-1960s, a period of "pre-history," preceding the development of the field of women's history. This was a time of data gathering, the bringing together of disparate facts when no conceptual framework had been created for the study of women's history. Stage two came in the 1960s, "birth and infancy" of the field in United States history, "when historians began to see their material through feminist eyes—that is, to probe the history of women's rights and interests."[1]

Rapid growth of "adolescence" came in stage three during the 1960s, when historians interpreted not only the constrictions but also the benefits that women had gained from their religious beliefs and institutions. The fourth period, "maturity," in Sklar's developmental scheme, emerged at the turn into the 1980s and continues today. Recognition of the centrality of class, community, ethnicity, and race were central to this period in studies of women and religion.

Sklar correctly forecast that in a fifth stage historians would continue to focus on and combine approaches developed in stages three and four. This has happened as we move into the twenty-first century. However, the fact that mainstream Protestant Christianity dominated the studies of women and religion by the early 1980s was not acknowledged when she predicted future directions. Nor was it seen how quickly religious pluralism would come to the fore in North America and in religious studies. In this *Encyclopedia of Women and Religion in North America*, we have emphasized women's experience within Christianity, Judaism, and other world religions in North America, as well as new developments in women's religious movements and racial and ethnic diversity related to women and religion. The inclusion of essays and primary sources representing these emphases in our three-volume *Women and Religion in America* and *In Our Own Voices*, published in the 1980s and 1990s, signaled new directions in the study of women and religion that distinguish this fifth stage.

The work on women in the many religious traditions now present in North America is, of course, uneven and much more remains to be done. The largest number of essays in this volume focuses on women in the tradition of Protestant Christianity. They represent the greatest depth and breadth of scholarship because most of the work to date has been done in this area. At the same time, this encyclopedia marks a beginning in scholarly work on the history of women in religiously plural traditions in North America. We hope that it will stimulate more research in these broad areas. Some traditions, such as those of Native Americans, have been studied primarily by non-natives and only recently have begun to educate women scholars from within the traditions. Others, such as Buddhism, have produced a notable roster of scholars and feminist reforms of the traditions, but these are largely by Western women converts rather than by women in the communities for whom Buddhism is traditional. The work of Buddhist women converts and women in traditional Buddhism communities have become two different and parallel histories that often have had little contact with each other.

Scholars in smaller communities, such as Sikhs, Jains, and Zoroastrians who can reflect on the tradition from women's points of view have only begun to emerge. These few women scholars are often overworked, with many demands on their time. Thus the struggle to adequately represent the many religious traditions in North America both historically, over four hundred years, and contemporaneously, across the whole range of traditions, has been a profound challenge. As editors we are painfully aware of the gaps in portraying all the religions in their own histories and in relation to each other adequately. Yet the fact that so many women historians now exist, and so much work on women in the many religions by both women and men has developed, represents a revolution in scholarship. The time to create an encyclopedia of women and religion in North America is now.

This introductory essay provides an interpretive framework for integrating the wide worlds of women's religious experience in North America presented in the volume. Many people will come to the encyclopedia to gain data and analysis about a specific area of women and religion in North America. Others will seek an overview of this large and wide ranging subject. The purpose of this essay is to provide a context both for interpreting the whole of women's experience related to religious institutions surveyed here and for understanding how specific sub-topics fit into the broader field.

The essay is divided into four parts. The first part, "Methodologies in Writing Women's Religious History," introduces the eight articles on "Approaches to the History of Women and Religion" in the opening section of this volume. Each of the essays employs several if not all the approaches, some more overtly than others.

A second short part of this essay details the six Native American, Aframerindian, and African Caribbean essays in this volume. A third, longer section interprets the evolution of "Women in the Protestant Christian Traditions." Women's experience in Protestantism is presented in several sections of the volume. Protestant women's experience in North America has broader implications than simply for the Protestant tradition. It illustrates the goals women set, the barriers they confronted, and the means they employed to come into their full identity from the colonial period until the present day. This is an important foundation for understanding the content of the religious lives of women in North America.

Protestant Christianity was the primary religious movement in the United States for the first two hundred years of its history, and it continues in part to maintain that dominance in Canada and the United States today, even though Protestant church membership has dwindled to less than half of the American population. Protestant women's experience provides patterns that were often adapted by Catholic and Jewish women and by the broader spectrum of females in the religiously plural context of North America. Its influence also seems larger than its present numbers because far more historical work has been done on Protestantism than in any other area of women and religion on this continent.

The fourth part of the essay turns to "Women in Catholic and Orthodox Christianity, and in Jewish, Muslim, Asian, and Newer Religious Movements." Catholics, Orthodox, and non-Christian religions now comprise over 100 million North Americans, rivaling the numbers of Protestants. However, these figures still leave a third of North Americans unaccounted for (World Almanac figures, 1999). Doubtless many of these other 100 million North Americans have roots in and affirm some relationship with Protestant, Catholic, or Orthodox Christianity, as well as non-Christian religions, but are not counted in official membership figures.

Bringing together Catholics, Orthodox, Jews, Muslims, Asian religions, and Newer Religious Movements in one section of this introduction is problematic. Indeed the section on Catholic traditions precedes that of Protestant women in this encyclopedia in recognition of the historical priority of Catholic over Protestant arrival in North and Central America. Yet given the cultural predominance of Protestantism, especially mainstream Protestantism in religious scholarship in North America, the wider worlds of non-Protestant and non-Christian religions can be seen in their differences, but also in their adaptations of the patterns set by Protestants. The experience of Protestant women is interpreted chronologically over the four centuries since colonization on American soil. To follow this approach in relation to Catholic, Jewish, Muslim, and Newer Religious Movements is now beginning to be possible.

Eight themes are raised in this introductory essay and developed in depth throughout the essays that follow. They are presented here in a series of questions to give guides to follow in reading either the entire work or a selection of the essays. Readers of this encyclopedia may find other major points that occur throughout the volume that speak to her or him.

1. What does it mean for women to "gain their own voices" in a religious tradition? How did they claim their voices? What were the barriers confronted in this quest?

2. What is the significance of scriptures to women in various traditions? How have sacred texts been liberating or constricting? Have women working out of a feminist perspective gained courage and empowerment from these texts to understand God's will for them or their own personal fulfillment?

3. What is the relationship between gender and race? How have experiences of women of different races paralleled each other or been different? How have women crossed racial boundaries to work together, and how have they remained separated by racial divisions?

4. How do the experiences of the "True Woman" and the "New Woman" provide interpretations for women in Protestantism and, by extension, to women in Catholicism, Judaism, and other faiths? How have the lines been blurred to create an evolution from the True Woman to the New Woman in the North American experiences? What does it mean to say that both roles continue to exist today in different denominations and religions?

5. What is the significance of community for women? How have gender-separate societies been outlets for the spiritual energies of women and given them support and training to gain authority and leadership? What has happened when women have been integrated into structures with men in larger religious structures and bureaucracies?

6. How has the leadership of women expanded from the home into church structures such as missionary work and orders of nuns and deaconesses and finally into ordination? How have leadership patterns of women differed from those of men?

7. How have women been empowered by their religious commitments? What do we learn from their vocational journeys that enable persons today to identify with their foremothers and to be empowered by them?

8. In what ways have the contributions of women been essential to the maintenance of religious traditions and institutions? How have these roles of women in churches and social reform been liberating or constricting to them?

These questions are aids to help readers integrate the worlds of women's varied religious experiences in North America, as well as to probe more deeply into particular sub-topics in this volume. We now turn to the first section of the worlds of women's religious experience in North America.

I. Methodologies in Writing Women's Religious History

Of the eight articles on "Approaches to the History of Women and Religion," Rita M. Gross's essay, "Women and Religion: Methods of Study and Reflection," develops the broadest perspective. Two primary methodologies are used: first, *descriptive* accounts of women's religious lives, cross-culturally and historically, and, second, *critical analytical* accounts of what religions say about women and the opportunities opened or closed to them. Presenting the facts and data about women's participation and experience is essential because a religion and culture cannot be understood if only men are studied. Analysis involves both critique and visionary reflection regarding constructive options that need to be open for women. Writers in this volume generally combine these approaches, with a stronger focus on particular stories of women's lived experience within social institutions than is given in brief entries in traditional encyclopedias. These biographical accounts describe and analyze how women's lives were constricted by social norms and how women claimed their own moral voices within these institutions, transforming them or moving outside and creating new movements.

Females must be at the center of creating such radical change. Leadership by women in the public sphere, including religious institutions, must be a natural and valid option for women as well as for men. Ann Braude, in her essay "Religions and Modern Feminism," traces how women have gained a public voice through three waves of feminism that challenged the status quo beginning in the mid-nineteenth century. Until the 1980s a small group of middle class, white, Christian Western women had described their experience as "women's experience," failing to recognize that they were universalizing their way of life by applying it inappropriately to women in general. Over the last two decades, feminist studies have emerged across races and religions to demonstrate within each tradition a belief that there is no liberty for women unless there is liberation for other oppressed groups. Religious language of "conversion" to a feminist consciousness at the heart of women's faith traditions is common among them.

Gender is an essential category for analysis of how women's roles have been socially constructed, rather than divinely prescribed, throughout history. In her essay "Gender and Social Roles," Susan Hill Lindley describes the change that has taken place over the last third of the twentieth century as scholars have made the distinction between sex and gender. Prior to the development of gender analysis, social roles of women were understood to be naturally and divinely given, unchanging and unchangeable because they were determined by sexual biology. Women were seen as naturally nurturing, emotional, sensitive, and subordinate, while men were naturally active, rational, aggressive, and dominant. A focus on gender is essential from a religious viewpoint because roles, both descriptive and normative, are considered to be determined by God. Women were designed to be wives and mothers in the private sphere of life, while men were meant to function in the public world as the decision makers and governors in social, political, and economic institutions. Consequently, public roles of leadership for women had no place in God's unalterable plan; women were meant only to exercise indirect influence within the home.

In their essay "North American Women Interpret Scripture," J. Shannon Clarkson and Letty M. Russell advocate a method to interpret the sacred texts of their Christian tradition. Since colonial times, the socially designated interpreters of the Bible have been men in positions of power and leadership. This has resulted in a patriarchal paradigm of authority based upon domination, the sanction of men in power to interpret scripture for those dependent upon them: women, children, and slaves. Within the last thirty years, women in the Jewish and Christian traditions have claimed their right and voice to interpret scriptures out of a new feminist paradigm based on authority within community. Women in other faith traditions in North America, including Muslims, Hindus, and Buddhists, have begun to take the lead in their religious cultures to interpret their own sacred texts. Women gather in community circles to interpret scripture and to advocate for the full humanity of all persons, not only oppressed women, because of their race, ethnicity, sexual orientation, or physical disability.

Mary Farrell Bednarowski describes a complementary analytical approach as "Women's Religious Imagination," in her essay by that title. This imagination finds inspiration through women's own life experience and in the substance and symbols of their own religious traditions, including scriptures. Women's religious imagination produces many varied fruits: world views, rituals, beliefs, moral codes, narratives, institutions, and spiritualities about the meaning and nature of life. Only recently has attention been given to the relationship of gender to religious imagination, leading women to ask what it is about being a female that awakens or inhibits that creative force within them. Historically, women's religious imagination has been powerfully motivated by their insider/outsider status: insiders to religious traditions and institutions by their greater numerical presence and indirect influence over men and children,

outsiders who were denied power and not allowed to discover their own voices and distinctive experiences. Religious imagination has provided women strategic insight to overcome restrictions on their full participation in communities, given them flashes of insight to perceive the oppression they have long experienced, and led them to an "elaborative imagination" to construct new visions for a just and loving world.

The issue of justice is at the heart of Marilyn J. Legge's approach to "Social Ethics, Women, and Religion." Her approach emphasizes, first, that a person must take charge of her or his own life, by affirming the God-given power and potential to seek one's own good. Secondly, a person must commit oneself to transform oppressive structures affecting human relations and the social order. Religious women have engaged the great social questions of their day by giving attention to women's lived experience and seeking justice in shared respect and power for and between women and men. Feminists, within Christianity and inter-religiously, have asked similar kinds of questions that focus, first, on their empowerment and second, on their faith commitment to the world. From a social ethics standpoint, feminists are concerned about what kind of people women ought to be; how meaning in their lives is constructed; whose interests they are serving; and what kind of world is envisioned for women and their communities.

A social analysis of women's rights and purpose must be held in healthy, fruitful tension with female psychic identity, as Ann Belford Ulanov develops in "The Psychology of Women's Religious Experience." Through the lens of the psyche, the study of the soul or spirit, she focuses on new trends in depth psychology and women's religious experience. Ulanov probes to find a theology that grows directly out of the feminine experience, not to construct a theology of the feminine. There is no one route by which women experience God, but there are common qualities at the heart of the spiritual journeys of females of diverse races, cultures, and circumstances. Women need to accept their religious experience as gendered, while rejecting the inherited sexism of submission and second-class status culturally assigned to women. They should embrace the essential connection between the soul and the body and affirm their emotions as necessary at the heart of their passion for personal and social justice. Finally, they need to understand that religion is rooted in the personal and is incarnational in relationships with God and other persons in the midst of all the ambiguities of life. Such a theology of the feminine can lead to an experience of resurrection: an invasion of God's grace into the ordinary round of life that delivers one from old solutions that no longer work.

Rosemary Skinner Keller's essay "Women's Spiritual Biography and Autobiography" concludes this encyclopedia's introductory overview of approaches to the study of women and religion. Understanding vocation to be at the heart of one's spiritual journey, she focuses on the vocational journey of Georgia Harkness, the first woman who was a professional theologian to teach at a seminary in the United States. Through episodes in Harkness's life, Keller makes the point that people may experience closer "vocational kinship" with persons with whom they experience commonality in spiritual journeys than with their own blood kin. Many writers in the encyclopedia incorporate biographical sketches into their essays. This article provides categories and an example of calling, career, and community to probe the spiritual and vocational journeys of one woman and of our own autobiographies. The themes developed in detail by other contributors to this section emerge in this essay's descriptive accounts of the relationship between one woman's personal spiritual identities and commitments to justice in religious and other social institutions, along with a feminist, gendered analysis of her life. Readers will not necessarily find identity with this particular woman, but guidelines to experience and interpret vocational kinship with countless other women in this volume and beyond.

II. Women in Native American, Aframerindian, and African Caribbean Religious Traditions

Even though the section of the encyclopedia on women in Native American, Aframerindian, and African Caribbean religious traditions comprises only six articles, historically they take priority over Catholic, Protestant, and Orthodox forms of Christianity, as well as Judaism, Islam, Asian religions, and Newer Religious Movements. Native Americans as the "first nations" of the Americas existed for thousands of years before European colonization in the sixteenth and seventeenth centuries. This priority needs to be recognized as such, even though their numbers have dwindled to less than 2 percent of the population of North America (itself the expression of a five hundred–year process of physical and cultural genocide). Those who turn to this section of the encyclopedia expecting colorful descriptions of customs, beliefs, and rituals of the more than six hundred tribal groups, eight different language groups, and nine cultural areas will be disappointed. Our decision was to privilege Native American women's voices over those of cultural anthropologists from outside Native American communities, however valid the work of such scholars may be.

This concern to have Native American women speak in their own voice had certain results. Some of the essays commissioned were never completed. This absence itself speaks volumes. It testifies to the enormous difficulties Native American women have to overcome the handicaps of racism, poverty, and oppressive education, as well as multiple work roles in their communities, in order to engage in academic knowledge production. It also expresses the somewhat alien nature of such academic knowledge production to truthful presentation of Native American religious cultures. As Laura Adams Weaver makes clear in her essay "Native American Creation Stories," such stories are inseparable from ceremonial enactments in sacred sites. Stories in the context of ceremonies are intended to renew the affirmation of "who we are," and are distorted when they are turned into positionless accounts of "what they believe." Moreover many Native American foundational stories within ceremonies were understood as internal to the community, and even privileged knowledge of religious leaders. They were not supposed to be told to "outsiders." Sometimes Native American informants deliberately falsified the accounts of their stories to missionary and anthropologist inquirers to prevent wrongful appropriation by such persons.

Privileging the indigenous voice also means that the history of genocidal violence and abuse predominates in many of these essays. Although this history may be shocking to many non-Native peoples, it is integral to the Native American story as it was and is being told in the twentieth and early twenty-first centuries. This expresses not a stance of victimhood but of resistance. By documenting the stories of massacres, of constant breaking of treaties that promised some land base to Native Americans, the appropriation of more and more land by whites, cultural genocide in the banning of native ceremonies, and the forced assimilation of Native peoples through federal and church-run boarding schools, one gives voice to the silenced cries of a people. This documentation lays the basis for protest, resistance, and the call for reparations, vindicating indigenous claims to autonomy and sovereignty and the renewal of submerged languages and cultures.

Kim Stone's essay "Native American Women and Christianity" describes the high level of parity of Native men and women in pre-colonial cultures and the concerted efforts to subordinate Indian women to Indian men, as well as to white society, by white colonialists and missionaries. Female divinities in Native cultures were systematically suppressed by those who sought to "Christianize" indigenous peoples, even though most Native cultures saw the cosmos and their own people as originating with a primal mother or pair of male and female deities. Matrilineal patterns were altered for patrilineal inheritance and lineage, women chiefs and leaders discounted, and Indian social structures changed to conform to Christian male dominance. Nevertheless Indian women have sometimes found ways to adapt Christian symbols to native cultures and to use Christian service institutions to aid them in their struggle for survival.

In the essay "American Indian Boarding Schools," Andrea Smith describes the brutal alternative to physical extinction of Native Americans through war and massacres; namely, forced cultural assimilation. By taking children away from their parents at an early age, making them stay in schools or with white families until early adulthood, washing their mouths out with soap if they spoke their own languages, and preventing them from learning from their elders, whites hoped to obliterate indigenous cultures and turn Native Americans into a lower class labor force within white society, doing farm labor or domestic service for white households. These schools did worse than this. They were often marked by physical and sexual abuse, malnutrition, and neglect of health, creating both early death and also a pattern of social disfunctionality that was carried over into Indian societies as the children raised in such schools returned to their own communities as adults.

Smith's essay "Appropriation of Native American Religious Traditions" expresses a key area of protest among Native Americans today against what they see as the latest assault in the long tradition by which whites sought to exterminate Indians physically and culturally, while at the same time "playing Indians" by imitating Indian dress and styles of life as hunters and warriors; appropriating cultural traditions, such as sweat lodges and vision quests; and claiming to teach esoteric traditions conveyed to them by some unnamed or fictitious Indian sage. As Smith makes clear, it is not that American Indians reject white interest in their culture, but such interest must be expressed in a manner of authentic respect. This means joining with Native Americans in their struggle to survive, not appropriating their traditions for fun and profit.

Patrick Neal Minges's essay "Religious Exchange in Aframerindian Life" tells the fascinating and largely unknown (in white U.S. history) story of the intermarriage, cultural exchanges, and mergers that took place from the sixteenth through the nineteenth centuries between Native Americans and Africans. Fleeing from slave ships and plantations, African slaves often found refuge in Indian communities, where they found both welcome and a congenial culture similar to their African traditions. To replace fallen Indian braves, African men were adopted into tribes and married to Indian women, whose matrilineal traditions made the offspring of such unions full members of the tribe. When whites defined all Indians and blacks east of the Mississippi as slaves, and removed Indians to territories west of the Mississippi, Aframerindians chose to go with their Native kin to avoid re-enslavement. Thus these two marginalized and exploited peoples of North America often have an unknown common history. In many an African American lineage there lurks the Indian grandmother.

Finally, Dianne M. Stewart's essay "Women in Afri- can Caribbean Religious Traditions" turns to the history of the islands of the Greater and Lesser Antilles where Native and African peoples also merged and mingled, but in a way that submerged the Natives beneath what became a predominantly African-descended population. These peoples brought with them African religious traditions that continue to define the religious cultures of black Caribbean peoples, both directly, as African-descended traditions, and by reshaping the Christianities brought to these regions by missionaries. A third tradition of post-Christian traditions, such as Rastafarianism, represents an African-identified protest against white dominance. This enlightening chapter provides a transition from Native to African traditions in the Caribbean, and provides vital background for much of the work in this encyclopedia on black Christianity.

III. Women in the Protestant Christian Traditions

"A full-throated presence wherever their worship community's witness is heard" is the goal feminist Protestant women have sought for their lives, their sisters, and other minorities who have been deprived of voices in the religious communities, denominations, and movements of which they are a part. Cynthia Grant Tucker applies this vision specifically to Unitarian Universalist women, declaring that it was implicit in the principles of their liberal religious tradition since the denominations' seeding in North American colonies in the seventeenth century. She recognizes further that even in the Unitarian denomination the "founding fathers, blinded by the prevailing myths of male privilege, failed to see . . . the concept that all persons had equal worth and the right to express themselves freely . . . also applied to their mothers, wives, and daughters" (Tucker, "Women in the Unitarian Universalist Movement"). To varying degrees, this statement describes the experience of women in all traditions in the United States and Canada, whether liberal, mainstream, or conservative, as they have sought to claim rightful presence of voice and leadership in North American churches and society.

This encyclopedia's extensive descriptions of women's experience provide the particularities of their in-depth experience in each Protestant Christian tradition. (The reader will note that the essays referenced below appear in various parts of the encyclopedia.) However, Tucker's words invite the questions and themes that frame the broad evolution of religious women's experience in Protestantism over four centuries in North America. What have been the boundaries and barriers that have constrained women's active presence and leadership in church and society? How have these boundaries been stretched and even broken down? How have women taken initiative and responsibility for their own lives? How has religious faith been empowering for women?

The interpretation of sacred texts provides the foundation for divine and social sanctions about women's roles in church and society. Hebrew and Christian scriptures have been both limiting and liberating for women in North American Protestantism since the founding of the American colonies in Massachusetts and Virginia. Feminist scholars of the past thirty years have emphasized that all interpretations are biased. The dominant theological interpretations in a society are developed by those in power and are rooted in their social location, class, gender, and race.

Drawing upon New Testament texts, such as I Timothy 2:11,12 and I Corinthians 14:34,35, both of which admonished women to be silent in church and submissive to men, Puritan fathers followed the patriarchal tradition they brought from Europe that prohibited women from speaking and preaching in churches and from exerting authority over men. Prescriptions for proper female conduct by colonial women were basically the same for women throughout the American and Canadian colonies. The home was the "Little Church," where the wife was under her husband's authority, shared in supervising children, servants, and slaves, and was the primary religious educator. The image of the good colonial woman was well portrayed in the words inscribed by her husband in 1675 upon the tombstone of Lucy Berkely, a member of the established Church of England in the South: "She never neglected her duty to her Creator in Publick or Private. She was Charitable to the poor; a kind mistress and indulgent mother & obedient wife" (Lyerly, "Southern Colonial Protestant Women," also see Cook, "Women in the Anglican Church in Canada"; Hirsch, "Protestant Women in the Mid-Atlantic Colonies"; Clarkson and Russell, "North American Women Interpret Scripture").

From the same early decades of colonial settlement, small groups of women reading Christian scriptures out of the liberating tradition of Galatians 3:28 and Titus 2: 3–4 found courage to speak in their own voices in church and society. The examples of Ann Hutchinson and Mary Dyer illustrate the types of bold leadership Protestant women have sought over four centuries to speak and lead in public, confident in their God-given gifts and right to freedom of speech. Ann Hutchinson was banned from the Massachusetts Bay Colony in the 1630s because she claimed the authority of the Holy Spirit to interpret scripture and teach men and women in her home. Mary Dyer, one of the first Quaker missionaries sent to Massachusetts from England, was first deported and then hung in the Boston Commons because she persisted in seeking to convert people to her

Quaker faith (Larson, "Women and Protestantism in Colonial New England"; Zikmund, "Women in the United Church of Christ").

During the seventeenth century there was little effort to spread Christianity among slaves and to baptize them. White colonists feared that God did not approve of slavery and that baptism would grant slaves full personhood, necessitating their freedom. Further, slaves clung to native African beliefs and were not interested in joining a church that permitted slavery. As true between white women and white men, black women were more responsive to Christianity than black men, perhaps out of the hope that the Christian faith would benefit their families and themselves. Further, the style of worship and theology of revivalism was more appealing to African Americans than was the more formal Church of England. The evangelical style of revivalism stressed conversion as a singular momentary experience, not a lengthy, slow process. Revival songs embraced emotion and body movement, more in the character of their African religious experience (Harris, "America's Evangelical Women"; Martin, "Women and African American Denominations"; Kirk-Duggan, "African American Hymnody"; Lyerly, "Southern Colonial Protestant Women").

The revivals of the First Great Awakening in the 1730s and 1740s, followed by the Second Awakening in the early nineteenth century, were strongly grounded in the conservative and liberating consequences of the colonial experience. Among its liberating effects, revivalism began to break down the rigid boundaries constricting both white and black women's public roles. Central to the revival faith was the belief that the immediate work of the Holy Spirit in one's conversion experience gave each individual the power to discern the state of her or his soul, without aid of clergy, a doctrine heretical to the early Puritans. Many women of the Church of England embraced this "New Light" revivalism initiated in the Presbyterian Church. Other strong voices of revivalism came from the Separatist Baptists, who were formidable foes of the orthodox Church of England in the South and opened liberating doors to women. Within self-governing congregations where members developed their own articles of faith, particular Baptist churches allowed women to vote and to hold positions as elderess and deaconess. Some congregations also opposed slavery and showed more respect to women and slaves, enabling them to participate freely in worship services (Lyerly, "Southern Colonial Protestant Women").

The nineteenth century was the era of evangelical dominance in North American religious culture, emphasizing personal conversion, the fruits of the spirit, and religious activism, along with social responsibility for the poor and oppressed. Such theological grounding provided a strong base to encourage women to pursue ministries of their own. This meant, first, that women focused on their role as spiritual nurturers of men and children in the home. However, it also empowered them to share the gospel, going out of their homes both to bring persons to Christ and to improve the material lives of those in need.

By the early nineteenth century, the "true woman" and the "new woman," two contrasting gender roles of women grounded in the theology and experience of the colonial period, emerged and have characterized the constriction and expansion of women's place in church and society ever since. The true woman was primarily seated in the home. Her four defining qualities were domesticity, purity, piety, and submission to her husband and to other male authority figures. Her function of "republican motherhood" was to train the men of her life—husbands, sons, and brothers—in religious and ethical precepts to make them worthy public leaders in the new age of industrialization and urbanization. Her place in the church was similarly restricted. The true woman related in a supportive and submissive way to male authorities, whether clergy or lay. Leadership roles of preaching and ordination were beyond her boundaries.

The new woman began to come into her own by the second half of the nineteenth century, first as she emerged in secular society and then in the churches. She claimed public roles in denominations long designated as the sole province of men. Deaconesses, who were the first professional women in churches, claimed the initial distinction of being new women in Protestantism. However, the new woman was seen as one who primarily sought leadership conferred by ordination after the Civil War period.

The distinction between the true woman and the new woman could not be so neatly and clearly separated in practice. Most Protestant women did not overtly question that their primary functions should be in the home. Still, throughout the nineteenth century, they stretched the boundaries of the true woman's role, and, in time, some began to take their places as new women. Countless Protestant women brought together the rationale of true womanhood with their Christian commitments to make socially needed and personally meaningful contributions to churches and society. Through their volunteer activities, they began to gain voices of their own and to find wider spheres of purpose and usefulness outside their homes.

Formation of gender-separate societies of converted women seeking appropriate outlets for their spiritual energies began as early as the first Great Awakening in the mid-eighteenth century and steadily increased during the second Great Awakening in the early nineteenth century. Women organized within congregations and towns to study the Bible, raise money for benevolence and mission needs in their own local areas and in distant lands, and work for social reform in the name of their religious commitments. Missions became the earliest and most popular cause joining women together. In turn, women created community for themselves, social outlets and support networks enabling them to develop skills as teachers, evangelists, social workers, and even physicians, midwives, and nurses. By the 1830s peer groups, determined by age, ethnicity, race, and social standing were forming. These services were all consistent with women's maternal natures and natural extensions of their true womanhood. They were also appropriate responses to Jesus's command to go into all the world and spread the gospel (Keller, "Leadership and Community Building in Protestant Women's Organizations"; Robert, "Protestant Women Missionaries").

After the Civil War, women expanded their gender-separate groups, particularly for mission purposes, onto regional and national levels. First organizing inter-denominationally in 1861, women in all mainline white Protestant denominations in the United States and Canada, including Congregationalists, Baptists, Methodists, Disciples, Christians, Episcopalians, Presbyterians, Lutherans, and the Anglican Church in Canada, developed their own denominational societies during the final quarter of the century. Women in African American churches, particularly the African Methodist Episcopal, African Methodist Episcopal Zion, and National Baptist, also organized strong denominational separatist societies (see articles under part 4, "Protestantism").

Still consistent with the ideology of true womanhood, these women were not preaching in mixed groups, "promiscuous assemblies" as they were called. They were nevertheless breaking down the boundaries between true womanhood and new womanhood. While they sought to reach men as well as women in evangelizing for Christ, their mission outreach focused on "women's work for women" and children. White denominational societies raised money and sent female missionaries to India, China, and Japan. Black church women's organizations commissioned women to South Africa to teach native females to read the Bible, improve their health, and educate and empower them to fight against oppressive customs. Women in missionary and benevolence societies, both in world and home missions, were getting their first experiences of leadership: leading meetings, administering programs and vast financial resources, speaking and praying in public. They built schools, orphanages, hospitals, and dispensaries in North America and in foreign lands staffed primarily by women. By 1909, one in ten missionary physicians were female. Further, women developed evangelical partnerships with indigenous women. Women's societies supplied funding for three times as many native women to teach the Bible to their sisters as Western missionaries (Robert, "Protestant Women Missionaries"; Hartmann, "Women in Protestant Church Societies and Bureaucracies"; Keller, "Leadership and Community Building in Protestant Women's Organizations"; Harris, "America's Evangelical Women").

Since the late nineteenth century, Hispanic women have been active in missionary work in the United States. In the Baptist and Methodist churches they created a host of services, particularly for women and children: providing Christian education for persons of all ages, establishing clinics and relief agencies for families, raising funds for Hispanic students to gain a theological education, and advocating for women to be ordained and function as pastors.

By the 1880s, the deaconess movement became prominent in most Protestant denominations. Usually single, these women were the Protestant equivalent to Roman Catholic nuns. Taking vows of full-time Christian service, most became home and foreign missionaries as evangelists, teachers, medical personnel, and social workers. They lived in deaconess homes, wore special uniforms, attended training schools, and worked with the most needy in society. Becoming a deaconess may have been an acceptable substitute for some church officials and laity who did not approve of ordaining women. At the same time, the deaconess movement provided the first professional status for women in churches and invited them into full-time ministerial-type work (Jurisson, "The Deaconess Movement").

The lines between the true woman and the new woman blurred in the deaconess movement. Lucy Rider Meyer, founder of the Chicago Training School, the first deaconess home and training school in the Methodist Episcopal Church in 1884, wrote that the "the world needs mothering" and that the deaconess provided that caring function. She also defined the deaconess as the "new woman of Protestantism." Rather than justify this role within the more conservative prescriptions of the true woman, she noted the wide fields of professional work opening in secular society for women, including positions of physicians, editors, and hospital superintendents. "Her field is as large as the work of woman, and the need of that work," Meyer wrote. She also pointed out "that the 'new woman' is not an invention of the last decade" but goes back at least to Hilda, Abbess of Whitby (b. 614 A.D.) who founded a double monastery for monks and nuns, one of the best seminaries of its day from which six bishops of the early church came forth.[2]

The same blurring of purposes in training for deaconess work was found in the origins of seminaries and colleges for women, founded around the middle of the nineteenth century by Emma Willard, Catherine Beecher, Mary Lyon, and others. They were justified at their beginnings by the ideology of the true woman and republican motherhood in Protestant faith: a better education would enable women to create better homes. Stretching this ideology into the creation of the new woman, they emphasized rigorous academic study, development of leadership skills, and commitment to the Christian faith to prepare them to teach in Sunday schools and public schools and to enter missionary work. Further, women educators also encouraged their sisters to do advanced scholarly work and to train to become physicians. Finally, they provided an environment of sisterhood and support among pioneer women entering higher education. The earliest women's colleges, all of which were begun by churches and have become distinguished, included Mount Holyoke, Vassar, Wellesley, Smith, Bryn Mawr, and Radcliffe in the East, Rockford in the Midwest, and Mills in the far West (Hurty, "Protestant Women's Colleges in the United States"; Brereton "Protestant Sunday Schools and Religious Education").

"The new woman of Protestantism" was identified primarily as one who stepped forward to preach and to be ordained. The religious enthusiasm of evangelicalism in the Second Great Awakening opened the doors for individual women to preach in camp meetings and revivals, if not in regular worship services. No woman could find herself immune to criticism as a true woman after she spoke in any setting of a "promiscuous assembly." In the first half of the nineteenth century, women initially sought to preach, not to be ordained, contending that they had special gifts and extraordinary abilities that the churches needed. They were simply asking for the freedom to do what God called them to do. In 1796, Elizabeth, the first black woman who claimed a right to preach, described herself as ordained by God, not men, and no barriers were raised against her. Amanda Berry Smith, early evangelist in the Methodist tradition, spoke at revivals and camp meetings in the United States, England, and Africa, and converted countless persons to Christianity. Most of the early women who preached and witnessed to their faith identified with the Baptist and Methodist traditions, where questions of propriety were raised but their efforts usually were not blocked (Zikmund, "The Protestant Women's Ordination Movement"; Martin, "Women and African American Denominations"; Brekus, "Protestant Female Preaching in the United States").

The first woman to receive ordination to the ministry was Antoinette Brown in 1853. Ordained in the Congregational Church by a single congregation, she did not confront the denominational barriers of general conventions and synods that had laid down broad strictures by the latter half of the century. The difficulty of acceptance by the congregation she served after her ordination led Brown to resign after one year. Later in life she moved into the more liberal Unitarian Church. Olympia Brown and Augusta Chapin were the first to be ordained into a connectional church system, the Universalist Church, a decade later. Most denominational bodies are connectional, meaning that regional or national structures, rather than local congregations, set the conditions of who can be ordained. By the 1870s, the justification for ordination began to shift to that of the "new woman of Protestantism": women should be ordained because of God-given gender equality. Use of biblical texts and theological arguments for women's rights were employed after the first women's rights convention at Seneca Falls, New York, in 1854. Resistance was strong and most denominations would not approve ordination of women. Lone women can be identified as ordained by the African Methodist Episcopal Zion, the National Baptist, and the Methodist Protestant churches in the 1880s and 1890s (Zikmund, "The Protestant Women's Ordination Movement"; Martin, "Women and African American Denominations").

At the same time that women began to seek leadership through ordination and to build separatist women's communities within national church structures, the new women of Protestantism also entered the world of social reform. Some may have moved into social reform because they were denied the opportunity to preach, to be ordained, or to work alongside men in mission organizations and other lay governing bodies of the churches. They also saw social sins, including slavery, militarism, and drunkenness, as institutional evils and passionately desired to address these wrongs themselves. Out of a sense of duty as moral guardians of society and a conviction of their rights as women, they first sought to work in reform societies organized by men. While women were welcome to form auxiliaries or make donations to these male-led organizations, leadership was generally denied them. These conditions and motivations led to the formation of women's reform movements, socio-religious organizations outside the churches in which the leadership and much of the membership were women who understood reform work as an expression of their faith (Riggs, "Lifting as We Climb").

The anti-slavery and abolitionist movement became the first cause that led women to organize through creation of the Anti-Slavery Convention of American Women in New York City in 1837. They justified abolitionism by their reading of the precepts of God's will in the Christian scriptures and their own participation in a political and public cause as a religious and moral imperative placed upon all people. Black and white women participated and established the immediate connection of slavery's abolition to women's God-given right to a public voice in plenary presentations. Women who became prominent reform leaders gained an initial experience of leadership at this convention. However, the interracial vision of the conference broke down and set the pattern for the future in two negative ways. First, the opportunity for black and white women to work together did not hold. The first women's rights convention in Seneca Falls, New York, eleven years later was attended only by white women. Second, the right of women to present their cause publicly was immediately challenged when clergy of the Congregational Churches declared the Grimke sisters' public defense of abolition to be a misjudged and ungodly action (Speicher, "Antislavery, Abolitionism").

The initial peace societies, which began as early as 1815, did not admit women to membership but only to auxiliary functions. The first organization to be open to women was the New England Non-Resistance Society, initiated one year after the 1837 women's anti-slavery convention. Women who became leaders in the women's rights and other reform movements gained training here. Women's pacifist groups also formed. Almost every major reformer in the women's movement worked for peace as one of their Christian reform missions (Ziegler, "Women and Peace Movements in North America").

Both in Canada and the United States, the heyday of volunteerism in social service and social justice movements came after the Civil War when the Social Gospel, a new theological perspective in both evangelical and liberal Protestantism, gained pre-eminence. Out of their recognition of the sinfulness of social systems and individuals, the Social Gospelers sought to establish the "Kingdom of God" on earth. Political, economic, and social institutions had to be converted. Traditional views of the movement have cast male clerics as leaders, placed women in their familiar roles as givers of charity, and almost totally ignored the work of the African Americans (Lindley, "The Social Gospel").

However, women entered fully into the movement, experiencing their faith as an imperative for action and forming separatist societies through which to channel their action. Many of their emphases were reforms to benefit women and children, such as laws effecting working conditions and hours in factories and sweatshops, compulsory education, temperance, and low income public housing. Definitive women's organizations, which arose in Canada and the United States and combined religious and social objectives of the Social Gospel, included the Young Women's Christian Association and the Settlement House Movement (Denomme, "Abundant Life for All"; Stebner, "The Settlement House Movement").

The Women's Christian Temperance Union (WCTU) is a notable example of the socioreligious nature of a

Protestant women's Social Gospel organization. Begun in 1887, it became the largest women's organization of the era, with chapters and 200,000 members in Canada and the United States by the turn of the century. It was known as a "Crusade" and its members the "Crusaders." The WCTU published a journal entitled *The Call* that brought members in disparate far-flung locales together in a community of a sisterhood of reform. Temperance was its central reform, but with a change in focus from the salvation of the individual male drunkard to the socially sinful institution of the liquor trade and the damage inherent to wives and children. Its president and driving force, Frances Willard, moved the organization to a "Do Everything Policy," engaging members in a broad activist reform agenda, including issues of peace, the double sexual standard, women's health and dress reform, urban problems of poverty, and working conditions for women (Gifford, "Nineteenth- and Twentieth-Century Protestant Social Reform Movements in the United States").

The broadening scope of concerns pointing toward social commitments in the twentieth and twenty-first centuries is found in the work of women in the Social Gospel movement. Barriers of religion, class, and gender were often broken down or at least significantly shifted. Some Protestant organizations began to work cooperatively with Catholic and Jewish women. Alliances, however tenuous, were formed between middle-class reformers and working-class women in some movements. Women and men engaged in more effective partnerships in some programs for community improvement and political rights. Women were trained and grew in leadership skills through voluntary associations, setting the groundwork for women of the next generations to establish themselves in professional positions (Gifford, "Nineteenth- and Twentieth-Century Protestant Social Reform Movements in the United States").

Less success was gained in race relations. Most white women's reform movements reflected the same racist attitudes held by society in general. Many refused to admit African American women to their membership or allowed only branches of women of color. African Americans developed parallel societies of their own, in part because of exclusionary policies of white women's groups, but also because they desired and saw greater gain for their own purposes by organizing in black women's communities. The black women's club movement emerged at the turn of the nineteenth century within church denominations and on the secular scene at local and national levels. The National Association of Colored Women and the National Council of Negro Women were the largest and strongest secular societies that were also religious movements. They were formed in response to racial conditions of the day, a time known as the nadir in United States racial relations, and as an outgrowth of the general trend among women to organize at the end of the nineteenth century. In composition of members, motivation of leaders, and theological grounding in the black religious experience, these organizations represented the collective commitments of African American churches. Female leaders believed their clubs were called by God to challenge the evils of racism in society; understood their personal religious beliefs led them into vocations of social activism; and developed analyses which cut to the core of race, gender, and economic oppression (Riggs, "Lifting as We Climb").

Women in the Social Gospel movement gave notable services in the name of their Christian faith and democratic ideals. However, their leaders identified another purpose of immeasurable value to the women leaders and organizations themselves. Frances Willard wrote that the Women's Christian Temperance Union's most important work may have been reconstructing the ideal of womanhood. Women's organizations of the day upheld aspects of preceding generations' True Womanhood, particularly that women had a higher moral nature than did men and that they needed to expand their mothering role into the public and national scene. But also, they were avowedly grooming strong and independent women who accepted no gender limitations to their sphere of action. In the same vein, Vida Scudder, a major leader in the settlement house movement, stated that the movement might have been more vital for the residents than for the immigrant neighbors. White middle-class women, many among the early college graduates, found significant personal ties and professional opportunities essential to the meaning of the New Woman. The creation of these communities for women only gave them a sense of purpose and usefulness as they established roots in the wider public world. A community of women provided networks of support and vocational motivation for themselves that could no longer be found in their families of origin (Gifford, "Nineteenth- and Twentieth-Century Protestant Social Reform Movements in the United States"; Lindley, "The Social Gospel"; Stebner, "The Settlement House Movement"; Keller, "Leadership and Community Building in Protestant Women's Organizations"). The early decades of the twentieth century brought significant losses in the structures of separatist societies in churches that women had created in the latter half of the nineteenth century. Many denominations within mainstream Protestantism in the United States and Canada began to place women's boards of missions under the control of general boards of each church body. National women's missionary organizations were dismantled and forced to merge into larger church agencies. Restructuring was justified in the name of "efficiency" and as a progressive move to integrate women into wider church bureaus. The gains made in building autonomous networks of support among women, controlling expenditures of funds, and commissioning their own female missionaries to national and international sites, were lost or receded in most denominations (Hartmann, "Women in Protestant Church Societies and Bureaucracies"; Robert, "Protestant Women Missionaries"; Cook, "Women in the Anglican Church in Canada").

Two denominations provided notable exceptions, the Methodist and the Episcopal churches, in which women maintained control of finances while being fully integrated into wider mission boards. The Women's Division of the Board of Global Ministries in the United Methodist Church continues to maintain that independence and power today. In the Episcopal Church by the 1970s the administrative and financial control by women was undone and women's base was dissolved. The constriction of women's separatist societies in the second half of the twentieth century by church officials was attributed to the rise of feminism and the fear of women's ordination (Schmidt and Myers, "Methodist Women"; Thompsett, "Women in the American Episcopal Church").

After a century of agitation for ordination in mainline Protestant denominations, the barriers finally began to come down in the 1950s. Still, it took longer in relatively liberal denominations for women to be ordained than it had taken for women to gain the vote in national elections. Women received the vote, with passage of the nineteenth amendment, in 1920, seventy-two years after the First Women's Rights Convention in Seneca Falls, New York, in 1848. Comparatively speaking, women were granted ordination in the Methodist Church in 1956, seventy-six years after Anna Howard Shaw and Anna Oliver first sought to be ordained in the Methodist Episcopal Church in 1880. Two major African American communions granted ordination to women at the mid-twentieth century, the African Methodist Episcopal Church in 1948 and the Christian Methodist Church in 1954, followed by the Presbyterian Church USA in 1955, and the Methodist Church the following year. Two major Lutheran denominations, the Lutheran Church of America and the American Lutheran Church, approved ordination for women in 1970. In 1976, the Episcopal Church granted ordination at the discretion of diocesan bishops, and finally in 1997 mandated that women could be ordained in all dioceses. The United Church of Canada first ordained women in 1936 but a married woman was not ordained until 1965 (Zikmund, "Women in the United Church of Christ"; Boyd, "Presbyterian Women in America"; Martin, "Women and African American Denominations"; Trothen, "Canadian Women's Religious Issues"; Airhart, "Women in the United Church of Canada").

Women were more successful in gaining ordination in decentralized denominations in which individual congregations made their own decisions about who should be ordained. The Congregational Church, a predecessor of the United Church of Christ, ordained the first woman in Protestantism in 1853. Even in the conservative Southern Baptist Convention, approval for local congregations to ordain women was passed in 1964 and over one thousand women have been ordained since then. Leadership of the denomination became increasingly fundamentalist after 1979, refusing to approve women in positions of authority and strongly discouraging ordination (Zikmund, "Women in the United Church of Christ"; Blevins, "Baptist Women").

Female leaders for the rights of women in the churches have spoken out and challenged Protestant churches throughout the twentieth century, long before the feminist activism of the late decades. Madeline Southard, president of the International Association of Women Preachers, lamented in 1925 that the church was the last social institution to embrace the growing spirit of what she termed "sex-democracy" (Zikmund, "The Protestant Women's Ordination Movement"). Just over a decade later, Georgia Harkness, the first woman to teach in a Protestant seminary in the United States, described the church as the most impregnable stronghold of male dominance in society. Both were speaking out of their personal commitments to work for the ordination of women.

As late as 1977, only 17 percent of the clergy in the ten largest Protestant denominations were women. Over 50 percent of the women who were ordained by that date were in Holiness, Pentecostal, evangelical, and military styled denominations such as the Salvation Army. From its origins in the United States in the late nineteenth century, the Salvation Army fully commissioned women as preachers, pastors, and administrators, and deployed them to types of work, such as selling newspapers in saloons, which contradicted traditional norms of female behavior. The centuries-long tensions between the true woman and the new woman, as they have co-existed side-by-side in American history, have been striking and overt in the Salvation Army. In its early years, the Army sent forth two kinds of women's forces, women warriors and slums angels. Women warriors were exemplary of the new woman who was to use her talents in all spheres and ways needed by society and to vindicate women's equality with men. Slums angels were representative of the true woman, who upheld gender distinctions of feminine modesty and employed the motherly activities of nursing, cleaning, cooking, and caring for children in immigrant urban neighborhoods. At its outset, the Salvation Army embodied a revolutionary view of gender, pushing women's roles to the limits of equality. As the century progressed, continuity of the organization prevailed, causing the Army to adopt language that deployed women in more socially acceptable ways (Winston, "Women in the Salvation Army").

In the conservative arm of Protestantism, three movements arose in the late nineteenth and early twentieth centuries that struggled with the same tension between emancipation and constriction of women's roles. Pentecostalism, founded in its initial fervor in 1906, affirmed women as "Eleventh Hour Laborers" before the dawning of Christ's Second Coming. Women, along with men, were to exercise any spiritual gift for the conversion of the world and of individuals. The more fluid world of the early movement gave way to questions of authority and order as fledgling denominations grew up, and women's work became more constricted into roles supporting male preachers and pastors. In the Hispanic Pentecostal movement, Trinitarian Pentecostals have continued to be open to women as preachers and as leaders over men, while the Oneness branch has strictly limited women's participation to support of male leaders (Blumhofer, "Women in Pentecostalism"; Espinosa, "Hispanic Pentecostal Women").

Similarly, when fundamentalism arose at the end of the nineteenth century, particularly among Baptists and Presbyterians, some male leaders who believed in the imminent arrival of Jesus' Second Coming condoned female evangelists. However, the deeper conviction was an anti-feminist bias based upon belief in the biblical precepts of a divinely ordained gendered hierarchy prohibiting women to speak in religious assemblies or to exercise authority over men. By the end of the 1920s, fundamentalist male leaders were increasingly suspicious of women, realizing that women were not automatic allies in support of masculine dominance and female obedience. Resistance to women in leadership has continued throughout the century, as fundamentalism has equated women's issues with feminism and theologically liberal ideas (Bendroth, "Fundamentalism").

Arising in the second half of the twentieth century, the charismatic movement was a natural legacy of the Pentecostal and fundamentalist movements. Stressing the baptism of the spirit, issuing in spiritual gifts of healing and speaking in tongues, more women than men participated in the movement by a ratio of ten to one at its founding at mid-century. Male pastors immediately focused attention on developing and strengthening men's organizations, notably the Business Men's Fellowship International, a precursor of Promise Keepers. Women Aglow, now Aglow International, became the major women's arm of the movement. In language that sounds similar to that of the Puritan fathers, wives were to submit to husbands, pastors, and other men in leadership, not as slaves but through their gracious choice to adapt to male headship (Griffith, "The Charismatic Movement").

The tensions that have been at the heart of gender differences in North American Protestant churches since colonial times are still present today: spiritual equality vs. social inequality of men and women, male domination and female submission, and the models of the true woman and the new woman. Women and men of all denominations confront the realities of their everyday lives in ways that heighten these tensions as never before. No matter what theological perspective a woman and man may hold, more women work outside the home than ever before, some in highly successful career positions in which they hold authority over men. In turn, they send their children to day-care centers, and husbands and wives share in care of their children in ways not experienced even one or two generations ago. The old paradigms are breaking down at all places on the continuum from conservative to liberal allegiances.

The ideology of the new Religious Right and the neo-evangelical sub-culture today, which continues to stress the ideal woman as committed to being a submissive wife, nurturing mother, and deferential church member, directly clashes with the daily experience of the majority of its female adherents. Too, women in conservative as well as liberal congregations, in both Canada and the United States, today acknowledge the background and present experiences of divorce, single parenthood, domestic abuse, and drugs in their less than idyllic family lives. Further, the rise of women as ordained pastors, preachers, and evangelists across the spectrum of Protestantism directly affronts and challenges the doctrine of female submission men and women continue to hold, some more overtly than others (Olson, "New Religious Right"; Blumhofer, "Women in Pentecostalism"; Harris, "America's Evangelical Women"; Griffith, "The Charismatic Movement"; Trothen, "Canadian Women's Religious Issues").

Conservative forces, among women as well as men, in the Religious Right remain strong. Home schooling provides a notable example. Two million elementary- and secondary-age children, representing one million households, are educated at home today, with mothers being their major teachers. Rejecting public school education because they believe it is based on secular humanism, home schoolers revive the concept from colonial American times that the home is a little church or seminary in which good academic education and religious training are inseparable (Carper and Ray, "Conservative Christian Strategies in Education").

At the same time, women are gaining their own voices and making striking breakthroughs in churches early in the twenty-first century. In conservative denominations, such as the Disciples of Christ, the number of women clergy continues to grow, even though most are associate pastors. One-third of the students in Disciples schools are women in Master of Divinity programs. At the far left of the continuum, the number of women in ordained and lay leadership positions in Unitarian and Universalist churches has slightly surpassed men, and the ratio of women to men studying in the denominations' divinity schools is three to one (Long, "Christian Church/Disciples of Christ Tradition and Women"; Tucker, "Women in the Unitarian Universalist Movement").

As have African American churches, Hispanic/Latino congregations are creating public space to resist cultural domination by predominantly white churches and social institutions. In the Evangelical movement among radical United States Hispanic Protestants, women take their places beside men in resisting ways of preaching, worshiping, and believing that white Protestant churches have pressed upon them. They are seeking to sensitize and train conservative Hispanic Protestant believers to bring renewal to their churches and to improve life within their communities, particularly for the survival of children and families (Conde-Frazier and Martell Otero, "U.S. Latina *Evangélicas*"; Sauceda, "Race and Gender in Latina Experience").

In mainstream Protestantism, women are making steady gains in leadership. In 2000, the African Methodist Episcopal Church elected its first female bishop. In the United Methodist Church, of its fifty-one bishops, eleven are women and three are women of color. Thirty-six percent of its delegates to the 2000 General Conference were women. In the Presbyterian Church USA, a woman was elected moderator of the 211th General Assembly in 1999. Though women do not hold equal leadership with men in any denomination, there are few national offices that women have not held.

One of the most encouraging signs is the way in which women are taking responsibility for themselves, and gaining support of collegial males, to speak in their own voices, change long-held traditions that have excluded them, and move into leadership positions in churches, theological education, and society. The changing demographics of theological education today is a key barometer. Women now make up 35 percent of the students in the 243 North American schools of theology in Canada and the United States, compared to 10 percent in 1972, with similar increases in the Master of Divinity programs. One-half of these women are in evangelical and Roman Catholic seminaries, communions in which many cannot yet be ordained. With 25,000 women and 47,000 men studying in theological schools today, the 31 percent increase of women and 12 percent increase of men over the last decade establishes that the increase of women is rapidly outpacing that of men. The number of women in faculty positions and top administrative positions of president and dean has also increased,

though not at the same pace as that of students. Too, the Association of Theological Schools has supported initiatives related to "Under Represented Constituencies," primarily racial and ethnic, and "Women in Leadership" in theological schools over the past decade (McLean, "Women in Theological Education").

Among Asian Pacific American Protestant women, Chinese and Korean women organized among themselves at the turn of the century to support solidarity with their nationality groups in the United States and women's rights within Korean and Chinese groups and in American society at large. More recently, Asian American women have stood out as leaders advocating social justice for women and their nationality groups (Brock and Kim, "Asian Pacific American Protestant Women").

A further encouraging advance is the way in which women are creating new forms of worship; they recognize that freedom and equality of women with men in religious institutions must be expressed in the most sacred space of worship. Countless groups of women at the grass roots level throughout the country have come together to develop countercultural worship services to those in which everything—leadership, decision-making, language and symbols—has been dominated by men. To express their own spirituality, women have developed experimental processes of worshiping together in new ways. The "New Feminist Ritual" movement is young but already changes have been introduced into some churches and synagogues (Walton, "New Feminist Ritual").

The use of inclusive language is another initiative championed by Christian and Jewish women to transform the English usage of language so that women and men, persons of color, handicapped individuals, gays and lesbians, and other persons excluded by traditional patriarchal patterns of language are fully and equally represented in words that name them. The movement for inclusive language has strong roots in mainline Protestant churches, including the United Church of Christ, Presbyterian USA, and the United Methodist Church, Episcopal Church, and American Roman Catholic Church, as well as the Metropolitan Community Church, demonstrated by resolutions passed in their governing bodies, educational materials, and use in churches' common life (Thistlewaite, "Inclusive Language").

In the last decades of the twentieth century and the beginning of the twenty-first, Christian-Jewish relations have been revolutionized, and Protestant women, along with Catholic and Jewish females, have been prominent in the changes taking place. A field of Jewish-Christian relations come into being: scholarly academic studies in Bible, theology, and history have unsettled conventional conclusions between the traditions. Agencies, institutes, and networks have been created. Churches and synagogues now offer joint study groups bringing lay people together for inter-faith discussions. While male office holders in Christian and Jewish institutions have overshadowed women in their public recognition, this new public field owes much to the contribution of women over the past several years. Women's commitment is advancing previously unknown reconciliation between the faiths (Boys, "Women's Contributions to Jewish-Christian Relations").

While Protestant women are making breakthroughs in churches and in Jewish-Christian dialogue at the turn of the twenty-first century, they are also stepping forth into public life to provide leadership for social causes in the name of faith. Their leadership echoes that of nineteenth-century women reformers, such as Frances Willard and Elizabeth Cady Stanton, and Freedom Fighters, including civil rights leaders of the 1960s. The context of their leadership is distinctly different, however. Earlier women reformers were grounded predominantly within a Protestant Christian culture, while modern progressive women work in religiously diverse and multicultural settings, including Protestant and Catholic Christian women along with Jewish, Muslim, Hindu, Buddhist, and broadly "spiritually directed" women. They can be found addressing complex social issues, including homelessness, poverty, HIV/AIDS, crime, and domestic violence. Many of these women of diverse faith traditions have found religious institutions to be inwardly directed and self-caring, and describe their commitment to social justice to be growing out of their broader religious callings or vocations. Their voices and actions come at a time when liberal Christianity as a whole has taken little public leadership in comparison to that of the Religious Right (Henderson, "The Public Leadership of Women of Faith").

Despite notable gains, the question remains how far the women's movement toward equality and inclusiveness in Protestant Christianity will go. Even as women find many doors open to them, old patterns of men in leadership and women in supportive roles continue to flourish in countless structures of local church congregations, church bureaucracies, seminaries, and other religiously related institutions. Further, drawing younger women into mainline church membership is increasingly difficult. More conservative non-denominational and fundamentalist churches are more aggressive and successful in bringing young adults into churches today, growing at more rapid rates than Protestant denominations (Hartmann, "Women in Protestant Church Societies and Bureaucracies"). Too, many younger women and supportive men take for granted the gains in churches and society that have been made, do not realize the struggles that enabled this progress, and fail to rec-

ognize that without continued commitment and diligence by their generation the new day for women will fade. History is marked by steps forward and steps backward, and this cycle could repeat itself in relation to women in Protestantism today.

IV. Women in Catholic and Orthodox Christianity, and in Jewish, Muslim, Asian, and Newer Religious Movements

Virtually all religions depend heavily on the contributions of women to maintain the religious tradition, even if these are largely invisible from the perspective of its officially credentialed leaders, priests, ministers, teachers, and organizational authorities. Women not only birth the children who are to carry on the tradition, but are the first to introduce these children to the prayers and beliefs of the tradition through observances in the home. For Catholics, this has meant saying the rosary, hanging holy pictures or a crucifix on the wall, perhaps creating a home altar. Home altars have been typical of some Catholic ethnic groups, especially Hispanic women (Rodriguez, "Latina Popular Catholicism").

Jewish women have had major roles in the home in both encouraging men and boys to fulfill their responsibilities for prayer and study and also in keeping the purity laws, a kosher kitchen, and in preparing the festival breads and other foods key to a Jewish home. They also wash and wrap the body in preparation for burial. In Islam the home is the primary space for women, who are largely excluded from the public arena. This is also the place where women can relax with one another. Hindu women also gather in a separate space in the home for female puberty rites, wedding preparations, and prenatal and birthing rites. Other domestic duties include keeping a home shrine where lamps are lit and incense, prayer, and food are offered to the deities; organizing votive rituals; and preparing for feasting and fasting festivals (Narayanan, "Hinduism in North America").

Buddhism traditionally was divided between laity and monks. Since monks were almost all male, women's religiosity lay outside the practice of meditation and philosophical teaching associated with monks. Monks are dependent on the laity for economic support. It is women who are the donors, and givers of food that feed monks, as well as the keepers of home altars and reciters of daily prayers that belong to lay Buddhism. Since Buddhism has been studied by Western scholars primarily in terms of the intellectual systems of monastic life, lay Buddhism, where almost all women lived their religious lives, has been largely invisible (Gross, "Women's Issues in Contemporary North American Buddhism").

Christians are accustomed to thinking of the local religious institution, such as the parish church, as being a virtual extension of the home where women play the major support roles. Women clean the building and arrange the flowers, care for the linens, teach Sunday school, and hold suppers and bazaars to raise money for the parish. Catholic women did such work as members of the Altar and Rosary Societies, although many such groups became primarily social gatherings. They also gathered in women's or mixed groups as members of sodalities (associations focused on particular devotions, such as the Sacred Heart). But much of this work of women in parishes is recent even among Christians— eighteenth century—and reflects the development of the parish church, not simply as a place where one goes to passively attend rituals performed by male priests and ministers, but as a community center.

This kind of women's work in parish churches, established as traditional by Protestant churches, and later by Catholic churches, then tended to become standard for other religious groups whose local institution did not usually function in this way. This development of the synagogue, mosque, temple as community centers is impelled not only by imitation of Christian institutions, but also by the need of minority religious groups for survival and resistance to assimilation by dominant North American Christianity. Fashioning the synagogue, temple, or mosque as a community center becomes a means of preserving both religious and ethnic identity for minority communities that have been displaced from settings where their religion and culture were dominant.

Thus Greek Orthodox churches become places not only for liturgy but also to teach Greek so that the children do not forget their national language. Likewise Buddhist temples become places where Japanese or Chinese is taught to children in danger of losing their ethnic language and identity. Celebration of traditional festivals with special foods is another way the community keeps alive its distinct ethnic culture in North American enclaves.

Already in the early nineteenth century Jewish synagogues began to expand from being study schools primarily for men, where women had limited access, to playing a variety of roles designed to keep Jewish identity alive by recreating Jewish community. Mixed choirs that included women were allowed in nineteenth-century Reform temples, something forbidden in traditional Judaism. Libraries, fund-raising events, and weekend schools developed, with women as the primary organizers and teachers.

More recently Islamic mosques have undergone a similar development into community centers. Traditionally in Islamic societies women were not expected to attend Friday prayers and cannot enter the prayer space if they are menstruating. In North America the very definition of a mosque is expanded to include a community center accessible to women. Auditoriums are fashioned to be shared by men and women, school rooms added where women take responsibility for religious teaching, kitchens and dining rooms used for fund-raising suppers and festivals. Prayer is still gender segregated in most mosques, with women praying either behind men or in a balcony. In many cases women have a separate room, but this also allows women's prayer leaders (Mattson, "Women, Islam, and Mosques"). Gender segregation in religion has an ambivalent effect on women. It can be experienced as an exclusion of women from the more valued male functions and roles, or it can be experienced as a women-centered space where women are in charge of their own religious life.

Buddhist monasteries and Hindu temples likewise have expanded their roles. In the Pure Land Buddhist tradition, a lay Buddhism has fashioned community centers that often function much like churches in North America. Again women care for the space, arrange flowers, prepare for festivals, and may be the primary religious school teachers for children. With married rather than monastic leadership, the wives of Buddhist ministers sometimes play key roles as counselors for women, developing organizations and social services for women, children, and families (Tabrah, "Religions of Japanese Immigrants and Japanese American Communities"). Similar developments bring new roles for women in Hindu temples in North America.

Women's prayer or social service organizations begun on the parish or local community level soon expand to regional, national, and even international levels. In the process women's organizational skills and roles expand from the home to the local community to the larger society without ever directly challenging women's "traditional sphere" as defined by the religious culture.

Following the lead of Protestant churches, Catholic lay women began to develop benevolent societies that initiated outreach to the poor and the morally "fallen." Prayer groups, such as sodalities, also drew women into inter-parish organizations beyond the local level. Such development of social service organizations was limited for Catholic lay women by the existence of highly organized and active women's religious orders that carried out most of this kind of work. From the eighteenth century into the 1960s the Catholic Church in America depended on women's religious orders, either imported from Europe or founded on this continent, to teach catechism to children, and to found orphanages, old-age homes, and hospices for the needy (Poirier, "Godmothers and Goddaughters"; Folk, "American Catholic Women, 1820–1900"; Sharp, "Determined Builders, Powerful Voices").

Nuns also were the major developers of hospitals and Catholic health services that still dominate much of the health services available in communities in North America. They also founded schools from the primary to the college level. Nuns were missionaries who spread Catholicism across the North American continent, following and ministering to unchurched Catholic immigrants as they moved west. This missionary work of women's orders expanded from North America to Asia, Africa, and Latin America in the twentieth century, with new women's orders, such as the Maryknoll sisters, playing a key role alongside Maryknoll priests (Dries, "American Catholic Women Missionaries, 1870–2000"; Schier, "Catholic Women's Colleges in the United States"). Only in the 1970s did the numbers of women in religious orders begin to drop in North American Catholicism and more and more educated laywomen began to take on roles as catechists, organizers of Catholic social services, and even missionaries.

Lay organizations for Catholic women and men above the parish level began to grow in the 1930s. The Catholic Worker movement gathered dedicated Catholic women and men into impoverished urban areas where they fed and aided the poor. From the 1950s the Catholic Family Movement trained lay couples to analyze their social environment and to seek transformative social involvement. Catholic Action brought Catholic youth, women and men, together, using the methodology of "see-judge-act." Catholic settlement houses, such as Friendship houses, brought enthusiastic young graduates of Catholic women's colleges into the cities to work with African Americans against the dominant racism.

National organizing of Catholic women did not always spring from women's initiative or embrace a progressive agenda. Organizations such as the National Catholic Council of Women developed after the winning of women's suffrage (mostly opposed by the Catholic bishops), intended to use Catholic women's new political influence to advocate for conservative "Catholic values" against birth control, secularism, socialism, and feminism (Campbell, "American Catholic Women, 1900–1965").

Jewish women in nineteenth-century America paralleled Protestant women's patterns to expand educational and social service outreach on the city, regional, and national level. Jewish women organized orphanages, outreach to immigrants, religious school movements, and hospitals. These institutions were designed to gather Jews together and prevent their assimilation into the dominant Christian society that was ready to provide them with their social services that carried an implicit if not explicit proselytizing intent. Organizations like the National Council of Jewish Women expressed both the exclusion of Jewish women from the Christian-dominated Women's Club movement and created an arena for Jewish women's national leadership. In the 1930s, some women's organizations became international, reaching out to the growing Jewish *Yishuv* (national community) in Palestine (Ashton, "Jewish Women's Service Organizations").

In recent decades American Muslim women have been developing national and international organizations. Some of these organizations respond to the pervasive hostility of the American Christian environment to Islam. They are designed to educate Christian churches, public schools, and communities about Islam and to overcome anti-Muslim religious bigotry. Other women's organizations respond to the abuse of Islam by militant fundamentalists, who justify harassment of women, forced veiling, and even violence, such as "honor killing," in the name of strict Islamic observance. The use of Islam for forced repression of Muslim women is opposed by arguing that such discrimination against women is contrary to the true nature of Islam as set out in the Qur'an. Thus Muslim women become both apologists for Islam in the larger community and defenders of women in the name of Islam within the Muslim community (J. I. Smith, "Women's Issues in American Islam").

Traditional patriarchal religions often allowed a space for exceptionally talented women to exercise religious roles through special charisms (spiritual gifts). Christianity allowed that women could be prophetic vehicles of God on occasion. Charismatic gifts, however, do not change the roles of women as a whole. In North American Catholicism women, often from a working class background, have claimed Marian visions and become the center of special veneration. Among Protestants, women have often functioned as charismatic revival preachers, although this did not readily translate into credentialing such women as regular ministers.

New religious movements often had a woman prophet as founder. Mother Ann Lee, founder of the Shakers, Mary Baker Eddy in Christian Science, Barbara Heinemann for the Amana Inspirationists founded their leadership on claims of prophetic revelations (Ruether, "Women in Communitarian Societies"). Mary Baker Eddy reserved the roles of Supreme Prophet and Leader to herself, choosing men to manage the institution. Women, however, have predominated as Christian Science practitioners, a role that depends on both training and healing gifts (Cunningham, "Christian Science").

Women leaders who claim revelatory experience have abounded in metaphysical movements, such as Theosophy, New Thought, and New Age (Wessinger, deChant, and Ashcraft, "Theosophy, New Thought, and New Age Movements"). Spiritualism, very popular in the second half of the nineteenth century in North America, typically made use of female, often youthful, mediums who were seen as passive vehicles for messages from the dead, including famous men (Gutierrez, "Spiritualism"). Afro-Caribbean religions, such as Vodou and Santería, center on spiritually receptive persons, often female, who become the vehicles of deities and ancestral spirits (Stewart, "Women in African Caribbean Religious Traditions"; Cardoza-Orlandi, "Vodou, Spiritism, and Santería").

Special charisms that give a sacred status to exceptional women are also found in Asian religions. In Tibetan Buddhism an American woman has been recognized by monastic leaders as a bodhisattva, a reincarnation of a great Tibetan teacher (Lavine, "Tibetan Buddhism"). Among Jains, a strict asceticism that avoids pollution and killing of any form of life is highly valued. Most of those who choose this ascetic life are female (Vallely, "Women and Jainism in North America").

The women's movements of the nineteenth and twentieth centuries have brought new challenges to the segregated gender roles of traditional religions. Seeking to enter seminaries and theological schools to train for ministry, women sought to change the rules of their religious organizations to allow them to be ordained. Protestants, as we have seen, began to make such overtures in the mid-nineteenth century. Catholics in North America began to organize to call for women's ordination in their Church in the mid-1970s, founding the Women's Ordination Conference. Despite the increasing vehemence of Vatican pronouncements that the ordination of women is both historically and ontologically impossible and not even to be discussed among faithful Catholics, the Women's Ordination Conference has continued to grow and even to become international (Fiedler and Pomerleau, "The Women's Ordination Movement in the Roman Catholic Church").

The priesthood for women also has been debated in the Mormon churches. The mainline Church of Latter-day Saints has rejected women's priesthood, insisting on complementary roles for women as wives, and excommunicates those who push to change the tradition. The Reorganized Church of Latter-day Saints has reflected more closely the developments in Protestantism and accepted the ordination of women in 1986, carrying out the first ordination in 2000 (Bushman, "Mormon Women"; Lester, "Women in the Reorganized Church of Jesus Christ of Latter-day Saints").

Orthodox Christians generally accept the view that women cannot be ordained a priest, although the Vatican arguments that the priest represents Christ and thus must be a male are in conflict with their own traditions in which the priest represents the assembled Church, not Christ as head of the Church (Karras, "An Orthodox Perspective on Feminist Theology"). The primary movement in Orthodoxy for women's ordination takes place around the restored female deaconate. This form of women's ordination to service, teaching, and assistance to the priest in baptism of women and visitation of the sick is well attested in the Orthodox tradition as late as the twelfth century and has never entirely died out.

Among Reformed Jews, recognition that women could be rabbis began in the mid-nineteenth century, although the practice did not happen until 1972 for the Reform tradition and 1974 for the Reconstructionist tradition. In the Conservative tradition the first ordination of a woman to the rabbinate took place in 1983. Thus Orthodox Judaism is the primary hold-out against this development (Goldman, "Reform Judaism"; Schwartz, "Tradition and Change"; Greenberg, "Orthodox Jewish Women in America"). Jewish women have also gained the training and been credentialed in other important congregational roles, such as cantor.

In the Buddhist traditions, ordained leadership is monastic. A highly advanced student is ordained by a monastic teacher as a lineage holder in a succession of teachers. When Buddhism was founded, women were reluctantly accepted into monastic life, although rules were set up that strictly subordinated nuns to monks. It was said that the very existence of nuns would cause a shortening of the historical existence of Buddhism. Nuns did not receive the economic support from the lay community on which monks depended for their existence. The result was that women's monastic orders died out in Theravada Buddhism and only marginally continued in Mahayana Buddhism, the two major groupings of Buddhism.

Thus organizing for the recognition of ordained women in Buddhism has focused on the restoration of women's monastic lineages. Since women traditionally did not enter monasteries, they had no opportunity to gain the training to be accepted as teachers. This pattern changed in the West where Eastern monastic teachers accepted both male and female students. This has allowed women, many of them converts to Buddhism, to gain the training and become increasingly accepted as teachers, abbesses, and lineage holders in the American Buddhist centers (Levering and Schireson, "Women and Zen Buddhisms"; Boucher, "The Way of the Elders").

Among Sihks, Jains, and Zoroastrians there is little push for women to become ritual leaders, although they are increasingly taking positions as organizers of community life. Among Hindus the ritual functions have to be carried out by a male of Brahmin caste. Since these priests are not seen as educated professionals and are defined by their ritual roles, the position is not highly valued for Hindu men and there is little interest among women in taking on this role.

Gaining credentialed leadership depends on first gaining the requisite education for such leadership. Since women were traditionally excluded from the theological schools that prepared men for ordained leadership, women had to first gain access to such schools. Already in the nineteenth century Protestant and Jewish women became the primary religious educators who taught the basics of the tradition to children. They often did so without formal training. Only in the twentieth century did religious education emerge as a trained profession for Protestant and Jewish women. For Catholic women, professional catechetical education has been primarily a development since the Second Vatican Council in the mid-1960s and is more and more in the hands of trained laywomen rather than nuns (Putrow, "Women and Catechetics in the Roman Catholic Tradition").

Jewish women have grown in numbers in Jewish theological schools, first to become teachers of children and then to obtain education for the rabbinate in those traditions that ordain women (Kaufman, "Women and Jewish Education"). Catholic women find their presence in Catholic diocesan seminaries contested but more welcome in seminaries run by religious orders. They are generally directed to take non-ordination degrees, and those who insist on taking the Master of Divinity, the ordination degree, are treated with suspicion. They are usually excluded from the *practicums* that train seminarians for sacramental roles, hearing confession, and saying mass, and only with reservation allowed to enter preaching classes.

By contrast, from the beginning of Buddhism in America, women convert Buddhists were able to gain training from monastic teachers without any organized efforts, since these teachers who migrated from Asia to the United States simply accepted women students because they assumed this was the Western custom.

Once women gain access to the higher education of a religious tradition, they soon become acutely aware of the teachings that inferiorize women and exclude them from ordained leadership and public teaching. This inevitably leads some theologically educated women to become feminist theologians, that is, to critique and seek to reinterpret patterns in the tradition that negate women as a gender group. For Catholic women (and Christians generally) this takes the form of questioning the literalness of speaking of God in exclusively male terms, of defining males as the normative human beings and privileged "images of God," of defining Christ's maleness as necessary to his representation of humanity, and the related argument that only males can represent Christ as priests. Soon Catholic women realized that the whole framework of traditional theology has to be shifted from an androcentric framework to one that is inclusive of both genders.

Orthodox Christian women generally do not feel it possible to reform the theological tradition in any way that would be defined as a modern change, but are able to reclaim patterns from the church fathers that offer a more inclusive view of God and humanity. Orthodox women cite the teachings of Eastern Church fathers, such as Gregory Nazianzus and Gregory Nyssa, who rejected gender essentialism for both God and humanity. God was said to be neither male nor female and able to be imaged as a female, although this was seldom done in practice. Likewise gender was not seen as essential to humanity, but an accident of fallen humanity to be shed as humanity becomes redeemed and assimilated into the divine nature as soul in a risen body. Thus, for Orthodoxy, there is no gender difference that prevents women from attaining equal holiness (Karras, "An Orthodox Perspective on Feminist Theology").

Jewish women struggle less with theory than with practice which defined the normative Jew as a male: for initiation rites (circumcision), puberty (bar mitzvah), and the counting of a quorum for a synagogue (*minyan*). This status of the male as normative Jew defines the very giving of Torah by God to male Jews only, and pervades the androcentric nature of Jewish laws. Thus feminist Judaism has taken the form primarily of devising equal rites for girls and women, for initiation, adult status, and the *minyan*, as well as arguing that women can observe the prayers traditionally demanded only of men (Plaskow, "Jewish Feminism"; Diner, "Jewish Women and Ritual").

Islamic feminist thought has concentrated primarily on the distinction between the actual text of the Qur'an, seen as infallible, and the later tradition of the laws that can been seen as possibly corrupted and unfaithful to the original revelation. Emphasis has been put on the creation stories, where men and women are defined as created equally by God. The second creation story where Eve is created from Adam's rib, the basis for Christian arguments for women's inferior and sinful nature, is lacking in the Qur'an. Thus Muslim feminists argue that much of the Islamic legal tradition that inferiorizes women has been based on borrowing this biblical story from Christianity and therefore this is an illegitimate development since this story is not present in the Qur'an.

Considerable argument both within Islamic and non-Islamic communities in the North American setting has focused on the mandate for Islamic dress for women. Arab feminists in Egypt and other Middle Eastern societies rejected the veil in the early twentieth century as an expression of women's subordination. But the adoption of Western dress by Muslim women now often is seen as an expression of a capitulation to Western lax sexual morality. Thus Muslim dress in public in the United States and elsewhere in the West is claimed by many Muslim women to be an expression of their religious identity, and a protection against sexual exploitation. Muslim women become acutely aware that they are subject to discrimination in schools and employment when they wear Muslim dress. Thus the wearing of Muslim dress without being discriminated against becomes a question of the equal rights of religions in the Western context (McCloud, "African American Muslim Women"; J. I. Smith, "Women's Issues in American Islam").

Buddhist women generally see Buddhism as "essentially" non-sexist in its core world view. Since Buddhism does not believe in a personal God, there is no male deity to privilege males as normative humans. There are both male and female images for meditational visualization, but these are not accorded the status of objective existence. Gender in humans likewise is seen as non-essential, in a tradition that sees the self as non-substantial; that is, lacking permanent being. Therefore there is no basis for according males higher status than females. Nevertheless Buddhism has taken on various religious arguments for gender discrimination, most notably the view that femaleness itself is evidence of bad karma due to poor conduct in a previous life that justifies bad treatment of women in this life. It is also argued that a woman's inferior bodily and spiritual nature makes it impossible for her to be enlightened as a female. Thus a woman must await reincarnation as a male to become fully enlightened. Buddhist feminists seek to contest these sexist teachings, reinterpreting them or discarding them as late accretions that do not reflect true Buddhism.

In addition to sexism within the religious traditions, non-Protestant religious traditions, each in different ways, struggle with the experience of religious, and racial-ethnic, discrimination within North America, historically dominated by white Anglo-Saxon Protestantism. In the nineteenth and first half of the twentieth century, Catholics felt the sting of anti-Catholic bigotry from Protestants that sometimes took the form of violence, such as the burning of convents or harassment of nuns on the street. Much of this overt hostility faded in the second half of the nineteenth century, but continued with pervasive assumptions that Catholics were not quite "American" until the 1960s, when John F. Kennedy became President.

Jews also experienced widespread anti-Semitism in America in job, housing, and educational discriminations, although never as viciously as in Europe (Prell, "Anti-Semitism").

Today it is primarily Muslims that feel religious and ethnic discrimination against their communities in the United States, ranging from a pervasive assumption that Islam is fanatical and culturally inferior to a stereotyping of Muslims as "terrorists," especially since the September 11, 2001, attacks on the World Trade Center towers and the Pentagon. In the wake of these attacks some Muslims or people thought to be Muslims, such as

Sikhs, were physically assaulted and even killed by other Americans assuming they were taking vengeance on "terrorists." Thus the right to be both Muslim and fully American is a key issue for Muslims.

Other religions, such as Buddhism, Sihkism, Jainism, and Hinduism, have been judged by Christians as lesser or even wrong religions not acceptable as "American" faiths. Some religious groups have also experienced historical discrimination based more on ethnicity and race than religion, most notably African Americans and Latinas, particularly Latinas of "mixed" ancestry that includes indigenous, African, Asian, and European. Native Americans have perhaps experienced the most severe discrimination, based both on being regarded racially as "savages" and the exercise of their religion forbidden as morally repugnant (A. Smith, "Appropriation of Native American Religious Traditions").

Thus many religious and ethnic groups retain memories of persecution and struggle with questions of being fully accepted in the United States in their own right. This means resisting the demands for assimilation to the white Protestant norm and the principled pursuit of an American identity in which there is no one normative race or religion, and all races and religions are accepted as equally American. Clearly this is a major revolution in American culture, and one that has only been partly understood in its full ramifications by most Americans of both larger and smaller ethnic and religious groups.

This question of the "right to difference" in one's religious and ethnic identity vis-à-vis white Christianity, also affects discourse among feminists of different ethnic and religious groups. Jewish feminists discern patterns among Christian feminists, as well as "Goddess" feminists, that reiterate anti-Semitic views of Judaism in feminist terms (Prell, "Anti-Semitism"). Both Womanist (African American) and *Mujerista* (Hispanic) feminists claim the need to form distinct groups and do anti-sexist reflection in their particular ethnic contexts, both because the men of their communities have failed to accept their anti-sexist critique, and also because white feminists have been insensitive to their differences (Townes, "Womanist Theology"; Isasi-Díaz, "*Mujerista* Theology").

Euro-American feminists, from the beginning of new-wave feminism in the late 1960s, have affirmed the principle that feminist critique is not just about gender hierarchy. Feminists must see gender within class and race and seek to overcome these inter-structured hierarchies of oppression (Tatman, "Euro-American Feminist Theology"). Yet African American and Latina women often find that, in practice, Euro-American feminists slip into treating "women's experience" as generic, based on their own class and racial identity, and fail to recognize the distinct experiences of women who come from different class and ethnic contexts. This myopia needs to be continually criticized in order to bring about a truly pluralistic consciousness of women's diverse realities.

More and more American women are emerging from a variety of religious and ethnic identities and gaining the education to speak authoritatively about their particular traditions. Women in diverse religions are becoming lay leaders, ordained ministers, and teachers in theological schools that train the next generation of ministers, priests, and rabbis. Yet there still remains a widespread inertia in the religious institutions that resists real change to include women as equals. In some cases this has taken the form of explicit backlash that vilifies feminists and feminism as "heresy" and even as "pagan." This sense that "the more things change the more they stay the same" in relation to religious institutions has led some women to despair of a real transformation of these institutions that fully overcomes sexism. For some feminists this is expressed in forms of separatism in which women develop their own religious assemblies where they can freely develop prayers and rituals that affirm them as women.

The emergence of separate women's worship communities has taken place particularly among Catholic and Jewish women. Catholic women have shaped the "woman-church" movement where they create their own feminist rituals, sometimes based on the Catholic mass, sometimes branching into new life-cycle rituals, such as puberty and menopause, or healing from different kinds of abuse (Hunt, "Women-Church"). Jewish feminists have been active in developing women's *minyanim* (gatherings) where they can do their own *Haggadad* (biblical interpretation) and develop feminist versions of traditional rituals, such as seders, or life-cycle liturgies (Plaskow, "Jewish Feminism"; Diner, "Jewish Women and Ritual").

Most of these separate feminist worship groups among Christians and Jews do not intend to break fully from their traditions, but rather to find a separate creative space for women that can exist alongside membership in the dominant institution. They may hope that developments in the women's groups may be absorbed by mainstream institutions. Some American feminist women, however, have felt the need to break with patriarchal religions entirely and to seek a women's religion untainted by patriarchy. Many of these women have turned to some forms of neo-pagan or Wiccan religions in the belief that patriarchy itself and its religious expression is a relatively recent development of the last six thousand years of human history. Prior to the emergence of patriarchy there existed matriarchal or egalitarian societies where women either ruled or were equal with men. These pre-patriarchal cultures worshiped a Goddess or a combined Goddess and God. It is possible to recover and/or rein-

vent this religious world view and practice today (Eller, "Ancient Matriarchies in Nineteenth- and Twentieth-Century Feminist Thought"; Fox, "Women in the Wiccan Religion and Contemporary Paganism").

Some forms of neo-paganism are exclusively for women (Dianic witchcraft), others believe that men and women can come together to worship the Great Mother and her son-consort in ways that overcome patriarchy and allow both genders to develop their full humanity. Such neo-pagan religions focus on life-cycle and year-cycle liturgies (i.e., summer and winter solstices, etc.) as well as liturgies of healing and personal affirmation. They typically see the Goddess as an immanent divine power permeating the earth or cosmos and make a strong connection between the redemption of humanity from patriarchy and the healing of the earth from ecological devastation. Some of these groups have become social activists who join with others in struggles against militarism and ecological abuse (Christ, "Rebirth of the Religion of the Goddess").

The notion that God is exclusively male, thus privileging the male as representative of God, is seen by post-Christian feminists as the central problem of patriarchal religions. Yet in theory few traditional religions actually see the divine as exclusively male. Judaism has seen God as above gender and able to be imaged as male and female. The Wisdom traditions imaged God as manifest in a female-personified Wisdom, and Jewish Kabbalah created a tetragrammaton of Father-Mother-Son-Daughter. Christianity likewise has claimed that God is not literally male. Residual traditions that image God as feminine, especially as Wisdom, remain in its tradition. Islam also claims God is beyond gender and does not include Father among its names for God. Zoroastrianism sees God as dual gendered, while Hinduism worships an array of male and female deities.

Yet the actual existence of these female-personifications of deity does not seem to have alleviated the patriarchal patterns of the religion. Some traditional veneration of the feminine, such as Catholic Marian devotion, even seems to reinforce male discrimination against actual women. Often when feminine images for God that exist in the tradition are revived today to create more inclusive language for God, such as the use of Wisdom in the Christian women's "reimagining" conference in 1993, this development is vilified by mainstream church leaders as heresy and paganism.

Thus the extent to which traditional religions can be either renewed or reformed to overcome sexist discrimination fully in theology and practice remains in doubt at the beginning of the twenty-first century, despite the extraordinary development of scholarship about women in all the religious traditions and the emergence of more and more women as credentialed leaders in many religious institutions.

The words of Catherine A. Brekus in closing her essay "Protestant Female Preaching in the United States" best bring together our effort in concluding this overview. She writes that because of the vast amount of work done in recent years to recover the history of women and religion, as evidenced in publication of this encyclopedia, we can now begin to "understand that the debates over women's religious leadership stretch deep into the American past, and they have been deeply inspired by the poignant stories of the women who went before them." In 2000, when Vashti McKenzie was elected to be the first female bishop of the African Methodist Episcopal Church, she explained,

I don't stand here alone, but there is a cloud of witnesses who sacrificed, died and gave their best.

Rosemary Skinner Keller
Rosemary Radford Ruether
August 2005

Notes

1. Kathryn Kish Sklar, "The Last Fifteen Years: Historians' Changing Views of American Women in Religion and Society," in *Women in New Worlds*, eds. Hilah E. Thomas and Rosemary Skinner Keller (1981), 52.

2. Rosemary Skinner Keller, "Laywomen in the Protestant Tradition," in *Women and Religion in America, Vol. I: The Nineteenth Century*, eds. Rosemary Radford Ruether and Rosemary Skinner Keller, 281, 282.

Part I

~

Approaches to the History of Women and Religion

WOMEN AND RELIGION: METHODS OF STUDY AND REFLECTION
Rita M. Gross

WHAT IS ROUTINE as we enter the twenty-first century—systematic study of and reflection about women and religion—was unheard of when the current senior scholars of women and religion began graduate training and careers. We, too, had been trained to use androcentric (male-centered) models of humanity and the generic masculine mode of language and research. If it occurred to us to inquire about *women* and religion, we were told that such inquiries were unnecessary; women were included in the generic masculine and therefore were already being studied. Alternatively, we were told that religion was something men did, so there were no data about women and religion we could study. If not put off by such answers, and we persisted in our inquiries, ridicule of our concerns was quickly followed by hostility and threats of loss of our careers.

But with the second wave of feminism afoot, the desire to study and reflect about women and religion could not be thwarted. The earliest publications, articles by Rosemary Ruether and Valerie Saiving and *The Church and the Second Sex* by Mary Daly, came out in the late 1960s. The first meeting of the American Academy of Religion (the professional organization of professors of religious studies) to solicit papers specifically on women and religion was in 1972. Literature about women and religion increased exponentially during the 1970s. By 1980, two landmark anthologies had appeared, one in each of the emerging subdivisions within the field. *Womanspirit Rising* (1979) gathered early writings of many of the most prominent feminist theologians. *Unspoken Worlds: Women's Religious Lives* (1980) is a descriptive account of women's religious lives in a wide variety of cultural contexts. Since then, study of and reflection about women and religion have only intensified and diversified.

To understand what is at stake, methodologically, in the field broadly called "women and religion," it is important to recognize that it encompasses two distinct subfields whose methods are quite different. If this distinction is not recognized, endless problems, both political and intellectual, are inevitable. On the one hand, the subject matter "women and religion" involves descriptive accounts of women's religious lives and roles, cross-culturally and historically. This enterprise is fact and data oriented; the only value that comes into play is the claim that one cannot understand a religion or culture if one studies only its men. The question of what women's religious lives and roles would be in a just and ideal world does not come into play when doing this

kind of research. On the other hand, the subject matter "women and religion" also involves critical analysis of what religions have said about women and the options they have offered to women as well as constructing alternatives that are more just and appropriate. Such work, often called *feminist theology*, is value laden and controversial. Like descriptive studies of women and religion, these critical and constructive reflections about women and religion are relevant for all religions, but they are often restricted to Christianity and Judaism.

However, both subfields owe their historical genesis to the second wave of feminism and depend on the same theoretical and methodological breakthrough that, though now commonplace, was difficult to envision in the early years of the study of women and religion. The early feminist critique of the field of religious studies was, in many ways, the first "postmodern" critique, although feminists have rarely been credited with this achievement. Simply put, the early feminists pointed out that universal ideas about "mankind" put forth by thinkers of the European enlightenment were, literally, about men. Women were only discussed as objects of men's curiosity, manipulation, or enjoyment, not as human beings who had lives and ideas of their own. Typically, men's religious ideas or ritual practices were described in great detail. The religious ideas or lives of women were almost never discussed, and their ritual practices were mentioned only when men required or allowed women's presence in their own ritual space. Furthermore, such descriptions were always from the men's points of view, never from women's. Yet on that basis scholars claimed to have described religion in its entirety and to be in a position to present universal claims about "mankind."

Very quickly, feminist scholars and thinkers labeled this construct *the androcentric model of humanity* and proposed alternatives. Coming to the insight that the received model of humanity within which scholars and theologians were expected to work was androcentric, not universal, was conceptually difficult, however. It involved a major paradigm shift, a major psychological reorientation, and relearning how to use the English language for the generation that first became conscious of androcentrism in our theories and our use of the English language. Eventually, this critique was fleshed out to consist of three main points. First, it was shown that androcentrism collapsed the human norm and the male norm, making what seemed to be the norm for men into the human ideal as well. Early studies in which people were asked to pick the ideal traits of an adult male, an adult female, and an adult human, sex unspecified, demonstrated that people usually said that the same traits that were desirable in an adult male were also desirable in an adult human, whereas they claimed that the opposite traits were desirable in an adult female.

NANCY AUER FALK AND RITA M. GROSS

Unspoken Worlds

Women's Religious Lives

The second wave of feminism stimulated the desire to study and reflect about women and religion. Anthologies of women's writing on religion, such as *Womanspirit Rising* and *Unspoken Worlds, Women's Religious Lives* became enormously popular. From *Unspoken Worlds, Women's Religious Lives*, 3rd edition by Falk/Gross. *Reprinted with permission of Wadsworth, a division of Thomson Learning.*

Second, because the ideal human and the ideal male were thought to be the same, it was assumed that one could study only men and achieve understanding of the human. Data about women were irrelevant to understanding the human because women did not conform to the human norm. Third, since men and women were not the same in all regards, women did need to be mentioned sometimes. But because they did not conform to the human norm, they needed only to be discussed as objects of some interest to normal humans—men—or as objects with whom men sometimes had interactions. Thus, women had the same epistemological and ontological status in androcentric thought as trees, unicorns, deities, and other nonhuman objects that needed to be discussed to make men's experience intelligible.

Consensus regarding a name for the corrective to the androcentric model of humanity was never achieved, although there is widespread agreement that inclusive models of humanity are needed. Phrases that gained widespread currency indicate well what feminist scholars and thinkers wanted instead of androcentrism. Regarding women as subjects within their own worlds, not merely as objects described and evaluated by the men in their worlds, became a dominant theme. Investigating how women were active players in their worlds, not

merely beings who were acted on by others, also became important for research on women and religion. Finally, whether we were investigating women of other cultures and other times or whether we were critiquing and reconstructing our own traditions, the claim that women had "named reality" and could "name reality" became a central theme. Women were not merely passive recipients of what others named for them; they also had opinions about reality, even if those opinions often had not been recorded. And in our own time and place, we definitely were not going to accept what we had been told about ourselves, history, scripture, deity, or ultimate reality by the men who had thought that androcentrism covered all the bases. We were going to see for ourselves, and we did.

However, despite its clear agenda, the movement to study and reflect about women and religion has encountered several serious methodological obstacles. The first obstacle involved a dispute over whether the *variety* of women's voices was being properly represented. This issue was especially serious in the theological wing of women's studies because most practitioners of that discipline had no significant cross-cultural study or experience. Some critics claimed that the rallying cry of studying "women's experience" had been co-opted by a small group of women, mainly white, middle-class, Western women, who were inappropriately speaking for women in general. What the early leaders of the movement to study and reflect on women and religion were saying did not ring true to many women from other racial, cultural, and economic backgrounds. This critique led to a great deal of diversification in the feminist theology movement in the 1980s, as black, Hispanic, Asian, and lesbian feminists wrote feminist theologies nuanced to represent their particular situation. In becoming more sensitive to racial, cultural, economic, and other diversities, however, feminist theology has lost its earlier sensitivity to religious diversity. Christian, and to a much lesser extent Jewish and pagan, women can get a hearing in feminist theological circles, but Muslim, Buddhist, and Hindu women, women from indigenous groups, and women from other small religious traditions often do not feel particularly welcome or comfortable at gatherings of feminist theologians. Despite the fact that frustration over not being included in the generic category "mankind" led to explicit study of women and religion, nevertheless, being fully inclusive of the variety of women's religious voices has been very difficult, and failures to do so have caused pain, frustration, and resentment on many fronts.

The second methodological obstacle is somewhat the opposite. Thoroughgoing postmodernism claims that feminist critiques of androcentrism and patriarchy are themselves an attempt at a necessarily flawed "grand narrative." There are only particularities, it is claimed, and so any attempt to claim that women's voices should be heard is itself nothing more than a universalizing and therefore false claim. On what grounds can it be claimed that the feminist project to bring women's voices into the mainstream is superior to, more valid, or better than the silencing of women's voices that has been more common throughout much of the world for many centuries? In that sense, the initial feminist project to overcome the false universalism of the androcentric model of humanity by showing that it does not apply to all humans has backfired. Stressing the particularity and variety of diverse human beings and human cultures, if taken to its extreme, gives no grounds for preferring feminist values to patriarchal values. Needless to say, very few people concerned with the study of and reflection about women and religion are willing to go to this extreme of postmodern thought.

Although historical origins and methodological problems are common to both facets of the field of women and religion, it is helpful to consider descriptive accounts of women's religious lives and roles separately from the normative, critical, and constructive discussions that are often labeled "feminist theology." As already stated, the enterprise of studying women's religious lives descriptively is fact and data oriented. The only value that comes into play is the claim that one cannot understand a religion or culture if one studies only its men. Separating descriptive studies of women's religious lives from feminist theology is strategically crucial for several reasons. Fundamentally, scholars in women studies can make very strong arguments that it is necessary to study the women of a religion or culture to have a better and more complete understanding of the religion under discussion. These arguments are completely independent of the preferences and politics of other scholars in the discipline. In other words, the project of descriptive women studies in religion cannot be rejected because of antifeminist beliefs on the part of some scholars in the field. To understand his subject matter, even an antifeminist scholar of religions would have to include data about women. Once this is understood, a large portion of the material studied in the broad field of "women and religion" becomes nonnegotiable data necessary to the field rather than a bone of contention between disagreeing segments of the theological world. In a certain sense, even what feminist theologians have been saying then also becomes data in the field, and their books must be read, whether or not the scholar or professor in question is personally a feminist. Because the discipline of women studies has so often been considered a political rather than an academic enterprise, it is important to remove it from the realm of personal preferences as much as possible and to emphasize its centrality to understanding the subject matter under discussion, beyond politics and personal preferences.

When studying women and religion descriptively, one may find oneself consumed by historical questions and the discipline of history, or one may find oneself more concerned about the present, whether in familiar or unfamiliar cultures and religions, pursuing questions familiar to the disciplines of anthropology and sociology. Each pursuit presents its own set of questions and problems.

In historical research, the main problem is that the records are often highly androcentric, and it can take great effort to ferret out information on women. Often one encounters four layers of androcentric record-keeping practices. First, at any given time, a religious community is more likely to keep records about its men than its women. Second, records about women of earlier times that may have been kept are often deemphasized by later generations of that religious tradition. Third, the Western scholarship on that tradition may well have studied primarily the men of the past. Fourth, contemporary practitioners of the religion being studied may well downplay the significance of women in their tradition when talking with scholars.

Nevertheless, after a scholar experiences the transformation of consciousness that occurs when the inadequacy of androcentrism is recognized, new questions are asked of the historical records, and resources that were previously ignored by historians often come to light. In the worst-case scenario, at least historians would note and point out the absence of women in the historical records, rather than giving their students and those who read their scholarly work the impression that such omission is normal and unproblematic. The historian may notice that conventional history has been interested mainly in powerful people—military leaders, royalty, and religious authorities—who tend to be men. One new question is *why* the bias of historians is to be more interested in such people than in less powerful, ordinary people. Why are kings, wars, popes, and parliaments more interesting than peace, ordinary people, mystics, and domestic technology?

Simply deciding to investigate women and religion historically, however, does not immediately answer questions as to what kind of data about women are most important to remember. In the development of women studies, the first record to be brought to light was rather depressing. A history of misogynist and male-dominant attitudes and practices surfaced first when people began to ask what had been going on vis-à-vis *women* and religion for all these centuries in all these different cultures, simply because it was closest to the surface in the records historians generally used. This history did provide ample evidence for feminists' claims that religions had treated women unfairly and needed to change. But it did not provide much inspiration. Then began the quest for great women and women's movements whose records had largely been hidden and overlooked for centuries. Such research was more satisfying and provided many role models, but it still left two questions unanswered: What had ordinary women's lives been like? Could any accurate accounts of their lives be pieced together? Finally, could we discover a more sophisticated and subtle history of the attitudes toward women that had been prevalent in the various religions and historical epochs? Surely, given all that women had actually accomplished, cultural attitudes surrounding gender must have been more complex than the simple misogyny that was so often repeated, in part because it was so extreme and shocking. For example, it is easy to find and repeat misogynistic statements in the scriptures of early Buddhism. However, the full range of attitudes, revealed by the existence in early Buddhism of the nuns' order and the literature produced by these nuns, is much more variegated and complex than simple and pervasive misogyny.

The central question for a historian seeking to go beyond androcentric accounts of any religious tradition is how to balance on the tightrope of seeking a past that is both *accurate* and *usable*. Accuracy, of course, means conforming to what the data actually reveal. This is im-

portant in any history, and feminist historians contend that a history that records only men is simply not accurate. But rewriting history also provides a trap into which many previously disempowered groups fall. The lure of a *desired* past sometimes overpowers the accurate past. This often happens when historians seek to discover what happened before "the fall," before our group became disempowered. One of the most controversial topics in women's religious history is what many would call the "myth," using that term in its popular rather than its technical meaning, of the matriarchal past. Many feminist neopagan groups believe it to be "gospel truth," but most scholars and historians of religion have at least some reservations about its accuracy. Most scholars of religion and theologians would also claim that adhering to an inaccurate but pleasing account of the past actually does more harm than good to the cause of writing women back into history.

The claim that history is usable is anathema to many conventional historians, but their fury obscures the fact that historical records are used all the time to affect what happens in the present. It also obscures the fact that any history is an *edited selection* of all the events that happened in the past and that what gets edited in or edited out makes a great deal of difference to how people view themselves in the present. To talk about Christopher Columbus discovering America, for example, writes the entire Native American population out of history, is highly distorted, and can contribute to a negative self-image among Native Americans. Similarly, for the most part, women have been written out of religious history.

What happened historically is so important religiously to women because all religious communities constitute themselves in the present on the basis of the *past* that they remember, recall, and reenact in religious rituals. Historical memory is especially critical to the so-called historical religions, those that claim that the deity has acted decisively in history, especially Judaism and Christianity. For them, what happened in the past is normative in a way that it is not normative to religions, such as Hinduism and Buddhism, that do not base themselves so completely on the religious significance of certain "historical" events, such as the Passover or the death and resurrection of Jesus of Nazareth. Because of this religious significance of history, a great deal of effort has been devoted to researching the "Jesus movement" and the formation of early Christianity, as well as other important historical moments in these religions. It makes a great deal of difference to people alive today if, for example, one remembers a Jesus who had only male disciples or if one ascertains that he also had female disciples that the early church chose to downplay and eventually to forget. It makes a great deal of difference if one finds that only men functioned as priests and religious leaders in the early church or if one finds that women also functioned as priests and religious leaders early on in Christian history. The one remembered past provides the warrant for a contemporary male-dominated church; the other remembered past would encourage, if not require, that all Christian denominations allow women to take on all priestly and leadership roles that their churches offer. With this example, it also becomes clear just how completely intertwined are the issues of an *accurate* past and a *usable* past.

When the focus shifts to the cross-cultural and contemporary study of women and religion, other issues come to the fore. Students of the present cannot complain that they lack data. Women are part of all religions and cultures, and they can be studied, if not by men, given the mores of many traditional societies, then by women. The reason why women were usually so absent from early accounts of contemporary religions and cultures is that these cultures were studied only by men, not because the women were not doing anything interesting or important to the culture.

Androcentric presuppositions affected the study of women in contemporary religious worlds differently from how they affected historical studies. Although information about women was not missing or impossible to obtain, many androcentric scholars were interested in women only when they came into male view, were interested only in what men thought about women or in cultural norms prescribed for women. Alternatively, it was sometimes thought that one could answer questions about women and religion by talking about goddesses. But all such investigations treat women as objects to others, not as subjects in their own right. To come to the realization that *women themselves*—their religious lives and thought—deserved study was somewhat difficult and was resisted by the field of religious studies.

Thus, at least three interrelated areas of study come into play when the subject matter is "women and religion" in contemporary contexts. The most essential and the most likely to be overlooked is women themselves as subjects—their lives, their interests, their strategies, their agendas, and their interpretations of the religious matrix they share with their men. It is so much easier, given androcentric consciousness, to investigate what people think women should be like than to investigate what women think about and do with their lives. Nevertheless, for a *human* account of religion, it is essential to put women center stage, to ask how the world and their religions look to them, to ask what they do with the demands and opportunities that their religions and cultures offer to them. Although this possibility was initially extremely conceptually difficult for most scholars of religion to imagine, by the beginning of the twenty-first century, immense progress had been made in this direction. Countless monographs have been produced that actually look into the religious lives and concerns of women, both ordinary women and women religious leaders in a wide variety of religious and cultural contexts. The literature on the religious lives of Muslim and Hindu women is especially large.

If cultural attitudes toward women and gender are not mistaken for women's *own* lives and attitudes, they are important information for scholars studying women and religion. Many things suggest themselves as research topics for the scholar interested in cultural norms about women: Their prescribed roles, expectations and limits placed on them, stereotypes about them, their status relative to men, how women should behave and feel, symbols of femininity, and the effect of these symbols on both women and men are all legitimate topics for research. Furthermore, studying these materials would be necessary in studies of women's religious lives because their lives are so deeply affected by these norms. Usually, it is not difficult to find these data; the more complicated problem is assessing how much and what kind of impact they actually have. For example, Hindu norms about the subservience required of women to male relatives in all phases of her life cycle are repeated frequently in textbooks on world religions. These norms require a woman to be subservient, first to her father, then to her husband, and finally to her son. They also require her to be devoted to and honor her husband, no matter how cruel, inconsiderate, or inadequate he may be. The average North American student reading this material might easily conclude that Hindu women are virtual slaves. But these norms do not tell us the whole picture about Hindu women at all. Although passive acceptance is culturally prescribed, Hindu women participate in many rituals that give them some sense of being able to affect the circumstances of their lives. Through various religious practices, a Hindu woman actively seeks a good, kind and long-lived husband, a prosperous household, and healthy offspring. Furthermore, as they move through the life cycle, Hindu women *gain* power, unlike their Western counterparts, and older Hindu women are much more powerful than younger women. Unfortunately, this information does not make it into basic textbooks on world religions anywhere nearly as frequently as the culturally prescribed passive subservience.

Finally, if they are not confused with or substituted for information about women's religious lives, the various goddesses that are so common in so many religious contexts are important to study. In fact, probably no other topic in the study of women and religion has changed more since the advent of serious women studies scholarship. Before the paradigm shift in models of humanity brought about by women studies, goddesses were usually regarded as exotic and primitive. All of them were lumped into one category, "the mother goddess." No serious theologian would begin to imagine that feminine imagery of the divine could be relevant or possible in modern Western religions. When androcentrism is considered normal and appropriate among humans, it is not surprising that among deities male deities would be considered "more normal." The absence of feminine imagery in Western monotheism conditioned early comparative scholars to portray goddesses as exotic and foreign in a way that they never portrayed male deities of nonmonotheistic religions.

All this has now changed radically. Slowly, it has become clear that goddesses are found in almost every religious context. If anything needs explaining, it is not the presence of goddesses in most religious contexts but their relative absence in only one religious context—monotheism. More in-depth research, however, reveals that there have been many times and places within monotheistic contexts in which feminist imagery of the divine has proved very attractive, not the least of them the struggle over various goddesses in ancient Israel and the presence of Lady Wisdom in late biblical and intertestamental literature. In addition, contemporary religious thinkers and theologians have begun serious exploration of the ways in which feminine imagery of the divine makes sense in contemporary North American contexts. Some of these explorations occur within Jewish or Christian contexts; other explorers want nothing to do with Christianity or Judaism.

In terms of data about goddesses, the two richest mines are Western antiquity and the religions of India, especially contemporary Hinduism. Both areas have been explored in depth in recent decades, but unfortunately almost no scholarly or popular authors have been able to span both these areas of research. Scholars looking into each of the two areas also usually have somewhat different agendas. Those doing research on the goddesses of Western antiquity are often interested in some version of the prepatriarchal hypothesis, discussed earlier. Thus, their work often has a more "political" tone than does scholarship on Hindu goddesses. In the last fifteen years of the twentieth century, many fine books on Hindu goddesses, based on field research, were published.

Given that research, both historical and cross-cultural, about women and religion had, by the beginning of the twenty-first century, gone on for thirty years, can any generalizations or conclusions be drawn from that research? Such generalizations and conclusions might help set the research agenda for future decades.

First, in line with postmodern thinking, notions of a universal and monolithic patriarchy have broken down. There are many forms of male dominance in different times and places. It is also questionable whether all societies are or have been "patriarchal." Both historical and anthropological research indicate that some societies are more egalitarian, not in the modern sense that

gender roles do not apply and anyone can do anything but in the sense that men's and women's spheres of activity are more balanced and complementary. Women and men may have a great deal of autonomy in their separate spheres, which are evaluated as equally important by the culture. Early feminists, still caught up in concerns with hierarchy and dominance, were not well equipped to notice this pattern. While the reality of "matriarchal" prehistory is highly questionable, it is likely that prepatriarchal societies were more egalitarian and that patriarchy or male dominance, in its various forms, is a historical development, not an eternal norm rooted in human biology. It is also clear that many indigenous and small-scale traditions cannot be labeled *patriarchal* or *male dominated*. Separate, complementary spheres of roughly equivalent importance are quite common.

The so-called world religions are all formally male dominated. However, the word *formally* is crucial. Public norms and religious texts of these traditions state that men should be in charge, should be religious authorities and leaders, and are superior and preferable human beings. However, studies of these traditions "on the ground," rather than "in an armchair" armed with classical texts, often reveal a different picture. Women actually have a lot to do with what happens, and their power is known and acknowledged. Anthropologists have introduced a distinction between *authority* and *power* that is extremely useful for discussing what actually happens in many religious situations that are formally male dominated. Men do have an acknowledged authority, but, as in the example of Hindu women cited earlier, that is not the whole story. Women give formal deference to men, and they can be subjugated by determined men. Nevertheless, women have a great deal of power in many subtle and not-so-subtle ways. Usually, they have a great deal of power within their own households and seek other strategies to have some impact on affairs outside their households as well.

Furthermore, there is considerable variety in the extent and kind of male dominance found in the major world religions. Ways of classifying these religions seldom take women's involvement in them into account; but if it were taken into account, it is unlikely that the current geographical and historical classifications would occur. Instead of classifying religions as Western, Indian, and East Asian, which is very common in religion textbooks, we might classify religions as to whether they are mainly oriented to the family and other social units or whether they are oriented to individuals, in which case they usually also have monastic institutions. Religions that are family oriented usually praise women as mothers but allow them few, if any, religious options other than motherhood. Religions that are more oriented to the individual often are suspicious of women's sexuality, but usually women have the religious option of a non-domestic lifestyle, although it is often more difficult for women than for men to exercise that option. If the world's religions were classified by these categories, religions from each of the three major geographical areas would be found in each category, and the variety in forms of formal male dominance would be much more apparent. To date, no textbook has been so organized, probably because of lingering androcentrism among textbook authors and publishers.

Finally, some generalizations concerning developmental patterns in religions may be warranted. In many times and places, there seems to be drift toward greater male dominance, which may then be questioned or overturned by new developments. The anthropology of religion provides a version of developmental patterns that is more accurate than the idea of matriarchal prehistory. Generally, though not universally, women have more independence, are more central to economic and political systems of their society, and have more significant religious roles in foraging and horticultural societies than in agricultural or early industrial societies. Foraging and horticultural societies usually also display more complementary gender roles than those dominated by agriculture and industry. Clearly a postindustrial economy seems to be presenting more egalitarian possibilities again.

It is easier and less grandiose to demonstrate this developmental pattern in the origins of some of the world's major religions and in the emergence of reform movements within those religions. Scholars have frequently argued both that Christianity improved the status of women, when compared to other contemporary cultures, and that it was much more egalitarian and open to women in its earliest forms than it was later. This same thesis has been argued, less systematically, for Islam and for Buddhism. Whether these religions improved women's situations vis-à-vis the surrounding cultures may be questionable, but it is clear that the status of women declined as these religions became more established and powerful. In addition, especially for Christianity, where more research has been done, scholars have demonstrated that many reform movements included an attempt to improve the status of women and that women themselves often take leading roles in these movements. In general, it can be demonstrated that in new situations, such as new movements within religions or when a religion crosses cultural frontiers, women often take on roles and responsibilities that they later relinquish or are forced to concede. Furthermore, in "marginal" nonmainstream religious movements, women often have more power and autonomy than in the majority religions. This pattern is extremely important for understanding women and religion in North America.

Scholars using different methods and asking different questions have developed the other major subfield concerned with women and religion, the critical and constructive discipline often called *feminist theology,* which analyzes whether women have been treated appropriately in religions of the past or present and suggests correctives that would make the religions more just and equitable. Because this enterprise is critical and constructive, it is more controversial than more descriptive aspects of the study of women and religion. As has been demonstrated, those cross-cultural and historical studies only demand that women's religious lives be included in the database of the field of religious studies, which could be a controversial expectation only if one were to claim that men alone constitute humanity. The theological and normative disciplines, however, evaluate all major world religions as having failed women and offer sometimes radical alternatives to them. Separating these two different concerns regarding women and religion is important to ensure that the descriptive aspects of women studies in religion are not entangled in or endangered by political fights over the validity of feminist criticisms of the religions.

Feminist critique and reconstruction are relevant to all major world religions. Nevertheless, because of North American dominance in the field of feminist theology, these discussions are far more advanced in the religions dominant in North America—Judaism and Christianity—and among North Americans who have renounced Judaism or Christianity for neopagan feminist spirituality. In academic circles, Christian feminist theology is often the only feminist religious voice present, even though Buddhists, Hindus, and Muslims, among others in North America, have made significant feminist critiques and reconstructions of their traditions. This problem of Christian dominance in the field of feminist theology has only recently been addressed at the beginning of the twenty-first century.

In terms of theological method, the major fault line among feminist theologians concerns whether they will continue to identify with one of the existing major world religions, seeking to transform it so that it is more equitable for women or whether they will decide that such transformation is impossible. Some of the more prominent feminist theologians of the later twentieth century, such as Mary Daly and Carol Christ, began their careers as Christians but decided at some point that, for them at least, Christianity was beyond repair. Male dominance, they argued, was so deeply embedded in its fabric that Christianity without patriarchy would be unrecognizable, would be so different from conventional Christianity that it could not be called by the same name. Probably more important in their decision to abandon Christianity, however, was the practical decision that, given the power of male authorities in the established

Christian churches, any significant transformation of Christianity was extremely unlikely. In addition to being frustrated with the extent to which men held authority in the churches, these theologians also argued that the male imagery of deity so omnipresent in Christianity and Judaism was unhealthy for women (and for men). Seeking different ways of handling religious authority and female imagery of the divine, many of these theologians left more mainstream religions for some version of neopaganism, often an explicitly feminist form of neopaganism. In these neopagan feminist movements, academically trained feminist theologians are a distinct minority, and their voices are often not fully represented in feminist theological circles.

The ranks of feminist theologians who have chosen to seek to transform their traditions from within are large and diverse. Nevertheless, they employ common strategies across the lines of different traditions, not only among the various Christian denominations but also among various major world religions. In a brief synopsis, this strategy employs the critical practice of "interpretation." These feminists claim that male dominance in its various forms, which is so pronounced in their traditions as currently constituted, is not a *necessary* doctrine or practice of the tradition but an unfortunate accretion due to historical and cultural conditions that no longer apply (if they ever did). They also claim that the tradition shorn of its male dominance is actually truer to its core teachings and core vision. Thus a feminist theological interpretation, rather than undermining the tradition, actually unlocks the power and relevance of the tradition that previously had been lost to patriarchal interpretations.

A strategy especially important to text-based traditions, such as Christianity and Islam, is to look closely at the sacred texts themselves in their original languages. In such traditions, certain passages of the sacred text are used as warrants for male dominance and sometimes for misogyny. Often these interpretations have become so familiar that adherents of the tradition cannot imagine any other way of reading the text. However, if parallel passages that encourage the opposite attitudes toward women can be found, as is almost always the case, then one is forced to rethink how seriously passages that disfavor women need to be taken, and one is also forced to ask why the tradition has, for so long, preferred to stress passages in its sacred texts that favor male dominance over passages that favor egalitarianism. Another tactic is to point to mistranslations; in the original language, the text may be more egalitarian than is an old, long-standing translation. The advantage of this strategy is that it engages the tradition on its own terms, taking the sacred text seriously, rather than denying the validity of something central to the tradition, such as the authority of its sacred texts. If one wishes to *transform* a tradition, it will be necessary to retain and work within its central categories, rather than abandoning them altogether.

A cluster of issues concerning ritual is faced by feminists in all major religions. Often the language used in liturgies is in the generic masculine, and the tradition's rituals are more oriented to men than to women. These problems are compounded by the fact that religious leaders and authorities are presumed to be men in all major religious traditions. Once the sheer magnitude of women's exclusion from most dimensions of all major religions was felt, women's movements in the various traditions became inevitable. Among the earliest issues taken up by many women's movements within religions was the issue of leadership. Most religions have faced, some more successfully than others, the problem presented by a male lock on positions of religious authority and leadership. At the beginning of the twenty-first century, most liberal Christian and Jewish denominations ordain women as clergy persons. However, conservative denominations, such as Orthodox Judaism and the Roman Catholic Church, seem to be further from that possibility than ever. However, simply putting women in front of the congregation did not satisfy many religious feminists. What good is it to have a woman leading a liturgy that uses generic masculine language, presiding over rituals that may not be relevant to women or that do not ritualize life experiences that are important to women? The language of many a favorite hymn or biblical reading used in the liturgy stood out as unacceptably androcentric after people became more sensitive to the issue of gender-inclusive language. Although there were many fights and offended traditionalists, many religious groups have issued new translations and versions of their liturgies. Imitating the ritual creativity of feminist neopagan movements, many women's groups have also devised new rituals especially for women.

The most powerful strategy is to analyze the central teachings and doctrines of a religious tradition, asking whether they support male dominance or egalitarianism. Feminist theologians who seek to transform a tradition from within will necessarily argue that the central insights of their tradition support egalitarianism, although sometimes they may also argue that some of the symbols that carry those insights need fine-tuning or adjusting. Such a case has been made by Jewish, Christian, Muslim, and Buddhist feminist thinkers. Thus, Christian feminist theologians may point to a core message of liberation from bondage, Jewish feminist theologians to the deity's covenant with the whole people, Muslim feminists to the radical equality espoused by Islam, and Buddhist feminist thinkers to the fact that egolessness and emptiness are beyond gender. At the same time, many point out that important transformations of their traditions are required to make these gender-neutral and gender-inclusive core teachings more apparent. For example, many Christian and some Jewish theologians now agree that using only male language and imagery for deity is incompatible with egalitarian, gender-neutral, and gender-inclusive praxis. It is no longer shocking or radical in many circles to use many other images and analogies for the deity. Buddhism, a nontheistic religion, does not face the problem of androcentric imagery for its ultimate reality, but it does face almost as serious a problem. The spiritual teacher or guru is central to many forms of Buddhism, and historically most spiritual teachers have been men. In some segments of North American convert Buddhism, about half the spiritual teachers are now women. Finally, feminist critical thinkers in many traditions have explored links between patriarchal theologies and other major social problems, such as the danger of environmental devastation. Most feminist thinkers would argue that feminist theologies are more amenable to helping solve some of these critical social problems than are conventional theologies. The ecological theologies of feminist theologians in a number of traditions are a significant case in point. Concepts of deity more likely to promote the human well-being of women are also often more likely to promote the well-being of the planet. Others have explored links between male-dominant theologies and images of deity as a warrior-king with religious sanctions for violence. Buddhist feminist thinkers, who do not propose alternative images of deity, tend to emphasize an interpretation of interdependence that encourages concern for the environment and a lessening of violence through moderation of both consumption and reproduction.

At this point, looking toward the future, several issues are critical. Perhaps most important is the question of how much the topic of women and religion, whether in its descriptive or its normative modes, will remain distinct and separate and how much the results of its scholarship and thinking will become part of the mainstream. At the beginning of the twenty-first century, women studies classes are still commonly filled mainly by women and for women to be researched mainly by women scholars. Such recognition easily falls into tokenism, in which women studies is given its little cubicle but does not have much effect on the academy or the religions at large. Such an outcome would betray the vision of feminism. To insist that mainstream scholarship and religious institutions incorporate the findings and recommendations of the women and religion movement is important. One tactic for accomplishing this goal is to insist that more classes and teaching materials be genuinely gender neutral and gender inclusive. Another is to support genuinely inclusive research in gender studies.

Another critical issue concerns the definition of the field of "women and religion." At present, many who research women and religion cross-culturally or historically do not identify with the discipline of women studies in religion. This is especially the case for those who do research on women and "non-Western" religions primarily for one reason. Women studies in religion has become too closely identified with Christian feminist theology, leaving little place for those whose interests in women studies in religion lie elsewhere. Even theologians and critical thinkers from other religious traditions often do not identify with the discipline of women studies in religion for the same reason. The breadth and richness of the entire field of women studies in religion need to be more clearly recognized and acknowledged. As we move into a more religiously diverse future in North America, the discipline of women studies in religion would be immeasurably enriched by reflecting that religious diversity.

SOURCES: Carol P. Christ, *Rebirth of the Goddess: Finding Meaning in Feminist Spirituality* (1997). Carol P. Christ and Judith Plaskow, eds., *Womanspirit Rising: A Feminist Reader in Religion* (1979). Paula Cooey, William R. Eackin, and Jay B. McDaniel, eds., *After Patriarchy: Feminist Transformations of the World Religions* (1991). Mary Daly, *Beyond God the Father: Toward a Philosophy of Women's Liberation* (1973). Nancy Auer Falk and Rita M. Gross, eds., *Unspoken Worlds: Women's Religious Lives* (1980; 3rd ed., 2001). Rita M. Gross, *Feminism and Religion: An Introduction* (1996). Barbara J. MacHaffie, *Her Story: Women in Christian Tradition* (1986). Rosemary Radford Ruether, *Sexism and God-Talk: Toward a Feminist Theology* (1983). Arvind Sharma, ed., *Women in World Religions* (1987).

RELIGIONS AND MODERN FEMINISM
Ann Braude

FEMINISM, THE VIEW that society should be transformed to include the full participation of women, has been a key factor influencing the distinctive shape of religious life in modern America. Incorporating the idea that power discrepancies between men and women have distorted human relationships and institutions, feminism has caused religious communions to rethink their history, their polity, and their theology. It has inspired transformations of religious language, symbols, and rituals, as well as influenced decisions about religious affiliation and disaffiliation. In addition, religious women, organizations, and motivations have played important roles in the feminist movements that have helped shape modern American society. While many essays in this encyclopedia focus on feminist transformations of religions, this essay will focus on the recip-

rocal interconnections between religions and modern feminism.

The term *feminism* was first used in the early twentieth century and has been applied retrospectively to the nineteenth-century woman's movement that has become known as the "first wave" of feminism. Beginning with the first women's rights convention in 1848, the first wave culminated in the passage of a constitutional amendment giving women the right to vote in 1920. The resurgence of a mass movement to advance the status of women in the 1970s is often referred to as "second wave feminism." A "third wave" of concern about justice for women emerged in the 1990s, fueled in part by the dramatic testimony of Anita Hill concerning sexual harassment at the confirmation hearings of Supreme Court Justice Clarence Thomas. Each wave of feminism originated among women whose involvement with struggles for racial justice inspired them to apply a similar analysis of inequality and discrimination to their experience as women.

Historically, religion and feminism have had an intimate, sometimes sympathetic, but often troubled, relationship. Many women have come to feminism as an extension of their religious faith. Liberal religious bodies have at times embraced and promoted feminism, coming to understand the assertion of the full humanity of women as part of their religious mission. Other groups have condemned feminism, interpreting it as an attack on God-ordained gender roles and therefore incompatible with true faith. A third group of religions owes its origins to feminism, having arisen in response to women's and men's dissatisfaction with traditions they perceived to be irredeemably sexist. For a fourth group of religions, those recently transplanted to the United States by immigrants, confronting feminism and its fruits constitutes one of the most challenging aspects of the encounter with American culture.

The majority of religious feminists in all these groups engage in an ongoing struggle to reconcile the promises of feminism with the promises of their faiths. And in all, including those opposed to feminism, the challenges raised by movements for women's liberation have served as sources of vitality, stimulating lively theological debate, renewed interest in scriptural criticism, liturgical and ritual creativity, and institutional innovation. To some extent during the nineteenth century and to a greater extent in the twentieth, every religious group has had to grapple with feminism in one way or another. Each has been changed by the encounter, whether by the embrace of feminism or by its rejection. No religion could ignore feminism, making it one of the key issues in the self-definition of modern religious organizations and communities.

Feminist movements, likewise, have been troubled by the issue of religious faith. And, likewise, they have been unable to ignore this persistent feature of modern American culture. Some activists have assumed that religious women are apologists for patriarchy who suffer from false consciousness or that their allegiance to religious communities or organizations makes them incapable of authentic advocacy on women's behalf. This view fails to acknowledge the diversity of American religions or their spectrum of opinions on women's issues. It also fails to acknowledge the substantial role of faith and faith communities in women's lives and culture throughout American history. If religion and feminism are antithetical, then feminism can never have the sweeping impact for which its proponents hope. In contrast, religious feminists see the transformation of consciousness embodied in the feminist transformation of faith traditions as one of the movement's most far-reaching and revolutionary results.

Religion and Feminism in the Nineteenth Century

The first comprehensive argument for women's rights penned by an American woman took the Bible as its focus. Sarah Moore Grimké's *Letters on the Equality of the Sexes* (1838) stressed the equal creation of man and woman and attributed biblical arguments against women's equality to the bias of male translators and interpreters. Ten years later, in 1848, Elizabeth Cady Stanton and Lucretia Mott called the first women's rights convention to consider the "social, civil, and religious conditions and rights of woman" (Stanton, Anthony, and Gage, 67). When the convention assembled in Seneca Falls, New York, it passed a "Declaration of Sentiments" that Stanton and Mott had modeled closely on the Declaration of Independence. Claiming for women the same political, economic, and civil rights claimed by male colonists declaring independence from England, they added attention to religious rights, which had not been addressed. While male colonists had complained of grievances against King George, Stanton and Mott addressed "the repeated injuries and usurpations on the part of man toward woman." "He allows her in Church, as well as State," they wrote, "but in a subordinate position, claiming Apostolic authority for her exclusion from the ministry, and . . . from any public participation in the affairs of the Church. . . . He has usurped the prerogative of Jehovah himself, claiming it as his right to assign for her a sphere of action, when that belongs to her conscience and her God" (71).

The above statement embodies the double role that religion would play in American feminism. It simultaneously depicted male church structures as sources of inequality *and* claimed an authentic relationship with God as authorization for combating those inequalities. Closely following the logic of the movement for the abolition of slavery, Stanton and Mott attributed discriminatory practices in church and society to theological errors that jeopardized the souls of those who usurped the rights of others, as well as harming those whose rights were usurped. The "Declaration of Sentiments" shows the churches both as a source of disenfranchisement and as a source of validation for women's independent humanity. Neither the word *church* nor the word *God* appeared in the Declaration of Independence, but for the women and men who signed the Declaration of Sentiments at Seneca Falls, both needed to be included if women's rights were to be secured.

In addition to the religious rights of women in general, the convention specifically endorsed the ordination of women. Participants resolved unanimously that "the speedy success of our cause depends upon . . . the overthrow of the monopoly of the pulpit." In the final resolution discussed on its first day, the convention concluded:

That, being invested by the Creator with the same capabilities, and the same consciousness of responsibility for their exercise, it is demonstrably the right and duty of woman, equally with man, to promote every righteous cause by righteous means; and especially in regard to the great subjects of morals and religion, it is self-evidently her right to participate with her brother in teaching them, both in private and in public, by writing and by speaking, by any instrumentalities proper to be used, and in any assemblies proper to be held. (71–73)

In this resolution, the convention took on the scriptural teachings most often offered to oppose women's equal role in Christianity, the Pauline letters urging wives to be subject to their husbands, to be silent in church, and to refrain from teaching men (1 Corinthians 11:3–12, Colossians 3:18–19, 1 Timothy 2:11–12).

In a sense, Paul's prohibitions set the agenda for the feminist struggles within the Protestant denominations in both the nineteenth and twentieth centuries. Because of these prohibitions, women (except among the Quakers) were excluded from theological education, from ordination, and from lay rights. These issues would all become focal points of activism among religious feminists. The first woman ordained in a Protestant denomination, Antoinette Brown Blackwell (1853), viewed her preparation for and participation in the ministry as part of the women's rights movement and played an active role in the campaign for women's suffrage. Similar views motivated Anna Howard Shaw, the first woman ordained to the Methodist ministry (1880), who served as president of the National American Woman Suffrage Association from 1904 to 1915. Both Blackwell and Shaw, like many women ministers who would follow them, concluded that deep-seated sexism made it impossible for them to function as ministers within their churches and devoted themselves instead to advancing the status of women.

The only religious groups to overtly embrace women's rights in the nineteenth century joined theological dissent to dissent from normative notions about women's roles. Radical Quakers believed that women's religious leadership and public voice were authorized by their conviction that every individual had access to divine truth by looking within. Spiritualist conventions provided a platform for some of the most radical feminists when they could find few other receptive audiences. Many women's rights activists gravitated toward Theosophy and Christian Science, two movements founded by women that rejected the notion of a patriarchal deity. Mormons, often assumed to advocate patriarchy because they practiced polygamy before 1890 and admit all men but no women to the priesthood, were vocal advocates of women's suffrage. When the exclusively Mormon Utah Territorial Legislature approved woman suffrage in 1870, it enfranchised more than 17,000 women, the largest population of female voters in the world. When the women of Utah were disenfranchised by federal antipolygamy legislation in 1887, they were outraged, calling it an affront to religious freedom, states' rights, and women's rights. "The Rights of Women of Zion, and the Rights of Women of All Nations" on the masthead became the motto of the *Woman's Exponent*, a newspaper published by the Relief Society, to which all Mormon women belong.

Elizabeth Cady Stanton, the intellectual giant of the women's movement, turned her attention to religion once again in the 1880s, concluding that the fight for equality could never be won as long as it had to be waged among "men who accept the theological view of women as the author of sin, cursed of God, and all that nonsense" (Kern, 1). She assembled a group of women's rights advocates to produce *The Woman's Bible* (1895), which provided commentary on biblical passages used to define woman's role. But while Stanton appreciated the fundamental role of religion as a source of women's inequality, she did not see change within the churches as a solution to the problem. Instead, she hoped that a diminution of organized religion's role in American society would aid women's advancement. In the other great publication she undertook during this period, *The History of Woman Suffrage*, she sought to recast the women's movement as focused exclusively on political and constitutional, rather than religious, issues.

As Gerda Lerner has observed concerning *The History of Woman Suffrage*, "The strongly secular bias of its editors and their disenchantment with the organized churches ... are reflected in the way they ... disregard[ed] the importance of feminist struggles in the various churches during the last century" (*The Creation of Feminist Consciousness*, 269). This bias is reflected in the tendency of subsequent historians of feminism to focus on figures like Stanton and Susan B. Anthony rather than on figures like Frances Willard, the powerful president of the Woman's Christian Temperance Union (WCTU), Helen Barrett Montgomery, the suffragist who became a leader of the women's missionary movement and president of the Northern Baptist Convention, or African American women's rights activists who led the black women's club movement. Willard, a devoted Methodist, described her adoption of the suffrage cause as a conversion experience that occurred while she knelt in prayer. Following this conversion, she led her entire organization, the largest women's organization in the United States, to endorse suffrage. When the WCTU endorsed suffrage, it became the largest organization to do so, far outnumbering both the tiny National Woman Suffrage Association led by Stanton and Anthony and the somewhat larger American Woman Suffrage Association led by Lucy Stone (which showed its religious sympathies by repeatedly electing popular preacher Henry Ward Beecher as president). Helen Barrett Montgomery, a proponent of the Social Gospel, became the leader of the largest women's movement in the United States when she was elected president of the National Federation of Women's Boards of Foreign Missions in 1917. Her book *Western Women in Eastern Lands: An Outline Study of Fifty Years of Woman's Work in Foreign Missions* (1910) described the efforts of the women's missionary movement to improve the status and conditions of women around the world as a direct continuation of the work for women's rights that began at Seneca Falls.

Leading advocates for black women's rights operated within a Christian framework for much of the nineteenth and twentieth centuries. As African American men lost voting rights with the emergence of the "Jim Crow" laws in the late nineteenth century, the National Association of Colored Women appealed to Christian beliefs to advance the claims of both men and women of color. For example, the Association's first president, Mary Church Terrell, asked the National Council of Mothers to teach their children not to be racists by noting that "the Father of all men will hold them responsible for the crimes which are the result of their injustice" (Terrell, 1).

Second Wave Feminism in Religious Organizations

When the terms *women's liberation* and *feminism* emerged during the 1960s, religious women recognized them immediately as describing elements of the goals they had long pursued within denominational and ecumenical organizations. During the 1950s and 1960s, Protestantism, Catholicism, and Judaism served both to ignite the discontent with women's limited options that Betty Friedan described in *The Feminine Mystique* (1963) and to nurture subcultures that inspired rebellion against it. While the religious climate of the period generally encouraged traditional gender roles, each religion included within it a social justice tradition that inspired feminist foment and leadership.

Unlike their secular counterparts, religious feminists did not have to build women's networks from scratch. Each group included women's organizations that cultivated a cadre of well-trained leaders with ready access to a large constituency. When *The Feminine Mystique* was published, it was immediately assigned to the 175 national leaders of Methodist women whose 1963 meeting was devoted to "Women in a New Age." Those women used what they learned to lead the 1.2 million members of United Methodist Women. In contrast, it would be another six years before Betty Friedan joined in founding the National Organization for Women (NOW) to advance the concerns raised in her book, and NOW's membership would never match that of United Methodist Women. Just as Frances Willard committed the Woman's Christian Temperance Union to suffrage in the nineteenth century, religious feminists hoped to carry the ideas of women's liberation to the average "middle-American" woman. "She's highly suspicious of women's liberation in general, but she'll often listen to a church woman—even when she's preaching the same message," Patricia Kepler, of the United Presbyterian Church's Task Force on Women, told journalist Judith Hole in 1971 (Hole and Levine, 373).

Among Protestants, the Social Gospel tradition of the early twentieth century continued in large and vibrant women's organizations that grew out of the women's missionary movement. Ironically, at the very moment that feminism came on the scene, many of these were losing their autonomy and being subsumed into general denominational structures. The loss of a voice in denominational affairs increased receptiveness to feminist analysis and legitimized making it a priority in women's organizations. The American Baptist Convention, for example, saw a 50 percent decline in the number of women on the professional staff of their state conventions during the 1960s. In 1964 a traumatic denominational restructuring forced Methodist women to relinquish control of programs that they had founded, funded, and nurtured for decades. "Out of long commitment to women and our recent restructuring, the Women's Division understood at once what the secular feminists were struggling with and in revolt against," recalled Theressa Hoover, the African American feminist who led the Women's Division of the United Methodist Church from 1968 to 1990. "Their analysis deepened our understanding of the systemic oppression of women. Their determination to revise patriarchal culture and politics energized us," she recalled (Hoover, 34).

Thus energized, in 1968 Methodist women successfully petitioned their denomination to examine "the extent to which women are involved at all structural levels in . . . policy-making channels and agencies of the United Methodist Church." When the Women's Division was asked to pay for the study, it refused, asserting that the male-dominated church structures should be responsible. Frustrated by the lack of a voice within their church, the Women's Division made its own recommendations to the denomination's Structure Committee, stressing both the desire for the return of its previous enterprises and its role in combating "ecclesiastical sexism." The 1969 statement described women's experience in the church through the categories of feminist analysis: "We have observed that where organized women's groups have been removed from a visible policy-making

and power sharing role . . . a) Male chauvinism increases; b) The status of women declines" (Hoover, 41–42).

The United Methodist Women's Division was particularly successful in promoting feminism because it succeeded in maintaining fiscal autonomy when other Protestant women's groups lost control of their own funds. Nevertheless, by 1969, the language of women's liberation could be heard at the national meetings of most liberal Protestant denominations. Both the United Presbyterian Church in the USA and the American Baptist Convention passed resolutions calling for the church to work toward equality for women both within its own structures and in every aspect of social and economic life. *Presbyterian Life*, the magazine of the United Presbyterian Church, devoted its February 1971 issue to women's liberation. Louise Orr, a church elder from Greenville, Tennessee, used the language of modern feminism to demonstrate that women's liberation was a Christian issue. "Paul meant *now* when he wrote" that "there is neither male nor female, for you are all one in Christ Jesus," she explained, criticizing her church's tendency to interpret Paul's statement only in an otherworldly sense. The decisions of the Lutheran Church in America and the American Lutheran Church to begin ordaining women in 1970 reflected a new commitment to women's equality.

The generation gap that appeared in the 1960s divided the women of some denominations over the issue of feminism. For example, in 1967 the General Division of Women's Work of the Episcopal Church took the position that their work should be integrated into other structures of the church and that specific representation of women's voices was not a priority. By the time these recommendations were to be implemented in 1970, a meeting of Episcopal women convened to critique their church's failures on women's issues. "The institutional Episcopal Church is racist, militarist, and sexist," began the resolution they adopted. They called on the church "to remedy the historical discrimination against women and its destructive effects in the Christian community" by ordaining women and by enforcing Title VII of the Civil Rights Act of 1964 with regard to employment in the church (Doely, 111–114).

Challenges to the autonomy of women's organizations also sparked feminist concerns among Latter-day Saints (LDS). In 1970 the Relief Society, in which all Mormon women participate, lost control over general and local funds, the authority to develop its own programs, and the authority to produce its own publication. A black-bordered notice in the June 1970 *Relief Society Magazine* announced that it would cease publication "in accordance with the directive of the first Presidency." After 100 years of independent publishing by LDS women, this sudden loss precipitated the founding of several unofficial, and explicitly feminist, publications. *Exponent II*, founded in 1974, described itself as "the spiritual descendent of the *Woman's Exponent*" that supported woman suffrage in the nineteenth century. Founded by the members of a Boston consciousness-raising group, the paper claimed feminism as part of an authentic Mormon heritage. Editor Claudia Bushman described the paper's purpose in its opening issue: "*Exponent II,* posed on the dual platforms of Mormonism and Feminism, has two aims: to strengthen the Church of Jesus Christ of the Latter-day Saints, and to encourage and develop the talents of Mormon women. That these aims are consistent we intend to show by our pages and our lives."

The assertion that feminism would strengthen their church reflected two distinctive elements of Mormon feminism. First, as members of a faith that still occupied something of an "outsider" status in the United States, they were part of a tradition that had experienced its own share of prejudice and did not want to add to that. Second, they believed that feminism was part of their history and heritage and an integral part of the Mormon faith. This latter view brought them into occasional conflict both with official church policy and with feminists who believed that LDS theology and ceremonies contained essential patriarchal elements. In contrast, Mormons for ERA, founded by Sonia Johnson in 1978, worked both for the passage of the Equal Rights Amendment (ERA) and to expose the efforts of the Mormon Church to defeat it. Johnson was excommunicated in 1979 for disobedience to her Stake president's instructions to abandon work on behalf of the ERA. The following decades witnessed the excommunication of a long list of Mormon feminists, including, in 2001, Maxine Hanks, editor of *Women and Authority: Re-emerging Mormon Feminism* (1992).

Feminists constituted a small minority among evangelical Christians, but the existence of even small groups of organized feminists elicited a dramatic response among theological conservatives committed to biblical literalism. Evangelicals encountered feminism just a few years after liberal Protestants encountered it. In 1974 Letha Scanzoni and Nancy Hardesty argued that feminism found support in the Bible in *All We're Meant to Be: A Biblical Approach to Women's Liberation.* Dispensationalist *Eternity Magazine* named this the most important book of the year. In the same year, at the 106th Annual Convention of the Christian Holiness Association, held in Louisville, Kentucky, Donald and Lucille Sider Dayton (later Groh) presented a historical defense of women's ordination. Dayton was one of eight women at Chicago's North Park Theological Seminary (Evangelical Covenant Church) who had been meeting regularly to study what the Bible says about women. They helped start the Evangelical Women's Caucus, which held the first conference on biblical feminism in 1975, and founded the periodical *Daughters of Sarah* the same year.

For Christians alienated by the Pauline Epistles, evangelical feminism brought a sense of reconciliation with God and the Bible and often with the church. It also brought a transformed gender consciousness. *Daughters of Sarah* was produced according to feminist principles of the day: Anyone who showed up at the meetings became part of the editorial collective that decided the content of the next issue, and every other month the group gathered in the basement of Lucille Sider Dayton's home to collate, staple, and mail the new issue. The tension between biblical texts and feminist principles came to a head at the 1986 meeting of the Evangelical Women's Caucus, when members voted to acknowledge the presence of a lesbian minority and endorsed "civil rights protection for homosexual persons." The result was the formation of an additional organization, Christians for Biblical Equality, dedicated to the view that the Bible teaches the equality of all believers regardless of race, class, or gender but rejecting homosexuality as unbiblical. Headquartered in Minneapolis, Christians for Biblical Equality produces a scholarly journal, *Priscilla Papers,* as well as a quarterly newsletter, *Mutuality.*

The question of whether feminism was best pursued inside or outside existing religious structures was especially salient for Roman Catholics. Many hoped that Pope John XXIII's call to bring the Church up to date in the Second Vatican Council would include recognition of women's equality. Disappointed on that front, emerging Catholic feminists were nevertheless inspired by a new understanding of the Catholic Church as constituted by "the people of God" rather than by the hierarchy of the institutional Church. Both laywomen and women religious formed a network of Catholic organizations advancing the feminist movement.

Catholic women's religious orders were perfectly positioned to provide participants in the developing feminist movement. Reaching their peak of membership in 1966 (180,000), they had raised sisters' educational level significantly as a result of the Sister Formation movement during the 1950s. When women's liberation hit the scene, they constituted a formidable community of educated, working women who had just been encouraged by Vatican II to leave their convents and engage the social issues of the day. Profoundly affected by their involvement with the civil rights movement, the peace movement, and movements for liberation in Latin America and elsewhere, they applied their concerns for justice to themselves and to other women. Committed to habits of daily prayer and reflection and to biblical mandates to work to end oppression, the Roman Catholic sisters who adopted feminism brought a disciplined and energetic cadre to the movement.

One of the first signals of changing understandings of authority among Catholic women religious came in 1971, when the Conference of Major Superiors of Women, against official advice from Rome, changed its name to the Leadership Council of Women Religious (LCWR). The LCWR endorsed the Equal Rights Amendment and supported more radical organizations like Network, a Washington-based lobbying group of sisters concerned with social justice and feminist issues. In 1978 the LCWR announced a five-year plan of study, prayer, and action for women's empowerment. In 1979 Sister Theresa Kane, president of the LCWR, took the opportunity of a public greeting to the pope to urge him "to be mindful of the intense suffering and pain that is part of the life of many women . . . [and] to hear the call of women . . . to be included in all ministries of our church" (Weaver, *New Catholic Women*, 86). This dramatic departure from the traditional deference of women religious toward the patriarchal hierarchy of the Catholic Church shocked many Catholics and heartened others who hoped that it would bring much needed attention to the role of women in the Church. The latter group was disappointed when Kane's statement received neither response nor acknowledgment.

While the Leadership Council of Women Religious represented the majority of American Catholic women's orders, smaller groups focused more specifically on feminist issues proliferated during the 1970s and 1980s. Las Hermanas (The Sisters), the national organization of Latina nuns, held its first convention in Houston, Texas, in 1971. Closely identifying itself with the interests of La Raza (the people), the group criticized the Catholic Church's paternalism both toward women and toward the Mexican American community. Nevertheless, Las Hermanas included as its final goal "to interest more Chicana women to choose religious life" (Basso, 64). In 1970, the National Assembly of Women Religious formed as an organization of nuns promoting "ministry, social justice, and justice for women." This group in turn gave birth both to Network: A National Catholic Social Justice Lobby (founded and staffed by women religious) and to the Women's Ordination Conference. In 1975 the Women's Ordination Conference held a historic gathering in Detroit at which 1,200 people addressed "Women in Future Priesthood Now." Nadine Foley expressed the mood of the conference when she described the failure to ordain women as evidence of "the conflict between official Church pronouncements and the spirit of the gospel with its message of freedom of persons through the redemptive activity of Jesus Christ" (Patrick, 177).

Ecumenical as well as denominational organizations participated in the rise of feminism. The National Council of Churches, Church Women United, and the Young Women's Christian Association (YWCA) produced net-

works of women leaders committed to promote women's rights both within and beyond their organizations. African American women provided more substantial leadership in feminist initiatives emanating from these groups than they did in most of the predominantly white movements that gave rise to feminism, perhaps because African American denominations made up a quarter of the church members represented in the National Council of Churches, the country's largest ecumenical organization, in the 1960s and 1970s.

Many of the most important black feminists, however, did not come from predominantly black denominations. United Methodists Theressa Hoover and Anna Arnold Hageman and Presbyterians Joan Martin and Emily V. Gibbes were among the black feminists who led units of the National Council of Churches. Historian Susan Hartman has recently argued that black women played a larger share in the leadership of feminist initiatives associated with the National Council of Churches than in secular feminist organizations and that as a result racial issues were more central to the agendas of these groups. The interlocking boards of directors of the National Council of Negro Women, the Young Women's Christian Association, and other denominational, ecumenical, and civil rights organizations suggest continuity between the religious content of the nineteenth-century black women's club movement and groups that contributed to second wave feminism.

Church Women United served as an umbrella organization for denominational women's groups and individuals related to the National Council of Churches. In 1965, a year before the founding of NOW, Church Women United sponsored a Committee on the Changing Role of Women that insisted on the need to make "a radical challenge to the Church . . . and raise the question of why the Church is not practicing what it preaches" (Hartman, *The Other Feminists*, 93). In 1969, at the General Assembly of the National Council of Churches of Christ held in Detroit, a women's caucus began its statement with "an affirmation of support for the movement to liberate women." They went on to challenge the assembly to view its own predominantly male composition as inconsistent with its goals of fostering a quest for meaning and wholeness in modern society. The search for community, the statement said, "will be futile if we do not now face up to what it means that God created life in 'our' image—male and female" (Doely, 97–100).

Religious Motivations of Feminist Activism

While religious organizations served as a fertile seedbed for the emerging movement for women's liberation, important feminists active beyond religious circles traced their activism to religious motives. "Without taking Christianity seriously I would never have been prepared to accept radical feminism," recalled Catholic author and activist Sydney Callahan. "Christianity taught me to reappraise the world I knew with a different eye. . . . The value of each individual whom God loved was not to be ignored, suppressed, or harmed in any way" (Doely, 37). Christian existentialism, the student Christian movement, and the civil rights movement, as well as social justice traditions within Catholicism, Judaism, and Protestantism, served as paths to feminism. The sex-segregated organizations and communities in which religious women imbibed these ideas also provided leadership training and experience.

In 1970 the National Student Council of the Young Women's Christian Association voted "One imperative: to eliminate racism wherever it exists by any means necessary." This decision committed hundreds of thousands of young women across the country to a critique of hierarchical social structures and to eliminating discrimination both within their own ranks and in the rest of society. Because the student Christian movement included parallel leadership structures for men and women in YWCAs and YMCAs (Young Men's Christian Associations), it was an important training ground for female activists. Early leaders Casey Hayden and Charlotte Bunch, who helped women's liberation emerge out of the New Left as an independent movement, recalled that women received more encouragement for leadership and self-expression in the student Christian movement than they did in leftist or antiwar groups like Students for a Democratic Society (SDS).

Charlotte Bunch was president of the University Christian Movement when she became one of the organizers of the first women's liberation conference in 1968. When she learned that *Motive*, the magazine of the Methodist Student Movement, was planning a special issue on women, Bunch suggested that Joanne Cooke, the only woman on the editorial staff, attend the conference. Using the language of her tradition, Cooke called her acquisition of feminist consciousness at that event a "conversion," just as Frances Willard spoke of her "conversion" to woman suffrage nearly a hundred years before. "All this is clearly Christian," she wrote about women's liberation. "It assumes brotherhood and sisterhood, with a radical call to mutual concern, involvement and commitment. It assumes working for justice and equality and dignity 'on earth.' And if fighting injustice, inequality and exploitation means a change basic enough to be called a revolution, . . . Amen" ("On the Liberation of Women," 4–5).

What resulted was the "Women's Liberation Issue" edited by Cooke, Bunch, and feminist poet Robin Mor-

gan. An important early collection of women's movement statements (including, for example, Naomi Weisstein's landmark article "Kinder, Kuche, Kirche as Scientific Law: Psychology Constructs the Female"), the issue made a sensation among its primarily Methodist readership. "Churchmen in business suits started coming to the office to demand an explanation," Cooke recalled. "Letters started pouring in, people started inviting me to speak to their church groups, and the issue started selling so fast we had to reprint it." The issue was so successful it was reprinted the following year by Bobbs-Merrill as *The New Woman: A Motive Anthology on Women's Liberation*. While Cooke came to her feminism out of Christian faith and found a vehicle and an audience for its expression within her faith community, "The Women's Liberation Issue" of *Motive* caused an uproar among Methodists and led to the magazine's demise. This scenario would be repeated regularly: Faith commitments led to feminism, but faith communities rejected the fruit they bore.

In *Personal Politics: The Roots of Women's Liberation in the Civil Rights Movement and the New Left* (1980), Sara Evans noted that virtually all the white women active in the earliest years of the civil rights movement came to it first through church-related activities and that it was among this group that feminism emerged. Even pioneers who were not active Christians often found themselves working in Christian groups. Jo Freeman, for example, began her political activism working with the Southern Christian Leadership Conference and worked for the Urban Training Center for Urban Mission sponsored by the United Church of Christ when she became one of the founders of the women's liberation movement in Chicago.

Religious feminists also played a role in founding the National Organization for Women. NOW's founding board included the Roman Catholic nuns Sisters Joel Read and Austin Doherty, and Pauli Murray, the civil rights attorney who became the first African American woman ordained to the Episcopal priesthood, as well as Anna Arnold Hageman from the National Council of Churches and Rev. Dean Lewis, a Presbyterian. In its early years, NOW included religion as an arena of feminist activism. NOW's Ecumenical Task Force on Women and Religion sponsored worship services and advocated for the rights of religious women. Similarly, *Ms. Magazine*, from its inception, reported on feminist activity within religious groups. In 1974, for example, the December issue featured the first ordination of women in the Episcopal Church as well as an excerpt from Mary Daly's *Beyond God the Father*, while the July issue included the response of three religious Jews (Paula Hyman, Audrey Gellis, Bracha Saks) to the question, "Is it Kosher to be a Feminist?"

The Formation of Feminist Religions

While some believers succeeded in reconciling women's liberation with the teachings of their faith traditions, others did not. Feminist concerns have contributed to the formation of new religious movements throughout American history. In the nineteenth century, both Spiritualism and New Thought, for example, emerged as movements blending spiritual and political concerns about women's rights. In the twentieth century, spiritual explorations and expressions pervade cultural feminism, which some see as the dominant form of feminism in the 1980s and 1990s. The insight that gender hierarchies can affect everything from personal identity, relationships, and sexuality to workplace environments and international politics has had profound explanatory power. Seeing the world anew through this interpretative frame has shifted perceptions of reality so fundamentally that many women and men have experienced a spiritual dimension to feminism itself. The view that feminism can mend personal, social, environmental, and cosmic ills resulting from sexism has given rise to new religious movements that place women's issues at center stage.

In 1971, Mary Daly, an assistant professor of theology at Boston College, published a trenchant critique of patriarchal assumptions embedded in Christian doctrine and called on feminists to move *Beyond God the Father*. This invitation served as a catalyst for a new religious movement of women from a variety of backgrounds who concurred with Daly's assertion that "if God is male then male is God" and soundly rejected both propositions. While Daly's theological critique of sexism in Christianity impelled many to seek alternative faiths, an emergent feminist witchcraft provided just such an alternative. Hungarian immigrant Zsuzsanna Budapest, who founded the Susan B. Anthony Coven #1 in Los Angeles, made an explicit connection between modern feminism and pre-Christian religious practices in Europe. In *The Feminist Book of Light and Shadows* (1971) she provided instructions for spells that she traced to traditions passed down through the women of her mother's family in Hungary. The nascent religious movement took inspiration from the translation of Monique Wittig's satiric fantasy *Les Guérillères* (1971), in which a tribe of women warriors overthrows patriarchy. "There was a time when you were not a slave, remember. . . . Or, failing that, invent" (89). Wittig wrote, and the words became a popular aphorism among those who felt the need of historical models for women's spiritual power to undergird contemporary feminism.

Feminists who followed Budapest in believing that they were participating in the revival of a pre-Christian religion with historical roots in Europe found support in Marija Gimbutas's publication *Gods and Goddesses of Old Europe* (1974) that interpreted the archeological record of Goddess figurines as evidence of a matriarchal religious past. Gimbutas, a Lithuanian émigré who received her doctorate from the University of Tübingen and joined the archeology department at the University of California at Los Angeles in 1963, provided the basis for much subsequent discussion of Goddess religion, including Merlin Stone's *When God Was a Woman* (1978). Feminist witchcraft, or Wicca, found its most effective American exponent when Starhawk published *The Spiral Dance: A Rebirth of the Ancient Religion of the Great Goddess* in 1979. Born Mariam Simos, Starhawk described herself as a religious child who became alienated from Judaism because it lacked models of female spiritual power. After meeting Budapest in Los Angeles and participating in Wiccan rituals, she provided instructions through which women remote from knowledgeable or sympathetic peers could learn to practice "the craft."

During the 1980s, several bestselling books popularized the idea that humanity lived at peace with itself and in harmony with nature during a Goddess-worshiping, woman-led prehistory. Marion Zimmer Bradley's feminist retelling of the Arthurian legend, *The Mists of Avalon* (1983), presented the idea that Christianity imposed intolerance, male authority, and sexual repression on a more harmonious, Goddess-centered, pagan world. In *Jambalaya: The Natural Woman's Book of Personal Charms and Practical Rituals* (1985), Luisah Teish introduced the idea that the Caribbean and West African traditions she grew up with in New Orleans provided access to a worldview devoid of patriarchal dualisms. Similar views concerning indigenous cultures of North America appeared in *The Sacred Hoop: Recovering the Feminine in American Indian Traditions* (1986) by the Pueblo/Lakota literary scholar and poet Paula Gunn Allen. The Unitarian Universalist Department of Education produced a popular adult education curriculum that brought Goddess spirituality to its members. The ten units of *Cakes for the Queen of Heaven* (1986) by Unitarian Universalist minister Shirley Ann Ranck became the basis for feminist spirituality groups within the denomination and contributed to the formation of the Covenant of Unitarian Universalist Pagans in 1987. Riane Eisler's immensely popular *The Chalice and the Blade* (1988) portrayed the rise of patriarchy 5,000 years ago as the source of evil in human civilization and as a historical development that is perpetuated through socialization. *The Partnership Way* (1990), a study guide designed to be used with *The Chalice and the Blade*, offered "new tools for . . . healing our families, our communities and our world." Carol Christ, a scholar who wrote several popular books about feminist spirituality, left the academic world to direct the Ariadne Institute, offering pilgrimage tours to Goddess sites in Greece.

Feminist religious movements are also in evidence among established faiths. In the United States, Judaism, Catholicism, Protestantism, and Buddhism all include new movements of which feminism is a central component. Jewish Renewal, a network of about fifty synagogues and communities across the United States, emerged out of a convergence of Jewish feminism with neo-Hasidism, the urge for more intimate and participatory Jewish worship expressed in the *havurah* movement, and concerns for social and racial justice. *Havurah* is the Hebrew word for "fellowship." A *havurah* is a small group that gathers to celebrate Jewish holidays in the home. Arthur Waskow suggests that Jewish renewal embraces "the emergence not only of a movement for equality of women and men in existing Jewish life but more deeply for their equality in shaping what Judaism is to become" (Waskow). The Woman Church Convergence emerged out of Roman Catholic feminist concerns but has come to encompass Christian women from across the religious spectrum. Likewise, Protestant women founded the Reimagining Community to respond to the goals of the World Council of Churches' Ecumenical Decade: Churches in Solidarity with Women but eventually incorporated other Christian and non-Christian participants. The trend toward ecumenism characterizes many feminist religious departures. The Evangelical Women's Caucus changed its name to the Evangelical and Ecumenical Women's Caucus to acknowledge the participation of non-evangelicals, and the National Council of Women Religious became the National Council of Religious Women for similar reasons. Sandy Boucher documented attempts to combine Buddhism and feminism in *Turning the Wheel: American Women Creating the New Buddhism* (1988).

Religious Feminists and Identity

Early on in second wave feminism, African American activists observed the futility of struggling for liberation as a woman unless one simultaneously works for liberation of other oppressed groups to which one belongs. At many points, minority women have chosen to locate their activism within movements of their own groups, rather than within the women's movement. The Black Sisters Conference, for example, participated in several coalitions of women's groups but maintained closer ties to the National Office for Black Catholics. During the 1980s, this concern gave birth to a new religious development, womanist theology. Beginning with Katie Cannon and Delores Williams, theologians, more than any other group, adopted Alice Walker's term *womanist* to articulate a distinctive black religious feminism. Taking the historic oppression of black people as their point of departure, they placed the moral agency of African American women at the center of religious ethics and theological reflection. The term has been adopted primarily by academic theologians and ethicists but has also been used by sociologist Cheryl Townsend Gilkes and historian Elsa Barkely Brown. Plumbing historical and literary sources as well as cultural and oral traditions, womanists use the wisdom of African American women as a resource for religious thought.

Whereas black women had long struggled with the impossibility of choosing whether to identify as blacks or as women, the insight that such oppositions could and should be actively rejected spread to other groups during the 1980s and 1990s. The publication of *Hispanic Women: Prophetic Voice in the Church* (1988) by Cuban-born Ada María Isasi-Díaz and Chicana Yolanda Taranga continued the work of Las Hermanas in articulating a distinctively Latina religious feminism. Following the example of African American theologians' use of the term *womanist*, Isasi-Díaz adopted the term *mujerista* to describe her perspective. The Chicana theologian Maria Pilar Aquino preferred to call herself a "Latina feminist" because of the negative connotations of "mujerismo" (the feminine stereotype complementing *machismo*) in Latin American feminism.

For religious feminists who had felt a conflict between feminism and participation in their faith communities, the new focus on "difference" had a special salience. Members of new or small religious movements, as well as recent immigrant groups, had to balance concern for gender justice with their group's struggle for acceptance in American society.

Muslim feminists looked within their own religious tradition for support for women's rights in the United States. *Karamah*: Muslim Women Lawyers for Human Rights was founded in 1993 by Azizah al-Hibri, professor of law at the University of Richmond, who had also been one of the founders of *Hypatia: A Journal of Feminist Philosophy* in 1986. Taking the Arabic word for "dignity" (*Karamah*) as its title, the group asserts that "the Qu'ran states that God has endowed human beings with dignity. This dignity extends to us all, regardless of race, status, or gender" ("Karamah Means Dignity"). It views Islamic law as an important resource for the defense of women's rights and advocates the use and enforcement of marriage contracts as a way to protect women's property and status. Because Islamic law represents a point of agreement between Muslim feminists and male religious authorities, it is seen as an avenue to the promotion of women's rights that does not conflict with the needs of a community struggling for acceptance in American society. They advise Muslim women both on matters of Islamic law pertaining to gender and on matters of American law pertaining to the free exercise of religion. This reflects their dual goal of addressing discrimination experienced by Muslim women both within their own communities and from non-Muslims.

Jewish women's prominence both as leaders and among the rank and file of feminism far exceeds what would be expected given that Jews comprised no more than 3 percent of the U.S. population. Betty Friedan, Gloria Steinem, Bella Abzug, Letty Cottin Pogrebin, Phyllis Chessler, Vivian Gornick, Shulamith Firestone, Robin Morgan, Andrea Dworkin, and Meredith Tax are among the nationally known Jewish founding figures. Most of this group did not initially connect their religious background with their feminist activism. However, many credited the experiences and values of their Jewish heritage with inspiring their feminist orientation. Friedan, for example, attributed her feminist stirrings to her "passion for justice, which originated in my feelings of the injustice of anti-Semitism" (Schneider, 504).

As the initial political urgency of feminism led into a period of greater introspection and focus on deeper issues of meaning and identity in the 1970s, many of the founding mothers either returned to their Jewish roots or experimented with religious practice for the first time. Beginning in 1976, a veritable "who's who" of the movement gathered annually at feminist Seders to explore how Judaism and feminism could deepen each other. In *The Telling* (1992), participant E. M. Broner chronicled their experiments with retelling the story of the Exodus from the point of view of the Jewish women who fled slavery in Egypt and filling a cup for Miriam, the sister of Moses, rather than for the prophet Elijah. Feminist Seders, widely attended by women not otherwise active in Jewish rituals, continue to enjoy immense popularity.

Although religious feminists played a role from the beginning, activists beyond religious arenas felt pressured to hide or ignore their faith commitments. Jewish women felt a special sting as they participated in international women's conventions where Israeli representatives were attacked as "racists" and resolutions called for the elimination of Zionism "along with colonialism and apartheid" (U.N. General Assembly Resolution 3379, Nov. 10, 1975). In 1982, Letty Cottin Pogrebin decried "anti-Semitism in the Women's Movement" in an article in *Ms. Magazine* (vol. X, no. 12 June 1982: 45–49, 62–72). There she paralleled anti-Semitism and sexism as twin oppressions and noted the prevalence of anti-Semitism on the Radical Left as well as the Political Right, within the African American community, and among religious feminists. While Christian feminists saw sexism as a problem of the Hebrew scriptures that is solved by the New Testament, she wrote, post-Christian Wiccans and Goddess worshippers blamed Jewish monotheism for the demise of Goddess cults and polytheism.

Antifeminism

While the new movement of feminism in the 1960s and 1970s found some enthusiasts within every religious group, it also found serious detractors. Some denominations that nurtured feminist minorities in the 1970s became less sympathetic, or even antagonistic, in the 1990s. Just as the women's movement reinvigorated religious faith and practice among its adherents, it also inspired renewed religious commitment among those who opposed it. Opposition to feminism united faith communities that had rarely found common cause, mobilizing them to new levels of public activism.

Feminist endorsement of reproductive freedoms and especially of the legalization of abortion served to coalesce vague concerns about feminism into a vigorous religious response condemning the movement. As Jane Mansbridge demonstrated in *Why We Lost the ERA* (1986), the Equal Rights Amendment was relatively uncontroversial when it passed the U.S. Senate 84 to 8 in 1972. It was only after the Supreme Court's *Roe v. Wade* decision legalized abortion in 1973 that women's legal equality and legal abortion, the two chief goals of the National Organization for Women, became linked in the public mind. The pro-life and anti-ERA campaigns were the first in which women's issues forged a coalition between conservative elements of the Republican Party (the party platform had long supported the ERA) and previously apolitical religious activists. This coalition included highly successful women's organizations launched by Christian activists, notably Phyllis Schlafley's Eagle Forum and Beverly LaHaye's Concerned Women for America. LaHaye was stirred to action by a 1979 television interview with Betty Friedan, which introduced the former NOW president as representing American women. Concluding that "the feminists' anti-God, anti-family rhetoric did not represent her beliefs, nor those of the vast majority of women," LaHaye founded Concerned Women for America, the highly effective organization she calls "the nation's largest public policy women's organization," and its magazine *Family Voice.*

The response to feminism in the Southern Baptist Convention illustrates its role as a catalyst for polarization. While few Southern Baptist women supported feminism, they participated in the social trends that accompanied it: increased workforce participation, increased educational levels, and delayed marriage and childbearing. As an expanding array of vocations opened to young Baptist women, an unprecedented number experienced a call to ministry. In 1964 Addie Davis became the first Southern Baptist woman to be ordained. By 1988, 500 had followed her example. They had their own organization, Southern Baptist Women in Ministry, where meetings had a decidedly feminist atmosphere. Business was done by consensus, inclusive language was extended not only to worshipers but also to God, and unconventional worship styles including liturgical dance (a radical innovation for Baptists) were introduced. In 1985 an entire issue of the official Southern Baptist student magazine, *The Student*, was devoted to women in ministry. Articles encouraged the ordination of women and concluded that biblical texts on women's submission should be taken no more literally than those instructing slaves to obey their masters.

The trend toward women's equality in Southern Baptist ministry contributed to a movement for greater uniformity that eventually led to fundamentalist ascendancy in the country's largest Protestant denomination. As tensions grew between moderate and fundamentalist Baptists, the ordination of women became symbolic of divisions within the denomination. When fundamentalists gained control of the Southern Baptist Convention, one key victory was a 1984 resolution prohibiting the ordination of women, an unprecedented departure from the long-standing Baptist principle that only local congregations decide whom to ordain. Conservatives made opposition to women clergy a litmus test for leadership, sometimes barring individuals from official positions for merely participating in congregations that ordained women as deacons.

For Southern Baptists, as for Orthodox Christians and Jews, opposition to the ordination of women is part of resistance to liberal modernity, including the liberal commitment to gender equality. In 1986 a coalition of evangelical theologians joined with Southern Baptists in forming the Council on Biblical Manhood and Womanhood to counter "the increasing promotion given to feminist egalitarianism." A 1987 meeting in Danvers, Massachusetts, produced a manifesto, a pamphlet that became known as the "Danvers Statement," endorsing "the glad harmony portrayed in Scripture between the loving, humble leadership of redeemed husbands and the intelligent, willing support of that leadership by redeemed wives."

The religious coalition formed in reaction against feminism left a permanent mark on both political and religious culture in the United States. It has also wearied some whose efforts to create more inclusive religious institutions still meet resistance after decades of discussion. The evangelical feminist magazine *Daughters of Sarah* published its last issue in 1996, and the National Assembly of Religious Women ended twenty-five years of existence in 1995. To some extent, these developments reflect feminism's transition from a small avant-garde to a broad movement that has dispersed onto "the

long march through the institutions." Activists who formerly focused on feminist organizations now lead churches and synagogues, social service groups, seminaries, universities, and denominations. But such developments also reflect the persistence of religious outlooks as determining factors in American debates about gender.

While some organizations of religious feminists that began in the 1960s and 1970s have closed their doors, others have sprung up in unexpected places. During the 1990s some of the most vibrant feminist undertakings have occurred in religious arenas. The energetic response to the 1993 founding of the Re-imagining Community by Christian women "who feel exiled from their tradition and want to find a way back home" and the successful conferences held by the Jewish Orthodox Feminist Alliance beginning in 1997 demonstrate continued interest in feminism in religious groups where it has already had an impact as well as its emergence in new locations. In some cases, discouragement to feminism, such as that offered by the Roman Catholic Church, seems to be a stimulant to continued activity, whereas in others it has the effect of alienating sympathizers from their religious communities. In any case, religion continues to form an important context for the exploration of feminism's impact.

Historians of feminism often describe four types of feminism: radical feminism, liberal feminism, cultural feminism, and socialist feminism. Religious feminists can be found in organizations and activities associated with all four. In some ways, a focus on religion and the vantage point of the twenty-first century draws these categories into question. For example, how would one categorize the feminism of the popular and prolific writer and activist Joan Chittister? A Benedictine nun, she has written over twenty books on feminist theology, the ordination of women, and Benedictine spirituality. Her 1998 book *Heart of Flesh: A Feminist Spirituality for Women and Men* illustrates the ways in which her thought bridges the four categories of feminism. Analyzing the history of patriarchal thinking, she shows how its tendency toward violence, authoritarian domination, and dualistic theology diminishes both women and men. This places her squarely in the camp of radical feminism, usually defined as the view that sexism is the cause not only of women's oppression but also of all forms of hierarchical dualism that result in the dehumanization of and discrimination against particular sectors of society. However, Chittister could easily be considered a liberal feminist, because she is a loyal Catholic whose goal is to reform an institution she views as patriarchal by calling it to its own highest truth. She works for the ordination of women, a classic liberal goal of gaining equal access for women to leadership roles within existing structures. Chittister has for decades lived as part of a community that rejects both private property and the commodification of female sexuality, that is composed exclusively of women, and that is committed to economic justice for the poor—all positions that could identify her with the socialist feminist view that economic class and gender definitions work together to support capitalism and oppress women. A number of her books, such as *Life Ablaze: A Woman's Novena* (2000) and *The Story of Ruth: Twelve Moments in Every Woman's Life* (2000), could be seen as expressions of cultural feminism because they emphasize the benefits of women's distinctive experiences and attributes.

As Chittister's example demonstrates, the inclusion of religious activists may require a reassessment of the categories used to analyze the history of feminism. The historical record demonstrates that religion and feminism are not antithetical forces in American society. Nor do they enjoy an entirely sympathetic relationship. Rather, the stories of religion and feminism are intimately intertwined, tangled in the many webs of meaning through which Americans experience and invent their history.

SOURCES: On the nineteenth century, see Sarah Moore Grimké, *Letters on the Equality of the Sexes* (1838); Gerda Lerner, *The Feminist Thought of Sarah Grimké* (1998) and *The Creation of Feminist Consciousness* (1993); Kathi Kern, *Mrs. Stanton's Bible* (2001); Elizabeth Cady Stanton, Susan B. Anthony, and Matilda Joslyn Gage, eds., *The History of Woman Suffrage* (1881); Mary Church Terrell, "Greetings from the National Association of Colored Women," *National Association Notes* 2 (March 1899): 1, reprinted in Nancy F. Cott et al., *Root of Bitterness*, 2nd (1996), 406–408; Donna A. Behnke, *Religious Issues in Nineteenth-Century Feminism* (1982); and Nancy Isenberg, *Sex and Citizenship in Antebellum America* (1998). While the primary sources on religion and second wave feminism are far too numerous to mention here, the only historical accounts to date have been written by detractors, for example, Donna Steichen, *Ungodly Rage* (1991), and Phillip G. Davis, The *Goddess Unmasked* (1998). For sympathetic accounts, see Judith Hole and Ellen Levine, *Rebirth of Feminism* (1971), and Sarah Bentley Doely, *Women's Liberation and the Church* (1970), which contains feminist resolutions passed by several denominations as well as Sidney Callahan's essay "A Christian Perspective on Feminism." On Catholicism, see Mary Jo Weaver, *New Catholic Women* (1986) and *What's Left: Liberal American Catholics* (1999), which includes Anne E. Patrick's history of the National Assembly of Women Religious, "A Ministry of Justice." Weaver has also edited *Being Right: Conservative Catholics in America* (1995). Feminism in the National Council of Churches is treated in Susan M. Hartman, *The Other Feminists* (1998) and "Expanding Feminism's Field and Focus: Activism in the National Council of Churches in the 1960s and 70s," in Margaret L. Bendroth and Virginia Leison Brereton, *Women and Twentieth-Century Protestantism* (2002). On women in the Southern Baptist Convention, see Nancy Ammerman, *Baptist Battles* (1990); Carl Kell and L. Raymond Camp, *In the Name of the Father* (1999); and Grady

Cothen, *What Happened to the Southern Baptist Convention* (1993). On evangelicals, see David Harrington Watt, *A Transforming Faith* (1991). *The Wisdom of the Daughters* (2001), edited by Reta Halteman Finger and Kari Sandhaas, reprints articles that appeared in *Daughters of Sarah*. Theressa Hoover tells the story of feminism in the United Methodist Church in *With Unveiled Face* (1983). A broad sociological survey of feminist religiosity is Miriam Therese Winter, Adair Lummis, and Allison Stokes, *Defecting in Place* (1995). On the involvement of early second wave feminists in religious campaigns for racial justice, see Sara Evans, *Personal Politics: The Roots of Women's Liberation in the Civil Rights Movement and the New Left* (1980), and Constance Curry et al., *Deep in Our Hearts* (2000). Sister Teresita Basso's "The Emerging 'Chicana' " is reprinted in Alma Garcia, *Chicana Feminist Thought* (1997). Arthur Waskow's "What Is Jewish Renewal? A Definition in Process" appears on the Web site http://www.shalomctr.org. *Karamah*'s mission statement and "Karamah Means Dignity" appear on their Web site http://www.karamah.com. The special double issue of *Motive* "On the Liberation of Women" is in vol. 29, nos. 6–7, March–April 1969. On Jewish feminism, see Susan Schneider, *Jewish and Female* (1984); Letty Cottin Pogrebin, *Deborah, Golda, and Me* (1991) and "Anti-Semitism in the Women's Movement," *Ms.* (1982); and Blu Greenberg, *On Women and Judaism* (1981). On feminist spirituality, see Cynthia Eller, *Living in the Lap of the Goddess* (1993), and Naomi Goldenberg, *Changing of the Gods: Feminism and the End of Traditional Religions* (1979). Mormon feminism is described in Maxine Hanks, ed., *Women and Authority: Re-emerging Mormon Feminism* (1992).

GENDER AND SOCIAL ROLES
Susan Hill Lindley

IN ROUGHLY THE last third of the twentieth century, "gender" as a category for scholarly analysis became increasingly prominent. *Gender* is distinguished from *sex,* the latter being a biologically based reality, whereas the former is socially constructed and is thus largely cultural and psychological. Self-conscious separation of "sex" and "gender" represents a significant change, since for much of human history gender and social roles were presumed to be as "natural" and unchangeable as biological sex. Intellectual, spiritual, and psychological abilities and characteristics were viewed as inevitably rooted in the particular biology of male and female. For example, it was widely assumed that women are "naturally" nurturing, emotional, and sensitive to others, whereas men are "naturally" aggressive, active, rational, and dominant.

Historical and cross-cultural studies and their result in increased historical and cross-cultural sensitivity were major factors in challenging the inevitability of certain cultural gender patterns. It became obvious that while virtually all human groups assigned particular roles to

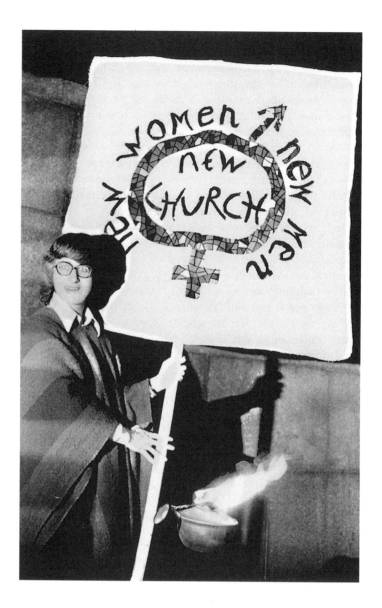

Many scholars, church leaders, and laypeople have begun, within the last few decades, to study and view religious beliefs and practices through a gender lens.
Copyright © Bettye Lane Studio

males and to females, those roles could be drastically different over time and across cultures. Such studies undercut any argument that biological differences alone invariably result in particular roles for men or women. Feminist scholars also questioned the rigidity, "naturalness," and purpose of gender roles, especially since they so frequently were asymmetrical: Women's roles were secondary, subordinate, less valued, and less rewarded.

But if gender is a social construction, not a biological necessity, why has some form of gendered social roles been so virtually universal in human history, and why, despite real variations across time and culture, have the asymmetry and some roles and characterizations been so widespread? A common suggestion for the origin of gendered social roles is found in a combination of biology and the survival needs of early hunting and gathering societies. A division of labor emerged, it is speculated, because of women's unique role in pregnancy

and nursing. Women thus specialized in child care and in those activities that could be performed in a relatively limited range of space, like gathering and early forms of agriculture. Men, on the other hand, had greater mobility and less interrupted time blocks (and quite possibly greater size and strength) and thus could specialize in activities like hunting and defense of the group. Over time, the division of labor led to division of spheres and differentials of power and value. Such gendered patterns of division and, typically, female subordination were culturally elaborated and enforced well beyond whatever biological and subsistence needs had generated them. Furthermore, when identification of one's own biological offspring was valued, men developed social rules and structures to ensure their paternity, which was less obvious than women's maternal connection with the children they bore.

Yet even those who concede such possible origin of

gender roles raised serious questions about their elaboration and development, their functionality in drastically different times and social situations, and the widespread devaluation of female activities and restriction of female power. At the same time, feminists challenged the implicit androcentrism of much of human and especially Western culture: that *man* is assumed to be the norm, a "neutral" term interchangeable with *human* and that women are, in some sense, deviants from that norm. As feminist philosopher Simone de Beauvoir suggested in *The Second Sex*, women have been perceived as the "Other." Uncovering and challenging that assumption of male as norm—the term *man* as both sex specific and putatively generic—thus required attention to gender as distinct from sex and to the forms of social control and enculturation that not only made sharply differentiated—and restrictive—roles seem natural but reinforced the asymmetry of female subordination.

Over the last few decades, scholars have come to different conclusions about a number of questions. Is "sex" itself at least partly a social construction rather than an immutable biological reality? Is the traditional binary division of male and female overly simplistic, ignoring not only homosexual persons but also those who are bisexual or transgendered? How does such biological sexual diversity interact with gender categories and assumptions? How are gender categories, roles, and identities interstructured with other forms of social and cultural division like race, ethnicity, and class? What is the balance of identity and difference, the individual as autonomous and as embedded in social groups and categories? To what degree *are* gender roles biologically based, or are they *purely* matters of cultural construction? If gender is constructed, can—or should—it be completely deconstructed? At one end of a "nature/nurture" assessment of a gender roles spectrum are "essentialists" who argue that while some elements of gender roles and identities may clearly be cultural constructions that vary over time and space, there are other important biologically based elements of gender that extend across time and cultures, giving women a common identity and making some sorts of gender roles or traits not only inevitable but desirable. At the other end are radical deconstructionists who argue that gender is wholly a social construct that can and should be eliminated as a social category, that emphasizing commonalities of "woman" obscures wide differences among women, especially across cultures, classes, and races, and that gender polarization combined with androcentrism is detrimental to individual humans, male and female, but especially to women who have been controlled and subordinated as a group. In addition, scholars studying gender place varying emphases on psychological, social, or cultural causes for persons' development of a gender identity. Wherever one stands on such a spectrum, though, it seems clear that self-conscious attention to gender as, at least in part, a social construction and to gender roles—their origin, impact, and persistence—can no longer be ignored in any serious attention to the "human condition," past or present.

Attention to gender as a category for investigation is particularly important in religious studies, not only because religion deals so centrally with human history, values, experiences, and social worlds, and because male religious experiences and pronouncements have been portrayed as normative and (falsely) neutral, but also because religion for so long provided the most important sanctions for setting and reinforcing gender roles through symbol, myth, law, tradition, and ritual. God (or the gods) created male-female differences in nature and roles. They are thus both divinely ordained and "natural"—and therefore those who deviate from assigned gender roles and identities are not only "unnatural" but also rebels against divine authority. In modern times, there has been a shift in some circles to argue that "science" or evolution is the source of "natural" biological differences, which then justify a wide range of cultural and social differences; such ideas were manifest in the late twentieth century in sociobiology or prenatal hormone theory. Still, for many people even in the twenty-first century, religious justifications for distinct gender roles rooted in the divine creation of male and female remain operative.

Insisting that gender must be taken as a central category in religious studies is not to suggest either that there are no commonalities in the religious beliefs and experiences of men and women or that there are not sometimes greater variations among women and among men than there are between the two genders. In other words, a gender approach to religious studies, in the sense of looking self-consciously and explicitly at those social constructions and their impact, is critical but not comprehensive. "Gender" is a relevant and unavoidable category. To be oblivious of historical and current differences between men and women, whether one believes them to be rooted in nature, the divine will, science, or culture, is dishonest and perpetuates the androcentric assumption of man as norm: *Homo religiosus* has in fact meant religious man, not religious person. But gender as the only approach risks overlooking complexities and the importance of other categories and could result in a new and sophisticated, but still reductionist, affirmation that biology was or is destiny.

Moreover, in trying to study gender roles in a particular religious tradition, one must be constantly aware of the tremendous variety within that tradition, depending on time, subgroup, geographical area, and so forth. Self-conscious and critical use of sources is also imperative. Written traditions—scriptures, laws, stories—have been central in much study of religion, and there is no question that they have hugely shaped traditions and hold continued contemporary authority. They cannot be ignored for questions about gender. Yet most—not all—written sources have been produced by men and thus often have failed to report much about women's religious ideas and experiences, assuming an androcentric norm; furthermore, when dealing with women's nature and roles, male writers at times have been more wishfully prescriptive than descriptive of actualities, let alone of women's perspectives on such matters. Thus more careful and nuanced reading of what is in those sources—and what is between the lines—is critical, as is attention to women's own writings and alternative sources like oral tradition, ritual, or art in order to reconstruct a more comprehensive and inclusive picture.

The remainder of this essay will focus on gender and social roles for women in religious groups in North America, although, except for Native Americans, this must include attention to religious foundations elsewhere. What gender and social roles have been prescribed for women by particular religions? Where do they come from, and what purposes do they serve? What authority is cited to give them weight? What limitations do they impose on women? What constructive or rewarding possibilities, images, and actions do they allow? How have women accepted, reinforced, and used such roles? How have women challenged or rejected gender and social roles? How and why have they changed over time?

Even before looking at social roles, however, it is helpful to consider gendered images of the divine, for these have had significant implications for psychological and social understandings of women's and men's natures and roles. In the Western monotheistic traditions, Judaism, Islam, and Christianity, the overwhelming evidence of images and language presents a male Supreme Being, despite periodic insistence by some voices in those traditions that God is spirit, ineffable, beyond human characteristics like gender. Recent feminist scholars have mined these traditions for alternative feminine symbols or representations, like the Shekhinah or "presence of God" in some Jewish traditions or the figure of "Lady Wisdom" or Sophia. Roman Catholic and Orthodox Christianity have strong traditions honoring Mary and female saints, and while they were, officially, to be venerated rather than worshipped and not to be seen as equal to God, these presented believers, both men and women, with female images for devotion and gave women opportunities for identification. In Buddhism, there is no "God" in the sense of a supreme deity, but there have been female savior figures or bodhisattvas like Prajnaparamita or Kuan Yin. Yet these are far less common than male figures; and, indeed, in some parts of

the tradition, a female must first become male before achieving Buddhahood.

Other religious traditions, including Hinduism and various Native American traditions, provide numerous female images of divinity along with male ones, providing men and women alike with gendered models and symbols. Some of the new religious traditions emerging in North America consciously symbolized divinity as both Mother and Father, notably the Shakers and the Christian Science of Mary Baker Eddy. The theology of the Church of Jesus Christ of Latter-day Saints formally and necessarily includes a "Mother in Heaven," but functionally her role has remained peripheral and minimal, although some contemporary Mormon feminists have endeavored to reintroduce and emphasize this imagery.

What is the impact of gendered—or ungendered—images and symbols of the divine on humans and their roles in a given tradition? The issue is a complex one, and much contemporary scholarship suggests that a single simplistic answer is both inadequate and misleading. On the one hand, the preponderance of male images often has been used to sanction and reinforce male privilege: Men's greater resemblance to God is frequently cited or assumed as endorsing men's "natural" religious and cultural leadership and their superior spirituality. Current resistance to "God-She" in many circles, even by those who agree that, of course, God isn't literally male, suggests a close identity of male images or symbols with divine reality for many believers. Furthermore, the presence of goddesses or other female divine figures does not necessarily translate into consistently egalitarian gender roles and value in religious and cultural practice. Given the reality of female symbols in some traditions and the search for recovery of female images and symbols by contemporary feminists, one might suggest that some form of female symbolism for the divine is a necessary, but not a sufficient, condition for more positive and egalitarian views on women's nature and roles. On the other hand, one cannot dismiss the degree to which the presence of Mary and the saints in Catholic tradition, female bodhisattvas in Buddhism, or female figures in Hinduism has allowed believers, especially women, to identify with and to focus their spirituality on symbols that affirmed their own gendered being. Moreover, women's own perception of female figures in myth and legend may not have conformed to official male orthodox interpretations. Thus while gendered symbols have often undoubtedly reinforced culturally defined gender and social roles, they have also—for different people and at different times—provided justification for challenging or reinterpreting those roles.

Symbols of the divine or ultimate reality undoubtedly impact gender roles in a given tradition. Equally important are the sources of authority that include such symbols but a great deal more in terms of myth, stories, history, and directives for human life, including significant material on gender roles. In many cases, such authority is found first in a written scripture: the Torah for Jews, the Christian Bible, the Qur'an for Muslims, the Vedas (*sruti*—"that which is heard") for Hindus, or the Pali canon for Buddhists. In addition, these traditions or streams within them have developed further written authorities like the Jewish Talmud, hadith literature in Islam, the Book of Mormon, Tibetan tantra or Zen commentaries in Buddhism, or literature known as *smriti* ("that which is remembered") like the Ramayana, Mahabharata, Puranas, and the Manusmriti in Hinduism. Questions then arise not only about the content and relative authority of written traditions but also about who has had or now has the authority to interpret foundational writings. Historically and predominantly, it has been men, although occasionally women have presented alternative readings. Today many feminists who wish to remain within a religious tradition turn to the foundational writings to find more positive and egalitarian elements and to critique later male interpretations, which are often more restrictive on matters of gender than were the original texts. Further questions arise in situations either where there is not a specific or uniquely authoritative written source or when additional sources of authority exist, like a religious leader who may either receive additional revelation, as in the case of Mormons, or can pronounce an authoritative interpretation of tradition, like the pope. Thus study of religion and gender is, on the one hand, *descriptive*: What, indeed, have been gender roles in the history of a given tradition, recognizing the diversity that has existed within every tradition, however much some leaders may wish to minimize that diversity in the interests of a single, consistent pattern? But study can also be *normative*: What might or should gender roles be?

Finally, gender roles have been decisively shaped by perceptions of the essential nature(s) of men and women and how that impacts not only activities in this life but also one's potential for salvation, however salvation is understood. In a number of religious traditions, there is significant ambivalence about whether males and females share the same essential human nature. One part of Christian tradition has insisted that while both men and women have a spiritual nature, women's subordination to men is part of the original order of creation, a subordination then intensified by Eve's greater guilt in the Fall. As a result of pervasive dualism in the early years of the Church, women were believed to be more carnal and less spiritual than men, identified with the inferior "material" aspect of reality. Some women could overcome that disadvantage by denying their more sexual female nature and remaining celibate, thus becoming "male." Yet other strains in Christianity suggested that "in Christ" there is neither male nor female, insofar as both sexes have souls, can be baptized, and may become saints, the highest honor for a human being. By the modern period, one can distinguish two streams challenging the superiority of male nature: One, influenced by the Enlightenment, insisted on the same essential human nature of men and women; the other proposed that men's and women's natures were equal but different ("complementary"). Furthermore, some Christians (and some post-Christians) argued for a kind of female superiority where women were seen as, by nature, more pious, peaceful, and moral.

Whether or not Christians believed in women's essentially different nature, the vast majority were convinced that differentiation and hierarchy for men and women were ordained by God and necessary in this life. For example, while the Puritans affirmed spiritual equality, they denied the possibility that it should translate into equal social roles or eliminate women's subordination. The Society of Friends was unusual, as its founders George Fox and Margaret Fell argued that female subordination in this world was a result of the Fall, but with redemption in Christ, such subordination was overcome, and the religious and social roles they endorsed, though not perfectly egalitarian, were much more radical than those allowed by other Christians of their day. Nor has the debate ended in contemporary America. A number of fundamentalist or evangelical groups, such as the Southern Baptists, affirm both different natures and a divine mandate for women's subordination (though insisting this does not undermine women's equal worth in the sight of God). Other Christians, including many feminists, take a position that women and men share the same essential human nature and reject both hierarchy and restrictive gender roles in church and society. Still others, again including some feminists, propose some form of essentialist view: Women do have a different nature than men, one that is, if anything, superior, and it should be valued and its impact increased in the public world.

Whatever their views on essential nature or social roles, most Christians believed not only that women could be saved but also that gender divisions and roles would be overcome in heaven. The same was not true for the Church of Jesus Christ of Latter-day Saints: Both men and women can be saved and achieve the highest level of heaven, but that is reserved only for those married "for time and eternity" as Mormons in this life; thus, families, gender identity, and gender roles continue in heaven. Streams within other traditions, too, claim that woman's place in an afterlife, if not the possibility of salvation, depends on her earthly marital situation. In an Orthodox Jewish tradition, a woman's place in heaven is dependent on her husband: The more she can enable his spiritual growth, the higher both will be. Traditional Hindu law suggests that a woman's place in heaven is dependent on her obedience to her husband. Faithful marriages will continue in heaven, although the husband, not the wife, has the possibility of multiple partners. In addition, questions of nature and salvation are complicated, as they are in Buddhism, by the doctrines of karma and reincarnation: Rebirth as a man is seen as "higher" in the progress toward *moksha*, or nirvana, if not actually a necessary condition for release from the cycles of rebirth.

Nevertheless, Judaism, Hinduism, Buddhism, and Islam, like Christianity, are multivocal about woman's essential nature and possibilities for salvation. While Judaism clearly endorses distinctive roles for men and women, it generally affirms the essential sameness of human nature and equal opportunities of salvation for the faithful Jew. Much of Hindu tradition affirms that women do, indeed, have different natures than men, closely tied to their different female bodies with implications for purity and pollution, but there are also sources like the Upanishads and the Bhagavad-gita that downplay essential differences in nature and stress the existence of the infinite divine spirit, or brahman, in human nature, regardless of sex, even though that identity of nature does not translate into similar or equal gender roles. In Islam, the dominant tradition rooted in the Qur'an is that women and men are equally human, equal in their obligation to submit to Allah's will, and equally responsible for their actions at the day of judgment; both men and women can become saints. Yet parts of the later hadith literature portray women as having an inferior mental and moral nature—and in both traditions, different gender roles in this life are commended. In the Buddha's original teachings, the goal and possibility of salvation are open to both men and women, but some later traditions diverged, with a few insisting that only monastics or only men can attain enlightenment. As religious traditions thus give no single "answer" on woman's nature (positive or negative), so they all present both positive and negative images of women, often but not always tied to how well women fulfill the cultural roles set largely by men and to whether women help or retard male identity and functioning. Thus "nature" is tied to gender roles, and in most cases both are viewed from male perspectives and to male advantage.

The roles most widely sanctioned for a woman across religious traditions are those of wife and mother, not merely as two among many human social functions but as her dominant identity. In traditional Judaism, marriage is the norm for both men and women, and a clear division of gender roles is rooted in halakah, or law. Woman's sphere is the home; man's, ideally, public religious leadership and study, although women participated and were commended for involvement in economic activity as an extension of the home, particularly if this enabled their husbands to pursue religious study. Not surprisingly, given that division, education was much more limited for girls, focused on what was needed for their domestic religious roles and, perhaps, economic functioning—not the scholarly study that was the highest goal and honor for men. Many mitzvoth, or commandments, applied equally to men and women, but, significantly, the reason women were exempted (traditionally if not universally in practice) from certain "timebound positive mitzvoth" was their domestic responsibility, and the three particular commandments for women (blessing the Sabbath bread before baking, lighting Sabbath candles, and observing ritual purity around menstruation) were directly related to their familial roles. In Hindu law, women were always to be under the control of a man—father, husband, or son—and while men, too, were expected to marry, the ideal for them was to progress beyond the first stage of student and the second stage of householder to the third stage of forest dweller and the fourth of renunciant—that is, one who embraces poverty and chastity and renounces ties to family and community. There were, indeed, some women who became ascetics and were honored as such, but the option was much more rarely taken than it was by men, and a woman who remained with her husband as he chose to become a forest dweller did so primarily to continue to serve him. In one tradition, the woman who culminates her devotion to her husband by becoming suttee, joining her deceased spouse on the funeral pyre, was not only honored in the community but expected to rejoin him directly in heaven. As in Judaism, a woman's education in religious matters was generally limited to what was necessary in her domestic role, so that in both traditions, the religious leadership that demanded substantial knowledge of sacred texts and commentaries was held by men with only rare exceptions. In Islam, too, marriage is the norm for both men and women; gender roles are both distinctive and hierarchical; woman's sphere is the home; and education for girls has traditionally been more limited than that of boys. Yet it is important to note that in modern times and particularly, though by no means exclusively, in North America, some of these traditions are being challenged: Marriage itself is still highly valued, but there is a move to deemphasize hierarchy and commend complementarity, if not mutual reciprocity in roles, as well as to encourage further religious education for women, for their own spiritual benefit and to enable them to better educate their children in religious traditions.

Occasional respected religious alternatives to woman's primary domestic role have existed in Judaism, Hinduism, and Islam, but they have been neither widespread nor systematic over the history of these traditions. In Buddhism and Christianity, however, there have been systematic and institutionalized alternative religious roles to wife- and motherhood, primarily asceticism or monasticism, generally seen as a higher spiritual way of life. Both Orthodox and Roman Catholic Christianity have offered to women, since the early centuries of the Church, a supported and commended option of celibacy and membership in a religious order. Thus Protestant Christianity's general rejection of monasticism impacted women particularly in reducing their respectable role options to one: wife and mother. A woman's single state was presumed to be a matter of misfortune, not choice, although Protestant women in the nineteenth century developed functional alternatives such as a religious career as a missionary or deaconess for those who felt called to a life of religious service outside of marriage. Buddhism, too, has a tradition of female monks dating back to its founding, although that tradition continued in Mahayana Buddhism in China, Taiwan, Vietnam, and Korea, while it died out in areas that embraced Theravada Buddhism or was replaced by a kind of semimonastic option embraced by some women. The Vajrayana tradition, primarily in Tibet, continued to have both male and female monastics and also developed distinctive roles for laymen and laywomen as teachers or gurus. The choice of the ascetic or monastic life in both Christianity and Buddhism offered to women not only greater spiritual rewards but often also greater opportunities for education, and consequently numerous women attained a certain spiritual authority for other believers. Yet even as nuns, women remained subordinate to male authority. There were, to be sure, occasional Christian abbesses in the early medieval period who exercised authority over dual houses— communities of men and women—but even they, and certainly most nuns and sisters in subsequent centuries, remained under the authority of a male clerical hierarchy. Gautama himself may have founded monastic groups for both men and women, but later tradition at least attributed to him a certain reluctance in doing so and an insistence that even the highest female monastic was subordinate to any male monk. In later tradition, since the prayers of male monks were seen as more valuable than those of women, lay support for the women was substantially less than that for men. Some Buddhist traditions also developed laywomen's groups that focused on devotion and doing good works, thus "making merit" (building up karma), but this role was not an ordained one and could complement a woman's domestic roles.

Even when a religious tradition offered alternatives to women, structural or exceptional, the majority of women still found their primary roles in home and family, and it was there that they developed a distinctive religious identity, an identity shaped by a combination of official (male) religious authority and their own perspectives, developments, emphases, and reinterpretations. While particulars varied across religious lines and over time—and within individual religious traditions due to factors like ethnicity—home-based rituals compensated women for those more public roles and activities from which they were excluded or, at least, discouraged from participation. Frequently women's domestic rituals were keyed to important female life cycle events and focused on the well-being of other family members, but they also enabled women to develop a distinctive spirituality and informal communities of women through prayer, ritual, and story. At times, this might take the form of more central focus on the female figures who were present but less central in the dominant male tradition: For example, Christian women sometimes focused their piety not only on Mary but on female saints; and *tkhines*, prayers developed by medieval Jewish women, invoked the matriarchs Sarah, Rebecca, Rachel, and Leah and other biblical heroines. Kuan Yin, the female manifestation of the bodhisattva in China, was seen as especially responsive to women's concerns of health, fertility, and family roles and restrictions. *Vratas* (vows), available to both men and women in Hinduism, were more frequently practiced by women. Involving fasting, mantra repetition, or other ascetic practices, vows might be undertaken with other women in one's household or in the community—and without a male priest—for the well-being and safety of their families. Women also took advantage of alternative quasi-public forms to supplement domestic religion and limited participation in central worship forms dominated by men: For example, in Roman Catholicism, Islam, Buddhism, and Hinduism, women went on pilgrimages or sought out shrines of saints.

Using gender as a central category of investigation in religious studies provides significantly more nuanced answers to questions like the nature of the divine, the nature of human beings, salvation, and social roles that are religiously sanctioned and enforced, even as further study suggests that the actualities of women's spirituality, religious activities, and self-understandings may have diverged from male perceptions of them. Another important question concerns religious leadership: How did (and do) women exercise religious leadership in those major historic traditions where most formal leadership and the highest religious authority were restricted to men, and how have these changed in some groups in recent times? What parallel forms of leadership have existed for women? What roles for women have been offered in more recently formed religions?

As suggested above, women have exercised religious leadership for other women, whether informally in home-based settings or communities of women or in a more officially recognized capacity. Women in Catholicism and Buddhism exercised authority within women's monastic communities. In medieval Judaism, a woman more learned in Hebrew and religious law known as a *firzogerin* might lead prayers for women in their own section of the synagogue. Protestant Christian and Reformed and Conservative Jewish women in America developed and led women's groups or sisterhoods that paralleled male-led religious bodies and engaged in study, fund-raising, and benevolent activities. Vegetarian societies developed by Chinese laywomen that combined communal devotion with charitable activities were brought to North America by Chinese women immigrants. In the early twentieth century, a movement known as Brahma-Kumaris (Maidens of Brahma) emerged with exclusively female leadership and mostly women members. They operate centers throughout India and abroad that prescribe a strict regimen of yoga and meditation practice to prepare for the imminent destruction of the world at the end of the *Kali*, or fourth period of the Hindu time cycle. Although in most of these examples women were ultimately subject to some male authority, they still held acknowledged positions of leadership and in practice were often able to exercise considerable functional autonomy (especially as men benefited from the funds they raised or the services they provided).

Some women have also been able to exercise a certain spiritual authority over both men and women due to an unusual degree of religious learning, mystical experience, or divine revelation: Prophetesses in Jewish and Christian scriptures; mystics like St. Catherine of Siena or Julian of Norwich in Christianity or Rabia al-Adawiyah in the Sufi tradition of Islam; Yeshe Tsogyal, a woman who was instrumental in the spread of Buddhism in Tibet, a teacher and sage; Bengali mystic and teacher Anandamayi Ma, who by the time of her death in 1982 had established some twenty-eight Hindu ashrams, or monasteries, for disciples who practiced her teachings.

In modern times and in some traditions, women have gained access to formal roles of religious leadership previously restricted to men. Reformed and Conservative Jews have women rabbis; women have been ordained in most Protestant groups; women function as spiritual leaders in predominantly Euro-American or African American Buddhist groups like some Zen centers and Tibetan Buddhist organizations—women like Pema Chodron, a fully ordained Buddhist nun who is the director of Gampo Abbey in Nova Scotia. In other traditions, however, the most prominent formal leadership roles are not open to women: Orthodox Judaism has no female rabbis; Roman Catholic and Eastern Orthodox Christianity and some branches of Protestantism

do not ordain women; the role of iman is not open to Islamic women. While Hindu women can be and have been gurus, or spiritual leaders, they have not traditionally been priests, ritual experts, although there is some movement in India to train women for such roles. Ironically, as women have moved into de jure if not de facto equality with men, in terms of participation in public worship and of leadership, some distinctively female traditions, rituals, and groups have been diminished or marginalized, a loss welcomed by some women but regarded with more ambivalence by others.

It is hard to generalize about the religious traditions of indigenous North Americans because of significant variations among tribal groups, the impact of European culture, and the lack of foundational religious texts, but some conclusions may be suggested. Virtually all Native American tribes affirmed the religious, cultural, and economic importance of women's roles as wives and mothers and, in many cases, viewed these gender roles as complementary rather than subordinate to those of men. Women then exercised significant religious leadership in specific female groups but also sometimes for both men and women: For example, women could be shamans, those religious figures whose special knowledge and power can help other humans to right and balanced relationships with the natural world and the spirit world. Today, a number of Native American women are searching for resources within their own tribal traditions that reaffirm women's religious experiences and leadership, just as contemporary Christians, Jews, Buddhists, and Muslims search for a usable past in their own foundational scriptures and early traditions. In addition, some non-Indian religious bodies begun in America have offered women as well as men opportunities for religious leadership since their founding, like the Shakers, Christian Science, or Theosophy, although others like the Mormons have followed more traditional patterns, allowing women quasi-parallel roles but restricting the priesthood to men. Finally, self-consciously post-Jewish or post-Christian forms of women's spirituality and Goddess religion emerged in the last third of the twentieth century whose leadership and membership were either predominantly or exclusively female.

Using a gender lens to study religion reveals some broad commonalities in women's religious roles, like the importance of female domestic rituals, but it also reveals significant diversity between and within traditions, ambivalence about woman's nature and spiritual potential, and frequently a disjunction between official male expectations and women's own behavior and perspectives. In addition, such study often uncovers marked asymmetry: Polygyny was condoned but not polyandry; divorce was much more difficult if not impossible for women in traditional Judaism or Islam to initiate than

it was for men; male adultery was not regarded as seriously as female unfaithfulness; men and women were
both expected to marry in traditional forms of Judaism,
Hinduism, or Islam, but that role constituted only a part
of male identity, whereas it was a woman's whole; men
and women in Christianity and Buddhism were both
offered a monastic alternative, yet women monastics frequently had lower status and remained in some way under male control.

Rarely are gender categories and questions the exhaustive explanation or single interpretive key for a religious topic, but they have added new and significant
dimensions in a number of recent studies. One such
fruitful application of gender questions and categories
concerns "fundamentalism." Initially, attention focused
on classic American fundamentalism as it emerged in
the early decades of the twentieth century. Those fundamentalist groups and leaders retreated from the relative openness to women's religious (not political or familial) leadership that marked the early years of
evangelical churches and Bible schools. They explicitly
repudiated "feminized" theology and recruited men to
join churches and take places and leadership therein;
they deplored the images and activities of the "new
woman" and idealized the gender roles of the Victorian
family. More recent study of fundamentalist resurgence
not only has continued to identify a crucial link between
Christian fundamentalism and a conservative ideology
of gender but also has proposed extension of the term
fundamentalist to other religions' manifestations of revitalized conservatism or traditionalism. That further
step has not been without controversy, as some scholars
have rejected the use of a term they consider to be historically incongruous and inherently pejorative.

Nevertheless, even if the term *fundamentalist* is rejected, there appears to be widespread congruence between conservative religious resurgences and a return to
or reaffirmation of clear and traditional gender roles.
Not only has the New Christian Right consistently opposed the feminist movement and issues like the Equal
Rights Amendment and abortion; it has also championed female submission to male headship in family and
church. Internationally, some Islamic societies' renewed
emphasis on restriction of women in terms of dress,
social customs, employment possibilities, and public activity has frequently accompanied Islamist resurgence.
While the more extreme actions in, for example, Af-
ghanistan, are not paralleled among North American
Muslims, there are tensions and controversies over matters like traditional dress and social customs. Does
"modest" dress require the wearing of traditional clothing, including the *hijab,* or head covering? Should
daughters be allowed to "date"? Is it appropriate for a
Muslim woman to leave her children in the care of others, especially nonfamily members, in order to pursue a

career? Among Muslims generally and in North America
in particular, preference for traditional roles and dress
for women is often linked to a rejection of certain Western cultural values like materialism and sexual freedom.
Furthermore, as loss of one's faith is tied to weakened
cultural identity, women, as traditional bearers of culture and centers of family life, become the foci for preservation of religious tradition and identity.

Nor is the issue either new or unique with Islamic
immigrants to America, as ethnic and religious immigrants both past and present have wrestled with the
problem of "Americanization": How much is necessary
for sheer survival? What changes and new opportunities
are seen by some immigrants as desirable but by others
as dangerous? At what point does Americanization become a threat to one's very Catholic or Jewish, Buddhist
or Muslim identity, as individuals or as a group? When
a decision is made to resist such Americanization by
ways that disproportionately affect women, might there
be differences in men's and women's motivation? If
some men display a need to control the female "Other"
when other aspects of their world appear to be beyond
their control, as Stratton suggests in his introduction to
Fundamentalism and Gender, might some women supportive of or attracted to such movements be motivated
not only by internalization of the gendered expectations
and symbols of the faith but also by a wish to claim
honor and respect for their traditional "female" roles
and values? Such a motivation appears plausible particularly when women perceive their traditional roles as
being under attack by other women or by social, cultural, or political authorities. Still other women may be
searching for changes they believe to be compatible with
the essence of their faith. Tensions and controversy in
situations where individual and group identity are perceived to be at stake are hardly surprising. Careful use
of gender analysis and recognition of diversity may help
scholars to avoid simplistic analyses or reductionist interpretations.

A second example of the significance of a gender lens
for a contemporary issue in American religion concerns
formal religious leadership. As ordained women in Protestant and Jewish groups in America became more than
a token few, questions were raised about their career
opportunities from initial placement through advancement and about whether women, as a group, would
bring different gifts, styles, and goals to the ordained
ministry. These questions present a variation on the
theme of "feminization" of American religion raised by
scholars like Barbara Welter and Anna Douglas about
Christianity in nineteenth-century America. Their concept of feminization included two major claims: first,
that women became by a decided margin the majority
of active church members, despite their exclusion from
its highest levels of formal leadership; second, that

the content of religion became more "feminine," more privatized and domesticated, emotional or even sentimental.

As different Christian and Jewish groups in America considered female ordination in the second half of the twentieth century, there were some observers who, noting the preponderance of women as active members in existing congregations, feared that allowing women to assume formal leadership might complete a female takeover of religion and drive men from the pews and the (now devalued) profession. Other observers wondered if ordained women would truly be accepted by congregations and their professional peers. By the late 1980s and into the 1990s, it appeared that while proportions of women studying in seminaries and being ordained had grown substantially, men had not abandoned the profession but continued to seek ordination and ministerial careers. Nor did women have a particularly more difficult time than men in finding an initial placement, once they had graduated or been ordained. But as a few women reached high-status jobs (senior minister or rabbi of a large congregation, bishop, etc.), others found it more difficult to advance up a career ladder, whether this was because of a "stained glass" ceiling or because of personal choices (e.g., choosing a smaller or more relational setting for ministry, or preferring to balance professional work and family responsibilities). Time, statistics, and research by social scientists will begin to answer questions about this aspect of "feminization," that is, whether religious institutions that ordain women will become overwhelmingly female in both membership and leadership.

More subtle but equally interesting is the question of feminization in terms of content. For most male leaders in the late nineteenth and early twentieth centuries and for many scholars studying the phenomenon, the term had a pejorative connotation: A feminized religion was soft, sentimental, and lacking in theological and intellectual rigor. By the end of the twentieth century, the perspective had undergone a dramatic shift. Some who saw women ministers, priests, and rabbis bringing a different and distinctive approach to ordained leadership, one more attuned to cooperation, empowerment, and equality, welcomed and commended the change. Indeed, they even argued that a change in the nature of religious leadership that would result from women's ordination was a strong argument in favor of that move. Such arguments would appear to have elements of an essentialist approach to matters of gender. Others, both advocates within religious traditions and some social scientists, have disagreed. In his study, Edward Lehman found some differences between male and female clergy but fewer than "maximalists" expected. More significant differences in ministerial style, he found, are related to one's ethnic or racial identity, when she or he attended seminary, or the type of position held. While both statistical studies and anecdotal-experiential evidence will probably continue to fuel debates on the question of a "feminine" style or approach to ministry, the range of persons and situations involved will likely preclude a simple answer.

Attention to gender and to social roles dramatically expands our understanding of human religious experience even as it displaces the falsely universal *homo religious*. Yet certain cautions are appropriate to any claim of exhaustive explanation. First, at a descriptive level, despite real gains and innovative use of resources, there are unavoidable limitations due to lack of evidence, particularly in early periods that would enable scholars *fully* to understand what women themselves thought and did beyond male views and prescriptions. Even more significant concerns arise as one moves from the descriptive to the normative. For example, a radical deconstructionist approach might seem to devalue women's social roles and thus dismiss the religious experiences of many women, historically and even today, who embrace "traditional" roles. On the other hand, a thoroughgoing essentialist approach runs the risk of ignoring or dismissing individuals or communities, different times or traditions, that do not fit expected patterns or values. While the descriptive and the normative cannot be neatly and consistently separated any more than a *purely* objective stance is possible for the scholar, the attempt to maintain some distinction is critical, lest feminist scholars find themselves ironically in a position similar to that of those men who, historically, presumed to describe but really prescribed women's roles and nature. To preclude a new false universality, scholars making use of the gender lens must recognize the significant diversity in thought and practice within each religious tradition as well as among them, keep racial/ethnic and class differences in mind, and balance insider and outsider perspectives with self-consciousness and awareness of their own limitations as they report and analyze women's religious experiences.

SOURCES: On fundamentalism and gender, see John Hawley Stratton, ed., *Fundamentalism and Gender* (1994), with papers representing a cross-cultural approach. On the feminization of religion in America, see Barbara Welter, "The Feminization of American Religion, 1800–1860," in *Insights and Parallels: Problems and Issues of American Social History,* ed. William L. O'Neill (1973); and Ann Douglas, *The Feminization of American Culture* (1977). Edward C. Lehman, Jr., explores the relationship between gender and ministry style in *Gender and Work: The Case of the Clergy* (1993). Sandra Lipsitz Bem, *The Lenses of Gender: Transforming the Debate on Sexual Inequality* (1993), and Judith Lorber, *Paradoxes of Gender* (1994), focus on broad debates in gender theory. Among works focusing on gender and religion are Caroline Walker Bynum, Steven Harrell, and Paula Richmond, eds., *Gender and Religion: On the*

Complexity of Symbols (1986); Ursula King, *Religion and Gender* (1995); William H. Swatos, Jr., *Gender and Religion* (1994); and John C. Raines and Daniel C. Maguire, eds., *What Men Owe to Women* (2001). Other works that focus on gender in a particular religious tradition include Leila Ahmed, *Women and Gender in Islam: Historical Roots of a Modern Debate* (1992); Yvonne Yazbeck Haddad and John L. Esposito, eds., *Islam, Gender, and Social Change* (1998); T. M. Rudavsky, *Gender and Judaism: The Transformation of Tradition* (1995); and Mary Stewart Van Leeuwen et al., *After Eden: Facing the Challenge of Gender Reconciliation* (1993).

NORTH AMERICAN WOMEN INTERPRET SCRIPTURE

J. Shannon Clarkson and Letty M. Russell

NORTH AMERICAN WOMEN have been interpreting the Bible since colonial times. In hearing or reading the Bible, both women and men tried to understand the meaning of these sacred writings for their lives. This understanding, and its relation to faith and action, has been rooted in particular religious traditions, but it also has been shaped by language, culture, social structures, and historical events of a particular era. Although there were early attempts to translate the Bible into Native American languages, most of the time the scriptures were read in European languages and their message mediated through those translations.

The cultures of the dominant groups doing the interpretation were patriarchal. The assumption was that women's status was derived from the race, class, and culture of their fathers, husbands, and sons and that women were not capable of ordering and interpreting their own lives. Dominant men of European descent interpreted the scriptures for those dependent on them: children, women, slaves, and those of the underclass. They taught that the patriarchal social structures reflected in scripture were to be emulated in daily life and that domination and subordination were part of God's design for creation. According to this way of thinking and acting, women were created out of man's rib to be his helper. Women sinned first and had always to be controlled to keep from falling into temptation.

In the North American context the scriptures interpreted were mainly the Hebrew and Christian scriptures. Although this began to change as people of many religious traditions became citizens of Canada and the United States, this essay focuses on the developments in Jewish and Christian interpretation, especially in the last thirty years. Both writers of this essay have been involved as white, Protestant women from the United States in the various phases of this recent development.

In these years, what is known as feminist interpre-

tation has become a key area in the struggle of women for full human dignity. Such interpretation reflects the growing realization among women that they have a voice to speak their own meaning and interpretation of scriptures. This contrasts with the patriarchal interpretations of past and present that reflect the androcentric bias of the writers and their texts even when they claim to be objective. Feminist interpretation recognizes that all interpretation is biased, reflecting the questions, assumptions, and theology of the interpreter. This interpretation proceeds from particular historical contexts and social locations of power, education, ethnicity, sexual orientation, and ability and advocates for the full humanity of all women together with all men and for the integrity of all creation. The outpouring of biblical scholarship and the participation of women in the leadership of their congregations make it possible for women and men to be critical of their own cultural and contextual understanding while still searching for ways the scriptures can be life giving in ever-changing contexts.

This new development was, of course, built on the knowledge and experience of both women and men in other centuries. Of particular note are the early attempts of women of all colors in North America to use their own biblical interpretations to counteract the traditions of domination that rendered them dependents in their families and hemmed in their lives.

The Woman's Bible

The last third of the twentieth century is not the first time that women have been aware that their subordination in American society was linked to religious traditions that gave divine sanction to male domination. In fact, almost from the moment the Pilgrims landed, bringing their scriptures and doctrines with them from Europe, women began to speak out in opposition to the subordination imposed upon them by scripture interpretations. Their primary texts were Galatians 3:28, "there is neither male nor female," and Titus 2:3–4, which encourages older women to instruct younger ones. Anne Hutchinson (1591–1643), who contended with the Massachusetts Bay clergy in 1637, is perhaps the most famous of these early women dissenters, but a careful examination of the records shows that she and many other women questioned and defied the authority of the clerics. Several women met with dire consequences for their views; Hutchinson was banished from her community, and Mary Dyer (1611–1660), a Quaker missionary, was hanged in 1660 on Boston Common. Eventually the witch trials in Salem, Massachusetts, brought an end to open dissent by women, for fear they might be accused of witchcraft.

Yet the questions did not totally cease. Jerusha Om-

The Women's Bible

Chapter. II.

by

Elizabeth Cady Stanton

Genesis II 21—25.

> 21 And the LORD God caused a deep sleep to fall upon Adam, and he slept; and he took one of his ribs, and closed up the flesh instead thereof.
> 22 And the rib, which the LORD God had taken from man, made he a woman, and brought her unto the man.
> 23 And Adam said, This is now bone of my bones, and flesh of my flesh: she shall be called Woman, because she was taken out of man.
> 24 Therefore shall a man leave his father and his mother, and shall cleave unto his wife: and they shall be one flesh.
> 25 And they were both naked, the man and his wife, and were not ashamed.

As the account of the creation in the first chapter, is in harmony with science, common sense & the experience of mankind in natural laws, the enquiry naturally arises why should there be two contradictory accounts in the same book, of the same event? It is fair to infer that the second version, which is found in some form, in the different religions of all nations, is a mere allegory, symbolizing some mysterious conception of a

Elizabeth Cady Stanton and her co-workers who edited *The Woman's Bible* in 1895 and 1898 believed that the Bible could be excised of its patriarchal bias. *Courtesy of the Library of Congress.*

pan, an Algonquin woman from Martha's Vineyard who died in 1711, raised questions about Adam and free will and the implications of original sin for future generations. Much later in that century, Judith Sargent Murray (1751–1820) was a strong voice contesting the dominant interpretation of a Genesis text. In her essay "On the Equality of the Sexes" (1790), she offered her own interpretation of the Adam, Eve, and Serpent story. She concluded that both Eve and Adam were disobedient to God, but asserted that Eve's motives were higher: Eve was trying to gain more knowledge, whereas Adam was acting out of his "bare pusillanimous attachment to a woman!" (Collins, 12–13). Murray admitted that she considered many biblical texts to be metaphorical and thus capable of carrying more than one meaning, an understanding many generations ahead of her time.

In the early nineteenth century, white women who joined in the abolitionist struggle against slavery came to recognize the links to their own struggles for emancipation. Out of this came the first wave of women's struggles for full liberation in North American society. Some women realized that the interpretation of the scriptures was a significant impediment in the cause of both women's rights and their antislavery work. Sarah Grimké (1792–1873), in 1837, extensively analyzed the scriptures to support her contention that men and women were created equal. She accused translators of misinterpreting the texts and asserted that only the original version would be her standard. The very outspokenness of some women abolitionists led to accusations against them that they were marring the sanctity of a woman's place, which was in the home. This conflict emerged even among women in the abolitionist community. Angelina Grimké asserted that Christianity, as she understood it, was a powerful witness for truth and reform, whereas Catharine Beecher argued that women should not step beyond their own spheres of hearth and home to campaign vigorously for the abolition of slavery since it would contradict their roles as Christian women.

The cult of womanhood that put white women on a pedestal was certainly a tactic used by men, and some women, to keep women docile. Yet some black women who had not gained the privilege of white women used biblical texts referring to the role of women as mothers and heros to justify their own leadership. In the 1830s Maria Stewart (1803–1879) proclaimed, "Did [God] not raise up Deborah to be mother, and a judge in Israel? Did not Queen Esther save the lives of the Jews? And Mary Magdalene first declare the resurrection of Christ from the dead?" (Giddings, 52–53). She also critiqued Paul, saying that although Paul might have objected to women speaking in public, Jesus did not (1 Corinthians 14:34–35). Perhaps the most well known defender of the right of a woman to speak her mind in public was Sojourner Truth (1797–1883) whose famous declaration

"Ain't I a woman?" was uttered at a women's rights meeting in 1851, where she asserted that Jesus came from "God and a woman—man had nothing to do with it" (54).

Such battles led the white women reformers to reflect on their own rights as well as those for whom they were fighting. They joined their African American sisters in reflecting on the scriptures, which could be interpreted either to strengthen their resolve, as Galatians 3:28, or to quicken their desire to reinterpret the patriarchal use of texts like I Corinthians 14:34–35, which admonished women to keep silent in the church. Anna Julia Cooper (1858–1964) advised the black clergy gathered at a conference of the Protestant Episcopal Church in 1886 to be as concerned and proactive in training young women for the ministry as they were about young men. She was born into slavery, yet in 1925 she earned a doctorate from the Sorbonne, becoming the fourth black woman in the United States to achieve that degree.

Eventually some women did take up the challenge to learn Hebrew and Greek and begin to examine the biblical text, while others carefully studied the English text and raised questions about the reigning interpretations. One who did so was Antoinette Brown (1825–1921), the first woman officially ordained (by a Congregational church) in the United States. While at Oberlin College she published an exegesis of 1 Corinthians 14:34–35 and 1 Timothy 2:11–12 in the *Oberlin Quarterly Review* in 1849 that questioned the interpretation of the Greek terms used for "speaking" and "silence." Emma Willard (1787–1870), writing forty years later, still bemoaned the fact that too few women were reading and interpreting the scriptures. An early proponent of women's education, she founded the Troy Female Seminary in 1821. Like many others of her time and earlier, Willard felt that the male interpreters had done considerable damage to women's ability to have a full and independent life. Men continued to use the Bible as a manual for the submission of women. This idea of early women reformers that a scholar's gender can make a difference was well over a century ahead of its time. Not until the last three decades of the twentieth century did this idea gain followers. Today there are still those who claim that biblical exegesis is an objective enterprise and that gender or race has no bearing on the interpretation. To this point, two seminarians commented, "It may be His-tory but it is Her-meneutics" (Erin Croddick, Kathryn Ott, Feminist Hermeneutics class, Yale Divinity School, October 27, 1999).

Some nineteenth-century feminists were not as hopeful that having linguistically trained women translate and interpret the scriptures would be liberating because they viewed the texts themselves as overwhelmingly biased in favor of men. Neither Matilda Joslyn Gage (1826–1898), women's rights advocate who wrote

Woman, Church and State (1880), nor Elizabeth Cady Stanton (1815–1902) and her coworkers who edited *The Woman's Bible* in 1895 and 1898 believed that the Bible could be excised of its patriarchal bias. Nonetheless, both women continued to struggle against the negative effect a patriarchy based in a religious tradition could have on the populace. Stanton called together a group of women who set out to comment on all biblical texts having to do with women. The further they progressed, the more certain she became that to disentangle the Bible from its patriarchal overlay would be impossible. Eventually she decided that the better task would be to set out afresh and create a new belief system that would assert that women were equal to men.

Over half a century later, Margaret Brackenbury Crook (1886–1972), a professor at Smith College, proposed an analysis of the biblical texts and interpretations of women in Judaism and Christianity to see exactly what the role of women had been and how this had shaped the relationship of the sexes ever since. Her call, and that of others in the mid-twentieth century, began a trickle of feminist biblical scholarship that was eventually to flow forth in the last decade of that century.

Liberating the Word

One cannot think of feminist biblical interpretation, or even biblical interpretation, without thinking of translation issues. Although some might believe that the scriptures are the inspired word of God, that word is one that has been transmitted through centuries and mediated by scribes and scholars. The text has evolved along with the development of writing and printing. Throughout the ages, the actual words have been matched with similar words in languages not yet born when the biblical words were first spoken (English, for instance). The work of the translators choosing these words involves not only linguistic skill but courage as well. William Tyndale (1494–1536), who first translated the scriptures into English, met with severe opposition. In fact, his New Testament was referred to as an "untrue translation," and many copies were burned. Eventually, he himself was executed and burned at the stake.

As shown previously, a segment of women in North America has always distrusted interpretations and translations of scripture prepared solely by men. Early calls to look more carefully at biblical interpretations were raised by women whose lives were circumscribed by societal mores based predominantly on religious ideas. In the late eighteenth and nineteenth centuries, there were calls by women encouraging women to study the biblical languages so that the traditional words might be analyzed with new eyes. Perhaps because the New England communities were established by Europeans seeking religious freedom, the role of religion in those communities was quite strong. Ironically, the persecution in Europe they sought to escape became a characteristic of many early colonial towns. Those who disagreed with the people in power suffered for their opposition. In particular, white women and Africans, both free and indentured, were ridiculed or, worse, tried in public places by the authorities.

However, threats were not sufficient to silence everyone, as noted earlier. Beginning with Anne Hutchinson and Jerusha Ompan on down through Elizabeth Cady Stanton and Anna Julia Cooper, the women of the first two centuries of U.S. history sought a new understanding of the scriptures. Thus the task of biblical interpretation became a quest to justify human rights for all, or at least laid the groundwork for such a search. In fact, the late twentieth century witnessed movements for new interpretations coming from a variety of viewpoints. White women feminists, Latin American liberation theologians, African American women and men, gays, lesbians, bisexuals, transgender persons, Asian Americans, and persons with disabilities all participated in a growing interest in a more contextual biblical interpretive endeavor.

Unlike the Qur'an, whose words cannot be changed from their meaning in the original Arabic, the scriptures used by the Jewish and Christian communities in North America can be changed through translation. In the broader United States culture, some confusion exists about the transmission of the Bible through the ages. The Christian community is much more likely to be unaware of language issues than the Jewish community, many of whom know the original language of the text, the Hebrew used for reading scripture in the synagogues. Some Christians, on the other hand, even believe that the words printed in red in their New Testaments are the actual words spoken by Jesus Christ.

Although such an assumption seems quite naive, a second large group of Christians believes that the current translations of the King James Version (KJV) of the Bible (presently two are available, the KJV and the New King James Version [NKJV]) are the actual translations written by the scholars assembled in England in 1611. They are unaware that since that time four major editions and hundreds of minor revisions have been published. Between the first translation and the version of 1769 (a period of 156 years), which was the last major version before the NKJV, over 24,000 changes were made in the text. The versions of the KJV available today have many differences, as the book is no longer under copyright restrictions.

The twentieth century saw a number of new biblical translations, beginning with the American Standard Version published in 1901. The second major translation was the Revised Standard Version (*RSV*) published as a complete edition in 1952. Like its predecessors, a group of scholars prepared the translation and the National Council of Churches of Christ (NCCC) was the authorizing agency. Publication took place during the height of the McCarthy era, a particularly conservative and anticommunist period in the United States. The RSV was issued in a bright red cover, which its detractors were quick to point out. Many maligned the translation as a Communist endeavor, and one pastor went so far as to attempt to publicly burn his edition during Sunday morning worship. Although he could not get the book to ignite, he later sent a canister of ashes of his Bible to the National Council of Churches of Christ. Like the reception given to Tyndale and other early translators, public resistance to "tampering with" the word of God is often vicious. Yet none of these translations was undertaken with a planned thought to "remedy" misinterpretations, other than updating vocabulary and occasionally adding a word or phrase in light of archaeological discoveries.

Not until the Division of Education and Ministry of the National Council of Churches decided in 1974 to produce a volume in which feminist scholars discuss the question of inclusive language in relation to biblical translation did a major effort emerge in response to women's calls 200 years earlier. Emily V. Gibbes (1915–   ), director of the Division, in anticipation of a new translation of the RSV wanted to gather feminist biblical scholars to consider the issues so that church members might be engaged in the conversation also. *The Liberating Word* was published in 1976, offering readers ways in which the biblical materials might be interpreted in less sexist fashion as well as giving information for creating nonsexist study and worship materials. Six years later, the Division appointed a group of six men and six women to produce the three-volume *An Inclusive Language Lectionary* (a systematic three-year collection of biblical texts read each week in Protestant, Roman Catholic, and Orthodox worship). When the first volume appeared in 1983, the Division of Education and Ministry was unprepared for the firestorm of criticism that greeted its publication. In fact, so much hate mail was received and some of such a vicious nature that the Federal Bureau of Investigation was called in to protect the writers and their families.

The next step of the NCCC was to publish a new translation of the RSV, to be called the New Revised Standard Version (NRSV) of the Bible. The committee that had translated the RSV was reconstituted and several new members added. The RSV committee had only one woman, but the NRSV brought in three additional women, all Old Testament scholars, as the New Testament was nearly finished before the new women were added. No persons of color were included. The instruction to the committee was to provide a translation that eliminated masculine-oriented language whenever pos-

sible. The language for the deity was not to be changed, as it had been in the *Inclusive Language Lectionary*. Many feminists thought the NCCC had shirked its duty, although most of the translation committee members felt they had gone as far as the current religious climate would permit. As their translation efforts proceeded, they additionally attended to issues of racism, anti-Semitism, discrimination against the handicapped, and homophobia. Five years after the publication of the New Revised Standard Version, an edition of the New Testament and Psalms appeared that included the principles used in the *Inclusive Language Lectionary* translation and thus treated references to the deity in inclusive language. Several other mainstream versions of the biblical text have been issued since with at least some attention to inclusive language.

The claim from earlier generations of women that the translators' gender makes a difference was illustrated in an incident at a conference of feminist biblical scholars, sponsored by the NCCC, titled "Biblical Interpretation Beyond Patriarchy." One of the participants, an Old Testament professor, asked another of the presenters who had been on the New Revised Standard Version translation team why the interpretation of the woman in Hosea changes so distinctly after chapter nine. The response was: That was where the committee was in the translation when she joined the team! The suspicion of those early critics of gender bias in biblical interpretation seems right on target. Recent interpretive work that attends to race also indicates that the social location of the translator has a bearing on the outcome of the translation as well. Thus the questions raised by women of color and white women two centuries ago seem to be valid critiques of a clerical and societal system that used a particular interpretation of the scriptures to control certain groups.

Feminist Interpretation of the Bible

In the ten-year period following the publication of *The Liberating Word*, women scholars began to publish full-length interpretations of the Bible and to organize themselves into groups so that they could develop the discipline of feminist interpretation and publish such collections as *Feminist Interpretation of the Bible*. Phyllis Trible, Old Testament professor emerita at Union Theological Seminary in New York City, published *God and the Rhetoric of Sexuality* in 1978 using literary analysis of the Hebrew Scriptures as a way of recovering old treasures, discovering new ones, and resisting texts that reinforce violence against women. Trible built on her earlier articles on Genesis 1–3 to revisit the creation of woman and man. Describing the first use of *adam* in Genesis 2:2–3 not as a name but as a reference to an undifferentiated earth creature, she showed how the text describes God's fashioning of sexuality and thus of both male and female. In reclaiming this story, Trible showed that the idea of fashioning Eve from Adam's rib had to do with partnership, not subordination. She also clarified that the term *helper* in verse 18 is used elsewhere to speak of God as helper and signifies that Eve is a partner, not a servant, of Adam (Psalm 33:20). Like other scholars such as Old Testament scholar Phyllis Bird, Trible affirmed that the creation story in Genesis 1 speaks of male and female created in God's image as representatives of God in the care of the earth (Genesis 1:26). She also made clear that Adam was with Eve in the garden, heard the conversation of the snake, and was able to make his own decision about obeying or disobeying God's command. These and many other changes struck at the heart of the patriarchal interpretations of the inferiority and sinfulness of women and are reflected in subsequent exegesis and translation by other scholars such as the New Revised Standard Version Bible published in 1989.

Jewish scholars who came from a tradition that did not emphasize Eve's sin, but nevertheless accepted the subordination of women as part of the Torah, were also at work on reinterpreting the story of Eve and on issues of violence against women. The early midrash or textual interpretation and elaboration on this story, "The Coming of Lilith: Toward a Feminist Theology," was published by Judith Plaskow in 1979, professor of religious studies at Manhattan College, and suggested that a second woman who had refused to do Adam's bidding, Lilith, joined in sisterhood with Eve to see what could be done with Adam's dominance in the garden (Kvam, Schearing, and Ziegler, 422–430).

In 1983 a second groundbreaking interpretation of scriptures was brought out by Harvard Divinity School New Testament scholar Elisabeth Schüssler Fiorenza. *In Memory of Her: A Feminist Theological Construction of Christian Origins* used methods of historical reconstruction to lift up the presence of women in the community of disciples around Jesus and in the early missionary communities reflected in Pauline texts. Of particular importance in Schüssler Fiorenza's work, and in her many subsequent books, was the emphasis on "discipleship of equals." The word *disciple* means "learner" in Greek and designates someone whose allegiance is to the vision and commitment of a teacher or a movement. "Equals," according to Schüssler Fiorenza, is a democratic concept that underscores the equality in diversity of those who follow Jesus. Reconstructing the lives of women and men around Jesus, she is able to claim the possibility of a radical, democratic vision that welcomed women as followers and leaders in the Jesus movement. This way of structuring religious life is opposed to hierarchical systems of domination whether they appear in the biblical stories of women's lives or in the lives of contem-

porary women struggling for full participation in their religious communities of faith (Russell and Clarkson, 70–71).

The annual meeting of the Society of Biblical Literature, an association of professors, students, and persons interested in the study of the Bible, celebrated its centennial in 1980. The meeting included the first session ever to be devoted specifically to women's scholarship. The session was organized by Phyllis Trible to explore "The Effects of Women's Studies on Biblical Studies" (*Journal for the Study of Old Testament*, 22). Two results of this meeting were that the organization's Centennial Publications Committee was pressured to include a book reflecting women's experience, feminist exegesis, and interpretation. This volume, published in 1985 as *Feminist Perspectives on Biblical Scholarship*, was edited by Adela Yarbro Collins, Old Testament professor at Yale Divinity School. Following a cooperative pattern of Jewish and Christian women's interpretation, the book came out of group meetings on this topic organized as a regular section of the Society of Biblical Literature beginning in 1981.

The second result of the centennial panel was the formation of an ongoing group of biblical scholars and theologians who met to clarify the distinctive character of feminist interpretation. In 1985, papers from this ongoing discussion were edited by Letty M. Russell and published under the title *Feminist Interpretation of the Bible*. The group learned that feminist interpretation embraces a variety of methodologies and disciplines. But the methods used do not make an interpretation feminist. Second, they agreed that the various methods used by scholars to unlock the meaning of the text are biased. For this reason it is impossible to delay the feminist critical perspective until the exegesis is finished, as a sort of theological afterthought. Their third common insight was that feminist interpretation is to be discovered in the approach taken to the scripture.

In the view of this group the critical principle of feminist interpretation, that which makes it distinctly feminist, is its advocacy for the full humanity of all women together with all men and critical suspicion of any text that evokes divine sanction to dehumanize persons because of race, class, gender, sexual orientation, ability, or any other form of difference. This general agreement did not settle the questions of the authority of the scriptures in faith communities for those who chose to work at the development of feminist interpretation. Some women scholars found authority for their interpretation in the liberating dynamics of the Bible. Others found it by interpreting scripture in terms of its reality in the lives of women struggling for liberation both in ancient times and in the present. In both cases, an appeal to the authority of the experience of women struggling against patriarchal oppression was a critical component.

In social structures, faith communities, and scholarly communities that had assumed that patriarchal authority was divinely established, women in the 1980s were still being questioned about the source of their authority for interpretations that included women's voices and perspective. Their interpretations called into question what it means for a particular collection of writings to be named sacred because they speak with the authority of divine presence in the lives of believers. This perspective was resisted by at least three groups of both women and men: faith communities that interpreted scripture according to their established androcentric, or male-centered, religious traditions; scholarly communities who used androcentric paradigms of academic authority; and women of many faiths and no faiths who in rejecting such androcentric authority had rejected the authority of scriptures.

The authority of scriptures is a key issue in contemporary societies where radical social change and the meeting of many different religious faiths and cultures challenge the assumption that the white, Western, male-dominated traditions of scripture are normative to the faith and behavior. Authority is a form of power that works by evoking the consent of those who accept a particular person, teaching, law, or writing. Human beings looking for guidance and a sense of security turn to authorities in their lives to fill these needs. Scriptures have this authority when they evoke consent of those who read, hear, and digest their messages.

One way of establishing scriptural authority is to show how the text is connected to its source or original author. Thus the canon in the Hebrew Scriptures and New Testament provided an approved collection of books believed to be a source of divine revelation. The Jewish community decided on the contents of its canon after the destruction of the second temple about 70 C.E. Christians accepted this canon as their own until about the second or third century C.E. when different Christian churches began to select additional writings to include as sacred. The list of books has never been totally agreed upon, yet many people consider the canon of their tradition to have a closed number of writings. For Judaism the first five books of the law of Moses (Torah) were the most sacred, as they witness to the origins of their faith. In the same way, Christians turn first to the gospel accounts about Jesus. The New Testament books were considered sacred because the church communities used them in worship and life as the apostolic witness to Christ. The idea of a closed canon (list of books) and of direct divine inspiration of the text evolved in a patriarchal world as a way of establishing a hierarchy of authority.

The prevailing way of thinking about authority in male-dominated religions is one of authority as domination. In this framework, all questions are settled with reference to what is considered to be the highest authority. Creation is assigned a divine order, with God at the top, men next, and so on, down through dogs, cats, plants, and so-called impersonal nature. This paradigm establishes authority over community and refuses to admit ideas and persons who do not fit into the prevailing male hierarchies of thought or social structures. It is easy to see why North American women of all colors and classes have usually found their interpretations of scripture challenged because patriarchal authority assumes their ideas are to be subordinate.

The feminist liberation paradigm is one of authority in community. This way of thinking seeks to raise questions of legitimacy based on the needs of those who are at the bottom of the patriarchal pyramid of oppressions. The liberation model emphasizes the use of authority with others as the community seeks meaning that resists dualistic either/or thinking, works interdependently through shared connections rather than hierarchies of truth. This renewed effort of women to interpret scriptures in the Jewish and Christian traditions has been full of disagreements and different ways of thinking, but women have sought to use a paradigm of authority that would welcome difference rather than subordinating or destroying it. For instance, the group working on feminist interpretation of the Bible did not agree on the configuration of the authority of the Bible, but they sought a way in which women's critically reflected experience, faith tradition, biblical witness, and intellectual research could all enrich each other. To the question, "What has the ultimate authority: bible, tradition, experience, or reason?" many scholars answered that all of them together can have authority as they lead women to understand and respond to the divine presence in their lives.

Depatriarchalizing

Feminist interpreters are not alone in recognizing that biblical texts are historical and conditioned, requiring careful and critical analysis of their context and development. But feminist interpreters pay particular attention to the way the biblical literature was shaped by patriarchal culture, worldview, and interpretation. Their starting point is a hermeneutic of suspicion about the model of reality that is buried in the texts. As early as 1976, Phyllis Trible published a paper on Genesis 2–3 under the title "Depatriarchalizing in Biblical Interpretation." This agenda became a key topic in women's interpretation of the scriptures all through the 1980s as women asked if it is at all possible to remove the Bible from patriarchy or patriarchy from the Bible.

What is it that the word *patriarchy* is used to indicate concerning the assumption of male domination that is so embedded in scriptures, religions, cultures, and social life? In feminist theory, patriarchy is used as an analytical tool for making sense of women's reality by naming, understanding, and reinterpreting the contradictions in their lives and their experience of oppression. *Patriarchy* is understood in two different senses: first, as a name given to a variety of social systems of domination and subordination in which women's realities are defined by the status (race, class, country, religion, etc.) of the men to whom they belong as daughter, wife, and mother; second, as an interpretive framework or paradigm of a dualistic social system in which authority as domination is understood as a description of social reality that justifies the domination of subordinate groups by those who are dominant. Although there are many patriarchal patterns in the long history of the Hebrew Scriptures and the New Testament, the relationships between men and women are characterized by a hierarchy of power in which women, along with children and slaves, were the property of the dominant male, and women were understood as passive recipients of male semen and mothers of male descendants. According to Paul and other writers, this is the natural, established order (1 Corinthians 11:7; Ephesians 5:21–6:9).

Many women, such as Carol Meyers, Duke University biblical studies professor, questioned the use of the term itself, finding it much too general a term to be applied to the variety of the Bible's literary contexts. Others, such as Susannah Herschel, Jewish studies professor at Dartmouth College, objected to the anti-Jewish stance of Christian scholars who blamed patriarchy on the teachings of Hebrew Scriptures. Delores Williams, professor of theology at Union Theological Seminary, and others have said that patriarchy was used by white women to cover up what is really demonarchy, the rule of white women and white men who use their power to destroy the lives of African American women and their families. Responding to this, Elisabeth Schüssler Fiorenza has sought to broaden the definition of scriptural oppression so that it clearly applies to women of all colors, cultures, classes, and contexts by speaking of "kyriarchy" to emphasize the rule of all lords or masters and not just the "fathers."

In spite of these important corrections of the term, *patriarchy* still has served as a way of constructing women's experiences of domination and the work they are about in reclaiming the scriptures of their faith traditions. Not only Christian and Jewish women have been about this task. For instance, Riffat Hassan, professor of religious studies at the University of Louisville, contradicts later Muslim traditions of women's inequality by showing that the descriptions of human creation in the Qur'an speak of an undifferentiated humanity in which man and woman are equal. Among other women, Rita Gross, professor emerita of comparative studies in religion at the University of Wisconsin–Eau Claire, writing in *After Patriarchy: Feminist Transformations in World Religion* (1991), points out that Buddhist teachings are not misogynist or patriarchal. Although the institutions of Buddhist life are male dominated, the basic teachings of Buddhism as currently constituted do not in any way condone gender hierarchy. Lina Gupta, professor of philosophy at Glendale Community College, has tried to show how Hindu tradition upholds the position of women through the model of Kali and her many manifestations at the heart of Hinduism.

However they name the reality of hierarchy, gender, dualism, and male domination in scriptures, women scholars have to deal with ancient texts that are saturated with an unacceptable perspective as long as they are understood to have authority in the lives of their religious communities as a witness to the divine. Depatriarchalizing is important work, for failure to change the assumed patterns of interpretation often invites continued divine sanction for subordination, rape, and violence against women and marginalized groups. This work is also risky since it questions teachings that have been an important source of authority in faith communities. Success sometimes invites the wrath of the establishment, loss of jobs, and so on. That no male biblical scholars joined *The Woman's Bible* project is no accident, nor that in 1976 there were still only a few women in the biblical guild able or willing to take the risk of publishing in *The Liberating Word*. Even now, it is often difficult for a woman to receive academic promotion if her writing takes up such "marginal work" as feminist hermeneutics.

Patriarchal biblical texts seem to repeat themselves in our lives. For instance, the experience of Miriam in her confrontation with Moses is not such a distant reality. In Numbers 12:2 we read one of the fragments left from her suppressed story of leadership as the Priestly writers do their best to dismiss the authority of this uppity woman. Thus with Aaron she confronts Moses for marrying a non-Israelite woman and for refusing to share the prophetic role, saying, "Has the Lord indeed spoken only through Moses? Has [God] not spoken through us also?" Not afraid to confront patriarchal authority, Miriam appears to claim her own prophetic role advocating a more inclusive form of leadership to serve the needs of the community. Her story in Exodus 1:2 and Numbers 12:20 has been interpreted by Phyllis Trible in her *Bible Review* article "Bringing Miriam Out of the Shadows" (vol. 5:1 Feb. 1989, pp. 14–25, 34), reminding us what patriarchy looks like in women's lives.

Mary Ann Tolbert, professor of biblical studies, Pacific School of Religion, and others have moved ahead with Trible's project of depatriarchalizing the Bible, suggesting that this work is in some ways similar to the project of demythologizing the New Testament undertaken by scholar Rudolf Bultmann in the 1950s. As Tolbert says: "The question Bultmann asked was how a pervasively mythological and Hellenistic document could continue to communicate anything of value to a scientific age" (Tolbert, 125). The question feminist interpreters asked in the 1980s was how "a pervasively patriarchal document" can communicate good news to those who reject this paradigm of domination. Bultmann carried out his project by separating what he considered to be the essence of the good news from the mythological language of apocalypse, miracle, and resurrection. He sought to make the gospel more acceptable to the nonbeliever by relating it to the personal, existential history of the believer.

Along with most contemporary scholars, feminists reject this method on the basis that it is impossible to separate essence from context; one cannot move ideas from one culture to another without shifting their meaning. They use interpretation to deal with what is in, around, and behind the text and recognize many biblical theologies or clues to meaning that are embedded in the texts. They do, however, emphasize another of Bultmann's ideas, that of the hermeneutical circle of interpretation in which we see that the questions we ask determine the answers that follow. In interpretation as well as in theology, what we see depends on where we are standing!

What is it that feminist interpreters saw from where they were standing? They saw patriarchy as an unacceptable worldview of cultures of the ancient Near East. Unlike mythology, however, patriarchy is alive and well in North America and appears among us in many different forms. The patriarchy of the Bible still makes perfect sense to many people. It does not even occur to them that a God who is sexist is not seriously imaginable to women who believe that God is one who created them in the image of God. What is needed is not just a translation but an elimination of this form of dehumanization and domination. What is needed is a way of explaining the Bible not only to nonbelievers but also to those whom liberation theologians call nonpersons: a way of explaining what it means for women who find themselves oppressed and marginalized by their gender, then endure double and triple marginalization because of their class, race, nationality, or sexual orientation. The interpreter stands with the one who has become a nonperson and struggles with the text like Jacob and the angel, seeking to find its blessing in full awareness of its possible curse (Genesis 32:24).

Although it was clear that patriarchy cannot be taken out of the scriptures because they were written in patriarchal cultural contexts, it was just as clear that many different methods needed to be used to reclaim the scriptures for those who considered them a source of meaning in their lives. In the beginning of the development of contemporary feminist hermeneutics, women

sought to reclaim texts about women that had been used against women such as the stereotypes of Eve and Mary. They also worked to identify liberating themes like those of justice and jubilee in order to show that women also were called to inherit the promise. Other women scholars took up the work of reconstruction and sought to uncover the patriarchal dimensions of the text. In the 1980s and beyond, as Katharine Sakenfeld, Old Testament professor at Princeton Theological Seminary, has pointed out, this later work of reconstruction was developed into at least three methods (*Theology Today*, 1989, 154–168). The first is formal literary criticism and focuses on the textual narrative with interpretive constraints provided by the perceived literary design and by the grammar and syntax of a text. The rhetorical criticism of Phyllis Trible is the best-known example of this approach. A second approach is a culturally cued literary approach. Although it also uses literary criticism, it concentrates on reading the text as a product of its own culture, exposing patriarchal structures and values. The work of Esther Fuchs, Renita Weems, and Drorah Setel are among those who take this approach. The third approach, historical reconstruction, uses data from other ancient Semitic cultures, as well as comparative sociological models and archaeology, to reconstruct a clearer and more reliable picture of women's lives. Phyllis Bird and Carol Meyers are included in this group of scholars working on historical reconstruction.

In these and other methods, the hermeneutic of suspicion about what might be going on in regard to the androcentric bias of the text is the beginning point in the struggle for reinterpretation. But the hermeneutic of suspicion must be complemented with a hermeneutic of commitment if it is to have any future. Commitment to act together with others in a community of faith and struggle is what sustains women when they wrestle with the scriptures of their faith tradition.

Searching Scriptures

In the 1990s and into the new century, women have been searching their scriptures for signs that they can be full participants in interpreting their meaning and in shaping religious beliefs in the growing multifaith context of North America. Women in synagogues, mosques, temples, and religious circles of all kinds are creating liturgies and religious traditions and working with their traditional scriptures. More and more tools are available to them and to those studying scripture through cooperative publication of commentaries and collections of articles on biblical interpretation.

The *Women's Bible Commentary*, edited by Carol Newsom and Sharon Ringe, was published in 1992 in celebration of the one hundredth anniversary of *The Woman's Bible*. It was the first one-volume biblical commentary written expressly by and for women from a feminist perspective. The anniversary was also celebrated in 1993 and 1994 by a two-volume commentary, edited by Elisabeth Schüssler Fiorenza, *Searching the Scriptures*. Biblical scholar Athalaya Brenner also began to bring out a ten-volume work on *The Feminist Companion to the Hebrew Bible*. Other scholarly collections appeared as well, such as *Women in Scripture: A Dictionary of Named and Unnamed Women in the Hebrew Bible*, the *Apocryphal/Deuterocanonical Books*, and the *New Testament*, edited by Carol Meyers, Toni Craven, and Ross S. Kraemer.

The *Women's Bible Commentary* was republished in an expanded version with the Apocrypha in 1998. In addition to interpretive essays, there are chapters on each book of the Bible and Apocrypha that deal with materials particularly relevant for women as well as with resources for a feminist interpretation of that book. *Searching the Scriptures* moves beyond the established canons of the Jewish and Christian traditions and searches for scriptures outside these texts as well. After introductory articles in "A Feminist Introduction" in volume 1, it moves to "A Feminist Commentary" in volume 2 that includes many ancient texts as well as those from the New Testament in an intentional transgressing of canonical boundaries. Thus Schussler Fiorenza pushes the boundaries of the traditional canon by exploring writings women in the first centuries might have heard as their own "scriptures." These texts witness to ancient religious experiences of women.

Rather than accept the shape of a canon authorized by a patriarchal church, the commentary problematizes the whole idea that there can be only one authoritative set of texts that can speak of the divine in women's lives. Schüssler Fiorenza chooses to speak of scriptures rather than the Bible because such sacred writings can have authority for women whether or not they are in a canon. She also chooses to use the term *searching* in order to indicate the ongoing task of women to address structures of domination by being suspicious of the texts but also to use their imagination to recover the traditions of texts for use in our own time. Lastly, Schüssler Fiorenza prefers the term *feminist interpretation* as a political term indicating all women rather than the term *women's interpretation*. What it means to be a woman is socially constructed in each society and age. What a woman's gender means is learned growing up in a particular culture. In our contemporary world the nature of woman is continually in dispute, so there is no way to say what a particular woman will think of a particular text.

This has been brought home increasingly as womanist, *mujerista*, Asian American, Native American, and lesbian feminists have continued to develop their own interpretative voices from different social locations. Af-

rican American womanist interpreters have led the way to understanding how patriarchy looks from the perspective of those who often struggle against the triple burden of racism, sexism, and classism. In New Testament studies, Clarice Martin, associate professor of philosophy and religion at Colgate-Rochester University, has provided insights into the ways that Pauline household codes concerning submission of slaves and wives in Ephesians 5:21–6:9 and elsewhere are texts to be resisted because they were drawn from the cultural norms and not from Paul's early letters. She calls for equal rejection of both these codes in African American churches. In the Hebrew Scripture, Renita Weems, associate professor of Hebrew Bible at Vanderbilt University Divinity School, evokes the story of Sarah and Hagar in Genesis 16:1–16; 21:1–21 to make clear that although women share the experiences of gender oppression, they are not natural allies when one group has economic, racial, political, and educational power and privilege, and the other is oppressed by this privilege. In her 1995 book, *Battered Love: Marriage, Sex, and Violence in the Hebrew Prophets*, Weems has gone on to show how social critical interpretation can expose the use of the metaphor of women's harlotry in Hosea and the later prophets to reinforce violence against women.

Similar critiques of white feminist interpretation are leading to new multicultural perspectives. For instance, Ada María Isasi-Díaz has shown that *mujerista* theology is based in the daily struggles of Latina women living in North America and not in the study of biblical texts. Yet their collective interpretation of the Bible as women is in itself revolutionary in a culture where they often had little education and very little voice. Kwok Pui-Lan, professor of Christian theology and spirituality, Episcopal Divinity School, has taken up this critique and reconstruction from an Asian feminist perspective in her book *Discovering the Bible in the Non-Biblical World* (1995). She makes clear that there are other sacred scriptures, and other non-Western perspectives, that call for new methods of reading that lead to new insights into multifaith hermeneutics and postcolonial discourse. These latter two perspectives have become a cutting edge of feminist interpretation as more and more women join in a conversation that is no longer North American but worldwide.

Joining in this ever-expanding conversation are lesbian feminist writers who seek to examine the issues of gender and sexuality in scriptures and in contemporary cultures. They, too, look at the Genesis account of Adam and Eve as a "text of terror" because it is used as an archetype of domination and subordination. It is the foundation of all arguments that homosexuality is against the order of creation because of the commandment to multiply. To counteract this tradition, Bernadette Brooten, professor of Christian studies, Brandeis University, in 1996 published *Love between Women: Early Christian Responses to Female Homoeroticism*. She uses gender analysis to show that the existence of female homoeroticism and its rejection was an unnatural blurring of gender roles by male interpreters, including Paul (Romans 1:18–32). This theme of women and their culturally assigned gender roles is developed as well by Ross Kraemer, professor of Judaic studies, Brown University, and Mary Rose D'Angelo, associate professor of theology, Notre Dame University, in *Women and Christian Origins* (1999) and becomes a basic theme for the reconstruction of Jewish traditions by Rebecca Alpert, professor of religious studies, Temple University, in *Like Bread on the Seder Plate: Jewish Lesbians and the Transformation of Tradition* (1997) and *Engendering Judaism: An Inclusive Theology and Ethics* (1998).

The creativity and insights that are part of the story of North American women interpreting scripture are abundantly available to all who are willing to read and ponder. There are indeed so many voices that it is often difficult even to hear and to be heard. Nevertheless, the themes in this search of scripture continue to be those of our foremothers before and during the time of *The Woman's Bible*. Domination and subordination of women and all oppressed or marginalized groups are still with us in our sacred texts and their interpretations. As women seeking to hear and understand what the scriptures say to us about the urgings of the divine in our lives, a major resource continues to be the communities of sisters who gather round to discern what is life-giving for women. The challenge continues to find a way to practice hospitality, to entertain all the voices and perspectives that are shared.

The Future of Women's Interpretation of Scripture

As long as women find that the texts of their traditions remain scripture or holy writing for them, they will continue to interpret scripture seeking to find its message for their lives and continue to read it out of their life experiences as well as their faith traditions. Others, for whom the scriptures no longer have authority to evoke consent and action in their lives, will continue to interpret them as well, in order to counteract the ways they are harmful to women's health and seek out meaning that might be life-giving for women. Some interpreters will use a canon within the canon speaking of the prophetic and liberating message of the scriptures in texts such as Galatians 3:28 that include women in the good news that all are welcome in God's intention for a mended creation. Some will continue to appeal from more recent interpretations to more ancient texts

and to the words of the creators of their faith traditions such as Moses, Jesus, and Mohammed. Others will move beyond the limitations of patriarchal creation of canon and doctrine and appeal to the lives of women in all centuries and cultures as the center of the continuing interpretation of scripture's meaning.

The perspective taken and the methods used in the interpretations will depend a great deal on the paradigm of an interpretative group concerning the relation of the scriptures to divine revelation. For instance, in Christian traditions, those who believe that the Bible is the word of God because it is inspired by God and is a complete and unchanging record of events and truths communicated directly by God to God's people will interpret the texts about women's subordination as divinely established. Yet as women they, too, will look for texts in the scriptures that confirm ways that women can flourish as companions of men and nurturers of the family.

Those who believe that the Bible contains the word of God, conveyed by inspired writers for their own time, seek to interpret the messages of texts that are hidden in the cultural and political context of ancient societies through historical and cultural reconstruction. A third group of women who believe that the Bible becomes the word of God will point to its divine source and search out the way its meaning can come alive in their own contexts. In this perspective, as Nirmala Vasanthakumar, one of the first women ordained by the Church of South India, puts it, "The Bible is only an instrument to disclose the revelation of God, and as such it witnesses to the word of God" (*In Search of a Round Table*, 42).

Feminist interpreters are found in all three positions, and many more, as they wrestle with how scriptures can be life-giving for women. These many forms of interpretation will have a future in religious communities and academic research only if women continue to do the work. As in the nineteenth-century movement for women's liberation, the movement of the twentieth century could die out as it grows and changes unless women see it as a priority in their struggles for human dignity. Women will need to make it a priority unless the culture of North America and the traditions of its religions transform the patriarchal structures and ways of thinking. If that change comes about, then the work of feminists will become foundational in a new paradigm of partnership or community in which hierarchy and dualistic perspectives on gender, race, and class will no longer dominate the way we live, think, and believe.

In the meanwhile, we can ask what future feminist interpretation will have. Will it not generate a body of literature that leads beyond the canon and toward the creation of new nonpatriarchal traditions? Most certainly this is the result for many feminist men and women who no longer find the biblical message or the

Christian or Jewish traditions to be life-giving for them. But many others make a choice over and over again to continue "God wrestling." They join with Phyllis Trible in saying that the Bible teaches us that nothing is hopeless, not even patriarchy.

The Bible is more than patriarchy. It also speaks of repentance, forgiveness, passion, and hope and provides us with a memory of God's intended future that is an impulse for change in the present. In the same way that Miriam's story did not end with being stricken with leprosy, feminist interpretation does not end when depatriarchalizing yields ever new dimensions of misogyny. As Trible points out in "Bringing Miriam Out of the Shadows," the community of Israel does not abandon Miriam (42). Even though she is shut outside the camp for seven days, they wait until she is "brought in again" (Numbers 12:2–14). She continues to journey with them and they with her. Her role as the prophet of liberation at the Reed Sea, still remembered in the one surviving verse of triumph in Exodus 15:21, is honored and preserved by the community in the writings of the later prophets such as Micah (6:4; Jeremiah 32:4). The communities of faith today also must wrestle with this prophecy, as they seek to journey through the patriarchal wilderness. They don't give up because the memory of God's intention to mend the creation points toward a future in which all can live as whole human beings in partnership among ourselves and with God and all creation.

The search for critical principles for feminist interpretation will continue as women seek out what makes their work distinctive. One characteristic that will be important for the future of this work will be women's commitment to continue their evolving model of working together in community. The early work had to be accomplished in community because no one knew enough to do their work alone, but now there is a new generation of feminist scholars. These women will need to find ways to integrate their knowledge and skill in biblical interpretation with a style of cooperation that continues to make a community of scholars possible. If they avail themselves of academic success through competition, they will have been co-opted back into the patriarchal model. A communal and cooperative approach to biblical interpretation is what could be called "biblical interpretation in the round." Interpreting the Bible as partners is a distinctive characteristic of women who seek to discover ways to become partners even in the midst of patriarchy.

A second critical aspect of women's interpretation is the commitment to keep the circle of research, discussion, and publication open by breaking down the barriers that divide women from women here in North America and around the world. We have seen this happening as the work of white, Euro-American scholars is challenged, corrected, and deepened by contributions from womanist, *mujerista*, Native American, Asian American, and lesbian feminist scholars who join together to do "Interpretation for Liberation"(*Semeia* 47, 1989). Another critical aspect of the widening circle of future interpretation is more extensive cross-cultural and multifaith dialogue as voices from the margin speak out of very different contexts (*Voices from the Margin: Interpreting the Bible in the Third World*).

A final critical aspect for future collaboration is continued work and research concerning interpretation and translation of words for the divine and of religious symbols in sacred writings that continue to reinforce patriarchal hierarchy. When texts are understood to convey a life-giving message, the words used that may demean women continue to be important to how the message is heard.

Keeping these critical principles in mind, the heritage of women's interpretation of scriptures will continue into the twenty-first century and will lead to ever new questions and issues that call for new methods and new voices. Working collaboratively "in the round" will at least assist women in all walks of life as they struggle with the scriptures. Even though the challenge of androcentric writings continues, women have found many new possibilities for reading the scriptures that allow them to make sense in their lives. In some feminist communities of interpretation we could say that Jacob's ladder has slowly become Hagar and Sarah's circle and now is joined by a whole crowd of liberation singers and dancers in Miriam's circle. And the good news is that women and men together are invited to the dance.

SOURCES: A comprehensive source for the many types of feminist theologies is the *Dictionary of Feminist Theologies* (1996), edited by Letty M. Russell and J. Shannon Clarkson. Serinity Young has edited a volume that focuses on world religions titled *An Anthology of Sacred Texts by and about Women* (1993). Sources representing a variety of Christian, Jewish, and post-Christian approaches to this topic include Rosemary Radford Ruether, *Sexism as God-Talk* (1983); Judith Plaskow, *Standing Again at Sinai: Judaism from a Feminist Perspective* (1990); Judith Plaskow and Carol P. Christ, eds., *Weaving the Visions: New Patterns in Feminist Spirituality* (1989); Adela Collins, *Feminist Perspectives on Biblical Scholarship* (1985); Paula Giddings, *When and Where I Enter: The Impact of Black Women on Race and Sex in America* (1984); Kirsten E. Kvam, Linda S. Schearing, and Valarie H. Ziegler, *Eve and Adam: Jewish, Christian, and Muslim Readings on Genesis and Gender* (1999); and Adolf Bultmann, *Jesus Christ and Mythology* (1958). Other sources on world religions include: Diana L. Eck and Devaki Jain, *Speaking of Faith: Global Perspectives on Women, Religion and Social Change* (1987); Rita M. Gross, *Buddhism after Patriarchy: A Feminist History, Analysis, and Reconstruction of Buddhism* (1993); Ursala King, ed., *Reading and Gender* (1995); Arvind Sharma, *Women in World Religions* (1987); and Amina Wadud-Muhsin, *Qur'an and Woman* (1992). Examples of writing by womanist, mujerista, and Asian feminist theologians include Delores S. Williams, *Sisters in the Wilderness: The Challenge of Womanist God-Talk* (1993); Ada María Isasi-Díaz, *En la Lucha (In the Struggle): A Hispanic Women's Liberation Theology* (1993); and Kwok Pui-Lan, *Discovering the Bible in a Non-Biblical World* (1995). The growing contributions of women from Asia, Africa, and Latin America can be seen in Virginia Fabella and Mercy Oduyoye, eds., *With Passion and Compassion: Third World Women Doing Theology* (1988); Mercy Oduyoye and Musimbi R. A. Kanyoro, eds., *The Will to Arise: Women, Tradition, and the Church in Africa* (1992); and Elsa Tamez, ed., *Through Her Eyes: Women's Theology from Latin America* (1989).

WOMEN'S RELIGIOUS IMAGINATION
Mary Farrell Bednarowski

WHATEVER ELSE IT may be, religion, like politics, science, art, or economics, is a vast and dynamic arena of human creativity. As the instigator, nurturer, and negotiator of this creativity, the religious imagination has produced many and complex fruits: worldviews, rituals, beliefs, moral codes, narratives, institutions, spiritualities, roles and always-further-unfolding questions about the nature and meaning of life. Just as the artistic imagination draws upon color, form, and perspective, so does the religious imagination find its inspiration in the stuff of life experience and in the substance and symbols of religious traditions. Until recently, there has been almost no attention paid to how the exercise of religious imagination is related to gender and not much notice of the fact that the fruits of the religious imagination we know most about have been cultivated primarily by men. What is it, we now need to ask, about being a woman that inhibits the religious imagination or awakens it and encourages it along one path or another?

One of the most powerful stimulants to the religious imagination of American women has been the historical persistence of their insider/outsider status. Women have been insiders in their religious traditions in terms of numerical presence and indirect influence since the middle of the seventeenth century. At the same time, they have been outsiders in terms of public presence and authority. Possessed of intimate knowledge of their communities through participation in rituals and service and fellowship groups, women nonetheless have been deprived of access to centers of power. Accustomed to hearing the preacher or teacher speak to them and about them, women traditionally have not been encouraged to discover that they have voices of their own and distinctive experiences to contribute to their communities.

When this conflicting reality of women's experience of religion becomes acute, as it has particularly over the last forty years, women begin to tell stories about com-

ing to see themselves as outsiders in communities where they have been involved for a lifetime. But women tell stories, as well, about what they have received from their traditions by way of histories and rituals, spiritual companions, and ways of looking at the world. Lutheran theologian Gail Ramshaw speaks for many women when she describes herself as "paradoxically richly nurtured by a church that constrained me" (Ramshaw, vii). Out of this dual and often volatile experience, women's religious imagination has blossomed, an imagination that is both critical of religion and involved in its ongoing construction. This gendered imagination looks to see whether there is still living water in the well, blessings yet to be found. It pushes hard at boundaries by redefining them, extending them, and often, ignoring them. In undertaking these multiple and demanding enterprises, women's religious imagination historically has taken an immense variety of forms and continues to do so into the present. Three of the most prominent are the strategic imagination, the imagination that expresses itself in flashes of insight, and the elaborative imagination that opens up religious themes inspired by women's experiences of their lives and their religious communities. All three forms demonstrate different configurations of women's insider/outsider status.

The Strategic Imagination: Subversion and Indirection

At any given moment in North American religious history, there is evidence that women use the strategic imagination to overcome restrictions on full participation in their communities. The women who devise these strategies may ultimately demand, "How do we change the entire system?" But for the short term they are more likely to ask, "How do we gain more access to participation and public authority?" There are innumerable contemporary examples, but it is even more compelling to look to history as a reminder of how long women have needed to employ such strategies and how much creative energy has been expended to convince their communities that they are fully capable and fully human.

One of the most broadly illustrative examples is that of Sor Juana Inés de la Cruz (c. 1649–1695), acclaimed in her own time the most learned woman in Mexico and the author of thousands of pages of sacred and secular writings. In the famous *La respuesta*, a letter to the bishop of Puebla, who had admonished her for a theological essay published without her knowledge, Sor Juana offers her spiritual and intellectual autobiography and a defense of herself as a woman endowed by God with great intellectual gifts. Including examples of biblical women, female saints and scholars, and learned women of her own time, she takes on the Apostle Paul's

Some women, like artist and former Roman Catholic contemplative nun Meinrad Craighead, leave behind the institution but not the inspiration of its symbols and rituals or "the community." *Copyright © Gay Block.*

prohibition against women speaking in church and insists that even though women cannot preach and teach publicly, they should be able to do so privately. She cites domestic space as an arena for acquiring both scientific and spiritual knowledge and suggests, "Had Aristotle cooked, he would have written more" (Sor Juana, 75). Finally, she cites Paul's letter to Titus (also invoked by Anne Hutchinson in her defense earlier in the century in Massachusetts Bay) encouraging older women to teach those younger. In short, she uses all the imaginative strategies of her time and culture to circumvent restrictions placed on her as a woman. She is an obvious insider to Roman Catholicism, a member of a religious order, who by virtue of "body" is also an outsider judged to be a dissenter when she speaks up.

Contemporary women recognize all Sor Juana's imaginative strategies: drawing from the narrative authority of her own experience; exercising a "hermeneutics of suspicion" by asking whose self-interest a particular textual interpretation serves; seeking out a usable past; finding ways to expand restrictions. That they are so familiar confirms that women's religious imagination as a subversive tool, used by insiders to the system, cannot yet be put aside as a function of past needs. History is full of examples. Nineteenth-century female Spiritualist mediums almost always spoke publicly in trance, in contrast with male mediums. Thus, they were able to say by implication, "I am not doing this of my own volition. I am a passive channel through whom the spirits of the dead have chosen to speak." Women in the nineteenth and twentieth centuries who worked for social causes frequently described themselves as extending the boundaries of the home into the outer world. Their public work could then be seen as "domestic" and therefore role appropriate. Black and white women preachers whose communities accepted their public preaching as based on a call from the Holy Spirit, a call that overrode gender role restrictions, made it clear that they did not seek equal authority with men.

All these women functioned as insiders but remained outsiders as well by virtue of body and limited authority. They crossed boundaries and accomplished work in public by breaking gender rules indirectly. In fact, "indirection" is another imaginative strategy by which women have achieved their own authority. They have "preached" the weekly sermon at home to male family members who did not attend services. They have exercised financial power over congregations by earning or bequeathing money for various projects and—again, indirectly—influenced decisions about how it would be spent. Even though they could not be ordained, women have offered essential support to male clergy or denied it. They have made their desires known to husbands and sons who served on decision-making bodies. While indirection has given women certain circumscribed authority, it also has a negative side. African American and Jewish women, for example, relate stories of pressure exerted upon them not to criticize their communities for fear that they will threaten social stability and survival.

Flashes of Insight: Inversion and Confrontation

A narrow view of the realities of women's lives suggests that acts of the strategic imagination are grounded in desperation rather than creativity, adequate primarily to maneuver a little within male-dominated religions. A more provocative interpretation sees them as imaginative acts of courage that have led to major shifts in thought and practice. However they have managed, for centuries women have found ways to preach, teach, study, and celebrate rituals. By doing so privately and publicly, even in a limited fashion, they have made the point that it is not lack of ability that has prevented women from doing these things more widely.

Historically, a growing experience of outsider status has stirred women's religious imagination in new ways, as women have recognized the inherent conflict between the qualified rhetoric of gender equality offered by most religious traditions and the realities of exclusion, restriction, and silencing. Eventually, the accumulation of dissonant experiences produced probing questions about why things are the way they are for women and how they could be otherwise. Why have women so often been kept from full participation when it is obvious that lack of ability is not the issue? Why has women's virtual silence been so little noticed and women's voices so little missed? Why have women's contributions to their communities been so seldom acknowledged publicly or so little valued that they have almost never warranted inclusion in history? The response to questions like these often takes the form of flashes of insight about the status of women, powerful acts of seeing and saying what has been the case all along. These insights appear to emerge suddenly, although further investigation usually reveals that the ground has been well prepared by the struggles of women in previous eras. Their emergence demands getting enough critical distance from the assumptions about gender roles that a whole culture takes for granted as so absolutely real and right that a community is actually incapable of seeing, much less questioning, them. The significance of these insights is that they open up whole new arenas of inquiry about the roles of women in religion and in society, and they unleash the religious imagination in multiple directions. Four such insights emerged fairly early in the contemporary women's movement when women were beginning to feel particularly their outsider status.

When Valerie Saiving suggested in a 1960 essay that for many different reasons women experience life and religion differently from men, she made the first move in constructing a new category of inquiry and authority in religion and theology. Over the years this category came to be called "women's experience." One of her particular examples focused on men's and women's differing understandings of "sin." If men, said Saiving, un-derstood sin in traditionally defined ways as pride, defiance of God, and alienation, women were more likely to experience it as the temptation to stay silent and hidden, to expend their energies in diffuse and trivial ways, and to dissipate their creativity in excessive attention to others' needs. In effect, Saiving's insight brought to light the reality that nobody—individually or institutionally—was asking, "What is it like to be a woman in this or that tradition?" "What do women, who are more than half the population of most religions, have to say about the sacred or human life or nature or religious institutions?" And hardly anyone had ever noticed this silence or caught on to the reality that if women's experiences had never been incorporated self-consciously into their communities' self-understanding, then those communities were not whole. This recognition stirred women's religious imagination to the absolute importance of telling stories about their own experiences of their traditions, positive and negative. And the telling of stories has led to creative speculations about how traditions must and will change if women's experiences are included in the shaping of religious practices and theological interpretations. Over the years, the term *women's experience* clearly became much too general a concept to bring to light the very different realities among women caused by race, class and economic status, ability, sexual orientation, and age. This powerful and often painful discovery expanded Saiving's original insight much more broadly as women of many communities began offering increasingly distinctive descriptions and analyses of their particular experiences.

Another major insight about women's place in religion emerged from the recognition that the dominance of maleness in the structures and content of Western religions had relegated women and the feminine to lower, nonsacred status. Post-Christian theologian Mary Daly's (b. 1925) terse analysis that when God is male, the male is God was her way of saying something profound about the nature of language and of naming. The languages we speak compel us to see (and not see) the world in particular ways. Languages that have no words to convey images of women's religious leadership or their connection to the divine fetter the religious imagination of the entire community with circumscribed visions of women's identity and role. Languages that associate concepts considered less spiritual, intellectual, and transcendent—earth, emotion, flesh—with the feminine shape a worldview in which women are "other" than the preferred norm. The early response by women to this insight was a combination of surprise, bewilderment, and outrage along with the realization that language both reveals and constructs power relationships in society. The ongoing significance of this insight has been the recognition that we are not at the mercy of language. Language is a tool of creative play for the religious imagination. One of Daly's strategies for demonstrating this reality has been reversal. She turns language and reality upside down. That which has been devalued becomes transvalued. Words like *hag, crone,* and *witch* take on positive rather than negative connotations. Daly is far from alone in her play with language. Witness all the creative work women have done with new images for the divine, with gender-inclusive language, with poetry and liturgy. She has, in fact, been criticized for replacing one pole of a classical dualism—male/female—with another and for being too optimistic in asserting that a female-centered language will alter reality and transform the world. But her early pivotal insight into language as a tool of both power and play has been a forceful impetus to women's religious imagination.

Women have been just as absent from history as they have been from language. American colonial historian Laurel Thatcher Ulrich, a feminist and lifelong Mormon, came to the conclusion in her study of seventeenth- and eighteenth-century women that "nice women don't make history." Those women, she discovered, who upheld their communities' expectations for virtuous behavior—insiders—have not been remembered by historians. Their names do not appear in books, and their portraits do not hang in gathering places and seminary libraries. Ulrich's insight, now so popular that it appears on bumper stickers, points to another, corollary pattern in American religious history: Women whose names have survived the filtering process of history—Anne Hutchinson, Mary Dyer, Mother Ann Lee, Mary Baker Eddy, Ellen G. White—have been regarded as dissenters, outsiders, women who are "not nice" by mainstream standards. Also missing from the history books are women's previous struggles for full participation, a fact that accounts for the surprise contemporary women experience at encountering the efforts of a woman like Sor Juana. As historian Gerda Lerner has pointed out, women have failed to develop a historical consciousness. Therefore, successive generations of women have to start over and over again in their struggles for full participation. These insights have functioned as jolts to the religious imagination that raise questions about history and send historians off in new directions. Who writes history? Who is remembered by historians and for what reasons? What kinds of new histories need to be written? What previously untapped resources, perspectives, and values will be their foundation? How do women cultivate a sense of themselves as historical actors with obligations to preserve evidence of their efforts for future generations? If women are indeed insiders to North American religion, what would religious history look like if it were written as if that were true?

A fourth insight that has been slower in emerging offers a different kind of challenge to women's religious imagination. This is the reality that no matter how irrefutable the evidence of gender injustice in religion, there is no guarantee of quick or even certain change for the better. The transformation of worldviews, social structures, values, and practices requires the ongoing work of many generations, not just one or two. Here women's religious imagination is confronted with the issue of persistence—with keeping on keeping on, as African American women have phrased it, and with avoiding the weariness, despair, and cynicism that are temptations to those who begin to realize how long and hard the struggle really is. As Gerda Lerner has pointed out, women's movements historically have tended to fade away and to skip several generations before starting over again—nearly from scratch. Whether awareness of this pattern is enough of an imaginative impetus at this moment in history to keep this erasure from happening again and whether there has been enough integration of women into positions of public leadership in their traditions to make the movement last—these are questions that are wide open at the beginning of the twenty-first century.

The Elaborative Imagination: New Themes Emerging

The insights described here have had their origins in women's critique—as outsiders—of the status quo. As these critiques are acknowledged and confronted and their causes and implications analyzed, the religious imagination is freed to roam into the territory of "otherwise"—to construct new visions for a just and loving world. In making this move, women's religious imagination has not left critique behind. Critique is its own kind of imaginative work and should not, in fact, diminish if historical consciousness is to be maintained. But women's religious imagination is not satisfied with exercising only one aspect of its capacity. In the immense outpouring of women's religious creativity over the last forty years, there is obviously a growing confidence and delight in women's play with religious ideas. There is a boldness with which women replace destructive assumptions about how things are or should be that do not make sense with what they know from their own lives. These elaborations are the fruits of women who are operating very much as insiders, not so much in the institutional sense but insofar as they have deep roots in the worldviews of their traditions. Women have a facility with the symbols and rituals of their communities. They have been shaped by participation in liturgies, by exposure to centuries-long echoes of the meaning of sacred texts and devotional practices. Their religious imaginations are both grounded and capable of imaginative flight. At the same time, the experience of being outsiders is never absent from the creative process.

Among the most intriguing of the new themes emerging from women's religious imagination is that of ambivalence, a highly charged combination of affection and anger, loyalty and disdain, gratitude and bitterness. This natural and powerful outcome of women's insider/ outsider status is a tremendous catalyst for the religious imagination. There is an ambivalence that comes from imbibing a tradition's assurances of equality combined with experiences of exclusion. These contradictory experiences, once thought to be an obstacle to participation in a community or a state of mind in need of resolution one way or another, have begun to function as a foundation of theological method, even to be seen as a virtue—a way women can proceed as both dissenters and participants.

Many Christian women speak of "defecting in place," that is, staying within the institution but pursuing not just reform but radical change. Muslim women are candid about how various forms of Islam have oppressed women, but they continue to see the Qur'an as a source of liberation and work to interpret it on behalf of women. Jewish theologians describe themselves as critics of Judaism's silencing of women but also as participants in the tradition. Theologian Rachel Adler says, "If I were not a feminist, I would not feel entitled to make theology." But she also makes it clear that "[i]f feminists reject the categories and content of the tradition, how can they claim that what they create in its place is authentically Jewish?" (Adler, xv, xix–xx). Some women, like artist and former Roman Catholic contemplative nun Meinrad Craighead, leave behind the institution but not the inspiration of its symbols and rituals or "the community," which she sees as transcending the boundaries of the institution. Former Christian Emily Culpepper compares her early life as a southern Protestant to "compost," since *roots* does not adequately convey her experience of radical discontinuity. Her description offers a perfect example of an organic metaphor for ambivalence: "It [her Christianity] has decayed and died, becoming a mix of animate and inanimate, stinking rot and released nutrient. Humus. Fertilizer" (Culpepper, 91).

In a postmodern age, women's creative use of ambivalence makes a particular contribution to religious institutions in general. Religions are human institutions, vehicles, hopefully, of transformation but never free of human corruption and distortion. Ambivalence, women say, is a highly appropriate stance to take toward a religious community just as it is toward other forms of institutional life in American culture. Informed ambivalence, as women well know, requires that members of a community work always to conserve what is best in a tradition without failing at the same time to point out and call to account its excessive and shortsighted tendencies.

Immanence, the conviction of sacred presence permeating the universe and accessible to humankind, is another of the themes that women elaborate. This claim works at the strategic level and has multiple theological implications as well. To say that "the divine dwells within—our very beings, our communities, our nature, and every atom of the universe"—is an empowering claim for women to make. Denied public leadership and authority as well as assurances that women's bodies are holy rather than sources of temptation, women have called upon the divine within as the undergirding of their own authority and goodness. At one level, women's emphasis on immanence relies on the strategy of reversal, holding up as full of positive meaning a concept that for centuries has taken second place to transcendence (the divine as far away and "other") and even regarded as dangerous.

What becomes clear through women's imaginative elaboration of immanence is that it is not just a strategic move but a reorientation of understandings of the sacred. If the sacred is experienced as more near than far, more accessible than remote, the religious imagination finds that it has many new places to go. Religion, in fact, comes down to earth. Roman Catholic women have begun to see the Virgin Mary not as a faraway heavenly intercessor whose total obedience has given her an entree to God but as a companion in the struggle for justice—an earthly and earthy Mary who is "with us." Buddhist women are reorienting their tradition in an earthbound way by insisting that Buddhist practice is meant to enhance this life rather than to foster renunciation of everyday life and preparation for death. Mormon women are seeking to expand the image of Heavenly Mother, the wife of Heavenly Father, and to promote institutional devotion to her. They see the need for this imaginative work as a way to speak to the lives of women and to enhance their role in Mormonism. Mormon feminists claim that the tradition cannot be whole until the Mother of Mormonism is fully acknowledged—until she comes down to earth and finds a place within the hearts of both women and men. In other words, the theme of immanence cuts across many different traditions and finds distinctive expression within them.

Women's imaginative elaboration of immanence has led to yet another prominent theme, that of the sacredness of the ordinary and the ordinariness of the sacred. This dual theme is another manifestation of reversal and, like immanence, has both strategic and theologically expansive functions. Insisting on the sacredness of the ordinary has served women by calling for more imaginative theological attention to the value of those tasks that are life sustaining, essential to the survival of the community, and traditionally carried out by women. They are typically performed on behalf of others who are thought to be doing more important things, accomplished far from the public eye, with little public acclaim, and perceived as having little historical significance. To care for children, to cook, to go to work, to wash clothes, to garden—all these tasks, whether performed by women or men, can be looked upon as religious practice if performed mindfully. And according to women of many different traditions, *the ordinary* refers not only to the domestic. The religious imagination of women has expanded the very meaning of the category to include a variety of ethical issues by pointing to how very ordinary it is for many people to lack life's necessities or to be suffering from a variety of physical and emotional ills.

Women's expansion of the sacredness of the ordinary has also inspired reflections on the ordinariness of the sacred. This theme, too, works at the strategic level to provide more access to the sacred and to demonstrate how the sacred has roots in ordinary life rather than in that which is remote, mysterious, and institutionally regulated. Such an approach has been especially fruitful in the arena of ritual. Roman Catholic women, for example, have been asking for several decades what it would mean for their tradition and for the role of women (who at present cannot be ordained to the priesthood) if the Eucharist, that is, communion, were looked upon as an ordinary meal open to all rather than an extraordinary one. What would happen, asks Buddhist Rita Gross, if more ordinary goals were set for Buddhist practice and more ordinary interpretations offered for its benefits— the household seen as a place where mindfulness and detachment can be practiced rather than as a place of distraction from one's spiritual obligations. This might, she suggests, bring about a reorienting of Buddhist practice toward individual sanity, peace, and comfort that would contribute to the well-being of the community and the earth. Overall, in this double-edged theme of the sacredness of the ordinary and the ordinariness of the sacred, it is possible to see a dual effort fostered by women's religious imagination. The first is to resacralize—to make holy again—daily life and work that are undervalued and considered "secular" and restore its power to be revealing of the sacred. The second is to demystify, that is, to render accessible and more comprehensible teachings and rituals in which women have been forbidden to participate fully.

Relationality is a fourth major theme in the repertoire of women's religious imagination. Understood broadly, it is the assumption that at the very heart of reality is a cosmic web of relationships and that everything that exists or has ever existed is somehow interconnected and interdependent. Women from many different communities claim that the moral vision underlying this assumption is much more compelling than that of a universe made up of separate, autonomous parts, endlessly circling each other but never connecting. The imaginative fruits of this vision have moved women in a variety of directions. Ecofeminists of many persuasions point to the similarities between exploitation of women and exploitation of the earth. They point to the interdependence between human and nonhuman, animate and nonanimate, as a worldview more conducive to justice and survival. It is a vision that sets aside hierarchical rankings and works to value and protect the needs and contributions of the most vulnerable. Goddess feminists claim "relationship" as basic to their understanding of reality, and they depict the Goddess as She Who will restore and sustain harmonious relationships between humans and the natural world. Christian theologians use the theme of relationality to reimagine new interpretations for traditional doctrines. Protestant Marjorie Suchocki rejects traditional understandings of sin as primarily defiance against God or as the act of one person against another. She insists on the relational nature of sin as violence to any part of creation. Elizabeth A. Johnson transforms the traditional Roman Catholic doctrine of the Communion of Saints from a hierarchical system of patronage whose workings require those on earth to seek favors from saints in heaven who are closer to God. She sees it instead as an inclusive symbol that "relates disparate cultural groups around the world at any one time, and women with men, and the most socially marginalized with the most powerful, all within an egalitarian community of grace, but also the living with the dead and the yet to be born, all seekers of the divine" (Johnson, 262).

Healing is a fifth theme that has stimulated the religious imagination of women. This theme is related to larger, pragmatic questions about what religion is for, how it works, and what its focus should be. The emphasis on healing repeats from another angle the contention that religion needs to come down to earth. Religion is for here and now, to find and relieve the causes of unnecessary suffering and to offer hope and support to those who are experiencing the inevitable suffering that comes with being human. Historically, women have found healing to be an outlet for exercising religious creativity and authority. During the second half of the nineteenth century, several healing religions emerged in American culture, Christian Science, founded by Mary Baker Eddy, being the most prominent. Usually begun by women and drawing disproportionate numbers of women members, these religions demanded a change in consciousness about the nature of reality as a prerequisite for healing. By doing so, healing religions or "mind cure" religions (as they were often referred to negatively) changed the arena of struggle from "the world" to "mind," a platform much more accessible to most women and one that tended to minimize dependence on clergy and physicians.

Early in this second wave of feminism that began in the 1960s, "healing" was used most frequently to refer to women's own need for healing—spiritual and psychological—from the effects of male-dominated religion and culture. By the beginning of the twenty-first century, the imaginative uses of healing have been opened up much further and have functioned to inspire new ways to think about traditional religious ideas. For example, womanist (African American) theologians like Delores Williams refute theologies of the Atonement (Jesus' suffering and death on behalf of humankind) that glorify surrogate suffering African American women have taken on for others—fieldwork, child care, sexuality—to the great detriment of their own well-being. She offers instead a theology of redemption that insists that African American women deserve abundant life. Her work is an example of women's conviction that religious doctrines must alleviate pain rather than cause it.

Imaginative interpretations of healing foster hope and wholeness often in collaboration with the artistic imagination. Minnesota artist Julia Barkley, an Episcopalian, began to paint in middle age—huge, multicolored, light-filled canvases of goddesses, women's bodies, and mythic figures. Barkley experienced her own version of the insider/outsider phenomenon. In the 1970s her paintings were rejected by a Minneapolis woman's art gallery because they were too religious, and by religious institutions because they were too threatening to orthodoxy. Now they hang prominently on the walls of United Theological Seminary of the Twin Cities. Barkley describes her chance to paint her emerging theology as healing: "To be able to say all the things—with my brush—that were formerly forbidden to say, has been an experience of greatest joy. Women have truly walked on water to overcome" (Bozarth, Barkley, and Hawthorne, 46). Chickasaw poet Linda Hogan calls one of her books *The Book of Medicines*. In the poem "Sickness" she writes, "I saw disease./ . . . It went to work./ It tried to take my tongue./ But these words,/ these words are proof/ there is healing" (63).

Ironies of the Insider/Outsider Imagination

Along with its more straightforward contributions to North American religion, an imagination grounded in a paradoxical identity—insider and outsider—is bound to produce some ironies also. At least four deserve comment here. First, the rigorous and often angry critique that women have imposed on religions and religion has certainly not destroyed religion. It has had both a vitalizing and a conserving, although not conservative, effect. Contrary to a dominant impulse in American religious history for reform to pare down, purify, get back to the basics, women's religious imagination has acted to ex-

pand boundaries, to open up new territory. If more than half the community is just starting to be heard from, there is obviously a lot left to say.

Second, there is the strange truth that in a postmodern age so focused on divine absence from the cosmos, women, because of their emphasis on immanence, have found themselves creating new ways of defining and experiencing sacred presence. By bringing religion down to earth, they have demonstrated, again, that there is much more to be said about religious symbols that for centuries had depended for their power on a supernatural reality that existed outside the world. Women have been demystifying institutional religion, but in the process they have been resacralizing the universe, pointing to new ways to understand and experience the very meaning of "sacred."

Third, at a moment in history when there is so much gloom about the decline, particularly, of the mainline churches, women—often to their dismay—have demonstrated the strength of these institutions to resist change. A highly optimistic interpretation of this reality might suggest that religious communities will learn from women's efforts that they should put more energy into embracing innovation change than into resisting it.

Finally, there is the irony that the very consciousness of outsider status may well be what has unleashed the most creative aspects of women's religious imagination. If indeed nice women still do not make history—or theology either, for that matter—women may have reason to hold to their outsider status to some extent and with it the imaginative possibilities of ambivalence. Women may resolve not to lose the creative edge that comes with holding two conflicting but dynamic identities together.

SOURCES: Choosing sources for a broadly inclusive concept like "women's religious imagination" is a matter of selecting texts that will frame historical and theological backgrounds and that will offer compelling examples from what have become, thankfully, innumerable possibilities from many different communities of women. Some texts that speak generally to issues of history and theology are Mary Farrell Bednarowski, *The Theological Imagination of American Women* (1999); Ann Braude, "Women's History *Is* American Religious History," in *Retelling U.S. History*, ed. Thomas A. Tweed (1997); Catherine A. Brekus, *Strangers and Pilgrims: Female Preaching in America 1740–1845* (1998); Gerda Lerner, *The Creation of a Feminist Consciousness* (1993); Sor Juana Ines de la Cruz, *The Answer/ La Respuesta Including a Selection of Poems*, ed. and trans. Electa Arenal and Amanda Powell (1994); and Laurel Thatcher Ulrich, "Vertuous Women Found: New England Ministerial Literature, 1668–1735," *American Quarterly* 28 (1976). Examples of women's religious creativity as it has emerged from particular communities include Rachel Adler, *Engendering Judaism: An Inclusive Theology and Ethics* (1998); Alla Bozarth, Julia Barkley, and Terri Hawthorne, *Stars in Your Bones* (1990), which includes paintings and poetry; Carol P. Christ, *Rebirth of the Goddess* (1997); Emily Culpepper, "The Spiritual, Political Journey of a Feminist Freethinker," in *After Pariarchy*, ed. Paula M. Cooey, William R. Eakin, and Jay B. McDaniel (1991); Mary Daly, *Beyond God the Father* (1973); Rita M. Gross, *Buddhism after Patriarchy* (1993); Linda Hogan, *The Book of Medicines* (1993); Ada María Isasi-Díaz, *Mujerista Theology* (1996); Elizabeth A. Johnson, *Friends of God and Prophets: A Feminist Reading of the Communion of Saints* (1998); Gail Ramshaw, *God beyond Gender* (1995); Delores S. Williams, *Sisters in the Wilderness: The Challenge of Womanist God-Talk* (1993); Gisela Webb, ed., *Windows of Faith: Muslim Women Scholar Activists in North America* (2000); and Terry Tempest Williams, *Leap* (2000), a Mormon woman's spiritual journey.

SOCIAL ETHICS, WOMEN, AND RELIGION
Marilyn J. Legge

THE TWENTY-FIRST CENTURY has ushered in a period of complex and enormous change and encompassing transformation. What is the nature of such fundamental world restructuring? What is happening to the fragile planet, the earth community? How do women under particular conditions suffer, and why? What kind of world do women yearn for? What, for example, ought women of different classes, cultures and ethnic groups, races, and religions do? How do justice and caring relate? How can women use their power in creative and collective ways, across public and private spheres, with respect for the ecosystem? How do women contribute to shaping virtues, values, obligations, and visions of the good life, to seeking justice and love, rooted in religious life, in their everyday lives and communities and on earth? These are some of the questions raised by religious social ethicists in North America as they refashion what counts as the deepest issues in ethical theory and practice and how these might best be addressed in light of diverse women's experience.

Social ethics addresses questions of moral agency (having power or potential to act), structures of human relationships and social order, and norms for action. Moral standards (criteria, measures, or norms) emerge from critical reflection on concrete moralities practiced in communities, including religious. Reflection on the rightness of interpersonal, communal, and public arrangements and practices is social ethics. The wider context stimulates ethical consideration of social, political, and economic issues (e.g., reproductive choices and technologies, health-care accessibility, work, the AIDS pandemic, ecological destruction). Social ethics generally deals with issues of social order: What is good and right, and what ought we do in the organization of human communities and the shaping of social policies? Hence,

the broad subject of social ethics is moral rightness and goodness in the shaping of persons and societies within earth communities.

Religion is about the meaning and purpose of life, the wider world, and cosmos. *Religious social ethics* refers to the wide-ranging work of religions that shape public practices and standards. Religious social ethics rely on varied and particular sources (e.g., religious leaders, scripture, and tradition) and norms (e.g., justice and love). In North America, while Christian social ethics has historically dominated, there are some comparable movements in other religions, in particular, Judaism and Islam.

The academic study of social ethics first emerged within the field of Christian theological study. It is usually traced to the course in social ethics taught at Harvard University in 1883–1884 by Francis Greenwood Peabody. This course gave rise to the development of the discipline of Christian ethics; the study of Christian social ethics became part of mainstream theological studies and some departments of religion. Today ethics is central to theological and religious studies because of the need to respond to practical and social questions about the contemporary relevance of religion in a context where religious belief is contested in an intensely pluralistic and complex world.

Women's Voices, Feminism, and Religious Social Ethics

Religious women are engaging the great social questions because both religion and the sustainability of life in a shared earth home require it. There is a wide array of approaches that have developed in relation to the activism of the women's liberation movement. By no means does all this movement define itself as feminist but instead communicates breadth, diversity, passion, and informality in the ways women work for radical change. Women move in surprising and unpredictable ways to overcome their disadvantaged and relatively powerless positions, which include economic and sexual use and abuse, as well as cultural and religious devaluation and marginalization. While there are women doing religious social ethics who do not claim the term *feminist*, the social and political nature of religion is most prominent in feminist work because it is linked with women's social movements for transformation.

Feminist approaches to social ethics ask critical questions about power relationships in any situation, looking for relations of domination and exclusion. For example, they examine gender relations between women and men or between straight and lesbian or bisexual women. Feminists ask "Where are the women?" to focus on women's lived experience; they seek justice based in shared personal respect and power for and among

The mission of the Women's Inter-Church Council of Canada Ecumenical Network for Women's Justice is to work for social justice, women's issues, ecumenism, and women's spirituality. *Courtesy of Women's Inter-Church Council of Canada, Gwyn Griffith, photographer.*

women and between women and men. Some feminists argue that a gender-based analysis is too limited to do justice to how women's lives are shaped not only by gender but as lived at the intersections of such vital factors as culture, ecology, geography, race, class, sexuality, and religion. This multidimensional approach to social ethics aims to account for, empower, and sustain women's lives in diverse social and ecological settings.

Women in different religious contexts use specific sources and interpretive questions to construct a viable social ethics: For example, Jewish feminists turn to the Torah and ritual (e.g., Judith Plaskow), Muslims to the Qur'an (e.g., Riffat Hassan, Amina Wadud), Goddess worshippers to female-centered traditions and earth-based spiritualities (e.g., Starhawk, Carol Christ), Buddhists to practices of release from suffering through mindfulness and compassion and a reconstruction of Buddhist institutional life with women in mind (e.g., Rita Gross and S. Boucher); Protestant feminists draw heavily on the Bible, Social Gospel, women-oriented, prophetic, and liberation traditions; Roman Catholic women have developed feminist moral theology as a distinct discipline related to a revised ethics of natural law, that is, interpretations of "human nature" as divinely created for meaning and purpose and how the moral goods that are constitutive of happiness are indeed knowable by human reason.

Ecumenically (intra-Christian) and interreligiously, feminist social ethicists ask: What sort of people ought women to be and become? How is meaning constructed? For example, in reading scriptures, are they enabled to read them in ways that are life giving in terms of women's lived experience, local culture, class, race/ethnicity, gender, and sexuality? Whose interests are served by a particular reading, doctrine, or social policy? What kind of world does this social ethics envision for women, their communities, and a sustainable environment?

Generative Women's Voices

Women's involvement in nineteenth- and early-twentieth-century struggles for justice in social, political, legal, and religious institutions has served as inspiration to feminists doing social ethics a century and more later. While there was a wide range of theological stances among this "first wave" of reformers who advocated for women's emancipation and participation in religious and public life, the evangelical spirit of their religious faith sparked powerful intellectual and morally persuasive activity. The early women's movement drew its strength from its relation to wider social issues: moral reform (by which they meant the closing down of brothels and curbing of men's sexual appetites); temperance (abstinence from drinking alcohol); antislavery (which moved from colonization of slaves outside of the United States to gradual emancipation and then abolition within the United States); and women's rights (which included rights to vote, to divorce and have custody of children, and to own and inherit property). White women of religious motivation included Lucretia Mott, the sisters Sarah and Angelina Grimké, Elizabeth Cady Stanton, Frances Willard, and Jane Addams in the United States and Nellie McClung, Alice Chown, Francis Marion Beynon, and Louisa McKinney in Canada. While left-wing evangelical Protestant Christianity fueled women's moral passion to rectify some injustices, the racism of white feminists was obvious in their later separation of women's rights from black enfranchisement.

Nineteenth-century African American women who were forerunners of black womanist ethics (feminist ethics based upon African American women's intergenerational experience) include Anna Julia Cooper, Amanda Berry Smith, Ida B. Wells-Barnett, Sojourner Truth (especially her historic 1851 "Ain't I a Woman" speech), and Frances Ellen Watkins Harper. What characterized these early women's reform activity was their clarity about women's dignity and humanity and their assurance that women had the capacity to act effectively for women's and "the Race's" emancipation. This confidence is evident in Anna Julia Cooper's open criticism of the racism of white feminists, challenging white Victorian opinion that a black woman could not be a lady and pressing to make black women visible in the white women's movement.

In Canada, Nellie McClung (1873–1951) is remembered as one of the formative political and religious activists of the Social Gospel movement. McClung, a fervent Methodist, championed suffrage, old age pensions, mother's allowances, public health nursing, free medical and dental care, birth control, divorce, and property laws for women. McClung was one of the "Famous Five" who successfully challenged the 1867 British court ruling that declared women are "persons in matters of pains and penalties, but are not persons in matters of rights and privileges" and therefore could not be appointed to the Senate. The lives of all Canadian women were affected by the landmark Canadian Supreme Court verdict of 1929 that declared women are indeed persons.

In the twentieth century Nelle Morton (1905–1987) was a forerunner shaping the discipline of religious social ethics. Born in Tennessee, Morton was a Christian who pioneered strategies for facing the social ethical challenges of what she named the sins of war, poverty, pollution, colonization, racism, and sexism. She asserted that the Christian prophetic faith was born, kept alive, and spread not necessarily by the impact of one person on another but by committed groups striving together to make God relevant to their total life and work. Mor-

ton's unique contributions to feminist social ethics, teaching, and learning are noted especially in three elements that enable and support critical consciousness: active listening and, as she put it, "hearing one another into speech"; images and concepts; and the church's work for social change. Morton defined the task of theology as "creating the path by journeying" where "road-building becomes inseparable from the journey itself" (Morton, 127, 67, xviii). A new model of doing social ethics began to emerge when women took their experience seriously as a key source of religious and social knowledge and wisdom.

Shaping Feminist Religious Ethics

In the late 1960s, as part of a general resurgence of grassroots women's activism known as "the second wave" of the women's liberation movement, an unprecedented explosion of feminist ethical debate took place. The term *feminist ethics* had emerged by the late 1970s and early 1980s. Feminist philosophers and academics began to develop two intertwining strands of ethical work: Some attended to practical contemporary ethical issues raised by social life, whereas others worked on the male bias and patterning of traditional ethical theory. Early feminist theorists such as psychologist Carol Gilligan at Harvard University challenged the traditional separation of justice and care, with the former being associated with the categories of male, mind, public, world, and self; and care with female, body, private, nature, and other. Theorists showed how these categories were organized into pairs or dualisms that functioned hierarchically; that is, the upper lot (those associated with justice) had more social power and value and thus dominated the lower categories (those associated with care). One practical outcome has been the argument that the family should be seen as a school for justice applicable to relationships in areas of life beyond it and that caring for others is not the special responsibility of women or the private sector. Care and justice, then, are not considered mutually exclusive virtues but should be important aspects of any social ethic. The principal insight of feminist ethics is that injustice against women is morally intolerable and wrong. Injustice can be practiced as oppression or domination and experienced in various forms—as exploitation, marginalization, powerlessness, cultural imperialism, and systematic violence.

As they participated in women's movements, religious feminists influenced first theological and biblical studies and then more gradually other fields in religion such as education, liturgy, religious studies, spirituality, and ethics. The first generation of academic women who developed the field of feminist social ethics were in Christian departments of theology or seminaries such as Beverly Wildung Harrison of Union Theological Seminary in New York and Margaret A. Farley of Yale Divinity School. These women were among the pioneers at work clearing spaces in the academy and religious institutions, along with other notable academics like Mary Daly (Boston College), Eleanor Haney (who asked in 1980, "What is Feminist Ethics?"), and Anne McGrew Bennett (who founded the Center for Women and Religion at the Graduate Theological Union in Berkeley, California).

Religious feminists constructed a new way of doing ethics by making the starting point women's experience of oppression and agency. By placing the full dignity, action, and personhood of women—their moral agency—central to moral reasoning, they redefined the scope and process of religious social ethics. *Moral agency* means that persons have the capacity to make sense of themselves as creatures who act "morally," that is, to discern actions, consider implications, be held responsible for one's choices and actions, and act on the values one hopes to embody. Early on, for example, Margaret Farley, professor of ethics and a Roman Catholic, built a feminist ethics on the conviction that women are fully human and are to be valued as such. She drew creatively on the natural law tradition central to Catholic moral theology. Natural law theory presupposes natural and intelligible goods that orient virtuous activity in the practical realms of life. Her work created a Christian feminist ethics with two criteria: one that would satisfy a feminist critique of the profound discrimination against women in religious patriarchy and at the same time develop grounds for the universal relevance and intelligibility of its own moral claims. To empower women's agency, she turned to the Catholic standard of the egalitarian participation of all human beings in the common good as the route to justice, an equitable sharing of goods and services necessary to human life and basic happiness. Further, she endorsed the ethical principles of embodiment, mutuality, equality, freedom, and respect for persons. She affirmed that justice and care are correlative norms and that autonomy, a traditional ethical ideal, is ultimately for the sake of relationality and community.

Beverly Wildung Harrison was also formative in shaping feminist religious ethics. Rooted in white, middle-American Presbyterianism, she developed a dynamic voice pioneering Christian feminist liberationist ethics. In her groundbreaking 1985 inaugural lecture as professor of Christian ethics at Union Theological Seminary, New York, "The Power of Anger in the Work of Love," she identified love with the making of justice or right relation and defined anger as a feeling signal that all is not well in relation to other persons, groups, or the world. She named three base points for an emerging feminist social ethics foundational to love: activity, embodiment, and relationship. Harrison commends how justice is a praxis "that realizes conditions that make my fulfilment and yours possible simultaneously, that literally creates a common good." Her definition of justice is radical equality and mutuality in community; it is the shared capacity for relationship and a quality of humanness that calls forth connection and solidarity. Acting for change toward justice in the uncertainty and messiness of living is to take courage together: in actions that are always partial and limited but nonetheless real. Theologically, she celebrates that "passion for justice, shared and embodied, is the form God takes among us at this time" (Harrison, 8, 39, 263).

A feminist religious ethics, at the same time personal, social, and political, is therefore deeply and profoundly worldly, one that delights in a spirituality of sensuality and acts for mutuality in living relationships with others and the world. Hence, love, justice, and power are substantial principles emerging out of struggles to meet basic needs. Attention to social class—how dominant economic power structures personal, social, and global relations—can illuminate how and why some benefit from, and others are burdened and marginalized by, reigning social arrangements and the varied roles religion plays in them, for good or evil.

The formation of feminist religious ethics grew predominantly out of white, middle-class women's experience and primarily in relation to Christianity. These formative developments in feminist moral theory all recognized that objectivity, traditionally understood to preclude loyalties and biases, was suspect. Instead feminist ethicists argued that one's vision is always perspectival: The problems seen and the solutions imagined cannot be separated from one's ecosocial location (the recognition that power relations swirling amidst factors of class, culture, race, gender, geography, sexuality, and family background shape how and what one knows). To acknowledge directly one's interests and actions and the willingness to be open to be changed by critique and relationship with others is crucial for critical self-awareness. Neutrality is neither possible nor desirable when historical structures are not objectively out there but are actively forming the ongoing dynamics of the present. In short, critical appreciation of women's experience was placed at the heart of the moral enterprise, neutrality and objectivity were denounced, and justice as mutual power in relation—human-divine-cosmic—emerged as the central norm or standard.

For a norm to be just, everyone who follows it must, in principle, have an effective voice in its consideration and be able to agree to it without coercion. Hence, for a social condition to be just—for right relation—it must enable all to express and meet their needs, especially the most vulnerable, and to exercise their freedom. Embracing the fragile and finite character of life is key to protesting the assaults of injustices due to racism, class elitism, sexism, and homophobia, to name but a few. Faith, according to a religious social ethics, can be construed, therefore, as facing tragedy with a trust in an enduring process of liberation and transformation, linked with choices in solidarity with the most vulnerable rather than with the powerful.

Differentiating the Field

An array of feminist social ethics has been developed by those who worked alongside, expanded, and challenged this legacy. The early feminist focus on power-in-relation required explicit recognition of differences among women. Since the 1980s a "third wave" of women's movement in religious social ethics has been working to specify women's experience, especially as rooted in particular mixes of class, culture, race/ethnicity, religion, and sexuality. Initially this task was taken up by scholars such as womanist Katie Geneva Cannon, *mujerista* Ada María Isasi-Díaz, and Janet Silman, from, respectively, African American, Hispanic, and aboriginal Canadian communities. In recent years, the question of difference has become a key theme in the work of women and religion. There are many reasons for this—the changing composition of Western societies, the increasing spread of economic globalization, and the impact of new social movements with networks of women being at the forefront. No longer can women's experience be approached as the primary source for women and social ethics as if it were an innocent foundation, that is, as if power does not shape the relations among women, as well as between women and men. Some feminists have insisted, therefore, that gender injustice does not stand alone. It is inevitably maintained at the conjunction of multiple relations of power that perpetuate racism, classism, heterosexism, and other oppressions. Compelling questions have been raised: Which women's experience counts? What power and potential for action are operative for women under different conditions, in particular relations and diverse contexts? The roots of the proliferation of difference are deeply embedded in the "postmodern condition" of vast, broad changes of a global scale affecting all areas of life.

Postmodern Conditioning of Power and Difference

The postmodern era is characterized by ambiguity, diversity, plurality, and especially the system of global capitalism that for the majority world impoverishes cultures and destroys communities. Postmodernism has involved the questioning of key categories in feminist theory, for example, of woman, nature, human, divine, and culture. These are seen not as innate, essential, or given but rather as humanly generated and socially con-

structed in history. Emergent movements of women have contested key theories in feminist frameworks (previously categorized as liberal, cultural, Marxist, and socialist). Ecofeminists contest categories of "nature" in feminist theory to reassess how best to conceive of human and nonhuman being, to illuminate human location within relationships of dependence on "nature," and what social ethics will preserve the environment as fundamental to social, economic, and personal wellbeing. German moral theologian Dorothee Soelle provides theoretical principles for good work: self-expression, social-relatedness, and reconciliation with nature. Connecting nature, the economy, and justice is a pressing agenda for religious social ethics.

The issue presented by difference and engaged through activism is not simply one of the invisibility of certain women, however: The very nature of experience itself is contested by those whose difference is constructed not in common with, but in divergence from, the assumed norm of white, heterosexual, middle-class woman. Women under postmodern conditions negotiate rather than receive their identities, communities, and moral agency. One regards the subjective, the personal, in terms of having multiple, coexisting selves rather than having a given, unified, and stable self within an assumed grand or master narrative. People belong to multiple communities simultaneously, requiring ongoing negotiation of identity, community, and religious life. Attention to the differences among women (whether aboriginal, Asian Canadian, bisexual, disabled, Buddhist, poor, etc.) exposes false universalisms (generalizations) in ethics. It is now uncommon to use the term *woman* to have a unified, common, or shared meaning, and women's experience is acknowledged to be a contested, even ambiguous and unreliable, guide to feminist action.

Christian womanist ethicist Katie Geneva Cannon asks, What are possibilities of moral agency when one is not free? What moral wisdom is created by black women in the face of oppression? Moral agency for black women cannot be understood apart from the continuing social matrix of women's lives that has been formed by the history of chattel slavery and ongoing forms of bondage under white patriarchal supremacy. To simply *exist* in the face of relentless powerlessness, black women have had to carve living space out of an intricate web of racism, sexism, and poverty. Their primary moral and religious challenge is, therefore, survival. Virtue for these women is best described not in terms of responsible uses of power (as designated in mainstream ethics). Rather, virtue for persons and communities without power is about developing strategies that allow them to persist with dignity. Cannon and others reframe traditional categories of ethics to account for moral agency in specific conditions, relating the choices available to moral formation (conscience, freedom, accountabilities).

The process of attending to and learning from diverse voices of women is an ongoing and necessary task. To see the flaws in shared systems of values, behaviors, and social, political, and economic arrangements requires difference, a thorough engagement with other communities, and with other ways of acting and knowing. The challenge of diversity has been well put by womanist theologian and ethicist Delores Williams with her notion of "multidialogics." If justice is to be nurtured in oneself and the wider world, persons will need to advocate and participate in dialogue and action with diverse social, political, and religious communities concerned about human survival and the productive quality of life for the oppressed. Similarly, feminist activist and scholar Sharon Welch, referring to the Rainbow Coalition, remarks that their aims of equality and respect are met by highlighting differences among the heterogenous groups, not by transcending them. Some feminists, such as Christian social ethicist Gloria Albrecht, theologically affirm difference in community to embrace the fullness and mystery of God and to challenge, therefore, any suffocation of particular voices. It is urged, therefore, that feminists ought to ask, What does the multiplicity invoked by difference contribute to the tasks of interdependence, collaboration, and solidarity within critical social ethics? Insofar as religious, cultural, geographical, political, economic, and technological structures divide, how can and does difference empower religious groups and various publics?

Justice and Solidarity in Particular

Ethicist and theologian Ada María Isasi-Díaz in developing a *mujerista* social ethics among Latina women living in the United States discusses the parameters of justice—"un poquito de justicia"—needed for moral agencies based on the value of human persons and their sustainable environments. She upholds interactive friendship, a form of neighbor love across difference, as central to participating in concrete, historical forms of justice. She insists that practices of solidarity are built by moving away from the false notion of disinterest, of doing for others in an altruistic fashion, and moving toward common responsibilities and interests that necessarily arouse shared feelings and lead to joint action. Such commitment is a praxis of mutuality. Justice includes the distribution of wealth, income, and other material goods but is wider than seeking to liberate an abstract individual, as liberal theory teaches, to define her or his own ends. Justice instead focuses not on individual wrongdoing but on collective, systemic injustice and how those most affected can participate in deliberation and decision making.

One example is the struggle of aboriginal women in Canada for reinstatement as full members of their community. In June 1985 the Canadian Parliament passed a bill that ended over 100 years of legislated sexual discrimination against native Indian women. The passage to amend Section 12 (1)(B) of the Indian Act marked the culmination of a long campaign to regain their full Indian status, rights, and identity. The remarkable story of the Tobique women at the heart of this struggle, which included a hearing by the United Nations Human Rights Commission, is told in *Enough Is Enough: Aboriginal Women Speak Out*. As Mavis Goeres put it: "We've had a long, hard struggle. I think what kept us going was our heritage and our sticking together. Maybe we didn't have all the same ideas, but we all had the one main goal in mind: equality for women" (Silman, 217). Various religious and women's groups were invited into solidarity and were politicized in the process of changing the law. Religious social ethics undertaken by women therefore has a twofold emphasis: to embrace responsibility for taking charge of one's own life and to make a commitment to transform oppressive structures.

Women in the Economy

A key area in religious social ethics is making women visible in the world of work and the dynamics of class, that is, how women's lives are defined by a particular economic system of production. The effect of current globalization of capital and of the restructuring of the world's economy on land, resources, and community has been noted in a growing body of gender-sensitive research that provides compelling evidence of the pronounced and multiple gendered impacts of this restructuring. A 1997 study conducted for the U.S. Agency for International Development shows that everywhere poverty is increasingly gendered, that is, affecting women most acutely. Women are impacted in five fundamental ways: First, female-headed households and elderly women are made poor or poorer. Second, women act as "shock-absorbers" during restructuring adjustments, both by curtailing their own consumption and by increasing their work to compensate for household income loss. Third, women tend to be more directly affected by reductions in social welfare spending and public programs. Privatization and welfare cuts simply mean that social services are shifted from the paid work of women in the public sector to the unpaid labor of women in the domestic sphere. Fourth, gains made toward the goals of gender equity during the 1970s are being lost with fewer good jobs for women and reductions in child care, education, and retraining programs. Finally, budget cuts within the public sector have a direct impact on women's employment when issues of pay and job equity are dropped.

In ecological and ethical terms, major agents in financial and government decision making have decided to value short-term accumulation of profit and capital at the expense of permanently writing off many individuals, depressed communities, and the environment. The shift to wealth accumulation in service and computerized technologies means that many in North America lack the requisite skills for this new economic model, and gender, class, and racial discrimination block avenues for retooling to meet new industries' demands. When computers are not available to working-class or underclass children, they enter school with a new kind of disadvantage. And unorganized women in the garment industry, working at below minimum wage, sew the sleeves for jackets that sell in high-end stores for hundreds of dollars. In short, globalization destroys peoples and environments; there is an *oikumene*, world household, of competition, domination, and possessions at the expense of an *oikumene* of sharing, cooperation, and solidarity.

The importance of retaining a knowledge of the dynamic of class relations under global capitalism needs to be stressed in a culture that increasingly emphasizes identities of consumption rather than production. There are more and more signs indicating that the fundamental structural shifts are propelling the poor, the elderly, aboriginal people, and others of color, and always more women and children, into a spiral of social neglect. Social and economic policies are forcing women to work more for less pay, to take on the care of the sick and elderly, and to depend on public assistance, food banks, and shelters. Social ethicists Barbara Andolsen, Pamela Brubaker, Elizabeth Bounds, Mary Hobgood, Joan Martin, Carol Robb, and Emilie Townes focus on what is at stake for particular women's lives in this emerging new world order. They are among religious social ethicists who focus on giving accounts of the burdens imposed on women by current economic conditions and showing implications for religious thought and practice.

In short, women's struggles for moral agency and communities of well-being are complicated by issues of power under conditions and dynamics of postmodern globalization. As an increasingly differentiated field, social ethics from diverse women's perspectives in religion aims to listen to and engage with multiple voices for wisdom and insight; to critically appropriate scriptures and traditions; to use the fullest range of emotion, reason, and imagination; and finally to discern truth and goodness in specific cultural and political contexts.

Sites of Feminist Religious Ethics

The women's movement has developed important coalitions of aboriginal women, women of color, labor feminists, lesbians, professional women, church and religious women, women with disabilities, poor women, and other activists. New forms of political action, focused on gender, sexuality, race, postcolonialism (all cultures affected by the imperial process), poverty, peace, the differently-abled, animal rights, and the environment have included strong cultural and sometimes explicit religious elements and practices. The women's movement is diverse. The movement has worked on such issues as equal pay for work of equal value, lesbian rights, abortion and reproductive choice, pornography, and peace, and it has evolved new social and cultural theory and feminist social ethics.

Feminist religious social ethics, as a form of socially oriented praxis, aims to bridge communities of religion, the academy, and various publics. Coalition building thus has been, and must continue to be, the mode of practice most needed. Religious social ethics committed to women's flourishing is nourished and participates in plural, ongoing projects and is careful not to distinguish too sharply between academic and activist grassroots work. Thus there are various ways of functioning as religious feminist ethicists. Feminists work in volunteer and paid ministries as chaplains, with congregations, community agencies (such as the battered women and shelter movement), in "outreach ministries" with refugees, in prisons, as staff of church bodies, and as engaged scholars and academics. There are numerous centers and networks of activism dedicated to seeking justice for women in religious and other communities. This work involves ethical practice: It situates specific moral problems faced by women in various religious communities and traditions; it analyzes existing social power and policies and develops potential alternatives to determine a "normative moral sense" or best judgment of what ought to be done in the current social context.

The aim of Catholics for a Free Choice (CFFC), established in 1973, has been to resist the Catholic hierarchy's opposition to abortion and to demonstrate that there is an authentic pro-choice Catholic position that supports reproductive rights and the primacy of conscience. Now an international agency, CFFC engages in research, analysis, education, publishing, and networking in relation to women's rights and reproductive health, population policy, gender equality, and sexuality. Mobilizing participation in public policy debates, communication and distribution of resources, and policy analysis and provision of data to policymakers are the core programs of CFFC USA, while CFFC-Canada focuses largely on advocacy. CFFC publishes a quarterly journal, *Conscience*.

The Justice for Women Program Ministry of the National Council of Churches staffed in New York City focuses on leadership, program and resource development, empowerment, and advocacy toward justice for women in church and society. Areas of work have included women in prison, prostitution, women, faith and economic justice, and women's health. Plans are under way to continue building the skills and resources developed during the Ecumenical Decade of Churches in Solidarity with Women (1988–1998), that provided a framework within which World Council member churches could critique their structures, teachings, and practices with a commitment to the full humanity and participation of women. It was also an impetus for churches to engage with and reflect on women's lives in society and to stand courageously with women in their struggles for justice and dignity.

Leaven was founded in 1987 in Michigan by Eleanor Morrison and Melanie Morrison, a mother and daughter team, to provide education and resources in the areas of spiritual development, feminism, antiracism, and sexual justice and to enable people to explore the connections between personal and social transformation. Work also includes advocacy for lesbians and gay men, spiritual direction, and consultation with congregations, church agencies, and nonprofit organizations. Leaven is committed "to providing support, nurture, and education for those who seek to be leavening agents for change—resisting oppression, engendering hope" (Leaven).

Sacred Web is a western Canadian–based project that invites women to reflect on the relationship of women, land, and spirit through art, story, justice making, and ritual. Inspired by the music of Carolyn McDade, the project's vision is to connect singing, reflection, and creative expression as part of the work of creating right relationship and sustainable ways of living with each other and the land. At regional gatherings and gatherings of women from across the western Canadian provinces, participants have shared stories of pain and vision and initiatives for healing, including sustainable agriculture and economic development. The project has generated a CD/cassette, *We Are the Land We Sing*, recorded with Carolyn McDade, and an anthology of writings, *Running Barefoot: Women Write the Land*, about women's connection with land and spirit.

WATER, the Women's Alliance for Theology, Ethics and Ritual, is a feminist educational center and justice network cofounded in 1983 by Mary Hunt and Diann Neu in Washington, D.C. Committed to an inclusive church and society, WATER supports theological, ethical, and liturgical development by and for women. Local, national, and international work includes programs and projects, publications, and workshops, counseling, spiritual direction, and liturgical planning, all aimed at implementing feminist religious values and social change. WATER welcomes visiting scholars, interns, and volunteers and shares resources with women in Latin America through its "Women Crossing Worlds" pro-

gram. *Waterwheel*, the Alliance's quarterly newsletter, includes liturgical and study resources in each issue.

The Women's Inter-Church Council of Canada (WICC), established in 1918, has representatives from eleven church partners. WICC's mission is to work for social justice, women's issues, ecumenism, and women's spirituality. Its Ecumenical Network for Women's Justice offers a framework to build a creative movement among people concerned with gender justice in the Canadian churches. The Network's mandate includes antiracism work; coordination of the Canadian churches' participation in the World March of Women against poverty and violence against women; and support of women's theology and spirituality. The ecumenical feminist journal *Making Waves*, a metaphor of advocacy for women's egalitarian participation in church and society, focuses on these concerns and networks.

In academic work, there are a number of well-established sites that engender attention to women and social ethics. The most influential are the American Academy of Religion (AAR) and the Society for Biblical Literature (SBL), where issues of women scholars in religious and biblical studies are addressed by their Committees on the Status of Women in the Profession. Activities include an academic advice column, sexual harassment policy, organization of special topics forums at the Annual Meeting of the AAR, and publication of *Guide to the Perplexing: A Survival Manual for Women in Religious Studies*. Several sections and groups at the AAR deal with topics related to women in religion: the Women and Religion Section; Feminist Liberation Theologians' Network; Feminist Theory and Religious Reflection Group; Lesbian-Feminist Issues in Religion Group; Womanist Approaches to Religion and Society Group.

In Canada, advocacy and networking among academic women happen at the annual Congress of the Social Sciences and the Humanities, the national meeting of all academic societies, especially in the Women's Caucus of the Canadian Society for the Study of Religion (CSSR). In North America, the Society for Christian Ethics has been a site of networking and explicit development of social ethics with respect to women.

One final example of religiously based activism is the Women's Theological Center (WTC) in Boston, which exists to nourish women's spiritual leadership and communities for liberation movements. WTC's programs and services focus on analysis of systemic oppression and exploration of the connections between theology/spirituality and social justice. WTC has a strong emphasis on antiracism work, offering training workshops and accessible resources.

Women in struggle "conspire" together, in search of new alternatives and ways of living with dignity. Women's religious social ethics accompanies the urgent struggles of women's lives that fund its religious, intellectual, spiritual, and moral agenda.

Challenges Ahead, Grounds for Hope

Feminist social ethics are, therefore, part of a constructive, evolving social movement that is shaping a multidimensional approach to integrate gender, race, class, and imperialist dynamics. The multifaceted nature of feminist struggle begins with examining women's own lives in communities to discover how people are alienated, used, and turned away from the ongoing healing power of right-relation and love amid the flawed and holy moments of relation. Then strategies emerge, where ambiguity and limits are acknowledged and taken seriously, and women are encouraged to live their lives more fully. Womanist ethicist Emilie Townes is among those who cogently articulate that the long, hard work of resisting injustice, apathy, and despair is ongoing, alongside the constant acknowledgment that the burden of changing an unjust and violent society falls most heavily on those who are most oppressed.

To act in compassionate solidarity across difference, while keeping one's own needs for liberation in mind, is a continuous challenge. In an increasingly fragmented and violent world, Sharon Welch proposes an ethic of risk for those with some power to enter the unfamiliar terrain of others:

Within an ethic of risk, actions begin with the recognition that far too much has been lost and there are no clear means of restitution. The fundamental risk constitutive of this ethic is the decision to care and to act although there are no guarantees of success. Such action requires immense daring and enables deep joy. It is an ethos in sharp contrast to the ethos of cynicism that often accompanies a recognition of the depth and persistence of evil. (Welch, 68)

Janet Jakobsen develops theories of agency and alliances that might work amidst the complexities of seeking justice across diverse agendas, particularly around questions of United States public policy and sexuality.

A primary vigilance, especially for those belonging to dominant/majority elements within networks of praxis, therefore, will be to not make their own and/or their group's experience into the norm and expect or persuade everyone else to think and behave like themselves. Often attempts to include those different from themselves may be with good intentions but actually alienate and silence those who are not just like them. Even if this additive form of inclusion is well-meaning, it nonetheless oppresses those being included. Inclusion is granted only on the basis of long-established rules and regulations that define the character and conduct of the community. No space is made available for new voices, practices, or visions to change the agenda or ways and means of association and proceeding. Instead, a multidialogical strategy toward solidarity teaches white feminists, for example, to take up the challenge of dismantling their privilege of white skin in antiracist work.

An intersecting challenge for women in religious social ethics is to deal with the current backlash of religious and cultural sex negativity and fear, as expressed especially in the powerful Christian Right "family values" organizations. Several historical reasons promote this attack on those who do not conform to patriarchally defined heterosexual family norms. Certainly the power of sexuality in Christian tradition has been dealt with mostly by denial and repression, and the key message, in both Protestant and Roman Catholic churches, is that women and sex are evil. Deep discomfort, especially in Christianity, is traced to the dualisms of mind over body, spirit over flesh, men over women, white over black, human over natural world. Women's bodies continue to be places where social conflicts are played out.

In the context of a broad cultural crisis, sexuality and the family have also become key issues for religious and public policy. Traditionally, sexuality was embedded in the marital relationship, and especially the child-centered family, as the central institution blessed by the "household of faith." The relation between religion and the family is (and always has been) intimate and complex. Religion has sanctified the family, most recently, the nuclear model; when this norm has been challenged, it has become a moral and political symbol, over-burdened with fear and fraught with conflict. Hence, the Christian right wing promotes "family values" to reassert a social order against feminism, abortion, and all those who do not conform to the norm of patriarchal, heterosexual marriage and its purpose to procreate (e.g., those who are single or live in alternative household patterns, those without children by choice, or those who are publicly gay, lesbian, bisexual, or transgendered).

Work by religious women in social ethics shows how matters of sexuality and family, including violence against women and children, are understood to be invariably spiritual, social, and public, not simply private, matters. Feminist religious scholars Lisa Sowle Cahill, Kelly Brown Douglas, Christine Gudorf, Judith Plaskow, and Traci West are among those who work to reframe sexuality and family with norms of survival and flourishing. In sum, social ethics among women's voices in religion is a multivocal and polycentric, practical and moral, inherently evaluative, and interdisciplinary practice. Women will need to embrace this character of ethical work to make systemic changes required for women's and the earth's well-being. Various religious and intellectual traditions and strategies will be called upon to share in domestic, secular, and religious arenas where people come together to nurture life, to renew spirits, to sustain hope, and to make a lived-world politics of radical change a lifelong practice. This work goes far beyond a critical passing on of scholarly and religious traditions. Women's religious social ethics is grounded in the stories and struggles of those who despite varied oppressions resist and survive appalling brutality and hostility. The twin challenges are interreligious dialogue and collaboration for justice and empowerment and staying connected with social movements, local and global, for vital civil societies through the creation of different relationships and new, nonoppressive, social structures. Diverse social and religious projects nourish women doing religious ethics. Emilie Townes offers norms and sources of hope for pro-active women's work in religious social ethics in "Women's Wisdom on Solidarity and Differences." Lament and hope are intertwined threads of an ethics of resistance and risk. Women in religion and social ethics will be accountable

for using the power that is theirs. Collaborative ventures among women doing religious social ethics envision vibrant communities attentive to difference, shared power, and political, social, and economic justice for a world of compassion and peace.

SOURCES: The early tillers in the field of feminist religious ethics include Margaret A. Farley, *Personal Commitments: Beginning, Keeping, Changing* (1986); Beverly Wildung Harrison, *Making the Connections: Essays in Feminist Social Ethics*, comp. Carol S. Robb (1985); Karen Lebacqz, *Justice in an Unjust World* (1987); Nelle Morton, *The Journey Is Home* (1985); Judith Plaskow, *Standing Again at Sinai: Judaism from a Feminist Perspective* (1990); and Sharon Welch, *A Feminist Ethic of Risk* (1990; rev. ed., 2000). Co-laborers were at work also, such as Katie Geneva Cannon, Mary Hunt, Ada María Isasi-Díaz, Carol Robb, and those represented in the collections edited by Barbara Hilkert Andolsen, Christine E. Gudorf, and Mary D. Pellauer, *Women's Consciousness, Women's Conscience: A Reader in Feminist Ethics* (1985) and by Lois K. Daly, *Feminist Theological Ethics: A Reader* (1994). Differentiation continues in the field; see, for example, Elizabeth M. Bounds, *Coming Together/Coming Apart: Religion, Community and Modernity* (1997); Lisa

Sowle Cahill, *Sex, Gender and Christian Ethics* (1996); Janet Jakobsen, *Working Alliances and the Politics of Difference* (1998); Janet Silman, *Enough Is Enough: Aboriginal Women Speak Out as Told to Janet Silman* (1987); and Emilie M. Townes, *Breaking the Fine Rain of Death: African American Health Issues and a Womanist Ethic of Care* (1998). The closing excerpt from Townes's "Women's Wisdom on Solidarity and Differences (on Not Rescuing the Killers)," *Union Seminary Quarterly Review* 53. 3–4 (1999): 153–164, evokes the passionate work of women doing religious social ethics. Also see Web sites: www.catholicsfor choice.org;www.viewitthere.com/cath4choiceCCFFC-Canada; http://leaven.org; www.hers.com/water.

THE PSYCHOLOGY OF WOMEN'S RELIGIOUS EXPERIENCE
Ann Belford Ulanov

THIS ESSAY CONCENTRATES on new trends in depth psychology and women's religious experience. The focus is not on the explosion in psychology about women as different from men, nor on clinical practice with women, nor on the birth of feminist theology, nor on sociological studies of the construction of gender. Important as all these areas of study are, this essay focuses on women's religious experience seen through the lens of the psyche.

Focusing on the psychology of women's religious experience means assembling dominant motifs that occur and recur in women writing out of themselves in relation to God, motifs that suggest a human mode of being that has been called feminine, thus finding a theology in the feminine rather than constructing a theology of the feminine. Such writing by North American women about religious experience springs from many large groups of women, both professional academics and lay workshop leaders, Roman Catholic, Protestant, Jewish, Muslim, and Asian feminist theologians. Women pastoral counselors make up these new groups, as do women liturgists, spiritual directors, Mormon women, scripture scholars, women psychoanalysts interested in spirituality, bishops, retreat leaders, women pastors and priests, women witches and Goddess worshippers, and psychics and tarot card readers. All these make up the large body of writings about women's spiritual experience, as well as spurring the recovery of the works of women mystics of other centuries and countries who bequeath us documents about religious experience of the highest caliber.

What, then, do we perceive as the commonalities that emerge in religious experience as represented by North American women? What phenomena present themselves as characteristic of women in this area? In a way this phenomenological approach treats the feminine mode as itself symbolic of one kind of exchange.

There is hardly only one route by which humans experience God. Nonetheless, to assemble common qualities that surface in women's religious experience of God introduces us to discernible, valid markers along this spiritual journey.

First and foremost, women encountering the sacred accept it as gendered. Conscious of their selves as woman, they discover and explore a feminine mode of experiencing God. For some women that means God comes to them as female, although they avoid the fusion of image and reality that insists God be equated with woman. Instead, they accept the gap between all human images of God and God. Nonetheless, feminine images of God's breasts or nurturing lap or motherly embrace grant a symbolic lens to perceive all of God, not some added-on aspect or attribute to balance heretofore exclusively masculine symbols for the divine. Just as any symbol falls far short of what it symbolizes, so feminine symbols function merely as pointers—but as pointers to the whole mystery of God. To speak of God as mother does not exhaust or define God, nor does it encompass the full range of women's experience, much of which has nothing to do with maternity. Any woman knows that she never knows what God will present to her, yet she perceives this annunciation through the lens of her female gender. For example, one woman was astonished that at the heart of intensely seeking God's will for her life came the certainty that she should come out as a lesbian, to live this self she was created to be fully in the world.

Conscious of the lens of gender, North American women writing out of their own experiences of God are also committed to rejecting the sexism embedded in the inherited constructions of female identity found in society and its cultural life, including religion. They want to risk new interpretations and perceptions of their experience in order to affirm their own worth. Refusing the old binary system of first and second class, of dominant and submissive, of hierarchy and lower status, women find themselves pointing out new markers on their religious journey. Any religion can be tested by its response to suffering and human destructiveness. This is no less true of the process of knowing, doing, being, creating, expressing in symbols religious encounters associated with a feminine mode of being human, a mode that belongs to all of us, men and women.

Instead of repudiating the body and all it symbolizes in this world's social, political, and material life, women's religious experience always includes the body, literally and symbolically. Body means bodiliness—the concrete and personal aspects of living in the flesh in this world, hence subverting and transmuting former doctrines of incarnation as a static descent of the divine into the human. Women affirm the worth of embracing the flesh and the religious experience that comes

The feminine mode always places wisdom next to love in the figure of Sophia. "Icon of Sophia—Divine Wisdom" by Eileen McGuckin. *Courtesy of Eileen McGuckin.*

through the flesh and in the flesh. Their spirituality may grow out of facing addictions to drugs or food or compulsive routines of work or obsessive goals of perfection. Religious freedom does not consist in conquering the addiction by leaving it behind to progress upward to God but instead by finding freedom by entering into its toils to hear the message from the beyond that can only find entrance through a wound to the flesh of this life here and now. The Canadian psychoanalyst Marion Woodman says that without her wounding food addiction she never would have discovered the numinous presence of Sophia.

The body must be honored. That God appears in the flesh means also my contemporary flesh now, ushering me through suffering to a more complete sense of body. For example, instead of pressuring oneself to fit the fashion stereotype of what a woman's body should look like, trying to alter or even discard the body one is given, the feminine mode accepts the body one actually has. No longer fused with collective images that dictate the right shape to be, one goes down into one's actual given body and even deeper in imagination to primordial images of humanity that are diverse. Women are fat, large, slight,

supple, with hairdos or bald, with pert or hanging breasts, with breasts taken off for battle, with breasts given to each other in comfort. Women as warriors, women as virgins, one-in-themselves, untouched by man-made cultural forms, giving birth out of themselves in direct congress with ineffable spirit, women as sisters bound in blood and heartfelt emotion. Here are psychic resources for contemporary women to support improvisations of their identities as children of God composed of physical body, social conditioning, historical location, family custom, and personal longing. These primordial images may challenge and surpass all one has inherited and been influenced to be.

Body signifies inwardness and modesty in unguessed ways. With internal sexual organs, invisible but felt, emphasis falls in the girl child on an inward realm of affect, instinctive impulse, imagined spirit, intuition of the infinite. She cannot check out her intimations against visible reality, as a boy can. Hence her fears of body damage, body invasion, or something just wrong inside can hold greater sway and instigate comparable defenses to combat such fears. A level of judgment grows up within that has been called *matriarchal superego* in contrast to the more familiar and differently positioned *patriarchal superego* that more easily identifies with social institutions like law. The matriarchal mode of judgment grows from an embedded instinctual impulse, blood ties to family members, and passionate attachment to models found in teachers and tribal elders. Flowing from this inward connection to others is a religious ethic characterized by fierce loyalty felt in the flesh. Fervent anger on behalf of the vulnerable and vehement retribution in the name of justice are based on intense emotional relationship rather than on abstract principle applicable to everyone universally.

Modesty belongs to this level of religious action and perception because the body enforces it, not only with the inward location of sexual organs but also because ideals are not as easily detachable from unseen body parts and sexual affects. This level of matriarchal superego grows as well in boys, but their ability to reality test their fears of mutilation or arousal against visible body parts makes outward declarations of their positions on matters of consequence more accessible. Women's religious experience includes a knowing that is mixed simultaneously with not knowing. The categories are less discrete and more enriched by embodiment in a matrix of unconscious and physical experience. Hence energy builds that can burgeon to powerful proportions. The danger in this style of knowing lies in energy accumulating outside a woman's ego that can sweep away her conscious stance or leave the articulation of her point of view fuzzy. The asset of this style of knowing lies in the tremendous power that, when harnessed through her conscious abilities, can astonish with its compelling perception of truth.

This emphasis on body in women's religious experience includes the life she lives with others, too. Body also means political and social body and the mystical body of Christ. Hence the accent falls on religion as relational, not single, not withdrawn, and on religion as inclusive of all parts of herself, the healthy and the wounded. In psychoanalytical literature a notion of creative illness has proved helpful in understanding the neuroses of its founders—Freud's discovery in himself of the oedipal conflict (as well as his addictions to cocaine and to cigars), Jung's six-year period of tremendous psychic upheaval. Such a time-out from daily chores, to be ill creatively, depends on a woman in the man's life holding the fort. But women need to interrupt their creative illness to cook dinner, do the laundry, see to the children. Thus women's religious experience conducts itself in the midst of ordinary life, with taxes to be paid, kids to get to school, houses to be cleaned, and so on. This means women's emotions and body life partake of religious experience. Childbirth forms a numinous in-breaking of God for many women, as does barrenness or the death of a child. Sexual arousal and

satisfaction, eros connection, anger and despair, passions of all kinds characterize this feminine mode of religious living.

Inclusiveness and relationality go together. If a woman accepts all her emotions as part of her religious experience, so that no despair or anger, no anxiety attack or depressive mood, no secret hope or lavish loving, no outsized ambition or unguessed tender support of another is excluded, then that fullness extends, indeed spills over, into her perception of others. In therapy a nun reported that Jesus said, "I want you to be all of the passionate woman you can be." These words touched on a different way to live her sexuality than the more conventional route with a partner. What she heard for herself became what she sought for others—to live with one's whole heart and soul and mind, here and now, all of it.

In this mode of perception, mutuality comprises the model for relationship more than equality, or of one over against the other. Mutuality allows for differences as well as intimacy, for unique improvisation as well as for support for everyone. We recognize the other in ourselves and ourselves in the other. Jesus is lover and also friend, brother, and an intimate "you" to whom we each owe all our attention.

If we each are all we can be, including wounds and destructiveness as well as fortitude and talent, then we connect with all of ourselves and want to connect with all of "you," whether the "you" is God or another person. Connectedness in the concrete is another mark of women's religious experience. The traditional divisions of spirit and flesh, this world and the next, love of self and love of neighbor, are not so much bridged as subverted, abrogated by a kinship that precedes separation. Spirit dwells in the flesh and translates into a style of action toward others that emphasizes being one with them. Doing is done by identifying with the other's point of view.

If left unbalanced by also standing as a separate self with another, perceiving limits, differences, devising strategies of action, this style of identifying with another can approach the danger of giving too much or not respecting another's limits and choices. But this mode of being with another can be priceless: as the touch of a cool hand on another's feverish forehead, or warmly holding the hand of one approaching death, or giving solace to one who is a refugee. This mode of spirit in the body also means exciting the other's mind to risk new imaginings and to harness the energy needed to bring them to fruition, whether that issues in a novel mathematical formula or surrendering one's drinking problem to a higher power.

This mode of connection does not occur in the abstract, a kind of never-never land, but in concrete location in this body, this residence, this time and place as we actually are. This spiritual inflection grants place to the particular, the specific, the person in front of you, the problem to be solved in this set of circumstances, the religious vision mixed with these private personal details. A hospice nurse said her task is how to facilitate a blessed death with this person with the weight of his or her history, not an ideal death but what is possible and what is worth risking hope and passion for in this situation. No room exists for sentimentality. A kind of unflinching seeing what is there and what is not there is what is required. This kind of seeing is like the gaze of contemplation on what is; it nurtures basic connectedness among us, aligning us on the same side as we face common problems and possibilities of how to live in relation to our sexuality and aggression, our destructiveness and creativeness. From such connectedness, a sense of community builds.

The religious dimension is rooted in the personal, incarnated in this relationship, this neighborhood, at this month. Perfection is out of the question. The weight of history is too great. We never start with a clean slate but always crowded by the problems and complexes of our mother and father, our ancestors and tribe. The aim of religious life in this mode of perception does not consist in having a goal nor reaching it perfectly. For example, Ruth Simmons, the first African American woman president of a major university in the United States, whose own teachers in the poor rural South lent her their clothes for her first college interview, says that education does not exist to get you a job; education exists to feed your soul. This mode of spirituality concerns itself with food, food for the heart, the body, the soul, the connection to neighbor and to the divine lover, who may come in the most abstract form of devotion to a cause, or in being a hundred percent present in this moment, or in uncovering the secrets of nature in the discovery of radium. The cause may be abstract, but the relation to it is personal. The living of it as best we can, not resisting the joy of it, being entered and filled fully to overflowing right now, that is the shift, in the feminine mode, to the long haul of living and making our way over into death, living right up to death. The feminine mode of religious perception makes what is perceived real. God is the center point where inner and outer coincide and the world blossoms. Blooms.

No single model offers itself as the way to be in religious experience for women or anyone else. The commonality we share lies in our differences. Old symbols can acquire new meanings; new symbols can arise. No dictating of attributes or roles to each sex occurs, as indeed the feminine mode symbolizes ways of perceiving, of action, and of thought, in men as well as women. Emphasis in this feminine mode of religious experience falls on continuity of symbols rather than overthrowing them to name new ones; on building from social and

biological experience rather than reversing it or discarding it; on exploring states of being rather than outlining discrete stages of making progress; on indwelling in those states of being rather than trying to move through them to the distant goal; on reconciling opposites through paradox rather than conversion to an opposite state of mind. Women's religious experience accents the continuity of the whole journey even in the midst of surprising insights that differ from conventional views. A Ph.D. student in religion and depth psychology counters the traditional discrimination of Christianity's idea of the stage of union with the divine, as distinct from the Hindu or Buddhist, which asserts that in the latter the individual is absorbed into the cosmic, whereas in Christianity the separate sense of self uniting with the divine is preserved. This student, writing out of her own religious experience and that of her parishioners, explores whether the merger does not in fact take place between human and divine, and only after the ecstatic moment do we resume consciousness of our small but definite sense of self in relation to the infinite. We are both absorbed and distinct, merged and separate, a living paradox to ourselves.

The feminine mode of religious experience reveals another commonality. Emphasis falls on the soul being fed by God rather than on understanding the soul's relation to God, so religious women stick close to their original experience of God and are willing to wait, sometimes for years, to realize in words what has been lived in vision or hearing, in sense of taste or touch, even in smell. These women adhere to what has happened even though they do not understand it. This indwelling bubbles up in appreciation, wonder, fierce resolve to aid neighbor, including the earth and all its inhabitants. Such lives are manifest more as spirituality than denominational religion, the whole rather than the specific part.

Recognition of commonality may occur across differences, between those at opposite extremes of churched and unchurched, of different religions, which on the surface exclude each other over competing doctrines, of different times in history and different modes of expression. Zora Neale Hurston, for example, found sustenance in Vodou tradition as a potential source of liberation for African Americans through reconnection to their African roots. At the same time, she could write about the "Shoutin Church" of Christianity: "Shouting is a community thing. It thrives in concert. It is the first shout that is difficult for the preacher to arouse. After that one they are likely to sweep like fire over the church. . . . It is absolutely individualistic . . . the shouter may mix the different styles to his liking, or he may express himself in some fashion never seen before" (Hurston, *The Sanctified Church*, 91).

The broad base of spirituality, as it feeds specific religious denominational expression, makes clear another commonality of women's religious experience, the accent on assertion as well as reception, on claiming as well as offering self, on coming into one's own as well as opening in service to others. What Valerie Saiving began in 1960 in her "feminine viewpoint" of the human situation continues. Sin for women is not puffing up the self in pride but in losing the self, in not finding and bringing self into effective being, in sloth. The dangers for women of distraction, diffuseness, not harnessing aggression into effective focus, as well as self-denigration, can be combated by religion's message of deliverance. These forms of bondage afflicted women's religious experience in the early twentieth century. For later decades we may add the danger is getting stuck on one note, a different kind of distraction, cut off from other parts of one's personality. We have seen the breakup of the feminist movement into fractious sections—those pro-family versus those who seemed to disparage it, those urging new paradigms for conceiving sexual differences versus those defending old ones. Women's religious experience can reach across these factions by reaching the whole of us, all of us, all women (and men) in the company of God, a living God. So to the one and two of us trying to relate to each other is added the third space between us where the divine spirit blows and engenders new life, followed by the shock that a fourth partakes of this relationship, this conversation of all the parts with the whole. The fourth is the whole, all of us as parts of the living God, like the different stains of color of a Helen Frankenthaler painting or the jolt of Joan Mitchell's tree painting that could be seen as an example of the full growth of the tiny mustard seed to nest all life. The "eccentric" combining of sounds from daily life in the musical compositions of Pauline Oliveros makes audible the Spirit in her deep listening.

Finally we come to the vision of how the new comes in from the point of view of the commonalities of women's religious experience. Historically, the advent of new roles for women in religion has ushered into traditional precincts and professions more recognition of this feminine mode of perception. Women are ordained priests and pastors and are fighting for expanded professional roles in denominations that deny them authoritative jobs. Women pastoral counselors make up a large majority in this religious-psychological profession. Women professors in theological seminaries and religion departments of colleges and universities also bring a new presence to these traditional studies. Putting women in top jobs will always make a decisive difference, as it is the psyche of the leader at the top—the teacher of the class, the head of the lower school, the pastor of the church, the chief executive officer of the company—who makes possible and impossible what that organization can envision and pursue. The commonalities discussed here are increasingly apt to turn up in these professions' territories.

For example, in the early years of this twenty-first century, it is generally accepted that differences between men and women exist and that women have different routes and different results in their ways of knowing, doing, thinking, acting, meditating. What still presses as new, not yet widely acknowledged and digested by women or men, is that the feminine mode of being human describes a way of being that belongs to men as well. Difference needs to join with sameness now. Girls have a different way of reaching moral authority, but that different way belongs to boys too, and it may even be predominant in some boys, as a masculine mode of being may predominate in some girls more strongly than in their brothers. Specific location in family, culture, historical time, and political situation combine to make up variable differences, nuances, in any given person. But feminine still, for too many, degenerates into sign, instead of enduring securely as symbol. Our interaction with and response to that symbolic mode of discourse belongs to all sexes, all permutations of sexual combination that make up the many different kinds of human beings.

To accept consciously that we all possess at least two modes of being human and that each of us works out our own unique mixture comprises a wondrous task for this twenty-first century that would markedly contribute to the reduction of discriminatory practices against women. Unconsciously, images of different ways of being arise in all of us and traditionally have been linked symbolically to men and women. Instead of rejecting these archetypal phenomena as a shrinking of cultural and personal differences into a prescribed set of categories assigned to each gender, to embrace these archetypal sources gives more elbow room to improvise and construct the variety of our own identities. Neither men nor women are ever one single thing but always a bundle of things—and never in their stereotyped roles. *Archetype* refers to a dynamic process, to energy patterns that each of us, originally and persistently throughout our lives, translate into individual variations. The greater access to archetypal energy, the more our individual personalities will show supple openness to the new.

Into the mix of cultural influences that we take inside ourselves so thoroughly that we think and imagine in terms of images dominant in our cultural time—for example, images of what it is to be a woman or to be a man, what it is to be religious or antireligious—we must now add recognition of the psyche's contribution. What primordial images of man and of woman arise in us, which probably differ even from those influencing sisters and brothers in the same family? These images come from a deep unconscious layer of our psyche and enter our ego awareness. We greet such images with surprise, knowing we did not invent them, nor did we produce them out of a collective cultural consciousness. Hence the psyche gets a vote, too, not to inject prescriptions of how we must be but to make us aware of our capacity to access other times and places in history as resources for living in the contemporary moment. A seminary Ph.D. student, clearly involved in an intellectual focus of high order, finds robust renewing energy watching TV's *Xena the Warrior Princess*, an updated version of the comic book *Wonder Woman*, who is herself a modern version of the ancient image of the Amazon, devoted to the feminine as one in herself, not defined by her relationships to man. She is an independent, self-sustaining woman fighting for right and might. A woman in therapy, permeated with unshed tears of sadness over afflictions suffered in childhood, was surprised by a dream of the *mater dolorosa*. Working with the image, she felt she was being offered a larger, less personal container for sorrow in which she could differentiate the tears she needed to shed and be done with from the ongoing suffering in the world carried by this primordial figure.

In religious experience the feminine mode of approach to suffering is not to flinch. Suffering is not solved nor done away with but entered, digested. We differentiate what belongs to ourselves and what we can metabolize and do something about. The rest, the big rest of so much suffering in our world, is not discarded but entrusted and confided to God. We stay in unsentimental relation to the suffering of others, alert to the moment of action to ameliorate it, but without letting the joy of life lived to be crushed, for good exists too and is mixed paradoxically with the bad. A woman from the Seneca tribe in northern New York State, named Mother of Nations, was responsible for bringing the Onondaga tribe into the newly formed confederation of tribes (Mohawk, Oneida, and Cayuga) brought about by a man called the Peacemaker who preached a peaceful and ordered society. She proposed a solution convincing to the Onondaga, who then entered the fold. That war broke out again later does not annul the value of the reconciling work she accomplished.

Similarly, the feminine mode in religious experience faces destructiveness. Entering, digesting, acknowledging one's part in it, energy is gathered to fight or transform or get over it, to plant again, to feel again, to love again. Destructiveness does not destroy when accepted as part of the complete picture. Indignant at injustice, wrathful at the persecution of the vulnerable, determined to fight desolation, to keep hope alive in hopeless conditions, to mourn until all the mourning is done, these are all powerful responses to destructiveness in this mode of approach. To be in an experience without solving, resolving, avenging, or forgiving is symbolized by the women at the foot of the cross. Left imageless, all their projec-

tions onto God smashed, they continue to abide in that forsaken place, ready to care for the body of God whom they loved.

In that contemplative action lie seeds of a human relation to God that grows into a new realm of religious experience. Here we see we must care for God. Here we behold the good and know that it is good for nothing and good for nothing in the world. Good is not conquered by evil, nor does it do away with evil. At that conscious level, good and evil vie, compete, coexist. At the deeper realm we are ushered into the unkillable creative power as the living God rises up from the other side, crossing the gap between death and life, unquenched, undaunted, calling us by name, revealing to us that this reality exists at this central depth in all time and has all along.

We are granted a new vision of God's prior action that fosters our ability to grasp this new ungraspable antecedent reality. God has been there and continues to be, surviving our worst efforts to rub God out through our colossal ignorance of this abiding presence. In depth psychology a mysterious force in transference-countertransference relationship shifts the analysand's sense that acceptance must be earned by good behavior to the stunning discovery that some total acceptance precedes all our actions. For example, the child who gets attention by hitting other children in the face only sees the wrongness of that strategy in light of his new relation to the therapist. She does not give him attention because he bashes other kids. She gives him attention (that survives his destructive behavior) because they are already in a relationship devoted to his growth. The analyst's relationship to her little patient symbolizes what is already offered to all of us by God, a relationship devoted to our growth, love, well-being. God's love comes toward us antecedent to our earning it by good behavior; from that love we derive ourselves prior to any law of how to behave to secure what we need to live. Only in this light do we really discern what is good and what is bad, this light whose dark radiance also stands against destructiveness.

The feminine mode contributes to our seeing this gift of grace by helping us open to the reality that breaks in upon us, whose light makes us clearly see that what we thought was reality before is now exposed as smaller, dimmer. In religious language, we are as walking in darkness. The suffering of our present world with all its destructiveness is unavoidable. We cannot finally end this and indeed fall into what psychoanalysts call repetition compulsion when we insist that we can cure all ills. What the feminine mode of approach leads to is a perception of the resurrection from this state of affairs. We do not deny the existence of suffering and destructiveness by fleeing into spirit, as if the hurt we do to each other does not matter. Nor do we sink into despair, giving up on any effort to combat hurt, as if caught in flesh.

The feminine mode shows us resurrection occurs in ordinary life when we feel the invasion of God's grace to deliver us from the repetition of old solutions that do not solve. The whole basis of being changes; the images change. Now we feel flowing waters that bring alive dead places; we see that we are fed from a table set before us even in the shadow of death; all the humiliating hierarchies of talent and inferiority, of poise and ineptness, of status and homelessness are leveled. The whole context is changed, is new: Being loved for merit has ended. We are just loved. The feminine mode always places wisdom next to love, for example, in the figure of Sophia.

What is astonishing about this route is the upending of the practicality, the earthiness of the feminine mode always locating in the concrete and particular over the abstract and universal. We would expect to be delivered into maxims or motives or practices that prove eminently useful, practical, expedient to make a difference here and now. Instead, we are escorted toward an imaginal realm or a psychic realm to dwell in its reality. To arrive there does make a huge difference, but not by translating into actions in the world we already know. Instead, we live in an additional world, a reality of presence that multiplies in varied and numerous ways, like a spice flavoring a whole dish or a lilt of music changing an entire film or a scent of perfume infiltrating all the atmosphere. That is the feminine mode—subtle, supple, forceful in its effects, but a surprise. In religious terms, it is the woman bathing Christ's feet with her tears and drying them with her hair, or the woman who empties the whole jar of ointment to anoint Jesus' feet for his death. Lavish, modest (she remains unnamed), she typifies this feminine mode of being (which we find also in the love poems of St. John of the Cross) that leads us to the daring act of recognizing and touching the suffering of God.

A last mark of the feminine approach concerns what grows out of living in this additional reality, this imaginal or psychic realm or, to use a more traditional term, the contemplative realm of being. Located in concrete, particular, embodied, and relational reality of our lives here and now, which this mode of being always accents, leads us to follow down to its roots to perceive that the creator God goes on creating now, a kind of continual creating from all time, forward into all time, and now. This perception convicts us of the reality of a living God to whom we are in relation now and to whom we make a difference in the created acts going on now; we have been a part of them all along, but only now do we see that, become conscious of our involvement.

Our roots grow deeper than we thought. They touch something completely other than our ideas about roots.

This is scary and calls on all the fierce aggression of the feminine mode to withstand and to enjoy. We see ourselves standing on a moving current, not on solid ground. The down-to-earthness of the feminine mode gives way to the eternal current—is it water? air? energy?—of God's love where matter and psyche are two aspects of the same reality. Embodied concreteness means knowingly participating in the ongoing moving current of God's love, where solid moves and invisible energy takes on visible form. Opposites coinhere, and everything we know, we do not know.

From this new place, this approach offers some clues (not definitive statements) about how the varied and multiple images for God and the divisiveness of religions might be reconciled. If we each go down far enough in our own traditions, we reach this same current, this same energy, this same self-communicating presence that invades every society and culture, and indeed every person if we become conscious of it. Meeting there gives us appreciation and compassion for all our efforts to frame this incomprehensible but ever near reality. From this depth, all our diversity can be integrated.

SOURCES: Roberta C. Biondi, *In Ordinary Time: Healing the Wounds of the Heart* (1996). Caroline Walker Bynum, Steven Harrell, and Paula Richman, eds., *Gender and Religion: On the Complexity of Symbols* (1986). Carol Gilligan, *In a Different Voice: Psychological Theory and Women's Development* (1982). M. Esther Harding, *Women's Mysteries, Ancient and Modern* (1935). Zora Neale Hurston, *Mules and Men* (1935). Zora Neale Hurston, *The Sanctified Church* (1983). Elizabeth A. Johnson, *She Who Is: The Mystery of God in Feminist Theological Discourse* (1993). Margaret Lawrence and Dorothy Martyn, *The Man in the Yellow Hat* (1992). Dorothy Martyn, "The Intersection of Two Disciplines in Group Therapy," *Union Seminary Quarterly Review* 51 (1997): 3–4. Ana-Marie Rizzuto, *The Birth of the Living God* (1979). Valerie Saiving, "The Human Situation: A Feminine View," *Journal of Religion* 40 (1960): 100–112. Marion Woodman, *Addiction to Perfection: The Still Unravished Bride* (1982). Ann Belford Ulanov, *The Female Ancestors of Christ* (1994, 1998). Ann Belford Ulanov, *The Feminine in Jungian Psychology and in Christian Theology* (1971). Ann Ulanov and Barry Ulanov, *Primary Speech: A Psychology of Prayer* (1982, 2001). Ann Ulanov and Barry Ulanov, *Religion and the Unconscious* (1975). Ann Ulanov and Barry Ulanov, *Transforming Sexuality: The Archetypal World of Anima and Animus* (1994).

WOMEN'S SPIRITUAL BIOGRAPHY AND AUTOBIOGRAPHY
Rosemary Skinner Keller

THE FEMINIST MOVEMENT begun in the early 1960s transformed the reading and writing of women's lives.

Biography, as traditionally understood, had meant "stories about the lives of prominent male subjects, written with an emphasis on the external and usually historical events of their lives, praising the subjects rather than questioning their characters" (Martin, 1).

Both the writers and subjects of biography had long constituted a "men's club." Most biographers were men, and their subjects were imposing male figures whose lives overshadowed those of common people. They were exceptional or extraordinary individuals, not models by which persons might discern meaning, purpose, and possibilities for their own lives. Biographers were instructed to write objectively and to keep a distance from the subjects of their writing. Male gender issues were not considered. The focus was on men's outward achievements and their success in the public arena, with little attention given to their private lives. When a man's personal experience, such as his place in his family of origin, marriage, and fathering of children, was included, it seldom was related to his public life.

Out of this traditional concept, many women also wrote biographies of males or narrative histories that featured biographical studies of men. Barbara Tuchman interpreted biography as a prism of history and wrote engrossing historical studies, humanizing and person-alizing public events through the lens of a male political or military figure's life. In 1979, after the feminist movement was well under way, she described her methodology in these words: "[B]iography is useful because it encompasses the universal in the particular" (Tuchman, in Oates, 95). Tuchman captured the essence of men's public lives and historical periods. However, she was blind to the reality central to the feminist movement that, in analyzing women's and men's experience, there is no universal that could be encompassed in the particular. Women's experience is not the same as men's, and their lives cannot be interpreted through men's.

Catherine Drinker Bowen, who wrote biographies of six men, including John Adams, Sir Edward Coke, and Francis Bacon, stated why exceptional women, such as herself and Barbara Tuchman, wrote about men instead of women. Asked why she never wrote a biography of a woman, Bowen answered that she did not dare to honestly respond that "I have, six times" (Bowen, in Heilbrun, 22). She wrote about men because their experiences represented the way countless women wanted to live their lives. She could not write about women because so few would admit their desire to find purpose and achievement by stepping forth boldly into the public world.

Georgia Harkness (1891–1974), the first female theologian to teach in a Protestant seminary in the United States, was active before the feminist movement's discovery of women's stories and so did not write an autobiography for publication. The biographer, however, who reads the public and private accounts of her experiences and studies her advocacy of social justice causes finds a woman called by God and strongly resolute to lead her own life. *John Bennett Archives.*

Through the 1950s, women were told to stay in their places within the home, to put fathers, husbands, and sons at the center of their lives, and to commit their private lives to advancing the destiny of males in the public realm. Biographies of men enabled women writers and readers to be ambitious and accomplished vicariously. By reading the stories of men's lives, women were able to venture outside the conventional roles that society prescribed for them. But to write of women who sought their rightful space in the public world was a highly suspect act.

The rise of the feminist movement in the 1960s and 1970s brought a new consciousness about the kind of women who could be subjects of biographies and the way in which their stories could be told. Carolyn Heilbrun's *Writing a Woman's Life* (1988) became the groundbreaking book calling biographers of women to develop a feminist perspective for writing and reading women's lives. She described two kinds of women in American society. First, the "unambiguous" woman lived out of the traditional female ideology of the woman's place in the home in order to promote the public purposes of men. Heilbrun contrasted this traditional role with the "ambiguous" woman, who sought a life of her own in both the public and the private spheres of life out of a desire to gain power, achievement, and self-control. In finding a new way to write women's lives, Heilbrun wrote that the

> choices and pain of the women who did not make a man the center of their lives seemed unique, because there were no models of the lives they wanted to live, no exemplars, no stories. These choices, this pain, those stories, and how they may be more systematically faced, how, in short, one may find the courage to be an "ambiguous woman," are what I want to examine in this book. (31)

Secular biographers, including Linda Martin-Wagner, Sara Alpern, Joyce Altner, Elizabeth Perry, Ingrid Scobie, Carol Ascher, Louise DeSalvo, and Sara Ruddick, as well as Carolyn Heilbrun, applied feminist ideology to call for profound changes in the methodology of writing biography. They declared the falsity of a universal human experience and placed gender at the center of analysis. These feminists understood that women's interior lives, their experiences within the private sphere of the home, and their movements into the public square were all interwoven and had to be interpreted in relationship to each other.

New questions, based on gender analysis, guided their research into women's lives. Feminist biographers asked what social influences caused women to submerge their lives in men's purposes. What led some women to

break out of the traditional social molds and claim their right to the public domain, power, and control of their own lives? How did the female life cycle, including birth, childhood, relationships with parents and siblings, marriage and motherhood, options of unmarried women, and female friendships and networks, affect their movement into public life?

Feminist authors also challenged the objectivity or detachment that traditional biographers thought necessary for writing the lives of male heroes. They wanted to bring their readers close to the women whom they wrote about. To write a woman's life, the author needed to interpret her inner self and her feelings. These writers believed that they could empathize with their subjects while maintaining a critical perspective on their lives. As new women stepped forward to seek equality and inclusiveness with men in public life, they wanted models of women who had sought the same rights and opportunities for their own lives but whose stories had not been told. Feminist biographers were naturally drawn to write about such figures because they, too, were seeking adventurous models for themselves.

They said it was appropriate for women to identify with, learn from, and seek to emulate qualities of their foremothers' experience. Whether consciously speaking out of a feminist perspective or not, Eleanor Roosevelt wrote in the introduction to her autobiography in 1950:

> Autobiographies are, after all, useful only as the lives you read about and analyze may suggest to you something that you find useful in your own journey through life.... There is nothing particularly interesting about one's life story unless people can say as they read it, "Why, this is like what I have been through. Perhaps, after all, there is a way to work it out." (*The Autobiography of Eleanor Roosevelt*, xviii, xix)

Biographers described the affinity women readers feel with subjects of female autobiographies and biographies, appropriating or identifying with the experiences of women whom they read about. They contended that this close tie led to a vocational bond at the heart of women's purpose in reading other females' life stories. Acknowledging that many late-twentieth-century women were seeking something more for their lives than the traditional gender prescriptions allowed them, Heilbrun described their effort to summon the courage to live out of the fullness of their own lives:

> [W]ith highly gifted women, as with men, the failure to lead the conventional life, to find the conventional way early, may signify more than having been dealt a poor hand of cards. It may well be the forming of a life in the service of a talent felt,

but unrecognized and unnamed. This condition is marked by a profound sense of vocation, with no idea of what that vocation is. (52, 53)

Emerging feminists of the late twentieth century claimed gifts, talents, and greater expectations for their lives than their mothers had believed were possible to attain, these writers stated. Women's awakenings and their determination to create alternative visions for their own lives led modern females to seek vocations that they themselves chose and not ones that were prescribed for them. However, these secular feminists stopped short of explaining the meaning of vocation, where it had come from, and where it was taking women.

These new biographers also failed to address other issues. They were white, middle-class women who did not mention differences in females' experiences resulting from race and class. In effect, they were universalizing women's experience just as traditional biographers had said that women's lives could be understood through men's.

Further, many feminist biographers dismissed spiritual calling as nonfeminist. Of the above authors, only Heilbrun even referred to it. She understood a Divine Being as something of a substitute for a man in sanctioning women to a vocation or calling. "One must be called by God or Christ to serve in spiritual causes higher than one's own poor self might envision, and authorized by that spiritual call to an achievement and accomplishment in no way excusable in a female self." Heilbrun contended that religious women see their identity "grounded through relation to the chosen other. Without such a relation, women do not feel able to write openly about themselves" (23, 24). Well into the twentieth century, she pointed out, an accomplished woman claimed in her public autobiographical writings that God brought a cause to her and laid it at her feet to appropriate. She did not admit to going out on her own to seek it. Only in her private writings of letters and diaries would she admit her ambition or claim to achieve.

Religious women find their deepest identity through their spiritual relationship with God, as Heilbrun states. Considering the social constraints long laid upon females, it is understandable that women, prior to the feminist movement, would be reticent to admit their own ambition to achieve in the social arena. They would naturally seek a circuitous route, justifying their entrance onto the public scene as God's work, not their own, as a means of societal acceptance.

Feminists of a religious persuasion in the late twentieth and early twenty-first centuries readily acknowledge this right in their public as well as private writings. They hold that God wills the abolition of gender barriers and that women have a God-given claim to the same places in society as held by men. In their autobiographical and other public statements, they make no excuses for seeking inclusiveness and equality as women's due. Religious feminists also reject the traditional secular ethic of individual gain and advancement traditionally associated with male advancement on the career ladder. Out of their faith perspective, they hold that calling releases them from adherence to the secular ethic of individual gain and advancement and leads women, as well as men, into vocations of service to God's people and the entire creation.

This essay explores the nature of feminist spiritual autobiography and biography. It introduces a methodology of writing religious women's lives based on the bond that women of faith experience through vocational kinship. Women on their own spiritual journeys are drawn to the subjects of biography and autobiography because they "compel an inescapable identification," in the words of Eleanor Holmes Norton in her introduction to Pauli Murray's autobiography, *Song in a Weary Throat* (1). Women do not read the stories of other peoples' lives through a distant lens. That identification does not necessarily grow out of a likeness of women's experiences with their foremothers and other women whom they may meet for the first time in this encyclopedia. Vocational kinship cannot be defined that narrowly.

Vocation traditionally means a regular occupation or profession, especially one for which a person is particularly suited or qualified. *Kin* usually refers to the person or persons closest in blood relationship. In bringing the two words together, *vocational kinship* is a shared identity growing out of a commitment to mutual purpose and values that binds people together in such close ties that they become kin.

Although it does not necessarily mean that one enters a religious order or is ordained, *vocation* has a religious connotation. Nor is it equated with work, whether in a sacred or secular occupation, in the public or private sphere of life. Vocation means the way a person lives the whole of her or his life as a response to God or a Divine Being, not just the kind of work one does or the way she or he may do it. Kinship can be a relationship with a person or community of persons with whom one feels such affinity and intimacy that they become a self-created or self-chosen family. A deeper bond of vocational kinship may be established with persons with whom one has no blood ties than with her own ancestors.

To learn about the essence of biography, simply to study its methodology is not sufficient. One must immerse oneself in reading biographies. This essay explores the compelling quality of autobiography, biography, and vocational kinship by re-creating through a feminist perspective the vocation of one religious woman, Georgia

Harkness (1891–1974). The first female theologian to teach in a Protestant seminary in the United States, Harkness was also a social activist who pushed the churches, including her own Methodist denomination, to abolish the evils of racism, sexism, and militarism in society and within their own structures.

A prefeminist of the early and mid-twentieth century, Harkness did not write an autobiography for publication. "Days of My Years," an unpublished autobiographical sketch, written when she was over sixty years old for the Pacific Coast Theological Group—several scholars and pastors in the San Francisco Bay Area—is central to the interpretation of her life and work. When read along with secondary sources, this personal memoir and her extant private correspondence make it possible first to discern how she interpreted her own life and empowerment by God, then to explore vocational kinship with her. The biographer who reads the public and private accounts of her experiences and studies her advocacy of social justice causes finds a woman called by God and strongly resolute to lead her own life.

The focus in this essay is on stories within her experience that illuminate the essence of Harkness's vocation. The themes and questions growing out of feminist gender analysis emerge naturally out of these stories: social influences that constricted her life; conditions that enabled her to break out of the traditional social role of women and to claim her own rights; her life cycle; and relationships that were critical in her movement into public life. Underlying all of these themes is her religious faith and the way in which her spiritual commitments influenced her experiences and vocation.

Harkness experienced a sense of mission, which she identified at times as a calling from God, that opened her to deeper personal self-realization through a life of service and justice for her sisters and brothers. Similarly, she led a nonconventional life by forging a career that was an alternative to the individualistic, upwardly mobile, secular careers that have come to define success in the United States. Finally, Harkness developed a personal community that expanded the meaning of her calling and career beyond work into the private areas of her life.

It is not presumed that all readers would experience a sense of vocational kinship with Georgia Harkness or with any other individual woman in this encyclopedia. Rather, this essay introduces vocational kinship as a theme and method of reading and writing women's spiritual autobiography and biography, which has not previously been developed. Affirming both personal identification and critical distance, vocational kinship becomes a window for better understanding other peoples' and our own spiritual journeys.

Calling from God

When Georgia Harkness was almost thirty years old, she was in a Ph.D. program in philosophy of religion at Boston University. She had decided that her vocation was to teach in higher education. However, she faced two severe roadblocks in her path: She lacked financial resources during the third year of her program; and she felt the need to return to her family home to care for her aging parents and their farm. Her mother enabled her liberation. She gave Harkness the small inheritance she was to receive on her parents' death. Further, her mother told her that her parents could get along without her assistance: "You have your own life to lead" ("Days of My Years," 7).

On the surface this story emphasizes a mother's gift of freedom to her daughter to choose her own life and work. For Harkness, that gift marked a profound vocational moment in her life. To be released from her parents' expectations was a call from God to continue forward on her vocational pursuit. She had long experienced a spiritual calling. However, it had never been given by God in a neat package to simply unwrap and put into practice, as some theological traditions in Christianity interpret it to be. She did not receive a once-in-a-lifetime summons from God to which she had no choice but to say yes. Harkness had to respond, not out of her parents' prescriptions but from within herself, as she struggled to determine what her calling was, whether she would accept it, and how she would live it out. At thirty years of age, Harkness continued on her vocational journey. She would travel in further search for many years to come.

Harkness had known ever since childhood that she had a calling from God. The language and experience of calling and conversion were part of her upbringing. Born in the final decade of the nineteenth century, she was raised in the tiny hamlet of Harkness, in rural upstate New York, named after her grandfather. She described her vocational roots, planted from childhood in this village, through the intertwining of her family, church, and school.

The conservative Methodist Episcopal Church of the community was her extended family. Long before she had any conception of what *vocation* meant, those deep roots were set by her parents, Lucy Merrill and Warren Harkness, when she was one week old and they took her to church in their arms. As a child, she reached out to the church in countless ways. Even today, over 100 years after her birth, the Sunday School record board remains on the church wall, listing her name with stars beside it for her regular attendance as a child.

When Harkness was over sixty years old, she humorously described her annual childhood conversion experiences. Her first conversion, followed annually by similar ones, came when she was seven at a revival meeting held every winter in her church. That summer, and in subsequent ones, she would backslide and be ready for conversion again. At seven, she wanted to be baptized and become a member of the congregation, but her mother insisted that she wait until she was old enough to know what she was doing. Playing the one hymn that she knew, "Trust and Obey," Harkness regularly substituted for the organist during Sunday morning services. Her "definitive conversion" came at fourteen when she decided to be baptized and join the church, an experience different from the dramatic conversions of her younger years.

Calling grew out of conversion for Harkness. Her first encounter with calling may have been a negative experience: simply to strongly question the traditional lifestyle of the women she observed all around her. By the age of twelve, pondering her mother's daily life within the home, she knew that a woman's typical domestic function was too narrow for her. She was not meant to be a traditional wife and mother.

Harkness always identified calling and vocation with work and sought the kind of occupation she could enter in response to her calling. That her parents, lifelong residents of rural New York, supported her disinterest in a traditional woman's role and encouraged her professional exploration was extraordinary in her day. They, too, must have realized that she had special gifts.

From high school through her doctoral program at Boston University, Harkness considered several professions that she identified as callings from God. Along with the influences of family and church, her vocational journey was rooted in her love of learning begun in the Haddock Hall Elementary School housed on weekdays in the church building. Since childhood, she had expected to be a high school teacher, probably in rural or urban New York State. Her father had sought this profession for himself but gave it up when he needed to take charge of the farm for his family. Both parents thought their two daughters had greater intellectual abilities than their two sons. Again, extraordinarily, they planned to send the two sisters, rather than the brothers, to college at the nearby teacher training school. The elder sister, Hattie, first received the mantle to become a high school teacher, but she died tragically when she was sixteen years old and Georgia was six. To be as smart as Hattie Harkness and to follow in her footsteps was the expectation placed on Georgia.

Pleasing her parents and herself, Harkness received the one Regents' Scholarship given to a high school graduate in her county to attend any college or university in the state. They chose the top institution in New York, Cornell University. While at Cornell, she became interested in philosophy through Dr. William Creighton, her philosophy professor. If she dreamed of becoming a college professor, she never recorded any aspiration of pursuing a doctorate. She left no indication that Dr. Creighton or any other teacher had encouraged her to pursue college teaching. Even though she had high grades and was a member of Phi Beta Kappa, Harkness probably had no mentor who suggested the idea. This was a period of blatant sexism and discrimination against women in higher education. The few women in a class were seated separately from the male students, and men were not allowed to speak to female students as they walked across the Cornell campus.

In college, Harkness consciously thought about a career that grew out of her church and educational roots and that expressed a calling from God. She joined the Student Volunteer Movement (SVM) originated by John R. Mott to encourage college students to dedicate their lives to missionary service in non-Christian lands. Feeling accepted in the SVM, it became her home while she was in college. Along with thousands of college students of her day, Harkness took its pledge: "My purpose, if God permits, is to become a foreign missionary." She had thought about this calling in high school but told no one, probably because she felt the idea was far-fetched for a young girl from a rural, isolated village. Like her father, Harkness rejected the calling to the mission field because she believed family needs necessitated that she remain closer to home.

Harkness tried for two years to follow her parents' chosen vocation for her to become a high school teacher. She taught in two towns near her family home but was clearly a misfit. She did not like high school teaching and was not effective in it. Reading about a new profession for women in the form of religious education work in local churches, she decided that "if I could not be a missionary, this was my calling" ("Days of My Years," 99). Also learning of a training program at Boston University School of Theology, she became one of the first students to enroll.

While in her Masters in Religious Education program, she returned to her love of philosophy and took courses in philosophy of religion at Boston University. In her words, she "fell under the spell of Dr. Edgar Brightman's kindling mind" and decided to pursue a Ph.D. Discerning her calling to be teaching religion to college students, "I asked Brightman if he would take me on as a candidate for the PhD." He tried to dissuade her, telling her that "I had the preparation, probably the brains, but that I lacked the stick-to-it-iveness. I told him that if that was all, I would see to that" (18). She summoned the courage and completed her degree successfully.

Harkness was Brightman's first Ph.D. student. In

evaluating her entrance into a doctoral program, he did not have the experience to judge her ability to successfully complete the advanced scholarly degree. In a day when few women held doctoral degrees or even entered Ph.D. studies, he probably had difficulty discerning, or even admitting to himself, that a young woman was capable of fulfilling the requirements to become a Professor of Philosophy of Religion. After completing her doctorate, Harkness and Brightman became valued colleagues and friends. They exchanged over 200 letters until Brightman's death in the 1950s that remain in the archives of the Boston University Library. In the correspondence, they discuss both personal and professional matters close to both of them. Even so, Brightman held an unacknowledged sexism in relating to Harkness. Later she confronted him with it.

After considering at least four different occupations—high school teaching, foreign missionary work, Christian education in a church, and teaching in higher education—Harkness chose college teaching, the profession that was least accessible for women in her day. She believed that God opened different opportunities for her and interpreted all these professional options as callings. She also knew that she was making her own decision in choosing her vocation. At age thirty-three, it appeared that she had settled in to a lifelong undergraduate teaching career, spending the next fifteen years at Elmira College in Elmira, New York, and two further years at Mt. Holyoke in Holyoke, Massachusetts. However, she had much further to go in living out her career as a calling.

The Call of My Career

Her mother's words that "You have your own life to lead" continued to challenge Harkness throughout her career. While her parents released her from their expectation that she become a high school teacher, the longer struggle of her adult years lay in establishing herself and gaining stature as a woman in her chosen profession of college and seminary teaching dominated by men.

Harkness always understood career foremost as a calling from God. She was primarily motivated by the question, What did God want her to do with her life? Out of her religious commitment, she made radical choices about what it meant to serve God's people. Those decisions were not driven primarily by a desire to climb the professional ladder to gain a higher salary or greater status as a professor in higher education. Rather, they were responses to a prophetic call from God to combat the blatant evils of militarism, racism, and sexism. As a college and seminary professor, she did solid and responsible work in the classroom as a teacher. In turn, her teaching and writing became a platform providing her with a public voice that gained attention. She was continually called outside the walls of her in-

stitutions to speak against the "isms" that oppressed God's people. At odds with the views of mainstream American and Christian culture, she raised prophetic social positions out of God's call and her personal conscience, views intended to challenge the church rather than advance her career.

In North American secular culture today, career is popularly thought of as advancement in a particular profession a person follows throughout his or her entire life course. To be successful in a career means to be upwardly mobile, to receive monetary advancement, higher status, and greater prestige. The person who runs fastest on the career track or climbs highest on the career ladder is considered the most successful, for that person gives most of his or her life to career advancement.

Some of the connotations of *career* held in modern North American secular culture apply directly to Harkness's vocational experience. As one of the early women to teach in colleges and as the pioneer woman theologian, all her colleagues were men. She was in a highly competitive professional situation with them, daily having to prove herself, not only as a professor but as a female. She was successful in her occupation, and she rose on the career ladder. However, that success was gained by running hard and fast on a career track.

As a pioneer, hers was the race of a lonely long-distance runner. When she accepted Garrett Biblical Institute's appointment in 1939, she was at a different place occupationally than professional women today. Most career women of the early twenty-first century are entering fields now occupied by a critical mass of females. However, it is striking how many of the same experiences of Harkness apply to women who still confront obstacles to leading their own lives in church, education, and business fields.

The reality of sexism confronted Harkness time and again. After only one month in her first college teaching position at Elmira College, she received a letter from Edgar Brightman that began with the question: "My dear Miss Harkness, or should I say, 'Professor'?" (October 20, 1923). As if responding to her former mentor's query, she took little time to establish herself as a professional woman to be reckoned with. By the end of her second year at Elmira, Harkness was identified as a key member of the faculty, taking the kind of leadership that would characterize her entire professional career. She led a faculty fight that resulted in a long overdue revision of the entire curriculum. Writing Brightman, she said that she "decided it was worth fighting for to try to smash the whole system and get a new one. . . . The result is a complete victory for the forces of reform. Our pernicious former system is now defunct" (May 2, 1924).

Despite her aggressive leadership on the Elmira faculty, she never called Brightman into question for the way he greeted her in his correspondence. Until his death seventeen years later, he always began his letters to her "Dear Miss Harkness," while she greeted him with "Dear Dr. Brightman." What would have happened had she told him to address her as "Professor" or "Dr. Harkness"? Was he blind to the difference of status between the salutations? Or, unconsciously, did he still see them in the male professor–female student relationship of traditional superior and subordinate status?

The most blatant case of sexism, in the way in which Brightman related to Harkness, came a few years later, in 1928, when she asked him to write a letter of recommendation for her to receive a Sterling Fellowship for a year of postgraduate study at Yale University. His recommendation was supposed to be sent directly to the Scholarship Committee of the University. He graciously responded to her request but, by mistake, sent the original copy of his recommendation directly to her, with the intent that she would send it on to the Committee.

After his extremely positive evaluation of her as a scholar and a teacher, Brightman referred to Harkness's "lack of feminine charm." She undoubtedly interpreted his comment as a reference to her large body and her physical awkwardness, as well as her feeling of discomfort and social inferiority in relationships with men, a condition she had long experienced. She wrote back, telling him that she knew what he meant and was not offended by it, although she undoubtedly was offended. She asked him directly "[i]f something less dangerous could be substituted for this half-line," because she feared that "a committee might be prone to read this as suggesting freakishness, or at least a conspicuous masculinity of dress or manner. And if so, the fellowship would probably go elsewhere" (January 27, 1928). Brightman apologized personally to Harkness for the grossly inappropriate words in his letter of recommendation, but he did not rewrite the letter to omit the pointless statement. Despite his faux pas, Yale granted her the year's fellowship.

When Harkness entered college teaching at Elmira in 1922, she probably envisioned herself as a classroom teacher who intended also to become a scholarly writer in her initially chosen fields of philosophy of religion and religious education. Her effectiveness at Elmira, both as a leader among the faculty and as a young published scholar, testify that she reached that goal early in her career. Other study leaves at Harvard University and Union Theological Seminary, as well as at Yale, enabled her to publish four books in philosophy of religion and ethics.

Harkness's career escalated rapidly during her years at Elmira and Mt. Holyoke in the 1920s and 1930s, probably much more quickly and successfully than she would have conceived or even desired. That pace and momentum continued after she became a seminary professor at Garrett and Pacific School of Religion for ten years each between 1940 and 1960. Her prominence as a teacher, writer, and progressive church leader brought her public recognition and resulted in more invitations to speak, nationally and internationally, than she could handle while simultaneously maintaining good health. Theologically, she became an evangelical liberal, balancing a strong personal commitment to Christ with a socially prophetic witness to the church.

Being ordained a local deacon in the Methodist Episcopal Church in 1926 and a local elder in 1938, she spent the next decades mounting a finally successful campaign in 1956 for the full conference membership of women, amounting to their ordination as elders along with men. As early as 1939, she wrote that "to close the door to any persons possessing spiritual and mental qualifications is, in effect, to say that sex is a more important factor in Christian vocation than character, spiritual insight, or mental ability" (*World Outlook*, January 1939, 30). Full rights of ordination for women were granted in 1956 as a result of a petition campaign, organized by Harkness and others, by local chapters of the Women's Society of Christian Service throughout the country. Simultaneously, she pressed, until her death in 1974, for the opening of equal rights for women in executive leadership positions on boards and agencies and for their right to sit on governing boards of local congregations.

Harkness addressed racism as well as sexism in challenging the Methodist Church throughout the mid-twentieth century on its policies of segregation. She opposed creation of the Methodist Church from its predecessor denominations in 1939 because the merger established a Central Jurisdiction for all black members beside the five geographical jurisdictions for white members. She contended that the concept of a jurisdictional system defied the church's unity in Christ and proposed that the jurisdictional system be abolished. The legislation had no chance of passing because it required the votes of clergy and lay delegates whose views were firmly entrenched in their racial and regional configurations. The Central Jurisdiction was not eliminated until 1972, four years after the Evangelical United Brethren and the Methodist Church merged to form the United Methodist Church. Harkness was one of the strongest advocates for its abolition, contending that the segregation within the denomination was a clear contradiction of Christian morality.

Harkness was one of the most important witnesses for social justice in the Methodist and Christian churches during the twentieth century. The personal reality was that work was the sum and substance of her vocation during many of these years. She experienced the reality that countless women who work outside the home today know: Their lives are juggling acts. Gaining a balance between responsibilities within the home and in the public workplace is difficult for women to achieve, whether they live alone, are single parents, or are part of a dual-career marriage.

For many of her midlife years, Harkness lived alone, responsible personally to no other adults or children. The juggling that her life demanded, and the heavy toll that it took on her emotional and physical health, came as a result of the fast track of her career advancement and the consuming quality of her professional vocational commitments. Harkness became *the* spokesperson for women and to women at church events throughout the world. Invitations to lecture and preach at women's groups, church meetings, and worship services came at a heavier rate than she anticipated. She was a delegate to countless national and international conferences, including both the Oxford and Madras meetings of the World Council of Churches in the 1930s. Requests continually came to her to write articles for a wide variety of church publications, at the same time that she was writing one or two books a year.

Brightman wrote her a letter in which he expressed his pleasure that she had been invited to speak in the Duke University Chapel, noting that she must represent all the women of the church. His words conveyed the distinction and the burden placed upon her one set of shoulders. Another time, she made a four-minute speech at the Oxford Meeting of the World Council of Churches on the role of women in the churches in which she described the churches as "the most impregnable stronghold of male dominance." The speech was transmitted to the United States, and she received so many invitations to speak at women's gatherings that she said, "I ran myself ragged in the attempt to keep up my school work and accept even a few of them" ("Days of My Years," 25).

That Harkness was the spokeswoman for liberal, prophetic-minded women throughout the churches is one way of highlighting the call of her career during her midlife years. Another way is captured in a picture taken in 1950 of the Dun Commission on Obliteration Bombing, sponsored by the Federal Council of Churches. In the photograph, Harkness is the lone woman among male theologians of her day. Standing in the middle of the front row, she is flanked by eminent professional colleagues, including Paul Tillich, Reinhold Niebuhr, John Bennett, and Robert Calhoun, distinguished professors at Union Theological Seminary and Yale Divinity School, and Bishop Angus Dun of the Episcopal Church. Harkness was dressed appropriately in a man-tailored suit with a straight skirt, plain white shirt, and "sensible" tie shoes.

She stood out on the Commission in another way, also. Harkness and Calhoun, professor of theology at Yale Divinity School, were the only members to contend that the United States should use atomic weapons under no circumstances, either as first strike or as retaliatory bombing. Many today might agree with a statement made later in his life by Bennett, professor of ethics and president of Union Theological Seminary when serving on the Commission. He said that he would have taken this unconditional position held by Harkness and Calhoun, had he realized the massive destructive power that atomic and hydrogen weapons would have. Harkness's witness on the Commission was the outcome of a stance she had taken as early as the 1920s and 1930s when she traveled in Europe to observe the devastation following World War I. The shock and grief that she experienced for the war's innocent victims, she wrote after returning from the continent, led her to profess that "I became a pacifist forever" (Harkness to Edgar Brightman, September 21, 1924).

A favorite story that Harkness loved to tell about her career took place at a meeting of the World Council of Churches in 1948. It captures her sense of humor, along with her eminence, as she enjoyed an hour of triumph that stayed with her throughout her life. The theologian with whom she had been in dialogue did not enjoy the recollection as much as she did:

> One incident from the Amsterdam Conference may be worth relating. With a few other men, Karl Barth chose to participate in the section on the Life and Work of Women in the Churches. At the beginning of the discussion Sara Chakko, the Chairman, asked me without warning to state its theological basis. I said briefly that it is in the O.T. It is stated that both male and female are created in the image of God; in the N.T. Jesus assumed always that men and women were equal before God, and in our Christian faith is the chief foundation of sex equality. Barth claimed the floor; said that this was completely wrong; that the O.T. conception of woman is that she was made from Adam's rib and the N.T. that of Ephesians 5, that as Christ is the head of the Church, so man is the head of woman. Then followed a lively interchange in which I did little but to quote Galatians 3:28, but the room buzzed. Barth convinced nobody, and if I have been told he was trying to have some fun with the women, his joke back-fired. A year later when a friend of mine asked him if he recalled meeting a woman theologian from America, his cryptic reply was, "Remember me not of that woman!" ("Days of My Years," 28)

Called to Community

To represent the women of the churches, to stand as a lone female among the premier male theologians of her day, to challenge the church to fulfill its prophetic purpose, to take down a notch the esteemed Karl Barth—the call of Georgia Harkness's career is capsuled in these experiences. She had a public career of service lived out of an alternative vision to the long-held American individualistic success stories of men in the professions. There is also a personal side to her professional advancement. Her commitment to her career caused Harkness's life to be consumed by work, good as that work was. And she ran herself ragged! Her life was transformed when she came to grips with the reality that work was the sum and substance of her existence. New purpose came when she discerned that vocation was more than work and that she could share herself personally in community with others.

In her late forties, Harkness entered the depth of loneliness in a dark night of her soul that extended for almost eight years, from 1937 until 1945. Her father's death in 1937 marked its opening stages, a time at which the strains of work were taking a heavy toll on her. The man whom she idolized told her on his deathbed, within an hour of his death, that he knew she had written good books, but he wished she would write more about Jesus Christ. His words shook the foundations of her vocation. Now at midlife, having taught philosophy of religion and religious education for a decade and a half and written seven books, relatively arid, sterile textbooks on ethics and philosophy of religion, she seriously questioned the direction of her years to come.

Over the next decade, clinical depression manifested itself physically, mentally, emotionally, and spiritually. She developed serious back problems, could not concentrate to work effectively, and felt bereft of the presence of God in her life. Her healing, which occurred gradually over several years, came from physical treatment, psychological counseling, and theological redirection. The basic cause of her cure and new sense of vocation came because she gained the community of family and friends in her mature years.

One concrete step she took to change her way of life was to buy a simple cottage on Lake Champlain that she named "Hate to Quit It." The cottage, with its name printed over the door, still stands today. A steady stream of family and friends visited her there during summers. Now she had a space, a home, that meant something more than work. And she did most of her writing in this setting, more quiet, peaceful, and relaxing than her office. The nature of her writing changed also. For the rest of her life, she focused in her books on questions of Christian faith, from prayer and meditation to theology to social justice and international issues, books especially directed to laypersons in churches. Representative titles include *The Dark Night of the Soul* (1945), *Prayer and the Common Life* (1947), *Understanding the Christian Faith* (1947), *Be Still and Know* (1953), *Beliefs That Count* (1961), *The Methodist Church in Social Thought and Action* (1964), and *Women in Church and Society* (1971). Her last book, *Biblical Backgrounds of the Middle East Conflict*, completed by Charles Kraft and published in 1976 after her death, continues to hold much truth related to the struggle in the Middle East today.

Vocation beyond work was introduced into Harkness's life through the pastoral presence of Ernest Fremont Tittle, minister of the First Methodist Church in Evanston, Illinois. After joining the faculty of Garrett Biblical Institute in 1940, she became a member of the church and a close friend and confidante of Tittle. Observing her strained condition, Tittle introduced her to Verna Miller, a musician, an administrative secretary with a firm in Chicago, and a new member of the congregation who had recently moved to Evanston. He told Harkness that it might be good for her to get better acquainted with Verna and possibly for them to live together. He recognized that Harkness was shy and had difficulty making friends, that she was too detached from other people and kept too much to herself.

Harkness and Miller, almost the same age but of very different personalities, became friends immediately. Miller, who had a wonderful sense of humor, could bring out a previously undisclosed lighter side in Harkness. They soon began to share a home, a partnership that continued for thirty years until Harkness died in 1974. Miller took primary responsibility for the house, cooking, and handling financial matters. Colleagues on the faculties of Garrett and later Pacific School of Religion described Miller as a good tonic for Harkness. Miller was well accepted by friends on both faculties and accompanied her to all seminary functions.

In 1959, when Harkness was almost sixty years old, she and Miller together picked up their roots in Evanston and moved to Berkeley, California, the first time that Harkness had not moved alone. She joined the faculty of Pacific School of Religion (PSR) as professor of applied theology, the same title she had held at Garrett.

Friends in the PSR community who knew them during their ten years in Berkeley provide intimate and discerning insights into the new and mature life that Harkness gained during these years, capsuled in the words of Wayne Rood, professor of Christian education during her years on the faculty, and Helen, his wife. Helen saw her as a person much at peace with herself. Whatever struggles Harkness had gone through, Helen believed she had come to accept who she was. Wayne stated the paradox at the heart of Harkness's being: "I encountered her right from the beginning as an aloof, analytical, rational scholar in a warm, caring, compassionate person" (Interview, Rosemary Keller with Wayne Rood, June 27, 1991).

Time and again, Harkness's pastoral side came to the

fore, as she supported students who experienced life as outsiders on the seminary campus. One was a young man who was suspected of being a homosexual and was dismissed from school by the president. Harkness and Miller helped him support himself by giving him odd jobs around the house and on Harkness's car, seeing him through at least a year after his dismissal until he moved toward primary school teaching. Carmen Pak must have felt like an outsider when she graduated from Pacific School of Religion shortly after the Methodist Church voted in 1956 that women could receive ordination with full conference membership. The bishop in their area, Gerald Kennedy, strongly discouraged Pak from seeking ordination. Harkness, on the other hand, insisted to Pak, "No matter what you do, be your own person," words reminiscent of Harkness's mother to her (Interview, Rosemary Keller with Harry Pak, September 7, 1990).

Miller took a traditional caretaker wifely role toward Harkness, although she spoke with vigor and authority to her partner. While Harkness and Miller shared some domestic responsibilities with equity, Miller was the business manager of the home. She enabled Harkness to be released for public service and distinction. Miller may have overly sacrificed her own selfhood through all that she gave to Harkness. Another colleague on the faculty, Durwood Foster, asked a profound question about them: "Verna seemed to be oriented to supporting and expediting Georgia's work in whatever way. You know, was she too much the servant and companion of Georgia? I guess I could look back on the relationship and wonder, 'Did Verna have a life of her own?'" (Interview, Rosemary Keller with Durwood Foster, June 26, 1991).

Moving once again in retirement in 1968 to the more southern Claremont, California, Harkness and Miller remained there until Harkness died in 1974. They lived vigorous and healthy lives together during these final years. Harkness regularly led an adult Sunday School class at the Claremont United Methodist Church while lecturing and teaching throughout the United States. Together, they went to Hawaii six times, had a trip to the Middle East, and during the last six months of Harkness's life, visited Alaska. They also traveled extensively in the United States, driving in Harkness's large hydraulic Pontiac and successive cars.

Harkness's primary community, one of family, was Miller. The love and care that they so generously gave to each other demonstrate that Harkness had found her own life to lead, one much fuller than that of career, which dominated so many of her years.

The larger institution of the United Methodist Church was also a community for Harkness. Until her death, she kept her membership in the tiny church in Harkness, New York, where she was first taken by her parents when she was three weeks old. Harkness challenged her denomination on hard issues of social inclu-

siveness throughout her life and was revered by church leaders and grassroots participants for her courage and conviction. Both her vital mind and her warm and caring personality kept her young for her age until she died.

Harkness's eighty-first birthday came during the last General Conference of the United Methodist Church, which she attended in 1972. In a move that surprised her, the entire conference delegation rose and sang "Happy Birthday" to her. In response, Harkness acknowledged that she could "hardly find words to express my gratitude and it is perhaps unusual for me to fail to find words," an opening that brought laughter throughout the house. "But above all the things that have come to me, you touch my heart deeply. This is the greatest. It might be said I'm a hardy perennial" (*Daily Christian Advocate,* April 22, 1972, 345).

Her self-description as a "hardy perennial" conveys the essential Harkness better than any accolades penned on public citations. Over her eighty-three years, she transplanted her sturdy roots from the Northeast to the Midwest to the far West. With each geographical move, and with changes within and without, Harkness kept sprouting, experiencing the fruits of maturity and conceiving new and fresh life.

The themes of calling, career, and community emerge from the autobiographical and biographical studies of Georgia Harkness, enabling a person to follow her vocational journey and perhaps to enter into her experience as vocational kin. The stories told in this essay shatter the stereotypes associated with calling, career, and community in relationship to vocation.

Calling is often identified in the Roman Catholic tradition as placing a person in a religious order of nuns, priests, or monks, perhaps even in cloistered orders, where she or he can live a holy life not subject to the temptations of the secular world. In the far different sphere of the evangelical tradition, calling is associated with a summons, perhaps coming only once in a lifetime, in which God gives a clarion call to an individual to change his or her way of life or do an entirely different kind of work. Customarily in many branches of Christianity, calling has been identified with persons who are ordained.

For Harkness, none of these understandings apply. A wide range of religious persons will relate to her vocational motivations and spiritual struggles and may find a vocational kinship with them. Calling from God came over an extended period of many years in her life. It was at the heart of her inward spiritual journey and required a response, even a wrenching one, that involved deep personal soul searching. Harkness was actively involved in responding to her call, discerning what it should be and how it changed several times.

Calling was not only an inward spiritual experience but also required that she evaluate and reevaluate the work and career path that she would follow. Further, it led her to commit her life to the wider sectors and needs of God's people by entering the struggle for social justice. God's call was tremendously empowering to Harkness, leading her into more purposeful and vital living than she had conceived previously.

Harkness's career grew out of her calling, leading her in a different direction than the stereotypical career race or career ladder would have taken her. Career is a middle-class possibility because it relates to work in professions, such as the ministry, law, medicine, social work, or business. The call of her career was to find a profession that gave meaning to her day-to-day work life, work given to the greater good of service and justice to persons who are dispossessed or in need.

Harkness's career was complex. Foremost, she was a teacher and a scholar in higher education, shifting from undergraduate to seminary teaching in midlife. Although she was a major figure in writing theology for both laity and clergy and was the only distinguished female theologian of her day, Harkness was always an outsider looking in, never "one of the boys" in the scholarly network. Her career also included her social activism, as she unrelentingly challenged the church to be what God called it to be in serving and seeking justice for all God's people.

Community has no stereotypical understanding related to vocation because vocation is normally seen as an individual experience. Calling is given to an individual, and an individual selects a career. However, community expands the nature of vocation beyond any previous individual and professional understandings. That expansion of the meaning of vocation came because Harkness experienced that she was called to more than work. Her work life defined her calling only for a part of her vocational journey. Finally, she experienced vocation more broadly than could be equated with work, through her personal relationship with a partner with whom she established the community of a family. Harkness came to experience calling as a way of responding to God with the whole of her life.

Calling is at the heart of vocational kinship as developed in this essay. It grows out of a relationship with God, which changes the focus of one's life from personal achievement to the larger good of God's people. Career, as a response to calling, becomes a search for work that commits oneself to seeking the welfare and justice of all, not one's own gain of money or prestige. For all the good that a person may do through her or his career, calling enables that person not to confuse having a career with having a life. It brings the experience of community to the center of one's existence. For God does not call people into abstract communities but enables women and men to enter into community in their closest day-to-day personal and professional relationships.

While vocation may be dissected into the three experiences of calling, career, and community, finally these experiences are not separate entities. Together they enable a person to discern her or his vocation and to have vocational kinship at a deeper spiritual and social level than they could have conceived without their conscious relationship with God.

SOURCES: Important collections of essays on the art of writing biography include Stephen Oates, ed., *Biography as High Adventure* (1986), and Marc Patcher, ed., *Telling Lives: The Biographer's Art* (1979), and books by Paul Murray Kendall, *The Art of Biography* (1985), and Catherine Drinker Bowen, *Biography: The Craft and the Calling* (1969). James William McClendon, Jr., in *Biography as Theology* (1974), uses biography as a way of doing theology. Feminist methodology on the writing of women's biography is found in Carolyn Heilbrun, *Writing a Woman's Life* (1988); and Linda Wagner Martin, *Telling Women's Lives: The New Biography* (1994); along with essay collections *The Challenge of Feminist Biography* (1992), edited by Sara Alpern, Joyce Antler, Elisabeth Israels Perry, and Ingrid Winther Scobie; and *Between Women* (1984), edited by Carol Ascher, Louise DeSalvo, and Sara Ruddick. The major manuscript collection of Georgia Harkness, containing her unpublished biographical sketch "Days of My Years," along with many letters, manuscripts, printed clippings, and published articles, is housed in the United Library at Garrett-Evangelical Theological Seminary. Over 200 letters exchanged between Harkness and Edgar Brightman are contained in the Edgar S. Brightman Papers, Mugar Library, Boston University. Harkness wrote over forty books and countless articles, many of the articles found over several decades of publication in the *Christian Century*, *Christian Advocate*, and *Zion's Herald*. Rosemary Keller's *Georgia Harkness: For Such a Time as This* (1992) is the only biography of her.

Part II

~

Women in Indigenous and African Traditions

NATIVE AMERICAN CREATION STORIES
Laura Adams Weaver

COMING FROM MORE than 600 tribal groups, divided into at least eight major language families, and living in nine distinct culture areas, the creation stories of indigenous peoples in what are now the United States and Canada represent an incredibly diverse and richly textured body of thought. Although many of these tribes' stories are similar to some degree, any generalizations must acknowledge the tremendous variety that results from differences in language, geography, and social structure. In addition to the number of stories from different tribes, within a given tribe there are also variations. Each individual tribe or nation has its creation stories, in the plural, both in the sense that there can be multiple versions of their creation and that each single reiteration is another event and thus another story.

Despite the tremendous variety in these tribal accounts, two basic models predominate—earthdiver stories and emergence stories. Earthdiver stories begin in a world covered with water. To help make a place for nonaquatic beings, an animal dives down to the bottom to secure a small dab of mud and returns with it to the surface, where it expands to form the lands of this world. In emergence stories, the people enter this world from one or more lower worlds. With the great diversity of people and places, however, there are certainly stories that follow different narrative patterns. Earthmaker, the creator in one version of the Maidu stories, sings the world into being. Whatever the type, creation stories are etiological, explaining how we came to be here, now, in this place. In *God Is Red*, Vine Deloria, Jr., notes that Native stories, less concerned with establishing the event as a beginning in time than as a beginning in place, are narratives that explain the origin of "an ecosystem present in a definable place." In simpler terms, he distinguishes between stories that depict an experience of reality "as 'what happened here' or 'what happened then' " (78). Grand cosmogonic stories (such as the biblical Genesis) describe the ordering of the universe at the beginning of time, stressing "then" rather than "here." By contrast, Native American creation stories are geomythological, intricately bound up with a given people and their particular land base.

As one might expect, earthdiver narratives are common among tribes where water is a central feature of the landscape, such as the Anishnaabe (Ojibwe) in the Western Great Lakes region or the Innu of the Quebec-Labrador peninsula in the North Atlantic. The earthdiver narratives of the Iroquois Confederacy are good examples. At its inception in 1452, it consisted of five nations—Mohawk, Oneida, Onondaga, Cayuga, and Seneca—with the Tuscarora admitted later to form the present-day Six Nations. The Confederacy was headed by fifty sachems, or clan leaders, who were in turn nominated by clan mothers. Iroquois are traditionally matrilineal, with all property inherited through the mother. The strong female presence in Iroquoian social life is reflected in the power manifested by Sky Woman and her daughter Earth Woman in the formation of their world. Although each tribe has one or more versions, the different tellings of "The Woman Who Fell from the Sky" remain remarkably similar in many respects. The Seneca version collected in the mid-1880s by ethnographers Jeremiah Curtin and J. N. B. Hewitt, a Tuscarora, provides a starting point.

As it is told, in the time before this world, people lived in another world above what we know as the sky. It was a beautiful world, resting on a thin layer of earth that floated like a cloud, and the sky people who lived there did not know what was underneath. In the center of their world, there was a great tree that provided corn for the people. The sky world had a powerful leader, called Earth Holder or the Ancient One. He had a daughter who became terribly ill, and no one knew how to heal her. A friend of the Ancient One was given a dream, and he instructed the father to lay his daughter beside the great tree, which must be uprooted. She was taken there, and the people started to dig into the thin layer of earth holding the tree in place. It was not long before it fell, leaving a hole in the earth through which they could see the sky below. A young man came along, and he was angry at what he saw. He shouted at the people that it was not right to destroy the source of their food, and he pushed the Ancient One's daughter through the gaping hole.

She fell down through the sky toward this world, which at that time was entirely covered with water. Its only inhabitants were fish and birds and animals that could swim. Ducks looked up and saw the woman falling in the sky. Many of them laced their wings together to break her fall, and she was placed on Turtle's back to rest. The creatures of this world determined to make a place where a human woman could live, so they decided to dive down deep and find some earth at the bottom of the water. After much debate, Toad was chosen to go. He swam down a long way, and just when he reached the point of exhaustion, his nose touched the mud that lay beneath the water. He brought a tiny bit back to the surface and smeared it on Turtle's back. The bit of earth grew until it formed all the lands of this world.

Sky Woman recovered from her illness and made herself a home in her new world. Not long after, she gave birth to a daughter, who grew tall and learned things quickly. Some time after she became a young woman, she conceived twins by the breath of the West

Part of a larger painting by Michael Kabotie and his assistant Delbridge Honanie titled "Journey of Human Spirit." In Kabotie's view all cultures and spiritual institutions have a place of beginning or birthing. The Grand Canyon represents this place for the Hopi. The ladder extending from the Hopi kiva, the underground religious chamber, symbolizes the *sipapuni*, the passage that was for their emergence into this world. *Copyright © 2001 Michael Kabotie and Delbridge Honanie. Used by permission of the artists.*

Wind. Several days before they were born, she heard the two arguing about who should be firstborn and from what place they would leave their mother. Djuskaha (Little Sprout) left her body the usual way. Othagwenda (Flint) pierced an opening under his mother's arm and emerged from there, killing her. After the death of her daughter, Sky Woman returned to the above world. Earth Woman's two sons vie for the control of the lower world. Djuskaha's contributions to the world are beneficial and imaginative, useful plants and animals, whereas Othagwenda's additions are malicious and ultimately destructive. Djuskaha eventually bests his brother and wins control of the world.

In Native American creation stories, the universe is rarely formed ex nihilo, out of nothing. The basic elements are already there, and the creators simply give them a new shape, forming mud and water into lands and seas. Frequently, as is the case in the Sky Woman stories, another world precedes this one. Except for its location, the newly formed world in Iroquoian stories is not markedly different from its celestial counterpart, where human like people coexist in recognizable family and community groups. Creation for Native American peoples is local, explaining not so much how we came

to be but rather how we came to be *here*. Also, the stories stress the collective aspect of creation. Rarely do they describe a lone creator. Creation in Native thought is a continuing process, so while the story might begin with a single figure, others soon come along to help. The cycle of creation is typically a collaborative affair, with many beings of all kinds combining their efforts to produce this world. Male and female, human and animal—a variety of forces are needed to bring the world and its peoples into being.

In most cases, multiple accounts of one tribe's creation have been collected and published, which underscores the difficulties of accurate translation and the problem of resolving discrepancies between the voices of informants and collectors. *Seneca Myths and Folk Tales* by Arthur C. Parker, an archeologist of Seneca ancestry, includes two versions that differ in key ways from Curtin and Hewitt's. For the most part, it is the narration rather than the structure that is affected. Parker's language is much more sophisticated and nuanced. Seneca language names are used throughout, so that the figures described seem more personal rather than emblematic. He offers considerably more detail, and key actions in the narrative are repeated for emphasis. In the Curtin-Hewitt account, Toad is the only animal that tries and succeeds the first time. As Parker tells it, many creatures try to reach the bottom before Muskrat finally makes it. That Duck dies in the attempt underscores both the difficulty of the task and the extent of the sacrifice the creatures make to shape a world for Sky Woman.

Most of the differences are aesthetic, but at least two key changes influence the narrative structure, a distinction that ultimately diminishes or strengthens the power granted to female beings. As with the animals' efforts to find earth, Parker's account of Sky Woman and Earth Woman goes into much more detail. In this case, the telling reinforces the integral role of Sky Woman and Earth Woman in shaping the world. The Curtin-Hewitt account focuses more on the conflict between the Twins, and Sky Woman and her daughter appear to be passive participants in the action. Sky Woman's expulsion from the sky world provides the occasion for earth's creation by the animals, but she herself contributes nothing. Earth Woman gives birth to twin sons, but it is they who create the plants, animals, and human beings that populate this world. Parker's version relates several key actions that are omitted in the previous account. As Sky Woman is forced out of the hole, she grabs at the base of the tree and falls to earth with handfuls of seeds. These mix with the mud that she spreads on Turtle's back, and a rich plant life springs up from the newly formed lands. After she is killed by Flint, Earth Woman is buried, and from the ground above her body, plants of all kinds—corn, beans, squash, and potatoes—start to grow. The two women are responsible for creating plant life, so that their story accounts for the origin of agriculture.

Another variable is the initial conflict that sets things in motion. As noted previously, creation stories are etiological, exploring causal relationships in the ordering of the world and explaining not only the way things are but also how they should be. Each of the three versions begins with a different situation that significantly changes how the narrative ascribes culpability for a crucial act of destruction—uprooting the great tree. In Parker's primary version, recounted in the main text, the Ancient One grew dissatisfied with his aging wife, and he replaced her with a young woman he found more appealing. After his taking a wife, he discovered that she was already pregnant by the potent breath of another man. (Traditional stories often tell of women who were impregnated by Wind.) The man is given a dream that instructs him to uproot the tree to punish Sky Woman. After that, she becomes obsessed with staring down the hole into the world below. Although the aging husband's actions ostensibly precipitate the event, his young wife's

intense curiosity is blamed for both the tree's demise and her expulsion from the sky world:

> Again his anger returned against her, for she said nothing to indicate that she had been satisfied. Long she sat looking into the hole until the chief in rage drew her blanket over her head and pushed her with his foot, seeking to thrust her into the hole, and be rid of her. . . . Again the chief pushed the woman, whose curiosity had caused the destruction of the greatest blessing of the up-above-world. (Parker, 61)

Pandora-like, this female thirst for knowledge threatens the existing world.

In a footnote, Parker briefly alludes to another version that significantly changes Sky Woman's situation. As in the Curtin-Hewitt variant, she was not the second wife of the Ancient One but rather his daughter. The old man who desired her is one of her father's rivals, who murdered her father and hid the body in the trunk of the great tree. Parker states that the old man "took her in the manner here related" (59), which implies that the Sky Woman's pregnancy is what sparks the man's anger. She is given a dream telling her where to find her father's body, and the tree is uprooted during her search. In this variant, the narrative arc describes the consequences that follow upon the murder of a leader rather than the cost of female desire for knowledge. In the Curtin-Hewitt version, disease precipitates the loss of the tree and Sky Woman's descent. Not entirely, however. The narrative reinforces the primacy of the collective. While solving a father's murder or curing a daughter's mysterious illness both explain the desire to uproot the great tree, Sky Woman and the Ancient One act on personal motives and put their community at risk.

In the Southwest, where water is a precious commodity, creation stories tend to be emergence narratives, such as those of the Diné (Navajo) or the Acoma Pueblo. The Hopi tell how the people migrated up through several lower worlds and entered this, the fourth world, through an opening in the ground. Understandably in a matrilineal society, the world is in large part shaped by a powerful female—or females, in some versions—either Hurúing Wuhti (Hard Beings Woman) or often Kóhkang Wuhti (Spider Woman). As it was told to Harold Courlander, in the beginning was only Tokpella (endless space), and only Tawa the Sun and other powerful beings lived then. To alleviate the sense of emptiness, Tawa infused elements of endless space with part of his own substance to shape the First World. The first inhabitants were insect beings, and Tawa found himself disappointed by their limited comprehension and by the dissension among them. He sent Spider Woman to guide them into the Second World. When they arrived, they saw that Tawa had changed their shapes along the way, so now they were different kinds of animals. At first, they were pleased with the new world and their new forms, but after a time, they began to fight among themselves again. Once again Tawa sent Spider Woman to guide them, and as they traveled, he created the Third World. When they arrived, they found their shapes had changed yet again; this time, they had become people.

Spider Woman told them that Tawa had made this place for them to live together without discord. The people learned to grow corn, and Spider Woman taught them to weave blankets for warmth and to shape clay into pots to store food. They were thankful for what they had been given, but there was very little light or warmth in their new world, so they were cold, and their crops grew poorly. Without heat to bake the clay, the pots they fashioned stayed soft and fragile. One day, a Hummingbird came to them, sent by Maasaw, the caretaker of the Fourth World. He had seen how difficult it was for the people to live without warmth, so he sent Hummingbird to teach them to use fire. They learned to make fires to warm their fields, to cook their food, and to harden clay to strengthen their pots. Those who had been given the knowledge of fire counted Maasaw as their relative. The gift of fire improved life for the people in the Third World, but once more there was discord. *Pokawas,* or witches, began to work among them, making medicines to harm others. Under their influence, the people started to neglect their responsibilities to each other and the land, causing disharmony and corruption through their world.

Tawa was dismayed by the people's actions, and once again he sent Spider Woman to advise them. She told them of Tawa's displeasure and instructed them to leave the wicked ones behind and find a new place where they could honor their obligations. The people had heard someone walking above them, and they fashioned four birds out of clay to fly up and discover if there was another world above the sky. First they sent Swallow, then White Dove, then Hawk, but each one grew tired before the task was done. The fourth time, Catbird flew up through a hole in the sky and found Maasaw there. When told what was happening in the Third World, Maasaw said that his world had no light and no warmth except for fire, but there was land and water, and the people could come if they wished. Spider Woman and her two grandsons devised a way for the people to reach the *sipapuni,* the opening in the sky to the next world. They called on Chipmunk to plant seeds: First a sunflower stalk, then a spruce tree, then a pine tree grew into the sky, but none were tall enough. Chipmunk planted a fourth seed, bamboo, and the people sang as

the stalk grew. Whenever they stopped to breathe, the growth halted, but it started again whenever they sang. Finally it grew tall enough to pass through the *sipapuni.* Their way was long and hard, but the people climbed up through the sky of the Third World and pushed up through the ground and entered the Fourth World.

As they emerged, Spider Woman watched as Yawpa the Mockingbird gave each a name and a language. One would be called Hopi and speak that language. Another would be called Diné and speak that language. Another would be called Apache and speak that language. Ute, Paiute, Lakota, Pima, Zuni, Comanche, Shoshone, White Men. Yawpa named them all and gave them a language. When all the people of good heart had emerged, the bamboo was dislodged so that the wicked could not follow. Then Spider Woman's grandsons helped give shape to the Fourth World. Flat, muddy ground was formed into mountains and mesas. Spider Woman helped the people to fashion Sun and Moon to bring light and heat. Yawpa gave varieties of corn to the people, and the Hopi chose the short blue corn, which meant their life would be hard, but they could survive it. They stayed near the *sipapuni* for four days, and when one of their number became ill and died, they discovered that a *pokawa* had entered the Fourth World with them. The dead child's father wanted to throw her into the *sipapuni,* but she pointed to where his child, no longer dead, played below them in the lower world. The people debated what to do with her but decided to let her stay. Good and bad are present in all places, and returning the *pokawa* to the lower world would not change that. None wanted her to come with them except the Bahanas, White Men, who respected her knowledge and were not afraid of her. Finally, the time came for the different peoples to separate and travel to their respective homelands. As the Hopi prepared for their migration, Spider Woman counseled them never to forget the *sipapuni,* and she covered it with water. They were to remember this was Maasaw's land, so they would always be in the presence of death. She told them to make songs and sing them to remember, because the ones who forgot why they came into the Fourth World would become lost and would themselves be forgotten.

Like all such stories, this version of the Hopi emergence narrative explains origins and causes of various things in the world. It tells why bamboo grows in segments or how the sun and moon were made so that there was light and heat in this world. It also establishes relationships between different clans or explains why different tribes speak different languages. Unlike the universal accounts provided by cosmogonic narratives, however, the geomythical explanation focuses more on local concerns. The Eden described in the biblical Genesis has no particular location. This brief summary of the Hopi account omits many details, but the original telling as recorded by Courlander describes and names the creation of specific mountains visible in the present-day Hopi landscape, providing an explanation not only for the Fourth World in general but especially for their immediate environment.

Another consideration in the study of tribal creation stories is the problem of context. In tribal settings, creation stories are often told or enacted as part of a larger ritual. Any single creation story functions performatively, in a complex of stories that provide a sense of individual and collective identity. Outside that complex, a story's meaning is altered. Most people will encounter creation stories out of context, translated from their original language and relocated to an extratribal setting. Any change in context effects a change in meaning, either subtly or dramatically, depending on the degree to which the frame intrudes into the story. Tribal sources may have had very little control over the ultimate disposition of the text. Some collectors make every attempt to respect both the people and the story, whereas others misuse the texts for personal gain or profit. Even the most careful translation, however, significantly changes the narrative utterance, so that the story of "who we are" becomes one of "what they believe."

The primacy of orality foregrounds the speech act, whereby the teller and moment of telling are integral parts of the story. On some level, collected stories require readers to attend to at least two narrative voices, the informant and the collector. Any translation from one language to another, from one context to another, requires a shift of perspective. It may be simply a matter of word choice. In Courlander's text, Maasaw (Masauwu) is called as "Ruler of the Upper World, Caretaker of the Place of the Dead, and Owner of Fire" (19). Words like *ruler* and *owner* appear to be foreign to a Hopi perspective, where power and property are shared. While the Hopi acknowledge his great power, in English they often refer to him simply as "The Caretaker of this World."

Courlander's version differs strikingly from another version published by missionary Heinrich (Henry) Voth in 1905. This telling is not simply a variant on the same emergence narrative but rather a different account of creation altogether. In the story told to Voth, the world in the beginning was covered with water. Hard Beings Woman in the East together with a second Hard Beings Woman in the West created a stretch of dry land between them. After Tawa the Sun commented that nothing lived there, the two formed creatures out of clay and sang them to life, birds and animals of all kinds. They also created First Man and First Woman, giving them writing and language. Spider Woman decided to create other pairs of beings and gave each a different language, explaining the origin of various tribes as well as the Spanish and the English.

Different clans, societies, or families often tell different versions of a particular story, and sometimes accounts told by men and women are likewise distinctive. In *The Fourth World of the Hopis*, Courlander suggests that Hopi traditions are an amalgam of stories and songs from different clans and groups that eventually came together to form the Hopi people. His explanatory note acknowledges that the contradictory accounts exist and have long been debated among Hopi people, although more Hopi than not accept the emergence narrative.

The Hopi's story of Voth, however, may prove more instructive than Voth's story of the Hopi. In the 1890s, Voth spent nine years working as a Mennonite missionary. His obsession with documenting the intricacies of Hopi culture and religion was decidedly at odds with his ostensible mission to convert his informants. Voth gained access to Hopi ritual, which suggests that his relations with the tribe initially earned him some degree of trust. Increasingly, though, he relied on his studies to provide financial support for his family, using what he learned to produce cultural displays and replicas of Hopi altars in museums and tourist sites. Once they learned that Voth was publishing detailed information about their rituals, the Hopi community grew to distrust the missionary's motives. In the mid-1960s, one informant from Oraibi told Courlander that Voth's actions were not right: "Instead of doing what he was supposed to, being a church man, he got into all the secrets, stole them and some of the altar things too, and revealed all the sacred things in his books." Similarly, another informant from New Oraibi describes Voth as someone who "did not stay in the back. He always pushed to the front, anywhere he wanted to be, even in the kivas. Nobody could stop him. . . . Most of the stories they told Voth is because they didn't want to tell him the true story" (Courlander, 230). Among the documents produced during this period were over 2,000 photographs. At the time of this writing, Hopi tribal leaders are seeking to extend the logic of the Native American Graves Protection and Repatriation Act (NAGPRA) to litigate the return of photographs and other artifacts taken by the man who would not stay in the back.

Cosmogonic narratives focus on the formation of the universe and its inhabitants over a relatively limited span of time. Once cosmos, earth, and people are in place, the act of creation is complete. By contrast, creation as recounted among Native American peoples is a series of acts extended over time and space. The cycle of Navajo creation stories does not end after the formation of the universe and the people's emergence into this, the Fifth World. Their cycle continues to describe the birth of Changing Woman and her twin sons, the slaying of the monsters, ending with the gathering of the clans that form the Navajo nation. In tribal thought, creation narratives are trifold, recounting the formation of the world, the people in it, but most especially their way of life.

Corn was a staple in the diet of many Native American peoples, so the story of its origins is one of their most sacred etiological narratives. Diverse tribes, from the Muscogee, Cherokee, and Natchez in the Southeast to Penobscot in the Northeast, tell the story of Corn Mother to explain the source of the grain. It is a story rooted in violence and sacrifice but just as deeply rooted in female power. Among agricultural people, food and economy are one, so Corn Mother is not simply the source of food. She is the wellspring of the culture. Although there are numerous local variations from tribe to tribe, the Cherokee version, recorded by James Mooney among the Eastern Band in the mid-1880s, may be considered representative.

As it is told, Kanati (Lucky Hunter) and his wife Selu (Corn Mother) lived with their two sons when the world was new. During a time when food was scarce, Kanati was away for long stretches of time in search of game. Although they had no meat, the woman and her children always had enough to eat. At length, the boys grew curious as to the source of this bounty of corn and beans. The next time Selu went out to the storehouse where she got the food, the boys contrived to spy on her. They removed a bit of mud from a chink in the wall of the building and waited. They watched their mother place a basket in the middle of the floor and stand over it. She rubbed her stomach, and corn sloughed off into the basket. She rubbed her armpits, and beans tumbled off her. Upon seeing this remarkable sight, the young boys concluded that their mother was a witch.

When the youths returned to the house, Selu could tell that they had discovered her secret. Confronting them, she said, "So you are going to kill me?" The boys replied, "Yes. You are a witch" (Mooney, 244). Knowing she was to die, the mother then instructed her children about what to do with her body after death. They were to clear a piece of ground by the house and drag her body around the perimeter seven times. Then they were to drag it over the ground inside the circle seven more times. If they did as she said, she promised that they would always have plenty of corn.

The pair killed Selu. Instead of clearing a large plot for their cornfield, however, they grew lazy and cleared only seven tiny spots. For this reason, corn now grows only in a few places rather than over the whole earth. The boys dragged their mother's corpse around the circle, and wherever her blood flowed out, corn sprang up. But they grew tired and lazy again, and rather than dragging it across the field seven times, they only did so

twice. This is why corn grows only in its seasons and not year-round.

In a variant recorded in Oklahoma in 1961 by Cherokee ethnographers Jack and Anna Kilpatrick, there is no matricide. Rather, once her power is discovered by the boys, the woman immediately loses vitality, becomes ill, and takes to her bed to die. Before her death, however, she explains what her sons were to do with her body. Similarly, in a Penobscot version, set down by Penobscot Joseph Nicolar in 1893, First Mother begs her husband to kill her, since it was the only way to provide food for her family during a famine. In all cases, Corn Mother gives to her sons both the crops and the rituals necessary to organize their planting, thereby preserving her people's way of life. For the societies that tell this narrative, Corn Mother also explains women as the primary agriculturalists.

Inuit creation myths tend to be local, but one story that is common among various Inuit peoples across the circumpolar region is that of Sedna (She Down There). Like Corn Mother, her story is one of violence and sacrifice, but it explores the darker side of female power. One important version was recorded by Franz Boas on Baffin Island in 1884, and Knud Rasmussen, himself Inuit, collected a second telling in Greenland during the early 1920s.

As it was told, an old widower lived with his beautiful daughter Sedna. Although the young woman had many Inuit suitors, she refused to marry any of them because she had been beguiled by the sweet song of a seagull. Despite her father's protests, she agreed to marry the bird-man and return with him to the land of his people. Contrary to her new husband's promises of luxury and beauty, Sedna found his domain repugnant. Their home was a crude tent made of fish-skins that did little to keep the elements out. Her sleeping mat was uncomfortable walrus hide. Instead of delicious meat, she was forced to eat raw fish that the birds brought her. In desperation, she cried out for her father to come get her.

When spring came, the old man went to visit his daughter. Seeing the miserable state of her existence, he determined to rescue her and have revenge upon her husband. When the seagull returned home, the father killed him and fled in his kayak with Sedna. The other gulls, however, pursued the pair and, once they spotted the boat, caused a violent storm to break out on the ocean. Panicking, the old man threw his own daughter overboard in order to save himself, but Sedna clung to the edge of the craft.

The crazed man then took his *ulu* and sliced off Sedna's fingertips. These fell into the water and became whales. Still the woman hung on to the boat. Still the storm raged. Terror-stricken, the father tried again to dislodge his now dreadful cargo, cutting her fingers off down to the first joint and then to the second. They fell into the sea and became seals and walruses. According to the story recorded by Knud Rasmussen among his own Greenlander Inuit people in the early 1920s, Sedna was at last forced to relinquish her grip, and she sank beneath the waves.

In Boas's account, however, the gulls departed, thinking she had drowned, and the storm subsided. Her father then pulled her back into the boat. Father and daughter arrive home without further incident. Sedna, however, still deeply resented her father's actions. At the first opportunity, she set her dogs on the sleeping man, and the dogs gnawed off his hands and feet. The old man cursed his daughter, the dogs, and himself. At that moment, the ground opened beneath them, swallowing their hut and all inside it.

Sedna became Mistress of the Sea and the ruler of the underworld. From there she controls the sea creatures formed from her flesh. When human beings anger her, she withholds these sources of food, and the people suffer. In order to placate Sedna and keep her happy, Inuit shamans travel to her realm and comb her tangled hair because, without fingers, she cannot do so herself. According to Rasmussen, Sedna's father is in charge of chastising those who have been wicked in this world before they can enter the land of the dead.

As in the Cherokee narrative, a male figure or figures dismember a female body, and her remains undergo a transformation that provides food for the people. Where Corn Woman recognizes the necessity of her death and exerts some measure of control by instructing her sons how to dispose of her body, Sedna's sacrifice is not of her own making. In one sense, this narrative of productive female sacrifice is appropriate among the Inuit, whose harsh environment necessitated population control that sometimes took the form of female infanticide. The power ascribed to Sedna is much like that of Corn Woman, however, in that her story explains tribal economics. Sedna exerts control over all the whales, seals, and walruses in the sea, which are the primary source of meat, oil, and skins needed by the Inuit to survive.

The handful of examples discussed here are but a tiny sample of the many Native American creation stories in which women figure prominently. Given that balance between male and female is a key principal in most tribal structures, stories of female creators are the rule rather than the exception. White Buffalo Calf Woman gives to the Lakota nation the pipe and seven sacred ceremonies that order their lives. For the Tlingit and Haida, the first two women made by Raven critique his creation and decide that one of them should be a man, thereby re-creating humanity. For the Mescalero Apache, 'Isánáklésh was one of the five sacred beings present at creation, and her power brought the people trees, plants, and medicinal herbs. For the Laguna, Thought Woman is the creator that gives shape and name to all things through the power of her imagination. In the words of Laguna poet Leslie Marmon Silko,

Ts'its'tsi'nako, Thought-Woman
    is sitting in her room
and whatever she thinks about
    appears.
(Excerpted from Silko's *Ceremony*, 1)

SOURCES: Collections with a range of creation stories from various tribes in North America include Stith Thompson, ed., *Tales of the North American Indians* (1929); Richard Erdoes and Alfonso Ortiz, eds., *American Indian Myths and Legends* (1984); Ella Elizabeth Clark, ed., *Indian Legends of Canada* (1960); and Susan Feldmann, ed., *The Story-Telling Stone: Traditional Native American Myths and Tales* (1965). Most of these stories are reprinted, retold, or compiled from one or more earlier sources, with varying degrees of contextualization. For an analysis and examples of different tribal creation stories, see Jace Weaver, *American Journey: The Native American Experience* (1998). Vine Deloria, Jr., in *God Is Red* 2nd ed. (1992), provides a comparative analysis of Native, Christian, and Jewish accounts of creation. Further study should focus on tribally specific materials. Hopi sources are Harold Courlander, ed., *The Fourth World of the Hopis* (1971), and H. R. Voth, ed., *The Traditions of the Hopi* (1905). Edmund Nequatewa in *The Truth of a Hopi* (1936) offers a Hopi account. Iroquoian stories of Sky Woman include David Cusick [Tuscarora], *Sketches of Ancient History of the Six Nations* (1827); Jeremiah Curtin and J. N. B. Hewitt [Tuscarora], "Seneca Myths and Fictions" (1918); and Arthur C. Parker [Seneca], *Seneca Myths and Folk Tales* (1923). The story of Corn Mother is found in James Mooney, *The Myths of the Cherokee* (1900), and a Cherokee perspective can be found in Jack F. Kilpatrick and Anna G. Kilpatrick, *Friends of Thunder: Folktales of the Oklahoma Cherokees* (1964). Sedna accounts are given in Franz Boas, *The Central Eskimo* (1888), and in Knud Rasmussen [Inuit], *Across Arctic America: Narrative of the Fifth Thule Expedition* (1927). Leslie Marmon Silko, *Ceremony* (1971), incorporates stories of Thought Woman in a novel about Laguna life during the mid-twentieth century.

NATIVE AMERICAN WOMEN
AND CHRISTIANITY
Kim Stone

WHILE STEREOTYPES PREVAIL that Native women in the Americas were subordinate to Native men, recent scholarship consistently indicates that Native women were equal to men in their communities. However, the status of Native women eroded after Christian colonization utilized four strategies: diminish female tribal deities, dismantle tribal sociopolitical structures based on gender egalitarianism, confiscate and break up tribally owned lands, and destroy clan structures. Despite the negative effects of Christian colonization, Native women did not just passively accept the erosion in their status. They often used Christianity against their colonizers to assert indigenous sovereignty.

Native Women's Status Prior to Christianity

Among North American aborigines, all creation is believed to be connected, existing in a nonhierarchical cycle of renewal and change. This framework is in direct conflict with the hierarchical epistemology inherent in mainstream Christianity. As prominent Native scholars Vine Deloria, Jr., and Paula Gunn Allen have argued, the Christian notion of time is chronological and flows in a predictable line from the past to the future. Direction of time is established through acceptance of a religious timetable of events, such as Christ's birth and crucifixion, as evidence of a divine, irreversible plan for

humanity. Power and authority extend from a male source and filter down hierarchically to other men. In Christian tradition, the first woman was created from the first man. In Native creation stories, a woman was frequently held to be the first human and demonstrated the power of creation in her reproductive and nurturing abilities. A continuation of that tradition is demonstrated among the Mohawk, Cherokee, and many other tribes that organized along matrilineal family lines. Clan affiliation is passed through women, although some tribes are also patrilineal. Traditional tribal households were composed of related groups of women of the same clan and their children. Husbands came from other clans and families. In keeping with first human creation traditions, women were valued for their reproductive abilities. They were also honored for their productive labor in farming, gathering, and the creation or processing of resources into clothing and shelter. Among the Plains tribes, for instance, men may have been the chiefs, but women owned the tipis in which men lived. Thus, labor roles enabled Native women to provide for

Kate McBeth (far right, back row) had followed her sister Susan to Idaho in 1879 and set up the first woman's missionary society among the Nez Percé. Targeting women for Christian conversion was useful in Euro-American infiltration of Native communities. *Courtesy of the Presbyterian Historical Society.*

a major portion of sustenance, making them invaluable to tribal well-being. Therefore, tribal lifestyles tended to be egalitarian. Even though women and men often had distinct roles, these roles were generally accorded equal status. In addition, Native societies were not based on a fixed binary gender system. Many Native communities had particular roles for women who lived their lives as men and for men who lived their lives as women. These roles often had important ceremonial significance.

Regardless of some variability in political involvement, depending on the tribe, Native women held direct positions of authority and power because of their social contributions. In many cases, women enjoyed separate but equal positions of power. It was common for Native women to lead or play roles as political advisers. For example, there were many women chiefs such as Wetamoo of the Wampanpag, Magnus of the Narraganset, and sub Chief Winema of the Modoc. There were also well-respected and influential women like Nancy Ward of the Cherokee and Sarah Winnemucca, a Paiute. Additionally, Native women were active in other public positions, such as trading and healing. Tlingit medicine women were both feared and respected. But in early Euro-American society, women did not enjoy equal human rights and were seen as dependent on men. Men were constructed as the controllers of resources, including women's reproduction and productive labor. Furthermore, women did not appear in positions of political leadership or authority. Consequently, European colonizers in the United States consistently attempted to diminish the social and political power of Native women, by devaluing and ignoring Native women's authority and contributions. In addition, missionary, explorer, and other non-indigenous sources of Native societies downplay the role of Native women, thereby erasing the histories of communities and female leadership that would challenge the notion of patriarchy as universal. As Nancy Shoemaker demonstrates, because Europeans would not recognize the leadership of Native women in negotiating parties, Native societies then began to devalue female leadership as relationships with Europeans assumed greater importance. In fact, Europeans often ridiculed the prominence of women in Native governing structures by terming them "petticoat governments."

Native Women and Christian Colonization

Christianity played an essential role in suppressing the political and social power of Native women by weakening Native values and traditions, the underpinnings of their egalitarian societies. Since the arrival of the first European visitors, the conquest of the Americas has always been accompanied by Christianization. The earliest Spanish and Portuguese explorers brought Catholic priests to establish missions for the enlightenment and conversion of Native people. But Bartholomé de las Casas documented the subsequent violence against Native people in his *Devastation of the Indies*. He chronicled the constant sexual assaults of Native women in front of their communities, the butchering of Native women and children, and the practice of hanging Indian peoples in groups of thirteen to commemorate the Last Supper of Christ with his twelve apostles. Spanish colonization focused on enslaving Native peoples into a system of tributary labor and land apportionment called the *encomienda*. It separated Native peoples from their homes, forced them to work for the owners of the plantation where they were enslaved, and forcibly Christianized them. Native peoples were generally worked to death because they could easily be replaced by other Natives. This system eventually became known as the mission system in California, where Native peoples were forced to work at Christian missions in order to support the military. Sexual exploitation of Native women was epidemic in these missions.

As brutal as Spanish colonization was, British colonization was even more genocidal. Unlike the Spanish, the British had no interest in Native peoples as a labor force. Infused with Puritan ideology that held that Native peoples were simply "Canaanites" who needed to be exterminated to establish the "New Israel" in the Americas, the British simply wiped out indigenous peoples. Again, sexual violence was a central tactic in this colonization process, so much so that even the British colonizers commented that unlike the British, Native peoples "never violate the chastity of their prisoners."

In addition to the violence suffered through military contact, European missionaries intentionally undermined gender equality in Native communities in their missionary activity. In her book *Chain Her by One Foot*, Karen Anderson reveals that Jesuits held women to be a source of potential evil and impure sexual passion, thus a threat to men's pursuit of godliness. To the Jesuits in New France, the authority and independence of Montagnais and Huron women made them dangerous. However, some Native people did convert to Christianity in the hope it would be useful for solving the social problems that European contact and colonialism brought. Warfare and disease weakened aborigines' ability to adequately provide resources for survival. In 1646, Hiacoomes, a Chappaquiddick Wampanoag on Martha's Vineyard, became a Christian convert. When he failed to contract a deadly plague that swept through the New England colonies, it seemed to his tribe that he had been protected by his new faith. From 1651 to 1675, "Praying Indian" settlements were established in New England. But the failure of Native religions to resolve new conditions of strife, or to ward off further settlement into tribal territories, left tribes decimated throughout the colonization period. Native women possessed power within tribes and families. So they were often resistant to Christian indoctrination, as Christianity accorded women lesser value and challenged women's authority. Native women's continued independence in the face of tribal crisis, coupled with continued denigration by priests and ministers, contributed to the targeting of Native women as the source of evil and misfortune. For instance, priests often complained about Montagnais and Huron women's blatant defiance and accused women of practicing witchcraft. Demonized and devalued, it seemed reasonable and justifiable for men to control and dominate Native women for the well-being of the tribe. By relegating women to an inferior status, missionaries were relentless in their punishment of defiant Native women. Beatings, starvation, and imprisonment were commonplace, as well as the missionaries' manipulation of Native men into enforcing church dictates upon Native women. In many cases, Native women's voices were eventually restrained in the public and political spheres and placed under the power of men. Without authority, Native women became the pawns of men seeking to align with Europeans for economic benefit and for clergymen who sought to establish their own authority.

This colonial degradation of Native women's status was concurrent with colonial efforts to appropriate indigenous lands and resources. Dishonorable deals and practices in making treaties, access to land, depletion of resources, and the unrelenting growth of the non-Native population served to undermine the status of Native men as hunters and warriors and in their ritual and political relationship to women. Christian religion was at the forefront of these relations, with priests and other religious figures serving as self-interested liaisons and interpreters between Native and non-Native people. *Jesuit Relations* (1632–1673) is an example of the Jesuit agenda. A collection of reports on New France by Jesuit missionaries, the *Relations* reveal the overriding goal of Jesuits among Native people was to stamp out the Antichrist and his pagan followers in New France. The Jesuits wanted to limit Satan's influence and wrote extensively of their efforts to gain converts by living among and settling nomadic aboriginal communities. Both Catholic and Protestant churches planned to overthrow idolatry and establish God-fearing communities among Native people. Conversion to Christianity provided the clergy with a fresh flock to educate and guide in the principles and practices of Christianity as the only true faith. This provided the church with a "mission," a justification for being among Native people. Missions require a base from which to serve, which translates to a requirement for land and resources. Through these relations, the churches negotiated not just for souls but for more land and resources. Racist thinking among Eu-

ropean clergy led to the view of Native peoples as dirty, savage, and impure, which justified the missionaries' importance in salvation as well as the necessity of the presence of missions.

Targeting women for Christian conversion was useful in Euro-American infiltration of Native communities. First, Christianity gained prominence in the public sphere by exercising control over the private sphere. For instance, Christian missionaries insisted that male-female relationships be sanctified through the church. In this model, Native women became the property of their husbands, whereas previously women were free to leave marriages in many tribes. Since Native women were often encouraged to marry non-Native men, they then became the property of white society. The church enabled Christian converts to participate in marriage rites that sanctified unions. Their property, which traditionally would have been passed to their daughters in matrilineal tribes, was then passed down through their sons. This shift from matrilineality to patrilineality then increased white access to land and resources through marriage to Native women. Native men as well also gained power through subjugating Native women. Over time, the status of Native women gradually diminished through a social transformation of Native politics and religion to a patriarchal system.

Displacement of Female Deities

Christianization encouraged tribal communities to displace the female creator in their religious systems to a male God who becomes the ultimate source of power, authority, and legitimacy. For example, Aztec myths of creation focus on the primordial male and female force, a dual personification called Two Lord and Two Lady (thought to predate Aztec theology). This entity generated the primary gods and goddesses, with others continuing to be born of female deities. But only the work of one goddess and the blood of all gods were needed to create humans. These relationships reflect Aztec understanding of female sacred forces as a primary source of life. Among the Iroquois, Sky Woman fell from the sky to earth and became the first human. But she is now said to receive her ideas and power from her deceased father. Likewise, in many Cherokee legends, Thunder, a masculine entity, has replaced River Foam Woman. In the midst of these subversions of female deities, missionaries competed against tribal healers and shamans for spiritual power. Christian symbolism and artifacts were used to undermine the aborigines' faith in tribal traditions. Male missionaries demonstrated their power, and the power of their male god, by predicting eclipses, interpreting visions, and using healing rituals such as bleeding. Eventually sacred role models for Native women were replaced with Christian saints and martyrs.

Two examples are the Virgin Mary, who symbolizes purity, and Ruth, whose life signified conversion, devotion, and obedience. Christian converts were also lured through the Vatican's canonizing of the Iroquois woman Kateri Tekakwitha. Still, the Church called her the "Holy Savage." Consequently, Native women were divinely ordained as subordinate, while female deities were replaced by less powerful Christian saints. It is important to note, however, that the role of women in Native cosmologies did not disappear. In many cases, it has continued underground and through indigenous oral traditions, particularly as the United States government made outright expression of Native traditions illegal through the Indian Religious Crimes Code. The Code made illegal any traditional ceremony or activity that could be construed as interfering with the civilizing of Native people. Since exposure to and adoption of Christianity was part of the civilization technique, the teachings of medicine (native religious tradition) people and even the Lakota messiah, Sacred Calf Pipe Woman, were forbidden. Sacred Calf Pipe Woman appeared to the Lakota shortly after they were pushed to the Plains from the Midwestern forests by the Ojibwa. She brought lessons of respectful conduct, and, among other things, bravery, generosity, and honesty—lessons that have helped the Lakota survive through their most difficult periods.

Destruction of Egalitarian Sociopolitical Structures

Missionaries often argued that Native peoples were not competent to truly practice Christianity because their languages and cultures were inherently incapable of articulating Christian concepts. Complained Jonathan Edwards: "The Indian languages are extremely barbarous and barren, and very ill fitted for communicating things moral and divine, or even things speculative and abstract. In short, they are wholly unfit for a people possessed of civilization, knowledge, and refinement." Consequently, missionaries, ministers, and the federal government all agreed that Native societies had to be transformed into the European model for Native peoples to be able to understand Christianity. One central civilizing tactic was the introduction of boarding schools in which Native children were forcibly taken from their homes to attend these schools on a full-time basis. Native children were forced to follow Christianity, thus depriving them of their traditional spiritual and cultural practices that were based on gender equality. In addition, the epidemic rates of violence against Native children in these schools contributed to the internalization of gender violence within Native communities.

The destruction of tribal governing strategies and their institutions (clans, societies, and councils) was also essential in reordering Native culture. The church has been instrumental in assimilating Native people to ensure their allegiance to colonial superiority and power. By the early 1820s, there was great pressure for Native people to assimilate and forget their traditions for the sake of peace. In order to receive federal recognition and protection, tribes were later required to develop democratic forms of government and to elect officials as dictated by the Indian Reorganization Act of 1934. After the new governmental bodies were established, positions of power went to men. Yet before this reorganization, women were renowned as warriors, chiefs, and healers. They kept the peace, made decisions to wage war and deal with captives, held council, selected chiefs, and spoke for their people.

Destruction of Tribal Land Systems

As the non-Native population expanded westward, there was nowhere to relocate Native people to make room for non-Native homesteads. In 1887, the Dawes Allotment Act sidestepped tribal authority, allotted reservation land in Indian Territory among individual Native families, and forced U.S. citizenship upon tribal groups, in exchange for opening the balance of most tribal land west of the Mississippi to non-Native settlement. In effect, the Dawes Act destroyed communally owned tribal lands and the traditional governance structures (although some tribes continued to function through these structures, they were generally not recognized by the United States). The gradual destruction of tribal governing and traditional institutions frequently made women's authority illegitimate and often undercut their social and political power. In addition, by individualizing landholdings, Native families became more isolated from each other. Such isolation then created the conditions by which violence and abuse thrive. That is, domestic violence happens more easily where the victim of violence is isolated from those who can intervene. Prior to colonization, violence against women was relatively rare in part because Native communities were so interconnected; it was difficult for abuse to happen without someone intervening in the situation. However, as Native families became more isolated from each other because of the Dawes Act, it became easier for men to abuse women without accountability.

Native people have seen their lands gradually stolen and their resources and economic livelihood dwindle. Moreover, they have been forced to change all strategies for maintaining their rituals, philosophy, and subsistence. Part of the church's goal to civilize Native people and make them more pliable involved encouraging them to take up lifestyles similar to colonists and settlers. This changed women's economic roles from farming production to domestic production. Without land and resources, Native women were deprived of their specialized role as agriculturists and often lost their right to participate in the tribe's government as well. These changes made Native women dependent on the male-dominated church for resources and economic assistance. In 1850, John Ross, an elected Cherokee leader, went on to establish the Cherokee Female Seminary. It was located at Park Hill in Indian Territory, which is now Oklahoma. The school became a principal tool for the Christian conversion, assimilation, and attempted subordination of Cherokee women and girls. In their new territory, the male-dominated Cherokee National Council sought to make their women over in the image and disposition of Caucasian Victorian women. Many tribes also became dependent on non-Native institutions as a means of survival. If survival demands male dominance as the primary and legitimate tradition or social value, submission to the laws and customs of the dominant culture and their religions becomes a factor in receiving assistance. Dan George, a former mission boarding school pupil and Coast Salish chief once stated, "The white man came and all he had was the Bible; now the white man has everything, and all the Indian has is the Bible" (Gizothe).

Erosion of Clan Structures

Eventually, men began to replace women as heads of clans in many tribes. Subsequently, men began to be elected to all political positions, resulting in the further domination of women. Additionally, many churches attempted to integrate Native women into white communities. The practice of intermarriage or forceful cohabitation allowed non-Native men to seek out relationships in powerful Native families, often with church blessings. Taking control of the Native wife's lands or other resources, the non-Native exploited the woman and her holdings for his benefit, sometimes killing her and selling her land. Also, the removal of women from the head of the family allowed for the disenfranchisement of women marrying non-Natives. In this way, the government would not have to recognize these women or their children as eligible for tribal and government benefits or other recognition. Furthermore, this strategy helped to silence women's voices as sources of authority and in passing on traditions and knowledge that would keep the culture and people alive.

Clearly, Christianity has been instrumental in the destruction and reformation of Native law and traditions. Because these traditions were based on gender equality, their erosion spelled the simultaneous erosion of Native women's status. However, many Native peoples are actively decolonizing their societies by restoring Native women to their rightful roles within Native communities.

Parallels in Other Countries

South American indigenous women experienced Christian control over their public and private lives in ways that mirror the experiences of Native women in the Northern Hemisphere. In order to fully examine the experience of Native women in America, one must take into account the experiences of Native women outside of current national boundaries. The traditional territories of Native people often overlap and were established long before the arrival of Europeans. Redrawing national boundaries has not changed the tribal status of aborigines or their widespread experience with colonialism and Christianity. For example, the traditional lands and social practices of Canadian aborigines extended beyond the borders established by non-Native governments. Today, the St. Regis Reservation extends over the U.S.-Canadian border into New York State. At one time, the Ojibwa stretched across Canada and the northern United States, from the Atlantic to the Pacific Oceans. Today, they are scattered between a few Canadian and U.S. reservations. They speak different dialects, but their experience under European patriarchy has been similar. In Canada, religious indoctrination was intense. The crusade for Christian converts among the aborigines was carried out with the same zeal. The denigration of women and their sexuality was apparent in long-standing misogynistic doctrines of the Catholic Church and in the Church's glorification of the virginity of Kateri Tekakwitha and Mary. Manuscripts and original accounts of priests in Canada detail their missionary work among Tekakwitha's Iroquois people and other Canadian aborigines. In later years, boarding schools, known as residential schools in Canada, functioned under the direction of Anglican, Catholic, Methodist, and Presbyterian denominations. As in the United States, physical and sexual abuse was widespread.

The invasion and conquest of Latin America occurred in the same historical period as that of North America. However, Pope Alexander VI decided that in the interest of Christianity, Native nations were to be overthrown and converted to the faith. In 1510, the Spanish developed a pre-battle document, called *The Requerimiento*, designed to notify Natives that they were about to be conquered and that it was their fault. In *The Requerimiento*, Native peoples were advised (in Spanish) that they must convert to Christianity or else the Spaniards had the divine right to kill them and take their lands. By 1511, Dominican Friars Antonio de Montesinos and Domingo de Betanzos questioned whether Native people were human, had souls, or should be allowed to receive holy sacraments. He and other mission friars claimed that Native people were subhuman beasts, incapable of being educated, or of accepting Catholicism.

Moreover, they held that God's plan for Native peoples was eventual extinction. Back in Spain, Franciscan Bishop Juan de Quevedo of Barcelona based his argument for Native people's inferiority on the Aristotelian theory that enslavement of inferior beings is natural and normal (Harjo, 20–21). These assumptions sanctioned the alienation of women and Native people and justified oppressive political institutions such as slavery and patriarchal dominance. Regardless of religious theorizing, large numbers of Native women throughout Latin America resisted colonization and ethnic cleansing. Anacaona, Janequeo, Fresia, Ambimany, Chisa, and other women served as warriors and leaders of resistance. Meanwhile, Spanish and Catholic missionaries introduced sexually charged notions of shame and honor. These concepts became racialized in the New World, mostly affecting women. Sexual honor relates to control of women's sexuality; thus in the public sphere, the social construct of public women permitted their sexual objectification. In the private sector, women were pushed toward domesticity and motherhood. Spanish concern with purity of blood was assured by controlling women's reproductive powers and offspring through religiously sanctioned marriage and the legitimacy of heirs among the dominant class. Regardless of the degree of assimilation demonstrated by Native people, many Spaniards and Church officials continued to view Natives as inferiors and potential slaves. Thus, European greed, in combination with religious fanaticism, allowed non-Natives to intensify misogynistic viewpoints, enslave, murder, and pillage throughout Latin America for several centuries.

The Conquistadors' pride, virility, and conquerer mentality became the foundation for the Latin masculine stereotype of machismo. *Marianismo* is a creed that arose from an absence of acceptable female role models in Latin American society. It is not to be mistaken for the cult of the Virgin Mary; rather, it is based on attributes associated with her. The essential character of *marianismo* is women's reproductive, life-giving abilities. It holds that women are semidivine, with moral and spiritual superiority to men. Because of this, women are seen to possess an inherent ability for humility and self-sacrifice. Other virtues are premarital chastity, patience, and submission to immediate male relatives. It is a direct contrast to the male stereotype of machismo. *Marianismo* attitudes and behaviors are thought to be found in all social classes of multiethnic Latin Americans.

Latin American Native groups experienced conversion pressures from both Catholics and Protestants. In Guatemala, the Mayans were removed and restricted to segregated communities, where they were both colonized by Spaniards and converted to Christianity by Catholic missions. As Mayan dissatisfaction with the co-

lonial government grew in the nineteenth century, Protestant missionaries began to receive state support, in spite of long-standing Catholic economic and political power. When the Jesuits were expelled in 1767, Mayan religion and traditions were revived in a patriarchal form. By the 1870s Protestantism had reshaped Mayan communities and culture. Mayan women found Protestantism acknowledged some degree of women's inherent spirituality. This allowed Mayan women to invoke gender stereotypes in order to manage problematic male behavior, like drunkenness and violence. Amidst years of subjugation, political upheaval, and economic depression, affiliation with new Protestant groups assisted Mayan women in regaining some autonomy.

Bolivia also engaged in a long history of suppression and religious conversion of Native people. By the early 1900s, the small, wealthy upper class and their subordinate officials ruled in close alliance with the Catholic Church. Ruthless suppression of non-Catholic beliefs and Native practices was common. Accordingly, urban migrants attempted some assimilation by adopting various aspects of the dominant culture while maintaining traditional beliefs. With the coming of Protestantism, churches helped aborigines to cope with the effects of social migration, poverty, and crisis-ridden communities. Even though Native women may play important roles in church women's organizations, they remain prohibited from careers or employment within the church. The kinship bonds Native women lose through migration and conformity to the Christian, patriarchal family model provide evidence of objectives to replace the female creator and wipe out the matriarchal clan structure. On the other hand, Native women have been empowered by strict evangelical rules that prohibit abusive male behavior. Evangelical denominations also seek to control male drunkenness and sexual harassment as shameful behavior. Thus, Puritanical attitudes demonstrated in many congregations are allowing women to develop greater self-esteem. Today, for example, many Quechua women in Bolivia and other countries are reclaiming their public voices and holding positions on town councils.

Clearly, there are parallels to be found among the experiences of aborigines in the United States, Canada, and Latin America. In spite of providing some support for women's concerns, Western religion has also played a predominant role in sabotaging Native women's autonomy. Conditions of colonization, ethnic prejudice, poverty, economic strife, and political chaos show that the cultural loss of aborigines is a reality and can be found among many reasons for conversion to the Catholic and Protestant faiths. Even when Christianity is found to be useful in domesticating men, converts (both male and female) are not necessarily loyal to the faith. Additionally, there seems to be some reluctance to admit that even though Native women may have attained some new version of authority and prestige, they have nevertheless experienced an erosion of their traditional autonomy through the influence of patriarchal religion.

Native Women's Response to Christianity

South American Native women experienced control over their public and private lives in ways that mirror the experiences of Native women in the Northern Hemisphere. In the early years, Native groups responded to missionaries in a variety of ways. Irate communities often expelled priests who jeopardized culture and security. However, Native people have always borrowed deities and rituals from neighboring groups, so Native peoples did not necessarily oppose all Christian practice and belief. There were many similarities between Catholicism, Protestantism, and Native beliefs. Common spiritual themes and honored biblical characters, like prophets and mothers, fit similar roles in Native traditions. Native beliefs in supernatural spirits also made it easier for them to relate to the concept of the Holy Spirit. Eventually, Christianity became an alternative resource for some aborigines. Some tribes turned to Christianity when their own traditions failed to protect them from the disease and famine resulting from contact with Europeans. Other Native people turned to various denominations for protection from the abuses of explorers, colonists, and settlers. Aborigines often hoped that alliances with missionaries would protect them from their enemies and further settlement of tribal lands. They listened to missionaries without being persuaded to convert. Regardless of the priests and ministers who strove to replace Native culture and religions, there were Dominican friars and Russian Orthodox monks and Protestant missionaries who were outraged by the exploitation of the aborigines. For example, in Mexico, the friars reformed the labor practices of Spaniards that enslaved the Aztec. Monks in the Pacific Northwest defended the Aleut and Tlingit, who were also virtually enslaved by Russian trappers and traders. Protestant sects sometimes evangelized while actively supporting the aborigines' rights to the land. Eventually, Native women discovered ways of using Christianity as a tool for resistance.

Although Christianity was damaging to Native women's status, it did offer a means of resistance through the use of celibacy as an alternative to marriage and motherhood. Native women were able to avoid undesirable husbands by taking vows of chastity. Kateri Tekakwitha may have been an example of this practice. Because of a smallpox epidemic in the 1600s, Tekakwitha's eyesight was weak. Her farming and other productive labor abilities would have been compromised by her visual problems. In her environment, women's labor was vital to survival. Tekakwitha would have had some difficulty fulfilling her role as a wife. Since men depended on women for sustenance, Tekakwitha's diminished capabilities would not have made her the best candidate for marriage. Thus, her suitors would not likely have been drawn from the men of best skill and behavior. So it is not surprising that she avoided the matchmaking attempts of her relatives and was recorded to have hidden in the fields to escape meeting her family's choice. By asserting a vow of chastity, she could co-opt the Christian virtues of virginity and purity as a reasonable means of removing herself from subjugation to a spouse.

Catherine Brown provides an early example of blended faith. As a Protestant convert in the early 1800s, she became another symbol of Christianity's civilizing power. However, Brown's interest in Christianity may have been misunderstood. Brown prayed, meditated, and fasted as a Christian. However, she did so in Cherokee fashion, alone and outdoors. Furthermore, she visited and prayed in places where traditional Cherokee sought spiritual guidance. Her evangelism may have been more an expression of her community orientation than an interest in her personal salvation. Among the Cherokee, community welfare was a religious and cultural concern. Moreover, Brown's attachment to her Christian sisterhood would have been an aspect of her heritage, considering the gender segregation in Cherokee society at that time. Choosing a mission community would have incorporated Brown back into a community at a time when Cherokee women were being excluded from the institutions of their own society. Even though she was sent away to school to take advantage of non-Native education, she remained connected to her family. Brown even accompanied her brother in a healing ritual as would be expected of her as a clan member. Regardless of her religious conversion, Brown remained connected to the traditional practices of her tribe.

Native people learned skills through education in mission schools. Adaptation to Christian lives and Euro-American standards helped some Native people to infiltrate colonial society and develop "civilized" reputations that allowed them to interact on some business and social levels. Native women were creative in adapting new forms of labor into their societies. As women's farming production gave way to Euro-American domestic practices of sewing and crafting, Native women began to produce goods for sale. For example, Iroquois beaded souvenirs in the form of small purses, pincushions, and other whimsical items became popular. Also, Cherokee quilts were highly prized. Income from the new pursuits offset farming as a means of food production. Other Native women engaged in less feminine labor, such as ranching, livestock trading, and the purchase of farming equipment. By the early 1900s, records show that Yakima women were more active in trading horses and cattle than the men. But conversion to Christianity, industriousness, and adoption of Euro-American culture failed to bring Native people acceptance among Euro-Americans or autonomy within their tribes. So Christianity was often discarded as a useless artifact of white society. The 1835 removal of Native people east of the Mississippi to land west of the Mississippi became a death march known as the Trail of Tears. Roughly 100,000 Natives in Michigan, Louisiana, and Florida were coerced and taken to Indian Territory by the military. Their land and possessions were confiscated, in spite of prior treaties. Thousands died along the trail. After removal and continued betrayal through abrogation of treaty rights, most Native people returned to their old religions and rituals.

In spite of the presence of some devoutly Christian aborigines, the majority have demonstrated a blended faith. Christianity has been seen as a white man's religion and essentially irrelevant to Native people. But just as missionaries once sought to transform Native society through Christianity, many aborigines have found methods of transforming Christianity and its symbols for application to Native society. Christian values like love, forgiveness, generosity, patience, and disapproval of aggression have become new resources in validation and support of similar Native traditions. Priests and ministers loosely fit roles as shamans. The story of the Virgin Mary and Saint Anne are used to support the importance of motherhood and the instillation of social values through child rearing. Crosses, stars, and crucifixes are worked into religiously significant Native designs. In effect, Christianity has become a tool for the reculturation of Native culture. The Methodist and Episcopal churches, for instance, have developed programs for ordaining women as ministers and priests. The Methodist church in particular has recognized an absence of Native clergy and has enacted plans to ordain Native peoples. There are also Christian organizations performing beneficial work in health care, domestic violence, education, substance abuse, and hunger. Misogyny and women's subordination still exist in Christian institutions and Native communities. But many Native communities have received valuable and appreciated services by Christian organizations to individuals and families. The results of these efforts have often produced positive outcomes on social and economic problems faced by Native people.

Thus, the relationship between Native women and Christianity is complex. Many Native women completely reject Christianity as a colonizing religion. Other women completely embrace Christianity and do not follow their traditional practices. Still other women practice both Christianity and their traditional spiritual beliefs. Even though it is clear that Christianity has negatively impacted their status, Native women have never simply acquiesced to Christian colonization. However, they have either resisted it or used it in various ways to support the sovereignty of Native peoples.

SOURCES: Historical perspectives on aboriginal women, their status, and the effects of European colonization upon gender relations can be found in Karen Anderson, *Chain Her by One Foot: The Subjugation of Native Women in Seventeenth Century New France* (1993); Carol Devins, *Countering Colonization: Native American Women and Great Lakes Missions, 1630–1900* (1992); and Nancy Shoemaker, ed., *Negotiators of Change: Historical Perspectives on Native American Women* (1995). Native American perspectives on colonial relationships are discussed in Robert Warrior, "A Native American Perspective: Canaanites, Cowboys, and Indians," in *Voices from the Margin: Interpreting the Bible in the Third World*, R. S. Sugirtharajah, ed. (1991), 277–285, and in *Who's the Savage?* David Wrone and Russell Nelson, eds. (1982). Essays on the roles of Native American women in Native tradition are found in Paula Gunn Allen, *The Sacred Hoop: Recovering the Feminine in American Indian Traditions* (1992). Research regarding the Native American response to Catholicism in the New World is detailed in Fernando Cervantes, *The Devil in the New World: The Impact of Diabolism in New Spain* (1994), and Rámon Gutíerrez, *When Jesus Came, the Corn Mothers Went Away: Marriage, Sexuality and Power in New Mexico, 1500–1846* (1991). Brenda Child, *Boarding School Seasons: American Indian Families, 1900–1940* (1998), and Devin Mihesuah, *Cultivating the Rosebuds: The Education of Women at the Cherokee Female Seminary, 1851–1909* (1993), both examine boarding schools' use of Christianity to promote sexism and racist ideology, as well as Native women's use of Christianity in resistance to domination. Quotation from Chief Dan George is discussed in Mardy Grothe, *Chiasmus in History and History in Chiasmus* at http://www.chiasmus.com/archive/msg00019.html. The cooperation between Protestant churches and the State and the subsequent impact on Native people is described in Robert H. Kellar, Jr., *American Protestantism and United States Indian Policy, 1869–82* (1983). Research on the views of the Catholic missionaries concerning Native people in Latin America are discussed in Maria Paz Harjo, "Religious Orders, the Indian and Conquest: Fifty Years of Dispute and Contradiction" in *Encounters* 9 (1992).

AMERICAN INDIAN BOARDING SCHOOLS
Andrea Smith

DURING THE NINETEENTH and into the twentieth century, American Indian children were forcibly abducted from their homes to attend Christian and U.S. government–run boarding schools as a matter of state policy. This system had its beginnings in the 1600s when John Eliot erected "praying towns" for American Indians where he separated Indians out from their communities to receive Christian "civilizing" instruction. However, colonists soon concluded that such practices should be targeted toward children because they believed adults were too set in their ways to become Christianized. Jesuit priests began developing schools for Indian children along the St. Lawrence River in the 1600s.

The boarding school system became more formalized under Ulysses S. Grant's Peace Policy of 1869–1870. The goal of this policy was to turn over the administration of Indian reservations to Christian denominations. As part of this policy, Congress set aside funds to erect school facilities to be run by churches and missionary societies. These facilities were a combination of day and boarding schools erected on Indian reservations.

Then, in 1879, the first off-reservation boarding school, Carlisle, was founded by Richard Pratt. He argued that as long as boarding schools were primarily situated on reservations, then (1) it was too easy for children to run away from school; and (2) the efforts to assimilate Indian children into boarding schools would be reversed when children went back home to their families during the summer. He proposed a policy where children would be taken far from their homes at an early age and not returned to their homes until they were young adults. By 1909 there were twenty-five off-reservation boarding schools, 157 on-reservation boarding schools, and 307 day schools in operation. The stated rationale of the policy was to "Kill the Indian and save the man." Over 100,000 Native children were forced into attending these schools. By 1926, 83 percent of Indian children were in U.S. government- and/or church-run schools.

Interestingly, Pratt was actually one of the "friends of the Indians." That is, U.S. colonists, in their attempt to end Native control over their landbases, came up with two general policies to address the "Indian problem." Some sectors advocated outright physical extermination of Native peoples. Meanwhile, the "friends" of the Indians, such as Pratt, advocated cultural rather than physical genocide. Carl Schurz, at that time a former commissioner of Indian Affairs, concluded that Native peoples had "this stern alternative: extermination or civilization" (Adams, 15).

When Pratt founded off-reservation boarding schools, he modeled Carlisle in Pennsylvania on a school he developed in Ft. Marion Prison, Florida, which held seventy-two Native prisoners of war. His strategy: Separate children from their parents, inculcate Christianity and white cultural values, and encourage/force them to assimilate into the dominant society. Attendance at these boarding schools was mandatory, and children were forcibly taken from their homes for the majority of the year. They were forced to worship as Christians and speak English (Native traditions and languages were prohibited). In addition, children were often forcibly separated from their siblings who were in the same school in order to disrupt familial bonds that might help preserve traditional practices and beliefs.

Economic Racism

Of course, because of racism in the United States, Native peoples could never really assimilate into the dominant society. Hence the consequence of this policy was to assimilate them into the bottom of the socioeconomic ladder of the larger society. For the most part, schools primarily prepared Native boys for manual labor or farming, whereas Native girls, according to the Indian Affairs Office, were to be "systematically trained in every branch of housekeeping" (Adams, 30). Children were also involuntarily leased out to white homes as menial labor during the summers rather than sent back to their homes. Indian girls learned such useful skills as ironing, sewing, washing, serving raw oysters at cocktail parties, and making attractive flower arrangements in order to transform themselves into middle-class housewives. As K. Tsianina Lomawaima points out, very few Native women were ever in a position to use these skills or become housewives. She states:

An economic rationale of placing Indian women in domestic employment does not account for the centrality of domesticity training in their education. An ideological rationale more fully accounts for domesticity training: it was training in dispossession under the guise of domesticity, developing a habitus shaped by the messages of subservience and one's proper place. (Lomawaima, 86)

The primary role of this education for Indian girls was to inculcate patriarchal norms and desires into Native communities so that women would lose their places of leadership in Native communities.

To further the assimilation process, Richard Pratt also instituted the "outing" system. Rather than return Indian children to their homes, the outing program placed them with a white family during the summer months, where they would perform either manual labor (boys) or domestic service (girls). The outing system was a microcosm of Pratt's greater vision for addressing the Indian "problem," which would have been to send every Indian child permanently to a white home. The idea of the outing system was to inculcate Victorian family ideals into Indian children. In practice, however, it became another form of slavery. Particularly in the West, children were often leased in gangs to work for farmers and ranchers under grueling working conditions. This practice of outing continued in another form after the boarding school era—child welfare agencies deemed Indian parents inadequate and turned over Indian children

During the nineteenth and into the twentieth century—as a matter of state policy—American Indian children were forcibly abducted from their homes to attend Christian and U.S. government–run boarding schools, such as this one in Tuba City, Arizona. *Courtesy of Cline Library, Northern Arizona University.*

to white foster care or adoptive homes. In 1978 Congress passed the Indian Child Welfare Act, which allows tribes to determine the placement of children taken from their homes. During the congressional hearings for this act, Congress reported that 25 percent of all Indian children were either in foster care, in adopted homes, or in boarding schools. In Minnesota, Indian children were 500 times more likely to be in foster care or adoptive care than non-Indian children; for South Dakota the rate was 1,600 times higher; for Washington, 1,900 times higher; and for Wisconsin, 1,600 times higher. Eighty-five percent of these foster care and adoptive homes were white. The hearings also found that the reasons children were taken from homes were often vague and generally ethnocentric. For instance, in North Dakota, physical violence was present in only 1 percent of the cases of children taken from their homes. Reasons that might be given for removal included children "running wild" (Congressional Hearings, Indian Child Welfare Act, 1978).

Medical Neglect and Starvation

U.S. policymakers' rationale for choosing cultural rather than physical genocide was often economic. Carl Schurz concluded that it would cost a million dollars to kill an Indian in warfare, whereas it cost only $1,200 to school an Indian child for eight years. Secretary of the Interior Henry Teller argued that it would cost $22 million to wage war against Indians over a ten-year period but would cost less than a quarter of that amount to educate 30,000 children for a year. Consequently, administrators of these schools ran them as inexpensively as possible. Children were overcrowded in these schools and given inadequate food and medical care. Furthermore, school staff had access to food of much better quality and in greater quantity than did the children. Disease epidemics frequently hit schools. For instance, in 1912, the U.S. Congress conducted a study that found that close to 70 percent of Indian children in Oklahoma boarding schools were diagnosed with trachoma. Compounding the health problems of Native children was that while they were denied access to Western medicine, they were also deprived of access to traditional forms of healing in their community.

As a result, children routinely died in mass numbers of starvation and disease. In addition, children were often forced to do grueling work in order to raise monies for the schools and salaries for the teachers and administrators. It is difficult, however, to ascertain the accurate death rate in boarding schools because schools only counted, at best, children who died in the schools. Oftentimes, if children appeared to be on the brink of death, they would be dismissed from school in order to lower the apparent death rate. In addition, survivors of boarding schools now testify to many mysterious deaths of children that were not accounted for. For instance, it was reported that at one school in the Plains area, children often heard the sounds of babies crying. Later, the school was demolished, and the skeletons of babies were discovered in the school walls (Oral Testimony of Boarding School Healing Project).

Violence

Sexual/physical/emotional violence was rampant in boarding schools. As one example in the Walker River Agency School in New York, the superintendent ordered ten girls to be publicly stripped to the waist and then flogged with a buggy whip as a result of a theft of a can of baking powder. Particularly brutalizing to Native children was the manner in which school officials involved children in punishing other children. For instance, in some schools, children were forced to hit other children with the threat that if they did not hit them hard enough, they themselves would be severely beaten (Oral Testimony of Boarding School Healing Project).

While sometimes perpetrators of the violence were held accountable, generally speaking, even when teachers were charged with abuse, boarding schools refused to investigate. In the case of just one teacher, John Boone at the Hopi school in Arizona, Federal Bureau of Investigation investigations in 1987 found that he had sexually abused over 142 boys but the principal of that school had not investigated any allegations of abuse (Goodbye BIA, 19). Despite the epidemic of sexual abuse in boarding schools, the Bureau of Indian Affairs did not issue a policy on reporting sexual abuse until 1987 and did not issue a policy to strengthen the background checks of potential teachers until 1989. While not all Native peoples see their boarding school experiences as negative, it is clear that much, if not most, of the current dysfunctionality in Native communities can be traced to the boarding school era.

This system was replicated in Canada in the form of the residential school system. Recently, the death toll of Native children in residential schools is reported to have run as high as 50,000. The list of offenses committed by church officials include murder by beating, poisoning, hanging, starvation, strangulation, and medical experimentation. Torture was used to punish children for speaking aboriginal languages. Children were involuntarily sterilized. In addition, in some areas, church clergy, police, and business and government officials were involved in maintaining pedophile rings using children from residential schools. The grounds of several schools were also found to contain unmarked graveyards of children who were murdered, particularly children killed after being born as a result of rapes of Native girls by priests and other church officials in the school (Fournier).

Native Children and "Hygiene"

Facilitating the rampant sexual violence that occurred at boarding schools were the practices in these schools that ideologically framed Native peoples as inherently dirty and impure. Children were forced to cut their hair, ostensibly because it was assumed they were lice infested. They often had their mouths washed out with soap if they spoke their Native languages. They were forced to clean their schools constantly such as by scrubbing bathrooms with toothbrushes. All these practices reinforced the notion that Native peoples were inherently unclean. As has been noted in writings on violence against Native women, the notion that Indian bodies are inherently dirty forms the justification for their sexual violation because such bodies are also seen as inherently rapable and violable. Only the rape of a body that is seen as clean counts as a rape in patriarchal societies (so, for instance, the rape of prostitutes is often not recognized as rape because they are viewed as inherently violable at all times). Consequently, colonizers were able to sexually violate the children in boarding schools with impunity.

Resistance

It is important to note that Native families did not simply acquiesce to this system. Parents frequently hid their children; sometimes entire villages refused to hand over their children. Government agents often responded by arresting the parents or withholding rations. Parents often assisted children in running away from school. When children returned home, communities would consciously undermine boarding school instruction by inculcating traditional teachings. Students also resisted boarding school indoctrination by running away from school, setting the school on fire, stealing, and other forms of defiance. Children ran away in significant numbers. For instance, about 130 children ran away from Chilocco Indian School, Oklahoma, in a four-month period in 1927; almost half of the children who were discharged from Carlisle Indian School in 1901 were runaways. At the Phoenix School, a group of Yavapai boys left the school and traveled 100 miles to their home without water or food and in freezing rain and snow (Adams).

Contemporary Boarding Schools

Today, most of the schools have closed down. Nevertheless, some boarding schools still remain. While the same level of abuse has not continued, there are still continuing charges of physical and sexual abuses in currently operating schools. In fact, in 2003, sixteen-year-old Cindy Gilbert Sohappy died while being held in a holding cell at Chemawa Indian School in Oregon. The investigation into her death is still pending.

Continuing Effects of Boarding School Policies

While not all Native people viewed their boarding school experiences as negative, it appears to be the case that, after the onset of boarding schools in Native communities, abuse becomes endemic within Indian families. For instance, Randy Fred (Tseshaht), a former boarding school student, says that children in his school began to mimic the abuse they were experiencing. After Father Harold McIntee from St Joseph's residential school on the Alkali Lake Reserve was convicted of sexual abuse in 1989, two of his victims were later convicted of sexual abuse charges. In Canada, a number of continuing effects as a result of residential schools have been documented, including physical and sexual violence perpetrated by survivors, under- or unemployment, depression, suicide, substance abuse, loss of language, and loss of cultural and spiritual traditions (Truth Commission). While some churches in Canada as well as the Canadian government have taken minimal steps toward addressing their involvement in this genocidal policy, the U.S. government and churches have not because there is not the same level of documentation of abuses. Similar continuing effects are currently in the process of being documented in the United States. Meanwhile, the United States has not instituted any policies that could address these effects, such as language and cultural revitalization programs, counseling and other healing services, or culturally sensitive economic development programs.

Gender and Boarding School Abuses

The continuing effects of boarding school polices are gendered in a number of ways. First, by mandating Christianity in schools, the U.S. government and church officials supplanted what were generally gender-egalitarian spiritual systems in indigenous communities with the patriarchal systems in Christianity. In addition, one of the values that colonizers attempted to instill in Native peoples was the concept of private property. In fact, the boarding school era coincided with the era of allotment in U.S.-Native relations. In 1887, Congress passed the Dawes Allotment Act, which divided tribal properties into individual allotments. Generally, the heads of household (men) received 160 acres of land, with everyone else receiving 80 acres. Remaining tribal lands (which was about 80 to 90 percent of the land) were then turned over to the U.S. government. Euro-Americans equated private property with civilization, and hence the division of tribal lands into private lands was integral to their "civilizing" mission. Many "friends of Indians" similarly argued that transforming the basis of Indian societies into monogamous nuclear families was critical to privatizing Native communities. With the monogamous marriage, Native women became then seen as the private property of their husbands.

Second, through the constant physical, emotional, and sexual violence committed against Native children, widespread domestic and sexual violence becomes internalized in Native communities. Native men begin to brutalize Native women and children in the same way they were brutalized in schools. Native counselors note that if one traces the genealogy of abuse and dysfunction in many, if not most, Native homes, the beginnings can often be traced to the first generation that attended boarding school. Interestingly, however, scholarship on U.S. boarding schools tends to minimize the gender violence that existed in boarding schools, particularly sexual violence. One reason may be that survivors are reluctant to talk about the abuse. However, this trend may be changing, as increasingly survivors are beginning to speak out more frequently about this violence.

Third, the education Native girls received did not prepare them for higher education; rather, it generally tracked them into domestic work and other stereotypical female work. At the same time, this type of work was devalued in the dominant society. While Native men and women may have traditionally engaged in gender-specific roles prior to colonization, these roles were accorded equal status. In boarding schools, girls were taught to engage in domestic work *and* were taught that their gender accorded them second-class status.

And fourth, boarding schools became an important avenue for white women to engage in civilizing missions in a manner that could elevate their status. As white women often had little power in society and were deemed subordinate to men, one way in which they could assert their power and influence was by engaging in civilizing work among people of color. Many white women were able to escape bonds of marriage or gain some measure of independence by working at boarding schools. Unfortunately, their independence was gained at the expense of Native peoples who were victimized by this process. Of course, the independence white women gained was only relative—women working in these schools were controlled by the men who ran the bureaucracy. In addition, women frequently suffered sexual harassment from their male coworkers.

Boarding Schools and Contemporary Indigenous Organizing

In 2003 a class-action suit was filed against the U.S. government. This case is largely based on violations of the "bad man clause" contained in certain treaties with U.S. tribes. This clause holds that if a "man" acting on behalf of the U.S. government harms Native peoples, and the injured parties complain to the United States with no redress, then they are entitled to redress. This case would only impact boarding school survivors who belong to tribes that have such clauses. In addition, these clauses only cover survivors who went to school on lands that are covered under the treaty *at the time it was written* and lived on those same lands as well. Thus, it is an important first step but does not cover most survivors of boarding school abuses.

An alternative approach to seeking redress for boarding school abuses in the United States is the Boarding School Healing Project (BSHP). The focus of this organization is a collective rather than individual remedy. Its four primary areas of work are:

Healing. Healing Native communities and individuals from the continuing effects of boarding school abuses.

Education. Educating non-Native communities about boarding school abuses and Native communities about the importance of healing from these same abuses.

Documentation. Documenting both the abuses perpetrated in boarding schools and the continuing effects of these abuses.

Accountability. Developing a movement for collective reparations from the U.S. government for boarding school policies.

What is unique about the BSHP is its feminist perspective on reparations struggles. That is, one of the human rights violations perpetrated by state policy in the forms of slavery and boarding schools has been sexual violence perpetrated by both slave masters and boarding school officials. However, the continuing effect of this human rights violation has been the internalization of sexual and other forms of gender violence *within* African

and Native American communities. Thus, the challenge is, Can affected communities form a demand around reparations for these types of continuing effects of human rights violations that are evidenced by violence *within* communities but are nonetheless colonial legacies? The question the BSHP raises for reparations activists is: How can an analysis be framed that recognizes gender violence as a continuing effect of human rights violations perpetrated by state policy for which the state needs to be held responsible?

SOURCES: There are numerous books that address the history of boarding schools. David Wallace Adams's *Education for Extinction* (1995) is perhaps the most thorough analysis of the U.S. boarding school system. It suffers, however, from an inadequate gender analysis. K. Tsianina Lomawaima's *They Called It Prairie Light* (1993) focuses on the Chiloco Indian School. While it has a well-developed gender analysis, its picture of boarding schools is colored by the fact that her research is drawn primarily from the Chiloco Alumni Association and thus is drawn primarily from those who are more likely to have a positive view of the school. The stories of those who ran away or did not survive are not as present in this narrative. Celia Haig-Brown's *Resistance and Renewal* (1988) provides a narrative of a Canadian residential school through interviews. Unlike the other two books, it more directly addresses gender violence, albeit briefly. The Truth Commission, an organization that conducted an inquiry in Canada, published a report on Canadian residential abuses in *Hidden from History: The Canadian Holocaust* (2001). Much of the current information on boarding school abuses is found in newspaper articles rather than books such as Suzanne Fournier's "Gatherers Mark School's Grim Litany of Death," *In the Province,* June 4, 1996. In the United States much information for this entry is based on oral testimony in the process of being collected through the Boarding School Healing Project.

APPROPRIATION OF NATIVE AMERICAN RELIGIOUS TRADITIONS
Andrea Smith

THE APPROPRIATION OF Native American spiritual/cultural traditions by white society has a long history in the United States—from colonists dressing as Indians during the Boston Tea Party to the Young Men's Christian Association (YMCA) sponsoring "Indian Guide" programs for youth. In contemporary society, this practice of "playing Indian" is particularly notable in the New Age movement in which American Indian spirituality, with its respect for nature and the interconnectedness of all things, is often presented as the panacea for all individual and global problems. An industry has developed around the selling of sweat lodges or sacred pipe ceremonies, which promise to bring individual and global healing. Supposed Indian spiritual leaders or those who claim to have been taught by Indian spiritual leaders sell books and records that purportedly describe Indian traditional practices so that anyone can be a practitioner of Native spiritual traditions.

These self-proclaimed spiritual leaders are commonly described as "plastic medicine (wo)/men." Some plastic medicine (wo)men make no claims to be indigenous but do make false claims about being mentored by a spiritual leader. One prominent example is Lynn Andrews, the author of several books, including *Medicine Woman* (1998) and *Jaguar Woman* (2002). She claims to have been mentored by a Cree medicine woman, Agnes Whistling Elk. However, her book contains a description of a hodgepodge of pan-Indian cultural practices, and no one by the name of Agnes Whistling Elk lives in the community Andrews claims to have visited. Some plastic medicine (wo)men actually claim to be indigenous, such as Brooke Medicine Eagle and Dhayani Yahoo, although the tribes in which they claim membership do not recognize them. And finally, some plastic medicine (wo)men actually are recognized members of a Native nation, but they do not have the authority within their tribe to act as a spiritual leader. One of the most famous such figures was Sun Bear, who became famous on the New Age lecture circuit but whose teachings were generally denounced by Native communities.

On the surface, it may appear that Native spiritual appropriation is based on a respect for Indian spirituality. Consequently, it often comes as a surprise to many non-Indians that Native communities have become increasingly vocal in opposing this appropriation. Of course, not all Native peoples have the same viewpoint on this issue, and in fact some are actively involved in this industry, but generally speaking, Native nations are becoming increasingly organized against the practices of spiritual appropriation. Most Indian activist groups have written position statements condemning the use of their cultural traditions by outsiders. Hopi, Cheyenne, and Lakota elders have also issued statements against it. One Oakland-based group named SPIRIT exists only to expose such thievery. Indian nations are even using the legal apparatus of intellectual property rights to file lawsuits against those who make a profit by stealing Indian culture.

One reason this conflict between those who appropriate Native religious traditions and Native communities arises is that many non-Indians often hold Christian assumptions about how all spiritual practices should operate. One common assumption is that indigenous religious traditions are proselytizing traditions—that is, Native spiritual leaders want non-Indians to know about and to practice Native spiritual traditions. In fact, however, Native traditions are linked to particular land ba-

Haunani-Kay Trask, Native Hawai'ian activist, argues that colonizers destroy the cultural base from which indigenous people resist colonization by commodifying it to meet Western consumerist needs. She terms the phenomenon "cultural prostitution." *Copyright © Christopher Brown.*

ses. Unlike Christianity, Native spiritualities depend on the land base that gave rise to them; they cannot easily be transplanted to another geographical area. Many ceremonies must be performed at specific locations.

Christian colonizers have had a much different relationship to the land than have Native people. Christians have often regarded the land as something to be controlled and subdued. Christian understandings of land are reflected in Genesis 1:28: "God blessed them, and God said to them, Be fruitful and multiply, and fill the earth and subdue it; and have dominion over the fish of the sea and over the birds of the air and over every living thing that moves upon the earth." Because Christian traditions have often regarded land simply as something for human use, land generally does not figure prominently in religious practice. By contrast, because Native peoples regard the land as their relative, they believe it is critical that land be respected ceremonially. Just as the land provides for the people so that they can live, so must the community care for the land ceremonially so that she can live. As a result, unlike Christianity, Native traditions are not proselytizing. Traditions are seen as applying specifically to the land base from which they arise; they do not apply to peoples from other lands.

Because Christianity is a proselytizing religion, its adherents generally attempt to "spread the Word" to as many potential followers as possible. The desire is to inform as many people as possible about the Christian religion so that individuals will want to convert to the faith. Also, because Christianity often emphasizes the individual believer's relationship to God, it is important that every individual understand the doctrines and practices of the faith. Native traditions, by contrast, often stress communal rather than individual practice. Consequently, it is not always necessary or even desirable for every member of a nation to engage in every ceremony or to have the same level of knowledge about the spiritual ways of a tribe. The reason is that all the members know that the spiritual leaders are praying for the well-being of the whole tribe. As Supreme Court Justice William Brennan once stated in his defense of Indian religion: "Although few tribal members actually made medicine at the most powerful sites, the entire tribe's welfare hinges on the success of individual practitioners" (Smith, i, 13).

Not only is it not always necessary for all members of a tribe to be equally knowledgeable about all ceremonies; because, as mentioned previously, the ceremonies only apply to the people of a specific land base, in many cases, ceremonial knowledge must be kept secret. Consequently, many tribes prohibit nontribal members from coming to their lands when ceremonies are performed. The New Age image of the all-wise shaman going on the lecture circuit to teach indigenous traditions to everyone is antithetical, then, to the manner in which Native traditions are actually practiced. To make these acts of spiritual appropriation even more problematic, most plastic medicine people charge for their services. True spiritual leaders do not make a profit from their teachings, whether it is through selling books, workshops, sweat lodges, or otherwise. Spiritual leaders teach the people because they have the responsibility to pass what they have learned from their elders to the younger generations. They do not charge for their services. In fact, they generally do not describe themselves as spiritual leaders at all. They are just simply known by the community as being one. To quote one Native activist, "If someone tells you they are a spiritual leader, they're not."

It might be easy to dismiss the appropriation of Native spiritual traditions as a petty annoyance. It might seem that even if those who appropriate Native traditions do so problematically, at least they have a sincere interest in Native communities. Many people think that the primary problem Native peoples face is ignorance; that is, non-Indians oppress Indians because they are ignorant about the value of Native cultures. Under this paradigm, if only non-Indians knew more about Indians, they would be nicer to them. Thus, even when attempts to know more about Indians are problematic, they are at least benevolently intended.

However, perhaps the primary reason for the continuing genocide of Native peoples has to do less with ignorance than with material conditions. Non-Indians continue to oppress Indians because Indians occupy land resources that the dominant society wants. The majority of energy resources in this country are on Indian land (LaDuke). The United States could not stop oppressing Indian people without fundamentally challenging its own hegemonic position or multinational capitalist operations. If we frame Native genocide from a materialist perspective, then we have to rethink our analysis of ignorance about Native cultures on the part of non-Natives. This ignorance becomes a willful ignorance. The larger society will never become educated about non-Indians because it is not in their economic interest to do so. Thus, these efforts to appropriate Native traditions seem less than benevolent in their intent and effects.

As mentioned previously, Native spiritualities are land based—they cannot exist without the land base from which they originate. When Native peoples fight for cultural/spiritual preservation, they are ultimately fighting for the land base that grounds their spirituality and culture. In addition, Native religions are practice rather than belief centered. Christianity, for instance, is generally defined by belief in a certain set of doctrinal principles about Jesus, the Bible, and so on. Evangelical Christianity holds that one is "saved" when one professes belief in Jesus Christ as one's Lord and Savior.

Native traditions, by contrast, are practice centered; that is, what is of primary importance is not so much the ability to articulate belief in a certain set of doctrines as taking part in the spiritual practice of one's community. Thus, it may be more important that a ceremony be done correctly than for everyone in that ceremony to know exactly *why* everything must be done in a certain way. As Vine Deloria (Dakota) notes, from a Native context, religion is "a way of life" rather than "a matter of the proper exposition of doctrines" (Deloria, 16). Even if Christians do not have access to church, they continue to be Christians as long as they believe in Jesus. Native spiritualities, by contrast, may die if the people do not practice the ceremonies, even if the people continue to believe in their power.

Native communities argue that Native peoples cannot be alienated from their land without suffering cultural genocide. This argument underpins (although usually to no avail) many sacred sites cases before the courts. Most rulings do not recognize the difference between belief- and practice-centered traditions or the significance of land-based spiritualities. For instance, in *Fools Crow v. Gullet*, the Supreme Court refused to overturn a lower court ruling (1983) against the Lakota who were trying to halt the development of additional tourist facilities. The ruling declared that this tourism was not an infringement on Indian religious freedom because although it would hinder the ability of Lakota to *practice* their beliefs, it did not force them to relinquish their beliefs. For the Lakota, however, hindering the practice of traditional beliefs destroys the belief system itself. Consequently, the Lakota and Native nations in general argue that cultural genocide is the result when Native land bases are not protected.

When we disconnect Native spiritual practices from their land bases, we undermine Native peoples' claim that the protection of the land base is integral to the survival of Native peoples and hence undermine their claims to sovereignty. This practice of disconnecting Native spirituality from its land base is prevalent in a wide variety of practices of cultural and spiritual appropriation, from New Agers claiming to be Indian in a former life to Christians adopting Native spiritual forms to further their missionizing efforts. The message is that anyone can practice Indian spirituality anywhere. Hence there is no need to protect the specific Native communities and the lands that are the basis of their spiritual practices.

In addition, the assumption that Native knowledge is for the taking has fueled multinational corporations' continued assault on indigenous knowledges. Because current intellectual property rights law only respects individual ownership and not community ownership of cultural property, nonindigenous entrepreneurs have been able to gather knowledge about indigenous plants,

medicines, music, and other forms of cultural knowledge because this knowledge is legally understood as "public" property. These individuals are then legally empowered to gain individual patents for these forms of indigenous knowledge and thus profit from it. As Laurie Whitt describes in the case of indigenous music:

> While others are free to copy the original indigenous song with impunity, were someone to attempt to copy the "original" copy (now transformed into the legally protected individual property of a composer who has "borrowed" it from the indigenous "public domain"), he or she would be subject to prosecution for copyright infringement. This includes any members of the indigenous community of the song's origin who cannot meet the requirement of "fair use." (Whitt, 151; also see Greaves)

The genocidal impact of this appropriation is clear in indigenous struggles to protect sacred sites. Many white New Agers mistakenly think that Indian people want to share traditional practices with non-Indians because they assume Indian traditions are proselytizing traditions. Consequently, they flock to Indian sacred sites, prevent Indian people from accessing their own sites, and destroy its habitat. They have the notion that Indian sacred sites are somehow "magic" places that can fill them with spiritual enlightenment. Despite pleas from Indian communities to leave their traditions in peace, non-Indians flock to sacred areas for quick spiritual fixes. In doing so, they ironically take part in destroying the religious practices of Indian people that they claim to embrace.

Thus, as Rayna Green argued in her germinal essay "The Tribe Called Wannabee," the long history of white people "playing Indian" is the practice of genocide. At the same time that whites have committed acts of genocide against Native communities, they appropriate what they see as Indian culture in order to fashion themselves as the true inheritors of "Indianness," now that real Indians have supposedly disappeared. After all, the assumption that a community can and should take on the cultural practices of another community rests on the presupposition that the community in question is no longer intact or able to practice their traditions themselves. In addition, becoming "Indian" often becomes the way even progressive whites attempt to disassociate themselves from their whiteness. By opting to "become Indian," they can escape responsibility and accountability for white racism. Of course, whites want to become only partly Indian. They do not want to be part of Native peoples' struggles for survival against genocide, and they do not want to fight for treaty rights or an end to substance abuse or sterilization abuse. They do not want to do anything that would tarnish their romanticized notions of Indianness.

Furthermore, the relationship between indigenous communities and the dominant society that wants to know more about them is structured by colonialism. Haunani-Kay Trask, Native Hawaiian activist, argues that colonizers destroy the cultural base from which indigenous people resist colonization by commodifying it to meet Western consumerist needs. She terms the phenomenon "cultural prostitution."

> "Prostitution" in this context refers to the entire institution that defines a woman (and by extension the "female") as an object of degraded and victimized sexual value for use and exchange through the medium of money. . . . My purpose is not to exact detail or fashion a model but to convey the utter degradation of our culture and our people under corporate tourism by employing "prostitution" as an analytical category. . . . The point, of course, is that everything in Hawai'i can be yours, that is, you the tourist, the non-Native, the visitor. The place, the people, the culture, even our identity as a "Native" people is for sale. Thus, Hawai'i, like a lovely woman, is there for the taking. (Trask, 185–194)

In Trask's model, exchanges between Native and non-Native cultures are governed by the interests of non-Natives. Natives are there to meet the needs of non-Native peoples regardless of the impact on indigenous communities. Many white New Agers continue this practice of destroying Indian spirituality. They trivialize Native American practices so that these practices lose their spiritual force, and they have the white privilege and power to make themselves heard at the expense of Native Americans. Native voices are silenced, and consequently, the younger generation of Indians who are trying to find their way back to the Old Ways become hopelessly lost in this morass of consumerist spirituality.

These practices also promote the subordination of Indian women to the needs of those from the dominant society. Natives are told that we are greedy if we do not choose to share our spirituality. It is presumed to be our burden to service white people's needs rather than to spend time organizing within our own communities. White peoples' perceived need for warm and fuzzy mysticism takes precedence over our need to survive.

It is particularly sad when this kind of colonial practice is perpetuated by white feminists in their efforts to heal from the wounds of patriarchal violence. They do not consider how such practices may hinder Native women from healing as well. Native counselors generally agree that a strong cultural identity is essential if Native people are to heal from abuse. This is because a Native woman's healing entails healing not only from any personal abuse she has suffered but also from the patterned history of abuse against her family, her nation, and the environment in which she lives (Justine Smith [Cherokee], personal conversation, February 17, 1994). When white women appropriate Indian spirituality for their own benefit, they continue the pattern of abuse against Indian cultures. The one thing that has maintained the survival of Indian people through 500 years of colonialism has been the spiritual bonds that keep us together. When the colonizers saw the strength of our spirituality, they tried to destroy Indian religions by making them illegal. From the point of contact, European colonizers theologically rationalized the conquest of Indian lands by the fact that Indian people were not Christian. Since then, American Indian religions have never benefited from the First Amendment's protections of free exercise of religion. Particularly during 1880–1930, the U.S. government pursued policies intended to destroy Native spiritual practices. In the 1800s, the government placed entire reservations and Indian nations under the administrative control of church denominations in an effort to Christianize and civilize them. The motto: "Kill the Indian to save the child." Interior Secretary Henry M. Teller ordered an end to all "heathenish dances" in 1882. Two years later, the Bureau of Indian Affairs (BIA) mandated thirty days' imprisonment for Indians who participated in traditional rituals. Indian males were also required to cut their braids. Also in 1890, Sioux Ghost Dance worshippers were slaughtered at Wounded Knee. In 1892, the BIA outlawed the Sun Dance religion and banned other ceremonies. Indians were made citizens in 1927, but the outright ban on the right to worship was in effect until 1934 during John Collier's reforms in BIA policies during Franklin D. Roosevelt's presidency.

The colonizers recognized that it was our spirituality that maintained a spirit of resistance and sense of community. Even today, Indians do not have religious freedom: In recent rulings, *Lyng v. Northwest Indian Cemetery Protective Association,* 485 U.S. 439 (1988), and *Employment Division v. Smith,* 494 U.S. 872 (1990), the Supreme Court has determined that American Indians are not protected under the First Amendment. Thus, ironically, the dominant society appropriates Native religious traditions while denying Native communities themselves from practicing these traditions.

This exploitation has a specific negative impact on Native peoples' ability to heal from abuse. Shelley McIntyre, formerly of the Minneapolis Indian Women's Resource Center, complains that Native women who try to heal from abuse have difficulty finding their rootedness in Native culture because all they can find is Lynn Andrews and other such "plastic medicine wo/men" who masquerade as Indians for profit (Personal conversation, 1993). It is unfortunate that as many white women attempt to heal themselves from the damage brought on by Christian patriarchy, they are unable to do so in a way that is not parasitic on Native women. They continue the practice of their colonial fathers who sought paradise in Native lands without regard for the peoples of these lands.

Spiritual practices that are healing to Native peoples are not only appropriated in the dominant society but sexually colonized as well. As Will Roscoe notes, colonizers have a long history of attempting to document what they see as sexual perversity in Native ceremonies in order to suppress them. He points to the efforts to undermine John Collier's attempts to protect Native religious freedom in the Southwest through the spread of rumors "that Zuni men and women imitated sodomy in a dance, that boys and girls were put together for unrestricted sexual intercourse; that the Taos Indians sacrificed two boys per year" (Roscoe, 187). Coupled with this horror of sexual perversity deemed to be taking place in Native ceremonies is this incessant desire of whites to know as many details as possible about Native sexuality. Roscoe reports that William Johnson, former special officer of the Indian Office, in his desire to spread "knowledge" about Indians to as many as possible,

> wrote a letter to the *New York Times* in 1924 attacking John Collier's policies by charging that boys and girls returned from Government schools are stripped naked and herded together entirely nude and encouraged to do that very worst that vileness can suggest; that at Zuni little girls were debauched in these dances; that Indian mothers, wives and daughters [are] ravished before hundreds of yelling, naked savages; and that little girls, too young and tender to be ravished, have been whipped naked until their little bodies were bruised and covered with purple welts . . . and Indian boys were being withdrawn from government schools for a two years' course in sodomy under pagan instructors. (Roscoe, 188)

This historical correlation between Native spirituality and sexual exploitation continues into contemporary attitudes about Native people, as seen in columnist Andy Rooney's description about Native spiritual traditions. They involve "ritualistic dances with strong sexual overtones [which are] demeaning to Indian women and degrading to Indian children" (Rooney, *Chicago Tribune,* March 4, 1992). Along similar lines, Mark and Dan Jury produced a film titled *Dances: Sacred and Profane* (August 1994) that advertised that it "climaxes with the first-ever filming of the Indian Sundance ceremony." This so-called ceremony consists of a white man, hanging from meat hooks in a tree, praying to the "Great White Spirit," and is then followed by C. C. Sadist, a group that performs sadomasochistic acts for entertainment (Lockhart, 10).

Self-described Cherokee porn star Hyapatia Lee directs a pornographic film framed as a documentary on *Native American Love Techniques* (1991). The film begins with the words "Each of the girls is of Cherokee ancestry with teachings offered to all people." Each scene depicts one of these "Cherokee" girls copulating with a white man. Lee offers a narrative preface to these scenes: "I'm mostly Cherokee Indian. I was taught to worship nature and honor my traditional religion. They knew [past tense] how connected everything is."

The film then attempts to transform Native cultural/spiritual traditions into pornography. For instance, one scene begins with Lee expounding, "Because we don't see ourselves as superior to animals, we can learn from them," which is followed by a couple having sex "doggystyle." Other scenes depict couples smudging each other or smoking a pipe before engaging in sex. In one scene we are informed, "The Indian culture teaches us the medicine path." Viewers are then called to "honor the four directions, more commonly known as 69."

Further trivializing women's status in Native communities, one scene begins with a talk about how Native communities respected women and men equally. "Father Sky wraps around Mother Earth." "Christians," continues Lee, "don't understand women's power"—at which point the woman proceeds to perform oral sex. Thus, symbolically the equality of men and women in Native societies is subordinated to the dominance of white men.

Finally, after repeated scenes of various pornographic sexual acts, the "documentary" ends with: "We hope this will be helpful for all our Anglo brothers. The teachings are meant for all. They are meant to keep us on the sacred path." In this conclusion, we see how "knowledge" about Native communities is explicitly tied to sexual exploitation. Native communities have no boundaries, psychic or physical, that the dominant society is bound to respect. What Native peoples have and know are not under their control; it must be shared with all, particularly our "Anglo brothers."

Thus, Native communities, in which violence against women was relatively rare, become depicted as hotbeds of abuse and violence. This reversal becomes internalized within Native communities themselves. This trend is evident in the proliferation of plastic medicine men who are often notorious for sexually abusing their clients in fake Indian ceremonies. Jeffrey Wall was recently sentenced for sexually abusing three girls while claiming this abuse was part of American Indian spiritual rituals that he was conducting as a supposed Indian medicine man ("Shaman Sentenced," A2). David "Two Wolves" Smith and Alan Campnhey "Spotted Wolfe" were also charged for sexually abusing girls during supposed "cleansing" ceremonies (Melmer, 1).

Bonnie Clairmont, a Ho-Chunk based in St. Paul, Minnesota, is doing groundbreaking work in bringing attention to the sexual exploitation that is done by those claiming to be spiritual leaders. Unfortunately, not all these spiritual leaders are obvious wannabees; some are Native men who do have respect in their community. Because she has not been afraid to denounce this kind of violence, she has been widely criticized, but she continues to hold conferences and speak out on abuses. At one conference that she co-organized, one elder made the interesting point that the New Age movement has had a large part in creating conditions ripe for sexual exploitation within "traditional" spiritual ceremonies. That is, the New Age movement promises the quick-fix solution by the all-knowing and all-powerful shaman. As a result, people seeking guidance learn to surrender their authority to these so-called leaders and learn not to listen to the warning signs when their boundaries are violated. This leader concluded, "I am no one special. When you come to see me, don't leave behind your common sense." The fact that legitimate spiritual leaders have been forced to issue statements proclaiming that "no ceremony requires anyone to be naked or fondled during the ceremony" (Michael Pace, in Melmer, 1) signifies the extent to which the colonial discourse attempts to shift the meaning of Indian spirituality from something healing to something abusive. A site that is a mode of resistance becomes yet another site of sexual violation.

Respecting the integrity of Native people and their spirituality does not mean that there can never be cross-cultural sharing. However, such sharing should take place in a way that is respectful to Indian people. The way to be respectful is for non-Indians to become involved in our political struggles and to develop an ongoing relation with Indian *communities* based on trust and mutual respect. When this happens, Indian people may invite a non-Indian to take part in a ceremony, but it will be on Indian terms.

It is also important for non-Indians to build relationships with Indian communities rather than with specific individuals. Many non-Indians express their confusion about knowing who is and who is not a legitimate spiritual teacher. The only way for non-Indians to know who legitimate teachers are is to develop ongoing relationships with Indian communities. When they know the community, they will learn who the community respects as its spiritual leaders. This is a process that takes time.

While it is often easier to see the problematics of spiritual appropriation in New Age circles, it is also important to examine how these practices are replicated within academic circles as well. Academics assume that if they want to study Native communities, the communities must want that as well. The assumption that knowledge about Indians is inherently positive undergirds academic treatments of Native religious tradition. As Cree historian Winona Wheeler (Stevenson) notes: Western-based academics places a high-value on procuring "knowledge" or the "truth" as a goal in and of itself. By contrast, she argues, within Native communities, knowledge does not confer the right to communicate that knowledge to outsiders:

One of the major tenets of Western erudition is the belief that all knowledge is knowable. In the Cree world all knowledge is not knowable because knowledge is property in the sense that it is owned and can only be transmitted by the legitimate owner. . . . You can't just go and take it, or even go and ask for it. Access to knowledge requires long-term commitment, apprenticeship and payment. As a student of oral history, in the traditional sense, there is so much I have heard and learned yet so little I can speak or write about, because I have not earned the right to do so. I cannot tell anyone or write about most things because it has not been given to me. If I did it would be theft. So I'll probably be an Old Lady before I am allowed to pass it on. By then, I'll have learned all those rules of transmission and will probably feel impelled to keep it in the oral tradition and not write it down. (Stevenson, 11–12)

Researchers presume that Native communities support their quest to know more about them. As a result, researchers have not often asked the questions, "Do Native people want others to know about them?" or "Do Native communities find this research helpful to them?" Tired of these colonial practices, tribal communities are placing tighter restrictions on what information can be provided to outsiders. Many are developing protocols regarding research of any kind to be done in their communities. For example, at a 1998 conference on biopiracy held at the Salish/Kootenai College in Montana, representatives from the tribal community reported that a researcher visited their reservation, reporting that he had been given a grant to study them—although he had not shared his research proposal with the community before he received funding. The tribal council called the agency who funded this individual and convinced the agency to redirect its funds to the tribe so that it could conduct its own research.

Most people studying Native religions (hopefully) do so to support Native communities; however, as Wheeler's statement informs us, we have inherited a colonial model of teaching, researching, and learning that undermines these efforts. There is often a very sharp disjunction between the way Native people learn spiritual knowledge in their communities and the learning models we use in teaching college classes. Within the community, one always hears elders say, "If you want to learn, be quiet and pay attention." Only through being part of the community over a period of time and developing trust does the knowledge come to you, and even then it comes very slowly. Meanwhile, in the classroom setting, we are encouraged to present the information very quickly and completely so that students can learn it for an exam. Consequently, we promote the misperception that Native traditions are learned quickly, easily, and outside of a community context. It is important to start imagining pedagogies that might more closely resemble indigenous methods of learning.

I would like to close with an Ojibwe story I was told to share with others because it hints at such an alternative approach:

A young man went to an elder and said he wanted to know more about the traditions behind rock paintings. The elder said fine and told him to meet him the next day. After they met up, the elder put him to work for several hours in tending to these paintings. Afterward, the elder talked to the young man for a little while about their significance but would then send him on his way and tell him to return the next day. When the young man returned, the same thing happened—the elder would repeat the same process, only talking to him a little at the end of the day, then send him on his way. This practice went on for awhile, when finally the young man became very irritated with the elder. "I'm not stupid," he said to the elder. "You can tell me more than you're telling me at one time. I'll be able to understand what you're saying." To this, the elder replied, "I know you're not stupid and that if I told you more, you would understand. However, it is not enough for you to understand the traditions—you must learn how to respect them."

SOURCES: Works that provide a critical analysis of spiritual appropriation and cultural appropriation include Rayna Green, "The Tribe Called Wannabee," *Folklore* 99 (1988): 30–55; Philip Deloria's *Playing Indian* (1998); Laurie Anne Whitt, "Cultural Imperialism and the Marketing of Native America," in *Natives and Academics: Researching and Writing about American Indians*, ed. Devon Mihesuah (1998); Tom Greaves, ed., *Intellectual Property Rights for Indigenous Peoples: A Sourcebook* (1994), Haunani-Kay Trask, *Notes from a Native Daughter* (1993); and Vine Deloria, Jr., *God Is Red* (1993). Some works that focus on issues of Native Americans and Indian Religious Freedom include Jace Weaver, ed., *Native American Religious Identity* (1998) and Andrea Smith, *Sacred Sites, Sacred Rites* (1999). See also Vine Deloria, "A Native American Perspective on Liberation," *Occasional Bulletin of Missionary Research* 1 (July 1977): 16. Winona LaDuke, "A Society Based on Conquest Cannot Be Sustained," in *Toxic Struggles*, ed. Richard Hofrichter (1993), 98–106. Jim Lockhart, "AIM Protests Film's Spiritual Misrepresentation," *News from Indian Country*, Late September 1994. David Melmer, "Sexual Assault," *Indian Country Today* 15 (April 30–May 7, 1996). Andy Rooney, "Indians Have Worse Problems," *Chicago Tribune*, March 4, 1992. Will Roscoe, *The Zuni Man-Woman* (1991). "Shaman Sentenced for Sexual Abuse," *News from Indian Country*, Mid-June 1996. Winona Stevenson, "'Every Word Is a Bundle': Cree Intellectual Traditions and History" (unpublished paper, 1998). Ongoing debates about spiritual appropriation can be found in Native newspapers.

RELIGIOUS EXCHANGE IN AFRAMERINDIAN LIFE
Patrick Neal Minges

THE FIRST RECORDED encounter between Africans and Indians in the southeastern United States was that of the "Queen" of the Cofitachiqui people and a "slave of Andre de Vasconcelas" who accompanied sixteenth-century explorer Hernando de Soto. Even though she offered de Soto her "sincerest and purest goodwill," he imprisoned her and forced her to lead his expedition into the interior coastlands in search of gold (Jameson, 172). As they approached the "province of Chalaque," she escaped and took with her a group of runaway slaves from the expedition. The queen and the slave of Andre de Vasconcelas fled to the mountains of North Carolina, where it was "very very sure that they lived together as man and wife and were to go together to Cutafichiqui" (172). They soon made their way to the village of Cofitachiqui on the banks of the Savannah River near Silver Bluff, South Carolina. There they began a new life together, and their children would form the core of a new Aframerindian community in what would become "a very celebrated place" (Bartram, 199).

This first contact between the Spanish conquistador and the Yuchi queen was perhaps an unusual one on the colonial frontier, but the encounter between the slave and the "Beloved Woman" was not at all unprecedented. As the traditional leader within what the colonists would later come to call a "government of petticoats," it was her responsibility to decide the fate of those captured in conflict. Her "voice was considered that of the Great Spirit, speaking through her"; and with the wave of her hand, a person could meet imminent death (Foreman, 7). Just as she had the power of death, the Beloved Woman could also bestow the gift of life

Sarah Lue Bostick's (1868–1948) paternal grandfather was a Native American, probably a Choctaw, and her paternal grandmother was an African American. African Americans and other persons of color participated in the Disciples of Christ tradition from its beginning, but found their activities within the tradition severely limited. *Courtesy of Disciples of Christ Historical Society, Nashville, Tennessee.*

and demand that the person be adopted into the clan structure of the community to replace the lives of those lost in battle. In addition, the captors could take these persons back to their home and force them into a life of servitude to the community without the bonds of clan; these were the "persons without a place."

To exist without the ties of kinship within nations of the American Southeast such as the Cherokee or the Mvskoke was to be without identity; one existed outside the sacred order. Indigenous culture found expression within a tapestry of structured relationships woven together to create a beloved community rooted in a harmonious balance of interdependent actors and activities. For Keres/Cherokee literary scholar Paula Gunn Allen, the concept of kinship is critical to the traditional worldview:

> The American Indian sees all creatures as relatives (and in tribal systems relationship is central), as offspring of the Great Mystery, as cocreators, as children of our mother, and as necessary parts of an ordered, balanced, and living whole. . . . This concept applies to what non-Indian Americans think of as the supernatural, and it applies to the more tangible (phenomenal) aspects of the universe. . . . The circle of being is not physical, but it is dynamic and alive. It is what lives and moves and knows, and all life forms we recognize—animals, plants, rocks, winds—partake of this greater life. (Allen, 60)

This sacred order of relationships extended beyond the human community to the bear, the turtle, the moon, and the savannah. All relationships within the natural order were coexistent and codependent; the harmony within any particular community reflected the basic structure of the universe.

To live one's life on the periphery of the community was the plight of the "person without a place." Yet even the person without a place was cared for within the perimeter of the "sacred hoop" in order to preserve the dynamically interconnected network of mutuality that made up what were known as the "old ways." Key elements in the old ways of traditional culture were communal ties to the land, shared responsibility for the working of that gift, and the communal distribution of the proceeds from such. As primary responsibility for

agricultural production rested with women, they maintained an economic system rooted in the well-being of the community. The good of the people relied on the ability of each to contribute to the shared effort, so even the disadvantaged were provided for within the social network. Even the weakest link was still a critical part of the beloved community.

However, the arrival of colonists from Europe in the early seventeenth century introduced the Indians of the American Southeast to a new kind of social relationship. These strangers declared themselves superior to the original inhabitants of the land and claimed divine right to all that belonged to the Native peoples, including their very person. When the vast riches they had envisioned were not readily available, the invaders seized the indigenous peoples and made them a commodity on the open market. Caravans of slaves trekked from the interior forests to the coastlands of the Atlantic, where dark and disease-ridden carriers made the middle passage to the West Indies or New England where a life of servitude awaited the captives. By the end of the seventeenth century, the Indian slave trade eclipsed the trade for furs and skins and became the primary source of commerce between Europe and the southeastern colonies. Fueled by the passion for material goods, indigenous nations were set against each other in an orgy of slave dealing that decimated the economic, political, and social structures of traditional societies. It was indeed a new world.

In 1619, a different kind of settler landed at Portsmouth, Virginia; indentured servants from Africa arrived as part of a fledgling project to finance the colonial mission. When these Africans had worked off their period of indenture, they fled from the population centers and sought out those persons most like themselves with whom they could settle. Among the indigenous peoples of southeastern Virginia, these Africans found persons who shared a culture similar to their own—one rooted in a sacred relationship to the subtropical coastlands of the middle Atlantic. Within the nexus of this new community, a unique synthesis grew in which African and Indian people shared a common religious experience. They forged ties of kinship and bonds of community into a culture that would forever change the spiritual landscape of the southeastern colonies.

There were, indeed, great affinities between West African traditional religions and those of the indigenous peoples of the American Southeast. In fact, it is perhaps erroneous to speak of West African traditional religion as if it were a singular entity existing outside of social and cultural contexts. Within these traditions, the existence of the sacred permeates all planes of existence; there is no clear-cut distinction between the sacred and secular, the religious and the nonreligious, the spiritual and the material. Wherever Africans are, they carry with them an appreciation of the sacred relationship with the place in which they find themselves and the active forces that shape their immediate environment. However, this relationship often finds its most profound expression within a particular place and among a certain people; in some places where the connection between the people and their environment has extended over thousands of years, a powerfully reverential relationship is established. As each person respected their own ties to land and to community, they also respected these same traditions within other peoples and communities. In this, the indigenous peoples of Africa and North America found common ground.

Africans and Indians each emphasized the circle of life—both with the environment and within one's community; each stressed the importance of sacred order and the power of ritual to affect and overcome disorder. Both attached great significance to kinship in their social organization, and each was rooted in a communal economy based on subsistence agriculture. As John Mbiti notes, traditional societies in Africa thrived on a structured system of interrelationships: "[T]he ideal for them has been . . . conformity to the life led by one's fellows, seeking to gain little or no wealth or position in a carefully egalitarian world where personal gain above the level of the accepted norm would be a source of unhap-

piness or danger, since exceptional achievement could be only at the expense of one's neighbors" (Mbiti, 267).

Therefore, many of these new African immigrants to the Southeast found a home among the Mvskoke, Cherokee, and Powhatan peoples in places such as Galphintown, Kituwah, and Weyanoke. As these societies were primarily matrilineal, Africans who married indigenous women often became members of their spouses' clan and citizens of the respective nation. The seventeenth-century trade in Indian slaves created great numbers of enslaved women; many of these Native women took enslaved Africans as their partners. By the early years of the eighteenth century, the number of Indian slaves in the Carolinas was nearly half that of African slaves. J. Leitch Wright suggests that the presence of so many women slaves from the southeastern nations where gynarchy was the norm helps to explain the prominent role of women in slave culture (148). As these relationships grew, the lines of racial distinction began to blur, and the evolution of black/Indian people began to pursue its own course. The cultures intertwined in complex ways in the colonial Southeast, and the emerging Aframerindian culture reflected the blending of these two peoples.

Based on their observations of the world around them, indigenous peoples built their societies and cultures to resemble the processes of the natural world. The people measured time not in the linear sense, but cycles were counted according to responsibilities entailed in the sacred relationships or as significant events that fell outside the ordinary. Lunar calendars such as the Ishango Bone from the Congo recorded the planting moon, the drying grass moon, and the harvest moon; ceremonial feasts and festivals corresponded to certain times, and community dances and rituals affirmed the continuity of all life. Elders becoming ancestors kept passage of time, and new births bespoke the promise of future generations with naming rituals paying respect to the continuity of life. Cherokee author Marilou Awiakta describes the cycle of life: "The pattern of survival is in the poetics of primal space. Balance, harmony, inclusiveness, cooperation—life regenerating within a parameter of order. . . . Continuance in the midst of change, these are cardinal dynamics that sustain the universe" (Awiakta, 181).

Mythopoetic traditions among persons such as the Mvskoke and the Ashanti celebrated the numerous spirits, sacred beings, forces of nature, creatures both animate and inanimate, as well as fellow inhabitants within the surrounding environment. The spider, as weaver of the web of life, the rabbit, as trickster figure, and the buzzard, as healer, took on great significance in both cultures. Through storytelling, animals and plants assumed anthropocentric qualities in order to spread the lessons of life across multiple generations. Fire and water became the focal points for rituals in which the bonds of community were celebrated and through acts of purifications and cleansing, a broken community made whole. With song and dance, natural history took form and presence within the midst of the people, and the workings of the natural order could be celebrated. Through community ritual, one could transcend one's individuality, and by connecting with the internal ancestor, the fire that was danced around and the fire that one's ancestors danced around became one.

Among the first peoples of Africa and the Americas, there were religious specialists who took the form of priests, traditional healers or shamans, and even conjurers and "witches." Coming from either gender and of any age, most had specific training handed down through the generations. Priests led religious ceremonies and rituals; traditional healers helped individuals deal with disease or communities with disorder; conjurers helped persons deal with the vicissitudes of daily existence. These persons were at the center of the traditional community because they were repositories for the knowledge and practice of traditional religion. Without them, the "old ways" would have vanished.

As peoples from Africa and the Americas bonded, the landscape of the early colonial frontier began to change dramatically. In areas such as southeastern Virginia, the Low Country of the Carolinas, and around Savannah, Georgia, communities of Aframerindians arose. In many places, Europeans found themselves outnumbered by persons of color, and the need to set these persons against one another became a critical factor in colonial policy. The notion of racial supremacy emerged as a convenient methodology of oppression, and by the middle of the eighteenth century, race became a critical aspect of identity. A 1740 slave code from South Carolina reveals the importance of this newfound ideology: "[A]ll negroes and Indians, (free Indians in amity with this government, and negroes, mulattoes, and mustezoes, who are now free, excepted) mulattoes or mustezoes who are now, or shall hereafter be in this province, and all their issue and offspring . . . shall be and they are hereby declared to be, and remain hereafter absolute slaves" (Williams, 290).

Some 100 years after Africans arrived on the shores of Virginia, a young woman named Nanye-hi of the Cherokee people made a name for herself among the people as a distinguished "war woman" during a battle with the Mvskoke. When a Mvskoke bullet felled her partner-in-life, Nanye-hi picked up his gun and "fought as a warrior throughout the rest of the skirmish" (Foreman, 21). When the battle was over and the fate of the prisoners was decided, Nanye-hi selected an African American Mvskoke whose life would be given to her, as was custom, for the life of her partner. Through this act, Nanye-hi exercised her power as war woman in accor-

dance with the old ways to protect and promote life regardless of race. Nanye-hi would later become Nancy Ward, one of the most important and influential figures in Cherokee history.

In the middle of the eighteenth century, an enthusiasm for political and religious liberation began to sweep through the nascent settlements from the European continent; this movement became known as the Great Awakening. John Marrant, a young African American musician from South Carolina, was converted by evangelist George Whitefield and dedicated his life to the Christian gospel. When his family rejected his newfound fervor, he fled to the wilderness and took up with a Cherokee hunter who taught him the Cherokee language. When he returned with the hunter to his village, he was seized by the Cherokee and imprisoned. While imprisoned, he spoke with the headman's daughter and convinced her that she was under "deep conviction to sin"; praying together before the headman, the black minister and the young Cherokee woman performed a miracle "and a great change took place among the people" (Marrant, 7). With the support of the Cherokee leadership, Marrant engaged in missionary efforts among the Mvskoke, the Catawba, and the Housa people. This pioneer African American missionary was perhaps the first Christian missionary to the indigenous peoples of the American Southeast; however, he would not be the last.

By the end of the eighteenth century, tremendous changes were sweeping through the Five Nations that would have a profound impact on traditional culture that would forever affect life among the people. With the settlement of hostilities following the Revolutionary War, the newly established federal government inaugurated its "program to promote civilization among the friendly Indian tribes." A critical element in the "civilization" program would be the shift from the community-based low-intensity agricultural collective that had been at the center of traditional society to the colonial model of an individually owned labor-intensive farm. This dramatic shift in the culture of the peoples of the Southeast could not be accommodated without first altering the social, political, and religious structures of traditional societies. Toward this end, the missionaries of the Christian churches would prove quite effective.

From the very beginning of U.S. policy toward the Indians, missionaries were to play a critical role in the "civilization" of the southeastern Indians. The missionaries, believing that a stable plantation society promoted both a self-sustaining church and orderly civil government, introduced European agricultural practices to the Indians by giving plows, livestock, and gristmills to the men and cloth and spinning tools to the women. In addition, these same agents asserted that a dominant part of the civilization program should be the death of that part of the "old ways" that centered on ties of matrilineal descent. Intermarriage with whites was becoming common, and this intermarriage radically affected traditional matrilineality and communalism; real economic inequality was first introduced among the southeastern Indians. Progressive Natives who spoke English began to adopt the social, economic, and political patterns of the dominant culture; one by one, the old ways were being undermined.

Gradually, the "Five Civilized Tribes" (Cherokee, Mvskoke, Choctaw, Chickasaw, and Seminole) developed a landed elite, and a small group of "white Indians" formed a bourgeois element that became dominant in national affairs; among this group of the rich and powerful, the practice of plantation slavery became most accepted. For traditionalists, slavery represented the quintessential evil of European "civilization." The people had seen the terribly destructive influence that the Indian slave trade had played on their own economic and social institutions; that civilization in the United States was being built on a system of racial inequality, and the implications of such for themselves were inescapable. When the leading men of their own culture began to abandon traditional teachings and embrace this alien and threatening ideology, forces were set in motion that could not be constrained.

Throughout the Five Civilized Tribes, a rebellion erupted against the civilization movement. Especially in the light of a pan-Indian religious awakening that spread among the nations in the early nineteenth century, many of the conservative members of the southeastern nations rebelled against acculturation by reasserting the old ways. In movements such as "White Path's Rebellion" among the Cherokee and the "Red Stick Revolt" among the Mvskoke, traditionalism reasserted itself and challenged the spread of "civilization." This left little room for colonial institutions, including slavery, among large populations of the conservative members of the southeastern Indians who did not adopt plantation agriculture and mercantile capitalism. In addition, from the earliest periods of the institution of slavery, Africans fled enslavement along the same routes that Indians had used to escape slavery in earlier times. The Mvskoke and the Seminole accepted these runaways and incorporated them into their nations because the African Americans were well skilled in languages, agriculture, technical skills, and warfare. Throughout the South, a powerful force of resistance was building.

At the beginning of the nineteenth century, the Second Great Awakening was sweeping through the South, taking the form of camp meetings and revivals led by circuit riders and itinerant preachers. Affinities between Baptist and Methodist liturgical practices and the rituals of traditional religion promoted the spread of evangelical religion among even the conservative members of southeastern Indians. Camp meetings and revivals, being social as well as religious functions that promoted direct participation in singing, shouting, and prayer, were well suited to those accustomed to traditional methods of worship. The preference of oratorical capabilities and oral tradition over literacy and competence in doctrinal sophistries also promoted the spread of the evangelical message. When accepted into the congregation, the symbolic rite of baptismal immersion was quite similar to the ancient Cherokee purification ritual of *amo':hi atsv': sdi* ("water: to go and return to, one") (Kirkpatrick, 397).

As many of the missionaries did not speak the Native languages, they relied on the multilingual and multicultural Aframerindians to spread the gospel message. According to early missionary Daniel Buttrick, as many African Americans as Native Americans attended the worship services of the American Board of Commissioners for Foreign Missions. The missionaries referred to their "Sabbath schools" as "our Black Schools," because of the presence of Africans as both students and teachers. In 1818, a Cherokee entering the Chickamauga mission was found "able to spell correctly in words of 4 & 5 letters. He had been taught solely by black people who had received their instruction in our Sunday School" (*Chickamauga Journal*, in Malone, 142).

Not only did Africans share with Native Americans; the process of cultural exchange went both ways. From the slave narratives, we learn the role Native American religious traditions played in African American society:

> When I wuz a boy, dere wuz lotsa Indians livin' about six miles frum the plantation on which I wuz a slave. De Indians allus held a big dance ever' few months, an' all de niggers would try to attend. . . . As soon as it gets dark, we quietly slips outen de quarters, one by one, so as not to disturb de guards. Arrivin at de dance, we jined in the festivities wid a will. (Kyles, in Works Progress Administration, n.p.)

Native Americans also played roles in the development of a different kind of institution. Throughout the awakening, brush arbors were the center of the "invisible institution." These were hastily constructed churches made of a lean-to of tree limbs and branches where people would steal away for worship. Brush arbors of this sort had long been a prominent part of the southeastern traditional religion; they formed the circle of clan structures that surrounded the sacred fire at traditional ceremonies. The brush arbors that formed the core of slave religion were borrowed from the architecture of the "stomp grounds" of southeastern traditional religious practices.

Over the years, these brush arbors grew into churches.

The first Negro Baptist Church was established near Silver Bluff, South Carolina, on the banks of the Savannah River. This place was, at the beginning of the nineteenth century, a center not only for economic trade with the southeastern Indians but also political and social discourse. George Galphin, the owner of the settlement, was a gregarious Irishman who had at least four wives, including Metawney, the daughter of a Creek headman, and two Africans, the "Negro Sappho" and the "Negro Mina." Members of Galphin's family were patrons of the Negro Baptist Church at Silver Bluff. One of the organizers of Silver Bluff Baptist Church was a free black from southeastern Virginia who had spent many years among the Mvskoke and Natchez people. Another nearby church, the First African Baptist Church of Savannah, was led by a former slave "whose mother was white and whose father was an Indian" (Sernett, 49).

The area around Savannah was not the only center for Aframerindian religion. From the southeastern marshlands of Virginia, triangulating around the cities of Richmond, Petersburg, and Williamsburg, arose another set of independent "black" Baptist congregations. This was also an area in which there was extensive mixing of the races; the Mattaponi, Gingaskin, Pamunkey, and the Nottoway people of the Powhatan Confederation all intermarried with Africans. Thomas Jefferson noted that among the Mattaponies there was "more negro than Indian blood in them" (Porter, 314). In an area on the James River where blacks and Indians still outnumber whites two to one, the Bluestone African Baptist Church was organized on the plantation of William Byrd in 1756. By the end of the century, there were numerous mixed congregations in this area.

Born in Powhatan County, Virginia, "mulatto" John Stewart decided to become a missionary after an Indian slave told him it was folly "to pretend to turn the Indians from their old religion to a new one" ("Two Negro Missionaries," 400). Another famous resident of this area was Aframerindian John Chavis, who ministered to slaves until he was stripped of his right to preach in the wake of Nat Turner's 1831 rebellion in neighboring Southampton County. Many Powhatan of mixed heritage in this area "were driven away in 1831 during the excitement occasioned by the slave rising under Nat Turner" (Swanton, 175). Within the slave community, having mixed blood meant something:

> My mother had Indian in her. She would fight. She was the pet of the people. . . . She was whipped because she was out without a pass. She could have had a pass any time for the asking, but she was too proud to ask. She never wanted to do things by permission. (Badgett, in Works Progress Administration, n.p.)

Further south, even greater trouble was brewing. Asi Yahola, the leader of the Seminole, of Florida had run afoul of the law after his African wife had been captured and returned to slavery. In order to punish those who enslaved his wife and imprisoned him, Asi Yahola led a revolt that would become the Second Seminole War; the resistance movement soon spread. American Board missionary Sophie Sawyer reported that during a sermon among conservative mountain Indians the question of slavery came up. "God cannot be pleased with slavery," said one of the Cherokees. There followed "some discussion respecting the expediency of setting slaves at liberty." When one of those present noted that freeing the slaves might cause more harm than good, a Native Baptist preacher replied, "I never heard tell of any hurt coming from doing right" (Walker, 299).

In 1835, a formal movement was put into motion by several influential persons within the Cherokee Nation to emancipate Cherokee slaves and receive them as Cherokee citizens. The following December, the Treaty Party of the progressive slave-owning Cherokee signed the Treaty of New Echota with the United States, relinquishing all lands east of the Mississippi and agreeing to migrate to the Cherokee lands beyond the Mississippi. According to American Board missionary Elizur Butler, the Treaty of New Echota prevented the abolition of slavery within the Cherokee Nation. Throughout the United States, the federal government set about its policy of forced Indian removal. As Andrew Jackson put it, "The consequences of a speedy removal will be important to the United States, to individual States, and to the Indians themselves. The pecuniary advantages which it Promises to the Government are the least of its recommendations" ("President Andrew Jackson's Case," in Jennings, n.p.).

In the minds of most people of the United States, especially among those inhabitants of the Southeast, the issues of slavery and removal were indissolubly linked. In the first issue of *The Liberator*, an abolitionist newspaper, the path to the slave auction block was littered with copies of trampled Indian treaties; "[F]rom the Indian to the Negro, the transition was easy and natural. . . . [T]he suffering of the Negro flowed from the same bitter fountain" (Green, in Hershberger, 39). Among the reasons for removal was the presence of "another class" of citizens of the nation—the African Americans who posed a significant threat to the whites and opportunity for runaway slaves. Among the Mvskoke people, the question of removal was deadly serious. Blacks knew that they were considered the property of those from whom they, or their ancestors, had fled, that the burden of proof lay upon them, and that their losing to the U.S. government meant they would become the property of whoever claimed them. Indian removal was serious business, indeed, ridding the country of its Aframerindian threat and opening up vast areas of the Old South for plantation slavery.

The southeastern Indians faced what was most certainly one of the cruelest times ever imposed upon the people; a soldier was to later note, "I fought through the Civil War and have seen men shot to pieces and slaughtered by thousands, but the Cherokee removal was the cruelest work I ever knew" (Mooney, 124). As they prepared to face what lay ahead, a revival swept through the camps:

> They never relaxed from their evangelical labors, but preached constantly in the fort. They had church meetings, received ten members, and one Sabbath, June 17, by permission of the officer in command, went down to the river and baptized them (five males and females). They were guarded to the river and back. Some whites present affirm it to have been the most solemn and impressive religious service they ever witnessed. (Jones, in *Baptist Missionary Magazine*, 236)

Even on the road the worship continued:

> We collected together, in the midst of our camps, and surrounded the Lord's table. The brethren and sisters apparently enjoyed the presence of God. Several came forward for prayer. In the many deaths which have taken place on the road, several of the members of the church were called from time to eternity, and some evidently died in the full triumph of faith. (Bushyhead, in Rister, 77)

Aframerindians blazed the route to the Indian Territory: "[M]y grandparents were helped and protected by very faithful Negro slaves who . . . went ahead of the wagons and killed any wild beast who came along" (Willis, n.p.). In spite of the fact that slaves were given the responsibility to guard the caravans at night with axes and guns, few made their escape. What for the southeastern Indians First Peoples became known as "the Trail Where We Cried" was for the Africans an exodus. Large numbers of slaves and free Africans fled with the Indians to the Indian Territory; they realized that as rough as life on the trail could be, there was no life for them in the Old South. By the outbreak of the Civil War, the African American population of the Indian Territory was about 20 percent.

Aframerindians were also guides to a different promised land. Among the Mvskoke people where the African presence was particularly strong, black Baptist preachers led worship services even on the "Trail Where We Cried." The blacks who fled west with the Indians "se-

cretly held their meetings, baptizing after midnight in the streams, with guards posted to keep from being surprised and arrested" (Hamilton, 98). At the heart of the Baptist gospel message was the universal language of freedom that arose within the prophetic religion of the Aframerindian Baptist churches. This folk community practiced an "art of resistance" that constituted the core of their religious beliefs and practices and was a community whose very existence constituted a challenge to the ideology of racial supremacy. As they traveled on a trail watered by their own tears and marked by their own graves, their faith in each other gave them the spirit to endure.

And whenever Indians gathered around the sacred fire, there were Africans present. When there were dances to celebrate, lost children to mourn, or seasons passing to be marked, there were Africans present. In addition, we must never forget that on the "Trail Where We Cried," there were also African tears.

SOURCES: Paula Gunn Allen, *The Sacred Hoop: Recovering the Feminine in American Indian Traditions* (1986), 60; Marilou Awiakta, *Selu: Seeking the Corn-Mother's Wisdom* (1993), 181; Joseph Samuel Badgett, in Works Progress Administration: Arkansas Writers Project, *Slave Narratives* (1932); William Bartram, *The Travels of William Bartram*, edited with commentary and an annotated index by Francis Harper (1998), 199; Carolyn Thomas Foreman, *Indian Women Chiefs* (1976); Beriah Green quoted in Mary Hershberger, "Mobilizing Women, Anticipating Abolition: The Struggle Against Indian Removal in the 1830s," *Journal of American History* 86, 1 (1999): 39; Chickamauga Journal quoted in H.T. Malone, *Cherokees of the Old South: A People in Transition* (1956), 142; Robert Hamilton, *The Gospel among the Red Men* (1930), 98; J. Franklin Jameson, ed., *Original Narratives of Early American History: Spanish Explorers in the Southern United States* (1907), 176; Alan Kilpatrick, "A Note on Cherokee Theological Concepts," *The American Indian Quarterly* 19 (June 1995): 394; Preston Kyles, in Works Progress Administration: Arkansas Writers Project, *Slave Narratives* (1932); Letter of Andrew Bryan to Reverend Doctor Rippon, in Milton Sernett, ed., *Afro-American Religious History: A Documentary Witness* (1985), 49; Letter from Rev. Evan Jones, in *Baptist Missionary Magazine* 18 (1838): 236; Jesse Bushyhead, quoted in Carl Coke Rister, *Baptist Missions among the American Indians* (1944), 77; John Marrant, *A Narrative of the Life of John Marrant, of New York, in North America with [an] account of the conversion of the king of the Cherokees and his daughter* (n.d.). 5–7; John S. Mbiti, *African Religions and Philosophies* (1970), 267; James Mooney, *Myths of the Cherokee and Sacred Formulas of the Cherokees* (1972); 124, Theda Perdue, "People without a Place: Aboriginal Cherokee Bondage" *Indian History* 9.3 (1976): 31–37; Kenneth Wiggins Porter, "Notes Supplementary to 'Relations between Negroes and Indians' " in *The Journal of Negro History* 18.1 (January 1933): 321; Kenneth W. Porter, *Relations Between Negroes and Indians within the Present United States* (1931), 314; "President Andrew Jackson's Case for the Removal

Act; First Annual Message to Congress, 8 December 1830" in Patrick Jennings, *North American Indian Removal Policy: Andrew Jackson Addresses Congress*, http://www.synaptic.bc.ca/ejournal/jackson.htm; Statutes of South Carolina quoted in George Washington Williams, *History of the Negro Race in America from 1619 to 1880: Negroes as Slaves, as Soldiers, and as Citizens* (1882), 290; John Swanton, *The Indians of the Southeastern United States* (1946), 175; Robert Walker, *Torchlights to the Cherokees* (1931), 298–299; Nathaniel Willis, *Indian Pioneer History Collection* [microform], ed. Grant Foreman, (1978–1981); J. Leitch Wright, *The Only Land They Knew: The Tragic Story of the American Indian in the Old South* (1981), 148.

WOMEN IN AFRICAN CARIBBEAN RELIGIOUS TRADITIONS
Dianne M. Stewart

THE CARIBBEAN REGION is composed of the Greater and Lesser Antilles, encompassing an extensive archipelago of islands with diverse populations after centuries of conquest, exile, and resettlement. Beginning in the late fifteenth century, Europe's expansion into the Caribbean region occasioned a history of genocide, enslavement, and colonization, bringing together peoples of indigenous, African, European, and Asian descent. With time, the British, Spanish, French, Dutch, and Danes claimed sovereignty over the vast collection of islands that compose the Antilles. The significance of most Caribbean islands to slave economies accounted for the disproportionate number of Africans in virtually each island when compared with dwindling numbers of indigenous people and sparse numbers of Europeans.

African women were introduced into the Caribbean for the purpose of breeding enslaved offspring. They were also central to the labor structure on the plantations across the Caribbean. There is ample evidence that women (as did men) began to resist bondage as soon as they were captured. As white men assaulted African women during the Middle Passage, many resisted with devastating consequences; others did so by refusing food and attempting suicide. Enslaved women's resistance could also be noted throughout the period of slavery. Overall, slave records that document women's defiance and insubordination in the day-to-day structures of plantation life contest the natural passivity often associated with the female gender. Women were punished more often than men for infractions such as intentional destruction of sugar cane, neglectfulness, and excessive insolence. Moreover, pregnancy did not shield them from undergoing the most brutal forms of punishment, from solitary confinement and iron collars to hand and foot stocks. They also participated in and led insurrections.

On the Caribbean plantations, African women endured the double burden of exploitation in terms of their rates of production as enslaved laborers and reproduction, both of which were essential to making Caribbean slave societies profitable. The conditions under which women labored did not change much throughout the period of slavery. For example, enslaved women in seventeenth-century Barbados were compelled to work only two weeks after giving birth. This pattern was still observable in the nineteenth century, the only difference being that the planters allowed for the attendance of an African midwife during childbirth.

The experiences and roles of women in the plantation economy varied greatly from island to island and fluctuated in accordance with modifications in labor size and economic stability during various stages of slavery. On many islands, women shouldered the triple burden of carrying out personal domestic duties in addition to field or domestic slave labor, farming their allotted provision grounds, and marketing their produce. Although the maintenance of personal provision grounds and market produce and brutal fieldwork allowed women a certain degree of independence denied to those working in the plantation houses, the enslaved woman was perpetually dispossessed of her liberty to create the most desirable life of meaning and purpose for herself and her children.

African Caribbean Religious Traditions

In most Caribbean islands Africans outnumbered Europeans from the inception of their arrival as bondspersons. Over the years the gap increased exponentially as slavery became the defining economic institution of the Caribbean. Although under extreme duress and inhumane circumstances, enslaved women and men from a number of West and Central African societies shaped the cultures of the Caribbean. The music, food, art, and dance of the Caribbean as a whole bear indelible traits of African civilizations that are centuries old. In addition, many Caribbean religions have a distinctive African ethos and identity whether historically rooted in emergent slave societies or in postemancipation movements.

The aggregation of European, Asian, and African religious traditions in the Caribbean has allowed for sundry religious expressions among people of African descent. African Caribbean religious traditions can be classified under three major trajectories that sometimes overlap or converge in terms of influence: (1) African-derived religions, (2) black Christianity, and (3) post-Christian religious movements.

Iyalorisha Melvina Rodney heads Egbe Orisha Ile Wa, one of the two central Orisha organizations in Trinidad, and is recognized as the country's supreme Orisha leader. *Courtesy of Funso Aiyejina, University of the West Indies.*

African-Derived Religions

African-derived religions are continental-based African traditions that were reconfigured under various systems in the Caribbean islands during the period of enslavement. Some of the more popular and better documented traditions include Haitian Vodou; Cuban Lucumi, Santería, and Palo; Jamaican Kumina; Trinidadian Orisha or Shango; and the British Caribbean-wide practice of Obeah. These traditions have West and Central African antecedents in countries such as Republic of Benin, Democratic Republic of Congo, Nigeria, Togo, and Ghana.

African-derived religions are often interpreted as "syncretistic" religions because they tend to incorporate elements of Euro-Catholicism or Protestantism in their symbol systems, rituals, and beliefs. They have also been maligned as evil magic and barbaric practices of primitive Africans that continue to pose serious impediments to the progress of civilization among blacks in the Caribbean. Devotees of African-derived religions have withstood centuries of persecution including official legal opposition, social stigma, and condemnation by the Christian church. There is evidence that most of the African-derived religions exhibit a principle of openness to ideas and symbols from Western Christianity or, at times, Asian religions such as Hinduism in Trinidad. However, across the board, they remain African oriented in both ethos and structure. Overlooking their inclusive and flexible approach to religious expression, the Christian church and colonial authorities vilified and attempted to destroy African-derived religions in the Caribbean because their defining features contravene Euro-Christian orthodoxy and aesthetics. These include (1) a communotheistic as opposed to a mono- or polytheistic conception of the divine; (2) ancestral veneration; (3) divination and herbalism; (4) mediumship and possession trance; (5) food offerings and animal sacrifice; and (6) a pervasive belief in neutral mystical power that can be accessed by humans for multiple purposes.

A second set of religious traditions has been termed *Afro-Christian* and is composed of devotees who tend to identify as African Christians—some more forthrightly than others. In Jamaica two groups known as Revival and Zion evolved from the earlier-nineteenth-century African-derived religion Myal and a Christian-influenced Myal-based society known as the Native Baptists. Revival groups are popularly called "Pocomania" and have also been referred to as "Pukkumina" by some scholars. The term, however, is not used self-referentially by devotees. Eastern Caribbean countries such as Trinidad and Tobago, St. Vincent, Grenada, and Barbados have also been home to devotees of Spiritual and Shouter Baptist traditions. The Spiritual Baptists are more commonly identified as the "Converted" in St. Vincent. Each of these groups upholds a similar religious practice that remains inconsistent with the orthodox teachings and liturgy of the established Christian church. Indeed, they incorporate any number of Christian traditions and sources into their ritual life and spiritual outlook. However, practitioners interpret religious phenomena and relate to the visible and invisible world domains through a traditional African approach to knowledge and reality, as opposed to modern Western Christian lenses. This set of religious expressions can be classified as well as African based because each tradition is structured upon the six defining features of African-derived religions mentioned above. In addition, Revivalists and Zionists maintain close connections with Kumina devotees, who practice one of the most explicit African-derived religious systems in Jamaica. Similarly, many Spiritual and Shouter Baptists affiliate freely with and partake in the Yoruba-based Orisha religion in Trinidad.

BLACK CHRISTIANITY

Christian missions to the Caribbean followed no central pattern of organization and dissemination. The Christian religion was introduced into the region in the early sixteenth century. During his voyages to the islands, Christopher Columbus saw tremendous possibilities for Christian evangelization among the indigenous populations. At his suggestion, King Ferdinand and Queen Isabella of Spain appointed Friar Bernardo Boil as the first Vicar Apostolic of their Caribbean territories. Boil and his assistants arrived at his post in 1493. His mission was soon aborted, ending in illnesses, death, and expulsion from the region. The Spanish continued to send missions to convert the indigenous communities and enslaved Africans in their colonies, often performing massive christenings of African captives as they disembarked in the Caribbean.

Wesleyans and Moravians were among the first wave of Protestant missionaries in the Caribbean during the mid- to late eighteenth century. The Wesleyans worked extensively throughout the eastern Caribbean, establishing missions in islands such as Trinidad, Grenada, St. Vincent, St. Christopher (now St. Kitts), and Antigua. Their work also extended to Jamaica in the Greater Antilles. The Moravians initiated their Caribbean missions in the Danish island of St. Thomas in 1732 and established missions in Jamaica, St. Christopher, and Barbados by 1788. The Church of England neglected to establish missions among the enslaved populations in the British West Indies until 1825, just thirteen years prior to Emancipation, and never attracted a significant membership among African populations. Another group of missionaries and settlers did, however, make a tremendous impact on black Christianity in the Caribbean. In the 1780s African American missionaries were among more than 4,000 black loyalists to resettle in Jamaica

after the American Revolutionary War. Most prominent among them was George Liele, evangelist to one of the oldest Baptist denominations in the United States, the Silver Bluff Baptist Church in South Carolina (1750), founder of the Yama Craw Baptist Church in Georgia (1777), and founder of the Black Baptist tradition in Jamaica (1780s). A similar development occurred after 1812 in Trinidad when African North American soldiers, many of them Baptists from the South Carolina region, were resettled in village communes across the island.

POST-CHRISTIAN AND RASTAFARIAN

The collaboration between colonial powers and the Christian establishment in the Caribbean created the environment for a third major trajectory in African Caribbean religions. Mission-based Christianity, established primarily under European authority, proved to be tolerant of slavery and colonial rule. During the 1930s a collective of African Jamaican men began to meet, preach, and disseminate information about the divinity of Ethiopian Emperor Haile Selassie (1930–1975), born Tafari Makonnen in 1892. Rejecting Christianity as oppressive, they named themselves after Selassie's title and birth name Ras Tafari (*ras* denoting nobility) and advocated black repatriation to Africa.

There are three major Rastafari groups: the Nyabinghi House, Bobos, and Twelve Tribes of Israel. The Nyabinghi are the most popular and influential of the three. The Bobos are virulent black supremacists, while the Twelve Tribes of Israel is the most liberal Rastafarian group. The Rastafari of Jamaica have spawned an international movement that might be characterized as primarily religious but encompasses a broader cultural, linguistic, and aesthetic orientation—what they call the *livity*. Rastafarianism has attracted adherents in other Caribbean islands like Trinidad and Tobago, Antigua, and Barbados as well as in the Caribbean diaspora of the United States, Canada, and Great Britain. The tradition also claims a following in other European countries and parts of the Pacific. Rastafarians are ardent pan-Africanists who levy piercing critiques of white supremacy and European colonialism with its attending trappings, which they label "Babylon." They believe in the supreme divinity of Haile Selassie and in the divine nature of all Africans. Many of their religious beliefs and practices are biblically inspired by their post-Christian, pro-black interpretations of scripture. They object to normative Christian interpretations of the Bible, which have traditionally been antiblack and therefore enslaving.

Rastafarians strive to bring themselves and their communities into alignment with nature and Jah's (God's) law. They adhere to a number of taboos and rituals to aid in this process. Of primary significance is the creation of a specific language that when uttered enhances positive vibrations and energies. Their diet of *ital*, or natural food, the ritual use of "the herb" ganja (marijuana), and their maintenance of locked hair are also essential to Rastafarian spirituality and cultural consciousness. Despite its decentralized structure, Rastafarianism has expanded and strengthened over the past sixty years as one of the most vociferous expressions of black nationalism in the twentieth century.

African-Derived Religion as Obeah

While any number of West and Central African cultures have contributed to the formation of African-derived religions in the Caribbean, scholars have determined that Congolese, Yoruba (Nigeria, Benin, Togo), Fon (Benin), and Akan, especially the Asante (Ghana), civilizations have provided the foundational structures and salient ingredients in the various compositions of African-derived religions in places like Cuba, Trinidad, Jamaica, Haiti, St. Vincent, and St. Lucia. Obeah, a practice of divination and assertion of mystical power, is the most common and popularly referenced African-derived practice in the Caribbean. Obeahists are consulted for their clairvoyance and skills in healing and problem solving via herbalism and mystical power. Obeah is not a religion per se with devotees but a component of classical African spirituality that became equally significant to enslaved African communities in the Caribbean. Obeah specialists, both male and female, operate as solo practitioners, using diverse elements, states of matter, and paraphernalia to access the invisible world domain, including water, fire/candles, stones, jars, plants, and esoteric writings. Obeah is principally viewed as "evil magic" and feared by the average person until some treacherous personal circumstance compels an individual to forfeit her/his suspicions and seek counsel from the nearest well-known Obeahist. Obeah owes its negative reputation to the missionaries, Protestant and Catholic, who, in establishing the authority of the Christian church, launched a vehement campaign against all vestiges of African religions in the Caribbean. Obeah proved to be most troublesome and was ultimately employed as a generic label to signify and discredit all African religious traditions in the region.

Feminine Conceptions of the Divine in African-Derived Religions

Indeed Obeah and other religious systems survived centuries of Christian condemnation and legal proscription. The most-well-established traditions are Yoruba (Lucumi, Orisha) in Cuba and Trinidad and Tobago, Vodou in Haiti, and Kumina in Jamaica. Although the sources of these three traditions converge and diverge in any number of configurations, as African-derived religions they share a common theological and philosophical foundation. Orisha/Lucumi, Vodou, and Kumina devotees venerate a community of divinities, which includes a variety of deities and departed ancestral spirits who represent aspects of the supreme creator deity and serve as emissaries of Olodumare (Yoruba), Bondye/'Le Bon Dieu' (Vodou), or Nzambi (Kumina).

African-derived religions are practical religions that emerge from a classical African cultural foundation with a particular philosophical framework informing its guiding assumptions, epistemological orientation and values, and the common structure and purpose of the various religions we currently find in operation across the Caribbean and other parts of the African diaspora. First, African Caribbean practitioners understand religion as *ebo* (Yoruba), that is, as work or duty and a life of service and deed but not as a religious experience that culminates in a confession of faith in a divinity, religious institution, or set of doctrines. African-derived religions are both imbued with and expressed through ceremony—dance, music, song, and communal feasting. This entails a great deal of pageantry and meticulous preparation in accordance with an aesthetic norm that involves the use of natural elements, vivid colors, food items, and flora and fauna. All are endowed with ritual meaning and associated with spiritual power.

Practitioners engage in extensive rituals in order to maintain constant intercourse with the divine community and balance within the universe. These might be conceived of differently, depending on the tradition, but are generally thought of in terms of the distinctions and correlations between two world domains and their respective constituents. The visible domain is home to humans (the embodied living), animals, trees, plants, mountains, rivers, and other forms of creation, while the invisible world domain is the locus of the divine community, including the ancestors (the disembodied living) and other spirits, some of which are potentially harmful. Practitioners utilize material aspects of creation, including their own bodies, in daily acts of devotion to the divine community and in special ceremonies honoring a particular divinity or the ancestors. Their focus is always pragmatic and concrete. Of chief concern is the preservation of health and well-being, livelihood, and extended life/relationships within and across world domains. Through divination, specific rituals are often prescribed for expelling misfortune and disease, for inviting hospitality, and for the flourishing of creation. Mutual responsibility between humans and venerated powers is a prerequisite for sustaining the proper balance needed for rituals and transformative power. Thus, divine and human agency together allow for the efficacy of ritual performance and concrete human endeavors.

Devotees of African-derived religions have a positive outlook regarding what they perceive to be the natural, correct, or normative relationship between humans and venerated powers. In other words, their powers exist to serve and help devotees, not to harm and destroy them or their cosmic, natural, or social environment. Although disturbing experiences may be interpreted as signs from the divine community that devotees need to give attention to their ritual or social responsibilities, it is assumed that the divine community operates in the best interest of humankind. African practitioners do not hold to absolutist notions of good and evil. They subscribe to concepts of situational ethics where a person's or community's context—the means by which and intentions with which they act—determines their moral status. Ultimately, African-derived religions promote concepts of moral relativity, neutrality, and flexibility within the realm of human action. The divinities remain outside the purview of ethical deliberation and are assumed to act in coherence with the governing laws of the universe. Consequently, African-derived religions are premised upon a philosophical outlook that sees infinite potential for many possible outcomes in human affairs, even when tools and mediums of spiritual guidance such as divination implements and oracles appear uncontestable. The possibility for negotiation is omnipresent in the world of African-derived religions. This includes openness, dynamism, and the potential for modification in divination interpretations, human thoughts, choices, and deeds, the relationships between humans and venerated powers, and all occurrences in the visible and invisible world domains. African-derived religions situate the devotee in a world permeated with spiritual power and assign responsibilities and expectations to both the devotee and the divine community in order to sustain reciprocity, harmony, and a hospitable environment for all creation.

The divinities are both male and female, at times with an androgynous head, as in the case of Olodumare (Yoruba), or with a counterpart of the opposite sex, as in the case of Danbala Wèdo and his wife Ayido Wèdo, who represent the collective unknown ancestors in Haitian Vodou. Each divinity is affiliated with a force of nature as well as any number of personal attributes and symbols such as colors, animals, body functions, and material devices. They are presented with particular ritual food offerings that may vary from island to island. For example, the riverine divinities are typically female and represent various natural sources of water. Osun is the goddess of the river. Her association with rivers dictates that her devotees perform offerings and ceremonies at river streams and canals. She is also associated with economics, aesthetics, and fecundity. Osun's color is gold/deep yellow in the diaspora and in Nigeria, with the exception of Trinidad, where most Orisha practitioners associate Osun with the color pink.

In the Caribbean, Yemoja is associated with the sea and is considered the maternal Orisha (divinity). She governs motherhood in all creation and is the consummate nurturer and wise woman. Her color is royal blue. Olokun, although conceived of as male in Cuba, is a female divinity in West Africa. Olokun is the keeper of secrets, the owner of mysteries, and is represented by the ocean's substratum. While Yemoja is also associated with the ocean, she is only associated with the top layers of the ocean. Olokun is very important to her devotees in the Caribbean and other parts of the African diaspora because she rules the ocean floor, which became the premature grave for innumerable Africans during the Middle Passage across the Atlantic Ocean. Like Yemoja, Olokun is also linked with the color blue; Olokun's blue, though, is the deepest shade of royal blue, several shades darker and richer than that generally used for Yemoja.

Oya is the Orisha of wind. She is the guardian of the cemetery and governs the powers of transformation. Oya is a fierce Orisha like the potent cyclone that can destroy within seconds. She is also the calm breeze that soothes and relaxes. Oya's color is purple. She is sometimes associated with an assortment of purples, blues, and pinks, purple being the dominant base color and the most pronounced in the mixture.

Vodou also retains a significant collection of divine female personalities, including Azacca's (divinity of agriculture) wife Kouzinn, the market woman with an acute business sense; Ezili Dantò and Ezili Freda, both of whom are associated with fertility, motherhood, and child rearing; and Lasyrenn, the mermaid who summons devotees to trace the depths of their past. These female Lwa (Vodou spirits or gods) claim both male and female devotees, as do their Orisha counterparts. Kumina devotees recognize a supreme divinity, Nzambi, and maintain a strong attachment to their female and male departed ancestors through an extensive ritual life of constant veneration. Devotees in the Revival Zion tradition of Jamaica also revere the Rivermaid, a female "Spirit Messenger" with characteristics, tastes, and accoutrements resembling those of her riverine counterparts in Orisha and Vodou.

The Haitian context provides the most exaggerated example of the concrete and pragmatic foci underlying African-derived religion. As the second country to establish independence in the Western Hemisphere (1804), Africans in Haiti possess that which no other African populace possesses in the Caribbean—a civilization rooted in the horizon of classical Africa's turbulent triumph over French–European expansionism. Thus, for two centuries, African culture has defined Haiti's national, official, popular, orthodox, mainstream, subterranean, central, and peripheral markers of civilization: from mythology, music, dance, and art to religion, aesthetics, language, and culinary traditions. The saliency of African culture in the construction of post-

Columbian Caribbean civilization is unparalleled in the region, and it could be argued that Vodou is the blood running through the veins of Haitian civilization.

With a history immersed within revolutionary zeal, Vodou has been the subtext for everything Haiti accomplished as an independent nation and digested from bewildered and offended world powers in the Western Hemisphere. The Vodou Lwa inspired Africans to revolt against slavery in the eighteenth century. Among them were female entities and participants who were instrumental to the African struggle against death and annihilation on the French plantations. Kita-demanbre, the female Lwa also known as Marinèt-limen-difé (light-the-fire), is associated with fire, pimento, and kerosene. She is paired with the revolutionary leader Dessalines, who, over time, was canonized as a powerful Lwa. They often appear together during Vodou ceremonies, for Kita-demanbre ignited the cannons used by Dessalines and his regiments during the revolution.

Classical African myths disclose the importance of reciprocity, symbiosis, and mimicry in African theism. Reciprocity and mimicry are also manifested in the relationships between the divinities and their devotees in the Caribbean. Haiti, more than any other Caribbean country, offers the perfect ingredients for their hyperbolic expression in Vodou. Kita-demanbre, like the African woman in Boukman's portentous dream that appeared waving a cutlass above her head, commanding resistance while standing over a black pig, defies modern Western notions of femininity and ideal womanhood. She replicates the militancy of the enslaved African woman in Haiti. As the French military leader Donatien Rochambeau remarked in his correspondence with Napoleon: "If France wishes to regain San Domingo, she must send hither 25,000 men in a body, declare the negroes slaves, and destroy at least 30,000 negroes and nègresses—the latter being more cruel than the men" (Dayan, 33–35). It is hardly known that Boukman, a *houngan* (priest), was coupled with a *manbo* (priestess) who officiated over the ceremony with him and reportedly held more authority in leading the rituals at Bois-Caïman that incited the revolt. Her name has escaped the records that managed to preserve Boukman's, although twentieth-century scholarship suggests that she could have been Cécile Fatiman, an enslaved mulatto *manbo* who, at the very least, did play a role in the Bois-Caïman ceremony, was married to revolutionary military commander and Haitian president Luis Michel Pierrot (April 16, 1845–March 1, 1846), and lived to see 112 years of age.

African Caribbean Christian Thought

The Christian church gained ascendancy as the official religion in the Caribbean by the twentieth century.

Nevertheless, popular religion among blacks in the Caribbean was always saturated with African religious practices and anchored in an African spiritual foundation. Over the past five centuries, African Caribbeans have joined innumerable Christian institutions from the Catholics, Anglicans, Baptists, and Methodists to the Salvation Army, Jehovah's Witnesses, Mormons, and Baha'i. With the exception of the Baptist and Pentecostal denominations, the Eurocentric character of these traditions has remained dominant with little, if any, evidence of African influences on official church liturgy, doctrine, theology, and piety. A critical period of reformation in the black Caribbean Christian experience took place in the postcolonial era, concurrent with the rise of black consciousness in the African diaspora. This reformation was theological in nature and part of a larger movement called *liberation* or *contextual theology*, inaugurated by African North Americans in the United States and Latin Americans in South America. Led by theologically trained scholars and clergy, it called for a contextualization of Christianity in the Caribbean region. Contextualization demanded a critical review of colonial missionary Christianity and its Eurocentric legacy in the islands. The proper corrective would include a reformation of church liturgy, piety, ministry, and theology that would eschew colonial values and practices in favor of practices and beliefs that addressed the needs of Caribbean people, especially the poor and suffering, and that celebrated and promoted their African heritage.

The success of this movement is difficult to establish in part because it is still charting the course for an adequate reformation. Colonial models of Christianity are still rampant alongside the movement to contextualize and decolonize Christianity in the islands. Still, efforts of forerunners such as Idris Hamid and George Mulrain of Trinidad and Tobago, Lewin Williams and Noel Erskine of Jamaica, Adolpho Ham of Cuba, and Cortwright Davis and Noel Titus of Barbados to make Christianity relevant to the Caribbean have included serious reflections on, and recommendations for addressing, the problems of racial discrimination and color consciousness as well as the trivialization and dismissal of popular religion, which is, to a large extent, a carrier of African spirituality, aesthetics, and cultural norms. This is not to say that all the contributors to liberationist Caribbean Christian thought are of African descent. While a good number of them are, their major preoccupation with emancipation from the manifold dimensions of colonial Christianity has led to serious considerations of the African religious experience in the Caribbean and its import to the Christian traditions in the region.

Although this group has been in the making for more than thirty years, women's perspectives are virtually absent from their literature. To date, there is no developed feminist position that attempts to reconcile Christianity to the life situations of black women in the Caribbean, although there is some indication that black feminist theological reflection will come to voice in the twenty-first century. While women remain active in various ministries of the church, they rarely are encouraged to pursue formal theological studies and academic credentials for professional teaching. An exception would be the work of Theresa Lowe-Ching, which argues for the compatibility between feminist theory and contextual theology, which rejects universals in theological discourse and seeks to relate theology to the particular social, political, and cultural context of a given Christian community.

Women's Roles in African Caribbean Religions

African-derived religions have sustained high numerical proportions of female participation and strikingly high numbers of women in leadership positions when compared with the low numbers of women leaders in the Christian traditions across the Caribbean. Considering the dynamic representations of African Caribbean religions, women's predominance as religious leaders and teachers is most conspicuous in the African-derived traditions. In Vodou, Orisha/Lucumi, and Kumina women hold high titles and officiate over the key ceremonies of each tradition. Women's authority as *manbo* (Vodou), iyalorisha (Orisha/Lucumi), queen or mother (Kumina) is normative and uncontested, even when compared with the status of their male counterparts. Thus, the priestess in African-derived religions is often the head of her congregation and carries out her responsibilities as leader of her shrine with the same status and authority as any priest. Although reliable statistics are lacking, some data suggest that the number of women leaders in the Kumina tradition of Jamaica is higher than the number of men. In the case of Vodou, women are duly represented among the priesthood as well, especially in the capital city Port-au-Prince, where urbanization carries with it better economic opportunities for women. Among Orisha practitioners in Trinidad the two central Orisha organizations recognize women at the top levels of leadership and authority. Egbe Orisha Ile Wa is actually headed by Iyalorisha Melvina Rodney. Iya Rodney was trained by one of Trinidad's most distinguished Orisha priests and was recognized by the international spiritual Yoruba leader, the Ooni of Ife in Nigeria, as Trinidad's supreme Iyalorisha during his visit to the island in 1988. She is viewed by Orisha practitioners as the most authoritative Orisha leader in Trinidad and holds that status on the Council of Orisha Elders, which is currently composed of three women and three men.

Vodou and Orisha traditions have elaborate initiation rites, which women must undergo before acquiring the title of priestess. In Kumina, there is no formal initiation process as such. However a Kumina queen is one whose entire life from birth to adulthood has been saturated in the rituals and practices of the tradition. This is so because the knowledge that a Kumina queen must possess includes fluency in Kumina's particular BaKongo-derived language, which devotees call "African." In rare cases, as with the now-deceased but well-celebrated Kumina queen Imogene Kennedy, one may receive a calling into the tradition later in life, but it is usually still early enough for the devotee to achieve leadership status. In the case of Kennedy, she received her calling at the age of twelve. In 1983 the Jamaican government awarded Kennedy an Order of Distinction for her "service in the development of African Heritage" (Chancery of the Order of Distinction, 35–36, 87, 123). Kennedy is the only Kuminaist to have earned one of Jamaica's highest awards.

The office of priestess or queen involves presiding over major ceremonies associated with one's shrine, conducting initiations for protégés, offering divination readings for devotees and noninitiated clients, acquiring expertise in herbalism, and performing rituals for clients and devotees, including animal sacrifice and the preparation of food offerings. In Trinidad, for example, the practice of holding an annual "feast" (*ebo*) is central for priests and priestesses who maintain shrines. Feasts take place over the course of seven days, beginning on Sunday and terminating on Saturday. Priestesses are responsible for organizing many of Trinidad's feasts. Even those presided over by a priest have extensive female participation in both official and unofficial capacities, contributing to their ultimate success. Women tend to make up a significant percentage of the choirs that perform to call down the Orisha during ceremonial feasts. Women also receive the Orisha when they manifest at ceremonies, providing them with their special implements, favorite foods, and substances and carrying out their requests. Finally, women become the vehicles through which the divinities manifest, including the most potent and revered male divinity, Shango, God of thunder, lightning, and fire.

The Revivalists ("Pocomania" or "Pukkumina"), Zionists, Spiritual, and Shouter Baptists have complex leadership structures of which women are central, predominant, and authoritative. The late twentieth and early twenty-first century has been a period of modification and accommodation, as these groups are increasingly incorporating aspects of Orthodox Christian traditions into their organizational structure and leadership patterns. Thus, male leadership is quite prevalent as men hold titles such as priest, pastor, and bishop. Among the Spiritual and Shouter Baptists, for example, women are not officially excluded from the office of bishop. Still, most bishops are men. The achievements of the women who have managed to hold such high titles have not gone unnoticed. Women like Bishop Barbara Burke and Archbishop Monica Randoo have gained prominence within the religion and the larger society for their leadership roles. Bishop Burke is also distinguished through her senatorial office in the Parliament of Trinidad and Tobago. Women devotees have also written and published monographs about the Spiritual Baptist tradition. The Reverends Hazel Ann De Piza and Patricia Stevens have each authored texts on the Spiritual Baptist faith. Both women have advanced degrees in religious studies and remain active in the Spiritual Baptist tradition.

The more common roles that women hold in these traditions pertain to the ritual life and spiritual development of their congregations. This is true in Jamaica, Trinidad and Tobago, Grenada, St. Vincent, and Barbados. Among the numerous female offices are Mother, Shepherdess, Matron, Mother Diver, Midwife, and Nurse (Spiritual/Shouter Baptists); and Mother, Governess Nurse, River Maid, and Coal Maid (Zion and Revival). Each title is associated with specific responsibilities and supervision of spiritual work, which may involve subordinate female devotees. This includes mundane tasks like sewing, bathing, and cooking, that take on ritual meaning in the religious milieu. Women are also responsible for preparing herbal medicines and feasting tables and performing principal tasks in the core rituals of the religion: baptism, mourning, and healing. In each case, women often function in some official capacity either as leader or as assistant. For example, during the ritual of mourning, "pointing mothers" have the knowledge and skills to guide their pilgrims through their spiritual journeys in the mourning room. Women also perform spiritual work for a clientele that reaches far beyond the parameters of their religious communities.

From its inception, Rastafari has been characterized by an explicit male ethos in virtually every dimension of the tradition. The general doctrines and practices of Rastafari would indicate that women are subordinate to men. Since the mid-1970s, however, Rastawomen have become more outspoken and assertive in challenging notions of gender and established practices that undermine women's liberation. An important and radical figure in such conversations has been Sister Ilaloo, a Rastawoman who advocates abandonment of old traditions (many of which are biblically based) that are oppressive to women. Rastawomen (known as "daughters" or "sistren" among devotees) have also begun to emerge as practitioner-scholars who are documenting the experiences of women and conducting studies on the construction of gender among Rastafari communities. Imani Tafari-Ama and Maureen Rowe are pioneer con-

tributors to this important development in the academy and the Rasta community. As Rastawomen, they have existential and experiential knowledge of women's status in their tradition. While there is no organized Rastafari feminist movement, Tafari-Ama brings to light the Rastawoman's silenced struggle to achieve equal status and respect in the tradition. Rowe's research documents female membership and political activism in the Rastafari movement as early as the mid-1940s. It also suggests that women maintained their independence, authority, and agency during the early stages of the movement without many of the rigid gender restrictions or taboos currently observed that impede women's authority and progress in the tradition.

For more than three centuries, African-derived practices have been pervasive throughout black grassroots communities in the Caribbean within structured religious systems, popular medicinal therapies, and cultural traditions. African-derived religious systems emerged within three contexts, one of which is currently in the making: (1) slavery, (2) the postemancipation era, and (3) black consciousness movements, which can also be described as a post-Christian African diasporic phenomenon.

Women have always been and continue to be active leaders and participants in African Caribbean religions. Although there are no extensive studies on the status of women in African-derived Caribbean religions, preliminary ethnographic data suggest that women continue to retain the highest levels of authority, leadership, and visibility in African-derived religions (such as Vodou, Orisha/Lucumi, and Kumina) with superficial or minimal connections to Christianity. Women also hold prominent and central posts in the African-derived traditions with a Baptist orientation. However, male leadership is increasingly prevalent among the Revivalists, Zionists, and Spiritual and Shouter Baptists as they adapt to the patriarchal leadership styles established by traditional Christian denominations.

On the whole, female members of African-oriented Christian and post-Christian movements have not enjoyed the same levels of authority and degree of exposure as those involved with African-derived religions. Nevertheless, there is strong evidence that in both Rastafari and the Caribbean contextual theology movement, nascent female contributions to the study of gender and women's experiences will be crucial to the next phase of scholarship on women in Caribbean religions. Historically, women in African Caribbean religions have come from the lower echelons of society. While the socioeconomic status of women in the various African Caribbean traditions has not changed much over time, increasing numbers of middle-class women are becoming members of African-based traditions, especially among the Rastafari and Orisha practitioners.

SOURCES: Leonard Barrett, *Soul-Force: African Heritage in Afro-American Religion* (1974). Dale Bisnauth, *History of Religions in the Caribbean* (1989). Edward Brathwaite, "Kumina—The Spirit of African Survival," *Jamaica Journal* 42 (1978). Barbara Bush, *Slave Women in Caribbean Society: 1650–1838* (1990). Chancery of the Order of Distinction, *The Order of Distinction* (1988). Barry Chevannes, *Rastafari: Roots and Ideology* (1994). Joan Dayan, *Haiti, History and the Gods* (1995). Leslie Demangles, *The Faces of the Gods: Vodou and Roman Catholicism in Haiti* (1992). Hazel De Peza, *Call Him by His Name Jesus: Spiritual Baptists: Christians Moving into the 21st Century* (1996). Maya Deren, *Divine Horsemen: The Living Gods of Haiti* (1953). Sylvia Frey and Betty Wood, *Come Shouting to Zion: African American Protestantism in the American South and British Caribbean to 1830* (1998). Howard Gregory, ed., *Caribbean Theology: Preparing for the Challenges Ahead*, (1995). Marietta Morrissey, "Women's Work, Family Formation and Reproduction among Caribbean Slaves," in *Caribbean Slave Society and Economy: A Student Reader*, ed. Hillary Beckles and Verene Shepherd (1991). Maureen Rowe, "Gender and Family Relations in Rastafari: A Personal Perspective," in *Chanting Down Babylon: The Rastafari Reader*, ed. Nathaniel S. Murrell et al. (1998). Edward Seaga, "Revival Cults in Jamaica," *Jamaica Journal* 3.2 (1969). Patricia Stephens, *The Spiritual Baptist Faith: African New World Religious History Identity & Testimony* (1999). Imani Tafari-Ama, "Rastawoman as Rebel: Case Studies in Jamaica," in *Chanting Down Babylon: The Rastafari Reader*, ed. Nathaniel S. Murrell et al. (1998). Mary Turner, *Slaves and Missionaries: The Disintegration of Jamaican Slave Society, 1787–1834* (1982). Maureen Warner-Lewis, *The Nkuyu: Spirit Messengers of the Kumina* (1977). William Wedenoja, "Mothering and the Practice of 'Balm' in Jamaica," in *Women as Healers: Cross-Cultural Perspectives*, ed. Carol Shepherd McClain (1989). Joseph Williams, *Voodoos and Obeahs: Phases of West India Witchcraft* (1932).

Part III

~

Catholicism

WOMEN IN NORTH AMERICAN CATHOLICISM
Rosemary Radford Ruether

CATHOLICISM IN NORTH America (Mexico, the United States, and Canada) is the largest Christian church in this region. In the year 2002 Catholics were 62.4 million in the United States, 12.5 million in Canada, and (at least nominally) about 89 percent of Mexico's 102 million people. Catholics in these three countries are ethnically diverse and bring a variety of distinct ways of being Catholic from different cultural backgrounds. The earliest form of Catholicism in North America was brought by the Spanish who colonized Mexico in the sixteenth century. The indigenous peoples of Mexico had enjoyed a rich culture under the pre-Hispanic empires that developed over 2,000 years before colonization. The Spanish arrival was a violent collision with these traditional cultures. Magnificent temples and palaces were destroyed, codices of learning were burned, and vast numbers of people died from disease, war, and exploitative labor.

Native people who survived were incorporated into a Catholic Christianity that often harbored remnants of their religious beliefs and practices under the surface. Religious leadership, as clergy or nuns, was monopolized by Spanish-born or Mexican-born Spaniards (Creoles). Catholicism was slow to allow indigenous people to join the priesthood or women's religious orders. But by the late sixteenth century, some women from the Indian elites were allowed to become nuns. In addition to convents, there were also less formal types of vocation as *beatas*, or holy women, who adopted a religious lifestyle in their homes and served local parishes (Myers, "Religious Women in Colonial Mexico). Confraternities and sodalities were organized on a parish basis around patron saints, and women exercised leadership in these local religious organizations.

From New Spain, Catholicism spread into the North American continent from Florida to California. Missionary churches dotted these areas, bringing Spanish settlers and evangelizing local indigenous peoples. The descendants of these people were incorporated into the United States in the early to mid-nineteenth century through purchase or conquest of territory claimed by Spain and then by Mexico.

The second major form of Catholicism in seventeenth-century North America came from France. New France or French Canada became the base for French colonization and missionary work that spread southward along the Mississippi River from Detroit and Chicago to St. Louis and New Orleans. French settlers tended to be fur traders and often married Native

women. Frenchwomen arrived as nuns and founded schools and hospitals in Quebec and Montreal. Missionary outreach also brought indigenous people into the church, and some were elevated as saints and role models of devotion. French Canadian Catholics spread down the East Coast from Maine to Boston in the eighteenth and nineteenth centuries, seeking work opportunities.

English Catholics also arrived in the seventeenth century, seeking escape from religious repression in England. English Catholics in Maryland promoted a practice of religious tolerance in contrast to anti-Catholic discrimination in England but ironically were themselves disenfranchised at the end of the seventeenth century when the Church of England became the established church of the colony. In Maryland Catholic laywomen played the major role in keeping the faith alive by leading devotions in their households and evangelizing servants. To attract landed settlers English Catholic women were given the opportunity to become landholders in their own right. Both indigenous people and enslaved Africans would become Catholics through these colonial households, with the mistress of the household often serving as godmother for these Indian and African converts (Poirier, "Godmothers and Goddaughters: Catholic Women in Colonial New France and New England").

Catholics came to the United States in successive waves. They came primarily from England in the seventeenth and eighteenth centuries, from Ireland and Germany in the mid-nineteenth century, and from other parts of Europe and also the Middle East in the late nineteenth and twentieth centuries. Each of these groups brought distinct cultural forms of Catholicism. Significant numbers of Irish women migrated as single women, rather than dependent wives, and sought employment as servants and factory workers. In New England and along the Atlantic coast Irish people often encountered hostility from Protestants. Many jobs were advertised with the phrase "No Irish need apply," and Catholics often had difficulty finding housing, loans, and adequate schools for their children. This hostility was sometimes directed at Catholic nuns, the most visible group of Catholic women. Some anti-Catholic literature portrayed convents as dens of iniquity where women were forced into sexual servitude by priests. The burning of the Ursuline convent in Charlestown, Massachusetts, in 1834 by a Protestant mob was an expression of this hostility and fear.

Most Catholic immigrants came from poorer classes who migrated for economic reasons, yet hostility to Catholicism was fomented by portraying Catholics, especially nuns, as representing aristocratic traditions alien to American values. Still some middle-class Protestants patronized Catholic schools because the education there was seen as giving their daughters an upper-class "polish," learning French and social graces. Thus Catholic nuns in antebellum Protestant America were caught between both religious and class tensions. These tensions eased somewhat as a result of the service of nuns and priests during the Civil War. Many Catholic nuns opened their convents as hospitals or traveled into war zones to volunteer as nurses for both the Northern and Southern armies, serving selflessly without political bias to either side. The Union government recognized their service by giving the nuns pay and official status as nurses (Folk, "American Catholic Women: From the Jacksonian Period to the Progressive Era 1820–1900").

From the 1880s into the early twentieth century, new waves of immigrants from eastern and southern Europe, especially Poles and Italians, would bring a major expansion in the Catholic population, increasing the ethnic diversity both of Catholicism and of the American urban landscape. There was a revived anti-Catholic "nativist movement" in the late nineteenth century, with groups such as the American Protective Association. In the 1920s the Ku Klux Klan revived, as this increased Catholic immigrant population began to threaten Protestant majoritarian status. The Catholic population by 1890 was 8 million and largely working class. They were seen as a source of labor unrest, through organized union movements. Catholic working-class women, especially Irish women, also participated as important labor leaders in both local unions and the national union movement, serving as organizers in the American Federation of Labor. The temperance movement also targeted Catholics as promoters of saloons and heavy drinking. Again Catholics were suspect as carriers of antidemocratic values.

The hostile environment tended to cause Catholics to withdraw into their own religious and ethnic enclaves. The bishops promoted parochial education and mandated that every parish build a school in order to remove Catholic children from public schools that were seen as de facto Protestant institutions. Religious women were recruited as the major teachers for this expanding system of Catholic parochial education. Catholic laywomen as wives and mothers were also the mainstays of sustaining the distinctive Catholic ethnic cultures, doing much of the work for pageants and festivals, as well as maintaining home altars and devotions. Women also predominated in the membership of many of the parish-centered sodalities. The work of cooking the special foods and making the decorations for community events fell largely to women. The development of national churches allowed different ethnic groups to gather in their own parishes. Here preaching in German or other European languages could be maintained along with distinct ethnic customs.

Nuns were the primary women professionals among Catholics in the nineteenth century. They were educated and self-supporting. They received little financial support from the hierarchical Church, raising their own funds from their own labor and from donations from laypeople. Living very frugally themselves, they were able to acquire property and build convents, schools, hospitals, orphanages, and homes for delinquent girls and the aged in community after community across the United States. Virtually all the social service of the Catholic Church was done by these religious women.

Twelve religious orders of women were founded between 1790 and 1830 and another 106 between 1830 and 1900. By 1900 there were 40,000 nuns in the United States, outnumbering priests four to one. By 1950 there were 177,000 nuns in 450 different congregations, running thousands of schools from elementary to college level and hundreds of hospitals and other institutions of social service. Religious women were often among the first pioneers on the frontiers of the United States as Americans expanded west from Texas to Colorado and the Pacific Northwest. Some carried guns as they braved dangerous conditions and made friends with settlers, Indians, and even outlaws. Italian-born Sister Blandina Segale, a sister of Charity of the Incarnate Word, was famous for her friendship with Billy the Kid. Frontier leaders often favored their presence as bringing both social services and a pacifying presence.

Catholic nuns working under pioneer conditions sometimes found themselves in conflict with the hierarchy and official Church law that had been shaped for religious women in Europe. Rules of strict cloister and restrictions on activities outside the convent had been made for elite women who bought large dowries to the communities. This did not suit the American situation where nuns came from poorer backgrounds and had to do all kinds of work from teaching to sewing, laundry, cleaning, cooking for themselves and for priests, and even agricultural labor to support themselves. They also needed to deal directly with laypeople without clerical intermediaries.

Some bishops and priest counselors urged them to observe cloister, heavy clothing, and strict monastic regimes of prayer unsuited to these realities, while other bishops wanted them to teach boys as well as girls, contrary to their order's constitutions. Women leaders of congregations had to negotiate these conflicts with the hierarchical Church, sometimes risking the wrath of a bishop. Some congregations voted with their feet by moving to another diocese where a bishop was more amenable to their views. Others split from their European foundations in order to adopt a new constitution more suitable to the American situation.

Until 1908 the United States was regarded as a mission territory by the Vatican. Nuns who came from European congregations or founded communities in North America saw themselves as missionaries in a non-

Catholic environment, seeking to maintain the faith of Catholic immigrants or draw back the unchurched to church attendance. Thus the history of Catholic women missionaries starts within their work in the United States itself. From these frontiers American nuns gradually expanded their work beyond these borders, to areas such as Jamaica and Hawaii. The first women religious went to Hawaii to aid in the work with lepers there. In the twentieth century women religious expanded their missionary work to China, Africa, and Latin America. The Maryknoll Sisters, an American order that sprang up as an "auxiliary" to the Maryknoll Fathers, pioneered missionary work in China.

Female missionary orders often were in tension with male missionaries on the definition of their role. The men wished to see the sisters as aiding them in their work, sometimes even by doing domestic work for them. The women saw themselves as full-fledged missionaries in their own right. Also the sisters found themselves restricted by traditional rules that forbade women religious to serve as doctors or even as midwives to deliver babies. Rules restricting women's medical training, based on the notion of female modesty, hampered all women who aspired to the medical profession. These were even slower to change for women religious. Only in 1936 were such restrictions modified to allow nuns to receive medical training and serve as doctors. Nuns found themselves serving in roles in health service and even as teachers at home and abroad for which they had received inadequate preparation (Dries, "American Catholic Women Missionaries, 1870–2000").

The work of nuns in founding colleges and medical schools often arose from the need not only to train laywomen but also to give adequate training to their own sisters as teachers and hospital staff. Many nuns were pressed into service as primary or secondary school teachers without a college degree. Many bishops and priests assumed that sisters did not need higher education to teach children. Sisters struggled to upgrade their own education with little support from the male hierarchy. As late as the end of the 1960s some sisters teaching in Catholic parochial schools were attending summer school to finish their college degrees and gain state teaching credentials in what was called "the twenty-year plan."

Many Catholic women's colleges were developed as an upgrade of high school–level education in Catholic girls academies, as was the case with women's colleges generally in the nineteenth century. Others were founded directly as colleges. Among the major Catholic women's colleges one can note institutions such as Trinity College in Washington, D.C., Saint Mary-of-the-Woods, Indiana, St. Mary's, South Bend, and the College of New Rochelle, New York. Some Catholic women's colleges paralleled male Catholic institutions, such as

Catholic University in Washington, D.C., and Notre Dame in South Bend, Indiana. By 1968 there were 170 Catholic women's colleges in North America.

Catholic nuns were among the first college presidents in the United States at a time when there were few women college presidents in Protestant or secular institutions. Catholic women's colleges often shaped their curriculum around perceptions of distinctly "feminine" virtues and saw themselves as preparing girls for religious life or marriage, rather than professions, but this changed in the second half of the twentieth century to standards of education competitive with secular colleges. Also in the post–Vatican II period, many Catholic colleges opened their doors to men, becoming coeducational, or were absorbed into male institutions. Others kept themselves afloat by offering innovative programs, such as weekend courses to appeal to working women (Schier, "Catholic Women's Colleges in the United States").

By the early twentieth century, some Catholic laywomen were aspiring to more professional employment, reflecting the rise to middle-class status of the Catholic population generally. Daughters of Irish or other immigrant groups whose mothers were domestic servants or factory workers were becoming librarians, teachers, and journalists. The growing Catholic press relied on many women writers and editors, although usually not in the top positions. Catholic women also produced Catholic sentimental novels, counteracting the anti-Catholic novels written by Protestants and defending traditional Catholic piety and practices. Catholic women writers in this period often took an antifeminist and antisuffrage position.

The position of Catholic women reflected the views of the Catholic hierarchy who generally opposed women's suffrage and identified feminism with socialism, atheism, and other "evils," such as birth control. Suffrage was seen as the cause of established Protestant women's groups that were often implicitly, if not explicitly, anti-Catholic. Catholic women also found themselves, like blacks and Jews, unwelcome in the Women's Club movement and thus founded their own Women's Clubs, reading circles, and settlement houses. Thus defense of Catholicism was seen as implying an antisuffrage position and defense of the primacy of women's roles as wives and mothers, even among women professionals who hardly exemplified this lifestyle themselves (Campbell, "American Catholic Women, 1900–1965").

But Catholic laywomen also found themselves marginalized in Catholic organizations to promote social reform. A case in point is the temperance movement. Catholic priests and laymen founded Catholic temperance organizations, such as the Catholic Total Abstinence League, to counteract the identification of Catholics with drinking and saloons. As Catholic women were not allowed to join these organizations, some Catholic women affiliated with the Women's Christian Temperance Union (WCTU), a far more radical temperance movement that supported suffrage, pacifism, and socialism.

Different immigrant ethnic groups formed insurance and mutual benefit societies to tide their communities over in times of economic adversity and communal clubs to preserve their cultures and languages. Often immigrant women were excluded from major leadership in these groups, although allowed to form women's auxiliaries. Some immigrant women's societies, such as the Polish Women's Alliance, arose as independent organizations to support working women of their community. Thus Catholic women often found themselves negotiating between two forms of discrimination, as Catholics among Protestants and as women among Catholics. One response was to found separate Catholic women's organizations, another was to join in nonsectarian or secular movements, such as the WCTU, or labor unions, like the American Federation of Labor.

The 1930s saw new efforts internationally among Catholics to train and support Catholic lay leadership. This was reflected in the Catholic Action movement that organized laypeople as students and workers. Reconciling itself to the separation of Church and state of liberal societies, the Catholic Church saw itself as penetrating secular society with Catholic values through laypeople trained in the faith. New Catholic lay movements also arose through more radical involvement with the labor movement, the urban poor, and interracial justice. The most notable of these independent Catholic movements was the Catholic Worker movement founded by Dorothy Day and French peasant philosopher Peter Maurin in 1933. The Catholic Worker combined a tradition of voluntary poverty with urban living and service to the poorest in American cities. They opened Houses of Hospitality where they fed and housed people and held lively discussions. In the 1930s the Catholic Worker identified with the radical anarcho-communitarian wing of the labor movement. It also rejected the just war tradition of Catholicism for an ethic of total pacifism.

Catholics founded many settlement houses in urban areas, paralleling the settlement house movement of Protestant leaders, such as Jane Addams's Hull House in Chicago. Catholic settlement houses sought to counteract what was seen as an effort of this Protestant movement to draw the Catholic immigrant working classes away from the Church. A few Catholics in the late 1930s and 1940s began to realize that interracial work (improved relations of whites and African Americans) was the major frontier for social justice work in American cities. Friendship Houses, founded by Russian émigré Catherine de Hueck, typically staffed by young white Catholic women graduates of Catholic women's colleges, sought to pioneer improved interracial relations through founding settlement house communities in urban areas. A few black Catholic women joined in the leadership of Friendship Houses (Moore, "African American Catholic Women").

The Catholic population continued to become more ethnically diverse in the twentieth century. Hispanics increased as the United States took over the Mexican Northwest (Texas, Arizona, New Mexico, California) in the mid-nineteenth century. These Spanish-speaking peoples did not cross the U.S. borders; rather, the borders crossed them. But new immigrants, especially from Mexico and Central America and smaller numbers from South America, continued to flow into the United States. The takeover of Puerto Rico after the Spanish-American War (1898) made this population U.S. citizens, and they flocked to major cities, especially New York. The Cuban revolution in 1959 drew large numbers of migrants from this island that gained easy access to U.S. residence as "refugees from Communism."

Hispanic peoples each brought distinctive regional forms of Catholicism with patron saints, festivals, and home devotions, with women playing a major role in preserving these traditions. For Mexican Americans three major family- and community-based observances were important to the preservation of their Mexican Catholicism: the veneration of the Virgin of Guadalupe, creating home altars, and the celebration of Días de los Muertos (Day of the Dead) when the living communed with dead relatives. These practices took on an additional intensity in the United States where Chicanos/as experienced racial-ethnic discrimination and sought to reinforce their own distinct sense of ethnic identity (Rodriguez, "Latina Popular Catholicism"). In the 1980s some Chicana women artists and writers also claimed the distinct Goddess traditions of pre-Hispanic Mexico and made explicit the images of these Goddesses buried beneath the figure of the Virgin of Guadalupe. Veneration for the Virgin of Guadalupe became many different things to different Chicana women—traditional piety and feminine identity for some women and empowerment as bold, independent women for others. For both, La Morenita, the "little Dark One," was beloved as a compassionate mother and sister whose help could be sought in the varied circumstances of life for Mexican women in the United States.

In the 1970s and 1980s Mexican women in Mexico were seeking new leadership flowing from Church renewal, inspired by the Second Vatican Council and Latin American liberation theology. Base communities (*comunidades ecclesiales de base*) created new face-to-face faith communities largely led by laypeople or religious sisters. These base communities, promoted by more progressive Mexican bishops, such as Sergio Mendez Arceo in Cuernavaca, provided a method of popular Bible reading in which laypeople studied the Bible from their own experiences and applied their reflections to projects of social service and reform. For some Catholics these base communities were seen as a new democratic way of "being church." Although slow to take on "women's issues," such as sexual and domestic violence and reproductive rights, many communities were predominantly female and might be led by laywomen as well as by nuns.

In 1979 at the meeting of the Third Latin American Bishops Conference in Puebla, Mexico, the organization Women for Dialogue (Mujeres para el Diálogo) was founded in an effort to influence the bishops to recognize specific issues of women in the Church and society. The group managed to succeed in inserting some small statements supporting women's equality in society and leadership roles in the Church in the Final Document of the Bishops Conference. The Women for Dialogue group continued after the conference as a major expression of feminist theological reflection and activism in the Mexican Church.

Ethnic diversity among Catholics was further increased in the twentieth century through new waves of Asian Catholic immigration, particularly Filipinos and Vietnamese, the two Asian countries with major Catholic populations. The first received its Catholicism from Spanish colonization from the sixteenth century and the second from French colonization in the nineteenth and twentieth centuries. Small numbers of Catholics also came from India, China, Japan, Korea, Sri Lanka, and other Asian countries. Generally Asian Catholics came to the United States or Canada from populations that were already Catholic in Asia, rather than being converted in the United States. Of course, Asian immigrants also brought with them Protestant forms of Christianity, as well as other religions, such as Islam, Hinduism, Buddhism, Sikhism, and Jainism.

From the 1980s Asians, particularly from Japan, Korea, and Hong Kong, gained the reputation of being the "model minority." Cultivating strong traditions of filial piety, family and community solidarity, hard work, and educational aspirations from their Confucian traditions, Asians, including Asian women, became increasingly prominent as students and teachers in American universities, as well as skilled professionals. Asian Christian women also attended theological seminaries and began to network as Asian American feminists across the United States and with their sisters from their countries of origin.

Catholic Asians, especially from the Philippines and Vietnam, however, often came with considerable economic handicaps. Filipinas migrated in large numbers to the United States, but many had been poor in the Philippines. They experienced racial discrimination in the United States as a people colonized by the United

States at the same time as Puerto Rico. Filipino women came particularly as nurses and medical personnel and became a major group working in American hospitals and nursing homes, often at low salaries. Vietnamese arrived in large numbers as refugees in the wake of the failed American intervention in Vietnam. Many had a hard struggle to gain economic upward mobility. Each community brought distinct forms of ethnic Catholicism with their own forms of devotion. Both communities also have major communities of religious women shaped in the home country that migrated with their people to the United States (Azada, "Asian and Pacific American Catholic Women").

The Second Vatican Council, held in Rome from 1962 to 1965, brought a surge of Church renewal to American Catholicism. The liturgy was to be celebrated in the vernacular with the priest facing the people and a new emphasis on community participation. Americans tended to interpret the Vatican II emphasis on the Church as "people of God" in the democratic sense of "we the people." Vatican II renewal was seen as promoting equal citizenship for all Church members, rather than the view of the Church as a clerical "perfect society" run by the hierarchy, in which laypeople were defined as "subjects" whose role was to "pay, pray, and obey." This redefinition of the Church contained the seeds of increased polarization among Catholics in the post–Vatican II period, as sectors of the clergy and laity sought to restore what they saw as the "true" Catholicism of the pre–Vatican II period.

Enthusiastic reception of Vatican II renewal in the United States and Canada had its seedbed in reform movements in North American Catholicism in the 1950s. One of these was the Catholic Family Movement (CFM) that began in 1949. Following the Catholic Action methodology of "see, judge, and act," Catholic married couples learned to reflect on the issues of their social context and decide on their own responsibilities for action. The Catholic Family Movement was an autonomous lay movement that accepted advice but not control from its clerical pastors and advisers.

During Vatican Council II, dissent from official Catholic teachings on contraception increasingly surfaced from the laity. Paul VI separated the issue from explicit discussion during the Council by setting up a separate Birth Control Commission that included not only clerical moral theologians but medical and population experts. Three married couples from France, Canada, and the United States who were leaders of the Catholic Family Movement were invited to be members of the Commission to bring in the perspective of the married laity.

Pat and Patty Crowley, leaders of CFM in the United States, polled their membership on birth control and brought dramatic testimony to the Commission of married couples' suffering under the traditional restrictions of Catholic teachings that allowed only the "rhythm" method of family planning. This testimony had a major effect on the discussion of the Commission. Many celibate clergy, accustomed to pronounce on this subject, had never before heard this criticism from married people. The result was a majority decision to change official teachings to allow any medically approved method of contraception within marriage. This decision, however, was rejected by Paul VI, under pressure by several moral theologians whose position had been rejected by the Commission.

The papal encyclical *Humanae vitae* (1968) reaffirmed the Church's traditional teachings on birth control. The result was a major crisis among members of CFM, as well as other progressive Catholic laity and clergy, who declined to accept the reaffirmed "old" teachings. This conflict over birth control represented a new phenomenon of dissent among modern Catholics in which an official teaching was publicly "not received" by some Catholic lay and clerical leaders. The majority of the laity ceased to comply with the anticontraceptive teachings in practice. Unlike the pre–Vatican II period, few parish clergy continued to pursue the issue of birth control through sermons or confessionals. This tacit permission to allow Catholic laity to follow their own consciences on the issue of birth control was aided by the decline of the practice of private confession after Vatican II.

The struggle over reproductive rights among Catholics shifted primarily to the issue of abortion, although the anticontraceptive position continued to be emphasized by Pope John Paul II in the last decades of the twentieth century and into the twenty-first century. But the hard line against dissent focused on the issue of abortion. No criticism of the Church's view that abortion is murder from the first moment of conception was allowed. Catholic clergy, nuns, and even laity could lose their jobs or be expelled from religious orders for any questioning of this teaching. A small Catholic women's organization, Catholics for a Free Choice (Católicas por el Derecho a Decidir in Mexico), carried the issue of dissent on the abortion issue, branching out into questioning the treatment of issues of women and sexuality in Catholic hospitals and health-care institutions. CFFC-CDD also took the fight internationally, confronting the Vatican on reproductive rights issues at gatherings of the United Nations, among other venues (Kissling, "Women's Freedom and Reproductive Rights").

Two other movements in North America also became important seedbeds for an increasingly explicit Catholic feminism. One was the Sister Formation Movement, which challenged the practice of placing nuns in Catholic school teaching without adequate education. The Sister Formation Movement demanded that religious women complete their college degree and teaching certificate before going into teaching and promoted graduate-level studies for religious women. Religious women and increasingly Catholic laywomen began to aspire to a high level of education, often pursuing their studies at first-rate secular institutions, such as Yale, Harvard, and the University of Chicago. This has resulted in an increasing educational gap between Catholic women and Catholic clergy, with the clergy still shaped by traditional Catholic formation, while lay- and religious women became accustomed to critical historical approaches to religious ideas.

Another important renewal movement was the Grail, a laywomen's religious community begun in Holland in the 1930s, which migrated to the United States in 1940. Always emphasizing women's capacity for Church leadership, the Grail became explicitly feminist in the 1970s. In retreats and college- and seminary-level courses, the Grail promoted the development of feminist theology in its headquarters in Loveland, Ohio, as well as other centers in the United States and internationally (Weaver, "American Catholic Women since Vatican Council II"). Feminism had been defined as unacceptable for Catholics in the pre–Vatican II period, but increasingly it was incorporated as part of the justice mission of the Church by feminist Catholics. Catholic women as teachers of religious studies and theology in Catholic and ecumenical religious studies departments and seminaries assumed major leadership as shapers of feminist biblical studies, theology, social ethics, liturgics, and Church history (Tatman, "Euro-American Feminist Theology").

From the mid-1970s, some Catholic women religious became explicitly feminist in public statements and study materials. Organizations of nuns, such as the Conference of Major Superiors of Women (later the Leadership Conference of Women Religious), took a feminist position critical of the traditional exclusion of women from ordained leadership and rejected the theological anthropology that defined women as unable to "image" Christ in the ordained priesthood. In addition to reproductive rights, women's ordination became a major flash point between Catholic feminist women and men and the reaffirmation of women's exclusion from ordination by the Vatican. The Vatican increasingly insisted that this question of women's ordination could not even be discussed by Catholics and made compliance with this position a criterion for promotion of Catholic clergy and even lay teachers of theology in Catholic colleges and seminaries.

The Women's Ordination Conference, sponsor of the first major conference on women's ordination in the Catholic Church, in Detroit in 1975 became the major institution carrying dissent on the ordination question. The leaders of this group both shaped theological perspectives to counteract the theological rejection of women's ordination by the official Church and agitated for women's ordination at bishop's meetings and ordinations of men. In 1978 lobbying at a Catholic bishop's conference in Washington resulted in the bishops accepting a three-year process of dialogue with the Women's Ordination Conference on issues of women in the Church. This dialogue, in turn, resulted in a decision to write a Bishops' Pastoral Letter on women in the Church.

The first drafts of this letter condemned "sexism as sin" and promoted a "partnership model" of women and men in the Church, family, and society. But intervention of the Vatican to insist on the traditional anthropology of complementarity, and on explicit condemnation of birth control, abortion, and women's ordination, resulted in a document that became increasingly unacceptable to the progressive wing of women and even some bishops in the Church. The result was the tabling of the Pastoral Letter by the bishops. This failure to agree on an official document on women in the Church signaled the growing polarization of North American Catholicism on issues of women (Weaver, ibid.; Fiedler and Pomerleau, "The Women's Ordination Movement in the Roman Catholic Church").

Women involved in the Women's Ordination movement and Catholic feminist theology became more and more doubtful whether ordination was even an appropriate goal for Catholic women, given the repressive system of control by the hierarchical Church over both the laity and the clergy. Catholic feminists began to look instead to the idea of "women-church," a feminist-based community movement where women could design their own liturgies and reflect on their aspirations as women in the church and in society, as the place for their spiritual nurture and support (Hunt, "Women-Church"). The Women of the Church Convergence networked Catholic feminist organizations, both women-church groups and lay feminist organizations, such as Catholics for a Free Choice, the Women's Ordination Conference, and WATER (Women's Alliance for Theology, Ethics and Ritual, a Washington-based group promoting Catholic feminist thought and practice in the United States and internationally.)

Religious women and laity in African and Hispanic Catholic communities also began to shape their own distinctive forms of feminism. Among African American women, religious, feminist or womanist reflection grew within the movements that began to meet together to shape their distinct perspectives as black Catholics. Hispanic women also joined with Hispanic men to shape a distinct perspective as Catholic Hispanics in the United States. But Catholic women religious, with increasing numbers of laywomen, also developed Las Hermanas to question how women were treated, not only by the larger Catholic Church (including white Catholic feminism) but also within Hispanic Catholicism itself (Medina, "Las Hermanas").

As the Vatican became increasingly vigorous in its efforts at retrenchment and restoration of pre–Vatican II forms of Catholicism, against feminist and democratization movements, progressive Catholic movements, such as Women of the Church Convergence, the Women's Ordination Conference, and Call to Action, a lay progressive movement, began to take on the aspect of a parachurch within North American Catholicism, gathering in its own liturgical communities, sometimes with ex-priests, sometimes with lay presiders. These groups developed their own media of communication, newsletters, and newspapers and organized national conferences to continue to promote their reform perspectives.

At the same time conservative Catholicisms developed that defined these dissenting Catholics as "no longer Catholics," claiming to be the only true representative of faithful Catholicism. This polarization has taken on the dimensions of an impasse where dialogue is not only not possible but officially not allowed on the critical issues, such as birth control, abortion, women's ordination, and even an anthropology of "partnership," rather than masculine-feminine complementarity.

The future of this polarization is uncertain. It may result in an increasing departure of Catholics to other Christian groups or to secular identities. Many Catholic women who wish to be ordained are leaving Catholicism for Protestant churches that ordain women. Catholicism may become a smaller, more unified, conservative denomination. Yet Catholic reform organizations may be able to maintain their existence and create, over a period of time, a new synthesis of traditional and progressive Catholicism. That Catholicism in North America will return to a public consensus on issues of women and sexuality any time soon appears unlikely. Catholic women in North America have worked within and alongside the official Church—and occasionally in opposition to it. In these various relations to the Church, women have been guided by a vision of what the Church should be.

SOURCES: All sources cited in this essay are other essays in *The Encyclopedia of Women and Religion in North America.*

RELIGIOUS WOMEN IN COLONIAL MEXICO
Kathleen Ann Myers

FOR MORE THAN three centuries the Roman Catholic Church influenced nearly every aspect of life in Spanish

America. The Church carried out the "spiritual conquest" of indigenous populations, sent clergy to the New World, granted licenses for building universities and churches, controlled publications, and established rules for behavior. Whereas men dominated the early years of the conquest and the evangelical missions in the sixteenth century, by the seventeenth century women became important partners in the institutional Church. Dozens of centers for lay religious women and nuns (beaterios, recogimientos, and convents) were founded. By 1650 nearly 20 percent of Lima's female population lived in religious houses. Other lay holy women (beatas) lived within their own homes or in those of pious patrons.

Many of these nuns and *beatas* were considered prestigious members of society, offering prayers and counsel to the community. Some became the focus of posthumous sacred biographies, portrayed as exemplary Christians and symbols of the New World's contribution to the Church. Nearly a hundred biographical *vidas* of religious women were published in Mexico alone. The

Spanish American Church thus provided an arena for devout women to exercise significant influence in colonial society. A closer look at the lives of Mexican religious women illustrates that women were integral partners—though not equals—in the building of Church and society. Recently rediscovered autobiographical letters, confessional journals, and official Church biographies illuminate the details of their lives.

After independence from Spain, many Latin American countries dropped religious women from their official histories. The only two religious women who remained visible in most histories were America's first saint, Rosa of Lima (1585–1617), and Mexico's star poet-nun, Sor Juana Inés de la Cruz (1648–1695). Both worked to support traditional Church teachings. In the viceroyalty of Peru, Rosa of Lima symbolized Christianity's triumph over infidels and was America's heir to the popular medieval Italian mystic Catherine of Siena. As a third-order Dominican and mystic, Rosa resembled Catherine, but her story included how through the power of her prayers she fought off Dutch pirates in

Although Mexico's star poet-nun Sor Juana Inés de la Cruz supported traditional Church teachings, she did not passively submit to clerical demands that she renounce her literary career. In fact, she secretly rebuilt her library after being commanded to dismantle it. *Courtesy of the Artes e Historia, Mexico City, Mexico.*

Lima's port and converted Andean populations. Sor Juana personified the culture and learnedness abounding in Spain's other viceroyalty, New Spain, centered in Mexico City. For the Church she served as a model nun who ultimately rededicated herself to a prayerful, penitential life.

Feminism and new cultural histories of the colonial period have uncovered material that has significantly revised our views of women and religion. "Recovered" documents reveal, for example, that Rosa was not as unlettered as Church portraits paint. On the contrary, she made a collage that reveals her knowledge of the mystic process. Sor Juana did not passively submit to clerical demands that she renounce her literary career. In fact, she secretly rebuilt her library after being commanded to dismantle it. Scores of women created spiritual lives in a range of places—at home, in patrons' houses, and in large and small convents.

As Spain was solidifying its colonization of Mexico in the mid-sixteenth century, Rome—with Spain as its ally—was deeply involved in its fight against the Protestant Reformation. Codified in the documents produced by the Council of Trent (1545–1563), the Counter-Reformation emphasized the sacraments, the role of the saints, increased episcopal power, the prohibition of many Church texts in the vernacular, mandatory enclosure of nuns, among many other measures. Trent deeply influenced the development of the Church in New Spain. The first convents in Mexico were founded as the rules of Trent were being promulgated. By the time women were becoming well integrated into the Mexican Church in the seventeenth century, Counter-Reformation guidelines for female spirituality were strictly enforced.

Tridentine regulations limited the public sphere of visionary women's influence and prohibited books about their individual spiritual practices. As a result, women who needed to validate the orthodoxy of their spiritual paths relied either on clergy or on their own experience of God's voice in their lives. Approved practices known as recollection (*recogimiento*) and mysticism required little ecclesiastical education and provided avenues for spiritual development beyond rote prayer. Because mysticism led to direct experience of the divine, new paths to spiritual authority opened for the practitioner. Beliefs about women's bodies and spirits emphasized women's natural ability to be a conduit for divine communication, even as the Church insisted on confessors monitoring spiritual activity to detect heretical practices. Confessants were to observe the all-important feminine virtues of obedience, humility, and holy silence. The possibility of women having knowledge of God's will through direct experience, coupled with the mandate that this experience be expressed according to Church norms for feminine behavior, created a complex

dynamic in which women reflected on their lives and spoke or wrote about them so they could be evaluated by clergy. The Counter-Reformation established the limits to behavior by way of the canonization process and the Inquisition, but it was the sacrament of confession that provided the vehicle for most people to formulate narratives about their lives.

This institutional process resulted in first-person life narratives that were used for confession, Inquisition cases, beatification of holy people, and exemplary biographies. The process helped women to forge individual identities and public personas. Three women working with the famous Bishop of Puebla, Fernández de Santa Cruz, bishop for Mexico's second largest city, along with a fourth woman who escaped conventional religious life, illustrate the dynamic possibilities for women in and outside the Church. Posthumous pious biographies promoted the three religious women as symbols of the flourishing of Christianity. And yet if we were to meet them today we would see great differences in their personalities, race, class, education, spiritual paths, and accomplishments. María de San José (1656–1719) lived as a lay holy woman on her family's hacienda but later became a prestigious nun, mystic, and author. In contrast, Mexico's most celebrated woman, Sor Juana Inés de la Cruz (1648–1695), became a nun in an order that allowed her to own a library and write secular poetry. Catarina de San Juan (c. 1600–1688), an illiterate woman of color, could enter the convent only as a servant. She chose instead the active life of a lay holy woman who helped the poor and worked for the Jesuits making communion hosts. Finally, Catalina de Erauso (1582–1650) fled the convent, became a soldier, and later received the pope's permission to live dressed as a man. Such distinct portraits illustrate how women carved out a rich variety of life paths and how the Church integrated them into the system.

In one of twelve volumes of confessional writings, the Augustinian Recollect nun María de San José (Juana Palacios Beruecccos) describes her call to the religious life. She depicts her daily spiritual life in more detail than any woman writing during the colonial period, both her secular life—thirty years living with her family, twenty of those as a lay *beata*—and her thirty years as a mystic nun and convent founder.

María was born on a hacienda, a half-day's journey from Puebla, to devout Christian *criollos* (people of Spanish descent) Antonia Berruecos and Luis Palacios. The seventh child and sixth daughter, María was reared by her mother until age five. Her mother, who had married at age fifteen and had experienced almost annual pregnancies, breast-fed María for five years in the hopes of avoiding further childbearing. When two more sisters were born, María was turned over to the care of older sisters. Her carefree life changed dramatically at age eleven, after her father died. She explains in her journals that she saw a frightening vision of the devil, who exclaimed: "You are mine. You will not escape my clutches." A subsequent vision of the Virgin Mary, offering to wed the young girl to Jesus Christ if she accepted the monastic vows of poverty, chastity, and obedience, led María to a religious life within a bustling household. She built a hut in the garden with the help of a family servant and began the life of an ascetic. Following spiritual practices similar to those of Rosa of Lima, María began a rigorous schedule of mental prayer, fasting, penance, and household tasks. Because of the relative isolation of the hacienda, María's only guidance came from a few books and occasional consultations with Franciscan friars who traveled through the area.

María's vocation both received support and provoked conflict. Although Church and society promoted the religious calling of young girls, the choice often upset family routines and financial plans. María blamed her tense family situation for a seven-year illness that brought her to the brink of death. By age eighteen, María recovered and was of age to become a nun. She dreamt of living in a convent, guided by a confessor and the rules that governed all activity throughout the day and night. But the lack of the substantial 2,000- to 4,000-peso dowry required for entrance into the convent and the objections of siblings who wanted her to remain on the hacienda thwarted María's efforts. A dozen years later, upon hearing news that a convent for "virtuous, poor, and entirely Spanish, with no mulatto, *mestiza* or any other mixture of race" would be opened, María begged Bishop Santa Cruz for entry. Because she was one of dozens of women clamoring for a dowered place in the convent, he initially denied her request. Only with the influential connections of María's brothers-in-law did the bishop change his mind and allow her to take the veil.

In 1687, at age thirty-one and after twenty years of living as a *beata* associated with the Franciscans, María entered the Convent of Santa Monica, first as a novice and then as a full-fledged choir nun (the highest rank in the monastic hierarchy and one who sang the Divine Office). María lived in a reformed convent modeled on Teresa of Avila's Carmelite reforms, which encouraged small communities of women (about twenty-four nuns and as many servants or slaves) and strict observance of monastic vows. María now had to obey all Church superiors, own nothing, and see family members only through an iron grate. She became "dead to the world" and a "bride of Christ." The highly regimented life of community prayer, shared meals, and regulated work proved difficult for her. From 5:00 A.M. until 10:00 P.M. her life followed a traditional monastic schedule. When she failed to wear the religious habit correctly, or to eat at designated hours, or to arrive at choir on time, she

was punished. She developed hives, felt tormented by the devil, and suffered ridicule from her religious sisters. In addition, she had difficulty speaking during the mandatory weekly confession of faults. In spite of these trials, María delighted in having her own little cell with a primitive bed, chair, and set of devotional books. To a woman who had shared a bed with six sisters on the hacienda, having her own space "was like a little bit of heaven."

During these years, the nun experienced frequent visions of heavenly figures. After four years of being unable to confess these visions to her confessor, in 1691 María began to reveal this inward spiritual life. Concerned about her visionary activity, her confessor consulted Bishop Santa Cruz, who urged the nun to write about her experiences. At first painfully but later with confidence, she wrote about the "gifts and consolations" God granted her. María's written accounts of her active visionary life ultimately changed the bishop's mind about her spiritual capacities: He supported her career as a mystic writer and chose her to found a new convent.

In 1697, María and four other nuns traveled to Oaxaca to start the Convent of Nuestra Señora de la Soledad. There María as novice mistress trained women to be nuns and experienced a new round of challenges. While the city had provided funds for the convent and welcomed the founders, controversy soon began to sour relationships. The five nuns, all from Puebla, were perceived as outsiders. They were accused of stealing the city's patron statue, the Virgin Nuestra Señora de la Soledad, housed at the convent's church, of refusing local women's applications to the convent, and giving precious dowered positions to women from Puebla. The controversy was quelled only after years of ill will and appeals to the bishop and viceroy.

Despite these conflicts, the convent—and María in particular—enjoyed the support of the bishop of Oaxaca, Angel de Maldonado. He appointed his own confessor to be María's spiritual director, and the two men ordered the writings of more than half of María's extant journals. Bishop Maldonado saw in her an "erudite chronicler" for the Church and asked her to record a history of the convent, life stories of clergy and nuns, visionary encounters, and prophecies. After more than twenty years of working to build a new community through teaching, writing, and praying, María died in 1719.

By the time of her death, María's importance to the local community and Church was clear. Period accounts describe throngs of people at her funeral mass. Bishop Maldonado ordered a biography to be written, based on María's own journals. He himself wrote a Latin tract to the pope proposing her canonization. María's visionary account of the Virgin Mary leading the nun through the Stations of the Cross was also published. María had succeeded in her efforts to follow Church prescriptions and to create a path for her own experience of the divine. Speaking as the official voice of the New Spanish Church, María's biographer Sebastian Santander y Torres describes María as a "new conquistador" and an "enclosed missionary," who worked on the behalf of the universal Catholic Church and New Spain in particular. In the preliminary pages to the biography, Church theologians unanimously conclude that María had indeed experienced mystic union with the divine, which gave her spiritual authority and reflected well on the Church. She was lauded as a product of the "New Eden" founded in the Americas.

Such official approval clearly suited María's desire to follow an approved path—one that María says God Himself endorsed by telling her, "Your road is very similar to St. Teresa's." Ironically, closely following institutional norms may have damaged her candidacy for sainthood. Although María adhered to Counter-Reformation models of female sanctity, and her biographer carefully cast his subject into this paradigm, Church officials in Rome may have felt she had not demonstrated "extraordinary virtue" or performed the required miracles to qualify for sainthood. By the time the bishop's petition reached Rome in the 1720s, scores of women like María had been proposed—and rejected—for candidacy. The fact that María led a life of enclosure may also have hurt her cause. The only two American female saints, Rosa of Lima and Mariana de Quito (1618–1645), were *beatas* and, therefore, more visible in the daily life of the larger community. Only one nun from Spanish America, the Puebla Carmelite María de Jesús Tomelín (1574–1637), advanced to the first stage of consideration for sainthood.

More significantly from our perspective in the twenty-first century, the Church's institutionalization of María de San José through a series of devotional publications based on her life and writings led to a muting of her own voice. The recent discovery of María's confessional journals allows us to compare them with the Church's publication of her works. The difference is startling to modern-day readers who are accustomed to the use of quotation marks to indicate a verbatim citation of a work. The didacticism that dominated colonial Church texts and citations preferred a spiritual truth to the exact words of the original. When María's own meditations on the Stations of the Cross were published, for example, priest editors deleted sections about her emotions to create a more acceptable text. When María's biographer quotes her journals, he often conflates his words with hers by adding entire sentences to her "quote" and then adds editorial comments that change the original meaning.

These published works became the official texts that represented religious women's lives and symbolized the success of Catholicism in America. For centuries they informed the public's perception of these lives, while the women's original accounts rarely were read. María's own journals reveal a more dynamic picture: She details how a *beata* and prestigious nun negotiated Church rules to validate her life path. María de San José earnestly followed the model of an obedient, humble nun who imitated the lives of Christ and his saints, but she also established a unique position for herself in the long tradition of saintly women in the Church.

The crucial element of clerical mediation of religious women's lives and the promotion of model feminine virtue deeply inform Sor Juana Inés de la Cruz's formulation of her life path. Instead of adhering to these norms, however, Sor Juana redesigned them and created an alternate model. In several recently discovered letters and in her famous autobiographical letter *The Answer*—written within a year of María de San José's account and also addressed to Bishop Santa Cruz—Sor Juana argues with clergy about the interpretation of God's will for women: Women were not destined to be silent and obedient to confessors that often failed to exercise good judgment. Sor Juana's strident stance ultimately led to a controversy that spanned the Atlantic; supporters in Spain published her work, while the archbishop of Mexico censured her literary pursuits.

Born in 1648 to a Spanish captain, Pedro Manuel de Asbaje, and a criolla woman, Isabel Ramírez, Sor Juana lived on her grandfather's farm with five siblings. By her own account in *The Answer*, Sor Juana portrays herself as precocious and independent: At age three she tricked a teacher into letting her attend an *amiga* (a girls' school for rudimentary education held in a private home). Later, she learned Latin in fewer than twenty lessons and wanted to disguise herself as a man and study science at the university in Mexico City. Instead, she devoured her grandfather's library. At about age ten, Sor Juana left home to live with relatives in Mexico City.

Within a few years, Sor Juana's wit and charm won her a place as a lady-in-waiting in the viceregal court. For five years she participated in ceremonial and social activities at court. Sor Juana's phenomenal gift for writing verse and accumulating knowledge became widely known. The viceroy himself decided to test (and perhaps display) Sor Juana's erudition by assembling forty of Mexico's learned men to examine her through a series of questions; the young woman's answers astonished them all.

By 1667, Sor Juana began to take stock of her situation as a highly gifted woman who longed to pursue her intellectual vocation. She was against the idea of marrying and decided to become a nun because the convent offered a degree of autonomy for study. After consulting her influential Jesuit confessor Antonio Núñez de Miranda, Sor Juana entered the prestigious but strict order of the Discalced Carmelites. Within months, however, she left due to illness. Two years later, in 1669, Sor Juana made a second attempt, this time in a regular order, the Hieronymite Convent of Santa Paula. Given a dowry by her godfather, Sor Juana took final vows. Like other choir nuns, her duties included praying the Divine Office and helping run the convent, serving as an accountant and music teacher for the girls' school annexed to the convent. The nuns at the Convent of Santa Paula observed the same rule as María's order, but they did not follow it to the letter. As many as several hundred women were housed in the extensive convent complex; they lived comfortably and received visitors. Sor Juana owned a two-story "cell" (more like a condominium) within the convent walls, had her own slave, maintained one of the largest libraries in New Spain, held regular conversations with Church and court officials, and continued to write poetry.

From within the cloister, Sor Juana actively participated in religious, civic, and cultural celebrations in viceregal Mexico. Commissioned to write poetry of etiquette, popular musical religious verse, courtly love poetry, and one-act sacramental plays, Sor Juana's corpus covers the range of popular and erudite, profane, and sacred baroque literature. Beyond these official petitions, she wrote about her quest for knowledge and about human relationships, devoting her most touching verse to her close friends the vicereines and her most barbed satire to relationships between men and women: "You foolish and unreasoning men/ who cast all blame on women,/ not seeing you yourselves are cause/ of the same faults you accuse" (*Poem 92*). Her stunning 900-line silva, *First Dream*, elaborates the abstract discursive journey of her soul as it attempts to comprehend the nature of the universe. Simultaneously inscribed within and breaking poetic conventions, Sor Juana's work appealed to her contemporaries. Her first collection of secular and sacred verse, *Inundación Castálida*, was published in Spain by the vicereine in 1689.

Sor Juana's record of intellectual questing and her copious secular verses led to the controversy of 1690–1691, the writing of *The Answer*, and, by 1693, her withdrawal from public life. Nearly ten years before she had already experienced a serious conflict with her confessor over her literary pursuits. In a letter rediscovered in the 1980s, we see that Sor Juana broke with Antonio Núñez de Miranda. He advocated that nuns be like "widows of Christ" and sacrifice "self will, freedom, and soul." Núñez urged Sor Juana to renounce her literary pursuits. She responded in a *Letter to Father Núñez* by defending her choice and questioning his authority: "Have they [women] not a rational soul as men do? Well, then, why cannot a woman profit by privilege of enlightenment as they do? . . . What rule dictates that this salvation of mine must be by means of Your Reverence? Cannot it be someone else? Is God's mercy restricted and limited to one man?" (Scott, 429–438). After the break with her confessor, Sor Juana continued to write with the protection of the viceregal court and even the encouragement of some members of the clergy.

Two letters written ten years later (1690–1691), the *Letter Worthy of Athena* followed within two months by *The Answer*, reveals that differences of opinion between the nun and Church hierarchy over religious women's roles had again come to a head. Bishop Santa Cruz was the probable catalyst for Sor Juana's first letter in the series; she had first described her arguments to him before someone asked her to write them down. The *Letter Worthy of Athena* is a scholastic refutation of a Jesuit's sermon about Christ's greatest *fineza*, or gift, to humankind. Sor Juana cleverly dismantled the sermon and proposes her own theological interpretation. As a woman who defended her right to pursue God-given talents, she presented Christ's greatest gift as that of the "beneficios negativos"; that is, despite being all powerful, God allows individuals to use free will and thus to grow in virtue.

When Bishop Santa Cruz both published Sor Juana's piece and admonished her for writing about the strictly male enterprise of theology, she answered with a highly crafted rhetorical letter, *The Answer*. Taking Bishop Santa Cruz's suggestion that she follow in Teresa of Avila's footsteps with her writing, Sor Juana echoes Teresa's clever narrative strategies to justify her path and urge readers to reconsider conventional precepts about women's religious lives. The Mexican nun begins her life story at essentially the same point as her sisters—that of the Divine call (*vos me coegistis*)—and follows much of the same process—that of the *imitatio Christi*—but she deliberately chooses a nonconventional way to justify her path. She shuns the culturally acceptable practice of following the mystic's path. Instead, Sor Juana underscores that a woman who has been bestowed with intelligence should use it to fashion her life, just as the visionary uses her gifts to define herself. After all, she argues, "All things proceed from God, who is at once the center and circumference, whence all lines are begotten and where they have their end."

In fact, Sor Juana proposes, much as Teresa and María de San José did in their life stories, that men often are poor spokespersons for God. Whereas her religious sisters in their confessional writings subtly instruct confessors through examples of good versus bad spiritual directors, Sor Juana says men have corrupted Church texts, in particular, Martin Luther: "This is what the Divine Letters became in the hands . . . of that wicked Luther, and all other heretics." Drawing on the didactic potential of spiritual autobiography (the *vida*), Sor Juana suggests that if women could share in the pursuit of truth, such difficulties would diminish: "Oh, how many abuses would be avoided in our land if the older women were as well instructed as Leta and knew how to teach as is commanded by St. Paul and my father St. Jerome!" As proof, she presents an impressive catalog of learned women from classical Antiquity and Christian history. By rewriting conventions for nuns, Sor Juana added to the debate about women's learning.

Although Sor Juana had supporters, the controversy continued, and by 1693 measures were taken to officially silence the nun. The archbishop initiated a secret process against Sor Juana, requiring the renunciation of her literary career (including the selling of her library) and a renewal of her religious vows. Within two years Sor Juana was dead from an epidemic. Upon her death, the Church immediately effected a redefinition of her life. A collection of the nun's works, weighted toward her religious verse, with an introductory hagiographic version of her life story, *Fama y obras pósthumanas* (1700), was published at the archbishop's request. The biography highlighted Sor Juana's keen mind but emphasized her "voluntary" rejection of her literary career and renewal of her religious vows. In addition, throughout the next century Sor Juana's most published work in New Spain was her *Spiritual Exercises*—not her secular poetry. Sor Juana became widely known as the "Phoenix of America," a symbol of the learned achievements in New Spain, and as a nun who ultimately followed the Church ideal for religious women. As in the case of María de San José's writings, however, new archival finds in the last five years have radically altered this official portrait. An inventory of Sor Juana's cell upon her death notes that she had started rebuilding her library, and she had several notebooks of writings. Although Sor Juana deviates from the conventional visionary path of her contemporaries, in the end her life is similar. The convent offered women the possibility to write, interact with high-ranking officials, hold offices (as abbesses, accountants, teachers, etc.), and become important symbols for the Church. A shift in the political or religious climate, however, could effect a dramatic change in the promotion or censuring of a person's life.

In the same years that Bishop Santa Cruz served as a catalyst for change in María de San José's and Sor Juana's lives, he promoted veneration of another religious woman in Puebla by authorizing the publication of a hagiographic biography about the Asian-born-slave-turned-holy-woman Catarina de San Juan. By the time of her death in 1688, a local cult to her had developed. Within a year, many of the highest-ranking local Church officials had endorsed her as a legitimate holy woman and approved the biography of her Jesuit confessor Alonso Ramos. Sor Juana's ex-confessor Núñez, also an official for the Inquisition, wrote a ten-page preliminary letter heralding Catarina's cause. Although the biography would grow to be three volumes and represent the longest work published in the colonial Americas, the Inquisition in Spain banned all three volumes as soon as the last one came off the press. "It contains revelations, visions, and apparitions that are useless and improbable and full of contradictions and improper, indecent, and dangerous comparisions—*que sapiunt blasphemias* [that are almost blasphemous]" (*Archivo General de la hacin in Mexico, Ramo Inquisition v. 678*), it said. A second, brief biography was published in its place, but within a year, the New Spanish Inquisition banned the veneration of Catarina's portrait and closed the popular oratory devoted to her. Notably, however, the Mexican Inquisition failed to observe the prohibition of Ramos's biography for a full four years.

Because Catarina de San Juan was illiterate, we have no autobiographical source for her own voice, but the politics involved in the representation and veneration of her life illustrate the significance a lay holy woman could have in colonial Mexico and the threat she might pose. History confirms few facts with regard to Catarina, but her biographers concur on significant events of her life. All accounts plot a compelling story: Born of pagan royal parents in the Mogul empire of India, Catarina (born Mirrha) was said to have been singled out at birth for special favors by the Virgin Mary. Among other incidents, she was miraculously saved as a toddler after having fallen into a river more than three days before. Within a decade of her birth, however, local wars forced Catarina and her family to flee to the coast, where the child was kidnapped by Portuguese slave traders. Taken to Manila, Catarina came into contact with Jesuit missionaries and converted to Christianity. In 1619, the Portuguese took the adolescent girl to Acapulco to sell her as a slave. A childless couple from Puebla bought her and made her a privileged domestic servant. Upon her master's death in 1624 and her mistress's subsequent decision to enter the convent, Catarina was given her freedom and offered a place in the convent as a lay servant, which she chose not to accept. She became a servant for the noted priest Pedro Suárez, who at one time served as confessor for Puebla's most famous local holy woman, the nun María de Jesús Tomelín. Although Catarina had already taken a vow of chastity and had prayed (successfully, according to the accounts) to look old and ugly in order to ward off men's advances, Suárez ordered her to marry his Asian slave Domingo. She now fought heroically to maintain a chaste marriage with an abusive husband.

By the 1640s both husband and master had died, and Catarina at last was free to devote her entire life to Christ. She took no formal religious vows but lived a life of reclusion, prayer, and penance in a small room that a wealthy neighbor had given her across from Catarina's favorite church, El Colegio del Espiritu Santo, run by the Jesuits. She appears to have supported herself by sewing and confecting chocolate. Within these confines, Catarina exemplified Christian virtue. She dedicated her life to works of charity and prayer. Biographers report her generosity with beggars, supernatural powers for reviving moribund dogs, and wise counsel to people who sought her guidance. Yet the majority of her time was spent praying for the larger Christian community, experiencing visions of a host of heavenly figures, and making prophecies about Jesuit souls, important political and ecclesiastical figures, and occurrences in the Spanish empire, such as the arrival of ships from Spain and the outcomes of battles in Europe. She lived the last four decades of her life under the protection of the Jesuits, following this charitable, contemplative, visionary path. Nearly blind and half-paralyzed by a stroke, Catarina died in 1688. Upon her death, commoners and high-ranking officials alike declared that the octogenarian had died in the "odor of sanctity." Crowds fought to see her one last time before her burial; many reportedly tried to tear off a bit of her tunic in order to have a personal relic as a powerful link to this charismatic woman.

New Spain's Church officials wavered in their response to this cult. Catarina personified the cultural and racial mixture prevalent in Spanish America and the promise of Christianity: that a lowly, nonwhite ex-slave woman could become a holy exemplar of the faith and a powerful intercessor for a community of believers. New Spain wanted its own saint, but the Counter-Reformation's guidelines for sanctity, together with Urban VIII's extensive reforms, made proclamation of sainthood difficult. The profile of a saint recognized by the Church in this period generally was of a white person associated with a powerful religious order and living in Spain or Italy. Madrid's own attempt to censure Ramos's work may also have been meant to send a political message about maintaining the status quo, which was dependent on "purity" of bloodlines to well-established white Christian Spanish families.

A closer look at Ramos's three-volume biography also reveals that he flew in the face of Counter Reformation guidelines for more humanistic orthodox narratives. Ramos grants Catarina significant spiritual authority and records his conversations with her about sensitive Church doctrine, such as the status of unbaptized souls on Judgment Day and the nature of mystical encounters with Christ. In a telling scene, he records one of Catarina's visions: When the Christ child appeared naked and asked her to clothe him, she insisted that he return later and fully dressed: "The charity and love for her beloved and dear Spouse grew with this vision, almost to the point of causing a rapture, and rendering violent her impulse to clasp the Child God in her arms, to no longer

be held back by the shackles of her virginal reserve, being frightened by the nakedness of her only and divine Lover." Ramos's exotic, at times erotic, rendition of Catarina's life was silenced after several years of debate in New Spain, and a second, more conventional biography, *Compendium of the Life of Catarina de San Juan*, by José Castillo de Graxeda, was promoted. In this work, Catarina is a model of humility and obedience. Little mention is made of her visionary experiences or ideas about Church dogma.

There was no monolithic Church response to religious women in New Spain. The official interpretation of lives tended both to silence and to promote local holy people. Whereas new documents allow us direct access to some of Sor Juana's and María's thoughts, Catarina's voice will probably never be heard without the filter of official (and not-so-official) biographies. We are left to read between the lines in order to gain a glimpse of the real woman.

The life of a fourth woman shows how lives were often rescripted to fit convention and, at times, actually publicized because of their deviations from convention. After living for years in a convent in San Sebastian, Spain, the fifteen-year-old Catalina de Erauso fled before taking irrevocable religious vows. She donned trousers, cut her hair, and embarked for America, where she became a soldier and later an outlaw. Catalina reports in her alleged autobiography: "My inclination was to wander and see the world." Successful in her disguise for two decades, she finally revealed her true identity to a bishop when confessing to a murder. Her status as a virgin saved her; Catalina reports that after matrons examined her, the bishop was so impressed he pardoned her, saying: "I esteem you as one of the more remarkable people in this world, and promise to help you in whatever you do, and to aid you in your new life in service to God." Not content with returning to the convent as the bishop wished, Catalina returned to Europe to petition the king for financial reward for her military service and the pope for a license to remain dressed as a man. Both petitions were granted, perhaps because she had successfully presented her "singular" case as an individual who had demonstrated the highly prized masculine virtue of valor and the feminine virtue of chastity. Earning the nickname of the Nun Ensign, Catalina ended her days living as Antonio Erauso, a muleteer who transported goods in Mexico. Nonetheless, even in this more extreme case of a woman who deviated dramatically from exemplary feminine behavior, the Church and society rewrote Catalina's life story upon her death: She was simultaneously exalted for her "singularity" and drawn back into a more traditional role. In Juan Perez de Montalban's famous play *La Monja Alférez*, the woman Catalina has fallen in love with marries a man in the end; Diego de Rosales's

Jesuit history of Chile claims that after fighting for Christianity Catalina ended her days as a penitential nun; a 1653 Mexican broadside announces the Nun Ensign's death with an apocryphal account of the burial of her remains with the saintly Bishop of Puebla Juan de Palafox y Mendoza. The extraordinary life of this woman, even when it did not follow the Church's ideal, became a tool for building local histories and identity.

This sampling of portraits of religious women during the colonial period helps us see how the Catholic Church was instrumental in developing and controlling women's spiritual lives. Within a set of rigid guidelines for female spirituality, women still managed to negotiate places for themselves as mystics, authors, convent founders, counselors, teachers, and even soldiers. The contrast we have seen between official Church texts about these women and their own autobiographical writings helps us to appreciate the variety of responses by both men and women to period norms.

By 1750, with the Bourbon Reforms and the increased secularization of society, monasticism declined and the search for local saints waned. The nineteenth-century Mexican reform initiated by Benito Juárez—and its closing of convents—and the twentieth-century Revolution further loosened the Church's hold over national projects. And yet several of these same religious figures, still venerated today in some communities, have been used to create a new identity for a culturally rich Mexico. María de San José's two convents have been restored and opened as colonial art museums. Sor Juana Inés de la Cruz's convent is a university, and her secular works are widely published. A folkloric statue of Catarina de San Juan, affectionately renamed as "La China Poblana" (Puebla's Asian woman), greets visitors to Puebla and highlights the exotic racial diversity of colonial Mexico. The lives of New Spain's religious women and men provide a rich source for understanding the intricate relationship between Church and society, between individuals creating their own life paths and institutional requirements, between the changing interpretations of rules for ideal Christian behavior and the early modern process of producing hagiographic and confessional life narratives. Through this complex dynamic, people articulated and authorized identities for themselves and their communities as they established European beliefs in a New World, beliefs that continue to impact society in the twenty-first century.

SOURCES: For lengthier studies of the women mentioned in this essay, see Kathleen Ann Myers: *Neither Saint Nor Sinner: Writing the Lives of Spanish American Women* (2003). See also Asunción Lavrin, "Women and Religion in Spanish America," in *Women and Religion in America: The Colonial and Revolutionary Periods*, ed. Rosemary R. Ruether and Rosemary S. Kel-ler (1981), 2: 42–78; and Josefina Muriel, *Cultura femenina novohispana* (1982). Antonio Rubial studies canonization attempts and biographies in *La santidad controvertida* (1999). For a full-length study and translation of María de San José's journals, see Kathleen Myers and Amanda Powell, *A Wild Country Out in the Garden: The Spiritual Journals of a Colonial Mexican Nun* (1999). Recent publications and translations of Sor Juana Inés de la Cruz's works include *Obras completas*, ed. Alfonso Méndez Plancarte (1994); *A Sor Juana Anthology*, trans. Alan S. Trueblood (1988); *The Answer/La respuesta*, trans. Electa Arenal and Amanda Powell (1994); Nina Scott, " 'If You Are Not Pleased to Favor Me, Put Me Out of Your Mind . . . ': Gender and Authority in Sor Juana Inés de la Cruz and the Translation of Her Letter to the Reverend Father Maestro Antonio Nuñez of the Society of Jesus," *Women's Studies International Forum* 2 (1988): 429–438; "Carta de Serafina de Christo, Convento de N.P.S. Gerñonimo de México en 1 de febrero de 1691 años," ed. Elías Trabulse, trans. Alfonso Montelongo, in *Sor Juana & Vieira, Trescientos Años Después*, ed. K. Josu Bijesca and Pablo A. Brescia (1998), 183–193. The original biographies about Catarina de San Juan are Alonso Ramos, *De los prodigios de la Omnipotencia y milagros de la Gracia en la vida de la venerable Sierva de Dios Catharina de S Joan* (vol. 1, 1689; vol. 2, 1690; vol. 3, 1692), and José del Castillo Graxeda, *Compendio de la vida y virtudes de la venerable Catarina de San Juan* [1692] (1987). Catalina de Euraso's alleged autobiography has been published in the original Spanish and translated: *Vida i sucesos de la Monja Alférez: Autobiografía atribuida a Doña Catalina de Erauso*, ed. Rima de Vallbona (1992), which includes selections from the petitions, play, history, and broadside; *Lieutenant Nun: Memoir of a Basque Transvestite in the New World. Catalina de Erauso*, trans. Michele and Gabriel Stepto (1996).

GODMOTHERS AND GODDAUGHTERS: CATHOLIC WOMEN IN COLONIAL NEW FRANCE AND NEW ENGLAND
Lisa J. M. Poirier

CATHOLIC WOMEN, BOTH laywomen and women religious from European countries, were among the first colonists of North America. This is partially because the European colonization of North America not only was a mercantile venture but also was a fundamentally religious enterprise. Conflicts between Catholics and Protestants, both in France and in England, were the backdrops against which French and English colonial policies were formulated. In the case of France, initial colonial efforts by Huguenot merchants were actively undermined by Cardinal Richelieu, who decreed in 1625 that only Roman Catholics might colonize New France. In addition, the deployment of religious missions to Native Americans eventually became a major factor in the French colonial enterprise. For English Catholics, the establishment of colonies in which religious tolerance would be practiced was a central impetus for colonization. Lord Baltimore himself was primarily interested in creating a haven for the toleration of Catholicism when he established a colony in Maryland. The differing motivations of French and English Catholics directly affected the proportion of women to men in French and English Catholic colonies; differing colonial policies also produced variations in the relative prominence of laywomen in relation to women religious in each colony.

While French colonial policy maintained that the establishment of permanent habitations was of primary importance, in reality, the economic support necessary for such an undertaking was slow in coming. Instead, due in part to the post-Tridentine Catholic revival in France at the beginning of the seventeenth century, early financial support from French sources (particularly from pious laywomen) was directed toward the establishment of missions. Thus, women religious were among the first French Catholic women inhabitants of New France. Because English colonial policy and English sources of financial support for the colony of Maryland were directed toward the implantation of permanent settlements under a form of governance that included religious toleration, laywomen, as members of Catholic families, predominated in the early years of that colony.

However, the story of Catholic women in North America during the colonial period is not simply a tale of immigration. Because of the Jesuit zeal for missions, which was foundational in both French Catholic and English Catholic colonial undertakings, many of the first Catholic women in both colonies were Native Americans converted by these missionaries. Unfortunately, many general histories of Catholics in North America in the colonial period tend to overlook or to minimize this important fact. (One notable exception to this lack of attentiveness to Catholic Native people is Jay P. Dolan's *The American Catholic Experience: A History from Colonial Times to the Present* [1985].) Special attention is

This painting by Louis Glanzam depicts Margaret Brent arguing before a court of law. Brent, a large landholder in colonial Maryland and an astute and savvy estate administrator, was the first woman in the New World to demand suffrage. *Courtesy of the National Geographic Society.*

given to Native Catholic women in the present essay—but not simply in a spirit of redress. Rather, an examination of the interactions between Catholic immigrant women and Catholic Native women will emerge as a key to understanding the experiences of women, as Catholics, in New France and in New England. To further enhance this brief portrait of Catholic women during the colonial period, interactions between Catholic immigrant women and women of African origin will also be explored.

A greater understanding of these relationships can be achieved by recognizing that many Catholic women were brought together sacramentally by means of the godmother/goddaughter relationship. Although the godparent/godchild paradigm is certainly reflective of colonialism's paternalistic understanding of Native and African people, godmother/goddaughter roles served as a means through which women of disparate cultures were brought into familial relation. As in France, the godparent/godchild relationship was taken seriously. Goddaughters were named after their godmothers, and godparents had definite responsibilities. Godparents were charged with the moral and spiritual guidance of the godchild and were expected to raise the child, should the child become orphaned. Godparents also provided a route of appeal and a source of refuge for the child, should the parents prove unable to carry out their parental duties. In many cases, during the early colonial period, the primary means of establishing intercultural relationships between women was religiously motivated and sacramentally mediated. With the passage of time and the growth of the European-descended population and with the introduction of slavery, the relation between godmother and goddaughter diminished in its potential to serve as an intercultural mediator. By the end of the colonial period, godmothers were most often family members or close friends of the same cultural background.

New France: Canada

Although in the papal bull *Inter caetera*, Pope Alexander VI had divided the whole of the Americas between the countries of Spain and Portugal, in 1533 French King Francis I convinced Pope Clement VII to interpret this bull as not pertaining to lands claimed or "discovered" by European countries subsequent to the issuance of the bull. This opened the door to French colonization of the Americas, which began with the voyages of Jacques Cartier. Permanent settlements were not established until 1605, when Pierre de Gua, Sieur de Monts, obtained a monopoly of settlement and trade from Henry IV and founded, with Samuel de Champlain, the habitation of Port Royal on the Bay of Fundy. Three years later, the habitation at Quebec was founded. Que-

bec, and later settlements in the area, such as Tadoussac and Trois-Rivières, were conceived and administered as fur-trading posts. It was not until the arrival of Recollet Franciscan priests and, subsequently, Jesuit missionaries that France's colonial venture took on its distinctly missionary character.

In 1615, the Recollets were sent to New France. Over the next ten years, operating primarily out of the settlement at Quebec, their efforts produced little in the way of converts (a mere fifteen Native converts over a twelve-year period have been documented), but they must be credited with establishing the groundwork for missions in New France. Like most early missionary efforts in North America, Recollet evangelization was directed toward Native men, given the European cultural assumption that males were heads of households, and their families would follow in conversion. Of course, this was not necessarily the case—some of the Native cultures the Recollets and later missionaries would encounter (notably, the Huron/Wendat) were matrilocal and matrilineal, with uncles (mother's brothers) having more familial influence than fathers of children.

The population of French Catholic women in New France was also extremely low throughout the first quarter of the seventeenth century. By 1627, of approximately 100 inhabitants, only 11 were women. Yet some of these women are very much worthy of mention. Louis Hebert (d. 1627), an apothecary who had been granted a seigneury in 1617, and his wife Marie (Rollet) Hebert (d. 1649) were one of the few families to establish a secure homestead in this early period. The Heberts, along with their three children, Anne (m. Etienne Jonquest 1618, d. 1619), Guillemette (m. Guillaume Couillard 1621, d. 1684), and Guillaume (d. 1639), and Marie's brother, Claude Rollet, built a stone house on their land in Quebec. The Hebert-Couillard household was a large one. It comprised not only blood relations but two Montagnais girls, Charité and Espérance, who had been adopted by the navigator Samuel de Champlain; a black servant boy from Madagascar, Olivier LeJeune, who had arrived on an English ship; and several other Native young women who had been placed in the care of the Jesuits. The Hebert-Couillard household was a gathering place for many of the early inhabitants of New France. Indeed, Marie Hebert's garden was once a source of nourishment for all of the colonists of Quebec; during the winter famine of 1628–1629, she distributed her last two barrels of peas—providing seven ounces daily to each person until the supply was gone.

The first formal baptism of a Native young man in Quebec (as opposed to earlier and frequent baptisms of the sick and dying) was celebrated with a banquet at the Hebert-Couillard household. The young man, Naneogauchit, son of the Montagnais chief Chomina, was given the name "Louis" by his godparents, Marie Hebert and Samuel de Champlain. The banquet, said to have consisted of fifty-six wild geese, thirty ducks, twenty teal, two barrels of biscuits, fifteen or more pounds of prunes, six baskets of corn, and even more, was prepared by Marie Hebert herself.

This celebration is of particular significance because of its relevance to the role of Catholic women in New France. The conversion and baptism of Native people was, of course, the primary goal of the Jesuit missionaries, who had been given responsibility for the mission in New France after the Recollets had departed. Although the Jesuits, like the Recollets, were primarily interested in converting Native men, even male converts required both a godfather (*parrain*) and a godmother (*marraine*) for a proper baptism. Over a period of years, Marie Hebert and her daughter Guillemette (Hebert) Couillard served as the godmothers of dozens upon dozens of converts, including the servant boy Olivier Le-Jeune and the Native young women who resided in their household. Through the religious role of godmother the first and perhaps the most enduring familial relationships between Native people and French women were forged. The relationship between godparent and godchild seems to have functioned well in New France and appears to have been integrated easily by Native converts. This is perhaps because many Eastern Woodlands Native cultures themselves sealed alliances and created trading relationships through the exchange of gifts and the celebration of banquets, which then resulted in the establishment of fictive kinship bonds.

The Hebert-Couillard women were not the only godmothers in New France, although they were indeed the earliest. As mentioned, the Catholic revival in mid-seventeenth-century France caused many French women to develop an interest in missions. Some funded Jesuit and other missions; others chose to become missionaries themselves. Most notable were Marie-Madeleine de Chauvigny, Marie Guyart, Jeanne Mance, and Marguerite Bourgeoys.

Marie-Madeleine de Chauvigny (1603–1671) became Madame de la Peltrie upon her marriage to the Chevalier de Gruel, Seigneur de la Peltrie. She was widowed at the age of twenty-two and was urged by her father to remarry. Having been caught up in the religious fervor of the time, she did not wish to marry again but vowed to serve the mission to New France. In 1639, after inheriting her deceased father's fortune, in addition to that of the Seigneur de la Peltrie, she chartered a ship and arranged for three Ursuline sisters and a postulant to accompany her to New France. She is recognized as the founding patroness of the Ursulines of Quebec. Madame de la Peltrie remained in Quebec for the remainder of her life and was especially interested in the conversion and education of Native girls. Her devotion to the evangelization of Native girls was evident from the moment she arrived. Just days after disembarking, she visited Sillery, a Jesuit-administered Native Catholic settlement outside Quebec. She kissed every child she saw, and before the day was over, Madame de la Peltrie served as godmother at the baptism of a Native girl.

Marie Guyart (1599–1672), widowed at nineteen, entered the Ursuline convent at Tours at the age of twenty, taking the name Marie de l'Incarnation. She accompanied Madame de la Peltrie to New France; with Madame de la Peltrie's financial support, and with her own business acumen and deep spiritual devotion, Marie de l'Incarnation founded the Ursuline convent and school in Quebec. A prolific writer, Marie de l'Incarnation produced two accounts of her spiritual life, another account of her vocation to mission work in New France, notes from retreats, notes from instructions on the catechism, notes from conferences, dictionaries in Iroquoian and Algonquin languages, a catechism in the Huron language, and an extensive correspondence that is estimated to have consisted of over 13,000 letters. She also wrote, with the Jesuit Father Jerome Lalemant, the constitution of the Ursuline order in New France, which established the autonomy of the sisters. The primary mission of the Ursulines in Quebec was made clear in this work: "to employ themselves to the best of their ability in working for the salvation of their neighbor . . . especially in the instruction of girls and women, in particular, the Indians" (Lapointe, 1). Although in her correspondence she does mention several "spiritual" sons and daughters (godchildren), it is clear that Marie de l'Incarnation's role, which she perceived as parental, centered on the academic and religious education of girls, both French and Native. Acculturation of the Native young women was her goal, and in this she was only partially successful. There is only one Native young woman (Marie-Madeleine Chrestienne) who attended the Ursuline convent school who is known to have married a French man and remained in Quebec.

Jeanne Mance (1606–1673), like Marie Guyart, was strongly compelled to mission work in New France. She deftly arranged for sufficient financial backing for a hospital, and upon her arrival in New France in 1641, she established the Hôtel-Dieu de Montreal at fort Ville-Marie, which fort would later become Montréal. Marguerite Bourgeoys (1620–1700), the foundress of the uncloistered Congrégation de Notre-Dame de Montréal, dedicated her life to the education of the girls of New France. In 1658, she began her school, located in a stone stable, for all the French children of Ville-Marie. Later, the boys were taught by priests, and Bourgeoys's congregation of nuns educated the girls. When the *filles du roi* (young women sent by the benevolent Catholic group called the Société de Notre-Dame, and later by the French court, as prospective brides for the colonists) arrived in Ville-Marie, Bourgeoys housed them and attempted to educate them on the finer points of managing a household in the environment of New France. In 1676, she established a boarding school for noble and bourgeoise French girls and later began domestic training schools for other girls at Lachine, Pointe-aux Trembles, Batiscan, and Champlain. Bourgeoys also began a mission school for Native girls at Montagne. Both Mance and Bourgeoys served as godmothers for many of the French infant girls of Ville-Marie.

As mentioned, Native women were among the first Catholic women in New France. Marie Aonetta was the wife of Joseph Chihoatenhwa, the favorite convert of the Jesuits at Ossossané, a Huron village. Beginning in 1634, the Huron villages suffered from wave after wave of contagious European diseases. The Huron people, in attempting to understand the origins of such decimation, often blamed the Jesuit missionaries for these deaths, especially since the sacrament of baptism generally was performed only for the sick and dying. Chihoatenhwa himself was baptized in the midst of his own illness, in 1637. Unlike most of his kin, Chihoatenhwa believed that baptism possibly could heal his condition. Chihoatenhwa recovered and proceeded to evangelize his family; within months, his two sons, three nieces, a nephew, a sister-in-law, and her baby had been baptized. The next March, Joseph's wife Aonetta, who appears to have hesitated for some time, was baptized and given the name of Marie. Directly after her baptism, Chihoatenhwa and Marie Aonetta were married in the Church—the first Catholic marriage performed by the Jesuits in Huron country. In 1639, the Jesuits built a central mission called Sainte-Marie, about three hours' walking distance away from the village of Ossossané, but Chihoatenhwa remained and served as the administrator of the Jesuit chapel and longhouse in his village, although both he and Marie Aonetta were ridiculed as "believers" by their friends and neighbors. In 1640, Chihoatenhwa was killed, most likely by other Huron men who regarded him as traitorous. After Chihoatenhwa's death, Marie Aonetta remained a faithful Catholic and continued to evangelize in Ossossané. She sent one daughter, Theresa Oionhaton, to be educated by the Ursulines in Quebec, but on her return home, the young woman was taken captive by Mohawk raiders. She became the wife of the Mohawk man who adopted her upon her arrival in his village; although the Jesuit Isaac Jogues attempted to negotiate her release, Theresa Oionhaton remained with her new kinspeople. In 1654, the Jesuit Simon LeMoyne encountered Joseph Chihoatenhwa and Marie Aonetta's daughter, who had retained her Catholic faith. Theresa Oionhaton spoke to him about her evangelization of a woman who was of the Neutral Nation and who also had been taken captive by Mohawks. LeMoyne baptized the woman as Theresa, using her godmother's name.

Kateri Tekakwitha (1656–1680) is perhaps the most famous Native Catholic woman of New France. After having conversed with Jesuit missionaries and Native converts in her home village of Gandaouagué, Tekakwitha sought baptism from the Jesuit priest Jacques de Lamberville. He baptized her a year later, in 1676, giving her the name Kateri (Catherine). Kateri Tekakwitha desired to join a religious order, or perhaps to found one for Native women, but was dissuaded by the Jesuit priests. She is said to have joined with other Native Catholic women (including her spiritual role model Anastasie Tegonhatsiongo) in the performance of extreme bodily mortifications in a quest to lead a holy life. Kateri Tekakwitha was singled out by the Jesuits for her virginity and purity. In 1679, she became the first Iroquois woman permitted to take a vow of chastity. After her death, Fathers Cholenec, Chauchetière, and Charlevoix memorialized her in their writings, attributing revivals in piety, healings, and miracles to the intervention of Kateri Tekakwitha. Kateri Tekakwitha is not documented as having served as a godmother. Her Jesuit hagiographers, in attempting to illustrate her exceptional nature by emphasizing her virginity and her desire for holy orders, may have deemphasized her familial relationships. Clearly, the Jesuits themselves viewed Kateri Tekakwitha as exceptional, both in her piety and in her spiritual nature; they elevated her above other Native women by creating a narrative of her life that placed her firmly within the European tradition of saintly ascetic virgins. She was beatified by Pope John Paul II in 1980. A strong devotion to Blessed Kateri Tekakwitha has arisen, particularly among Native Catholics in the United States and Canada. Her relics at Kanawake, Quebec, and a shrine to her memory in Auriesville, New York, are pilgrimage destinations for many contemporary Catholics.

Many other Native Catholic women and French Catholic women shaped the colonial environment of New France by simply living their lives as devoted members of the Church. These women attended mass, supported the Church materially and financially, sent their children to be educated by priests or sisters, joined religious confraternities, served as godmothers to each other's children, and sometimes took holy orders themselves. However, documentation about these women is sparse, particularly because contemporary records were most often kept by men, who were not interested in or privy to the details of women's lives.

In the case of immigrant Catholics, we do know that one of the primary relationships in New France was that of *premier voisin*, or "nearest neighbor." In the new environment, immigrants relied on their neighbors in time of hardship and shared with them in time of abundance. When families grew, baptisms of children were, whenever possible, celebrated in the presence of neighbors and friends. While godparents of children were sometimes relatives of the parents, many new colonists did not have a pool of relatives from which to draw; in these cases, neighbors and friends (sometimes shipboard friends made during voyages of immigration) were selected. In choosing nonrelations as godparents, mothers forged sustained familial relationships between their daughters and their women friends and neighbors, ensuring a continuity between families into the next generation.

New France: Louisiana

In the last quarter of the seventeenth century, the explorations of Louis Jolliet, Father Jacques Marquette, Robert Cavalier de la Salle, Henri de Tonti, Pierre LeMoyne d'Iberville, and Jean-Baptiste LeMoyne de Bienville greatly extended the territory of New France. The expanded New France now included Louisiana, which stretched south from Detroit, continued throughout the Mississippi valley, and terminated in the port of New Orleans. Louisiana did contain some important fortified settlements, including Detroit, Vincennes, Cahokia, Nouvelle-Chartres, and Kaskaskia, but south of Illinois country, few outposts existed. The southern settlements consisted of Mobile, Biloxi, and New Orleans.

The forts in the Illinois country were populated almost entirely by soldiers and by men involved with the fur trade; while these men often married Native women, and had their children baptized by mission priests, there is little recorded about the women they married. While many marriages were contracted à la façon du pays, with no sacramental validation, some were formally consecrated by mission priests. The children of these marriages are most likely to have been baptized. As a result of these marriages, numbers of Catholic Native women are likely to have formed communities within and around the forts. Native families who were converted by the Jesuits also lived within and around the missions in Illinois country. Father Jean-François Buisson de Saint-Cosme, reporting back to the Bishop of Quebec on his visit to one such mission, wrote of Fort St. Louis on the Illinois River:

> The Illinois mission seems to me the finest that the Jesuits have up here . . . there are many grown persons who have abandoned all their superstitions and live as perfectly good Christians, frequenting the sacraments and who are married in the Church. . . . We saw . . . some Indian women married to Frenchmen who edified us by their modesty and by their assiduity in going several times a day to the Chapel and pray. (Shea, 47)

It is quite possible that these women sometimes served as godmothers to each others' children, especially since there were few, if any, French Catholic women within these communities. At Kaskakia, for instance, twenty-one children were baptized between 1701 and 1713. Of these, eighteen had Native mothers. It appears, then, in upper Louisiana, the godmother/goddaughter relationship did not function as a cultural mediator as it did in Canada.

The southern portion of Louisiana was quite different in composition, especially in regard to the number of French women present. From its beginnings in 1718, New Orleans was conceived as a tobacco colony. Administered by La Compagnie des Indes, the city was immediately populated with French colonists (approximately 7,000), some of whom were forcibly recruited, and with slaves (approximately 1,900). Extremely high mortality rates and continued importation of African slaves dramatically changed the composition of the initial population, so that by 1731, the New Orleans census counted fewer than 1,000 French men, women, and children but over 3,600 African slaves. Among the approximately 100 French women in New Orleans in that year were seven Ursuline sisters, led by Marie Tranchepain de Saint-Augustin, who had established a convent and a school for girls in 1727. This school also provided for the instruction of Native and African American girls, but like the other orders in New Orleans (Jesuits and Capuchins), the Ursulines were themselves slaveholders.

The *Code Noir* was revised and applied to Louisiana by Louis XV in 1724. Although the *Code Noir* decreed that all slaves must be converted to Catholicism, current scholarship has demonstrated that this element of the *Code* (as well as many other aspects) was adhered to only loosely. In practice, conversion of slaves was achieved merely by administering the sacrament of baptism. Although the *Code Noir* provided guidelines for the humane treatment of slaves, these guidelines were often ignored by individual masters and by the society as a whole. Thus, although slaves were baptized, and although in the early years of New Orleans, godmothers of slaves were almost always French women, the intercultural familial relationships engendered by godmothering in other parts of New France may have been but nominal in New Orleans.

It is important to note that in the early years of New Orleans the godparents of slaves were generally not their masters or mistresses but other French men and women of the community. This may attest to a persisting (although, even under the *Code Noir*, unenforceable) regard for the godparent as a route of appeal and source of mediation in the case of unconscionable mistreatment of the godchild. Although slaves in New Orleans certainly were regarded as the property of the slaveholder,

New Orleans law advised that slaves should be cared for and disciplined as if they were the children of the master. Perhaps, then, the practice of selecting godparents from outside the master/slave relation may have served, in some cases, a protective function, although a necessarily tenuous one. In later times, godparents of slaves were most often other slaves, which altogether eliminated the possibility of such protection, at least in legal terms.

Within white New Orleans society, French women did take the role of godmother seriously. Through the selection of godparents, New Orleanians established kinship relationships with persons not related through blood. Most often, the godparents themselves were from two different families, thus creating quasi-familial ties between one generation and the next and also providing the godchild with two distinct sources of protection, should she or he be orphaned. The protective role of godparents appears to have been taken seriously in New Orleans, particularly after Louis XIV's secularization of the institution of godparenting into official "civil tutorship." Tutors were able to sue on behalf of their wards in order to protect the financial interests of their godchildren. In sum, godparenting in the context of widespread slaveholding reduced its protective function for slaves but held increasing significance for French families concerned with community formation.

New England: Maryland

The colony of Maryland, established by George Calvert, Lord Baltimore, and his son Cecilius, may be said to owe its origins in part to Lady Baltimore, who advised her husband to seek a charter for the lands around Chesapeake Bay after a failed attempt at colonizing Newfoundland. In the early years of Lord Baltimore's colony, Catholic women were allowed the same rights to claim land as were Catholic men. The wealth and prestige of a few of Maryland's early Catholic women settlers is perhaps best reflected in the lives of two notable women, Mary and Margaret Brent, who were given adjoining land grants from Lord Baltimore. Margaret Brent and her sister and two brothers left England to settle in Maryland in 1638. Margaret and Mary's grant, the "Sisters Freehold," was composed of 70 acres located in the colony's capital. Margaret expanded her holdings by paying for the transportation of ten men to the new colony, which investment was rewarded by another land grant and, later, by being deeded another 1,000 acres by her brother. She soon became the most powerful woman in Maryland.

In 1647, during the Protestant revolt against the Catholic government, Governor Leonard Calvert, Cecilius Calvert's brother, had hired mercenaries from Virginia in order to defend the colony. Upon the governor's death, the soldiers remained unpaid and underfed and were on the verge of mutiny. Governor Calvert had named Margaret Brent sole executrix of his will; it was her duty to resolve this critical situation and thereby to maintain the security of her own fortunes. Brent was a woman experienced in the administration of estates. As an unmarried woman of property, she had previously filed suits and had acted as an attorney-in-fact for others in the Maryland court. Brent put her experience as an administrator, trader, and legal claimant to work, importing corn from Virginia to feed the troops and using the late governor's estate to pay much of the money owed to the soldiers. Brent then used the deceased's power of attorney over his brother Cecilius's holdings to acquire and sell some cattle, using the proceeds of the sale to pay the soldiers in full. Most famously, in 1648, Brent applied for two votes for herself in the Maryland Assembly, one her own as a landholder and one as Lord Baltimore's attorney. Although she was denied both votes, the Assembly commended Brent for her expertise in handling the Calvert estate, and Brent remains the first woman in the New World to have demanded suffrage.

There has been some speculation as to why Margaret and her sister Mary never married, especially given the shortage of women in the Maryland colony. It has been ventured that the Brent sisters may have taken vows of celibacy, although no evidence exists in support of this theory.

Margaret Brent was also notable for her relationship with a particular Native woman. Mary Kitomaquund, daughter of the Piscataway *tayac*, or chief, was brought in 1640 by Jesuit Father Andrew White to be educated among the English at St. Mary's, the capital of the colony. Margaret Brent and Leonard Calvert were Mary Kitomaquund's legal guardians, and when Mary Kitomaquund was baptized in 1642, it is almost certain that Brent also served as her godmother. In what was possibly a bid for more land (that held by the Piscataways) and power, Brent's brother Giles married Mary Kitomaquund and relocated to lands in Virginia. The Brent sisters followed their brother and Mary Kitomaquund, purchasing a new plantation that Margaret dubbed "Peace." Margaret died there around the year 1671, bequeathing her many properties to her brother and to her nephews and nieces.

Brent's role as godmother to a Native woman appears to relate her to other Catholic women in the early colonial period in North America. While Giles Brent's marriage to Mary Kitomaquund may have been one of expediency, it is quite plausible that Margaret Brent took her position as godmother quite seriously. She appeared in court as Mary Kitomaquund's guardian more than once, and it is assumed that Mary Kitomaquund lived in Margaret and Mary Brent's household for years before her marriage to Giles.

Summary

During the colonial period in the Americas, Catholic women of European origin incorporated themselves into the vast and varied geographies of the Americas in many ways. They served as missionaries, philanthropists, workers, farmers, hostesses, members of religious societies, and household managers. They were the mothers, daughters, sisters, and wives of men of disparate rank and station. While godparenting may not have been their only, nor their most obvious, religious commonality, observing their participation in and judicious use of the sacrament of baptism does help us to understand the worlds through which they traveled. Most often, the institution of godparent was used to construct and formalize extended families of care and cooperation. The formation of ties of fictive kinship enabled women to negotiate the challenges of the new relationships that came into being as a result of colonialism and slavery in the Americas. Many times, the role of godmother accentuated hierarchical relationships, with the godmother clearly standing superior to her godchildren, whose Native or African cultures were held to be inferior. Sometimes, however, women's use of this institution enabled them to bridge cultural divides by establishing relationships of kinship with others apparently unlike themselves. In every case, the godmother and godchild relationship serves as an interesting lens through which to view the lives of Catholic women in the colonial Americas.

SOURCES: As mentioned, James J. Kenneally's *The History of American Catholic Women* (1990) is an excellent source. Primary materials relating to Catholics in colonial New France are found in Reuben Gold Thwaites's edition of the *Jesuit Relations and Allied Documents* (1898), in Irene Mahoney's edition of *Marie de L'Incarnation: Selected Writings* (1989), and in Gabriel Lapointe's edition of *Constitutions et règlements des premières Ursulines de Québec* (1974). Recent secondary works include Hubert Charbonneau et al., *The First French Canadians: Pioneers in the St. Lawrence Valley* (1993); Leslie Choquette, *Frenchmen into Peasants: Modernity and Tradition in the Peopling of French Canada* (1997); Micheline Dumont et al., *Quebec Women: A History* (1987); W. J. Eccles's classic study *The French in North America, 1500–1783* (rev. ed., 1998); and Patricia Simpson, *Marguerite Bourgeoys and Montreal, 1640–1665* (1997). For those without the time or language competence for Marcel Trudel's magisterial *Histoire de la Nouvelle-France* (1963), his work is accessible in abbreviated form in an English reissue of his *Introduction to New France* (1997). Charles J. Balesi's *The Time of the French in the Heart of North America, 1673–1818* (1992) is devoted to that part of New France known as Louisiana; primary materials relating to that geography are collected in John G. Shea's *Early Voyages Up and Down the Mississippi* (1861). New France's southernmost extreme is explored in Thomas N. Ingersoll's *Mammon and Manon in Early New Orleans: The First Slave Society in the Deep South, 1718–1819* (1999). The Maryland State Archives hold primary materials on Margaret Brent and her family; Lois Carr Green's "Margaret Brent—A Brief History" is available on their Web site at http://www.mdarchives.state.md.us/msa/ under "Special Collections." Finally, insight into the institution of godparenting as it was constructed by European Catholics is provided by Agnès Fine in *Parrains, marraines: La parenté spirituelle en Europe* (1994).

AMERICAN CATHOLIC WOMEN, 1820–1900: FROM THE JACKSONIAN PERIOD TO THE PROGRESSIVE ERA
Holly Folk

A SERIES OF tensions troubled American Catholic women in the nineteenth century. Some of them were internal divisions between laywomen and nuns, between immigrants holding on to their Old World culture and their native-born coreligionists, and between "cradle Catholics" who could be somewhat casual about their practice and converts whose commitment to their new faith manifested itself in an evangelical zeal. By far the most troubling issue was that of assimilation: Catholics were torn between their desire to emulate Protestant success and their need to oppose anything "non-Catholic." As women tried to work their way through this maze of issues, they were constrained by idealized models of Catholic femininity. Although most women at this time sought fulfillment through marriage and motherhood, their religious affiliations gave them different ways to understand themselves within these roles. Protestants had a model historians have dubbed "the cult of true womanhood," which kept women domestically happy by valorizing their spiritual natures. Catholic women, on the other hand, were expected to replicate "the Holy Family." Ironically, the Virgin Mary was upheld as a model of motherhood in a religious tradition that had a deeply embedded perception of women as corrupt temptresses. Catholic women, who usually had many children, were to aspire to the virtues of a woman with one divine child and were to do so within a Church that defined them as immature beings in need of surveillance. Whether women chose marriage or the convent, they were expected to be under male control. The stereotypes about women being more devout than men were played out partly in attempts to keep women contained. At the same time, women outperformed men in religious observance and, by working from the margins of the institution, were able to shape American Catholicism in significant ways.

Laywomen in the Antebellum Period

In the 1700s, the American church was primarily defined by an elite class of English Catholics, most strongly based in Maryland. By the 1820s and 1830s, the arrival of immigrants from Europe brought dramatic changes. The result was a shift in religious style, away from sacraments and toward devotions focusing primarily on Mary, Jesus, the Sacred Heart, and the Blessed Sacrament. Devotional Catholicism, distinctly a women's religious culture, espoused traditionally feminine values, such as emotionality, sentimentality, and receptivity to the supernatural, and cultivated submissiveness in a lay population formerly accustomed to governing itself through trusteeship, the system whereby frontier churches called their own priests and made other decisions outside diocesan control. Practices such as reciting the rosary took place in the home, where women held the responsibility of maintaining their families' shrines and altars. Women also comprised the majority of members in the charitable sodalities and devotional societies that created a sense of community vital to parish life.

As devotionalism flourished, Catholics consecrated the American landscape by establishing a series of shrines across the United States. In the 1850s, Adele Brice founded the Chapel Shrine of the Immaculate Conception (the "Wisconsin Lourdes") in Robbinsonville after the Virgin Mary appeared to her. When Mary commanded Brice to begin preaching, the young laywoman aroused the ire of the male clergy. She and her followers protected themselves by becoming lay members of the Third Order of Saint Francis.

Yet Catholics often seem conspicuously absent from the history of American women before 1900. This omission reflects not only long-standing biases in the field but also the increasingly sectarian nature of nineteenth-century Catholicism, which made laywomen ambivalent about participating in changes affecting the Protestant mainstream. Furthermore, the incorporation of Protestant values by Catholic women tended to reflect the distinct priorities of their faith and occurred in a delayed manner that sometimes looked behind the times.

While their numbers increased substantially in later decades, a handful of Catholic writers emerged alongside the Protestant women who discovered fiction writing and journalism as early career possibilities. The first such novel was *The Two Schools: A Moral Tale*, written

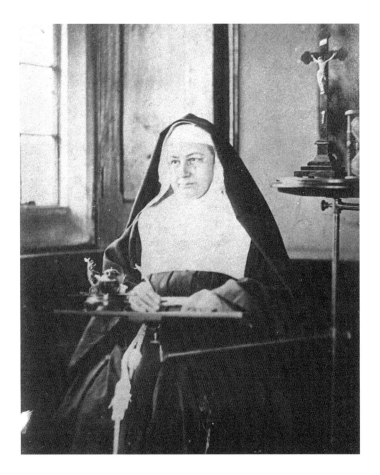

Margaret Cusack, the Irish founder of the Sisters of Saint Joseph of Peace, accused the male clergy of ignoring the needs of the poor, and was censured by the bishops of New York and Newark, Michael Corrigan and Winand M. Wigger. When Archbishop Wigger threatened to refuse admission of postulants to her order, Cusack resigned as Mother Superior and eventually chose to leave the Church rather than cease her protest. *Courtesy of the Sisters of Saint Joseph of Peace.*

by Mrs. Mary Hughs and published in 1835. In addition, some Catholic women adopted the Protestant assumption that women were to be the guardians of their society as an extension of their domestic roles and organized female benevolent societies, like the Mary-Marthian Society in Baltimore, which served poor and sick whites but not blacks, and the Catholic Female Benevolent Society of Detroit, founded in 1834 to assist orphans and the "worthy poor." In the 1850s, Catholic women established the Women's Protective Emigration Society to help Irish girls in danger of becoming prostitutes. By and large, however, the basis for the charity efforts of Catholic women was the parish group rather than the Protestant "moral reform" society or temperance organization. Catholic laywomen raised money for orphanages, hospitals, and other projects and often established "ladies auxiliaries" to assist the efforts of sisters devoted to these causes. The charitable activities of individual Catholic laywomen were also directed toward their faith. Sylvia Parmentier (1793–1882), an immigrant from Belgium whose husband Andre designed the Brooklyn Botanical Garden, was a prominent donor to German Catholic pioneers. Her philanthropy was continued by her daughters, Adele and Rosine, who supported projects to aid sailors, Indians, and African Americans and helped raise money for a girl's Catholic high school in New York City. The Parmentiers' financial support was essential to the growth of American Catholicism.

In some cases, converts were among the most zealous servants of the faith. The daughter of an Ohio senator, Sarah Worthington King Peter (1800–1877), raised money for numerous charities. Rose Hawthorne Lathrop (1851–1926), the youngest daughter of writer Nathaniel Hawthorne, founded the Dominican Congregation of St. Rose of Lima in service of terminal cancer patients. Ellen Theresa Gavin (?–1922) supported the Jesuits and foreign missions and worked for prison reform, which was a favored cause of converts Emma Forbes Carey (1833–1916) and Katherine Conway (1853–1927) as well. Ironically, during the nineteenth century, Protestant-Catholic relations were characterized both by periods of anti-Catholic nativism and by the conversion of significant numbers of Protestants to Catholicism. As many as 40,000 Protestants had joined the Church by 1900. While the majority were immigrants from predominantly Catholic countries, the conversions of educated and affluent Protestants were especially prized by the Catholic hierarchy. Some converts, like Mary Gove Nichols (1810–1884), were proponents of the social causes associated with liberal Protestant culture, such as dress reform and Spiritualism. Others, including Sophia Dana Ripley (1803–1860) of Brook Farm, had ties to liberal Christian movements like Transcendentalism. Many of these converts cited Catholicism's rich history

and intellectual theology as attractions; for some, the Church even seemed to have had an aristocratic cachet.

Catholic Women Religious before 1860

Even more than their counterparts in the laity, women religious played a direct role in the growth of a Catholic institutional infrastructure. Before 1829, only a small number of women's congregations existed, but by the late 1830s, nuns outnumbered priests; in 1859, there already were fifty-nine communities of nuns and sisters in the United States. Because even more communities were founded after the Civil War, there is a tendency in most histories to see the late nineteenth century as more important than the antebellum period. The earlier decades, however, reveal significant patterns in the lives of nuns and sisters in the United States.

American communities of women religious differed from European congregations in several ways. The official status of American sisters was that of "pious ladies" rather than women religious, until their communities were ratified by a papal statute in 1864. Even then, however, American women religious usually took "simple" rather than "solemn" vows, meaning greater freedom in public life but a lower status in the eyes of the Church. The life of American nuns was almost universally focused on service over prayer. Wherever they moved, they consecrated the landscape with schools, hospitals, orphanages, and other institutions. Owing to the vast needs of the Church in North America, most orders were uncloistered, a concession that facilitated their service beyond convent walls, although in later decades, the question of enclosure became progressively more complicated, sometimes with major consequences to the services sisters could perform.

Not only were American sisters more activist than their European counterparts; they also were more egalitarian. Old World, class-based distinctions between "lay" and "choir" sisters, whereby some members of continental religious communities functioned as domestic servants, were seldom espoused. In general, American novices were not expected to bring dowries to the convent when they joined. Before the Civil War, widows and even divorced women were allowed to join convents.

American Catholicism's lack of rigidity in class distinctions did not extend into the question of race relations. In the antebellum period, although free black women founded two orders, the Oblate Sisters of Providence in Baltimore and the Sisters of the Holy Family in New Orleans, virtually all orders of women religious were racially segregated. Some Southern convents even relied on slave labor. Nevertheless, for white women, the unique circumstances of the Church in America meant greater opportunities to pursue a religious life. As a result, increasing numbers of Native-born women aspired to become sisters, although the majority of women's orders were extensions of European congregations (91 of 119 established in the nineteenth century), and Europe continued to supplement the population of American convents into the 1870s.

Some American women appear to have joined convents in an effort to reject traditional expectations of marriage and motherhood. Sister Clementine of Wisconsin, the former Anna Martin (1869–1935), recalled, "I always had in mind to be a sister. I never could stand menfolks. I ran whenever I could to get out of their way." Quite often, nuns seem to have been attracted because of the social connections and bonds felt with women who already were sisters, as Katherine Silberz (Sister Pancratia, 1858–1939) remembered: "My mind was so captivated with them [with the sisters] that I almost adored every thread on them; my mind was soon made up to join them." Ironically, the strength of such friendships had the potential to be socially divisive for women who pursued them; many women who were expected to care for older parents or younger siblings faced familial opposition to their taking of vows (Deacon, 30, 47).

Without dowry requirements or support from established parish communities, American convents faced frequent financial hardships, which were worsened by nuns' tendency to put what money they had into their service projects. The sisters' living conditions were often deplorable. One mother superior cautioned a candidate: "Inconvenience in everything, especially our lodging . . . food that is often disgusting . . . severe cold, prostrating heat, and practically no spring weather. God alone and the desire of His glory: nothing else matters" (Kenneally, 51). Accordingly, women religious were forced to turn to innovative means to make ends meet. The most important source of income was the tuition earned from the schools they operated. Sometimes, nuns raised livestock or grew crops. In St. Louis, Missouri, they sold hand-stitched gunpowder bags for a cent apiece. The need for money forced many communities to turn their attention away from poorer Catholics and market their abilities to wealthier Protestants. Nuns capitalized on their familiarity with "genteel culture," selling handmade lace and embroidery or teaching such skills to the daughters of Protestant families. As a result, nuns were associated in the Protestant imagination not only with poor immigrants but also with a European elitism that had joined forces with the American upper class.

The alignment of Catholic women religious with the American Protestant bourgeoisie is important background to the events at the Mount Benedict Convent of Ursulines in Charlestown, Massachusetts. In August 1834, amid vicious rumors of novices being held against their will and with the vocal encouragement of prominent Protestant minister Lyman Beecher, the convent

and its elite girls' school were burned by a mob of angry working-class Protestants. Historians note the burning of Mount Benedict as one of the most grotesque examples of anti-Catholicism, but recent scholarship suggests that hostility against Boston's upper class was as much a factor in the violence as anti-Catholic nativism. The effect on the Ursulines' project, however, was devastating. Within a year, the small community of nuns had left Boston entirely.

The Ursulines' involvement, direct or indirect, in class conflicts may help explain why women religious were so often the targets of nativist hostility during the antebellum period. Convents in Baltimore, St. Louis, and New Orleans also were attacked. Their authoritarian structure made convents subject to the criticisms that non-Catholics registered against the "antidemocratic" nature of the Church. Nuns also challenged Protestant ideals of womanhood, by virtue of their celibacy and independent lifestyles, which were seen as destructive of the family. Nuns were so frequently described as immoral that the Carmelites and Ursulines wore secular dress in public to avoid harassment.

By the 1850s the Know-Nothing Party introduced legislation in Massachusetts and Maryland to prevent the abuses and immoralities associated with nunneries. That such attempts at legal oversight of convents were only marginally successful should not obscure wider anti-Catholic sentiments, illustrated by one woman's implication in the hostilities against Mount Benedict. In 1831, a Protestant woman named Rebecca Theresa Reed (1812–1838) converted to Catholicism and joined the Mount Benedict convent as a novice shortly after. Four months later, she left under acrimonious circumstances; Reed herself acknowledged that she found it nearly impossible to adapt to the discipline of convent life. After the torching of Mount Benedict, Reed was publicly blamed for inciting the riot. In response, she published an exposé of her experiences there, titled *Six Months in a Convent* (1835). Reed's work was decried in Catholic publications, but she also was excoriated by Protestants for "social-climbing": paradoxically, convents were sometimes seen as avenues to social mobility.

Neither Catholic nor Protestant criticisms were able to prevent Reed's book from selling 50,000 copies. It became a cornerstone of a popular genre of anti-Catholic literature, the most successful manifestation of which was Maria Monk's *The Awful Disclosures of the Hotel Dieu Nunnery in Montreal* (1836), selling 500,000 copies and remaining in print through much of the nineteenth century. While Reed's book reported abuses such as nuns being forced to kiss the floor (a common sign of humility in European Catholicism), *The Awful Disclosures*—which was largely ghost-written by several Protestant ministers from New York—spread rumors of priests and nuns carrying on illicit sexual encounters, with the resulting children murdered behind convent walls. In a fusion of religious intolerance and public entertainment, women claiming to be "escaped nuns" confirmed such abuses to a credulous and prejudiced American public. Sister Isabella, whose exit from the Carmelite convent in Baltimore sparked a riot in 1839, was one of many popular speakers on public lecture tours.

In addition to anti-Catholic bigotry, however, Reed's case also calls attention to the fact that despite a surplus of celebratory literature a nun's life was often quite difficult. The ambition of postulants could be incompatible with the expectations of humility and obedience placed on them. Communal living presented its own set of problems, too, especially in terms of interpersonal conflict. Attrition rates from convents often were quite high. Conflicts within religious orders have yet to be given adequate historiographic attention, but in many cases, they precipitated actual schisms. Often these were over issues such as proposed mergers with other communities or the implementation of an order's rules. In 1846, some of the American Sisters of Charity chose not to join with the French Daughters of Charity, because the merger meant refusing to teach boys. As a result, thirty-three out of fifty sisters withdrew from the community to organize a new order under Elizabeth Boyle. Later, in 1852, out of eight Sisters of Charity in Cincinnati, three left to return to the mother house in Emmitsburg, Maryland, while the remaining five became the nucleus of a new community, under the leadership of Mother Superior Margaret George.

Communities of women religious were troubled more frequently, however, by uneasy relationships with the male clergy. Unlike priests who had free housing, nuns usually had to pay for their rent and heat. Unequal compensation, the expectation that sisters would do the domestic work at seminaries and rectories, and disagreement about control of projects undertaken by sisters were additional sources of strife. The autonomy of women's congregations depended significantly on the capabilities of their Mothers Superior, who had the power to withdraw nuns from parishes and seminaries and reassign them to other duties. The clergy could retaliate by refusing to administer the sacraments or intercepting the sisters' mail. Both Mother Theodore Guerin (1796–1856), founder of Saint Mary-of-the-Woods in Indiana, and Mother Rose Philippine Duchesne (1769–1852), who established the Society of the Sacred Heart and was the fifth American canonized a saint (in 1938), faced excommunication by their bishops. Women's congregations sometimes found a buffer against the power of their local bishops by aligning with the national churches of some immigrant communities, which were themselves at odds with the American hierarchy. They also attached themselves to the rules of

certain orders of parish priests, like the Jesuits and Dominicans, and became "third-order" congregations directly affiliated with the Vatican. Such papal congregations, such as the nuns who in 1873 affiliated with male Franciscans in La Crosse, Wisconsin, often found greater freedom than that available within the diocesan structure.

In the history of American Catholic women, the opening of the American West tends to receive scant attention, although sisters were part of the narrative of expansion from the very beginning. Mary Rhodes (1783–1853) founded the Sisters of Loretto in Bardstown, Kentucky, in 1812 with the help of two friends and a Belgian priest, Charles Nerinckx. Mother Rose Philippine Duchesne led four sisters from France to St. Louis, Missouri, in 1818 to establish the first school for girls west of the Mississippi River and later served as a missionary to the Pottawatomi Indians in Kansas. The French Sisters of St. Joseph of Carondalet also had an early presence in St. Louis, arriving in 1836 to open a school for the deaf. As more Americans migrated westward, nuns increased their efforts. The Sisters of Loretto arrived in Kansas in 1847. In the wake of the California gold rush, the Sisters of Mercy established a presence in San Francisco by 1854. Under the leadership of Mother Superior Mary Baptist Russell (1829–1898), they staffed hospitals, schools, and shelters for the elderly and poor women.

Catholic Women in the Civil War

The Civil War interrupted the founding of orders of women religious, which only resumed in the 1870s. Furthermore, the war had a series of consequences for Catholic Americans, which came out of the roles they played in the conflict, as well as the social, economic, and demographic changes it precipitated. For all these reasons, the Civil War represents a break in nineteenth-century Catholic history.

Until the moment of seccession, Catholics generally were absent from the debate over slavery and abolition. American Catholics' precarious minority status muted their response to such a divisive political issue. Furthermore, long-standing tenets within Catholic theology regarding the naturalness of servitude, sharp social differentiation, and the separation of earthly and temporal powers contributed to a disinclination to take a stand. Unlike Protestant women, who were vital contributors to the religious justifications of the Civil War, few Catholic women participated in the abolition movement.

Once the fighting was under way, the Church's neutrality allowed Catholic women to serve the interests of both the Union and the Confederacy. A laywoman named Rose O'Neal Greenhow (1815?–1864) was one of the most effective spies for the South. Dubbed the

"Bread Woman of New Orleans," Margaret Haughery Gaffney (1814–1882), a former laundress and dairy owner, used the proceeds from her successful bakery to help Confederate soldiers as well as poor girls and orphans. In the North, Mary A. Brady (1821–1864) founded the Soldiers Aid Association of Philadelphia in 1862. Ellen Ewing Sherman (1824–1888), wife of General William T. Sherman, became well known for her fund-raising on behalf of Union soldiers.

Most important, almost 640 sisters from twelve orders tended to sick and injured soldiers on both sides. Women religious saw tending the sick as a religious vocation, not a menial task or social outlet to pursue for a few years before marriage. Their devotion to the suffering often came at the expense of devotional pursuits; necessity sidelined their recitation of the daily office and sometimes even attendance at daily mass. The work they performed included giving medicines and dressing wounds, bathing and feeding patients, doing laundry, cleaning, and even assisting with surgery. Nuns also tended to the dying on the battlefield, both physically and spiritually. A Daughter of Charity stationed in Richmond described her experience:

> Day and night our Sisters constantly administered by turns to soul and body; nourishment, remedies and drinks to the body and as best as they could "living waters to the soul." Indeed, as far as possible, our dear Sisters subtracted from food and rest, the dying and suffering state of these poor men, causing them to make all sacrifices to them even joyfully, regarding such sacrifices as only a drop or cipher compared to the crying duties before them. While they were attending to some, others would be calling to them most piteously to give their wounds some relief. (Maher, 120)

Records from the war attest to many deathbed conversions, which came as a result of the sisters' ministrations.

The lives of sisters, emphasizing poverty, humility, obedience, and community, made nuns emotionally and socially equipped for the hardships of wartime life. Not surprisingly, their aid was often requested by military medical personnel. Sometimes women's congregations decided independently to send sisters where they perceived there to be a need. Their autonomy in matters such as choosing when and where to participate was further reflected in the sisters' general unwillingness to suffer a financial loss for their services. While bishops and doctors were pleased by the nuns' tendency to accept lower wages than Protestant nurses, women religious usually demanded board, rations, and appropriate clothing when serving for a long time.

The fact that nuns assisted the Union and the Confederacy reflected both American Catholicism's politically neutral stance and the sisters' long-standing ethic of relieving human suffering. Sometimes their impartiality subjected sisters to suspicion and criticism, and instances of anti-Catholicism did erupt. Protestant reformer Dorothea Dix, celebrated for her own nursing work during the war, was not only unwilling to collaborate with the sisters in hospital efforts; she refused to work with Catholic women in general. More often than hostility against the nuns, however, their service during the war won them tremendous public approval, permanently changing Protestants' impressions of nuns and the Catholic Church.

Catholic Women in the American West, Post-1865

The end of the Civil War meant an immediate freeing up of military resources to facilitate accelerated westward expansion. Nuns were often among the earliest arrivals on the shifting frontier, where services initially were directed toward Native people. Nuns were seen as good role models for Indians because of the ongoing perception that they were humble and obedient. In 1874, as part of Ulysses S. Grant's "Peace Policy," two Sisters of Charity were sent to the Fort Totten reservation in North Dakota to start a school for the Devil's Lake Sioux. After 1890, when federal Indian policy changed again and most religious organizations abandoned or were forced out of projects on reservations, the Grey Nuns stayed on at Fort Totten for ten more years as official government employees. Other groups of women religious also began projects with tribes on the Great Plains, including the Irish Sisters of Presentation, Swiss Benedictines, and German Sisters of St. Francis. In South Dakota Katherine Drexel (1858–1955), founder of the Sisters of the Blessed Sacrament for Indians and Colored People, established the St. Francis Missionary School and the Holy Rosary Mission for the Oglala Lakota (Sioux) in 1886 and 1888, respectively. Drexel was canonized in 2000.

The interactions of sisters and Native communities are best described as mixed. Recent scholarship has brought to light many negative aspects of the relations between Native peoples and the Catholics, Protestants, and Mormons sent to convert them. Furthermore, the children's experience in Catholic boarding schools has become the subject of particular criticism. Discipline was often quite harsh, and students were expected to do much of the manual labor to keep the schools operating. Missionaries and Native Americans, however, faced similar hardships associated with boarding school and reservation life, such as inadequate food, housing, and clothing and rampant epidemics associated with close living spaces. Tuberculosis was a major killer among both nuns and indigenous people.

In keeping with the assumption that nuns exerted a "civilizing" influence, they soon were expected to address the rowdiness of non-Indian culture as well. Both the Presentation and Benedictine Sisters added parish schools for whites soon after arriving on the reservations. Other orders skipped reservation work entirely, moving directly to providing services to fledgling Catholic parishes. The Sisters of Loretto opened a school in Denver in 1864. After their arrival in Colorado in 1877, the Sisters of Saint Joseph opened several schools, hospitals, and orphanages. The service of nuns to non-Indians is one sign of a nascent Catholic presence in the West, where Irish, German, Italian, and French Canadian labor was needed for mining and railroad work. By the 1870s, at least 1,200 Catholics had settled in Arizona. As many as 6,000 Catholics lived in Colorado at the turn of the century. In Denver, especially, Italian Catholic women seem to have been active in creating a solid parish life. As few records exist, it is difficult to portray life in these communities.

Because the lives of individual Catholics afford better information, the history to date has tended to focus on unusual Catholic women, like Nellie Cashman (1850–1925), who was a prospector in the Southwest and later in Alaska. When not looking for gold, she ran several restaurants in Arizona. Cashman also financed and organized the building of the first Catholic church in Tucson. Arguably the most colorful woman religious on the frontier was Sister Blandina Segale (1850–1941?). An Italian immigrant who joined the Sisters of Charity's Cincinnati mother house at sixteen, she was sent to Trinidad, Colorado, in 1872. There, Sister Blandina gained recognition for her acquaintance with the outlaw Billy the Kid, a friendship documented in her book *At the End of the Santa Fe Trail*. Later, she founded a trade school for Indian girls and a hospital for railroad workers in Santa Fe, New Mexico. In her autobiography, she reflected, "I wish I had many hands and feet, and a world full of hearts to place at the service of the Eternal. So much one sees to be done, and so few to do it. I have adopted this plan: Do whatever presents itself, and never omit anything because of hardship or repugnance" (Segale, 33). In keeping with her motto of "To teach and meet emergencies as I see them," Segale returned to Cincinnati in 1894 to work with Italian immigrants. There, she founded the first Catholic settlement house three years later.

The "New Immigrants": Working-Class Catholic Laywomen

Nineteenth-century Catholic culture was primarily urban and coastally oriented. Census records from 1890 show that 48 percent of Catholics lived in cities of more than 25,000 people. This demographic pattern coincided with the tremendous influx of immigrants, now not only from Ireland and Germany but increasingly from eastern and southern Europe. Their arrival swelled the ranks of American Catholics, so that by the 1890s there were 8 million Catholics in the United States and 2,000 churches. Yet immigration created a crisis for the Catholic hierarchy, frustrated by the lack of familiarity of newcomers with basic rituals as well as their indifference to supporting the Church financially.

The immigrants were heterogenous in their devotional lives. They revered different saints, often tied to their unique cultures. The Irish focused on St. Patrick, and the Poles on St. Stanislaus. Public displays of worship also varied; the Germans were fond of pageants and processions, while Italians and eastern Europeans favored festivals devoted to the patron saints of their particular communities. Yet these diverse groups shared the common experience of relying on women to guard their religious and cultural distinctiveness. Just as saints were intermediaries between God and human beings, women were the intermediaries for their families to the saints. They served as representatives of their families in visits to the Church, where they presented gifts to protective figures on behalf of their relatives, and performed ritual acts of sacrifice such as allowing themselves to be dragged down the aisles. Women prepared the foods associated with certain holidays, like the Polish babka bread of Easter or the Italian fish supper on Christmas Eve. They maintained shrines in their homes and continued to be the majority of members of sodalities and devotional organizations.

While the Irish-controlled American hierarchy strived to build a single model of religious life, the new immigrants fragmented into national churches, where services were performed in the languages of their home countries, and culturally based institutions such as the German Central Verein, the Polish National Union, and the Sons of Italy. By the turn of the century, many of these groups had created or accepted ladies' auxiliaries or independent women's organizations like the Daughters of Isabella or the Polish Women's Alliance. Yet women's rights tended to be addressed only tangentially: Rather, their concerns were subordinated to ethnic ones and placated by the promise of a trickle-down gain of benefits. Some immigrant women also formed mutual-aid societies, although men's groups were much more prevalent. The first female insurance organization, the Ladies Catholic Benevolent Association, was founded in 1890; twenty-one years later it had 121,000 members.

The new waves of immigration precipitated several waves of anti-Catholic nativism, beginning in the 1870s and continuing throughout the remainder of the century. Catholic women were often unfairly caricatured for both their ethnicity and gender, as was Catherine O'Leary, whose cow was blamed for starting the Great Chicago Fire in 1871. Nativists, especially the American Protective Association, often associated Catholics with labor unrest as well. Yet through most of the nineteenth century, lay Catholic labor activism took place without the approval of the Church, which was vehemently anticommunist and strongly defended the principle of private property.

The Church was especially ambivalent about women in the paid workforce, because they represented a threat to Catholic expectations of womanhood. The hierarchy's continuing preference that women keep to their feminine roles as wives and mothers had the potential to invite disastrous consequences for the urban Catholic working class where poverty was widespread. Nor was the clergy able to prevent Catholic workers from organizing. In the 1880s, female Bohemian cigar workers went on strike in New York City. "Big Mary" Septak led Polish, Italian, and Hungarian women armed with rolling pins and fire pokers as they stood with their husbands in an 1897 Pennsylvania coal strike.

Several Catholic women became prominent leaders in the labor movement, beginning with Augusta Lewis (1840–1920), who organized the Women's Typographical Union in 1868. Ten years later, Elizabeth Flynn Rodgers (1847–1939) established the first women's union in Chicago and was elected a delegate for the Knights of Labor in 1881. Leonora Barry (1849–1930) also worked for the Knights of Labor, as a female investigator of labor conditions. When a group of priests derided her as a "lady tramp," Barry defended her right to organize as "an Irishwoman, a Catholic, and an honest woman" (Foner, 1:200). The Chicago Teachers Federation was founded in 1897 by two Catholic women: Margaret Haley (1861–1939) and Catherine Goggin (1855–1916).

The most famous Catholic woman labor activist was Mary Harris ("Mother") Jones (1830–1930), one of the founders of the Chicago-based union the Industrial Workers of the World (the "Wobblies"), who later participated in strikes in the railroad, steel, textile, and coal industries. Although she once worked as a convent school teacher, Jones was highly critical of the Church, which she saw as otherworldly in focus and detached from the real needs of working people: "I never saw more moral cowards in my life than those sisters . . . they are simply owned body and soul by the Rockefeller interests" (Hennessey, 215). Yet Jones's activism was strongly rooted in a revolutionary interpretation of Christianity rather than Marxist atheism. Her recommendation that workers "pray for the dead and fight like hell for the living" presaged the "liberation theology" movement of the late twentieth century. Despite her

fractious relationship with Catholicism in life, Jones arranged her own burial with a full church service.

Outreach of Nuns to Immigrant Catholics

The Catholic hierarchy's conservative stance on the labor question reflected their tendency to be indifferent to the plight of the urban poor. By and large, the male clergy did little to respond to the needs and priorities of immigrant Catholics. Rather, they left institutional Catholicism's responsibilities to nuns and sisters. With their services so much in demand, women's orders recruited heavily in both Europe and the United States. Although only 1,334 sisters served in the United States in 1850, at the end of the century, more than 40,000 women religious staffed hospitals, orphanages, asylums, and schools across America.

By 1870, women religious had opened seventy hospitals in the United States. Thirty years later, the number had quadrupled, and six orders of nuns staffed almost half the private charity hospitals in New York City. Hospital work often required a broad interpretation of religious rules. In New York, for example, the Sisters of Saint Dominic were considered a cloistered order until 1896, but their cloister was extended to encompass St. Catherine's Hospital in Brooklyn. The hospital work done by Catholic women religious generally has been seen as an extension of their role as nurses during the Civil War, but some historians have suggested that the care provided in later years was less than adequate. Catholic ideas regarding sexuality and the body precluded innovative treatment of certain conditions, such as childbirth and venereal disease. Nuns also were sometimes accused of being more interested in saving souls than bodies—for example, withholding medicine from sick children in order to "make them angels." In at least one case, a priest was summoned rather than a doctor to attend to a hemorrhaging patient. Two historical developments converged to become the major factors affecting the quality of care in Catholic hospitals. In the late nineteenth century, nursing adopted new standards of professionalization; at the same time, the Catholic Church sought to reinforce traditional values regarding religious life that kept sisters from taking advantage of new methods and thereby upgrading their skills. As expectations of enclosure became more widespread, male doctors' nighttime access to hospital wards was often curtailed, with obvious consequences for their patients.

In 1910, 52,000 children were being raised in 285 Catholic orphanages, although this number represented boys being cared for by male brothers as well as children raised by nuns. Like Protestant and municipal homes for children, Catholic orphanages were racially segregated, but their racial profile was not their only significant demographic point. As the numbers of the working poor swelled, these facilities began to serve fewer children whose parents had died. Instead, they housed the children of immigrants who could not afford their care.

Several orders of women religious ran protective associations aimed at keeping poor women from entering prostitution, as well as maternity homes and domestic violence shelters. Such endeavors became a special mission for the Sisters of Mercy and Sisters of Good Shepherd; the latter operated 150 homes for wayward girls and poor women by 1893. Yet of all the activities undertaken by women religious, no issue was more controversial than sisters' outreach to women. Priests and bishops tended to regard not only prostitutes but also working women as so beyond the pale of salvation that they questioned the value of helping them at all. Nuns responded to the male clergy with varying levels of defiance. Perhaps the most extreme criticism of priests came from Margaret Cusack (1829–1899), the Irish founder of the Sisters of Saint Joseph of Peace. In the 1880s, Cusack accused the male clergy of ignoring the needs of the poor and was censured by the bishops of New York and Newark, Michael Corrigan and Winand M. Wigger. When Archbishop Wigger threatened to refuse admission of new postulants to her order, Cusack resigned as mother superior and eventually chose to leave the Church rather than cease her protest. She defended herself in a spirited autobiography: "I have a duty to God, to the church, and above all, to those who have confided their alms to me so often and so generously. I know that they have a right to be told why I have been unable to carry out a work so necessary for the poor, and for working girls. . . . It has certainly taken me a very long time to realize that there was no justice for me, and no use in persevering, but I have realized it at last" (Cusack, 483). That Cusack was not the only foundress to clash with Corrigan suggested that her frustrations against the clergy were valid. Mother Frances Xavier Cabrini (1850–1917), who established the Missionaries of the Sacred Heart, faced opposition when she began her outreach to Italian immigrants. Cabrini used traditional Catholicism to defend herself: "If the mission of announcing the Lord's resurrection to his apostles had been entrusted to Mary Magdalen, it would seem a very good thing to *confide* to other women an evangelizing mission" (Kenneally, 97).

Cabrini was vindicated when she became the first American citizen to be canonized. Ultimately, however, priests and bishops were victorious in their campaign against the aid of nuns to poor women. In 1884, the Third Plenary Council of Baltimore's call for universal religious education channeled the labor of most sisters into parochial schools, with services to adult women sacrificed to the greater goal of educating Catholic youth. Catholic schools quickly became the major philanthropic endeavor of the Church; between 1880 and 1900, the number of children attending Catholic elementary schools more than doubled, to 850,000 students. Parochial schools became the backbone of an educational system that flourished well into the twentieth century. Yet the nuns who staffed the schools as teachers and administrators were not simply conductors of diocesan Catholicism; they often contributed to the perpetuation of ethnic distinctiveness. The Polish Felician sisters who arrived in Wisconsin in 1874 helped socialize immigrants to American culture, but the schools they ran also helped create a coherent Polish American identity, one essential to the later movement for national churches. A comparable situation was found in southern New England, where "Grey Nuns" from Canada became a powerful force for the preservation of French Canadian culture, the movement known as "la survivance."

American Catholic Women in the Age of Progress

Parochial schools spawned a new interest among Catholics in education; the late nineteenth century witnessed the proliferation of a diverse array of initiatives to educate adults. In the wake of the establishment of several Catholic colleges for men by priests, nuns began to found colleges for women, beginning with the College of Notre Dame in Maryland in 1896. The capstone of their endeavors was Trinity College in Washington, D.C., established in 1900 by two School Sisters of Notre Dame de Namur: Sister Julia McGroarty (1827–1901) and Sister Mary Euphrasia Taylor (Ellen Osmonia Taylor, 1855–1918). The sisters' cause was aided by growing support in the United States for women's higher education, as well as a widespread sense that Catholics of both genders would do better to learn in religious institutions, a sign of the continuing cultural divide between Catholics and Protestants. Yet many Catholics, including a good portion of the clergy, remained suspicious of the need for women's colleges. Questions also were raised about whether female students at Trinity would distract the men at nearby Catholic University. Ironically, this concern was balanced by the recognition that Trinity could serve as a segregated alternative to coeducation. Both McGroarty and Taylor wrote pleas invoking Catholicism's tradition of intellectual women as justification for their cause. Sister Julia asserted that nineteenth-century Catholic women possessed "every facility for becoming as brilliant lights in the intellectual world as those who have shown in ecclesiastical history in 1586 bygone ages—the Hildas, the Liobas, the Marcellas, the Paulas, the Eustochiums, the Catherines, and hosts of others" (Hayes, 84). Ultimately, objections to the establishment of Trinity were only resolved when the Vatican declined to condemn the nuns' proposal.

In 1884 at the last national meeting of the Catholic Church in Baltimore, the Third Plenary Council issued a call for Catholic adult education, which encouraged lay Catholics to initiate grassroots projects, including evening classes, literary societies, and summer schools. At first, these groups were all male, but they quickly became popular among women, beginning with the Ozanam Reading Circle for Women, organized in 1886. Three years later, the *Catholic World*, the Catholic newspaper in the United States, started publishing lists of books appropriate for group reading and discussion. The column, known as the "Columbian Reading Union," linked reading circles across the country. Catholics also copied the Methodists' Chautauqua program and brought guest lecturers and cultural events to locales across the country. The Catholic Summer School of America was launched in New London, Connecticut, in 1892. The following year, Cliff Haven Summer School held its first session in New York. With several hundred attendees at each program and as many as 10,000 a year, Cliff Haven was the largest and best known Catholic summer school and served as a model for schools in Wisconsin, Louisiana, and Maryland. Because three-fourths of its participants were female, the curriculum at Cliff Haven showed a particular orientation to women, and prominent women Catholic writers were frequent lecturers.

Concerns about threats to Catholic identity proved to be the salvation of these organizations, which were criticized for their embrace of inappropriate, "modern" attitudes about gender. Some Catholics complained that the institutes were simply places where young people sought each other for romantic encounters. In response, two noted conservative women, Katherine Conway and Eliza Allen Starr, pointed out that the Columbian Reading Union was a successful preventative to mixed marriages with Protestants. In a letter printed in the *Catholic World*, a woman named Julie E. Perkins justified reading circles: "Many young ladies who are graduated from Catholic academies and other schools feel when school time is past, a mature desire for self-improvement. They seek a more advanced course of Catholic reading" (June 1889, 416).

Perkins's defense of the reading groups contained a new concern with respectability and self-cultivation, Protestant attitudes that were adopted by American Catholics as they entered the middle class. As increasing numbers of Catholics, mostly "lace-curtain" Irish Americans, made economic gains, Catholic women also were confronted with the expectations of a new domestic ideology championing the values of purity, piety, domes-

ticity, and submissiveness. For Catholics, as for Protestants decades earlier, this model of women's identity offered new opportunities for action within the public sphere even as it reinforced traditional expectations that women's public lives would be circumscribed by standards of appropriate conduct.

The adoption of middle-class values and changes in gender ideals coincided with two other changes within American Catholicism. A "lay renaissance" in the late nineteenth century afforded Catholic women an increased voice in defining their faith; and the Third Plenary Council's call for Catholic education created a need for more Catholic literature, which in turn caused a booming religious press. These developments made it possible for dozens of Catholic women to pursue careers as novelists, journalists, and editors. Family magazines and religious newspapers emerged as alternatives to secular pulp fiction. The *Ave Maria* was the first such publication but was quickly followed by others, like the *Boston Pilot*, *Catholic Home Journal*, and *Catholic World*. In 1865, the year of its founding, the *Ave Maria* had a circulation of 6,000; by 1891, subscriptions had more than quadrupled. Its success was largely due to Angela Gillespie (1824–1880), mother superior of the Sisters of the Holy Cross and head of St. Mary's Academy at Notre Dame, who worked for the paper as an "editorial assistant" from 1865 to 1889.

Although ostensibly run by priests, Catholic newspapers often employed women behind the scenes. The *Sacred Heart Review*, for example, was staffed primarily by young Irish women; by 1880 its circulation had climbed to 40,000. These women had a great deal of editorial power but were obliged to temper its public demonstration. As a result, although women writers were strongly represented in the Catholic press, their published work tended to reaffirm traditional Catholic themes. Novels by writers like Anna H. Dorsey (1815–1890), Mary A. Sadlier (1820–1903), and Eleanor C. Donnelly (1836–1917) were usually didactic, aimed at glorifying the Church and pointing out the dangers of non-Catholic society. These works often portrayed female characters as suffering figures of redemption, whose self-sacrifice "tamed" men. Similarly, many of the essays and opinion pieces published by prominent women such as Eliza Allen Starr (1824–1901), Madeline Vinton Dahlgren (1825–1898), and Katherine Conway (1853–1927) were highly conservative.

Collectively, these writers reflect how, in the late nineteenth century, American Catholic women found more opportunities to express their views publicly but were nonetheless expected to refrain from challenging traditional gender roles. It cannot be said that these women were not sincere in their religious beliefs or visions for American womanhood, but their lives and work still suggest that many profited personally by taking a reactionary stance on the "woman question," best illustrated by their opposition to the suffrage movement. In the 1860s, Ellen Ewing Sherman, known for her charitable work on behalf of Union soldiers, successfully circulated an antisuffrage petition to members of the U.S. Congress. In the following decades other women followed in her footsteps, sometimes carving successful careers by opposing women's rights. These included ex-socialist Martha Moore Avery (1851–1929), journalist and Irish American nationalist Margaret Buchanan Sullivan (1847–1903), and Ella B. Edes (1832–1916), a convert working for the Congregation of Propaganda who spent several years in Rome as a reporter on the Vatican. Even the most vehement antifeminists, however, often were selective in their conservatism. Eleanor Donnelly was strongly pro-education; Eliza Allen Starr urged greater involvement of women in the arts. Madeline Dahlgren cosponsored Ellen Sherman's petition to Congress and campaigned against suffrage for twenty-five years but also supported the right of women to work.

Antisuffragists found a willing audience among American Catholics, even though at the local level, voting was often a priority for Catholic women. By 1888, for example, between 6,000 and 7,000 Catholic women cast ballots in school board elections in Massachusetts. As a group, however, Catholics of both sexes opposed suffrage. In part, this stance reflected their alienation from mainstream Protestant priorities. Non-Catholic perception that the Church was antidemocratic pervaded the feminist movement. In her book *Modern Society*, Julia Ward Howe attacked Catholicism. During the 1890s groups like the Independent Women Voters in Massachusetts joined with the American Protective Association to promise that native-born women voters would drown out the voices of immigrant women, should suffrage be attained. Other factors contributed to Catholic perspectives, too. Although Bishop John Spalding of Peoria, Illinois, supported women's right to vote because he believed their enfranchisement could help elevate society, more commonly the hierarchy perceived suffrage as a threat to idealized female domesticity. The legacy of Pauline theology and the fact that suffrage was linked to the birth-control movement also made Catholics reluctant to pursue women's rights.

Except for Jane Campbell (1854–1928), who founded the Philadelphia County Woman Suffrage Association, there were few prominent Catholic women feminists in the nineteenth century, and some Catholic supporters of women's rights were as conservative as their opponents. Elizabeth Blanche Murphy (1845–1881) argued that liberation would make women better wives. Mary Elizabeth Blake McGrath (1840–1907) supported the suffrage movement but was better known for her involvement in dress reform and "moral cleanliness." Still, support for the vote could be found among individual women whose nonconformity made them distinctive, such as writers Charlotte Perkins Gilman (1860–1935) and Mary Agnes Tincker (1835–1907), who were ambivalent about or even hostile to the Catholic Church. Others had unusual affiliations to Protestant social activism: Writer Alice Timmons Toomy was connected to Jane Addams's settlement house movement, and labor activist Leonora Barry Lake (1849–1930) went on to work for both suffrage and temperance.

Despite the activities of these women, few cooperative endeavors between Catholics and Protestants emerged during the Progressive Era. Both middle-class Catholics and Protestants were concerned about immigrants' lack of familiarity with American ways and saw in their poverty a lack of civilized behavior, but Catholics hoped to protect the preexisting religious commitments of immigrants, while Protestants often viewed their conversion as essential. Consequently, Catholics and Protestants pursued parallel, rather than collaborative, projects; for example, Catholics had founded twenty-seven settlement houses by 1915. Catholic women's participation in the temperance movement ran somewhat counter to this model, however. Because Catholics were alienated by the nativist undertones of organizations like the Anti-Saloon League, the Catholic Total Abstinence Union (CTAU) was established in 1872. For six years it refused to admit women as anything more than "honorary" members and barred them from participating in conventions until 1887. Many Catholic women therefore joined the Women's Christian Temperance Union despite its Protestant profile. In 1890 Sally Moore was chosen as the third vice president of the CTAU, and women's participation in the organization increased substantially thereafter. By 1902, 16 percent of the participants in the Catholic temperance movement were female.

Catholic Women's Prospects at the Turn of the Century

The settlement house, temperance, labor, and suffrage movements all enjoyed some of their greatest successes between 1900 and 1930. It is difficult, therefore, to focus on any of these developments as a historical end point for the nineteenth century. Nor does the "Americanist Controversy," a common standard demarcating the period, work for American Catholic women, because the pseudoconflict had little impact on their lives. Two other events may better showcase the distance American Catholic women had come in the nineteenth century and how far they still had to go. In 1893, although Catholic women did not participate in the

World's Parliament of Religions, numerous laywomen delivered position papers and staffed the women's pavilion of the Catholic Congress, held in conjunction with the Columbian Exposition in Chicago. Similarly, a papal bull issued in 1900 ratified the accomplishments of women religious, albeit with mixed consequences for American sisters.

At the Catholic Congress, many women presenters reaffirmed the conservative perspectives that had made them famous. Eleanor C. Donnelly gave a paper titled "The Home Is Woman's Sphere" in which she lamented:

> To throw aside the tiresome details of home-keeping; to board, or live in a flat; to slaughter the unborn innocents; have a free foot, unfettered by duty to house, husband, or children, are not these the crying demands of *fin de siecle* women? . . . They dress like men, they talk like men. They force themselves into the manliest avocations of men, and strive to fill them, loud-voiced and aggressive, to the criminal neglect of their own bounden duties. . . . All that is gentle, attractive, womanly withers under the hot sun of publicity and notoriety. (*Catholic World*, August 1893, 680–681)

Nonetheless, other speakers issued a call to support women's achievements and goals on a variety of fronts, including education, work, and social engagement. Antifeminist journalist Katherine Conway, one of whose papers was titled "Woman Has No Vocation to Public Life," reinforced traditional prohibitions on women's religious leadership but suggested that their individual abilities determine their access to careers in medicine, law, industry, and the humanities. Conway's vision was articulated even more strongly by Rose Hawthorne Lathrop, who urged women "to arise and defend your rights, your abilities for competition with men, in intellectual and professional endurance" (Kenneally, 91).

Women's exclusion from the World's Parliament of Religions reflected their ongoing marginalization in both American society and their own religious tradition. Yet their presence in the Catholic Congress announced not only an imminent arrival in the American mainstream but a determination to arrive as Catholic women, committed to promoting "the genuine good of humanity in accordance with the principles of the Catholic Church" (92). The forum offered new opportunities for collective action: Participants passed a resolution encouraging the development of societies to aid young working women. The most successful such initiative was the Catholic Women's Association of Brooklyn, which grew into an extension center of the State University of New York. The Catholic Women's League also was launched by women at the Catholic Congress. Led by honorary president Eliza Allen Starr and with headquarters in Chicago, the league opened day-care centers, job services, and shelters for poor girls. Eventually, the organization joined the suffrage battle on the side of women's rights.

Seven years later, American nuns announced their figurative arrival within Catholicism, when the papal bull *Conditae a Cristo* formally recognized congregations of sisters with simple vows. For American nuns, this declaration had mixed consequences. While acknowledging the authenticity of their religious commitments and their contributions in building an American Catholic infrastructure, American women religious were required to adopt more stringent rules of cloister, thereby assuming a more European profile. The new imposition of scrutiny of behavior and expectations of propriety ushered in by *Conditae a Cristo* suggest that it did not translate to a real empowerment of women religious but rather to a loss of autonomy. The experience of the Sisters of Notre Dame in Massachusetts offers one example of this pattern. Beginning in the 1890s, the nuns' ability to leave the convent was vastly curtailed. All manifestations of a "normal" social life came under ecclesiastical control, including social visiting, shopping, and attending to the sick. After 1908, these nuns found themselves limited to their church, convent, and school. Social visits were totally prohibited unless excused by special permission of their cardinal. American sisters had "arrived" in international Catholicism, but this meant new expectations of conformity to tradition.

Both the presence of women at the 1893 Catholic Congress and the 1900 declaration reflected the new roles and opportunities that had emerged for Catholic women inside and outside the cloister over the nineteenth century. In some ways, however, Catholic women's history at the turn of the century is best understood as an unfinished narrative. Lay or religious, Catholic women had yet to successfully challenge their secondary status in religious and secular life.

SOURCES: Toward the end of the nineteenth century, women writers were frequent contributors to the *Catholic World*, making it the best set of original sources. Several of the speeches from the women's forum at the Columbia Exposition were reprinted in the August 1893 issue. For individual quotations and general information, see James Kenneally's book, *The History of American Catholic Women* (1990), as well as James Hennessey, *American Catholics: A History of the Roman Catholic Community in the United States* (1981). The *U.S. Catholic Historian* has run many articles on the history of Catholic women in the United States, including Mary Hayes's article "The Founding Years of Trinity College, Washington, D.C.: A Case Study in Christian Feminism" (10 [1989]: 79–86). For biographies of individual women, see Louise Callan, *Philippine Duchesne: Frontier Missionary of the Sacred Heart, 1769–1852* (1957); Sister Blandina Segale, *At the End of the Santa Fe Trail*

(1948); and Margaret Anna Cusack, *The Nun of Kenmare: An Autobiography*, ed. Maria Luddy (1998). On Leonora Barry, see Philip Foner, *Women and the American Labor Movement*, vol. 1 (1979). Dissertations by Florence Jean Deacon, "Handmaids or Autonomous Women: The Charitable Activities, Institution Building and Communal Relationships of Catholic Sisters in Nineteenth Century Wisconsin" (University of Wisconsin, Madison, 1989); and Mary Ewens, "The Role of the Nun in Nineteenth Century America" (University of Minnesota, 1971), have addressed the lives of women religious in this period. For the service of nuns during the Civil War, see Mary Denis Maher, *To Bind Up the Wounds: Catholic Sister Nurses in the U.S. Civil War* (1989).

AFRICAN AMERICAN CATHOLIC WOMEN

Cecilia A. Moore

THE FIRST KNOWN Catholic of African descent in North America was not a woman. His name was Esteban, and he was a slave. In 1536, he accompanied a band of Spanish explorers surveying an area now known as Florida, Texas, and Arkansas. Esteban's story is important to the history of African American Catholic women because it manifests the presence and contributions of black Catholics from the earliest days of Catholicism in the New World. His enslavement was a harbinger of over 300 years of African American Catholic experience. There can be no understanding of the history of African American Catholics without an acute sensibility to the ways in which slavery shaped African American Catholics' experience and engagement with their faith. Esteban's story is important to the histories of African American Catholic women because it adumbrates themes particular to their experiences. His role as an explorer is symbolic of the innovations and initiatives in religious life, social justice, education, and religious and cultural expression that are the hallmarks of African American Catholic women's history.

By the mid-sixteenth century, Spain was aggressively colonizing the Caribbean and the southernmost part of what is now considered to be the United States. Hoping to build an empire based on the agricultural riches of these areas, the Spanish enslaved Africans to work for the plantations they established. Young men of sturdy constitutions were most desired for slavery, but women were also imported to work side by side with the men and to bear new generations of slaves. Sacramental records from Florida and the Caribbean indicate that Catholic masters tended to abide by the requirements of the Church that slaves be baptized in the Church. Africans were also married in and buried from the Roman Catholic Church. By the eighteenth century communities of enslaved black Catholics existed.

But Africans did not arrive in North America stripped of religious sensibilities or convictions. The transatlantic voyages and consequent bondage did not destroy their religious traditions, values, beliefs, and principles. And while it is imprudent to claim a monolithic African religion, it is possible to identify characteristics West African religions share in common. Among these are faith in the gods and ancestors, the primacy of family and community over the individual, corporate worship, belief in the efficacy of prayers of the living to the dead, sacrifice to the gods, the idea of death as passage to a greater life, and adaptability in religious practice. African women held significant roles in West African religions. In some cases women served in priest-like roles. Elderly women enjoyed reverence because their communities regarded them as wise in spiritual and temporal matters. Women also served as healers, leaders of religious rituals, and the primary religion teachers of their children.

One way Europeans convinced themselves that they were justified in enslaving Africans was by asserting that slavery was a way to bring Christianity to Africans, whom they considered to be heathens. Skipping over the fact that Christianity has a much older history in Africa than in the West, Europeans contended that slavery was justified by bringing the light of true faith, faith in Jesus Christ, to a people doomed to damnation without it. Catholic Europeans involved in the slave trade particularly believed that Catholicism would save the Africans. Many Catholic masters felt a spiritual urgency and religious obligation to have those they enslaved baptized. The less fervent had their slaves baptized to stay in the good graces of the political interests of the time. Still others thought greater coercion over them could be exercised by controlling slave religious practice and theology.

Some Africans already may have been Catholic when they arrived in the New World, although this is not likely. But it is clear that not all Catholic slaves converted only because required to do so by their masters. There were slaves who freely chose Catholicism because they believed in its message. For these women and men, Catholicism may have resonated with their African religious beliefs, practices, and principles. Roughly parallel to their beliefs about the gods and the ancestors was the Roman Catholic communion of the saints. The centrality of the family and community over the individual in West African traditional religions was similar to the primacy of the Church over the individual in Catholicism. The Catholic mass replete with elaborate vestments, incense, Latin chant, liturgical movement, and mystery evoked the light, color, music, rhythm, and splendor of West African religious celebrations and rituals (Brown).

From the sixteenth century to the nineteenth century, African American Catholicism grew in areas where Ca-

that her religion would not be interfered with she was quite happy" (O'Neill, 44). After emancipation, Mitchell went to live with an African American Catholic family in Richmond, and at age seventy-three the daily communicant became a Franciscan tertiary. She died in 1912 and was buried from St. Joseph's Catholic Church in Richmond, the church for which she had prayed. St. Joseph's Catholic Church was one of the first parishes established especially for African Americans in Virginia.

The quality of Mitchell's devotion was not uncommon for black Catholic women. Throughout the eighteenth and nineteenth centuries, one may find women fully engaged with their faith in all manner of religious activities and charitable activities. These women joined sodalities, established and endowed schools and orphanages, created religious communities, and even petitioned Pope Pius IX to come to the aid of African American Catholics neglected by racially prejudiced American priests and bishops. They worked within and for the African American community. Slavery complicated, but did not deter, their endeavors, and these women succeeded in creating a strong and resilient Catholic identity and community.

At age fifteen, Anne Marie Becroft, a freeborn African American Catholic Washingtonian, started her first school for African American girls in Georgetown in 1820. Becroft had studied at the Potter School and the New Georgetown School in Washington, D.C., until the racist sentiments and intensified Southern fears about the dangers of educating blacks forced the schools to dismiss her. Becroft ran her day school for girls until 1827, when the pastor of Holy Trinity Catholic Church, a white parish with African American members, asked her to start a Catholic day and boarding school. With the help of Visitation Sisters, Becroft did so, and the school was an immediate success. Students hailing from Virginia, Maryland, and Washington, D.C., paid a dollar a month. Becroft ran the school until 1831 when she became a member of the Oblate Sisters of Providence, taking the name Sr. Aloysius. One of her students took the school's helm after Becroft's departure.

At about the same time, in Louisiana another laywoman established a Catholic school. Born in Guinea, West Africa, Marie Bernard Couvent was enslaved as a child and brought to Haiti. How she achieved her freedom is not known, but once free she went to live in

tholicism and slavery prevailed. This meant African American Catholic communities established roots in Florida, the coastal regions of Alabama and Mississippi, Louisiana, and Maryland. In these areas the numbers of lay and religious Catholic slaveholders were significant. Maryland Catholics were particularly conscientious about having their slaves baptized, especially if they were children. Catholic slave children could have either black or white godparents and sometimes one of each. A significant number of Maryland slaves did marry in the Church, and Catholic masters tried to arrange Catholic spouses for their slaves.

The value of Catholicism to African American slave women is revealed in informal community recollections. Emily Mitchell is regarded as the first African American Catholic in Richmond, Virginia, and reportedly in the whole state of Virginia. She was born in Baltimore in 1824 to John and Priscilla Mitchell, Catholic slaves. In 1846 the non-Catholic Breeden family bought Mitchell for the purpose of caring for their children. The fact that the Breedens were not Catholic gravely troubled Mitchell. "It was a great worry to her that she might not be allowed to practice her faith, but after an assurance

New Orleans. There she married a prosperous free black man named Gabriel Bernard Couvent. When he died, he left Marie a good deal of property that she donated to start a school for free orphans of color in New Orleans. Couvent, called the "Widow Couvent," became well known and respected during her lifetime in the city for her acts of charity. Her generosity continued after her death in 1832. In her will, she directed that the money she left be used to establish a Catholic school for free children of color. It was finally ready in 1848 and was called L'Institution Catholique des Orphelins Indigens. It was open to all children, not just orphans. The school gained a reputation for excellence, and later New Orleanians called it the Couvent School.

Father John F. Hickey kept the *Journal of the Commencement and of the proceedings of the Society of Colored people; of the approbation of the Most Rev. Archbishop Samuel and the Rector of the Cathedral Revd. H. B. Coskery* as a record of the weekly meetings of an African American Catholic society in nineteenth-century Baltimore. This document reveals ways in which African American Catholic women prayed and engaged in works of charity. Of the 250 African American Catholics who made up the Society of the Holy Family from 1843 to 1845, 170 members were women. One of the four society officers was a woman named Mary Holland. Holland served as first counselor, and her responsibility was to establish policy for the society.

The Society of the Holy Family met on Sunday evenings at 7:00 P.M. They prayed the rosary and had lessons in doctrine and spirituality. On occasion members would offer spontaneous prayers. Father Hickey noted, "Jane Thomson came out with the Gospel of John by heart" and "Jane came out with something about the rock of Peter" (Davis, 87). Society members' weekly dues were used to pay rent to the cathedral and to have masses said for deceased Society members. They also developed a lending library of religious and inspirational books. The Society of the Holy Family was short-lived, commencing in 1843 and ceasing in 1845. Some white Catholics took exception to the meetings in the Cathedral's hall, and the Society of the Holy Family was informed that it was no longer available. Without a place to convene, members disbanded and distributed the remainder of its financial holdings to the poor.

Racial resentment was a reality that all nineteenth-century African American Catholics experienced in their Church. As the United States drew closer to the Civil War and as the Catholic population boomed in the nineteenth century, principally from immigration from Ireland, racial resentment grew. New Catholic immigrants settled primarily in the northeastern cities and lived on the literal and figurative margins of society. They found work that no one else wanted and lived where no one else wanted to live. And though many had never seen an African American, they learned to fear them and what the emancipation of African Americans would mean for their own precarious social and economic standing. Catholic priests and bishops shared these fears and overwhelmingly voiced their public support for the continuation of slavery.

This situation inspired Harriet Thompson to write on behalf of a group of twenty-six other African American Catholics to Pope Pius IX in 1853. They wanted the pope to know about the terrible injustices black Catholics experienced within the Church with the consent of priests and bishops, most of whom were of Irish descent. They feared that the Catholic Church's neglect of African Americans threatened the souls of their people. Thompson explained, "It is a great mistake to say that the church watched with equal care over every race and color, for how can it be said they teach all nations when they will not let the black race mix with the white" (Davis, 95).

Thompson's reference to race mixing had to do with Catholic education. Writing from New York, Thompson knew of Archbishop John Hughes's battle against the public schools and their Protestant underpinnings and of his work to establish Catholic schools in New York to protect Catholic youth from the "Protestant" public schools. But she also knew that Archbishop Hughes did not intend black Catholic children to attend the Catholic schools. In fact, Thompson believed that Hughes's ill will toward African Americans was so great "that he cannot bear to come near them" (96). Because Catholic schools would not admit black children, this opened the door wide for Protestants to make inroads among African Americans.

Thompson shared the belief of many Catholics that faith and education were intertwined and that the Catholic Church was an educational institution as well as a spiritual institution. Denying African Americans the educational ministry was devastating to the Catholic Church's spiritual ministry because education planted the seeds of faith and reason. African American Catholic children had to attend the "Protestant" public schools. In the public schools they learned "that the Blessed Eucharist is nothing but a wafer, that the priest drinks the wine himself and gives the bread to us, and that the Divine institution of confession is only to make money and that the Roman pontiff is Anti-Christ" (Davis, 95). To Thompson and to those for whom she wrote, the priests and bishops who willfully neglected blacks were responsible for this situation.

Harriet Thompson was a devout Catholic representing a faithful group. She was not the first Catholic to present a pope with grievances against the clergy, but neither was her action commonplace. That an African American Catholic community, represented by a woman, would presume to send such a letter is evidence of two things. First, it indicates the strength of this community in the nineteenth century. Committed to their faith, they were prepared to demand justice from the Church. Second, the letter reveals the leadership roles African American Catholic women exercised in the nineteenth century. The letter testified to the fact that black Catholic women's voices were so respected that they could represent their community before the highest authority in the Church.

Concern for maintaining family ties was something most African American Catholic women shared in common. Slavery was particularly devastating to black family ties as slave parents and children could be sold apart from one another at the will and discretion of the slave owners. Catholic slaveholders were not above selling parents and children apart as well as husbands and wives, despite the primacy the Catholic Church assigned to families through its regard for marriage as an indissoluble sacramental union. The Metoyer and Tolton family histories provide insights into how some African American Catholic women kept their families together and Catholicism at the center of their family identities during slavery.

Coincoin Metoyer was born into slavery in 1724 in Natichioches, Louisiana. Her baptismal name was Marie Therese, but her parents called her by the African name Coincoin. As a young woman, Coincoin became the lover of a French merchant named Claude Metoyer. Together they had seven children, all baptized in the Roman Catholic Church. In 1778, Metoyer purchased Coincoin and their children and then freed Coincoin and their youngest son. He also gave her 68 acres of land, to which she added over 600 acres in 1794. With her freedom, Coincoin became an entrepreneur, a slaveholder, and a founder of a black Catholic community. She dealt in tobacco, indigo, and bear grease, and her mission was to secure the freedom of all her children.

By 1793, she had accumulated enough wealth to purchase all her children but one. Although she was not able to free this daughter, she did purchase the freedom of her daughter's children. Ironically, Coincoin and her descendants became the largest black slaveholding family in the United States. At their peak, they held 500 slaves, 20,000 acres of land, and a dozen plantation manor houses. Coincoin instilled a strong commitment to Catholicism in her children and made church and family ties the defining features of Isle Breville, the Cane River community they created. After her death in 1816, her son Augustin became the head of Isle Breville, where he built St. Augustine's Catholic Church, one of the oldest black Catholic communities.

Catholicism and family ties were also defining features of the Tolton family. In 1863, Martha Jane Chisley Tolton decided to row her family of three small children from slavery to freedom. A Kentuckian and a slave by birth, Martha became part of her master's daughter's dowry in 1849 and moved with her new mistress and master to Missouri. Two years later, Martha married Peter Paul Tolton, who was a slave on a nearby plantation and a Catholic. Their marriage was witnessed by a priest in St. Peter's Church in Brush Creek, Missouri. Their three children were baptized in this church as well. When the Civil War broke out in 1861, Peter Tolton determined to join the Union army. He planned to rejoin his family once the war was over, but he never returned. Believing that her husband had died in the war, Martha Tolton pursued freedom for their family by rowing a makeshift vessel across the Mississippi River to Illinois. She and the children had stolen away at night and with the help of Union soldiers were successful in escaping the slave catchers. Their dangerous journey brought them to Quincy, Illinois, where they settled.

Tolton raised her children in the Catholic Church, and her son, Augustus Tolton, became the first known African American priest in the United States in 1886. When Father Tolton started his ministry in Chicago's African American community in 1889, Martha Tolton accompanied her son and helped him found the first African American parish in the city.

African American laywomen clearly played important roles in the Catholic world, but African American sisters were the most visible embodiment of Catholicism in the African American community from the nineteenth century through the early twentieth century. Between 1828 and 1916 African American women founded three successful religious communities: the Oblate Sisters of Providence (1828), the Sisters of the Holy Family (1842), and the Franciscan Handmaids of the Most Pure Heart of Mary (1916). Black women were among the first in North America to establish native religious communities. The religious zeal that inspired the foundations of these communities is captured in a prayer attributed to Sr. Henriette Delille: "I believe in God, I hope in God. I love and I want to live and die in God." The charisms and missions of these religious communities reflected the values and needs of the African American community. Education and assisting the poor, the orphaned, and the elderly were the fundamental missions of the black sisters.

Race was also a factor in the foundation of these religious communities. White religious communities did not accept African American women until the twentieth century. The idea that African American women could live moral and chaste lives committed to God, as did white women religious, was unacceptable to many Catholics.

In 1872 Sister Marie called on Archbishop Napoleon Perche of New Orleans to show him her community's new habit. As this sister had a fair complexion, the archbishop mistook her for a white woman. Upon learning that she was a Sister of the Holy Family, he ordered her to take off the habit. The habit was a sign to the world that she had consecrated her life to God just as white sisters did. He called her "proud" for deeming herself the moral and spiritual equal of white sisters. The archbishop could not accept such equality.

As early as 1824, African American Catholic women took their first steps toward religious life in Kentucky. Father Charles Nerinckx, a missionary frontier priest to Kentucky, tried to establish a community with three free black women in association with the Sisters of Loretto, a white religious community. But Nerinckx's community fell apart shortly after he established it, and he left Kentucky in the same year. Four years later in Baltimore, Maryland, Elizabeth Clarisse Lange and Jacques Hector Nicolas Joubert, a French Sulpician priest, founded the Oblate Sisters of Providence. Elizabeth Lange was one of the thousands of Haitian émigrés who came to Baltimore in the late eighteenth and early nineteenth centuries. Most of these women and men were Catholic, and their presence greatly increased the black Catholic community of Baltimore. Father Joubert, also a Haitian refugee, worked among the black Catholic community that worshipped in the basement of St. Mary's Seminary. This is how he met Elizabeth Lange, who conducted a school for girls in her home.

And by 1828, she, Madeline Balas, and Rosine Boegue had already begun to live a religious life informally. Their commitment to teaching children and desire for religious life prompted them to found a community with Joubert that would be devoted to the education of African American children, especially girls. Archbishop Whitfield of Baltimore approved the creation of the Oblate Sisters of Providence, saying he believed it was the work of God. But many Catholic Baltimoreans opposed the foundation of a black order. In the annals of the Oblate Sisters of Providence, Joubert recorded, "I had myself heard much talk. I knew already that many persons who had approved the idea of a school for pupils disapproved so strongly that of founding a religious house, and could not think of the idea of seeing these poor girls (colored girls) wearing the religious habit and constituting a religious community" (Morrow, 39).

On July 2, 1829, Elizabeth Lange, Madeline Balas, Almedie Duchemin Maxis, and Rosine Boegue made their first professions as religious. The women called themselves the Oblate Sisters of Providence because they regarded their mission of providing education, especially to African American girls, to be a manifestation of God's care for African American people. For their motto they took *Providentia Providebit,* which means "God will provide." It gave them inspiration and confidence as they cleared one hurdle after another as they established their community and pursued their mission.

One of the highest hurdles faced was raising the money to keep their ministries and community alive. Like all religious communities, they had to find ways to support themselves and their schools. Unlike other orders, the Oblates did not enjoy the patronage of the Church and its members. To support themselves in the early years, the sisters did embroidery work, made vestments for priests, and worked as domestics. The Oblates agreed to work as domestics for the Sulpician Seminary on the condition that their housekeeping responsibilities not interfere with their educational mission or with their practice of religious life. In 1835 the Oblates wrote:

We do not conceal the difficulty of our situation as persons of color and religious at the same time, and we wish to conciliate these two qualities in such a manner as not to appear too arrogant on the one hand and on the other, not to miss the respect which is due to the state we have embraced and the holy habit which we have the honor to wear. Our intention is not to neglect the religious profession which we have embraced. (Morrow, 51)

Accepting the housekeeping work presented the Oblates with a twofold "difficulty." Housekeeping presented the challenge of meeting their religious and teaching commitments while working in a field that was not regarded with respect. The Oblates were black women living in a society that did not deem them fit for any life other than that of servitude. Without explicitly stating so, the Oblates called the Sulpicians' attention to this reality. The sisters wanted a guarantee of the protection and respect that all sisters merited because they consecrated their lives to God. The Sulpicians agreed to the Oblates' terms, and for many years, the Oblates worked as the housekeepers for the seminary while continuing to develop their educational mission and live out their religious calling.

In 1842 a second African American religious community took root, this time in New Orleans, the Sisters of the Holy Family. The primary forces behind this foundation were Henriette Delille, Juliette Gaudin, and Father Etienne Rousselon. Born in 1813, Delille was a free woman of color, a race and class unto themselves in New Orleans. Considered neither black nor white, they enjoyed privileges not accorded to free blacks or slaves. Most free persons of color had white fathers and mothers of African and mixed heritage. Such persons were most often the result of *placage,* a form of marriage usually between French men and free women of color. *Placage* was not legal or acknowledged by the Roman Catholic Church, but it was sanctioned by the Creole culture that dominated in New Orleans. Quite often *placage* relationships lasted for lifetimes. The fathers of children born to these unions provided support for their families and left their *placage* wives and children property in their wills. Often, the men were legally married to white women and supported the wives and children of these marriages as well. Within Creole culture, *placage* was considered an acceptable way of life for a free woman of color, and mothers often groomed their daughters for such a life.

As a young and beautiful free woman of color, Henriette Delille determined to reject *placage* and to serve God by pursuing religious life. Her biographer Audrey Detiege explained that "when other young women of their class were concentrating on their dancing lessons, gossiping about the latest scandals of the town, and dreaming of the balls and men, Henriette and her friends were coming into contact with the stark miserable realities of poverty and the sordid conceptions of slavery which indeed caused them to mature rapidly" (Detiege, 19). To Delille *placage* was an offense to God because God's law required men and women to be united only in the sacrament of marriage. Delille and her sisters challenged the practice and advocated for legal and sacramental marriages of free people of color.

Delille's involvement in social work, something that was not expected of a woman of her class and status in society, made her aware of the horrors of slavery and poverty in New Orleans. She gained this experience through her work with the Sisters of Soeur Ste-Marthe, a French nursing order that conducted a school for free girls of color and a night school for slaves. Through this religious community, Delille met Marie-Jeane Aliquot, a French woman who had pledged her life to serve blacks when a black man saved her from drowning. In 1836, Aliquot tried to establish an interracial religious community, calling the order the Sisters of the Presentation. Delille and Juliette Gaudin joined the Sisters of the Presentation, and they worked for the interests of poor blacks. However, the community's bright promise did not survive for long because of laws requiring racial segregation in Louisiana. Two years later, Delille received permission to organize an informal sisterhood of colored women that would be devoted to instructing slaves in the Catholic faith. This was another step along the way to the foundation of the Sisters of the Holy Family.

In November 1842, Delille and Gaudin took private vows before Father Etienne Rousselon. At Father Rousselon's behest, the women took the name Sisters of the Holy Family. Soon a third member, Josephine Charles, joined them. The charisms of the Sisters of the Holy Family are education and service to the poor. Between 1842 and 1862, when Delille died, the Sisters of the Holy Family conducted a school, an orphanage, and a home for the aged. They taught catechism to free children of color and slave children as well. They also helped to nurse New Orleans through a terrible cholera epidemic.

Both the Oblate Sisters of Providence and Sisters of the Holy Family indirectly contributed to the foundation of the third order of African American sisters, the Franciscan Handmaids of the Most Pure Heart of Mary, founded by Father Ignatius Lissner, of the Society of African Missionaries, and Barbara Williams in 1916. Williams had been a member of the Sisters of the Holy Family, a member of a short-lived black Franciscan community in Louisiana, and a postulant of the Oblate Sisters of Providence, before founding the Handmaids.

In the early 1910s, Father Lissner established several Catholic schools in Georgia for African American children and staffed the schools with white sisters. This arrangement worked until 1913 when the Georgia state legislature began to consider legislation making it illegal for whites to teach blacks. Fearful that such laws would spell the end of the African American Catholic schools, Lissner invited the Sisters of the Holy Family and the Oblate Sisters of Providence to take charge. But neither order could help at that time because of other teaching commitments elsewhere. Lissner began exploring the possibility of establishing a new community of African American women religious, especially for the mission in Georgia. This was when he learned about Barbara Williams and her desire for religious life.

In 1916 Williams became the first member of the Franciscan Handmaids of the Most Pure Heart of Mary, taking the name Theodore and becoming the Mother Superior. Soon she was joined by a small but committed group of women to take charge of the Georgia schools. However, the Georgia legislature did not pass the proposed legislation that would have prevented whites from teaching blacks. The white sisters continued to teach at the schools Lissner founded. The Franciscan Handmaids did teach at a new school Lissner founded in Savannah, but it did not provide enough income for the sisters to maintain themselves. They lived in poverty and took in laundry to supplement their resources. For six years, the sisters struggled to keep the order alive.

Lissner had left Georgia soon after the founding of this order. Despite losing their ally and supporter, the Franciscan Handmaids persevered. In 1922, the Franciscan Handmaids of the Most Pure Heart of Mary accepted Patrick Cardinal Hayes's invitation to begin a new mission in Harlem. Thus the Franciscan Handmaids became part of the Great Migration of African Americans who moved from the South to the northern and midwestern industrial centers seeking better lives. And Harlem was the destination of many of these pilgrims. Before blacks made their homes there, Harlem had been the home of many European Catholics. These Catholics established numerous parishes and schools. As the African Americans moved into the neighborhood, the Catholics began to move away. Concern for these Catholic parishes and a desire to provide for the spiritual needs of Harlem's newest residents prompted Cardinal

Hayes's invitation. He wanted the sisters to be a Catholic witness in Harlem and to establish a day nursery for the children of working families. The sisters accepted the invitation, relocated their motherhouse to Harlem, and established the St. Benedict the Moor Day Nursery in 1923. They became involved in a variety of educational and charitable endeavors in the neighborhood.

The work of African American Catholic sisters and laywomen paralleled and intersected in the twentieth century as they worked to make Catholicism a vital force in the African American community. They launched initiatives in social justice, education, literature, music, and theology. As they sought to make Catholicism known to the African American community, which was overwhelmingly Protestant, they also endeavored to make African American heritage and experience properly understood and appreciated by Catholics. Laywomen like Mollie Moon and Anita Rose Williams became the backbones of Catholic Interracial Councils and African American Catholic women's groups. They worked to bring about racial justice in the United States and in the Roman Catholic Church. Young African American Catholic women began integrating Catholic institutions of higher education in the 1940s and 1950s. Elizabeth Adams wrote *Dark Symphony*, Helen Caldwell Day, *Color, Ebony,* and Ellen Tarry, *The Third Door: The Autobiography of an American Negro Woman*. They published these conversion narratives to educate and inspire African Americans.

After spending time with Dorothy Day at the New York City Catholic Worker House, Helen Caldwell Day founded a Catholic Worker House in Memphis, Tennessee. Similarly, Ellen Tarry became involved in the Friendship House movement, whose goal it was to forge understanding, friendship, and ultimately interracial justice between African American and white Catholics. Tarry went on to help found the Chicago Friendship House and to write articles and essays about the African American Catholic experience and the need for racial justice. She also developed educational programs to foster pride in African American children about their heritage and also to educate Catholics about African American history and culture. While a student at St. Francis de Sales High School in Rock Castle, Virginia, Tarry converted to Catholicism. The Catholic tradition's emphasis on the equality of all people before the altar of God inspired her conversion and her life's work for racial justice and understanding.

In 1968 African American women religious as a body took up the work for racial justice, understanding, and empowerment through their creation of the National Black Sisters' Conference (NBSC). Sr. Martin de Porres Grey, a Sister of Mercy of Pittsburgh, Pennsylvania, initiated the National Black Sisters' Conference. The members were African American sisters from predominantly white religious communities as well as sisters from the three historically African American religious communities. The NBSC was founded during the civil rights movement and on the cusp of the women's liberation movement. In 1968 the United States was in turmoil, and African Americans were in shock and grief over the assassination of Dr. Martin Luther King, Jr. African American women religious looked for ways in which Catholicism could make a positive difference in these circumstances. According to M. Shawn Copeland, a member of the 1968 gathering, "in a most proactive way, the NBSC promoted and advocated an 'image' of the black Catholic sister and her mission in terms of liberation. The Conference understood and presented itself as a *grassroots* organization concerned with the interests, protection, and development of the individual sister" (Copeland, 123).

In an effort to bring African American sisters together, Sr. Martin de Porres wrote to 600 superiors of religious communities in the United States to ask for their help and prayers. Only a third of the communities replied, but the lukewarm response of the superiors did not deter Sr. Martin de Porres, who enjoyed the support of her community. She described her motivation to go forward with the first meeting.

> It was important that we get together so we could evaluate our roles as participants in the Church and come to a deeper understanding of our own people's position and the creative tension now circulating in the black communities. We also hope to create ways of developing a living relationship between black and white. The core of the racial problem is basically spiritual and this is where the Church claims that the creative power of God is effective. ("An Awakening to Black Nun Power," 48)

Sr. Martin de Porres saw the primary purpose of the NBSC as educational. She thought black sisters had to educate white clerics and religious about the causes of racial problems in the United States. Providing them with an understanding of African American history and culture was key. Sr. Martin de Porres also thought the NBSC would help black sisters take on more leadership roles in the Catholic schools, especially Catholic schools in predominantly African American neighborhoods. And the NBSC was also a means for African American sisters in predominantly white orders to have the chance to gather to discuss their experiences. Even though many religious communities had accepted African American women, there was still a subtle racism at work in most communities.

The NBSC held its first meeting in August 1968 at Mt. Mercy College in Pittsburgh. Over 150 sisters from seventy-nine religious congregations from the United States, the Caribbean, and Africa convened for a week of prayer, deliberation, and planning. The NBSC invited some African American clergy and laity to attend and discuss interpretations of black power and the condition of African Americans. The women also discussed their relevance as religious sisters to the African American community, how to become more effective leaders in their communities, and how to incorporate black cultural traditions into the Roman Catholic mass.

By the early 1960s, internationally acclaimed jazz composer and pianist Mary Lou Williams was at work developing enculturated music for the Catholic Church. Inspired by the Vatican Council II and her own conversion experiences, she saw jazz as a means of spiritual conversion. Williams became a Catholic in 1957 after a spiritual journey she had embarked on at the height of her career. Because she was feeling "distracted and depressed" in 1954, a friend suggested that she read Psalm 91 for encouragement. She sat down with a Bible and read all the psalms. Of them Williams said, "[T]hey cooled me and made me feel protected" (Balliet, 85). After secluding herself in France for six months, Williams returned to the United States, determined never to play jazz again.

Her spiritual journey eventually led her to pray at the Church of Our Lady of Lourdes in New York City. Of this experience Williams said, "I just sat there and meditated. All kinds of people came in—needy ones and cripples—and I brought them here [to her home] and gave them food and talked to them and gave them money. Music had left my head and I hardly remembered playing" (85). All she wanted to do was to devote her life to prayer and to serving the poor. In 1957, Williams and Lorraine Gillespie, the wife of Dizzy Gillespie, took instructions from Father Anthony Woods and were received into the Catholic Church.

Not long after her conversion, Williams established the Bel Canto Foundation to help musicians recover from alcoholism and drug addiction. To support the foundation, Williams called on friends from the jazz community for donations of clothing, shoes, and other goods to sell at a thrift store. Williams ran the thrift store herself, stocking it with the finest shirts and shoes from Louis Armstrong and his wife, designer dresses from Lorraine Gillespie, and novelties like a mink tie and a hand-painted pool cue from Duke Ellington. She dreamed of buying a country house as a retreat for recovering musicians, complete with soundproof practice and meditation rooms.

Encouraged by Father Woods, Williams began to play jazz again. He told her that "its *your* business to help people through music." Williams, performing in jazz clubs, also began to write hymns for Catholic worship. Eventually she composed four jazz masses, the most fa-

mous of which she called "Mary Lou's Mass." Williams saw jazz as her sacred gift to the Catholic Church. To her it was also prayer and a way to serve others. She explained, "I am praying through my fingers when I play . . . I get that good 'soul sound,' and I try to touch people's spirits" ("Prayerful One," 59).

Williams's desire to serve the Catholic Church through her secular vocation was characteristic of African American Catholic women in the twentieth century. At age sixty-one, Dr. Lena Edwards fulfilled a lifelong dream of becoming a Catholic medical missionary. After marrying, establishing a successful medical practice in gynecology and obstetrics in Jersey City, New Jersey, and raising a family of six children, Dr. Edwards went to live and work among Mexican migrant workers in Hereford, Texas. Originally, she hoped to do a mission in the South for poor African Americans, but her son, Brother Martin Madison, a Franciscan friar, told his mother about the medical needs of these migrant workers. In January 1961 she arrived at St. Joseph's Mission in Hereford to serve as the only doctor. She decided to focus her work on prenatal care for mothers and children's health initiatives, the greatest needs in the migrant community. Edwards learned Spanish and tried to live as much like the migrant workers as possible. She kept the same hours they kept, ate their diet, dressed as they dressed, and worshipped with them.

To better meet the migrant workers' medical needs, Edwards built Our Lady of Guadalupe Maternity Clinic, which took care of women and their children in all stages of maternity and infancy. She contributed over half of the funding for the construction, and the people of Hereford gave the rest. Edwards also became an advocate for justice and education for migrant workers. She had planned to spend the rest of her life at the mission. The illness of her ninety-one-year-old mother and her own failing heart caused her to leave Texas in 1965. But Edwards continued to advocate on behalf of migrant workers.

In an address to the National Conference of Catholic Bishops in 1989, Sister Thea Bowman challenged bishops to come to confront the Catholic Church's history of racism in the United States and to embrace the gifts of African Americans to the Catholic Church. Sister Thea was a Franciscan Sister of Perpetual Adoration, a college English professor, and a faculty member of the Institute for Black Catholic Studies at Xavier University of Louisiana. Like her African American Catholic foremothers and forefathers, she too experienced a form of bondage. Cancer bound her to a wheelchair and to extreme pain. Although she lacked physical freedom, she was able to make a positive difference for the entire American Catholic community.

In her songs and stories, Sister Thea spoke of the need to come to moral terms with history, of the persistent need for social and racial justice, and of the ultimate need for forgiveness, acceptance, and redemption. Of being a black Catholic, Sister Thea said:

What does it mean to be black and Catholic? It means that I come to my church fully functioning. That doesn't frighten you, does it? I come to my church fully functioning. I bring myself, my black self, all that I am, all that I have, all that I hope to become, I bring my whole history, my traditions, my experience, my culture, my African-American song and dance and gesture and movement and teaching and preaching and healing and responsibility as gift to the church. (Cepress, 32)

Bowman's message and mission were not new. She inherited them from the generations of African American Catholic women who preceded her. She added a statement that reflects the perspective of African American Catholic women as they enter a new century. Bowman spoke of the need for the Catholic Church to accept African Americans as "fully functioning" members of the Church. African American Catholic women continue to celebrate their racial and religious heritage and continue to seek a place of equality at the Catholic table.

SOURCES: *The History of Black Catholics in the United States* (1990), by Cyprian Davis, is the most comprehensive study of African American Catholic history. Davis includes a chapter on African American women religious and provides many examples of other significant African American Catholic women in his study, too. *To Stand on the Rock: Meditations on Black Catholic Identity* (1998), by Joseph A. Brown, and *Slave Religion: The "Invisible Institution" in the Antebellum South* (1978), by Albert J. Raboteau, are essential for understanding the role of slavery in African American Catholic experience. *Black Women in America: An Historical Encyclopedia*, 2 vols. (1993), edited by Darlene Hine Clark, Elsa Barkley Brown, and Rosalyn Terborg-Penn, features many articles about individual African American Catholic women. "No Cross, No Crown: The Journal of Sister Mary Bernard Deggs" (*U.S. Catholic Historian* 15 [Fall 1997]: 17–28), by Cyprian Davis, Virginia Meachum Gould, Charles E. Nolan, and Sylvia Thibodeaux; *Henriette Delille: Free Woman of Color* (1976), by Audrey Detiege; "The Sisters of the Holy Family and the Veil of Race" (*Religion and American Culture: A Journal of Interpretation* 10 [Summer 2000]: 187–224), by Tracey Fessenden; "A Cadre of Women Religious Committed to Black Liberation: The National Black Sisters Conference" (*U.S. Catholic Historian* 14 [Winter 1996]: 121–144), by M. Shawn Copeland; "An Awakening to Black Nun Power: Catholic Sisters at Pittsburgh Confab," published in *Ebony* (October 1968: 44–49); *Violets in the King's Garden: A History of the Sisters of the Holy Family in New Orleans* (1966), by Mary Frances Borgia Hart; *Response to Love: The Story of Mother Mary Elizabeth Lange, O.S.P.* (1992), by Maria M. Lannon; "Outsiders Within: The Oblate Sisters of Providence in 1830s Church and Society" (*U.S. Catholic Historian* 15 [Spring 1997]: 35–54), by Diane Batts Morrow; and *The Oblates' One Hundred and One Years* (1931), by Grace Sherwood—all are essential reading for understanding the unique contributions of African American Catholic sisters. *Dark Symphony* (1942), by Elizabeth Laura Adams; *Color, Ebony* (1951) and *Not Without Tears* (1954), by Helen Caldwell Day; and *The Third Door: The Autobiography of an American Negro Woman* (1992), by Ellen Tarry, are four twentieth-century autobiographies of African American women who converted to Catholicism. These books give insights into how African American women perceived Catholicism and their places in the Catholic Church in the United States. " 'My Spirit Soared': Ellen Tarry's Conversion to Catholicism" (*Sacred Rock: Journal of the Institute for Black Catholic Studies* 2 [Summer 1999]: by Cecilia Moore, looks at how Catholicism influenced Tarry's life as a writer and activist for civil rights. "Profiles: Out Here Again," published in *The New Yorker* (May 2, 1964, 52–85), by Whitney Balliet; "Prayerful One," published in *Time* (February 21, 1964, 58–59); and Tammy Lynn Kernodle's "This Is My Story, This Is My Song: The Historiography of Vatican II, Black Catholic Identity, Jazz, and the Religious Compositions of Mary Lou Williams," *U.S. Catholic Historian* 19.2 (Spring 2001): 83–84—these are important sources for understanding Mary Lou Williams and how jazz and Catholicism mutually transformed her life. *Sister Thea Bowman, Shooting Star: Selected Writings and Speeches* (1993), edited by Celestine Cepress, provides insight into the work Thea Bowman did to integrate African American cultural and spiritual traditions with Roman Catholicism. Other important works concerning African American Catholic women are *The Forgotten People: Cane River's Creoles of Color* (1977), by Gary B. Mills; *Some Outstanding Colored People* (1943), by Michael O'Neil; "Papists in a Protestant Age: The Catholic Gentry and Community in Colonial Maryland, 1689–1776" (Ph.D. diss., University of Maryland, 1993), by Beatriz Betancourt Hardy; *Motherhood, Medicine, and Mercy: The Story of a Black Woman Doctor* (1979), by M. Anthony Scally; *Soul on Soul: The Life and Music of Mary Lou Williams* (2004), by Tammy Lynn Kernodle; and *Persons of Color and Religious at the Same Time: The Oblate Sisters of Providence, 1828–1860* (2002), by Diane Batts Morrow.

LATINA POPULAR CATHOLICISM
Jeanette Rodriguez

ACCORDING TO THE U.S. Census Bureau, the Latino/Hispanic population in the United States has surpassed 32 million persons. As of October 1, 2000, the estimated number of Latinos was 32.7 million, making up 11.9 percent of the total U.S. population. The number of Hispanic women totaled 16.3 million, accounting for 49.8 percent of the total Hispanic population. Despite increasing conversions to mainline Protestant denominations and other groups, this population continues to identify itself as Catholic, "a mi moda" (my way). By 2005, the number of Latinos is projected to be 38.2 million. Mexican women represented the largest portion of Latina women (63.3 percent of all Latina women are Mexican, 10.1 percent are Puerto Rican; 4.5 percent, Cuban; 14.9 percent, Central and South American; and 6.8 percent, other). More significant than these statistics is the role Latina women have traditionally played through the centuries in the creation and transmission of religious formations and beliefs:

> Among Latinos, a persistent element is the centrality of women's endeavors in the religious sphere. Besides being a creative force, the matriarchal core is also a repository of moral and family values, and for this reason it takes on added importance as a stabilizing element in a community in transition. (Diaz-Stevens, 253)

Popular Religion

Inherent in those cultures that served as influence for the Latina are religious worldviews. These worldviews— or assumptive worlds—include sixteenth-century Span-

ish Catholicism with Native Amerindian and African indigenous religions. For example, Mexican American women inherit the legacy of the Spanish conquest, which was motivated, facilitated, and sanctioned by religion. Religion inspired the Spaniards to seek not only wealth for the Spanish crown but also souls for God. Religion facilitated the conquest through missionaries who assimilated the Indians into a church structure that controlled them. Religion also sanctioned the conquest in that the Spaniards believed that they were doing the will of God. Given the pervasive role that religion and the Church had in the colonization of Latin America and the Caribbean, it could be argued that the impact that religion had upon other institutions such as the family was even greater than what it may have been elsewhere. A religion forged from the combination of sixteenth-century Spanish Catholicism and Indian religion would influence the faith of many Latina women.

"From the very beginning," argues U.S. Hispanic theologian Orlando Espin, "the Christianity received and understood by the people (i.e. popular Catholicism) was molded by the experience of vanquishment as its

Before her surgery, Guadalupe Favela (left) and her sister Socorro Favela Rivera visited Our Lady of Guadalupe's shrine in Mexico City to pray for a safe recovery and restored health. The sisters' strong ties to their native country and thus to the Guadalupe story of resistance against the dominant power is shown on Socorro's skirt, which has an eagle devouring a serpent—the symbol on the flag of Mexico. *Courtesy of Dr. Gabriella Gutierrez y Muhs.*

constituting context. All other cultural, religious, constitutive elements of popular Catholicism (including doctrinal contents, ethical demands, and symbolic expressions) depended completely on this one context" (Espin, 11).

As in many transitional social orders, women were the primary carriers of the religious belief system. The very nature of the Roman Catholic Church's hierarchy and traditional teachings called for women to be subordinate to men, but this system did not preclude them from playing an active role in the practice of popular religion. *Popular religion* has been defined many ways. For the purposes of this essay, popular religion is considered home-based, non-cleric-led expressions and celebrations of faith. This also includes such practices as pilgrimages, processions, fiestas, and community-created sacred shrines. People celebrate these spontaneously because they want to and not because they have been mandated by the official hierarchy. *Catholicism* here, in relationship to the Latino culture, refers not to the institutionalized version of Catholicism but to popular Catholicism, handed down through generations more by the laity than by the ordained clergy. Although Hispanic popular religion has its historical roots in sixteenth-century Catholicism, it has evolved a life of its own that captures the identity and values and inspirations of the people.

A wonderful illustration of this is Maria's account. Her maternal grandmother lived in a small province in Mexico, in the state of Jalisco. Her relatives on her mother's side have been involved with Los Cristeros (1927), a religious revolutionary movement that fought against the government when the government tried to repress religion. Her life was simple: She woke at 5:00 A.M., swept the sidewalk and cleaned the house, and by 6:00 A.M. went to early mass. Breakfast by 7:30, lunch by 11:00, dinner by 3:00. The smell of roasted *chiles de arbol* and *tomatillos* always permeated the kitchen and the patio, to her family's delight. By evening, neighbors would drop by and start chatting. Then they would make plans for the social events of the town. First priority was given to anything related to El Patron del Pueblo, San Miguel. The women talked about going to *La Peregrinación,* a walking journey to the next town ten miles away. The walk would culminate in the *atrio* (church front court). From the *atrio,* the women's journey would continue on their knees until they were in front of the altar of the church. At that point, the person might feel impelled to pray to God out loud and make any special petitions she/he had. Maria did the *Peregrinación* several times. There would be people who after requesting something from God would do it as a *manda* (pledge, commitment). What she remembers clearly about the *Peregrinaciónes* was the way people bonded with each other during those journeys. They would stop at any *rancheria* about lunchtime, and would be invited for lunch. If the owners were wealthy, they would have *mole* or other delicacies (a *mole* is a special dish containing chiles and chocolate); if they were poor, they would have fresh *frijoles de la olla* (beans cooked with salt in a clay pot) with tortillas and *queso fresco* (fresh cheese). It is very important to understand that these beans cooked in a clay pot, and the fresh cheese, are more than just dishes offered to pilgrims. These food items are the poor people's basic diet. Women would have beans cooking all day in preparation for any unexpected guests who would arrive, adding salt and water to the basic recipe. Fresh cheese was made from the leftover milk of the cow and eaten on a daily basis. They are the soul foods of Mexicans, given with *corazón* (heart). The pilgrims were always treated like longtime friends.

Popular religion continues to exist because for the poor and marginalized it is a source of power, dignity, and acceptance that adds to and fills out their experience of the institutional church. Popular religion is not celebrated by a few but by the majority of the people. It is an expression of faith that has survived over a considerable period with roots in the historical beginnings of Hispanic culture. Above all, popular religion is active, dynamic, and lived and has as its objective to move its practitioners, the believers, to live their faith. That is, the people's own history, both personal and cultural, their own possibility for being saved in history, is expressed. Popular religion not only narrates a people's own history, but it also represents and acts it out. The life of the people is life as a human-divine drama in which natural and supernatural claims are intimately intertwined.

Popular religion also functions as a form of resistance to assimilation. At the Catholic Theological Society of America (CTSA) Conference of 1989, Orlando Espin and Sixto Garcia pointed out that popular religion is an important guardian of culture, history, and identity; without it, Hispanics in general and Latinos in particular would not be the people they are. "Our Identity as an integral part of the Catholic Church would not have survived the frequent clashes with the non-Hispanic— and often, anti-Hispanic—ways of the Church in America" (Espin and Garcia, 71). Faith expressions of popular religion are readily accessible to anyone without exception, and no one is excluded from participating. They provide a deep sense of unity and joy, while providing a forum for shared suffering. They are participatory, and everyone takes an active role. For those who participate in the realm of popular religion, religious experience permeates all space and time. They are spaces and times of special strength and power that are part of the religious experience.

Women traditionally have been expected to socialize their children into the belief system of their specific culture and to instill in them the religious belief system, including the teachings of the Roman Catholic Church as they have understood them. For many people in the Hispanic/Latino community, and for most people who have been similarly marginalized on many levels, the religious worldview is their only worldview. They understand everything within a religious context. Latina women have been marginalized as women and as *mestizas* (of mixed racial ancestry); thus religion is a significant dimension of their human experience.

For this population, religious and cultural oppression plays a major role in the formation of their assumptive world. For example, the history of the Mexican American woman is a legacy of conquest and resistance. This has shaped the uniqueness of her perceptions, emotional states, images of self, values, gender roles, and expectations—all of which affect her relationship with what she deems divine.

In Hispanic culture, everything is interrelated, interconnected, and interdependent. People identify themselves through their relationships to others. These relationships between people also apply to the relationships between people and the divine. The saints are Jesus' friends and therefore friends of mine; Jesus is my brother, God is my father, Guadalupe is my mother. This parallel dichotomy of identity of self and other is a legacy of the institutional Church's separation of genders within the lay clergy continuum. For while consecrated males held the liturgical powers of the sacraments, women developed a unique, deeply religious parallel spirituality. Outside the convent's cloister, too, the male centeredness of politics, economics, and other secular pursuits afforded women opportunities to forge their identities and self-expression within the domestic sphere. The power of women, then, to formulate and express religious consciousness in the home was both a result of oppression and an expression of liberation. This dynamic parallelism of clergy and laity results in a uniquely feminine spirituality that ensures a cultural legacy in spite of being "hidden." This spirituality of relationship is one that is uniquely feminine, emphasizing the possibilities of being fully human within an extended community. This community is a network of extended social relations, bound by mutual obligations articulated by the matriarchs of the various families.

Within popular religion, social organization is predominantly horizontal, with temporal responsibilities that do not separate persons or give unequal weight to functions. In preparation for Las Posadas, Holy Week, Día de los Muertos, or All Souls' Day, everyone plays a role and each is important, whether their task is to make the tortillas or proclaim the Word. In celebrating these rituals, social organization is paramount in that elders are recognized as spiritual leaders and children are trained to assume those roles. All are essential to the celebration; all are valued and affirmed. The presence of clergy, although desired, is not required, and the fiesta could easily take place without them.

Día de los Muertos: Day of the Dead

One day is not always the next, but another time.
—Simon Ortiz

No one living in society is free from some form of ritual. Ritual and ceremony are elements and expressions of being human. One of the most common forms of ritual involves acting or dramatizing religious stories. The ritual of Passover, for example, commemorates a meal eaten by the Jews the evening before they left the land of slavery in order to reach the Promised Land, a land promised by the God of their fathers and mothers. This meal is recounted in the Haggadah, the narrative expressed in the book of Exodus, read (or recited) during the Seder meal. The purpose of the Haggadah is to pass on this memory of liberation and to affirm that there is a continuity between the past and the present and that the God of the ancient Israelites is the same God of contemporary Jews. Hence there is a solidarity between contemporary Jews and the ancestors who went before them.

The Christian Passover celebration is also a reenactment of a particular moment in time, Jesus' last supper with his apostles. It carries with it a meaning that a whole believing community wishes to memorialize. This communion connects the communion of saints who have gone before, who stand with each other today, and includes a consciousness of those who will follow.

Rituals are times when people step outside of what is called ordinary time in order to connect with past events, events that transcend time and space and offer future directions. Ultimately, rituals are ways of entering the realm of the sacred. They allow believers to participate in the sacred moments of the past that call forth an affective response in the present in order to illuminate the believers for the future. There is one moment in the human journey that significantly challenges us in terms of mystery and sacredness, and that is the moment of death and dying.

While every culture has its own unique way of dealing with death, some cultures have special holidays to celebrate and honor the memory of relatives and friends who have died. In Mexico, Día de los Muertos and the celebrations that take place during the last days of October and early November correspond to the combined Roman Catholic liturgical feasts of All Saints' Day and All Souls' Day. It is a celebration for which people attend to details with the utmost care. The whole extended family takes part in the preparations. Specific types of flowers, goods, and decorations made both at home and purchased in special markets are brought together. The house is tidied, and a special altar within the home welcomes the spirit guest to a meal with new plates, favorite foods, colorful flowers, memorable photographs, decorations, and gifts. These gifts are called *ofrendas* and stand side by side with things that the dead enjoyed in life, that is, special toys, sweets, food, and flowers.

Once a year the portals of time are opened, and communities of believers gather to remember those who have gone before them, to be cognizant of those who are with them, and commit themselves to those who will follow. Warmed by candles, consoled by the company of the living, and the spirits of the loved ones who have gone before them, many parts of Latin America, and in particular Mexico, will celebrate all night in cemeteries for Día de los Muertos. Families go to cemeteries to clean and decorate graves. Altars are erected in homes and filled with the favorite things of the deceased, while the women of each family clean their house, make candles, prepare great quantities of chicken, tortillas, hot chocolate, a sweet corn dish called *atole,* and a special bread baked in the shape of little animals. The men of the family build a small altar of clay on which they place offerings of food and/or toys for the *anjelitos*—"little angels"—children of the family who have died. Mexicans acknowledge, affirm, and nurture the relationship between the living and the dead.

In Mexico, the Day of the Dead is a cultural event marked throughout the country but observed primarily in the most populated indigenous regions. In this essay, the focus is on the celebration particular to Mexico for its unique syncretistic manifestation. Día de los Muertos is a custom that is a mix of Mexican indigenous rites and Old World Roman Catholicism. The day is an optimistic remembrance sprinkled with a mocking approach to death.

Although there is a very visible and public aspect at the community level, the core of the celebration of the Day of the Dead takes place within the family home. It is a time for family members to come together, not only for those who have gone before them but also for the living. For a few brief hours each year, loved ones are brought into the realm of the physically present to remember and reunite. The souls that return come in a spirit of love and peace and come from another world that, for many Mexican Indians, is very like this one. These worlds for the living and the dead exist in a state of permanent interaction (Carmichael and Sayer, 14).

This celebration is known by different names: Día de los Muertos, Día de los Difuntos (Day of the Deceased), Día de las Animas Benditas (Day of the Holy Souls), Todos Santos (All Saints). The central notion of the celebration is kinship. It is a time to "re-member" home and to bring together the essential elements of community. Through the awareness of real and ritual kinships, therefore, the deep and intricate web of dependency on people and the awe of life become transparent.

Ideally, mindfulness of death is a countercultural consciousness. It may also be a key element in an awakened spirituality because it holds enormous potential for personal conversions, reminding us not to take each other for granted and to live each moment to the fullest.

Just as there are categories of life, so too death has categories that are recognized by the Hispanic/Latino cultures: those who died of natural causes; those who were sacrificed, died in battle, and died in symbolically related activities (as befitted societies so much concerned with bloodshed and death); those who died in connection with water, the natural elements, and symbolically related activities; and possibly those who died young (Nutini, 57).

The dead are the bridge to the divine. They bring with them the power to protect, care for, and bring grace to the living. Since they are part of the liminal reality of life's passage, they negotiate the path to the divine. Prior to Christianity, these "demi-gods" mediated the uncontrollable elements of the agriculture, social, economic, and other systems. Similar then, to Roman Catholic saints, they could intercede for human beings to God. The private family-centered elements of the contemporary ritual are likely rooted in the pre-Christian tradition. After Christian contact, the liturgy of the Roman Catholic Church assumed a public context for the rites. The vestiges of the old rite, however, are still seen in the home tradition.

A contemporary preparation and celebration of the Day of the Dead is told by Cleo. Cleo begins her celebration by remembering her friends and loved ones who have died. She says that her reclaiming and resurrecting the ritual of the Day of the Dead in her home took place after the death of her very close friend Ermelinda. Cleo grieved for this friend, and in sharing her grief with other Latina friends, she concluded that it was time to resurface and re-create the traditional Day of the Dead ceremony. She and her friends had traditionally practiced the yearly cemetery visits to those who had died. But Cleo wanted to remember Ermelinda in a special way, and with her friends, she designed a way of remembering that was not only healing for Cleo but became a process of healing and reclaiming the tradition and remembering that took a new form. The first time they celebrated the ritual, the focus was on Ermelinda. As they progressed in their preparations, the other friends began to bring pictures of their loved ones, and they decided to practice this ritual every year. As Cleo states, there are distinctive steps to the preparation. It begins with remembering, followed by networking with other friends in the planning, then beginning the variety of ritualistic practices. They start with the preparation of the food.

For the celebration of the dead, Cleo prepares a traditional dish called *posole* (dried corn similar to hominy). It is an indigenous dish but also reminds Cleo of a Native couple who died, whose recipe she uses. In the preparation of the meal itself, she is remembering dear friends. *Posole* is served with tortillas and refried beans, as well as enchiladas and tamales. The food preparation is shared among the Latina women, and everyone contributes in a communitarian spirit to the potluck meal. There are no formal invitations to this celebration, but by word of mouth, people come. Cleo is never quite sure how many are coming, but there always seems to be enough for everyone. *Frijoles de olla* are always simmering.

She taps the wisdom of her elders, of her sisters, of her girlfriends, of her *comadres,* in the preparation, design, and implementation of the ritual. In setting up the altar, Cleo makes sure that there is water for the spirits, candles to light the darkness, and flowers to adorn the altar. Especially important is the presence of marigolds. (Marigolds—*cempazuchitl* or *sampoal*—represent the ancient cultures, traditions that have been practiced for thousands of years in celebrating life after death; it was the flower of the dead in the Nahuatl culture.) Upon this altar the pictures of those who have gone before, as well as their favorite food, or special mementos are placed. People bring a variety of things to the altar. Many times they leave them at the altar and with Cleo to place on altars in the years to come: beads from someone's grandmother, a poem written about another's grandfather, pictures of relatives and friends who have died, and *papel picado* (colorful cutouts of skeletons).

The ritual itself begins by asking the matriarch of the extended family to lead the opening prayer. People stand before the altar and share stories of the people they have brought to the altar. At times the grief of individuals is so great that they are unable to speak. In one particular celebration, a woman who had just lost both her parents could barely speak of them, and in an intimate, delicate moment, the children of this mother stood up and spoke for their mother. They spoke of their grandparents and the impact they had, not only on them but on their mother, and the gift and the wisdom transmitted to them as a legacy through their mother.

What was particularly interesting about Cleo's sharing of this celebration is how it extended beyond a New Mexican/Colorado–mediated cultural experience. That is to say, that individuals who were not even Catholic, or Latinos, began to come to the celebration and partake of the ceremony, signifying that although this ceremony is mediated in particular through the Mexican culture, deeply universal and human needs and aspirations are addressed.

Tonanzin-Guadalupe

In the Christian liturgical calendar, Advent, the four weeks prior to Christmas, is a time of waiting and anticipation. It is a time when the prophets of the Hebrew scriptures, who ask us to believe God's proclaimed promises, are recalled. Voices are raised in prayer to this God who not only proclaims but also fulfills their promises. For many Latinos in the Americas, and in particular Mexico, the feast of Our Lady of Guadalupe, December 12, is the beginning of Advent. The narrative image of Our Lady of Guadalupe, while mediated through a particular culture, is a story that nevertheless makes God's presence known in the world. This story is about betrayal and trust, destruction and hope, death and resurrection. In many ways it contains the Pascal mystery of the Mexican people and their resurrection into a new creation through the mediation of Tonanzin (Guadalupe).

The year is 1531. The "Nican Mopohua" recounts this story, situating it ten years after the Spanish conquest of the indigenous peoples of the Americas. This document is the Nahuatl narrative published in 1649 by Luis Lasso de la Vega, chaplain of the Guadalupe hermitage from 1646 to 1656. The title "Nican Mopohua" is taken from the first phrase of the document (variously translated as "Here it is told" or "In good order and careful arrangement"). Theologian Virgilio Elizondo helps us to understand the depth of this clash of cultures when he writes:

> Each had its unique ways of approaching truth, expressing beauty, and communicating with ultimate reality. Each was guided by different value systems, different systems of logic, different anthropologies, and different mythologies. Europeans had known of the great mysterious differences between themselves and the people of some other great continents, but they had not even suspected the existence of the continents they ran into in the beginning of 1492. Here they encountered not only an unsuspecting continent, but a different humanity. (Elizondo, xiv)

The protagonist of the story is a fifty-two-year-old Christianized indigenous person named Juan Diego. The story takes place on a Saturday morning, December 9, 1531. Juan Diego is on his way to catechetical instruction. On his way there, he passes over the hill of Tepeyac, the ancient site of the great earth goddess Tonanzin. Tonanzin, however, is not a name but a title in

Nahuatl; it means "mother." As he passes over this mound, he hears beautiful music. Following this music, he encounters a woman, a woman who speaks to him not in the language of the conquistadors but rather in the language of his people, Nahuatl. She says to him, "Juan Diego, the smallest of my children, where are you going?" It must have been something about her that he recognized, because the story says that he falls on his knees and says to her, "I'm going to *your* house, in order to hear of the divine things our priests tell us." Tonanzin-Guadalupe responds,

> Know and understand, you the smallest of my children, that I am the holy virgin Mary, mother of the true God, *por quien se vive,* for whom one lives. I have a great desire that there be built here a *casita* so that I may show forth my love, my compassion, my help and my defense, to you, to all of you, to all the inhabitants of this land, to all who call upon me, trust me and love me. I will heal your pains, your sorrows, and your lamentations, and I will respond.

With this introduction, time stopped, and Juan Diego entered into a space of intimacy and consoling presence. Then Tonanzin-Guadalupe said to Juan Diego, "In order for this to happen, you must go to the bishop and tell him that it is I, the Mother of the True God, who speaks."

With that, Juan Diego goes to see the bishop, who listened to him kindly, but, as Juan Diego says, "He did not believe me." He further goes on to suggest that perhaps Guadalupe should send one of the more esteemed persons, so that they might believe, because "I am a nothing, and no one, a pile of old sticks. You have sent me to places I do not belong." Tonanzin-Guadalupe's reply is that, yes, she has many messengers, but it is imperative that *he* be the one to take this message. This reflects upon our own tradition that demonstrates a God who consistently chooses people the world has rejected in order to manifest God's power and presence in the world. She sends Juan Diego once again to the bishop, and this time with a sign, a diversity of roses, that blossomed in the winter on a lifeless hill. Juan Diego returns to the bishop and reiterates all that he has seen and heard. At the moment Juan Diego drops his *tilma* (cloak) with a shower of flowers; as they fall to the ground, the image of Tonanzin-Guadalupe appears on the *tilma,* which hangs in the basilica of Mexico City today.

This story is filled with sensory pleasures: music, flowers, song, processions. One only needs to reflect on the many popular Guadalupe songs to get the key points of the story and the tone of intimacy and trust. Two songs illustrating the essence and time of the story are "Desde el Cielo una Hermosa Mañana" and "Mañanitas a la Virgen de Guadalupe."

Verse one of the first song recounts the time and place of the "encounter." It was dawn, and the morning was beautiful! Guadalupe's arrival fills them with joy, light, and harmony. All this in the language that they are familiar with and on a site that is sacred to them. The Virgin tells him that it is this hill that she has chosen to construct her altar. Everything about her was Mexican, even how she held her supplicant's hands (verse 5). On her tilma, flowers were painted, and her beloved image chose to stay (verse 6). The last two verses explain why the Mexican is a Guadalupano, and to be Guadalupano is essential. The song ends in a final prayer: Mother of the Mexicans, you are in heaven, pray for us.

The second song is also popular. Dedicated to Guadalupe, it is used as a birthday song. Speaking in the first person, the people address the beautiful Virgin of the Valley of Anahuac and tell her that her children have come to greet her. The chorus asks Guadalupe to awaken, to look at the dawn, and receive the flowers that they have brought her. They avow their love for her and congratulate her on this great day of her apparition. The song ends with the devotees once again prostrating themselves for her blessings.

The image of Guadalupe is filled with signs and wonders, an iconography that opens portals into a different understanding of who God is, who we are, and how the world might be. First and foremost is how she identifies herself. The titles Guadalupe uses to introduce herself in the official account of the "Nican Mopohua" are that she is the Mother of the God of Truth, Mother of the Giver of Life, the Mother of the Creator, the Mother of the One Who Makes the Sun and the Earth, the Mother of the One Who Is Near—these coincide with the names given the ancient Mexican gods. These titles, well known to the Nahuatl people, introduced her and stated who she was and where she came from, using the symbology, iconography, and cosmovision that were understood by the people. The woman who speaks in their native tongue touches the deepest beliefs and longings of the human heart: the desire to be seen, heard, understood, accepted, embraced, and loved. Guadalupe represents even more than compassion and belief. She is the one who defends the marginalized and the poor. She identifies herself as Mother of the True God for Whom, Through Whom, One Lives.

She is the symbol of a new creation and a new people. She addresses a deep desire for dignity and restoration of self. The encounter with Tonanzin (our mother) Guadalupe for all devotees who come to her is one of unconditional love and an affirmation of a people's place in salvific history. More significantly, it affirms a need to experience a maternal face of God. This maternal face of God is partly made visible by the key words Guada-

"Desde el Cielo una Hermosa Mañana" (Popular)	"From the Heavens One Beautiful Day"
1. Desde el cielo una hermosa mañana Desde el cielo una hermosa mañana La Guadalupana, La Guadalupana, La Guadalupana bajo al Tepeyac.	From the heavens one beautiful morning From the heavens one beautiful morning The Guadalupe, the Guadalupe, The Guadalupe descended upon Tepeyac.
2. Su llegada lleñó de alegría Su llegada lleñó de alegría De luz y armonía, de luz y armonía De luz y armonía todo el Anahuac.	Her arrival was filled with happiness Her arrival was filled with happiness Of harmony and light, of harmony and light, Of harmony and light throughout Anahuac.
3. Por el monte pasaba Juan Diego Por el monte pasaba Juan Diego Y acercose luego, y acercose luego, Y acercose luego al oir cantar.	Through the mountain journeyed Juan Diego Through the mountain journeyed Juan Diego He then approached, he then approached He then approached upon hearing song.
4. Juan Dieguito la Virgen le dijo Juan Dieguito la Virgen le dijo Este cerro elijo, este cerro elijo, Este cerro elijo para hacer mi altar.	Little Juan Diego the Virgin told him Little Juan Diego the Virgin told him I choose this mountain, I choose this mountain, I choose this mountain for my altar.
5. Suplicante juntaba las manos Suplicante juntaba las manos Eran Mexicanos, eran Mexicanos Eran Mexicanos su porte y su paz.	Beggingly she joined her hands Beggingly she joined her hands They were Mexican, they were Mexican, They were Mexican her demeanor and her peace.
6. Y en la tilma entre rosas pintada Y en la tilma entre rosas pintada Su imagen amada, su imagen amada, Su imagen amada se dignó dejar.	And on his cloak painted among roses And on his cloak painted among roses Her image appeared, her image appeared, Her image appeared for all to see.
7. Desde entonces para el Mexicano Desde entonces para el Mexicano Ser Guadalupano, ser Guadalupano, Ser Guadalupano es algo esencial. Ruega a Dios por nos.	Since then for Mexicanos Since then for Mexicanos Being Guadalupano, being Guadalupano, Being Guadalupano is at our core. Pray to God for us.
8. Madrecita de los Mexicanos Madrecita de los Mexicanos, Que estás en el cielo, que estás en el cielo Que estás en el cielo, ruega a Dios por nos.	Blessed Mother of the Mexicans Blessed Mother of the Mexicans Who is in heaven, who is in heaven, Who is in heaven, pray to God for us.

lupe uses. She is here to demonstrate her love, compassion, help, and defense; she hears and heals the people's miseries and suffering. She does not bring her presence or message to the center of power and domination but to the poor and the abandoned.

Guadalupe makes herself present in the roses Juan Diego gathered from the mountains, a presence ushered in with the music he hears as she approaches. The encounter sustains the larger symbolic culture of Indians since for the Nahuatl flower and song—*flor y canto*—together manifest the presence of the divine.

In the world of the Nahuatl people, botanical elements were and continue to be used to express the concept of truth. The beauty and fragrance of flowers can

"Mañanitas a la Virgen de Guadalupe" (Popular)	"Mañanitas* to the Virgin of Guadalupe"
Oh Virgen la mas hermosa Del valle del Anahuac Tus hijos muy de mañana Te vienen a saludar.	Oh most beautiful Virgin Of the Valley of Anahuac Your children bright and early Have come to greet you.
Coro:	*Chorus:*
Despierta, Madre despierta Mira que ya amaneció Mira este ramo de flores Que para ti traigo yo.	Awaken, Mother awaken See the sun has now come up See this bouquet of flowers That for you I have brought.
Madre de los mexicanos dijiste venias a ser pues ya ki ves, Morenita Si te sabemos querer.	Mother of the Mexican people You said you'd come to be You can see now, We know how to love you.
Coro:	*Chorus:*
Despierta, etc.	Awaken, etc.
Recibe Madre querida nuestra felicitación, por ser hoy el dia grande de tu tierna aparición.	Blessed Mother please receive Our best wishes to you, For today is your big day Of your graceful appearance.
Coro:	*Chorus:*
Despierta, etc.	Awaken, etc.
Recibe Madre querida nuestra felicitación, miranos aqui postrados Y danos tu bendición.	Receive, dear Mother Our best wishes to you, See we're here to stay, look at us here prostrated, And receive your blessing.
Coro:	*Chorus:*
Despierta, etc.	Awaken, etc.

*Mañanitas does not have a direct translation but refers to a joyous celebratory song.

only come forth if they emerge from a healthy root, and since God is the ultimate and definitive root of truth, of all stability, then flowers were God's way of showing God's self to the world, the most delicate evidence that human thought can rise toward God, overcoming limitations and providing an opportunity to enter into communion with the heart and body of God.

This faith experience of Our Lady of Guadalupe stands in opposition to the scientific, objective, and rational assumptive world of the dominant culture. Therefore, this experience of Our Lady of Guadalupe is perhaps not the most effective medium by which to communicate with the dominant culture the possibilities of merging two different cultures and creating something new. But the story and experience of Our Lady of Guadalupe has been at its very core a resistance to and a way of surviving in that dominant culture and its world for generations of Latinas.

The story, belief, image, and cultural memory of Our Lady of Guadalupe help Mexican Americans to envision a different world. In Christian terminology, it is an eschatological experience. In this experience, the marginalized have a special relationship with God, one that is profoundly meaningful for a people who have no other relationship with anything powerful in this world.

Home Altars

Plaster saints, artificial and/or real flowers, family pictures, scented candles—these are but a few of the elements of home altars. The frequency of home altars can be found among a cross section of Latinas, whether they are Puerto Rican, Colombian, Mexican, or Cuban. The home altar has a visible and significant place in the domestic sphere as both a religious and a ritual symbol. The home altar is focused on the extended family, immediate community, saints, and women's relationship to them.

Home altars are located in a variety of places within the home: a few feet from the front door, in the bedroom, in the family room. There may be one home altar; there may be several in the same dwelling place. Home altars can be permanent or, in some cases, "portables." That is, a woman may display her altar at significant times, then fold up the altar and put it back in her bureau.

These altars form the basis for home devotion and are maintained by the mother and other adult women in the house. It is primarily the mother who takes upon herself the responsibility to teach the children the altar's purpose and maintenance. The focus of the home altar is to draw attention to the secular world's dependency on the divine. The creator of the altar brings together sacred icons in a sacred place of the home. This actively negotiates women's personal relationship with the creator and the pantheon of sacred people.

One would place on their altar the saints and/or the Marian image that one has developed a relationship with through family tradition. There may be pictures of loved ones. These may be people still living, to whom prayers are directed for protection or healing. Or a picture of a loved one who has died, so that they too might be able to intercede for the family. There are candles lit as a ritualistic gesture of petition. There are flowers, perhaps rosary beads, special mementos symbolic of the family's experience. Decorative items may include jewelry and even money. The objects themselves may be inexpensive, but the meaning ascribed to those objects gives them a priceless value. What is significant about the objects is

that through them one is fostering, deepening, and developing one's intimate relationship with God and the saints.

The *dicho* (saying) "La mujer es el alma de la casa"— the woman is the soul of the house—underscores the importance of the religious role of women in the home. This practice was well established even in the early days of colonization. Ranchos of the Spanish period, for example, give evidence of the important role that home religion played in resisting the invader and maintaining traditional values.

The altar tradition is learned informally and passed down generation after generation through the female lineage of the family. A distinction is made between the church altar, which is the central focus of worship for the Christian community and the home altar, which is, in more intimate terms, referred to as "El Altarcito" (The Little Altar). To examine these home altars is to see reflected the specific history, hopes, experiences, and needs of the families. At the heart of this altar tradition is the relationship to a particular saint, the Virgin in any of her manifestations, or groups of saints who serve as a woman's personal intercessor before God. The saints and Mary are represented in contextual human forms and are given a place of honor so that they may be known and appealed to in the most human and intimate way. The mother brings their presence into the home and makes them part of the family.

A woman creates a place for the family before these altars. This is a sacred place, where the family may sit and make themselves known to God and feel God's response to them through the intercession of the saints or a particular Marian devotion. A charming story surrounding this tradition of home altars is presented by researcher K. F. Turner. The assumption of being privileged with God at home was made clear to her at a gathering of neighborhood women. They had met to view Pope John Paul II's speech in Mexico City. "In response to his adamant refusal to accept the possibility of sanctioning women priests in the formal church hierarchy," one of the women responded, "Who needs it? We are our own priest at home." The researcher reports that everyone laughed, nodding their heads in agreement (Turner, 30).

SOURCES: T. K. Turner's *Mexican American Women's Home Altars: The Art of Relationship* (1990), explores unexamined Catholic folk traditions maintained and transmitted over the centuries by Latina women. Primary fieldwork was done in south Texas. Turner applies feminist theory to the examination of the tradition of home altars and its critical contribution to the art of relationship. Elizabeth Carmichael and Chloe Sayer's book, *The Skeleton at the Feast: The Day of the Dead in Mexico* (1982), describes one of the most important festivals in Mexico, Día de Los Muertos. This book reviews the historical origins of the feast and its contemporary cultural manifestations.

Hugo G. Nutini's article "Pre-Hispanic Component of the Syncretic Cult of the Dead in Mesoamerica Ethnology: An International and Social Anthropology," *Journal of Culture* 27.1 (1988), examines the pre-Hispanic component of this cult of the dead. Orlando Espín's *The Faith of the People: Theological Reflections on Popular Catholicism* (1997) and his article, co-authored with Sixto Garcia, "Lilies of the Field: A Hispanic Theology of Providence and Human Responsibility" (1989) are invaluable sources for understanding the popular religion of the U.S. Latina population in the United States. A. M. Diaz-Stevens's "Latinas and the Church" in *Issues and Concerns* (1994) explores the role and influence that these women have had in the Roman Catholic church. Jeanette Rodriguez's *Our Lady of Guadalupe: Faith and Empowerment Among Mexican-American Women* (1994) offers an interdisciplinary method for exploring the faith that empowers Mexican-American women. See also Virgilio Elizondo, *Guadalupe: Mother of the New Creation* (1997).

ASIAN AND PACIFIC AMERICAN CATHOLIC WOMEN

Jocelyn M. Eclarin Azada

ASIAN AND PACIFIC American Catholic women are a diverse group who trace their origins back to more than fifty countries and Pacific states in the Asian continent including Cambodia, China, India, Japan, Korea, Laos, the Philippines, Samoa, Tonga, and Vietnam.

The first Asian women immigrated to the United States in the mid-1800s, often accompanying Asian men in their search for a livelihood and expanded options in a new America rich with opportunity. Asian men—from China, Japan, Korea, the Philippines, and India—provided manual labor for San Francisco's gold rush, the Transcontinental Railroad, Hawaii's sugar plantations, and the seemingly limitless agricultural fields of the West Coast. No less than the men, Asian women in the United States also worked and contributed significantly to the establishment and stability of their communities. They managed households *and* contributed to the family income through grueling fieldwork alongside their husbands and even entrepreneurial home-based enterprises such as taking in laundry and cooking for single male laborers.

Cultural constraints as well as immigration quotas restricted the numbers of women in the first wave of immigration from Asia to the U.S. mainland from the turn of the century until World War II. The men came from poor, uneducated, and rural backgrounds. Promising work, high wages, and even adventure in the United States, recruiters for American railroad and agricultural companies presented a way out of debt and poverty for these men. They came as sojourners—planning to work for a short period of time and then return to their homelands, having saved enough of their earnings to pay off their family's debt or start their own family. Upon arriving, miners and farmers found back-breaking working conditions at subsistence-level wages. American society did not welcome them. They were segregated, physically abused, and denied the rights to become citizens, to own property, or to intermarry with whites.

Generally, women came in far fewer numbers to the mainland. U.S. immigration policy discouraged the permanent settlement of Asian workers. Culturally, a single woman was not permitted to travel alone, and a married woman stayed at home to care for the children, and sometimes her husband's parents, while he was away. Furthermore, companies recruited single men without families to lower labor costs and provide migratory labor that could move from season to season. Thus, in 1900, only 5 percent of the Chinese and 5 percent of the Filipino populations on the mainland were women. The percentage of women in the Asian Indian population in California's Imperial Valley to the south and Sacramento Valley to the north was approximately 1 percent. The Japanese community was the exception to this pattern, as women in Japan, who were both educated and wage earners in their own country, had played a key role as factory workers in that country's industrialization and could travel without censure. Between 1911 and 1920, women were 39 percent of the Japanese immigrants to the United States. Women made up 34.5 percent of the Japanese population on the mainland, concentrated in California, Washington, and Oregon. They worked as unpaid field laborers on family farms and provided other paid services, taking in cleaning, sewing, and washing, in addition to domestic responsibilities in their own homes.

Legislation closely regulated the flow of Asian immigrant labor. The makeup of each immigrant population—the work they did, their respective numbers of women and men, the families they formed, and where they landed—was determined by balancing economic need against racial and political considerations with the sending countries. The earliest Asian immigrant communities experienced racial hostility and violence. Chinese women were among the first targets of racist laws. While prostitutes from Europe, Mexico, and even South America worked in California's gold rush frontier, Chinese women were particularly singled out as immoral and "heathen." In fact, many of the approximately 4,000 Chinese prostitutes came from destitute families and were either kidnapped or tricked into prostitution. By 1875, the Page Act was passed to prohibit the entry of Chinese women, all presumed to be prostitutes who would engage in "criminal and demoralizing purposes" (Asian Women United, 3). In 1882, the Chinese Exclusion Act extended the ban to all Chinese for ten years.

1920 women were approximately 46 percent of the Japanese and 20 percent of the adult Korean population in Hawaii.

Of the Koreans who came to Hawaii through 1920, a majority were from urban areas; 70 percent were literate, and 40 percent were Protestant Christians. These migrants were encouraged by American Protestant missionaries in Korea to go to Hawaii for the religious freedom and economic opportunity unavailable to them in Korea, which was fighting for its independence against Japanese imperialism and also suffering under severe conditions of famine and drought. Many of the Korean women who emigrated were "picture brides," so called because they married men already in Hawaii through brokered marriages. A man would initiate the proposal by sending his photograph to a friend or relative of a woman, who would then choose to marry him or not. Many women opted for marriage as an alternative that would increase their own life options.

> When my neighbor showed me a photograph of a man who had been in America, I decided to marry him right away. Because I was raised in a poor family in Kyungsang province, in the southern part of Korea, honestly speaking, I was more interested in his money than in his appearance.
>
> My intention was to leave my prospective husband for study as soon as I arrived and return to Korea with a higher education.
>
> After we exchanged photographs through my aunt's friend, who had also come as a picture bride, I became determined to come because of Japanese oppression, even though my parents disapproved. I just had no freedom. (Asian Women United, 54)

Filipino immigrants to Hawaii also brought their wives with them, though in fewer numbers than Japanese and Koreans. By 1930, women were 16.6 percent of the Filipino population in Hawaii, allowing the formation of a more permanent and stable Filipino community. The Filipino laborers were primarily from poor, farming families and were Christian as well; 90 percent of them were Catholic.

The central event of Japanese American history—the relocation of Japanese Americans to internment camps in California, Washington, and Oregon—occurred dur-

In 1907, another law conditioned the immigration of Asian women and men. The Gentleman's Agreement Act between the United States and Japan banned further immigration of Japanese and Korean men but did permit Japanese and Korean wives to join their husbands in the United States; this law profoundly impacted the settlement and stability of these communities, particularly in Hawaii.

Hawaiian plantations followed a different recruitment strategy that encouraged Japanese and Korean women to migrate along with their husbands and guaranteed employment and housing that could accommodate families. Plantation owners thought that men with families were more motivated workers who were less likely to patronize and attract brothels and gambling halls, which catered to single male workers on the mainland. Women played major roles in these communities, working within the home and without. Japanese immigrant, or Issei, women became the majority of wage-earning women a few years after arriving in Hawaii and maintained this position for decades. The vast majority worked in sugar fields, performing the same tasks as the men, such as weeding, irrigating, cutting cane with a knife, and loading cane onto trucks. As one woman described herself: "I did anything that the men did. . . . I did any and all kinds of work." A labor report likewise characterized these women: "not strong physically, but perform hard and exhausting work, keeping up through sheer force of spirit" (Asian Women United, 140). By

ing World War II after the Japanese attack on Pearl Harbor. By the 1930s Japanese Americans established solid communities in California, Washington, and Oregon, with thriving businesses, civic organizations, social clubs, athletic leagues, and church groups. As a result of Executive Order 9066, 120,000 persons of Japanese descent on the West Coast were incarcerated in relocation centers, and all their private property was taken.

After World War II, wives and family of American military personnel were permitted to enter the country under the War Brides Act of 1945. As a result, 200,000 Asian women immigrated to the United States from the Philippines, Korea, and Japan between 1945 and 1965. A period of settlement of Asian American communities occurred until the Immigration Act of 1965, which prompted another surge of Asian immigration with markedly different characteristics than the first.

The Immigration Act of 1965 abolished country quotas and allowed professionals and families entry into the United States. Unlike the Asian immigrants of the first wave, these second wave immigrants were highly skilled and trained in technology and service occupations. Unlike the first wave, figures were low for Japanese immigration during this wave, a fact attributed to an expanding Japanese economy with a need for skilled workers. From 1965 to 1970, the majority of Chinese, Filipino, Korean, and Asian Indian immigrants were admitted as professionals in industries ranging from health care to engineering. Bringing along their families, they intended to settle as residents raising their children in this country. Finally, high percentages of women immigrated. In contrast to the earlier immigrant communities of the first and second waves, between 1975 and 1980, women comprised more than half of all Asian immigrants.

As a result, Chinese, Filipinos, Koreans, and Asian Indian communities increased dramatically. For example, the Korean population grew from 10,000 in 1960 to 500,000 in 1985. Similar increases are observed for the Asian Indian community, which saw its population increase from 10,000 in 1965 to 525,000 in 1985. From the late 1970s to the present, migration consisted mainly of family members from Asian countries who followed their relatives to America. Between 1990 and 2000, China and the Philippines ranked first and third in annual numbers of immigrants to the United States.

Southeast Asians came to the United States beginning in the mid-1970s. Most were political refugees from Vietnam, Cambodia, and Laos, fleeing wars in their homelands. As political refugees, they had experienced war, disruption of their lives, and stays in refugee camps before coming to the United States. Vietnamese refugees had the highest levels of education. Many were professionals, managers, and technicians prior to their arrival in this country; accordingly, they became the most pro-

ficient in English. Cambodians and Hmong came from rural areas and were farmers and fisherfolk with few years of schooling; not surprisingly, these groups have the highest rates of illiteracy and unemployment in the United States. Vietnamese and Laotians are more likely to have come from urban areas. The Hmong have come from primarily rural regions; Cambodians come from both rural and urban backgrounds. Vietnamese refugees typically traveled by boat to this country. Cambodians and Laotians, on the other hand, walked across the border to Thailand; often, they waited many months in crowded refugee camps there and in the Philippines before coming to the United States.

From 1975 to 1979, refugees tended to come from the elite, well-educated, and professional classes. The demographic profile of refugees after 1980 changed dramatically, however, as later waves of refugees were poor, with low levels of education and few transferable skills. Additionally, those who arrived later had suffered more trauma before and during their escape as war conditions escalated. Southeast Asians are geographically concentrated in urban areas and states in the West. Almost half of all Southeast Asian immigrants reside in California; throughout the rest of the country, Cambodians have mainly resettled on the East Coast, Laotians in the Midwest, and Vietnamese in the Gulf states.

Asian American Women in 2000

Information from the 2000 U.S. Census provides a demographic sketch of the Asian American population. Asian Americans numbered 11.9 million or 4 percent of the total U.S. population. Chinese are the largest subgroup of Asian Americans, with 2.7 million people, followed by Filipinos and Asian Indians, with 2 million people each. There were approximately 1.2 million Vietnamese, 1.1 million Koreans, and roughly 800,000 Japanese. Over half, 57 percent, live in the western part of the United States, and 75 percent live in ten states: California, New York, Hawaii, Texas, New Jersey, Illinois, Washington, Florida, Virginia, and Massachusetts. Ninety-six percent reside in metropolitan areas.

Asian American households tend to be larger, as 23 percent claim more than five members, compared to 13 percent for non-Hispanic white households. Eighty percent of Asian American families are headed by married couples, and 13 percent are headed by single women. One-third of Asian American families have incomes greater than $75,000; at the same time, 21 percent of Asian American families have incomes less than $25,000.

Sixty percent of Asian American women in 1999 worked outside the home. Asian American women were more likely than non-Hispanic white women to have less than a ninth-grade education (17 percent and 12 percent, respectively) and more likely to have a college degree than non-Hispanic white women (39 percent and 25 percent, respectively). Asian immigrants in general are employed in both the highly paid, highly educated sector of the workforce and in the lower-paying service and manufacturing jobs. Women are prominent at both ends of the spectrum, with the growth of high- and low-paying female-intensive industries such as the service, health-care, microelectronics, and apparel manufacturing industries. They also play a key role in family-owned businesses such as restaurants and small grocery stores. According to the 2000 U.S. Census, 36 percent of Asian American women are employed in managerial and professional occupations; 32 percent in technical, sales, and administrative support occupations; 11 percent as operators and laborers; and 3 percent in production and craft occupations.

Asian American Women and the U.S. Catholic Church

Few of the Chinese and Japanese immigrants at the beginning of the twentieth century were Catholic. In the hopes of obtaining conversions, the Catholic Church established missions to minister to these immigrants. Not until fifty years after the arrival of the first Chinese to California, however, was a mission established for Chinese immigrants. Asian religious sisters played important roles in these missions, located in Los Angeles, San Francisco, and New York, starting schools with special language and cultural preservation classes for second and third generations of Chinese and Japanese. In 1903, Old St. Mary's Church in San Francisco's Chinatown was established by Paulist Fathers. However, the church was without a Chinese pastor who could minister to the people in their own language. Records from the Archdiocese of San Francisco indicate that in 1904 a native Chinese religious sister, Mother St. Ida, arrived with a group of the Sisters of the Helpers of the Holy Souls to work with the Chinese at Old St. Mary's.

In 1912, the first Japanese mission church in the United States was established in Los Angeles by Fr. Albert Breton. He credits Japanese sisters with the most impact on the work of that mission:

> 1915. But the work of the Japanese Catholic Mission in Los Angeles got its real start when four Japanese Sisters of the Visitation arrived from Japan in March 1915. . . . In the Fall of 1916 I went to Japan to recruit some young Sisters. In the spring of 1919 I went again for the same purpose. The Sisters of the Visitation were eleven at their highest point. (Burns, Skerrett, and White, 235)

In the 1920s, the Church ministered to the predominantly single male population of Filipinos through clubs that offered social services and positive social events. In 1925, a mixed Japanese and Filipino parish, Our Lady Queen of Martyrs, was established in Seattle, and in 1947, the only national parish for Filipinos, St. Columban's was started in Los Angeles.

The firsthand account of a second-generation Japanese woman, Antoinette Yae Ono, tells of life in the Manzanar War Relocation Center during the Japanese internment. Ono, a convert to Catholicism and a Maryknoll sister, performed her ministry in the camp and was assisted by two Japanese Maryknoll sisters, Sisters Susanna Hayashi and Bernadette Yoshimachi. Ono wrote:

> In May, two Japanese Maryknoll Sisters, Srs. Susanna and Bernadette, arrived in camp with more of the evacuees. The Sisters voluntarily interned themselves seeing the opportunities that would come their way to help their own people spiritually. The Sisters were given one room like the rest and a number, a number by which each family was recorded. The Sisters found it very difficult at first for camp life meant using the shower, etc. with the rest. . . . From the very first week that the Sisters arrived catechetical work was started beginning with the children and soon afterwards the adults were under instructions, also. Each Saturday catechism lessons were held for any children whose parents did not object to their attending catechism. Individual instructions were given during the week for those who were actually interested in the faith. Srs. Bernadette and Susanna taught the older Japanese in their own language. The younger people were taught by older boys and girls who volunteered to help the Sisters in teaching the catechism. . . . The Sisters not only did catechetical work but they also visited the sick and taught in the hospital and helped many persons who came to them for their own personal difficulties. (Burns, Skerrett, and White, 247)

In the second half of the twentieth century, U.S.-born and foreign-born Asian Americans made up 2.6 percent of the U.S. Catholic Church in 2000. Thirty dioceses counted more than 100,000 Asian Americans as members; the five dioceses with the highest numbers of Asian Americans are Los Angeles, Honolulu, Brooklyn, San Jose, and Oakland. The two largest Asian American Catholic communities are the Filipino and Vietnamese communities. Eighty-three percent of Filipino Americans and 30 percent of Vietnamese Americans consider themselves Catholic.

In November 2001, the U.S. Conference on Catholic Bishops issued a pastoral statement on Asian and Pacific Islander Catholics, titled *Asian and Pacific Presence: Harmony in Faith*. Divided into four major sections, this statement describes the history, practices, contributions, and challenges of Asian and Pacific Islander Catholics. As a starting point, the pastoral notes first the diversity captured by the term *Asian American,* which spans at least twenty different ethnic groups, more than 100 languages, and includes U.S.-born second-generation citizens, recent immigrants, and those whose families have been here for generations. The pastoral statement also touches on the common history that Asian American Catholics claim—a rich heritage in Asia that endured persecution, has been led by laypeople, and continues to be practiced close to the hearts and lives of the faithful here in the United States.

European missionary activity beginning in the sixteenth century spread Catholicism throughout Asia. Tradition has it that Christianity began in India in the first century with St. Thomas the Apostle. European missionaries arrived centuries later and established schools, hospitals, and churches. In 1991 slightly over 1 percent of India's population was Catholic. Conversions eventually led to conflict with Confucian doctrine in China, Korea, and Vietnam and suspicion of European political and military agendas in Japan. Consequently, the Japanese imperial government banned Catholicism, with 3 million converts, from 1637 to 1865. During these 200 years, the faith was not eliminated but practiced in secret by laypeople who passed it down from generation to generation; 20,000 *kakure kirishitan,* or hidden Christians, were still practicing their faith by the time the ban was lifted. The Church in Korea was initiated by laypeople in the late eighteenth century—scholars who were converted simply by studying Jesuit and Chinese missionary Mateo Ricci's *True Doctrine of God,* an explanation of Catholicism in Confucian terminology. Within ten years, there were 4,000 converts—the result of laypeople's efforts—all before the first Catholic priest arrived in Korea. Since Korean Catholics refused to perform ancestor rites, a foundational expression of Confucian filial piety, more than 10,000 Koreans were martyred from 1801 to 1871. In 1984, 103 Korean martyrs were canonized by John Paul II. Persecutions of Catholics began for the similar reasons in Vietnam in 1798 and continued until the twentieth century. Over 130,000 Vietnamese were martyred for their faith, and in 1988, 117 Vietnamese martyrs were canonized.

Only in the Philippines, where today 85 percent of the population is Catholic, did Western Christianity take solid hold. Wholesale conversions to Catholicism in that country were the religious dimension of a total political colonization by the Spanish in the sixteenth century that thoroughly altered Philippine society and lasted 400 years. Native Filipinos also found parallels with their own indigenous traditions in the religion of the missionaries, and so practiced Catholicism outwardly while retaining their own beliefs.

According to the pastoral statement, a strong tradition of lay leadership stems from the mission-based history of the Catholic Church in Asia. Laypeople were encouraged—and needed—to build and sustain the Church in countries like Vietnam or Korea, where less than 10 percent of the population is Catholic, and in the Philippines, where there is a shortage of clergy. Catechists—laypeople of strong faith and trained in the basic teachings of Catholicism—are familiar to Catholics in Asia as teachers of the faith and leaders in prayer. Today, in churches, dioceses, and even at the national level in the United States, Asian American Catholic women continue this tradition of building and sustaining the Church as visible leaders in liturgical, social service, hospitality, and ethnic ministries. Kim Le, a Vietnamese woman in Los Angeles, exemplifies this leadership.

I was born Catholic. My mom converted to Catholicism from Buddhism, and then both of my parents converted. When I was young, I was involved in Eucharistic ministry. I went to mass every day, but I didn't realize what everything meant. In 1975, South Vietnam collapsed and my dad was sent to reeducation camp, which means prison. My brother was sent to the United States. I said to God, "Why did you let my family be in this situation?" I didn't go to church for 2 or 3 years, thinking that if a God exists, he wouldn't let something like this happen. But then I went to charismatic seminar and received a grace to know that God exists and loves me. I became a catechist; I loved mass. Then my sister escaped, but she passed away. In 1977, I was a catechist in Vietnam for children who were homeless. I learned Catholic doctrine, and I learned about the Bible. In 1999, when I left Vietnam, I was a catechist, a leader for the prayer group, and a leader for the youth group. Now, I am the General Secretary of Youth Ministry for the Archdiocese of LA.

Another lay catechist in Vietnam, Annie Trang, became active in her parish as a catechist and member of the choir after resettling in this country in 1989. She shares her leadership experiences in a refugee camp:

We escaped together with 9 seminarians, and we still keep in touch with email to our friends. At reunions, we cry a lot. . . . The camp was Panat Nikhom, Thailand. In camp people are sad; they give up a lot. . . . Before camp, I was very shy, I didn't do anything. I'm very quiet and shy. In camp, no leader. In 10 months we created a group. We train a lot of people. We organized them with seminarians and other young people; we play together, pray together; study. In camp we taught the children about God, the Bible. The kids' situation was that they left Vietnam without parents. . . . I remember there were 3 girls, about 9 and 10 years old, whose parents were killed and they were raped by Thai pirates. . . . We were really active with other young people, and helped a lot of people, a lot of kids. There were 13,000 Vietnamese kids who came to us every day. I was 23 years old.

Asian American women are very active in leadership roles within the institutional Church. For example, Sr. Lucia Tu began working with ethnic ministries in the Archdiocese of Los Angeles in 1987, when she was the Secretariat of Ethnic Ministries. At that time, ethnic ministries was construed in terms of African American and Hispanic ministries. In 1991 she initiated the addition of the Asian Pacific ministry. In recent years, this office has expanded to include Native American and Arab-speaking Catholics. Last year, the importance of the largest Catholic Asian Pacific community in Los Angeles was recognized with a special office for Filipino pastoral ministries. This office is staffed by a Filipino, Sr. Mary Christina Sevilla, RGS, Good Shepherd Sister.

The practice of Asian American Catholics is community based and family centered. Sacraments and rites of passage such as baptisms, weddings, and funerals are culturally nuanced practices that preserve ethnic culture. Popular devotions to Mary and the saints intertwine with the joys, concerns, and sufferings of life, with prayers of petition and thanksgiving for family, health, and financial blessings. Attending mass and family prayers strengthen and nurture the primary Asian value of the family. A second-generation Indian American nurse who lives in Florida and is active in her parish, Jeanette Campos Phan, portrays the underpinning of faith and family:

Growing up with my grandparents and extended family in Hyderabad, being Catholic was very important. My grandparents, aunts, uncles would say prayers, novenas and the Rosary with all of us cousins—about 20 or 30 of us would be in the room. That rich heritage growing up, I associate being Catholic with family, it was part of family life and family culture. Now, my cousins and I, years apart and all over the world, hold ties together because of our sharing that in our formative years. . . . I have been Catholic all my life. I appreciate the rich history of 400 years of Catholicism in India and treasure that aspect of my faith. Now, there is this connection between being of Indian heritage and this great heritage of being Catholic and sharing that with my family.

Finally, the pastoral points to the gift of an Asian spirituality and culture that values harmony with God, other people, and the whole universe. Asian American Catholic practice and beliefs are enriched by the perspective of practicing the faith in dialogue with non-Western culture, with other religious traditions in Asia, and with the poverty experienced in their homelands. Indeed, the very questions of our globalized world—of interreligious dialogue, relating across cultural identities, and global justice—are part of the natural experiences of Asian American Catholics. A Filipino immigrant in Chicago relates her faith to her Asian spirituality:

I am a practicing Catholic, and strongly Asian in spirituality. Going to mass, believing in Jesus Christ, Catholic rituals—they give me spiritual growth. But I feel close to the spirits of my ancestors. To me, that's very Asian. As a Christian, every time I pray, I pray for the dead. I talk to them and they communicate with me through dreams, especially when I go through major decisions and changes in my life—the communications are so detailed! When my mother prays, she prays for the dead and puts food on the altar at home. . . . it's a meeting of both.

Similarly, Cathy Cheng, a medical doctor and second-generation U.S.-born Chinese American living in Chicago, describes her Catholic faith in relation to the Chinese cultural practice of honoring ancestors:

I practice cultural Chinese Buddhist practices at home by paying respects to ancestors with the shrine and the incense. A lot of Chinese can totally reconcile being Catholic and doing these rituals. It's a meaningful way for me to remember my grandparents—I was close to two of them—it's something that ties me to my heritage. . . . For me, the symbol of the community of saints—those who have gone before us—as definitely an active part of our faith life is important.

By their own experiences and also through family members in their homelands, many Asian American Catholics are personally connected to the poverty throughout the global South and can challenge the U.S. Church. A Filipino immigrant and community leader in Chicago, Susan Gonzales, remembers:

In the Philippines, the sermons are connected to social justice; the sermons are political, social commentary. When I was an activist in the Philippines, I was accustomed to Christians of all denominations, especially Catholic religious, speaking out and being persecuted.... I have not observed that here as much.

A Vietnamese immigrant woman who now lives in Texas recalls her experience in a refugee camp:

Life in camp very difficult. . . . I had to survive. . . . No electricity. . . . A lot of people, a lot of soldiers. . . . There was not enough food to eat. I did not have money. At that time, I usually go to chapel and sit on these and cry.

A Vietnamese immigrant woman in southern California reflects on the different economic realities encountered in the United States and in Vietnam:

In Vietnam, we're very poor. Here, there is a lot of materialism, you work hard to get pay, and life is the many things around you. Materialism makes it harder to care about God, and to see the poor people around you.

Finally, an immigrant from China who converted to Catholicism in her adulthood, Tingting Cai, expresses her concern for the poor in her poem "Lord, You Are Too Far Away" (see box at right).

Filipino American Catholic Women

An estimated 1.5 million out of 1.8 million Filipino Americans are Catholic. Filipino Catholics bring with them a traditional faith that was born from the Hispanic Catholicism of the missionaries. Devotional practices are distinctive of Filipino Catholicism rooted in the Spanish Catholicism of the sixteenth century. Filipinos are drawn to objects, actions, practices, places, and special times to help them become more aware of Christ's presence. Examples of these devotional practices include blessings of homes; actions such as kneeling, bowing, making the sign of the cross, and touching statues; novenas, litanies, and saying the Rosary; objects such as rosaries, scapulars, crucifixes, statues, and holy water; places such as churches and shrines; special times, such as Advent, Holy Week, and feast days. Through these practices, they exhibit a desire for God and a faith that God is involved in their daily lives. Sally Alimboyoguen, a nurse and Filipino immigrant in San Diego, describes the importance these practices have for her:

I've been a Catholic since birth. My parents and grandparents were Catholic. My grandmother would say the rosary with the grandchildren, always at 6 pm. The rituals that are important to me are going to church, praying the rosary at

Lord, You Are Too Far Away

You say, "I am hungry"
But your voice cries out from North Korea
It is too far away for me to know your
hunger

You say, "I am naked"
But your voice travels from Africa
It is too far away for me to see your
nakedness

You say, "I am thirsty"
But your voice comes from Far East
It is too far away for me to realize your thirst
You say, "I am sick and imprisoned"
But your voice echoes from nowhere
It is too faint for me to recognize your
loneliness

Dear Jesus, when can I be near enough
To share my rice with you in your hunger
To spare my clothes for you in your
nakedness
To offer you a drink
And to visit you when you are lonely?
I ponder it in silence

home, praying novenas, having statues of the St. Nino, Sacred Heart, and the Blessed Mother. When I pray with other Filipinos, we say the rosary, share our experiences, offer thanks and pray with and for each other. When we share our devotional prayers, we are sharing our love of the Lord with friends and praying for continuous growth in our faith.

Another immigrant Filipino in Chicago describes how her faith helps her deal with difficulties in life:

There are times when I feel overwhelmed by problems—financial problems and missing my family—and a short visit to the church to give thanks for my blessings and pray for strength always helps me.

Filipino Catholic women are the main bearers of family faith. Grandmothers, mothers, and sisters are family evangelizers. In the United States, this practice lives on, as Filipino Catholic women take on the role of transmitters of faith. Vickie Arirao, a Filipino nurse and professor of nursing in New York City who immigrated in 1970, remembers her mother:

My mom walked to daily mass here in Harlem. When she was in her late '70s, my mom was giving holy communion to sick people, shut-ins. . . . She was old and frail herself, yet she walked up seventeen flights of stairs to give communion to those people in the neighborhood she knew could not get to mass.

Inspired by her example, Vickie herself is active in lay ministries as a soup kitchen volunteer, Eucharistic minister, and organizer of medical missions to the Philippines in which doctors and nurses from the United States donate their services and also medicine primarily in rural areas.

Puri Lahoz, a teacher and Filipino immigrant in Chicago, discusses a family ritual among three generations of women in her household:

My mother is the spiritual leader for the religious rituals in the house, and they're very Catholic and very traditional. She's part of a group that brings a special rosary here, and they sing every decade. . . . Angela, my 10-year-old daughter, is committed now to saying the rosary, too.

Filipino American women are also leaders within the institutional Church at archdiocesan, diocesan, and parish levels. Their contributions strengthen their own immigrant community and enhance the larger Church community at the same time. A Filipino pastoral leader, Lena Tolentino, at Our Lady of Mercy Parish in Chicago, discusses how small faith communities in her church meet the pastoral needs of Filipino parishioners:

The goal of small faith communities in the archdiocese depends on the needs of the community. Family ties in the Philippines are so important, and some of the people are here alone. So the goal of the small faith community at Our Lady of Mercy is to provide moral support, somebody to listen, somebody to pray with and for in times of difficulty, someone to cry with.

In the Archdiocese of San Francisco, Noemi Castillo works with the Office of Ethnic Ministries and was instrumental in initiating a program for Filipino pastoral ministries in the Bay Area. Terisita Nuval is the director of Asian Pacific Ministries in the Office of Ethnic Ministries in the Archdiocese of Chicago.

Filipino women religious from several congregations like the Religious of the Virgin Mary (founded in Manila by a Filipino woman religious), Religious of the Good Shepherd, Dominican Sisters of Sienna, and the Scalabrini Sisters have served and continue to serve in the United States as teachers and administrators in parochial schools, nurses and administrators in hospitals and hospices, social workers, and counselors in parishes, diocesan social service programs, and many other fields of ministry.

Vietnamese American Catholic Women

French missionaries came to Vietnam in 1615. Conversions in the seventeenth and eighteenth centuries were followed by almost two centuries of persecution by the Vietnamese government, perceiving Catholicism's challenge to filial piety to be a threat. Vietnamese refugees and immigrants in the United States are followers of various religious traditions: the indigenous religion called Caodism, Animism, Buddhism, Confucianism, Taoism, and Christianity. Although Catholics constitute only 8 percent of the total population in Vietnam, in the United States, they make up at least 30 percent of Vietnamese Americans. Due to past experiences of religious persecution, a high proportion of Catholics fled the country, beginning in 1975 after the fall of Saigon. Among the earliest arrivals were 200 Catholic priests and 250 sisters. Today, approximately 325,000 Catholics are among the 1.1 million Vietnamese Americans. Seventy-five percent of Vietnamese Catholics belong to primarily Vietnamese parishes or multicultural pastoral centers. In parishes and multicultural centers, women and men can practice faith in their own language and culture. They also participate in pastoral care, catechesis, Bible studies, and prayer services.

Vietnamese American Catholics are noted for their fervent devotion to faith. Their religious institutions and beliefs are integral to their lives as individuals and are central to their families and communities. One Vietnamese woman describes her family's practices of faith:

My parents are both Catholic; we prayed as a family every night and went to church every single day in Vietnam. My mom was in the choir in Vietnam, and now everyone in my family is in the choir at our parish. My husband and I now, with our son, pray every night at home in front of the statue of Holy Mary.

Elaborate weddings, funerals, and ancestor commemoration rites link religious tradition with ethnic culture. Celebrations of holidays and religious feast days also preserve ethnic identity. These festive celebrations include Tet, the lunar new year celebration in late January and early February; November 24, which honors the Vietnamese Martyrs; and a celebration for Our Lady of La Vang, the name given to Mary when she appeared in La Vang, Vietnam, to comfort those being persecuted for their faith. The most significant change among the Vietnamese American Catholics over the past two decades is the more active participation of the laity including women.

Religious vocations from Vietnamese Americans are among the highest of any ethnic group. In 1995 alone, 300 Vietnamese priests were ordained, and 450 Vietnamese sisters entered religious orders. There are about twenty Vietnamese female religious societies in the United States. These religious congregations hold annual retreats together to build up a spirit of community among all the Vietnamese sisters. The largest is the Congregation of the Lovers of the Holy Cross (Dong Men Thanh Gia), the first congregation for women established in Vietnam in 1670. It began as a congregation for Vietnamese women religious to serve the Vietnamese people and now has twenty-four independent congregations in Vietnam and Los Angeles.

The history of the Congregation of the Lovers of the Holy Cross in the United States began on August 1, 1975, when Sr. Cecilia Chuyen Nguyen visited the Vincentian nuns in Philadelphia to request a space for their community to continue their religious and community life of prayer, meals, recreation, and ministry. Her hopes to establish their community in America became a place where older sisters could be cared for, where younger sisters could complete their training, begin ministry with Vietnamese refugees, and find candidates for their community.

> Our sisters want to stay together so that we can continue the religious and community life which we had in Vietnam. But in Vietnam, most of the Sisters were school teachers or school administrators. In America they can not do school work because of language difficulties. Still, our Sisters are healthy and strong, and they can do hard physical work. They can mop floors, clean, cook, do dishes, scrub pots and pans, take care of the sick and the elderly.

The order gradually reestablished its ministries and its identity as a Vietnamese women's religious congregation in the United States. Most Vietnamese women's religious communities in America focus on pastoral, educational, social, and hospital work.

Generation X Asian American Catholic Women

Asian Americans are a highly diverse group, not only by country of origin, status in the home country, and circumstances of migration but also by generation. Second-generation Asian American women, mostly children of Asian immigrants who have come as a result of the Immigration Act of 1965, face different challenges than their parents. Immigrant or refugee Asian women have faced the stresses of leaving their homelands and extended families, adapting to a new culture, and surviving economically. Second-generation American-born Chinese, Filipino, Indian, and Korean women in the United States have typically achieved high levels of education and high median incomes. For these women, a primary challenge is to integrate their two cultures—ethnic and American culture. Conflict occurs internally and between generations, as these women respond to cultural expectations that they uphold traditional values and also conform to racial and gender stereotypes while living in the larger multicultural society.

In their twenties and thirties by the year 2000, these women are members of Generation X, the cohort born between 1961 and 1980 that was shaped by such social changes as the civil rights, feminist, and environmental movements, communication and transportation technologies that make globalization possible, and the influence of entertainment media. Interest in this group within the Catholic Church has been prompted by a distinct Generation X spirituality manifested by this generation. Generation X Asian American women's voices also resonate with this spirituality.

These young Catholics emphasize religious experience and spirituality and are on a personal spiritual journey. The teachings of Jesus instill a desire for equality and justice. Maria Ferrera, a thirty-three-year-old Filipino American, clinical social worker, and University of Chicago Ph.D. candidate, describes what is meaningful to her about her faith:

> The rituals that are important to me are the mass, contemplative prayer and Taize prayer. . . . Advent and Lent and taking the time to think about what the journey means, letting the self-centered parts of me go. I chose my profession, social work, as a ministry. I think about Jesus as a gentle, compassionate spirit and how I want to live as he did.

Soyun Kim, a twenty-eight-year-old Korean American who lives in Chicago and has worked for the Passionist Lay Missioners, a lay volunteer program, makes connections between the journey from Korea to the United States and her own personal journey.

> I was fairly young, maybe 13, when I realized that God was involved in my life in a concrete way. The turning point came when my parents were deciding to bring us to the States. I remember having a conversation with my mom, and she was

asking, "Where is God calling us, what does God want us to do?" I remember thinking, "God wants us to go to America." In the patriarchal culture of Korea, I was aware that my options were limited. I felt I wouldn't be able to fulfill my potential if I stayed in Korea. And I felt that that's not what God wanted. . . . I am culturally Catholic and remember my family going to church, praying morning, lunch, and evening prayers with me. . . . The Eucharist is very important to me and liturgy in general, with the liturgical year following the seasons, winter solstice and spring equinox. The cross is a reminder that Jesus is not this removed person, his opposition to injustice, his commitment to social justice, this is a symbol of communion to me.

Generally, they find religious institutions suspect and question Church teaching and institutional hierarchy, as Juhi Ryo, a Ph.D. student at the University of Chicago and an adult convert to Catholicism, resonates with this perspective:

At age 13 I immigrated to the U.S. I had a difficult time "fitting in" either in the Korean speaking churches or English speaking churches. . . . When I was 14 or 15, I rebelled and quit going to church on Sundays. I thought I should arrive at some sort of revelation about God on my own, just one-on-one with God, at my most honest moments. . . . Even though I didn't attend a church, I always thought myself a Christian.

As a generation exposed to many different nationalities, cultures, and lifestyles, this group values tolerance and pluralism. They are also open to many different religious traditions. Finally, community, another deeply held value by Generation X Catholics, is a group of people with a common spiritual purpose and commitment. A Korean American woman comments on her spiritual practice individually and with a community:

I also practice yoga and sit in silence for meditation. What is meaningful to me in my practice with others is a circle of people sharing symbolism of giving birth to light and the divine.

Asian American Catholic women have been instrumental in shaping and preserving Catholic teachings, practices, and institutions within their communities. From the beginning of Asian immigrant history in the United States at the middle of the nineteenth century to the beginning of the twenty-first, women have been primary role models of faith at home with their families, in internment camps and refugee camps, in their par-

ishes, in the institutional Church, and in their work in the communities where they have settled.

SOURCES: An important treatment of Asian American history from women's perspective can be found in the anthology *Making Waves: An Anthology of Writings By and About Asian American Women* (1989), edited by Asian Women United of California. A highly readable collection of essays, this book is written for a general audience with great attention to presenting the voices of the women. Quotes by and about Japanese women on Hawaiian plantations as well as the Korean picture brides come from essays in this book. References to the early Chinese and Japanese mission churches, Catholic outreach to the first Filipino communities on the West Coast, and the work of Japanese religious in World War II internment camps come from a recent book explicitly concerned with Asian immigrants and the U.S. Catholic Church titled, *Keeping Faith: European and Asian Catholic Immigrants* (2000), edited by Jeffrey M. Burns, Ellen Skerrett, and Joseph M. White. The book is a valuable collection of primary historical documents, ranging from diocesan, parish, and clerical commentaries on ethnic groups to firsthand accounts by members of the groups themselves. An extensive collection, it covers European groups from the beginning of the country's history to the influx of Irish, Italian, and German immigrants in the nineteenth century, to the Asian immigrants of the twentieth. Quotes by Asian American Catholic women without reference to published material are taken from personal interviews conducted for this essay from 2000 to 2002. Ms. Cecile Motus, Coordinator for Ethnic Ministries, Office for the Pastoral Care of Migrants and Refugees at the United States Conference for Catholic Bishops in Washington, D.C., contributed her research about Vietnamese American Catholic Women to this article.

AMERICAN CATHOLIC WOMEN, 1900–1965
Debra Campbell

THE YEARS BETWEEN 1900 and 1965 ushered in unprecedented turbulence and change for American women, including Catholic women. What made Catholic women's experience profoundly different from that of their female counterparts in other American religious groups was the unique centralized character of the Catholic Church, including its (all-male) hierarchy of bishops and priests who looked to the Vatican in Rome for leadership and guidance. The clerical leadership and hierarchical structure of the Church determined how Catholic women could respond to social, economic, and political change in America. Women who wished to remain Catholics in good standing with access to the sacraments had to pay attention to the Church's directives conveyed through parish priests, local bishops, and official statements issued by the Vatican. As they responded to technological, political, and social changes, twentieth-century American Catholic women became embroiled in complex conversations that had been under way within the American Catholic community for over a century—debates about how assimilated Catholics could become without endangering their faith and the sanctity of the family, and veering toward Protestantism or secularism. Clergy and bishops enjoined all Catholic educators, from priests and professors to mothers and members of women's religious congregations, to emphasize what made Catholics different from others: the Church's claim to be the most direct and certain path to salvation. Meanwhile, for the most part, Catholic leaders downplayed difference and diversity within the Catholic community in order to underscore the universal character of the Church and the obligations of individuals and local churches to conform to the teachings and practices endorsed by the Vatican.

When the twentieth century began, the massive waves of European immigration that had sharply increased the American Catholic population and transformed its ethnic composition were reaching a climax. Between 1901 and 1910, 2 million immigrants entered the United States, double the number in the preceding two decades. In 1910, the American Catholic population swelled to over 16 million, an increase of 12 million since 1870. Catholic numbers rose to almost 18 million in 1920 and over 20 million in 1930. The Johnson-Reed Act (1924) curtailed the rapid growth of southern and eastern European Catholic ethnic groups, with a quota system that favored northern Europeans. The Great Depression that followed shortly thereafter kept immigration numbers relatively low. Two prominent exceptions to this pattern were the steady influx of Mexican Catholics in the West and Southwest throughout the twentieth century and the accelerating rate of Puerto Rican immigration, which reached massive proportions after World War II.

At the dawn of the twentieth century, Catholic women were a far more diverse population than is generally acknowledged. During the first two decades of the century, a period often described as the closing years of the "immigrant church," most Catholic women of recent immigrant origins worked for wages, as they had during

Mother Mary Alphonsa, born Rose Hawthorne, daughter of Nathaniel Hawthorne, converted to Catholicism in 1891 in the midst of an unhappy marriage. She later founded the order of the Servants of Relief for Incurable Cancer, dedicated to providing personal care and kindness to the terminally ill, poor, and indigent. *Courtesy of Holy Cross College Archives.*

the previous century. Polish immigrant women, like their nineteenth-century Irish counterparts, initially chose domestic service. French Canadian and Italian immigrant women figured prominently in the textile industry and frequently remained in the workplace after they married and had children. These women resisted pressure from bishops and clergy who, bolstered by Pope Leo XIII's social encyclical *Rerum Novarum* (1891), insisted that factory work posed a dual threat to women's virtue and family life and thereby endangered the foundations of a Christian society.

In fact, Catholic women represented an important bloc within organized labor and assumed positions of leadership in labor unions. The legendary Mary Harris "Mother" Jones (1830–1930) resolved any tensions she perceived to be posed by her Catholic background and her primary commitment to justice for workers by distancing herself from the Church during her long career as a labor organizer. Nonetheless, Jones conformed to her own definition of a Catholic and left explicit plans for a Catholic requiem mass in Washington, D.C., and a public interment in the Union Miner's Cemetery in southern Illinois. Subsequent generations of female Catholic labor leaders acknowledged no incompatibility between their Catholic faith and their work as organizers. Agnes Nestor (1880–1948), a glove maker with an eighth-grade education, helped organize and administer the International Glove Workers Union, served as president of the Chicago Women's Trade Union League from 1913 to 1948, and remained a member of its national executive board from 1907 to 1948. Nestor openly practiced her Catholic religion, accepted an invitation to chair the National Council of Catholic Women's committee on women in industry, and received an honorary Doctor of Laws degree from Loyola University in 1929. Mary Kenney O'Sullivan (1864–1943), who, in 1891, became the first female organizer in the American Federation of Labor, represented a model for devout Catholic women who wished to combine motherhood with an eventful public career as a labor organizer. Elizabeth Maloney, an Illinois Catholic who founded the waitresses union in 1903 and lobbied for eight-hour and minimum-wage legislation, kept a picture of the Sistine Madonna in union headquarters to remind union members about self-respect.

At the other end of the socioeconomic spectrum at the turn of the century was the growing segment of the female Catholic population born into middle-class comfort and prosperity, for whom paid employment outside of the home was deemed inappropriate, even "unnatural." For these women, mothers' and wives' most important duties revolved around the home: making it a clean, orderly, inviting place for the husband's return at the end of the day and a domestic shrine in which they could teach their children the fundamentals of the faith.

Virtually all middle-class Catholic homes at the turn of the century contained sacramentals, that is, rosaries, statues of the Virgin and the saints, and crucifixes. It was the mother's responsibility to procure and arrange these visible accoutrements of the faith and to use them in teaching the children what Catholics believe.

Catholic women's responsibility to make their homes holy and Catholic crossed class and ethnic lines. Working women of Italian, Polish, and Mexican descent maintained household shrines to patron saints from the homeland and conducted domestic rituals imported from the old country to commemorate seasonal and liturgical cycles, heal illness, and provide protection from malevolent powers, such as the evil eye. These domestic rituals, which remained in the hands of immigrant mothers and their daughters, are powerfully evoked in fictional works such as Francine Prose's novel *Household Saints* (1981) and in Robert Orsi's ethnographic study *The Madonna of 115th Street* (1985). Both within specific immigrant Catholic communities and within American Catholic society in general, women's powerful presence as spiritual leaders and teachers in the home remained a point of contention. In the wake of World War I, American Catholic bishops and clergy launched a drive from the pulpit and in popular Catholic magazines to reinstate fathers as the heads of Catholic households. This was the beginning of a recurring effort that continued intermittently and without success for half a century, until the massive changes ushered in by Vatican Council II (1962–1965) completely changed the context in which men's and women's roles in the Church were to be considered.

The opening decades of the twentieth century were a time of institution building and centralization on the parish and diocesan level. Bishops and clergy who encouraged the proliferation of new organizations and initiatives were responding to the needs of the most recent immigrants and the growing American Catholic population, but they were also reflecting a new emphasis upon centralization of power that had emanated from the Vatican during the late nineteenth century. Organizations for the laity represented a Catholic response to secularism and socialism, deemed threats to the natural complementarity of the sexes and the sanctity of the nuclear family. Bishops and clergy hoped to provide a whole range of options for Catholics who wished to participate in educational, social, and charitable organizations, so that they would not be tempted to join non-Catholic or nonsectarian ventures.

There was a vast selection of parish societies and clubs for women to choose from: sodalities (devotional societies organized by sex and age group); service groups such as the Altar Society and the Queen's Daughters (a Catholic version of a widespread Protestant society called the King's Daughters); women's auxiliaries to men's societies such as the Catholic Foresters and the St. Vincent de Paul Society; reading circles; and women's industrial clubs. By the late nineteenth century, an increasing number of women within the Catholic community no longer needed to work for wages, so they gradually expanded their arena of responsibility from the domestic to the public realm. When they attempted to join the Catholic Total Abstinence Union or the charitable ventures of the St. Vincent de Paul Society, they were directed instead to the female auxiliaries affiliated with the men's organizations, which offered prayers and financial support, without the benefits or responsibilities of full membership. At the 1901 national convention of the Catholic Total Abstinence Union, retired labor organizer Leonora Barry Lake (1849–1930) confronted the assembled clerics and laymen on the issue of women's exclusion from active temperance work:

> Who have built the churches? If you answer truly you must say "the women." Who makes the man go to Mass of a Sunday morning? Who sends the children to Sunday School? The women. Good priests and laymen—bring the women into our movement. (Gibbs, 152–153)

Many Catholic women chose to work in non-Catholic women's movements, such as the Woman's Christian Temperance Union, instead of Catholic organizations, whose autonomy was constrained by the virtual veto power of bishops within organizations calling themselves Catholic, and the requirement that a priest-chaplain be assigned to each organization. Nevertheless, there were pioneering ventures in which Catholic women broke new ground in serving the Church and society, often with the help of enterprising priests who believed in expanding women's role. In 1910 Thomas Augustine Judge, a Vincentian mission priest, provided opportunities for six devout laywomen to serve as parish visitors to the poor and unchurched in St. John the Baptist Parish, Brooklyn, where Italian immigrants' anticlericalism made the women far more effective outreach ministers than priests would have been. After one year, the small group reported over 1,000 home visits, many baptisms, and even deathbed conversions. Judge was soon transferred, but he left the group, named the Cenacle after the upper room in Jerusalem where the apostles had prayed, in the able hands of one of the original members, Amy Marie Croke, a teacher at a New York secretarial school. By 1912 the movement spread to Baltimore, site of its first residential facility where members could serve the poor and unchurched and provide temporary housing for young women in need.

Meanwhile, in his mission work in the South, Judge saw new opportunities for Cenacle workers. In the tiny mill town of Tallassee, Alabama, he encountered Mrs.

John O'Brien serving as pastor to twenty-five local Catholics: leading communal recitations of the rosary, teaching catechism, organizing services featuring prayer, hymns, and the stations of the cross between monthly visits of the itinerant priest. In 1916, a small core group of Cenacle women joined Judge in eastern Alabama. Despite much local resistance, the Cenacle served a tiny, beleaguered, racially mixed Catholic community, nursed many victims of the Spanish influenza epidemic of 1917–1918, and opened St. Peter Claver School for black children.

The same features that made the Cenacle movement unwelcome in some dioceses also made settlement houses suspect in the eyes of some priests and bishops. Autonomous, activist women planning their own social reform movements did not fit into the larger strategy of the bishops and clergy who envisioned a Catholic united front, centralized and controlled from above. Still, the settlement movement made famous by Jane Addams of Hull House in Chicago produced some offshoots within the Catholic community. Santa Maria Institute (1897), established by the legendary Cincinnati Sister of Charity Blandina Segale at the request of her bishop, was among the first Catholic settlements. From modest origins in a basement, it developed into the Santa Maria Educational and Industrial Home and sponsored a kindergarten, nursery, residence hall, and eventually, an Italian-language magazine. In the next two decades, Catholic settlements sprang up across the country to provide educational, vocational, and social programs in immigrant neighborhoods, including: Brownson House, established by Mary Workman for Mexican and Italian immigrants in Los Angeles, and Weinman Settlement, launched by Josephine Brownson for Syrian immigrants in Detroit. In 1906, Marion Gurney, a convert active in St. Rose's settlement for Italian immigrants sponsored by a Dominican parish in New York, established a religious order, the Sisters of Our Lady of Christian Doctrine, devoted to settlement work.

Catholic settlements were often short-lived, underfunded parish outreach programs run by priests and sisters as well as laywomen. They were never as numerous, and rarely as rich in cultural and educational programs, as nonsectarian women's residential settlements such as Hull House. One major reason why Catholic settlements were not as popular or numerous as non-Catholic settlements was that many Catholic women who might otherwise have chosen settlement work opted instead to enter the convent. The first two decades of the twentieth century witnessed phenomenal growth in Catholic women's religious communities, both transplanted European congregations and new orders founded in the United States. It was an age of pioneering sisters. Mother Frances Cabrini (1850–1917) arrived in America in 1889 with six Missionary Sisters of the Sacred Heart and an open-ended mandate from the Vatican Congregation for the Propagation of the Faith to help Italian immigrants. While they were not the first Italian women to act as missionaries, Cabrini's congregation was the first to bear the title. When a Roman cleric maintained that missionaries had always been men, Cabrini, equally insistent, replied: "If the mission of announcing the Lord's resurrection to his apostles had been entrusted to Mary Magdalene, it would seem a very good thing to confide to other women an evangelizing mission" (Sullivan, 266). Cabrini's missionaries dealt with all facets of immigrant life. They encouraged Italians to baptize their children, return to the sacraments, and have marriages regularized by the Church, but they also helped with legal aid, repatriation, child care, jobs, and groceries. They worked in urban and rural settings, taught in schools, nursed the sick, provided recreation programs, and served as prison chaplains. They paid special attention to those whose needs had been overlooked by Church and state alike, such as children released from orphanages at fourteen and the children of miners and transient workers.

Three innovative sisters at work early in the twentieth century were Mother Mary Katharine Drexel (1858–1955), a Philadelphia heiress who founded the Sisters of the Blessed Sacrament for Indians and Colored People (1891); Mother Mary Alphonsa (1851–1926), who established the Dominican Congregation of St. Rose of Lima, also known as the Servants of Relief for Incurable Cancer; and Mother Mary Josephine Rogers (1882–1955), who started the Foreign Mission Sisters of St. Dominic. Drexel served as superior of her new order from 1907 to 1937 and oversaw the establishment and administration of schools and missions for blacks and Indians all across the country. In 1915 she founded a teaching college in New Orleans that became Xavier University (1925), the first Catholic college for African Americans in the United States. When other Catholic philanthropists ignored the educational and spiritual needs of the Indians and the government stopped subsidizing Indian mission schools in 1900, Drexel remained the primary financial supporter of Indian missions and schools. Mother Mary Alphonsa, born Rose Hawthorne, daughter of Nathaniel Hawthorne, converted to Catholicism in 1891 in the midst of an unhappy marriage to George Lathrop, from whom she was separated in 1895. In 1900, two years after her husband's death, Rose Hawthorne founded the order that she called the Servants of Relief for Incurable Cancer, dedicated to providing personal care and kindness to the poor and indigent who were terminally ill. Mary Josephine Rogers attended public school and graduated from Smith College in 1905. When she returned to her alma mater in 1906 as an assistant in zoology, she also agreed to teach a mission study class for Catholic stu-

dents. Preparation for the class put her in contact with James Anthony Walsh, director of the Society for the Propagation of the Faith in Boston. In 1912, when Walsh established Maryknoll Seminary for missionary priests near Ossining, New York, Rogers moved to Maryknoll, where she soon emerged as leader of a group of women that would become the nucleus of the Foreign Mission Sisters of St. Dominic (also called the Maryknoll Sisters), officially recognized by the Vatican in 1920.

Cabrini, Drexel, Lathrop, and Rogers were pioneers, but they were not alone. There were over 40,000 sisters in America at the dawn of the twentieth century. Sisters had responded with energy and imagination to the monumental challenge posed by the American Catholic bishops who had decreed at the Third Plenary Council in Baltimore (1884) that each parish build a school near its church. Because bishops and pastors depended almost exclusively on sisters to staff the new schools on very tight budgets, the decree put enormous pressure on sisters, who were also engaged in nursing, social work, and providing homes and care for orphans, wayward girls, and unwed mothers. The pressure was exacerbated by the accelerating health-care needs of the Catholic immigrant community. The number of Catholic hospitals in America rose from approximately 75 in 1872 to approximately 400 in 1910, and nursing sisters were the backbone of these hospitals.

Meanwhile, the many congregations with European roots grappled with questions posed by Americanization. In 1908, in response to the pressures of the American environment, the Sisters of St. Joseph of Carondelet, whose roots were French, abolished the class-based distinction between choir sisters (who governed the order, taught in schools, and cared for the poor) and lay sisters (who did domestic chores and manual labor.) Other congregations with European origins and traditions were moving in the same direction. This kind of adaptation was crucial in the opening years of the twentieth century when American-born sisters and candidates for admission to religious orders soon outnumbered those born in Europe and when European congregations could be suspect in the eyes of non-Catholic Americans. During World War I, for example, the School Sisters of Notre Dame, which still had European ties, struggled to achieve a delicate balance between loyalty to their European heritage and American patriotism. They reached a spirit of compromise in their two-pronged fund drives for American Liberty Bonds and relief efforts for German, Hungarian, and Austrian war victims.

Sisters were among the first to promote Catholic women's higher education. During the nineteenth century, female academies founded and run by sisters had served a variety of purposes. They had provided the kind of advanced education deemed appropriate for Catholic women of the middle and upper classes, and because they were private schools for tuition-paying students, they also helped the sisters to raise money to pay their living and educational expenses. By the beginning of the twentieth century, as the training of teachers became increasingly specialized and certification standards began to rise, there was a growing need for Catholic women's colleges to make continuing education possible for the sisters who staffed the parochial schools. Mother Austin Carroll of the Sisters of Mercy formulated a plan for an American Catholic women's college in New Orleans in 1887, but the project met with strong clerical opposition and faltered.

In 1899, the College of Notre Dame of Maryland, an academy that extended its curricular offerings to the college level, celebrated the graduation of its first six seniors, the first graduates of a Catholic women's college. In 1900 Trinity College in Washington, D.C., a Catholic women's college modeled on Vassar, Radcliffe, and Bryn Mawr, accepted its first students. It was followed five years later by the College of St. Catherine in St. Paul, Minnesota. Like their counterparts at the most exclusive non-Catholic American women's colleges, sisters who would become professors at Trinity and the College of St. Catherine completed graduate programs at Oxford, London, the University of Chicago, and other premier research universities. By 1915 there were nineteen Catholic women's colleges in the United States; by 1925 there were thirty-seven more.

Not every Catholic woman who attended college selected a Catholic institution. In 1906 there were sufficient Catholic students at Radcliffe for Emma Forbes Cary (1833–1918), a convert from a blueblood Boston family, and the sister of Elizabeth Cabot Cary Agassiz, founder and early president of Radcliffe, to establish the Radcliffe Catholic Club. Sometimes bishops and clergy intervened and aggressively promoted Catholic women's colleges. Boston mayor John F. Fitzgerald was about to send his daughter Rose (who upon her marriage would become Rose Fitzgerald Kennedy) to her first choice, Wellesley College, until Archbishop William O'Connell insisted that he send her to a Catholic women's college instead. O'Connell's preference for Catholic education for women was part of a larger agenda, the hierarchy's response to the "new woman," which expressed itself most clearly in the controversy over woman suffrage.

During the two decades leading to the ratification of the Nineteenth Amendment in 1920, a vocal segment of the Catholic Church, including bishops, priests, laymen, and laywomen, speaking in the press and from the pulpit and public platform, warned their coreligionists that woman suffrage was only the tip of the iceberg. Woman suffrage, contraception, atheism, anarchism, and socialism—these were simply different names for the same immanent threat to motherhood and the traditional

family. Martha Moore Avery, a former Socialist soapbox speaker who had converted to Catholicism in 1903 because she believed that only the Church could reverse the decline of the family and safeguard the sanctity of motherhood, entered the public opposition to woman suffrage with the blessings of the archbishop of Boston. Avery tirelessly denounced woman suffrage before the Massachusetts legislature in 1908, 1910, 1914, and 1915 and engaged in public debate with National American Woman Suffrage Association president Anna Howard Shaw. Katherine E. Conway (1853–1927), author of fiction, nonfiction, self-help books, and editorials for the Boston Catholic newspaper *The Pilot,* which she served as editor from 1905 to 1908, opposed the ballot in her writings and as a member of the Massachusetts Association Opposed to the Further Extension of Suffrage to Women. Neither Avery nor Conway saw any contradiction in mounting the public platform to decry women's entry into public life.

By the beginning of the twentieth century, many Catholic women supported woman suffrage, including a growing constituency of middle-class teachers, social workers, officeworkers, and volunteers in charitable organizations who sought the vote to protect the same values that Conway and Avery saw threatened by woman suffrage. Sara McPike (d. 1943), an executive secretary at General Electric and cofounder of St. Catherine's Welfare Association of New York, supported extending the vote to women, along with legislation providing equal pay for equal work, as part of a larger agenda to improve the plight of women and children. St. Catherine's members collaborated with Carrie Chapman Catt and the National American Woman Suffrage Association, especially its efforts to win Catholic clergy and laywomen to the pro-suffrage camp. In 1917, McPike led 500 Catholic women in a suffrage parade. Margaret Foley (1875–1957), a former Hat Trimmers Union officer associated with the Boston Women's Trade Union League, used the skills that she had developed as a labor organizer to promote the work of the Massachusetts Woman Suffrage Association and later, in 1918, as chair of the Organizing and Industrial Committee of the Margaret Brent Suffrage Guild, composed of Catholic suffragists.

Lucy Burns (1879–1966) was a rare figure among suffrage activists: a self-identified Catholic suffragist. Burns, a member of the Vassar class of 1902, had seemed destined for a distinguished academic career until she encountered the Pankhursts and other militant English suffragists while doing graduate work at Oxford in 1909. Back in the United States, Burns and fellow suffrage activist Alice Paul established the Congressional Union for Woman Suffrage, which aimed to win the vote by federal constitutional amendment instead of the state-by-state campaigns envisioned by the National American Woman Suffrage Association. In the Congressional

Union and its successor, the National Women's Party, Burns worked strenuously to implement Paul's strategies. She led demonstrations against President Wilson ("Kaiser Wilson") during World War I. Burns, who spent more time in jail than any other American suffragist, went on a hunger strike and was force-fed in prison in 1917. In 1919, she rode in the "Prison Train" with other formerly jailed National Women's Party members to publicize the suffrage cause. When the Nineteenth Amendment finally passed in 1920, Burns retired from public life.

An important factor that had led to the ratification of the suffrage amendment was women's crucial, highly visible performance during World War I. Women took new jobs in industry left vacant by soldiers. They stepped in to provide public services, such as driving street cars and cleaning the streets. They raised crops in the Woman's Land Army. They nursed the sick at home and abroad. The war also provided the occasion for yet another echelon of American Catholic organizations on the national level, beginning with the National Catholic War Council (NCWC), launched in 1917 to provide an official Catholic voice and organizing mechanism in America during the war. Among the Council's seven subcommittees was a committee on women's activities run by a male cleric, assisted by his male secretary. The women's committee coordinated local Catholic women's war activities and provided housing, recreation, and employment facilities for the expanded female workforce. It also launched the National School of Social Service on the Catholic University of America campus, which prepared women for social work both in America and overseas. To outsiders, the graduates, who promised to abstain from alcohol, eschew makeup, and wear distinctive uniforms, may have resembled a quasi-military religious order, and this assessment would not have been far from the truth. Before departing for duty overseas, School of Social Service graduates attended mass as a group and pledged themselves to the service of Jesus Christ and the National Catholic War Council. Some 127 volunteers staffed twenty-four centers in Belgium, Italy, Poland, and France and cared for the needs of refugees, orphans, nurses, and Red Cross personnel.

After the war, the NCWC retained its acronym but renamed itself the National Catholic Welfare Conference and in 1920 launched among its subsidiary organizations the National Council of Catholic Women. The National Council of Catholic Women, administered by a board of clergymen and assisted for decades by its long-time secretary Agnes Regan (1869–1943), attempted to provide on the national level the same kind of top-down organization and oversight of women's social reform activities that bishops and archbishops had begun to achieve on the diocesan level. In the educational campaigns of the National Council of Catholic Women and

diocesan Leagues of Catholic Women, the hierarchy sought to mobilize the energies of articulate laywomen to create the impression of a Catholic consensus on controversial issues such as contraception, the Equal Rights Amendment, and the child labor bill of 1924. Sometimes the National Council of Catholic Women's agenda was almost indistinguishable from that of other conservative Christian churches. In 1927, for example, it passed a resolution "against those violations of womanly dignity known as beauty contests, against the moving pictures, the magazines, the books, that lower the dignity of the Christian girl and the Christian mother" (Brown and McKeown, 141).

The postwar years witnessed great strides made by Catholic women working in the secular arena, such as public school teachers, social workers employed by state agencies, and gradually, doctors, lawyers, and professional writers and journalists. At the same time, laywomen faced a backlash against the prospect of women's autonomy and advancement within the Church or in Catholic organizations, including parochial schools and social welfare organizations. The *Bishops' Program of Social Reconstruction,* published in 1919, had set the tone for the years ahead. It had urged that as many female workers as possible hastily vacate their wartime occupations, which threatened their health and morals, but also recommended that the few women who might remain in the same work as men should receive equal pay. The bishops' efforts to centralize and oversee Catholic women's public vocations and activism did not always succeed. Both sisters and laywomen could, on occasion, resist clerical efforts to co-opt or control Catholic women's property and successful ventures in social reform. When Boston's Cardinal William O'Connell sought to place all Catholic institutions under diocesan management and ownership, his bid to take over Carney Hospital failed because the provincial council of the Daughters of Charity composed the hospital board. When, in a similar effort to consolidate diocesan property and power, San Francisco's Archbishop Hanna tried to absorb the St. Margaret's Club settlement house, members refused to cooperate and were banned from the property. St. Margaret's Club appealed directly to the Vatican, which sided in its favor. In 1927, Hanna gave the club an unconditional deed to the property.

Sisters were pushed in two directions after the war. By 1920, American sisters had created or maintained approximately 500 hospitals, over fifty women's colleges, and over 6,000 parochial schools, serving 1.7 million schoolchildren in every region of the country. As early as 1915, the year the Catholic Hospital Association held its first annual convention, sisters from at least thirty congregations had sponsored about 220 nursing schools based at Catholic hospitals. Bishops, parish priests, and Catholic hospital administrators depended on the energy and expertise of sisters to keep the ever-expanding system of schools and hospitals running. Sisters' lives were complicated, however, by the revised Code of Canon Law issued by the Vatican in 1917. The new Code emphasized the importance of the cloister, that is, the preservation of strict, impermeable boundaries between the sisters and the secular world, which included their students, patients, and families.

Canon law stipulated that a sister who ventured out of her community for classes, or even medical appointments, be accompanied by a member of her community, a requirement that made earning advanced degrees logistically difficult. Canon law also restricted sisters' contact with their students and students' parents and forbade access to radio broadcasts and newspapers that might have furthered their education and helped them to understand the world their students inhabited. In the 1920s and 1930s, sisters were under pressure from both Church and state to advance their education and earn college degrees. Pope Pius XI's 1929 encyclical *On the Education of Christian Youth* called on sisters to prepare themselves even more rigorously to educate Catholic youth. Rising state certification standards and the goal of providing secondary education for all Americans made the question of continuing education for sisters all the more urgent.

Starting in the mid-1920s, the American Catholic community crossed a demographic threshold that took them beyond the age of the immigrant church and into an era of newfound economic stability and middle-class status for a visibly growing segment of the Catholic population. Like their Protestant counterparts, Catholics began to move out of the cities and into the suburbs, an exodus that would only accelerate after World War II. This meant that sisters, who had joined the convent with a vocation to educate and Americanize a church of working-class immigrants and their children, gradually found themselves teaching in a distinctly different environment. Increasingly, with each decade that passed, sisters were being asked to make more severe sacrifices, and even engage in part-time fund-raising, to subsidize parochial schools for a prosperous, middle-class constituency. There were moments during the depression when this pattern was suspended, but the upward mobility of the Catholic community continued apace from the 1920s onward.

Some sisters found enclaves where they could work with the poor in situations that permitted a greater degree of autonomy and more opportunities to adapt their methods and skills to meet the needs of the people they served. Starting in 1920, the Maryknoll Sisters worked among the Japanese in California and Seattle and within the next few years, laid the foundations for an extensive network of foreign missions in Asia, Africa, and Latin America. They lived among indigenous peoples to learn how they could help them and introduced the Catholic faith to those who expressed an interest, but always in ways that fit into the context of the local culture. They could not have pursued this modern and fruitful approach in America, where they would have been forced to work within the constraints of the revised canon law. Because they worked on the fringes of the Church, far from what were perceived to be centers of money and power, the Maryknoll Sisters were able to preserve and implement the vision of their founder, Mother Mary Joseph Rogers.

The career of another missionary, Mother Anna Dengel (1892–1980), shows how insights gained in the foreign mission field could occasionally inform Vatican policy and thereby improve the lives of female Catholic missionaries and countless women all over the world. Dengel, an Austrian-born laywoman, started out as a Catholic missionary doctor dedicated to providing medical care for Muslim women in India, whose religious tradition forbade access to male medical doctors, except family members. Dengel soon became aware of the emotional and spiritual burnout that afflicted isolated female missionaries without any larger support community, a situation exacerbated by the Vatican policy against allowing sisters to be medical doctors or midwives. Dengel envisioned teams of laywomen, doctors and nurses, traveling together. On a fund-raising visit to the United States in the 1920s, she encountered a priest who helped her to outline a plan for a religious community of laywomen working in medical missions. Dengel's group took a private oath in 1926, since making public vows in an officially recognized religious order would mean giving up medical or nursing careers. In 1936, aided by her ally Cardinal Dennis Dougherty of Philadelphia, Dengel finally persuaded the Vatican to change canon law to permit sisters to practice medicine and assist at childbirth. The change meant that Dengel's Society of Catholic Medical Missionaries could become a religious order. Within ten years, Dengel's mission sisters numbered over 100, at work throughout the world, including in clinics in the United States.

The Maryknoll Sisters and Dengel's Medical Missionaries represent exceptions to the general pattern of constriction in the lives of American sisters between the 1920s and the mid-1960s. The same period brought some new opportunities for laywomen to expand and diversify their role in the Church and society. The Depression awakened the consciences of Catholic women and men, many of whom sought to provide for the growing number of poor and homeless within the framework of the existing Catholic charitable societies, which had become centralized within the National Conference of Catholic Charities (1910). Meanwhile, Pope Pius XI's social encyclical *Quadragesimo Anno* (1931) gave papal support to the already widespread impulse among the upwardly mobile urban Catholic population to mitigate the suffering of the poor. This impulse was bolstered by a popular theological movement propagated in the American Catholic Church by the writings of the Catholic intellectual revival, made available by Sheed and Ward Publishers, which opened a branch of their London-based firm in New York in 1933. Those who kept up with the new releases by Sheed and Ward, the works of neo-Thomistic philosophers Etienne Gilson and Jacques Maritain, and Catholic authors G. K. Chesterton, Hilaire Belloc, Sigrid Undset, François Mauriac, Caryll Houselander, and many others, became aware of three rising strains within the Church that intensified the commitment to social activism among the laity. Women proved especially responsive to these three themes that dominated popular Catholic theology and spirituality in America from the 1930s through the mid-1960s: Catholic Action, the image of the Church as the Mystical Body of Christ, and a renewed emphasis on the communal nature of the liturgy.

Catholic Action, a concept and popular motto embraced by Pope Pius XI (1922–1939), referred to the participation of the laity in the spiritual work primarily delegated to the clergy, such as teaching, preaching, and caring for the poor and sick. In the fundamentally egalitarian, action-oriented world inhabited by educated (or self-educated) American Catholics, the attraction of Catholic Action stemmed from its participatory, activist character more than the opportunity that it provided to implement the strategies of bishops and pastors. Papal emphasis on Catholic Action made laypeople's direct engagement in efforts to promote justice and Christian values in society acceptable, even desirable, in the eyes of otherwise hesitant pastors and bishops. It empowered certain bishops, priests, and individual laypeople to launch ambitious social experiments that sought to infuse the modern world with Catholic values.

On June 29, 1943, Pope Pius XII issued an encyclical titled *Mystici Corporis* (Of the Mystical Body of Christ). Those who read Sheed and Ward publications were apt to interpret the metaphor of the Church as Christ's body as support for their emphasis on the organic and cooperative nature of the Church rather than the hierarchical, institutional dimension. Like Catholic Action, the theology of the Mystical Body had special appeal in the American setting because it provided a way to articulate a growing hunger on the part of the laity to be integral, not auxiliary, to the work of the Church. Closely related to the revival of the Mystical Body was the liturgical renewal that accompanied it. Because the Church constituted a real body, with interdependent members, the secular world inhabited by the lay members remained as open to sanctification as the cloister, the monastery, and other Catholic institutions. Moreover, the mass, which provided the spiritual energy for the Christian body, represented a celebration of the unity and value of the entire body.

Although priests presided over the mass, laymen and laywomen viewed their participation in the mass as a crucial component in their attempts, under the rubric of Catholic Action, to remake the world in the image of Christ. At Manhattanville College, a women's college run by the Society of the Sacred Heart, Mother Georgia Stephens and Mrs. Justine Ward established the Pius X School of Liturgical Music in 1916, an early expression of the liturgical renewal as it was embraced by Catholic women. As laypeople became more involved in the liturgy and reflected deeply on their role in the Christian body, it was only a matter of time before they raised questions concerning the laity's own priesthood and women's potential to act as priests. By the 1950s, these questions, raised implicitly by Catholic Action, the Mystical Body of Christ, and the liturgical renewal, were being discussed openly by American Catholic women. These conversations sparked anxieties about women overstepping their boundaries and prophylactic efforts on the part of some clergy who promoted family liturgies that reinforced the father's natural role as the head of the family.

Catholic Action assumed a variety of forms. It inspired individual women who founded and managed bookstores that sold Sheed and Ward publications and other (mostly European) works spawned by the Catholic intellectual revival. Sara Benedicta O'Neill at St. Benet's Library and Bookshop in Chicago (1933) and Evangeline Mercier, Mary Stanton, and Martha Doherty at St. Thomas More Lending Library and Bookstore in Cambridge, Massachusetts (1936) were part of a whole network of women and men who promoted local discussions of Catholic theology and its practical social and political implications. In ways similar to the feminist bookstores of the late 1960s and 1970s, these Catholic bookstores were grassroots universities; they gave their patrons both intellectual tools and a support group in which to ask new questions and discuss individual and communal answers to those questions.

The publishers, Maisie Ward (1889–1975) and her husband Frank Sheed, who appeared on the Catholic lecture circuit sponsored by Catholic bookstores and colleges from the 1930s through the 1960s, also sought to encourage Catholics of both sexes to propagate the faith in public settings under the auspices of the Catholic Evidence Guild. Ward had begun street preaching for the Guild in London's Hyde Park in 1919. When she lectured at Catholic women's colleges in the United States in the 1930s, she urged students to form branches of the Guild. At Trinity College in Washington, D.C., and at Rosary College in River Forest, Illinois, her message and example bore fruit, and students engaged in street preaching. The Rosary College Catholic Evidence

Guild stands out because it sponsored several generations of student missionaries to the South from 1935 to the late 1940s, when there were few priests and parishes and much residual prejudice against Catholics. The Rosary College students spent summers in Oklahoma, Louisiana, and North Carolina, where they gathered outdoor crowds by singing "You Are My Sunshine" and "The Bells of St. Mary's," explained fundamental Catholic teachings, and answered impromptu questions from the audience. They even staged a Catholic baptism, using a plastic doll, to dispel false notions of Catholic sacraments. The students collaborated with a priest, but they were solely responsible for planning, publicizing, and delivering their presentations.

Another Catholic Action movement that spread to and through Catholic women's colleges by the early 1930s was the Catholic Association for International Peace, the first official Catholic peace organization in the United States, established in 1927. At the instigation of its secretary, Elizabeth Sweeney, various student societies, such as Catholic Action, Catholic Students Mission Crusade, and International Relations, at a number of Catholic colleges, read, distributed, and discussed pamphlets published by the Association and helped to subsidize their production. Prominent faculty members at Catholic women's colleges, such as Elizabeth Morrissey at the College of Notre Dame in Maryland and Vincent Ferrar, O.P. at Rosary College, played important roles in Catholic Association for International Peace.

Catholic college students (male and female, from Catholic and non-Catholic institutions) comprised a core group in two ambitious Catholic social justice movements founded in the 1930s by Catholic women in New York City: the Catholic Worker movement and Friendship House. The Catholic Worker movement was established in 1933 by Dorothy Day (1897–1980), convert and former radical journalist, and an itinerant, working-class French philosopher and social prophet, Peter Maurin (1877–1949). Day had been part of the community of communists, anarchists, and assorted leftists congregated in Greenwich Village before World War I. She was incarcerated with the suffragist Lucy Burns in 1917, when she set out to protest the fact that Burns and the other jailed suffragists were being denied their rights as political prisoners. After her conversion in 1927, Day become frustrated with what she considered the Church's passive, bourgeois approach to poverty and injustice, which she pronounced less Christian than the communists' activist approach. The Catholic Worker movement represented her attempt to provide a radical activist alternative within the Church.

The Catholic Workers sponsored a penny paper, the *Catholic Worker,* which they hawked on the streets and sent to a growing list of subscribers across the country.

They established Houses of Hospitality, where volunteers lived among the poor, and provided them with food and clothing. The movement spread from New York to Chicago, Buffalo, Boston, Seattle, and beyond. Houses of Hospitality, as well as a few Catholic Worker farms, made it possible for Catholics from different socioeconomic and educational backgrounds to confront poverty and injustice, both by feeding the poor and by participating in the formal and informal discussions of theology, Catholic Action, liturgy, and literature that took place over coffee, soup, and bread. When conversations turned to pacifism, Day accepted no compromises. From the Spanish Civil War through Vietnam and into the age of nuclear deterrence, Day publicly opposed war unequivocally and declared it incompatible with Christianity.

On the question of war, or any other matter of conscience, Day was not afraid to disagree publicly with priests and bishops. In 1963 she wrote to a group of Los Angeles Catholic activists:

> We must follow where the spirit leads. So go ahead, . . . don't look for support or approval. And don't always be looking for blame, either, or see opposition where perhaps there is none. . . . I beg you to save your energies to fight the gigantic injustices of our times, and not the Church in the shape of its Cardinal Archbishop. (Piehl, 92)

Catholic Workers also broke new ground in their witness against racism, both in American society and within Catholic institutions. In 1951, Helen Caldwell Day, an African American convert from the South who had been involved in the Catholic Worker movement while in nursing school in New York in the late 1940s, wrote to the *Catholic Worker* to protest the segregated masses still being celebrated in Mississippi. In her autobiography *Color, Ebony* (1951) Helen Day shows how the Catholic Worker experience gave her a new framework in which to interpret and protest segregation. When a parish priest explained to her that he was being prudent in keeping the mass segregated, in the hopes that white parishioners would support a school for black students, Day displayed the same candor and clarity people had come to expect from her:

> The only thing [the pastor] forgot was that that kind of prudence has no place in the Mystical Body of Christ, in the life of the Church. He forgot that the Church is One, Holy and Universal, and that the Mass is for all, so that no baptized person can lawfully be forbidden to hear and offer it, to satisfy the prejudices of a few, or of a majority. (176)

On Valentine's Day in 1938, the Baroness Catherine de Hueck (1900–1985) established the first Friendship House in Harlem, with financial assistance from Columbia University's Newman Club. De Hueck, a Russian émigré, had launched a Friendship House in Toronto in the early 1930s to provide a Christian alternative to communism for impoverished Canadian immigrants. In Harlem and in the new branches established in Chicago, Washington, D.C., Portland, Oregon, and Shreveport, Louisiana, from the 1940s through the early 1950s, the anticommunist message was replaced by an assault on racism. Friendship House volunteers lived together in black neighborhoods in voluntary poverty, working to promote desegregation and social justice. Catholic students flocked to the Harlem Friendship House from Columbia University, Hunter College, New York University, Manhattanville College, and St. John's University and from as far away as St. Benedict's College in Minnesota. When the baroness married Edward ("Eddie") Doherty, a journalist, in 1943, and turned her attention to the Madonna House center of lay spirituality in Combermere, Ontario, the volunteers took over leadership of the original movement. They published a newspaper, *The Catholic Interracialist,* and sponsored a network of fellow travelers called the Outer Circle. The character of the Outer Circle varied from place to place. In New York, it was an intense, interracial discussion group on racism that met in Maisie Ward's apartment; in South Bend, Indiana, black and white couples visited each others' homes for study and social service projects.

Many Catholic college students who were active in the Harlem Friendship House were already aware of the racism in the Church and the surrounding society. After a lecture in the spring of 1933 by George Hunton, who was soon to establish the Catholic Interracial Council of New York (1934), Manhattanville College students had produced the "Manhattanville Resolutions." These eight resolutions formulated by female college students combined Catholic teachings with democratic principles and represented the first step toward an Interracial Program for Catholic colleges. When, in 1938, Manhattanville prepared to admit its first African American student, a group of socially prominent alumnae protested. Manhattanville's president, Mother Grace Damman, R.S.C.J., responded in a powerful address titled "Principles versus Prejudices," in which she declared that it was time for students, faculty, and alumnae to live integrated lives, fully Catholic in every area and aspect. Other premier Catholic women's colleges followed Manhattanville's example and worked toward integration in the 1940s. As late as 1944, however, administrators at Webster College opted to retain the old segregationalist policies, in large part because they feared the financial implications of integration.

Still another movement that focused the activist energies of female Catholic college students and alumnae and served as midwife to Catholic women's expanding roles from the 1940s through the 1970s was the Grail. Jesuit Jacques van Ginneken founded the movement, originally called the Society of Women of Nazareth, in the Netherlands in 1921. The Grail was rooted in the premise that women had the special spiritual qualities required to lead the modern world away from sin and back to God. It was transplanted to America in 1940 by Lydwine van Kersbergen (1904–1998) and Joan Overboss (1910–1969), two experienced veterans of European Catholic Action with the ambitious goals of nurturing liturgical renewal and the idea of the Church as the Mystical Body of Christ among young American Catholic women. They worked in a variety of venues: at the movement's first American home, Doddridge Farm, owned by the Diocese of Chicago at Grailville; the movement's permanent headquarters, in Loveland, Ohio; and by the early 1950s, at urban outposts and missions throughout the world. By the late 1940s and early 1950s, the Grail had trained generations of American Catholic women to be leaders and spokeswomen for change.

The Grail originally made its reputation in America as a rural center, part of the "back to the land" movement that captured the imaginations of a small but intense segment of the American Catholic community in the decades immediately following World War II. The special programs sponsored by full-time Grail members for an endless stream of visitors sought to achieve a monastic balance between work and prayer. The work could be gardening, baking bread, fixing the tractor, or staging the group reading of *Brideshead Revisited* that so impressed its author, Evelyn Waugh, in 1949. The prayer might be plain chant, liturgical dance, or a meditation on baking bread, gardening, or dance. Generations of Catholic women learned from the Grail that work is prayer, that laywomen could be primarily responsible for the work and prayer of their own community, and that their community was coterminous with the world.

Starting in Brooklyn in 1948, the Grail launched a series of city centers specializing in urban outreach. By 1961 there were centers in Manhattan, Cincinnati, Philadelphia, Queens, Detroit, Toronto, Lafayette (Louisiana), and San Jose. City centers developed programs intended to meet local needs and make the best use of the talents of the Grail volunteers in residence. They launched experiments in cooperative living, efforts at ecumenical and interracial dialogue, educational programs, theater and dance companies, and family service projects. In 1946, Mary Louise Tully left for China to become the American Grail's first missionary overseas. Four years later, the Grail established its foreign mission training program. Teams went to Uganda and Basuto-land in 1953. By 1957, the Grail offered a fifteen-month training program for missionaries who already had competence in nursing, teaching, social work, or medical technology.

By 1963, over 100 Grail missionaries were at work in Africa, Asia, and Latin America. There was a growing hunger for this kind of full-time service among Catholic baby boomers, and the Grail, along with Catholic women's colleges, provided necessary guidance for potential missionaries. An important experiment in mission placement for laywomen originated at Regis College in Weston, Massachusetts, in 1950. Between 1950 and 1975 the Regis Lay Apostolate sent 425 lay missionaries to work in Catholic schools in ten South and Central American countries and the Caribbean, as well as Mexico, Taiwan, and nine southern and western states. The Regis College Lay Apostolate emerged almost by chance, out of a circle of sisters from different religious congregations who corresponded with Sister John Sullivan, an English professor at Regis. It involved the collaboration of Sister John, her students, and some local laywomen who were drawn into her orbit. The story of the Regis missionaries shows how a small movement that started at a Catholic women's college could expand organically, mostly by word of mouth, to include Catholic women from all across America.

Sisters' lives were beginning to change in the 1950s, catalyzed by a now-famous speech, "The Education of Our Young Religious Teachers," delivered by Sister Madeleva Wolff (1887–1964), president of St. Mary's College in South Bend, Indiana, at the National Catholic Educational Association's annual meeting in 1949. Sister Madeleva had already broken precedent in 1943 when she had established the Graduate School of Sacred Theology at St. Mary's to make it possible for women, who were not accepted in existing graduate programs in theology at Catholic universities, to do doctoral work in theology. This time she spoke candidly about the crisis in sisters' education that had been brewing for decades so that it now required decisive action. During the late 1940s, the beginning of the baby boom, the parochial school system was expanding far too quickly for sisters to meet the need for adequately trained teachers, and the trend would continue through the 1950s. Sister Madeleva sketched out an ambitious plan to begin to remedy the situation, which gave rise to the Sisters' Educational and Professional Standards Commission (1952), a grassroots organization armed with a $50,000 Ford Foundation Grant, to produce strategies to improve sisters' educational and spiritual formation. Two years later the Commission was renamed the Sister Formation Conference.

Sisters' reform efforts coincided with the agenda of Pope Pius XII, who urged an international assembly of teaching sisters gathered in Rome in 1951 to be open to changes that would make them more effective in their work. The pontiff insisted that modernized, simplified habits, as well as other innovations, even motorcycles, might be compatible with a sister's vocation. The Sister Formation Conference and the Conference of Major Superiors of Women, established in 1956, endorsed the idea of change and encouraged individual congregations to inaugurate wide-ranging discussions and long-range planning. A cadre of leaders emerged, and women's religious congregations sent potential leaders to study for doctorates so that they could teach in their own colleges and train other sisters. Graduate education and increasing dialogue among sisters laid the foundations for the sisters' networks and Catholic women's networks that would be so important by the late 1960s and 1970s.

Changes in sisters' lives accelerated rapidly during the 1960s. When, early in the decade, the Vatican asked sisters to volunteer for work in Latin America, 20,000 sisters responded. Around the same time, the Conference of Major Superiors of Women petitioned Rome requesting representation on Vatican commissions that made decisions concerning sisters lives but was rebuffed. Vatican roadblocks did not reverse the drive for autonomy within women's religious orders. When the American edition of Léon-Joseph Cardinal Suenens's *Nun in the Modern World* appeared in 1963, it prompted passionate discussions in convents across America. In the summer of 1965, American newspapers published photographs of sisters in new, modified habits. The older habits, based on European prototypes centuries old, had symbolized, and even enforced, the cloister. The new habits signified the dawn of a new age in which a growing number of sisters believed that everything, including the very notion of the cloister, was on the agenda for discussion.

The new age was invigorating for sisters who, thanks to the Sister Formation Conference and the Conference of Major Superiors of Women, as well as the dialogue that had begun in 1949, were ready to enter the world as trained professionals. In 1965 nearly 50 sisters marched in Selma, Alabama, with civil rights protesters. Nursing sisters in Detroit stood by, on duty, during voter registration drives. The *Catholic Directory* reported that there were 177,354 American sisters in 1963. Some 13,618 sisters staffed approximately 803 hospitals in 1965. The tide was turning, however. The mid-1960s marked the beginning of the exodus of sisters from the convents, a trend that would only become more dramatic in the following decade. Entrance rates started to fall in 1963, as the rate of departure from religious life rose. In 1965, 1,562 sisters left the convent, a number that grew to 4,337 two years later.

The years between the late 1940s and the mid-1960s witnessed profound changes in the lives of American laywomen. Women in the Catholic Workers, Friendship

House, the Grail, and serving as lay missionaries across the globe were asking new questions about their place in the Church and in American society. We will never know how many women were involved in the small groups (cells) of the Young Christian Workers, a European Catholic Action movement that was embraced by many American Catholic students and working women from the late 1930s through the 1950s. The Young Christian Workers, founded by Belgian priest Joseph Cardijn in 1913, emphasized a ministry of "like to like" (workers to workers, students to students, wives to wives). The movement promoted a three-part "inquiry method" (observe-judge-act) through which cell members sought to address specific social problems and thereby reverse the secularization of modern society. Cells sprang up in munitions factories, among secretaries in office buildings, at Catholic secondary schools and colleges, and by the mid-1940s, among middle-class businessmen and their wives. Single women's cells grappled with sexual harassment and racism in the workplace. Married women's cells experimented with "pre-Cana" classes for couples engaged to be married.

Out of the Young Christian Workers emerged the Christian Family Movement, in which cells of married couples tested the usefulness of the inquiry method for their lives. At the Christian Family Movement's first convention in 1949, thirty-seven couples representing cells from eleven cities elected the first executive couple, Pat (1911–1974) and Patty Crowley (1913–   ) from Chicago, pioneers in the movement. The Christian Family Movement was a grassroots enterprise in which married people learned to think, act, and judge for themselves on a variety of issues. Cells established credit unions, helped needy families, transported the elderly and handicapped, conducted housing surveys, and lobbied for low-cost housing. In 1956, the entire movement focused on racism; later Christian Family Movement couples organized to march in Selma and helped with voter registration drives. In 1961, the movement reached its peak with 40,000 member-couples.

The Crowleys sat on the Birth Control Commission established in 1963 by Pope John XXIII. They polled their membership and recommended that the Church reverse its prohibition of the birth-control pill, condoms, and other "artificial" means of contraception. Members of the Christian Family Movement had learned to trust their consciences. When, in 1968, Pope Paul VI issued the encyclical *Humanae Vitae* reaffirming the traditional position outlawing all means of birth control except for the rhythm method, the Crowleys and their constituency were demoralized, but they did not doubt their own judgment. Surveys conducted in the 1960s showed that Catholic women were using forbidden contraceptives and often still receiving the sacraments.

Vatican Council II, which convened in Rome on October 11, 1962, did not bring about the autonomy and confidence that was becoming so visible among Catholic women, sisters and laywomen alike, by the early 1960s. Instead, it catalyzed changes that had been under way for over a decade. Like the Birth Control Commission, it raised expectations and gave Catholic women an opportunity to articulate new aspirations and strategies for fuller participation, even leadership, in the Church. There were no women among the 2,600 official delegates (all bishops) at Vatican II, but by the final session in 1965, there were twenty-three female auditors, including ten sisters, present. In 1962, Gertrud Heinzelmann, a Swiss lawyer acting on behalf of St. Joan's Alliance, petitioned the council's preparatory commissions to discuss the possibility of women priests. (St. Joan's, an English Catholic suffrage organization, founded in 1911, rededicated itself in 1959 to working for women's rights within the Church.)

Heinzelmann's petition was no more successful in producing immediate change than the Conference of Major Superiors of Women's petition or the Birth Control Commission's recommendation. Nonetheless, seen in retrospect, it helped to spark the beginnings of the feminist revolution launched later in the decade. In the December 20, 1963, issue of the liberal Catholic journal *Commonweal*, Rosemary Lauer, a philosopher at St. John's University in New York, reflected upon Heinzelmann's petition. Lauer briefly outlined the history of sexism in the Church and affirmed its incompatibility with the scriptural portrait of Jesus. Then, drawing upon Thomas Aquinas's writings, she maintained that "women's soul does not differ from man's and therefore can receive the sacramental character of ordination as well as his" (Lauer, 367). Lauer's ideas resonated with those of a vocal segment of female *Commonweal* readers, whose upbringing in democratic America and experiences in the postwar era convinced them that an all-male priesthood was an unfortunate anachronism.

Mary Daly, who would soon emerge as a pioneer Catholic feminist theologian, was then at work on a doctorate in philosophy at the University of Fribourg in Switzerland. She wrote the editors of *Commonweal* applauding Lauer's article. She went on to lament Catholic women's "sub-human status" in the Church and the absence of articles and books on the subject. She ended with a "prophecy and promise" that set the agenda for the decades ahead: "[T]he beginnings of these articles and these books are already in the minds and on the lips of many of us. And . . . they will come" (Daly, 603).

SOURCES: Passages quoted come from Joseph Gibbs, *The History of the Catholic Total Abstinence Union* (1907); Mary Louise Sullivan, M.S.C., "Mother Cabrini: Missionary to Italian Immigrants," *U.S. Catholic Historian* 6 (Fall 1987): 266; Dorothy

M. Brown and Elizabeth McKeown, *The Poor Belong to Us: Catholic Charities and American Welfare* (1997); Mel Piehl, *Breaking Bread: The Catholic Worker and the Origin of Catholic Radicalism in America* (1982); Helen Caldwell Day, *Color, Ebony* (1951); Rosemary Lauer, "Women in the Church," *Commonweal* 79 (December 20, 1963): 367; and Mary Daly, "Letter to the Editors," *Commonweal* 79 (February 14, 1964): 603. Important secondary treatments of American Catholic women's experience from 1900 to 1965 include James K. Kenneally, *The History of American Catholic Women* (1990); Karen Kennelly, C.S.J., ed., *American Catholic Women: A Historical Exploration* (1989); and Mary Jo Weaver, *New Catholic Women: A Contemporary Challenge to Traditional Religious Authority* (1995). For the history of American sisters, see Patricia Byrne, "In the Parish But Not of It," in *Transforming Parish Ministry* (1989), by Jay P. Dolan, R. Scott Appleby, Patricia Byrne, and Debra Campbell; and Carol K. Coburn and Martha Smith, *Spirited Lives: How Nuns Shaped Catholic Culture and American Life, 1836–1920* (1999). Notable among the many important specialized studies are Paula Kane, *Separatism and Subculture: Boston Catholicism 1900–1920* (1994); Mary J. Oates: *The Catholic Philanthropic Tradition in America* (1995); and Mary J. Oates, ed., *Higher Education for Catholic Women: An Historical Anthology* (1987).

AMERICAN CATHOLIC WOMEN SINCE VATICAN COUNCIL II
Mary Jo Weaver

CATHOLIC WOMEN HAVE been major players in the historical development of their Church throughout the centuries, reflecting the central preoccupations of the hierarchy even as they created new possibilities for themselves on the margins of the institution. As the essays in the section show, women in a variety of colonial situations—Spanish, French, and English—not only did what was expected of them, by populating and founding religious orders, but they also invented new modes of religious expression and overcame overwhelming odds to become effective contributors to a developing religious community in a new and often hostile environment. Catholic women in black and Hispanic communities, who had to find space for themselves in an uncongenial Church, were pioneers whose heroism has only recently been rediscovered and is now being replicated by Asian Pacific women in the American Catholic Church. European immigrant women in the nineteenth century were part of an expanding Church that had to overcome anti-Catholic bigotry and join the great task of preserving and passing on the faith to new generations troubled by conflicts over how much they could assimilate into a new country while maintaining a Catholic identity. The women's movement of the nineteenth century and the great crisis points of the early twentieth century—two world wars and the Great Depression—gave Catholic women opportunities to expand their identities. As policies of backlash and constraint followed those years of national crises, Catholic women searched for new ways to express themselves within an increasingly conservative Church. When Vatican Council II (1962–1965) coincided with the new wave of the women's movement, the two events conspired to raise a contemporary challenge to traditional religious authority.

Catholic women since the Council have been remarkably active on a number of fronts, including women's ordination, the women-church movement, and reproductive rights. In general, however, it is fair to say that Catholic women in the last half of the twentieth century have revisited an old conflict about the teaching role of the Church, a battle between those who seek change and those who defend tradition. Meriol Trevor, a historian of the modernist controversy, called these two groups "the prophets and the guardians." Rosemary Haughton, communitarian and essayist, in a more metaphorical approach, speaks of Mother Church (the fierce, protective lawgiver) and her wild sister Sophia (the unruly, daring mystic). In nineteenth-century American Catholicism, this dialectic was between those who urged immigrants to become more American and their opponents, who believed that ethnic particularity was crucial to keeping the faith. Among women in the postconciliar Church, the battle lines were drawn between accommodation and resistance to feminism.

The teachings of Vatican II and the imperatives of the women's movement have inspired those Catholic women who urge accommodation. They work toward greater inclusiveness in the Church, an amelioration of liturgical language, and the rights associated with American values, that is, freedom of expression, self-determination, and equal opportunity. Those who resist such accommodation have taken their cues from Vatican officials who hope to replace the *aggiornamento* (updated) Catholicism of Pope John XXIII (1958–1963) with the *restoration* Catholicism of Pope John Paul II (1978–2005). These women urge obedience to the pope, eschew dissent, and accept the traditional teaching about women's roles in Church and society. Feminism is the flash point around which this battle most often occurs. Since the Council, a majority of Catholic sisters and many lay organizations have embraced the values of the women's movement as a cultural expression of the spirit of Vatican II. Antifeminist Catholic women, however, find the seeds of religious destruction in the women's movement and tend to give the documents of Vatican II their most conservative reading. The general outline of the conflict can be traced in the lives of both laywomen and nuns.

Women who do not want to be ordained, but find the sexist language of the liturgy too painful to attend regular worship services, sometimes meet and celebrate the Eucharist together in defiance of the Church's ban on ordination. *Used by permission of Woven Word Press.*

Lay Catholic Feminists

The American Catholic Church has always counted on women. In every conceivable setting—urban, rural, and suburban—women have been the mainstays of the congregation, the tireless supporters of parish life, hospitals, and schools, whose labor-intensive projects have sustained the institution. Nor is there much evidence that women in the past were inclined to rebel against a system that consistently defined their roles as auxiliary to those of men. The second wave of the feminist movement in the 1960s gave Catholic women a new perspective and a means to interrogate the system. By denying traditional sex-role stereotypes, feminist critics invited women to define their own experience and find a sense of solidarity that could lead them to understand the power of collective energy. Contemporaneously, Catholics had been invited to a similar sense of empowerment within their Church. The documents of Vatican Council II gave laypeople a new sense of mission in the Church and seemed to invite insights from experience into the dialogue about the future. Would it welcome women's experience?

Because the documents are sometimes ambiguous, capable of progressive and conservative readings, there has been an ongoing argument within Roman Catholicism about the intention of the Council. Catholic feminists read the documents as a charter for structural change, universality, collegiality, and social justice. In decrees on ecumenism and religious freedom, they have found a mandate to learn from other religions and to be sensitive to cultural diversity. Conciliar constitutions called for collegiality within the Church and seemed to invite genuine institutional modifications that would allow power to be shared at all levels. Finally, the Council's emphasis on social justice and new roles for the laity seemed to invite Catholic women to place their own goals within an ecclesiastical program equity aimed at marginalized groups. Many women hoped that social justice would eventually include feminist goals.

One example of a Catholic women's organization that used the combined energy of the Council and feminism to transform itself was the Grail movement. This initially hierarchical group of single women dedicated to the lay apostolate was not a feminist organization until after the Council. As it followed the spirit of Vatican II and became increasingly democratic and collegial in its governance, the Grail gradually embraced feminism. Although Grail had espoused specifically antifeminist views in the 1950s, it began to reassess its own positions in the early 1960s. Over the next few years Grail changed its organizational model to a completely decentralized self-government shaped around three task forces. Grail members were dedicated to the bonding of women, committed to search for God in traditional and nontraditional ways, and open to new waves of theology focused on liberation of and identification with the poor, especially in Third World countries. Grail also opened its membership to include married Catholic women, then Protestant women, and eventually became a totally inclusive center for women and women's issues on both theoretical and practical levels.

For the last thirty years, the Grail has been a conference center and meeting place for those who want to be involved in women's issues, liturgy, and global awareness. In the early 1970s, the Grail joined the Protestant Church Women United to sponsor conferences of theological exploration for an ecumenical group of women and to host "Seminary Quarter at Grailville," an intensive set of theology courses that gave graduate credits to its participants. This program, particularly, involved women from seminaries and universities who were searching for and creating a theology in which women's concerns were central rather than peripheral. In July 1982, the Grail sponsored a national conference that brought together an ecumenical group of feminist thinkers and activists for a week of talks and workshops designed to make connections between women and poverty, ecology, and social justice. The conference also aimed to raise the consciousness of participants about varieties of racism, homophobia, and injustice and to

celebrate women's bonding through rituals designed to help participants imagine alternative futures. In 1995, in keeping with its mission of aiding women to find their theological voices, the Grail Women Task Force began a consultation that eventually led to "Woman Defined Theologies," a weeklong, interdisciplinary living-learning experience with the option either for academic credit or for personal enrichment. The singularity of the title is meant to honor each woman's experience as a theological starting point. Today the Grail is a small but significant forum for Catholic feminist thought and experience. Its members live throughout the world and work in a variety of programs aimed to overcome poverty, violence, and injustice toward women. Its liturgical life—centered on the celebrations of Holy Week—is explicitly feminist and inclusive, blending traditional Roman Catholic rituals with new sensibilities, ecological awareness, and social justice imperatives.

In various progressive movements of the 1960s—peace, civil rights, antipoverty—women found themselves welcome only so long as they did not raise "women's issues" or attempt to take on "men's jobs." In the American Catholic Church of the 1960s, women participated in renewal with passion and dedication: They worked on ecumenical committees and interparish educational projects to enhance renewal of familial, liturgical, sacramental, spiritual, and social life within Catholicism. Yet when women in the parish began to question Catholic attitudes toward and treatment of women, they encountered either a chilly silence or a rehearsal of traditional Catholic teaching. The Church supports traditional gender roles in its doctrine of complementarity, a belief that sexual differences between males and females testify to a divine intention about their respective roles.

The first feminist voices raised in the Catholic Church—those of Mary Daly and Rosemary Radford Ruether—criticized the texts and traditions about women, finding in them a deep well of prejudice against women that had been upheld as a manifestation of God's will for centuries. With their strong critical voices and constructive alternatives to patriarchy, Daly and Ruether were foundational for the next generation of feminist critics in the Church. In the 1980s, feminist theologians such as Elisabeth Schüssler-Fiorenza, Anne Carr, and Elizabeth Johnson opened new veins of scholarly discourse urging a "hermeneutics of suspicion" about the ways in which scripture, systematic theology, and religious language had violated divine intent by discriminating against women. In sharp contrast to traditional Catholic teaching, Schüssler-Fiorenza coined the phrase "a discipleship of equals" to describe the intentions of Jesus and the early Christian community. In two magisterial books (*In Memory of Her* [1983] and *Jesus: Miriam's Child, Sophia's Prophet* [1994]), she raised questions of Christian origins that forced scholars to widen the scope of their work to include the women who played crucial roles in the early years of the Christian Church. Anne Carr, building on the generative work of Karl Rahner (1904–1984), created a feminist systematic theology in *Transforming Grace* (1988) that opened new approaches within traditional theological categories. Thanks to pioneers like Ruether, Daly, Schüssler-Fiorenza, and Carr, Catholic feminist theology at the turn of the century was an expansive discipline able to raise fundamental questions within the heart of Catholic teaching. An impressive example of a second-generation feminist theologian is Elizabeth Johnson. In *She Who Is* (1992), Johnson connects classical theology and feminist thought using traditional thinkers such as Thomas Aquinas to explain why one must think about God in female categories.

> In the end, this exploration points toward God with the coinage SHE WHO IS, a divine title signifying the creative, relational power of being who enlivens, suffers with, sustains, and enfolds the universe. SHE WHO IS points to holy mystery beyond all imagining who created women as well as men to be *imago Dei*, the grammar of God's self-utterance and participants in her liberating care for this conflictual world and all its creatures. (13)

Other feminist voices among Catholic women came not from professional theologians but from women whose experience in local parishes led them to take critical stands within the Church or radical action on its margins. In the nineteenth century, Cardinal John Henry Newman described ecclesiastical life as a dialectical interplay among theological, devotional, and hierarchical elements, all of them essential to the Church. Since women were not permitted to study theology until after Vatican II and since they are still not permitted to be priests or bishops, it is not surprising that a major focus of feminist energy has been on the "devotional" or liturgical elements of Catholic life. For nearly fifty years, Catholic women petitioned for ordination to the priesthood, but to no avail. Before the discussion could even begin, the Vatican issued a decree stating emphatically that women had never been ordained in the past and could not be ordained in the future. When supporters of women's ordination raised questions about ecclesiastical authority, the pope issued a second, more stringent decree saying that the question could no longer be discussed. In the face of this rejection, some Catholic women have left Christianity to seek religious alternatives elsewhere. Others, who have been active in the movement toward women's ordination but see that change is unlikely to occur, have left the Catholic

Church in order to be ordained in other Christian communities. Women who do not want to be ordained, but find the sexist language of the liturgy so painful that they cannot attend regular worship services, sometimes meet in defiance of the Church's ban on ordination to celebrate the Eucharist together. Although they do not believe that such celebrations constitute an ultimate solution to the problems that confront them, those women who seek spiritual wholeness need a way to share their pain and loneliness and a space in which they can offer their gifts, prayers, and liturgical aspirations. They believe that "what is coming already makes a claim on the present" and so gather in faith and anticipation to find solidarity in their mutual love of the Church and their hatred of its injustice toward them (Dierks).

In a variety of ways, Catholic feminist women are claiming responsibility for their own spiritual lives. A nationwide survey of 7,000 American Catholic women in the early 1990s was published as *Defecting in Place*. Survey participants believe that women and religion are at a crossroad. "If women are not taken seriously and their talents recognized, there will be serious consequences. I've had three daughters and they are not drawn to current religious traditions. They see no place for women. Why join such confusion?" (Winter et al., 12). Most of the women in the survey meet regularly for ritual sharing in a variety of feminist spirituality groups. Some of them, like other Catholic feminists, have turned to the mystical tradition of the Church and have adopted practices of meditation and the guidance of a spiritual director as they try to negotiate their way through a recalcitrant patriarchal tradition. Since spiritual direction privileges experience and seeks to pay attention to what God is doing in the individual heart, women have seized an opportunity to explore their spiritual lives within, but not constrained by, the institutional Church.

Antifeminist Catholic Laywomen

Three developments in the last fifteen years demonstrate the unwillingness of institutional Catholicism to come to terms with feminism. The debacle of the bishops' pastoral letter on women in the Church, the attempts of the Vatican to stifle any discussion about women's ordination, and the organized energy of right-wing Catholics united against feminism show that the hierarchy and a vocal segment of the laity believe that feminism is incompatible with Roman Catholicism. Since these Catholics continue to define women in terms of complementarity, they are incapable of understanding women's issues as a legitimate part of the social justice agenda of the Church.

A committee of American bishops began to work on a pastoral letter on women in the Church in the early

1980s. Although the bishops consulted nearly 75,000 women over many years, each draft of the letter showed evidence of a decreasing confidence in the project. After ten years of listening sessions and four drafts of the proposed letter, the initiative came to a halt. In the listening sessions for the first draft of the proposed letter, most of the women consulted expressed feminist views. They raised questions of equality, due process in the regulation of religious life, inclusive language, and women's ordination, as well as the issues that have become the most sensitive in debates between conservative and progressive Catholics—that is, birth control, divorce, homosexuality, and abortion. When the first draft reflected some of these concerns, conservative Catholic women who had felt marginalized since Vatican Council II were galvanized into action. Many of them, who considered themselves loyal and faithful Catholics, felt betrayed by the Church because all the markers they had counted on to describe their faith before Vatican II—dogmatism, Latin, a lack of ambiguity in moral teaching, set forms of worship, unchanging moral codes, and papal power clearly invoked and cheerfully obeyed—seemed to be in a process of erosion. When they tried to explain why traditional Catholicism had lost valuable ground, they tended to blame the women's movement, which, in their interpretation, meant "radical feminists" who, they believed, were antimotherhood lesbians bent on the demise of the family and the destruction of the Church.

Led by Helen Hull Hitchcock, a recent convert to Catholicism, six women joined together in 1984 to form Women for Faith and Family (WFF), a group concerned that the listening sessions sponsored by the bishops would not produce an accurate picture of American Catholic women. As this group interpreted the process of the proposed pastoral letter, it privileged a small minority of Catholic women in sessions that were designed to elicit complaints. The process seemed to discourage participation from women whose Catholicism included obedience to the pope and a willingness to accept his teaching on all issues, including traditional understandings of women's roles.

Although Women for Faith and Family was begun as an ad hoc response to the controversy surrounding the proposed pastoral letter, the organization assumed that there were thousands of women who agreed with them and needed a forum for their views to be heard. The perceived climate of dissent—over papal teaching on birth control coupled with the *Roe v. Wade* decision—focused media attention on Catholics who did not agree with Church teaching. WFF therefore aimed to provide a way for those who opposed dissent in general and feminism in particular to organize their voices. For example, when Catholics for a Free Choice sponsored a full-page ad in the Sunday *New York Times* (October 7, 1984) calling for discussion about abortion in the Cath-

olic Church, WFF saw it as evidence of a fundamental divide between traditional Catholic teaching and feminism. Conservative women were thus moved to organize to give testimony of their faith to the bishops.

Women for Faith and Family was created to find and amplify the voices of women who affirm traditional Catholic teaching. Its goals were to assist orthodox Catholic women in their effort to provide witness for their faith; to help them deepen their understanding of that faith; to find ways to provide fellowship for such women; and to serve as a channel of communication between orthodox Catholic women and the hierarchy. Their first project was the "Affirmation for Catholic Women," an eight-point statement and petition meant to gather signatures of women who agreed that women's nature was distinct and meant for childbearing (nuns are considered to be spiritual mothers) and that papal teaching was to be upheld in all matters of human reproduction. They also recognized as legitimate the subordination of women in service of the family and supported the sanctity of life. Finally, they condemned sex education in schools, ideologies that deny the distinct nature of women, and any attempts to secure priestly ordination for women. The "Affirmation for Catholic Women" gathered 70,000 signatures in two years.

By 1992, when the bishops were to vote on a final draft of the letter, there were so many disparate voices in the air that no letter was ever published. It could be argued that this outcome would have been predictable, had the bishops consulted American Catholics on almost any topic. Since the bishops in the 1980s did not hesitate to publish controversial pastoral letters on peace and the economy, it may be concluded that the subject matter—the very idea that complementarity was a maladaptive arrangement of gender roles—was the culprit. In their letters on peace and the economy, the bishops reflected the positions of the pope. Given the pope's views on women, there was no way the bishops could produce a pastoral letter that raised feminist questions and supported positions that the Vatican did not even want discussed.

The failure to issue a pastoral letter on women in the Church is a clear example of the great divide within American Catholicism over religious authority. Antifeminist Catholic women are religious conservatives who resist accommodation to the modern world and prefer the role of "guardians" of the tradition. They understand their own identities in terms of complementarity, believing that men and women have a *spiritual* equality that is experienced in this world in God-given, gender-specific roles. The pope champions this position when he addresses women or women's issues and so makes it impossible for priests and bishops to hold any other public view. Pope John Paul II has also made opposition to women's ordination and support of traditional teaching against artificial birth control a litmus test for priests who hope to ascend to the rank of bishop.

Conservative Catholic women, a small but vocal minority within American Catholicism, represent a point of view that has always been present within the Church, one that is necessary for the dialectical health of the institution. Their expression of that view, however, is unusually hostile. Perhaps their perception that the Catholic Church is under siege from a coalition of dissenters led by feminists accounts for the vitriolic nature of their rhetoric. Donna Steichen's *Ungodly Rage: The Hidden Face of Catholic Feminism* (1991) claims that Catholic feminists have adopted paganism as their spiritual center because they seek to replace God the Father with a goddess of their own making. Her angry book argues that Catholic feminists are motivated by "vengeful rage" and their movement is one of the "poisonous spiritual fruits" of Vatican II. Deeply worried about perceived connections between feminism and witchcraft, Steichen claims that the ultimate objective of feminists is the obliteration of Christianity. Anne Roche Muggeridge's book *The Desolate City: Revolution in the Catholic Church* (1990) is a more encompassing indictment of contemporary Catholicism that, among other things, describes nuns who seek change in their lives as having souls "like empty houses into which wandering devils enter and dwell. There is a real stink of brimstone at gatherings dominated by feminist nuns," she says, "especially their liturgies, a creepy neo-paganism with strong suggestions of sexual perversion" (141). Helen Hull Hitchcock's defense of masculine language in the liturgy, *The Politics of Prayer: Feminist Language and the Worship of God* (1992), claims that feminists hate the Church and that their "thirst for power combined with deep resentment" gives rise to their overwhelming desire to destroy it (xxv).

An unusual arena for antifeminist rhetoric can be found in contemporary Marian apparitions. Mary's appearances in the United States since the Vatican Council have been coupled with messages from heaven that countermand the women's movement. Sandra Zimdars-Swartz, aware that Marian devotion is a complex phenomenon with a complicated history, has nevertheless shown that in the last thirty years, since the rise of the women's movement, Marian apparitions in the United States have eclipsed similar appearances in Europe as popular pilgrimage sites. Although Mary's message continues to underscore traditional Catholic piety—prayer, repentance, and conversion—it has also tended to take on the rhetoric of family values and conservative social agendas, including a tacit condemnation of feminism. Mary has appeared in Conyers, Georgia, and South Phoenix, Arizona, as a loving mother with a threefold message: the need to venerate mothers, to end abortion, and to return to traditional gender roles.

Catholic Sisters Inspired by the Women's Movement

American sisters, like their counterparts in other countries, have been confined to certain roles by way of sex-role stereotyping. Their lives, wardrobes, spirituality, and behavior have been set for them by far-removed males; and they have had power in the Church only insofar as they conformed to traditional expectations. Their problems were exacerbated by their history of isolation from one another and from laywomen in the Church. Before Vatican Council II, sisters lived in consecrated space closed off from contaminating contact with "the world" and were effectively discouraged from dialogue with other women. In some ways, they projected an image of superiority, women chosen by God to be brides of Christ. Heroically dedicated to a materially austere and spiritually rich life, they enjoyed a quasi-clerical status despite the fact that they were technically defined by the Church as "laywomen," with no priestly powers.

Ironically, these isolated and etherealized women in the Church were the first ones prepared to become leaders of the feminist movement in Catholicism through a series of Vatican directives in the 1950s aimed to modernize religious orders to make them more serviceable to the Church. Unlike women in the parish whose coalitions were local, sisters had national networks and impressive organizational skills. By the time Vatican II ended, they were already reassessing their traditional roles as dutiful daughters of the Church. Although initially organized in the mid-1950s to support institutional initiatives, by the 1960s the Conference of Major Superiors of Women (CMSW) was asking to be represented on commissions dealing with the lives of sisters, governing bodies composed exclusively of male clerics. As sisters modified the internal structures of their own congregations, replacing obedience with processes of discernment, and sharing a more representational form of government, they were ready for both Vatican II and the women's movement.

In 1971, the Conference of Major Superiors of Women changed its name to the Leadership Conference of Women Religious (LCWR), a public acknowledgment that their structural self-perception no longer found its best expression in notions of "superiors." Although the Vatican did not welcome this change, the sisters persisted and received official recognition for the name change three years later. In the meantime, the Leadership Conference of Women Religious endorsed and supported Network, a Washington-based lobbying group of sisters interested in social justice and feminist issues. LCWR also initiated a large-scale collaborative conversation of national sisters groups in "Sisters Uniting" and supported the Center of Concern, an independent, interdisciplinary team engaged in social analysis, religious reflection, and public education around questions of social justice. Their executive officers began going places besides gatherings of sisters: They attended meetings of American bishops as observers, went to Russia to explore the plight of Soviet Jews, and sent representatives to International Women's Years sponsored by the United Nations. LCWR endorsed the Equal Rights Amendment (ERA), joined the ecumenical committee for support of the ERA, sponsored workshops on economic justice, wrote and distributed consciousness-raising packets on world hunger and feminism, and grew increasingly interested in Third World issues. Their work with religious conferences in other countries helped to make social justice a global concern for the American Church.

As they became more aware of themselves as women—as outsiders in the official Church—American sisters represented by the Leadership Conference of Women Religious requested the appointment of women to the Synod of Bishops and repeated their desire to serve on Vatican commissions that oversaw women's religious life, requests routinely ignored. In 1976, LCWR unveiled a five-year plan to promote study, prayer, and action on women's issues. The new decade began with the organization's president, Sister Theresa Kane, publicly urging the pope to hear the call of women to be included in all ministries of the Church, including priesthood. Throughout the 1980s and 1990s, LCWR worked with bishops and with men's religious orders on a variety of issues (leadership, diminished vocations, and retirement). Although these exercises of cooperation were cordial, the sisters were increasingly and painfully aware of the entrenched patriarchal underpinnings of the Catholic Church. In her 1999 presidential address, Nancy Sylvester, I.H.M., said that relations between the official Church and women religious were "at an impasse."

If American Catholic sisters faced an uncertain future, they did so with the same unflinching nerve that has characterized their presence throughout American history. For example, although Network now has a staff that is more than 50 percent laypeople, they are optimistic about the future. As they see it, the prophetic charism of nuns has effectively called laypeople to positions that were formerly filled by sisters. Put another way, if Vatican II issued a "universal call to holiness," then religious women have an obligation to bring everyone to the ministry of justice in the Church. American sisters today continue to be pioneers—only the frontiers have changed. In the nineteenth century, they helped to settle the West, today sisters are involved in a complex, international network of social justice initiatives. President Bill Clinton honored Carol Coston, a Dominican sister, on January 8, 2001, with the Presidential Citizens Medal, the second highest civilian honor given by American presidents "in recognition of citizens who have performed exemplary deeds of service for our nation." Coston helped to found Network in 1971 and served as its director until 1982. She chaired the Interfaith Center on Corporate Responsibility and in 1989 helped to found Mary's Pence, a Catholic foundation that finances projects to assist poor women. Today she directs Partners for the Common Good, an alternative loan fund sponsored by religious institutions. Its lending pool of more than $8 million supports housing and entrepreneurship in low-income neighborhoods.

The number of sisters may be declining, but they are neither in a panic about it nor hoarding their reserves. Rather, they are putting money into alternate investments and projects for the poor. Sandra Schneiders, the most articulate interpreter of the present and possible future of religious life in America, believes that the emergence of a responsible adult laity may be the most important renewal movement in the history of the Church. In *Finding the Treasure* (2000) she uses the spiritual framework of St. John of the Cross (the dark night of the soul) to chart the transformation of religious life.

A surprising sector of feminist consciousness in religious life has occurred in some contemplative groups of American nuns. Unlike their sisters whose lives are shaped around some work in the world, contemplative sisters are cloistered. They have dedicated themselves to lives of prayer, separated from the outside world by way of grilles and veils and sealed into monasteries where no one from the outside comes in and no one from the inside goes out except as dictated by the laws of enclosure. After Vatican Council II, some of these sisters wanted to modify enclosure, to show that a deeply contemplative life was possible without strict enforcement of medieval laws of enclosure. Although isolated for centuries even from other sisters in their general communities—Carmelites in one part of the country had never met or talked with Carmelites in another part of the country, for example—some contemplative sisters in the 1960s believed that renewal would require collective vision and energy. Their issue was a familiar one: They wanted some control over their own lives, reasonable changes based on their experience that would break the iron connection between enclosure and contemplation.

Perfectae Caritatis (October 28, 1965), the conciliar decree on the renewal of religious life, called for modifications in cloistered life and said that the Church should give consideration to the wishes of the monasteries themselves as nuns adjusted themselves to the conditions of the times. Less than a year after that decree, however, and just as nuns were considering some changes, a new "Instruction" was published by the Vatican, which restricted the extent to which the cloister could be modified. In other words, it reinforced external cloister regulations just as some sisters desired to change them. After some contemplative nuns attended one Conference of Major Superiors of Women meeting in 1965, they were forbidden to attend another one, and the president of the organization was told not to allow contemplative nuns to become even associate members. As sisters in various contemplative orders met for mutual support in 1966, they were told that they could hold no future meetings and seek no further consultation. When a national gathering for contemplative sisters was planned for August 1969—in Woodstock, Maryland—and after the invitations had been sent out, Cardinal John Carbury, chairman of the Pontifical Commission for Contemplative Religious in the United States, wrote to all contemplative communities to discourage them from attending such meetings. Nevertheless, 135 contemplative nuns made their way to Woodstock, and as they arrived, a new Vatican directive, *Venite Seorsum,* virtually forbade sisters to attend meetings. Obviously issued without consultation of the sisters themselves, *Venite Seorsum* was meant to intimidate the nuns at Woodstock. When the nuns who attended the seminar studied a Latin text of the document, they signed a letter of protest. At that same meeting, they founded the Association of Contemplative Sisters (ACS), an organization that has never been approved by the Vatican.

The Association of Contemplative Sisters sponsored six-week educational forums for four successive years in the 1970s. It stimulated feminist discussion within contemplative communities that were trying to renew themselves according to the documents of Vatican II and to gain some control over their own lives. The association welcomed laywomen contemplatives first as "friends," then as associates, and finally, in 1986, as full members. ACS, therefore, became a place for Catholic women who were following a contemplative path in their own lives. As ACS moves into the twenty-first century, its membership is predominantly laywomen, and it has become a nurturing space where women can explore the contemplative dimensions of their lives and see their journeys reflected in the lives of others.

The renewal process stimulated by Vatican II and the women's movement, whether experienced in contemplative environments or in the public forum of political involvement, has been one of increasing radicalization. Sisters and nuns have expanded the horizons of their experience and have a strong sense of themselves as women of the gospel. Organizations and individual communities have made significant contributions to the future of religious life, whether or not that life continues in its present forms. As even a casual use of a Web search engine will disclose, hundreds of books on specific religious orders—their history and future, their heroism and tragic decline, their hopes for the future—have been published in the last thirty years. Many religious orders have Web sites that can be found through the links provided on the LCWR home page.

By the end of the twentieth century, most American sisters had either abandoned or modified their traditional garb, their medieval schedules, and their workplaces. Sisters who before Vatican Council II typically chose vocations that would place them in schools and hospitals today work in women's shelters, in prisons, and in the private sector as lawyers, university professors, and community organizers. Many no longer live in convents but share an apartment with one or two other sisters. In place of traditional vows of poverty, chastity, and obedience made in the presence of the bishop, many of these sisters make promises to their communities to lead lives of material simplicity that are open to the promptings of the Holy Spirit. These changes privilege experience and community over episcopal oversight and conservative doctrinal interpretation.

American Sisters Inspired by Traditional Teaching about Women

Although the Leadership Conference of Women Religious represents most religious orders of sisters in the United States, it does not speak for all of them. The Institute for Religious Life founded in 1974 by John Hardon, S.J., is a national organization of bishops, priests, religious, and laypeople who support traditional vocations to and expressions of religious life. It has the support of the Sacred Congregation for Religious in Rome as it seeks to convene those who wish to "promote the teaching of the Church on consecrated life" or "authentic religious life." Sisters in this group represent more than 100 religious communities and a dozen communities of laypeople. The Institute holds annual national meetings and publishes a quarterly newsletter, *Religious Life.* Although its preoccupations are doctrinal—the Trinitarian context of consecrated life was the theme of its annual meeting in 2000—the Institute takes every opportunity to speak against the aims of the women's movement and to promote the traditional Church teachings that are decidedly antifeminist. In 1977, the Institute began to publish *Consecrated Life,* an English translation of the Vatican periodical for religious published twice each year

In 1992, some of the leaders of the Institute for Religious Life and other groups founded a new organization for nuns who share a commitment to traditional understandings and embodiments of religious life for women. Adapting the name abandoned by the Leadership Conference for Women Religious in the early 1970s, it became the Council of Major Superiors of Women

Religious (CMSWR). In 1995 the pope approved the council as a national association of women religious in the United States, an alternative to LCWR. The conservative Council of Major Superiors of Women Religious publishes a monthly newsletter and sponsors a House of Studies in Rome where sisters can learn theology while living in a traditional convent. Contrary to national trends in other religious orders, vocations in those groups who belong to CMSWR are on the rise. Whether increasing vocations in this sector testifies to the vitality of the tradition or to the fear of the alternatives proposed by the women's movement is not altogether clear. Women who enter the orders represented by the Council of Major Superiors of Women Religious agree to four tenets: freely given obedience to the pope and the Church; wearing of a distinctive religious habit as a sign of poverty and consecration to God; the importance of community life as essential to common prayer and spiritual growth; and active participation in community-based ministries that bring Christ to the young, the sick, the poor, and those who seek a deeper relationship with God.

Sisters, priests, bishops, and laypeople involved with the Institute for Religious Life and the Council of Major Superiors of Women Religious are primarily interested in promoting vocations to traditional religious life for women. The structures, leadership concepts, formation programs, and daily schedule of traditional sisters have not changed very much. On the one hand, in an ideal world, sisters in traditional convents and those in congregations that have been more radically touched by the women's movement would be good dialogue partners, preserving the tension between the "prophets and guardians" that has been a leitmotif of ecclesiastical history. On the other hand, precisely because the leadership styles are so different—one accepting male authority, the other insisting on defining its own experience and conditions of life—such a conversation does not appear to be possible in the foreseeable future.

The Legacy of Catholic Feminists

In the years since Vatican Council II, Catholic women who embraced feminism have not had much success on the institutional level. Some laywomen and nuns who were enthusiastic and hopeful supporters of the women's movement as an agent for change have left the Church to seek an alternative religious path. Sisters, who were leaders of the feminist movement within the Church in the thirty years since the council, have seen their communities get older while attracting few new vocations. Perhaps no one foresaw what Gene Burns concluded in his sociological analysis of Catholic ideology—that even though American sisters and laywomen

managed to institute *a de facto* pluralism within the church . . . they did not create a church of dialogue in which women are central participants. Instead, they encounter[ed] more of a polite standoff in which they do not have power to move further and Rome is unwilling to move further or allow the bishops to do so. (*The Frontiers of Catholicism: The Politics of Ideology in a Liberal World,* 1994, p. 197)

The question has become not whether the Church will welcome feminism but whether Catholic feminists can nourish their religious lives and refuse to capitulate to the "love it or leave it" mentality that greets any suggestion that the Church might take feminism seriously. Yet however liberating it may be to ignore the institution from time to time, members of a Church cannot withdraw themselves entirely and still hope to maintain the kind of resolute presence that moves obstinate authorities. Catholic feminists often find opportunities for bonding and experimentation on the margins of the institution but understand that change requires creative engagement. It is not unusual, therefore, to see Catholic women cite the story of the tenacious widow in the Gospel of Luke (18:1–8) as a model of the kind of persistence Catholic women must maintain in the face of injustice. The vision of a discipleship of equals that is undermining for patriarchal Church structures is one that Catholic feminists know can be made effective only through determination.

As the twentieth century ended, religious studies scholars, historians, and sociologists were interested in what appeared to be increasingly severe divides between peoples in similar religious traditions. Foundations provided funding for massive international studies of fundamentalism and for conversations between liberal and conservative believers. This author's own experience with such a conversational attempt suggests that Robert Wuthnow is right when he says that as liberals and conservatives come to know more about one another, they find it impossible to engage in any dialogue whatsoever, preferring to glare at one another across an unbridgeable chasm.

Historically, the Catholic Church has been able to open itself to varied and sometimes threatening voices that have led it to new understandings of itself, but seldom at the time those voices were raised. Feminists in the Catholic Church are part of a very long story in which thirty years constitutes a miniscule time frame. Whether contemplative communities will continue to exist with a feminist consciousness, the willingness of such nuns to organize in the face of official hostility made it possible for cloistered women to share their lives in ways the institutional Church has yet to imagine.

Whether or not American sisterhoods continue to attract feminists, those sisters who came together to establish the Leadership Conference of Women Religious and to heighten awareness of global injustice have laid down a legacy for young people in the Catholic Church who are increasingly attracted to some kind of social justice work. If many Catholic women in the parish have grown tired of fighting for feminist ideals, their persistent voices have raised a series of issues that continue to be discussed within the Church and, given the cultural climate, cannot be ignored forever. If Catholic feminists today sometimes seek extraecclesial sources of spiritual nourishment, they do so partly as warriors preparing for a long campaign. Military language is not out of place here; the Catholic Church and the army are similarly hierarchical institutions insistent on obedience that harbor different forms of protest. As Mary Fainsod Katzenstein has shown in *Faithful and Fearless: Moving Feminist Protest Inside the Church and Military* (1998), women in the military have turned to the courts and Congress, whereas feminists in the Church have used "discursive" protests. Catholic feminists write books and articles, organize workshops and conferences, conduct quiet protests, and join spirituality groups to explore radical pathways toward faith and justice. Most of the women who participate in such activities consider themselves members of the Catholic Church who are fearless in their attempts to reshape the institution. Perhaps they are best understood as guerrilla fighters within a recalcitrant institution with a very long history. If they sometimes appear to be underdogs or to occupy marginal positions within the institution, it would nevertheless be unwise to dismiss their vision of the future. In the late 1960s, during the Vietnam War, when someone asked Ho Chi Minh what he thought of the French Revolution, he is reputed to have said, "It is too soon to tell."

SOURCES: Papers from the groundbreaking Grail conference (1982) can be found in Janet Kalven and Mary Buckley, *Women's Spirit Bonding* (1984). For an introduction to Catholic feminist theology, see Susan Ross, "Catholic Women Theologians of the Left," in *What's Left? Liberal American Catholics,* ed. Mary Jo Weaver (1999). Pope John Paul II prohibited any discussion of women's ordination in *Ordinatio Sacerdotalis* (May 30, 1994), English translation in *Commonweal,* June 17, 1994. A collection of liturgical prayers and comments about women celebrating Eucharist can be found in Sheila Durkin Dierks, *WomenEucharist* (1997). A more extensive study of this phenomenon is Miriam Therese Winter et al., *Defecting in Place: Women Claiming Responsibility for Their Own Spiritual Lives* (1994). Helen Hull Hitchcock's article "Women for Faith and Family: Catholic Women Affirming Catholic Teaching," describing the emergence of antifeminist Catholic women, and Sandra Zimdars Swartz's article "The Marian Revival in American Catholicism: Focal Points and Features of the New Marian

Enthusiasm" on contemporary Marian apparitions, can both be found in Mary Jo Weaver and R. Scott Appleby, eds., *Being Right: Conservative Catholics in America* (1995). A survey of contemplative practice among laywomen is Virginia Manss and Mary Frolich, *The Lay Contemplative: Testimonies, Perspectives, Resources* (2000). Extensive bibliography and history of the women's movement in the Catholic Church can be found in Mary Jo Weaver, *New Catholic Women: A Contemporary Challenge to Traditional Religious Authority,* 2nd ed. (1995).

DETERMINED BUILDERS, POWERFUL VOICES: WOMEN AND CATHOLICISM IN NINETEENTH- AND TWENTIETH-CENTURY QUEBEC AND CANADA
Carolyn Sharp

SIX MILLION ROMAN Catholic women live in Canada. Three million are found in French-speaking Quebec where they represent more than four-fifths of Quebec women. One and a half million Catholic women live in Ontario, Canada's most populous province, where they form one-third of the female population. While most of these speak English, nearly one-third speak French as their first language, and many others are recent immigrants to Canada. The remaining one and a half million Canadian Catholic women live in Canada's other eight provinces and three territories. They are predominantly English speaking, except in New Brunswick where nearly two-thirds of Catholic women are Acadians who have French as their primary language.

Any discussion of Roman Catholic women in Canada must begin by recognizing the fundamental duality of this experience. French-speaking women, especially in Quebec and Acadia, have historically found themselves in a homogeneously Catholic society in which religion and language are markers of a shared cultural and political identity within an English-speaking and Protestant-dominated continent. Even today, despite the increasing levels of religious disaffection within Quebec society, the cultural influence of Catholicism continues to shape the religious horizon of most women. In English-speaking Canada, whatever their linguistic and ethnic origins, Catholic women have been members of a religious minority, a factor that has shaped their historical and contemporary experience. Throughout the nineteenth and early twentieth century, most English-speaking Catholic women were of Irish origin. The increasing diversity of Canadian immigration in the latter part of the twentieth century has changed this, especially in Ontario. The arrival of Catholic immigrants, primarily from eastern and southern Europe, but also from

Catholic nuns such as Mother Benedicte of the Sisters of Providence (Cluny, Alberta) found themselves traversing the broad plains of Canada to attend to rural, isolated families, providing health care, education, and spiritual guidance. *Courtesy of the Glenbow Archives.*

Latin America, Asia, and Africa, have led both to a growth in the Catholic population and an ethnically diverse Catholicism. By the end of the twentieth century, Roman Catholics had become the largest religious group in English-speaking Canada.

Women in Canadian and Québécois Catholicism, 1831–1901

Producing a New Catholic Order: The Role of Religious Congregations of Women

In August 1833, Magdalen O'Shaughnessy sailed into the harbor of Saint John's, Newfoundland. At the invitation of Michael Fleming, the Roman Catholic bishop of Saint John's, O'Shaughnessy and three other Irish Presentation sisters, Xaverius Lynch, Mary Bernard Kirwan, and Mary Xavier Maloney, came to this small British fishing colony to establish a school for girls. Their arrival opened a new chapter in the history of Catholic women in what is now Canada. For the remainder of the century, the rapid growth of religious congregations provided the workforce that allowed the Roman Catholic clergy to establish and consolidate the institutional presence of the Church in Canadian society. In English-speaking Canada, the establishment of women's religious congregations was central to the creation of a Catholic minority culture that challenged Protestant domination of Canadian society while carving a space in which Catholics could thrive and flourish. In French-speaking Canada, and especially in Quebec and Acadia, the work of religious congregations allowed for the survival of a society in which religion and language became the markers of collective identity. In both contexts, women's religious congregations were crucial to the development of an ultramontane Catholic order in British North America. The dominant ideology within the French-speaking and English-speaking Catholic Church in Canada, ultramontanism was an antiegalitarian and antiliberal vision of Church and society that emphasized a centralized and hierarchical ordering of authority and power within the Church, and especially the absolute authority of the pope, while jealously defending the Church's rights and privileges within society, particularly against the perceived threats of nondenominationalism and secularism. It promoted a vision of women's place in family, Church, and society that emphasized their subordination to male authority.

Newfoundland: The Implantation of an English-speaking Catholic Church

In the 1830s, Newfoundland was a small and isolated colony, dominated by British merchants and traders. Half of its population were Irish Catholics who had labored under the civil and legal discriminations of the anti-Catholic Penal Law until Emancipation in 1828. Responsible government was only beginning; the first legislative assembly met in 1833, the year Magdalen O'Shaughnessy and her companions arrived. Denominational control of education was at the heart of the tension over the rights and place of the growing Catholic population in Newfoundland society. For the bishop of Saint John's, the arrival of the Presentation sisters provided a way both to meet the educational needs of the Catholic community and to further his combat for Catholic rights in education. He sought not only to provide free schooling to the daughters of predominantly working-class Catholic Newfoundlanders but to provide it in sexually segregated classrooms, unhindered by the influence of Protestant or liberal thought. The cloistered Presentation sisters whose rule dedicated them to the teaching of poor children were ideally suited to this task. In a decade, more than a thousand students studied within their convent walls in Saint John's, and they soon sent members to open similar schools in other communities. At the same time, they undertook the training of laywomen teachers who worked throughout the colony, most notably in the fishing outports, carrying on this work until the creation of the Island's Normal School in the early twentieth century. The Presentation sisters were thus crucial in the creation of the publicly supported Catholic denominational school system that prevailed in Newfoundland until 1997.

In 1842, under the leadership of Mary Anne Cree-don, a second group of Irish women religious arrived in Newfoundland, the Sisters of Mercy. Their beginnings in Newfoundland were marked by the fragility of the enterprise. Due in part to tensions with the local bishop, the two Irish women who had accompanied Creedon left Newfoundland. A relative, Maria Nugent, joined the small congregation, but in 1847 she died of typhoid fever caught while nursing famine refugees. Creedon carried on her work alone, living as a solitary Sister of Mercy, even while she sheltered the sisters of the Presentation following the destruction of their convent by fire. In 1848, her Irish-born niece Agnes Nugent joined the congregation, and in 1854 Anastasia Tarahan became the first Newfoundlander to join the congregation. When Creedon died in 1855, the small congregation counted only four members. Fifteen years later, in 1870, forty Sisters of Mercy carried out a wide range of activities.

Bishop Fleming had purposely recruited the Sisters of Mercy to run schools for the daughters of the Catholic middle class where fine needlework, music, and dancing were taught alongside catechism and basic reading and writing. By providing a suitable education to the daughters of the middle class, the Sisters of Mercy played an important role in the social promotion of Catholics in a society dominated by a Protestant elite. Well beyond their homes and parishes, the women they educated played a role in weaving the cultural fabric of Catholic life. They established among themselves networks that fostered music, theater, and good works. The Mercy convent schools thus helped to lay the foundation for the colony's nascent cultural and social life. Moreover, unlike the Presentation sisters, the Sisters of Mercy were not cloistered and were thus able to carry out a variety of charitable roles outside the convent. In addition to their work in the field of education, they nursed the sick, visited prisoners and the poor, and cared for orphans and the elderly, as well as educating the daughters of the middle class.

The same pattern established in Newfoundland, where a local bishop sought to establish women's religious congregations for his diocese, was also found in Upper Canada (Ontario) and the Maritimes. In 1849, four women arrived from New York to found the Sisters of Charity of Halifax. The bishop of Toronto recruited the Sisters of Loretto from Ireland in 1847 and the Sisters of Saint Joseph from Philadelphia in 1851. In 1854, Honora Conway founded the Sisters of Charity of the Immaculate Conception in Saint John, New Brunswick. French-speaking congregations in Quebec sent women to work among both English-speaking and French-speaking Catholics, establishing new provinces of already existing congregations and founding entirely new congregations, as in the case of the Sisters of Providence

of Kingston in 1861. From these foundations, French-speaking and English-speaking women religious moved out across the country, establishing schools, building hospitals, starting orphanages, and organizing social services. Unlike in the United States, many of these institutions received some form of government funding.

QUEBEC: THE REORGANIZATION OF THE FRENCH-SPEAKING CHURCH

During the French regime, seven congregations of women religious had been implanted in Canada. In 1639, under the patronage of Madame de La Peltrie, the Ursulines and the Augustines came to Quebec City from France. In 1658, Marguerite Bourgeoys founded the Congrégation de Notre Dame in Ville-Marie (Montreal). In 1659, at the behest of Jeanne Mance, the Religieuses hospitalières de Saint-Joseph came to Ville-Marie from France, and a second monastery of Ursulines was founded at Trois-Rivières. In 1701, the Augustines founded a second monastery and hospital in Quebec City. In 1737, Marguerite d'Youville founded the Soeurs grises, or Grey Nuns, in Ville-Marie. At the end of the eighteenth century, a few hundred women belonged to these congregations. They ran five hospitals, educated girls in convents and parish schools, and carried on charitable works.

The period immediately following the capture of Quebec in 1759 and the end of French rule in New France was one of disorganization. On the one hand, the British had recognized the rights of the Canadiens to maintain their language, their religion, and their civil law. On the other hand, the British did not intend that a distinct culture should survive nor that Roman Catholicism thrive in this newly acquired British possession. They developed assimilationist policies designed to bring the Canadiens into the Protestant fold. The continued existence of Roman Catholic clergy was tolerated, but they made the appointment of new bishops difficult, barred the arrival of priests from Europe, and forbade new members in men's religious congregations. Similar restrictions did not apply to congregations of women religious. Recognizing the usefulness of their work, the British colonial government allowed them to continue their activities unimpeded. Indeed, the British colonial elite sent their daughters to schools run by the Ursulines and the Dames de la Congrégation, where they learned French and needlework, music, and drawing.

The excommunication by the clergy of those who took part in the popular uprising called the Patriots' Rebellion (1837–1838) convinced the British colonial government that the support of the Roman Catholic clergy was necessary to the maintenance of colonial rule. Just as in 1774 they had offered guarantees with regard to religion, language, and law, in 1840 they made concessions that recognized the Church's institutional prerogatives and denominational control of the education system. The Church used these concessions to establish itself as the unifying institution of a demoralized people. Under the leadership of the ultramontane bishop of Montreal, Ignace Bourget, the groundwork of antiliberal clerical nationalism was laid. In Roman Catholic schools, hospitals, and social services, women's religious congregations provided much of the labor required to create and maintain the Church's cultural hegemony in French Canadian society.

The nineteenth century saw an extraordinary expansion of women's religious congregations. In 1800, 300 women were scattered throughout seven existing congregations. Forty years later, after the Patriots' Rebellion, the Grey Sisters of Montreal founded the Soeurs de la Charité de Saint-Hyacinthe. In 1842, at the behest of Bishop Ignace Bourget of Montreal, the Religieuses du Sacré-Coeur arrived from France. In the next 60 years, more than two dozen congregations of women religious came into being in French Canada. Unlike English-speaking Canada, where almost all religious congregations were imported from Europe, the United States, or even Quebec, the majority of these congregations were founded by French-speaking Canadians.

The experience of the founder of the Sisters of Saint Anne, Esther Blondin, provides a striking example of how the tensions between the institutional priorities of the clergy and the women's own hopes and aspirations marked the lives of women religious. Born in 1809, at a time when the education system was dismal, Blondin was unschooled as a child and only learned to read and write as an adult. As a lay teacher, she ran a flourishing school on the outskirts of Montreal that not only provided for the basic education needs of parish children but trained boarders for teaching. At a time when the hierarchy opposed sexually mixed schooling, she understood that in rural areas only schools that accepted both girls and boys could overcome the high illiteracy rates crippling French Canadian society. Having long aspired to the religious life, she gathered around her women who shared her commitment to educating the children of the poor and in 1850 founded the Sisters of Saint Anne. The congregation grew and in Blondin's lifetime spread throughout North America. In spite of this success, Blondin herself was marginalized. The congregation's overbearing chaplain contested her leadership and obtained the support of Bishop Bourget of Montreal to remove her from leadership. Her role as founder was ignored, and she ended her days as the congregation's sacristan and laundress. Notwithstanding this conflict, Blondin's commitment to education shared in the ultramontane view that the nondenominational education favored by liberal thinkers threatened the Catholic faith and French Canadian culture. So, too, the spirituality of self-denial that figured so prominently in nineteenth-

century Catholicism marked her acceptance of her own fate.

The attraction of religious life endured well into the twentieth century, reaching its peak in the 1930s. The groundbreaking work of the historian Marta Danalewcyz has provided a framework for understanding the explosion of religious life in French Canada, clearly establishing that the factors at work were sociological as well as religious. In a society in which women had extremely limited life choices and almost no possibility for professional activity, religious life offered an alternative path. In religious life women were able to find an outlet for their professional talents, economic security outside of marriage, and social status outside of family.

It would be wrong, however, to idealize the freedom of action and choice enjoyed by religious women. The difficulties encountered by Esther Blondin were not unique, nor were they limited to French Canada. In 1876, the meddling of the bishop of Halifax threatened the education work of the Sisters of Charity, forcing them to seek protection from the bishop of Antigonish. As a result, they were placed under his jurisdiction. Religious life did allow for the deployment of women's professional talents and creativity in areas of Church and society from which they were otherwise excluded. Yet, by and large, the work of women religious as educators and caregivers was an extension of the feminine role in society. Nor did all members of religious congregations find themselves in professional roles. Indeed, several communities were founded for the express purpose of keeping house for the clergy. Thus, while for many women religious life was a means of social promotion, between and within religious congregations, class distinctions remained. The congregational structures of the Ursulines clearly mirrored the larger society's inequalities. Three classes of religious existed within this cloistered teaching congregation: Choir nuns (the elite) were the teachers; cloistered converses (or lay sisters) did the menial tasks within the cloister; and the Angelines, a separate group of lay sisters named after Angela de Merici, the Italian foundress of the Ursulines, lived in a separate community outside the cloister and were responsible for those tasks that required leaving the cloister. Drawn from the daughters of families who could not afford to educate them nor provide them with a suitable dowry, the Angelines occupied the lowest rung within the hierarchy of the congregation.

Reproducing the Catholic Order

Ontario: The Spiritual Promotion of Catholic Motherhood

Most Catholic women in Canada were laywomen, married and mothers. Only a few worked voluntarily outside the home. The prevailing order defined their proper sphere as that of the parish and the hearth where their lives were dedicated to reproducing the ultramontane Catholic order. Historian Brian Clarke has shown that the promotion of parish-based devotional associations played an important role in fostering women's participation in the Church's understanding of their roles as protectors of the domestic Catholic order. While promotion of personal piety was the explicit aim of these associations, like denominational schooling, they worked to reinforce the boundaries of Catholic identity. For the English Canadian Church, this reinforcement of boundaries was crucial, both warding off the dangers of religious assimilation into the dominant Protestant culture and facilitating the integration of newly arrived Catholic immigrants into the already existing Catholic community. Through the promotion of monthly communion, the rosary, and devotional prayer, these associations contributed to an inwardly directed religious identity, loyal to the Catholic Church and respectful of its authority.

Women formed the overwhelming majority of the members of devotional associations. Devotional associations encouraged women to maintain Catholic households that integrated and respected the teachings of the Church in all aspects of life. They championed the role of Catholic mothers in raising the next generation of Catholics. At the same time, they advocated the moral values of self-denial, service, patience, and suffering typical of feminine subordination and promoted an ideology of separate spheres that enclosed women within the household. Paradoxically, the vision of women as the guardians of faith and morals created a tension within the household. A devout Catholic woman obeyed her husband and the Church, as represented by her priest. When the two came into conflict, it became her duty to convince her husband to accept the clerical positions. Such conflicts were recurrent and often involved questions of personal morality, alcohol and temperance, and sexuality and contraception.

QUEBEC: HEROIC MOTHERHOOD

In Quebec and throughout French-speaking Canada, women were similarly enrolled in the work of reproducing the Catholic order. In a context of concern for collective survival as a French-speaking people in North America, the idealization of motherhood encountered the more specific sense of urgency of expanding the French-Canadian population. These two forces coalesced in a mythic commitment to large rural families in which the language, honor, and faith of New France could be maintained and nourished. The work of nineteenth-century novelist Laure Conan celebrates this heroic motherhood, serving both Church and people in a spirit of sacrifice and devotion. The tremendous ex-

pansion of the French Canadian population throughout the nineteenth century was the fruit of women's numerous maternities, a period when most French Canadian women had six or more children.

While many women shared in the worldview that saw children as gifts of divine providence, sexuality and reproduction were often a source of tension, pitting the clergy against laity, the Church against women. While birthrates remained high throughout the nineteenth and early twentieth centuries, they were also declining. Before the invention of modern contraception, extravaginal ejaculation and other traditional methods were employed to limit family size. Hostile to these practices, the clergy railed against them, using parish retreats to remind men of their conjugal duties and the confessional to chastise women for their failure to produce sufficient numbers of children. For married people, even abstinence was frowned upon. While the overwhelming Church presence in French Canadian society could not guarantee the success of its campaign against contraceptive practices, as evidenced by the dropping birthrates, it did ensure an increasing pressure on the everyday lives of women and foster a climate of guilt in which defiance was most often covert. Sexual knowledge and pleasure increasingly became suspect. Bishop Bourget forbade the reading of books about sexuality and contraception and opposed the presence of novels in Montreal's public library. Thus the stage was set for one of the most important cultural conflicts of the twentieth century, the conflict between women and the Church over the question of sexuality.

Women and Canadian Catholicism, 1901–1970

REFORMING THE CATHOLIC ORDER: WOMEN AND SOCIAL CATHOLICISM IN QUEBEC

In Quebec, the tightly controlled ultramontane Catholic order lasted well into the twentieth century, fully disappearing only in the 1960s, during the period of social transformation known as the Quiet Revolution. Yet the life of the social reformer and early feminist Marie Lacoste Gérin-Lajoie shows that the forces of change were already at work from the beginning of the twentieth century. Gérin-Lajoie was the daughter of a prominent Montreal bourgeois family. Her sister Justine Lacoste founded Saint Justine's Hospital, the first French-speaking hospital for children. Gérin-Lajoie published a critique of family law and worked to inform women of their existing rights. Advocating a comprehensive legal reform, she campaigned to improve married women's rights, in particular their right to control their own salaries, to have a say in the sale of family property, and to inherit from intestate husbands. Gérin-Lajoie's social action was grounded in a sense of bourgeois duty, inspired by the teaching of Leo XIII's encyclical *Rerum Novarum*, and motivated by a concern for women's welfare. She advocated a "Catholic feminism" for whom social action outside the home was a natural extension of women's maternal role and whose central focus was the protection of women's rights as wives and mothers. This vision led her to participate in the foundation of the Fédération nationale Saint-Jean-Baptiste (FNSJB). Among the FNSJB's priorities was the right to vote, making it perhaps the only Catholic women's suffrage organization in North America.

Throughout Canada, English-speaking Protestant women led the struggle for the right to vote. Gérin-Lajoie and the other founders of the Fédération nationale Saint-Jean-Baptiste initially participated in the Montreal Local Council of Women, whose membership consisted primarily of English-speaking Montreal Protestants. When women obtained the vote in federal elections in Canada in 1917, the provincial vote was left to the discretion of provincial parliaments. In Quebec politicians used its distinct French-speaking Catholic culture as a pretext to deny women the provincial vote until 1940. Indeed, in spite of initial support from the bishop of Montreal for the Fédération, Gérin-Lajoie quickly encountered the Church's opposition to women's suffrage. In 1922, the episcopate forced her to abandon the suffrage campaign. When women's rights activists Idola Saint-Jean and Thérèse Casgrain stepped into the breach, they encountered strong hostility from Quebec's political, cultural, and ecclesiastical elites. In 1990, fifty years after women obtained the provincial vote, the Assembly of Quebec Bishops formally apologized for its unjust opposition to women's fundamental right to participate in the democratic life of Quebec society.

Gérin-Lajoie's most successful battle was access to university education for women. While the English-language McGill University first admitted women in 1884, the French-language universities, all Roman Catholic, continued to exclude women. For Gérin-Lajoie, this was a personal as well as a political battle. Determined that her daughter Marie would undertake university studies, she found an ally in one of her daughter's teachers, Mère Sainte-Anne-Marie (Aveline Bengle). Nurturing the dream of an undergraduate program for women, Sainte-Anne-Marie and several other members of the Congregation of Notre Dame had prepared themselves for the task of teaching young women the strenuous *cours classique* leading to a bachelor's degree. Convincing the bishops of the wisdom of this course of action was extraordinarily difficult. The clergy was ideologically invested in the development of the recently founded domestic arts schools that corresponded to their idealized vision of women as wives and mothers. Conscious of her prestige and status, Gérin-Lajoie threatened to send her daughter to McGill University, a precedent the bish-

ops certainly wished to avoid. In the meantime, a Montreal newspaper carried an advertisement announcing the opening of a French-speaking nondenominational women's school. These threats to their control of women's higher education forced the bishops to give in. However, Gérin-Lajoie and Sainte-Anne-Marie also found themselves forced to make compromises. Courses in philosophy, literature, Greek, and Latin were complemented by courses in the domestic arts, thus emphasizing that even university-educated women's true destiny was in the home.

In 1911, the young Marie Gérin-Lajoie received her Bachelors of Arts, graduating with the highest provincial matriculation mark. The authorities decided not to publish the results and granted the first-place prize to the (male) student who finished second. She went on to found the Soeurs de Notre-Dame du Bon Conseil, a congregation of religious women whose primary work was social action, especially with impoverished women and immigrants. She was also one of the founders of professional social work in Quebec. In 1913, Sainte-Anne-Marie received her licentiate in philosophy from Laval University and went on to an influential teaching career.

While urban elite women formed the Catholic feminist circles in which Marie Lacoste Gérin-Lajoie moved, other women were also organizing to take charge of their lives, although often in less explicitly feminist ways. Among the women's associations that emerged in the beginning of the twentieth century were the Cercles de fermières and the Jeunesse ouvrière catholique féminine (JOCF). Established by the provincial Ministry of Agriculture in 1915, the Cercles de fermières formed a movement of rural women, committed to the development of their expertise in crafts and horticulture. In the context of the increasing industrialization and urbanization of Quebec, the organization was a means to stem the rural exodus. Heavily influenced by the clergy's idealization of agricultural life and its promotion of large families, it was pervaded by a conservative nationalism that nonetheless recognized the economic importance of women's labor to the survival of rural society. Understanding men's and women's spheres as complementary, but equally necessary, the personal and intellectual development of women was a means to further the well-being of their families and of society as a whole. Homogeneously Catholic and French speaking, this secular organization was parish based and, by and large, receptive to the clergy's views on women, opposing the right to vote, promoting large families, and mistrusting feminism. Nevertheless, it represented a breach in the existing Catholic order. Its decision-making process was independent of Church authority, women controlled their own finances, and it had no spiritual objectives. Indeed, the women even chose their own chaplains. The clergy made several attempts to establish a Catholic movement of rural women under their control, but found it difficult to compete with the success of the Cercles de fermières. Ironically, when the clergy did successfully create a confessional rural women's movement in the 1960s, the Association féminine d'éducation et d'action sociale, this new organization challenged the Church's traditional teaching, quickly adopted feminist goals, and played an important role in raising consciousness around women's social and economic rights.

If the Cercles de fermières represented an effort by the State to promote rural life, the Catholic Action youth movement for Jeunesse ouvrière catholique féminine, founded in 1932, represented an effort by the Church to respond to the challenges facing urban working-class women. Known in English as Young Catholic Workers, it was modeled on the movement founded in 1925 by the Belgian priest Joseph Cardijn. Brandishing slogans like "Safeguarding young workers for Christ," its social Catholicism was overtly anticommunist and opposed to the U.S.-based nonconfessional trade unions, promoting instead the creation of Catholic trade unions. Moreover, while concerned with the morals of young women, the movement was neither devotional nor focused on individual conversion but concerned with the sanctification of social structures. Through the see-judge-act method of systematic social analysis, its members learned to make the connections between the social teaching of the Church and the concrete circumstances of their own lives. Union organizers, community activists, and members of cooperatives, they dedicated themselves to the improvement of living and working conditions. At a time when young working-class women had no access to secondary or postsecondary education, the movement was an important training ground where they gained confidence in themselves, developed their intellectual and political skills, and acquired a critical understanding of their society. Members called it the University of the Streets. Gradually the original corporatist vision valuing interclass cooperation gave way to a more radical vision that integrated notions of class struggle and the transformation of capitalist society. It thus helped to lay the groundwork for the strong social-democratic orientation of Quebec's Quiet Revolution and also for Quebec Church's emergence as a strong voice for social justice.

The Catholic order created in the nineteenth century retained its hold on Quebec society through much of the twentieth century, taking its final breath in 1959, with the death of the conservative and very Catholic provincial premier Maurice Duplessis. Yet the experience of women in the early twentieth century betrayed cracks from which the revolution in women's lives would emerge. Throughout the first part of the twentieth century, laywomen's organizations in English-speaking Canada retained an inwardly directed orientation, which strayed little from the vision of the nineteenth-century devotional association. The minority status of Catholic women hampered their presence in social and political debates outside their homes and parishes. In Quebec, the Church's dominance of society as a whole slowed down women's emancipation, but it also favored the emergence of outwardly directed Catholic movements whose collective energies were directed toward the transformation of women's place within the existing order.

THE REFORM AND DECLINE OF WOMEN'S RELIGIOUS CONGREGATIONS

The growth in religious life, begun in the nineteenth century, continued unabated through the first half of the twentieth century. In 1960, 60,000 Catholic women in Canada belonged to religious congregations, 45,000 of them in Quebec. Yet as the changes in the Church brought about by the second Vatican Council began, these numbers hid the first signs of decline. For social and cultural reasons, fewer and fewer women were attracted to religious life. The emancipation of women meant that they no longer needed to turn to religious life in order to realize the professional and personal accomplishments that it afforded previous generations. The religious disorientation and disaffection of an increasingly secular society further contributed to this decline. For women religious who lived through this period, the time was one of paradoxes. It seemed that women's hopes and aspirations, gifts and talents, would finally triumph over the institutional priorities of the clergy. Many of the expectations for reform, however, faltered on the hierarchy's resistance to change and continued abuse of power. Moreover, the exodus of large numbers of women religious and the failure to draw new members brought into question the very future of women's religious congregations. At the turn of the millennium, 22,000 women belonged to religious congregations, most of them over seventy-five years of age. Fewer than 200 are under forty-five.

The experience of Irene Farmer, superior general of the Sisters of Charity of Halifax, provides a striking example of the challenges facing women religious as the congregations entered into a period of reform and decline. Born and raised in Alberta, with a business school education and a successful professional career, Farmer was in her late twenties when she entered religious life in 1937. At the time, every moment of religious life was meticulously regulated, every behavior scrupulously prescribed. Rapidly thrust into leadership positions, Farmer was conscious of the ridiculous and harmful nature of this fastidious spirit. Already in the 1950s she was involved in reform efforts. In the 1960s, as superior general, she rewrote her congregation's constitution and emerged as a major voice in organizations such as Canadian Religious Conference and the International Union of Superior Generals. Farmer's reform eliminated outdated customs and removed the protective wall and structures that isolated religious women. It also renewed the understanding of mission, allowing for the expression of individual talents and interests and radicalizing the congregation's commitment to justice and equality for women. Even this sort of reform, however, could not stem the tide of decline. During the "great exodus," one-quarter of the Sisters of Charity left religious life. Of the 1,200 remaining members, 400 were elderly and fewer than 100 were under forty. In 2000, the congregation had 335 members whose average age was seventy-six.

Farmer knew that the great transformation of women's lives was not limited to religious congregations. The Sisters of Charity founded Mount Saint Vincent as an academy for girls in 1873. In 1951 it became the only independent women's college in the British Commonwealth. In 1966 a new charter transformed Mount Saint Vincent into Canada's only women's university. This renewal of the congregation's commitment to the education of girls and women under Farmer's leadership reflected a desire to participate in women's advancement. In 1985 the Mount was granted one of five Chairs in Women's Studies created by the Canadian government, an eloquent recognition of its contribution to the lives of women in the Maritimes.

In 1967 Farmer was also a coauthor of the Canadian Religious Conference's brief presented to the Royal Commission on the Status of Women, presided by Florence Bird. The brief advocated improvements in the education of girls and women, equality in employment, government-subsidized child care, and measures to address the discrimination faced by natives and immigrants. This brief foreshadowed the ongoing support of many women's religious congregations in Canada for much of the feminist social agenda. Farmer herself models the major shift in the spirituality and praxis of Canadian women religious. The nineteenth-century spirit of self-abnegation had disappeared. In its place had emerged an active and dynamic faith, committed to the experience of God's love for the world and concern for the poor and marginalized.

Disrupting the Catholic Order:
Feminist Activism, 1970–2000

By the end of the 1960s it was clear that every aspect of women's lives was undergoing dramatic and irreversible change. The publication of the report of the Royal Commission on the Status of Women in 1970 provided the Canadian government a blueprint for the institutionalization of this social revolution. Within the Roman

Catholic Church, although the 1960s had also been a time of change, women committed to full emancipation remained unsatisfied, calling for a "Council for the second sex." In 1971 two groups of women, one in Alberta, the other in Quebec, called on the Canadian bishops to review the status of women in the Church. Central to their concerns were the recognition of women's full and equal humanity in Church and society, women's participation in Church leadership and decision making, and the Church's understanding of sexuality.

A certain optimism motivated these appeals. Prominent members within the Canadian episcopacy, including Cardinal George B. Flaliff of Winnipeg, were known to support changes in the Church's teaching on women. In response to the devastating news of *Humane Vitae*, the encyclical reiterating the Vatican's opposition to contraception, the Canadian bishops had issued a statement on the importance of conscience. Many Canadian Catholics chose to follow theirs. In 1972, the Canadian Conference of Catholic Bishops established a committee of bishops and women on women's role in Church and society, chaired by Corinne Gallant of New Brunswick. The committee's 1974 report received no formal follow-up. In 1976, the Congregation for the Doctrine of the Faith published *Inter Insigniores,* confirming women's exclusion from the ordained priesthood. The time for optimism was finished. The changes women had gained in society would not easily find their match within the Catholic community.

Those who hoped for change, however, were not so easily deterred. In 1976 a group of French-speaking women created the feminist collective l'Autre Parole. This network of feminist-based communities nurtures alternative spiritual and liturgical practices among its members and provides a platform for the feminist analysis of issues of concern to women. In 1981 the Canadian Conference for Women's Ordination came into being, changing its name in 1988 to the Canadian Network for Women's Equality. Born of a commitment to the ordination of women and the development of women's theological voices, the network has popularized the work of feminist theologians through conferences and workshops. In 1982 women employed by the Church in a wide range of pastoral roles created Femmes et ministères. In addition to building an important network of solidarity, the group has sponsored important studies of women's working conditions within the Church, receiving support from the federal Secretary of State for the Status of Women for their work in the field of employment equity. In 1986, a group of women religious in Quebec created the Association des religieuses pour la promotion des femmes. Concerned with the impoverishment of women and multiple forms of violence they face, this organization has provided a bridge between religious women and the secular women's movement.

These groups have formed the core of an ongoing feminist activism within the Catholic Church in Canada and Quebec. They have made it possible to name and treasure women's gifts and talents, to challenge the ongoing male and clerical dominance of the Catholic Church, and to develop innovative practices for nurturing women's spiritual well-being.

In spite of the increasingly difficult situation for women within the Roman Catholic Church throughout the world, Canadian and Quebec women have been able to make some headway in bringing about change. At various Roman synods, the Canadian bishops have consistently, at times courageously, spoken out in favor of women's emancipation. In liturgy, the English-speaking sector of the Canadian Bishops has produced an inclusive-language policy and published an inclusive-language lectionary, although this remains a source of tension with the Vatican. In Quebec the assembly of bishops has established a status of women officer in each diocese, responsible for promoting women's equality, and created a provincial structure for the coordination of their work. In addition, in 1989 the bishops published a landmark document on wife battering, *A Heritage of Violence?* This document affirms the need to develop an appropriate pastoral response to conjugal violence and also adopted a feminist analysis, acknowledged the way the Church itself has contributed to this phenomenon, and recognized the important role the women's movement has played in raising awareness and formulating solutions. The Canadian Conference of Religious, as well as individual women's religious congregations, have supported politically and financially the women's movements struggle to eradicate the feminine face of poverty and violence against women. The Canadian Catholic Organization for Development and Peace has adopted a policy commitment in the area of gender and development, incorporating it into its overseas development work and its development education work in Canada.

In spite of these gains, the spirit of optimism that prevailed in the early 1970s has not returned. Indeed, many feminists have become increasingly discouraged and disillusioned. In the 1980s Joanne McWilliams, one of the first Catholic women theologians to obtain a doctorate, joined the Anglican Church of Canada. She is now an ordained Anglican priest and a member of the Primate's Theological Commission. In the 1990s Mary Malone, a theologian renowned for her feminist positions and a close associate of the Canadian bishops, publicly withdrew from the Roman Catholic Church, because she could no longer profess a belief in the God it preached nor display a confidence in its ability to renew its faith so as to be inclusive of women and their spiritual wholeness.

In English-speaking Canada, feminist women have had to confront the rise of a Catholic Religious Right.

As elsewhere in North America, these groups promote the identification of feminism with abortion and of Catholic identity with a commitment to the recriminalization of abortion. (In 1988, the Supreme Court of Canada struck down the Criminal Code section dealing with abortion, leaving Canada with no federal abortion law. The provision of abortion services and their funding, including coverage by provincial health insurance, is regulated by the provinces.) The Religious Right portrays the moderate openness of Canadian bishops to the women's movement as an implicit support for abortion rights and as contrary to the Church's official teaching. In addition to abortion, these groups mobilize around the opposition to publicly funded child care, employment equity, welfare, and government support for single mothers. In some cases, these groups have been able to rally support of various bishops for their political agenda, most notably in the case of their opposition to the recognition of the civil rights of gays and lesbians. They have also convinced Toronto, Canada's largest English-speaking diocese, to withdraw funding or support from Catholic organizations when these have created strategic alliances with the women's movement around issues such as violence and social welfare policy.

In Quebec the growing social disillusion with the Church itself presents a challenge. Most Québécois continue to identify themselves as Catholics, yet a growing number of women and men have abandoned nearly all forms of religious practice. This dramatic religious disaffection is in part due to the disjuncture between a society that identifies equality between women and men as one of its shared public values and a Church that continues to exclude women from positions of leadership and decision making. So, too, in spite of its enduring Catholic identity, a deep rift separates this sexually permissive culture from many of the Church's positions. While Catholic religious education is offered in public schools, sexual and contraceptive education are required by the provincial curriculum. Divorce is widely accepted, and one-quarter of all couples live in common-law unions. The provincial human rights code forbids discrimination on the basis of sex, family status, or sexual orientation, and the province recognizes the civil union of gays and lesbians. The public health system provides universal access to publicly funded abortion. Moreover, much of Quebec popular culture, television, films, and novels display a rejection of the Church's previous domination of family, sexuality, and conscience.

This profound schism between Church and society has placed ethics at the center of feminist theology. Monique Dumais has argued that the contemporary women's movement in Church and society represents a shift from a heteronomous morality to a self-determined liberative praxis. She questions the capacity of present hierarchical structures to fashion an adequate response, one that can in inventive and prophetic ways integrate women's contemporary ethical experience while giving women an equal voice in shaping the Church's reflection on substantive issues. Louise Melançon has raised similar questions in her analysis of the ethical questions surrounding the question of abortion.

Research on Women and Catholicism in Quebec and Canada

At the end of the 1970s and beginning of the 1980s, feminist theology emerged among both French-speaking and English-speaking women. From its beginning, this theology has been fashioned by a mixture of intellectual, activist, and ecclesial concerns. Monique Dumais, Marie-Andrée Roy, and Louise Melançon are founders of l'Autre Parole. Ellen Leonard was a founding member of the Canadian Conference for Women's Ordination. Lise Baroni, Yvonne Bergeron, Micheline Lague, and Pierrette Daviau are closely associated with the work of Femmes et ministères. Working in a variety of theological disciplines, feminists have developed both critical and constructive frameworks for challenging the pervasive patriarchalism of Catholic theology and proposing alternative visions grounded in women's emancipatory praxis. The work of these women has in turn incited younger theologians to respond to the challenge of doing theology in a feminist key. Denise Couture has challenged older feminists to rethink their categories in light of the experience of younger women who, having enjoyed the benefits of the formal equality gained by a previous generation, now face the challenge of living out that equality. In the fields of liturgy and religious education, Miriam Martin has explored the importance of integrating feminist insights for the personal and spiritual development of young women. Heather Eaton has opened new paths through her work on ecofeminism.

In Quebec the historical importance of the Roman Catholic Church has stimulated research on women and Catholicism in fields other than theology and religious studies. Feminist historians, sociologists, and political scientists have sought to understand the impact of the Church's promotion of patriarchal social structures and women's subordination within the Church on the whole of Quebec social, political, and cultural institutions. The work of sociologists Nicole Laurin and Danielle Juteau is indicative. They have produced an institutional sociology of women's religious life that highlights the economic and social dimensions of women's religious contribution to Quebec society. Relatively little historical or

sociological work has been done on the history of Catholic women in English-speaking Canada. As women, they are a footnote in Church histories, mainly visible as members of religious congregations. As English-speaking Catholics, they are nearly invisible in feminist histories that focus on the experience of Protestant women in English-speaking Canada and Catholic women in French-speaking Quebec. Thus, for example, while substantial research exists with regard to the roles played by Protestant churchwomen in the women's suffrage movement as well as the resistance encountered by Catholic women from Quebec's Roman Catholic bishops, there is little or no research on English-speaking Catholic women and the vote. Similarly, while feminist historians and sociologists in Quebec have identified the experience of women's religious congregations as important to a more general understanding of women's lives, in English-speaking Canada, such research is usually done for the congregations themselves, by researchers working with limited resources outside the universities, although there are some signs that sociologists and historians have begun to become interested in these questions.

SOURCES: Studies of the lives of individual women and histories of women's organizations are an important source of information. See Mary James Dinn, *Foundation of the Presentation Congregation in Newfoundland* (1975); Hélène Pelletier-Baillargeon, *Marie Gérin-Lajoie* (1985); M. Williamina Hogan, *Pathways of Mercy in Newfoundland* (1986); Yolande Cohen, *Femmes de paroles. L'histoire des Cercles de fermières du Quebec, 1915–1990* (1990); Geraldine Anthony, *Rebel, Reformer, Religious Extraordinaire: The Life of Sister Irene Farmer* (1997); Christine Mailloux, *A Woman in Turmoil* (1997); Lucie Piché, "La Jeunesse ouvrière catholique féminine et la dynamique du changement social au Quebec, 1931–1966" (Ph.D. diss., Université du Quebec à Montréal, 1997). Several studies focus on a particular aspect of Canadian women's experience of Catholicism. See Marta Danylewcyz, *Taking the Veil: An Alternative to Marriage, Motherhood and Spinsterhood in Quebec, 1840–1920* (1987); Monique Dumais and Marie-Andrée Roy, *Souffles de femmes: Lectures féministes de la religion* (1989); Nicole Laurin et al., *À la recherche d'un monde oublié. Les communautés religieuses de femmes au Quebec de 1900 à 1970* (1991); Louise Melançon, *L'avortement dans une société pluraliste* (1993); Lise Baroni et al., *Voix de femmes, voies de passage: Pratiques pastorales et enjeux ecclésiaux* (1995); and Brian P. Clarke, *Piety and Nationalism: Lay Voluntary Associations and the Creation of an Irish-Catholic Community in Toronto, Montreal* (1999). Information on women and Catholicism in Canada and Quebec can also be found in survey books. See Micheline Dumont et al., *Quebec Women: A History* (1987); Alison Prentice, *Canadian Women: A History* (1996); and Terrence Murphy et al., *A Concise History of Christianity in Canada* (1996).

Part IV

❧

Protestantism

COLONIAL PERIOD

WOMEN AND PROTESTANTISM IN COLONIAL NEW ENGLAND
Rebecca Larson

PROTESTANTISM WAS A pervasive force in the development of colonial New England, and religion was central to the female experience. During the period from 1620 to 1775, the practice of piety provided a framework of meaning for New England women's lives and spiritual sustenance to endure hardships. Female membership predominated in the region's Congregational churches for many decades, and in a dissenting sect, the Quakers, women were active in the ministry. The prevailing Puritan theology assigned women specific roles in the family and in the church that restrained egalitarianism, but Protestant spirituality also opened certain avenues of power and authority to women.

The settlement of New England was part of the English colonization of North America. Women participated from the inception of permanent European habitation in this region. In contrast to the English plantation in Virginia (1607), where most settlers were young, unmarried men, New England colonists arrived primarily in families, resulting in a closer male/female ratio. Religion was an important motive for the migration of early New England settlers, who were nonconformist Protestants in conflict with the Church of England as it was then established. Many women and men ventured across the Atlantic to New England fueled by intense concern for their spiritual salvation and that of their families. Colonist Mary Angier recalled, "[T]hinking that her children might get good [participating in the ordinances of a godly church] it would be worth my journey" (Selement and Woolley, 66). After suffering persecution in England, they sought a refuge on the far margins of the English world, where they could worship according to Reformed Protestant beliefs.

The religious disputes in England underlying this exodus to the New World were an outgrowth of the Protestant Reformation. The women and men in the Puritan movement, motivated by Protestant reforming zeal, wanted to "purify" the Church of England by purging elements that deviated from the apostolic Christianity described in scripture. Henry VIII had founded the Church of England by severing its ties to the Roman Catholic Church, rejecting papal authority. The king had been impelled less by Protestant convictions, however, than by his aim to establish the state's authority over the Church and his need for a divorce. Under succeeding monarchs, Anglicanism continued to closely resemble Catholicism with its elaborate ceremonial forms and an ecclesiastical hierarchy headed by bishops. The Puritans, a varied group of dissenters, sought further ref-

This woodcut from Nathaniel Crouch's book *The Kingdom Darkness*, entitled the "Salem Devil Dance," reflects the Puritan view that the New England wilderness was the devil's domain, void of servants of God. *Courtesy of The Connecticut Historical Society.*

ormation by eliminating these vestiges of Catholicism, which they regarded as man-made corruptions of the faith. They shared a Reformed emphasis on simplicity of church organization, with worship services dominated by the sermon, and called for a return to godly conduct.

An active English laity of devout women and men risked fines or imprisonment by dissenting from Anglican practices. The Protestant Reformation had encouraged each believer's direct relationship with God through prayer and reading of the Bible (the revealed Word of God), although lay reformers were assisted on their spiritual quest by ordained, educated clergy. Dissatisfied with the "hollow" formalism of Anglican services, Puritans held private meetings in their homes to discuss theological matters or went to hear nonconformist ministers preach according to Puritan tenets. They were harassed by the Church of England leadership, backed by civil authorities, attempting to enforce religious uniformity.

According to established Christian theology, women were excluded from the ministry on the basis of Apostle Paul's directive that females not usurp authority over men but remain silent in church (1 Timothy 2:12). Eve's role in the fall from God's grace suggested that a woman was intellectually weaker, vulnerable to Satan's enticements, and dangerous in her power to seduce man. Yet

Eve also had been created in God's image to be a meet ("suitable") help for man, and Protestant theologians accorded new respect to marriage. By eliminating the celibate caste of priests, monks, and nuns, reformers centered religious education in the household. This spiritualization of the family affirmed the authority of the patriarch but also elevated the laywoman's status. Under her husband's rule, a Puritan woman could be honored as a pious spouse and a guardian of grace in her children.

Taking as their motto a pamphlet, *Reformation without Tarrying for any*, a small minority of radical "Separatists" concluded that the Church of England was so corrupt they had to separate from it entirely. Members of this group (later known as the Pilgrims) sailed to Plymouth aboard the *Mayflower* in 1620. But the majority of Puritans rejected formal separation from the Anglican Church, trying instead reform from within. The opposition of Charles I and William Laud, the archbishop of Canterbury, as well as a belief that divine judgment was about to befall the sinful English nation, eventually prompted many Puritan families to seek religious renewal in America.

Some 20,000 Puritans crossed the Atlantic in the "Great Migration" between 1630 and 1643, as what had been a reform movement in England became the establishment in New England. John Winthrop (1588–1647), the leader of the Puritans founding Massachusetts Bay Colony in 1630, described their purpose in a sermon on board the *Arbella*: They were to be a "city on a Hill," an example to the world of a Christian society. The New England Puritans characterized themselves as a people in covenant with God, comparable to the tribes of ancient Israel. In order to receive God's protection, the Puritans sought to create a "Bible commonwealth" where obedience to God's Word was preeminent. The colony's laws were based, as much as possible, on biblical precepts, and every town was organized around a meetinghouse where families worshipped.

A New England colonial woman gained certain protections in comparison with her English counterpart as a result of the Puritan reforms. In the Bible commonwealth, theoretically, a husband's authority was limited: It was illegal for him to strike his wife or command her anything contrary to God's laws. Marriage was newly defined as a civil contract, rather than a sacrament. A marital union, therefore, could be ended by divorce if either spouse neglected a fundamental responsibility (as in cases of adultery, desertion, or cruelty). However, a married woman in seventeenth-century Massachusetts retained her "feme covert" status under English common law: Subsumed within her husband's legal identity, she was unable to own property or sign contracts. According to Puritan theory, a woman's role in society was divinely ordained and revealed in scripture. She was subordinate to her husband whom she was to honor and obey but a coauthority over their children and servants. A well-ordered family was viewed as the foundational unit of Puritan society. Hierarchically arranged by rank and gender, the Puritan household was "a little Church" and "a little Commonwealth."

Although Puritan reformers upheld a patriarchal order in a conservative social system, they promoted a radical theology that acknowledged the equality of souls before God. Women, as well as men, were required to testify to an experience of "conversion" in order to gain membership in the New England churches. A wife might be among the spiritually "elect," even if her husband were not. The New England Puritans gradually severed their ties to the Church of England; their form of church government was "Congregational," with authority localized in each congregation. Church attendance was required of all inhabitants. But in contrast to the Church of England's birth-based membership, Puritan church membership was restricted to "visible saints": believers whose "conversions" through God's grace evidenced their inclusion among God's "elect." Influenced by the writings of Reformed theologian John Calvin (1509–1564), Puritans believed in the doctrine of "predestination": that God in his infinite wisdom had elected some to eternal salvation, while others were fated to damnation. Calvinist theology emphasized the original sin of Adam and Eve, an essential flaw in human nature that only God's mercy could correct.

The conversion narratives of applicants for church membership in Cambridge, Massachusetts, between 1638 and 1645 (transcribed by the minister Thomas Shepard) reveal that ordinary women and men were well versed in the Puritan clergy's tenets of regeneration. The testimony of a maidservant (identified only as "Katherine, Mrs. Russle's Maid") exemplifies the rigorous self-examination, familiarity with the Bible, and knowledge of the stages on the way to salvation that were required. After recognizing her sinful nature, Katherine agonized for several years whether or not she was among God's elect: "I knew the Lord could [pardon sin], but yet I question would He [for me]?" She recounted "looking into the word [Bible]" for solace until finally ready, with faith, to "close with Christ in a promise" (Selement and Woolley, 99–101). New Englanders of every rank were a "people of the Word," most of whom read their Bibles regularly. Yet in 1650 only an estimated 30 percent of the women and 60 percent of the men also knew how to write. Most seventeenth-century New England white females were taught to read as a prerequisite for religious edification, but writing was considered a specialized, work-related skill, primarily taught to males. Women were excluded from the university education mandatory for clergy—the scholarship that was a primary source of religious authority for Puritans.

Puritan ministers encouraged the active piety of laywomen as recipients of their teachings, but females were not to be definers of the faith. An early theological challenge was posed by Anne (Marbury) Hutchinson (1591–1643), a clergyman's daughter and wife of a prominent merchant. After Reverend John Cotton immigrated to New England, Hutchinson felt "there was none then left [in England] that I was able to hear, and I could not be at rest but I must come hither" (Hall, 337). Troubled by the "falseness" of the Anglican Church, Hutchinson sailed with her family from England to Boston, Massachusetts, to join Reverend Cotton's transplanted Puritan congregation. Hutchinson soon created a division in the Bay Colony when she accused the other New England Puritan clergy of preaching "a covenant of works" (salvation achieved by external propriety) rather than a true "covenant of grace" (God's gift of inner regeneration). Hutchinson led weekly scriptural discussions at her home, attracting a sizable following of women and men. Colony leaders feared that Hutchinson's criticisms were undermining trust in the Massachusetts social and theological system, legitimized by claims of fidelity to God's tenets. Additionally, they were threatened by her assumption of religious authority, which violated the hierarchical order favoring men. Asserting that they upheld the "true religion," the Massachusetts magistrates opposed the toleration of conflicting religious opinions.

In 1637, Hutchinson was brought to trial before the General Court. Among the charges, Governor John Winthrop declared that she had maintained an assembly not "fitting" for her sex by teaching both women and men (312). A clergyman contended, "You have stept out of your place, *you have rather bine* [been] *a Husband than a Wife and a preacher than a Hearer*" (383). Hutchinson learnedly cited Bible passages in her defense: "I conceive there lyes [lies] a clear rule in Titus [2:3–5], that the elder women should instruct the younger," denying that men were present at her meetings (315). But her assertion that the Holy Spirit had spoken to her by "an immediate revelation" conflicted with the Puritan teaching of *Sola Scriptura* (Scripture alone) and was seized upon as proof of her heretical delusion (337). In 1638, Hutchinson was excommunicated and banished from the colony. The conflict Hutchinson engendered became known as the "Antinomian controversy." Hutchinson's adversaries accused her of "antinomianism"—the belief that God's grace absolved Christians of responsibility for obeying moral law.

New England records yield other lesser examples of women dissenting from the Puritan ministry on the basis of independent scriptural judgment, refusing to inhabit the passive congregant role. The majority of New England colonial women, however, did adhere to the theological positions prescribed by Puritan clergymen. The writings of Anne (Dudley) Bradstreet (1612–1672) reveal a Puritan woman of faith whose orthodox theology eased the harsh realities of her world: the sufferings of childbirth, illness, and death. In a poem mourning the destruction of her home by fire, Bradstreet recalled the spiritual promise: "Thou hast an house on high erect /Fram'd by that mighty Architect, /W[i]th glory richly furnished /Stands permanent tho: this bee fled" (McElrath and Robb, 237). But in a devotional legacy to her eight children, Bradstreet recorded her anguished wrestlings before arriving at conviction. She had questioned the existence of God and the doctrines she had been taught: whether He was "such a God as I worship in Trinity, and such a Saviour as I rely upon" and "why may not the Popish Religion bee the right?" Yet she finally had rested her faith on "this Rock Christ Jesus" (218). As the daughter of the second governor of the Bay Colony and the wife of a magistrate, Bradstreet held an honored position in Massachusetts society. Unusually well educated for a woman of the era, Bradstreet found expression in the "masculine" domain of poetry writing despite neighbors' criticism ("I am obnoxious to each carping tongue,/Who sayes, my hand a needle better fits" [7]). Her admiring brother-in-law, a Puritan minister, carried Anne's poems to England to be published as *The Tenth Muse Lately Sprung up in America, or Severall Poems, compiled with great variety of Wit and Learning, full of delight . . . By a Gentlewoman in those parts* (1650). These were the earliest published poems by a Puritan colonist of either sex.

The Congregational Way spread to other parts of New England as Puritan settlers moved to the areas that now form Connecticut, New Hampshire, and Maine. Disparaged as "the latrine of New England" for accepting religious outcasts, Rhode Island was the only colony in the region founded as a refuge for those who conflicted with the Puritan orthodoxy. The colony was established by minister Roger Williams (whose assertion that civil officials should not have power over an individual's religion led to his banishment from Massachusetts in 1635). Rhode Island's charter guaranteed freedom of worship.

Women experienced new religious latitude when political, social, and spiritual upheaval created a "world turned upside down" in England during the 1640s, influencing developments in New England. In the turmoil surrounding the outbreak of the English Civil War, radical sects arose in which some women preached, prophesied, and voted on church business. The Quakers, a religious group that emerged amid the unrest of mid-seventeenth-century England, believed that both women and men were qualified to preach when inspired by the Holy Spirit. Rejecting a paid, learned clergy, Quakers practiced an egalitarian worship during which individuals attentive to the Inward Light (John 1:9) might spontaneously come forth in a vocal ministry. Puritans insisted that such direct revelation by the Holy Spirit had ended with the apostles; the Bible was the final authority in religious matters. The Quakers honored scripture as inspired revelation but believed that God's immediate speaking, the ultimate source of religious authority, never ceased in any age.

The Quaker invasion of New England began in 1656 when two English female evangelists, Ann Austin and Mary Fisher, arrived in the Massachusetts Bay Colony. The Quaker women were carefully searched for witches' marks (any unnatural growths where, it was believed, witches suckled their imps), imprisoned for five weeks, and deported from the colony. New England Puritan leaders viewed Quakers as heretics who would not only lead listeners astray religiously but erode the social order with their leveling attitudes. Quaker missionaries persisted in proselytizing in Massachusetts, using Rhode Island as their base. In 1658, legislation was passed banishing nonresident Quakers from the Bay Colony upon pain of death. Four Quaker missionaries, three men and one woman (Mary Dyer, a former supporter of Anne Hutchinson), were executed between 1659 and 1661 before Charles II forced the Puritans to abolish this law. The failure of the Massachusetts policy to prevent Quaker incursions effectively ended the Puritan ideal of a religiously unified society. Quakerism, with its inclusion of women in religious leadership, gathered adherents even in New England's least tolerant colony.

Puritanism remained the dominant religion in New England, but the failure of many church attenders, baptized children of the "elect," to experience conversion as adults led to a crisis in the Congregational churches. The Halfway Covenant of 1662 was a ministerial compromise to keep as many inhabitants as possible within the Puritan fold. The Halfway Covenant extended baptism to the unregenerate grandchildren of church members. Some colonists viewed this religious innovation as a fatal compromise of the pure church of "visible saints," and a scattered Baptist movement coalesced into a church in Massachusetts. Baptists rejected infant baptism, believing that testimonies of individual conversion were essential prior to both baptism and church membership. Baptist views, which had arisen in England under the Puritan umbrella, were considered a heresy by Congregational orthodoxy. Early Massachusetts Baptists, such as Lady Deborah Moody of Salem (excommunicated in 1642), had been persuaded to keep their opinions private or voluntarily leave the colony. Roger Williams and his followers formed the first colonial Baptist church in 1639 in Rhode Island. The laity leadership of the Baptists was patterned on the primitive Christian church. Any male church member could take a leading role in their meetings; female members may have been allowed to speak informally during time for exhortation. In contrast to Puritan women's exclusion from church governance, Baptist women were permitted to vote in some congregations. Rhode Island's policy of religious toleration contributed to the growth of dissenting religions, such as the Quakers and the Baptists, allowing greater experimentation with women's religious role.

Colonial New England women viewed the dangers posed by the frontier within a Protestant religious framework, contributing to a genre of writing known as the "captivity narrative." The Puritans' conception of the New England wilderness as the devil's domain, void of servants of God, justified their displacement of the Native American inhabitants. The expansion of white settlement provoked a succession of Indian attacks, when many colonists were killed or taken captive. In their accounts as Indian hostages, New England white women created narratives of spiritual salvation in which survival depended on faith in God. Since the Puritan clergy had characterized Indians as diabolical heathen representing the powers of darkness, the Christian captives cast their struggle in terms of spiritual warfare. The most popular narrative to emerge from King Philip's War (1675–1676) was authored by a minister's wife, Mary Rowlandson, *The Sovereignty & Goodness of God, Together with the Faithfulness of His Promises Displayed; Being a Narrative of the Captivity and Restoration of Mrs. Mary Rowlandson* (1682). Clergymen also used captives' stories in sermons to unify the orthodox community. Puritan divine Cotton Mather elevated Hannah Duston (who had killed Indians to escape captivity in 1697) by comparing her to the biblical heroine Jael (whose murder of a Canaanite military commander helped to save Israel).

In 1692, the infamous episode of witchcraft hysteria at Salem Village in Massachusetts led to the imprisonment of over a hundred suspects and the execution of twenty people. Witchcraft was a capital crime in seventeenth-century New England, as it was in early modern Europe. In the colonies, most accusations occurred in New England where strong belief in God was accompanied by a fear of Satan's evil influences. In contrast to the outbreak at Salem (where tensions may have been heightened by the commercializing of the economy and its attendant inequities), colonial witchcraft cases typically involved only one suspect, and relatively few ended in an execution. Witches in theory could be of either sex, but approximately 78 percent of those accused were female. In Puritan teaching, women were not inherently more evil than men, but they were weaker physically and intellectually and, therefore, more vulnerable to assault by the Devil. Also linking women with witchcraft in colonists' minds were submerged assumptions derived from pre-Reformation European tradition: that women were malicious and envious, dissatisfied with their societal limitations, and likelier than men to collude with Satan to achieve power. Pagan forms of supernatural belief (in witchcraft and other superstitions) persisted among seventeenth-century New England colonists, coexisting with their Christian faith. But by 1701, official support for witchcraft prosecutions had ended in New England, and the Massachusetts authorities overturned all the Salem convictions.

The preponderance of New England white women were not Jaels slaying Indians on the frontier or accused witches but pious "daughters of Zion" filling the Congregational pews to worship. After 1660, women noticeably outnumbered men in Congregational church membership. Lamenting a decline from the founders' religious zeal, Puritan ministers warned that many New Englanders were seeking worldly, not heavenly, rewards. They concluded, however, that Eve's curse of childbearing had become women's blessing. Clergymen suggested that females had greater concern about their salvation than males because they risked death during childbirth. Additionally, church membership (identification as spiritually "elect") was one of the few public distinctions available to New England Puritan women. Religious teaching often elevated qualities traditionally thought to be female: transforming weakness into gentleness, obscurity into humility, changing worldly handicaps into spiritual strengths. Puritan ministerial literature, particularly funeral sermons, increasingly praised female church members, as clergymen sought to promote a vision of a godly New England. Their sermons in the late seventeenth and early eighteenth centuries improved the public image, if not the status, of women eulogized as obedient wives, devoted mothers, and charitable neighbors.

With the growth of trade and transatlantic shipping in the eighteenth century, residents of New England seaports became more cosmopolitan, exposed to other faiths. Enlightenment rationalism, advancing a scientific view of the natural world, helped to diminish fears of witchcraft. Passage of the Toleration Act (1689) in England had guaranteed freedom of worship for persecuted Protestant dissenters, such as the Quakers and the Baptists. Religious toleration was further mandated when Massachusetts received a new charter in 1691, placing the colony under a royal governor's authority and dictating suffrage based on property, not on Congregational church membership. Anglicanism, a dissenting religion in Puritan New England but powerful because of royal support, established a foothold in the region. Unlike Puritan, Quaker, and Baptist women, Anglican women had no background of dissent. Nor did Church of England membership rest on testimony of a conversion experience. The Anglican emphasis on ritual observance rather than inward transformation supported traditional roles and resulted in a moderate, rational piety. In the 1720s, Quakers, Baptists, and Anglicans gained the right to use church taxes to support their own congregations. Yet New England remained a region steeped in Puritan values: Church attendance was mandatory in eighteenth-century Massachusetts and Connecticut. The state-supported Congregational churches were organized to keep pace with population growth. By lobbying through their husbands, Puritan women often promoted the establishment of new meetinghouses in outlying areas. The founding of Harvard (1636) and Yale (1701) as clergy training grounds ensured a steady supply of ministers for the New England churches.

Quakerism, or the Society of Friends, was a minority religion on the periphery of Congregationalist New England, but in Rhode Island the Quakers were politically and economically powerful. Women continued to inhabit prominent roles in eighteenth-century Quakerism, providing important spiritual leadership and assisting in church discipline (Quakers held separate women's meetings for church business as counterparts to their men's meetings—an unprecedented inclusion of females in church government). Women's meetings supervised Quaker marriages and provided relief to the poor. Among the New England women who influenced the development of Quakerism in the region was Mary

(Coffin) Starbuck (1645–1718), known as "a wise, discreet woman, well read in the Scriptures," and "an oracle." The first Quaker meeting for worship on Nantucket was held weekly at Starbuck's house because of her "great reputation" among the islanders for knowledge in religious matters (Jones, 126). Nantucket Island became a Quaker stronghold.

New England Quakers were separated, to some extent, from their Puritan neighbors by their distinctive testimonies, including plain speech (usage of "thee" and "thou"), a simpler style of dress, and pacifism. In addition, Quaker meetings formally recognized particular women and men as ministers (those considered to be "called" by God to preach). The introspective orderliness of the "quietist" eighteenth-century ministers gradually replaced early Quaker missionaries' confrontational witnessing (interrupting church services or court sessions) and dramatic symbolism (appearing in sackcloth and ashes to urge repentance). The impact of Quaker women ministers such as Lydia Norton (fl.1706) of Hampton, New Hampshire, and Eliphal Harper (d. 1747) of Sandwich, Massachusetts, was not limited to their New England communities. Female Friends journeyed on religious visits approved by their meetings to wide-ranging destinations such as Pennsylvania, Barbados, and England, preaching to the general public as well as to Quakers.

In the 1730s and 1740s, a series of religious revivals known as "the Great Awakening" transformed the face of Puritan religion in New England. This spiritual revitalization temporarily generated a rise in lay power and new assertions of women's voices. The Awakening, an evangelical movement of intercolonial and transatlantic dimensions, was the most significant development in the spiritual life of eighteenth-century New England. Congregations divided into pro-revivalist New Lights and anti-revivalist Old Lights. New Separate churches arose, and the Baptist membership swelled with evangelical converts. Revivalist ministers of theologically diverse groups preached a "heart-centered" religion marked by emotional, dramatic sermons and public conversions. When famous English evangelist George Whitefield visited New England in 1740 at the zenith of the Great Awakening, his charismatic, extemporaneous preaching drew crowds as large as 30,000. New Englanders of all ranks—free blacks and slaves, as well as whites—were affected by the revivals. For the first time in the colonies, many African Americans were converted to Christianity.

The conversion experience, or "New Birth," quickened and intensified, was the goal of evangelicalism. Hannah Heaton, a Connecticut farmwife, recalled how she passed through terror, despair, resignation, and release into spiritual rebirth when she heard a fiery sermon in 1741. Sudden conversions under the influence of New Light clergymen's emotional preaching often resulted in listeners' ecstatic cries or physical convulsions. Prior to the Awakening, Puritan churchgoers had been expected to listen silently while ministers explained scripture and learnedly guided them through gradual, more rational conversions. But in the throes of New Birth, even women might interrupt church services by weeping, shrieking, fainting, or praising God, and revivalist ministers viewed these outbursts as evidence of the Holy Spirit's power. Old Light clergy, unconvinced that the Awakening was the work of God, asserted that the revivals were products of women's "passions." During the New England revivals, however, almost 50 percent of the new converts were male, signaling to New Lights that an extraordinary "great & general reformation" was occurring.

The communal quest for witness of the divine at revival meetings diminished distinctions of gender, wealth, and education, while emphasizing the division between converted and unconverted. New Light clergy criticized "unconverted" ministerial colleagues, asserting that formal theological education could not substitute for the religious authority of inner regeneration. This challenge to clerical tradition had the unintended effect of fracturing the boundaries between laity and clergy. Some evangelical converts felt empowered by the experience of grace to speak as lay exhorters. Lacking institutional authority, exhorters did not deliver formal sermons explaining biblical texts but publicly urged repentance.

The extent of female witnessing and exhorting during the revivals has been difficult to assess because of fragmentary and conflicting accounts. The Separates (radical New Lights who separated from the Congregational orthodoxy) allowed women to exhort but did not permit them to serve as pastors. Ebenezer Frothingham, a leading Separate minister, asserted that God had chosen some women and uneducated men to witness to the new outpouring of the Holy Spirit in America. Among the Baptists, women occasionally prayed aloud or exhorted in religious meetings. Congregationalist Bathsheba Kingsley (d. 1748) rode from town to town, warning people to repent of their sins, although her church did not allow women to exhort (or exercise authority over men). Kingsley ignored the disapproval of moderate New Light minister, Jonathan Edwards, whose account of local revivals, *A Faithful Narrative of the Surprising Work of God* (1737), had stirred interest in the Awakening. The Congregational church, consequently, barred Kingsley from receiving the Lord's Supper. Eighteenth-century female exhorters argued that they had transcended their gender by union with Christ, claiming that God had given them a special commission to speak his words. Certain that Mary Reed had been inspired by God, Reverend Nicholas Gilman of Durham, New Hampshire, read her prophetic utterances to his con-

gregation in 1742. He also consulted Reed for spiritual guidance.

The evangelical fervor of the Awakening temporarily loosened restrictions on women's religious speech. But gendered lines of authority within the churches were not ultimately changed. Reacting to revivalistic excesses, New Light and Old Light clergy increasingly shared concern about disorderly evangelical women, fearing that religious turmoil would lead to sexual improprieties. By the mid-1750s, even the Separates and the Baptists refused to permit women to pray aloud in church or exhort publicly. The Baptists disavowed their earlier egalitarianism in church governance in exchange for greater political power, evolving from a marginal sect into a respectable denomination during the eighteenth century.

Sarah Osborn (1714–1796), a Congregational church member, became an esteemed spiritual counselor through her evangelical network in Rhode Island but had to deny any pretension to clerical authority. Inspired by the preaching of George Whitefield and another revivalist, Gilbert Tennent, Osborn began a women's prayer group in 1741. A prodigious author, Osborn revealed doctrinal knowledge in gospel commentaries and evangelical tracts equal to that of many clergy. In 1766 and 1767, Osborn's residence in Newport became the center of a great religious revival. Hundreds of white women and men, free blacks, and slaves gathered at her home for weekly prayer meetings and religious conversation. A ministerial adviser objected to her "instruction" of men. Osborn claimed her activities did not usurp male leadership, believing that God had assigned her this work. She asserted, for instance, that the slaves had requested her assistance only because no minister was willing to serve them. Osborn's female circle of church members formed the backbone of the First Congregational Church. Although lacking voting rights, these women were instrumental in calling Samuel Hopkins, a protégé of Jonathan Edwards, to their pastorate in 1769.

Among New England Protestant groups, Quakers continued to be distinctive by allowing women's participation in the ministerial role. Friends had gained greater acceptance in New England society by the mid-eighteenth century, as a people of virtuous morals and respectable fortunes. Earlier, Quaker women ministers had been shouted down, at times, in public meetings by colonists insisting that the Apostle Paul had forbidden their preaching. But Enlightenment influences among the elite promoted religious toleration. In addition, a post-Awakening public familiarized with itinerancy was less respectful of educational qualifications and more sympathetic to a "calling" by the Holy Spirit. During her 1768–1769 tour of the American colonies, Rachel Wilson (1720–1775), an English Quaker minister, drew sizable audiences of men and women of various faiths.

When Wilson arrived in Boston, the *Gazette* (July 10, 1769) reported that she had preached to "a large audience and gained applause," displaying the benevolence characteristic of a "true christian." Ezra Stiles, a Congregational minister, later Yale College president, wrote in his diary that he had heard "an eminent Quaker Preacher," Rachel Wilson, deliver a sermon in Rhode Island. Despite his disapproval of female preaching within his own church, Stiles found Wilson to be "a pious sensible woman" (*The Literary Diary of Ezra Stiles*, 1:14).

On the eve of the American Revolution, the pacifist Quakers with their close ties to England increasingly were viewed with suspicion. The Anglicans also were perceived as Loyalists in New England in the 1770s. But Congregationalist, as well as Baptist, clergy offered powerful support to the revolutionaries, characterizing colonial resistance to Great Britain as a righteous cause. Women known as "Daughters of Liberty" newly participated in patriotic activities under church auspices; they wore homespun clothing, boycotting British goods. In 1774 a broadside titled "An Address to New England: written by a Daughter of Liberty" in Boston viewed the political crisis within the traditional framework of New England covenant theology, advocating repentance of sins in order to retain the Lord's protection.

Between 1620 and 1775, women inhabited a variety of roles, from "visible saint" to heretic, in New England Protestantism. Contained within Protestant tenets was the potential for greater female religious expression. Since women, as well as men, were part of a "priesthood of all believers," they were encouraged to read the Bible for themselves and participate in a direct, personal relationship to God. But traditional social hierarchies, such as the subjection of female to male, or laity to clergy, still were imposed in varying degrees in regional churches. In a culture that highly valued piety, however, women of spiritual achievement, who lacked explicit political and economic power, could wield moral authority and influence. At the close of the colonial period, most New England colonists continued to view their lives through a Protestant religious lens.

SOURCES: Marilyn J. Westerkamp, *Women and Religion in Early America, 1600–1850: The Puritan and Evangelical Traditions* (1999), and Laurel Thatcher Ulrich, *Good Wives: Image and Reality in the Lives of Women in Northern New England, 1650–1750* (1982), provide excellent overviews. The voluminous scholarship on Puritanism includes Edmund S. Morgan, *The Puritan Family: Religion and Domestic Relations in Seventeenth-Century New England* (1966), and Harry S. Stout, *The New England Soul: Preaching and Religious Culture in Colonial New England* (1986). For conversion narratives, see George Selement and Bruce C. Woolley, eds., *Thomas Shepard's "Confessions,"* in Colonial Society of Massachusetts, *Collections,* vol. 58 (1981). For Anne Hutchinson's trial, see David D. Hall, ed., *The Antinomian Controversy, 1636–1638,* 2nd ed. (1990), and Mary Beth Norton, *Founding Mothers and Fathers: Gendered Power and the Forming of American Society* (1996), chapter 8. See Joseph R. McElrath, Jr., and Allan P. Robb, eds., *The Complete Works of Anne Bradstreet* (1981), and Elizabeth Wade White, *Anne Bradstreet: "The Tenth Muse"* (1971), for the Puritan poet. On witchcraft in New England, see Carol F. Karlsen, *The Devil in the Shape of a Woman: Witchcraft in Colonial New England* (1987), and Elizabeth Reis, *Damned Women: Sinners and Witches in Puritan New England* (1997). For women and the Great Awakening, see Catherine A. Brekus, *Strangers and Pilgrims: Female Preaching in America, 1740–1845* (1998). On the dissenting sects, see Rebecca Larson, *Daughters of Light: Quaker Women Preaching and Prophesying in the Colonies and Abroad, 1700–1775* (1999); Rufus M. Jones, *The Quakers in the American Colonies* (1962); and Susan Juster, *Disorderly Women: Sexual Politics and Evangelicalism in Revolutionary New England* (1994).

PROTESTANT WOMEN IN THE MID-ATLANTIC COLONIES
Alison Duncan Hirsch

THE FIRST PROTESTANT women to come to the mid-Atlantic region were Walloons, French-speaking refugees from present-day Belgium who came to the Dutch colony of New Netherland in 1624. Within twenty years of this initial settlement of thirty families, New Netherland had become a cosmopolitan community that included Dutch, Swedes, Finns, Germans, English, and other Europeans, as well as enslaved Africans and Mohawk traders. Most of the Dutch colony's inhabitants were Protestant, although they did not always see their commonality as fellow Protestants, even in contrast to the small number of Catholics and Portuguese Jews, refugees from Holland's failed colony in Brazil. The Dutch and Walloon settlements along the Hudson and Delaware Rivers—in a widespread area that later became New York, New Jersey, Pennsylvania, and Delaware—were the beginning of the remarkable pattern of religious and ethnic diversity that marked the region and would come eventually to characterize North America as a whole.

The historical record is not nearly as diverse as the region's population was. Nearly everything written about women and religion in the colonial mid-Atlantic has been on the Quakers, not because they were the majority (they were that only briefly in Pennsylvania) but because they left the best records. With their own separate business meetings, Quaker women played a more public role in their sect than other women did. But women played a vital role in the early years of every

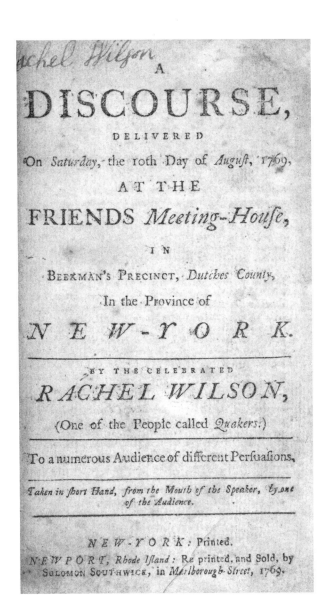

A DISCOURSE, DELIVERED On Saturday, the 10th Day of August, 1769, AT THE FRIENDS Meeting-Houſe, IN BEEKMAN'S PRECINCT, Dutches County, In the Province of NEW-YORK. BY THE CELEBRATED RACHEL WILSON, (One of the People called Quakers.) To a numerous Audience of different Perſuaſions, Taken in ſhort Hand, from the Mouth of the Speaker, by one of the Audience.

NEW-YORK: Printed. NEWPORT, Rhode Iſland: Re printed, and Sold, by SOLOMON SOUTHWICK, in Marlborough-Street, 1769.

Quaker Rachel Wilson, who toured the American colonies from 1768 to 1769, was a charismatic, revivalist preacher. Like Wilson, many Quaker women took active public roles. *Used by permission of the Houghton Library, Harvard University.*

congregation, even if the records are silent on their participation. Women were the majority of every congregation. They collected funds and donated money to build churches and hire ministers; as wives, servants, and tavern keepers, they fed, clothed, and housed ministers and traveling preachers; as mothers and schoolmistresses, they instructed children in their faith. They kept churches going through difficult times, and sometimes they were instrumental in splitting churches apart.

In 1643 a visiting Jesuit priest reported that the island of Manhattan had a population of "four or five hundred men of different sects and nations . . . men of eighteen different languages" (Jameson, 259–260). Undoubtedly a significant number of women, with a comparable degree of diversity, lived in the city, but most observers were interested only in the number of men, as a way of gauging military strength. This pattern of religious diversity held special challenges for women, particularly when it came to finding a husband and spouses for children among members of the same church. But the region also came to hold out opportunities for women who wanted to preach or perform other public roles in church, as well as for those who chose celibacy over marriage—a formal option that the Protestant Reformation had taken away when it closed the convents.

By law the only public religious services in New Netherland were those of the Dutch Reformed Church, but for the most part the colony's leaders tolerated other religions, as long as dissenters did not erect churches or synagogues. One exception was the Quakers, who created almost as much of a stir in New Amsterdam as they had in Boston. In 1657, Dorothy Waugh and Mary Wetherhead, both in their twenties, disembarked from an English ship and soon began quaking with religious fervor in the streets. They were arrested and banished. But Lutheran, Huguenot, and Mennonite women and men held private services of their own or simply attended the Dutch church without ever becoming members.

In 1638, Sweden established settlements in the Delaware Valley and soon built several Swedish Lutheran churches to serve a small population of Swedish and Finnish peasant families. After the initial years, when soldiers—young, unmarried men—were a significant proportion of the population, both New Netherland and New Sweden had populations where the sex ratios were relatively equal, and women soon came to be a majority of church membership. The surviving historic records of these churches contain little information on women's roles but only note their presence in the vital records of births, marriages, and deaths. Church records focus on ministers and the formal, public institutions of religious life, and women's roles lay elsewhere, at the more intimate intersection of family and church. Documents note details about specific women only when they caused trouble or hardship; often the only women mentioned were minister's wives. The Dutch reported with some disgust the "impious and scandalous habits" of Swedish minister Lars Lock, or Lokenius, who served in the Delaware Valley from 1647 to 1688 (Jameson, 396). He had remarried without first getting a divorce from his wife, whose name and fate are unknown. But the name of another Swedish woman appears often in the records: Armegat Printz, the daughter of New Sweden's governor, defied her husband and refused to return with him to Sweden. She created further controversy when she sold a piece of property to some Dutch newcomers, particularly since the property included the Swedish church and its bell.

When the Dutch conquered New Sweden in 1655, the Swedish churches and most of their congregations remained in what is now Delaware, Pennsylvania, and southern New Jersey. In 1664, the Dutch themselves surrendered to the English, and New Netherland became New York. By that time, the colony had 9,000 or 10,000 European inhabitants. Only about half were Dutch or Walloon; the rest were Swedish, Finnish, or German, as well as about 2,000 English, most of whom had migrated from New England. Most famous of the New Englanders was Anne Hutchinson, who moved to a rural area north of New Amsterdam after her husband's death; soon afterward, in 1643, she and several of her children were killed in an Indian raid.

A series of English royal grants resulted in the formation of new colonies besides New York: by the 1670s, East and West New Jersey (they merged in 1702), and Pennsylvania and Delaware, granted to William Penn in the 1680s. In addition to the Swedish Lutherans already living there, New Jersey attracted many English Quakers, Scottish Presbyterians, and other Protestants. New Jersey, like New York, became ethnically and religiously diverse by historic accident rather than by design. Pennsylvania was unique in its self-conscious creation of diversity: William Penn invited women and men of all faiths to settle and invest in his colony in the hope that together they would create a Quaker "Holy Experiment." In addition to Quakers from England, Wales, Scotland, and Ireland, Penn's promotional literature brought Baptists and Anglicans from England, Huguenots from France, Presbyterians from Scotland and Ireland, German Lutheran and Reformed Church members, and a host of German, Swiss, and Dutch Pietist and Anabaptist sectarians: Mennonites, Amish, Brethren (Dunkers), Schwenkfelders, and Moravians. Catholics and Jews found greater civil liberties in Pennsylvania than anywhere else in the Atlantic world. This tolerant environment also fostered the development of new religious communities, including ones that exalted celibacy as a way of life for both women and men. Pennsylvania offered women a wide variety of ways, both usual and unusual, of expressing their faith.

In the Society of Friends (Quakers), women had their own formal institutions, women's meetings whose clerks kept minutes and account books. Quaker women left diaries, autobiographies, and other writings that were preserved by their meetings or descendants. Quakerism had grown out of the religious ferment of England's Civil War. In the 1650s, individual "Seekers" came together in the spirit of the early Christians, with a priest-

hood of all believers, the radical notion of spiritual equality among all believers, women and men. Critical to the development of the sect in England was the support of Margaret Fell, wife of a prominent Lancashire judge, who supplied traveling Quaker "ministers"—women as well as men—with food, lodging, and money. In 1666 she published a tract defending *Womens Speaking* in public on religious matters; early Quaker women, moved to speak in churches and public places, faced ridicule and persecution everywhere they traveled. Finally, Pennsylvania offered them an opportunity to speak without fear, although some chose to travel to other colonies and abroad in order to preach in hostile environments. Jane Fenn Hoskens (b. 1694) and Elizabeth Ashbridge (d. 1755) both came to Pennsylvania as indentured servants; raised in the Church of England, they joined the Society of Friends when its members literally befriended them. Hoskens became a schoolmistress and a public minister when she was still in her twenties. Traveling in the ministry required permission of the men's as well as the women's meeting, and the meeting paid her travel expenses on several trips throughout the English Atlantic world, including Ireland, Barbados, and most of the mainland colonies. She evidently was a charismatic speaker, but she took no personal credit, seeing herself as a conduit for God's message. After she spoke, she wrote, "The doctrine of truth descended as a small rain upon the tender grass, whereby many were refreshed, and a living greenness appeared" (Harris, 210). Ashbridge joined the ministry later in life and died while on a visit to Ireland, after patiently enduring "much bodily hardship in Traveling" and "much spiritual exercise in mind" (W. Andrews, 172).

The first Germans to arrive in Pennsylvania were Mennonite families seeking freedom from persecution; they settled in Germantown, just outside Philadelphia, in 1683. German Anabaptists shared much of the Quakers' ideology—pacifism, refusal to swear oaths, and the spiritual equality of believers—but their ideas about women were quite different. Mennonites, Amish, and Schwenkfelders all derived their church names from their male founders, and the official name of the Dunkers, the Brethren, betrayed that sect's male bias. Following the admonition of Paul, these German sectarians held that women should not speak in church, or anywhere else in public, for that matter. But women were essential members, since the family was the center of religious life. For the Amish, who never built churches, their houses were their meeting places, giving women even greater centrality in worship.

Dutch and German Pietists with more radical ideas about women began arriving in 1662, when Dutch Mennonites established a short-lived religious, noncelibate community on Delaware Bay (1662–1664). Bohemia

Manor, on the Upper Chesapeake, an ascetic, celibate community, had a longer life (1684–1728) as a colony of the Dutch-based Labadist society. These followers of the ex-Jesuit mystic Jean de Labadie had earlier found protection under Elizabeth, Princess Palatine of the Rhine, who also supported the Quakers. In 1694 a small group of men and women under the leadership of mystic Johannes Kelpius established a community on the outskirts of Germantown. Known as the Society of the Woman in the Wilderness—after the biblical woman who ran into the wilderness to await her bridegroom, Christ (Revelation 12)—they practiced celibacy and extreme abstemiousness. The community lasted less than twenty years, but, like Bohemia Manor, it provided ideas and members for the more enduring Ephrata community (1733–1796) in rural Pennsylvania, founded by the charismatic Conrad Beissel. In the mid-1720s, two sisters, Anna and Maria Eicher, left home to follow Beissel into his Lancaster County retreat. To avoid scandalous rumors of free love, his male companions built a separate cabin for the women, making them the first of his female followers to adopt the solitary life. At least two married women, Maria Christina Sauer and Maria Hanselmann, left their husbands to be "rebaptized in virginity." Another married woman, former Quaker Christina Höhn, secretly used her household money to support Beissel: "She clothed him anew," the records say (Alderfer, 46). She and other women influenced the entire group to adopt the Quaker plain style of clothing. By the 1730s, the group was organized into three "orders": married Householders, the Brotherhood of the Angels, and the Spiritual Virgins. In 1735, construction began on the first communal building, with cells on the first floor for men and on the third floor for women. The second floor contained rooms for meetings and love feasts and foot washing, rituals modeled after those of the early Christians. (Love feasts were simple fellowship meals, but outsiders suspected a sexual component.) Ephrata's women, both married and celibate, were responsible for much of the economic production of the community; they also wrote many hymns and created most of the illuminated manuscripts (*fraktur*) that merged art, poetry, and music into a holistic spiritual experience.

Throughout the colonial period, the majority of German immigrants to the region were Lutherans and Reformed Church members who dismissed the radicalism of the sectarians but shared similar ideas about women's place in the church. In the 1740s, another German group, the Moravians, arrived in Pennsylvania with very different ideas. The Moravians were the only other group from the period whose women left anywhere near the written record of Quaker women. Moravian women kept spiritual autobiographies that have been preserved by the church. Like Quakers, Moravian women spoke in public, held their own meetings separate from the men in their congregations, and handled the finances and charitable activities of their separate all-female organizations, or "choirs."

Even among the more radical sects in the mid-Atlantic region, public activity by women was the exception rather than the rule. Most sectarian women had more in common with their counterparts in the older denominations than either group would have liked to admit. As women, they shared common experiences throughout their life cycle, from birth through marriage and childbirth, possibly widowhood, and death. The first generation also shared the experience of immigration.

Immigration

Women in the first generation of immigrants rarely recorded their experiences; they were generally too busy with the daily tasks of building a life in a new world. Many women, like men, came to the mid-Atlantic colonies for religious reasons, although economic motivations also played a part in the decision to leave home for a dangerous ocean voyage and an unknown future. Quakers required that wives consent to emigrate: Husband and wife had to apply separately to their original men's and women's meetings for a certificate of clearness to take with them to their new meeting. Some women made the decision to emigrate alone. Elizabeth Haddon, a Quaker, felt a calling to manage her family's estate in what became Haddonfield, New Jersey, and was one of the few single women to come without her family. In 1685, Marie Ferree, a Huguenot, migrated with her family to the Palatinate, where her husband died. In about 1709, she immigrated to London and then to Esopus (now Kingston), New York, before finally settling in rural Pennsylvania. Barbara Yoder became the founder of the first Amish family in America when she arrived in Philadelphia in 1714 with her nine children; her husband had died at sea. Many other women undoubtedly made the trip against their will, forced to follow husbands, fathers, or brothers across the Atlantic. Others were kidnapped: African women to be sold as slaves and European women to be sold into servitude until the cost of their voyage was paid.

The voyage was difficult for women, especially if they were pregnant at the time. Mary Jemison, later renowned as the White Woman of the Seneca, remembered little about her childhood, but she did remember stories of how she was born at sea—a vivid memory for her Presbyterian mother. Women were thankful if they and their families arrived, as Susannah Wright (1697–1784) put it, "with all our lives and healths which with all other mercys I hope we shall never forget" (ms. letter to W. Crowdson, 1714, FLL). This young Quaker woman, only seventeen when she immigrated with her parents and younger sister, found her new land to be "the pleasantest as can be imagined." Older women like Hannah Penn (1671–1726) thought Pennsylvania a "desolate land" (Dunn and Dunn, 4:36); her voyage from England had taken nearly three months, and she gave birth to her first child a month after her arrival.

Birth, Childhood, and Education

From birth to death, the religious aspect of life was a highly visible aspect of daily life for women. Death in childbirth was a fear shared by women throughout the Atlantic world, and part of the responsibility of midwives was to pray for the life and health of mother and child. Susanna Miller, or Mueller (1756–1815), a German Lutheran midwife in rural Lancaster County, Pennsylvania, kept a record of the 1,667 infants whose births she attended; alongside the stark data of each birth—the date, the number of children born (single or twin birth), the father's name, and her fee—she copied verses from the Bible and German hymnals.

For Lutherans, Anglicans, Huguenots, and Reformed, infant baptism marked the child's formal initiation into the church. When frontier life or wartime prevented ministers from coming to perform baptisms, mothers brought their infants long distances to receive the rite. Thomas Barton, the pastor of Anglican St. James' Church in Lancaster, told of baptizing thirty or more infants a day during the Revolution, when Pennsylvania's military rule prohibited Loyalist men like him from traveling outside their own county. He went to the county line "where I was met by the women (who are not subject to the penalties of the law) with their young ones to be catechized and their infants to be christened" (Klein and Diller, 55). From 1776 to 1778, he reported, he baptized a total of 347 children and 23 adult converts. Black parents too sought baptism for their children, not always successfully. A Dutch minister reported in 1664 that "the Negroes occasionally request that we should baptize their children," but he refused because of "their lack of knowledge and faith" and their "worldly and perverse aim" of gaining freedom for their children. Other parents were just as adamant about not having their children baptized; this was true of Anabaptists, who believed in adult baptism, and sectarians like the Quakers and Mennonites, who did away with the rite altogether. In Hempstead, Long Island, whose residents were Reformed, Presbyterian, and "Independents," there was only one minister, a Presbyterian. Everyone attended his services, "but when he began to baptize the children of parents who are not members of the church, they rushed out of the church" (Jameson, 297).

Girls as well as boys growing up in Protestant households received their earliest education primarily from their mothers. They learned to read the Bible, and they learned by example as well as reading what the ideal behavior for a woman was. Ministers frequently credited their mothers with instilling religious faith in them. German Reformed pastor Philip William Otterbein paid tribute to his mother for her spiritual guidance. Wilhelmina Henrietta Otterbein of Dillenburg (now Weisbaden, Germany) became a widow when her eldest son was twenty; all six of her surviving sons became Reformed ministers, and her only surviving daughter married a minister. Henrietta gave her blessing when, in 1752, Philip decided to travel to America, where he served in a succession of churches in Pennsylvania and Maryland and became a leading figure in the revival movement that developed into the Church of the United Brethren in Christ.

Older children attended catechism classes, usually after Sunday church services, to prepare them for full-fledged membership in their parents' church. The Dutch Reformed Church in New York had forty-four boys and twenty-one girls, but in other churches the sex ratio was often reversed, with more girls than boys. The churches also operated primary schools for older children. In 1741, Benigna Zinzendorf, daughter of the Moravian leader, then just sixteen years old herself, opened a school for girls in Germantown, northwest of Philadelphia, where she soon had twenty-five students; in 1749, she began another school in Bethlehem that became a well-respected boarding school, with classes in religion, reading and writing in both English and German, and sewing. Sewing instruction incorporated religious ideals, as young girls practiced their skills on samplers with poems like these from Leah Gallagher's sewing school in Pennsylvania: "Martha Taylor is my name/Lancaster is my Habitation/Octorara is my dwelling place/& christ is my Salvation" (Ring, 411).

Marriage

In 1696, English Quaker Hannah Callowhill told her suitor, William Penn, that she had planned to live her life "to the Lord" as her husband. Perhaps she had planned on traveling in the ministry or serving as a leader of the women's meeting in her native Bristol, England. Penn assured her that in accepting his proposal "thou thus marryest him in me" (Dunn and Dunn, 3:428), referring to the in-dwelling spirit of the Lord that members of the Society of Friends believed was within each person. The Penns did marry a few months later, and she traveled with him to Pennsylvania in 1699. Thereafter, like most other Protestant women, her religious dedication most often took the form of service to husband and children. That service expanded after her husband's death (in 1718) to managing Pennsylvania's government as its "proprietress" until her children came of age. In this role, Hannah Penn found her spiritual mission in protecting the rights of the colony's Quakers against incursions by the crown and Anglican clerics.

After her non-Quaker husband's death, Margaret Fell married George Fox, who had become the most prominent Quaker leader. By that time, 1669, Quakers had established their own marriage procedures: The bride and groom appeared before the women's and men's meetings, respectively, to ask for approval, and the wedding ceremony took place at a regular meeting for worship, with no minister but an audience of fellow believers, who all signed the marriage certificate after the service. American Quakers continued this practice, which gave women an unparalleled public role in marriage ceremonies.

In 1762, Philip Otterbein married Susanna LeRoy, or King (c. 1736–1768), the daughter of French Huguenots who had settled in 1752 at Tulpehocken, Pennsylvania, where the thirty-five-year-old minister was serving two Reformed churches. Like most ministers' wives, she left little trace in the written record. Besides the record of her marriage at the age of twenty-six and her death six years later—as well as the noticeable absence of birth records for any children—we know only that she came into a substantial inheritance after the death of several male relatives. In addition to bringing their household labor into marriage, some women brought economic resources that made life more comfortable for poorly paid clergymen.

Susanna LeRoy also illustrates one way that women in smaller religious and ethnic groups dealt with the problem of finding a marriage partner: They married men of different national origins who were fellow Protestants in churches with tenets similar to their own. Marriage in a religiously and ethnically diverse society presented particular problems for women more than men, since marriage so totally defined a woman's life. In the 1690s, more than 40 percent of New York City's French Huguenots married English or Dutch spouses. In the first decades after the English conquest of New Amsterdam, when English women were scarce, many English and Scottish men married Dutch women and joined the Dutch Reformed Church.

Marriage across ethnic and denominational lines created a dilemma when children were born: Where would they be baptized and receive catechism? Often, mothers were apparently able to make the final decision. Among the forty-four boys and twenty-one girls in Sunday evening catechism class at New York's Dutch Reformed Church were four children of English fathers and Dutch mothers, all church members. In the city's French church, 20 percent of all baptisms were the children of interdenominational marriages.

Some women avoided marriage entirely, either by personal choice or by joining radical communitarian societies. Quaker women like Susannah Wright, Bathsheba

Bowers (c. 1672–1718), and Hannah Griffitts (1727–1817) chose the single life. Wright and Griffitts were part of a circle of friends who shared their thoughts through letters and poetry. Wright praised her niece, Elizabeth Norris, for rejecting marriage; she was a woman whom "no Seducing Tales Can gain/To yield obedience or to wear the Chain/But set a Queen & in your freedom reign" (Blecki and Wulf, 33). Bathsheba Bowers lived alternately as a recluse and as a public preacher, after she overcame an initial "fear of preaching" that "fiercely invaded me." Her home in Philadelphia was a small house furnished "with books, a Table [and] a cup," and it was "as if she lived in a Cave under Ground or on the top of a high mountain." There she wrote one of the earliest spiritual autobiographies by a woman published in America (1709), *An Alarm Sounded to Prepare the Inhabitants of the World to Meet the Lord in the Way of His Judgements* (Zweizig, 65, 67, 73).

Death

Protestant women prepared for death by praying, writing memoirs, leaving instructions for their funerals, and providing for the care of younger children. A Lutheran woman, Anna Margareth Meytzinger, asked that Henry Muhlenberg preach her funeral sermon, bury her in the graveyard of New Providence Church in rural Pennsylvania, and write her parents in the Palatinate to tell them of her death. She specified the three hymns that she wanted sung at her funeral. A few days after Meytzinger's demise, a fellow congregant, Regina Dober, died at age eighty-two. "She yearned for a blessed death," wrote Muhlenberg, "and had long since written down her funeral text." The pastor followed both women's instructions (Muhlenberg, 1:265–267).

When younger women lay dying, their primary concern was for the spiritual as well as physical care of their minor children. After Samuel Mueller left home during the Revolution, his Amish wife became fatally ill. According to family legend, on her deathbed she told friends: "I want my children reared in Christian homes—among a plain people" (Peachey, 30). Even young girls prepared themselves for death. In 1714, as Quaker Hannah Hill, Jr., eleven years old, lay dying in Philadelphia, her family recorded her "sayings" and later published them with a narrative of her illness and death as *A Legacy for Children*. "O Almighty God!" she called out. "Prepare me for thy Kingdom of Glory. I do freely Forgive all, and have nothing in my Heart but Love, to both White and Black." She exhorted her sister to be a faithful Quaker: "Dear Sister! My desires are, that thou mayest Fear God; be Dutifull to thy Parents, Love Truth; Keep to Meetings, and be an Example of Plainness" (Harris, 128–129).

Many women kept diaries of their spiritual progress

and, as they aged, wrote memoirs. Moravians formalized the process, with a surviving church member adding an account of the memoirist's final illness and death before the document was read aloud and distributed. Anna Rosina Anders (1727–1803) recalled attending Count Zinzendorf's children's meetings in Germany: "[T]hough I did not always understand him, yet it made an impression on my heart and I felt a desire to be happy." She went on to lead the Single Sisters' Choir in Bethlehem from 1748 to 1764 and later traveled to England, where she died. Before Martha Büninger (1723–1773) died, her husband added his comments to the life story of "my dear Martha," who had served with him at the Gnadenhütten Indian mission, where he functioned as "teacher and steward" and she, in his words, as "steward and cook" (Faull, 5, 31). They were among the few survivors in the 1755 massacre of the Moravian Indian community by non-Christian Indians.

Women customarily prepared the deceased for burial. As the colonial population grew in cities like Philadelphia and New York, women advertised their services to families of the deceased. Lydia Darragh, a Quaker, announced in the *Pennsylvania Gazette* that she would "make Grave-Clothes, and lay out the Dead, in the Neatest Manner" (quoted in *Notable American Women,* 1: 434). Women chose their own burial sites, often influencing the rest of their families. Deborah Franklin (1707–1774), a lifelong congregant of Christ Church, Philadelphia's first Anglican Church, was buried in its graveyard, while her husband was away in England, serving as an agent for the colonies. Benjamin Franklin never became a church member and, in fact, supported a number of the city's churches, but when he died nearly twenty years later, his grave was beside hers. Mary Alexander (1693–1760), a New York shopkeeper raised in the Dutch Reformed Church, was buried next to her husband in a vault at Trinity Church (Anglican). Circumstances forced other women to be buried alone. Mary Brant, the Mohawk companion of British Indian agent Sir William Johnson, fled to Canada during the Revolution and was buried at an Anglican church there. After Sir William's death, she could not claim the rights of a wife—including the right to be buried with him— because she had never been married in a church ceremony.

Women's Role in Schisms and Church Scandals

Although women could not vote in most churches, they were an important factor in the disputes and schisms that rocked nearly every denomination and congregation at some point during the colonial period. In 1691, women were in the thick of the controversy when Pennsylvania Quakers split over the ideas of George Keith, a Scottish Quaker and schoolmaster at Friends' School in Philadelphia. Keith had proposed a formal confession of faith for Quakers, which was voted down, and he urged Friends to free their slaves and to refrain from holding political office to avoid being complicit in supporting military activities. By 1692, Keith and his supporters were holding their own meetings, calling themselves "Christian Quakers," and other Friends had left the Society to join Anglicans, Presbyterians, or other churches. A contemporary list of the dissidents shows that women comprised nearly two-thirds of Keithians in Philadelphia, somewhat less in the surrounding towns.

In other schisms, women fought to preserve the status quo. In the 1780s, the Baptist minister in Pittsgrove, Salem County, New Jersey, introduced new ideas about the universal salvation guaranteed by an all-loving God. Some church members left for other churches, some remained in the now-Universalist church (later part of the Unitarian Universalist Association), but a group of thirteen women continued to meet separately, in homes or outdoors whenever itinerant preachers came to town. After ten years, the women regained the meetinghouse, and the congregation was restored to its Baptist origins.

In the case of the Ephrata Cloister, women were responsible for the preservation of the entire community when it was rent with conflict in its first decade. In the early 1740s, brothers Samuel and Israel Eckerling, leaders of the single men, set up a system of mills to make the community financially profitable—a goal clearly at odds with the community's ideals of poverty and charity. Ephrata was soon producing a variety of products for a large regional market: grains, logs, paper, printers' ink, textiles, tanned leather, shoes, and bookbindings. The Eckerlings overreached when they tried to pull the Householders into the communal economy. These married couples, who owned nearby farms, came to live in a new building, Hebron, and adopted the celibate life, with men and women living in separate sides of the building; they were to relinquish their farmlands to the community. On arrival, they were rebaptized and received letters of divorce in a mass divorce proceeding that flew in the face of civil authority.

The Hebron experiment lasted less than a year. The women in particular soon wanted to return to their farms, where they had left their children in charge of the farmwork. Eventually, the Householders went home, and the community burned all the letters of divorce. Maria Eicher and the Sisterhood were the deciding factor in the differences between Conrad Beissel and the Eckerling brothers, with the women opting for Beissel. The Sisters renamed themselves the Spiritual Order of the Roses of Saron and occupied the now-deserted building, which was renamed Saron.

Women could bring a minister down and cause his

ouster with accusations of misbehavior, especially sexual impropriety. In 1715, Francis Phillips of Philadelphia's Christ Church faced accusations that he had propositioned a female servant and had slandered three prominent women in his congregation (he boasted that he had slept with them). The authorities arrested him late one Saturday night, and the congregation found the church doors locked when they arrived for services on Sunday. A few hundred men marched to demand his release, and the servant recanted (she said that her master, the Anglican minister in Chester, Pennsylvania, had put her up to it), but Phillips was found guilty of slander and fined. The minister assembled an impressive list of supporters, including twelve women in his congregation, and the governor pardoned him. The bishop of London, who was responsible for appointing colonial priests, was less forgiving and removed him. The fact that one of Phillips's more prominent female accusers was related to the bishop probably did not help him.

In 1744, Margareta Christiaan, a black woman, accused the Lutheran pastor in Loonenburg (now Athens), New York, of getting her pregnant. Other scandals involving sexual misconduct brought down two Presbyterian ministers in Philadelphia: Samuel Eakin, whose child was born too soon after his wedding, and Jedediah Andrews, accused of "scandalous conduct with one Mary Holly, a married woman of an infamous character." He had served in the ministry for forty-nine years, but testimony by three women destroyed his career, and he died a year later. Another Presbyterian minister in Donegal, Pennsylvania, was accused of "unchaste behaviour" with a woman (Kocher, 15, 23–24). Even though witnesses denounced his female accuser for using profanity and practicing witchcraft, he was driven from office. The Swedish Lutheran minister of Raccoon, New Jersey, was accused of illicit relations with Katharine Persson; he drowned before the case came to trial. Rumors of scandalous behavior swirled continuously around Conrad Beissel, the charismatic founder of Ephrata, and around the love feasts there and in Bethlehem. Early Moravians married by lot and believed that sex within marriage was a "service to God," not just for the sake of procreation but also because it enabled believers to achieve the "innermost connection" with each other and the church (Faull, 30). This elevation of sex to the level of a religious ritual was highly suspect to critics.

The revivals of the Great Awakening created schisms in many mid-Atlantic colonial churches; it also created tensions between daughters and parents, wives and husbands. Women were on both sides of the disputes between Old Side and New Side Presbyterians and Old Light and New Light Congregationalists; while ministers engaged in heady theological disputes, women voted with their feet, often choosing more enthusiastic, evangelical preachers over traditionalists. Daughters and

wives left their family churches to join the Moravians, the Baptists, and the newly emerging Methodist movement. The region's awakening began in 1729 among the Scots-Irish and Dutch of New Jersey, where women were two-thirds of the new church members; most were under twenty-five and unmarried. Older women sought new spiritual inspiration as well. In the 1760s, Mary Cooper (1714–1778) of Oyster Bay, Long Island, visited Quaker, Anglican, Baptist, and New Light meetings. Raised in the Church of England, she had married a former Quaker-turned-Anglican when she was only fourteen. At age fifty-four, she became a member of the town's New Light Baptist Church (Congregationalists who practiced adult baptism), where her sister, Sarah Townsend (1719–1780), was a prominent member. In 1773, when the minister (Townsend's son-in-law) suggested merging with a traditional church, Townsend ran out of the meeting shouting, "Babylon! Babylon!" followed by a crowd of fellow dissidents. After months of contention, the congregation split, and Mary Cooper wrote that attendance fell sharply at meetings: "Not a horse or carrgge thare and a very few peopel thare. Alas, oh Lorde, how changed is the face of the church. How dissolate my soul is, rent with sorrow" (Cooper, xi, 69).

Other women were able to effect change that they viewed as positive. Barbara Heck (1734–1804), the traditional "Mother of American Methodism," was born in Ireland, the daughter of German parents who were refugees from the Palatinate. She and her relatives were among the first Methodists in Ireland, and in 1760 she immigrated to New York with her husband and others. They practiced their faith quietly until 1766, when Heck visited friends and family who were playing cards. She threw the cards into the fireplace and exhorted her cousin, Philip Embury, to once again begin serving as a lay preacher as he had in Ireland. She and her family led the campaign to build the first Wesley Chapel on John Street in Manhattan.

Toward the end of the eighteenth century, two women established new religious communities in rural, western New York, after facing a hostile environment in New England and coastal cities. The more famous is Ann Lee (1736–1784) because her Shaker communities became the most enduring American religious communities, in spite of long-lasting antagonism toward the group. Jemima Wilkinson (1752–1819), who called herself the Public Universal Friend, was more popular at first, but her movement and her community, New Jerusalem, disintegrated after her death. Wilkinson wore a long garment similar to a clerical robe, sometimes white or purple instead of the traditional black of male clergy. She discarded the use of gender pronouns, and her followers, both men and women, never referred to her as "she" but only by her adopted title, sometimes abbreviated as "P.U.F." or simply "the Friend." Women were among her critics and perhaps even among the mob that stoned her Philadelphia lodgings in 1787. Quaker men called her "an artful and designing woman"; Elizabeth Drinker commented that she and her "Deciples" had "occasioned much talk in this City . . . — her Dress and Behaviour, remarkable" (Crane, 1:404).

Both Lee and Wilkinson adopted celibacy, although Wilkinson was willing to have married as well as single "disciples." At the end of the eighteenth century, Shakers and Universal Friends embodied some of the most unusual possibilities for women to "live to the Lord" in the American region that had provided the greatest religious toleration and diversity for nearly 200 years.

SOURCES: Manuscript sources are in repositories such as the New York Historical Society, the Historical Society of Pennsylvania (Philadelphia), the Lancaster County Historical Society (LCHS), the Moravian Archives (Bethlehem, PA), the Quaker Library (Haverford College), Friends' Historical Library (Swarthmore College), and the Library of the Society of Friends, London (FLL). Modern editions of women's writings are *The Diary of Elizabeth Drinker,* ed. Elaine Forman Crane (1991); Margaret Hope Bacon, *"Wilt Thou Go on My Errand?" Journals of Three Eighteenth-Century Quaker Women Ministers* (1994); the diary of Elizabeth Ashbridge in William Andrews, *Journeys in New Worlds* (1990); Catherine La Courreye Blecki and Karin A. Wulf, *Milcah Martha Moore's Book: A Commonplace Book from Revolutionary America* (1997); Mary Cooper, *The Diary of Mary Cooper: Life on a Long Island Farm, 1768–1773* (1981); Katherine M. Faull, *Moravian Women's Memoirs: Their Related Lives, 1750–1820* (1997); and Sharon M. Harris, *American Women Writers to 1800* (1996). Tidbits of information on women are in editions like William Stevens Perry, *Historical Collections Relating to the American Colonial Church,* vol. 2, *Pennsylvania* (1871); J. William Frost, *The Keithian Controversy in Early Pennsylvania* (1980); and J. Franklin Jameson, ed., *Narratives of New Netherland, 1609–1664* (1909). Editions of men's papers include some material on women; see Richard S. Dunn and Mary Maples Dunn, eds., *The Papers of William Penn,* 3 vols. (1981–1986), and Henry Muhlenberg, *The Journals of Henry Melchior Muhlenberg,* trans. Theodore G. Tappert and John W. Doberstein (1942). For women's samplers, see Betty Ring, *Girlhood Embroidery: American Samplers & Pictorial Needlework, 1650–1850* (1993). Monographs include Catherine A. Breckus, *Strangers and Pilgrims: Female Preaching in America, 1740–1845* (1998); Rebecca Larson, *Daughters of Light: Quaker Women Preaching and Prophesying in the Colonies and Abroad, 1700–1775* (1999); E. G. Alderfer, *The Ephrata Commune: An Early American Counterculture* (1985); Dee E. Andrews, *The Methodists and Revolutionary America, 1760–1800: The Shaping of an Evangelical Culture* (2000); Joyce D. Goodfriend, *Before the Melting Pot: Society and Culture in Colonial New York, 1664–1730* (1992); and Patricia Bonomi, *Under the Cope of Heaven: Religion, Society, and Politics in Colonial America* (1986). Church histories include Samuel W. Peachey, *Amish of Kishacoquillas Valley, Mifflin County, Pennsylvania* (c. 1930); H.M.J. Klein and William F. Diller, *The History of St. James' Church* (1944); and Donald Ruth Kocher, *The Mother of Us All: First Presbyterian Church in Philadelphia, 1698–1998*

(1998). Important articles are Mary Maples Dunn, "Saints and Sisters: Congregational and Quaker Women in the Early Colonial Period," *American Quarterly* 30 (1978): 582–601; Jean Soderlund, "Women's Authority in Pennsylvania and New Jersey Quaker Meetings, 1680–1760," *WMQ,* 3d ser. 44 (1987): 722–749; Jane T. Merritt, "Cultural Encounters along a Gender Frontier: Mahican, Delaware, and German Women in Eighteenth-Century Pennsylvania," *Pennsylvania History* 67 (2000): 502–531; Beverly Prior Smaby, "Forming the Single Sisters' Choir in Bethlehem," *Transactions of the Moravian Historical Society* 28 (1994): 1–14; Ann Kirschner, "From Hebron to Saron: The Religious Transformation of an Ephrata Convent," *Winterthur Portfolio* 32.1 (1997): 39–63; and Janet Moore Lindman, "Wise Virgins and Pious Mothers: Spiritual Community among Baptist Women of the Delaware Valley," in *Women and Freedom in Early America,* ed. Larry D. Eldridge, (1997), 133. Articles on individual women include Alison Duncan Hirsch, "A Tale of Two Wives: Gulielma and Hannah Penn," *Pennsylvania History* 61 (1994): 429–456; Graham Russell Hodges, "The Pastor and the Prostitute: Sexual Power among African Americans and Germans in Colonial New York," in *Sex, Love, Race,* ed. Martha Hodes (2000); and Suzanne M. Zweizig, "Bathsheba Bowers (c. 1672–1718)," *Legacy* (Pennsylvania State University) 11.1 (1994): 65–73.

SOUTHERN COLONIAL PROTESTANT WOMEN
Cynthia Lynn Lyerly

THE FIRST PERMANENT Protestant colony in North America was Virginia, settled in 1607. Throughout the seventeenth century, both black and white women lived in a predominantly male world. In the 1630s, men outnumbered women by six to one in the Chesapeake, and even by the century's end, women were outnumbered in the tobacco colonies by three to two. Equally important, over half the women who immigrated to the southern colonies came as indentured servants, their labor bound to a master for an average of three to five years. Although the shortage of white women meant that many could marry men of higher status and wealth than themselves, the mortality rates also meant that half of all marriages ended within seven years by one spouse's death. Only 15 percent of all twenty-year-old women would reach the age of sixty, and two-thirds of all children lost one parent before they turned eighteen. Infant mortality was alarmingly high as well, with one-quarter to one-half of all children dying in their first year of life. Toward the end of the century, the tobacco colonies became less deadly, and white southerners could expect their marriages to last between eighteen and twenty years before one spouse died, which meant women bore more children, more of whom would live to adulthood. The imbalanced sex ratio and appallingly high mortality rates in the seventeenth-century South helped contribute to a rough and unstable environment. All southerners knew death personally, and mothers frequently faced the agony of burying their infants and toddlers.

Slavery came to the first American colony in 1619 when in exchange for supplies a Dutch ship captain traded twenty slaves to merchants in Jamestown, Virginia. Slaves constituted a small percentage of the unfree labor force until the 1660s, and it is unclear exactly when white Virginians began to assume that slaves were bound to serve their masters for life. What is clear is that the first law that singled out people of African descent for discriminatory treatment was aimed at women. In 1643, the Virginia legislature levied a tax on all male laborers sixteen and older and included a tax on "negro women" of the same age. White women, even indentured servants, were not "tithables"; "negro women" were. In 1662 the legislature further wrote slavery into law by declaring that a child would inherit the legal status of its mother. Thus children of free men and enslaved women would be slaves, including the children resulting from a master's sexual abuse of his bondwoman. The English had long believed that it was morally wrong to hold other Christians as slaves, so in 1667, the Virginia legislature declared that Christian baptism would not affect a slave's status; after this, white Christians could legally hold black Christians as slaves for life.

For many reasons, tobacco planters began preferring African slaves to white indentured servants in the last quarter of the seventeenth century. Although the tobacco colonies became large-scale slave societies gradually, slavery came to South Carolina already fully grown, as that colony was founded by Barbados whites who brought their slaves from the Caribbean to the North American mainland. By the beginning of the eighteenth century, slavery was entrenched in the southern colonies. Georgia was the only exception, for slavery was prohibited in the colony from its founding in 1733 until 1749. Slavery's impact on the social, political, and religious development of the southern colonies cannot be overemphasized.

The Church of England

For most southern colonists before the Great Awakening of the 1740s, the Church of England was their

Young Moravian Girl by John Valentine Hardt. The Moravians offer a vivid example of the range of women's religious experiences in the colonial South. Women could be ordained as deaconesses. Ministers and their wives were both considered *Arbeiteren*, workers for the Lord. The *Saal Dieneren*, church ushers and elders, were composed of men and women who were respected by their peers. *Courtesy of the Smithsonian Art Museum.*

spiritual home as well as the official church. By the laws of the colonies, church attendance was mandatory, only Anglican ministers could solemnize a marriage, and dissenters were taxed for the support of the Anglican clergy and establishment. The church not only baptized its members' children and attended to their religious needs but also served as a moral court and a social service agency. The vestrymen, composed of twelve planters, punished immorality of various kinds, from fining people who did not attend services to punishing couples accused of fornication. The latter happened in 1649 to William Watts, a white man, and Mary, a black servant, who were forced to stand in their local meetinghouse wearing white sheets and holding white wands—a traditional form of public penance—for having sex outside of marriage. Women in colonial Virginia were far less likely than men to be cited for not attending church services. The vestries also handled poor relief within their parishes. Women, especially widows, were prominent on the church relief rolls.

Little else is known about women's roles in the churches or their religious experiences for the seventeenth century. Several tombstone inscriptions hint at the role of religion in women's lives. Virginian Lucy Burwell, who died in 1675, was lauded as "virtuous" twice on her tombstone, which also told readers that she had "Exchanged this World for a Better one" (Tyler, "Inscriptions," 220). The husband of Lucy Berkeley who died in 1716 at the age of thirty-three saw fit to have the following inscribed on his wife's tombstone: "I shall not pretend to give her full Character; it would take [too] much room for a Grave stone; shall only say that She never neglected her duty to her Creator in Publick or Private. She was Charitable to the poor; a kind mistress and indulgent mother & obedient wife" (Tyler, "Old Tombstones," 244).

Evidence about Anglican women is more plentiful for the eighteenth century. The only official role for white women in the Church of England was as sextons. Sextons cleaned the parish churches, polished the silver used in communion services, and readied the churches for services. The majority of sextons were men, but a few women in the eighteenth century did serve in this capacity, some for decades. Although women occupied no other official church position, they were vital to Anglican parish life. There were never enough clergymen in the southern colonies; many parishes went years without a parson. Mothers took responsibility for raising children in the faith. Women prepared the dead for burial and made sure the church had proper vestments and silver for services. Since funerals and weddings usually took place in private homes, women were instrumental in arranging the spaces for these central church rituals. Anglican clergymen kept sporadic records, but those that survive suggest that women were more loyal to the church than men. The minister of St. Philip's Church in Charleston, South Carolina, kept an account of the parishioners who communed between May 1711 and May 1712. One hundred sixty-three women participated in the rite of communion in that church year; only eighty-two men in this same period took the sacrament.

Religion was very important to Eliza Lucas, a South Carolina gentlewoman who attended services at St. Philip's in the 1740s. Her thoughts were with God during times of illness and war, but she also praised "the great Author of all" (Pickney, 26) for the budding trees and mockingbird's song in the spring. She persistently advised her brothers to care for their eternal souls. When her brother Thomas was diagnosed with an incurable illness, she exhorted him to be resigned and commit himself to God, for "those that have a well grounded hope of a blessed immortality to come" could look forward to "as much happiness as a creature is capable of" after death (70). She married Charles Pinckney in 1744, and the couple had two sons before Charles died of malaria in 1758. Despite her melancholy state, she wrote her sons that "we are indebted to the infinitely wise and good God . . . for the most comfortable and joyous hope that we shall meet in Glory never never more to be seperated [sic]!" (95).

Anglican women were expected to be pious and upright and, if well-to-do, benevolent. The Reverend John Dixon's wife Lucy (d. 1769) fulfilled all these expectations. Her tombstone noted that "Her Exemplary Piety, Domestic Virtues, Liberal Charity Deservedly Caused her to be Highly esteemed, cordially beloved, sincerely lamented By The Public, Her Family, the Poor" (Tyler, 256). Elizabeth Stith, of Surry County, Virginia, also was cognizant of her duties as an Anglican woman. In her will of 1764, she began by praising God and noting that "I give my soul to him that made it trusting in a Happy Resurrection through the Merrits [sic] and intercession of my dear Redeemer Jesus Christ" (Stith, "Will," 114). Her will went on to distribute various rings and pieces of silverware to grandchildren and friends. But Stith did not forget the promises she had made in church to her godchildren. To three she gave 5 pounds each to buy engraved silver cups; to Martha Taylor, who must have come from a poorer family, Stith left 5 pounds to allow Martha four years of schooling. She left 50 pounds to her parish church for an altar piece of "Moses and Aaron drawn at full length holding up between them the Ten commandments." (115). To the local "Free School," Stith was even more generous, bequeathing 120 pounds, the interest on which was to be used to pay for the education of six poor children.

Stith's charity, however, did not extend beyond the white community. The same will that was so generous to local poor white children was callously indifferent to Stith's slaves. She ordered the sale of all the slaves she owned and singled out by name Hannibal, George, Joe, Lucy, Grace, Isaac, Isham, and Jemmey, whose purchase prices were "to be applyed towards Discharging the Legacys in my said Will" (116). Stith did not even ask her executors to attempt to sell slaves as family units, as a few legators of the century did. Stith's last will and testament illustrates the position of the Anglican church on slavery and the impact slavery had on white Anglican women. The Church of England viewed slaveholding as perfectly compatible with Christianity, so even a devout believer like Stith had no fear that her ownership of slaves would jeopardize her soul.

The Great Awakening

The Great Awakening had its roots in the southern colonies. In May 1738, the Reverend George Whitefield arrived in Savannah, Georgia, to assume the Anglican pulpit. Although he was there only a short time, by January of the next year, some Georgia Christians had stopped attending services in the Anglican church, opting instead to attend services conducted by Whitefield's converts. The colony's secretary lamented the divisions that New Lights in Georgia had caused, mentioning that even husbands and wives were differing about religion. The divisions in Georgia would be replicated in most of the other colonies in the decades to come. In the South, Whitefield and his followers had their greatest effect in Georgia and South Carolina. In Virginia, Samuel Davies, a New Light Presbyterian, and his followers had the greatest impact.

The differences between New Lights and orthodox Anglicans centered mainly on two issues. The first was doctrinal. Anglicans obtained salvation by being baptized, then later catechized and confirmed, attending church services, living a moral life, and attending to the "ordinances" (the holy rites, like the sacrament of communion, as well as daily duties, like prayer). New Lights believed that only those who had had a conversion experience, an immediate work of the Holy Spirit on a repentant heart, could go to heaven. The second, related, difference between New Lights and Anglicans was the role of the clergy. New Lights believed that each individual had the power to discern the state of his or her soul. Moreover, New Lights could achieve conversion without the aid of an ordained clergyman.

Catherine Bryan's route from Anglicanism to New Light belief was typical. A South Carolina gentlewoman, Bryan thoroughly accepted Anglican views of salvation. She made "it her practice to retire seven times a day, as did the holy David, to pray, and give praise to God," and she "sought diligently, by attending the ordinances, by fastings, and by doing good, &c. to prepare herself for the acceptance of God through Jesus Christ" (Bryan, *Living Christianity*, 10). But in 1739 Bryan became severely ill, and believing she was dying, she began to despair of her salvation. She followed the New Light path to conversion, becoming convinced of the "depravity and baseness of her corrupt nature, the pollutions of her soul, and the insufficiency of all her religious works and endeavours." Her escape from damnation was simple: "I . . . was forced out of myself to rely entirely on Christ, and begged of God to have mercy on me." (17–18). The "peace and comfort of soul" Bryan exhibited after her conversion so affected her husband that he, too, determined to travel the New Light path to heaven (10).

Bryan had read the sermons of George Whitefield, but she did not convert under New Light preaching and, indeed, needed no clergyman to find her way to heaven. The Anglican method—good works, prayer, and the ordinances—had proven "a wrong foundation." Bryan, who laid the blame for her ignorance on "the books I had read, and the doctrines I had heard preached by our clergy," began urging other Anglicans not to be thus deceived. She touted the benefits of the new birth and exhorted her sister to seek a "living" and "true faith," language that implied Anglicanism was a dead and false one (16–18). By emphasizing her complete dependence on Christ and the insufficiency of works and the ordinances, she highlighted how she no longer needed the guidance of an educated clergyman. God worked directly on her heart (branded "enthusiasm" by Anglican clergy), and she was so certain she had found the true path to heaven that she encouraged others to follow her.

It is clear from the debates between Anglicans and New Lights in the press that women were taking part in New Light services and that enough women were embracing New Light religion to worry the Church of England clergy. Some Anglican women, like Eliza Lucas, denounced the New Lights as deluded and clung to the rational faith of her family. Others, like Catherine Bryan, embraced the new religion of the Great Awakening. Since white women, it seems, had been the most loyal communicants in the Anglican church, clergymen on both sides of the divide fought to attract and keep them. On the heels of Whitefield and Davies, however, came more formidable foes of orthodoxy, the Separate Baptists.

Separate Baptists

The Reverend Shubal Stearns and some like-minded believers came South in 1755 and settled in Guilford County, North Carolina. From there, these earliest Separate Baptists spread the faith into Virginia and South Carolina. Separate Baptists are credited with forming a counterculture in the southern colonies, and that counterculture had profound implications for women. Baptists held to no universal creeds; each congregation was self-governing, and the members agreed on articles of faith. The rite of baptism was done by full immersion, and as only those who presented convincing accounts of their conversion could be baptized, the sect did not baptize infants or small children. Early Baptists in the South also practiced foot washing, the kiss of charity (in emulation of the early Christians, who greeted one another with a holy kiss), and extending the right hand of fellowship to new members. Every woman in the church was a sister, every man a brother. In some Baptist churches, women could vote; in many, women investigated offenses committed by other women. In Stearns's church, women were appointed eldresses and deaconesses and in these positions served as lay assistants to the minister. Stearns's sister Martha Marshall was a leader in her church, known for giving inspiring exhortations.

The Baptists forbade dancing, gambling, cardplaying, drinking liquor, and dressing ostentatiously; some congregations even opposed slavery. The ruling elite in the South feared the Baptists, for the Baptist worldview was the antithesis of gentry culture. The Baptists also granted white women and slaves more respect and more of a voice than was thought appropriate by the elite. For free women who joined the Baptists, the church offered a public forum in which they were respected and treated as individuals. For women used to being seen as some man's wife or some father's daughter, the opportunity to be recognized as an individual believer was empowering. While there is suggestive evidence that Whitefield's congregations included more women than men, there is definitive proof that in Separate Baptist congregations women outnumbered men.

African Americans and Protestantism

In the seventeenth century, little effort was made to spread Protestant Christianity to slaves. Many masters feared that Christian slaves would be harder to govern. Some did not believe their slaves capable of becoming Christians. The English settlers had also inherited a belief that it was unlawful for Christians to enslave other Christians, even after laws were passed—the first in Virginia in 1667—that explicitly declared baptism did not free slaves. Ironically, these laws were enacted not simply to protect slaveholders' property but also to encourage masters to have their slaves Christianized. This hope went largely unfulfilled. Some few slaves were baptized into the Church of England, but they represented only a tiny percentage of the entire enslaved population.

Church officials in England were dismayed by these poor efforts, and in 1701 the Society for the Propagation of the Gospel in Foreign Parts (SPG) was chartered, with one of its main goals the Christianization of slaves and Indians. In South Carolina, an SPG missionary reported in 1705 that he had twenty black communicants and a

thousand slaves under instruction. But these numbers represented a tiny percentage of the total slave population. Even the most dedicated SPG missionaries and Anglican parsons found masters reluctant to have their slaves converted. One elite woman asked a missionary if she would have to see her slaves in heaven; if so, she was against any efforts to preach to them (Raboteau, 103). Slaves, too, resisted efforts at their Christianization. Some clung to their African religious beliefs. Others had no interest in a church that sanctioned slavery and relegated even baptized black members to balconies or back pews.

When the Society for the Propagation of the Gospel ministers found cooperative whites, they sometimes met with better results. In 1713, the SPG offices in London officially recognized two Anglican women of South Carolina who had embraced the Society's goals. Mrs. Haigue and Mrs. Edwards decided to instruct local slaves in the faith. The SPG missionary found that fourteen slaves under these women's care could recite the Apostle's Creed, the Ten Commandments, and the Lord's Prayer and answered his doctrinal questions perfectly. He baptized all fourteen the next Sunday. That the Society would officially recognize these women for saving fourteen enslaved souls indicates how slow Anglican progress was among slaves. Although the percentage of slaves who became Anglicans was small, there is evidence that suggests a significant difference by gender. In several Virginia parishes, at least twice as many slave women sought baptism into the Church of England as men. After 1750, when Anglican priests turned their attention from converting enslaved adults to baptizing slave children, the sex ratio of blacks baptized as Anglicans evened out.

Slaves were far more responsive to New Light preaching, and New Lights were far more committed to Christianizing slaves. George Whitefield attracted blacks to many of his services, as did Samuel Davies. But it was the Separate Baptists who were the first Protestants to attract large numbers of slaves to their faith. Baptist congregations were, when compared to the wider world, relatively egalitarian. Black women were called sisters and given the right hand of fellowship when they became members. Slaves gave religious testimony in Baptist churches; enslaved men preached to all-black and mixed-race audiences. While no black women were designated preachers, the opening of pulpits to any black was a radical move. Church membership, which for Anglicans had meant memorizing creeds and catechisms, for Baptists was based on an individual's heartfelt conversion. Mass baptisms in rivers or lakes underscored the equality of all believers before God as well as converts' new birth in Christ. Some Baptist congregations disciplined slaveholders for abusing their slaves or for separating slave families.

Slave women were central to the development of African American Christianity. Among slaves, women outnumbered men in Baptist, and later, Methodist churches. Black women were essential in bringing evangelical religion to their families. Ecstatic experiences were part and parcel of evangelical worship. The Holy Spirit would work on hearts, minds, and bodies so that believers fainted, shouted, became entranced, and had visions. Black women were prominent among those who were possessed by the Spirit or inspired by God. While the secular world viewed black women as lascivious "wenches," black women in evangelical churches vividly demonstrated their holiness and connection to the divine.

Diversity

The southern colonies contained a diverse array of Protestants despite the fact that the official church in the southern colonies was the Church of England. In Georgia there were Salzburgers and Reformed Protestants. In South Carolina, there were Baptists and Presbyterians. In North Carolina, Lutherans, Quakers, and Moravians could be found.

Although the evidence about many of the women in these groups is lost, a few rich snippets survive. Hannah Dart belonged to a Congregational Church in Charlestown, South Carolina. Her pastor, Josiah Smith, a strong supporter of George Whitefield and New Light religion, published the funeral sermon he delivered at her burial service in 1742. Reverend Smith included a brief sketch of Dart's life in the sermon and apologized for not being able to portray her virtues in full merit. Dart was charming, intelligent, accomplished, and beautiful and possessed all "of the Ornaments of *her sex.*" In speech, she "at once *commanded improv'd* and *pleas'd.*" As a wife, mother, and mistress, Dart was an exemplar. She was pious from a young age and "made an *early Dedication* of herself to God." As a good Calvinist, she "had low Thoughts of *human Nature*, in its lapsed Condition" and believed that "Righteousness . . . is by *Faith alone.*" She was charitable to the poor and to the church's ministers and "looked *the last Enemy* in the Face, without shrinking," through a long, fatal illness. Her pastor told his audience she was undoubtedly in heaven now, meeting her first husband and Hannah Rowe, an English pietistic author beloved by Dart. She was lauded as a "Woman of such *Merit*, and excellent Endowments; such a *Wife*, such a *Mother*, such a *Mistress*, such a *Friend*, such a *Christian*, such an *Ornament* of Her *Sex*, such a *Beauty* and *Support* to Her *Church* and *Profession*" and mourned by many. Reverend Smith counseled his listeners to "rather *imitate* than *weep.* . . . Let our Conversation I mean be in *Heaven*, like *her's* [sic]"(Smith). Clearly, Dart was a respected member of her church to

have such a tribute made and then memorialized in print.

Dart was, except for belonging to a Congregational church, in many ways a conventional pious Protestant woman. The Moravians offer a vivid example of the range of women's religious experiences in the colonial South. In 1753, a group of Moravian men left Pennsylvania to found a settlement in backcountry North Carolina. Moravian women came to Wachovia in 1755. These Moravians, formally the Renewed Unitas Fratrum (Renewed Unity of Brethren), were European, especially German, Pietists who had come to America to escape persecution and establish societies apart from the world. The Moravians had many distinctive features. The one most noticed by outsiders was the choir system. Moravians were organized by age and marital status into smaller groups called choirs: infants, young boys, young girls, older boys, older girls, single brothers, single sisters, married couples, widowers, and widows. Each choir met several times a week for special singing, prayer, and worship services. Each choir had a spiritual leader (*Pfleger*, if a man; *Pflegerin*; if a woman) and a business leader (*Vorsteher*, if a man; *Vorsteherin*, if a woman). Women's choirs were led by women, but these were not the only leadership roles for Moravian women. Women could be ordained as deaconesses. Ministers and their wives were both considered *Arbeiteren*, workers for the Lord. The *Saal Dieneren*, Church Ushers and Elders, were composed of men and women who were respected by their peers.

Men and women were seated on separate sides of the *Saal*, or church, during services. The women who served as *Saal Dieneren* gave the wine and bread to female members during communion and the cakes and tea to them during Love Feasts, services that celebrated through food and drink the spiritual unity of the congregation. Single brothers and single sisters lived in separate houses and were not to be in contact with each other. Initially, North Carolina's Moravians pooled their resources into one *Oeconomie* (economy). These practices led critics to suspect Moravians of being antipatriarchal and antifamily. Neither was the case, although Moravian women were not bound solely to a patriarchal family because of the choir system. Moravians were encouraged to marry, but here, as elsewhere, Moravian practices were unique. Individual men and women were not to choose their own spouses. When a young man or woman was ready to marry, he or she approached the church elders and made the request. The elders would then use the Lot to determine the proper spouse for that person. The Lot was the Moravian system for determining God's will in important matters. The Lot usually contained three possible answers: yes, no, and a blank, which meant that the question was not to be decided yet. No Moravian was forced to marry against his or her will, and most abided by the Lot's decision, but it was forbidden to court outside of this system.

The choir system not only institutionalized leadership roles for women; it also provided a strong and vibrant community life. In addition to weekly meetings, each choir had a special festival or covenant day during the year. On May 4, 1770, for example, the single sisters in North Carolina celebrated. The day began with a prayer service, then a sermon by the minister, the receiving of new choir members, a celebratory lunch, a Love Feast, the reading of the choir's "memorabilia" (a record of the activities of the choir that year), a singing service, and a liturgical service that evening for all the Moravians at which the single sisters were remembered with special songs and prayers. A communion service for the single sisters ended the day. When members were dying, or "home going" as the Moravians termed it, a member of their choir was at the bedside with the family.

Anna Catherina Antes Kalberlahn Reuter left a memoir of her life as a Moravian woman. Born in Pennsylvania in 1726, Catherina joined the Moravians as a single sister in 1745. The elders and the Lot chose a spouse for Catherina in 1758, a physician named Martin Kalberlahn, and the two left Pennsylvania for the North Carolina settlement in 1759. She lost Martin to the plague after only twelve months of marriage. Catherina was assigned to take care of the girls in the nursery and joined the widows choir. In 1762, the elders and the Lot chose a new husband for her, the surveyor Christian Reuter. Soon after they were married, Catherina and Christian were chosen as *Saal Dieneren*. Catherina appreciated the choir system, noting that "I had been Single Sister, Married Sister, and Widow, and had learned the worth of having eternal truths presented as they were applicable to each group, and had enjoyed the intimate fellowship within each Choir." Catherina would join the widows choir again in 1776, would marry two more times before her death in 1816, and would be ordained a deaconess in 1786. On her tombstone she was described as a "Leader in Church and Community service" and her life as "A life spent in the service of others" (Fries, 158, 317).

Hannah Dart and Catherina Antes led very different lives because of their religious affiliations, and these lives highlight the wide variety of Protestant women's experiences in the colonial South. Dart was an elite woman who belonged to a distinct religious minority. She fulfilled her religious duties in her family, with the poor, in her church, and by facing death with fortitude. Antes also belonged to a religious minority, and though she was never wealthy, she was highly educated for a woman of her day. Antes fulfilled her obligations to God and her fellow Moravians in her family, in her various choirs, and as a leader. For both women, their relationship to God was embedded in relationships with the people around them. Both died in full hope of salvation and of reuniting with loved ones and friends who had died before them.

The Revolution and Southern Protestantism

At the close of the American Revolution, church and state were finally officially separated in the South. Women could now choose to worship in any church they wished and could be married by any licensed minister. Women continued to outnumber men in southern Protestant churches as the evangelical denominations, especially the Baptists and Methodists, came to dominate the religious landscape. If, as some historians suggest, America became a religious marketplace with various sects competing for members, women were critical to the movement away from High Church ritual toward evangelicalism in what would come to be called the nation's "Bible Belt."

SOURCES: Material for this essay was drawn from Lyon G. Tyler, "Inscriptions on Old Tombs in Gloucester Co., Virginia," *William and Mary College Quarterly* (April 1894); "Tombstones in Middlesex County," *William and Mary College Quarterly* (April 1904); Lyon G. Tyler, "Old Tombstones in Mathews County," *William and Mary College* (April 1895); Elise Pinckney, ed., *The Letterbook of Eliza Lucas Pinckney, 1739–1762* (1972); "Will of Mrs. Elizabeth Stith," *William and Mary College Quarterly* (October 1896); Hugh Bryan, *Living Christianity Delineated, in the Diaries and Letters of Two Eminently Pious Persons Lately Deceased* (1809); Albert J. Raboteau, *Slave Religion: The "Invisible Institution" in the Antebellum South* (1978); Josiah Smith, *A Funeral Discourse, Deliver'd in Charlestown, South-Carolina, April 25th 1742* (1742); Adelaide L. Fries, ed., *The Road to Salem* (1993). Other important works include Kathleen M. Brown, *Good Wives, Nasty Wenches, and Anxious Patriarchs: Gender, Race, and Power in Colonial Virginia* (1996); Joan R. Gundersen, "The Non-Institutional Church: The Religious Role of Women in Eighteenth-Century Virginia," *Historical Magazine of the Protestant Episcopal Church* (1982); Cynthia A. Kierner, *Beyond the Household: Women's Place in the Early South, 1700–1835* (1998); John K. Nelson, *A Blessed Company: Parishes, Parsons, and Parishioners in Anglican Virginia, 1690–1776* (2001); Daniel B. Thorp, *The Moravian Community in Colonial North Carolina: Pluralism on the Southern Frontier* (1989); and Mechal Sobel, *The World They Made Together: Black and White Values in Eighteenth-Century Virginia* (1987).

PROTESTANTISM IN BRITISH NORTH AMERICA (CANADA)
Marilyn Färdig Whiteley

IN 1765, LAWRENCE Coughlan, a follower of John Wesley, began preaching in Newfoundland. He continued with some success until 1773, when ill health forced him to return to England. William Black, a Methodist preacher from Nova Scotia, went to Newfoundland in 1791 to investigate the state of Methodism there. He reported with dismay that the work had virtually disappeared: The only traces he could find were a class of about fifteen women who met among themselves in Carbonear and one of twelve or thirteen women meeting in Harbour Grace. Where there had been a revival about twenty years earlier, this was all that remained.

Black's lament provides an example of why it is difficult to document the role women have played in Protestantism in British North America as elsewhere. These women of Newfoundland fishing villages had been impelled by their faith to keep alive their religious practice for about twenty years, but theirs was no official organization. Since the women only met among themselves, Black did not count their activity as evidence of a vital continuation of Methodism within the colony.

The failure of women to count is a situation that is played out with many variations in the story of Protestantism in British North America. Only with careful rereading of familiar sources and with the discovery and use of new sources are the varied contours of women's role beginning to be seen.

Women helped to bring Protestantism to the new land in diverse ways. During the eighteenth and early nineteenth centuries, some brought their faith when they came as settlers; others organized in support of missionary efforts to British North America; and a few immigrated in order to serve as preachers or missionaries. The shape of women's activities also depended on their denomination. In subsequent years, as churches were organized in the wilderness and then in the villages, towns, and cities of the developing colonies, women's participation again tended to follow the opportunities and constraints of their denominational heritage as well as the changing social patterns and expectations of so-

Eliza Barnes (1796–1887) was born in Boston but by 1827 was a missionary in Upper Canada (now Ontario). During her first years there, she traveled among several missions, teaching children and adults, and organizing the native women into Dorcas Societies. *Courtesy of the United Church of Canada/ Victoria University Archives.*

ciety. Some women nevertheless found ways to stretch these boundaries. Increasingly during the nineteenth century women expressed their faith by banding together in organizations, some denominational and others reaching beyond the confines of a single group. In 1867, several British North American colonies united to form the Dominion of Canada (then comprising Nova Scotia, New Brunswick, Quebec, and Ontario). Following this Confederation, the stage was set for a broad expansion of women's associational work and for the spread of women missionaries to new Canadian frontiers and to the world overseas.

Planting the Protestant Faith

In the early days of exploration and settlement, Roman Catholicism held sway over much of what later became British North America, while the British developed colonies to the south. The chief exception was the island of Newfoundland. For many years it was visited only seasonally as a base for European fishing fleets, but gradually settlements were planted, and occasionally preachers came to address the religious needs of those working and living there. Among them were two Quaker women, Hester Biddle and Mary Fisher, who preached on ships in St. John's harbor in 1656 and 1659. Thus even in the early days of Canadian history there are traces of Protestant women's activity.

Following the British conquest of French colonial power in the Atlantic coastal regions in 1710 and in Quebec in 1759, settlement of English-speaking and mainly Protestant immigrants increased. British North America consisted of the now-existing Canadian provinces of Newfoundland and Labrador, Prince Edward Island, Nova Scotia, New Brunswick, southern parts of Quebec and Ontario, and coastal portions of British Columbia. (The northern and western territories controlled by the Hudson Bay Company were not areas of Protestant settlement until after Confederation in 1867.)

Nova Scotia (which included what is now New Brunswick) welcomed British settlers and "foreign Protestants" from Germany and Switzerland. Attracted by the colonial governor's promise of religious freedom, "planters" from New England moved north. Presbyterians from Ireland and Scotland and Methodists from Yorkshire enriched the mixture before the turmoil of the American Revolution temporarily closed off immigration. Once peace returned, both disbanded soldiers and civilian Loyalists arrived in Nova Scotia and in New Brunswick, which became a colony separated from Nova Scotia in 1784. Loyalists also moved into Quebec, to the bank of the upper St. Lawrence River, to the shores of Lake Ontario in the area of Kingston and the Bay of Quinte, and onto the Niagara peninsula. They were followed by other settlers principally from the United States. By the early days of the nineteenth century, the English-speaking settlers of Canada were followers of a small number of Protestant traditions, mainly Church of England, Presbyterian, Methodist, and (especially in the Maritimes) Baptist.

Along with their clothing and their tools, these families brought their family Bibles and their less tangible religious traditions. One among them has been singled out as a shining example of the faithfulness manifest less dramatically in many others. This was Barbara Ruckle Heck (1734–1804). She was born in Ireland, a descendant of Germans who had fled persecution in the Palatinate. In 1760, Heck immigrated with family and friends to New York City. Six years later, according to the famous story, when she saw her fellow Methodists playing cards, she threw the cards into the fire. Her cousin, Philip Embury, had been a Methodist lay preacher in Ireland, and she urged him to preach. He did, the first Methodist Society in New York was formed, and Heck came to be regarded as the "mother of American Methodism."

Heck's activity did not, however, end in New York City. In 1770, the group moved north to New York's Camden Valley. The years of war were difficult as the Camden Valley men chose the side of the crown, and the Loyalists' farms were confiscated. Paul and Barbara Heck moved again, spending time in Montreal before settling in 1785 near what is now Prescott, Ontario. Here the Hecks and their neighbors soon formed a Methodist class. In these small gatherings, members assembled weekly under the supervision of a leader in order to seek salvation through group confession and instruction. While in most cases classes were created after a congregation had been established, here the settlers formed the small group well before the arrival of the first Methodist preacher in the region. Theirs is widely regarded as the first Methodist class in Canada, and thus Barbara Heck has been considered a mother of Canadian Methodism as well.

Methodists depended heavily on lay preachers and class leaders, persons who gained leadership status on the basis of their religious experience and on their ability to convert others; these things validated their ministry. Denominations less influenced by this evangelical ethos depended more heavily on leaders sent from their lands of origin. Male clergy were ordinarily selected and supported by members of a male ecclesiastical hierarchy. Sometimes, however, women played an extraordinary role in the process. Noteworthy were women in Edinburgh whose efforts shaped and supported the Presbyterian church in Cape Breton Island, Nova Scotia.

Isabella Gordon Mackay (1778–1850) and her husband were members of the Church of Scotland and supporters of the Edinburgh Auxiliary of the Glasgow Colonial Society. In the 1820s and early 1830s, Mackay's religious faith and sense of duty caused her to become involved with sending libraries of religious literature for circulation in Nova Scotia. Soon, however, she became convinced that more could be accomplished through concentrated effort. The chosen target of Mackay and her coworkers in the Ladies' Association (formed in 1832) was the Cape Breton mission. In 1833, the group's first missionary sailed for Cape Breton despite the reservations of some members of the Glasgow Colonial Society: The women had carefully chosen a Gaelic-speaking farmer-turned-preacher who could relate to the settlers. During the following years the women's choices and their support shaped not only the ecclesiastical but also the educational patterns of Cape Breton.

The Church of Scotland clergy were all men, as were those sent by societies connected with the Church of England. Although John Wesley had gradually moved toward using the leadership skills of women, the preachers sent to British North America by the Wesleyan Methodists of Britain and by the Methodist Episcopals of the United States were also male. New, smaller British Methodist denominations in the early part of the nineteenth century welcomed female preachers, however, and some of these continued their ministry in North America.

Among them was Elizabeth Dart Eynon (1792–1857). Born in Cornwall, she was a member of the first Bible Christian Society in England, formed in 1815. Soon she was a preacher for this new Methodist group. In 1833 she married, and she and her husband left England for their new mission on the northern shore of Lake Ontario. They shared a 200-mile circuit, conducting services sometimes individually, sometimes together. It was a difficult life, but she endured. After one journey she wrote, "I walked about six miles through the woods; on entering which I was tempted that fear would overcome me; but after I proceeded some distance, I felt not the least fear, and my soul was so filled with heaven and God, that I felt all within was joy and love" (Muir, 64).

During her later years ill health and advancing age may have curtailed Eynon's labors, but her earlier efforts should have secured for her an identity as a preacher. Yet the notices following her death do not speak of her preaching ministry. As denominations sought respectable social status, the story of their women preachers faded from memory.

Although women did not come from the Methodist Episcopal Church as preachers, some came as missionaries to indigenous people. Eliza Barnes (1796–1887) was born in Boston; by 1827 she was a missionary in Upper Canada (now Ontario). During her first years there, she traveled among several missions, teaching children and adults and organizing the native women into Dorcas Societies. These groups were named for Dorcas in the book of Acts and followed her example as one who was "full of good works and almsdeeds."

The native women made moccasins and gloves to sell for the support of the mission. Barnes also journeyed into the United States where she collected money for missions and again organized Dorcas Societies for their support.

Barnes also preached, and people came eagerly to hear her. In one instance, a doorway became her pulpit as she delivered a sermon to women who filled a house and to men standing in the front yard. In 1833 she married a widowed missionary, William Case, who, like many of his peers, did not approve of women preaching, and in later years this gifted woman settled down to a more traditional role.

Henriette Odin Feller (1800–1868) came with a very different mission. Feller was from Lausanne, Switzerland, where she gained experience in nursing and, after the death of her husband, in business. In 1835, Feller and a young man, Louis Roussy, began work as French-speaking evangelists among Roman Catholics in a new settlement at Grande-Ligne, south of Montreal. Feller displayed remarkable energy as well as deep spirituality. She taught, nursed the sick, and oversaw all parts of the mission's activity. Like Barnes, she organized groups of women in the northeastern United States for the support of this Baptist mission.

Denominations: Opportunities and Constraints

In the early decades of settlement, congregations in British North America found their organizational identity in church structures based elsewhere, and until the local groups became self-supporting, their ministers were often missionaries supported at least in part by these foreign churches. Gradually, however, this changed. Groups formed their own, Canadian, denominational organizations and increasingly produced clergy from within their ranks rather than relying on those sent from abroad. The role women played within these groups depended greatly on the continuing denominational traditions.

The Church of England stood in a different situation from the rest. For some time both colonial government and church leaders assumed that it was the established, or official, church of the British colonies. Presbyterians fought for coestablishment, and Methodists led in contesting the granting of such privileges. Eventually practice changed so that no denomination enjoyed a special status. Even so, Church of England and, in many cases, Presbyterian congregations often included a significant number of the social elite among their membership. Both denominations were governed by male hierarchies. Within the Church of England there was a strong awareness of episcopal rank and order, while the various branches of the Presbyterian tradition placed stress upon a well-educated clergy. Presbyterianism's more evangelical wing carried the potential for a larger role for women, but generally neither denomination offered scope for women's leadership.

Yet women in both groups felt called to express their religious faith, and it became easier to respond to this call as settlement became more economically secure and as urban centers grew. Some who enjoyed social and economic privilege exercised their Christian responsibility in benevolence. For many, the first step was private charity, but faced with such difficulty as that brought by the War of 1812, and the problems of increasing immigration, women recognized the usefulness of working together to fulfill God's requirement that they help those less fortunate. Some participated in societies devoted to the distribution of Bibles and Prayer Books, working within societies that included both men and women or forming groups of their own. In Malpeque, Prince Edward Island, for example, Presbyterian women formed a Female Society for Propagating the Gospel and Other Religious Purposes. Part of its mission was to distribute Bibles to the families of isolated fishermen.

Others engaged in aid of a more directly practical type. Members of the Ladies' Benevolent Society in Hamilton visited the poor and gave them aid. In Montreal, although nuns carried out much benevolence work, Protestant women also found scope for their labors. In 1815 a group of women began helping others in distress with such practical items as food, clothing, and firewood. The result of their efforts was a Female Benevolent Society that served an increasing number of immigrants and soon opened a House of Recovery for those in special need. This led to the founding of the city's first general hospital. Montreal women also opened a Protestant Orphan Asylum in 1822, as once more women organized in response to an urgent public need.

For many of the women, participating in benevolent activities provided them with an opportunity to express their Christian faith in ways that were acceptable to church and broader society, and such activities were especially attractive to women whose denominational traditions allowed them few outlets of expression. No doubt, most of these women operated within the roles expected of them. A few, however, such as Harriet Dobbs Cartwright (1808–1887), appear to have embraced such opportunities as an escape from the narrow confines of societal expectations regarding woman's role.

Harriet Dobbs was born in Dublin, Ireland. She was drawn to an evangelical strain of religion within the Church of England and struggled for years with a sense of her sinfulness until finally she experienced God's mercy. She wrote that her spirit "rose up triumphant . . . & ascended to the God of My Salvation, with psalms & hymns of joy & praise," and she remained in this euphoric state for "days and weeks" (McKenna, 291). In 1832 she married Robert Cartwright, a Church of En-

gland clergyman, and went with him to Kingston in Upper Canada. Upon her arrival she fulfilled the necessary social obligations, but then she quickly set about to shape what seemed to her an appropriate Christian life, far from society's expectations for a clergy wife. Over the next nine years she gave birth to five children, but during the first seven of those years she was aided in her domestic affairs by the presence of her husband's sister. Thus she was able to devote herself to teaching and supervising both Sunday and day schools, to organizing women to sew for the benefit of the poor, and to reviving Kingston's Female Benevolent Society.

Cartwright was aware of criticism that she neglected her home duties and claimed that she did not "advocate the intrusion of females upon spheres of action, not belonging to their station" (McKenna, 293). Nevertheless, she found ways to pursue what she considered "more useful occupations" that were much more satisfying to her sense of Christian purpose. Her husband died in 1843, but she did not remarry. She was active in the Orphan's and Widow's Friend Society and became interested in the treatment of women prisoners in the local penitentiary. Her final project before her death was an attempt to found a kindergarten school.

Women with Cartwright's independence and strength made opportunities even when the male hierarchies of their denomination offered them a limited role. The practices of Wesleyan groups meant that Methodist women faced a different set of needs and possibilities. Their preachers had no homes but continually moved from place to place with their possessions in their saddlebags. Enjoying little financial support from church or missionary society, they depended for food and shelter on the hospitality of settlers. The burden of this hospitality lay upon women, but the women's role in the success of this ministry has been all but invisible. One early-nineteenth-century preacher was delayed by ice and deep snow and only reached his stopping place at seven in the evening. To his dismay, he discovered that "the family had no bread or meal to make any of, till they borrowed some of a neighbor; so," he complained, "I got my dinner and supper about eleven o'clock on Saturday night" (Carroll, 1:78). His report shows no awareness of the family's own need, no sensitivity to what must have been both inconvenience and embarrassment to the woman of the household: borrowing from a neighbor and preparing a meal late in the evening. Such labors by women sustained the efforts that brought Methodism into a prominent place in the new land.

In evangelical groups like the Methodists and Baptists, more weight was placed on the individual's religious experience and his or her relationship with God. Here women were often freer to claim authority. Although preaching by evangelical women was never widespread in British North America, and declined as the nineteenth century wore on, women found other ways to express their faith within their congregational structures. Since Baptists placed authority in the local worshiping community, their practices might vary from one congregation to another. Central to their congregational life was the Saturday meeting where converts gave testimony, members reaffirmed their adherence to the church covenant, and those present arranged to visit candidates for baptism and those feared to be straying from the church's rules. Although women's participation was not universally approved, it is evident that in many congregations women took part in covenant meetings.

The various branches of Methodism, even those that did not encourage women's preaching, offered women a significant role. Methodist class meetings, mentioned earlier, required leaders. In larger congregations, groups were usually divided along gender and age lines. Women frequently led classes of women and girls, and also of young men, and sometimes they led mixed classes as well. Their leadership was valued. Groups of congregations that formed a circuit dealt with their official business at quarterly conferences. Membership at these meetings included local preachers, class leaders, and stewards. While most local preachers and stewards were men, class leadership gave some women entry into the decision-making body of the church.

Class meetings also gave women who were not class leaders an opportunity to testify to their religious faith. Testimony was a significant religious practice among Methodists and other evangelicals. It was considered to be of value not only to the person testifying but to those hearing, whether in class, prayer, or covenant meetings. As the 1840 obituary of Sarah Martin Davison stated, "The class meeting was not only the means of great spiritual benefit to herself, but it gave her the opportunity of testifying to those with whom she met, the wonderful dealings of the Almighty to her soul" (*Wesleyan*, January 13, 1840).

Some enterprising women gathered their neighbors for class or prayer meetings. In the winter of 1858–1859, young Annie Leake taught school in the remote community of Apple River, Nova Scotia. She discovered that there was "but one praying man" in the community and one other family that invited her to lead family prayer when she visited (Tuttle, 40). A preacher came only once every six weeks. But the mail driver was a religious man, and he came more often, so Leake organized a prayer meeting on the nights he remained in the village. She referred to this as her "aggressiveness in religion," and due to similar "aggressiveness" gatherings were held in many farmhouses and villages across the land.

Within all evangelical communities of faith, such religious aggressiveness was deemed appropriate. Women and men who had come into the church as a result of their own religious experience and decision assumed a Christian responsibility to lead others into the fold. Some might do this by their participation in revival services. Although the traditional picture of a camp meeting is of an audience focused on a man preaching from a platform, that image is incomplete. Occasionally there was a woman on that platform. Even when there was not, such services depended heavily on laywomen as well as men who exhorted sinners to repent and prayed with seekers who had not yet reached a new religious state. These assistants were ordinary people who were often less than ordinary in their dedication and zeal.

Concern for the souls of others was not limited to public arenas. For women especially, the home was a center of religious activity and obligation. During the nineteenth century there was a greater separation of the roles of men and women, and the realm of women increasingly became that of the home. Along with ordinary household duties, women took on the task of imparting religious knowledge and moral virtue to their children. Their ultimate goal was the child's own entrance into the life of faith. Bible reading, family prayer, and time spent in "the closet" in private prayer were tools of this activity, and many pious stories and laudatory obituaries in the religious press testified to how a mother's tears and a mother's prayers resulted in the salvation of her erring son.

A few groups maintained their life of faith in separated communities, chief among them the Quakers, members of the Religious Society of Friends. Their egalitarian beliefs had many consequences. Among these was the lack of hierarchical religious organization; they had no ordained or professional ministry. Affairs of the societies were managed by a system of women's and men's meetings where decisions were reached through consensus. The women's and men's groups each had their own areas of concern, but the women were not relegated to a lower level of responsibility. They had an unparalleled voice in the affairs of their church.

Similarly the Quakers might acknowledge the gift of ministry of any woman or man. The early preaching women in St. John's harbor had their descendants in women like Sarah Haight of Upper Canada and in Jemima Burson and Phoebe McCarty Roberts, both of Pennsylvania. During the fall and winter of 1821–1822, Burson led Roberts and two men to visit Quaker societies in various parts of Upper Canada. They visited families and attended meetings wherever they went, and Canadian Quakers welcomed the women's leadership.

North of Toronto they visited the Children of Peace, a dissident group of former Quakers. Brought together by David Willson in 1812, the members attempted to follow a purer and more primitive form of Christianity in preparation for Christ's return. This group, which persisted until 1890, provided a strong place for women both in its organization and in the worship life of the community. Their services included processions and musical instruments, producing an atmosphere far from the quiet simplicity of conventional Quaker meetings.

Organizing for Service

Smaller groups like the Quakers were a minor feature of the religious landscape of British North America. Most women were part of denominational traditions where even the role of class leadership was not open to women. But in the nineteenth-century era of voluntary organizations, countless women found within these groups an opportunity to use their talents in ways deemed appropriate to their social role. In churches with few resources, women organized to support their local congregations; they raised money to build churches and to provide a comfortable home for their minister. But women's groups also looked outward.

Adoniram and Ann Hasseltine Judson, from the United States, set forth as missionaries in 1812, and their work in Burma brought overseas missions to the attention of Protestants all across North America. Among those who espoused the cause of missions were Baptist women in Saint John, New Brunswick, who formed a Mite Society in 1818. Soon other Baptists in New Brunswick and Nova Scotia also began giving money to overseas missions.

By the middle of the nineteenth century, Canada had sent its first missionaries overseas. Various denominations formed their own societies for the support of foreign missions and mission work among natives and settlers on this continent. Women frequently served as collectors, faithfully gathering funds. Occasionally they took a more active role. A number of missionary societies and auxiliaries were formed by Methodist women in the 1820s and 1830s. Best documented is the small Cramahe Female Missionary Society in Upper Canada. They collected money by soliciting cash and the promise of subscriptions and by distributing mite boxes to those willing to place in them small amounts of money over a period of time. In 1842, at their fifteenth anniversary meeting, the women reported that they had also received the proceeds of a bazaar, a common way for women to raise funds.

These efforts for missions were the beginning of a movement that would become a major enterprise for women during the latter part of the century. Baptist women in Nova Scotia formed a society in 1870, and those in other parts of the country soon did the same. The 1867 Confederation of colonies into the Canadian nation caused churches to organize nationally. Presbyterian women formed a denominational missionary society in 1876; Methodist Episcopal women organized the same year, and those in the Methodist Church of Can-

ada in 1881. Soon women's missionary societies were supporting their own missionaries in Canada and overseas. The organizational work that provided the foundation for the female missionaries also gave participants the opportunity to develop their own leadership abilities.

The activity of women in the area of benevolence has already been noted. The emphasis for others, especially evangelical women, lay not in welfare work but in social reform. Their chief concern was temperance. Many women joined community temperance associations run by men, but as early as 1822, Mrs. John Forbes organized a temperance society in a settlement south of Montreal. In the following decades, women in such groups as the Montreal Temperance Society continued the work. By the time Letitia Youmans organized the pioneering Canadian local association of the Woman's Christian Temperance Union in Picton, Ontario, in 1874, temperance was a sphere of reform firmly espoused by many Protestant women.

Another common area of women's activity was that of Sunday Schools. Beginning as a movement to bring literacy and moral education to the poor, these nonsectarian institutions came to be replaced by denominational and interdenominational ("union") Sunday Schools. Generally under the control of male organizers, their success depended on a body of willing and capable women teachers who extended outside the home the religious nurture that was already part of their domestic role.

Scattered among the records, however, are many evidences of women's more prominent activity. When one Methodist minister remarked on the need for a Sunday School, one elderly woman in his church replied, "[P]oor dears, I will do what I can, they must not be let run wild." She and one of her friends collected children and some adults, and a Sunday School was begun (*Christian Guardian*, August 8, 1855). This scene was repeated many times in country, village, and city. Although their inclusion might be born only of necessity, women were not always excluded from leadership. In 1850, the Methodist press described a school organized and managed by two women. The account conceded "[t]hat ladies can be eminently useful, even if it be necessary in the superintendency," and urged other women to show similar leadership "where men, 'the *lords* of the creation,' will not take hold of the mighty work" (*Christian Guardian*, December 4, 1850).

The Ending of the Colonial Period

During the decade preceding Canadian Confederation, women recognized new opportunities. In 1860, a Miss Woodman was teaching Chinese immigrant men in British Columbia. During the same year, Jane Brodie from near Montreal went to a Labrador mission in what is now the Quebec-Labrador border area. She worked at this isolated outpost as a teacher and evangelist during much of the next twenty years. These women and their contemporaries were followed by a much larger number of women missionaries on Canadian soil during the latter part of the century, especially in the newly established western territories taken over from the Hudson Bay Company's control. Increasingly, too, the wives of missionaries made real contributions to the work of the church, although their husbands' names, and not their own, are inscribed on the records of the church. Among these was Jean Ross Hunter, wife of a Church of England missionary; both wife and husband produced translations of scripture into Cree. By the end of the century, missionary reports would be filled with the active contributions of missionary wives.

In 1867, Confederation brought the union of the British North American colonies of New Brunswick, Nova Scotia, and Canada (the latter an earlier union of Lower Canada and Upper Canada). The end of the colonial period brought a shift in how some of women's work was organized as the new nation inspired regional associations to unite as national bodies. This brought new opportunities that built upon a rich heritage of the religious expression of Protestant women in British North America. They found varying ways to express their faith within to the different denominational traditions and personal situations in which they lived, although traces of the women's activity are often hidden. Much more study remains to be done, but the faithful Methodist women in Newfoundland who met among themselves had many daughters of all denominations in British North America.

SOURCES: A general history of Canadian religion in the colonial period is found in John S. Moir, *The Church in the British Era* (1972), while *A Concise History of Christianity in Canada* (1996), edited by Terrence Murphy and Roberto Perin, includes more about the role of women. A general account of Canadian women's history is *Canadian Women: A History* (1988), by Alison Prentice and others. An important early account of Methodism is John Carroll, *Case and His Contemporaries* (1867–1877), and the Methodist newspapers the *Wesleyan* and the *Christian Guardian* are valuable primary sources. Annie Leake Tuttle's writings are published as *The Life and Letters of Annie Leake Tuttle: Working for the Best* (1999), edited by Marilyn Färdig Whiteley. Scholarship specifically about women and religion during this period is found in a number of books and articles. Elizabeth Muir, *Petticoats in the Pulpit* (1991), examines Methodist women preachers in Upper Canada. Katherine M. J. McKenna discusses Harriet Dobbs Cartwright in " 'The Union between Faith and Good Works': The Life of Harriet Dobbs Cartwright, 1880–1887," in *Changing Roles of Women within the Christian Church in Canada*, ed. Muir and Whiteley (1995). On Henriette Feller, see John Mockett Cramp, *A Memoir of Madame Feller* (1876). Other resources include Judith Colwell, "The Role of Women in the Nineteenth Century Baptist Church of Ontario," in Canadian Society of Church History *Papers* (1985); Elizabeth Jane Errington, *Wives and Mothers, School Mistresses and Scullery Maids: Working Women in Upper Canada, 1790–1840* (1995); Cecilia Morgan, "Gender, Religion, and Rural Society: Quaker Women in Norwich, Ontario, 1820–1880," *Ontario History* (December 1990): 273–287; Jan Noel, "Women and Social Welfare in the Montreal Region, 1800–1833," in *Changing Roles of Women within the Christian Church in Canada*, ed. Elizabeth Muir and Marilyn Färdig Whiteley (1995); Laurie C. C. Stanley, *The Well-Watered Garden: The Presbyterian Church in Cape Breton, 1798–1860* (1983); and Marguerite Van Die, " 'A Woman's Awakening': Evangelical Belief and Female Spirituality in Mid-Nineteenth-Century Canada," in *Canadian Women: A Reader*, ed. Wendy Mitchinson et al. (1996).

Denominational Traditions

WOMEN AND AFRICAN AMERICAN DENOMINATIONS
Sandy Dwayne Martin

CHRISTIANITY, PARTICULARLY ITS Protestant variety, has been of immense, even central religious, social, and political significance in the historical experience of African American women. This essay focuses on the largest black denominations but also addresses themes and developments that have often been equally applicable to black women in smaller black as well as mainly white denominations. The beginning of the story of the connection between African women and Christianity can be traced to the biblical and ancient world. Increased attention to the racial-ethnic dynamic of ancient Judaism, Christianity, and Islam reveals that all three religions developed in a racial-ethnic-culturally diverse world, where various peoples migrated, lived among and alongside each other, and interacted on varying levels. A closer study of Christian origins in particular reveals that African peoples were intimately involved in the origins and growth of the religion, including being central to its leadership. In other words, from the inception of the Christian movement, African peoples, by race and ethnicity, not simply geography, have been a part of the Christian movement. Egypt and northwestern Africa were important theaters of some of the earliest leaders, churches, and movements, some "orthodox," some subsequently judged "heretical," such as Gnostics, Arians, Monophysites, Montanists, and the Donatists. Ethiopia, or Abysinnia, joined Armenia and the Roman Empire as one of the earliest kingdoms to embrace Christianity as a state religion in the fourth century. The kingdom of Ethiopia and numerically minority communities in Egypt and other northern African areas have remained committed to the faith down through the centuries. In southern Egypt and Nubia, strong church communities resisted the tide of expanding Islam as late as the eighteenth century.

From Africans to African Americans

While a small percentage of Africans in the Americas may have embraced Christianity prior to their being sold and relocated for enslavement, the great majority entered their new worlds as practitioners of traditional African religions. A smaller but significant percentage (estimates range from 6 to 20 percent) of the victims of the Atlantic slave trade conducted by Europeans and their African partners came from Islamic societies. Thus, African American women adopted Christianity against backgrounds of mainly traditional African religions and secondarily Islam. We need greater research on the pe-

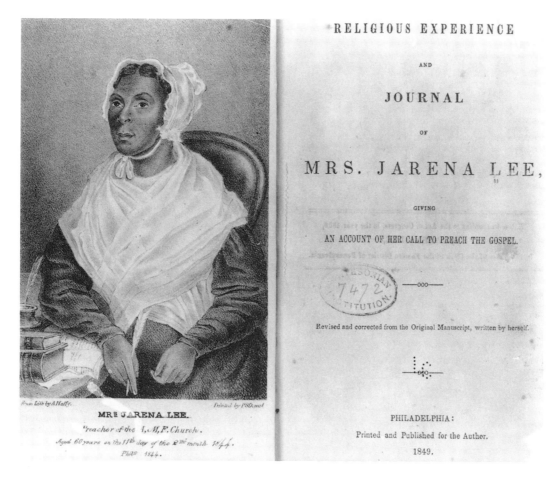

Jarena Lee, in her conflict with the African Methodist Episcopal Church, reflected the arguments used by black women to justify their right to preach the gospel. Lee spoke of her clear calling and direction from God and insisted that since Christ died for males and females, both should be free to preach the gospel. *Courtesy of the Library of Congress.*

riod from the contact of Europeans with Africans in the fifteenth and sixteenth centuries to the middle of the eighteenth century when Africans in what is now the United States joined the Christian movement in significant numbers. That these Africans entering the Americas, and the preindependent United States, continued to practice as best they could the traditions of their foremothers and forefathers is clear. Undoubtedly, as with any religious tradition, changes occurred in the face of new circumstances and challenges.

We must also bear in mind that traditional African religion manifested itself in a variety of ways on the mother continent and in the Americas since it varied from ethnic group to ethnic group. Nonetheless, there are central features that united the various ethnicities and facilitated easier synthesizing of their multiple, ethnic-based traditions. Speaking generally, with an appreciation for variations among the different groups, traditional African religion(s) were characterized by a belief in a Supreme Being who was the source of all

existence; a Vital or Spiritual Force permeating reality; deities of varied ranks and powers who superintended specific areas of existence; a deep respect or veneration of ancestresses and ancestors; the importance of sacred leaders such as priests, priestesses, prophets, and prophetesses; a belief in the sacred and central significance of community; the religious bases of life cycle rituals; and an emphasis on the importance of ethical behavior.

It was within this context of African traditional and occasionally Islamic religious traditions, the barbarous transport to the Western Hemisphere by means of the Middle Passage, and life in a strange physical, cultural, and religious environment that African women in America for the most part first encountered Christianity. More aggressive historical and archaeological research will yield a fuller picture of the attempt of African women during early colonial America to continue their traditional religious practices. The occasional involvement of African women in witchcraft controversies in the English colonies between 1647 and 1692 may reflect attempts by women such as Marja and Tituba to continue and/or adapt traditional African cultic practices in a new but (for them) a dangerous environment. Records reveal, however, that African women were embracing Christianity at a very early stage of their presence in English America. As early as 1641 one woman is known to have converted to Puritan Christianity. In 1683 a free African American woman, Ginney Bess, received baptism. In many instances the Quakers, or Society of Friends, showed themselves to be among the earliest friends of African Americans' quest for freedom from chattel bondage. In 1688 the Germantown Protest placed a community of Pennsylvania Quakers firmly in opposition to enslavement. The pronouncements of significant Quaker leaders, such as George Fox, Anthony Benezet, and John Woolman, both inaugurated and kept alive this passionate opposition to the enslavement of fellow human beings. Nonetheless, the number of African American conversions to the Society of Friends was quite small.

One of the earliest and most systematic efforts of a religious body to Christianize Africans in the English colonies appeared with the formation in 1701 of the Society for the Propagation of the Gospel in Foreign Parts (SPG), established by the Anglican Thomas Bray in England. This organization focused on Native Americans as well as African Americans. The impact of the SPG on the religious lives of black women was quite limited for a number of reasons: the continuing strength of traditional African religions; black distrust of missionaries who supported the system of slavery; a scarcity of missionaries and clergy to serve white colonists, Native Americans, or Africans; lack of financial resources of the organization; a lack of religious zeal among English clergy; a general ignorance or neglect of spiritual matters among the colonists in general; and a resistance, or in some cases a great hesitancy, on the part of enslavers to Christianizing the enslaved because they saw the principles and practices of the religion as antithetical to maintaining subservience to the slave system. During the 1720s the bishop of London attempted to speak to the last concern when, contrary to the sentiments of English common law, he promulgated the teaching that the baptism of the enslaved does not mandate the physical liberation of the individual.

African American Women and Evangelical Protestantism

Around the middle of the eighteenth century there occurred a profound change regarding Africans in America and their embrace of Christianity. This radically new openness to Christianity on the part of black women and men was further heightened in the early part of the nineteenth century when even greater numbers of blacks accepted Christianity. There were two principal sets of reasons for this change: one cultural and the other religious. Culturally, as time progressed English America witnessed the growth in the population of native-born, as opposed to immigrant, Africans. The natural increase in population, percentagewise, led to fewer Africans imported for slavery. With a greater acclimatization to North America in language and other social and cultural customs, blacks became more Americanized, to the extent that chattel slavery allowed such a reality. This Americanization increased with the closing of the African slave trade in the early nineteenth century. While people were still being smuggled into the country, the numbers of forced African immigrants decreased. To a great extent, Africa steadily receded to the background of conscious black memory and celebration, though by no means completely disappearing. Increasingly, black women and men became African Americans and less Africans in America.

This cultural development accompanied a religious development: the emergence and spread of revivalist Christianity. During the eighteenth century the First Great Awakening (c. 1720s to 1750s) emerged in the middle colonies, spread to New England, and eventually came to the southern colonies. The Awakening was a series of revivals that emphasized the individual's direct contact with God. Emphasis was placed on conversion to Christianity "on the spot" rather than by means of doctrinal learning or a catechetical process. Preaching was Bible based, often emotional and dramatic, and in keeping with the classical Protestant credo of the "priesthood of all believers," each person was expected to witness or testify to others about their experience with God and to engage in individual acts of piety and righteous living, such as loving deeds, Bible reading, and personal acts of prayer. Among many Christians, leadership in the community, such as preaching, was determined more by a personal, direct call by God to the individual with less priority placed on formal training. The Great Awakening had counterparts in, and influences from, the Pietist movement in central Europe and Anglican revivals. The denominations most affected were the Baptists, Congregationalists, Presbyterians, and the Anglican Church, with the latter's revival wing emerging as the Methodist Episcopal Church after the Revolutionary War.

At a culturally expedient time, African American women found a form of religion with which they could relate, identify, and find comfort. Whether struggling and impoverished (as most free people of color were) or enslaved and destitute (as the great majority of African Americans were), black women embraced a form of faith that affirmed their personal worth and placed on cosmic levels of significance their ordinary, routine acts of kindness, religious testimony, and personal and family devotions. As Africa, in conscious ways, receded to the background, African American women discovered a religion that united them with other like-minded peoples across ethnic African and even human racial lines. African American evangelical women had greater opportunities to exercise leadership in circles that increasingly emphasized appointment originating from God rather than formal training by people. John Wesley, the Methodist founder, during his preevangelical, Anglican years testified to the presence of enslaved women in services held in the Georgia colony during the 1730s. With the advent of evangelical Methodism in the United States, we find an enslaved woman named Betty as a member of Barbara Heck's society in New York City, a group that some term the earliest Methodist society in America. By 1808 records point to "Old Elizabeth," who engaged in lay witnessing and Bible study leadership. Born enslaved in 1766, Elizabeth secured her freedom around 1796 and twelve years later was leading a black woman's meeting in Baltimore. White Methodist leaders forced her to surrender control of the meeting to a male, but some time later we hear of her preaching the gospel even in some slave states, a gospel that included a condemnation of slavery. Although males were the clerical leaders in the independent black Baptist congregations founded in Silver Bluff, South Carolina, in the 1770s and the First African Baptist Church in the 1780s, women were vital members of both congregations as well as the oldest but not continuous independent black congregation on record, the Bluestone or First African Baptist Church in Virginia founded around 1758.

During the early decades of the nineteenth century, another series of revivals appeared in the United States, termed the Second Great Awakening. It differed in some fundamental ways from the first: There was a more positive, proactive attempt to start revivals rather than depending on them to occur spontaneously; there was an even greater participation of African Americans and women in the Second Awakening than in the First; and certain practices, known as "new measures," recognized the growing practice of women to participate in public prayer and give testimonials to their faith and Christian experiences. With the greater freedom to exercise public prayer and testimony, more instances of women, black and white, enslaved and free, becoming preachers or exhorters are recorded. In some instances making public testimony to one's faith and leading Bible study became in effect preaching of the gospel, although it was not called that and not done from the pulpit. In other instances, such as with Jarena Lee, Sojourner Truth, and Amanda Berry Smith, women owned the title of evangelist, exhorter, or preacher. Interestingly, during the

first half of the nineteenth century women did not seek "full" ordination, that is, the authority to pastor churches or conduct sacraments, but they did seek to be recognized as preachers.

Jarena Lee in her conflict with the African Methodist Episcopal (AME) Church reflected the arguments used by black women to justify their right to preach the gospel. Lee spoke of her clear calling and direction from God and insisted that since Christ died for males and females, both should be free to preach the gospel. To those who argued that preaching was a much more expository, refined public elaboration on doctrine and the faith than exhortation grounded in an individual's knowledge of God's salvation, Lee responded that perhaps this type of preaching had incorrectly gone beyond the activities of poor, unlearned fisher disciples of Christ. Sojourner Truth's name came to her from God and spoke eloquently about what the Reverend Truth's mission was: to sojourn or travel here and there, proclaiming God's truth. Truth's message was a gospel intricately and inextricably tied to preaching against the evils of slavery. After the Civil War, Amanda Berry Smith would survive the slights and neglect of her AME male ministers and play a very active role in proclaiming the gospel in the United States, England, India, and Liberia. That these women preachers and prayer leaders often traveled many miles by foot, experienced some of the crudest forms of verbal harassment, made choices between motherhood and traveling the preaching circuit, and suffered from economic want eloquently testifies to their dedication. While these women's use of the Bible was helpful in making their case for the right to preach, often the actual power and effect of their preaching upon people was what moved critics to accept, or at other times soften their opposition to, the legitimacy of their ministry.

Black Women, the Slave Church, and Independent Black Christianity

From the 1750s we witness two major contexts for the growth of black Protestant Christianity: one in enslaved territory and the other in the "free" states. The earliest independent black congregations began in the slave colonies and states, including First African or Bluestone Baptist Church in Virginia around 1758, the Silver Bluff Baptist Church during the 1773–1775 period, and the oldest, continuous congregation of black Christians, the First African Baptist Church, in 1788, in Savannah, Georgia. While some African Americans had a degree of autonomy in separate Southern black congregations, the increased abolitionist movement, including the first publication of David Walker's *Appeal* first in 1829, the revolt of Nat Turner in Virginia in 1831, and a new, more aggressive white antislavery movement during the 1830s, meant that these black churches had a great deal of their autonomy circumscribed or superintended during the thirty years leading to the Civil War. Besides, many of the congregants of these independent black churches were enslaved women and men. In addition, a good segment, if not majority, of black women and men Christians had to resort to the "invisible institution" to practice their faith with a larger measure of comfort and freedom. The *invisible institution* is a term describing all those beliefs, practices, and activities of enslaved people that went unobserved by whites. Meeting in slave cabins, the woods, and other secret places, black women were able to express their innermost and most profound feelings, thoughts, and prayers. Unseen and unheard by whites, black women joined black men and children in praying for freedom, worshipping freely with whatever exuberance they found necessary and appropriate, and listening to enslaved preachers who often contradicted the "slaves obey your masters" message heard when white people were present and, instead, preached a gospel for the downtrodden and the oppressed, emphasizing that God was on the side of freedom.

Apparently, men solely exercised the roles of "pastors" in both the visible and invisible institutions of black Christian life, but women played key roles in the secret worship services. With the conclusion of slavery, the black Christian community still had a place for these "mothers of the church," who served as religious leaders and advisers for the entire religious community. Significantly, there is often in evangelical circles a thin line between the substance of lay testimony and prayer leadership and the formal endeavor of pulpit ministry. While more research is required, it seems that "informally" black women were often de facto ministers in the invisible institution.

Beyond this freedom to worship more freely, African American women experienced a wholeness as people and even more particularly as women in Christianity, visible and invisible. In a very racially chauvinistic, enslaved environment African American women were seen first and foremost as blacks and secondarily as women. Generally their portraits vacillated between "Jezebel," a wicked, sinful woman tempting men (including white men) to succumb to sin, and "Mammy," the long-suffering, patient mother and adviser of white people whose love and dedication to white children and adults often superseded concerns for her own family. In Protestantism, black women found a means of measuring their worth and fidelity to God beyond that which whites of either gender or black males might attempt to impose on them. In the name of Christ, they enhanced positive self-concepts, rejected unfair and demeaning stereotypes, embraced motherhood as a sacred rather than as an exploitative economic activity, and found

comfort in the face of suffering and death. Black Protestant women found a wider Christian family and opportunities to be united and sometimes reunited with family and friends on the same or other plantations, farms, and households.

While some scholars might see indications of white-black female gender bondings between slaveholders and the enslaved, such observations entirely escape this researcher. Quite the contrary, black women, like their male counterparts, viewed slavery as sinful and contradictory to the will of God. They found it practically impossible to enjoy fellowship (even had it been offered) with or to value the purported Christian faith of anyone, white male or female, who either dealt out the harshness of oppression, approved of it, or remained ethically silent. In the face of attempts to degrade her, disrupt her family, even her parent-child relationship, the beatings and other atrocities executed with the same ferocity and humiliation as those delivered to black men, the African American woman found in Protestant Christianity the means of securing her human and gender worth and the internal strength to withstand and even triumph over adversities during and after enslavement.

The nineteenth century was an era of active efforts by religious ministers and laypeople, male and female, including and especially evangelical Protestants, to reform society along religious, humanitarian, and social lines. Voluntary societies were those organizations formed by a gathering of individuals usually from various denominations committed to the achievement of one goal: for example, distributing Bibles, conducting foreign or overseas missions, fighting prostitution, curbing the use and sale of alcoholic beverages, improving the penal system, and eliminating slavery. Often these groups envisioned the accomplishment of their single goal as the solution to all the other evils of society as well. Scholars speak of the interconnectiveness of these various societies as the "benevolent empire." African American Christians, including black Protestant women, were involved in these efforts as well. For most black women the number-one and most fundamental issue, aside from evangelicals' wish to spread Christianity, was the eradication of slavery. Obviously, women enslaved felt the immediate, painful reality of oppression. But even most free black women's lives were intricately tied to their enslaved brothers and sisters. Most free blacks had a history of personal enslavement and/or had relatives and friends who were still ensnared in the system. In addition to the sheer brutality of the slaveholders and their appointees' attacks upon the persons of the enslaved, the system of slavery itself represented for black Protestant women and other antislavery or abolitionist Christians the reservoir of various sins adversely infecting the morality of the slaveholder, the larger society, and sometimes the enslaved: greed, laziness (on the part of the slaveholders), adultery, hatred, inability to embrace and practice Christianity or to worship freely, kidnapping, and physical brutality. Therefore, the ministry of Sojourner Truth, which essentially equated the practice of Christianity with the elimination of slavery, echoed the views of black Protestant women in general. Aside from the elimination of oppression, the abolition of slavery also would help promote genuine Christianity rather than the hypocritical religion of the slaveholders which betrayed the teachings and spirit of Jesus Christ's gospel.

In addition to Sojourner Truth, women such as Harriet Tubman and Maria Stewart stepped into the public arena in order to combat slavery, racism, and at times sexism. Stewart, a Baptist, has the apparent distinction of being the first woman of color to give public addresses in the 1830s during a period when for women even to pray and make religious testimony in public and in gender-mixed assemblies was considered radical. Stewart raised her voice in opposition to enslavement and racial discrimination in the Boston area. In a sense her life adumbrated a wider connection between abolitionism and women's rights in the nineteenth century. That is, many women, especially white women, found an impetus to the struggle for women's suffrage and equal rights via their generally frustrated attempts to participate openly and fully in the battle against slavery. Tubman represents even more concretely the connection between enslaved and free African Americans. Born a slave, she escaped from Maryland, making her way north to freedom, later returning to rescue enslaved family members. She made more journeys into slavocracy to lead the oppressed to freedom. For these heroic efforts she was nicknamed "Moses." Tubman remains perhaps the most popularly known "conductor" on the Underground Railroad, that secret network comprising the enslaved, the free, whites, blacks, and persons of various religious backgrounds that provided directions, food, lodging, and haven for refugees seeking freedom in the North or Canada. A member of the young but growing African Methodist Episcopal Zion Church, Tubman was like Stewart and Truth motivated by her religious convictions and keenly committed to religious community.

Other Reform Activities

Clearly black women, while heavily involved in antislavery activities, had related interests: emigration and colonization, as well as missionary, humanitarian, and benevolent work. First, let us consider the domestic sphere of American society. Generally humanitarian and benevolent activities were closely connected and inseparable from the religious convictions of both African American and white Christians, as observed in women's antislavery and abolitionist activities. The earliest independent black organization in North America was not the denominational church but the Free African Society, a benevolent society formed in the 1780s in Pennsylvania that combined Christian piety and acts of service to humanity, such as aiding widows and orphans and providing for burial expenses. This was a type of voluntary society, made up of women and men from various denominations. Temperance in its origins referred to efforts to keep the consumption of alcoholic beverages within moderate use but eventually meant total abstinence. African American Christians, particularly in Protestant denominations such as the Methodists and Baptists, strongly supported temperance for a number of reasons: the religious conviction that it was sinful, the actual cost in family and economic terms caused by the reckless use of alcohol, and inclusive of the previous two reasons, the threat to racial progress that drunkenness represented. In a largely hostile white environment, any disorderly or irresponsible conduct on the part of even a few members of the African race justified in the minds of many whites the enslavement and second-class treatment of all blacks. Both African American Baptist and Methodist records indicate that women and men often expressed their commitment to eliminating the use of alcohol most strongly through agencies of the church as well as interdenominational moral reform societies.

Black women, as their male counterparts, spoke out forcefully in favor of other virtues and reforms. One was the necessity of blacks to acquire whatever education was available to them. With the great absence of formal schools for African Americans, many women and men sought training in apprenticeships, sometimes trading their labor or that of their children in exchange for training for themselves or their children; and many were self-taught. Even among the enslaved, reading was a much coveted skill, with some scholars of slave religion speaking of the enslaved's high regard for acquisition of literacy comparable in intensity to religious awe. Women Protestants, like their male counterparts, stressed the importance of free blacks' being gainfully employed and not given to idleness and laziness. With the negative stereotypes of black women so rampart in society, black Protestant women generally took the lead in efforts to curtail or eliminate prostitution and to insist that all Christian women conduct themselves with flawless sobriety. While the emphasis on hard work, sexual purity, and the acquisition of education might sound to many in the twenty-first century as black women's embrace of middle-class values, it must be remembered that these women were concerned with the very survival of the race in the face of many harsh critics and enemies who maintained that African Americans were best suited for slavery. Free blacks, therefore, felt a special obligation to survive and at times prosper not simply for their own sake but as proof to an often skeptical world that Africans had the same moral, spiritual, and cultural values and potentials as whites.

One means of dealing with enslavement and discriminatory treatment was the use of emigration or colonization as a means of escape from an unjust social order and the opportunity to help build a new, more humane society. African American women and men in the pre–Civil War America generally distinguished between emigration and colonization. Emigration was the decision on the part of an individual, family, or group to move to another part of the nation or to another country. Not only escaped slaves fleeing to the North or Canada fit this category but also free African American women and men in the South and the North who sought freedom and greater justice in other places. Black Protestant women uniformly approved of this voluntary relocation on black people's own terms. Colonization was understood as efforts organized and supported by whites to have African Americans, especially free blacks, removed from the country and relocated in Africa or some other land.

Most women and men of color, such as Maria Stewart, vigorously opposed colonization because they saw it as an effort to rid the country of free blacks. Such a removal would mean that the enslaved no longer would have a haven, should they be able to escape, would not have a visible example of black people's ability to survive as free people, and the antislavery movement would lose effective spokespersons for freedom. And just as important, black women and men insisted that the United States was as much their home as anyone else's. While they respected and supported the right of individuals and even groups to act in their own interests, most African American Christians saw colonization and sometimes even emigration as denying, in the face of proslavery and racially chauvinistic opponents, an important principle that blacks had the right to enjoy equal and just participation in American society.

Colonization and Christian Missions

Some African American women and men did venture overseas as colonizers and missionizers during the pre–Civil War period, mainly to Africa and Haiti. Women also accompanied the black loyalists who left the colonies during the Revolutionary War period and settled in Nova Scotia. By the 1790s many of these colonists had relocated to Sierra Leone, a British colony in West Africa for Africans escaping the slave trade, and established the first Baptist congregation on the African continent. The American Colonization Society, founded in 1816–1817 as a vehicle to transport African American slaves freed on the condition that they would emigrate, was the principal sponsor of African resettlement during this period.

Among the earliest settlers of the American colony of Liberia in the 1820s were two founders of the Richmond African Baptist Missionary Society, the Reverends Lott Carey and Hilary Teague and their wives and families. Thus, the Careys and the Teagues journeyed to Africa supported by three agencies: the Richmond Society, the national Triennial Baptist Convention, and the American Colonization Society. Sometimes whole congregations of African Americans were provided passage to their new African home. In addition to being settlers or colonists, these women and men ventured to Africa with the intention of doing missionary work among the indigenous African peoples, a dream that often did not come to fruition.

On the mission field, the husband, if a minister, served as preacher and pastor and the wife as Bible teacher or nurse. While missionary societies often listed only the husband's name, husbands and wives operated as teams in the field. Indeed, the wife generally interacted most intimately with women and children, whose numbers often constituted the majority of new converts. Besides, women would take sole responsibility in a mission field upon the death of a husband and the absence of another male missionary. During the 1850s, the black Baptists Joseph and Sarah Harden were sent by the Southern Baptist Convention to the Liberian mission field. In 1855 the convention transferred them to Nigeria. By 1869 with her husband, Joseph, dead and another male missionary leaving because of ill health, Sarah Harden assumed full responsibility for the local Baptist church. In an age when Baptist women were not licensed to preach and denied ordination, Mrs. Harden had become a de facto pastor in West Africa, a development that would recur throughout the history of missions.

Civil War and Reconstruction

The advent of the Civil War and the ensuing Reconstruction period signals a profoundly new day for African American women and men, including Protestants. A civil strife that arrayed Northern and Southern white men and women against each other served as the means to unite, and in some cases reunite, black women and men of the North and South. For the refugees from slavery, the abolitionists, and all black women and men, the freeing of African Americans enslaved in the Confederacy with the Emancipation Proclamation in 1863 and the subsequent Thirteenth Amendment to the U.S. Constitution legally eliminating servitude from the land represented a literal exodus of biblical proportions. They saw in these activities, despite all the inconsistent and self-serving efforts of human beings, the movement of God in history in answer to centuries of prayers and a culmination of painful efforts to secure freedom. Here was an opportunity for black women as well as men to perfect the political freedom promised by recent governmental actions. More broadly, it was an occasion to reconstruct a people for spiritual as well as temporal wholeness. It is no wonder that black males eagerly volunteered for service in the Union forces and women praised God that they at last had the opportunity to fight for a united and free nation.

Black women, free and soon to be free, educated and untrained formally, well known and the unknown, aided Union soldiers and came south to help in the uplift of their racial kin, and black men rejoiced. Many unknown women nursed soldiers, served as Union army spies or informants, set up schools to educate the recently freed, helped organize and reorganize churches, and raised funds for all needs. Harriet Tubman, Moses and chief of the Underground Railroad, served as a spy. Charlotte Forten journeyed south to establish a school for blacks and kept a valuable journal of her endeavors and experiences. Lucy Craft Laney, a Presbyterian born in Georgia in 1854, established a school for African Americans in Atlanta. Anna Julia Cooper attended Saint Augustine, an Episcopal college in North Carolina, and became a teacher and principal in Washington, D.C. While suffrage would remain elusive for most women of all races prior to the twentieth century, black women as a result of Union victory and the short-lived Reconstruction era had much to celebrate: physical freedom from chattel slavery, psychological freedom to be parent and spouse on their own terms, mental freedom to acquire new skills and knowledge, and greater legal freedom and protection of their person and property as a result of Reconstruction reforms in the states.

Given this new reality, African American Protestant women, as their male and female counterparts in both Protestant and Catholic Christianity, took bold advantage of these new opportunities. Many black women desired the establishment of black families along the model of whites, one based on patriarchy. Some women welcomed the opportunity to follow the more domestic, stereotypical activity of wife and mother. Although this may surprise or puzzle many contemporary readers, we must understand that black people, as whites, generally embraced familial and societal patriarchy. Furthermore, for many African American women chattel slavery had forcefully denied them freedom to select this traditional role. Also, racialist propaganda and prejudice during and after slavery, in the North and the South, had branded black people as morally deficient, an attack that greatly concerned African American women in the age of the cult of true womanhood. On the other hand, some women disagreed with this emphasis on domesticity at the expense of involvement in the public arena, and most women, whether they agreed or not, had little choice but to work outside the home. Just as slavery had

its harsh version of gender equity between black women and men (e.g., equally grueling work and brutal punishments), so the postslavery era for most blacks was marked by exploitation and deprivation exposing most black women to the same or comparable circumstances as their brothers.

African American Women and Pulpit Ministry

But the post–Civil War era was one in which women and men of color played a profound public role in society. Both labored to establish and maintain church and other religious institutions. Whereas the pulpit was virtually reserved for men, women such as Virginia Broughton, a Baptist, and Amanda Berry Smith, an AME Methodist, insisted on their right to preach, even if it did not entail full ordination or the right to pastor and serve the sacraments or ordinances of the church. Interestingly, Broughton in the late nineteenth and early twentieth centuries embraced a doctrine more commonly associated with Methodists, the principle of holiness, a belief that Christians should aim for and expect perfection, freedom from all conscious sin. Women and men, black and white, who embraced the holiness doctrine were most apt to recognize women's right to the pulpit. Smith during this era preached in England and served as a missionary in Liberia and India. While these two women did not insist on ordination, they stood firm in their conviction that God had called them to preach the gospel. As with their forerunners, these women defended their call to minister in writings and often found that the most obstinate opponents to women's preaching changed their mind after hearing a sermon preached by these women.

Other women ministers, particularly as we enter the 1880s and 1890s, more forthrightly requested absolute equality in the pulpit, including full ordination. These women and their male supporters faced stiff opposition because only a few mainline Protestant churches, white or black, approached ordination during this era. The Methodist Protestant Church and the Congregationalist denomination, mainly white groups, were two notable exceptions, but even the ordination of women in those bodies did not guarantee denominational-wide acceptance. What one local church permitted in Congregationalism might be disallowed in another; the Methodist Protestant Church explicitly left the matter of ordination to the decision of local annual conferences, that is, regionally drawn administrative divisions of the denomination. The United Brethren ordained a woman as elder in 1894, but the merger of this and other bodies that produced the Methodist Church in 1939 severely undercut women's pulpit freedom.

During this period, some black Protestant women, like their white counterparts, sought pulpit equality.

Sarah Ann Hughes in North Carolina during the 1880s received ordination as deacon from Bishop Henry McNeal Turner, a move later revoked by the AME denomination. It was in the African Methodist Episcopal Zion (AMEZ) Church that women, white or black, made their greatest, most unambiguous legal advances toward ministerial equality among mainline churches during the late 1800s and early 1900s. Not only were women ordained as deacons during the 1890s, but the Reverend Mrs. Mary Jane Small became the first woman to receive ordination as elder in 1898. Despite efforts to rescind her ordination and/or to restrict other women, the General Conference of the AMEZ Church upheld Small's ordination in 1900 and, thus, officially went on record declaring full gender equality in the church. Although other women ministers, such as the renowned Julia Foote and famous Florence Randolph, followed Small into full AMEZ ordination, prejudice against women obstructed the goal of true equality in the ministry.

While some nonmainline, Holiness/Pentecostal, and sometimes heterodox groups recognized women's right to the pulpit in the late 1800s and early 1900s, the AMEZ's actions were extremely rare among Methodists and other Protestants. Sister Methodists did not begin to follow suit with full ordination until midcentury: the AME in 1948, the Christian Methodist Episcopal (CME) in 1954, and The Methodist Church (later United Methodist) in 1956. Nonetheless, the greater insistence on the part of many women for greater rights in the church moved these denominations, even during this period, to create ever widening arenas for women's ministry and work. The AME, for example, created the office of stewardess in 1868, agreed to license women to preach while withholding full ordination in 1884, and established, like other Christian bodies, the office of deaconess in 1900. In addition, while the three major black Methodist groups preceded their mother church—the mainly white (but very diverse) United Methodist Church—in ordaining women, as late as summer 2001 the United Methodist Church and another predominantly white group, the Episcopal Church, demonstrated far greater receptivity to selecting black and white women as bishops than the black denominations.

Women in Baptist groups, such as the National Baptist Convention, USA, Incorporated (NBCI) (organized in 1895) and the National Baptist Convention of America (NBCA) (1916), and the Progressive National Baptist Convention (PNBC) (1961) have continued to encounter great opposition to ordination. During this turn-of-the-century era, neither the NBCI nor the NBCA went on record supporting women's ordination but generally stood quite opposed. The mainly African American group Church of God in Christ (COGIC), organized in the 1890s as a Holiness group and reorganized in 1907 as a Pentecostal body, held an ordination position dur-

ing this period roughly midway between the black Methodists and the black Baptists. Occasionally, a woman might become de facto pastor in place of her late husband. Officially and by practice, however, ordination as such was denied and the preaching freedom of women only recognized when performed under the categories of missionaries and evangelists. The fact that these categories did have the official approval of the COGIC denomination meant, though, that women in this body found greater legal and practical freedom in the pulpit than their Methodist sisters. Some Holiness and Pentecostal groups, though smaller, offered even greater pulpit equality for women. In some instances, black women formed their own independent denominations, such as Bishop Ida Robinson's Mount Sinai Holy Church, organized in Philadelphia in 1924 and which has remained a body under the authoritative control of women, and Elder Lucy Smith's All Nations Pentecostal Church, started in Chicago during the 1930s. All the activities regarding women's ministry during this period could be summarized by stating that by the 1950s and 1960s, prior to the greater number of ordinations of women in mainline Protestant bodies in the 1970s and 1980s, black (or white) women ministers in most instances were Pentecostal or Holiness, a few were Methodists, and even more rarely Baptists.

Other Forms of Religious Leadership

Despite having ordination largely denied them, black Protestant women during this era still contributed greatly to leadership in their respective denominations. By the early 1900s all the major black Methodist and Baptist denominations had inaugurated women mission societies. Of course some auxiliaries and societies devoted to domestic mission work date back prior to the Civil War, such as the Daughters of Conference of the AMEZ. With greater resources and organization for missions in the postwar era, women not only raised funds for male-led conventions, societies, and operations but insisted on establishing their own. For example, the women of the AMEZ organized what eventually became the Women's Home and Foreign Mission Society in 1880. Baptist women organized auxiliaries to state conventions, and Nannie Helen Burroughs led the way in founding the Woman's Auxiliary of the National Baptist Convention (later USA, Inc.) in 1900. With some women the formation of these groups reflected a rising feminist or protofeminist consciousness, demonstrated in the "Woman's Column" of the AMEZ's newspaper, *The Star of Zion*. In the 1890s the column writer Sarah Dudley Pettey, a native of North Carolina and wife of a progressive Zion bishop, supported women's quest for equality in both church and society. Some male ministers complained bitterly that they had received unpleasant pastoral assignments because they had crossed Mrs. Pettey. She appears to have operated in some ways as a co-bishop with her husband, Charles Calvin Pettey, who ordained the first woman elder in Zion in 1898. Women not only raised funds and organized mission societies, but like their prewar pioneering sisters, they also journeyed to domestic and overseas mission fields. Women from various denominations, black and white, for instance, traveled to Africa as missionaries. Sometimes they served as co-missionaries with their husbands. Other times single women ventured to the fields, often establishing new mission stations. These single women include the Baptists Lulu C. Fleming, who journeyed to central Africa, and Emma B. Delaney, who did mission work in southern and western Africa.

Outside the traditional church and denominational organizations, women during this period founded and/or participated in a number of "secular" or "quasi-religious" organizations, which on an individual basis included all or some of the following goals: delivery of social services to the disadvantaged, education, temperance, health issues, housing, employment opportunities, labor issues, black suffrage, women's suffrage, and fostering morality. These groups drew heavily on individuals with strong religious and moral commitments, maintained close communications with religious bodies, and placed morality and ethics as significant components of their overall activities. The black women's club movement is a fine example of organized efforts by women to make an impact on the community. By the 1890s there were an extensive number of local, separate, independent women clubs dealing with matters affecting the overall African American community as well as issues particular to women. In 1896 the National Association of Colored Women (NACW) was formed. This national body premiered in response to attacks on the morality of blacks in general as well as particular attacks on the moral and ethical character of African American women. In pursuit of issues, such as outlined above, the groups helped to establish schools, orphanages, kindergarten programs, and homes for the elderly. Mary Church Terrell, the first president of the NACW, set the pattern for promoting qualities such as the need for black self-enhancement, purity in morals, and temperance while also fighting segregation, lynching, and promoting women suffrage. The NACW enjoyed its greatest membership strength and influence prior to 1930.

The Urbanization Period

Between the years 1915 and 1954 we have a period in African American history that could be termed the *urbanization* age. African American women and men migrated from southern and rural areas to the urban North and urban South. By the 1950s the demographics of black America shifted from overwhelmingly rural and southern to an urban and markedly increased northern populace. A number of factors contributed to one of the greatest mass movements in the nation's history, factors that influenced men and women and affected whole families and communities. These included increased racial oppression through the means of Jim Crow segregationist laws, continued disfranchisement of most black male voters (and the nonenfranchisement of black women), lynching and other acts of racial terrorism, souring agricultural economy in some areas during the first two decades of the 1900s, and greater availability of jobs in northern and urban areas. In many instances this caused profound disruption of family life with husbands and fathers often journeying to the cities in search of better jobs and a better standard of living for their families. On the other hand, sometimes entire families and practically whole church congregations relocated to one or a number of places. Black women in churches, women's clubs, and humanitarian organizations played crucial roles in assisting migrants to adjust to their new environment. In the more densely populated urban areas, women who felt the call of ministry found it easier to establish their own congregations or even denominations, for example, the Mount Sinai Holy Church in Philadelphia.

During this urbanization era a number of other profound developments affecting black women occurred. Three wars—World War I, World War II, and the Korean Conflict—were fought during this period. Black women served as nurses and entertainers and in other ways supported American soldiers, especially African American men, during these conflicts. Black Protestant women, as American women Christians in general, strongly supported America's role in all these conflicts and, more than nonblack men and women, endorsed and honored their African American brothers' service in all these wars. Particularly with World War I and World War II, black Christians, women and men, insisted that African Americans be granted the right to serve in all branches of the armed services. Black women Protestants supported the wars for the same reasons as Americans in general: World War I was to make the world safe for democracy; World War II sought to stop the spread of Nazism and fascism; and the Korean Conflict aimed to curtail the spread of communism. In addition blacks, including women Protestants, fought any exclusion from military or military-related participation based on race and held to the conviction that loyalty and devotion to one's country in times of crises would assist in the struggle for full inclusion in American life. In denominational minutes, newspapers, and other media, women, at times more forcefully than their male counterparts, made very clear their support and rationale for American policy. During this urbanization period black Protestant women also continued missionary efforts both domestically and internationally, especially in Africa, maintained support for black schools and colleges, and continued the quest for equality in the churches. Women attained ordination in the AME and the CME in the 1940s and 1950s. Marcus Garvey's "back to Africa" movement—the first mass movement of African Americans—enlisted the support of many Protestant women, especially between 1916 and 1930, with the Black Nurses Corp being one example of Garvey's organizational attempts to include the skills of women.

Just as black women were well represented in the birth and growth of blues and jazz during this period, they also figured very prominently in the emergence and resiliency of gospel music. Beginning in the 1920s with Thomas A. Dorsey, a former musician for the blues legend Ma Rainey, gospel music was a marriage between traditional church music and blues/jazz. While in the early decades many churches looked with disdain on this new medium of musical praise and proclamation of the gospel, in time gospel music found welcome homes in the traditionally black Protestant denominations of Baptists, Methodists, and Holiness/Pentecostal. Women gospel singing greats included the Roberta Martin Singers, Albertina Walker, Dorothy Norwood, Shirley Caesar, and perhaps the most renowned of them all, Mahalia Jackson, originally of New Orleans. Since the 1980s the list of women gospel singers includes Tramaine Hawkins, CeCe Winans, Vanessa Bell Armstrong, and the group Mary Mary. Gospel singing has been a means for countless women and girls in local churches in communities around the country to witness to their faith and fortify the gospel ministry. In addition, many great secular singers began singing gospel music, including Gladys Knight and Aretha Franklin.

Black Protestant women also made their presence in the political arena known during the urbanization period. While the more mainline civil rights groups, such as the National Association for the Advancement of Colored People (NAACP) and the Urban League, both founded in the early 1900s, retained male dominant leadership, women played great roles in the founding, growth, and operation of these organizations, with Ida Wells-Barnett, the great newspaperwoman and leader in the fight against lynching, being a major player in the NAACP. Franklin Roosevelt's New Deal and Mrs. Eleanor Roosevelt's strong support of civil rights were both instrumental in changing the majority of African Americans' allegiance from the Republican to the Democratic Party by the 1940s. Mary McLeod Bethune's participation in Roosevelt's administration as the director of the Division of Negro Affairs in the National Youth Administration, which made her the highest-ranking African American serving in the government, exemplifies this new political turn. On the other hand, Nannie

Helen Burroughs, founder and corresponding secretary of the Woman's Auxiliary of the National Baptist Convention, USA, Incorporated, retained her Republican allegiance. Not until the 1970s with the Republicans' swing to the Right on racial and civil rights issues would the national Democratic Party's hold on African American supporters become consistently lopsided. Women suffrage for white women and northern black women had been federally guaranteed by the 1920s, but the southern black woman, for the most part, remained unenfranchised, like her disfranchised male counterpart. Sadly, some of the most vocal and vigorous white women suffrage supporters in the early 1900s, especially in the South, actually appealed to racial prejudice and white supremacy as a political argument for enfranchising white women.

The Modern Civil Rights and Post–Civil Rights Eras

While the 1910s would witness the start of a slow turn in the nation's legal stance back toward equal rights for blacks, with painstaking progress being made during the urbanization era, not until the modern civil rights period (1954–1968) would political, societal, and to some extent, economic improvements come to a great mass of African Americans. This period saw the passage of civil rights laws dismantling racial segregation, guaranteeing the right to vote, ensuring open accommodations, and more. In other words, the civil rights movement was very successful in removing legal (though not always de facto) obstacles to full citizenship for blacks and, most profoundly, forcing the nation to renounce racism and segregation as acceptable societal values and principles, however much the fight against discrimination remained necessary. With the emphasis on the male leaders of organizations such as the Southern Christian Leadership Conference, the NAACP, the Student Nonviolent Coordinating Committee (SNCC), the Urban League, the Congress of Racial Equality, and others, it is possible to miss the tremendous and indispensable involvement of women and girls. From the inception of the Montgomery Bus Boycott in 1955, women in the city played key roles in organizing and carrying out the project. Indeed, much of the groundwork and support for the Martin Luther King, Jr.–led movement came from the Women's Political Council of Montgomery, founded by Professor Mary Fair Burks of Montgomery State College in 1946. Women (and sometimes girls) figured prominently in organizing, recruiting civil rights workers, filing legal claims or lawsuits, participating in sit-ins and demonstrations, integrating schools and colleges, joining freedom rides, and conducting political and voter education projects as well as doing the "behind the scenes" duties traditionally classed as "women's work," such as making coffee and cooking. Because very often the civil rights movement was a mass participation activity, representatives of the entire black community found roles to play: the churched and unchurched, girls and boys, women and men, the professional and laborers, and educated and noneducated.

Unfortunately, many black men and women reflected the patriarchal thinking of the time that excluded women from more visible, organizational leadership positions. The Southern Christian Leadership Conference, for example, was a largely male and minister-dominated organization that consistently relegated women to marginal levels of leadership. While women focused on the overall progress of the black community, these acts of chauvinism and exclusion did not entirely escape notice or sharp attacks. Individual women delivered particularly harsh criticisms of the male clergy. In the last decades of the twentieth century, women and men historians have worked to present more gender-inclusive treatments of the movement. Thus, Diane Nash, Ella Baker, Mary Lane, Dorothy Cotton, Septima Clark, Unita Blackwell, Victoria Gray, Annie Devine, and many others are finally receiving recognition for their key contributions. Perhaps the most noted female civil rights leader was Fannie Lou Hamer, civil rights activist, recruiter of black voters, demonstrator, and fighter for economic justice. A former sharecropper in the Mississippi Delta, Hamer was a founder of the Mississippi Freedom Democratic Party, an organization that sent shock waves through the 1964 national Democratic Party convention and helped alter the state's Democratic Party radically. The civil rights movement was very strongly influenced by black Christian interpretation that saw the obliteration of racism and discrimination as requirements of God's will. Many churches did not join the struggle, but a significant, if not majority, portion of the support for the direct, mass-action approach derived from participating churches in terms of supplying volunteers, providing meeting places, and giving religious justification for the movement. Protestant women as well as men, laywomen as well as male clergy, even when they were most critical of the church and the ministers, understood the movement for justice as not only a constitutional and legal imperative but a religious one as well.

The era of Black Nationalism or Black Power rose in the late 1960s. Increasing emphasis was placed on pride of race, African and African American history, knowledge of black culture, and the importance of African Americans having control over those institutions and services in the black community. Also developing was Black Theology, a form of liberation theology academically popularized by Professor James Cone, who combined the nationalist pride and critiques of Malcolm X with Martin Luther King, Jr.'s liberationist understanding of Christianity. Black Theology insisted that at the heart of the Christian gospel was the mandate to free not only the spiritually but the temporally oppressed, with a focus on blacks in North America. In the 1970s women theologians began to point out the deficiencies in Black Theology, which at that time largely ignored the oppressed plight of women, and Feminist Theology, which said little about racial injustice. Womanist studies, the term *womanist* borrowed from the famous writer Alice Walker, extended beyond theology (represented, e.g., by Jacquelyn Grant and Delores Williams) to include ethics (Katie Geneva Cannon), sociology (Cheryl Towsend Gilkes), biblical studies (Clarice Martin and Renita Weems), and history combined with a focus on theology and ethics (Cheryl Sanders). This pursuit of gender and racial equality contributed to and occurred in the context of widening opportunities for African American Protestant women in church and society. While black Baptist national conventions and the Church of God in Christ lagged behind the black Methodist denominations in ordaining women, it was clear that in many quarters of those churches significant progress based on changing perspectives was taking place. Besides, black women, as their male counterparts, were proving themselves willing to join other religious groups, such as the United Methodist Church, that provided better leadership opportunities. Consistent with the religious practice of many other Americans during the last fifth of the twentieth century, this migration to other religious groups did not limit itself to denominations within a given form of Christianity or to historically black churches; many black Baptist women, for example, found welcome arms extended by mainly white Methodist and Presbyterian bodies. This migratory pattern was assisted by the fact that African American women since the 1970s were becoming a numerically significant presence as students, professors, and other personnel in black and white seminaries and divinity schools. Indeed, in some predominantly white institutions they constituted a majority of black students by the 1990s.

Conclusion

As with their white counterparts, black women in the first decade of the twenty-first century constituted the majority of church members in at least most denominations. To be sure, African American women were members of Roman Catholic and mainly white Protestant denominations, including the Presbyterian Church, USA, the United Methodist Church, the Church of Jesus Christ of Latter-day Saints (the Mormons), the Evangelical Lutheran Church in America, the Episcopal Church, as well as many others. By far the largest percentage of women were found in the historically black denominations, such as the National Baptist Convention, USA, Incorporated, the National Baptist Convention of America, the National Baptist Missionary Convention, the Progressive National Baptist Convention, the African Methodist Episcopal Church, the African Methodist Episcopal Zion Church, the Christian Methodist Episcopal Church, and the Church of God in Christ. There were smaller denominations, such as the Mount Sinai Holy Church, but the preceding list of denominations contains well over three-fourths of all black women Christians in the United States.

In the dawning years of the twenty-first century, the black community in the United States could relish advances in a number of areas: rising incomes for many, a higher percentage of home ownership, a political climate devoid of much of the race-baiting and hatred characteristic of many American communities only a few decades earlier, rising prominence in sports and entertainment, and in sum, a greater access to many social, economic, and political areas of American life long denied them. On the other hand, there persisted challenges, such as a continuance of poverty in certain sectors, racial prejudice and discrimination that were sometimes more insidious given their often "subtle" forms of expressions, inadequate education, lack of proper health care for many, high rates of divorce and children being reared in single-headed families, racial profiling, and violence. However long the march to full freedom, it was clear that African American Protestant women would be among the leaders facing the challenges and taking advantage of new opportunities, just as they had throughout American history.

SOURCES: John W. Blassingame, *The Slave Community: Plantation Life in the Antebellum South* (1972). Cain Hope Felder, ed., *Stony the Road We Trod: African American Biblical Interpretation* (1991). John Hope Franklin and Alfred A. Moss, Jr., *From Slavery to Freedom: A History of African Americans*, 8th ed. (2000). Paula Giddings, *When and Where I Enter: The Impact of Black Women on Race and Sex in America* (1984). Glenda Elizabeth Gilmore, *Gender and Jim Crow: Women and the Politics of White Supremacy in North Carolina, 1896–1920* (1996). Herbert G. Gutman, *The Black Family in Slavery and Freedom, 1750–1925* (1976). Evelyn Brooks Higginbotham, *Righteous Discontent: The Women's Movement in the Black Baptist Church, 1880–1920* (1993). Sylvia M. Jacobs, *Black Americans and the Missionary Movement in Africa* (1982). Dorothy Sharpe Johnson and Lula Goolsby Williams, *Pioneering Women of the African Methodist Episcopal Zion Church* (1996). Gerda Lerner, ed., *Black Women in White America: A Documentary History* (1972). C. Eric Lincoln and Lawrence H. Mamiya, *The Black Church in the African American Experience* (1990). Susan Hill Lindley, *"You Have Stept Out of Your Place": A History of Women and Religion in America* (1996). Bert J. Loewenburg and Ruth Bogin, eds., *Black Women in Nineteenth Century America* (1978). Sandy D. Martin, *Black Baptists and African Missions: The Origins of a Movement, 1880–1915* (1989). Sandy D. Martin, *For God and Race: The Religious Leadership of AMEZ Bishop James Walker Hood* (1999). Patricia Morton, ed., *Discovering the Women in Slavery: Emancipating Perspectives on the American Past* (1996). Albert J. Raboteau, *A Fire in the Bones: Reflections on African-American Religious History* (1995). Belinda Robnett, *How Long? How Long?: African-American Women in the Struggle for Civil Rights* (1997). Rosemary R. Ruether and Rosemary Skinner Keller, eds., *In Our Own Voices: Four Centuries of American Women's Religious Writing* (1995). Jack Salzman, David Lionel Smith, and Cornel West, eds., *Encyclopedia of African-American Culture and History*, vol. 4 (1996). Milton C. Sernett, *African American Religious History: Documentary Witness*, 2nd ed. (1999). Frank M. Snowden, Jr., *Blacks in Antiquity: Ethiopians in the Greco-Roman Experience* (1970). William J. Walls, *The African Methodist Episcopal Zion Church: Reality of the Black Church* (1974). Judith Weisenfeld and Richard Newman, eds., *This Far by Faith: Readings in African American Women's Religious Biography* (1996).

WOMEN OF ANABAPTIST TRADITIONS
Marlene Epp

THE TERM *ANABAPTIST* is a sixteenth-century phenomenon but is often used in contemporary settings to refer to those groups that distinguish themselves by adherence to adult or "believers" versus infant baptism. Sixteenth-century religious authorities, both Protestant and Catholic, referred to certain radical offshoots of the Reformation as "ana-baptists" because of their practice of "rebaptizing" adult believers voluntarily. The largest Christian denominations in the United States and Canada that claim Anabaptist roots are the Mennonites, Amish, and Hutterites. Of these, the Mennonites are the largest, with about 415,000 members. Their name derives from the sixteenth-century Dutch Anabaptist leader Menno Simons. The Amish separated from the Mennonites in the late seventeenth century, choosing to place greater emphasis on outward forms like plain dress and discipline of church members who deviated from tradition. Today, the Amish—numbering about 69,000 in the United States and just over 1,000 in Canada—generally represent the most conservative of Anabaptist groups. The Hutterites, another Anabaptist offshoot, are distinguishable by their belief in holding property in common. Today the Hutterites, with about 25,000 members, live communally in large colonies mainly in the American Midwest and on the Canadian prairies. In addition to these three, there are a number of small groups, such as the Brethren in Christ and Church of the Brethren, who also are considered part of the "believers church" tradition and have similar beliefs and characteristics. Most of the examples in this essay will be drawn from the Mennonites.

A number of general statements can be made about

Especially in the early years of pioneer settlement, the household was the social unit that shaped the identities of Mennonite and Amish women more so than the church. Women also played a primary role in nurturing kinship and other social relationships across huge geographic spaces, since migration inevitably divided Mennonite communities and quite often extended families as well. *Copyright © Dave Hunsberger.*

the experience and roles of women in these relatively small Protestant denominations. Because women in Anabaptist groups have in the past been part of a tradition that attempts to set itself apart from society, they were participants alongside men in a common project of establishing boundaries that would uphold separation ideals. Yet because religious authority was vested in male leaders, women had no official voice in establishing normative practice within their church communities. Anabaptist women thus actively participated in ordering their lives within ethnoreligious and sectarian communities, yet historically they were simultaneously subject to the constraints and proscriptions, often gendered in nature, of those groups.

As well, because the primary authority for religious practice among Anabaptist groups lies with the congregation, and because Anabaptists have a history of diversity due to geographic mobility and church schisms, there is a great deal of variance in the religious experience of women within these traditions. For instance, across North America, there are at least fifty different subgroups that would identify themselves as Mennonite. Then there are various groups of Amish, including the most identifiable Old Order, and moderately conservative groups such as the Beachy Amish. Along this continuum, there is variety in the extent to which religious beliefs and rituals shape everyday life. For women within

those conservative groups that eschew motorized transportation and modern household technology, religion undergirds and fashions their culture and daily lifestyle. At the other end of the spectrum are women who identify with many of the cultural traditions of their ancestors but are not actively involved in the religious aspects of the traditions. Within groups like the Amish or Hutterites, where cultural symbols like food, quilting, and dress are strong identity signifiers, women are important shapers of ethnic culture.

As well, the pace at which women have been brought into what were in the past exclusively male religious realms, such as pastoral work, varies according to denominational subgroup, locale, and degree of conservatism. As a result, one risks generalizing about the way in which religious belief is understood and practiced by Anabaptist women. Yet Anabaptist groups have common patterns in their histories and share a core of religious doctrines that shape the way in which women's lives are ordered and lived out.

Religious Beliefs and Historic Background

The primary and characteristic doctrine of the Anabaptists was a belief in a church community based on voluntary membership and thus a practice of adult baptism. The revolt against infant baptism was radical and heretical in sixteenth-century Europe because it removed religious belief and church membership from state authority. Anabaptists envisioned a church of believers set apart from the secular world, yet which also modeled Christian belief to those outside the church. Consequently, certain leaders placed substantial emphasis on a "pure church" including varying degrees of discipline toward church members who deviated from community norms. Anabaptists also rejected ecclesiastical hierarchy, the performance of sacraments, and paying for indulgences as a means to salvation.

Some analysts of the early Anabaptist movement have emphasized the equalizing potential of a movement that rejected the necessity of a clergy mediating between God and the individual and made the reading and interpretation of scripture accessible to the entire laity. The idea of a "priesthood of all believers" has sometimes been put forward to suggest that the Anabaptist movement offered women a more elevated position than was available in other Christian denominations. And indeed there were women within the movement who hosted clandestine worship services, interpreted and taught scripture to those gathered, traveled and evangelized to bring their faith to others, and were arrested and executed for heresy. Helene of Freyberg (d. 1545) was an Austrian noblewoman who purportedly sheltered Anabaptist fugitives on her estate and eventually separated from her own family to join the radicals. A collection of stories, *The Martyrs' Mirror* compiled by Thieleman J. van Braght, about 930 Anabaptists who were killed for their religious beliefs includes entries for about 300 women, leading some historians to suggest that women were active in the early stages of this radical religious movement. Among the Hutterites, an Anabaptist group that lived communally and held property in common, one's covenant with the church community took precedence over a marriage covenant. Thus, a woman who chose to join the Hutterites following a spiritual conversion had the freedom to leave her husband if he was not also a believer.

These possible equalizing tendencies in early Anabaptism were accompanied, and perhaps offset, by a strong emphasis on the Bible as the final authority for Christian thought and practice and, as well, literal readings of scripture passages. This biblical literalism, interpreted in particular cultural contexts over time, took at face value biblical admonitions that women submit to their husbands, remain silent in church, and keep their heads covered. As one historian described it, Anabaptist women were "peers in the faith [but] subordinates in marriage" (Marr, 347). That is, while the Holy Spirit made no gender distinctions in bringing spiritual rebirth to individuals, the social order of the earthly church and family was stratified according to sex. The tension between spiritual equality and social inequality continued

to shape the lives of Anabaptist women throughout the centuries.

Migration

Early in their history, Mennonites and Amish developed a tendency toward mobility and migration in search of locales where they could establish relatively isolated communities. Driven by persecution and/or beckoned by religious freedoms and economic opportunities, they often moved to geographical frontiers to reestablish themselves. One historian of Mennonites has argued that "migration . . . often gave women the occasion to exert high degrees of power and influence" in their communities (Loewen, 96). To the extent that uprooting and new settlement demanded full participation of all family members and allowed women to create things new, sometimes including new roles, this observation may be true. In pioneer agricultural communities such as were established in Pennsylvania and Ontario by Mennonite and Amish immigrants from Switzerland throughout the eighteenth and into the nineteenth centuries and on the Canadian prairies and the American Midwest by Mennonites from Russia beginning in the 1870s, there was a certain egalitarianism that often occurs when institutional structures are less a priority than the physical labor demanded of women and men, young and old, in subsisting. Women and men were equally engaged in milking, in making hay, in setting up sheaves of grain, and in filling the cellar with food for the winter.

Women frequently added to these sustenance tasks by generating income through the sale of garden produce or handmade goods. Women of course had the extra physical burden of bearing as many as twelve or more children. Large families were both necessary and useful for farm operations and for the establishment and growth of church communities. As household producers and reproducers, women's work was essential to the success of the rural household and may have "provided them with a significant degree of meaning, status, and power" to offset the patriarchalism of Mennonite church communities (Loewen, 344).

Especially in the early years of pioneer settlement, the household was in fact the social unit that shaped the identities of Mennonite and Amish women more so than the church. Women also played a primary role in nurturing kinship and other social relationships across huge geographic spaces, since migration inevitably divided Mennonite communities and quite often extended families as well. Because they possessed a high rate of literacy, Mennonites were prolific letter and diary writers, and women in particular nurtured kinship relationships across many miles through regular letter writing.

Many of the patterns that shaped women's lives in early immigrant communities continue to exist in the more rural, isolated, and sectarian communities, such as the Amish and other Old Order groups. Among conservative groups, where there is little distinction between the "church" and the "community," families play a major, indeed primary, role in passing on and expressing religious beliefs. For the Old Order Amish, who have no church buildings but hold worship services in homes and sheds, church and household come together most directly. It is argued that because the community, church, and household are so closely related among conservative Anabaptists, there is more gender equality and greater value attributed to women and their work. Furthermore, in pioneer settings of the past and where social boundaries today limit contact with the outside world, women frequently carry specialized roles such as midwife, chiropractor, folk healer, and undertaker.

In the twentieth century, agricultural opportunities in both Canada and the United States began to diminish, but Mennonite migration did not. For a large wave of Mennonite immigrants (about 21,000) to Canada from the Soviet Union in the 1920s, women became a significant source of family income. As families struggled to establish themselves in rural areas, many sent their daughters, some as young as thirteen, to nearby cities to fill the high demand for domestic workers. These young women then sent their wages home, a contribution that meant the difference between survival and not for some impoverished households. Fearful for the morality of young women amidst the perceived evils of the city, Mennonite churches created boarding houses that also functioned as employment bureaus and later formed the nuclei of urban congregations. Unmarried women like Helen Thiessen (1892–1977) and Helen Epp (1897–1983), each of whom worked for several decades as matrons and administrators of such "girls' homes" in Winnipeg, Manitoba, found opportunities for a church-related vocation that was unavailable in their own formal congregations. Thiessen immigrated to Canada from Russia in 1903, grew up in rural Saskatchewan, and spent her adult years working with immigrants at city missions and later at the Mennonite girls' home. Epp, whose mother died when she was a teenager, cared for nine younger siblings until she immigrated to Canada in the mid-1920s, working on a farm until she moved to Winnipeg. The young women within this Mennonite immigrant community were at the forefront of an urbanizing trend that continued through the twentieth century. As such they played a significant role in altering a Mennonite ideal that considered a rural lifestyle and agricultural vocation practically akin to religious belief.

A post–World War II migration of Mennonites to Canada also saw women play a pivotal role in family and church history. Among the approximately 8,000 Mennonites who arrived in Canada as refugees from Ukraine after the war was a high percentage of widows with children and an overall ratio of women to men of about two to one. This gender imbalance was due primarily to the arrest and exile or execution of large numbers of adult men during several waves of Stalinist repression in the 1930s and to losses on the warfront as Mennonite men were conscripted into both Soviet and German armies. With the loss of formal church leadership due to the closure of all Mennonite churches by 1935 and the fact that most ministers were in exile, women assumed responsibility for maintaining religious practice and ensuring that their Christian faith was passed on to their children. They gathered together in the secrecy of their homes and read from the Bible, sang well-known hymns, and took turns leading the group in prayer. In the absence of formal religious structures and institutions, women refugees developed what has been described as a "domestic religion" based on stories, relationships, and informal ritual (Klassen, *Going by the Moon and the Stars*).

When these female-headed families arrived in Canada, having survived horrendous wartime conditions as refugees, they posed a dilemma for Canadian Mennonites for whom the patriarchal nuclear family, with a male as proper head, was the norm. Mennonite churches that received a large number of postwar immigrants suddenly found a membership roster that was decidedly imbalanced in favor of women. For some congregations this meant new additions to their church buildings, increased financial responsibilities—such as a fund in British Columbia that allowed widows to purchase houses—and the formation of new women's organizations. In some cases, the large number of women as primary earners expedited the process of granting women a vote in church decision making, something that was not standard practice in the 1950s. Again, women played a decisive role in shaping Mennonite migrations and religious development.

Nonconformity

The pattern of some Anabaptist groups to migrate and resettle in order to escape persecution and obtain a degree of isolation has been accompanied by a general orientation of separation from the outside world, that is, from the behavior and thought that is outside the church of believers. For some groups that meant geographic separation, while for others it was manifest in nonconformity or disassociation with trends of the world. Anabaptists believed they should follow a lifestyle that was nonconformed to the rest of the world, based on their reading of Romans 12:2. A popular descriptive phrase for this stance was "separation from the world," a position deemed necessary for a truly holy and Christian life. This view manifested itself, for example, in abstinence from voting in political elections or refusal to swear an oath in a court of law, in establishing separate schools, in insisting upon the maintenance of the German language or related dialects, in disallowing marriage with people of other denominations, and in objections to the use of musical instruments, electricity, and motorized transportation. Today the majority of Anabaptist groups, except for those in Old Order groups, do not adhere to these obvious and outward forms of separation.

The setting of social boundaries around the church community has had particular implications for women. One aspect of nonconformity especially gender specific is that of dress. At different points in history, and to varying degrees for different groups today, Mennonite, Amish, and Brethren groups adopted distinctive dress forms that were applied with particular inflexibility toward women. Toward the end of the nineteenth century and at least up until World War II, Mennonites of Swiss background in both the United States and Canada developed dress codes that for women included the wearing of a cape dress—a kerchief or capelike attachment to the bodice of a dress—as well as a prayer covering and bonnet for the head. The prayer covering, also called a veiling or cap, was to be worn by all baptized women, following a literal application of 1 Corinthians 11, in which the apostle Paul commands that women have their heads covered during worship in recognition of their subordinate place in the universal order. The bonnet was prescribed partly because it preserved a plainness of dress in opposition to the sometimes outlandish modern turn-of-the-century hat. But it was also promoted because it was worn more easily over the prayer covering. Church leaders feared that should women discard their bonnets, the hat was sure to go next.

These dress prescriptions were enforced quite stringently in some locales, and women who chose not to wear the covering and bonnet might lose their church membership. In 1870 the Church of the Brethren decided that women who were unwilling to cover their heads during worship should be dealt with "mildly, but strictly," and those who wore hats, rather than bonnets, to communion would not be served communion (Brubaker, 27). Although certain dress guidelines were established for men, for the most part only clergymen adhered to them. While some women, wearing their coverings proudly, exalted their position as "brides of Christ," others resisted what they saw as a clear double standard whereby they were expected to carry the "banner of nonconformity" for the entire church (Epp, 237–257).

One often-told story is that of two American Mennonites who, en route to mission work in Turkey in the early twentieth century, reportedly tossed their regulation bonnets overboard. Observing the resistance of Turkish women to regulations regarding veiling of the face, one of these women wrote that "the Turkish women must be going through a process of liberation much as our Mennonite women have" (*Vision, Doctrine, War*, 251). In some communities, church splits occurred when conflicts arose over dress issues. At the root of such splits were differing interpretations of scripture and sometimes divergent views about women's place in relation to God and man.

While the most urbanized and assimilated of Mennonite groups gradually gave up distinctive dress practices after World War II, there are numerous conservative groups who still maintain certain aspects of separatism in dress. Usually some form of head covering, because of its biblical foundation, is for such groups a symbol of both nonconformity and female subordination. The Old Order Mennonites and Amish exhibit the greatest uniformity and traditionalism in dress, with women dressed in dark or plain-colored long dresses and aprons and with nineteenth-century bonnets and shawls. However, in these very conservative groups men also adhere to church-prescribed dress standards, and thus a certain gender equality is obtained.

Even for those Anabaptist groups who relinquished or never adopted particular dress forms, the emphasis on separation from "worldliness" sometimes focused on aspects of women's culture such as birth control, hairstyles, makeup, jewelry, and household technology. Ideals of separation were also behind the church's past rejection of various government social programs, some of which were crucial in helping widows and single mothers out of financial straits. For instance, in Canada family allowance checks were issued to all Canadian families beginning in 1944. While many other Canadian women hailed this program as a gesture toward greater autonomy in managing their households, some Mennonite churches feared potential government intervention in family life and warned their members not to accept the checks.

Pacifism

Anabaptists set themselves apart from the mainstream not only by establishing social boundaries but also by rooting their religious values in the doctrines of nonresistance. Again they took their cues directly from New Testament scriptures, believing that warfare is wrong because it is contrary to Jesus' command to love one's enemies. Historically, the most concrete expression of this belief was an unwillingness to participate in secular warfare, and thus much effort was expended in securing exemptions from military service and alternate status as "conscientious objectors" (COs) for Anabaptist men. The fact that women were not conscripted into the military, however, meant that women from these pacifist traditions have by and large been left out of the great stories of nonresistant expression. As one woman said: "Because the destiny of the Mennonites revolved around the way sons were involved in [conscientious objection] and not the way the women experienced the truth of scripture, women's contribution was not as significant" (Wiebe, 23).

On the one hand, wars often meant economic difficulty for women because their menfolk might spend significant periods of time away from the household, either to perform public service work or to spend time in prison. During both world wars, many women took responsibility for managing family farms or took the unprecedented step of entering the paid workforce. Women who lived in urban settings especially, and those whose plain dress identified their religious affiliation, frequently felt public censure because their menfolk were perceived to be shirking their duty to the country.

At the same time, challenges to the church's position also presented women with the opportunity to increase activity deemed appropriate to their particular sphere. Women of Anabaptist traditions expressed their nonresistance primarily by providing material relief, both to their own men in work camps for conscientious objectors at home and to war sufferers overseas. Not unlike women with men in the forces, pacifist women prepared care packages with writing paper, envelopes, warm socks and gloves, and home baking for their own men in CO camps. In the United States, a church-administered work program for COs called Civilian Public Service (CPS) also drew women in as nutritionists, nurses, and cooks and in other roles within the nearly 100 camps established across the country. Wives and girlfriends of COs also uprooted themselves to be nearer their menfolk in CPS camps and together with those employed at the camps were seen as morale boosters and nurturers. Those involved with CPS developed vocational aspirations and also a "sense of purpose and usefulness in time of war" (Goossen, 93).

During World War II, Mennonite women's organizations entered what has been described as a "golden era" because of the sheer magnitude of their activity. Women's groups collected new and used clothing, sewed and mended, knitted, assembled care packages, and canned food to send overseas to refugees and other civilians suffering from wartime deprivation. One relief worker in England suggested that Mennonite women in North America adopt the slogan "Non-Resistant Needles Knitting for the Needy." For many women, sewing clothing and quilts and knitting socks and bandages became a unique contribution to their country and their particular expression of nonresistant religious belief.

Women's activities sometimes went beyond supportive ones to small acts of activism against militarism. One young Mennonite woman disapproved of the military slogans molded onto pats of butter at the restaurant where she worked, and so she served the butter upside down! The importance of tangible pacifist expressions for women was one of the reasons behind the formation of the Mennonite Nurses' Association in 1942, when it appeared that American nurses might be drafted into the military to alleviate a critical nursing shortage during the war. Wartime service at CPS camps also drew women into vocational peace work in the postwar era as Anabaptist and other pacifist church groups created institutions and organizations that promoted relief and development work as an expression of active pacifism.

The "Quiet in the Land"

Although the concrete work of material relief provided Anabaptist women with a way to express the peace position held by their church, the ethos of "not resisting evil" may present other issues for women. Anabaptist groups were often described as "the quiet in the land" as a description of their agricultural orientation, their quiet piety, and their nonresistant demeanor. The German word *Gelassenheit* (yieldedness) is often used to describe a particular theological concept emphasized in varying degrees by the Anabaptist groups. It refers to a personal disposition of self-denial and complete submission of the individual will to God and to the community. This belief arose in part in response to the suffering experienced by the early Anabaptist church. In order to rise above the persecution and torture, and not give up their beliefs, individuals were called to yield themselves to God.

The observation has been made that for Anabaptist women especially, *Gelassenheit*, combined with nonresistant (pacifist) beliefs, can lead to a tendency toward passivity, submission, and obedience to authority out of proportion to any biblical emphasis on such. Normative notions of discipleship—following the example of Jesus—are also cited as supporting the silent role of women. Such an orientation may also reinforce stereotypical female characteristics of self-denial and docility. The extreme manifestation of such theology, argues one female theologian, conveys "a gendered message which perpetuates the conditions leading to violence against women" (Penner, 1). While there is no conclusive evidence that violence against women is more common in Anabaptist homes and communities than in society generally, neither is there any indication that pacifist religious beliefs necessarily result in nonviolent homes. What is especially relevant to women's lives is the ironic fact that peace churches in the past tended not to include the problem of violence against women in articulations of their theology. Beginning in the 1980s, this apparent contradiction began to be addressed by concern for and programs directed at addressing issues of domestic violence in society and within Anabaptist communities.

Institutional Roles

Elise Boulding, in her important exploration of the "underside" of history, asserted that early Anabaptists "practiced complete equality of women and men in every respect, including preaching" (548). Indeed, there are many examples like that of Elisabeth Dirks who was accused of being a preacher for her teaching and missionary activities and was drowned in 1549. If there is evidence for female leadership in the early decades of the Anabaptist movement, it is also clear that the cessation of persecution and the increasing formalization of church life resulted in fewer allowances for women particularly in such positions of leadership as preaching.

It is only in the last two decades of the twentieth century that Mennonite women have become leading ministers in Mennonite churches. An exception to this was the ordination of Ann J. Allebach (1874–1918), a teacher, mission worker, and suffragist, who was formally ordained as a Mennonite minister in a Philadelphia church in 1911. This example would not be a precedent, however. Whatever call to "prophecy" was granted to sixteenth-century women, the biblical admonition that women be silent became dominant in Anabaptist church life for the centuries that followed. Roles such as bishop, minister, and deacon could only be held by men, either through selection or election. And although the practice varied and still varies widely from one congregation to another, until late in the twentieth century women were not allowed to add their voice to formal decision-making processes in the church.

Sixty years would pass before another woman was formally ordained to pastoral ministry in North America. Emma Richards was ordained as a Mennonite minister in 1973 in Illinois and in Canada; Martha Smith Good was ordained in Ontario in 1978. The women's movement and "second-wave" feminism undoubtedly spurred Anabaptist churches and their female members to question prohibitions against women in senior ministry and other leadership positions in church bureaucracies. The reinterpretation by feminist theologians of biblical passages regarding women's right to preach and prophesy reinforced this development for certain biblically literalist Anabaptist groups.

Despite the increase in the number of women being ordained in Mennonite churches in the early twenty-first century, "pockets of strongly ingrained resistance to women preachers endure" (Klassen, "Speaking Out in God's Name," 242). Ironically, in Pennsylvania where Ann Allebach became a minister, there are certain groups still resisting the ordination of women despite strong pressure from women and men within those groups. One of the largest of the modern Mennonite subgroups, the Mennonite Brethren, at the end of the twentieth century did not sanction the ordination of women. And within the most conservative Old Order Mennonite and Amish churches and among the Hutterites, the few formal leadership roles that exist are held exclusively by men.

In contrast, women within certain modern Anabaptist subgroups are increasingly assuming prominent leadership roles within church institutions. In the 1990s, two major American Mennonite colleges chose female presidents—Lee Snyder at Bluffton College in Ohio and Shirley Showalter at Goshen College in Indiana. And in the year 2000, the Mennonite World Conference, a network of global Mennonite churches, named its first woman, Nancy Ruth Heisey, as president-elect.

If women have only recently been allowed roles as ministers and preachers, they have been very active in other sectors of church activity. Early in the twentieth century, a deaconess program for unmarried women existed, mainly in Virginia and in the American Midwest, that gave women opportunities to exercise both their religious piety and professional aspirations. In the latter locale, orders of deaconesses almost akin to Catholic religious orders were involved in health care in Mennonite-run hospitals. In the eastern United States, deaconesses had the mandate to visit women and children, enforce dress regulations, and assist women when certain church rituals were performed. Among the latter was the Anabaptist ordinance of footwashing whereby church members, usually separated by sex, would wash each other's feet in remembrance of Christ's similar act of service to his disciples. As well, women have been active as Sunday School teachers, as writers for church periodicals, as music leaders, and most notably, as church-sponsored missionaries, both on domestic and foreign fields.

In the late nineteenth century, as overseas missions were introduced to the program of Mennonite and Brethren churches, women found a way in which they could effectively function as religious leaders but far away from the watchful eye of church authorities. Initially it was mainly unmarried women who seized the opportunity to travel to distant places like Africa and India to preach, teach, and in other ways minister. Bertha Ryan (1871–1953) opened the Church of the Brethren's mission in India in 1894 where she started Sunday Schools and in particular cared for those suffering the effects of severe plague and famine. She spent six years in India but did not return after getting married while home on furlough. Indeed, some women from Anabaptist churches were so eager to express their faith in concrete vocational ways that they accepted overseas assignments from other denominations well before Mennonite and Brethren churches had developed a missions program. One of the most well-known missionaries is Annie Funk (1874–1912), who went to India as a teacher in 1906. When her mother became ill, Funk booked passage home on the *Titanic* and, according to oral tradition, gave up her place in a lifeboat to someone else and so lost her life at the age of thirty-eight.

Single women were also often the pioneers in opening inner-city missions in urban centers like Chicago and Toronto at the turn of the century. Women missionaries from "plain" churches faced unique dilemmas as they sought, out of evangelistic zeal, to bring people to Christian faith but in doing so were compelled to enforce Anabaptist peculiarities on newcomers to the church. Women had the special task of teaching converts the importance and nuances of dress codes, especially the wearing of a head covering. Christmas Carol Kauffman (1901–1969), fiction writer and mission worker in Chicago, expressed her dual roles of helping the poor and converting people to Mennonitism in a 1935 diary entry: "Dec. 16. Gave out one covering and fed two tramps" (151).

For women who did not assume church-related vocations, women's organizations offered a specifically female venue for women to express themselves within church life. It has been said that women's organizations within the Mennonite church function as a "parallel church" in which women exercise leadership in performing some of the roles that were historically unavailable to them in the main institution. Because Mennonite religious values included the maintenance of social boundaries, women were historically discouraged and sometimes prohibited from participating in the activities of women's organizations in wider society. Thus beginning in the late nineteenth century, they began to carve out a space for themselves under the umbrella of male-run Mennonite church institutions. In the context of their own organizations, often referred to as mission societies or sewing circles, women sewed and knitted for charitable causes and also engaged in Bible study, prayer, and devotional discussion.

This relatively autonomous women's activity did not progress without opposition. In the late 1920s, the Mennonite Women's Missionary Society, based in Ohio and led by Clara Eby Steiner (1873–1929), was effectively taken over by the church's mission board and its male leaders, who were threatened by women's success in raising funds and supporting overseas missionaries. They may have feared the potential influence this would give women in the area of missions overall. Without question, however, the grassroots material work and fund-raising of women's organizations have provided the foundation on which such Mennonite bureaucracies as Mennonite Central Committee, which engages in relief and development around the world, have been built.

Women of the conservative Anabaptist groups, such as the Old Order Mennonites and the Amish, do not have formally constituted organizations. But they nevertheless meet in each other's homes to quilt and sew for themselves, for sale to outsiders, and for charitable causes.

Women in North America who adhere to various Anabaptist traditions today find both strength and limitation in a history that offered new opportunities for the expression of faith while also delineating sometimes rigid roles for women within small sectarian communities. The working out of the tension, or balance, between spiritual equality and social inequality continues to be foundational to the diversity that exists for Anabaptist women today.

SOURCES: A good survey volume on women of Anabaptist traditions is Kimberly D. Schmidt et al., eds., *Strangers at Home: Amish and Mennonite Women in History* (2002); James C. Jahnke, *Vision, Doctrine, War: Mennonite Identity and Organization in America 1890–1930* (1989). For information about women in early Anabaptist communities, see C. Arnold Snyder and Linda Huebert Hecht, eds., *Profiles of Anabaptist Women: Sixteenth-Century Reforming Pioneers* (1996). For women as North American pioneer settlers, see Royden K. Loewen, "'The Children, the Cows, My Dear Man and My Sister': The Transplanted Lives of Mennonite Farm Women, 1874–1900," *Canadian Historical Review* 13.3 (1992): 344–373. On Mennonite domestics, see Frieda Esau Klippenstein, "'Doing What We Could': Mennonite Domestic Servants in Winnipeg, 1920s to 1950s," *Journal of Mennonite Studies* 7 (1989): 145–166. Material on Mennonite women in World War II includes Pamela E. Klassen, *Going by the Moon and the Stars: Stories of Two Russian Mennonite Women* (1994); Rachel Waltner Goossen, *Women against the Good War: Conscientious Objection and Gender on the American Home Front, 1941–1947* (1997); and Marlene Epp, *Women without Men: Mennonite Refugees of the Second World War* (2000). On women in the Church of the Brethren, see Pamela Brubaker, *She Hath Done What She Could: A History of Women's Participation in the Church of the Brethren* (1985). On peace theology and domestic violence, see Elizabeth G. Yoder, ed., *Peace Theology and Violence against Women* (1992). Studies relating to women in institutional church life include Gloria Neufeld Redekop, *The Work of Their Hands: Mennonite Women's Societies in Canada* (1996); Pamela E. Klassen, "Speaking Out in God's Name: A Mennonite Woman Preaching," in *Undisciplined Women: Tradition and Culture in Canada*, ed. Pauline Greenhill and Diane Tye (1997); M. Lucille Marr, *Anabaptist Women of the North*; and Royden K. Loewen, *Family, Church, and Market*.

WOMEN IN THE AMERICAN EPISCOPAL CHURCH
Fredrica Harris Thompsett

WHAT WE CHOOSE to notice has ethical and historical ramifications. It is important to frame this review of

Episcopal women within its colonial beginnings in a hemisphere that was already home to 300 societies of Native people. In the seventeenth century arriving European settlers and merchants forcibly enslaved and brought to these shores men, women, and children of Africa. The Church of England located itself in this context. Today we would call the colonial adherents of the Church of England "Anglicans." In postrevolutionary America, Anglicans reorganized themselves as the "Protestant Episcopal Church in the United States of America" (1789), the "Episcopal Church." While the broad history of Anglican and Episcopal women begins and continues to be predominantly an Anglocentric account, Native and African women must be visible. The pursuit of their stories and those of other women resembles archaeological recovery rather than institutional formality. It involves digging below the topsoil to reveal resources that have been neglected and ignored over time.

When the Church of England first established itself in Jamestown in 1607, the colonists carried a royal decree from King James I that advocated preaching and planting religion among "savages." In this legacy of ecclesiastical colonialism, the rites, doctrines, and other cultural assumptions of the Church of England displaced Native spirituality. Consider, for example, the familiar legend of the first Native American baptized in the English colonies. Romanticized notions of the "Princess Pocahontas" strain credulity. Instead, this daughter of a Native American chieftain was admitted to Holy Baptism in 1611 while being held hostage aboard a ship in Jamestown's harbor. The subsequent, short life of Pocahontas, whom the English called "Lady Rebecca," was tragically marked more by English greed than by grace.

Chroniclers of American Indians and missionary efforts by the Church of England record only glimpses of other women. There are records of an influential Creek woman, Mary Bosomworth (*sic*), who in 1740s Georgia helped her white missionary husband keep the peace. Molly Brant and her brother were Mohawk leaders in a sustained missionary episode among Mohawks in New York State. Yet, for the most part, Anglican and Episcopal efforts to convert Native Americans largely ceased until the second half of the nineteenth century.

The Anglican colony in Jamestown was important in another respect. It was a port of entry for slave ships into North America. In 1623 Jamestown was the site of the baptism of the first African slaves: servants named Anthony and Isabel and their child William. Planting Anglicanism among the early settlers in Virginia and elsewhere included evangelizing Native American populations and African slaves, although colonial Virginians made it clear that baptism was not a path to manumission. Anglicanism was the religion of the slaveholding plantocracy, and most of its missionary agents accepted slavery as a necessary part of colonial life. Prosperous southern white women were expected to teach and catechize their children, as well as their slaves and other servants. Colonial records from Virginia indicate that among adult slaves women were more likely to join the church. Persons of African descent lived in the northern colonies. Freed blacks resided in colonial Philadelphia and other cities where the Great Awakening's evangelical preaching also increased their number.

By the start of the American Revolution in 1775 Anglicans were the second largest denomination in the colonies, with a widespread representation from the Car-

Bishop Barbara Harris, the first ordained woman bishop of the Episcopal church, celebrates the Eucharist with, from left, Rev. Florence Oi-Tim Li, first female priest in the Anglican Communion, Rev. Carter Heyward, Rev. Margaret Bullitt-Jonas, and Rev. Joseph Pelham. *Courtesy of the Episcopal Diocese of Massachusetts.*

olinas to New England. This constituency included a disproportionate number of wealthy persons, poor persons and those of middling means, both freed blacks and those held in slavery, and a small percentage of Native Americans. Among this number women likely outnumbered men. Although their witness was clearly subordinate to men's and largely invisible in official church histories, women's activities were essential to the health and continuity of colonial religious life. Women could not hold any formal office in the Church of England or its transplanted colony. In this hierarchical church, governed by patriarchal assumptions, none of the ordained, preaching, or sacramental roles were open to women (nor would they be until the twentieth century). Women could not formally sit on a vestry, the governing body of a local parish. Instead, in accord with society's widespread expectation for women, the family was the site of women's spiritual authority, and the development of popular piety was largely in their hands. In their domestic sphere, laywomen were actively involved as teachers, responsible for family prayers, for religious education, and for the public events of baptisms, weddings, and funerals that were often held at home. With the revivals of the Great Awakening women often determined the family's choice of denomination. Although official participation was barred, there are instances of women taking the lead in establishing new parishes. This pattern of direct involvement in identifying the need for new congregations, funding buildings, and letting their voices be heard in calling clergy would continue throughout the nineteenth century. One historian describes the colonial church as an active female constituency set within a male hierarchy. In this regard, colonial Anglican women persistently shaped a sure, if prescribed, foundation for their nineteenth-century Episcopal sisters.

In Republican and antebellum America, the church struggled both with survival and with revival. The earliest decades of the Episcopal Church's life in the new nation were not promising. The church's total membership, estimated at 10,000 in post–Revolutionary America, stood in sharp contrast to its larger numbers and wealth on the eve of the Revolution. Episcopal Church leaders spent their energies rebuilding the institution's life and image, recovering from loss of property and revenues in colonies where their church had been established, and reordering its constitutional polity in ways that assured loyalty to democratic values rather than aristocratic traditions associated with British rule. The new Church's Constitution and Canons (1789) prescribed a hierarchical structure dependent on bishops, on regional diocesan meetings, and on national conventions of clergy and laymen.

The chaos following the Revolution challenged post-Revolutionary citizens and families. Women were put forward as the moral guardians of the Republic. Episcopal women found themselves in the position of defending both the nation and their church. Many labored in daily practice and in print to establish their image as faithful and loyal "mothers" of the Republic. While it is hard to hear conversations of ordinary women who survived these transitions, two literary remnants offer clues to the theological substance and energy of Episcopal women. Martha Laurens Ramsay (1759–1811) was a privileged woman of South Carolina whose testament, in the form of her posthumously published *Memoirs*, indicates a turbulent life grounded in the surety of God's gracious Providence. The daughter of a Revolutionary War statesman, Martha returned to a war-ravaged Charleston, where she married and had eleven children, eight of whom survived her death. Throughout illnesses, deaths, financial reversals, her own depression, and other challenges to her self-esteem, Martha recorded in her diary conversations with a God in whose rational Providence she was able to find grace and consolation. Her husband posthumously edited and published her diary, portraying her as a faithful and virtuous model for her family and nation.

A similar yet even more intimate testimony comes from *The Sabbath Journal of Judith Lomax, 1774–1828.* Estranged from her prestigious Virginian family and dealing with everyday economic survival on her own, Lomax described herself as an ardent yet "lonely Episcopalian" who was attracted to evangelical Christianity. Her life included enthusiastic attendance at worship on the Sabbath and during the week, listening as well to preachers of other denominations, teaching Sunday School, donating as she was able to the nearby theological seminary, and attending Episcopal (and other) Conventions. From 1819 to 1827 Lomax preserved her religious reflections in a Sabbath Journal. Theologically she reflected on complex issues including soteriology, Trinitarian theology, epistemology, and all "the wonderful works of Creation daily operating before our eyes" (Hobgood-Oster, 19). This newly available modern edition of an ordinary woman's theological reflections provides evidence that theology by laywomen is worthy of further study. Lomax's journal reveals that the so-called Second Great Awakening, strongest among Baptists and Methodists, influenced devout women of other denominations. Another Virginian and Episcopalian, Ann Randolph Page (1781–1838), was a wealthy plantation mistress. Page's life also changed when she was converted through evangelicalism to antislavery sentiments and actions.

Women's personal devotion to Protestant Christianity was expressed not only in their diaries, journals, and domestic affairs but through increasing efforts to rebuild and strengthen local congregations. Episcopal women, their efforts for the most part hidden behind the official actions of male vestries and clergymen, stepped forward in several ways to support and extend the witness of their parishes. Historian Joan Gundersen describes the period between 1780 and 1830 as the time when women shaped their own church through societies and philanthropic activities. Some projects focused on adding parlors, kitchens, and meeting halls as local congregations were literally remade to accommodate domestic values; other activities faced outward toward social service. Middle-class white women organized themselves into service guilds with fund-raising strategies and disbursements that they controlled. Some of these activities were interdenominational; many were not. All provided women with collective experience in developing programs and in shaping an expansive piety for their church. Before the Civil War an estimated 35,000 black Episcopalians were living in the South. Little scope was allowed for black female leadership, whether freed or slave. Yet scattered records give evidence of black women's activity in black congregations in Philadelphia and elsewhere. Black women, when they were able, were also benefactors of congregations. One example is Elizabeth Denison Forth (d. 1866), a Michigan woman born in slavery who, through hard work and careful investment, left a fortune to build a church where rich and poor Episcopalians might worship together.

The two primary centers of antebellum service that attracted Episcopal women, like many of their Protestant sisters, were education and mission. For women with no authority to evangelize, religious education provided opportunity for fulfillment and accomplishment. When the Sunday School movement blossomed early in the nineteenth century, Episcopal women helped finance these endeavors and were increasingly involved as teachers. For many white middle-class women, teaching outside the home provided a new experience of leadership. Although men formally led in institutionalizing the Sunday School movement and its interdenominational unions, by 1830 the majority both of Episcopal teaching staff and Sunday School students were women. Black women, dedicated to community development and the priority of education, functioned formally and informally in this vanguard of teachers. Despite laws in the South against teaching slaves to read, some women formed underground schools.

Teachers were also attracted to missionary service. Two Episcopal women, one black and one white, represent early exemplars of women's missionary service. Elizabeth Mars Johnson Thomson (1807–1864), a black woman, was known as one of the "best teachers" in the Episcopal missionary colony in Liberia. Thomson, along with her first husband, was educated for service in Liberia in the African Mission School formed by Connecticut Episcopalians. When her husband and infant son died shortly after their arrival in Africa, she married another Episcopalian working in the colony. With her husband (later ordained an Episcopal priest), Thomson helped to establish and teach in several schools. She reported in 1834 that she had "quite a flourishing school of about seventy children. . . . Some of them [the native girls], I think, are more intelligent than the Americans" (Burkett, 25). Thomson remained in Liberia for thirty-three years, one of the longest tenures among nineteenth-century Episcopal missionaries to Liberia. A missionary and educator in her own right, not by virtue of her marriages, Thomson was acknowledged as a leading figure in Liberian education. Another early missionary and religious educator with a long and dedicated tenure of service was Mary Briscoe Baldwin (1811–1877), who served in Greece and elsewhere in the Middle East for forty years. Baldwin, the first single woman to serve abroad, reported that her time was "always usefully occupied, & perhaps more so than in any situation I could find at home" (Gillespie, "Mary Briscoe Baldwin," 83). By 1855 there were thirty-one female Episcopal missionaries; eleven of this number were single.

These early missionaries and their successors were responding to the Episcopal Church's 1821 decision to establish itself as "The Domestic and Foreign Missionary Society." A thirty-member, all-male Board of Missions was in charge of planning, developing, and supporting the church's missionary efforts. Local missionary societies developed in response to this vision, and several of these were composed of women. In addition to supporting missionaries serving abroad, antebellum women encouraged the westward expansions of their church. Pre–Civil War reports, for example, about the midwestern missionary episcopate of Bishop Jackson Kemper mention single and married women (some of them wives of clergy) working as teachers, fund-raisers, and volunteers. Historian Joan Gundersen recounts how the Ladies Social Circle in a frontier Minnesota congregation developed, funded, maintained, and controlled their new parish, leaving the male vestry with little to do. While the recorded history of this parish is notable, women's leadership would prove critical throughout the century in establishing other congregations, particularly those from the trans-Mississippi west all the way to California. In this, as in other instances, Gundersen suggestively describes the local parish as a "female institution."

By the 1850s the Episcopal Church had grown to measure sixth in membership and third in property values. Women were the majority of church members as well as most of the volunteers or meagerly paid workers who staffed its educational programs and missionary outreach. They were the active mainstay, while clergy and laymen comprised the church's official leadership.

New ways of serving, laboring, growing, networking, and communicating among Episcopal women were all formally established between 1850 and 1920. Through this sustained process, churchwomen's organizations and the Episcopal Church were transformed. The first clear addition to women's ministries was the appearance of Episcopal sisterhoods, influenced by Anglo-Catholicism in England. The earliest, the Sisterhood of the Holy Communion, was founded in 1852 by Anne Ayres (1816–1896), who had been professed as Sister Anne in 1845. This sisterhood focused at first on providing nursing sisters for service in New York City and was instrumental in establishing St. Luke's Hospital. Over the next thirty-five years other sisterhoods followed. They offered single women the advantage of living a consecrated life of prayer, as well as being in the forefront of social service ministries. These included the Society of St. Margaret, founded in England and invited to Boston in 1873 to become part of Boston's Children's Hospital. The second American order, founded in New York by Harriet Starr Cannon (1823–1896), was the Community of Saint Mary. Its Memphis branch provided heroic nursing service during the yellow fever epidemic of 1878, thereby overcoming anti-Catholic prejudice. Gradually public support for women's orders increased, and the service institutions that they administered and staffed multiplied. By 1900 these included over eighty institutions: hospitals, schools, orphanages, retreat centers, homes for aged women, missions, and summer schools. Episcopal sisterhoods opened a new occupation for those women attracted to an ordered religious life and provided a church-related option for women. Other careers in church work would follow.

Notably, after the Civil War, increasing numbers of both black and white Episcopal women were drawn to teaching and founding educational institutions. The major impetus was educating freed slaves, yet betterment of their race had been a longtime priority for black women. The Episcopal Church, like other denominations, established a Freedman's Commission that recruited both black and white teachers. Some of these women were sent to educate freed blacks at St. Augustine's School in Raleigh, North Carolina, founded in 1867 (St. Augustine's later became a college and continues to educate black women and men). Local women's societies also sought teachers for freedom schools in the South. The result was that one-third of the new Episcopal missionary teachers were black women. African American historian J. Carleton Hayden identifies two of these missionaries as Cordelia Jennings Atwell and Mary Miles, both experienced educators. Miles, who had taught in Sierra Leone and Liberia, returned to Virginia to work with freed slaves. Even after support from the Freedman's Commission was withdrawn, Miles developed an extensive system of mission schools that eventually served 600 students in rural Virginia. Although she was from a prosperous black Virginian family, Cor-delia Jennings Atwell had to travel to Philadelphia to be educated. There she founded and served as principal of a private school, which later became part of the public school system. Atwell had followed the example of her mother, Mary M. Jennings, who had also returned to the South to establish freedom schools and Sunday Schools. Atwell's experience in heading Episcopal parochial schools, associated with the work of her clergy husband, led to starting schools in Kentucky and Virginia.

The dedication of Miles and Atwell to uplift their race through education was further mirrored in the lives of Elizabeth Evelyn Wright (1872–1906), whose labors to expand southern education eventuated in founding Voorhees College in Denmark, South Carolina, and by Frances Gaudet-Joseph (1861–1934), an activist in prison reform and juvenile justice, who founded in 1902 the Gaudet Normal and Industrial School for homeless black youth in New Orleans. In thanks for its early support, Gaudet-Joseph left her school to the local Episcopal diocese. The zeal for founding church-sponsored institutions extended to Hawaii where Queen Emma (1836–1885), a devout Anglican convert, was the benefactor of schools, churches, and missions that would later become part of the Episcopal Church. The best-known and most prolific Episcopal educator was Anna J. Haywood Cooper (1858–1964), a teacher at every educational level who began her studies at what was then St. Augustine's Normal School, earned degrees from Oberlin College, became the principal of the M Street High School in Washington, D.C., served as president of Frelinghuysen University (which educated working blacks), and earned a doctorate at age sixty-six from the Sorbonne. A lifelong Episcopalian and friend of the influential black priest Alexander Crummell, Cooper was an activist for the betterment of black people, an author, lecturer, and leader in black women's organizations and clubs. Yet one more exemplar of outstanding educational leadership was Artemisia Bowden (1879–1969). Bowden, also an alumna of St. Augustine's in Raleigh, taught at Episcopal parish schools and went on to found St. Philip's School (later an accredited junior college) in San Antonio, Texas. Bowden was enthusiastic about black women's contributions, asserting that women upheld the destiny of their race.

The tenacious and effective leadership of these women provided critical educational resources for students blocked by segregation from attending most Episcopal institutions. For example, many white women among early church workers were educated at Bishop Potter Memorial House (1867–1891), a residence and training school founded by Episcopal women in Philadelphia that offered education in nursing, mission work, and teaching in parish schools. The first training program for black Episcopal women, Bishop Tuttle School in Raleigh, was not opened until 1925. Black and white women workers in the Episcopal church were poorly paid. Most lacked sufficient financial means and required support from others to survive.

These and other needs were addressed by the Woman's Auxiliary to the Episcopal Church's Board of Missions. The Woman's Auxiliary would become the most influential framework of support for women's vocations in the Episcopal Church, as well as for encouraging churchwide missionary outreach. The Auxiliary was initiated in 1872 by an enterprising Massachusetts family of Episcopal sisters: most notably Mary Abbot Emery Twing (1843–1901) and Julia Chester Emery (1852–1922). Historian Mary Donovan has chronicled the vigorous missionary activity of the Emerys and their leadership in developing the Auxiliary from 1870 to 1920. Existing and new women's missionary societies were shaped into a centrally coordinated body. Auxiliary members participated at the parish level in devotional programs, education about mission, financial giving (including "boxes" of missionary supplies), and sponsoring specific missionary projects and persons. Starting in 1880, representatives of the Woman's Auxiliary convened nationally at the Triennial Meeting. Gathering every three years at the same time as the Episcopal Church's General Convention, Triennial would later be characterized as a parallel organization to the church's male hierarchy. The Emery sisters also contributed a section on "Woman's Work" to the national church's periodical *The Spirit of Missions*, sharing information from missionaries and building a worldwide network among Episcopal women. Mary Abbot Emery served as the Auxiliary's first general secretary. Resigning after her marriage, Mary Abbot Twing was succeeded in 1876 by her sister Julia Emery. A powerful administrator who served as general secretary for forty years, Julia established what would become not an auxiliary but rather an essential missionary structure of the church. From 1876 on a third sister, Margaret Theresa Emery, coordinated the provision of missionary "box work." Donovan depicts the Emery sisters' leadership as "self-effacing and subservient, their actions courageous and innovative. While deferring to authority, they generally managed to get their way" (3).

Meanwhile, Mary Abbot Twing championed other interventions that would prove critical in building a systematic program for mission. When some members of the Board of Missions became concerned about the Auxiliary's growing power, Twing responded by developing a structure that registered all women church workers, both voluntary and paid, in an educational and training program. The Board of Missions accepted this effort with enthusiasm, particularly as they did not have to fund it. Additionally, Julia Emery along with Ida Soule (1849–1944), an experienced organizer and leader of Auxiliary chapters, worked to establish a separate fund controlled by the Triennial Meeting. Inaugurated in 1889, the United Offering, today called the United Thank Offering (UTO), was a supplemental fund given by the Triennial to the Board of Missions for a designated purpose. In 1901, the United Offering Committee exclusively designated these funds for women's missionary work. Churchwomen, directly and indirectly, soon provided much of the Episcopal's Church's funding for mission. The Woman's Auxiliary now had the ability to recruit, train, deploy, and fund individual women missionaries, as well as a national structure to communicate news about these efforts. Not surprisingly, within ten years more women than men were deployed as foreign missionaries with education and medicine as their primary emphases. The Emery sisters had intentionally shaped and enlarged women's participation in mission.

Another strategy advanced by Mary Abbot Twing provided legitimation for women's professional work through the newly shaped ministry of deaconesses. These were women ecclesiastically "set aside" by pledging obedience to a diocesan bishop to serve those in need, particularly the sick, the homeless, and other distressed populations. Unlike a male deacon, the new American deaconess had no liturgical functions. Instead, her role was seen by men as submissive service under a bishop's direction (similar to domestic submission to one's husband). However, the women who took on this role soon viewed themselves as professional church workers. The bishop of Maryland in 1858, followed by the bishop of Alabama in 1864, first set aside small groups of women deaconesses. Other dioceses from Nebraska to New York followed with some women serving needs in parishes and most attached to charitable institutions. In Alabama, for example, the work of the deaconesses centered on the Church Home for Orphans. Although churchwide support for deaconesses was tenuous, this order had clear biblical precedents. Moreover, dioceses in England encouraged the deaconess movement and founded training institutes for candidates. Twing, with support from other early advocates of American deaconesses, used her publicity skills to campaign for national approval. In 1889 the General Convention finally passed a canon recognizing the order of deaconesses as a religious vocation for women. The New York School for Deaconesses (called St. Faith's) and the Church Training and Deaconess House in Philadelphia (later called St. Mary's) were founded in 1891 and provided educational resources. In Berkeley, California, the Deaconess Training School of the Pacific (later established as St. Margaret's House) was founded in 1908, and its alumnae began to serve western dioceses; the Chicago Church Training School opened its doors in 1917. At the New York School where she studied as a student, Susan Knapp (1862–1941) went on to become a teacher, a deaconess, dean of the School, and an international promoter of the deaconess movement. Knapp's independence apparently troubled the school's trustees. In 1916 she was replaced by a clergyman who knew little about the work of deaconesses. Knapp quietly resigned and moved to Tokyo where she taught Bible classes to Japanese students for twenty-five years.

In such insecure circumstances, continuing support from the Woman's Auxiliary and United Offering grants for training and funding individual women church workers and deaconesses were critical. Many of these women served in isolated places where clergymen seldom stayed for long. One such woman was Harriet Bedell (1875–1969), a deaconess who served over fifty years as a missionary and teacher among Native American populations in Oklahoma (where her initial salary was $400 a year), in Alaska, and lastly among the Seminoles in Florida. Deaconesses, largely funded by churchwomen, were particularly useful to missionary bishops. The early history of every western diocese was shaped by the presence of women missionaries helping to develop congregations and providing education, nursing, and parish administrative services. In many places, Utah and Nevada, for example, women also carried out the church's primary contacts with Native Americans. Native American women also formed chapters of the Woman's Auxiliary and sent in their contributions for missionary work in other parts of the world.

Meanwhile, Episcopal women were busy launching societies to meet other needs. In Lowell, Massachusetts, Emily Edson (1826–1908) called women from her parish together to help young women workers in urban centers find educational and spiritual resources. Through her efforts the first American chapter of the Girls' Friendly Society was founded in 1877. This Society evolved its own national structure with close ties to the Woman's Auxiliary. The Daughters of the King, begun in 1885 in a New York City parish, shaped a simple rule emphasizing evangelism and spiritual development. By the end of the century over 300 chapters were organized in local parishes and in several dioceses. Later, in the 1920s, the Daughters of the King began a productive fund to support women church workers. Circulating educational materials also attracted women's attention. The Church Periodical Club was organized in 1888 from a New York City parish by a Wells Fargo heir, Mary Ann Drake Fargo. Through its efforts Bibles, prayer books, and periodicals were "sent West" by train and stagecoach. By the century's end, the club was active in fifty dioceses. In 1891 two Connecticut women, dedicated to advancing mission education, founded a publishing house, eventually known as the Church Missions Publishing Company. The advantage women found in building na-

tional networks from local and diocesan bases also led local Altar Guilds to form a National Association early in the twentieth century. These and other associations expanded women's opportunities for work beyond their local parish. Through these efforts the vision of women and of the wider church became much less parochial.

The organizations noted above largely presented themselves as submissive and nonthreatening to churchmen, and they did not explicitly challenge dominant social and economic structures. However, various women working without official church sponsorship would instigate social change. Inspired by her friendship with Adelyn Howard, Emily Malbone Morgan (1862–1937) began the Society of Companions of the Holy Cross in 1884. The Companions started as a small group of privileged New England women concerned with the welfare of working women and grew into an international organization. Companions, while not living together in community, were bound by a rule emphasizing intercessory prayer, a simple lifestyle, and other Christian ideals including social justice and Christian unity. Black women, deaconesses, and overseas missionaries were among the early Companions.

Several Companions were active as founders, urban workers, and residents of settlement houses where Episcopal women, among others inspired by the Social Gospel, already exercised significant leadership. These included Ellen Gates Starr, a cofounder of Hull House in Chicago, Mary Simkhovitch of Greenwich House in New York, Helena Stuart Dudley of Denison House in Boston, and Mary Van Kleeck of the College Settlement Association, which recruited college women for settlement work. Interpersonal connections among Companions and conversations at annual conferences inspired many members of this activist sisterhood to address socially progressive issues. Two other Companions, Harriette Keyser and Margaret Lawrence, did most of the organizing work in support of the Church Association for the Advancement of the Interests of Labor (CAIL), founded in the 1890s. Keyser served energetically as CAIL's secretary for almost thirty years. The most prominent Companion was Vida Dutton Scudder (1861–1954), a professor at Wellesley College, socialist, writer, and reformer who in 1919 helped found the Church League for Industrial Democracy. Scudder, like other Episcopal women who made the Social Gospel a reality in the early decades of the twentieth century, emphasized the need for restructuring society to address economic inequalities. Scudder, Keyser, and others challenged the Episcopal Church to address social issues. Their efforts led to General Convention's appointment in 1910 of a Joint Commission on Social Service on which women—specifically Scudder, Simkhovitch, and Deaconess Knapp—served for the first time. In this and other actions, as well as through their own professional careers, individual Companions continued to challenge the social conscience of their church. According to historian Mary Donovan, Episcopal women lived the Social Gospel long before clergymen talked about it.

Overall, between 1850 and 1920, women's organizations, notably the Woman's Auxiliary, defined a parallel or shadow structure that advocated and authenticated churchwomen's service. Whether as missionaries or as dedicated leaders of social service projects in local parishes, as teachers and institutional administrators, as members of sisterhoods, as deaconesses with lives dedicated to service, or as professional women working outside the church to advance the Social Gospel, the Episcopal Church's missionary vision was transformed by the talents, organization, funding, and enterprise of its women. Most of the ministries, societies, and networks developed in the nineteenth century remain today.

In 1920 national suffrage was extended to women voters. However, if Episcopal women thought they were about to be admitted with equality to the voting and other leadership ranks of their church's national leadership, they were badly mistaken. The Episcopal Church, which includes both Catholic and Protestant components within its polity and sacramental life, traditionally adhered to an ordered ministerial hierarchy of bishops, priests, and deacons (not deaconesses) buttressed by gendered understandings of service. Women were relegated to the separate sphere that they had so fully developed in the previous century and men to continuing leadership in the political councils of the church. A biblical and theological affirmation of ministry based in baptism that explicitly included laity was not prominent in the church's life until the advent and use of the revised 1979 Book of Common Prayer. In this text "laypersons" are specifically included among the church's "ministers." This transformation in the theology of ministry and women's struggle for full participation shaped the twentieth-century Episcopal Church.

It took over fifty years of legislative wrangling before women were regularly admitted as diocesan deputies at national General Conventions. General Convention, meeting in 1919 on the eve of national suffrage, proposed that women elected by the Woman's Auxiliary serve on the new National Council (today called the Executive Council). This recommendation was defeated. The same convention underscored its gendered assumptions by a constitutional change noting that deputies must be "laymen." Along the way women were excluded from the church's national bureaucratic structures. They were, for example, refused appointment to the Commission on Holy Matrimony, which addressed such sensitive and pertinent issues as remarriage and exclusions from Holy Communion. There was one victory in 1935

when provision was made for four women on the National Council. Yet the troubling matter of women's voice and vote in General Convention did not go away; it reappeared perennially from 1946 until 1967. The Diocese of Missouri in 1946 chose Elizabeth Dyer as one of its elected deputies. She was seated with voice and vote for this convention only since, after further debate, the male deputies ruled that *laymen* was not an inclusive term. Still, in 1949 four more women were elected by diocesan deputations. When this convention offered to let them sit without voice or vote, these women emphatically declined this so-called courtesy. One of those elected, Ruth Jenkins, described the debate against seating women as "disgusting and heartbreaking." As late as 1969, Mary Eunice Oliver, a deputy from Los Angeles to the Special Convention of 1969, spoke of enduring "only by God's grace" the sexism and humiliation occasioned by her election (Darling, 78–79, 93). The decision to approve women deputies finally came at the 1967 General Convention, and following its required ratification by the 1970 Convention, forty-three women were seated as national representatives and legislators. General Convention finally caught up with local practices that from the 1950s onward (and earlier in some western dioceses) had permitted women's service on vestries and at diocesan meetings. By the 2000 General Convention, over 53 percent of lay deputies and almost 25 percent of clerical deputies were women. Moreover, during the last decade of the twentieth century, Dr. Pamela A. Chinnis served as the first woman president of the House of Clerical and Lay Deputies.

Another twentieth-century struggle for women's participation involved the Woman's Auxiliary, which had expanded from 1920 to 1960, led by Executive Secretaries Grace Lindley and later by Margaret Marston Sherman. The Auxiliary increased its involvement in religious education and social service. The Triennial meeting of the Auxiliary in 1922 designated funding for two new training houses for women. The first, Bishop Tuttle Training School, opened in Raleigh in 1925 as the National Center for the Training of Young Negro Women for Christian Leadership in Church and Community. It offered a high-quality, two-year educational program for black women until 1940. Women trained at Bishop Tuttle often became the mainstays of small black congregations, providing organizational, educational, and other leadership. In 1945 Bishop Payne Divinity School (established in 1878 for Negro men) added a Christian Education Department for women students. Historian Joyce Howard, who interviewed many of the pioneering black women leaders trained for Christian service in this period, has described their quiet yet persistent ways of struggling against racism with the church. Este Virginia Brown and Fanny P. Gross Jeffrey, two

Negro field secretaries appointed as national staff by the Woman's Auxiliary in the 1930s and 1940s, were critical in challenging racism at the local, diocesan, and national levels. It is not surprising, given their efforts, that Triennial in 1943 insisted that dioceses send one united deputation, rather than seating segregated chapters sent by some dioceses.

The other new school, with significant funding from the Woman's Auxiliary, was Windham House, opened in 1928 on 108th Street in New York City. Windham House residents lived, worshiped, and studied together, while most residents enrolled in nearby graduate schools to prepare for vocations as teachers, social workers, and missionaries. In the mid-1940s Windham House inaugurated a two-year program of academic and practical fieldwork study with courses (some taught by General Seminary faculty who had to travel uptown to teach the women) and field credit accepted toward religious education degrees awarded by Union Theology Seminary. One of the most able supporters of Windham House was Adelaide Teague Case (1887–1948), a professor at Teacher's College, Columbia University, who later served as the first woman professor in an Episcopal seminary (Episcopal Theological School in Cambridge, Massachusetts). On the West Coast, St. Margaret's House in Berkeley, California, offered future women church workers a graduate degree program with strong academic and practical resources.

In other respects, the period from the 1930s through the early 1960s marked the high tide of activity for the development of laywomen's work in the domestic Episcopal Church. Triennial funded and actively recruited women workers. A 1950s series of recruitment articles ran under the header "Why I Went into Church Work," as women described their vocational journeys. Women workers found employment in suburban and other parishes where appointments in Christian Education proliferated. A new organization, the Association of Professional Women Church Workers, was organized (1952) to develop professional standards. Then, as a result of administrative reorganization at the Episcopal Church Center in 1958, the General Division of Women's Work (GDWW) effectively replaced the administrative staff of the Woman's Auxiliary. Local chapters were boldly named Episcopal Churchwomen (ECW). The GDWW was a well-staffed, active national group with a governing Council elected by Triennial and several other women's associations.

Yet within a decade this administrative and financial structure was undone. Several factors led to dismantling separate structures for women. Some Episcopal seminaries, starting in the 1950s, began admitting women as students primarily in Christian Education programs. Women's training centers closed, believing that they had

served their purpose: St. Margaret's House in 1966 and Windham House in 1967. In a swift series of moves the General Division of Women's Work was dissolved. One stated rationale for integration was consolidating women's and men's lay ministries. Additional factors surely included economic pressures for massive staff cutbacks and the national administration's unstated reluctance to fund and share power with women. The result of these changes are evident in the career of Francis Young, who had risen within the ranks of the Woman's Auxiliary and was in 1960 appointed by the church's senior officer, the Presiding Bishop, to head the GDWW. In 1970 Young was effectively demoted from heading a division to staffing a single desk as "Lay Ministries Coordinator." She resigned in 1972. She would later write a text with the telling title *What Ever Happened to Good Old "Women's Work"?* Although Triennial leaders refused to disband, they had by 1970 effectively lost their budget, staff, and national representatives. The United Thank Offering survived as a committee subsumed into the national office for world mission, although soon its funding was no longer designated for professional women's salaries. The places set aside for women on the Executive Council were abolished, and General Convention elected fewer women. Historian Mary Donovan's provocative analysis of these events that resulted in "the complete dissolution of women's separate power base" emphasizes different gendered understandings of "lay ministry" with women envisioning "men and women working together in areas of social need," and men showing "little experience or interest in such action" (Prelinger, 227–228). In effect the women's leadership at first thought that their integration into the national church structures would give greater representation to women's work; they were later surprised when the reverse proved true.

Dismantling the women's division was not a story that caught attention in 1970. Instead, with the cultural rise of feminism and of its critics, the "problem" of women's ordination dominated discussions of women's ministries. Ordination is an important symbol of leadership and power in the Episcopal Church, and women's admission to the orders of deacon, priest, and bishop would be an indelible change. Without this representation, all women were second-class citizens. Within the Anglican Communion only one woman, Florence Li Tim-Oi, had been ordained a priest, and that was in 1944 by the bishop of Hong Kong. This action, however, was officially repudiated by international Anglican leaders. Within the Episcopal Church, women's ordination had been studied on and off since 1919. A major step toward priesthood for women was taken when the 1970 Convention approved a canon that retired the old "deaconess" language and acknowledged women "deacons."

This official approval for women deacons was actually preceded by Bishop James Pike's irregular investment of Phyllis Edwards in San Francisco in 1965. As of 1970 women deacons, like their male counterparts, were seen as clergy, entitled to be called "The Reverend."

In 1970, the same convention that approved women as deacons voted down opening the priesthood to women. Historian Pamela Darling tells the story of what happened next. The Reverend Suzanne R. Hiatt, a 1964 seminary graduate and the first woman ordained to the diaconate in 1971 under the new canon, was an early strategist and radical leader in the movement for the ordination of women to the priesthood and episcopate. In 1971 the Episcopal Women's Caucus (EWC) was formed as a network of laywomen, seminarians, and deacons supporting women's full participation at all levels of ministry. The Caucus, along with other groups, focused on canonical change at the 1973 Convention in Louisville. In 1973, although a majority of votes cast by clergy and by lay deputies were in favor of women's ordination, this motion did not receive the two-thirds majority needed in each order, clergy and laity. After Louisville, Hiatt and others engaged in various symbolic actions protesting women's exclusion from the priesthood. Unwilling to wait until 1976 for another potential defeat, she and ten other deacons seized the moment to "right a longtime injustice." On July 29, 1974, these women, who came to be known as the "Philadelphia Eleven," were ordained by three retired bishops at Philadelphia's Church of the Advocate. The service in a black church included strong parallels to the injustice of racism. Barbara Harris, Advocate's senior warden, led the procession as the crucifer. Dr. Charles Willie, the first black elected as vice president of the House of Deputies, preached. Most bishops responded with intense outrage that women and their supporters had acted without orderly permission. Bishops met in "emergency" session and, without hearing from the women, declared their ordinations "invalid," a verdict later changed to "irregular." A second service with four more "irregular" ordinations occurred in 1975 in Washington, D.C. Once again the Caucus and other political strategy groups lobbied for a positive vote at the next convention. There, despite a significant "traditionalist" (as they called themselves) minority in both bishops and deputies, the 1976 Minneapolis Convention approved women's ordination to the priesthood and episcopate.

The vote was clearly positive, yet acceptance in practice of women clergy was not assured. The presiding bishop, John Allin, set a reactionary tone at the 1977 Bishops' meeting by commenting that "women can no more be priests than they can become fathers or husbands" (Darling, 140). He and others shaped a "conscience clause" justifying their refusal to ordain women. At the same meeting, bishops expressed their fears about ordaining homosexuals. Women's assertion of authority and the specter of electing women bishops challenged the personal, sexual, and social relationships of these "Fathers" of the church. Yet in 1988 Barbara C. Harris, the crucifer for the Philadelphia ordinations and an outspoken advocate of social justice, was elected bishop by the diocese of Massachusetts. Standing by Bishop Harris's side at her 1989 consecration as the first woman bishop in the Anglican Communion was the first Anglican woman priest, octogenarian Florence Li Tim-Oi, and the feminist theologian Carter Heyward, one of the Philadelphia Eleven. By the end of the twentieth century there were nine Episcopal women bishops and approximately 2,000 ordained women, 14 percent of the total number of clergy. Included in this number are over 70 black women and much smaller representations of Native American, Asian American, and Latina women. In 2002, Carol Joy Gallagher, a Cherokee priest elected by the diocese of Southern Virginia, became the first indigenous woman bishop. As in other mainline denominations, contemporary clergywomen are visible, although few head the most prestigious parishes. By 2000 a handful of Episcopal dioceses continued to deny women access to ordination and professional ministry, despite legislation insisting that the canon approving women's ordination is mandatory, not "permissive." Bishop Barbara Harris, in a July 2000 address to the Episcopal Women Caucus, aptly portrayed the Episcopal Church as "a strange land where despite all the so-called progress, people of color, women and gays and lesbians continue to struggle to claim their place."

The history of Episcopal women's lay and ordained vocations, as evidenced in Bishop Harris's consecration, is replete with multigenerational connections. This is particularly true for Native American women whose stories and legacies are handed down from lay missionaries, deaconesses, from UTO-funded nurses, and from indigenous grandmothers to their granddaughters. Ginny Doctor, an Onondaga priest who once served the same Alaskan village as Deaconess Bedell, tells of extensive church and community services provided by her grandmother, Rena Thomas Doctor (1901–1985). The first Asian American woman ordained to the priesthood (1985) was Fran Toy. Sensitive to her ancestors' legacies, Toy recorded an oral history of Rose King Yoak Won Wu (1890–1982), wife of the first Chinese Episcopal priest in the United States. Toy celebrated her first Eucharist in True Sunshine Parish in San Francisco where the lively and industrious Rose Ru and her husband both labored. Latina women priests similarly value their lay predecessors.

Amid twentieth-century debates about what women "could do" in the church, Episcopal women have made preeminent contributions to church and society. Some of these women leaders are nationally well known, others less so. A brief list, for example, includes Frances Perkins (1882–1965) in the field of workers' rights and labor relations; Eleanor Roosevelt (1884–1962), advocate for social and civil rights, who was responsible for shaping the United Nations Declaration of Human Rights; Miriam Van Waters (1887–1974), an exemplary reformer of America's women's prisons; and Dr. Cynthia Clark Wedel (1909–1986), an ecumenical leader and first woman president of the National Council of Churches, who later served as president of the World Council of Churches. Less well known are two midwestern black leaders for whom political and religious activism were inseparable. Eva Del Vakia Bowles (1875–1943) was a longtime Secretary for Colored Work for the YWCA who, nationally and internationally, worked for equal services for Negro women and girls. Mattie Hopkins (1918–1988), a Chicago public school teacher and administrator, was a strong advocate for urban affairs in her church and in Illinois politics. Hopkins rightly emphasized the distinctive history of black women as a "continuous struggle, much failure, some success; one step forward, two steps back" (Hopkins). Black women continue to acknowledge their ancestors. When the Reverend Nan Peete addressed the international Lambeth Conference of Bishops, she dedicated her presentation advocating women's ordained leadership to her mentor, Mattie Hopkins.

Despite the ambiguities of women's contributions in a church where men still dominate the political and spiritual leadership, women's energetic witness has been central to the church's vitality. This is particularly true of their participation in local parishes. Historian Joanna Gillespie has researched the religious perceptions of ordinary women across three generations of women in four Episcopal congregations. She rightly emphasizes that the religious experiences of these women are central, complex, diverse in class, and multigenerational. Feminists, moderates, and those who think of themselves as more traditional enjoy the same parish's culture. Gillespie points to their open-mindedness, spiritual depth, and piety as resources for generations to come. Unlike their nineteenth-century sisters, however, contemporary women are more individualistically and locally identified.

Black women's history teaches somewhat different lessons. In this perspective, strength comes with being contributing members of the community. Service is expected, not optional. It is important to record and honor different legacies from various cultural histories. Lessons about social awareness, public service, theological wisdom, and respect for all ministries hold promise for the church's future leadership. The witness of Pauli Murray (1910–1985), the first African American woman priest, provides a fitting, closing testimony to past struggles and to the promise of a brighter future. Murray was a free-

dom rider in the 1940s, a civil rights lawyer, teacher, poet, writer, feminist, and (at the age of sixty-two) an Episcopal priest. She wrote that in her ordination:

> All the strands of my life had come together. Descendant of slave and of slave owner, I had already been called poet, lawyer, teacher, and friend. Now I was empowered to minister the sacrament of One in whom there is no north or south, no black or white, no male or female—only the spirit of love and reconciliation drawing us all toward the goal of human wholeness. (435)

SOURCES: Four recent books are central to understanding Episcopal women's history: Mary Sudman Donovan, *A Different Call: Women's Ministries in the Episcopal Church, 1850–1920* (1986); Catherine M. Prelinger, ed., *Episcopal Women: Gender, Spirituality, and Commitment in an American Mainline Denomination* (1992); Pamela W. Darling, *New Wine: The Story of Women Transforming Leadership and Power in the Episcopal Church* (1994); and Sheryl Kujawa-Holbrook, *Freedom Is a Dream: A Documentary History of Episcopal Women* (2002). Other resources directly used here are Owanah Anderson, *400 Years: Anglican/Episcopal Mission among American Indians* (1997); Joanna Bowen Gillespie, *Women Speak: Of God, Congregations, and Change* (1995); Joanna Bowen Gillespie, *The Life and Times of Martha Laurens Ramsey, 1759–1811* (2001) and "Mary Briscoe Baldwin (1822–1877), Single Woman Missionary and 'Very Much My Own Mistress',", *Anglican and Episcopal History* 57 (March 1988), 63–92; Laura Hobgood-Oster, ed., *The Sabbath Journal of Judith Lomax, 1774–1828* (1999); Mattie Hopkins, "Other Struggles Seducing Blacks," *Witness* 65 (March 1982): 114–116; Pauli Murray, *Song in a Weary Throat* (1987). Additional information is found in journal articles including Randall K. Burkett, "Elizabeth Mars Johnson Thomson, 1807–1864: A "Research Note," *The Historical Magazine of the Episcopal Church* (March 1986) 21–30 and Joan R. Gundersen, "The Local Parish as a Female Institution," *Church History* 55 (September 1986): 307–322. Other essential resources are the *Newsletter of the Episcopal Women's History Project* (now called *Timelines*); reports on black Episcopalians in 1980s issues of *Linkage*; and the Archives of the Episcopal Church, currently located in Austin, Texas.

WOMEN IN THE ANGLICAN CHURCH IN CANADA
Sharon Anne Cook

UNTIL THE ANGLICAN Church Synod of 1955, no church structure directly represented women. Nevertheless, Anglican women had worshipped and lived in their faith in Canada from at least the seventeenth century. Many English and Loyalist immigrants from the American colonies at the time of the Revolutionary War continued the Anglican tradition in small enclaves, worshipping and taking the eucharist with missionaries or military chaplains. In this process of day-to-day worship, women assumed much responsibility for spiritual growth, both in sanctified settings and within the home where religious sensibility had always been nurtured and sustained.

In addition to overseeing their children's religious instruction and creating a domestic setting where spiritual growth could occur, Anglican women carved out a role for themselves as "helpmeets" in many areas of church operation. For example, Anglican women in the nineteenth century established corps of "workers" to enlist subscribers for building funds, collect funds for other church activities, visit the sick and provide relief for the poor, even sometimes paying the rent to prevent the sale of the furniture, provide religious instruction of the

young, and beautify their sanctuaries, for example, through needlework.

Yet most of the official history of the Anglican Church in Canada excludes women and their vital religious role. Traditionally, that history has been seen to begin with the naming of Loyalist Charles Inglis as bishop of Nova Scotia in 1787, to be followed by the consecration of Jacob Mountain as first Lord Bishop of Quebec in 1793. His diocese extended from the Gaspe Coast to Windsor, Ontario, encompassing the newly defined provinces of Upper and Lower Canada. By 1860, there were six bishoprics—Nova Scotia, Quebec, Toronto, Fredericton, Montreal, and Huron—and these combined to form the Provincial Synod of the Church of England and Ireland in Canada. The Ecclesiastic Province of Ontario was created in 1912, followed two

Mrs. Roberta E. Tilton, a member of St. George's Church, Ottawa, spearheaded the founding of the first diocesan board of the Women's Auxiliary in 1885. Since that time the WA and its successor, Anglican Church Women, have played a leading role in the Anglican Church across Canada. *Courtesy of the Anglican Diocese of Ottawa.*

years later by the Ecclesiastic Province of British Columbia. Anglicanism was spread throughout this country, as in most others, through missionizing. These efforts were directed by the Society for the Propagation of the Gospel, founded in 1701; by the Church Missionary Society of 1799, which was renamed the Domestic and Foreign Missionary Society; and by the Missionary Society of the Church of England in Canada, established in 1905. The supreme legislative and administrative body of the church, the General Synod, was formed in 1893. The modern Anglican Church in Canada dates from 1955 when it took its modern name and organized itself into thirty dioceses in four provinces, each with a metropolitan archbishop.

Women's involvement in the structures of the Canadian Anglican Church did not occur until the late nineteenth century when their activism there was paralleled by women's organizational development in society at large. For example, the 1890s saw the establishment of the National Council of Women, women's missionary societies, the Young Woman's Christian Association, and the Women's Institutes. This expansion of women's organizations coincided with profound changes in Canadian society including rapid urban growth, industrialization, and increased immigration from Europe and the United States. All of these factors drew a variety of responses from the newly developing middle class and most especially from women. Some women channeled their energies into the founding and expansion of social service agencies, such as the Children's Aid Society and orphanages. Others, like the Woman's Christian Temperance Union (WCTU), sought legislative changes to protect society's most vulnerable members, women and children, during this period of instability. Still others worked to ameliorate economic and spiritual dislocation through denominational association.

By the twentieth century, various secular agencies had been established to take on many of the welfare tasks previously shouldered by denominational women's groups, including the support for and inspection of facilities for the indigent, orphaned, mentally ill and challenged, and criminal elements of the population. This did not mean that philanthropic initiatives were no longer needed; the change came in who would receive Anglican women's help. Where the objects of support in the nineteenth century had often been intemperate and immigrant families, gradually the focus shifted to missions in the west, north, and overseas, as well as especially exposed and/or pivotal members of their own community, including young working women, middle-class girls, mothers, and children.

At the same time, the twentieth century witnessed a marked expansion in the number of women's groups formed to protect these interests and a remarkable degree of solidarity among women engaged in such work. Typically, women maintained membership in several groups for several decades, working with trusted friends, neighbors, and kin on a variety of projects. Single women were always well represented. Furthermore, the groups never operated in isolation. Although each had a specific mandate, the leadership of these groups formed an interlocking network of highly principled, talented, and spiritually vigorous women. For instance, Roberta Tilton, one of the most celebrated Canadian Anglican women of the late nineteenth and early twentieth centuries, helped found the Woman's Auxiliary at the provincial and diocesan levels and was very active in the Girls' Friendly Society, the Mothers' Union, and the Girls' Auxiliary. Through her, and women like her, the connection was made to external women's groups. Tilton was a director of the Ottawa Protestant Orphans' Home and Refuge for Aged Women, where these most vulnerable of Ottawa's urbanizing society were housed under the same roof; she was one of the original founders of the National Council of Women and was a secretary of the Ottawa Local Council (of Women).

In briefly surveying selected Anglican women's organizations in the twentieth century, as well as some church societies in which women predominated, several gradual changes become clear. First, the nineteenth-century tradition of groups involving single adult women as leaders and members faded, with single women becoming increasingly invisible in the general membership. This trend is well illustrated by the histories of the Girls' Friendly Society and a nineteenth-century subgroup of the Woman's Auxiliary for single women called the Young Woman's Auxiliary. Second, women's perception of their appropriate position underwent a clear development from supportive "help-meet" for powerful male organizations, such as the Woman's Auxiliary for the Domestic and Foreign Missionary Society, to one of supportive status to the main body but women centered and women led in most activities. Third, while most Anglican women labored at the parish and diocesan levels, the romantic image of serving the church in western Canada was increasingly embraced by many. Few were able to become "lady missionaries," but many Canadian Anglican women supported such ventures through financial offerings and public admiration.

Founded in 1874 in Hampshire, England, the Girls' Friendly Society was devoted to preventing the working-class young woman from falling into sin by creating a "fighting fellowship" of middle-class and married "Associates" to befriend and guide the single and working-class "Members." The goal was to firmly instill appropriate behaviors so that the Member would monitor her own actions successfully. A portion of the "G.F.S. Candidates' Hymn" leaves little doubt as to how the virtuous working-class girl was to act:

Little maidens must be holy,
Pure in every thought;
By the previous blood of Jesus
Each one hath been bought.

Little maidens must be gentle,
Even in their play,
Modest in their words and ways,
Innocently gay.

Little maidens must be helpful,
Fly at mother's call,
Swift and joyous as the sunbeams,
Shining bright on all.

Chastity, humility, cheerfulness, and service were all expected of the pure young working-class Anglican woman. More than this, however, the proper Anglican girl must also be pious in all her thoughts and deeds with the fond expectation of salvation as her reward.

The Girls' Friendly Society was extended to Canada in 1882. Where the parent English Society had been much concerned with temperance and social purity issues, the Canadian organization added to these concerns more practical matters such as proper and safe accommodation, affordable holiday sites, supportive networks for young women seeking employment in unfamiliar areas, and sometimes employment bureaus. Originally there was a definite distinction between the status of the Associates and the young working-class Members, but predictably the result of this elitism that ascribed most important work to the Associates was difficulty in finding sufficient numbers of Members once the organization was transplanted to Canadian soil.

The Mothers' Union was founded in England in 1876; twenty years later, a Central Council, from which Diocesan Councils were established, was formed. The English group was reserved for married women, but eventually it adopted a structure similar to the Girls' Friendly Society, recruiting as well single women. Baptized Anglican mothers who declared their adherence to the Three Central Objects (upholding the sanctity of marriage, raising children to be responsible future parents, and organizing other mothers into Unions) were invited to become Members, while unmarried women professing an interest in children's spiritual welfare could become Associates. Childrens' spiritual growth was too often handed over to the church, and specifically to the Sunday School, asserted the Mothers' Union. In its view, since mothers cultivated their leadership within the family by providing examples of "purity" and "holiness," the prime duty for children's spiritual education was clearly the mother's. To act as spiritual mentors to their own children, Anglican Mothers' Union members required instruction for themselves and organization into support groups. This they provided through regular meetings, readings, and sponsored lectures.

The societal principles underpinning the Mothers' Union paralleled those of many other mainstream conservative women's groups, including the National Council of Women and the Woman's Christian Temperance Union. Women's knowledge, skills, and energies in defense of the nuclear family were privileged as society wrestled with the unsettling effects of consumerism, secularism, and the increasing numbers of mothers engaged in paid employment. A renewal of self-discipline of body, mind, and spirit by all members of the Anglican family was required, the members insisted.

The premier organization for Anglican women in Canada was organized in Ottawa, Ontario, in 1885. A group of seven Ottawa women led by Roberta Tilton (1837–1925) approached the bishop of Ontario with a request to establish a woman's auxiliary to the Domestic and Foreign Missionary Society. Even though the Woman's Auxiliary operated from the beginning as an adjunct to the Society with the motto "The love of Christ constraineth us," the specific functions of the Woman's Auxiliary were contentious for years. In general, they can be said to fall into four categories: community and missionary service, spiritual renewal, self-education, and youth leadership. By 1889, the Woman's Auxiliary women had defined their responsibilities as individual and united prayer for missions, financial support of the churches' "lady missionaries," the provision of education for the children of missionaries who lived too far from available schools, and financial aid for the Domestic and Foreign Missionary Society. This final and very important function is where the women of the Woman's Auxiliary Central Board and the men of the Board of the Domestic and Foreign Missionary differed.

In an era when all churches were concerned with finding money to support their rapidly expanding activities, especially in the mission field, the Board of Management of the Domestic and Foreign Missionary Society believed that the women of the National Woman's Auxiliary had undertaken to collect money for the Domestic and Foreign Missionary by house-to-house canvas in each parish. This was entirely consistent with a view of women as helpmeet to the parent missionary organization. However, the Woman's Auxiliary collected most of its money directly from its own membership at the parish and diocesan levels, as was common in women's missionary societies. That it raised its money in this manner was highly symbolic of the *personal* sacrifice that women made by contributing their own, often slender, resources of housekeeping money. Later the Woman's Auxiliary institutionalized this collection in the United and Diocesan Thankofferings and the Extra-Cent-A-Day Fund.

In the Woman's Auxiliary's view, because it raised its own money from its own women members, it should have the right to decide how that money would be spent in the mission field. Unfortunately, the Domestic and Foreign Missionary Society Board of Management rejected the National Woman's Auxiliary's request that it "designate" its contributions for particular areas of concern, for example, women and children in domestic missions. The battle was waged for years. Deeply frustrated, the Woman's Auxiliary had an opportunity to separate in 1905 when the Board of Domestic and Foreign Missions was dissolved and replaced by the Missionary Society. After a good deal of discussion, the National Woman's Auxiliary decided to remain an auxiliary of the new society, making it the oldest continuous national organization of the Church of England in Canada.

In addition to community service, spiritual renewal, and self-education, the Woman's Auxiliary/Auxiliary of Church Women has long devoted much energy and resources to educating the next generation. Women had served as Sunday School teachers from earliest days in most Protestant denominations, including the Anglican. But the mandate for women to undertake "Christian nurture" in the late nineteenth century required that additional efforts must be made to reach all children. Its youth program was always an important component, including the Babies' Branch, later renamed The Little Helpers and intended for children from five to seven, and the Junior Auxiliary, which extended membership to children from seven to twelve. However, the Girls' Branches, redefined in 1921 as the Girls' Auxiliary for young women between thirteen and nineteen, became its banner youth group. The Girls' Auxiliary also replaced the adult single women's sector, the Young Woman's Auxiliary (YWA).

As an outgrowth of the Social Purity movement, the Girls' Auxiliary was reorganized to address a deep concern about the safety and need for spiritual training of young women. The Girls' Auxiliary operated alongside of the Canadian Girls in Training, the Young Women's Christian Association, and the Girl Guides. Links with the Guides were so close that Anglican Guide Companies and the Girls' Auxiliary often worked in tandem, competing for badges in much the same way. But if the Woman's Auxiliary from the beginning had great success in its programs for girls and young women, it regularly expressed disappointment in its flagging efforts to reach young men. Beginning in the 1920s, the Woman's Auxiliary discussed the possibility of establish-

ing Boys' Missionary Clubs without much success. In addition, a Church Boys' League under Woman's Auxiliary auspices was organized, but this too failed to thrive.

To maintain this network of youth groups, many women within the Woman's Auxiliary were required to develop leadership and pedagogical skills. As the Girls' Auxiliary Handbook pointed out, the leader must act as "an interpreter of youth to the adults, a friend and guide and an instructor." If non–Woman's Auxiliary churchwomen could be found who were able and interested in leading a youth group, they would be required to join the Woman's Auxiliary at the earliest opportunity This was thought to be necessary to maintain a coordinated youth program firmly under female direction. In order that pedagogical skills and program information could be imparted to youth group leaders, much prescriptive literature was produced at the national and diocesan levels. A great deal was expected of the Woman's Auxiliary member as educator: She must provide a stimulating and a demanding program that balanced spiritual and material concerns for the children and young people in her care while remaining sensitive to individual differences, parish, and diocesan needs.

After having given distinguished service for eighty-one years, the Woman's Auxiliary (WA) was reorganized in 1966 into the Anglican Church Women's Association with much the same mandate as had evolved with the WA. Support continued for such causes as assembling bales (of clothing and other essentials) for residential missions, educating deaconesses through the Anglican Women's Training College in Toronto, Ontario (later combined into the Centre for Christian Studies), and financing church missionaries. Other initiatives, such as further strategies to support women's centrality in family life, were also undertaken.

Throughout much of the past two centuries, women of the parishes and dioceses have provided artistic service to the church through the network of guilds as affiliated members of the Woman's Auxiliary. Altar Guilds have committed themselves to provide equipment and linens for church services, hospitals, and institutions and to arrange for their laundering and storage. Embroidery Guilds have had a proud tradition of making and decorating altar linens, bookmarks, brocade for the surplice and stoles, frontals, burses, purificators, and hangings. Women with aesthetic gifts thus found an outlet for their talents in a religious culture that highly valued their skills. In addition, the guilds provided a further opportunity for self-education as women researched models and types of church embroidery, developing their own patterns to meet diocesan styles and changing forms of artistic expression.

The shortage of ordained clergy was a persistent

problem for the Anglican Church missionizing to white settlers in western Canada. In 1907 the Colonial and Continental Church Society first sponsored women to assist clergy through conducting the "Sunday School by post" with children in remote areas and working with isolated women and girls. In 1909 the Reverend George Exton Lloyd convinced the Ladies' Association of the Colonial and Continental Church Society to sponsor the emigration and training of Anglican women teachers for the government schools under the Colonial Teachers' Scheme. By 1916, Lloyd had established a separate church society to accomplish the same aim, under the title of the Fellowship of the Maple Leaf. The Fellowship of the Maple Leaf was heavily dominated by women. While Fellowship of the Maple Leaf teachers never attempted to establish a denominational school system, they did hope to infuse their teaching with a British tone and ideal and with Anglican rituals through instruction in scripture and prayer, as far as the provincial school authorities would allow. In addition to day-school teaching, Fellowship of the Maple Leaf teachers often conducted Sunday Schools, and sometimes also led youth groups such as the Girl Guides. They were supportive as well of the Sunday School Motor Caravans that traveled throughout the west during the summer, conducting Sunday Schools and conducting the "Sunday School by post."

The best known of the "vanners" was Eva Hasell who, with a dedicated team of women, spent each summer providing vacation Bible schools and Sunday Schools for more than fifty years. (Eva Hasell and Iris Sayle took out their last caravan in 1972 when Hasell was eighty-seven.) These devoted workers, many of whom partly financed their own excursions, were sponsored by the Archbishops' Western Canada Fund. The vanners were almost entirely female and British in origin in the early years. The mission continues today under the name "Western Canada Sunday School Caravan Fund."

Although the Canadian Anglican Church first accepted women as deacons in 1971 and as priests in 1976, the tradition of "lady preachers" was much older than these official dates would suggest. Drawing on the example of English women known as "bishop's messengers" who provided missionary and community service at the behest of diocesan bishops, a Canadian corps was organized in 1928, with a much broadened mandate. Teams of women, one of whom was theologically trained and the other charged with labor-intensive tasks, traveled throughout the West, acting as pastors, evangelists, educators, social workers, and administrators. Classified as a religious order, the group never commanded a huge following—in total, fifty-six licensed messengers served between 1928 and 1977—yet a significant number of other volunteers assisted them in a wide variety of educational initiatives.

From uncertain beginnings, the Canadian Anglican community has come to strongly embrace and celebrate women's ordination. In fact, this central difference with Catholicism has been noted as the chief stumbling block to discussions of church union. In their role as priests, Canadian women have benefited through such role models as Florence Li Tim-Oi, the first woman to be ordained in the world Anglican Communion. Ms. Li was ordained to the priesthood in 1944 in the diocese of Hong Kong when her pastoral services were required. However, after her elevation to the priesthood was criticized, she chose to resign her ministry in 1946. Until 1983, she served the church unofficially, defending it after the communist takeover of mainland China. In that year, she went to Canada to become an honorary assistant at St. John's Chinese congregation and St. Matthew's parish in Toronto. In 1984, the fortieth anniversary of her ordination, Ms. Li was reinstated as a priest. Until her death in 1992, she exercised her priesthood with faithfulness and dignity and in so doing forwarded the cause of other women seeking ordination. To honor her leadership in the international and Anglican community, Renison College at the University of Waterloo has established a full tuition award in her name and the construction of the Florence Li Tim-Oi Memorial Resource Centre and Archives, which will house Ms. Li's personal papers and other materials related to her life, as well as materials related to East Asian language and culture.

Widely recognized for their contributions through community service and education, women in the Anglican Church in Canada continue to struggle with the challenge presented by feminism to the church's liturgical and cultural life. With the battle for inclusive language in its liturgies and scriptural translations having been largely engaged, the "revelatory status of the Scriptures" with sexist imagery, misogynist narratives, and patriarchal directives remain a fundamental problem for many feminist Canadian Anglicans. Susan Storey writes that

[a] feminist vision of the church would not be of an institution charged with transmitting intact what it has received from the past, as entrusted wealth buried in the ground. It would be, rather, a vision of a community that remembers its history, for better and for worse, and opens itself to the wind of the Holy Spirit, to the breath of new life and the taste of new wine. (Storey, 176)

The history of the Canadian Anglican Church, which incorporates women's struggles, helps to remind us of the special contributions made by women to that history, most particularly in service to the church, education, and providing social amenities for Canadian women and children.

SOURCES: The author wishes to thank Fred Neal and Jack Francis from the Ottawa Diocesan Archives for their help and valued suggestions. See F. A. Peake, "Anglicanism," in *The Canadian Encyclopedia* (2000), 77–78; Leonard L. Johnson, "About People and Their Churches," in *Faith of Our Fathers: The Story of the Diocese of Ottawa*, Right Reverend Robert Jefferson and Leonard L. Johnson, eds. (1956); Anglican Diocesan Archives [hereafter ADA], Ottawa St. Alban's Association of Women Workers, *Second Annual Report*, (1869–1870); Sharon Anne Cook, "To Bear the Burdens of Others . . ." N.E.S. Griffiths, *The Splendid Vision: Centennial History of the National Council of Women of Canada, 1893–1993* (1993); Ruth Compton Brouwer, *New Women for God: Canadian Presbyterian Women and India Missions, 1876–1914* (1990); Rosemary Gagan, *A Sensitive Independence: Canadian Methodist Women Missionaries in Canada and the Orient, 1881–1925* (1992); Diana Pedersen, "Keeping Our Good Girls Good: The YWCA and the 'Girl Problem,' 1870–1930," *Canadian Woman Studies* 7.4 (Winter 1986); Margaret Kechnie, "Keeping Things Clean 'For Home and Country': The Federated Women's Institute of Ontario, 1897–1919" (Ph.D. diss., O.I.S.E., 1996); A. B. McKillop, *Matters of Mind: The University in Ontario, 1791–1951* (1994); Paul Rutherford, ed., *Saving the Canadian City: The First Phase, 1880–1929* (1974), chapter 1; Andrew Jones and Leonard Rutman, *In the Children's Aid: J. J. Kelso and Child Welfare in Ontario* (1981); Patricia T. Rooke and R. L. Schnell, "The Rise and Decline of Nineteenth-Century British North American Protestant Orphans' Homes as Woman's Domaine, 1850–1930," *Atlantis* 7 (Spring 1982): 21–36; Sharon Anne Cook, "*Through Sunshine and Shadow*": The Woman's Christian Temperance Union, Evangelicalism, and Reform in Ontario, 1874–1930 (1995); Richard B. Splane, *Social Welfare in Ontario: 1791–1893. A Study in Public Welfare Legislation* (1965), 56–58; and ADA, Associates' Minute Book of the Girls' Friendly Society and Ottawa Diocesan Council, January 6, 1894. The YWA mirrors other single women's organizations, such as the Young Woman's Christian Temperance Union, a subgroup of the WCTU. For more information on nineteenth-century Canadian organizations for single women, see Sharon Anne Cook, "The Ontario Young Woman's Christian Temperance Union: A Study in Female Evangelicalism, 1874–1930," in *Changing Roles of Women within the Christian Church in Canada*, Elizabeth Gillan Muir and Marilyn Fardig Whiteley, eds. (1995), 299–320; Mary Heath-Stubbs, *Friendship's Highway: Being the History of the Girls' Friendly Society, 1875–1925* (1926); Mary G. Woodward, *The Mothers' Union Golden Book* (1924); Woodward, *The Mothers' Union in Canada Handbook* (1960); Woodward, *The Mothers' Union Course of Twelve Lectures* (n.d.); Woodward, *The Mothers' Union Canadian Official Handbook* (1953); John Webster Grant, *A Profusion of Spires* (1988); Mrs. Willoughby Cummings, D.C.L., *Our Story: Some Pages from the History of the Woman's Auxiliary to the Missionary Society of the Church of England in Canada, 1885 to 1928* (1928); Sharon Anne Cook, "Beyond the Congregation: Women and Canadian Evangelicalism Reconsidered," in *Aspects of the Canadian Evangelical Experience*, ed. George R. Rawlyk (1997); Joint Committee on Girls' Work, "A Manual for Leaders of Anglican Girls," (1933); ADA, Diocesan Altar Guilds of Canada, *A Manual for Altar Guilds*; Marilyn Barber, "The Fellowship of the Maple Leaf Teachers," in *The Anglican Church and the World of Western Canada, 1820–1970*, ed. Barry Ferguson (1991), 154–166; F.H.E. Hasell, *Across the Prairies in a Motor Caravan* (1922); Vera Fast, *Missionary on Wheels: Eva Hasell and the Sunday School Caravan Mission* (1979); Alyson Barnett-Cowan, "The Bishop's Messengers: Women in Ministry in Northwestern Manitoba, 1928–1979," in *The Anglican Church and the World of Western Canada, 1820–1970*, ed. Barry Ferguson (1991); and Susan Storey, "Feminism and the Church: Challenge and Grace," in *The Challenge of Tradition: Discerning the Future of Anglicanism*, ed. John Simons (1997).

BAPTIST WOMEN

Carolyn D. Blevins

FREEDOM IS THE hub of Baptist theology. Baptists believe that each person is free to interpret the Bible for herself, that each person is free to relate to God directly, that each church is free to do what it believes is best, and that all people are free to worship or not worship as they please. Freedom leads to diversity, and Baptists can be quite diverse. Diversity for Baptist women covers the whole spectrum from the submissive wife to the proclaiming minister. Problems arise when one woman answers the call to preach and others believe women should not preach; or one church believes that having women ministers is biblical and other churches believe it is not. Freedom is the theology. Diversity is the outcome. Within this understanding of freedom, Baptist women have made a wide range of contributions.

Like others coming to the New World in the seventeenth century, Baptists came seeking, among other things, a place where they could worship without punishment. Baptists who settled in the Massachusetts Bay Colony soon discovered they were not welcome if they did not worship as the Puritans prescribed. Some Baptists moved to Pennsylvania and South Carolina to be able to worship freely. In search of a place where anyone could worship without civil interference, Roger Williams led a group of Baptists to establish the colony of Rhode Island. In Providence in 1639 he formed the first Baptist church in America. Several Baptist groups emerged in America over the next three centuries. In the 1720s Free Will Baptists, who opposed Calvin's doctrine of predestination and preached that any person could believe in Christ, originated in North Carolina. (Free Will Baptists stressed the freedom of any individual to accept Christ, opposing the Calvinistic Baptists who believed that only the elect could be saved. As Calvinistic Baptists moderated their views, the distinctions between the two groups faded.) Another group of Free Will Baptists emerged in New England in 1780.

Lottie Moon, one of the first single missionaries sent out by Southern Baptists, worked in China for almost forty years. Believing she was called to be an evangelist to all, Moon refused to be restricted to "women's work" such as teaching only girls and women. *Courtesy of the Southern Baptist Theological Seminary.*

On their way to India in 1812, Ann Hasseltine Judson (1789–1826) and Adoniram Judson became convinced of believer's baptism. No longer agreeing with the theology of the Congregationalists who had sent them as missionaries, they resigned from their Congregational assignment. Luther Rice, their companion, returned to the United States to raise funds from Baptists for their support. Rice's fund-raising efforts were successful, but he realized that fund-raising would be a continual necessity. A more efficient method of supporting missionaries was needed. In 1814 he was instrumental in the organization of the General Missionary Convention of the Baptist Denomination in the United States for Foreign Missions, popularly known as the Triennial Convention. Thirty-one years later in 1845 Baptists in the South left the Triennial Convention over the issue of slavery and formed the Southern Baptist Convention.

Baptists in Canada established their first convention, the Baptist Convention of Ontario and Quebec, in 1888.

In 1895 black Baptists organized the National Baptist Convention in the United States, Inc. During the twentieth century Baptists in the northern United States made significant changes. Several groups in the North united in 1907 to form the Northern Baptist Convention. In 1911 most of the Free Will Baptists in the North united with the Northern Baptist Convention. Northern Baptists changed their name in 1950 to the American Baptist Convention, then again in 1972 to American Baptist Churches in the USA. (For clarity this group will be referred to throughout this essay as American Baptists.)

Missions

The greatest contribution Baptist women have made to religious life in America and abroad is in the vast area of missions—missions in other lands, in America, in home towns. Small groups of women who gathered to pray for, learn about, be actively involved in, and give to missions were the foundation of mission work among Baptists. Without the long-term and determined effort of these groups, Baptists' strong identification with missions would have been rather meager. These small gatherings became linked in well-organized national mission societies headed by remarkable women who led the efforts to reach women and men around the world with a variety of ministries.

Mary Webb (1779–1861) organized the first mission effort among Baptists. Webb, a "hopeless cripple," had visions far beyond the limits of her wheelchair. In 1800 she gathered eight Baptist and six Congregational women to pray for and give to missionary work. With this group she formed the first mission society in America, the Boston Female Society. Webb's group became the model for other missionary societies. Her vision set in motion a movement among women that shaped the Baptist denomination into one of the largest missionary-minded groups in America.

Webb's young mission society soon discovered how necessary its efforts were. Life was changing in the new century and bringing new opportunities. The colonies had gained their independence from England. The American West was opening up, as was trade across the Atlantic. The revival movement of the late eighteenth and early nineteenth centuries so spurred Baptist growth that by the twentieth century it became the largest Protestant denomination in America. All these factors awakened Baptist interests in Native Americans, western settlers at home, and the "heathen" in foreign lands. This climate provided rich soil for Webb's society and similar groups that soon sprang up.

Many Baptist women and men in America became interested in missions; some even went to foreign lands themselves. Ann Hasseltine Judson found missions so compelling in 1812 that she left America with her new husband, Adoniram. Arriving in Burma, they discovered that men had very little contact with native women. Ann was able to visit in Burmese homes that her husband could not. Before long she was busy evangelizing, administering a small school, and translating the Bible into two languages. She had a great impact among the Burmese people, but her greater influence may have been in America. Ann was a faithful letter writer. Her letters to Ann Graves in Baltimore telling about the work and needs in Burma were passed eagerly from mission society to mission society. Ann educated Baptist women to the realities of life and work on the mission field. Through her letters mission interest among women grew rapidly.

By the nineteenth century Americans became more aware of peoples in other lands. The revival movement known as the Great Awakening inspired many Christians to take the gospel abroad. The societies soon dis-covered that they could do more for missions if they organized regionally and then nationally. Women missionaries working in home and foreign fields became the catalysts for missions organizations in America. Their pleas for financial support stimulated the formation of mission societies.

Free Will Baptists also formed mission societies. Rev. and Mrs. Eli Noyes, recently returned from mission work in India, eagerly told Free Will churches in 1841 of that country's needs. They settled in Providence, Rhode Island, where the first local Free Will Baptist Woman's Missionary Society was formed. In June 1847, a Free Will Baptist women meeting in Lisbon, New Hampshire, formed the first state mission organization among Baptists, the New Hampshire Yearly Meeting Benevolent Association. Four months later, in October at Sutton, Vermont, they organized the Free Will Baptist Female Missionary Society, the first national woman's missionary society in the United States. Marilla T. Hills (1807–1901), active in the antebellum Underground Railroad, was one of the founders of the Free Will Baptist Woman's Mission Society and wrote their constitution. "Mother Hills," as she became known, organized numerous local groups. To urge the advancement of women, she created networks for communication among groups. As a popular speaker for over sixty years she was the most influential woman among Free Will Baptists in the nineteenth century.

Baptist women in Canada also organized to support missionary work. The Canadian Baptist "Female Mite Society" formed in 1818 prepared the way. By 1820 Canadian women were allowed to pray, educate, and raise funds for missions, but the men controlled the boards and the appointments. When Hannah Maria Norris Armstrong (1842–1919) applied to the Canadian Maritime Baptist Foreign Mission Board in 1870, she was rejected due to lack of funds. The board encouraged her to get her "sisters" to support her with their egg, butter, and knitting money. Armstrong immediately went on the road in eastern Canada. In ten weeks she organized thirty-three Women's Mission Aid Societies, the first in that country. In 1876 A. V. Timpany, telling of the need for missions to women and children in India, urged Canadian women to organize regionally to meet that need. Women accepted the challenge. Mrs. T. J. Claxton led the Women's Baptist Foreign Mission Society East. Susan Moulton McMaster led the Women's Baptist Foreign Missionary Society West. In 1882 the women's societies appointed their own missionary, Mary J. Firth, to serve in India.

In the States women had a growing interest in supporting missions through mission societies. American Baptist women in Boston and Chicago formed the Woman's American Baptist Foreign Mission Society (WABFMS) of the East and the Woman's American Baptist Foreign Mission Society of the West in 1871. Three years later a similar organization was formed on the Pacific Coast. Joanna P. Moore (1832–1916), working among the freed people of the South, asked Christian women in the North for help. Her urgings prompted Baptist women to form the Woman's American Baptist Home Mission Society (WABHMS) in 1877.

A growing number of local and state mission societies in the South saw a need for centralizing their efforts and formed the Woman's Missionary Union (WMU) of the Southern Baptist Convention in 1888. Black Baptist women also organized. The Woman's Convention auxiliary to the National Baptist Convention, founded in 1900, was more broadly based in its scope, but its first project was to support the Foreign Mission Board's effort to send Emma DeLaney in 1901 to Africa. The last third of the nineteenth century saw the rise of many regional and national missions organizations.

As the number of state societies grew and national organizations formed, strong leadership was needed. In the South, Annie Armstrong (1850–1938) proposed that a national women's mission organization be formed that would not interfere with the management of the convention's missions boards, would not appoint or direct mission work, but would efficiently collect money and disburse information on mission subjects. Armstrong worked tirelessly to establish state organizations, encourage mission projects, and publish mission materials. The strong organizational start of the Southern Baptist Woman's Missionary Union was primarily a tribute to Armstrong, who from 1888 to 1906 devoted her life to building the new organization. A strong-willed woman, she refused to accept a salary and traveled at her own expense. When Charlotte Diggs "Lottie" Moon (1840–1912), a missionary to China, wrote in 1887 of crucial needs and suggested that women at home have a week of prayer for missions and take a special offering, Armstrong wrote letters to all the societies asking them to give to a Christmas offering to send to China. The $2,833.49 given was the beginning of an annual Southern Baptist Christmas offering. The annual Annie Armstrong Easter Offering for Home Missions honors her contribution in establishing the Woman's Missionary Union as a strong organization.

Once strong mission organizations were formed, missions education became increasingly important. The women developed programs and materials that informed Baptists about the other cultures, the people, and their needs. Although Mamie Steward was referring to black Baptist men, she spoke for all Baptists in 1898 when she said that men were often interested in missions, but women were missions' most ardent friends and advocates. Women wrote and published materials about mission work on this continent and others. Groups of young children, older girls and boys, and

women were organized to learn about, pray for, and give to missions at home and abroad. Women not only led these groups but also trained others to lead them.

Women organized for missions, women educated about missions, and women became missionaries. In some Baptist churches being a missionary is the highest spiritual calling a woman can attain. Women became career missionaries to a range of people from the Indians in North America to the Indians in Asia. On the mission field, women made major contributions in the areas of education, medicine, and church work, especially among national women. For example, in the United States women established work with Native Americans. Isabel Crawford (1865–1961) went as a missionary from American Baptists to the Kiowas in Oklahoma in 1893, beginning her work while living in a tent. Crawford organized a missionary society called "God's Light upon the Mountain." As a result of her work in Oklahoma the "God's Sunlight" mission was founded in 1901 in Arizona, and her response was, "God's Light upon a Mountain has borned a papoose!" (Crawford, 79). Crawford proved to be quite a tenacious Baptist, which ultimately caused her resignation. When on a Communion Sunday in 1905 the nearby minister could not come to administer the ordinance, Isabel suggested that a local man do so. The church voted unanimously to follow her advice, and a communion service was held. That such a good service would cause any kind of trouble never occurred to Crawford since every Baptist church is autonomous. However, the local Indian Baptist association believed that only "Jesus men" should administer communion. The prolonged dispute caused the Indians much pain. As a result, Isabel resigned, saying, "A church without the power to observe the Lords' Supper is not a Baptist Church! A church that bows to any authority higher than the Holy Scriptures is not a Baptist Church! . . . I resign. I cannot stay" (Brackney, 309).

Hannah Maria Norris Armstrong (1842–1919) was appointed by Canadian Baptists as a missionary to Burma in 1870, translating and writing in the Karen language, establishing a Bible school in Rangoon and a public library, mentoring local pastors, establishing orphanages, even serving as chaplain on a steamship to 3,000 Telugu workers. On furlough she also proved to be a very effective fund-raiser among influential Americans. Lottie Moon, one of the first single missionaries sent out by Southern Baptists, worked in China for almost forty years. Believing she was called to be an evangelist in China, Moon refused to be restricted to "women's work" such as teaching only girls and women. When crowds gathered around the "foreigner," she used the opportunity to read the Bible and tell the people about Jesus. When male missionaries complained that she was preaching, she replied that people wanted and needed to hear the gospel. She suggested that if the men did not like her sharing the gospel, they should send some men who could do it better! Ahead of her time, she did not try to impose Western culture on the Chinese but adopted Chinese culture to such an extent that she died of starvation because she shared her meager food supply with the Chinese. She prodded Baptist women at home to organize as the Methodists and Presbyterians had done. Through her letters and life, Moon has had immeasurable impact on Southern Baptist missions and women.

Louise "Lulu" Fleming (1862–1899) was the first black woman appointed as a career missionary by the Woman's American Baptist Foreign Mission Society and the first female medical officer sent out by Baptists. Fleming went to the Congo as a nurse. On furlough she went to medical school and returned to Africa as a physician. Fleming was instrumental in sending several young African women to the United States to receive an education.

Sent by National Baptists to Africa in 1901, Emma Delaney (1871–1922) was instrumental in establishing many schools in Central and West Africa. When she returned to the States on furlough in 1905, Daniel Malakebu, a native African boy who became a Christian under her teaching, accompanied her without her knowledge. Daniel sneaked away from home and wound his way through 200 miles of dangerous jungle to follow Emma back to America. Once he was in America, she encouraged him to attend medical school. After graduation he and his new wife returned to Africa, where he became the supervisor for missions of South, East, and Central Africa. Delaney's legacy was indeed far-reaching.

Increasingly Baptist women learned from missionaries that it was inappropriate for men to minister to women and children in many cultures. In some countries women had limited options for education and therefore limited opportunities in society. "Women working for women" was the belief that motivated Baptist women to help their sisters wherever they lived. Usually that began by empowering women to go to mission fields.

Social Work

All mission work was not thousands of miles away. Some was at the doorstep of many churches or in a nearby state. Industrialization and increased immigration from Europe brought many rural or international people into cities. These new workers often were poorly paid and lived in poor conditions. Women raised the consciousness of Baptists regarding the spiritual and physical needs of people in their own nation, in their own city, and in the very community where Baptists worshipped. Among white Baptists, pronouncements

about social problems often came from Convention leaders, but the day-to-day work of trying to solve those problems usually was by the women, especially in the South. Attending to social problems among black Baptists was a major concern for both genders, although women did most of the fund-raising.

Giving to the "poor souls overseas" was easier than getting involved with the poor or unfortunate person nearby. But learning about mission needs overseas opened women's eyes to similar problems at their doorstep. Child labor practices, racial prejudice, industrial oppression, poverty, and disease were local problems. Mary Webb, the earliest woman's mission society leader, discovered quickly that mission opportunities were just around the corner. In 1816 she established a mission in Boston for the poor and the criminals, sent a woman to work in the black community, and started Penitent Females' Refuge, a program to reform prostitutes. Webb organized nine other groups that focused on specific social needs.

All over America, Baptist women began to organize work among uneducated girls, poor mothers, immigrant families, older citizens, homeless men, and inner-city families. Social services became a crucial part of women's commitment. These services were usually initiated, staffed, and funded by local women. National and regional leaders encouraged women's groups to investigate the needs in their own cities or towns. Baptist women in the South and North learned about labor laws, educational levels in the community, and the prevalence of poverty and identified which social services were already available. As a result mission work varied: mother's meetings, sewing schools, day nurseries, boys and girls clubs, cooking schools, visiting in hospitals and prisons, providing services for mill workers, community Sunday Schools, and working to improve living conditions.

Annie Armstrong (1850–1938) urged white women in Baltimore in the 1880s to work with the poor, the indigent, the sick, and immigrants. Ahead of her time, she established work with the black community as well, then helped black women to organize a national women's organization. Helen Barrett Montgomery (1861–1934) served on the Rochester, New York, school board for ten years to influence the improvement of schools in inner-city neighborhoods. She and Susan B. Anthony raised the money needed to open the doors of the University of Rochester to women students.

At a time when Baptist men were engaged in vigorous debates over the social gospel, women established numerous social programs. Many Baptists believed that evangelism should be the emphasis in all ministry. Baptist women fervently believed in evangelism also. However, they insisted that ministry meant meeting the needs of people as well as preaching the gospel. Lulie P.

Wharton (1871–1948), a leader in the social work emphasis among Southern Baptists, said that women's contribution to the welfare of society could never be given full measure as long as the prevailing attitude was that "her thoughts, her feelings and her actions are of real worth only when they have been strained through a masculine percolator" (Wharton, 27). She advised women to be involved in personal service wherever they were.

Rather ironically, while the evangelism versus social gospel debate raged in male Baptist circles, the women were not debating but quietly and effectively making a difference in community after community. As some observed, the evangelists knew little, if anything, about the souls they converted, but the women knew the individuals they led to Christianity and whose life situation they worked to improve. Nannie Burroughs (1879–1961), noted leader of the Women's Convention of the National Baptist Convention, observed that the ministers preached "too much Heaven and too little practical Christian living," often exploiting the poor and uneducated rather than being involved in solving their problems (Higginbotham, 175).

Mission literature in the early twentieth century largely reflected women's views. Women insisted that while preaching the gospel was essential, it was not enough. Spiritual messages were more effective when physical needs such as food, clothing, housing, and health needs were addressed. Ministry was not merely talking about the gospel; it was living it as Jesus did. Kathleen Mallory stated the issue quite clearly in 1912 when she wrote an article titled "Has the Church Fulfilled Its Obligation When It Has Preached the Gospel?" In an effort to *be* the gospel, settlement houses as centers for social ministries were established in Chicago, Louisville, and Washington, D.C.

One of the greatest and most controversial problems facing society, especially in the South, was how to meet the needs of the newly freed slaves. People enslaved all their lives were suddenly thrust into a free society. For the first time they had to secure their own homes and find jobs. Such change was quite a jolt. Many Southerners, still dealing with their own Civil War wounds, were not rushing out to assist their black neighbors with that transition.

Joanna P. Moore (1832–1916), a Pennsylvanian, refused to accept the notions of racial inferiority and segregation. In 1863 she was the first woman appointed by the American Baptist Home Mission Society and was sent to Island No. 10 in the Mississippi River near Memphis, Tennessee. Later she worked in Arkansas and in Louisiana. George Gaines, a farmer and soldier, wrote Moore that white people often said hard things about black people: "But I for one am determined that shoe shall not fit me. I will try as you have so often told me

to choose for my companions the moral, the sensible, and especially the religious" (Brackney, 239). Until she died in 1916, Moore worked in black communities in the South teaching them to read, teaching them the Bible, helping them find housing and jobs, establishing mother's training schools, stressing honesty and trust, and working to improve racial relations. Northern women had little contact with black people. Moore and black women who visited the North challenged stereotypes of African Americans and informed them of black people's realities. As a result northern women became more interested in what black women often referred to as "woman's work for woman." The northern interest in race issues stressed the importance of women in solving the race problem nationally. "Woman's work for woman" connected Baptist women across racial, regional, and class differences.

In the meantime, some southern leaders had a growing interest in solving some of the South's social problems. In May 1912, 700 people from twenty-eight states met in Nashville, Tennessee, and formed the Southern Sociological Congress. Its annual meetings addressed the social, civic, and moral problems in the South. One of the early leaders was Fannie E. S. Heck (1862–1915) of North Carolina. The Woman's Missionary Union spurred Heck's interest in social action. Fifteen years before the Southern Sociological Congress, Heck started a department of "neighborhood mission work" in North Carolina. She also became involved in nonreligious benevolent efforts. When elected as the first president of the Woman's Club of Raleigh, she led the members to work on community health and sanitation issues. She also established and led the Associated Charities of Raleigh. But Heck became convinced that charity without Christ was lacking. As president of the Southern Baptist Women's Missionary Union, she inaugurated a program of "Personal Service" that encouraged local church societies to become engaged personally in addressing social problems. Under various names this program remains a vital ministry within Southern Baptist life.

WMU leadership's interest in the social reform movements of the South enabled women across the South, already involved in "personal service," to expand those services to the black communities. And in the North, Canadian Jennie Johnson started a mission in Flint, Michigan, in 1928 to feed the thousands of unemployed Americans suffering from the depression. Baptist women were being missionaries in the home land.

While many women in Baptist life are noted for their dedication to addressing social problems, thousands of other nameless women made significant contributions to improve physical and spiritual conditions in their community. Joanna Moore's words in the 1880s could be echoed again and again. "I wish you could know the great number of women who are doing real mission work within the bounds of their own home and their own church . . . holding mothers' and children's meetings, caring for the poor, reading the Bible in the homes of their neighbors" (Higginbotham, 93).

Women's societies among white Baptists tended to focus on missions at home and abroad. However, the Woman's Convention (National Baptist) had a much broader agenda: ending racial discrimination, curbing all violence, women's suffrage, equal educational opportunities, training for mothers, equal employment opportunities, child care for working mothers, better working conditions, and better wages. National Baptist women joined efforts with secular organizations to deal with the problem of urbanization. Nannie Burroughs believed that a church had no right to be in a community if it was not going to improve life in that community. The Woman's Convention actively promoted woman's suffrage, although their sisters in the Southern Baptist Convention WMU did not, fearing it would hurt their mission effort. When the Nineteenth Amendment to the U.S. Constitution securing woman's suffrage passed in 1919, Helen Barrett Montgomery warned that political questions on which Christians differed should be left to secular women's organizations. "But," she said, "questions affecting education, the protection of young girls, child welfare, the milk supply, and temperance are those on which the public opinion of the Christian church is overwhelmingly one" (Montgomery, in *The Baptist*).

Race was eventually an issue for most of the women's societies. As they became involved in the mission and education efforts for black people in the early part of the twentieth century, women in the North began to abandon their stereotypical views. From early in the century women in the South were prodded by their leaders to address racial issues. Literature continually dealt with racial issues. National conventions featured black speakers. Within their organization and within the convention, the WMU worked harder on this social cause than any other, but local response varied greatly. Leaders of the women's national societies, with few exceptions, spearheaded the efforts to end racial discrimination.

Fund-Raising

Baptist women demonstrated that giving amounts systemically was more effective than the occasional big offerings. Churches traditionally focused on certain times of the year, such as harvest time, to replenish the bank account. Women usually did not have large sums of money, but they did have the butter, egg, and knitting money to drop into empty sugar bowls. Women discovered that small amounts given regularly throughout the year produced larger annual amounts than once or twice a year offerings. Even the poor could experience the dignity of giving. Churches began to adopt the women's

system. In 1911 Lansing Burrows, a Baptist statistician, acknowledged the success of the giving plan of the women when he said that their method was the "power of that portion of the church which we have wrongly designated as the weaker sex" (Burrows, 115). Women taught Baptists how to give.

Often Baptist women's societies raised missions awareness and monies, while men took charge of dispersing funds and appointing the missionaries, although some Woman's American Baptist Mission Societies did appoint their own. In those societies where women did not appoint missionaries, women learned to exert influence when needed. When men in the Southern Baptist Convention refused to appoint single women to the mission field in the nineteenth century, the women's societies responded by suggesting that they withhold their offerings and pay for single women themselves. The appointing board promptly changed its policies. Although women were not allowed to vote in that convention or in most churches, they discovered money could be an effective voice.

The Lottie Moon Christmas Offering, initiated by Southern Baptist women in 1887, became an annual offering for international missions. The Annie Armstrong Easter Offering provides funds for home missions. Named in honor of women who inspired them, these offerings are the largest revenue source for both foreign and home mission boards, collecting millions of dollars each year for Southern Baptist missions. When organizing in 1888 the WMU of the Southern Baptist Convention stated in its constitution's preamble a desire to stimulate the grace of giving and to aid in collecting funds for missions. To accomplish these goals women were encouraged to practice self-denial, which the leaders and members regularly did.

Missions were not the only beneficiary of Baptist women's fund-raising efforts. In numerous instances, women financially sustained the denomination's work. When white society denied traditional services to the black community, the black church supported newspapers, schools, recreation, welfare services, and employment for the community. Fund-raising by black women enabled the church to be an effective force in racial self-help. During the depression of the 1930s, Canadian, American, and Southern Baptist women assisted denominational boards to pay off critical debts. Baptist women were not rich, but they gave their meager monies faithfully and sustained church work in many areas.

Education

Baptist women are teachers in many forums. Most Baptist women will teach at some time in their lives, many in their local church. Sunday School teachers in Baptist churches are predominantly women. Some women teach Sunday School for forty or fifty years, which means they influence many lives from birth to retirement. Through their regular preparation for classes, they become lifelong learners. Many Baptist churches have short-term summer programs such as Vacation Bible School or Backyard Bible Clubs. Women are the primary teachers for these activities.

Baptist women usually take these teaching responsibilities seriously, seeing them as a form of ministry. Some have a sense of call to teach. So crucial is the women's role that the teaching programs of most churches would collapse, were women to withdraw their services. Even when Baptists argue over women's role in the ordained ministry of the church, all sides agree that the churches could not function without the women. Since the faith of future generations is shaped by the church's teachers, the women's teaching role is likely their most influential one in any local church.

With the explosion of church-funded schools in the nineteenth century, many women entered the profession of teaching. Single women especially found respectability as well as steady income through teaching. Because many schools were single-sex schools, women found many job opportunities in the girls' schools from the primary grades through the college years. Not only did they teach; they also became school administrators. They even founded schools, thus shaping them from the beginning. Women at times taught younger children in boys' schools, as women were considered adept at molding the "plastic minds of the young." By the end of the nineteenth century some of these schools closed, reducing the teaching opportunities for women. However, in the twentieth century women began to teach in coeducational schools, mountain schools, college and graduate schools, and village schools in other countries. Since teaching often came with low wages and long days, it was a ministry to students, parents, and the communities.

Nannie Burroughs stunned a 1901 assembly of black National Baptist leaders when she proposed a school be established in Washington, D.C., for black women. When the leaders did not supply the funds, she raised the money herself and purchased the land. Six years later she informed the convention that the land was ready and she needed $50,000 to build and open the school. But the National Baptists did not have the money and discouraged such a large undertaking. In fact, Booker T. Washington advised Burroughs that placing a school in the nation's capital was not a good idea. Burroughs disagreed. She believed that the location was ideal because it was in the border state region. National Baptist men did not approve or support the plan, but National Baptist women did. With this backing, Burroughs opened her school in 1909 as the National Trade and Professional School for Women and Girls. Burroughs's school,

like many for black girls, stressed self-help. Burroughs's program was based on the 3 Bs: the Bible, the Bath, and the Broom. Emphasis was placed on clean lives, clean bodies, and clean homes. Education, morality, and productive economic skills were the goals of education at the school. The renamed Nannie Helen Burroughs School, a private school in Washington, D.C., for elementary and secondary age children, is still in operation.

Northern Baptists provided schools for black men in Atlanta and Richmond but none for black women. Black churches in each city pledged money for women's schools. In 1881 Sophia Packard and Harriet Giles of the Woman's American Baptist Home Mission Society established the Atlanta Baptist Female Seminary (later renamed Spelman) in a church basement. At Spelman and at other schools they established, black women stressed independence, self-help, and the "politics of respectability," which emphasized improving individual behavior and attitudes. Not only did respectability benefit the person, but it also improved race relations.

The Woman's Baptist Mission Society in 1881 founded the Baptist Missionary Training School of Chicago to provide biblical, medical, and domestic training. Elizabeth Church taught the biblical courses from 1886 and became the preceptress in 1904. Ellen Cushing (1840–1915) realized a need for a women's training school in Philadelphia. In 1892 she became a founder and the first principal of the school. In 1966 the school was renamed the Ellen Cushing Junior College and later merged with Eastern College. Using the Chicago school as a model, Woman's Missionary Union established the Woman's Missionary Union Training School, a tuition-free school in Louisville, Kentucky, in 1907. These schools prepared women for work in the mission fields. Their experience in the training schools also gave the young women valuable leadership skills in a single-sex environment.

Women's schools provided not only education for women but also professional opportunities in education. Sally B. Hamner was the president of Richmond Female Institute from 1877 to 1890. Modena Lowery Berry was cofounder and vice president of Blue Mountain College in Mississippi in 1873. Susan Moulton McMaster founded Moulton College in Canada. When founded in 1946, Lois Tupper became the director of the Women's Leadership Training School located in Hamilton, Ontario. She served in that position until 1968 when she became the first woman to hold a full professorship in a Canadian theological college, McMaster Divinity College.

Publication

Even when their public voice and vote were limited, women used the pen and press to speak, to teach, to inform, and to influence. In 1822 Ann Judson wrote *A Particular Relation of the American Baptist Mission to the Burman Empire.* As one of the first published records of an American foreign missionary, it stressed the role of missionary women in improving the social status of women in other lands.

Baptist women all over America provided significant literature. By the 1880s Baptist women were preparing literature for Sunday School teachers. In Baltimore, women led by Annie and Alice Armstrong launched a very effective Missions Room, enlisting women to write, publish, and distribute missions literature. Fannie E. S. Heck in *Royal Service,* Margaret and Jane Buchan in *The Canadian Missionary Link,* and Helen McMaster in *The Baptist Visitor* were leaders in this effort. Hundreds of women busily wrote missions and Sunday School curriculum materials, thus shaping both their denomination's missions education and theology. These efforts not only met the need for study helps but also demonstrated that such publications could be profitable and useful in building loyalty and cooperation in the denomination. The Boston Women's Society voiced the goal of other societies: that the literature would instruct thousands of children, thus creating an informed generation more willing to support missions than the current one.

Sallie Rochester Ford (1828–1910) and her husband worked as editors of the widely influential periodical *The Christian Repository* in the 1850s. In her fictional writings Ford addressed theological issues. She was also active in the publication of *Kind Words,* a monthly Sunday School paper for children. Ann Graves in 1843 wrote in her *Women in America: Being an Examination into the Moral and Intellectual Condition of American Female Society* about the plight of women and especially the lack of higher education. Agnes Osborne launched *The Heathen Helper,* a missions support magazine, in Louisville in 1882. Her sister-in-law Christine Osborne started *The Baptist Basket* in 1888 to promote the practice of tithing and benevolence.

Ann Hasseltine, Sarah Boardman, and Emily Chubbock were consecutive wives of Adoniram Judson, and all served with him as missionaries in Burma. Emily was a noted writer under the pen name of Fanny Forester when she married Adoniram in 1845. Emily wrote a biography of Sarah, a widely read literary work that portrayed a model for Christian women. Emily's work was also a model for authentic, realistic missionary biographies instead of the usual ones that portrayed missionaries only as saints.

Helen Barrett Montgomery's classic mission work *Western Women in Eastern Lands,* published in 1910, insisted, among other things, that there was a direct relationship between the advance of Christianity and women's rights. Education was the primary emphasis of her work; she saw education as essential to lifting women around the world out of their low status. Montgomery wrote five other books that promoted missions. She was the first woman to publish a translation of the Greek New Testament into modern English, the *Centenary Translation of the New Testament.* Montgomery believed that outdated expressions hindered the understanding of the Bible by the less educated; she determined to make her translation clear for young people and foreigners. Her new translation also provided explanatory notes to introduce the texts, making it user-friendly.

Denominational Work

Outside of women's societies, Baptist women have had few opportunities to make widely known contributions to their denominations. In less public ways, however, they have wielded significant influence. As is true in most churches, denominational agencies depend on women's daily work and support to complete their tasks. Clerks, secretaries, assistants, and associates carry out an important part of the work of an agency's or board's work. These contributions have yet to be fully measured.

Although few Baptist women held high office in Baptist denominations, many occupied executive positions in national women's work. Twentieth-century executives such as American Baptist's Violet Rudd and Elizabeth Miller and Southern Baptist's Kathleen Mallory and Alma Hunt exercised considerable influence on other Baptist boards' executives. Decisions about mission work and convention programs frequently were made in careful consultation with women leaders.

Valuable work is not always accompanied by a paycheck. Baptists have been blessed with nonsalaried professional women who made major contributions to the denominations and churches they serve. As already noted, at the denominational level some women have led the mission work as professionals. At the state, regional, and local levels that work was led by committed women who received no pay. They led meetings, workshops, and conventions. They encouraged struggling organizations. They spent hours writing letters, making telephone calls, and planning meetings to lead women in missions education and giving. Thousands of these women have been the backbone of missions success among Baptists.

Election to a national office has been rare. In 1921 Helen Barrett Montgomery became the first woman president of an American denomination when she was elected president of the Northern (American) Baptist Convention. In 1956 Mary Milne was the first woman elected to be president of the Baptist Convention of Ontario and Quebec. National and Southern Baptists have yet to elect a woman to this role. In 1963 Marie Mathis was elected as second vice president of the Southern Baptist Convention, the highest elective position a woman has held in the convention. Letha R. Casazza was the first woman to serve as a state convention president among Southern Baptists when she was elected president of the Baptist Convention of the District of Columbia in 1973.

Baptists Helen Barrett Montgomery and Lucy Peabody were instrumental in establishing one of the most successful ecumenical women's efforts when they organized the first World Day of Prayer in 1919, which continues to be observed annually.

Local Church

Although women have been movers and shapers in the founding of churches, their contributions often are omitted from official records. Only news accounts, diaries, and oral histories tell their stories. For instance, First Baptist Church of Dallas, Texas, owes its birth to a woman named Lucinda Williams, who did not give up when others were discouraged. Church histories, like that of the First Baptist Church, Nashville, Tennessee, and First Baptist Church, Richmond, Virginia, chronicle the numerous contributions women made to the many ministries of the church: providing benevolent funds, sewing to make money for missions or church causes, raising money for church indebtedness, making visits, sewing for orphans, providing for the poor, teaching inner-city children, and enlisting children in Sunday Schools.

The wives of Baptist ministers often have left an indelible mark on the congregation. Some women sensed a call to be a spouse of the minister. These women often were "ministers" in their own way, through missions leadership, music programs, Sunday School work, official hospitality, home visitation, leading conferences and workshops. Their contribution to the work and ministry of a local church was often invaluable.

Ministers

American Baptists, Free Will Baptists, and Canadian Baptists encouraged women in preaching ministry more frequently than did Southern Baptists and National Baptists. However, women did not hold positions of ministerial leadership in proportion to their membership in any of these groups.

Every Baptist church is free to call whomever it wishes as minister. As Baptist congregations favor men as senior ministers, women have had few opportunities to lead churches in that capacity. Yet from their earliest days in seventeenth-century England, Baptists have had churches with women preachers, scattered though they were. The earliest reference to a Baptist female preacher in America was to Catherine Scott, who influenced Roger Williams to establish the first Baptist Church in America in Providence, Rhode Island, in 1639. In the 1750s Martha Stearns Marshall, noted for preaching with fire and zeal, was jailed on at least one occasion in Connecticut. Hannah Lee Hall and Martha Clay, who was also jailed, preached in Virginia regularly. In the late 1700s Mary Savage and Sally Parsons were preaching in the New England area. By the early 1800s Clarissa H. Danforth, Martha Spaulding, and Salome Lincoln preached frequently in that region. Danforth, well educated, single, attractive, and from a respected family, held many revivals and influenced the founding of a number of churches.

The first Baptist group to ordain women to preach was the Free Will Baptists in 1815 when they ordained Danforth. In 1882 May C. Jones of Seattle, Washington, was the first woman to be ordained in the West. The first woman ordained by American Baptists was Edith Hill of Kansas in 1894. Canadian Baptists ordained Jennie Johnson in 1907, who preached in Chatham, Ontario, for twenty years. The Baptist Convention of Ontario and Quebec ordained a woman for the first time in 1947, Muriel Spurgeon Carder. African American women Sapphira Phillips and Grace Staten were ordained in Indiana by Free Will Baptists in 1907, as were three more black women four years later. In 1964 Addie Davis was the first Southern Baptist woman to be ordained. When she could not find a church to lead in the South, she pastored in Readsboro, Vermont. Druecillar Fordham in 1972 became the first black woman ordained in the Southern Baptist Convention and also the first to serve as pastor. The Black Ministers Conference of Baltimore and Vicinity admitted women preachers for the first time in 1979. All these women were pioneers in Baptist circles as they pushed open the heavy door of opposition to women clergy.

Both American Baptist and Southern Baptist women initiated Women in Ministry meetings in the early 1980s to provide support and networking opportunities for women ministers. American Baptist Women in Ministry held its first conference in 1980 and established the organization. Carolyn Weatherford led the Woman's Missionary Union to sponsor a dinner for Women in Ministry in 1982, which led to the organization of the Southern Baptist Women in Ministry. After several Southern Baptist Convention actions that restricted women's leadership in the 1980s, the organization dropped the name "Southern" and became Baptist Women in Ministry in 1995.

As in other denominations, women have served Baptist churches in various professional capacities. In the nineteenth century some churches paid a woman a hundred dollars a year to serve as music director or organist. Over the years job opportunities in local churches expanded. Whether the title was minister or director, they led music, education, youth, children's, recreation, senior adult, counseling, and hosting ministries. Their leadership in these positions not only benefited the programs they directed in their churches but also modeled women's leadership, especially to young people. The church secretary may be the most knowledgeable and influential professional woman in many Baptist churches.

A significant number of ordained Baptist women moved into chaplaincy, some because they felt called to that ministry, some because they could not find churches in which to serve. In hospitals, prisons, hospice programs, clinics, military units, and corporations, they make spiritual contributions often unknown to those outside the programs.

Theology

While men spoke frequently of the subservient woman, this idea was rarely expressed in women's writings and speeches. Women's work in missions led to an enlargement of the role of mothers and homemakers to that of world mother and community homemaker. The focus of many Baptist women was directed toward their obligations to other people, especially underprivileged or oppressed women and children. While they used Jesus' relationship to women as their model, they did not expend much effort working to achieve rights for themselves. Some Baptist women's groups have been criticized for lack of leadership in the suffrage and women's rights movements.

Baptist theological stress on the individual and the priesthood of the believer gave women the foundation to influence the lives of women missionaries. Every Baptist had a responsibility to respond to God's call. When boards resisted appointment of single women, women's mission groups brought pressure, often in financial form, to change the boards' policies. Mission societies also asked that missionary wives be given specific tasks based on their training. As Baptist women gained some rights in American society, they insisted on more rights for women serving overseas.

As teachers and writers, women continually influenced Baptist thought. Women taught the young people in churches during their formative years. Publishing gave them the opportunity to emphasize the basic doctrines of their churches. Baptist women often stressed the social gospel, expanding the traditional focus on evangelism as the real mission of the church. Because women were working with inner-city populations, immigrant families, Native American groups, and the poor, they understood the society in which these people lived. As they taught, wrote, and led groups, Baptist women stressed Jesus' nurturing ministries. Salvation was im-

portant but so were hunger, housing, and healing. Mission and Bible study materials pointed to Jesus as a model and indicated ways people could address these problems. Early in the nineteenth century Baptist women saw medical missions as a natural model of Jesus' ministry. Meeting the health needs of people was a ministry in itself. Medical missions was not merely a hook to attract people to the gospel; healing itself was ministry. A disciple of Christ should care about landlord abuse in the community, poor schools, unjust laws, hungry families, and the rights of others. This understanding became the basis for the work of Baptists, especially in inner cities.

As women moved into editorial positions, Baptist publications began to reflect their concerns. Family issues became a more frequent focus. Bible study materials began to include more passages about women. Gender-sensitive language replaced male-centered language. Readers discovered a Bible with more women than they had previously realized: There were now Bible study materials about Deborah as well as Gideon and illustrations that included interests of women as well as men.

Mary Cook, born a slave, graduated from State University of Louisville and later taught there. Cook used the black press, an edited anthology, and various speeches to extend the black church's theology to be more inclusive of women as modeled in the Bible. Virginia Broughton came from a privileged background, was raised as a free black, and graduated from college in 1875. Working as a teacher and missionary, she became a woman of influence among black Baptists. Cook and Broughton stressed Jesus' relationship to women as models for modern women. Women were encouraged to model the image of comforter and to assume the responsibility of preaching and sharing the gospel. Cook insisted that Jesus' conversation with the Samaritan woman set a new standard for respecting the intellect of women and encouraging them to be involved in the advancement of the gospel. Cook and Broughton shifted woman's primary allegiance from husband to God and advised male leaders that women expected more leadership roles in the work of the church.

As more women became interested in the doctrines of the church, some entered seminaries to study theology more intensely. Gradually female theologians were hired to teach in Baptist graduate schools and seminaries. Their presence caused these institutions to become more inclusive when taught by either male or female professors. Students benefited by being exposed to inclusive theologies, to androgynous views of God and scripture, and to supportive discussions of women in leadership.

Exercising the freedom of Baptist theology and amid much diversity, Baptist women repeatedly worked to serve God and their society in spite of the resistance they often faced in their own denominations. Their contributions to Baptist life range from the pen to the pulpit and from their homes to the other side of the world.

SOURCES: For additional reading, see Leon McBeth's *Women in Baptist Life* (1979) and Eleanor Hull's *Women Who Carried the Good News* (1975). Evelyn Brooks Higginbotham provides a fine history in *Righteous Discontent: The Woman's Movement in the Black Baptist Church, 1880–1920* (1993). Primary materials from Mary Webb, Isabel Crawford, Joanna P. Moore, and Helen Barrett Montgomery can be found in William H. Brackney's *Baptist Life and Thought* (1983). Additional information about Isabel Crawford can be located in her autobiography *Joyful Journey* (1951). For a more thorough discussion of the concept of personal service, see Mrs. H. M. Wharton's article in *Royal Service*, September 1925. Helen Barrett Montgomery's essay on civic roles was printed in *The Baptist*, August 28, 1920. To read more of Lansing Burrows' comments, see *How Baptist Work Together* (1911). See Catherine Allen's *A Century to Celebrate: History of Woman's Missionary Union* (1987) for a comprehensive history of the WMU, Southern Baptist Convention.

CHRISTIAN CHURCH/DISCIPLES OF CHRIST TRADITION AND WOMEN
Loretta M. Long

THE FUNCTION OF women in the Christian Church/ Disciples of Christ tradition (or the Disciples) has been a principal issue of contention from the movement's inception. It has rolled through the history of the tradition, also known as the Stone-Campbell movement, gathering enough weight eventually to divide its members and excite substantial debate even in the twenty-first century. Although essentially conservative for most of its early history, the Disciples' approach to the role of women still offers a narrative of extremes in viewpoints from the most liberal to the most conventional.

The divergent history of the Disciples of Christ tradition itself makes it difficult to draw clear lines around the experience of women within it, particularly in its earliest years. Several groups of Christians in the early-nineteenth-century United States shared similar theological convictions but operated independently in separate regions of the country. They communicated often with each other, and although the groups never officially joined, they may still be classified as part of one religious movement. These groups defined themselves by their emphasis on scripture as the only basis for authority, the primacy of the local church, and the spiritual equality of all believers. By the 1830s the Disciples of Christ, under the leadership of Alexander Campbell and Barton Stone, became the most numerous and well known of the groups. The name of their group generated controversy from the beginning, with Campbell preferring "Disciples" and Stone preferring "Christians." While their movement is frequently referred to as the Disciples of Christ in the nineteenth century, that would change after the splintering of the movement.

By the 1930s, the Disciples had spawned three separate traditions: the Christian Church (Disciples of Christ), the Churches of Christ, and the Independent Christian Churches. The first separation gained official notice in 1906 when the more conservative, predominantly southern, "Churches of Christ" requested separate listing in the religious census published that year. Leaders of the Churches of Christ such as David Lipscomb of Tennessee objected to expanding the central doctrine of Alexander Campbell, dedication to scripture as the only foundation of church practice. Lipscomb particularly disputed emerging Disciple practices such as the creation of missionary societies, the development of a denominational structure, and the support of women preaching, which he argued did not conform to scripture. The resulting ethos of the Churches of Christ emphasized radical congregational autonomy and a conservative reading of the New Testament as the foundation for church policy.

The Independent Christian Churches emerged by 1927 from a dispute within the Disciples body over the developing denominational structure of the church and the form it would take. The Independent Christian Churches, like the Churches of Christ, rejected denominational hierarchy particularly as the Disciples supported open membership within that structure (accepting unbaptized members into the Christian Church). After their departure, the remainder of the Disciples were commonly known as the Christian Church (Disciples of Christ), and by the twentieth century the term *Disciples* generally applied only to them. Most important, after 1906, one can no longer speak of the Disciples tradition in terms of one single movement.

Several factors contribute to the disparate attitudes toward women within the Christian Church/Disciples of Christ tradition as a whole. First, the traditionally decentralized nature of the structure they adopted explains much of the deviation. For example, within the Disciples of Christ umbrella, both supporters and detractors of women's preaching found a home together with those who favored equality for women and those who placed severe limits on women's role. The lack of an entrenched hierarchy prevented one dominant ideology regarding women's role and allowed each to reside in the Disciples of Christ tent.

Of the three main branches of the movement, only one, the Christian Church (Disciples of Christ), adopted any form of denominational hierarchy, so other parts of the group retained a locally focused tradition, allowing

With the ordination of Clara Babcock in 1889 and her subsequent twenty-five-year preaching career, the stage was set for the split between the Churches of Christ and the Christian Church (Disciples of Christ) in 1906. *Courtesy of Disciples of Christ Historical Society.*

that became final in 1906. In particular the debate over women's fitness to preach separated the two camps.

Women and Preaching in the Early Christian Church Movement

The multiple origins of the Disciples contributed to its diversity in views about the legitimacy of women preachers. The earliest and most active roots of the Disciples of Christ lay among the "Christians" of New England, led by Elias Smith, and a similar group, the "Republican Methodists," led by James O'Kelly of Virginia. Deeply influenced by the democratic enthusiasm following the Revolutionary War, both groups advocated a simple (Republican) form of Christianity freed of all denominational strictures and dependent on scripture only for authority—similar qualities to those that would later characterize the Disciples of Christ. Such doctrine removed many restrictions on women and left the door open for their broader participation in religious affairs.

Both the "Christians" and the Republican Methodists operated in a fluid, postrevolution social environment countenancing experimentation in gender roles. In the religious excitement that flooded the country after the American Revolution, women emerged as religious leaders celebrated for their speaking abilities and inherent moral nature. Taking their inspiration from Paul's affirmation that "neither male nor female" existed in Christ, the women preachers did not rely on the denominational authority of ordination but on their own skills to attract a following.

One of the first women preachers connected with the Christian Church/Disciples of Christ, Nancy Gove Cram (1776–1825), actually began her career as a missionary among the Oneida Indians of New York in 1812. She soon found working through an interpreter too difficult and moved to a nearby white community to continue her work. When those moved by her preaching and teaching wanted to found a church, the unordained Cram contacted three members of Smith's "Christians" who agreed to move to Charleston, New York, and establish a congregation. Cram's popularity mushroomed after the founding of the church and culminated in a four-year preaching tour of New England, making her the first female evangelist in the Disciples of Christ tradition.

When her meetings overflowed churches, barns, and all other venues in which they were held, other women

for different practices among various churches aligned with the broader tradition. Yet the existence of denominational newspapers allowed members to express their varied views as they debated the role of women. From preaching to writing to serving as missionaries and teaching Sunday School, the story of women in this tradition has been a diverse and intriguing one.

A second factor contributing to the variety of ideas regarding women in the Disciples of Christ tradition involves disagreement over the authority of scripture. While all the branches of the movement accepted the primacy of scripture in determining doctrine, disagreement arose over how scripture might be applied to a number of issues. The "Churches of Christ" favored a more literal interpretation of scripture's proscriptions about women's proper behavior. On the other hand, the more liberal Christian Church found a larger role for women by softening the rigidity of the Apostle Paul's New Testament commands and emphasizing the importance of understanding the context of those statements. By acknowledging the patriarchal nature of the world in which the church of the first century c.e. operated, the Christian Church found more room for women to participate in a nineteenth-century culture than loosening its bonds on women. This fundamental disagreement factored into the growing split between the two branches quickly followed in her footsteps. Abigail Roberts (1791–1841), converted by Cram in 1816, enjoyed a sixteen-year preaching career, converting hundreds and establishing at least four congregations throughout New England before deteriorating health forced her retirement. Nancy Towle (1796–1876) of New Hampshire began preaching in April 1821 delivering lengthy sermons at as many as six to eight meetings a week for years on end. Her eloquent oratory and persuasive presentation of the biblical message converted hundreds.

Because of their gender, all these women faced vigorous opposition from men in the communities where they preached and were often prevented from speaking. Their public speaking violated new ideas about women that have since been labeled the "separate spheres" ideology. In this system, women ruled the domestic sphere and men the public. Women's suitability for ruling the home rested on the commonly held belief that they were naturally more moral than men and could raise moral children to be responsible adults. Their moral nature could only be sustained by avoiding the corruption of public life (government, the workplace, etc.). Women's participation in public speaking violated this system of gender roles. Thus, their meetings were frequently interrupted by protests, some of them violent. Enemies accused the female preachers of violating their feminine nature and the sanctity of the home they existed to protect. These women often lamented that their call to preaching had demanded the sacrifice of family, friends, and social acceptance. But they did not renounce their calling. Nancy Towle records that "those females who have renounced every earthly enjoyment, for the sake of precious souls, I ever esteem the noble part of God's creation" (Towle).

These early efforts at women preaching did not take root. By mid-century the movement's coalescing structure left little room for female leadership in public worship. As the number and size of the churches expanded, hierarchies emerged, and women preachers found it more difficult to sustain a following. Every major denomination, including the Disciples, issued letters restraining women from preaching. After 1830 evidence of women preaching in the various traditions that shared the Disciples of Christ ideology declines, but the controversy did not disappear forever.

Disciple Motherhood and Education

Women's participation in the Disciples tradition took shape with the appearance by 1815 of Alexander Campbell, its most respected leader. His views of the role of women would hold significant sway until his death in 1866. Campbell's opinion of women's capabilities differed greatly from that of Smith and O'Kelly. Through-

out the 1820s, Campbell and his father, Thomas, as prominent leaders of the Disciples, emphasized the role of women as wives and mothers. Unlike Smith's "Christians" and O'Kelly's "Republican Methodists," the Campbells, recent immigrants from northern Ireland, were largely untouched by the egalitarian effects of the American Revolution. Operating from a less radical mind-set in dealing with social issues, Campbell believed that scripture did not allow women to preach to men. Instead, he suggested through his writings and speeches that women should serve a pivotal function in another area altogether.

Campbell argued that the role of women was to ensure the critical instruction of young Disciples in Christian doctrine as head of the "school of the home." He seemed influenced by the suggestion of Thomas Jefferson and others that motherhood was critical to the political future of the United States. Jefferson had argued that the new republic required virtuous citizens to secure a stable democracy; voters must exercise their rights with moral responsibility in order for the country to survive. Jefferson suggested that women, with their natural virtuous tendencies, would be the logical agents of this inculcation of republican virtues. Campbell adopted this reasoning and lent it spiritual significance. Thus, just as "Republican Mothers" found a new role in the early republic, Disciples women would find a new avenue to participate in the religious movement.

While restricting women from public church leadership, Campbell nonetheless reserved for women a role he deemed critical to the future, the evangelization of the next generation. His wife, Selina Huntington Bakewell Campbell (1802–1897), embodied this charge. While her husband traveled across the country preaching and teaching, he wrote to his wife often, thankful that she was raising their children to follow in his spiritual footsteps. Selina raised their six children in the strength of her faith, laying the foundation for their own Christian beliefs. She also supported this role for women in dozens of letters and articles she wrote for publication in Disciple newspapers. In a religious tradition that emphasized evangelism, this role for women drew them to the very heart of the movement and earned them respect from the men.

The most significant consequence of Disciple motherhood was its emphasis on the need for women's education. Disciples were among the first to found colleges to instruct women in their role as mothers and moral leaders. By 1838, the Disciples operated at least four female seminaries located mostly in Kentucky and Tennessee. Campbell's sister, Jane McKeever (1800–1871), for example, operated the Pleasant Hill Seminary in western Pennsylvania as early as 1840. Her involvement in education began with the opening of a school in her home in 1819. Although still dominated by "feminine" pursuits such as music and needlepoint, the curriculum she developed also included instruction in science and language that formed the core of a liberal arts education. Campbell spoke often to the women at the school and in the pages of his journal supported his sister's institution as well as a number of other schools for women. His own daughters attended McKeever's academy and P. S. Fall's academy in Kentucky. McKeever also participated actively in the Underground Railroad that ferried hundreds of slaves from bondage in the South to freedom in the North. Such activities distinguished her among the early women of the Disciples of Christ tradition.

Scripture and Disciple Women's Participation in Church Life

The availability of education spurred the growing demand of Disciples' women for broader participation in church life. They faced several obstacles. In particular, the emphasis on scripture as the arbiter of all disagreements about church doctrine made the issue of women problematic as each participant in the debate relied on different scriptures to establish their legitimacy. Controversy over women's public participation in church life centered on three main issues: preaching, participating in worship service, and serving as deaconesses. Unlike Nancy Cram and Abigail Roberts, whose public preaching was a manifestation of the egalitarian milieu associated with the American Revolution and described above, post–Civil War advocates of women participation in public worship relied on notions of gender difference to establish the practice.

By the 1850s, debate regarding women speaking publicly had revived. Many Disciples of Christ women and men now called for official recognition of women's right to preach. Among them, Barbara Kellison (1823–1879) of Des Moines, Iowa, argued forcefully for the practice in her 1862 pamphlet "Rights of Women in the Church." Kellison declared her belief that she had been called by God to preach and expressed her frustration with men who while claiming women their equals yet excluded them from participating fully in church affairs. This led her to turn to arguments outside scripture to sustain her position. Specifically, she relied on nineteenth-century societal assumptions regarding the emotional and spiritual nature of women in claiming their right to preach. Just as women's moral nature made them able mothers and wives, she argued, it should also make them the proper exponents of God's message to humankind. Her views echoed through the letters sent by her Disciple sisters to various newspapers that reopened a still unsettled debate.

Postbellum opponents of women preaching lost no time in marshaling ample support in scripture for prohibiting the practice. Newspaper editors like David Lipscomb in Tennessee especially emphasized Paul's statement to Timothy forbidding "a woman to teach or have authority over a man" (1 Timothy 2:12). They also challenged the use of women's moral nature to justify their right to preach. They believed a woman's modesty was violated, not enhanced, when she stepped into a pulpit. Campbell especially leaned on this scriptural position and responded to inquiries on the subject by declaring Paul's judgment final and unarguable. After Campbell's death in 1866, the debate would take on a new stridency. Dozens of letters, articles, and editorials littered the Disciples' major newspapers and sustained the issue throughout the 1880s and 1890s. With the ordination of Clara Babcock (1850–1925) in 1889 and her subsequent twenty-five-year preaching career, the stage was set for the split between the Churches of Christ and the Christian Church (Disciples of Christ) in 1906. Those of the Disciple fellowship who would soon form the Christian Church (Disciples of Christ) largely accepted women as evangelists; those who became the "Churches of Christ" uniformly rejected this innovation. Although the role of women was not the only issue that separated them, the Christian Church's desire to broaden the public participation of females in the church did not sit well with the more conservative Churches of Christ, who clung to the opinions of Campbell and others in limiting such activities. Yet if women were not to be preachers, what would their role in the worship service be? This question proved difficult to answer.

Women in the Worship Service

Scripture seemed to offer two different perspectives on the role of women in the worship service, and this was reflected in the arguments between various leaders of the movement. Some held that women should be allowed to offer prayers and testimonies of their own spiritual experience in their congregations, a practice the apostle Paul seemed to allow in the eleventh chapter of his first letter to the Corinthians. Others pointed to subsequent statements in the fourteenth chapter of the letter that apparently prohibited women from speaking in public assemblies of Christians. The debate raged in Disciples' newspapers throughout the post–Civil War era.

Several Disciple men spoke in favor of women's participation in the worship service, among them the prominent William Pendleton, son-in-law of Alexander Campbell and editor of the *Millennial Harbinger* after Campbell's retirement. He reasoned that women must not be denied the right to voice their prayers and sing songs of worship to God. He suggested that Paul's comment in Corinthians enjoining women to be silent in worship prohibited them from engaging in disorderly behavior during the worship service but left room for women's orderly participation. Few congregations accepted this interpretation.

Another proposal for settling the issue of women's participation in worship relied on differentiating between public and private worship. Public worship referred to corporate meetings in a building used for that purpose. Private meetings took place mostly in homes and were conducted separately from the official church. Pendleton, who opposed women's public preaching, acknowledged the difference between the two and allowed women to speak in a private meeting—particularly if only other women were present. He contended that Paul's New Testament injunctions applied to public worship only. Remove that circumstance and women's activities expanded. They were then free to pray, exhort, read scripture, and participate in a host of other activities as long as they took place in a private setting.

A few Disciple men rejected even Pendleton's comparatively minimal restrictions. Randall Faurot, for example, maintained that Paul's restrictions applied only to women's disruptive behavior in the church assembly occurring in the first-century Christian church and should not be interpreted to forbid the same activities allowed for men (praying, reading scripture, preaching) in the public service. Isaac Errett, editor of the most widely circulated newspaper in the Disciples tradition, the *Christian Standard*, weighed in with support for a wide variety of activities by women from teaching to praying and even occasionally speaking in public. These men, however, made up a small minority within the movement. The larger body of church members felt uncomfortable with women conducting these activities, and the role of deaconess, in particular, brought strong responses from both sides.

Women as Deaconesses

Many suggested scripture allowed women to serve in the role of deaconess, or official "servant," in the church. Part of the Disciples' emphasis on scripture found its expression in their desire to "restore" the practices of ancient Christianity to nineteenth-century North America. While this desire permeated most aspects of Disciples' religious life, it was especially evident in the debate over women's role as deaconesses. Many Disciples found in Paul's letters to first-century Christian churches' acceptance of, and even support for, the appointment of deaconesses in the local church. Deacons were a common sight in many Disciples churches, where they were responsible for meeting the needs of the poor. Many argued that women's natural sensibilities to such needs qualified them for official recognition in such a role.

Campbell had taken up the issue in 1827 in an article he wrote for his early periodical, the *Christian Baptist*. He expressed a conviction that the first-century churches had appointed women to the office of deaconess to perform tasks for the women of the church who were in need, citing instances of these appointments from 1 Timothy and Romans to support his position. While he did not advocate that every church adopt this office for women, his support for the role carried weight.

The most famous of the New Testament deaconesses was Phoebe, whom the apostle Paul introduced to the church at Rome in a most intriguing way: "I commend to you our sister Phoebe, a servant [deaconess] of the church in Cenchrea. I ask you to receive her in the Lord in a way worthy of the saints and to give her any help she may need from you, for she has been a great help to many people, including me" (Romans 16:1–2). Many Disciples leaders made occasional calls for the appointment of deaconesses in the church, and some churches did appoint women to meet the spiritual, emotional, or physical needs of the women of the church. The necessity of women performing these tasks reflected the belief of nineteenth-century Disciples that females operated in a different world from males. Thus, only women could minister to the special needs of other women.

Other Disciples took a different approach to church officialdom. Preachers from the Churches of Christ like David Lipscomb and E. G. Sewell had views of the proper role of deacons that also affected their perception of deaconesses. They took exception with the endowing of any member of the church with a particular office. Both Lipscomb and Sewell felt that those doing the work of deacons were deacons and did not need the label to justify their work. The Churches of Christ left the role of deaconess to women who met the needs of other women in the church without technically appointing them to an office. But soon they would be confronted with a change in societal perception of women in the form of the "new woman" that would threaten to alter their view of women all together. Lipscomb confronted these changes in the 1880s.

Silena Holman and the New Woman

Throughout his career, Alexander Campbell supported the role of all Christian women in active ministry, writing often of his deep respect for the moral, spiritual, and intellectual capabilities of women. His wife frequently referred to his comment that "men are the prose and women the poetry of humanity," and he warned those who would demean the abilities of women that God did not view them so (Campbell, 354). While he felt constrained by the apostle Paul's admonition that women should remain silent in the churches, he underscored women's other contributions to church life such as teaching, child rearing, and personal evangelism. His convictions foretold the emergence of a new kind of woman in American society, and in the Disciples, in the years following his death.

In the late nineteenth century, a fresh voice entered into the debate over women's proper role in American religion. Her medium was the written word, and through it she interacted with the most powerful men of the day within the Disciples tradition. Her name was Silena Holman (1850–1915), and her exchange with David Lipscomb over women's role in the church stirred much interest in the 1880s.

The wife of a lay leader in her congregation, Holman mothered eight children, wrote a number of articles for publication, and was active in her church in Fayetteville, Tennessee. She also served for fifteen years as the president of the Tennessee Women's Christian Temperance Union (WCTU) increasing its membership from less than 200 to more than 4,000. Her life demonstrates a profound dedication to Christian service and moral leadership.

Lipscomb, a prominent Tennessee preacher and editor who attracted thousands of Disciple readers through his editorship of the *Gospel Advocate*, frequently crossed swords with Holman in his newspaper. The interchange between Lipscomb and Holman began with a letter to the *Gospel Advocate* suggesting that Paul's command for women to be silent in the churches also prohibited them from teaching children in Sunday School. Lipscomb responded that women were not enjoined from teaching children or even their husbands as long as they did so in a modest manner and not in any domineering way. Before long, Holman wrote to preacher/editor Lipcomb in Nashville, probing the limits of his conception of women's role. Lipscomb published her letter and his response in the *Gospel Advocate* in 1888.

Holman's comments reflected a new trend among nineteenth-century Disciple women, the emergence of the "new woman." This new woman sought an expanded place in American religion and society, capitalizing on the perception of women as the natural moral leaders of society to demand a larger role in reform. Holman argued that the higher level of education enjoyed by women in the United States fitted them for a larger role than previously allowed.

Lipscomb generally supported the role of the new woman called for by Holman but with reservations. While he championed women's contributions as pious, submissive servants, he argued that their abilities were best demonstrated in a private setting. Never should a woman appear in front of a mixed audience. To do so was to violate her natural submissiveness and moral purity, he believed. There was plenty for them to do within the home to lead their children, their friends, and their husbands to greater piety and spiritual commitment.

Lipscomb went so far as to suggest that women who pursued public roles neglected their duty and thereby contributed to the moral breakdown of American society. Children raised without the proper supervision of their mothers developed bad character as a result.

Holman objected to the restriction of women to private action. She maintained that many educated women had much to contribute to church life. She believed women in particular should not be prevented from speaking publicly simply because they were women. Their participation in public affairs would not result in the neglect of children. Instead, their children would now have a better role model for emulation. Holman was the last of the Church of Christ women to participate in a public dialogue over their role in the church. Their voice would virtually disappear until the women's movement of the 1960s revived the issue.

Women and Missions in the Disciples of Christ

Much of the post–Civil War era women's participation in American religion focused particularly on a new area of concern in church life: missions. Women's voice would contribute fundamentally to missions activities among the Disciples of Christ branches. As Disciples women participated in the debate over their proper role, they found a variety of ways to serve their religious tradition. In the late nineteenth century the most dynamic of these roles lay in the area of missions. While the post–Civil War era saw a rise in sensitivity to the world's spiritual condition, missions had been a concern of most American religious traditions since the eighteenth century. Every major Protestant denomination, as well as Catholic and Jewish fellowships, had sponsored organizations to promote the spread of their beliefs both in the United States and abroad. At first, women contributed little to this effort, but by the end of the nineteenth century, the situation had fundamentally changed.

The first evidence of women's participation in missions within the Disciples of Christ was Selina Campbell's appeal to the women in her husband's journal the *Millennial Harbinger* in 1856. She sought to win support for the first female Disciples missionary, Mary Williams (1780–1858), who operated a school in Syria in the 1850s. Frustrated at the lack of concern among the male leaders of the American Christian Missionary Society, Campbell assumed personal responsibility for raising funds for her friend. Converted in 1835 at the age of fifty-five, Williams was in her seventies when she entered the mission field. She worked with tireless devotion to the children of the Holy Land. She died in December 1858 before returning to the United States. In spite of Williams's dedication and Campbell's fund-raising efforts, interest in missions among the Disciples remained minimal, a circumstance that did not change until the end of the Civil War.

In the post–Civil War era, the Disciples' interest in foreign missions expanded to encompass women around the world, particularly those in Asia and Africa. Supporters of missions, however, found two elements missing in these efforts. First, indigenous women usually could not be reached by male missionaries due to the social mores in these continents. Second, few funds were available to support missions efforts. These two circumstances hampered the missionary work sponsored by Disciples' churches. To solve these problems, Mrs. Caroline Neville Pearre (1831–1910), a resident of Iowa City, Iowa, commenced a letter-writing campaign in 1874 to engender interest in missions among her fellow Disciples. Her efforts met with significant success, and that same year the women of the Central Church in Indianapolis founded a society complementary to that formed in Pearre's hometown. Important as these early events were, the most important advance for women's efforts came when Isaac Errett took up their cause in the pages of the *Christian Standard*, a key journal among the Disciples. Errett called upon every Disciple to take an interest in missions, and he helped women organize a meeting in conjunction with the General Convention of the entire church in 1874.

After the 1874 convention, the Disciples women, following in the steps of their Congregational, Baptist, Methodist, and Presbyterian sisters, answered the increasing calls for women to enter the mission field and reach out to their sisters in other lands. They formed their own missionary society, liberated for the first time from the male-dominated American Christian Missionary Society and dedicated to raising funds for the support of female missionaries around the world. The organization took the name of the Christian Woman's Board of Missions (CWBM) and would enjoy great success in supporting missions efforts for the next fifty years. Its sister organization the Canadian Christian Woman's Board of Missions followed in 1887. The leadership quickly targeted four major areas of interest for the society: the American West, Jamaica, freed slaves in the American South, and Asia (especially India and China). By 1876 the women had raised enough money to send their first missionaries, Mr. and Mrs. W. H. Williams, to Jamaica.

Subsequent missionaries came from a variety of backgrounds, but one of the most intriguing was Sarah Lue Bostick (1868–1948). Her paternal grandfather was a Native American, probably a Choctaw, from Virginia, and her paternal grandmother an African American. Her mother was of black, French, and Native American ancestry. African Americans and other persons of color had participated in the Disciples of Christ tradition from its beginning but had found their activities within the

tradition severely limited. Bostick's efforts aimed to remedy this situation and inspire other ethnic groups. Widowed at the age of thirty-five, she was baptized shortly after her second marriage to the minister Mancil Mathis Bostick. She later would be ordained in the Christian Church and spend forty years as a missionary among the former slaves of Arkansas. Her work extended to providing educational opportunities to young African Americans, whom she encouraged to attend college. By January 1913 she had procured funds to start her own college, and the Jarvis Christian Institute (Arkansas) was born.

Other missionaries soon followed as the CWBM formed chapters in more than a dozen states and held annual conventions attended by thousands of men and women. With the money raised, the women supported hundreds of missionaries and several schools for women in places like the Holy Land and Asia. Women made their presence felt in missions in a way never contemplated. Often their fund-raising efforts outstripped those of the American Christian Missionary Society and established women as the premier financial managers of the churches. Soon women's efforts moved beyond missions into other activities.

Women and Reform

Churchwomen played major roles in late-nineteenth-century social reform, and Disciples women joined these efforts. The nineteenth century in the United States saw the rise of a new attention among women to the consequences of an industrial society. They viewed with concern the rise of poverty in the cities and the increasing numbers of orphans, widows, and the lame, all in need of care. In meeting these needs women found a new avenue of participation in American society, resulting in the formation of numerous associations, each addressing a specific social ill.

Disciple women participated in these reform movements in a myriad of ways. The women of the Churches of Christ, for example, avoided participation in most reform movements because of their opposition to any benevolence organization outside the local church. Instead, they focused their efforts on local needs and service. Nearly every congregation had a Widows Mite Society or Orphan Aid Society to help the needy in the immediate vicinity of the church. There were a few notable exceptions to the proscription against participation in national reform associations, however. Silena Holman, for example, as the president of the Tennessee WCTU, was very active in the movement to curb alcohol consumption and thus mitigate its effects on the most vulnerable in American society. In recognition of her efforts, her portrait was hung in the Tennessee Capitol, a privilege accorded to only a few women.

The women of the Christian Church (Disciples of Christ), on the other hand, embraced the reform movements openly. Numerous Disciples women worked in the WCTU, the suffrage crusade, the movement against child labor, and in most other contemporary reform movements. Of these, Zerelda Wallace (1817–1901) stands out. Stepmother of Lew Wallace, the novelist and Civil War general, Mrs. Wallace founded the Indiana chapter of the WCTU organization and as the wife of the state's governor brought public recognition to the cause. She was also a member of the Central Christian Church in Indianapolis that played a prominent role in the establishment of the Christian Woman's Board of Missions, an effort that received her enthusiastic support. Her participation in another pivotal reform movement of the day, suffrage, also distinguished her, although in this effort she would find much less success. Many Disciples had concluded that the defense of the home, the woman's ultimate duty, would be better sustained if women were given the vote. In 1880, Wallace embraced this movement when she headed the Department of Franchise formed under the national WCTU organization. She represented thousands of women in the Disciples of Christ tradition who moved easily from the temperance movement to the crusade for women's suffrage.

Disciples women also brought their interest in reform inside the doors of the church. In 1886 a group of women met at the First Christian Church in St. Louis, Missouri, to pray and discuss how the church must respond to the condition of the nation's poorest citizens. Sarah Matilda Hart Younkin (1843–1899) led women in establishing an organization that would eventually grow into the National Benevolent Association (NBA) of the Christian Church (Disciples of Christ), staffed, led, and directed by women. The NBA would respond to the needs of thousands of orphaned and neglected children throughout the United States by establishing orphanages and providing temporary housing for single mothers in need (mostly widows) and their children.

Following the 1886 meeting, Younkin traveled from town to town and from church to church, recruiting funds and organizational support. At first the National Benevolent Association received little help from the church hierarchy. The Annual Convention of the Disciples Denomination, for instance, allowed the women no participation in the official program. The NBA women responded by holding their own annual meeting where they continually expanded their strategies for meeting the needs of women in straitened circumstances. Not until 1899 would the church officially acknowledge the association as an important part of the Disciples' ministry. Women had constituted the organization's leadership since its inception, but in 1917 the NBA experienced a shift in its organizational structure.

Concerned that women could not manage such a large organization in the increasingly complex legal and financial environment, James Mohorter, a leader in the Christian Church, arranged the election of several men onto the NBA's board. Women soon lost control over their activities and never again exercised so much power over reform efforts among the Disciples.

Women's Loss of Autonomy

Women distressed by their experience with the National Benevolent Association found it repeated in a number of organizations founded and staffed by women. The second decade of the twentieth century saw most women's organizations subsumed under denominational umbrellas and stripped of their operational independence. Influenced by the rise of big business in the larger culture and the societal prejudices concerning women, churchmen determined to remove women from positions of leadership and place their activities under more direct male oversight.

This ended the dynamism of the women's reform movements of the nineteenth century and inaugurated a new era of businesslike church institutions that excluded nonprofessionals from participation in their management. Women's organizations retreated from the national level but survived as smaller, localized societies. Within the Christian Church (Disciples of Christ) alone, some 4,500 women's organizations including missionary societies, business guilds, and charities were founded during the first half of the twentieth century. These were invariably local and small in scale; the larger ecclesiastical organizations became the exclusive preserve of men.

The Conservative Years

The loss of national leadership plunged women into several decades of conservative reaction. Despite the division of the Disciples movement, in part because of the controversy over women's roles, a wide range of views remained within each branch. The basic differences stemmed from a different view of the legacy of Alexander Campbell's teachings. The Christian Church (Disciples of Christ) emphasized his efforts to unify the church and establish the Christian faith around the world. At times, this desire for ecumenism and evangelism eclipsed Campbell's emphasis on scripture as the ultimate foundation of the church, the underlying principle insisted upon by the Churches of Christ.

These differences in the interpretation of Campbell's teachings presaged differences in the entire Disciple tradition's perceptions of women's roles. Yet not all twentieth-century members agreed on the form women's participation in church life should take. While some in the Christian Church (Disciples of Christ) supported the ordination of women and openly accepted their activities in a wide range of church affairs, others mistrusted such a large role for women and worked to limit their influence in national church leadership. Similarly, while the conservative Churches of Christ feared women's dominance of church life and maintained severe restrictions on women's leadership, some of their number pressed for opportunities for women to contribute to worship and evangelism within the church. The shared challenge for women of both groups was a growing professionalization of religious life in the broader Disciples of Christ tradition that left women sidelined in many activities. Whereas women had once led the effort to address social problems such as the growing number of orphaned children and destitute women, they now found themselves closed out of such opportunities by men with advanced training in psychology and social work. Gone were the days of well-funded women's organizations and national conventions. These were replaced by professional organizations that emphasized education and government cooperation.

One prominent example of the loss of female autonomy involved the most prominent women's organization, the Christian Woman's Board of Missions. The society had survived its merger with the Christian Church hierarchy as the Christian Women's Fellowship after the loss of its independence in 1917. While it continued to raise money for missionaries around the world, its operations remained under the oversight of the United Christian Missionary Society, in which women had some input but no leadership positions. This established the pattern for most of the rest of the twentieth century as women's activities were confined largely to the local arena. The debate over expanding women's roles continued, but the voices were much quieter. An economic depression, two world wars, and economic expansion effectively muted the discussion.

While the churches of Christ remained much the same, the Christian Church experienced some significant change during these conservative years. The consolidation of their evangelistic efforts had contributed to women's greater participation in ecumenical movements and the development of a denominational structure. Such a structure provided a forum for the discussion of women's roles that resulted in significant changes.

By 1949 Christian Church (Disciples of Christ) women's organizations had become so fragmented that they often competed with one another, lacking any means to coordinate their overlapping efforts. Fortunately, Jessie Trout (1895–1990), a Canadian-born former missionary to Japan, soon provided the leadership necessary to transcend these boundaries and restore women's national religious activities. Trout had gained valuable experience as the national secretary of *World Call*, the magazine of the United Christian Missionary Society in the 1940s. In 1949, she organized a meeting of women leaders in the Society to plan a new organization that would merge as many of the local women's organizations as possible. Three years later the Christian Women's Fellowship (CWF) officially took shape, and the majority of women's organizations were eventually subsumed under its umbrella.

Accompanying the organization of the CWF was another landmark decision relating to the role of women. In 1953, the College of the Bible in Louisville, Kentucky, a major source of trained ministers for the Christian Church, announced its willingness to accept women for the Bachelor of Divinity degree that could lead to ordination. This controversial move was decried by many in the Disciples tradition who found little justification in scripture for such a practice. The ordination of women would also be one of the factors that contributed to the defection of the Independent Christian Churches from the Christian Church (Disciples of Christ).

In spite of the Christian Church (Disciples of Christ) women's success in regaining the leadership role, for the women of the Independent Christian Churches and the Churches of Christ, the middle twentieth century brought a more restricted role. The only major contributions of women in these groups came in the area of education. Women emerged as the teachers of children in Sunday School programs and the leaders of "Ladies' Bible Studies." Rarely did any woman find herself in the position of teaching men.

Women in the two breakaway segments of the Disciples tradition infrequently participated in national women's organizations. They mistrusted the power wielded by organizations like the CWF and felt more comfortable operating within their local congregations. In 1930 the *Christian Standard*, now representing the Independent Christian Churches, ran a series of articles on the success enjoyed by the Woman's Union at Long Beach, California, which it held up as an example of effective women's leadership. The articles described a locally focused women's group that consolidated all women's activities within the church into one women's union. From missions to benevolence to the organization of social activities for the entire church, the new entity united many of the formerly separate organizations that had at times found themselves in competition with one another. Possibly influenced by the trend toward consolidation and professionalization in the business world at the time, these women sought to concentrate their resources on the local level but evinced little interest in national efforts.

In the Churches of Christ, many women focused on their duties as mothers and homemakers. One of the most prominent representatives of this perspective was the journalist Winifred Mason Moore Showalter (1885–1956). Showalter began her career as a journalist in 1931 with a regular column, "Home Department," in the *Christian Worker* published in Wichita, Kansas. Her articles contained suggestions for women on caring for their children, maintaining good Christian behavior, and promoting a Christian household. She ended her column in 1947 only to shift her full attention to a larger project, the editorship of the *Christian Woman*. Under Showalter's direction, *Christian Woman* had begun publication in 1933 and shared the same purpose Showalter had demonstrated in her earlier columns. She hoped her journal would "be instrumental in leading some soul to the truth, in helping some mother to be more in love with her home and family, or . . . strengthen[ing] the faith of our young people" (Showalter, 9). Regular columns in the *Christian Woman* bore titles such as "Keeping Christian Women—Christian," "Ironing Day Meditation," and "Woman and Her Mission." The journal contained little or no mention of equality or a women's movement and was limited largely to devotions and household matters.

Apart from those in the Christian Church (Disciples of Christ), the women of the Disciples of Christ tradition disappeared from missions activism, reform movements, and female colleges. Instead, they swelled the ranks of Sunday School teachers, religious educational leaders, and religious curriculum specialists. Ironically, as women's educational levels rose, their level of participation in the Independent Christian Churches and Churches of Christ declined. The dissonance in the situation lay just beneath the surface and would erupt in later conflict over the issue.

The Rise of Feminism

The relative complacency of most women in the entire Disciples tradition came to an abrupt end with the women's movement of the 1960s. With the increasing calls for women's full participation in American public life by organizations such as the National Organization for Women (NOW), many Disciples churches found it difficult to reconcile their perceptions of women's proper role with the growing push for egalitarianism. While some, particularly those in the Christian Church (Disciples of Christ), welcomed the movement with open arms, the Independent Christian Churches, and especially those within the Churches of Christ, feared its impact on the church and the family.

Criticism of the women's movement came in many different forms. Some women in the still conservative Churches of Christ argued that women who worked eight to ten hours a day abandoned their home and family. Furthermore, the separate income women gained created barriers in marriage. Thus, career women, ac-

cording to articles in church publications, were responsible for the growing divorce rate and the resulting destruction of the family. Others feared the impact on the family when mothers would be drafted to fight in a war. The sizable conservative element of the entire Disciples movement thus reacted strongly to the Equal Rights Amendment (ERA) proposed in 1972. Their newspapers were flooded with articles condemning the amendment and warning of its consequences on church life and, most important, the family. They quoted women of the movement who labeled housework degrading and marriage a legally sanctioned method of control of women by men.

Such attitudes were deemed unbiblical by many Church of Christ and Independent Christian Church women who occasionally organized themselves in opposition to the amendment. For example, church publications carried notice of anti-ERA activities at the International Woman's Year (IWY) Conference in Houston, Texas, in November 1977. Some 11,000 to 18,000 women met at a Pro-Life convention elsewhere in Houston and vocalized their opposition to the policies adopted at the IWY Conference. The women of the conservative majority within the larger Disciples tradition expressed their support for this protest and counted hundreds of their number among the participants at the counterconvention.

Most members of the Disciples of Christ tradition breathed a sigh of relief when the ERA failed to receive the requisite number of state ratifications necessary for inclusion in the Constitution. Ironically, the end of the ERA movement did not spell the end of feminism's challenges to American religion in general and to the Disciples in particular.

Postfeminism

Even after the furor over the Equal Rights Amendment abated, women's issues remained at the forefront of church life. Women continued to make gains in American society, demanding equal opportunity in the workplace, the family, and the church. Even the most conservative churches within the Disciples of Christ tradition found it difficult to ignore the issue. Gender egalitarianism had permeated many aspects of American life, forcing the churches to confront it.

Members of the Churches of Christ continued to mistrust the women's movement for several decades. Irene Taylor (1931–) writing for the *Firm Foundation* in 1992 argued that the ERA movement had been a cover for an even more radical agenda to advance the legitimization of homosexuality. She expressed her understanding that many well-meaning Christian women had joined the movement to ratify the amendment, thinking that it would improve the condition of women but argued that the real plan of the amendment had become obvious. While many Americans celebrated the prospect of a new gender-balanced society, Taylor and other Church of Christ women feared the destruction of American society altogether.

In spite of such opposition to the organized women's movement, many churches in the Independent Christian Churches and the Churches of Christ reevaluated the position of women in the worship service and leadership of the church throughout the 1990s. Some commissioned women to perform functions once reserved solely for men, including leading public prayers and presiding over the Lord's Supper celebrated at Sunday morning services. Conferences on the role of women held within the Churches of Christ reinforced this trend. For example, in 1998 the Center for Christian Education, a preacher training school in Irving, Texas, with ties to the Churches of Christ, convened a forum titled "The Role of Women" and drew 400 participants from all over the country. Speakers at the conference included several university professors from church-affiliated schools, such as Abilene Christian University in Texas and other prominent preachers. The lecturers addressed the scriptural injunctions on female behavior and the historical role of women in their religious tradition. Most concluded that interpretations of scripture that favored the exclusion of women from public church life were unnecessarily strict. This left room for women to assume a more active role in the church worship service and church leadership. This conference and others like it have supported the gradual movement of women into new positions of prominence in the Churches of Christ.

Yet such changes do not mean that women have left behind their traditional roles within the Disciples of Christ tradition. The *Christian Chronicle*, one of the most widely circulated Church of Christ publications, observed in a March 1996 article that "in the calm of the storm" surrounding women's role in the church, women continued to participate in ministries to children, youth, and parachurch organizations like hospital and prison chaplaincies and maternal and children's homes. These activities have continued the activist reform orientation of women of the early twentieth century and maintain the fundamental heart of women's role as caretakers of the needy.

Despite the willingness of individual congregations and individuals to explore changes to the role of women, limits on women's activities remain uniform in the majority of Disciples churches. In both the Independent Christian Churches and the Churches of Christ, accepted roles for females include church secretaries, Sunday School teachers of elementary-aged children, and hospitality-related activities such as preparing food for large church gatherings. Yet a growing number of churches are poised to make changes in the role of women on a gradual basis, although most are still opposed to any plans for ordaining women.

Within the Christian Church (Disciples of Christ), the number of women clergy continues to grow. By 1984, 4.2 percent of Christian Church head pastors were women in addition to 32.8 percent of associate ministers. While the number of associate ministers had mushroomed since 1972, the number of women head pastors showed only a slight increase, up from half a percent, indicating some barriers remain. Currently, more than a third of students in Masters of Divinity programs at church schools are women, many of them seeking ordination. While women clergy still lag behind men numerically, they have succeeded in overcoming many of the obstacles that once prevented their broad participation in church affairs. They receive significant aid in their efforts from the Christian Woman's Fellowship, whose leaders have openly recruited more female clergy and offered emotional support to current clergy.

The women of the Christian Church (Disciples of Christ) are also very socially active. In addition to seeking a broader role for women in the church, they have also sought for gender equality in the larger society. For example, in 1988 the CWF launched a two-year campaign against domestic violence based on the example of Presbyterian and United Church of Christ women. In 1991, they shifted their attention to economic justice for women and spent several years seeking equal pay for women in the workplace and other changes. Such efforts figure often into the plans of Christian Church women's organizations and conventions and continue to shape the contribution of women to the church and society.

Two hundred years after its foundation, approaches to the role of women in the Disciples of Christ tradition remain remarkably varied. From the ordained women preachers of the Christian Church (Disciples of Christ) to the doctrinally constrained silence of the thousands of women who fill the pews of the conservative churches, the position of women in this tradition defies simple categorization. Yet few churches have completely escaped change in the midst of this heated debate. They enter a new millennium unwittingly unified by their struggle to reconcile their heritage with the exigencies of a culture immersed in concern about gender equity.

SOURCES: C. Leonard Allen, *Distant Voices: Discovering a Forgotten Past for a Changing Church* (1993). Fred Arthur Bailey, "The Status of Women in the Disciples of Christ, 1865–1900" (Ph.D. diss., University of Tennessee, 1979). Selina Campbell, *Home Life and Reminiscences of Alexander Campbell* (1882). Bertha M. Fuller, *Sarah Lue Bostick, Minister and Missionary* (1949). Bill Grasham, "The Role of Women in the American Restoration Movement" (unpublished manuscript available from the Center for Christian Education, Dallas, TX, 1998). Ida W. Harrison, *History of the Christian Woman's Board of Missions* (1920). Debra Hull, *Christian Church Women: Shapers* of a Movement (1994). Hiram Lester and Marjorie Lester, *In-asmuch . . . the Saga of the NBA* (1987). Loretta M. Long, *The Life of Selina Campbell: A Fellow Soldier in the Cause of Restoration* (2001). Winifred Mason Moore Showalter, "Just Between Ourselves," *Christian Woman* 5 (October 1957): 8–9. Nancy Towle, *Vicissitudes Illustrated in the Experience of Nancy Towle, in Europe and America*, 2nd ed. (1833).

WOMEN AND LUTHERANISM
Mary Todd

LUTHERANS COMPRISE THE third largest denominational family among Protestants in the United States and the fifth largest in Canada but have received disproportionately less attention in both the popular press and American religious history than those rankings might indicate.

Like so many other traditions, the history of the Lutheran experience in North America is largely a story of immigrants and their various adaptations to the American religious landscape. There is neither a simple nor a single Lutheran story but many. The context of those stories depends on the convergence of several factors: the period of history in which the immigrants arrived, their land of origin, their leadership, and the conditions of settlement. Although their names have largely been lost to history, women were players in almost all those stories.

Lutheran history parallels American history in that each has experienced three major waves of immigration. Lutherans came first during the colonial period, then in the antebellum period, and in the greatest number between the Civil War and World War I. Immigration by itself, however, is never enough to define the experience of a people, for their new homeland required them to make adjustments and accommodations. In the process they became Americans as well. And so the larger Lutheran story is one of identity, of understanding oneself and one's religious heritage over against a social context that in the twentieth century in particular reflected an increasing pluralism in religious belief and behavior.

If Lutherans have been paid little attention in the narratives of religious history, women have received similar treatment in Lutheran narratives. Yet, as in other denominations, women have played a significant role in North American Lutheran history. The best known women served as leaders of women's auxiliaries or were wives of clergy. Lutheran women came very late to either congregational or church governance and even later to the pastorate. Because only a generation has passed since Lutheran women could be ordained as clergy, women today continue to serve as "first-women," pioneers in breaking the stained-glass ceiling of the institutional church. But a far larger number of women remain anonymous in Lutheran history, women who, while denied roles of leadership, have been the greater number in worship, in the education of children, in tasks of mercy and caregiving, and in the financial support and ongoing life of the church. Women's lives, marked by the rituals of their church, reflect a steady faithfulness to their baptismal calling, whether their vocations be personal or professional. Their stories provide a consistent, though not always visible, thread in the tapestry of the larger Lutheran story.

Lutheran Roots

Lutherans understand themselves as reformers of the church catholic. Martin Luther (1483–1546), an Augustinian monk, never sought to start a new church when he posted ninety-five theses on the door of the castle church in Wittenberg, Germany, in 1517. His challenge was instead to Vatican practices he believed were inconsistent with biblical teaching. The debate he invited led not only to his own excommunication in 1521 but to the development of the multiple strands of Protestantism that quickly emerged in Europe over the course of the Protestant Reformation.

The primary statement incorporating the principles of Lutheran doctrine is the Augsburg Confession of 1530. Following a series of disputes among Lutheran reformers about interpretations of that confession, a larger collection of documents known collectively as the Book of Concord was published in 1580. These statements of faith, creeds, and catechisms form the confessional basis of Lutheranism.

Luther's preeminent contribution to Protestant thought is the concept of justification by grace through faith alone, apart from works. Lutheran theology can be summed up by a shorthand Lutherans call the *solas—sola fide* (faith alone), *sola gratia* (grace alone), *sola scriptura* (scripture alone). *Sola scriptura* recognizes the Bible as the sole authority for faith, the only source and norm for teaching. Lutheran self-understanding is based on adherence and subscription to scripture and the sixteenth-century confessional writings that explicate it.

The concept of paradox—both/and—is helpful in understanding Lutheran theology. Several key tenets of the faith depend on a creative tension between seemingly contrary notions. Lutherans strive to hold both law and gospel in balance without overdependence on one to the neglect of the other. When Luther spoke of being *simul justus et peccator* (at the same time both saint and sinner), he was describing one of the most challenging tensions for contemporary Lutherans—his conception of the two kingdoms, in which Christians live simultaneously in the realm of sin and the realm of faith. Lutheran understanding of the eucharist as the real pres-

Emmy Carlsson Evald founded the Women's Home and Foreign Missionary Society of the Augustana (Swedish) Lutheran Church in 1892 and served as its president until 1935. During her leadership, the WHFMS built 64 hospitals, schools, and nursing homes, including the New York Lutheran Home for Women, which she headed for many years. *Courtesy of the Evangelical Lutheran Church in America.*

ence—the bread and wine *are* Christ's body and blood—is a further example of paradox that is at the heart of the church's faith.

Luther rejected any notion of holy orders creating a clergy estate, but at the same time he believed firmly that the church needed a set-apart office of ministry, the pastoral office of Word and sacrament. The function of this ordained ministry was to represent believers publicly through preaching and administration of the sacraments of baptism and the eucharist. Yet Luther also recovered the baptismal theology of the church in his emphasis on the priesthood of all believers, by which he meant that every Christian, by virtue of baptism, serves as priest to every other Christian, obviating the need for a mediator between God and humanity. Both aspects of the Lutheran understanding of ministry stress the servant nature of the office.

Luther's contributions regarding education remain an essential component of Lutheranism. His *Small Catechism*, an explanation of the key tenets of the faith in question-and-answer format, serves as the primary tool for teaching doctrine; his favorite catechetical question, "What does this mean?" provides a useful standard for clarification and application of theological matters. Lutherans in America have made an important commitment to parochial or church-related education. Both the Lutheran Church–Missouri Synod (LCMS) and the Evangelical Lutheran Church in America (ELCA) have extensive systems of schools at every level, from preschool through college.

Finally, a signal contribution of Lutheranism has been its appreciation and creation of music. Beginning with the sixteenth-century chorales of composer Johann Sebastian Bach, and Luther's own hymns such as "A Mighty Fortress Is Our God," Lutherans have incorporated music into their worship through liturgy and sacred song sung by congregations and choirs, most often to the accompaniment of a pipe organ. Women's voices and musical gifts have contributed richly to this tradition, one on which they in turn have depended in their private devotional lives.

The Colonial Period

Lutherans began migrating to North America in the early seventeenth century. The middle colonies formed the locus of settlement for European Lutherans in that first century of colonization. A small group of Dutch Lutherans in New Netherland, along the Hudson River Valley, formed the first congregation in North America in 1649, though denied the pastor they repeatedly asked be sent them. Dutch governance of the colony included provision for Dutch Reformed religious practice only. In 1669, after the English had taken control and renamed the colony New York, Dutch Lutherans, though still a minority, established congregations in Albany and Manhattan that today remain active congregations in the Evangelical Lutheran Church in America. In New Sweden, along the Delaware River Valley, Lutheran settlers fared better because the state church of Sweden sent clergy to the colony.

German settlers found William Penn's "holy experiment" a refuge due to Penn's welcome of a variety of religious practice in his Pennsylvania colony. Many more Germans came to the English colonies in the early years of the eighteenth century due to the cumulative ravages of years of war on the continent. Germans known as Palatines, who included both Lutheran and Reformed believers, began arriving in 1708, coming from various regions of Germany. The two faith communities often shared "union churches" that allowed each worship space but at separate meeting times. Most Palatines settled in New York, but some traveled south along the eastern seaboard and established a community at New Bern, North Carolina. Even greater numbers of

Germans arrived in the first half of the eighteenth century, including those who settled in Halifax in 1750, the first Lutherans in Canada. Many of these later arrivals came as Redemptioners or indentured servants, reflecting the practice of contracting several years of labor for passage across the Atlantic that was integral to peopling the North American colonies.

Throughout the colonial period, the greatest challenge for Lutherans in North America was a serious clergy shortage. Entirely dependent on the churches in Europe to send pastors, the laity started congregations and built churches but could not fill the leadership void. Lay leaders labored to hold worship services and provide for the spiritual needs of the people, occasionally introducing innovation when Old World practice hindered their efforts. An important late-eighteenth-century American contribution was the training of catechists who could minister before being ordained.

A second problem was the lack of polity, or church governance. Because the European model of a state church was not transplanted into the varied religious landscape of North America, Lutheran churches were free churches. Colonists needed to create a structure but had no model on which to base it. The voluntary nature of religious practice in the colonies meant there would be neither tax revenue nor required membership, as had been the rule in Europe. Creative alternatives would be the unique contribution of the immigrants as they planted churches in their new homeland.

Language both united and divided colonists and often determined how and where colonial Lutherans worshipped. Swedes favored English, while Germans preferred their native tongue. In the Danish West Indies, where Danish missionaries beginning in the 1660s worked among the Africans imported as slaves, the majority African population called for worship in the Creole language, and the missionaries complied.

Most immigrants left their homelands for economic, not religious, reasons. What has been true of all waves of American immigration has been true of Lutherans as well. An exception in the colonial period was the Salzburgers, 20,000 Lutheran and Reformed believers who were expelled from Austria in 1734 by the local Roman Catholic ruler. Offered refuge in North America through the British Society for the Propagation of Christian Knowledge (SPCK), more than 300 became early settlers of the new colony of Georgia that had been founded in 1732. Salzburgers named their new community on the Savannah River Ebenezer and founded there the first orphanage and school in Georgia.

In 1742 a German pastor arrived in Pennsylvania who is generally recognized as the Father of American Lutheranism. Henry Melchior Muhlenburg (1711–1787) was sent from Halle, the academic center of Pietism, to minister to Lutherans in Philadelphia. Pietism is perhaps best understood as a personal expression of faith that stressed the need for individual regeneration and conversion, a personal "heart religion" affirming individual expression along with mission-mindedness. Muhlenburg, believing the disparate Lutherans in America should be gathered together on occasion, in 1748 established the Ministerium of Pennsylvania, the first permanent governing body for Lutherans in America. The Ministerium was a clergy gathering; not until 1792 was voting representation by laymen introduced. While providing a site for discussion of current issues and concerns, its primary concerns were, one, accommodating the various practices of different immigrant groups and, two, seeking solutions for the worsening clergy shortage that led not a few unqualified individuals to present themselves as clergy to colonists eager for a pastor. Such "pretenders" remained a persistent problem well into the early national period and heightened the need for trained clergy.

Throughout the colonial period, though excluded from theological debate, leadership, and governance in their churches, women remained faithful but anonymous members of growing Lutheran congregations.

The Nineteenth Century

The American Revolution and the successful war for independence from England opened a vast frontier for settlement. The first decades of the new nation were marked by interior migration far more than by the immigration that had established the former colonies. As Americans began to overspread the Transappalachian West, settlers established new congregations, and demand for clergy increased. Additionally, the greater territory brought with it a need for some sort of governing body or synod to provide oversight to congregations in outlying areas.

American religion in the first third of the nineteenth century experienced a shift that markedly altered the religious landscape, an embrace of evangelicalism that was sharply contrasted to structured European systematic theologies. The "democratization of American Christianity" that was born in the Second Great Awakening had mixed impact on Lutherans. Those in pietistic traditions responded more positively, while more orthodox Lutherans expressed dismay at the increasingly populist expressions of faith and their "new measures," such as camp meetings, anxious benches, and lay testimony, particularly that of women.

Two competing factors helped shape American Lutheranism between the Revolution and the Civil War. The transatlantic connection remained strong throughout the nineteenth century, even as Americans continued to develop a national identity of their own. Within that identity, religious adherents struggled to create a self-understanding as well, Lutherans no less than others. But, as in the colonial period, few models were deemed workable in the new nation. American independence and democracy offered a significant challenge to the European understanding of church.

When American Lutherans identified the need for a national governing body in 1820, the resultant General Synod was founded as advisory only, to alleviate concern over potential abuse of authority. Nevertheless, the new synod provided a forum for Lutherans to concentrate on their common interests and goals, including the need to establish seminaries and colleges for the training of pastors, while deemphasizing the differences among the member groups.

Authority remained a central issue as the century wore on. As the nation tested the limits of its own federal system, so its churches were tested by various adaptations introduced by Lutherans in America. To the more orthodox, like the Henkel family in the South, a governing body such as the General Synod appeared far too authoritarian. In founding the more confessional Tennessee Synod the Henkels created a synod based on theology rather than geography. But to its founders, the General Synod offered opportunity for Lutherans in America to create a cooperative venture despite theological distinctions. These two contrasting points of view—synodical and confessional—not only foreshadowed subsequent history but embodied a principal difference among Lutherans in America.

Samuel Simon Schmucker (1799–1873), a professor at the new Gettysburg seminary founded in 1826, and most responsible for organizing the General Synod, embraced several features of the evangelicalism that was transforming American Protestantism in the antebellum period. Schmucker felt the Augsburg Confession needed to be adapted for American Lutherans and that Lutherans needed to adapt to the changes in the social context that surrounded them. He sought a truly American church. His convictions led him to introduce the Definite Synodical Platform in 1855, a revision of the Augsburg Confession that was strongly opposed by more confessional Lutherans, especially those known as "Old Lutherans."

A second wave of German immigration to North America included groups who, like the Salzburgers, left Germany for religious reasons more than economic. Rejecting the rising rationalism of the times, orthodox Old Lutherans saw America as a refuge from the union with the Reformed they feared because of significantly different understandings of church and sacrament between the two groups. Old Lutherans shared an insistence and dependence on the sufficiency of the Lutheran confessions and an intention to transplant the doctrinal purity they felt was being lost in Europe in their new land. That intention often meant the establishment of separatist communities.

Old Lutherans came to America from Prussia and Saxony in the late 1830s, each migration following a charismatic leader who promised freedom from the persecution the believers had known under state consistories. The Saxons settled in Perry County, Missouri, 100 miles south of Saint Louis, the Prussians in Milwaukee and Buffalo. What should have provided them common cause in their new homeland—their shared commitment to the Lutheran confessions—instead led to an animosity that ruptured any potential relationship. Polemic would be the language introduced to America by the Old Lutherans, spoken in the German they believed to be the only proper means of transmitting the faith.

Both groups competed for the support of a clergyman whose influence is significant to American Lutheranism, although he never left Germany. Wilhelm Loehe (1808–1872), a pastor in Bavaria, responded to the lack of clergy in the United States by sending "emergency helpers" to join pastors of the Ohio Synod who were serving Germans in the American Midwest. These "Loehe men" joined with the Missouri Saxons to found the Missouri Synod in 1847. But Loehe's displeasure with the new synod's congregational polity, in which the synod was to be advisory only, aggravated his disagreement with the Missourians over their understanding of ministry, which they considered an office, and Loehe, a status. In the end, Loehe broke with Missouri and joined with the Buffalo group to found the Iowa Synod in 1854.

Conflict over ministry caused bitter dissension between the Old Lutherans. Beyond that, they were critical of the "New" Lutherans, the General Synod and those who not only spoke English but were influenced by American revivalism and other new measures. Patterns set in the early years by the various ethnic synods would influence their future relationships. One example was the refusal of the confessional Lutherans in Milwaukee to accept German clergy from the United Rhine Mission Society because the men served both Lutheran and Reformed believers. Those clergy founded the Wisconsin Evangelical Lutheran Synod (WELS) in 1850. Disagreements between German and Scandinavian congregations in Minnesota led to the formation of the Minnesota (German) Synod and the Augustana (Scandinavian) Synod in 1860. Each synod considered itself confessional, but differences of opinion about how that claim was understood kept them separate.

While remaining distinct from one another, six confessional synods in 1872 agreed to form an advisory Synodical Conference to cooperate in mission initiatives. The loosely confederated conference began the first intentional mission work among African Americans in 1877. The hope of uniting confessional Lutherans was shattered, however, when several of the member synods withdrew from the Synodical Conference following an especially vicious controversy over predestination in the 1880s.

While confessional Lutherans were experiencing both union and schism, other ethnic synods began to entertain discussions of merger. Norwegians led the way, forming the United Norwegian Lutheran Church (UNLC) in 1890 and the Norwegian Lutheran Church in America (NLCA) in 1917. Three synods joined to form the United Lutheran Church in America (ULCA) in 1918, three others formed the American Lutheran Church (ALC) in 1930. The twentieth century saw a dizzying succession of mergers as various immigrant church bodies sought common ground over historic difference.

Lutheran history from the first settlement in North America through the mid-nineteenth century remains a history dominated by individuals, all clergymen. To tell the story of women is also to tell the story of the laity. With rare exceptions, only after the Civil War are the contributions of individual women recorded. Most women's names are found only in church registers of official acts—baptisms, confirmations (the rite of passage to adulthood), marriages, and burials. Until the twentieth century, and even into it in certain rural locations, Lutheran women, like women in countless other churches in America, generally sat on one side of the church with the children, while the men sat on the other. It was not uncommon that women communed after the men and teenage boys, although celebration of the eucharist itself was an infrequent occurrence in the nineteenth century. The prevailing gender construct of separate spheres found its parallel in the churches, where women's work—for German women summed up as *Kinder, Küche, Kirche* (children, kitchen, church)—became an extension of their work at home. Women oversaw the teaching and nurture of children in the Sunday Schools, cleaned the church building, and contributed funds to the support of the pastor and teachers.

Pastors' wives were generally held in high esteem due to the leadership they often provided in the local parish. In the Missouri Synod, clergy wives sometimes filled in as the parochial schoolteacher in a parish, a role frequently also held by their pastor husbands. It has been said in critique of the Protestant Reformation that the only role created for women was the new position of pastor's wife, since Luther and the Reformers advocated closing the cloisters and Luther himself married Katherine von Bora, a former nun. But while marriage to a pastor may have conferred status on the clergy wife, at the same time it carried an increased sense of obligation to the congregation, often the result of demanding expectations on the part of parishioners. Emilie Lohmann

Koenig (1829–1854), who traveled alone at age twenty-four from Germany to Lafayette, Indiana, to marry a pastor, wrote of her life in a frontier parsonage, where "trying to visit all the women of the church, . . . something required of the pastor's wife, . . . keeps me very busy," and of her concern for her young husband, given "much unrest in the congregation, and bickering and quarrels between the members" (Koenig, 25, 33).

Deaconess Ministry

For single women there remained few options, but the nineteenth century offered a new opportunity in the reintroduction of the early church office of deaconess. In the first centuries of Christianity, deaconess (from the Greek *diakonia*) work was a ministry of service to women by unmarried, though not necessarily never-married, women. In 1836, Pastor Theodor Fliedner (1800–1864) and his wife Friederike (1800–1842) began a deaconess community in Kaiserswerth, Germany. The female diaconate appealed to and became an acceptable outlet for the single woman who wished to devote herself to a life of self-sacrifice and service to people in need. Though all deaconesses received nurses' training, their ministry was by no means limited to nursing. In the 1850s a training program was initiated in Neuendettelsau, Bavaria, by the same Pastor Loehe who had provided clergy to the Old Lutherans a decade earlier. Loehe's pietist interest in social concerns led him to establish a range of social welfare and assistance programs and institutions of care.

In America, Lutheran deaconess work began first in the General Synod and then spread to the ethnic synods. The first deaconesses came to the United States in 1849 to work under the direction of Rev. William Passavant (1821–1894), founder of the Pittsburgh Infirmary, the first Protestant hospital in America. In 1850 Sister Catherine Louisa Marthens (1828–1899), a member of Passavant's congregation, became the first woman consecrated as a deaconess in America. Marthens took special interest in work with orphans. Over the next several decades, deaconess work grew steadily as five motherhouses were established, and the Lutheran Deaconess Conference, started in 1894, became the first inter-Lutheran agency of any kind. The mercy work deaconesses provided was especially popular among Norwegian Lutherans in the United States, though each of the ethnic synods eventually had its own deaconess community.

Sister Elizabeth Fedde (1850–1921) traveled to New York City from Norway to provide ministry to seamen at the request of the Norwegian Relief Society. After establishing the Brooklyn Deaconess House in the city in 1885, Fedde was sent by Passavant to Minneapolis, where she founded the Deaconess Home and Hospital in 1888. She in turn appointed Sister Ingeborg Sponland (1860–1951), a deaconess traveling in America from her native Norway, as hospital supervisor in 1891. Sponland not only stayed in America but helped establish seven more hospitals in North Dakota and Minnesota. In 1906 Sponland moved to Chicago to serve as administrator of the Norwegian Lutheran Home and Hospital, a post she held for thirty years. Calling her work a "ministry of mercy," Sponland offered uplift and assistance to immigrants in the neighborhoods surrounding the hospital. Because she recognized the physical expansion of the building as essential to the growth of its services, Sponland fought for both more deaconesses and more space. The new Chicago Lutheran Deaconess Home and Hospital, dedicated in 1910, was funded in large part by the Ladies Auxiliary that Sponland herself had founded only two years earlier. In 1931, her dream of a deaconess home and training school was realized, the result of funds raised by the Women's Missionary Federation, an organization that also offered women opportunities for service and education. Sponland was fond of reporting what a pastor once said to her: "You women *do* the business, while we discuss it" (Sponland, 149).

In 1884 seven deaconesses, brought to America from Germany by prominent layman John D. Lankenau, arrived in Philadelphia, where they established a motherhouse three years later. Deaconesses founded and staffed orphanages, clinics, and charitable institutions. In 1910 the Board of Deaconess Work of the General Synod opened the first school to prepare women for full-time service to the church in connection with the Baltimore motherhouse. Deaconess ministry reached its peak in the first third of the twentieth century and began to decline thereafter, but the contributions of individual women continued. The gravestone of Sister Anna Huseth (1892–1929), who worked with Eskimos on the Seward Peninsula, reflects their dedication: "She hath done what she could" (Lagerquist, *From Our Mothers' Arms*, 122). In 1920, Sister Emma Francis (1875–1945) became the first woman of color to serve as a deaconess, both in St. Croix and in Harlem. In Chicago, Sister Caroline Williams (1870–1961), known as the "angel of the court," served as a social worker in the Juvenile Court from 1919 to 1945. In 1946 Sister Anna Ebert (1901–1997), of the Philadelphia motherhouse, was elected first president of DIAKONIA, the world federation of diaconal communities and associations. E. Louise Williams (b. 1945), executive director of the Lutheran Deaconess Association, was elected president of Diakonia in 2001. The merged deaconess community of the predecessor church bodies of the ELCA, for many years based in Gladwynne, Pennsylvania, relocated to Chicago in 2002.

In 1919 two Missouri Synod pastors, Philip Wambsganss (1857–1933) and Friedrich Herzberger (1859–1930), started the Lutheran Deaconess Association (LDA) as an outreach of the Synodical Conference. Herzberger's mother had been a deaconess for the General Synod before her marriage. The Missouri pastors were determined that their deaconesses would be differentiated from other deaconesses, who in their minds too closely resembled Roman Catholic nuns due to their dark garb and title of "Sister." A motherhouse was founded in Fort Wayne, Indiana, in 1922, where the deaconesses in the new program attended nursing school at the Lutheran Hospital. In 1935 the deaconess program was defined separately from nursing, and admission was limited to women who had already completed training as social workers, teachers, or nurses. In 1943 the program relocated to Valparaiso University, also in Indiana, and by 1946 its curriculum had been expanded to a full four-year degree in theology. The LDA had no restriction against its deaconesses marrying, but until the late 1960s, a woman was involuntarily retired as a deaconess when she became a mother.

In 1980, after Missouri Synod women in the LDA program grew uneasy over the movement of some deaconesses into the pastoral ministry, the synod authorized a separate deaconess training program at its college in River Forest, Illinois (now Concordia University). Women in both programs serve in congregational and institutional ministries, frequently as hospital chaplains.

Women's Associations

Until the late twentieth century, the activity or contribution for which most Lutheran women were recognized outside the home was their participation in women's associations affiliated with their local congregations. Lutheran women trailed their Protestant sisters in starting such groups, largely due to German attitudes about women's work and to clergy resistance. More pastors objected to women's organizing than supported them doing so. Where male opposition was high, especially in the South and Midwest, women's associations were slower both to organize and to gain status. Pastors' wives often took the lead in organizing. The earliest recorded association was of women who accompanied their pastor-husbands to conventions in the Frankean Synod of New York in 1837. Clergy wives invited women from their congregations to join them in sewing circles that did mending for parochial school teachers or made paraments for communion and baptisms. The informal nature of such groups served two purposes in the gendered structure of nineteenth-century society: It assured the men of the church that their wives were participating in an acceptable gathering, and it offered the women opportunity to form networks of friendship outside the home while engaged in work that benefited persons in need.

In the post–Civil War years, women's organizations

began to proliferate in American society. Churchwomen saw value in creating similar groups within their various denominations. Scandinavian Lutheran women began to organize in earnest much earlier than German women did. But whenever women expressed desire for an organization of their own, fear followed—fear of separatism (Lutherans sometimes refer to this as "a church within a church"), fear that the women might take over the church, fear that they would spend their time together idly in gossip. The men's fears were groundless, as the women took their gatherings and their mission seriously. Beginning with devotions and followed by business, the highlight of women's meetings often came afterward when they demonstrated their skills of cooking, baking, and hospitality in providing refreshments for the assembly.

Because women were doing women's work in the church as well as at home, their contributions were little noted. Despite the lack of recognition, women's societies devoted themselves to fund-raising, using their proceeds to purchase items for church and world. Mite societies depended on the voluntary offerings of their members to support mission work at home and abroad. Funds were gathered by individuals, in offering plates and mission boxes, and collectively, through the sale of donated goods or services such as cooking for men's meetings like the Lion's Club or the Rotary. Women's groups purchased hospital equipment, built buildings, and retired building debt. Due to women's efforts, congregations were able to purchase vestments, paraments, linens, communion ware, and other church furnishings. In addition to fund-raising, women's societies often donated clothing, quilts, blankets, and food to agencies and missions. Churches came to rely on their women to cover expenses that would have sorely stretched meager congregational budgets.

As women's societies expanded in number and activity, interest grew in linking congregational groups into a formal structure affiliated with the larger church. In 1879 the General Synod formed the Women's Foreign Missionary Society, the first federation of local missionary societies. One of the first federations of Norwegian women was the Hauge Mission Dove, formed in 1901 by the women of the Hauge Synod. Soon other churchwide groups were organized in the Norwegian synods. The United Church's Women's Missionary Federation was founded in 1911 in St. Paul, Minnesota. Emmy Carlsson Evald (1857–1946) founded the Women's Home and Foreign Missionary Society (WHFMS) of the Augustana (Swedish) Lutheran Church in 1892 and served as its president until 1935. During her leadership, the WHFMS built sixty-four hospitals, schools, and nursing homes, including the New York Lutheran Home for Women, headed by Evald herself. A suffragist, Evald started Lutheran Women's Leagues in several cities and

was called by one pastor the most powerful person in the Augustana Synod.

Each of these groups encouraged its women to practice spiritual discipline by contributing a thankoffering out of gratitude for blessings received. Yet the federations were more than fund-raising operations, for each also had an educational arm designed to heighten awareness of mission needs. The women of the WHFMS of the United Synod, South, began to organize in 1904. As they did so, local societies asked for materials to use in their meetings. This need led the organization's Literature Committee to begin an intentional effort to write, publish, and distribute studies, devotions, and tracts to their membership. The response overwhelmed the southern women, who, in the decade before World War I, found their publications in demand across America and in translation in both home and foreign mission fields.

During the same period, women's organizations such as the Women's Missionary Conference of the Joint Synod of Ohio sent speakers to congregations to alert members to mission opportunities. The General Synod organization encouraged women to take seriously their roles as spiritual nurturers of children and provided literature packets for congregations to develop cradle rolls for preschool children. What these organizations did best was remind Lutheran women of the sacredness of their dailyness.

As the ethnic synods merged in the twentieth century, their women's organizations scrambled to keep up with their parent churches. Along with church changes, women's organizations dealt with sociocultural changes and the problems all voluntary organizations experience in personality and leadership differences. In 1931 the American Lutheran Church Women's Missionary Federation was formed following the merger of the Joint Synod of Ohio, the Iowa Synod, and the Buffalo Synod. The question of leadership arose—should the executive director be paid or be a volunteer? A single woman who had to support herself could serve only if salaried. The answer would help define the organization's attitude toward woman's proper place in church and society. Katherine Lehmann (1876–1960), an unmarried leader of the Ohio Synod women, was appointed to the first paid staff position in the new organization.

Once federated, or granted official auxiliary status to a church body, women's societies contributed substantial funds to mission work. Fund-raising by a concentrated association of women's groups allowed for the construction of hospitals and old folks' homes. In Chicago, the Ladies Dime Savers Program significantly reduced the debt of the Altenheim, later the Lutheran Home and Services Ministry to the Aged. On the West Coast, the California Synod of the General Synod received such generous financial assistance to start mission congregations from the WHFMS that it was referred to as the Woman's Synod. First United Lutheran Church in San Francisco was founded in 1886 as Women's Memorial Lutheran Church, the fruit of mission work commissioned by the WHFMS.

The Missouri Synod had a men's organization and a youth organization before it authorized the formation of a women's auxiliary. Women had organized sewing circles and *Frauenverein* (ladies' aids) from the mid-nineteenth century to meet the needs of seminary students, orphans, old folks, and beginning at the turn of the century, foreign missions. Young women had eagerly joined the synod's youth organization, the Walther League, from its 1893 founding and became voting members in 1900. Clergy resistance and fear that women might usurp authority from men tended to keep the scattered local women's groups separate. But the pastors also recognized the fund-raising abilities of the women and regularly counted on their contributions to supplement congregational offerings.

The Missouri Synod had to overcome a decade of objection before it approved the formation of the Lutheran Women's Missionary League (LWML) as its official auxiliary in 1942. Still the clergy kept the organization within its sphere of influence—the League pledge, song, and first constitution were written by pastors, and the planning committee consisted entirely of clergy. The League adopted the familiar mite box for gathering mission funds, developed materials for Christian growth and leadership training, and began publishing the *Lutheran Woman's Quarterly*.

At the national and regional levels, women's organizations held regular conventions and rallies. But at the local level by the 1920s women sought more specific activities and gatherings. The new concept of "circles" met the needs of women who wished to associate with other women on the basis of shared marital status, age, or family situation. Younger women often preferred a group of their own. The NLCA responded in 1928 by organizing the Lutheran Daughters of the Reformation, young, single career women first organized on college campuses with a focus on Bible study. Also in the 1920s altar guilds became a new area of service for women as Lutherans experienced an increased interest in liturgy.

Women in Mission

Lutheran women did not just support foreign missionaries; in some cases, they became missionaries themselves, like young women in many Protestant denominations who dedicated themselves to work in foreign mission fields at the turn of the twentieth century. Serving as missionaries allowed single women to pursue ministry opportunities that would not have been available to them, had they remained in the United States.

Such women were supported by local women's organizations well before their denominations agreed to do so.

At the turn of the twentieth century, women like Dr. Anna Sarah Kugler (1856–1930) left North America and traveled to India, China, and Africa. Kugler arrived in India in 1883 and served forty-seven years as a medical missionary to Indian women, founding both a hospital and a medical college for women. Kugler remains the only Lutheran woman included in *Notable American Women*. Sisters Maud (1889–1980) and Annie (1891–1978) Powlas served as missionaries to Japan from 1918 to 1960. Other women went to Madagascar as translators, to Alaska to work among Eskimos, to Liberia to work as midwives, to China to work in orphanages. Their steady and steadfast commitment heartened the women at home, who eagerly attended events at which missionaries on furlough spoke.

Mission work was not always half a world away. It could be in one's own neighborhood. In 1917 Laura Mellenbruch (1871–1949), a practical nurse in San Juan, Texas, began mission work to Mexicans when she first gave Sunday School materials to Mexican children who lived near her home and later held Sunday School classes on her porch. Her devotion to the neighbors she served was evident when she wrote to a pastor asking his assistance in providing them a proper Christmas celebration: "You will likely think me an awful botheration. I am coming again about 'my' Mexicans" (Letter to Pastor Neumeister, December 1, 1920, Joint Synod of Ohio Mexican Mission Correspondence, ELCA Archives). Mellenbruch's ministry was the beginning of the Mexican Mission for the Board of American Mission of the Joint Synod of Ohio.

The Twentieth Century

Protestantism in the early decades of the twentieth century was torn by a controversy over, in general, how Christians were to respond to change and, in particular, how they were to understand the Bible. The dramatic changes of the late nineteenth century included the introduction from German graduate schools of a method of biblical study known as the Higher Method, a historical-literary scholarship that considered the Bible as both divine and human text. Theological modernists embraced the new scholarship as modernists in general had embraced science. Those who could not accept the liberalism of the modernists declared themselves fundamentalists, conservative believers who insisted on the inerrancy of scripture as the first of a list of "Fundamentals," primary beliefs about which there could be no argument.

Lutherans distanced themselves from the fundamentalist/modernist controversy primarily due to the fundamentalist belief in premillennialism (chiliasm), a conviction that the end of the world will be preceded by a literal thousand-year reign of Christ. Nevertheless, the influence of this early-twentieth-century controversy would be made clear in Lutheran struggles later in the century. Ultimately, American Lutherans would find themselves again divided on a core element of the faith—the Bible.

But Lutherans in the early decades of the century were working on overcoming division. One word explains much of the Lutheran story in the twentieth century—*merger*. Church fellowship, however, involves far more than a corporate model might suggest, as Lutherans have long held that there must be agreement on doctrine before there can be any union.

The exigencies of war in Europe altered Lutheran relationships twice in the twentieth century. Following World War I, American Lutheran synods, with the exception of the Missouri Synod, formed the National Lutheran Council as a cooperative agency to assist in postwar relief efforts. The war had impacted the Missouri Synod most directly. In 1917 the synod dropped the word *German* from its name and abandoned its use of the German language in worship and schools as German Americans suffered suspicion and persecution.

As World War I had led to the National Lutheran Council and subsequently to renewed discussions on fellowship, so the postwar period following World War II raised new interest in cooperation and fellowship. The 1950s were unparalleled in terms of church growth and church construction, especially in the new suburbs. As the number of congregations grew, so did the need for various agencies and boards within the synods. Lutherans again realigned with the formation of the American Lutheran Church in 1960 and the Lutheran Church in America (LCA) in 1962. The Missouri Synod alone retained its historic separation, given its belief that complete doctrinal agreement was necessary prior to any union or fellowship. Yet the spirit of openness introduced in the 1960s by the Second Vatican Council was reflected in a significant Lutheran cooperative venture—the formation in 1965 of the Lutheran Council in the United States (LCUSA), a pan-Lutheran partnership between the ALC, the LCA, the Missouri Synod, and the much smaller Wisconsin Synod.

The spirit of openness was not to last, as within a decade the Missouri Synod experienced an internal struggle that eventually led to schism. The controversy over the Bible as previously defined by the fundamentalist/modernist episode erupted at the synod's St. Louis seminary in the early 1970s and culminated in a 1974 walkout of 85 percent of the students and 90 percent of the faculty to form a seminary-in-exile called Seminex. The next phase of the crisis had to do with whether graduates of Seminex could be ordained and called to serve in the synod. In 1976, 150 congregations left the synod to form the Association of Evangelical Lutheran Churches (AELC), whose early goal was unity with other Lutherans. The AELC would persist in its dream. In 1982 a task force of seventy representatives from the three church bodies met as the Commission for a New Lutheran Church (CNLC), committed to representation from all constituencies in the church, including women and racial and ethnic minorities. The Evangelical Lutheran Church in America came into being in 1988.

Women in Ministries of Leadership

If the nineteenth century found Lutheran women organizing and meeting among themselves, the twentieth century saw them enter more fully into the life of the church, first at the congregational and later at the institutional level. The change in women's participation in churches paralleled the change in American society, most clearly evident in the campaign for women's right to vote.

In the 1910s, during the struggle for women's suffrage in the United States, a strong antisuffrage lobby developed that argued women did not need the right to vote, as they already had the greater power of influence. In some Lutheran churches, the grant of suffrage was seen as threatening the separate spheres of women and men; men of the German synods worried about the "feministic tendencies" they associated with suffragists. The General Synod and Augustana Synods had granted voting rights to women near the turn of the century. Danish and Finnish synods followed. A pastor's wife was elected voting representative to a church convention in 1911 in the Danish Evangelical Lutheran Church, also known as the Happy Danes. By the late 1950s most Lutheran women in North America had gained the right to vote in their congregations. As in other developments regarding women, the Missouri Synod was the last, only approving woman suffrage in 1969.

Over the course of the twentieth century, women's leadership in the various synods tended to be sporadic rather than consistent. Individual women served the church in positions of responsibility for extended tenures without necessarily increasing the visibility or numbers of women in staff positions. Mary Markley (1881–1954) was appointed in 1919 as the first woman staff member in the United Lutheran Church in America. In her position with the synod's Board of Education—the first of its kind in any American church—Markley administered the church's work with college students through the Lutheran Student Association of America. In 1927 she was tapped to be president when planning was begun for a Lutheran College for Women to be built in Wheaton, Maryland. The dream of such a college was never realized, however. Mildred Winston (1900–1980) served the LCA as director of the placement service for its Board of College Education and Church Vocation. Winston, widely known as an advocate for women, wrote *Women, a Resource in the Church* in 1947. In 1948 Cordelia Cox (1902–1997) became the first woman to head a major Lutheran agency when she was appointed director of the Lutheran Immigration Service. During her nine-year term, more than 57,000 refugees from the Baltic states and eastern Europe came to the United States. Another pioneer in postwar refugee work was Henriette Lund (1887–1984). Before joining the National Lutheran Council in 1943 to develop and monitor standards of Lutheran social service agencies, Lund had actively opposed the "orphan train" initiative in which East Coast child welfare advocates sent urban children to families in her native Midwest. Lund was awarded the United Nations Peace Medallion in 1975.

Florence Montz (b. 1924), president of the Lutheran Women's Missionary League from 1971 to 1975, was elected to the Missouri Synod's Board of Directors in 1983, despite the objections of men in her own North Dakota district who denied women the right to vote in their congregations. Montz was reelected, serving the maximum twelve years. Subsequently three more women have been elected to this board that oversees the synod's financial well-being.

A founding principle of the ELCA was equity. Forty percent of the membership of the Commission for a New Lutheran Church were women. When the new church elected its officers, it chose as vice president Christine Grumm (b. 1950) from the AELC. Dorothy Marple (b. 1926), former assistant to the LCA bishop and active in the women's division of the Lutheran World Federation, served as coordinator for the transition team for the new Lutheran church.

Women in Education Ministries

Women started teaching in the ethnic synods almost from their founding, though not officially. The Missouri Synod had a practice of starting a school and congregation together. The pastor was often also the teacher, and the pastor's wife was often the substitute teacher. The first woman to teach in the Missouri Synod was Elizabeth Damm (d. 1865), a widow who started a school in her New York City basement in 1852. As the century wore on, increasing numbers of women were teaching, though without training.

Parochial school teachers in the Missouri Synod needed to be trained in synodical colleges. Five women enrolled at Concordia College in Seward, Nebraska, in 1919. The synod reluctantly agreed in 1929 that women could be trained as teachers and, in 1938, began admitting women to Concordia College, River Forest, Illinois. Within a generation, women teachers outnumbered male teachers and continue to do so. The synod is second only to the Roman Catholic Church in the number of parochial schools in its system.

One woman stands out for her contribution to education in the African American community. Rosa Young (1890–1971) was a young Methodist woman who started a private school in a Methodist church in rural Rosebud, Alabama. When financial constraints threatened the survival of Young's school, Booker T. Washington suggested she appeal to the Synodical Conference. In response Young received not only funds but a pastor to begin a mission congregation. Young joined the new mission church and eventually started several additional schools, including the Alabama Lutheran Academy in Selma, now Concordia College.

Higher education in the first half of the nineteenth century was gender segregated. Prior to the Civil War, Lutherans had founded a number of female seminaries in both northern and southern states. The number of such schools grew following Roanoke College president David W. Bittle's 1851 "Plea for Female Education." Most of these were private institutions not under any synodical control. Because higher education was primarily directed at training an educated clergy, colleges enrolled only males until Thiel College in Greenville, Pennsylvania, founded by William Passavant, admitted three young women in 1866, becoming the first Lutheran coeducational institution. Very gradually other older Lutheran colleges began admitting women, while those institutions founded in the late nineteenth century opened as coed facilities. Most women who attended Lutheran colleges did so in order to prepare for church work as teachers or musicians. Carthage College was the first institution to grant a bachelor's degree to a woman, in 1874. At St. Olaf College, Agnes Larson (1892–1967) chaired the history department and had two sisters as faculty colleagues. Today there are twenty-eight colleges and universities affiliated with the ELCA and ten institutions in the Missouri Synod's Concordia University System.

The first woman to serve on a Lutheran seminary faculty was Jennie Bloom Summers (1869–1937), who taught Latin, German, English, and psychology to students at the Divinity School of the West in Portland, Oregon, later Pacific Theological Seminary, when it opened in 1910. The daughter of a pastor, Summers had studied at Harvard, the University of Chicago, and the University of Berlin before being hired to replace an ailing professor for one year. It would be much later in the century before women assumed leadership positions in theological education. The first woman to serve in primary academic leadership roles at Lutheran seminaries was Faith Rohrbaugh Burgess (b. 1935), dean at Lutheran Theological Seminary in Philadelphia from 1978 to 1991. In 1996, Rohrbaugh became president of the Lutheran Theological Seminary in Saskatoon, a school of the Evangelical Lutheran Church in Canada.

Women in Ordained Ministry

Women began attending the seminaries of the LCA and the ALC in the mid-1960s. As they neared graduation, the American Lutheran Church asked LCUSA in 1967 to study the question of the ordination of women. The ALC, believing it was important not to make a decision apart from the other Lutherans, hoped for agreement on the ordination of women by all the major church bodies. Lutheran women had been ordained in Europe since the end of World War II. Mainline Protestant denominations in the United States began to open public ministry to women beginning in the mid-1950s.

Following an eighteen-month-long study into the four primary categories of argument generally raised about the ordination of women—biblical, theological, practical, and ecumenical—the theologians agreed to disagree. They found neither a mandate in scripture requiring the ordination of women nor a conclusive prohibition on doing so. They believed, further, that Lutheran churches could differ in their practice without it threatening their fellowship. And so they reported their findings to their various church bodies in late 1969. Over the same period seminary faculties and the women's organizations of both the ALC and LCA had studied the same question and reached the same conclusion.

The following year, at their respective conventions, the Lutheran Church in America first, and then the American Lutheran Church, voted to ordain women to the ministry of Word and sacrament. Elizabeth (Beth) Platz (b. 1940), an LCA chaplain at the University of Maryland, became the first Lutheran woman to be ordained in North America. Platz still serves as campus pastor at Maryland. Only a month later, Barbara Andrews (1935–1978) was ordained by the American Lutheran Church. Earlean Miller (b. 1935) was the first African American Lutheran woman to be ordained in 1979. A woman enrolled at Concordia Seminary, St. Louis, was among the students who walked out in 1974. Two years later Janith Otte (b. 1947) was certified by the Seminex faculty for ordination and was ordained on Reformation Day 1977, the first female pastor in the Association of Evangelical Lutheran Churches. Otte served as chaplain at University Lutheran Church, Berkeley, California, and at a residential counseling program for young women in Oakland.

The Missouri Synod continues to base its opposition to women in ordained ministry on its understanding of two New Testament scriptures—1 Corinthians 14:34–35 and 1 Timothy 2:11–12. The synod depends heavily on the notion of "order of creation" to defend male headship and female subordination and thereby preclude women from the pastoral office. Every synodical convention since 1969 has been asked to clarify the inconsistency in interpretation concerning women's service in the church, as each congregation may determine its own practice with regard to women serving as lectors, communion assistants, and congregational officers. The synod appointed task forces on women in the 1970s and a President's Commission on Women (PCW) in 1983 to examine the status of women in the church. The PCW issued a report in 1986 expressing its concern that "the inconsistencies and uncertainties of what women can do is resulting in a church that is on a collision course with itself" (God's Woman for All Generations, 3–4).

The issues are very different for a church body that ordains women. In 1992 April Ulring Larson (b. 1950) became the first woman to be elected bishop by her synod, the Lacrosse (Wisconsin) Area Synod of ELCA. Only the second female Lutheran bishop in the world, Larson was one of three final candidates for presiding bishop of the ELCA in 1995, and one of seven candidates in 2001. Margarita Martinez (b. 1947), a woman of color, was elected bishop of the Caribbean Synod in 2001. The 2002 roster included seven women among sixty-four bishops in the ELCA and 2,573 clergywomen. That same year the Evangelical Lutheran Church in Canada (ELCIC) elected Cynthia Halmarson (b. 1954) as bishop of the Saskatchewan Synod.

Women's work in Lutheran churches until the last third of the twentieth century remained separate and distinct from men's. Once the ordained ministry was open to women, another realignment took place. If women could do everything in the church, what need was there any longer for a separate women's organization? Others argued that the need continued but required redefinition. Still others suggested that the changes in women's lives in society in general offered the churches and their women's organizations new opportunities, not only programmatic but in service.

Feminism

The inclusion of women in the life of the church has been the result of women's desire to serve God and neighbor. At the same time, the feminist movement in the last third of the twentieth century led some Lutheran women to ask questions of their church's position on women in church and society.

The Lutheran Women's Caucus (LWC) was organized by women in the Missouri Synod in the late 1960s and became a pan-Lutheran organization in the mid-1970s, as women sought to raise the consciousnesses of their church bodies to issues brought forward by women in the second wave of feminism. The Caucus published a newsletter called *Adam's Rib*, later *Well Woman*. At the 1971 convention of the Missouri Synod, Caucus members staged a daily street theater to demonstrate visibly women's limited roles in the church, inequity in parochial teacher salaries, and the representation of women in synodical publications. Their energies earned them the label of radicals who supported the ordination of women. But their persistence also earned individual members of the Caucus invitations from the synodical commissions to participate in dialogue and in the synod's first Task Force on Women. The Caucus ceased publication of its newsletter in the mid-1990s.

Since 1989, a tiny minority of women in the Missouri Synod has argued that the position of the church with respect to the service of women needs to be reexamined. Different Voices/Shared Vision held its first conference in St. Paul in 1989 and began publishing a newsletter the following year. Their stated intention was to study the biblical basis of understanding "who we are as God's children, male and female." The primary force behind this effort was Marie Meyer (b. 1938), a member of the first President's Commission on Women. Over the next decade, Meyer challenged the synod's reliance on the order of creation defense of a male pastorate and helped plan regional conferences on the woman question. Interested in engaging the synod in dialogue on its limitations on the service of women, the feminist activists reorganized in 1998 as Voices/Vision and continue to advocate for change in the Missouri Synod position through a Web site.

The decisions of the ELCA predecessor church bodies to ordain women in the 1970s left feminists in the new church body without the primary cause for which their Missouri Synod sisters were fighting. Margaret Barth Wold (b. 1919), director of American Lutheran Church Women in the 1970s, wrote a muted argument for feminism in her 1976 book *The Shalom Woman*. As the ELCA was taking shape, the women's organizations of both the ALC and the LCA had unanimously agreed that there be a women's organization in the new church structure. They were not agreed, however, as to the nature and status of such an organization. Some favored the more traditional auxiliary, whereas others desired a more issue-centered commission, a unit of the church whose task would be to address sexism and justice in church and society. Following a contentious and unresolved consultation, the new church made a deliberate decision to have both a women's organization, Women of the ELCA (WELCA) (a partner in ministry, not an auxiliary), and an advocacy arm, the Commission for Women. The Commission carries out its mandate through two focuses: to promote justice and full participation and to assist the church on issues of safety and justice as they impact the church. WELCA publishes *Lu-*

theran Woman Today, study materials, and other print resources.

Since 1988, nearly 95 percent of American Lutherans have affiliated with either the ELCA or the Missouri Synod. Canada parallels the United States, having two primary Lutheran church bodies, the Lutheran Church–Canada, formed in 1988 of former Missouri Synod congregations, and the Evangelical Lutheran Church in Canada, formed in 1986 in a merger of two Canadian synods. Aside from the obvious numerical difference—ELCA (5.2 million) has twice the membership of Missouri (2.6 million)—the historical difference is striking: The Missouri Synod has retained its autonomy since its founding, while the ELCA is a newcomer to the American religious landscape, an amalgam of many ethnic synods and previous mergers.

Observers both within and outside Lutheranism have attempted to reduce the differences among Lutherans to dichotomous either/or distinctions. Some have located the demarcation between orthodox and pietist traditions, others between depth of subscription to scripture and the confessions. At the beginning of the twenty-first century, Lutheranism in America remains far more complex doctrinally than such facile distinctions would indicate. Sharp divisions in each of the two major church bodies along conservative/moderate lines presuppose only continued struggle over identity, not eventual realignment. Amid this dynamic, one distinction is clear: One of the things that separates Lutherans in America is their difference of belief and practice on the service of women in the church. In a denomination whose theology depends on paradox, women today find paradox at the heart of their service to the church.

SOURCES: The archives of the ELCA are located in Chicago, the archives of the LCMS at the Concordia Historical Institute in St. Louis, and the archives of WELS on the campus of Wisconsin Lutheran Seminary in Mequon, Wisconsin. A bibliography of women and women's issues in North American Lutheranism was compiled by Betty DeBerg (1992). There is no general or comprehensive narrative of Lutheran women's history in North America. On Norwegian American women in the American Lutheran Church and its predecessor church bodies, see L. DeAne Lagerquist, *From Our Mothers' Arms: A History of Women in the American Lutheran Church* (1987) and *In America the Men Milk the Cows* (1991). Women's service in the LCMS is most fully recounted in Mary Todd, *Authority Vested: A Story of Identity and Change in the Lutheran Church–Missouri Synod* (2000). A useful community study is Carol Coburn, *Life at Four Corners: Religion, Gender, and Education in a German-Lutheran Community, 1868–1945* (1992). Articles by James Albers (1980) and Susan Wilds McArver (1994) in Lutheran Historical Conference *Essays and Reports* address the work of women's organizations, as does Ruth Fritz Meyer, *Women on a Mission* (1967) and Marlys Taege, *WINGS: Women in God's Service* (1991). On the variety of women's service, see Marilyn Preus, ed., *Serving the Word: Lutheran Women Con-*

sider *Their Calling* (1988); Emilie Lohmann Koenig's *As Thou Leadest Me* (n.d.). A most thorough account of deaconess ministry is Frederick S. Weiser, *Love's Response: A Story of Lutheran Deaconesses in America* (1962). See also Ingeborg Sponland, *My Reasonable Service* (1938). On women in ordained ministry, see Gloria Bengston, ed., *Lutheran Women in Ordained Ministry, 1970–1995: Reflections and Perspectives* (1995). The most complete narrative of American Lutheran history is L. DeAne Lagerquist, *The Lutherans* (1999), available in both student and library editions.

METHODIST WOMEN

Jean Miller Schmidt and Sara J. Myers

THE ROLE OF American Methodist women in the church originally derived from that played by British Methodist women, who became involved during the movement's initial stages in the eighteenth century. John Wesley, the founder of Methodism, had watched his mother, Susanna Wesley, minister to her own family and to the members of her husband's congregation when his father, the Reverend Samuel Wesley, was absent. As a result of his mother's influence, John Wesley allowed women to assist in the founding and expansion of Methodism, and his attitude helped shape the thinking of his male associates.

Lay leaders, both male and female, provided critical leadership in early Methodism as band leaders and class leaders. Wesley created bands and classes within the Methodist societies, or congregations, and designated the leaders of both groups himself. Bands were groups of two to four members, either all men or all women and all married or all unmarried, who met regularly to examine each other's spiritual lives. The classes, composed of about a dozen people, provided pastoral care for the members of the group and held each other accountable for their actions.

Band leadership offered many women opportunities to serve, due to the fact that the majority of Methodists were women and the bands were segregated by sex. On the other hand, since the classes contained men and women, men were more often appointed leaders. If, however, a totally female class was formed, a woman usually became the leader.

Wesley also introduced the role of sick visitor in the 1740s, which both men and women could fill. As sick visitors, Methodists had responsibility for attending to the spiritual and physical needs of the ill.

Women received encouragement from Wesley to speak in public about their faith through praying, testifying, and exhorting. Although most women found it difficult to pray in public, they participated more readily given the familiarity of the most common settings in which they prayed—their homes or female prayer meetings. Women and men testified in public about their faith and the gospel during Methodist love feasts, which included sharing simple meals as well as describing their spiritual journeys. Women also spoke publicly when they exhorted their fellow Christians to repent and believe in God. Exhortations took place in both classes and bands and often after an itinerant minister preached a sermon. Occasionally, exhorters, women and men, even took the place of ministers, when the latter were unable to perform services.

Eventually, Wesley supported women as preachers, which expanded their leadership options within the Methodist movement. He officially recognized several women as ministers before he died in 1791. However, after his death, women preachers faced the challenge of male church leaders who wished to consolidate the institutional gains of the church and opposed female preachers as too unorthodox. Even though women dominated the membership rolls by two-thirds to one-third, they had lost an important advocate for their role as leaders with Wesley's death.

Colonial and Early American Methodist Women

During the mid-eighteenth century in the American colonies, Methodist laypeople began arriving and establishing Methodist societies, even without official sanction from John Wesley. Robert and Elizabeth Piper Strawbridge organized the first Methodist society in the colony of Maryland in the 1760s. The meeting took place in their home since no other location was available, a typical situation during that time.

Barbara Heck, who lived in New York City, helped initiate the first society there in 1766. Heck, later called the mother of American Methodism, gathered a small congregation and asked Philip Embury, her cousin, to preach. Earlier, in 1751, she had joined the Methodist movement in Ireland at the age of eighteen, then later immigrated to North America, taking her religious convictions with her. By 1767, the membership of the society was of sufficient size to warrant renting a loft on William Street in which to hold services. The next year, Heck encouraged the society to lease a site on John Street, which they later purchased. In that location, they built Wesley Chapel, a "preaching house," which they dedicated on October 30, 1768. In 1769, Wesley appointed missionaries to the colonies for the first time. When they landed, they discovered that Methodism had already taken root.

About 1770, American women began to be appointed as class leaders, and probably, Mary Evans Thorn was the first. Although originally from Pennsylvania, she had moved with her family to North Carolina and joined the Baptist church. Her husband died in the late 1760s, after which she moved to Philadelphia. There she met several

Methodists who encouraged her to participate in their society. Joseph Pilmore, one of the missionaries sent by John Wesley to America, recognized her leadership abilities and appointed her a class leader. As a class leader, she was responsible for pastoral oversight of a group of approximately a dozen women who met weekly.

In the early Republic from the 1780s through the 1790s, Sarah Day, Elizabeth Burnet, and Catharine Warner all held positions as class leaders in New York. Baltimore also had three women serving as class leaders in 1792, appointed by Francis Asbury, the first bishop of American Methodism. However, by the beginning of the nineteenth century, all class leaders were men, reflecting, in part, the increasing institutionalization of the Methodist Church. Furthermore, male church leaders discouraged public speaking by women in church settings.

As Methodism expanded in the American colonies, biographical and spiritual records of the experiences of church members became increasingly popular. Church leaders supported Methodists who wished to share their religious journeys with others. Sometimes this occurred in church settings or meetings in the homes of church members, but stories were also written and published, both to celebrate the spiritual lives of individuals and to influence the conduct of others and to encourage them to lead godly lives. The conversion experience formed a particularly important component of such records. Methodists had the opportunity to share their stories in class and band meetings and during love feasts and to learn from the experiences of their fellow Christians.

The *Arminian Magazine* and *The Methodist Magazine*, early Methodist periodicals, included biographical descriptions of women and men who had lived holy lives and died feeling assured of salvation, according to their biographers. Although both men and women were subjects of these biographical documents, stories of women predominated, often poor and illiterate women. Methodist preachers as well as family members contributed accounts of church members whom they felt exemplified the Christian virtues and who could serve as models of proper behavior for the living.

In *The Methodist Magazine*, which was published in New York, the issues for the decade following 1818 contained obituaries or memoirs about eighty-four American Methodist women. The accounts had a formulaic regularity, including a woman's early experiences in the church or as an unsaved person, her recognition that she needed salvation, which often happened in her teens,

then a gradual strengthening of her faith, culminating in her assurance of salvation. Many women died young in childbirth or from disease, although some of the accounts were of elderly women.

Typically, the account of the woman's life would include her effort to return to good health, then her reconciliation to the inevitability of her death. She made whatever arrangements she could for those who would be left without her and urged her family, friends, and acquaintances to repent before it was too late. Her death became a testimony to a faithful life in the church, and her faith made her unafraid to die. The description of the last hours of Hannah Johnson's life was typical.

> She bore her affliction with patient submission, without a single complaint, and almost without a groan. From first to last she possessed her reason, and about fifteen hours before her death she was informed that the doctor thought her dangerous, but she seemed not at all frightened, and said she was willing to go if it was the Lord's will; manifesting at the same time that her only anxiety was to be more satisfied with the divine presence. (*The Methodist Magazine* [1825] 207)

Although early Methodist women depended on the entire Bible for inspiration, one passage in particular

The election of the first woman bishop, Marjorie Matthews, took place after the creation of The United Methodist Church. Matthews was elected in 1980 by the Central Jurisdictional Conference. *Reproduced with permission from the Methodist Collections of Drew University.*

served as a guiding principle, 2 Corinthians 12:9, "My grace is sufficient for you." The verse helped them to understand the Methodist doctrine of Christian perfection, holiness, or sanctification, and it also offered comfort to them in their daily struggles. Methodists defined Christian perfection, holiness, or sanctification as a state of grace achieved following conversion, almost a second conversion, but in no sense something that one attained automatically. Even though conversion might lead to joy at the assurance of forgiveness and a closer relationship with God, Christian perfection, holiness, or sanctification required a complete surrender to God's will. Methodist women prayed that they would demonstrate "grace sufficient" to gain the second level of conversion and agonized that they would disappoint God if they did not. Women who had not yet achieved Christian perfection wrote in their diaries that they felt unworthy. However, they never gave up hope of gaining that state of grace and continued to work toward it throughout their lives.

Methodist social gatherings such as the weekly classes, band meetings, and love feasts encouraged intense spiritual sharing. In spite of an outside world dominated by divisions based on class, race, and gender, early Methodism encouraged spiritual egalitarianism. Among women, one manifestation of this egalitarianism was the leadership role of influential females to whom others referred as "Mothers in Israel." The origin of the phrase came from biblical descriptions of Deborah in Judges 5:7. In Methodist circles, it referred to women whom the community recognized as spiritual leaders. Often, these women offered their homes as places where preaching could take place and where itinerant ministers could find food and lodging. In addition, many Mothers in Israel led class and band meetings and functioned as worship leaders in the absence of an ordained minister. In other words, they began to exercise leadership roles that transcended the traditional roles for women found in other denominations.

Methodist women welcomed the supportive community of other women, although many activities within the church, such as band meetings, were segregated by sex. Furthermore, women were denied official church responsibilities such as voting for and serving as trustees. Nonetheless, in a world where women's rights were restricted, the Methodist societies offered spiritual comfort and opportunities for women to develop self-esteem and to exercise power.

Some women joined the Methodist societies even though their husbands did not, or they became members long before their spouses. Once they joined, many of these women began evangelizing their families, friends, and neighbors in an effort to promote the Methodist societies.

An important role played by early Methodist women was providing hospitality to itinerant ministers. In the beginning, most Methodist preachers were young and unmarried, without homes of their own. Their preaching circuits took them over vast territories, which either lacked hostelries or had accommodations that cost more than their meager salaries could cover. Methodist women took these ministers into their homes for as long as they wanted to stay. Inevitably, some of the preachers viewed the women as spiritual mothers, seeking their advice and confiding their problems. In many memoirs written by ministers, the authors reflected their gratitude for the kindness these Methodist women had shown them.

Early to Mid-Nineteenth Century

In the decades preceding the Civil War, the Methodist Episcopal Church expanded into the pioneer West at the same time that it was consolidating its position as a major Protestant denomination in the North and the South. The church gained respectability and a voice in the public arena, but at a cost to women.

Increasingly, Methodist women found their sphere of influence retracting. As part of a much larger phenomenon in the United States, women came to be seen as the protectors of the domestic world, moral values, and family religious life. Their role in raising their children began to preoccupy their time. The *Ladies' Repository*, the first magazine published exclusively for Methodist women, helped promote the emerging female sphere with articles that described the model Christian home.

In the southern states, the ideal of female behavior also prevailed, but within a much more patriarchal society in which slavery was omnipresent. Women's responsibility for the religious life of the family extended to the slave population as well. Although the role of women in southern society expanded during and after the Civil War, the ideal of the charming, innocent, pious, and long-suffering southern lady continued to inform perceptions of women.

Still, many Methodist women accepted leadership positions as band or class leaders or as exhorters. Other women felt called to preach, in spite of societal expectations that they should limit their public role in the church. They began to itinerate, though as unordained preachers. In the first two decades of the nineteenth century, Jarena Lee and Fanny Butterfield Newell commenced preaching careers.

Jarena Lee (b. 1783), who was a free black in New Jersey, joined the African Methodist Episcopal Church, which was established in 1816. Although her pastor initially discouraged her from preaching, he eventually realized that she had a gift for public speaking and could be a significant force in gaining conversions. Her preaching career, which began in Philadelphia, eventually took her to upper New York State, New Jersey,

Maryland, Ohio, and several southern states. In her autobiography, she wrote,

> In my wanderings up and down among men, preaching according to my ability, I have frequently found families who told me that they had not for several years been to a meeting, and yet, while listening to hear what God would say by his poor coloured female instrument, have believed with trembling—tears rolling down their cheeks, the signs of contrition and repentance towards God. I firmly believe that I have sown seed, in the name of the Lord. (Andrews, 37)

Although she often encountered prejudice because she was black and female, she was allowed to preach to audiences that included both free blacks and slaves, males and females. After her preaching career was less active, the 1852 General Conference of the African Methodist Episcopal Church voted against a resolution that would have given women official licenses to preach. However, such actions did not stop women like Lee from following what they believed God had called them to do.

Fanny Butterfield (1793–1824), who was born in Maine, converted and joined the Methodist Episcopal Church at age fifteen. She felt called to preach in 1809, a year before she married the Reverend Ebenezer F. Newell. After their marriage, she traveled with him in Vermont and Maine, preaching when she could, although the church did not sanction her work. Like Jarena Lee, she accepted what she interpreted as authorization from God to preach, even though the church usually disagreed.

The Methodist Protestant Church, established in 1828, proved somewhat more amenable to women preachers. Hannah Pearce (1800–1868), an English-born woman, began preaching as a member of the Bible Christians when she was nineteen. Eventually, she moved to America to marry William Reeves, whom she had met in England when he was a Wesleyan Methodist lay preacher. In America, he had been ordained in the Methodist Protestant Church, and they both preached to the congregations where he served as the official minister. In 1831, the Ohio Annual Conference of the Methodist Protestant Church asked her to preach at their meeting, an affirmation of her skill in the pulpit. She declined their offer of a circuit appointment of her own but continued to work closely with her husband.

Originally, Methodist preachers were discouraged from marrying, and those who did usually left the itinerate ministry. Church leaders did not want preachers distracted by families, and the life of circuit riding was filled with physical hardships that few families could tolerate. However, as young men increasingly left the min-

istry to marry and start families, church leaders gradually changed their position. They reasoned that women, who were considered innately more religious than men, could provide critical assistance on a circuit. For women, life as a minister's wife became a way to have a Christian vocation, which was otherwise denied to them.

A specialized form of advice book emerged to help women prepare for life as the spouse of an itinerant Methodist minister. The advice books listed educational requirements and skills that the ideal minister's wife should possess. The books also warned that the future would contain much loneliness and long separations from loved ones. They also stressed the difficulties of raising a family in conditions that were sometimes primitive, since most circuits provided little in the way of housing. Furthermore, ministers usually served for only one or two years in a circuit, then they were moved to another location, resulting in constant packing, moving, and resettling.

Methodist ministers' wives found themselves with far more responsibilities than keeping house, raising children, and planting gardens. They established Sunday Schools, evangelized frontier pioneers, participated in revivals and camp meetings, served as church sextons, and accompanied their husbands to remote preaching appointments. Even though the work was demanding and unending, the role of minister's wife allowed many women to serve the church in ways that offered personal fulfillment and gave them an acceptable way to answer a call from God.

Beginning in the 1830s, a new movement emerged that allowed Methodist women to continue developing their positions of leadership in the church—the Holiness movement. Two women, Phoebe Worrall Palmer and Amanda Berry Smith, became well-known evangelists who preached the Holiness doctrine in the United States and in Europe. They insisted that if the Holy Spirit commanded women to speak in public, no man should try to prohibit them. Still, they faced opposition and criticism, both for speaking publicly and for relegating their domestic duties to a secondary place in their lives.

Phoebe Palmer (1807–1874) was born in New York City and had a conversion experience early in life. By 1835, Palmer's sister, Sarah Lankford (1806–1896), was in charge of women's prayer meetings at two New York City churches, Allen Street Methodist Episcopal Church and Mulberry Street Methodist Episcopal Church. The next year, Lankford combined the membership of the two groups and began holding the prayer meetings, which occurred every Tuesday afternoon, at the home where she and her husband lived with Phoebe and Walter Palmer. The prayer meetings became known as the Tuesday Meetings for the Promotion of Holiness.

Phoebe Palmer began sharing the leadership with her sister.

Her decision to become involved in the Tuesday Meetings resulted from the death of her young daughter in 1836. After that tragedy, she began praying intently, and asking others to pray for her, that she might achieve sanctification, the second conversion experience that Methodists deem so important for their spiritual well-being. In 1837, she experienced what she regarded as sanctification, and she believed she might lose it unless she spoke about her experiences publicly. Her sister left New York City, and Palmer took over the leadership of the Tuesday Meetings. A decade later, the meetings included men and women, laypeople and clergy, Methodists and those from other Protestant denominations. Anyone could receive the gift of sanctification, and those who did felt obliged to testify in public about it, regardless of gender.

Palmer began receiving invitations to evangelize about Christian holiness beyond New York City, and in 1840, she made her first such trip. She also began publishing accounts of her struggle to achieve holiness in an effort to guide others in the process that had worked for her. She became involved in mission work in the slums of New York City, having convinced the Ladies' Home Missionary Society of her church to tackle the project. They established the Five Points Mission with a chapel, schoolrooms, baths, apartments, a day school, and many social programs.

She continued to receive criticism for speaking in public, and she heard from other women that they did, too. In response, she wrote a book titled *Promise of the Father*, which argued that women and men received the gift of the Holy Spirit at Pentecost, thus giving both the right to preach. As she stated,

> Suppose one of the brethren who had received the baptism of fire on the day of Pentecost, now numbered among those who were scattered every where preaching the word, had met a female disciple who had also received the same endowment of power. He finds her proclaiming Jesus to an astonished company of male and female listeners. And now imagine he interferes and withstands her testimony by questioning whether women have a right to testify of Christ before a mixed assembly. Would not such an interference look worse than unmanly? And were her testimony, through this interference, restrained, or rendered less effectual, would it not, in the eye of the Head of the church, involve guilt? (Palmer, 28)

Palmer further based the arguments in her book on scriptural passages, the history of the early church, the record of eighteenth-century women preaching in the Wesleyan societies, the inconsistency of the Methodist Church regarding women's participation in church activities, and the practical reality that the church needed the contributions that women could make. She supported the right of women to pray, testify, and preach in church.

Amanda Berry Smith (1837–1915), who was born into slavery, also began her career as a Holiness evangelist in New York City. She worked as a washerwoman before she had a life-changing dream during a serious illness. In the dream, she was preaching at a camp meeting to a large audience. She became convinced that God had not only cured her illness but also had chosen her to become an evangelist. She experienced sanctification in 1868, which further encouraged her.

She began by conducting prayer meetings in her apartment and preaching to black audiences near New York City. Following the death of her husband, she left the city and expanded her evangelistic work, speaking at revivals and testifying at camp meetings. Eventually, she traveled to Britain, India, and Africa, supporting herself as an evangelist wherever she went. In 1890, she came back to the United States and started an orphanage in Illinois.

American women's lives changed during the Civil War years as they assumed many responsibilities that husbands, fathers, and other male friends and relatives had shouldered before leaving home to become soldiers. As well, women undertook new work in relief agencies and as nurses. As a result of the war, American society experienced major changes in all aspects of life, including the churches.

In the decades after the war, the various branches of the Methodist church moved away from their pioneer roots and became well established as part of the religious mainstream. While lay leaders, local preachers, and ordained traveling preachers had once shared responsibility for the care of parishioners, increasingly the ordained ministers were appointed to churches for longer periods of time. They also assumed a greater share of the day-to-day duties they had delegated when they were required to be on the road constantly.

The Late Nineteenth Century

Many middle-class women, including Methodist women, who had gained experience outside the home during the war were reluctant to return to their former lifestyles and sought new opportunities to use skills they had acquired. As one result, women began establishing voluntary associations exclusively for women, some to improve society and some for personal enrichment.

The first formal organization of Methodist Episcopal Church women took place in Philadelphia in 1868 with the establishment of the Ladies' and Pastors' Christian

Union. The goal of the organizers of the Union was to provide assistance to the poor and underprivileged in their city through women's auxiliaries in every local Methodist Episcopal Church. As the name indicated, they did not operate independently. Each auxiliary worked under the guidance of the church's pastor, who served as president. The Union's plans included visiting house to house, inviting nonmembers to church, helping the sick and the poor, and encouraging children to attend Sunday School.

The idea of the Union soon expanded beyond Philadelphia, and in 1872, the General Conference of the Methodist Episcopal Church endorsed the legitimacy of the Ladies' and Pastors' Christian Union in local churches throughout its jurisdiction. Furthermore, the General Conference approved the Union's constitution, appointed a Board of Managers, and encouraged all ministers to cooperate with the women of the church in establishing local societies.

The 1872 General Conference also voted support for the Woman's Foreign Missionary Society, for which women in Boston provided the organizational impetus. In March 1869, a small group of women gathered initially to hear reports of missionary work in India offered by Clementina Rowe Butler and Lois Stiles Parker, who were both married to Methodist missionaries. After hearing Butler and Parker, the Boston churchwomen decided to establish a society to help foreign missionary efforts aimed at women. The missionary wives had indicated that only other women could evangelize Indian women because of cultural restrictions on contact between the sexes.

Within a week the Methodist women of Boston had organized a society, adopted a constitution, and elected national officers. Almost immediately, they began publishing *Heathen Woman's Friend*, later *The Woman's Missionary Friend*, a monthly magazine that described conditions in the mission fields of the church and documented the work of the society in providing assistance to the missionaries. For example, in 1880, a letter from a missionary in Tokyo was published in *Heathen Woman's Friend* in which she wrote:

Oct. 21 was the anniversary of our arrival in Japan, and while a very long time seems to have elapsed since the good-byes were said in the home land, and God's afflictive dispensation has brought sorrow to our hearts, still on the whole it has been a happy year. More and more do I feel it a privilege to work for Christ in this land. Not that the gospel teaching is everywhere received with favor, or that the people flock to hear the truth proclaimed.... At Mito, where our mission has recently opened a work, our two helpers were attacked by a party of Buddhist priests and their friends, and badly beaten. (*Heathen Woman's Friend* [February 1880] 179)

The ordained clergy who ran the Missionary Society, the committee that funded and appointed the church's foreign missionaries, did not entirely approve of the women's organization. They invited the Woman's Foreign Missionary Society leaders to a meeting with the secretaries of the Missionary Society in early May 1869. At the meeting, they asked the women to send any money raised to the Missionary Society, since the secretaries claimed that women's fund-raising might decrease donations to missions in the church as a whole. The women declared that they operated independently, and they intended to raise and disburse monies for their own projects. They did say that they would not engage in activities that would draw funds away from the Missionary Society.

The women initially organized the Woman's Foreign Missionary Society into local church auxiliaries and a national administrative unit called the Executive Committee. Within the first year, they realized that another layer of organizational structure, regional branches, could provide important help for the local auxiliaries as well as better communication with the national body, and six regional branches were established. The regional branches, each with a corresponding secretary, proved instrumental in expanding the society, organizing various activities, and raising money. The corresponding secretaries provided the vital link between the local auxiliaries and the Executive Committee, especially since the latter met only once a year. The decentralized nature of the society gave women throughout the church a multitude of opportunities for participation and leadership.

In 1880 Methodist Episcopal women formed a successor to the Ladies' and Pastors' Christian Union, the Woman's Home Missionary Society. They planned to help those in need in the United States in contrast to the focus of the Woman's Foreign Missionary Society. Their work expanded beyond the urban agenda of the Ladies' and Pastors' Christian Union to include Native Americans, Mormons, African Americans, and poor whites in the South, Chinese immigrants in California, and anyone living in the territories beyond the western border of the United States.

Women in other branches of Methodism also formed missionary societies with goals similar to those of the organizations of the Methodist Episcopal Church women. In the Methodist Episcopal Church, South, which had separated from the Methodist Episcopal Church in 1844 over the issue of slavery, women founded the Woman's Missionary Society of the Board of Missions, later the Woman's Foreign Missionary Society, in 1878. Also, women established the Woman's Department of the Board of Church Extension, later the

Woman's Parsonage and Home Mission Society and still later the Woman's Home Mission Society, in 1886. Methodist Protestant women formed the Woman's Foreign Missionary Society in 1879 after listening to Lizzie M. Guthrie, the wife of a missionary in Japan, talk about her work. Women in both the Methodist Episcopal Church, South, and the Methodist Protestant Church had to struggle against male opposition to their efforts to raise money and spend it as they determined it should be spent, just as Methodist Episcopal Church women had done earlier. The men always advocated adding any revenue from the women's societies to the general missionary coffers of the churches, and they opposed any activities that would divert contributions from their own organizations.

Before the Civil War, women who wished to serve as missionaries had to go as the wives of missionaries, although sometimes they were allowed to stay and continue the work begun with their spouses if their husbands died in the field. The establishment of missionary societies resulted in women themselves becoming missionaries. After the founding of women's missionary societies, the leaders used the societies' financial resources to fund single female missionaries. They justified their actions because they had been told that in the mission fields men were not allowed to meet and talk with the women they encountered. While their wives would have been permitted to do so, they were overworked already helping their husbands and running their own households. Thus, the need for female missionaries seemed obvious.

The female missionaries embarked on pioneering careers, often operating independently by necessity and developing skills beyond the training they received before departing. The first two women sent by the Woman's Foreign Missionary Society of the Methodist Episcopal Church, Isabella Thoburn (1840–1901) and Clara Swain (1834–1910), sailed for India in 1869. In 1886, Thoburn, an educator, founded Lucknow Woman's College, the first Christian higher education institution for women in India, where she served as principal and taught classes. Swain used her medical training to improve the health and physical well-being of women and children in Bareilly, India.

Women in other Protestant denominations in the United States also organized missionary societies, raised funds to launch female missionary careers, and struggled with male church members over control of their work. Women believed in the superiority of their culture and their religion, and they were determined to evangelize the world, if not personally, then through the missionaries they sent. At the same time that female missionaries were expanding women's possible roles, the women who established the missionary societies also developed many new skills as they organized activities locally and nationally, raised money in ingenious ways, published magazines and mission literature, spoke publicly about their work, and negotiated with male church leaders.

The General Conference of the Methodist Episcopal Church that approved the Ladies' and Pastors' Christian Union and the Woman's Foreign Missionary Society in 1872 had to deal with other issues related to women as well. At that time, they established a Committee on Woman's Work due to the number of resolutions that were submitted. One resolution proposed that women be allowed to be licensed to preach and even ordained, but that failed to pass. Women did secure eligibility for lay offices in the church, such as Sunday School superintendent, when the language of the Discipline, which codified Methodist Episcopal Church law, became gender neutral. At the 1876 General Conference, resolutions in favor of licensing women to preach, licensing them to exhort, and allowing them to occupy pulpits on a temporary basis were proposed, though none passed.

Although the Northern Indiana Conference of the Methodist Protestant Church had ordained Helenor M. Davison by 1866, other branches of Methodism did not follow suit. However, in 1869, Maggie Newton Van Cott received a license to preach from the Windham Circuit of the New York Conference. Van Cott had been converted in 1857 or 1858 and joined the Methodist Episcopal Church in 1866. She led prayer meetings, taught Sunday School, and engaged in evangelism. After first receiving an exhorter's license, then a local preacher's license, she served as a substitute pastor in Springfield, Massachusetts. She traveled to California in 1874 to officiate at revival meetings. The clergy of the San Francisco District Conference recommended her for ordination, but Bishop Stephen M. Merrill of the California Conference refused. Her local preacher's license, though, continued to be renewed.

In 1880, the Methodist Episcopal Church received applications for ordination from two women, Anna Howard Shaw and Anna Oliver. They were both graduates of Boston University School of Theology and had local preacher's licenses. Furthermore, their local examining committees approved their candidacies. However, Edward G. Andrews, the bishop of the New England Conference, would not ordain them. The two women decided to appeal his decision to the General Conference, which also ruled against them as well as rescinding all local preacher's licenses that had been issued to women since 1869. The General Conference did not reverse the decision about licenses until 1920.

Disappointed but undeterred, Shaw followed the advice of a Methodist Protestant Church minister and applied for ordination in that church. The New York Conference approved her application, and she was ordained on October 12, 1880. Four years later, the General Conference of the Methodist Protestant Church ruled that her ordination was invalid, but the New York Conference continued to honor it. In 1892, the Methodist Protestant Church finally recognized full laity and clergy rights for women.

In the Methodist Episcopal Church, women gained limited clergy status in 1924, which allowed for their ordination to a particular church in an emergency. The Methodist Church, formed by the merger of the Methodist Episcopal Church, the Methodist Episcopal Church, South, and the Methodist Protestant Church in 1939, finally granted women full clergy rights in 1956.

Although late-nineteenth-century male church leaders opposed the ordination of women, they did approve another form of church-related employment for women—the role of deaconess. The deaconess movement in the Methodist Church began under the leadership of Lucy Rider Meyer (1849–1922) in 1885 in Chicago. She dreamed of a school that would train young women to become religious leaders in urban environments. While she received the support of local clergy, they took no responsibility for raising the money to initiate the project. Eventually, she gained the support of the Woman's Foreign and Woman's Home Missionary Societies as well as the clergy to start a training school and to rent a building in which to conduct classes. The school offered its first lecture in October 1885. Local ministers, teachers, and physicians taught courses, and the curriculum included theological study as well as practical training, including fieldwork in urban locations. Within two years, Meyer decided that her students were sufficiently prepared to begin living in a home in one of the poorer, immigrant neighborhoods of Chicago and ministering to the needs of the residents. The next year, the General Conference of the Methodist Episcopal Church received petitions to authorize deaconess work as an official ministry of the church. The General Conference acquiesced, and an administrative structure was established.

Meyer's Chicago Training School prepared two types of deaconesses: nurse deaconesses and missionary deaconesses. The two-year course of study included specialized courses for each type of deaconess, although all students took required courses in biblical studies, Methodist Episcopal Church discipline, church history, theological doctrine, and social service methods.

The Methodist Episcopal Church, South, also established the office of deaconess and founded a training school for deaconesses in 1892, Scarritt Bible and Training School, which was initially located in Kansas City, then later moved to Nashville. The Woman's Board of Home Missions administered the work of deaconesses in the southern church. When they graduated, the deaconesses usually lived together in deaconess homes and received in compensation only their room and board, uniforms, and a monthly allowance. Their uniforms—long black dresses and bonnets with white ties—served to identify them and protect them in the neighborhoods in which they worked. The women who became deaconesses hoped that their work would improve conditions for the urban poor. They visited tenement dwellers, identified needs, and returned with assistance.

The deaconesses often reported about their work in official publications of the missionary societies, providing Methodist churchwomen with firsthand descriptions of their wide-ranging activities. M. E. Smith, the deaconess in charge of the Louisville, Kentucky, Wesley House, wrote, "The clinic is a very important part of our work, and through it we reach many whom we could touch in no other way; for in ministering to the body we can often bring healing to the soul as well" (*Our Homes*, August–September 1909, 18). Margaret Ragland, a deaconess at St. Mark's Hall, New Orleans related, "There is a gratifying response to our free bath offer. We have three showers and one tub bath that we are giving the district. Wednesdays and Fridays we reserve for girls, and give the other days to men and boys" (21).

The deaconesses' work exposed them to the negative consequences of immigration, urbanization, and industrialization. They took the information gathered and shared it with churchwomen, and those women often used the data to promote important changes in society, such as child labor laws and better conditions for working women.

Another late-nineteenth-century issue was the question of whether laity rights should be granted to Methodist women, which, like ordination, often pitted women against men. Laity rights include serving as delegates to annual and general conferences and participating on churchwide committees, in other words, having a role in governing the church. Some men feared that they would lose their power in the church if women gained laity rights. Others argued that the Bible prohibited such rights for women, who should not be concerned with secular or church politics. However, their work in organizing missionary societies and establishing the deaconess movement convinced women that they needed a voice in the decision-making structure of the church.

Even laity rights for men were a relatively recent innovation in the late nineteenth century. The General Conference first admitted male lay delegates in 1872, with two delegates per conference plus the clergy members. A discussion took place at the 1872 General Conference about whether the term *laymen*, when referring to possible delegates, should include women as well as men. In 1880, the General Conference supported women as lay church officials, for example, stewards, class leaders, and Sunday School superintendents.

Women could also serve in the governing body of local churches that elected delegates to the electoral conference, which then chose delegates to General Conference. The next logical step was the election of women as lay delegates to General Conference, which did occur in 1888. However, these first female lay delegates were denied official seats at the Conference. The General Conference did agree to allow a referendum in which all members of the church would vote on the issue of female delegates. Although a majority voted in favor, the vote was less than three-fourths of the membership required to change policy. Additional maneuvering took place in 1892, but in 1900, the General Conference finally agreed that women could become delegates. The first officially sanctioned women delegates served at the General Conference of 1904.

The more democratic Methodist Protestant Church gave laity rights to white men as early as 1830 but not to women or blacks. The church split in 1858 over a disagreement about giving laity rights to black men. In 1877, the church reunited and resolved the issue of suffrage by allowing each annual conference to decide for itself. In 1892, four women served as delegates to the General Conference, though some opposed the action.

The Methodist Episcopal Church, South, delayed granting laity rights to women until 1922. Southern Methodist women became suffragists for church rights after the General Conference forced them to cede control of their missionary societies to the church's Board of Missions and to combine their foreign and home societies into the Woman's Missionary Council. Under the leadership of Belle Harris Bennett (1852–1922), southern Methodist women petitioned the General Conference of 1910 for laity rights, but they were denied. In 1914, they mounted a better campaign but still faced defeat because the bishops adamantly opposed them. The General Conference leadership changed during the next four years, and newer members did not oppose the women as their predecessors had done. Finally, in 1918, the women succeeded in winning laity rights.

The Early Twentieth Century

In response to the growing number of women in the workforce, Methodist Episcopal women established a new organization, the Wesleyan Service Guild, in 1921 as an auxiliary of the Woman's Foreign and Woman's Home missionary societies. Organized for women employed outside the home, the Guild had a Central Committee to conduct its administrative work, a constitution, and a newsletter titled *World Service Greetings*. The goals of the Guild included developing the spiritual life of its members, its primary purpose, providing opportunities for service, advocating Christian citizenship, and offering social and recreational activities. During the Great Depression of the 1930s, the Guild served as a support system for women who lost their jobs or faced salary reductions.

In 1920, the General Conference of the Methodist Episcopal Church once again began granting women licenses as local preachers, forty years after they had withdrawn that privilege. At the next General Conference in 1924, the church voted approval for a limited type of ordination for women, the right to be local elders, though not members, of an annual conference.

In the South, among the projects undertaken by Methodist women were efforts to assist blacks by sponsoring educational institutions and improving relations between whites and blacks. The women funded a program for women at Paine College in Augusta, Georgia, which had been started by the Colored Methodist Episcopal Church in 1883. Southern Methodist women also established social settlements in Augusta, Nashville, and elsewhere, which they called Bethlehem Centers.

To improve race relations, the Woman's Missionary Council of the Methodist Episcopal Church, South, voted in 1920 to form the Commission on Race Relations. The Commission sponsored a conference for white women leaders that year to which several black churchwomen were also invited, so that the former could hear firsthand accounts of the racial problems faced by southern black people. Although the conference helped begin a dialogue between the white and black women, it also reinforced the challenges they faced.

Middle to Late Twentieth Century

In 1939, the Methodist Episcopal Church, the Methodist Episcopal Church, South, and the Methodist Protestant Church united to form the Methodist Church. Representatives at the Uniting Conference defeated a motion for full clergy rights for women. In the Methodist Episcopal Church, the issue had been introduced beginning in 1828, and in the Methodist Episcopal Church, South, since 1926. Only the Methodist Protestant Church ordained women, and those women lost their status as full conference members with the uniting vote, though they could continue as unordained ministers. However, women and their male supporters began working in earnest to change the situation.

The Methodist Church received over 2,000 petitions requesting that women be given full clergy rights before the General Conference met in 1956. The petitions came not only from individuals but also from women's societies throughout the country. The Committee on the Ministry tried to limit clergy rights to unmarried women and widows, but the delegates voted against that restriction. Instead, they passed a motion that "[w]omen are included in all the provisions of the Discipline referring to the ministry" (The Methodist Church *Discipline* [1956] 115). Since then women have taken their place as full clergy members of the denomination.

The first woman to be granted full clergy rights as an ordained pastor was Maude Keister Jensen (1904–1998), which occurred while she was serving as a missionary in Korea in 1956. Jensen began teaching Sunday School at age twelve and felt called to ministry early in her life. She received a license to preach while she was a student at Bucknell University in Lewisburg, Pennsylvania. Soon after graduating in 1926, she left for the mission field in Korea. Her future husband, A. Kris Jensen, was also a missionary in Korea, and they married in 1928. She earned a Bachelor of Divinity degree from Drew Theological School in 1946, but when she applied for deacons orders in 1948, the bishop of the New Jersey area would not support her candidacy. She continued to seek ordination and was finally ordained as a local preacher in 1952 by the bishop of the Central Pennsylvania Conference, though full membership took another four years. She and her husband worked for almost forty years in Korea, and the Korean government honored her twice for her social welfare work. After her retirement, she earned a doctorate at Drew Theological School.

Gusta A. Robinette (1905–1996) was the first woman to be appointed a district superintendent in the Methodist Church. She was originally from Columbia City, Indiana, and was ordained in the Sumatra (Indonesia) Conference in 1956. Her appointment as district superintendent was to the Medan Chinese District in Indonesia in 1959.

Margaret Henrichsen (d. 1976) was the first woman district superintendent appointed in the United States, which occurred in 1967. Henrichsen, who was born in Plainfield, New Jersey, trained to become a kindergarten teacher. She and her husband managed a home school for girls who needed special care. When he died in 1943, she went back to school and earned a theological degree. Her first appointment was in Sullivan, Maine, where she pastored seven churches. She wrote a memoir of her experiences on that circuit in which she described some of the challenges of being a clergywoman.

From the beginning I enjoyed studying and preparing sermons. . . . The trouble was the fight for time. The pastoral work was increasing. The more families I got to know, the more people came to trust me, the heavier the load and the less time for study, meditation, and creative work. . . . What little time I could get for real study was further trespassed upon by glaring needs in the house; floors that had to be swept or washed, windows that had become so smoky they cried out to be washed, some ironing and mending. . . . The trouble was that having chosen to be the minister I also had to be "her wife." (Henrichsen, 136–137)

In 1968, the Methodist Church merged with the Evangelical United Brethren Church. The latter had been a union of the Evangelical Church and the Church of the United Brethren in Christ, which took place in 1946. The election of the first woman bishop, Marjorie Matthews, took place after the creation of the United Methodist Church.

Matthews (1916–1986) was elected in 1980 by the Central Jurisdictional Conference. Matthews was a native of Onawa, Michigan, who was employed by an auto parts manufacturer for many years. In 1967, she earned a bachelor's degree from Central Michigan University, followed by a Bachelor of Divinity degree from Colgate Rochester Divinity School in 1970, and a master's in religion and a doctorate in humanities from Florida State University in 1976. In 1965, she had been ordained an elder and served churches in Michigan, New York, and Florida. She served as a district superintendent before being elected bishop. As bishop, she presided over the Wisconsin Area for four years, then she retired in 1984.

In 1984, Leontine T. C. Kelly became the first African American woman elected a bishop. She was born in Washington, D.C., and received a bachelor's degree from Virginia Union University in 1960. She taught in the public schools, then decided to return to school and earned a Master of Divinity degree from Union Theological Seminary in Richmond, Virginia. She was ordained in the Virginia Annual Conference in 1972. After being elected bishop, she served in the San Francisco area until she retired in 1992. She has recently been a member of the United Methodist Council of Bishops' Initiative on Children and Poverty. Kelly welcomed three more African American women to the Council of Bishops in 2000—Violet Fisher, Beverly Shamana, and Linda Lee.

Sharon Brown Christopher was the first woman to become the president of the Council of Bishops, an office of one year's duration that began in May 2002. Christopher was educated at Southwestern University in Georgetown, Texas, and Perkins School of Theology, Southern Methodist University, Dallas. She was ordained a deacon in 1970 and an elder in 1972 in the Wisconsin Annual Conference. She served churches there until being elected a bishop in 1988. As a bishop, she was assigned first to the Minnesota Area, then to the Illinois Area in 1996.

By 2000, the United Methodist Church reported a total of 5,202 ordained women clergy under appointment in the United States. In addition, the church had thirteen female bishops, eleven active and two retired, ten of whom were white and three African American.

Methodist laywomen continued their active participation in the church after the formation of the Methodist Church and, later, the United Methodist Church. In 1940, the women's foreign and home missionary societies of the three denominations united as the Woman's Division of Christian Service under the Board of Missions and Church Extension of the Methodist Church. The Woman's Division constituted one of four divisions under the new Board. The women leaders of the missionary societies worked with local societies to ensure a smooth transition to the new structure. The Woman's Division had three departments, Foreign, Home, and Christian Social Relations and Local Church Activities, each with its own executive secretary. The responsibilities of the secretaries included establishing goals, drafting resolutions, planning conferences, and implementing programs. They ensured that the connectional system, which involved churchwomen at all levels, worked effectively and efficiently.

The Board of Missions reorganized in 1964, which resulted in the foreign and home mission work of the Woman's Division being moved to the World and National divisions of the Board. Women from the Woman's Division held seats on the boards of both the World and National divisions. The Woman's Division then included departments for Christian Social Relations, Program and Education for Christian Mission, and Finance.

In 1968, the women's organizations combined without major disruptions. The new Women's Division oversaw the work of the local auxiliaries: the Women's Society of Christian Service, for homemakers, and the Wesleyan Service Guild, for employed women. Also that year, the Women's Division requested that the Uniting Conference form a Study Commission on the Participation of Women in the United Methodist Church. At the same time, the Women's Division formed an in-house Ad Hoc Committee on Churchwomen's Liberation.

In 1972, the two types of auxiliaries were combined to create United Methodist Women with program areas called Christian Personhood, Christian Social Relations, and Christian Global Concerns. As well, the General Conference that year created the Commission on the Status and Role of Women at the urging of the Women's Division, which has played an important role in bringing women's issues to the attention of the church.

The 2000 General Conference offered a glimpse of the current activities and concerns of women in the United Methodist Church. The General Commission on the Status and Role of Women and the Women's Division, General Board of Global Ministries, submitted important proposals that were approved by the delegates to the General Conference. The Women's Division resolutions included reaffirmation of the use of diverse biblical metaphors and language reflecting diversity and inclusiveness in worship and church publications, opposition to recruiting and training children to be soldiers and to making children targets for sexual abuse and gender-based violence, and a call for the church to educate about and advocate against hate crimes. The General Commission on the Status and Role of Women supported resolutions and legislative proposals to increase efforts toward the eradication of sexual harassment in the United Methodist Church and its institutions, to ensure full and equitable participation of women at all levels of the church, and to recommit to eliminating sexual misconduct in all ministerial relationships, among other agenda items.

Since the establishment of Methodist societies in the United States in the mid-eighteenth century, the participation of women has been an integral aspect of church life. Furthermore, Methodist women have been involved in the changes and movements that have defined American society for almost two and a half centuries. Given the current activities of United Methodist clergywomen and laywomen, the contributions they make in the future will continue to shape their denomination and the broader world.

SOURCES: Jean Miller Schmidt's *Grace Sufficient: A History of Women in American Methodism, 1760–1939* (1999) is the most comprehensive history of the topic for the period before the establishment of the Methodist Church in 1939. William L. Andrews's *Sisters of the Spirit: Three Black Women's Autobiographies of the Nineteenth Century* (1986) includes the autobiography of Jarena Lee. *Women in New Worlds: Historical Perspectives on the Wesleyan Tradition*, vol. 1, Hilah Thomas and Rosemary Keller, eds. (1981), and vol. 2, Rosemary Keller, Louise Queen, and Hilah Thomas, eds. (1982), have essays on many important Methodist women. See also Phoebe Palmer, *Promise of the Father* (1859) and Margaret Henrichsen, *Seven Steeples* (1953). Web sites for the United Methodist Church are useful for current information about clergywomen's and laywomen's activities in and contributions to the church.

QUAKER WOMEN IN NORTH AMERICA
Mary Van Vleck Garman

THE QUAKER MOVEMENT emerged in England during the 1650s. Groups of religious seekers were attracted to the teachings of George Fox, who called on true Christians to abandon the "steeple houses" of the established church and to live authentic spiritual lives animated by the mighty power of God. Early Quakers espoused radical theological views about the immediate presence of Christ, available without the mediating agency of clergy, sacraments, buildings, or ritual. Civil authorities were offended when Quakers refused to participate in the military, swear oaths in court, or pay tithes to the state church. Equally insulting were the Quaker protests against traditions of social deference, such as removing one's hat in the presence of "superiors" or using titles of address and obsequious language.

In public Friends articulated their understanding of the gospel message in prophetic outbursts or strident tracts and pamphlets. Among the most controversial of their beliefs was the claim that God intended women and men to be "helpsmeet" to each other in all ways, both public and private. Quaker families and Quaker organizations were to serve as signs of the restored order that Christ came to establish. From the very beginning of the Quaker movement, women joined men in public preaching and teaching, organizing and writing, and the suffering that came as a consequence of violating both laws and customs.

When they met to worship, early Quakers waited together in silence, anticipating that the power of the Holy Spirit would inspire some to rise and speak to the group. Gradually Friends began to acknowledge, or "record as ministers," those men and women who spoke powerfully to the needs of the gathered community. Often these same ministers traveled from their home congregations, or Meetings, to represent Friends in the wider world. Convinced that there was "that of God" in every person, Quaker women and men in ministry were sent off with the blessing of their Meetings to offer their version of the Christian gospel to the world and to challenge the authorities in their own countries.

A distinctive style of governance, based on the same principle of waiting, developed as well in the early decades. When they gathered to make decisions, early Friends tested their ideas, which they often called "lead-ings," in conversation with one another. Instead of voting, they would seek prayerfully to find the best way forward based on the collective wisdom of the group. Friends rejected formal creeds and held instead to four main ethical principles: integrity, peacefulness, simplicity, and equality. All individual leadings to act or speak on behalf of the Society of Friends were tested against these four testimonies. Each group of Friends designated a "clerk," whose main responsibility was to listen carefully to the conversations, then to articulate and record for the group the "sense of the Meeting." This style of leadership and governance worked well in the early decades of the Quaker movement. Early Friends were frequently jailed for their views, which meant that new leadership had to emerge quickly. The patterns that were established in the early decades have been adapted to circumstances since but have been remarkably resilient in subsequent centuries and locations.

One of the most outspoken early leaders was Margaret Fell, the wife of Thomas Fell, judge of Assize. Her genius for organization, her willingness to open her home, Swarthmoor Hall, to traveling Friends, and her leadership during the years of persecution were pivotal for the survival of the movement. In an early tract, "Women's Speaking Justified" (1666), she challenged the Pauline prohibition against women's speech (1 Corinthians 14: 34–35). In fact, she and other early Quaker women argued that partnership between women and men was a sign of the redemption God intended for all of creation. The public ministry of women, they insisted, was indelible evidence of the power of the Spirit of God; thus women who claimed their right to public ministry were the faithful disciples, while anyone who set out to silence

Dinora Vasquez, a long-time Quaker activist from Mexico, attended the International Theological Conference of Quaker women at Woodbrooke in 1990. Out of that experience she felt a leading toward ministry, and came to study at Earlham School of Religion, Richmond, Indiana. After graduation she initiated a ministry with Mexican immigrants to East Central Indiana, in keeping with the Quaker tradition of work for social change. *Courtesy of Dinora Vasquez.*

them was interfering with God's wishes. Quaker women began to gather in the earliest days in a weekly "Women's Meeting," which organized relief efforts for families of members in prison.

The first Quakers came to North America during the seventeenth century, settling in Virginia, Maryland, and Carolina, and in Jersey, New York, Massachusetts, Rhode Island, Connecticut, and especially in Pennsylvania. Quaker women participated in all of the major turning points that Friends have faced on this continent. They adapted to the circumstances in North America and developed leadership skills within their own faith communities. These skills were in demand in the wider society, where Quaker women have consistently modeled female leadership.

Colonial Beginnings

In July 1656 two Quaker women arrived in Boston harbor. Ann Austin, who had left her husband and five children in England to make the journey, was accompanied by Mary Fisher, a young, unmarried woman of twenty-three. Their goal was to introduce the people of Boston to the gospel as Friends understood it. The civil authorities considered Quakers to be potentially dangerous to the well-being of the colony, and the two women were sent to jail. Their books were burned, and they were held without food, light, or bedding for five weeks. Quaker chronicler Joseph Besse revealed the depths of their suffering while in prison, where they were "stripped naked, under pretence to know whether they were witches" and "in this search they were so barbarously misused, that modesty forbids to mention it" (Besse, 178–179). Upon their release they were deported to Barbados. As they were leaving, another boatload of Quaker women and men arrived, continuing the "Quaker invasion" of New England.

The case of Mary Dyer illustrates Quaker persistence and Puritan brutality. She first came to Massachusetts in the 1630s and befriended Anne Hutchinson. Hutchinson infuriated the Puritan leaders by challenging their interpretation of scripture and teaching her understanding of the gospel to groups that included men and women. When she was convicted and banished to Rhode Island at her ecclesiastical trial in Boston in 1638, Dyer joined hands with her and shared her fate. Later, after Hutchinson and her family had migrated to Long Island, Dyer returned to England, where she joined the Society of Friends and began her career as a public minister. She returned to Boston in 1657 and continued to preach and to visit Friends in prison, for which she was arrested with two male companions and sentenced to death. After witnessing the hanging of her two companions, Dyer was reprieved and banished, under a stern threat of execution. Within two years she returned to

Boston, "in obedience to the will of the Lord," and in 1660 she was hanged, as her executioners said, "like a flag for others to take example from." Mary Dyer did become an example, but not in the way the Puritans had hoped. Her death so shocked King Charles II that he sent word to Boston that Quakers should no longer be executed for their beliefs. Although the threat of death was removed, Quakers continued to be whipped, imprisoned, and banished from Boston until the 1680s.

Elizabeth Hooten, the earliest female preacher among Friends, made three trips to North America during this period. In 1661, she and Joan Brocksopp journeyed via Virginia and Rhode Island, since ship captains were forbidden to transport Quakers to Boston. After surviving her subsequent punishment (abandonment, after two days' journey, in the wilderness) she returned to Boston with her daughter in 1663. They were arrested and convicted, stripped to the waist, tied to a cart, and whipped through the towns surrounding Boston. Hooten died, in 1671, on the island of Jamaica, preparing to undertake her third journey to North America.

As in England, Quaker women in North America understood themselves to be prophets sent by God to witness on behalf of the Truth. From time to time their actions were extreme, designed to provoke those in authority into harsh reactions. For example, Lydia Wardell, known among Friends as a "woman of exemplary Modesty in all her Behavior," appeared naked at the church in Newbury, Massachusetts. She was protesting the practice of publicly stripping and whipping women, sometimes until their bodies were permanently disfigured.

Quakerism spread throughout the southern colonies partly as a result of the ministry of Elizabeth Harris, who journeyed and preached throughout Virginia and Maryland in the 1650s. By the early 1660s regular gatherings for Quaker worship were also held on Long Island in New York, and in 1677 groups of Quakers founded a settlement in West Jersey. George Fox discovered, during his visit to North America in 1672, that men's and women's Meetings were caring for the poor and attending to other church business throughout the colonies. In 1676 Fox published an Epistle to all Friends, entitled "An Encouragement to all the Women's Meetings," in which he made a biblical argument on behalf of women's leadership. In the preface to this Epistle, an anonymous group of women Friends offered a "salutation of unfeigned Love" to the women of "Rode-Island, New York, and there-away." Clearly the Quaker women of England and those in the colonies felt themselves to be "dear Sisters" who were engaged in "Exercises of Love and Mercies to all that stand in need" (Fox, 5). Perhaps someday research will uncover the identities of these women.

By the end of the seventeenth century Friends were living and worshiping throughout the colonies of North

America. Friends met weekly for worship and monthly for business, so their local Meeting was called a "Monthly Meeting." Three or four times a year several Monthly Meetings in an area would meet for worship, business, and fellowship, and this gathering came to be called "Quarterly Meeting." The term *Yearly Meeting* was used to refer both to an annual gathering of Monthly Meetings from a particular geographic area and to the organization formed by these Monthly Meetings. The earliest Yearly Meetings were in New England (1661), Baltimore (1672), Philadelphia (1687), New York (1695), and North Carolina (1698). At these annual gatherings, Friends worshiped together, shared concerns, organized events, and also sought to deepen their spiritual lives. Each Yearly Meeting produced an Epistle that was sent to all other Yearly Meetings around the world. Separate Women's Meetings for Business, which were common among Monthly Meetings and Quarterly Meetings, were also established among Yearly Meetings throughout the seventeenth and eighteenth centuries. The Minutes and Epistles from these Women's Meetings offer researchers glimpses into the lives of Quaker women in North America.

In 1681, the king granted a section of land in North America to aristocrat-turned-Quaker William Penn, who named the colony in honor of his father. After the Glorious Revolution in England (1688), which brought the Protestants William and Mary to the throne of England, the persecutions of Quakers began to subside. The Delaware Valley became a haven for Quaker families, who made up between one-half and two-thirds of the population by 1683.

During the decades leading up to the Revolutionary War, Friends were caught in a series of dilemmas. Commitment to the peace testimony meant that Friends would not participate in militias, nor would they, in Pennsylvania, levy taxes to pay for England's European wars. At the same time, Indian attacks against settlers on the western border of Pennsylvania raised questions about the capacity of Quakers to sustain their vision of a "Holy Experiment"—a colony based on Quaker principles. By 1756 Friends in Pennsylvania resolved the crisis by withdrawing from public life and from their positions in the state Assembly. Throughout the colonies, Friends began to pay closer attention to the inner life. Each year they considered questions for self-examination—called "Queries"—that were designed to explain traditions and inspire more faithful adherence to the Quaker way of life. As members were disowned for deviations from those testimonies, some Friends began to worry about the future of the Society, while others rejoiced that a "spiritual reformation" was under way.

As revolutionary sentiments grew stronger in the colonies, Friends declared their intention to remain neutral.

Once the war began, a representative group of Friends gathered in Philadelphia to spell out their principles and to specify the ways they would support one another. Women Friends continued to travel in ministry, sometimes going great distances through war zones to visit and to offer encouragement. Their concern was for those who were suffering because of the war, no matter which side of the conflict they were on. The consequences of these choices were significant: Throughout the war Friends were considered traitors, and many households suffered as fines were levied against them. Other Friends rebelled and joined the short-lived "Free Quakers" who supported the colonial cause. Pennsylvania went through a period of acute upheaval, as Friends debated and struggled to remain faithful to their witness for peace.

Throughout this period, women and men continued the tradition of meeting together for worship and separately to attend to business. The earliest Women's Meetings in North America were established in Maryland (1672) and Pennsylvania (1681). This pattern was followed wherever Friends migrated. They used a Book of Discipline, which, while not a creed, spelled out the details of Friends' testimonies. For example, the Philadelphia Discipline explained the practice of having separate Women's Meetings by indicating that they had been established "in accordance with divine wisdom" and had been continued because "long experience" had shown that they were advantageous "not only to the society [that is, Society of Friends] but to the youth of their own sex" (*Philadelphia Book of Discipline*, 1796).

Friends in the colonies continued to rely for spiritual nurture on transatlantic relationships, which were maintained by remarkable preaching journeys, many of them made by Quakers like Mary Peisley from Ireland and Catherine Payton from England, who visited among North American Friends in the late eighteenth century, offering encouragement and guidance. Pairs of Friends from North America sometimes reciprocated, visiting and preaching among English and Irish Friends. The story of Hannah Barnard illustrates one such journey and suggests some of the theological issues emerging within North American Quakerism.

Born in 1754, Barnard was a powerful preacher who held strong views against war, considering it to be "a moral evil, which man creates to himself, by the misapplication of his powers, or, in other words, by the abuse of his free agency" ("A Narrative of the proceedings in America of the Society called Quakers, in the case of Hannah Barnard," 9). In 1797 Barnard and a companion were granted a certificate from Hudson (New York) Monthly Meeting to travel to Europe. Although well received in Ireland and in Scotland, when Barnard arrived in England in 1800, questions were raised about her beliefs, which some criticized as "not one with Friends." Her preaching and teaching, the British elders argued, had the potential to lead unsuspecting Friends into atheism. Barnard argued that God, in God's unchangeable nature, would never command humans to wage war. By saying this, she challenged the authority and unity of the Bible, implying that some biblical injunctions carried less eternal power than others.

Barnard argued that her ultimate source of authority was not the scriptures but was rather "the divine light" that God gave to all humans, along with intelligence and the power to interpret scripture. In making this argument, she was not breaking with Friends' tradition. Robert Barclay, the foremost Quaker theologian of the seventeenth century, argued in his *Apology* that Friends should rely primarily on "the Spirit of God which must give us the belief in the scriptures which will satisfy our consciences" (Barclay). Elizabeth Bathhurst, another early Quaker theologian, also argued against the idea of scripture as the highest or only source of authority for the Christian life, since the scriptures were "Publications in Testimony of that Creating Word of Power" and were not themselves the ultimate power ("Truth's Vindication," in Garman et al., 351). Nevertheless, Friends in Britain and in New York found Barnard's preaching dangerous and determined that she was threatening the unity of Friends.

After an unsuccessful effort to defend herself against these charges, Barnard returned home in 1801 to discover that the elders and ministers of Hudson Monthly Meeting would not allow her to present her account of her travels, removed her from the list of ministers, and disowned her as a member. During the next twenty-five years, Friends continued to struggle over the issues raised by her preaching.

Era of Expansion

Quaker families migrated westward from New England and Pennsylvania, and north from Virginia, Maryland, and the Carolinas, seeking to live apart from the practices of the slave trade and beyond the injustices shown to Indian people. In 1813 Ohio Yearly Meeting was established, and in 1821 Indiana Yearly Meeting became the second Yearly Meeting west of the Allegheny Mountains. Quaker families from the South (the Carolinas and Virginia) settled on the Blue River and near White Lick in the south central part of Indiana. The earliest minutes from these Meetings indicate the continuation of the tradition of partnership between men and women: Both men and women were appointed as elders, served on committees, and were recorded as ministers. Quaker families also settled in Iowa in the 1830s. Their numbers grew steadily until "a joint committee of men and women Friends" sent word to Indiana Yearly Meeting in 1858 that they wished to become an independent Yearly Meeting. The migration of Friends to Kansas was primarily motivated by their commitment to equality. In the 1830s the Shawnee were forced by the U.S. government to move from Ohio to a reservation in Kansas. The Shawnee Nation petitioned Ohio Friends to continue to support them, and some Quaker families responded by moving to Kansas and establishing a school in the area. Friends also went to Kansas in response to passage of the Kansas-Nebraska Act of 1854, which overturned the Missouri Compromise of 1820 and opened the possibility that, given sufficient pro-slavery voters, Kansas would enter the Union as a slave state. In 1856 seven Quaker families settled in Kansas under the care of Indiana Yearly Meeting's Whitewater Quarterly Meeting, and by 1872 Friends in Kansas were constituted a separate Yearly Meeting.

Careful attention was paid to following Friends' process in the Women's Meetings established among migrating Quakers. At Blue River Meeting of Women Friends in Washington County, Indiana, "Betsy Trueblood, Phebe Winslow, and Mary Draper," were appointed to bring the names of a suitable woman to serve as an Overseer "in the place of Martha Nixon, who requests to be released from that service" (1st of 8th month, 1835). The minutes of the Women's Meeting of Cane Creek (South Carolina) Monthly Meeting of Friends tell of marriages accomplished once there was "nothing to obstruct" and "clearness from all others" was established. Some women were subsequently disciplined when a baby arrived "too soon" after the marriage. However, those who were disciplined often "made satisfaction" to representatives of the Women's Meeting once they acknowledged their "sense of misconduct."

Another important responsibility of the Women's Meeting involved supporting those who felt a leading to travel in ministry. With the blessing of their Meeting in North Carolina in 1751, Abigail Pike and Rachel Wright journeyed 200 miles from Perquimans County to Cane Creek to help establish a Quaker Meeting there. The minutes of the Blue River Meeting of Women Friends record that Priscilla Cadwallader laid before her Meeting, in July 1829, her desire to make a missionary trip "to the inhabitant of the continents, and some of the West Indies." In 1851 the women of Newberry Monthly Meeting, Friendsville, Blount County, Tennessee, recorded their gratitude for the visit of "Our beloved Friend Rhodema Newlin" from South River Monthly Meeting in Warren County, Iowa. Further study of these minutes will reveal additional ways that Quaker women on the frontier developed as ministers and leaders and supported each other in these callings.

Once a year the members of each Monthly Meeting discussed, responded, and forwarded to the Yearly Meeting their answers to the Queries. Among the Women's Queries were questions about whether "love and unity are preserved amongst you" and if "Friends keep to plainness in every part of their conduct." It was assumed that Friends were "clear of purchasing, disposing of, or holding" any slaves, but that was not considered the end of their responsibility. Quaker women also had to consider their willingness to "look after the promotion and education of the Freedmen" in their communities. The full story of the role of people of color during this era is yet to be told; however, there is evidence that freed slaves accepted the "hand of Christian fellowship" and joined the Society of Friends in the 1870s and after.

Social Reform Movements and Quaker Women

As early as 1696 some Friends in North America began to organize against slavery and the slave trade, and finally in 1743 Philadelphia Yearly Meeting's Book of Discipline included a statement declaring that slavery was contrary to Friends' traditions and beliefs. The antislavery impulse among Friends was grounded in the testimony of equality: Quakers believed that all human beings had access to the divine. Friends condemned slavery as a violation of human dignity and also as an economic and political system that corrupted all who participated in it. Throughout the eighteenth century the "Quaker prophet" John Woolman and others worked tirelessly, calling on Friends to turn away from slavery, war, greed, and sin.

The minutes of Quaker Women's Meetings reveal their horror at the persistence of slavery and their awareness of the complexity of the political questions involved. Elizabeth Margaret Chandler contributed articles to the antislavery publication *Genius of Universal Emancipation* in the 1820s, and when she moved from the Philadelphia area to Michigan, she continued antislavery work there. In the 1830s and 1840s Quaker women from the East Coast to the western frontier offered financial support to free black families in their neighborhoods and throughout the nation. In Canterbury, Connecticut, Prudence Crandall antagonized both local citizens and state lawmakers when, in 1831, she admitted black children to her school for girls. The ensuing turmoil forced her to close the school, which she attempted to reopen in 1833 as a "High School for Young Colored Ladies and Misses." She was arrested and jailed briefly. Once she was released, her school became the target of boycotts, harassment, and arson.

As Friends increased their participation in the national movement for abolition of slavery, a number of Quaker women had opportunities to demonstrate their leadership skills. Angelina Grimké of South Carolina published an influential tract, *An Appeal to Christian Women of the South* (1836), and she and her sister Sarah moved to New England, joining the antislavery lecture circuit in the 1830s. Abby Kelley joined the New England and the American Anti-Slavery Societies. The minutes of Women's Meetings across the Society of Friends show that many Quaker women worked behind the scenes against slavery and on behalf of freed slaves in their communities.

Perhaps the most influential Quaker woman devoted to the antislavery cause was Lucretia Coffin. Raised in a Quaker community on Nantucket Island, she was active in her Meeting and was recognized as a minister. Coffin graduated from Nine Partners Friends School in New York at age sixteen and was then employed there as an assistant teacher. When she discovered that James Mott, another teacher, was being paid more than the experienced female teachers at the school, she protested and resolved to work against such injustices. After two years of teaching, she married James Mott, and they settled in Philadelphia to raise their family. Although she initially supported the colonization movement, which would have established settlements of freed slaves in Africa, deeper reflection convinced her to join the more radical movement to abolish slavery altogether. In 1833 she played a central role in organizing the Philadelphia Female Anti-Slavery Society. Four years later this group called together women from all over New England to meet in the Anti-Slavery Convention of American Women.

As the antislavery movement gathered adherents, their efforts became entangled with "the woman question." Some clergy and evangelical Christians expressed distaste at the presence of women in leadership positions, and the debate that ensued distracted people from the horrors and the persistence of slavery and required time-consuming responses. Prominent contributors to the American Anti-Slavery Society withdrew their support and formed the American and Foreign Anti-Slavery Society, which did not allow women to serve on committees or speak in public. The General Association of the Massachusetts Congregationalist Clergy issued a "Pastoral Letter" that warned against the threat to the "female character" that resulted from encouraging women to "bear an obtrusive and ostentatious part" in efforts to bring about social reform. The clergy in Massachusetts were particularly shocked at the speeches by two Quaker women from the South, Sarah and Angelina Grimké, who spoke before "promiscuous" (that is, mixed male and female) audiences about the particular horrors endured by slave women. The "Pastoral Letter" charged that "modesty and delicacy" should require women not to name such things in public.

While they were used to women in leadership positions, many Friends were uneasy with the national antislavery movement. Most Friends lived in communities that remained separate from what they called "the world's people." They still considered churches to be "steeple-houses" and referred to ordained ministers as "hireling priests." Friends were concerned that attendance at rallies or participation in organizations would be interpreted as endorsements of "worldly practices." Although they hated slavery and prayed and worked for its abolition, some Friends struggled to find ways to join in the national movement while retaining their distinctive identities.

Caught in the middle of these debates were many Quaker women who were drawn to the antislavery cause in spite of the uneasiness within the Society of Friends and the opposition of the national antislavery movement. In 1840 the World Anti-Slavery Convention in London denied women the right to participate in the meetings, even though Lucretia Mott had been sent as a delegate. She and Elizabeth Cady Stanton pledged to continue their antislavery work and to link it with their advocacy for the rights of women. They were joined by a number of other women, many of them Quaker, and the result was the Seneca Falls Convention for the Rights of Women, held in 1848. Throughout the next seventy years Quaker women all across the Society made significant contributions to the movement for women's suffrage.

After the Civil War, Quaker women provided much of the leadership in other major social reform movements of the nineteenth and early twentieth centuries. Beginning in 1865 evangelical preacher Rhoda Coffin organized on behalf of women prisoners in Indiana, determined that male guards would no longer be allowed to strip and whip women prisoners "in the presence of as many as wished to look on" (Coffin, 151). After years of lobbying for her cause, she became a "full-fledged woman suffragist" because, since she could not vote, Indiana lawmakers had dismissed her efforts. Quaker women also joined enthusiastically in the temperance movements of the nineteenth and twentieth centuries, both within the Society and through participation in the Woman's Christian Temperance Union.

The education of freed slaves in both the North and the South continued to be a high priority for Quaker women. Involvement in this effort offered them opportunities to use their skills as organizers, teachers, and administrators. Some Friends centered their work in the devastated sections of the South. Martha Schofield from Pennsylvania established a school in Georgia; in Virginia, Emily Howland founded a community for freed slaves, and Alida Clark and her husband Calvin opened a school in Arkansas, which became Southland College. Friends all around the world dedicated themselves to raising the funds necessary to support these educational institutions.

Quaker women worked through committees of concerned Friends, on boards, in the classroom, and as fund-raisers to establish and sustain Friends boarding schools, day schools, and colleges. Rebecca Jones, in the late eighteenth century, was a moving spirit behind the establishment of Westtown, a boarding school for Quaker youth, near Philadelphia. The indomitable Martha Tyson balanced her antislavery work with her commitment to higher education, and in 1869 Swarthmore College opened as a coeducational institution. Tyson made sure that Swarthmore's board included both men and women and that the curricular offerings for male and female students were the same. In 1884 M. Carey Thomas helped to found Bryn Mawr College as a sister institution to Haverford, where only men enrolled.

In the Midwest Quaker colleges were also established, often beginning as boarding schools and then becoming colleges. Malone College (1892) and Wilmington College (established in 1863 as Franklin College and purchased and renamed by the Quakers in 1870) served the Quaker youth of Ohio; Earlham College was established by Indiana Yearly Meeting in 1847; and in 1873 William Penn College was founded in Oskaloosa, Iowa. In 1889 Mary Mendenhall Hobbs succeeded in persuading North Carolina's Women's and Men's Yearly Meetings to join her in funding a residence for women at Guilford College (formerly New Garden Board School) in Greensboro, North Carolina. In the West, Friends founded Whittier College in California (1887), Friends University in Kansas (1898), and George Fox College in Oregon (1891). All of these schools were coeducational and included both men and women on their faculties. The full story of the contributions of women to Quaker higher education has not yet been told.

Theological/Cultural Splits

During the first half of the nineteenth century, North American Friends went through a period of theological upheaval. In 1827 there was a major split into two factions, each claiming to be the true heirs of early Friends. The debate initially centered around a Friend named Elias Hicks, who was born in New York in 1748. He was a recognized minister, strongly antislavery, and deeply attentive to the inner workings of the Spirit in his own soul. Hicks traveled and preached among Friends for decades before his views were considered controversial. He did not value theological reasoning or training because he feared that it was based on outward knowledge. He preached that all authentic knowledge came instead from the Inner Teacher, the ultimate source of truth.

Early in the 1820s some Friends, calling themselves "Orthodox," began to raise questions about Hicks's views, and the debates that followed were fierce. In 1827 the followers of Hicks withdrew from Philadelphia

Yearly Meeting and began to hold separate sessions. The split spread to Baltimore, New York, Ohio, and Indiana Yearly Meetings. Particularly distressing was the split Ohio Yearly Meeting in 1828 at Mount Pleasant, where something like a riot took place.

Understanding the Hicksite/Orthodox separation is made more complicated by factions within each side. Among the Hicksites were those Quietists Friends who advocated a lifestyle oriented around total reliance on the Inner Christ. Joining them were other followers of Hicks who accused the Orthodox of seeking to impose creeds that would constrain intellectual and spiritual freedom of Friends. Among the Orthodox Friends were those influenced by the emerging evangelical theologies of the day, as well as those who believed that Hicksites were dangerously close to Unitarians in their beliefs. Interpretations of these complex debates vary among scholars, but all agree that the divisions were distressing and painful.

The next series of theological conflicts that divided Friends erupted in 1854, influenced by Joseph John Gurney, an evangelical English Friend who traveled throughout North America especially among "Orthodox" Quakers. Some Friends began to incorporate aspects of Gurney's theology in their preaching and teaching and adopted practices similar to those used by other evangelical groups, such as revivals, prepared sermons, and hymns during worship. Their opponents followed the teachings of John Wilbur, a Quaker farmer from Rhode Island. "Wilburites" withdrew and formed their own small and inwardly focused Quaker groups. The result was a major schism within the "Orthodox" branch of the Society. As Holiness theology flourished and revivals spread, "Gurneyite" Friends began to predominate in the Midwest and the West, while "Wilburite" Friends were found mainly in Iowa, Virginia, North Carolina, and Ohio.

Despite the upheaval, the separations that fragmented Friends in the nineteenth century may not have been a "tragedy" for Quaker women (Nancy Hewitt, "The Fragmentations of Friends: The Consequences for Quaker Women in Antebellum America," in Brown and Stuard). Certainly Quaker women's roles in all branches of Friends continued to develop and expand as families migrated into the Midwest, the Plains, and the Northwest and Southwest. In 1858 Western Yearly Meeting's list of twenty-eight ministers included the names of thirteen women. Among them was Margaret Cox, whose gifts of ministry were recorded in 1859. Noted for the "quiet dignity of her bearing" and the "kindness of her heart," she was a prophetic speaker whose words were "ever so plain and pointed." Similarly, Iowa Yearly Meeting encouraged women to work in ministry and to accept positions of responsibility. In the first fifteen years, 110 ministers were recorded, with 43 of them women.

Between 1867 and 1878 there were 80 recorded ministers in Iowa Yearly Meeting, and of them 36 were women. In 1901 the General Superintendent of the Yearly Meeting wrote approvingly of the work of "thirty-two women who have been in the pastoral relations this past year." He concludes his report with words of encouragement for women in ministry and refers to the "well recognized fact" that both men and women can be called by God to this work.

The pattern of Quaker women's involvement in all forms of leadership continued as Friends moved westward to California and Oregon. Quaker minister Friends traveled throughout California in the 1860s, and by 1895, when California Yearly Meeting was established, nearly half of all pastors were women. When Oregon Yearly Meeting was set off by Iowa Yearly Meeting in 1891, a number of women from other Yearly Meetings served as traveling ministers. Rebecca Mendenhall Lewis and her husband David Lewis from Ohio settled there, as did Mary B. Pinkham, who came in 1870 for several weeks and returned in 1873. Rebecca Clawson and Elizabeth and Nathan White, all from Indiana Yearly Meeting, followed in 1874. The first session of Oregon Yearly Meeting was held in 1893 at Newberg, and women and men were equally represented in the committees of the Yearly Meeting, as well as among the visitors from other Yearly Meetings. In subsequent years Friends in Oregon continued to be served by "earnest, devoted, sanctified, consecrated men and women" who served as pastors throughout the Yearly Meeting. As with other Yearly Meetings the leadership was shared between men and women. However, in Oregon there never was a separate Women's Meeting for Business. Women participated in all aspects of Yearly Meeting life, but males filled the leadership positions. As the nineteenth century concluded, the Society of Friends was spread across the continent—and across a theological spectrum from liberal to conservative.

Turning Point—and Move toward Unity

In 1886 a group of Quaker leaders decided to address the growing tensions among Friends, with the goal of finding unity around key ideas of faith and practice. They invited Friends from London, New England, Baltimore, North Carolina, Ohio, Indiana, Western, Iowa, Canada, and Kansas Yearly Meetings to send representatives to a national conference. Two of the issues on the agenda involved the roles of women within the Society: missions and pastoral ministry.

North American Friends had begun foreign missionary work in the mid-nineteenth century when Sybil and Eli Jones of Maine traveled on behalf of Friends to Liberia in 1851, then to Syria in 1869, where they founded a school for girls in Ramallah. Similarly, Indiana Yearly

Meeting sent missionaries to Mexico in the 1870s, and other groups began to discuss whether Friends should establish a centralized missions committee to coordinate these efforts. Women's missionary groups had begun to meet in the 1880s, and some Friends were uneasy with that idea.

The desire for a pastoral ministry system among Friends emerged in the latter half of the nineteenth century, as some Quaker ministers began to attract large numbers of new adherents to the Quaker faith. Concern for the spiritual nurture of Quaker communities gave rise to discussions about establishing some form of paid and settled Quaker ministry. Some Friends began to wonder whether a pastoral system would continue to include both women and men.

Although the role of women at the 1887 conference has never been fully explored, they were well represented. Mahala Jay of Indiana Yearly Meeting presided at the clerks' table with Timothy Nicholson, and thirty-two of the eighty-six delegates from North American Yearly Meetings were women. The six members of the special delegation from Britain included two women. As Friends struggled to discern the best ways to remain faithful to their traditions and also to move into the future, they began to articulate their differing understandings of appropriate gender roles. Quaker women voiced opinions on all sides of the issues.

Friends discussed at length the question of separate women's missionary groups versus a joint and centralized committee on mission. Eliza Armstrong Cox of Western Yearly Meeting shared her vision for a national Quaker women's missionary organization that would be parallel to those found in other Protestant groups. Samuel Rogers of Canada Yearly Meeting applauded the example of the women Friends of Canada, whose diligence and creativity in missionary work had brought new life and energy to the Yearly Meeting during the early decades of their struggles. Mary Whitall Thomas of Baltimore Yearly Meeting, while somewhat attracted to the idea of Quaker women working together, pleaded with Friends to resist the idea of separate missions organizations. She argued that such a step would make Friends too much like other religious groups, where women were relegated to the margins of power and position. Other Friends, both male and female, responded with ardent appeals in support of women's organizations, not as a substitute for joint efforts but as additional ways to serve God.

Another issue under debate was the possibility of a paid pastoral system. Some expressed misgivings about Quaker participation in any sort of public preaching ministry, while others described the spiritual hunger of those newly attracted to Friends and the urgent need for pastoral care from a settled, rather than an itinerant, minister. Charles Hutchinson of Iowa Yearly Meeting

expressed uneasiness with the idea of women in the role of public minister, claiming that he "never knew of a woman being employed to do a man's work, except a man first backed down and left it for her to do" (Hutchinson, *Proceedings,* 118). Mary Whitall Thomas of Baltimore Yearly Meeting linked the trend toward the pastoral system with the idea of a centralized Quaker organization and claimed that both would undermine women's leadership possibilities over time. She reminded her listeners that "women among Friends hold a totally different position from women of every other church," (Thomas, *Proceedings,* 127) so they did not need to appropriate tactics from other Christian groups. Mary S. Thomas, also from Baltimore, argued that adopting a pastoral system would eventually lead Friends to establish a seminary for training ministers. A seminary, she implied, would automatically exclude women. Other friends feared that the pastoral system would damage the potential for women serving in ministry, since "large congregations will want men for their pastors" (Jay, *Proceedings*). Esther Frame, widely known for her successful preaching within Indiana and Ohio, argued forcefully on behalf of "the woman question," claiming that women as well as men were called to follow the Great Commission given at the end of Matthew's gospel (*Proceedings, 10th month 13th, 1887*).

Throughout these debates, some Friends opposed any innovation as a betrayal of traditional Quaker faith and practice, while others advocated openness to the workings of the Holy Spirit. By the conclusion of the conference, a statement of Christian principles, called the Richmond Declaration of Faith, was accepted. Friends also approved the possibility of Quaker missions, including separate women's organizations that would work jointly with a centralized Quaker missionary effort. The idea of Quaker pastors also received support, although many Friends continued to operate with no paid ministers.

Aftermath of the Richmond Conference

Every five years after the 1887 conference, Friends gathered for similar conferences, each time widening their circle of inclusion. In 1902 an official organization was established, called "Five Years Meeting." Its goal was to bring together Friends from across the continent and around the world and to offer them opportunities for fellowship, support, and encouragement. The transcripts from these gatherings include full texts of prepared speeches and also debates among Friends as they struggled to discover how to be faithful to Quaker traditions and also to respond to the world around them. Women were present as representatives to Five Years Meetings, but their voices gradually fell silent during many of the key debates. Most Meetings who joined in Five Years

Meetings began to hire pastors and adopt other innovations in worship practices and theological expression, with the hope of combining the prophetic zeal of the earliest Quaker decades with the evangelical revivals of the day. These Meetings became known as "programmed" or "pastoral" and were found mainly in the Midwest and the West.

Many Meetings continued to worship without pastors or liturgy. Often these Friends were attracted to liberal theological ideas, such as historical/critical methods of biblical study and ecumenical and interfaith dialogues. They hoped to renew the Society of Friends by bringing together the inward, mystical journey with the outward movement toward other religious traditions and toward action for social reform. In 1900 Friends General Conference (FGC) was established, made up mainly of Meetings from the eastern United States and some from the Midwest. FGC was centered in Philadelphia and met in alternate years for fellowship and consultation.

Given the wide variety of Quaker groups at the beginning of the twentieth century, the status of women cannot be easily summarized. The *American Friend,* a monthly journal of Five Years Meeting, published a series of articles by Emma Coffin that tell part of the story. She was born in the mid-nineteenth century in Indiana, and she and Charles Coffin were the first couple in Western Yearly Meeting to be married in the "new" style, that is, by a pastoral minister. During her long life she served as a pastor in Iowa, California, and Indiana Yearly Meetings and worked among Friends on committees and as an evangelist. Her articles in the *American Friend* were based on a survey of male leaders within the Yearly Meeting on the subject of women in ministry. What she learned surprised and worried her. Many respondents believed that women were "not strong enough" for pastoral ministry and were more suited to work in Christian education. Others suggested that most Meetings, given the choice, would prefer a man because "men and boys look for qualities in their leader which are not always found in a woman." Coffin pointed out the irony of the situation: Just as women were expanding their spheres of responsibility within other denominations and in society as a whole, Friends, despite their long tradition of equality, were closing doors to women's leadership. She expressed particular discouragement about young women, noting that most of the women in pastoral ministry were over fifty, and that many Meetings did not encourage young women to develop as ministers.

Emma Coffin was not the only person who was worried about the future of women's leadership among Friends as the twentieth century began. In 1919 a letter to the editor of the *American Friend* asked whether the place of women in the church was eroding. The author asked, "Shall [women] have to plead for our rights in the Friends Church as we have in our legislative halls?" Perhaps in response to these expressions of concern about young women and their leadership, a conference focused on women in ministry took place in Richmond, Indiana, during April 1919 at a local meetinghouse. Most of the participants were Earlham College students who came from the three Yearly Meetings (Wilmington, Indiana, and Western) closest to Richmond, although young women from the Richmond community also attended, as did one young woman from the New York Yearly Meeting.

They discussed the history of women's roles in Quaker organizations and were surprised to learn how many current Quaker committees had only one or no women on them. They developed a list of ways that women might be more involved in the leadership of the Society. First on their list was pastoral ministry, since they were "quite clear . . . that there is still a distinct place for women in the ministry, but the call must be direct from God, and trained and developed as much as possible." They also believed that women could serve as pastoral secretaries, teachers, or secretaries of religious education. At the conclusion of their gathering, they developed a letter outlining their concerns and conclusions and sent it to the Deans of Women at Quaker colleges and the women ministers of Indiana, Wilmington, and Western Yearly Meetings.

The impulse toward unity was also powerful during the middle of the century, especially among young Friends, so that by 1955 New York, Baltimore, and Philadelphia Yearly Meetings no longer recognized the old Hicksite/Orthodox/Gurneyite splits. Yearly Meeting minutes of this era indicate that women assumed important leadership positions at all levels of most Quaker organizations. The United Society of Friends Women continued to bring together Quaker women from across the country to work together in supporting missionary efforts around the world and in North America.

Motivated by their commitment to the peace testimony, Quaker women also became active in international organizations, such as the Women's International League for Peace and Freedom, founded in 1919. Emily Greene Balch, on the faculty at Wellesley College, joined the effort out of her concern for social justice and her training as a sociologist. Florence Kelley, also a social worker, and Lucy Biddle Lewis of Philadelphia Yearly Meeting joined Quaker sympathizer Jane Addams in this effort to apply the principles of urban social work to the effort to prevent war.

Beginning in 1917 Friends joined together to form the American Friends Service Committee (AFSC). The initial focus of the organization was to respond to the suffering of families in Europe during World War I and to offer young men alternative service to military participation. During the mid-twentieth century Friends deepened their involvement in addressing the suffering in Europe. Carolena Wood of New York Yearly Meeting traveled to France and then Germany in 1919 with Jane Addams and Alice Hamilton, and eventually the "Quäkerspeisung" fed millions of malnourished German children. Both the Women's International League for Peace and Freedom and the American Friends Service Committee offered Quaker women opportunities for service abroad and within the United States. Alice Shafer, a Friend from Illinois, after hearing Carolena Wood's account of her work in Germany before the war, was inspired to go to Berlin in 1939 to work with the Quaker International center. Shafer returned after World War II, and stayed until 1949. After that she worked all over the world, but mainly in Central America and Brazil, for UNICEF (United Nations International Children's Emergency Fund).

Other national and international Quaker organizations were established in the twentieth century to address particular concerns. In the 1940s Friends began to lobby in Washington, D.C., around Quaker concerns and formed the Friends Committee on National Legislation. Beginning in 1958, the Friends World Committee on Consultation was established to seek unity among Friends all around the world. As with the AFSC, from the beginning women were part of these organizations in leadership roles and in day-to-day work on behalf of others, but the full story of their involvement and contributions over the decades has yet to be told.

Division/Unity in the 1960s, 1970s, 1980s, and 1990s

By the middle of the twentieth century Friends in North America were spread across a broad spectrum of theological and ideological points of view. Some Friends, heirs to the Wilburite point of view, withdrew from the social and political influences as much as possible, retaining the "plain speech" and traditional ways of the earlier Friends. Other groups of Quakers found more in common with the growing evangelical theological and cultural outlook of other conservative Protestants. In 1963 Friends from Ohio, Colorado, Oregon, and California withdrew from Friends United Meeting (formerly Five Years Meeting) to form the Evangelical Friends International, with headquarters in Newburg, Oregon. Although the number of women in pastoral ministry within this branch of Friends declined, women did not disappear from leadership positions, especially in missions and in youth work.

Some Quaker women began to explore the connections between Quakerism and feminism; the complex issues raised by the "culture wars" came to the foreground. Conflicts developed as religious feminism was equated with Goddess worship, witchcraft, and the occult. Secular feminists were portrayed as antifamily, pro-abortion, pro-lesbian, and antireligion. Some Friends, even those who supported the tradition of women's equality with men, concluded that feminism was unnecessary or even dangerous because males and females were forced to engage in struggles that jeopardized the peace testimony. However, many other Friends, both men and women, celebrated the links between the feminism and Quaker traditions and practices. They urged women and men to ground themselves in the Quaker ideal of being "helpsmeet" to one another and to join in the movement for women's liberation.

Efforts to address the disunity among Friends continued, despite the ongoing tensions. In 1963 a Quaker seminary was founded at Earlham College to train all types of leaders for the Society of Friends. Although women students were rare in the earliest years of the school, during the 1970s this began to change, and by the 1980s the enrollment of women at the Earlham School of Religion reached 50 percent, where it has remained. Courses in feminist theology and an atmosphere that encouraged the ministries of women became part of the school's identity. Beginning in 1972, *Quaker Religious Thought,* an occasional journal, published articles by Quaker scholars across a wide theological spectrum. Over time the work of Quaker women scholars has been included in this journal.

In 1975 a group of young Quaker women toured some of the Yearly Meetings in North America as a "Quaker Youth Caravan." They engaged Friends in a series of dialogues about sexism and related issues, sparking serious conversations about gender, feminism, and power relations within the Society of Friends.

Among the women of Friends United Meeting, an organization known as "Quaker Women in Public Ministry" began in the 1980s, with the goal of offering support and encouragement to women engaged in any form of public ministry. Local groups meet regularly for support, and a number of national conferences took place in the 1980s and 1990s.

The occasional publication *The Friendly Woman* has been providing an outlet for Quaker feminists to share their views. The task of editing *The Friendly Woman* has rotated among a number of Quaker feminist groups around the country, and this shared approach has built a strong community of care and concern. During the sessions of Friends General Conference, beginning in the 1980s Quaker feminists came together to establish a Womyn's Center, a safe place for women to gather, sing, worship, pray, talk, and make connections. Strong and supportive friendships have been forged through these annual gatherings, and currently FGC women are discussing how to continue this tradition into the future.

Conclusions

The tradition of Quaker women's leadership is embedded in the history of Friends and has been a powerful factor as Friends migrated across North America and made their contributions to life on this continent. Nevertheless, at times Quaker women's voices have been muffled, their leadership has been thwarted, and their contributions have been discounted. A full exploration and analysis of how and why this happened will require more extensive searching of the minutes of Yearly Meetings and other Quaker organizations, the publications (including "Letters to the Editor") of monthly publications, and the diaries and journals of Quaker women across the country and the theological spectrum.

Some of the silencing came from within the Society and can be seen, for example, in the debates surrounding Hannah Barnard in the eighteenth century. She was thought to be a "headstrong" woman who was unwilling to defer to the elders of London Yearly Meeting and the leaders of Hudson Monthly Meeting. Although Lucretia Mott, in the nineteenth century, was recognized as a minister of long standing, she was also criticized and even disciplined by Hicksite Quakers for her radical views on political and theological matters and her forthright tone. Other Quaker women antislavery activists, like Abby Kelley Foster, left the Society of Friends in frustration. Quaker women have sometimes appeared to silence themselves. Mary Sibbitt, the temperance activist known as the "Kansas Cyclone," declared, after sitting through the sessions of Five Years Meeting in 1902, that her "heart was pained" at their silence and reminded them that "we cannot complain that the brothers do not give us a chance" (*Proceedings*, 322–324)

Although no one explanation suffices for the erosion of women's equality within the Society of Friends, perhaps it can be partly explained by some of the peculiarities of Friends' theology and organization. From the earliest days, Friends have expressed their view of the Christian gospel using a variety of words and concepts. They have not insisted on the use of any one combination of those words and have disavowed creedal statements altogether. In the absence of creeds, Meetings have relied on "seasoned Friends" to teach Quaker thought and to model Quaker traditions for both newcomers and each new generation. When there were not enough experienced Friends to accomplish this, a Monthly Meeting could easily drift toward borrowing the theological views and expressions found in other religious groups in the neighborhood. This may explain the wide variety of beliefs and practices that developed, over time, among Friends.

Ecclesiastically Friends have avoided hierarchical structures, such as may be found in other religious bodies, that can enforce discipline from a national level toward the local group. If a Monthly Meeting or other Quaker body appropriated beliefs or practices that departed from Friends' traditions, there was no accepted way to challenge those innovations, beyond disputes and separations.

Perhaps the mystery can be explained more simply: Friends became more like "the world's people" during their migration across the United States. They had to compete with other Protestant groups for followers, and maybe, especially in the climate of revivals and the rise of evangelical theological views, the presence of women in the pulpit and in leadership was perceived as embarrassing and a hindrance to the future of the Society of Friends.

Recent developments suggest that in the twenty-first century women's leadership roles are expanding all across the spectrum of Friends in North America. The *Friendly Woman* continues to be published monthly, giving opportunities for Quaker feminists to write and to be published. In 1990 the Earlham School of Religion cosponsored an international gathering at Woodbrooke in Birmingham, England, where seventy-two Quaker women from all theological perspectives met for ten days to learn together and to celebrate the theological diversity and unity of women in leadership among Friends. Women who attended that conference continue to explore their expanded vision for Quaker women's futures and the futures for all women.

Whether they risk being called "women's libbers," are labeled as "divisive and strident," or are accused of witchcraft, Quaker women in North America continue to speak up, and because of their courage and creativity, all sorts of new and renewed conversations are becoming possible. For example, two groups of Quaker women living in the Pacific Northwest have been gathering regularly for discussion and fellowship for more than ten years. This "Multwood Group" consists of women from Reedwood Friends Church, affiliated with Evangelical Friends International, and Multnomah Friends Meeting, an unprogrammed, nonpastoral Meeting. In their conversations they are discovering the beliefs and hopes they hold in common despite their differences and are celebrating their new awareness of the common tradition of empowerment that undergirds all Quaker women.

SOURCES: Early writings by Quaker women can be found in Mary Garman, Judith Applegate, Margaret Benefiel, and Dortha Meredith, eds., *Hidden in Plain Sight: Quaker Women's Writings, 1650–1700* (1996). Margaret Fell's *Women's Speaking Justified* has been recently republished (1980). Her collected letters, *Undaunted Zeal*, edited by Elsa F. Glines, were published in 2003. The story of Hannah Barnard is told in "A Narrative of the proceedings in America of the Society called Quakers, in the case of Hannah Barnard" (1804). Lucretia Mott's speeches and sermons can be found in *Lucretia Mott, Her Complete Speeches and Sermons,* edited by Dana Greene (1980). *Selected Letters of Lucretia Coffin Mott,* edited by Beverly Wilson Palmer, was published in 2002. A wealth of material by and about Quaker women can be found in archives and collections of Quaker colleges and organizations. For an overview of Quaker women in North America, see *Mothers of Feminism,* by Margaret Hope Bacon (1986). Bacon has also edited a collection of travel journals, *Wilt Thou Go on My Errand?* (1994). Rebecca Larson, in *Daughters of Light: Quaker Women Preaching and Prophesying in the Colonies and Abroad, 1700–1775* (1999), synthesizes the accomplishments of these remarkable women with the historical context. *Witnesses for Change* (1989), edited by Elisabeth Potts Brown and Susan Mosher Stuard, includes essays and documents relating to Quaker women. Emma Lapsansky has summarized the issues in "New Eyes for the 'Invisibles' in Quaker–Minority Relations," *Quaker History,* 90.1 (Spring 2001): 1–7. A conference held at Guilford College resulted in *The Influence of Quaker Women on American History: Biographical Studies* (1986), edited by John Stoneburner and Carol Stoneburner. Other sources include: Joseph Besse, *Collection of the Sufferings of the People Called Quakers,* vol. 1 (1753); Mary Coffin Johnson, ed., *Rhoda Coffin, Her Reminiscences Addresses, Papers, and Ancestry* (1910); George Fox, *An Encouragement to All Women's-Meetings in the World* (1676); and Robert Barclay, Proposition 3, "The Scriptures," *Apology* (1678).

WOMEN IN REFORMED CHURCHES
Rebecca Button Prichard

THE REFORMED CHURCHES in North America trace their family roots to the Swiss Reformation of the sixteenth century. The Zurich reformer Ulrich Zwingli held much in common with both the Lutheran and the Radical reformations, yet stood somewhat apart from them in theology, biblical interpretation, and political approach. Zwingli and Luther tilled the soil for a new generation of reformers, including the French-born theologian John Calvin. Calvin's reforming activity in Geneva and Strasbourg gave rise to those churches with Reformed roots, sprouting first in Europe—Scotland, France, Germany, and the Netherlands—then spreading to far-flung colonies, including those in North America. Then, as now, Reformed women did what they could to further the faith, to serve God, and to bear witness in both private and public spheres.

The marks of the early Calvinist churches are still important to Reformed Christians today. Reformed faith is rooted in the Word of God, both its preaching and its practice. The sermon is central to worship in these churches. Reformed Christians were urged to study the Bible in their own language, and mothers taught the faith to their children. For Calvin and his colleagues, scripture was of primary importance in teaching believers what they need to know to live the life of faith—more important than church tradition or human knowledge and experience. For Reformed women, this reliance on scripture has been both blessing and bane, depending on interpretation, for women's voices have been both encouraged and silenced by biblical teaching. Among the Reformed churches in North America there are communions that ordain women as leaders and those that still forbid any official role.

Calvin's majestic theology, laid out in the *Institutes of the Christian Religion*, has shaped the way Reformed Christians view all kinds of relationships, including the roles of women in church and society. God is Creator of all, mighty, transcendent. All creation, including human life, is designed for God's praise and glory. God sustains the created order and calls believers into faithful relationship with their Creator and one another. There is an ordered beauty to creation, yet human sin has contributed to the brokenness and confusion of that order. God offers mediation through Jesus Christ and spiritual power in the person of the Holy Ghost. Calvin's theology allowed for the possibility of women's involvement in church and world, but he was certainly no champion of women's leadership. By allowing for marriage among the clergy, women were offered new roles in church and home, albeit limited. An emphasis on the priesthood of all believers gave women a new kind of spiritual status within church and society. Calvin's reforms were supported and financed by women of wealth and power.

Calvin's Geneva was an experiment in Christian community. Reformers in Geneva and in other Reformed cities, such as Strasbourg, sought to reform both church and society. Reformed cities were safe havens for Protestant refugees fleeing persecution in Catholic regions. Calvinists in Scotland, Switzerland, Germany, and the Netherlands wanted to order society on Protestant principles, which they saw as less hierarchical than those of medieval Christendom. From the beginning, Reformed women took their part in serving the poor and needy, in educating the young, and in supporting the work of reformation. At times strong women, such as Katherine Zell in Strasbourg, and Marie Dentiere in Geneva, took on public roles, speaking out and bearing witness to their newfound faith.

From these early roots, Reformed Protestantism began to branch out. Reformers such as John Knox in Scotland, Martin Bucer in Strasbourg, Thomas Cranmer in England, and Guido de Bres in the Netherlands were all influenced by the teachings of Calvin. Yet the cultural contexts of these leaders shaped the churches that emerged in these diverse places. Politics and power had as much influence as the personalities involved. By the

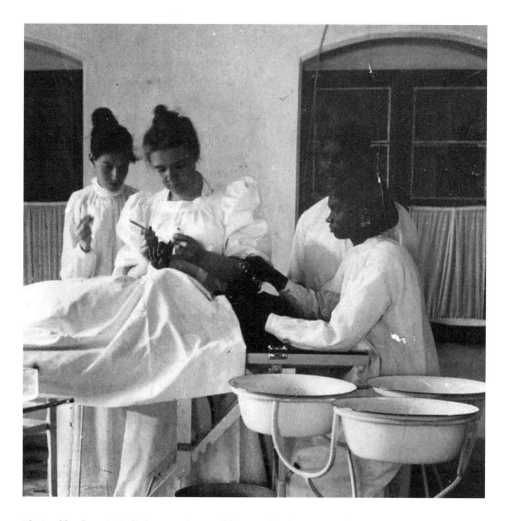

Ida Scudder, born in India in 1870, is a notable example of a woman called by God to minister outside traditional roles. After graduating from Dwight L. Moody's Northfield Seminary in Massachusetts, she went back to India as a short-term missionary. Ida had no intention of staying in India, yet one night, while caring for her ill mother, three Indian men—two Hindus and a Muslim—came to her, begging her to help their wives in childbirth. Their religions forbade male doctors from treating female patients. All three women died. Ida Scudder returned to the United States and became a doctor in order to serve the women of India. *Courtesy of Vellore Christian Medical College Board, New York City.*

end of the sixteenth century, Reformed churches were established in these and other places. Though all traced their roots to Calvin, they expressed their faith in a variety of forms—in worship, in doctrine, and in the ordering of their common life.

Whereas the Lutherans found a common statement of faith in the Augsburg Confession, it was typical of Reformed Christians to set forth their beliefs within a particular context. Reformed confessions proliferated in the sixteenth century, and no one document took precedence. The Scots Confession, the Belgic Confession, the Heidelberg Catechism, the First and Second Helvetic Confessions, the Confession of Geneva, even the Thirty-

Nine Articles of the Church of England reflected the influence of Calvin's teachings in a variety of cultural contexts. The First Helvetic Confession summarizes well a kind of tolerance within the Reformed family: "We wish in no way to prescribe for all churches through these articles a single rule of faith. . . . We agree with whoever agrees with this, although he [*sic*] uses different expressions from our Confession" (Leith, *Creeds of the Churches*, 127–128).

The urge to order belief and yet to allow for differences has become a reason for the continued branching out of the Reformed family. Often when there has been a move toward tolerance and ecumenism, there has been a remnant that chose tradition and order. Virtually all Reformed churches are representative and nonepiscopal in polity (though bishops govern the Hungarian Reformed Church); their doctrine is based on historic confessional statements. Presbyterian and Reformed churches share a polity that is based on a kind of representative democracy that sees the local congregation as part of a larger church organization. Other churches within the Reformed family prefer a more congregational polity. Laity and clergy share in the leadership and government of the Reformed churches. The tension between tolerance and tradition is reflected also in a tension between ecumenism and conservatism within the Reformed churches. It is not surprising that women's leadership has been valued in those Reformed communities that also value tolerance and ecumenism and that generally the more traditional remnant churches are less open to women's leadership.

Jean-Jacques Bauswein and Lukas Vischer, in their summary of the Reformed family, use the terms "Reformed," "Presbyterian," "Congregational," "Evangelical," and "United" to describe the variety of churches worldwide that are part of the family (*The Reformed Family Worldwide*). These terms refer to the family roots, to the organizational structure, and to the theological outlook of these churches. In their survey, they list eighteen Reformed denominations in Canada and forty-five in the United States. These include large mainline denominations and small "remnant" churches that have either split or refused to join unions. Most of these smaller communions do not allow for the ordination of women as ministers, although some allow for female deacons or elders. Still, women take an active part in the lives of these churches even when their official leadership roles are limited.

Those Reformed denominations that ordain women as ministers include all the larger mainline churches—the Reformed Church in America, the Presbyterian Church (USA), the United Church of Canada, and the United Church of Christ. The Christian Church (Disciples of Christ) also has roots within the Reformed tradition, but their noncreedal approach raises some question as to just where they fit in the family tree. Within these denominations are included the present-day offspring of Dutch, Scottish, English, German, French, and Swiss Reformed ancestors. The history of these North American churches is the history of the search for religious freedom, the transplanting of European culture and faith in the New World, and the struggle of women and men of faith to continue reforming both church and society. Included here are stories of women in a variety of these churches—Presbyterian, Reformed, and Congregational, including those that still limit the roles women can play, for Reformed women have found ways

to minister and serve in both official and unofficial ways in all these churches.

Matrones and Ministers' Wives

In the sixteenth century, Reformed theology and preaching found followers among women of many walks of life; queens, duchesses, refugees, and widows were among the faithful. Queens and noblewomen played public roles, as *matrones* (women of means), within the Reformed movement. The wives of pastors and reformers often played important roles. It is difficult to find evidence that female deacons served (at least officially) in Calvin's Geneva, but there are early instances of deaconesses, especially among the widows. The biblical account of Mary and Martha, which gives credence to a kind of ministry of hospitality, together with Paul's teachings about the widows' ministry of service, gave scriptural backing to possible diaconal roles women might play. The flow of refugees to Geneva, Strasbourg, and other Reformed havens demanded a network of caring and compassion. Women were called upon to open their homes and hearts as well as their purses.

Naturally, women of means continued to support their churches and the causes that grew out of their Reformed faith. In North America, a number of notable women contributed time, money, and support to Reformed institutions. Nettie McCormick, wife of Cyrus, who made his fortune in farm equipment, was involved in the support of McCormick Seminary in Chicago. Margaret Sage and Louise Carnegie, both Reformed churchwomen, gave money to mission, to the arts, and to educational institutions. Jane B. Smith, wife of Johnson C. Smith, supported the college that bears her husband's name, now a Presbyterian seminary, part of the Interdenominational Theological Center in Atlanta, which continues to train large numbers of African American leaders for the ministry.

The sixteenth-century Reformers began to question the traditional church teachings regarding sexuality and sin, which included the denigration of women as "carnal" and sexual intercourse as a necessary evil. In order to put into practice these changing views, Protestant pastors actually went into convents seeking converts; many newly "liberated" nuns became the wives of these reformers. Martin Bucer led many Strasbourg pastors to the altar, and he eventually convinced Calvin himself to marry the widow Idelette de Bure.

While many have noted that the move from the cloister to the kitchen was hardly "liberating," the role of pastor's wife within the Reformed communities carried with it some measure of freedom, power, and possibility for ministry. In most Protestant traditions including the Reformed, the role of pastor's wife, until recently, has been one of the few visible (albeit limited) positions available to gifted women. Although this new wifely role had its limitations, many of these women were strong characters who found ways to minister within the new domain they had been given. Wives and mothers were responsible for the Christian education of their children, for the spiritual nurture of the domestic realm. Certain ministerial duties that had often been carried on by women—caring for children, for the sick, for the welfare of the poor and the refugees—continued within the Reformed communities.

Katherine Zell, wife of Strasbourg pastor Matthew Zell, stands out as a great foremother for all the Reformed women who married pastors and served the church in this wifely role. She opened her home to refugees and students; she established a ministry to the infirm, including lepers; she had the courage to stand up to both church and civic patriarchs in calling for better conditions for the poor and sick. The ambiguous, limited, but very real power of the pastor's wife, of the caretaker of the domestic realm, has been available to Reformed women even in those churches where ordination remains unimaginable.

Sarah Edwards (b. 1710), wife of the famous Puritan preacher Jonathan Edwards (b. 1703), was a woman who exemplifies this wifely role. Sarah Pierrepont came from a family full of clergy and was the daughter of the minister of the Congregational Church in New Haven, Connecticut. She and Jonathan met there in 1723, when he was a graduate student and tutor at Yale. Jonathan was an only son with ten sisters; his mother was the daughter of a clergyman. In a famous description of Sarah, Edwards wrote: "She is of a wonderful sweetness, calmness and universal benevolence of mind" (Dodds). Sarah was well read, as well educated as a girl could be in those days. Some of the books she gave her husband influenced his thought. They married when she was seventeen and he was twenty-four, on July 28, 1727.

Shortly after their marriage, Jonathan became the pastor, "a learned, orthodox minister," for the new settlement in Northampton, Massachusetts. New England congregations paid close attention and scrutiny to the minister's wife. The Edwards had eleven children, the first a daughter, Sarah, born on August 25, 1728. All their children lived, remarkable in an age when infant mortality was high. Sarah was resourceful and taught her daughters the arts of homemaking. She was also known for her hospitality to strangers, and a steady stream of houseguests joined their family. Life in Northampton was demanding. Physical exhaustion, melancholy, and depression came upon her at times. Sarah went through a kind of conversion experience in January 1742, brought on by apparent depression followed by a spiritual awakening. Edwards describes Sarah's mystical ex-

perience as life changing. Sarah herself wrote these words about it: "I had for some time earnestly been wrestling with God. . . . I felt within myself great quietness of spirit, unusual . . . willingness to wait upon him, with respect to the time and manner in which he should help me, and wished that he should take his own time and his own way to do it" (Dodds, 97).

Eventually a series of controversies arose in the Northampton church surrounding Edwards's participation in the Great Awakening, his desire for a greater salary, and jealousy of Sarah among the widows of the town. Despite other offers, Jonathan wanted to remain a Congregationalist pastor, so they went to Stockbridge, Massachusetts. Their daughter Esther was married to Aaron Burr, who became the president of the College of New Jersey, later Princeton. When Burr died in 1757, Edwards agreed to become president but died of smallpox shortly thereafter, on March 22, 1758, as did their daughter Esther. While Sarah was arranging to take charge of the Burr children, she also passed on, of dysentery, on October 2, 1758. The descendants of Jonathan and Sarah Edwards include many ministers and missionaries.

Traditional role models have continued to shape the expectations of the pastor's wife in a variety of Protestant churches including the Reformed. The women's movement and the opening up of ordination to women have challenged these traditional expectations in the last fifty years. One well-known Presbyterian minister's wife who struggled with these changes is Catherine Marshall.

Catherine Marshall is best known through her writings, including the biography of her famous husband Peter, a Scottish immigrant who was pastor of New York Avenue Presbyterian Church in Washington, D.C. Catherine's own writings, especially autobiographical works such as *To Live Again*, tell of the drastic change in her life when her husband died. Peter Marshall espoused traditional roles for men and women in the church and in marriage. In a famous sermon, he sets forth those values: "No woman ever became lovelier by losing her essential femininity . . . to be sweet is far better than to be sophisticated. America needs young women who will build true homes." As a faithful wife and mother and homemaker, the Christian woman, "will know that she is carrying out the plan of God" (Boyer, 255).

As the pastor's wife, Catherine was called to embody those values. The literature of that time documents a great malaise among pastors' wives in living up to the expectations placed on them by the parish. In *A Man Called Peter*, Catherine wrote, "To say that the pastor's helpmate was expected to be gracious, charming, poised, equal to every occasion, would be a gross understatement. . . . There is a very real sense in which a church feels that its minister and his wife belong to *them*, and they want to be proud of their possession" (Boyer, 260). Yet Catherine sought to live up to these expectations, and found great fulfillment in her marriage.

As a widow and a single mother, however, Catherine's financial situation was, at first, precarious. Her successful writing career forced her to wrestle with the conflict between the traditional values she held as a pastor's wife and the vocational satisfaction she gained as an independent woman. She speaks of the gratification of her new work: "I began to experience the deep satisfaction and inner contentment known only to those who have found the right vocational spot. . . . It was as if I had come home to my own element" (Boyer, 265). Yet throughout her life she continued to long for the wholeness she had found in marriage.

It seems that Christian women, including Reformed women, have continued to wrestle with the conflicting demands that are placed on them in terms of traditional role expectations and the new opportunities that have opened up for women in church and society. Reformed Christians are not of one mind on how this struggle is to be resolved.

Missionaries

The role of the *matrones* carried over into the support of domestic and foreign missions of the church. Mission activity was a hallmark of most Christian churches, including the Reformed, during the nineteenth century. Women were at the forefront of the missionary movement, both at home and abroad. Women lent their financial support to those who served, and missionary societies sprang up throughout Europe and North America. A number of notable Reformed women stand out as great supporters of mission. Mrs. Sarah Doremus, of the South Reformed Church in New York City, appealed to women of all denominations to support mission. Opening her home for meetings and speakers, she became the first president of the Women's Union Missionary Society for Heathen Lands. Another notable Dutch Reformed woman was Mrs. Paul Van Cleef, who became the president of the Women's Executive Committee of the Board of Domestic Missions.

Among the German Reformed, a similar pattern emerged. Women became excited about mission and used their resources to support it—even in the face of opposition. In 1878, Sarah Herlacher of Hazleton, Pennsylvania, was among a group of German Evangelical women who wanted to form a mission society. The male leaders of their church forbade it. Sarah was quoted as saying, "Well, they cannot prevent our gathering funds and praying for such an organization" (Leith, *Reminiscences*, 15). The commitment of these women to pray and to pay for mission at home and abroad paved the

way for what is now the World Day of Prayer, an ecumenical observance of Church Women United.

It has been noted that the missionary movement closely paralleled the Victorian urge toward colonialism. Some have felt that Christian society effectively imposed its values on native peoples in the name of "civilizing" them. In retrospect, we see certain problems associated with this movement, not the least of which was shoring up traditional role models in which women's sphere of influence was limited to marriage, home, and children.

An example of this urge can be seen in the mission of the Canadian Presbyterians in Trinidad. The East Indian population was made up of slaves from India, many of whom were women. Indian tradition included arranged marriage; young girls were taught wifely ways by their husbands' mothers. This tradition did not carry over into the immigrant community. Women remained largely unschooled, even in domestic affairs. A Canadian Presbyterian, John Morton, came to Trinidad from Nova Scotia in 1868 and joined with others, including Scottish Presbyterians, to minister to the East Indian people. John's wife Sarah eventually took up the work of educating young girls, with a primary purpose of developing Christian wives and mothers, effectively taking the place of the Indian mother-in-law.

The Mortons developed both a school and a home for young East Indian women. Their hope was to provide wives for the teachers and catechists among the mission staff. Normally graduation from the school coincided with marriage. The home was closed in 1909 when Sarah Morton retired, but the work was continued by another Canadian missionary, Adella Archibald. Under her leadership, the emphasis began to change from grooming Christian wives to the general education of girls in Trinidad. Archibald established a home in Iere to the south. As times changed and education for girls expanded, academic excellence became increasingly important, a development that paralleled the British influence on the educational system in Trinidad. Over the years, the Women's Missionary Society in Canada, and later, the United Church of Canada, continued to supervise this educational mission. In time, the early emphasis on traditional female roles gave way to more modern thinking, and with Trinidad's independence in 1961, the Canadian and British patterns were replaced with a resurgence of Caribbean identity.

The women's missionary movement can also be seen as sowing the seeds of feminism, of opening to women ways to serve God not previously available to them. There are some remarkable stories, in various traditions, including the Reformed, that tell of the women who supported missions, overseas and at home, and also of the women who were called to serve as missionaries, sometimes in nontraditional roles. We can also see how the women's missionary movement paralleled movements for abolition and suffrage at home and how it paved the way for ecumenical cooperation.

One of the earliest alliances was a partnership between the Congregational, Reformed, and Presbyterian Churches, the American Board of Commissioners for Foreign Mission (ABCFM), founded in 1810. This organization was a successor to cooperative efforts among the Reformed churches as early as 1796. Despite a Calvinist belief in the doctrine of election, which emphasizes divine rather than human initiative in the process of salvation, Reformed missionaries sought to proclaim the good news of the gospel in North America and overseas. Yet it could be said that Reformed missions also placed a strong emphasis on serving human need, seeing service as part and parcel of the proclamation of the gospel.

One of the early missions of the American Board (ABCFM) sent Dr. John Scudder and his wife Harriet to India in 1819 to set up a medical mission. The Scudder family produced several generations of missionaries within the Reformed (Dutch) Church tradition. A granddaughter, Ida Scudder, became a notable example of a woman called by God to minister outside of traditional roles. Ida was born in south India in 1870. After graduating from Dwight L. Moody's Northfield Seminary in Massachusetts, she went back to India as a short-term missionary. Ida had no intention of staying in India, yet one night, while caring for her ill mother, three Indian husbands—two Hindus and a Muslim—came to her, begging her to help their wives in childbirth. Their religion forbade male doctors from treating female patients. All three of the women died, and Ida resolved to return to the United States and become a doctor in order to serve the women of India. After receiving medical training in Philadelphia and New York, she returned to Vellore, India, in 1900, where she established a women's hospital. Over time, Dr. Ida Scudder founded other hospitals and clinics as well as a medical school for women in India. She helped raise large sums of money among Reformed churches in America for this medical mission and her students have carried on her work in south India.

R. Pierce Beaver, in *American Protestant Women in World Mission*, speaks at length of the many single women who were pioneers in missionary service. One of these pioneers was Betsy Stockton, a black slave in the Princeton household of Robert Stockton. When Stockton's daughter Elizabeth married Dr. Ashbel Green, the president of Princeton College, Betsy came to live with them. Dr. Green was a Presbyterian minister and, with his wife, was deeply involved in support of foreign missions. Betsy was given her freedom at age twenty and encouraged by the Greens to serve as a missionary in Lahinah, Hawaii. Records of the American Board

(ABCFM) in 1824 indicate that she was the first single woman, other than a widow, to serve as a missionary overseas. Betsy continued to serve as a teacher and a churchwoman until her death in 1865.

The enthusiasm for mission among nineteenth-century women was not only for overseas mission. A number of notable women served as missionaries in North America. Susan LaFlesche Picotte was the daughter of an Omaha chief, Joseph, who became a Christian under the ministry of a gentle Presbyterian pastor, William Hamilton. Hamilton was particularly careful to work within the Native culture of the Omahas, and the LaFlesche family seemed able to integrate Christianity with their traditional ways. Susan became a doctor and a medical missionary. Like Ida Scudder, she studied at the Women's Medical College in Philadelphia, then returned to Nebraska to serve as a physician among the Omaha people. Susan became a missionary after her husband died, in 1905. She was also the first Indian appointed a medical missionary by the Presbyterian Board of Home Missions. In her ministry among the Omahas, she encountered many of the social issues and health-related problems associated with the changing ways of life brought on by exposure to European American culture. Susan taught public health and worked to build a hospital on the Omaha reservation.

The ABCFM sent "foreign" missionaries to fields in North America as well as overseas. Narcissa Whitman and Eliza Spalding, sent by the ABCFM to the Oregon territory in 1836, were the first white women to cross the Continental Divide. Marcus Whitman was a medical missionary who was introduced to Narcissa by a Presbyterian pastor keen on evangelizing the Indians. The ABCFM preferred married missionaries in teams that included at least one pastor. The Whitmans were accompanied by Henry and Eliza Spalding, Henry being a Presbyterian minister. As it happens, Narcissa had once refused an offer of marriage from Henry, a fact that contributed to difficult relations between the couples over the years.

When the foursome reached the Pacific Northwest, they set up two stations, one with the Nez Percé Indians, in what is now Idaho, and one with the Cayuse, further west. Marcus reluctantly played the role of pastor to the Cayuse, believing their primary mission to be one of service, medicine, and the development of agricultural skills among the Indians. The Whitmans were able to overcome their differences with the Spaldings and with the ABCFM, continuing their mission for over ten years. When an influx of settlers arrived in Oregon, relations with the Cayuse grew more difficult. After an outbreak of measles in 1847, the Whitmans and some of their coworkers were massacred by the Indians. The story of Narcissa Whitman and Eliza Spalding bears testimony to the courage and faith of these women but also to the complex and ambiguous relations that existed between church, board, missionaries, and Natives.

Canadian women also supported and served missions to Native Indians. As in other churches, the Presbyterian Women's Foreign Mission Society (WFMS) raised significant sums of money for mission. The Canadian Presbyterian women were especially successful in their fund-raising activities. As in other places, their work was often done along traditional female lines, "civilizing" the Indians, teaching, and nursing. Two Canadian Presbyterian women, Lucy Baker and Catherine Gillespie, illustrate the changing attitudes toward this approach. Lucy Baker is well known among Canadian Presbyterians for her educational efforts among the Indians in Western Canada. Her work reinforced traditional Victorian values. Her ministry was largely among Native children, teaching them the ways of the English-speaking world. Catherine Gillespie also engaged in mission work with Native Indians on behalf of the Women's Foreign Mission Society. A teacher at first, she also received medical training. She adapted herself to life on the plains, often breaking with traditional female roles. She was an accomplished horsewoman, making dangerous journeys at times to carry out her work. Catherine also took on managerial roles in the mission institutions, normally reserved for males. Together, these women demonstrate a transition in outlook that moved the church to a more critical understanding of missionary efforts. In time, the values of womanhood espoused in the Victorian age gave way to a kind of maternal feminism.

Donaldina Cameron is another Reformed woman who ministered on North American soil. Born in New Zealand, and coming to California as a child, she took up an urban mission among Chinese women in San Francisco. Her mission helped free these young women from prostitution; she worked with police to raid opium dens, brothels, and gambling houses. A Presbyterian mission in San Francisco's Chinatown, Cameron House, still bears her name.

Preachers

Because scripture is the central authority, preaching is pivotal to theology and worship within the Reformed churches. This was a double-edged sword for Reformed women who felt called to preach. Because Congregationalist, Presbyterian, and Dutch Reformed churches tended to take Paul's admonitions about women's silence literally, women's preaching was not always welcome. Yet there were women in these churches who felt called to speak, to teach, and to preach. Some of them were given an opening when they were able to justify their calls with scripture. Some Reformed women left these churches for others that were more open to female preaching.

Among the early Puritans, gender roles were clearly defined. Women's preaching was feared and forbidden among these seventeenth-century Calvinists as evidenced by the story of Ann Hutchinson. Ann was a Puritan woman, living with her husband in Boston, Massachusetts, who felt called to teach and preach. This began with meetings for women in her own home. These gatherings became more and more popular, and after a time men began to attend. Hutchinson was well versed in scripture and felt called by the Holy Spirit to this ministry. Eventually the church and civic leaders sought to censure her, and they succeeded, accusing her of false doctrine and exercising authority over men in a public gathering. She was exiled to Rhode Island, where she experienced a somewhat greater measure of religious freedom. Some of her sympathizers eventually joined with the Quakers.

The revivals in American Protestantism are often associated with the frontier and the religious movements of the lower class, but the middle-class Reformed churches also took part in the renewals referred to as the "Great Awakening." The Puritans, Presbyterians, and Dutch Reformed churches in the northern and middle colonies experienced revivals in the first half of the 1700s that reflected a similar wave of renewal in England and Scotland. These were occasions for spontaneous, Spirit-led preaching by laity and clergy alike, including some laywomen.

A century later, during the Second Great Awakening, a Presbyterian minister, Charles Grandison Finney, encouraged women to speak out about their faith, even in public gatherings. One of his students at Oberlin College was Antoinette Brown, a Congregationalist. On September 15, 1853, she became the first woman ordained in the United States, as pastor in a Congregational Church in South Butler, New York. In 1878, she moved from the Congregational Church to the Unitarian Fellowship.

It is true that there were not as many notable women preachers in the Reformed churches in the eighteenth and nineteenth centuries as there were in more evangelical movements. A stricter emphasis on orthodox theology than on charismatic gifts is one possible reason. Another is the insistence in all these churches on a well-educated clergy; women simply did not have access to seminary education. The Reformed, Presbyterian, and Congregational churches also tended to be middle to upper class in their makeup, a social location that encouraged traditional gender roles and expectations. Yet from church documents we learn that women wanted to preach and did preach in these churches, often causing controversy, dissension, and prohibition.

There were movements from within the Calvinist tradition that seemed to welcome women's preaching more than these mainstream denominations did. Often these women were part of reforming trends, as in the Restoration movement of the early-nineteenth-century American frontier. The Restoration movement began in the early 1800s. A number of Presbyterians, including Barton Stone, who migrated to Kentucky, and Alexander Campbell, ministering in Pennsylvania, became increasingly uncomfortable with the strictures of Calvinism, particularly the kind typified by the Westminster Confession of Faith. They joined with others, including some Baptist Calvinists, to "restore" the church to its earliest roots. The Stone-Campbell movement had at its center an ecumenical urge to move beyond the sectarianism of the Protestant churches. Their movement, which continues today in the Christian Churches, including the Disciples of Christ, is characterized by weekly communion, believers' baptism by immersion, and a strong ministry of the laity. The gifts of women were welcomed early on, though there was some resistance to allowing them to baptize and serve communion.

John and Philip Mulkey were Calvinist Baptists who began to question the doctrine of predestination, eventually leading their Kentucky congregations into the movement that the renegade Presbyterians, Stone and Campbell, had begun, rejecting human creeds and seeking to restore the church to its New Testament origins. One of the Mulkey daughters, Nancy, was a particularly powerful preacher—"a woman moved, and surely by the power of the Holy Ghost, to speak to the people," wrote Joseph Thomas in 1810, who was "astonished at her flow of speech and consistency of ideas" (Harrison, 24). Another eyewitness describes Nancy Mulkey's preaching:

> The youngest daughter in this remarkable family was a shouter, as then called. . . . She would arise with zeal on her countenance and fire in her eyes, and with a pathos that showed the depth of her soul, and would pour forth an exhortation lasting from five to fifteen minutes, which neither father nor brother could equal, and which brought tears from every feeling eye. (24)

Another frontier movement that seemed ready to welcome women's preaching was the Cumberland Presbyterian Church. This church began as a revival movement in the early 1800s, with concerns similar to those of the Restoration movement. In 1906, some of the Cumberland Presbyterians joined with the United Presbyterians, but a separate Cumberland Presbyterian Church continues today. In 1889, the Presbytery of Nolin, Kentucky, ordained Louisa Woosley (1862–1952) to the ministry of Word and Sacrament. She was a woman who had a keen sense of God's call in her life and who typifies many Reformed values. Woosley was hardly a renegade, though she believed deeply in the equality of women and men before God. Throughout her life she sought to balance her role as wife and mother with her call to minister. She worked always within the church's structure to seek affirmation of her call to ministry. For many years she tried to resist a call to preach, but through study and prayer, she accepted her call as God's will. She treasured the Bible and studied it intently. Over the years her ordination was argued and debated and even rescinded within the church, yet she served faithfully. She served as a pastor, an evangelist, and an officer within the church. In 1891, she published a book titled *Shall Women Preach?, or the Question Answered.* In this book she argues biblically and theologically for the equality of women in the church:

> Let the man and woman stand side by side, shoulder to shoulder, in defense of the cause of Christ. It necessarily follows, if they are heirs together of the grace of life, that each has a share (an equal share) in all that pertains to salvation through Christ; for the woman was created in the image of God just as was the man. And if she gains anything in Christ she gains equally as much as the man. (Hudson, 225)

In her ministry, which lasted over fifty years, Woosley preached in various churches and presbyteries in Kentucky, some 6,343 sermons.

In Canada, too, Christian women responded to the call to preach, often in frontier situations where ordained clergy were rare. Methodist, Presbyterian, and Anglican women took on ministerial roles, including preaching, among the Natives of British Columbia around the turn of the twentieth century. Records show that there was some controversy about women's preaching and constant effort to justify it biblically. Some women preachers, such as Bella Johnston, ministered primarily among women and children. Bella was matron of the Alberni Indian Girls' Home in British Columbia, Canada. Other Canadian Presbyterian women, like Mary Swartout and Elizabeth MacVicar, led Sunday services. Mary carried on her husband's ministry of teaching and preaching on Vancouver Island after his death. Records of these women preachers are scarce, but they demonstrate the way that women responded to a call to preach, that they had successful ministries, and that their work helped to change the church's views on the roles of women.

Ordination

Those denominations that have a congregational polity were able to ordain women long before those that have a more central form of government. For instance, the United Brethren and the Congregationalists ordained women a century before the United Methodists or the Presbyterians. It is also true that churches that value biblical authority, as the Reformed churches do, have been more resistant to women's ordination than those that value a kind of charismatic authority. Just so, frontier movements like the Disciples and the Cumberland Presbyterians were more open than those Reformed churches that still resist women's leadership such as the Christian Reformed Church and the Presbyterian Church in America. Although women's ministry has gained acceptance since the mid-twentieth century, the struggle has been ongoing in the Reformed family.

Reformed believers often speak of an inward and an outward call to ministry. The voice of God for an individual must be validated by the church. We have seen that Reformed women who felt the call to preach sought ordination as recognition of a call to ministry. For Antoinette Brown that call was validated by a Congregational church in Wayne County, New York, in 1853; she is generally considered the first woman in North America to be ordained in a mainline denomination. The Calvinist and Puritan roots of the Congregationalists and her association with Presbyterian Charles Finney place Brown within the Reformed family. Louisa Woosley's call to preach was also confirmed by the Cumberland Presbyterians who ordained her in 1889, though her official place within the church structure was questioned during her lifetime. Two ordinations within the Stone-Campbell tradition were reported in the early 1880s, but Clara Hale Babcock, ordained in 1888 or 1889, is generally considered the first ordained woman in the Disciples tradition.

Because of their representative polity, their insistence on seminary training for clergy, and a tendency to interpret scripture more strictly, the ordination of women in Presbyterian and Reformed churches was slower in coming. In those Reformed churches that have connectional rather than a congregational polity, women serving as deacons and elders paved the way for women's ordination as ministers. In the United Church of Canada, a diaconal tradition preceded the ordination of female pastors. The United Church of Canada was formed by a union of Methodists, Presbyterians, and Congregationalists in 1925. Both Methodists and Presbyterians had a tradition of deaconesses—single laywomen who were employed by the church. Their work included teaching, nursing, social work, and other forms of service that fit with traditional female roles. If a woman married, she was removed from her role as deaconess, marriage and motherhood being considered a higher calling. As the churches united, efforts were made to bring the role of deaconess into the new church. The work of deaconesses tended to be underpaid, undervalued, and overshadowed by the ministry of male clergy. During wartime many deaconesses served pastoral roles, but such roles were discouraged again, once the men returned from service. In 1938, the United Church of Canada ordained Lydia Gruchy as its first woman minister. Not until 1964, after years of organized struggle, were deaconesses granted full standing in the courts of the United Church, giving them, at last, a voice in the ministry of the church.

By the early 1900s there were women preaching and seeking leadership roles in the Dutch Reformed and the Presbyterian churches. These churches share a representational polity that calls for churchwide ratification of major constitutional changes. The Reformed Church in America and the Presbyterian Church (northern and southern) began debating the issue early in the twentieth century. These churches, which now enjoy full communion, also ordain laypersons as deacons and elders to share in the ministry of the church.

The Reformed Church in America (RCA) first considered a proposal to ordain women as elders and deacons in 1918. At that time their constitution required officers to be chosen from the "male members" of the church. The proposal asked only that the word *male* be deleted. The move was defeated that year and proposed again and again until, in 1972, the General Synod allowed for the ordination of women to the offices of elder and deacon. The question of ordination to the Ministry of the Word was first addressed in 1955. In 1973, a ministerial candidate, Joyce Stedge, was examined and licensed by the Rockland-Westchester Classis (regional governing body). That same year she was ordained and installed as pastor of a Reformed Church in Accord, New York. Her case and those of others, together with a general call for equality of men and women in the church, led to a series of debates and votes in the Reformed Church in America, which culminated in the decision to ordain women to the Ministry of the Word in 1979. Throughout the debates in the RCA, arguments against the ordination of women included a sense that "the time was not right," "men would abdicate their responsibility," and "it would divide the church." Some objected on scriptural grounds. In 1992, the General Synod of the RCA elected Beth Marcus, of Holland, Michigan, as its first woman president.

In 1983, the Presbyterian Church in the United States (PCUS) merged with the United Presbyterian Church in the United States of America (UPC). This reunion began to heal a breach dating back to the Civil War. In 1992, the reunited body, the Presbyterian Church (USA), added to its constitution a new Brief Statement of Faith, which finally gave confessional standing to the ministry of women by affirming that the Holy Spirit "calls women and men to all ministries of the church."

While women have served in leadership roles throughout the history of the Presbyterian Church, until recently those leadership roles were not officially sanctioned. To find that female leaders serving in "unofficial" ways paved the way for the "official" recognition of women's ministry in the Presbyterian churches is no surprise.

In the latter half of the nineteenth century there was a flurry of overtures (appeals from the local presbyteries to the national assembly) that indicate controversy surrounding women preaching and speaking in public. The first definitive action of the General Assembly regarding women's ordination was a negative one, concurring with an overture from the Presbytery of Brooklyn, New York, requesting

> that the Assembly accept and transmit to the presbyteries for their approval such rules as shall forbid the licensing and ordaining of women to the gospel ministry, and the teaching and preaching of women in our pulpits, or in the public and promiscuous meetings of the Church of Christ.

The UPC allowed for women deacons in 1915, for women elders in 1930, and for women ministers in 1956. The PCUS approved the ordination of women as deacons, elders, and ministers in 1964. The steps toward women's ordination involved political maneuvering paralleling that of other Protestant bodies; the key events for Presbyterian women took place in the late 1920s, early 1930s, and again in the 1950s and 1960s.

In the early 1920s, the UPC moved to subsume all women's boards under the structure of the national church. This caused not a little dissent among the women who had worked to raise money and to organize for mission and education. The now-famous Hodge-Bennett report, meant to address the causes of unrest among women in the church, was a result of this upheaval. The report led to a debate in the larger church and to the decision of the General Assembly to allow for the ordination of women as elders, authorized to serve in governing bodies of the church at all levels. The presence of female elders from 1930 until 1956 allowed many women to begin working within the power structures of the church; the groundbreaking work of these laywomen paved the way for women's ordination as ministers. Elisabeth Lunz notes that "without the power of persuasion and action of unordained women, ordination to the offices of elder and minister would not have been opened to women in either of the former denominations that now form the Presbyterian Church (U.S.A.)" (Brasfield and Lunz, 1).

An overture calling for women's ordination came to the UPC General Assembly in 1953 from the Presbytery of Rochester, asking the assembly "to initiate such actions as may be necessary to permit the ordination of women to the Ministry of Jesus Christ." In 1956, final approval was gained from the presbyteries to add the following sentence to the constitution regarding ordination as ministers: "Both men and women may be called to this office." In 1956, Margaret Towner, of Milwaukee, was the first woman ordained among the northern Presbyterians; Rachel Henderlite, ordained in Hanover, Virginia, in 1965, was the first in the southern church. Lois Stair, of Waukesha, Wisconsin, was the first female moderator of the General Assembly, elected in 1971.

Even while these Reformed churches ordain women as ministers, other churches still refuse or resist. For instance, the Christian Reformed Church (CRC), also part of the Dutch Reformed tradition, voted in 1990 to ordain women, pending a two-year period of reflection. In 1992, the General Synod voted 109–73 against final approval, an action that met with a demonstration in response. The vote has been a disappointment to those women in the CRC who have felt a call to ordained ministry. Other Calvinist churches that have refused to ordain women include the Reformed Church of Quebec, the Bible Presbyterians, the Free Reformed Churches of North America, the Korean American Presbyterian Church (KAPC), the Orthodox Presbyterian Church, the Reformed Presbyterian Church, the Canadian Reformed Churches, and the Presbyterian Church in America (PCA). The PCA left the Presbyterian Church (USA) in part over the issue of women's ordination.

The changing roles of women in the church, including those churches within the Reformed family, closely parallel developments within other Protestant churches and within North American culture at large. Despite cultural and spiritual resistance to these role shifts, faithful women have sought to serve and to hear God's call in a variety of ways. Some have chosen to serve within the bounds of traditional roles, and others have worked for reform. Many of the stories told of women within the Reformed churches echo those of other church traditions. Methodists, Anglicans, Baptists, and Catholics can surely tell of women missionaries, of frontier preachers, of teachers and principals, of nurses and doctors, of social workers, of wives and mothers, who put their faith into action, often in positions of leadership. Many of these women can tell us of the joy and satisfaction they found in serving; others can tell also of the discrimination they have faced.

There are elements of Reformed theology and politics, however, that have shaped the way Reformed women have struggled to serve. We have seen how those churches with a congregational focus have been able to move forward more readily than those with a representational structure. This is why Antoinette Brown was able to be ordained nearly a century before her Presbyterian sisters. We have noted also the way that social class and educational expectations have served to preserve traditional roles for women. Those churches that require a seminary education for their ministers, which most of the Reformed churches do, have been slower to welcome women into the ranks of seminary-educated clergy. Yet when women have sought education and training, they have advanced the cause of women in ministry.

A Reformed emphasis on the authority of scripture and the centrality of preaching has also been a mixed blessing for women in these churches. Those scriptures that seem to preclude women's authority in the church have been used to keep them from visible leadership roles, especially in churches that take a stricter approach to both Calvinism and the interpretation of scripture. Yet there has been found within Reformed biblical interpretation a warrant for women's equality and an affirmation of women's gifts in the early church. This belief in the equality of all believers, together with the many examples of biblical women who were leaders, prophets, disciples, and apostles, has encouraged women to take a more affirmative approach toward scripture.

Another issue that has affected the ministry of women in the Reformed churches has been a struggle in Calvinism between what we might call freedom and order, or even free will and determinism. One example of this tension is a disagreement about attitudes toward mission and evangelism. Reformed Christians who believe strongly in election, or predestination, may be wary of evangelism that seems to focus on emotional conversion experiences. This was one point of disagreement among Presbyterians during the Great Awakening. Another way this tension has surfaced is in discussions of social concern versus personal salvation. Some missionaries, such as the Scudders and the Whitmans, saw meeting human needs as a primary focus of missions, while others saw conversion as the primary goal. Freedom of conscience has also been a high value in Reformed thinking, yet there have always been those in the church who believe that theology and behavior should be subject to church order. The early Puritans who censured Ann Hutchinson clearly favored order. No doubt many Reformed women have been silenced or discouraged by this Calvinist tendency.

We have seen, for instance, how women encouraged the mission of the church, beginning early in the 1800s. Women financed mission; they opened their homes to mission societies that prayed for missionaries and heard their stories. Many women chose to serve at home and abroad. Reformed women seem to have been more involved in ministries of service than of evangelism per se. These women witnessed a change, and some of them led it, from mission that imposed English-speaking culture on native cultures to a kind of mission that sought to integrate traditional culture with education and self-development. These women's missionary societies formed the basis of the ecumenical movement and of women's associations and organizations in virtually all of these churches. These women's organizations have continued to be a rich and mighty resource for the church of gifts of time, talent, and treasure. Women's groups have often been on the forefront of calling the church to action on issues of national and global concern such as hunger, domestic violence, peacemaking, and women's rights.

Women in the church, including Reformed women, have continued to struggle with the competing demands and role models placed on them. Women employed by the church, including clergywomen, have faced the same struggles that women entering other male-dominated professions have faced. They bring concerns about child care, about balancing work and family, about gender roles in their marriages. Single and divorced women in ministry face subtle forms of discrimination as well. Clergy couples and ministers' husbands have to forge new roles in the church. Many ministers' wives no longer feel called to serve in the traditional way that women like Catherine Marshall did. Women often bring different styles of leadership to the ministry; these more egalitarian ways are not always welcome.

The theological and political differences of women in the Reformed churches are as diverse as the Reformed family, which ranges from progressive mainline churches to those churches that remain strictly Calvinist. Women have been agents of change in all these churches, and faithful women have heard the call of God to serve in a wide variety of roles, some in highly visible positions of leadership and others in quiet and gentle service to children, to the poor, and to the sick. A Reformed emphasis on the ministry of each member of the body of Christ encourages and values each of these roles as a call from God, enabled by the Spirit.

SOURCES: Jean-Jacques Bauswein and Lukas Vischer, *The Reformed Family Worldwide: A Survey of Reformed Churches, Theological Schools, and International Organizations* (1999). R. Pierce Beaver, *American Protestant Women in World Mission: History of the First Feminist Movement in North America* (1980). Paul Boyer, "Minister's Wife, Widow, Reluctant Feminist: Catherine Marshall in the 1950s," in *Women in American Religion*, ed. Janet Wilson James (1980), 253–271. Alice Brasfield and Elisabeth Lunz, eds., *Voices of Experience: Lifestories of Clergywomen in the Presbyterian Church (U.S.A.)* (1991). Elisabeth D. Dodds, *Marriage to a Difficult Man: The "Uncommon Union" of Jonathan and Sarah Edwards* (1971). Richard L. Harrison, *From Camp Meeting to Church: A History of the Christian Church (Disciples of Christ) in Kentucky* (1992). Mary Lin Hudson, " 'Shall Women Preach?' Louisa Woosley and the Cumberland Presbyterian Church," *American Presbyterians* 68.4 (Winter 1990): 221–230. John H. Leith, ed., *Creeds of the Churches: A Reader in Christian Doctrine from the Bible to the Present* (1982). John H. Leith, ed., *Reminiscences: Being a Record of Five and Twenty Years Progress in the Women's Home and Foreign Missionary Society of the United Evangelical Church* (1910). Also see: Catherine A. Brekus, *Strangers and Pilgrims: Female Preaching in America, 1740–1845* (1998). Jane Douglass Dempsey, *Women, Freedom and Calvin* (1985). Kristin Herzog,

"The La Flesche Family: Native American Spirituality, Calvinism, and Presbyterian Missions," in *American Presbyterians* 65.3 (Fall 1987): 222–232. Geoffrey Johnston, "The Road to Winsome Womanhood: Presbyterian Mission among East Indian Women and Girls in Trinidad, 1868–1939," 103–120, and Mary Anne MacFarlane, "Faithful and Courageous Handmaidens: Deaconesses in the United Church of Canada, 1925–1945," in John S. Moir and C. T. McIntire, eds., *Canadian Protestant and Catholic Missions, 1820s–1960s* [Includes articles cited by Grant, MacFarlane, and Whitehead]. Elizabeth Gillan Muir, and Marilyn Fardig Whiteley, eds., *Changing Roles of Women within the Christian Church in Canada* (1995). Rebecca Prichard, "*Grandes Dames, Matrones,* and *Femmes Fortes*: Reformed Women Ministering" in Catherine Wessinger, ed., *Religious Institutions and Women's Leadership: New Roles inside the Mainstream* (1996). James H. Smylie, "American Presbyterians: A Pictorial History," *Journal of Presbyterian History* 63.1–2 (Spring/Summer 1985). Jonathan Howes Webster, "The ABCFM and the First Presbyterian Missions in the Northwest," *American Presbyterians* 65.3 (Fall 1987): 173–185.

PRESBYTERIAN WOMEN IN AMERICA
Lois A. Boyd

WOMEN HAVE BEEN actively involved in Presbyterianism in the United States of America since the denomination's inception in the new country in 1789. Late-eighteenth- and early-nineteenth-century family histories, newspapers and periodicals, printed sermons, obituaries, illustrations, and other personal accounts give evidence of women's church membership and attendance, financial gifts, and personal piety, as well as their early zeal for missions and Christian education in their communities, in frontier America, and in foreign countries.

Women expressed their interests principally within the local church or, sometimes with their husbands, in nonsectarian organizations devoted to societal reform, missions, education, publication, and distribution of religious books. Some gathered in their own social groups—unaffiliated with one another—variously called cent, mite, or sewing societies. There they pledged their modest resources and studied scripture, prayed together, and sewed items for seminarians or missionaries. The groups appeared supportive but unassertive in the denomination, exemplified by one participant's view: "Let man then, exercise power; woman exert influence" (Boyd and Brackenridge, 2nd ed., 6).

Although the numbers of female participants on church rolls and in their associations increased, mention of women does not appear in denominational minutes or reports for more than two decades after the first Presbyterian General Assembly, or national governing body of the denomination, was formed in 1789. In 1811, and

then again in 1817, the minutes of the General Assembly of the Presbyterian Church in the United States of America recognized the "pious females" interested in education, religious mission, and moral issues. (The various strands of Presbyterianism that would evolve over the years are described in a descriptive sidebar at the end of this essay.)

Early Presbyterian clergy and scholars saw women as inclined toward religion but reiterated the church's traditional doctrine that claimed the subordination of woman and the supremacy of man as ordained by God. The language of the nineteenth century endorsed women's sphere, an arena of domesticity, maternity, nurture, and piety. While church leaders banned women from voice or vote in the local church or in denominational courts, they nevertheless urged them to exert moral and religious influence over their families.

The women's small societies foreshadowed the development of larger organizations and increased participation. This might have come about by their need for social engagement or, in part, by the revivalist atmosphere of the early century, which encouraged women's prayer meetings, for example. This alarmed some Presbyterian clergy, who feared that if females were allowed to pray together, they might also attempt to preach. At least as early as 1826, records show that an "itinerant female" (which implies a relationship to revivalism) preached in two churches, which compelled church officials to advise Presbyterian ministers and elders to be "watchful for the future and guard against such innovations" (Boyd and Brackenridge, 2nd ed., 94).

The 1832 General Assembly distributed a pastoral letter to all Presbyterian churches on revivalist practices. Within the longer letter were three sentences pertaining to women to which the church would refer as policy for most of the rest of the century:

Meetings of pious women by themselves, for conversation and prayer, whenever they can conveniently be held, we entirely approve. But let not the inspired prohibitions of the great apostle to the Gentiles, as found in his epistles to the Corinthians and to Timothy, be violated. To teach and exhort, or to lead in prayer, in public and promiscuous assemblies, is clearly forbidden to women in the Holy Oracles. (94)

During the 1800s, women became key in creating, sustaining, and staffing the increasing network of Presbyterian Sunday Schools. During the same period, many also continued to vest time, energy, and resources in women's groups. The early societies generally addressed local needs, but the growing denominational program for foreign missions in the 1830s led male church officials to solicit women's assistance for work abroad and

Maggie Kuhn, founder of the Grey Panthers, was also an activist within the Presbyterian Church. She formed a group of female Presbyterian professionals into a special interest group in 1966. *Urban Archives, Temple University Press, Philadelphia, Pennsylvania.*

for home missions. Within the context of the church's policy on women, clergy suggested their efforts should be "woman's work for woman," a phrase that evolved into "woman's work for women and children" in the literature of Presbyterian women's missionary endeavors. Accepting the challenge, women initially packed missionary barrels with clothes and supplies for individual missionaries and their wives and families as well as collected dollars for their support. The women's fund-raising acumen supplied considerable fiscal resources and gained recognition by the denomination for the efficiency of their management and distribution of the funds and goods collected.

Identifiable leaders emerged during the period that Presbyterian women developed larger associations. Mentioning only a few, in the Presbyterian Church in the USA, Mary E. James, who led that denomination's Woman's Executive Committee of Home Missions, a national organization, through the last decade of the nineteenth century and into the twentieth, combined an interest in missions with a keen political sense. Church periodicals indicate that she and her officers intervened at the highest political levels on issues such as polygamy and Native American poverty. Strong-minded, proud, and loyal, James declined an office near the male boards members during the 1900 General Assembly, preferring to stay with her office force. Her secretary said, "She does not need any prestige higher than the place she has

made for herself, and I fancy the 'big guns' will seek her even if she is not quartered in their midst" (Boyd and Brackenridge, 2nd ed., 25). In the Presbyterian Historical Society archives is a letter to a colleague in which James reminisced in her later years, "All along these years there has been continuous pushing forward, sometimes finding ourselves in debt at the close of the year, to our chagrin, and anxiety, again flourishing, in close sympathy with the Board, so that we suffered with it when the Secretaries were inefficient—oh how those years come before me!"

Also in the archives are scores of personally handwritten letters from Frances E. H. Haines, the first corresponding secretary of the Woman's Executive Committee, to missionaries, teachers, and local society members. In them she gave support and advice, including instructing the members of the women's groups on parliamentary procedures, where the presiding officer should sit, voting procedures, and even suggesting refreshments that could be served. Nettie Rogers Finks and her daughter Theodora were the only editors of the extremely popular periodical *Home Mission Monthly*, a self-supporting magazine that began in 1886 and ceased publication in 1924. Julia Graham was a well-known leader of the Ladies' Board of Missions of the Presbyterian Church of New York, one of the influential regional groups primarily dedicated to foreign missions.

Sarah Foster Hanna is said to have been the first

woman to address a Presbyterian assembly. She spoke to the United Presbyterian Church of North America General Assembly in 1875 concerning the founding of a women's missionary society. Hanna was a graduate of the Emma Willard Seminary at Troy, New York, and director of Washington Seminary in western Pennsylvania. Visitors of distinction visited the school, including John Quincy Adams in 1843, who was received and addressed by Hanna: "It was long before the time when a woman could speak in public without trampling on all conventional rules, and Mr. Adams was visibly affected" (*The United Presbyterian* [1903], Presbyterian Historical Society [PHS]).

Hallie P. Winsborough, longtime superintendent and then secretary of Woman's Work of the Presbyterian Church in the United States (southern), was the first female to speak on developments in women's work before that denomination's 1920 General Assembly, but not without considerable contention. Although controversy continued in the southern church for some time on whether a woman should be allowed to speak to the General Assembly, a ruling elder at the 1926 General Assembly said, "I would be most uncomfortable in facing my wife and daughter if I return home and do not hear Mrs. Winsborough read her own report" (Boyd and Brackenridge, 2nd ed., 129). Winsborough described herself as "a woman of no previous business experience, unknown to the great body of women in the Church, a woman laden with family cares and a member of the most remote church in our Assembly" (Boyd and Brackenridge, 1st ed., 220). This woman would serve the Presbyterian Church in the United States from 1912 to 1927 as superintendent of the woman's auxiliary, from 1927 to 1929 as secretary of woman's work, and from 1929 until 1940 as secretary emerita.

Katharine Jones Bennett spanned two centuries in her more than forty years as service as a Presbyterian administrator. She used the term "The Church Woman's Decade" to describe the emergence in the 1870s of women's programmatic, financial, and administrative commitments to home and foreign missions in the Presbyterian Church in the USA. A graduate of Elmira College, in 1909 Bennett succeeded Mary James as president of the Woman's Executive Committee. Her integrity and speaking, writing, and administrative abilities led her to become a spokesperson in the denomination. A tribute from Henry Sloane Coffin, prominent Presbyterian minister, writer, and educator, written March 24, 1941, and in the vault of the Presbyterian Historical Society in Philadelphia, says,

My mind goes back to those early days after the fusion of the Boards [women's boards co-opted into the denominational structure] when some of the masculine element found it difficult to think that women could be companions in wisdom. It always seemed to me in those days that you knew far more about the work and had a far sounder judgment than any man then on the Board, or, for that matter, who has come on since. Your patience with the somewhat overbearing males and your quiet conquest of their judgments has been a source of great joy to me.

As with other boards and agencies, the fund-raising of the women's organizations was tied to the country's economic condition, so its ongoing commitments to missionaries, teachers, schools, and hospitals mandated special appeals and borrowing money when necessary. Because their support was so central to mission projects, the General Assembly sometimes would ask the women to expand their programs in difficult times. In 1885, for instance, it urged the Woman's Executive Committee to include a Woman's Department of Work for Freedmen. Although apprehensive about assuming more fiscal responsibilities, the Committee allocated funds to build schools and support women teachers and missionaries in the South. Many notable female African American Presbyterian educators, physicians, and missionaries were related to these programs, one of whom was Lucy Craft Laney. A daughter of slaves (her father became a Presbyterian minister after the Civil War), she graduated from Atlanta University at the age of fifteen. Laney founded the Haines Normal and Industrial Institute in 1886 in Augusta, Georgia. As one minister described her, "We [the Board of Missions for Freedmen] cannot claim the credit of having the foresight to assign her to the position she is filling so well, for she has simply made the position for herself by her courage, her ability, her zeal, her self-denial" (*The Church at Home and Abroad* [1893] PHS). The Woman's Executive Committee also had programs among Hispanics, Native Americans, Asians, and newly arrived immigrants, from which came many women leaders.

During the late nineteenth and twentieth centuries, operating through the Presbyterian hierarchy, women blended their background of personalized philanthropy and cent-society models—emphasizing that even giving a small amount would result in a considerable accumulation—with increasingly sophisticated fund-raising methods. In the early days of the female home mission enterprise, letters to individual women and the local societies asked for funds for a single scholarship, a partial payment on a building, or the support of one young person, or even a portion of his or her care. This grew into other types of fund-raising, resulting in cumulative gifts in the millions of dollars. In 1924, Katharine Bennett reviewed Presbyterian women's work and gifts for home missions as a "vital asset in nation-building," and her colleague Margaret E. Hodge, the executive of the women's foreign missions program, who also served Presbyterianism for more than forty years, commended female support for a substantial contribution to the foreign missionary endeavor (Boyd and Brackenridge, 2nd ed., 23). Women in all the various Presbyterian denominations made similar efforts for missions during the nineteenth and early twentieth centuries.

During the second half of the nineteenth century, considerable debate on the so-called woman question, or women's status in the church, occurred in Presbyterian General Assemblies, presbyteries, synods, and local pulpits as women's lifestyles evolved into more participation in the national culture. During the Civil War, many Presbyterian females continued church activities but also worked in war-related programs and supported their homes, businesses, and properties. In an 1863 Presbyterian periodical, a male leader of the Board of Foreign Missions claimed that Christian women of America learned about the power of organization "in the hospital and sanitary operations of our Civil War" (8), while a female writer in 1890 felt that *the genius for organization*" (italics in original) among women had been "a surprise to themselves" (24). Urged on by social forces such as suffragism and women's access to higher education, they experienced widening professional opportunities, including as doctors, teachers, foreign and home missionaries, denominational administrators, and church educators.

In the 1870s, there was a significant increase of interest among females in pursuing mission careers. Influenced by the powerful women's missionary boards as well as by the wives of missionaries who had served as unpaid workers for years, a sizable number of women were appointed as missionaries. In fact, church leaders voiced their fear that the work at home and abroad seemed to be "going into the hands of the ladies" (72). Some writers have argued that women's move into church professions might have paralleled men's retreat from those jobs. This has not been documented in Presbyterian archives, but occasional informal observations alluded to males seeming to be leaving missions to women. Not to be ignored, however, was women's strong commitment to missions, as well as a desire for the vocational opportunities offered in evangelization, religious education, medicine, and social work.

Because of increased visibility, discussions arose on whether women should have an official role, specifically be allowed to vote, in church affairs. The 1891 Presbyterian Church in the USA General Assembly first formally acknowledged the need to define women's status. A committee looking at establishing the role of deaconesses felt that "a majority in the church are in favor of securing in some orderly way the services of godly women to assist in religious work, and are desirous of clothing them with some measure of authority." In 1892

the General Assembly approved letting local churches appoint women "for the care of the poor and sick, and especially of poor widows and orphans." The denomination also encouraged the establishment of institutions and training schools so that Presbyterian women could be adequately prepared for service. Although deaconesses served effectively, primarily as nurses and social workers, they were never a significant factor in Presbyterian life, especially after Presbyterian denominations modified their constitutions to allow women to serve in the office of deacon, an officer of the church for service. The various Presbyterian denominations approved the election of women as deacons on different timetables, as early as 1906 and as late as 1964.

In the latter part of the nineteenth century, some women, such as Edith Livingston Peake, a member of the First United Presbyterian Church of San Francisco, served as lay evangelists in the United Presbyterian Church in North America. Another denomination, the Cumberland Presbyterian Church, also permitted women evangelists and, in fact, was the leader in the debate on ministerial status for women. The central personality was Louisa Layman Woosley, who defended female ordination at the Cumberland General Assembly and in 1891 published a book titled *Shall Women Preach? or The Question Answered*. In November 1889, by action of Nolin Presbytery in Kentucky, Woosley became the first Presbyterian woman to be ordained to the ministry. Although the Cumberland church invalidated her ordination in 1895, Nolin Presbytery refused to comply and took steps that allowed her to retain her ministerial standing while dropping her name from the roll of presbytery. In 1911 the Leitchfield Presbytery, successor to Nolin Presbytery, added Woosley's name to its roster, and she was restored to the General Assembly's roll of ordained ministers in 1913 without challenge (*American Presbyterians* [Winter 1990]: 223–224). The 1921 Cumberland Assembly adopted a statement that ended restrictions regarding women's status.

Throughout the early twentieth century, there also are records of women serving without ordination but with the approval of individual presbyteries. One was Lena L. Jennings of Ohio, who began her ministerial career in 1923 and retired in 1950, still without ordination, although the Presbytery of Wooster bestowed upon her the honorary title of minister emeritus and provided her with a pension of $60 a month (Boyd and Brackenridge, 2nd ed., 124).

In light of educational, professional, and cultural changes in the early twentieth century, Presbyterian women's interest in traditional missionary organizations declined markedly. In 1929 Katharine Bennett noted in *The Presbyterian Magazine* that the young women of that decade belonged to a completely different world from that of their parents and were "a generation looking with unafraid eyes at all institutions, even ecclesiastical—and asking 'why?' of many accepted customs." A few years before she published this, a major reorganization in the Presbyterian Church in the USA in 1923 had dissolved the woman's boards and subsumed their work under the Boards of National and Foreign Missions. Church leaders assured women that this would elevate their status in denominational structures, since women would be represented on each of the boards by a fixed numerical formula and could participate and vote on a range of church policies. Moreover, women would have some representation on the General Assembly's General Council, the powerful executive committee of the General Assembly.

Despite the denomination's rationale, as well as support from some women leaders, the rank and file involved in Presbyterian women's organizations was outraged, resulting in the unleashing of long-held concerns. On the one hand, women expressed resentment toward the male church leaders for taking unilateral actions without consultation, limiting representation, and restricting fiscal control. On the other hand, some men intimated that the women's organizations constituted a "church within the church," which, in a letter of January 18, 1926, written to a colleague in Baltimore, Katharine Bennett interpreted as concern that women's giving through their organizations would cut down their gifts to the church (PHS Archives). Bennett wrote a pamphlet titled "Hold Steady," in which she urged women to continue their sacrificial giving. Margaret Hodge asked women to look forward to the new organizational structure (Boyd and Brackenridge, 2nd ed., 31–32).

In the face of continuing dissent, the General Assembly asked Bennett and Hodge to investigate discord among Presbyterian women. In response, based on data obtained from Presbyterian women throughout the country, Bennett and Hodge's 1927 report, "Causes of Unrest among the Women of the Church," was the first such critical analysis written by women rather than by clergymen. They said in their preface: "If by 'unrest among the women of the Church' is meant a far-reaching, organized, seething opinion, then we are discussing something which does not exist. . . . The women of the church are not a unit in their attitude toward the position accorded them in the Presbyterian Church" (Bennett and Hodge, 1). Nevertheless, their extensive research indicated that the underlying cause of dissension was triggered by the way the women's boards were terminated:

[W]hen the Church, by action taken by the men of the church with but the slightest consultation with the women . . . decided to absorb these agencies which had been built up by the women, the by-product of such decision was to open the whole question of the status of women in the church. Then women faced the fact that their sex constitute about *sixty per cent of the membership of the Presbyterian Church*, but that a woman as an individual has no status beyond a congregational meeting in her local church. . . . The women looked about into business and professional life and saw women rapidly taking their place side by side with men, with full freedom to serve in any position for which they had the qualifications. They saw the church, which affirmed spiritual equality, lagging far behind in the practical expression of it; they saw democracy in civic work, autocracy in church administrations. (10–11)

Bennett and Hodge wrote,

What they [females] do wish is the removal of inhibitions which constantly remind them that they are not considered intellectually or spiritually equal to responsibilities within the church. Most ask for no one thing, only, that artificial inhibitions that savor of another century having been removed, they may take their place wherever and however their abilities and need of the church may call. Woman asks to be considered in the light of her ability and not of her sex. . . . her mind rebels even if her heart keeps her tongue quiet. (27)

The findings, presented by Bennett and Hodge to the 1927 General Council, led that body to meet with fifteen women in November 1928, the first time that ordained male church leaders met with women specifically to discuss questions of gender equity in church government. Among the participants was Louise Blinn, an active Presbyterian from Cincinnati, who on her own initiative had generated two petitions to General Assembly, in 1924 and 1926, asking for sexual equality and the reinstatement of women's organizations. From detailed notes taken at the meeting, Blinn was quoted as saying "I have a fine intelligent girl in college, and she is going to have the finest education I can provide. I have served the Church for twenty years or more, but under the present conditions, I never would think of suggesting to her that she look to the Church for the outlet of her energy." As the daylong conference drew to a close, Blinn proposed a recommendation "that the right of the members of the Presbyterian Church to share and participate in defining its faith and determining its policy shall not be abridged because of sex" (Boyd and Brackenridge, 1st ed., 129).

After the conference, a four-person committee including Bennett and Hodge was charged to submit recommendations concerning the role of women in the church to the 1929 General Assembly. Initially, the two males on the committee focused on the question of status for women, while the two women reiterated the priority of reinstating women's organizations. Although the women acknowledged the desirability of a unified program in which men and women functioned as equals, they did not feel that official status would produce the same results as a power base supplied by a strong woman's organization. In the discussion on the issue of equality, however, Bennett and Hodge pushed for the removal of all discrimination against women.

On May 20–21, 1929, a Conference on Women's Status and Service in the Church met in St. Paul, Minnesota, not only to discuss, as Margaret Hodge wrote in *The Presbyterian Banner* of April 1929, removing "ecclesiastical disabilities of women" but also to recognize their service to the church. The women clearly wished immediate equality rather than a gradual process. In a letter written December 1, 1930, Stated Clerk Lewis S. Mudge responded to an inquiry from Judge Claude T. Reno in Allentown, Pennsylvania, concerning the eligibility of women to an ecclesiastical status. He analyzed the climate:

> Permit me to add that there was no *demand* on the part of our women whatever for an admission to the status of a minister, or for admission to that of ruling elder. There was, however, a very wide spread and insistent feeling that so far as the ruling eldership was concerned there was no good reason why women should not be admitted to it. . . . They have a voice today, they said, in the State on an equal basis with men, and in practically every other sphere of activity, excepting the Church, their equality was recognized. . . . Furthermore, some of our wisest and most conservative women said you may do as you please to our generation, but we warn you that our daughters will not stand for any such treatment. This was said not in indignation or with unkindly insistence, but it was said in solemn warning and was supported by facts. (PHS Archives)

Ultimately the General Assembly submitted three options to presbyteries: Grant full ecclesiastical standing to women as minister, elder, and deacon; ordain women as elders only; and provide for licensure of women as evangelists. The presbyteries approved only ordaining women as elders, which was sustained by the 1930 General Assembly. Ordination as elders enabled women to serve on all governing bodies and particularly on committees in which important decisions affecting the denomination were made. The first woman elder in the Presbyterian Church in the USA was Sarah Dickson, director of religious education at Wauwatosa Presbyterian Church in Wisconsin, ordained on June 12, 1930, very shortly after the General Assembly action (*American Presbyterians* [Winter 1990]: 246–248). Five female elders attended the 1931 General Assembly as commissioners, but Presbyterian women in significant numbers did not immediately enter the eldership, either because their congregations did not elect them or they themselves thought it improper to serve.

Even though governance was more inclusive, many Presbyterian churchwomen of the 1930s still wished to reconstitute a national women's association. In 1943, the General Assembly approved the organization of the National Council of Presbyterian Women's Organizations. In 1958, a union of the United Presbyterian Church of North America and the Presbyterian Church in the USA into the United Presbyterian Church in the United States of America dissolved this group into a new women's organization, United Presbyterian Women.

In the coming decades, issues of ecumenism, cross-culturalism, and feminism would profoundly influence traditional women's organizations. Presbyterian women became involved in the international and national discussions on women's status and liberation and were affected by such events as the 1963 President's Commission on Women, Betty Friedan's book *The Feminine Mystique* (1963), which articulated concerns of many women, and the organization of the National Organization for Women (NOW), which supported full women's rights.

Gender issues gained more attention after women had virtually no input concerning the denomination's adopting a new Book of Confession, participating in the Consultation on Church Union, and planning a radical restructuring of national boards and agencies. A group of female Presbyterian professionals led by Margaret E. (Maggie) Kuhn, later to become well known as the leader of the Gray Panthers, formed a special interest group, and she and others organized a seminar on the changing roles of men and women, with Betty Friedan as a resource leader, in the summer of 1966. The seminar prompted the 1967 General Assembly to appoint a committee to study "the status and participation of women in society and in the judicatories and agencies of the church." Two years later this committee produced a document, "Study of Women in the Church and Society," and recommended a further three-year study of women's status in church and society from which originated the first of the women's advocacy groups (Boyd and Brackenridge, 2nd ed., 52–53).

In the Presbyterian Church, United States, the women's local organizations had not joined into an assembly-wide auxiliary until 1912, and Janie McGaughey, an executive in that denomination's women's work from 1929 to 1956, noted in her 1961 book *On the Crest of the Present* that basic principles of organized women's work changed only in accordance with alterations to General Assembly structure and policies. In later years, these women saw their organizational structures dismantled in a sweeping denominational reorganization. A member of the board and a future moderator of the southern denomination, Dorothy Barnard commented on the church's 1974 restructuring: "We [the women's organization] went from an influential trend-setting board with adequate staff in three major program areas . . . to a staff where only one person was actually assigned to programmatic responsibilities for the Women of the Church. . . . How could we have foreseen such a loss?" (Chapman-Adisbo, 33).

Reunion of the northern and southern denominations into the Presbyterian Church (USA) in 1983 led to combining the two women's groups into Presbyterian Women in the Presbyterian Church (USA). Cleda Locey was the first moderator of the united organization, presiding over a churchwide gathering of Presbyterian women at Purdue University in 1988. The merged General Assembly created a new national structure with nine major ministry units, including a Women's Ministry Unit, composed of four constituency groups: Presbyterian Women, the Committee of Women of Color, Justice for Women, and Women Employed by the Church. In 1992 a downsizing of the administrative structure led to women's ministries being moved under the National Ministries Division and three of its constituent groups dissolved at the national level. Presbyterian Women maintained its organization and churchwide coordinating team. Also established was an Advocacy Committee for Women's Concerns, a function of the Office of the Executive Director of General Assembly Council, whose mandate dealt with the diversity of the church's membership.

Coinciding with this period of women's organizations was the discussion of women's having a full role in the church on an equal standing with men, including ordination as ministers. During the nineteenth century, Presbyterian church fathers spoke and wrote on the theological and scriptural issues of women speaking in church bodies, although whether that included preaching, teaching, lecturing, or praying, and in what venue, often was ambivalent. By the 1870s some men and women supported a more lenient interpretation of scripture and doctrine, probably influenced by the obvious: Women constituted a majority of most Presbyterian congregations, led strong mission, education, and benevolent organizations, raised substantial funds for the church, and in fact, were speaking in various church forums, although without ordination. Church doctrine and polity were gradually modified, and efforts to widen women's roles met limited success as the Presbyterians opened the diaconate and then the eldership to women. Women's ordination to the ministry, however, was de-

feated in 1930, and little public discussion ensued until the middle of the next decade.

In May 1946 Tamaki Uemura, an ordained minister of the Church of Christ of Japan, was invited to officiate at a communion service during a Presbyterian Women's Organization national meeting. The stated clerk and the moderator of the Presbyterian Church in the USA General Assembly ruled that she could not administer the sacraments at a denominational service, since the church did not recognize women's ordination to the ministry. The public and widespread effects of this incident led the executive General Council to propose to the presbyteries in 1947 that ministerial ordination be granted to women, but with neither national debate in the denomination nor organized support from the women's organizations, the issue failed.

The national social and political climate, the growing demands for trained church workers, and international cultural pressures predicted reemergence of the issue of ordination. More quickly than anticipated perhaps, it reappeared at the impetus of one Presbyterian woman, as described in her local church minutes and in an interview in 1981 with Presbyterian historian R. Douglas Brackenridge. An acknowledged feminist and suffragist since her days at Vassar College, Lillian Hurt Alexander, a ruling elder in the Third Presbyterian Church in Rochester, New York, learned that a friend's daughter, who had graduated from seminary, could not be accepted as a ministerial candidate in the Presbyterian church. Alexander drew up a petition recommending that the session of the Rochester church and the Presbytery of Rochester ask the General Assembly in 1953 "to initiate such actions as may be necessary to permit the ordination of women to the ministry of Jesus Christ." In her petition, she said, "When a woman is led of God so to dedicate her life, it would be difficult to discover truly Christian grounds to deny her request" (Boyd and Brackenridge, 2nd ed., 127–128).

The petition was sent to General Assembly on February 17, 1953. Because of union negotiations among three Presbyterian denominations, the church moved deliberately, but this time churchwomen threw their support behind the movement. The request for women's ordination needed a majority vote from the presbyteries. By March 1, 1956, the votes gave women full ecclesiastical parity with men, which would be incorporated into the merger of the Presbyterian Church in the USA and the United Presbyterian Church in North America as the United Presbyterian Church in the United States of America. In 1957, the southern Presbyterian Church presbyteries declined to ordain women as deacons and elders, but in 1964 they approved ordaining women at all levels—deacon, elder, and minister.

Margaret Towner, a graduate of Union Theological

Seminary, New York, and a director of Christian education, was the first woman to be ordained in the United Presbyterian Church in the USA on October 24, 1956, at the First Presbyterian Church in Syracuse, New York. Rachel Henderlite, a Ph.D. in Christian ethics from Yale Divinity School, who also had a background in Christian education, was the first woman ordained in the Presbyterian Church in the United States on May 12, 1965, at All Souls Presbyterian Church, Richmond, Virginia.

Despite the opportunity, initially few women in Presbyterian seminaries pursued a career in pastoral positions. In 1959, of sixteen ordained women, only three were in parishes, two in small rural churches in upper New York State and one in an inner-city congregation that participated in the East Harlem Protestant Parish in New York. More than half of the women were involved in Christian education. Two were in mission work, and the remaining women served either as chaplains or as counselors. The denomination initially provided little advocacy or support.

By 1969 General Assembly statistics noted that the northern denomination had 69 females among 12,865 males in the ordained clergy, and women constituted slightly more than 15 percent of the eldership and 40.8 percent of the diaconate. In a landmark event in 1971, a woman was elected moderator of the General Assembly, in which position one presides over the Assembly for a one-year term. Lois Harkrider Stair of Waukesha, Wisconsin, who had served as a Presbyterian leader on local, regional, and national levels, assumed this role at a time when the denomination faced issues of gender, race, and youth's disaffection with the church's social responsibility agenda. A strong supporter of minority issues who wished to blend diverse factions within the church, she forcefully articulated church unity (*American Presbyterians* [Winter 1990]: 269–283). Nine women have been elected to the moderator's position through 2000.

During the 1970s, the United Presbyterian Church in the USA initiated a five-year, half-million-dollar Women in Ministry project. Response to an initial questionnaire concerning women in ministry identified attitudinal issues at the presbytery and congregational level. Despite a shortage of pastors and although women enrolled in Presbyterian seminaries in record numbers, congregations seemed reluctant to select a woman for their pulpits. The newly formed women's advocacy groups in both Presbyterian denominations, the Council on Women and the Church and the Committee on Women's Concerns, addressed issues of women clergy and seminarians. For example, the Council worked on the recruitment, training, and placement of women in pastoral and administrative positions and monitored conditions for female seminarians. Presbyterian seminaries were encouraged to help women students in their fieldwork, internships, and postgraduate placement, to establish priorities in hiring women faculty, to evaluate patterns of discrimination reported by female students, and to reflect in their publications the contemporary roles of women. The Committee on Women's Concerns maintained contact with women seminarians, monitored seminary curricula and staffing, and annually published statistics on women ministers, elders, and deacons.

New forms of ministry involving clergy couples, with husband and wife both ordained, led to issues of role, status, compensation, location, and lifestyle. Single women often found it difficult to secure positions other than in small or struggling churches. Racial–ethnic clergywomen described a combination of gender and racial prejudice. Both Presbyterian denominations had advocacy groups for minority women in the 1970s and 1980s. The Third World Women's Coordinating Committee and its counterpart in the southern church, the Committee on Racial Ethnic Women, were consolidated in a Committee of Women of Color, upon reunion of the denominations.

A nationwide denominational survey in the late 1980s tested congregational attitudes on women clergy. Asked if the respondent's congregation would call a woman if recommended by the nominating committee, 79 percent responded affirmatively, an increase of 10 percent over a survey done earlier in the decade. To questions about the preference for a male or female pastor performing pastoral functions, 75 to 81 percent indicated "does not matter," again up nearly 10 percent from the previous survey. Despite such increases, other data demonstrated barriers in the employment and advancement of clergywomen, particularly relating to attitudes, with many congregations preferring a white male minister. As more women clergy appeared in pulpits, congregations seemed to become more receptive. Comparative statistics compiled for 1999 showed 3,420 Presbyterian women in active ministry at the end of 1999, comprising almost one-fourth of all active ministers. Jack Marcum, associate for survey research of the Presbyterian Church (USA), reported in October 2001 that by 2000 women were one in seven pastors and co-pastors, four in ten associate pastors, and six in ten of all other active ministers.

During its existence, from 1987 to 1993, the Presbyterian Women's Ministry Unit promoted attitudinal changes in local congregations. Presbyterian staff provided leadership for an ecumenical program, "Blindspots and Breakthroughs," that focused on regional and local judicatories and individual church members. Among other projects, it monitored compliance with gender inclusiveness and equality, proposed denominational discussion topics, and initiated programs to encourage wider participation of women in the Presbyterian church. Its annual reports to the General Assembly reflected such undertakings as the "Ecumenical Decade: Churches in Solidarity with Women, 1988–1998," featuring a global Colloquium on Women's Theology, an International Consultation on Economic Justice, and a project on Women in Ministry in the 21st Century; the first Committee of Women of Color National Consultation; publication of *Voices of Experience*, edited by Alice Brasfield and Betsy Lunz, which documented clergywomen's experiences; a study paper on family violence; a major conference on sexual misconduct in the church; and a comprehensive survey of the status of Presbyterian clergywomen. In its final report to the 1993 General Assembly as an autonomous administrative group, the Unit summarized its accomplishments in the areas of leadership development, education, spiritual nurture, and advocacy, while pointing out issues to be addressed, such as gender inequality, failure to attract and hold young women in church professions, and the inability to respond effectively to the needs of diverse groups of women, especially women of color (Boyd and Brackenridge, 2nd ed., 64).

An event of the 1990s, the "Re-Imagining . . . God, the Community, the Church" conference, especially polarized Presbyterians on issues relating to feminist theology. Held in Minneapolis in 1993, the conference was part of a series of events in the Ecumenical Decade program and brought together more than 2,000 persons from thirty-two denominations, forty-nine states, and twenty-seven countries. A number of Presbyterian women, including associate director for Churchwide Planning Mary Ann Lundy, attended.

The four-day event featured plenary sessions on Re-Imagining God and Community, preceded by presentations on Religious Imagination, as well as other offerings and workshops. Certain statements and events received wide dissemination. Particular interest focused on the use of Wisdom/Sophia as an appellation of God and a "Ritual of Sunday," which featured a liturgical sharing of milk and honey. The conference raised considerable tension and concern among many Presbyterians, with more than fifty communications from presbyteries and sessions and thousands of letters from church members reaching denominational headquarters. Pressure for Lundy's resignation resulted in her leaving in 1994. Voices heard in support affirmed the need to express the multiple and multicultural dimensions of the female experience (Boyd and Brackenridge, 2nd ed., 62–63).

Presbyterian Women, with its grassroots presence in local churches, continued its national publication, Bible study, financial support of the mission of the church,

and work for justice and peace. In 1999, estimating a membership of 300,000 to 350,000 members, the organization announced it intended to establish a fund to ensure financial support of women's programs at the General Assembly level to celebrate ten years as a unified organization.

Because of contested issues concerning women's ministries during the 1990s, the 1999 General Assembly requested a review of the Women's Ministries Program Area, including "the theological balance of [its] programming and material," by the end of February 2000. In February, the Council extended the timetable, because critics charged that the original review relied solely on input from the women's supporters. In June 2000 the Council affirmed the work of the Women's Ministries Program Area but called for the agency to be more broadly inclusive of the theological diversity around women's issues.

Over the years, Presbyterian women have been persistently loyal to their denominations, even in the face of disenfranchisement, controversies, criticisms, reorganizations, reunions, and their own lack of unanimity on various issues. In 1915, the officers of the Woman's Board of Home Missions affirmed that "Mrs. James brought us up with deference and obedience to the Assembly's [male] Board [of Home Missions]. 'Loyalty to the Board' was one of her re-iterated maxims, and when her mantle fell upon her associate Mrs. Bennett, the same policy was pursued" (Boyd and Brackenridge, 2nd ed., 24). Bennett's patience appeared tested, however, as she and Margaret Hodge examined their research in compiling their historic *Causes of Unrest among Women of the Church*. They wrote in that document, "It should not surprise anyone that among thinking women there arose a serious question as to whether their place of service could longer be found in the church when a great organization which they had built could be autocratically destroyed by vote of male members of the church without there seeming to arise in the mind of the latter any question as to the justice, wisdom or fairness of their actions" (Bennett and Hodge, 11). Despite such strong sentiments, these two women leaders, and many of the others who had voiced their concerns, urged cooperation between men and women.

Contemporary reports on the activities of Presbyterian women reflect continuing discussion on women's ministries. The historical context includes the participation of churchwomen in their homes, churches, and communities over the centuries, the "pious females" of the early period, members of the women's mission and educational associations of the nineteenth and twentieth centuries, wives of ministers and missionaries, female church school teachers and educators, lay volunteers, unordained preachers, foreign and home missionaries, church administrators and professionals, deaconesses, commissioned church workers, and women elders, deacons, and clergy.

SOURCES: The material in this essay is based largely on Lois A. Boyd and R. Douglas Brackenridge, *Presbyterian Women in America: Two Centuries of a Quest for Status*, 1st and 2nd eds. (1983, 1996), and is used with the permission of the Presbyterian Historical Society (PHS), Philadelphia, Pennsylvania. Sources include denominational minutes, reports, publications, record groups, periodicals, oral histories, and other materials at the Presbyterian Historical Society and the Historical Foundation of the Presbyterian and Reformed Churches at Montreat; information on the Presbyterian Church (USA) is from its Web site at http://www.pcusa.org/. A useful resource is Kristin L. Gleeson and Frederick J. Heuser, Jr., *A Guide to Women's Archival Resources in the Presbyterian Historical Society* (1995). Some early writings by Presbyterian women are Katharine Bennett and Margaret Hodge, *Causes of Unrest among Women of the Church* (1927); Katharine Bennett, *Status of Women in the Presbyterian Church in the U.S.A. with References to Other Denominations* (1929); Hallie Paxson Winsborough, *The Women's Auxiliary PCUS: A Brief History of Its Background Organization and Development* (1927) and *Yesteryears* (1937); Louisa M. Woosley, *Shall Women Preach? Or The Question Answered* (1891); and numerous articles in church periodicals. Other selected references are Annette Chapman-Adisbo, *Years of Strong Effort* (1998); Janie McGaughey, *On the Crest of the Present* (1961); Page Putnam Miller, *A Claim to New Roles* (1985); Elizabeth Verdesi, *In But Still Out: Women in the Church* (1973, 1976); and Verdesi Taylor and Lillian McCulloch Taylor, *Our Rightful Place: The Story of Presbyterian Women, 1970–1983* (1985). Essays involving women and the church are in various volumes of Milton J. Coalter, John M. Mulder, and Louis B. Weeks, eds., *The Presbyterian Presence: The Twentieth Century Experience*, 6 vols. (1990–1992).

The Presbyterian Church in the United States of America (PCUSA) was organized at the national level with the creation of a General Assembly in Philadelphia in 1789. Presbyterianism in America has encompassed various denominations calling themselves Presbyterian that have divided and merged. At the end of the Civil War, southern Presbyterians formed a denomination, the Presbyterian Church in the United States (PCUS). In 1906 the PCUSA and a majority of the Cumberland Presbyterian Church reunited. The United Presbyterian Church of North America, which was formed in 1848 through the merger of the Associate Synod, founded in 1753 by Covenanters, and the Associate Reformed Synod (Seceders), joined the PCUSA in 1958 to form the United Presbyterian Church in the USA (UPCUSA). A continuing denomination, the Associate Reformed Presbyterian Church, refused the merger. Another continuing body was the Reformed Presbyterian Church of North America. The Presbyterian Church in America was formed in 1973 by the withdrawal of conservative congregations from the PCUS. Other small groups maintain their separate denominational identities. In 1983, the UPCUSA and PCUS reunited into the present-day Presbyterian Church (USA). For further information, refer to Clifford Merrill Drury's *Presbyterian Panorama* (1952) and *Encyclopedia of the Reformed Faith*, s.v., "Presbyterianism in America," by Elwyn A. Smith.

WOMEN IN THE UNITED CHURCH OF CANADA
Phyllis D. Airhart

THE CREATION OF the United Church of Canada in 1925 brought together the Methodist Church (Canada, Newfoundland, and Bermuda), the Congregational Union of Canada, and all but a third of the Presbyterian Church in Canada. A number of local congregations already operating as union churches, most of them in western Canada, were also formally received into the new denomination. Inaugurated with approximately 8,000 congregations, 600,000 members, and 3,800 ministers, it has remained the largest Protestant denomination in Canada.

Supporters of church union shared the enthusiasm for Christian unity that was widespread as churches around the world looked for more effective ways to cooperate in their work. Union was also considered the most effective way to take care of the religious needs of new immigrants who were arriving in large numbers in the early twentieth century. For each denomination to try to cover the vast territory of the north and west where new communities were springing up seemed a terrible waste of already scarce resources. The plan to unite offered a solution.

But this first modern union across confessional lines in Western Christianity was accomplished only after a long and bitter round of negotiations drawn out over a period of nearly three decades, in the course of which both men and women formed strong opinions. Support among Methodists and Congregationalists was solid and approval quickly secured, with only Methodists in New-

Canadian Lois Wilson was the first woman to be elected president of the World Council of Churches, a position she held from 1983 to 1991. Regarded as an international authority on human rights issues, she was made an officer of the Order of Canada in 1984 and appointed to Canada's Senate from 1998 until her retirement in 2002. *Used by permission of Wolf Kutnahorsky, Berkeley Studio, catalogue no. 89.135P/98, Victoria University, Toronto, Canada.*

foundland voting to reject union. The story was different in the Presbyterian Church. After the General Assembly voted to proceed with union, an effective resistance movement drew strength from efforts at the local level. A congregational vote was held in each Presbyterian congregation to determine whether it would join the new church.

Although men were more visible in the controversy that erupted, the Presbyterian Women's League shrewdly organized family, friends, and other local support in anticipation of the vote and sponsored successful fundraising activities for the cause of resisting church union. Those who were against union were quick to recognize the potential of such an organization, particularly in congregations where the pastor had sided with the unionist cause. Women who favored church union did not form a separate organization but worked instead with the movement's male leadership.

In the years since 1925, the United Church of Canada has followed a trajectory familiar to other North American mainstream churches: significant public presence in the early decades, decline in membership and financial resources during the depression years, revival and new congregational development in the suburbs after World War II, and lower rates of membership and participation in recent decades. Throughout its history the church has upheld the importance of transformation of both individuals and institutions that was central to the evangelical piety of the founding traditions. The influence of the Social Gospel has been evident in the church's impulse to serve as the "conscience of the nation." The United Church of Canada has often claimed the latter when taking positions on political and social issues

viewed at the time as risky or debatable. Women in the denomination have drawn on this heritage in making the case for recognition of their place in its life and work.

With women ardently involved in local congregations as lay leaders, questions about status and roles were lively issues even prior to 1925. The three uniting churches employed women workers as deaconesses, although it is unclear whether the Congregationalists had ever formally approved formation of such an order as part of their polity. Despite calls in all three churches to ordain women, none had taken this step. Ordination of women was actually permitted under Congregationalist policy, and women had served as ministers in the United States, but by the time of union, no woman had yet been ordained in Canada. Methodism had a long history of allowing women to speak from the pulpit as lay preachers, but ordination was considered quite a different matter. Even after 1918, the year that women gained the same membership rights as men to serve on official boards or as delegates to the General Conference, motions to ordain women were defeated. Women could vote on local congregational matters in the Presbyterian Church but were prohibited from serving as members of the session (local) and could not be named as either presbytery (regional) or General Assembly (national) delegates.

Church union at first did nothing to change the policy of former Presbyterian churches. No names of Presbyterian women appear in the list of commissioners to the United Church of Canada's first General Council in 1925, which included four women: two former Methodists and two former Congregationalists. Reflecting the lingering reluctance to fuel controversy among former Presbyterians, the Basis of Union continued to refer to those eligible to serve as members of session as "men." It was not until 1932 that the General Council passed a motion to substitute the words "members in full membership" for "men," ratifying a change approved in a churchwide vote authorized in 1930.

Women's ordination quickly surfaced as a controversial issue as the new church began its work. As long as there were no women candidates seeking ordination, delaying consideration had been easy. That situation changed in 1923. The Presbyterian General Assembly received a request to ordain women who had "full theological training." Lydia Gruchy had recently graduated from St. Andrew's College in Saskatoon, Saskatchewan, and was working in a home mission pastoral charge. The 1924 General Assembly agreed to defer the request, since even ardent supporters of women's ordination such as Principal Edmund Oliver of St. Andrew's College saw church union as a higher priority. Neither Methodists nor Presbyterians wanted to provoke dissension by taking a step that even women in some local congregations did not support.

Once union was achieved, supporters of Lydia Gruchy and women's ordination quickly put the matter before the General Council of the new church. The report of the committee formed in 1926 recommended that no immediate action be taken on ordaining women to the ministry of Word and sacraments. Instead, the committee proposed that women be admitted to an *ordained diaconate* to preach, teach, and baptize where necessary.

For some, even this compromise went too far, for the door had been left open by the use of the phrase not to ordain women "at this time." A minority statement appended to the committee's report presented objections to women's ordination. One concern was specific to the particular form of ordination proposed: Since the order of deacon was in other churches understood to be an inferior and temporary order of ministry, the committee was thus consigning women to a position of perpetual inferiority. To remedy this "injustice," they argued, women ought not to be ordained to the ministry at all.

Other objections included in the minority report were typical of the case against women's ordination made over the next few years; indeed, some of the arguments were to surface again decades later in discussions of whether married women could serve as ordained ministers. The minority report claimed that women themselves did not favor such a move. Women could not serve in remote and difficult pastoral charges without "loss of that womanliness which is her greatest possession." Only single women could serve since married women would have to either remain childless or create the "not very edifying spectacle of the husband keeping house" ("Report of the Committee on the Or-

dination of Women," The General Council [of the United Church of Canada], 1927, Toronto). Since the church needed more rather than less masculinity, having women in ministry would undermine efforts to attract "strong virile manhood" to this work. Moreover, there was simply no demand for women's ordination.

Since the ordination of women required an amendment to the Basis of Union (which stated that "God calls men" to the ministry of Word and sacraments), a majority of presbyteries had to vote to change the reference to "men." Those who opposed women's ordination found some surprising allies in the ensuing debate. Although she was not expressing the official position of the Woman's Missionary Society, national president Janet MacGillivray implied that most members of that organization did not favor ordination. Some prominent Social Gospel leaders, notably Ernest Thomas in an exchange of published correspondence with social reformer Nellie McClung, also objected. The confusing vote of the presbyteries, reported to the General Council in 1928, did little to clarify the matter, serving only to delay a decision. The "no" vote outnumbered the "yes" vote by only two, but a quarter of the presbyteries did not vote at all. And since the question was over ordination to the *diaconate* (which many supporters of women's ordination considered unacceptable), how was a "no" vote to be interpreted? The church once again took the safe path and waited.

The discussion centered on the ordination of one particular woman, Lydia Gruchy. Opponents insisted there was no demand outside Saskatchewan to ordain women. Undeterred, Saskatchewan Conference reported to the 1934 General Council that unless the Council objected, Gruchy would be ordained. The next vote with its straightforward question "Do you approve of the ordination of women?" passed easily. The recommendation to ordain women was approved at the 1936 General Council, and shortly after, Gruchy became the first woman to be ordained by the United Church of Canada, the first denomination in Canada to do so.

The 1936 decision paved the way for the ordination of some women but left unresolved a number of questions. What to do with women who married subsequent to ordination was one of the first to be raised. The general assumption was that a married woman could not be an ordained minister or a deaconess, thus the appeal of "ordaining" women as deaconesses. Deaconess could be a temporary role, moved in and out of easily. Ordination to the ministry of Word and sacrament was another matter: Primary and lifelong service was assumed. On that basis, Margaret Butler, a married woman and a mother, was at first denied ordination in 1946. Most women simply avoided confrontation by marrying after they were ordained. Lois Wilson, the first woman to be elected as moderator of the United Church of Canada, recalls in her autobiography the tip of a friend who urged her to follow her own example; she had delayed marriage until after she was ordained (Wilson, 23). Wilson decided not to follow that advice. She was ordained in 1965, on her fifteenth wedding anniversary, with her husband Roy, an ordained minister, involved in the laying on of hands at the service (42).

A year earlier the way had finally been cleared for Wilson and many others to consider ordained ministry as a suitable vocation for a married woman. When Elinor Leard, a married woman, was ordained in spite of the objections of the United Church of Canada's moderator, General Council was asked to clarify "the relationship of an ordained woman minister to her work following her marriage." The Commission on Ordination, which was given the task of dealing with the problem, concluded in its report to General Council in 1962 that a married woman was unable to discharge her obligations to her husband and children and, at the same time, carry on the work for which she was ordained. Grappling with such issues as to whether there was something about the act of ordination that was unique and unrepeatable, and whether ordination could be suspended in some way or even revoked, the committee's report took a position that preserved traditional assumptions, recommending ordination only for unmarried women, widows, or those whose work in ministry would not interfere with their roles as mothers or wives.

Unwilling to adopt this recommendation when it was put to a vote, the General Council referred the report to its Executive for further deliberation. The Executive rejected the report's recommendation in 1963, upholding instead the practice of ordaining married women. The next General Council ratified the Executive's decision in 1964. But attitudes took even longer to change—even for the women ministers themselves. In her autobiography Wilson recounts that the local newspaper reported her as saying that she felt that "her ordination will give her a greater opportunity of helping her husband" in his work as minister. When the Wilsons served as team ministers, many in the congregation still preferred to have him preside at baptisms or funerals; some brides wondered if they were properly married when a woman conducted the wedding service (Wilson, 42–44).

A second unresolved issue concerned the standing of other women workers in the church, particularly deaconesses. A committee set up in 1926 to assess the working conditions of women workers identified nearly 1,000 such employees. More than one-third were missionaries supported by the Woman's Missionary Society; another 116 were deaconesses. Others held positions as social workers, educators, assistants to ministers or chaplains, or secretaries. All but a few dozen of the women who worked in congregations were in clerical positions.

Recruitment was a major objective of the committee,

but it was hindered in attracting new recruits by certain church policies and practices. Although working conditions and salaries varied, remuneration was generally far below the going rate for comparable services elsewhere. Other policies would give a woman pause for thought as she pondered becoming a candidate for diaconal ministry. To be considered, a woman had to be single and between the ages of twenty-three and thirty-five. The old practice of accepting only single women, borrowed in the early days from the model of Catholic sisters who lived in community, obliged a woman to withdraw from the order if she later married. It was not until the 1950s, coinciding with consideration of ordained women in similar situations, that deaconesses were allowed to continue as members of the order subsequent to marriage. Such policies gave the impression that diaconal work was temporary and inferior to the "lifelong" commitment of ordination. Too, a woman's natural and primary calling was considered to be marriage and motherhood.

The debate over whether to ordain women and efforts to recruit more women workers at first ran counter to the practical realities of church life in the 1930s. For a time the financial pressures of the Great Depression resulted in more limited opportunities for women. In 1938 the recently ordained Lydia Gruchy moved to Toronto, where she served for five years as executive secretary of a new committee on the Deaconess Order and Women Workers, which was to address the challenges faced by women employed by the church. By the early 1940s the expanded opportunities in congregational ministry, created by a shortage of ordained ministers during World War II, continued as congregations grew after the war and expanded into the suburbs. Plans for congregational development often included Christian education and community outreach, areas of work in which deaconesses specialized. Despite these new opportunities, questions of "status" were left unresolved until 1964 when deaconesses (later referred to as "diaconal ministers") gained the same standing in the courts of the church as ordained ministers. Even so, they were still technically counted as "lay" representatives until 1968, when both ordained and diaconal ministers were designated as "Order of Ministry."

The relationship between ordained and diaconal ministers (nearly all women) has remained unclear and at times been strained. Until the early 1970s, more women prepared to become deaconesses than ordained ministers. Diaconal ministry thus was and continues to be a significant form of women's ministry. But it begs the question: Why have two forms of ordered ministry? Attempts to have only one order of ministry—ordained—have repeatedly met with opposition from diaconal ministers themselves. Many see their particular form of ministry as a way of highlighting service and education—"ministry on the margins" as they put it. Some see diaconal ministry as a way of resisting what they consider to be the hierarchical assumptions of ordained ministry; it is an alternative style of ministry that involves a different approach to educational preparation. The Centre for Christian Studies (formerly named Covenant College and before that the United Church Training School) has played a key educational role in preparing women workers and continues to press the case for the diaconal ministry as distinct from ordained ministry.

While the church in Canada debated recruitment and ordination, the mission field continued to attract women in significant numbers. Women were more quickly accepted as missionaries than as ordained ministers, since the general assumption was that they could work more effectively with other women in cultures where the ideology of separation of the sexes prevailed. Despite the hard work and discomforts, missionary life offered professional opportunities in a number of fields, notably medicine, often well in advance of available secular options in Canada. The varied activities of women missionaries included evangelistic, educational, and medical work in home missions in Canada and foreign missions around the world.

Women missionaries, notably Katharine Hockin, were among those at the forefront of discussions to develop a new concept of partnership in mission. Her own life story represents the shift: As one who was initially "sent" by the United Church of Canada to serve as a teacher in China, she later promoted the policy of responding only to invitations from partner churches in other countries who required particular expertise or resources. When Hockin was born in 1910, her parents were serving as Canadian Methodist missionaries at the West China Mission. After studying and teaching in Canada from 1926 to 1940, she returned to China. Living through the upheavals of the Cultural Revolution, she watched as an "atmosphere of acceptance" of Westerners became "one of outright hostility, with expressions of resentment and hatred." Yet she came to realize that if she had been a Chinese youth, "I would in all probability hate me too!" Departing in 1951 with her own sense of mission tested, she resolved to help Canadians understand what was happening in China, even when they could not agree with communist practices. The final stage of what she called her "pilgrimage in mission" came with the recognition that "we may have moved from Clone to Companion": no longer expecting our partners in mission to imitate our practice of Christianity and instead working with, rather than for, them as friends (Hockin, 27).

Women who served the United Church of Canada as paid professionals were joined by those whose participation involved such volunteer activities as singing in the choir, church school teaching, community outreach, and other expressions of hospitality and care. The group identity of United Church women has been most prominently displayed in gender-specific organizations such as missionary societies, women's auxiliaries, and clubs for girls. After union denominational leaders were challenged to find a place in the emerging ecclesial structure for those organizations in which girls and women had participated prior to union. Some fit easily because denominational lines had already been blurred. Across the nation Protestant girls aged twelve to seventeen joined the Canadian Girls in Training (CGIT) to become, with Jesus' help, "the girl God would have me be." Organized in 1917, the organization had attracted nearly 30,000 girls by the time of church union. Other gender-specific groups operated with little disruption created by union except where congregational life was changed by the closing or merging of congregations. The locally administered Ladies' Aid societies continued to respond to such concerns as maintaining parsonages and reducing church debt. In 1940 these groups were succeeded by the Woman's Association (WA) of the United Church of Canada, a new organization that described its members as "the home-makers of the Church."

Most visible and influential among the various women's organizations were the missionary societies. Formed in the late nineteenth century, three denominational societies combined in 1926 to form the Woman's Missionary Society. At a time when similar women's organizations in the United States were merging with the largely male-led denominational mission boards, the Woman's Missionary Society chose instead to retain its autonomy for more than another quarter century. Until 1962 the society raised and allocated its own funds; had its own board, which cooperated with but remained distinct from the general board of missions; and oversaw the recruitment, placement, financial support, and ongoing encouragement of its missionaries working in Canada and overseas. The educational component was a crucial factor in the program's success. Women not only worked together but learned together as they explored the new worlds that study books, leaflets, and other regular publications such as *World Friends* and *The Missionary Monthly* opened to them. The Woman's Missionary Society worked not only with adults but with children and youth through affiliated Baby Bands, Mission Bands, Canadian Girls in Training groups, and Mission Circles. In addition to providing money to support those who served as missionaries at home and abroad, the Woman's Missionary Society allocated staff funding to develop programs for varied activities. Its personnel included Olive Sparling, assigned to the Woman's Missionary Society national staff to work as secretary for children's education. She later became a key member of the team that produced the New

Curriculum, an innovative program of church school materials that generated controversy for its liberal theological assumptions, launched in 1962 after a decade of planning and preparation.

In 1962 the Woman's Missionary Society and the Woman's Association merged to form the United Church Women (UCW). Creating a new organization was recommended by a committee formed in 1953 to study their relationship to each other and to the administrative structure of the denomination. In part the impetus had come from local groups, which saw no reason to support two different women's groups, often composed of the same members, at a time when employment outside the home left some pressed for time for such voluntary activities. The merger effected with the church's general mission board was also an acknowledgment of the confusion that had often resulted from efforts to support two sets of missionary personnel. Reba Patterson, the last woman to serve as president of the Dominion Board of the Woman's Missionary Society, and Jean Hutchinson, chair of the denomination's Board of Women, were instrumental in the organizational transition.

As part of the agreement to form the United Church Women, $6.5 million in funds along with property holdings were transferred from the Woman's Missionary Society to the new Board of World Mission. The new board was responsible for about ninety missionaries formerly supported by the Woman's Missionary Society (a depleted complement stemming from recruitment problems that had troubled the organization in its final years). In exchange for structural integration, the Woman's Missionary Society was promised at least one woman among the officers of the new missions board. Women were to make up a minimum of one-third of the lay members of the board and were assured of increased representation on other national church boards. Yet women remained significantly outnumbered by men on most committees, contributing to their sense of loss of administrative power. Autonomy had been one of the defining features of the Woman's Missionary Society. With that gone, the United Church Women tended to assume a role in most congregations similar to the one previously played by the Woman's Association. Those who treasured the educational dimension of the Woman's Missionary Society programming also lamented the lost opportunities for study.

Involvement in local United Church Women units peaked in the mid-1960s. Since then a number of factors can be attributed to membership losses and dwindling support for its volunteer activities, including the changing patterns of women's employment outside the home and a heightened sense of individuality that occasioned a more inward-looking and less altruistic approach to the religious life. Working women found it difficult to fit one more commitment into already busy schedules. They were now more likely to be invited to serve on presbytery and national committees, an acknowledgment of the promise that had been made at the time of restructuring of women's groups, but indicating in some cases the need to replace men who were no longer as willing to serve. In an attempt to address declining membership, the organizational shape of the church's programming for women was restructured in 2000 under a new name: Women of the United Church of Canada. Whereas the focus of the older United Church Women units had been fund-raising, hospitality, and study, the new organization will attempt to combine such activities with an attention to spirituality and the formation of support groups that have more recently emerged as program alternatives.

These organizational changes coincided with indications of the impact of cultural change evident in other major committee reports. The report of the Commission on the Gainful Employment of Married Women (1962) signaled the challenges the church would face over the next decades as it dealt with women's declining participation in volunteer activities. For instance, the report noted that the majority of women's group members were nonworking married women who were able to attend meetings during the day. But the census figures for 1961 disclosed a startling trend: 20 percent of married women were working outside the home, and nearly 50 percent of working women were married. A comparison with figures from the 1941 census indicated how dramatically the situation had shifted in just two decades; then the percentage of employed married women was only 5 percent, even though the country was at war.

Noting that its report was the first in Canada to consider the implications of married women in paid positions from a Christian perspective, the committee appears to have been refreshingly open to the direction of this trend—ironic in view of the recommendation of the Commission on Ordination that was put before the same General Council (though not approved) *not* to ordain married women. The report pointedly observed that a woman who taught school or worked as a hospital custodian might be using her time away from family concerns as profitably as one who filled her days with such idle amusements as bingo, bridge, shopping, or coffee-partying. The church was urged to counter the unsympathetic attitude toward working women that contributed to the sense of guilt that many experienced. The church could give some practical assistance for children of working mothers by providing lunch and other meals or after-school supervision of homework and recreation. The report also recommended that the government or a social agency study new policies that might be necessitated by the increased number of working mothers, specifically the need for financial assistance to young mothers who were working only because of financial necessity, a minimum wage law, and equal pay for equal work.

Through the decades women in the United Church of Canada have grappled with the implications of roles prescribed for them in these and other reports, some of which have created controversy in their wake. In the 1930s the church supported the notion of "voluntary parenthood," the euphemism of the day for birth control, in "The Meaning and Responsibility of Christian Marriage" (1932) and the "Report of the Commission on Voluntary Sterilization" (1936). The traditional spousal relationship presented in the "Commission on Christian Marriage and Christian Home" (1946) reflected the postwar desire for normalcy and family stability, whereas the reports of the Commission on Christian Marriage and Divorce (1960, 1962) recognized the failure of many to achieve lifelong marriage unions. By agreeing to perform marriages where one or both persons were divorced, the United Church of Canada took the brunt of criticism for a practice that a number of other denominations have since adopted with far less fanfare.

Other policies with ramifications for women have generated controversy. Greater awareness of the power of language to shape religious experience was evident by the 1970s. Much attention has since been given to sexism not only in relationships and employment but in the language of theology and worship as well. The church has also been concerned with the human rights of those in same-sex relationships. Even the contentious 1960 report on marriage and divorce, regarded as radical in its day, had explicitly condemned the practice of homosexuality. However, after considerable debate and study in the 1980s, women and men in same-sex relations were supported in the statement approved by General Council in 1988 that all persons who professed faith in Jesus Christ and obedience to him were welcome to be full members of the United Church of Canada, regardless of their sexual orientation, and as such they could be considered as candidates for its ministry.

The story of women in the United Church of Canada has been one of vitality and increasing visibility. Along with the countless women who have served in the congregations and courts of the church with little recognition, a number have gained prominence in the national church. Since 1980, when Lois Wilson became the first woman to serve as moderator, Anne Squire, Marion Best, and Marion Pardy have been elected to that position. Each has brought her unique gifts to the United Church while serving as its chief elected officer with responsibilities for providing spiritual leadership to the church, representing it at numerous public occasions,

and interpreting its policies. In 1994, Virginia Coleman was elected as secretary of General Council, the denomination's chief administrative officer, working in that position until 2002.

From the outset, women have found opportunities for service in the church's educational institutions. Winnifred Thomas, Gertrude Rutherford, Jean Hutchinson, Harriet Christie, and Gwyneth Griffith were among the women who provided strong administrative leadership as principals of the school that trained diaconal ministers. Women's leadership in preparing native students for ministry is recognized in the naming of one of the denomination's educational centers: the Dr. Jessie Saulteaux Resource Centre. Many have served with distinction far beyond denominational circles. Lois Wilson, for example, was the first Canadian to be elected president of the World Council of Churches, a position she held from 1983 to 1991. Regarded as an international authority on human rights issues, she was made an officer of the Order of Canada in 1984 and appointed to Canada's Senate from 1998 until her retirement in 2002.

Women are well represented numerically in the United Church of Canada. In the first census figures after church union (1931), women counted for 49.3 percent of its members. This percentage has edged up slightly in each subsequent census, with the most recent data (2001) indicating that 53.6 percent of the 2,839,125 Canadians who identify themselves as affiliated with the denomination are women. Statistics also reflect the sea change in professional opportunities for women in ministry. In 2003 the United Church of Canada reported that 34 percent of its 4,596 ministry personnel were women: 27 percent of ordained ministers, 94 percent of diaconal ministers, 54 percent of lay pastoral ministers, and 78 percent of staff associates. The continuing appeal of ministry for women is reflected in numbers as well. In 2003, 65 percent of the new ministry personnel in ordered ministry were women: thirty-four of the fifty-five ordained ministers, and six of the seven diaconal ministers. Whatever the future may hold for the United Church of Canada, these statistics signal that women will be at the forefront of those shaping it.

SOURCES: One of the early research projects on women in the United Church of Canada combines the stories of women as ministers, missionaries, and lay leaders along with analysis of their contribution. See Shirley Davy, ed., *Women Work and Worship in the United Church of Canada* (1983). The development of ordered ministry in the United Church of Canada is explored in Valerie J. Korinek, "No Women Need Apply: The Ordination of Women in the United Church, 1918–65," *Canadian Historical Review* 74.4 (1993): 473–509; Nancy Hardy, *Called to Serve: A Story of Diaconal Ministry in the United Church of Canada* (1985); and Mary Anne MacFarlane, "Faithful and Courageous Handmaidens: Deaconesses in the

United Church of Canada, 1925–1945," in *Changing Roles of Women in the Christian Church in Canada*, ed. Elizabeth Gillan Muir and Marilyn Färdig Whiteley (1995). Lois Wilson's autobiography, *Turning the World Upside Down: A Memoir* (1989), provides an engaging account of her multifaceted work as a denominational leader. Katharine Hockin reflects on the changing context of missionary activity in her autobiographical article "My Pilgrimage in Mission," *International Bulletin of Missionary Research* 12 (January 1988): 23–30. Mary Rose Donnelly and Heather Dau tell the story of Hockin's work in China and at the diaconal training school in Toronto in *Katharine Boehner Hockin: A Biography* (1992). Missionaries and the women in congregations who supported them are featured in Donna Sinclair, *Crossing Worlds: The Story of the Woman's Missionary Society of the United Church of Canada* (1992).

WOMEN IN THE UNITED CHURCH OF CHRIST
Barbara Brown Zikmund

ALTHOUGH THE UNITED Church of Christ (UCC) is predominantly a mix of traditions from the English Protestant Reformation, and several sixteenth-century European continental Protestant reform movements, it also draws upon faith and practice that is uniquely American. Some parts of the United Church of Christ are rooted in frontier revivalism, which sought to make religion reflect the "republican values" of the new nation. Others are nurtured by the rich religious legacy of African Americans. In the twentieth century the UCC has been enriched by the ideas and religious vitality of Native Americans, Asians, Pacific Islanders, Hispanics, and central Europeans, especially the Hungarians. Its history stretches from Puritan New England to the Hawaiian Islands. Its women have been and continue to be leaders in American religion.

Colonial Beginnings

The earliest colonial history of the United Church of Christ begins with Congregationalism in New England. Congregationalists came to the colonies seeking religious freedom. Most of them rejected the religious practices of the Church of England, which they believed was still tainted with Roman Catholic evils. Some early Congregationalists were "Separatists"—they thought that they needed to "separate" from the corrupt English church. But most Congregationalists were "Puritans," not "Separatists." They did not want to leave the church; they simply wanted to create a better church in the New World.

Their New England "Congregational" understanding of the church insisted that when faithful Christians gathered to worship under the guidance of the Holy Spirit, they were a complete church. They did not need pastors or bishops; they did not need "Books of Common Prayer" or guidance from some far-off authority. They believed that each individual "congregation" was under the "Lordship of Jesus Christ." Each member of the congregation was responsible for his or her faith. Theologically, most Congregationalists were "Calvinists" and stood firmly within the Reformed tradition, but ecclesiastically they were deeply committed to the radical idea that the essence of the church was found in the "gathered community of the saints."

Women within Congregationalism were theologically equal with men, equally lost in sin and equally in need of God's grace in Jesus Christ. They cared for their families, studied their Bibles, prayed and sought to live a godly life in hopes that God had predestined them for salvation. We do not know a great deal about many individual Congregational women, but we do know that most of them struggled with the state of their soul and took their religious life seriously. Church records, letters, and personal diaries document their religious fervor. Churches were filled with women. And writers like Anne Bradstreet and Phillis Wheatley capture some of their piety in poetry. Early Congregational women found their fulfillment as "good wives." Unlike religious traditions, which glorified celibacy, Congregationalism lifted up marriage as God's plan for men and women. A woman enabled a man to live a holy life. Her well-ordered family served as a model for church and state. During the colonial era the highest calling for many Congregational women was to marry a clergyman. As wives of key religious leaders, Congregational women often made silent but important contributions to their communities.

Unfortunately, historical records also reveal that when Congregational women, like Anne Hutchinson, deviated from supportive roles and became more assertive, they got into trouble. In 1636 Hutchinson, who tried to remain very respectful of her pastor John Cotton, made the male leadership of early Boston uneasy. She held meetings of women in her home to discuss theology and in the process criticized some religious leaders. Eventually her views were seen as heretical, and she was tried and banished from Massachusetts. Fifty years later, in the late seventeenth century, Congregational women (and some men) were condemned as "witches" in Salem, Massachusetts. A number of them were killed in the resulting hysteria.

Most Congregational women, however, were not radical enough to threaten authority. They lived out their lives as "good wives," and sometimes they inspired others. By the early eighteenth century male clergy began

Repeatedly the UCC General Synod has passed resolutions and expended staff resources to deal with issues of women and poverty, sexual harassment, racism, affirmative action, AIDs, sexual discrimination, genital mutilation, and all forms of violence against women and children. The denomination has worked closely with other organizations to pass national laws that will protect and support working women, minority women, and lesbians. *United Church of Christ, Cleveland, Ohio.*

publishing the memoirs of pious Congregational women to inspire people. "Women," they argued, "were crucial to the salvation of the church."

Congregationalism is not the only colonial legacy within the United Church of Christ. In the early eighteenth century, William Penn, an English Quaker, founded Pennsylvania—attracting many colonists from all over Europe. Thousands of peasants from the Rhine river valley, who wanted to escape from years of religious wars between Catholics and Protestants, and between Lutherans and Reformed Protestants, came to America looking for a better life. Most of them spoke German. They were not seeking religious freedom like the Congregationalists; they just wanted land and an opportunity to raise their children in a peaceful place. They saw America as the "promised land" for those who were willing to work hard.

Religiously, large numbers of these German immigrants were rooted in the moderate ideas of the Swiss German Reformation. They came from the Palatinate, the area around the city of Heidelberg. Their religious beliefs had been shaped by the moderate pastoral message of the Heidelberg Catechism. Their worship practices were simple and disciplined.

We know very little about the earliest German Reformed women. No doubt they spent their days and years tending to large families and doing what was necessary to maintain their homes and farms. They also participated in numerous German Reformed churches throughout colonial Pennsylvania and North Carolina. Initially German Reformed churches looked to the Dutch for ecclesiastical support. Yet, during the war for independence, German Reformed colonists embraced the patriot cause. In the midst of the hostilities the liberty bell was hidden in the Old First German Reformed Church of Philadelphia. German Reformed women and men felt that God had called them to a new life in a new place. They had no loyalty to the English crown or any other European authority. Shortly after the end of the war, they broke away from the Dutch church and reorganized themselves as a new independent church— the German Reformed Church in the United States. In that church, although women remained behind the scenes in supportive roles, we know that they were there. The graves of women fill the small neat cemeteries next to many United Church of Christ churches in Pennsylvania and North Carolina.

The relationship of Native American women to Congregational and German Reformed women during the colonial period was minimal. Except for a few Native women who befriended settlers and were idealized, like Pocahontas, European colonists did not look favorably on Native peoples. They generally pitied Native women and saw no hope for them or their people, except through conversion to Christianity. The work of John Eliot, an early missionary to the Indians, made Congregationalists more aware of Native Americans, but many decades passed before American Indian women began to find a place within the United Church of Christ.

Reflecting National Diversity

In the first half of the eighteenth century, the American colonies experienced a grassroots revival of religious enthusiasm known as the Great Awakening. Local pastors, such as Congregationalist Jonathan Edwards, called church members to deepen their faith and rediscover their salvation in Jesus Christ. Women and men responded in great numbers. Many women deepened their spiritual concerns and became more intentional as Christian mothers and wives.

After the Revolutionary War, as Americans began to move West, patriotic enthusiasm about living in a "republic" also democratized their attitudes about religion. They had thrown off the authoritarian power of the British Empire and its king, and they were eager to promote what they called "Republican religion"—that is, religion free of authoritarian assumptions and practices.

THE CHRISTIAN MOVEMENT

On the expanding frontier of the new nation some men and women left denominations rooted in European traditions to form new nonsectarian "Christian" groups. They rejected all denominational labels, believing that the true church should be known only as "Christian," and its only head was Jesus Christ. They embraced the Bible as their only rule of faith and practice, rejecting all creeds. Christian character was a sufficient test of faith.

Initially, so-called frontier Christians refused to affiliate with any wider ecclesiastical organizations. They promoted Christian unity and rejected denominational camps. They appealed to the independent spirit of expanding frontier society and participated in revivalism. Within the Christian movement there were a number of women who preached and founded churches. Although pioneer Christian women were never formally "ordained," these "female laborers in the gospel" were highly respected and effective. In the early nineteenth century Nancy Gove Cram of Weare, New Hampshire, and Clarissa H. Danforth of Vermont carried on effective itinerant ministries among Christians in northern and western New England. Abigail Roberts, one of the best known early Christian preachers, was reputed to have founded four churches in New York, Pennsylvania, and New Jersey during her short ministry in the 1830s.

Some branches of the frontier Christian movement became denominations that are known today as the Disciples of Christ and the Churches of Christ. Others called themselves the "Christian Connection, or Christian Churches." Small "Christian Churches" persisted in northern New England, in North Carolina and Virginia, and in Kentucky, Ohio, Indiana, and Illinois. They endured by resisting bureaucratic organization and spreading their ideas about the essence of Christianity and Christian unity through newspapers and magazines. In the early twentieth century a group of these Christian Churches recognized, however, that they needed to connect with the wider church. Eventually they merged with the Congregational Churches to create the General Council of the Congregational Christian Churches. Most people do not realize that the strong advocacy for women's leadership within the United Church of Christ comes from the history of the Christian Churches as well as from Congregationalism.

AFRICAN AMERICANS

The story of African American women in the United Church of Christ draws upon both Christian and Congregational history. First, the blacks in the South, especially in eastern Virginia and North Carolina, were influenced by the "Christian movement." Even before the Emancipation Proclamation slaves often organized informal "churches." In the worship and life of such groups, women's leadership was regularly exercised and honored. "Holy women" were part of the legacy of African culture. After the Civil War, white "Christians" in the South helped blacks organize "Afro-Christian Churches." In these Afro-Christian Churches Sunday Schools played a key role in educating and upholding the dignity of black men and women in the post–Civil War South.

Second, Congregationalists were deeply committed to the abolitionist cause. Unlike many denominations, such as the Methodists, Baptists, and Presbyterians that split into Northern and Southern denominations over the issue of slavery, Congregationalism was a Northern denomination, and it never split. Congregationalists tended to agree that slavery was wrong, in spite of the fact that they had great debates about how Christians should bring about its end.

Initially, moderate Congregationalists supported "gradual emancipation" through the American Colonization Society. Over time, however, most Congregationalists came to believe that only "immediate emancipation," or abolition, was a Christian position. Congregationalists worked through the American Missionary Association (AMA) to end slavery; and once slavery was abolished, they sponsored a great missionary effort to educate and uplift the newly freed slaves. Even before emancipation, Mary Ann Shadd Cary became one of the first black women lawyers in America and challenged the AMA and well-known black men of her time, such as Frederick Douglass, to recognize her ability and her commitment to education for her people.

After the Civil War hundreds of Congregational missionaries, female and male, white and black, went into the war-torn South to found and teach in schools for freed slaves. One such woman was Edmonia Highgate, a free black woman from Plymouth Congregational Church in Syracuse, New York. In the 1860s she taught in a number of schools in Virginia, Maryland, and Louisiana, and she also raised money for the work of the American Missionary Association. Many AMA schools only lasted for a few years until the basic literacy needs of former slaves were met. Others, however, grew into highly respected institutions of higher education, such as Fisk University and Dillard University. Not surprisingly, where American Missionary Association schools persisted, strong African American Congregational churches flourished. Black women and men, nurtured in schools founded by Congregationalists, adapted the legacy of Congregationalism to meet their needs in the new South. Many of the first black women in the United States to get a college education were graduates of American Missionary Association colleges and members of southern Congregational churches.

German Evangelicals

Women's presence in the United Church of Christ has also followed later patterns of immigration. Although it is impossible to list all of the immigrant groups that have come into the denomination, it is important to mention six: German Evangelicals, "Germans from Russia," Armenians, Hungarians, Hispanics, and Asian and Pacific Islanders.

The United Church of Christ is a union of the Congregational Christian Churches and the Evangelical and Reformed Church. These two denominations were themselves the products of two earlier church mergers. All in all, in 1957 four historical traditions flowed together to create the United Church of Christ. The Congregationalists, German Reformed, and Christians have already been mentioned. The "Evangelicals," which joined with the German Reformed Church to create the Evangelical and Reformed Church, are the fourth main group in United Church of Christ history.

The story of the German Evangelicals begins within Protestantism in northern Europe in the early 1800s. In that setting Lutheran and Reformed Protestants had been arguing and even fighting with each other since the sixteenth century. Rivalries between Protestant factions were fierce and sometimes petty. In that environment,

although many Protestants became discouraged, several things happened to give them hope.

First, in 1817 the ruler of Prussia declared that there would only be one "Evangelical," or Protestant, church in his realm. Lutherans and Reformed Christians would worship together and learn to live with their differences. Although at first his decision was controversial, over time many Protestants in that region came to see themselves simply as part of the "Evangelical Church of the Prussian Union," a blend of Lutheran and Reformed traditions.

Second, German Evangelicals were inspired by the principles of "Pietism," a movement to rediscover the personal and emotional aspects of Christianity. Pietistic Swiss Protestant missionary societies began to train and send missionaries to America to serve the religious needs of European immigrants.

And third, as millions of Germans became increasingly frustrated with the economic and political situation in Europe, they made personal decisions to emigrate. The flow of German immigrants into the Mississippi River valley during the first half of the nineteenth century brought people with many different attitudes toward religion. Some were totally secular, leaving their religious past behind. Others were zealously trying to preserve some pure form of religious dogma or ritual that they thought had been compromised. And still others simply sought comfortable ways to practice their piety and evangelical practice without being hassled.

German Evangelicals were part of this last group. They organized churches to provide support for their families as they established farms across the Midwest. Their churches were often served by missionaries from the Swiss missionary societies, and their moderate religious practices were respected on the prairie frontier. It is hard to document the role of women among German Evangelicals, except to say that they loved their churches and their pastors, and they did what they had to do to build a new life for themselves and their families in America.

In order to meet the needs of so many new German immigrants, not surprisingly, more established German denominations in America, such as the German Reformed Church in the United States, also extended itself into missionary work on the frontier. In the last half of the nineteenth century a number of new German Reformed Churches were also founded in the upper Midwest.

By the early twentieth century, the (German) Reformed Church in the United States and the (German) Evangelical Synod of North America (by that time both denominations had dropped "German" from their names) came together to form the Evangelical and Reformed Church.

GERMAN CONGREGATIONALISTS

European immigration to the United States continued throughout the nineteenth century and into the early twentieth century. In the 1880s and 1890s large numbers of ethnic Germans, who had lived for several generations in Russia under the hospitality of the czars, came to North America. These "Germans from Russia" were very independent, having run their own German towns, schools, and churches as ethnic enclaves in central Russia for decades. When they arrived in America, although they spoke German, they found that they had more in common with the Congregationalists because they organized their churches "congregationally." It was natural for German Congregational churches to affiliate with other Congregationalists. Women in the German Congregational churches were active parishioners, but there is little record of women's formal leadership among German Congregationalists.

ARMENIAN CONGREGATIONALISTS AND HUNGARIAN REFORMED CHURCHES

The story of women in the Armenian Congregational churches and the Hungarian Reformed churches is much the same. Due to the fact that the Congregational American Board of Commissioners for Foreign Missions did major mission work in Armenia, when the Armenians fled the Turkish assault on their culture in the early twentieth century, immigrant Armenians felt a special link to Congregationalists. As they organized new churches in America, they invariably sought affiliation with Congregationalists.

Hungarian immigrants, deeply loyal to their Reformed heritage, turned to the (German) Reformed Church in the United States. In the 1920s the Reformed Church in the United States signed an official agreement with the Hungarian Reformed Church (back in Europe) agreeing to provide support for Hungarian refugees in America. When the Evangelical and Reformed Church came into being a few years later, it created a special Magyar Synod for Hungarian churches; and when the United Church of Christ was formed, it carried on that obligation through an "acting conference" called the Calvin Synod. Women in Armenian and Hungarian churches in the United Church of Christ have helped to preserve these ethnic traditions within a predominantly Anglo-Saxon denomination.

HISPANICS, ASIANS, AND PACIFIC ISLANDERS

The United Church of Christ draws deeply from its European roots, but as it has matured, it has also benefited from the important contributions of Hispanics, Asians, and Pacific Islanders. Indeed, the presence of some of these groups in the history of the United

Church of Christ is as long standing as it is among several European groups.

Congregational missionary work in Mexico laid the foundation for the Mexican Congregational churches. The American Missionary Association, which did so much with African Americans in the South, also played an important role in Puerto Rico. Furthermore, the American Missionary Association sent missionaries to California and Hawaii to support the development of Chinese and Japanese Congregational churches. Finally, when the American Board of Commissioners for Foreign Missions turned its attention to the Pacific Islands and Asia, it sent Congregational missionaries to the Sandwich Islands (Hawaii) in the early nineteenth century. Today the United Church of Christ is the largest Protestant denomination in the state of Hawaii. Although Hawaiians should not be called "immigrants," their contributions, along with Hispanics, Japanese, Chinese, Filipino, Native Americans, and African Americans, have helped the United Church of Christ claim a twenty-first-century identity as a multiracial and multicultural church. In all of these groups women have played key roles by raising ethnic consciousness and pressing the leadership of the denomination to live up to its calling.

Mission Outreach and Service

The growing presence of racial and ethnic diversity in the United Church of Christ is only one way to tell the story of women in the UCC. Another way to remember women in the United Church of Christ is to lift up the role of women in the history of missions.

WOMAN'S BOARDS OF MISSIONS

For the United Church of Christ this history dates back to a woman named Mary Webb, who became personally concerned about the mission commitments of American Christians. In 1800 she gathered together some Congregational and Baptist women in her home to found the Boston Female Missionary Society for Missionary Purposes. This action marked the beginning of what came to be known as "female cent societies," based on the idea that any woman could save one cent a week for mission by denying herself some little thing. "Cent societies" were inspired by the biblical parable of the "widows mite," which reminded churchwomen that their small contributions for mission could make a big difference. In 1810, soon after the founding of the American Board of Commissioners for Foreign Missions (ABCFM), women's "auxiliary" mission societies began channeling their funds through the American Board. By 1839 there were 680 local "ladies associations" collecting funds for foreign missions. Although at its founding the

ABCFM involved several denominations, after other denominations established their own agencies for mission, the ABCFM carried on as the major foreign mission board for the Congregationalists.

Initially, the ABCFM refused to send unmarried women into the mission field. It was considered too dangerous, and it was not appropriate for a Christian woman to be unaccompanied. During the first half of the nineteenth century, therefore, Congregational women who felt a call to mission service could only respond by becoming a missionary wife. Many of them did.

After the Civil War, however, Congregational women were no longer content with the conservative stance of the ABCFM or with indirectly supporting mission through "auxiliary" organizations. In 1868 a group of Boston women met to hear returning missionary wives talk about "the needs of pagan women and children." Soon thereafter they affirmed their desire to help by establishing a Woman's Board of Missions (WBM). The WBM was an independent Board dedicated to personalizing the mission work of the church for women. Within several years three more Congregational "woman's boards" were founded in Chicago, in Hawaii, and in California.

Woman's Boards of Mission supported the needs of women. They raised funds in new ways, and they did not spend money until they had it in hand. Furthermore, they kept administrative overhead low by relying on volunteers. Not surprisingly, by the end of the nineteenth century over half of the Congregational missionaries in the foreign field were women. And although by the late 1920s the Woman's Boards were absorbed into the American Board in the name of efficiency, the contribution of women to the foreign mission work of Congregationalism was extraordinary.

Meanwhile, Congregational women who stayed at home carried out Christian mission locally. They organized maternal societies to help young mothers with infant care, they founded moral reform societies to rescue young girls from prostitution, and they taught in Sunday Schools to educate unchurched urban children. During the first half of the nineteenth century Congregational women were active in the abolition movement, and many supported runaway slaves on the Underground Railroad. Later they joined the Woman's Christian Temperance Union (WCTU) and worked to defend homes and families from the destructive consequences of alcoholism.

Deaconesses, Parish Assistants, and Directors of Christian Education

The mission work of German Evangelical women found its expression on the domestic scene. Building on a European revival of the biblical role of the "deaconess," in the 1880s German Evangelicals in St. Louis founded the Evangelical Deaconess Society. The society provided opportunities for single women to obtain training as nurses and to render important service to church and society. Deaconesses worked in hospitals and homes for the aged. Some worked in local parishes. Before 1930 thirteen additional Evangelical deaconess institutions were founded, and over 500 deaconess sisters trained. The German Reformed Church also established several deaconess institutions, and the Congregationalists in Illinois organized the American Congregational Deaconess Association.

Consecration as a deaconess did not entail a vow of celibacy, and many deaconesses left to marry after a few years. Those women who spent their lives as deaconesses, however, carried out a local but significant mission.

Although few Congregational women became deaconesses, in 1909 the Congregational Training School for Women provided yet another mode of mission service for women. The school, founded by Florence Amanda Fensham at Chicago Theological Seminary, enabled young women to prepare for urban social work, missionary service, and jobs as parish assistants in local churches. By 1919 there were 300 graduates of the school working in local congregations.

Eventually, the school expanded its training programs to introduce a Bachelor of Religious Education degree. Other Congregational institutions of higher education, such as Hartford Theological Seminary (Connecticut) and the Schauffler College of Religious and Social Work (Ohio), also developed curricula to prepare Congregational women for vocations in Christian education. By the 1930s larger churches in many Protestant denominations were regularly hiring professionally trained women to run their Christian education programs.

Empowering Laywomen in the Churches

Congregational and Christian Women

Congregational women organized their mission boards shortly after the Civil War. However, for women in the Christian movement formal organizations were slow to come. The general Christian suspicion of denominational bureaucracies meant that it was not until 1854 that the Christians established a national Board of Home and Foreign Missions and not until the 1886 quadrennial session of the American Christian Convention, in New Bedford, Massachusetts, that a Woman's Board for Foreign Missions was elected. Four years later, in 1890, at Marion, Indiana, the Christians organized a comparable Woman's Board for Home Missions.

When the Congregationalists and the Christians came together in 1931, a new Congregational Christian Women's Fellowship was created.

EVANGELICAL AND REFORMED WOMEN

Within the German Reformed Church the story was more complex. Although many colonial Reformed churches had "ladies aid societies" in local congregations, and some German Reformed churches formed "ladies auxiliaries" to support the ABCFM, they did not develop any independent "women's mission organizations" until after the Civil War. Credit must go to a local pastor's wife named Elvira Yockey. Beginning in the 1870s she argued that women needed to find their voice in the church. She believed that women's missionary societies not only raised money to support mission but also created sentiment and educated women and children about Christian mission. In 1877, under her leadership, the Woman's Missionary Society of the First Reformed Church of Xenia, Ohio, came into being. A little over five years later, in 1883, the General Synod affirmed the importance of women's work for mission. Finally, in 1887 the Woman's Missionary Society of the General Synod of the Reformed Church in the United States was organized in Akron, Ohio. Within a few years, the fears that an "unwomanly aggressiveness" might emerge in such organizations had faded, and there was nothing but praise for the work of women for the evangelization of the world. By 1923 the Woman's Missionary Society of the General Synod had a national journal and three full-time staff.

For women in the German Evangelical Synod of North America a national organization supporting women and mission was not created until 1921. During World War I the efforts of many Evangelical women within the American Red Cross convinced many people that the organized women of our church could become a power. To that end, they petitioned the General Conference, and in 1921, a convention was called to create the National Union of Evangelical Women. The "Union" affirmed all kinds of local women's organizations in the churches. It invited women to move beyond home and church to support programs for the "Kingdom-at-large." By 1925 its name was changed to the Evangelical Women's Union.

After the Evangelical and Reformed Church was formed in 1934, women from both churches came together in 1939 to form the Women's Guild of the Evangelical and Reformed Church.

WOMEN'S ORGANIZATIONS AND THE WIDER CHURCH

The legacy of independent women's organizations within the Congregational, Christian, Evangelical, and Reformed churches is an important story. However, after over 100 years of reaching for independence, in the 1920s that accomplishment began to be eroded.

The Congregational Woman's Boards of Mission were very successful. By the late nineteenth century the Woman's Boards were controlling 20 percent of the mission budgets. Male leaders feared that women might take over existing mission agencies or that women were collecting their money at the expense of denominational treasuries. Both of these allegations had little basis in fact. Furthermore, as national denominational bureaucracies became more centralized and professionalized, separate "woman's boards" were viewed as inefficient. Finally, there was still a healthy skepticism among men (and even among some women) that good Christian women could or should handle the increasingly complex bureaucratic and financial matters of their boards.

During the 1920s a debate over cooperation or consolidation began to dominate Congregational discussions about mission structures. The women upheld the importance of cooperation, while the male leadership of the church argued that consolidation was the modern way. In the end, in 1927 three of the four Congregational Woman's Boards of Missions (based in Boston, Chicago, and San Francisco) gave up their autonomy and were absorbed into the American Board of Commissioners for Foreign Missions. The women were not forced into this new arrangement, they debated its merits and risks, and after careful (and prayerful) discussion, the leaders of the Woman's Boards embraced it as progress. Many women thought that the circumstances that led to the founding of their independent boards had changed. They respected pleas from missionaries in the field that the current structures were redundant. They believed that now that women had the right to vote, younger women would not want "separate organizations." And finally, they admitted that existing structures were sometimes inefficient and perhaps even wasteful. With their vote, Congregational women lost control of their money and their direct connection to women missionaries. In return the women were guaranteed one-third of the seats on the governing board of the ABCFM.

Unfortunately, consolidation did not accomplish what it promised. In the decades that followed, many lamented that the incorporation of the Woman's Boards into the American Board only reinforced bureaucratic solutions and strengthened male-dominated leadership in the church. Yet Congregational women did gain greater visibility and influence in the decisions of the national mission board, something that women in other denominations could only dream of at that time. Fifty years later, when UCC women began to seek a more direct role in denominational decision making, the tradition of one-third laywomen's representation on the national mission boards gave women political leverage to bring about change.

The United Church of Christ

In spite of the demise of the national independent Congregational woman's mission boards, from 1927 to 1957 (when the UCC was formed) local woman's organizations flourished. The Women's Fellowship of the Congregational Christian Churches and the Women's Guild of the Evangelical and Reformed Church continued to provide resources and support for hundreds of groups of women who gathered monthly in their local churches to respond to God's mission. Stay-at-home wives and mothers flocked to local churches during the post–World War II "baby boom." At church they found support for their changing lives, and they also continued to educate themselves about Christian mission and to support the work of the church in the world.

However, when the United Church of Christ organized itself into a new denominational bureaucracy in the early 1960s, denominational leaders continued to argue that separate women's denominational structures were out-of-date. As a consequence, the United Church of Christ created a national Council for Lay Life and Work. Although a woman, Helen Huntington Smith, served as its national executive, there was no central office in the new church with primary concern for the needs of women. Local Women's Fellowships and Guilds simply continued to do what they had been doing at the local level without any national support.

The Modern Women's Movement

In 1963 Betty Friedan published a book titled *The Feminine Mystique*. Stimulated by that book and a flurry of "feminist" writers in the late 1960s, many American women began to question prevailing attitudes about women. In 1971 the General Synod of the United Church of Christ passed a "Resolution on the Status of Women in Church and Society." It stated that "God's love for all his children makes no distinction of worth between male and female. They are equal in value in God's sight; therefore, distinctions made by society which assume an inferior-superior relationship are contrary to the will of God." Recognizing that "women have been the victims of injustice resulting from cultural patterns which have greatly restricted their freedom in the performance of their sexual roles," the General Synod affirmed nine goals in the resolution: (1) to increase the numbers of women serving the church in ordained and lay leadership; (2) to develop educational materials to raise the awareness of women's contributions to history and culture; (3) to promote church involvement in social action programs concerning women's rights and expectations; (4) to eliminate discrimination in employment and compensation on the basis of sex; (5) to call on the United States to endorse the UN Convention on the Political Rights of Women; (6) to work for easier access to contraceptive information and access to physician-performed abortions; (7) to commend movements seeking to overcome the economic, cultural, and social injustices inflicted on women; (8) to affirm lifestyles that allow boys and girls to express their essential humanity and make free vocational choices; and (9) to recognize that further study is needed on the legal implications of the Equal Rights Amendment (*General Synod Minutes* 71-GS-24).

Soon thereafter, the president of the church appointed a Task Force on Women in Church and Society to study the situation of women. The Task Force did many things. It launched a new publication for women, *Common Lot*; it began giving the Antoinette Brown Award (an award named after the first woman ordained to ministry in a Congregational church) to two outstanding ordained UCC women at each General Synod; and it pressed the General Synod to use "inclusive language," asking that inclusive language be used in all future UCC publications. This was the first act of its kind in any American Protestant denomination.

In 1975 the Task Force presented a detailed report to the General Synod, documenting the situation of women in the UCC. The report examined the structures that served the needs of women in the churches, such as Women's Fellowships, Women's Guilds, and Task Forces; it described the situation of ordained women and laywomen employed by the churches; and it presented information about the growing numbers of women seminarians. In its conclusion, the report recommended ways to eliminate "the institutional and cultural sexism which permeates both the institutional church and the society."

The work of the Task Force on Women in Church and Society led to the creation of an Advisory Commission on Women, staffed through the executive offices of the church. In 1979 this interim structure was replaced by the Coordinating Center for Women in Church and Society (CCW), a center administratively attached to the office of the president of the church. Marilyn Breitling served as its executive. Also, in 1979 the first National Meeting of UCC women was held in Cincinnati, Ohio.

Women in the United Church of Christ had many needs. There were younger women with jobs and families who did not have time for traditional women's meetings and activities. There were older women who wanted help to maintain their local Women's Fellowships and Guilds. In 1982 CCW recognized all of these needs and initiated a national "membership organization" called the United Church of Christ Women in Mission (UCCWM). Local women's groups and/or individuals could join. Members received packets of materials to support local programs and to educate everyone about mission. The UCCWM sought to increase networking among women, to strengthen existing women's organizations, to celebrate the gifts of women, to enrich and deepen the faith development of women, and to forge a strong commitment to mission in the life of the church.

It did all of these things. It also began a pattern holding Honored Lay Women Luncheons at each General Synod to recognize the contributions of laywomen in church and society. Since 1983 over 1,000 women have been selected for this honor. In 1983 CCW also celebrated the election of Carol Joyce Brun as secretary of the UCC, the first woman to hold such a high position in any major mainline Protestant denomination. In 1984 it sponsored a second National Meeting for UCC women in Milwaukee. And in 1986 it established an annual Woman's Week, providing resources to help local women's groups highlight the gifts of women in local congregations.

Yet the future of a national United Church of Christ structure dedicated to serving the needs of women was by no means secure. The task force, advisory council, and coordinating center were all ad hoc entities attached to the president's office. By the mid-1980s a consensus began to emerge that it was time for the General Synod to establish a permanent denominational instrumentality to support the ministries of women. Finally, in 1987 the Coordinating Center for Women in Church and Society was formally approved as a permanent constitutionally authorized instrumentality of the church. Under the leadership of Marilyn Breitling, Mary Susan Gast, and Lois Powell, the Coordinating Center for Women persisted in that form until the denomination totally restructured in 2000.

Ordained Women

Historians generally believe that the first woman formally ordained to the Christian ministry by a mainline Protestant denomination in America was Antoinette L. Brown. "Nettie" Brown, as she was called, attended Oberlin College in the 1840s and became convinced that she was called to preach. When she finished the collegiate course at Oberlin, the faculty allowed her to continue her studies in the Theology Department, but they refused to grant her a theological degree.

Brown was well known as a lecturer on temperance, abolition, and other literary topics, and eventually a small Congregational Church in South Butler, New York, extended a call to her to become their pastor. In keeping with Congregational custom the South Butler church invited other nearby churches to participate in her ordination on September 15, 1853. It was not a big deal. The preacher affirmed that the church does not "make a minister" rather, God had called her; and that the churches, under the "Lordship of Jesus Christ," had gathered to celebrate that fact. Following traditional Congregational ecclesiology, the gathered community of the saints led by the Holy Spirit "set her apart by prayer and laying on of hands" to the Christian ministry.

Unfortunately, Brown's ministry in South Butler was short. After a few years she resigned due to ill health and doctrinal doubts. She later married Samuel C. Blackwell, brother of Emily and Elizabeth Blackwell, early women physicians. After her many children were grown, she devoted herself to writing and late in life returned to active ministry as a Unitarian. Brown's ordination was not followed by any great increase in Congregational women seeking to become local church pastors. In 1889, over thirty years after her ordination, there were only four ordained Congregational women listed in the annual *Congregational Yearbook*. By 1899 the number had risen to forty-nine.

In 1920 the National Council of Congregational Churches appointed a commission to investigate the number, standing, and need for women ministers in Congregational churches. The commission reported that in 1919 there were 67 ordained women out of 5,695 clergy in the denomination. Eighteen of the women were pastors of very small churches, 14 were copastors with their husbands, 14 were religious educators or church assistants, and 21 were employed outside the churches. The commission concluded that women presented no serious problem to the denomination, because they were "too few in number and too modest or at least inconspicuous in their form of service." At that time the commission was more interested in encouraging women to enter into the field of Christian education than parish ministry (*Minutes of the Nineteenth Regular Meeting of the National Council of Congregational Churches*, 1921, 39–41). By 1930 there were 131 ordained clergywomen, or 2.2 percent of all Congregational ministers.

Within the Christian Connection, the story was not much different. Although early Christians encouraged and celebrated the ministries of female evangelists, it was not until 1867 that Melissa Timmons (later Terrill) was ordained to the gospel ministry at Ebenezer (Christian) Church in Clark County, Ohio. The local Christian Conference stated that it did not approve of the ordination of women to the eldership of the church, "as a general rule," but Sister Timmons had been set forward to that position at the request of her local church. Therefore, the Conference treated her as an ordained minister in good standing in the Conference. By the time the Christians merged with the Congregationalists in 1931, there were 45 women among 917 Christian clergy. This was not as many women as the Congregationalists had, but it was a better percentage.

Within the Evangelical and Reformed traditions, concern about the ordination of women was not an issue during much of their history. There were always a few women who sought out clergy husbands and engaged in ministry as the wife of a pastor or as a missionary wife. After 1890, committed single women were consecrated as deaconesses. But the vocation of most Evangelical and Reformed women revolved around their responsibilities as wives and mothers at home and as active laywomen in their local churches. It was not until 1948 that the Evangelical and Reformed Church formally ordained a woman named Beatrice M. Weaver (later McConnell) to "a ministry of word and sacrament." Local German Reformed congregations often "ordained" lay elders. Although there were few female lay elders, the question of lay or clergy ordination of women was never an issue in the Reformed Church in the United States.

Weaver was a graduate of Ursinus College and attended Lancaster Theological Seminary in the 1940s. When she learned that a local Lancaster church gave a special scholarship to Ursinus graduates, she applied. She was awarded the scholarship and spent time as a seminarian teaching, preaching, and visiting in that congregation. When they asked her if she wanted to be ordained, she said yes. After her graduation from Lancaster (she was also the first woman to graduate with a divinity degree from that seminary) and her ordination at Saint Paul's Evangelical and Reformed Church, she served as assistant pastor there for six and a half years. In 1949 a second Evangelical and Reformed woman, Ann Blasberg, was ordained to be a chaplain to students at the University of Wisconsin. And in 1950 and 1951, two additional women were ordained by the Evangelical and Reformed Church.

As the issue of women's ordination gained a higher profile during the 1950s and 1960s in many mainline Protestant denominations, the United Church of Christ insisted that it had no problem with women clergy. By 1955 women accounted for 3.5 percent of the clergy in the anticipated United Church of Christ. Most of those clergywomen were Congregational Christian. In 1980, 9 percent of UCC clergy were women, and in 1990 that percentage had doubled to 18 percent.

When the Task Force on Women in Church and Society made its report to General Synod in 1975, it reported on the situation of 200 clergy women who had responded to its questionnaire in the early 1970s. Half of the clergywomen in that sample were ordained after 1960, half of them were married, and half were serving local congregations. Forty-six percent of them were over the age of fifty. Unfortunately, the salaries of those clergywomen were far below the average salaries of UCC clergymen at that time.

The Task Force report was a wake-up call, because it also disclosed that in spite of these inequities, more and more women were attending seminaries. Denominational statistics and the annual *Fact Book of the Association of Theological Schools in the United States and Canada* show that from the mid-1970s on enrollments of women in UCC seminaries climbed to between 50 and 60 percent. Female students actually helped seminaries by making up for sagging male enrollments, in spite of the fact that local churches remained ambivalent about their ministry. Yet UCC clergywomen would not be denied. Many entered alternative specialized ministries, and others developed "interim ministry" into a distinct vocation.

For UCC clergywomen the 1980s and 1990s were a time of expanded opportunities—and ongoing inequities. In the 1980s a group of UCC clergywomen created a National Network for United Church of Christ Clergywomen. It was a self-supporting association made up of ordained UCC women and women aspiring to ordination. Although one national meeting was held in 1984, the organization eventually was forced to disband. Two national church instrumentalities (the Coordinating Center for Women and the Office for Church Life and Leadership) carried on its work by focusing on the three issues that continued to concern clergy women: balancing the demands of ministry and family; developing a fair and user-friendly placement system; and correcting the dramatic differences between male and female salaries. In 1993 a newsletter titled *Called, Blessed and Sent* was launched to share information and assure clergywomen that they were not forgotten.

Clergywomen in the United Church of Christ by the end of the twentieth century were no longer scarce or questioned. Search committees regularly reviewed the profiles of women as they searched for new pastors. There were female conference ministers and strong lay support for women pastors. Although there were still fewer female senior ministers in multistaff congregations, and the differential between male and female salaries had not disappeared, things were much better. Like all professional women, clergywomen do not find it easy to balance the demands of their families and their ministry, but they manage. Some of them claim that things are easier in the ministry than in other professions. Mostly, however, younger clergywomen resist focusing on their gender. They simply seek to carry out their calling as ordained ministers of the church of Jesus Christ.

Advocacy for Women

The story of women in the United Church of Christ is not simply about women—who they were and what they did. It is also a history of active advocacy by the denomination for a number of causes related to women.

In 1970 the UCC Council for Christian Social Action drafted a statement titled "Toward Freedom of Choice in the Area of Abortion." It called for church action to support the repeal of overly restrictive abortion legislation and the expansion of sex education programs. This was the beginning of consistent advocacy for "reproductive choice" for women by the United Church of Christ. In 1971 the UCC General Synod passed a formal resolution on "Freedom of Choice Concerning Abortion," and from that time on it repeatedly took initiatives to protect women's freedom to choose on the basis of conscience and personal religious conviction, free from government interference. After the Supreme Court *Roe v. Wade* decision, the UCC General Synod reaffirmed its concern for women's reproductive rights in 1973, 1977, 1979, 1981, and 1989. Although there are people within the UCC that do not agree with this stance, and even a small advocacy group which is "pro-life," the national work of the UCC has maintained a clear pro-choice stand for over thirty years.

A second major area of advocacy related to women was around the Equal Rights Amendment (ERA). After Congress approved the ERA in 1972, in 1975 the UCC General Synod went on record declaring its support for the ERA and urging the whole church to work for ratification. Two years later it reaffirmed its support for the ERA and asked national instrumentalities and church agencies not to meet in states that had not ratified the ERA. This position was aggressively reaffirmed at the next two General Synods. In fact, as the June 1982 deadline for ratification approached, the 1981 General Synod held a candlelight vigil in Rochester, New York, in support of the ERA. Even after the amendment failed, in 1983 when the ERA was reintroduced into Congress, the UCC once again voted its endorsement.

The third major area of advocacy related to women surrounds the issue of "inclusive language." Very early in the 1970s some UCC women began to advocate for language that did not perpetuate the sexist patterns of the past regarding human beings and that explored more gender-balanced ways of speaking about God. In 1973 the General Synod passed a resolution that asked that a "concerted effort" be made by the instrumentalities, conferences, associations, and local churches to educate the membership of the United Church of Christ about the "issues and sensitivities" involved in writing and using inclusive language. New publications were to be "deliberately inclusive." In 1977 the General Synod instructed the Office for Church Life and Leadership to begin a process to develop a new "book of worship" for the denomination that would use inclusive language. About that same time, the president of the church offered a personal revision of the UCC Statement of Faith in an effort to make it more inclusive. Also in 1983 an official "Doxological UCC Statement of Faith," which avoided some of the pronoun problems in the original statement, was endorsed by the General Synod.

Over the years the debate about inclusive language

within the United Church of Christ became more, rather than less, divisive. Younger laywomen and clergywomen were most likely to be adamant promoters of inclusive language, while older laywomen and male clergy did not find the issue as important. Those who were more conservative about traditional doctrines, such as the "Trinity," insisted that changing language was a threat to the core beliefs of the church. Finally in 1989 the General Synod passed a conciliatory resolution. It called for "thoughtful theological reflection and reconciliation" between those who hold "different convictions of faith regarding language for God." It encouraged all members of the church to be "sensitive to one another's burdens" and to remember that they "share a common hope." It lamented the fact that "the way in which inclusive language is sometimes employed or ignored in the Church gives birth to pain or a sense of loss among us" (*General Synod Minutes* 89-GS-92).

In response to this conciliatory resolution the Office for Church Life and Leadership prepared a study guide titled "How Shall We Speak?" and suggested that after a period of study everyone might affirm an "Inclusive Language Covenant," 1993. The Covenant was honest. It noted that "language near and dear to some is experienced as excluding by others." It stated that "formulations of belief, like the Trinitarian formula, are not easily expressed in ways that are immediately or readily viewed as faithful by all." Yet after dialogue and study it encouraged those who did not agree with each other to make some promises to each other, ending with these words, "We will seek and enter into a respectful dialogue that engages ourselves with others to find, to create, and to use worship and educational materials and programs which further our understandings and capabilities to use language and imagery in ways that are faithfully inclusive."

In spite of these efforts at reconciliation, the inclusive-language debate continued to fester. In 1993, as a new hymnal dedicated to inclusive language was nearing completion, there was animated debate at General Synod about the use of the word *Lord*. The resulting *New Century Hymnal* did retain some language deemed part of the "memory bank" of the church, but most of the hymns and service language sought to be "deliberately inclusive." Although a small group of vocal theologians and pastors complained that church doctrine was being put at risk, most people in the United Church of Christ were happy with the new hymnal.

The fourth major area of advocacy related to women within the United Church of Christ falls under the area of human rights and social injustice. Repeatedly the UCC General Synod has passed resolutions and expended staff resources to deal with issues of women and poverty, sexual harassment, racism, affirmative action, AIDs, sexual discrimination, genital mutilation, and all forms of violence against women and children. The denomination has worked closely with other organizations to get national laws changed to protect and support working women, minority women, and lesbians. There have been times, on some of these issues, when the actions of the national staff, and even the General Synod, have not been appreciated by some people in the local churches. Most of the time, however, the membership of the churches has taken pride in this work and sent delegates to national meetings who vote with amazing consistency to make the world a fairer and safer place for women. It is an impressive record.

Denominational Restructuring

When the United Church of Christ was created in 1957, it was a delicate coming together of two ecclesiastical traditions with different understandings of accountability and institutional decision making. The new denominational blend was no longer purely "congregational," nor was it based on a "presbyterial" or representative system.

Over the years this hybrid mix of structures worked amazingly well. One leader of the UCC was fond of saying that the United Church of Christ was a church of "soft verbs": When the General Synod acted, it did not have "legal authority" to mandate compliance. Its work could only be accomplished by soft verbs: The General Synod "strongly encourages" or "urges." The General Synod "requests" or "asks." The General Synod "recommends" or "suggests." So-called hard verbs, such as "requires," "mandates," "demands," or "expects," were not part of the UCC vocabulary. The officers of the church did their work by persuasion. The various settings of the church (local, regional, and national) thrived when they respected and honored the work of the other parts of the church.

Yet the organizational energy expended to keep the United Church of Christ healthy, and the confusion and redundancy that often prevailed, continually raised the question of restructuring. As the denomination matured, the case for total restructuring, not merely constitutional adjustments, grew stronger. Finally in the early 1990s a Structures Committee was chosen and a timetable set in place to completely restructure the national setting of the church by the year 2000. The General Synod received a preliminary report in 1995. In 1997 it adopted a new constitution, reducing nine major instrumentalities to four. In 1999 new bylaws were approved and new leadership chosen.

Advocates for restructuring argued that the United Church of Christ was a church that valued mission and covenant over old structures and ideologies. They affirmed that restructure was a means to increase the church's effectiveness in carrying out God's mission in the world. They reminded everyone that the church exists for mission, and the mission of the church belongs to God alone. They argued that a totally new denominational structure built around four "covenanted ministries" would provide more centralized administration, regroup similar ministries into more focused teams, improve the sharing of information, reduce duplication, and allocate limited financial and personnel resources more equitably. The four new "covenanted ministries" are the Office of General Ministries, Local Church Ministries, Justice and Witness Ministries, and Wider Church Ministries. Coordination and decision making for the denomination are now led by a "Collegium" of five officers with equal authority elected by the General Synod (two of them are women).

As restructuring proceeded, women in the church were fearful that all of their hard-won efforts to make the Coordinating Center for Women a constitutionally established "instrumentality," with leverage in the budgeting process and visibility in the bureaucracy, might disappear. Yet they were also hopeful that the concerns of women might become more central in the work of the church. Although it is premature to tell how well the new arrangements are actually serving the needs of women, it is important to recognize several values that are influencing the ways in which the restructured denomination relates to women.

First, the concept of "covenant" is central. The new structure is not hierarchical; it is covenantal. The constitution states that

within the United Church of Christ, the various expressions of the church relate to each other in a covenantal manner. Each expression of the church has responsibilities and rights in relation to the others, to the end that the whole church will seek God's will and be faithful to God's mission. Decisions are made in consultation and collaboration among the various parts of the structure." (*UCC Constitution*, Article III, 1993)

Second, leadership of the new national structures believes that the best work emerges when partnerships are developed among the covenanted ministries. In serving the needs of women, the United Church of Christ Women in Mission, which has provided resources and support for women's groups and individuals for twenty years, has been revitalized. The program is now a "partnership" between Local Church Ministries, Justice and Witness Ministries, and Wider Church Ministries. Groups and individuals that join continue to receive the same benefits, *and* all of the dollars given to UCCWM go directly to mission work. Through the Women in Mission Partnership program, UCC women are able to develop more direct connections to the mission outreach of the United Church of Christ in many parts of the world.

Staff resources for women are now located in two places in the national UCC offices: In Local Church Ministries, Deborah Bailey serves as Minister for Women's Concerns within the Worship and Education Ministry Team. *Common Lot* continues to be published from her office. And in Justice and Witness Ministries, Lois Powell serves as Minister and Team leader for the Human Rights, Justice for Women and Transformation Ministry Team. The two women work closely with each other to educate and nurture women and to challenge and inspire women to Christian witness in church and society. Support for clergywomen flows through the Parish Life and Leadership Ministry Team within Local Church Ministries.

Under the new constitution concerns for women's issues and advocacy for women arise in various national offices. National staff not only work to build partnerships among covenanted ministries within the national setting of the United Church of Christ, but they also develop collaborative action plans with women in conferences, in associations, and in local congregations. Finally they stretch their commitments beyond denominational boundaries to advocate around issues important to women with dozens of ecumenical organizations and agencies.

Women in the United Church of Christ are diverse, drawing upon a rich theological, cultural, and ethnic history. Historically women have been, and remain, focused on God's mission in the world. Laywomen and clergywomen have found, and continue to find, many ways to carry out that mission in the contemporary world.

SOURCES: *Common Lot* is the newsletter established in the early 1980s for UCC women. Archive issues are available at the national UCC Office for Women's Concerns (in the Worship and Education Team of the Local Church Ministries). Recent issues are available online at http://www.ucc.org/women/commonlot.htm. A useful source is Louis H. Gunnemann, *The Shaping of the United Church of Christ: An Essay in the History of American Christianity* (1977, 1999). *Short Course on the History of the United Church of Christ*, previously published as a small paperback, is now available online at http://www.ucc.org/aboutus/shortcourse/index.html. Also see Barbara Brown Zikmund, ed., *Hidden Histories in the United Church of Christ*, 2 vols. (1984, 1987). Therein see chapters on deaconesses, the Chicago Training School, Woman's Boards of Missions, American Missionary Association work, German Congregationalists, Hungarians, Armenians, Japanese, and Chinese. Finally, see Barbara Brown Zikmund, ser. ed., *The Living Theological Heritage of the United Church of Christ*, 7 vols. (1995–2003).

WOMEN IN THE UNITARIAN UNIVERSALIST MOVEMENT
Cynthia Grant Tucker

A FULL-THROATED PRESENCE wherever their worship community's witness is heard, Unitarian Universalist (UU) women enjoy a status implicit in vows made well over 200 years ago when their "liberal religion" was seeded in North America. Achieving a voice and respect, however, did not come easily in a denomination convened by men accustomed to being the framers and centers of serious discourse. No matter how earnest the founding fathers' conviction that all people had equal worth and the right to express themselves freely, they were blinded by the prevailing myths of male privilege and failed to see that these principles applied to their mothers, wives, and daughters, as well as themselves. To empower the muted, tremulous voices and prod the liberal religious body to live up to all that its name implied, it took the reformist agitation late in the twentieth century. Some observers, citing the vestiges of the male aristocracy even now, and wary of history's way of repeating itself, suspect that the parity Unitarian Universalist women have won will be hard to maintain. Yet even the skeptics agree that the realignments since 1970 have brought remarkable changes, with women entering the new millennium with a statistical edge as local lay leaders, seminarians, ordained clergy, and elected trustees representing the roughly 224,000 members the denomination counted in 2002. Nor can anyone who is familiar with North America's social history diminish the transforming role UU women have played in the larger community by interpreting their religious beliefs more generously than their movement's founders and giving them broad and practical application.

Shaping Theology in the Pews

Despite the retention of Christianity's patriarchal structure, women had good enough reason for having higher expectations when liberal religion's progenitors, the Universalists and Unitarians, cast off the narrow and joyless teachings of Calvin—and Luther in Canada—to embrace a radically optimistic and democratic perspective. These two distinct groups—which moved closer in beliefs but remained institutionally separate until they merged in 1961—rejected the Reformation's position that humans were hopelessly flawed and that only those few whom God had "elected to grace" would be spared hell's fire and brimstone. They argued that all humanity, like everything else God created, was not only fundamentally good but perfectible. The universal Father was

In autumn 1907, women marched past the Boone, Iowa, Universalist Church. Unitarian Rev. Eleanor Gordon was near the head of the parade, and Rev. Mary Safford is believed to have participated. *Courtesy of the Iowa Women's Suffrage Collection, State Historical Society of Iowa, Des Moines.*

too wise and loving a parent to be playing favorites, saving a few of his children while damning the rest. Liberal clerics debated details but agreed that salvation was open to all and that the whole human clan would meet in the next life, secure in its Maker's embrace. For women, whose work of bearing new life and keeping families intact made separations especially hard when death took loved ones, the teaching that innocent children and longtime companions had not been consigned to the flames but were waiting for them in a better life eased their burden immeasurably.

Then, too, there was for these women the comfort of having their clandestine doubts about devils, the threefold makeup of God, and the literal truth of Jesus' miraculous birth and resurrection questioned by clergy who cherished the Nazarene's message. Moreover, regardless of how much traditional thought these women retained or rejected, they felt validated in hearing that people of faith must trust their own minds to adjudicate claims of religious truth and that being well read and informed was not contingent on gender but a universal imperative. The cerebral Unitarians held that reason and conscience, rather than scripture, must be the ultimate

tests of high truths. This radical trust in human discernment emboldened them to abandon the Christian belief in a supernatural Jesus and all the miraculous demonstrations of his divinity. The Universalists, slower to give up a literal reading of scripture and challenge the Bible's authority, were more reluctant to question such teachings as the triune nature of deity and God's intercession through Jesus' atonement. Yet in stressing perfectibility, they, too, put a premium on education, and gradually even these cautious cousins moved from strong pietistic roots to a more rationally grounded and flexible faith. As a consequence, women who had been censored elsewhere for using their questioning minds and feared they were flirting with heresy the first time they entered a liberal church were able to go home acquitted of what mainstream pulpits called pride and apostasy.

Even before the male leadership organized local societies into official denominations, women were taking the meaning and application of liberal theology into their own hands, adding new inflections and contours tailored to their particular needs. On the Universalist side, the first to leave her mark was Judith Sargent Stevens Murray (1751–1820), a native of Gloucester, Massachusetts, who found her life's work in explaining her faith as a writer. Born twenty-five years before the colonies banded together to form a new nation, and thirty years before the continent had its first Universalist church, this zealous defender of liberal thought was prepared for her calling by free-thinking parents who did more than most—though less than she wished when it came to her formal schooling—to help their children develop their minds and set an example of courage and honesty in their pursuit of religious truth. Before she was out of her teens, Judith had followed her elders in questioning onerous doctrine, a practice that led the Congregational church to suspend the family's membership. The Sargents's prayers for better guidance were answered in 1770, when roving evangelist John Murray came to the colonies to preach the doctrine of universal salvation as taught by James Relly in England. Relly's belief that all human beings were in effect already saved—because they had paid for their sins by being united with Christ in his death—found such fertile soil in Gloucester that Murray decided to settle there permanently. In 1780, he became the first minister of the colonies' first Universalist church, preaching his inaugural sermon in a meetinghouse Judith's father helped to build on a parcel of land the family contributed. In 1788, after her first husband, John Stevens, died, Judith—who for years had been using her pen to promote the new movement—married John Murray. The partnership was a blessing for both if mutual love and support, not financial security, were the measure. In the parsonage, Judith Sargent Murray furthered her literary career while assisting her husband's work.

Besides her keen intellect and a vast fund of erudition amassed primarily on her own, Judith displayed the passion of one who, by dint of experience, railed against the cruel aspects of orthodox teachings. When she was nineteen and her nine-year-old brother, Fitz William, was ill, the boy—repeating what he had been told by a tutor—tearfully blurted out that he was convinced God was going to send him to hell when he died and keep him from seeing his parents and siblings ever again. Horrified by these bleak expectations in someone so young, his sister Judith, using her strength of conviction, threw him a lifeline, a letter of rescue, to pull him out of needless despair to the ground of his family's religion of joy. As shown by her twenty letter books—now housed in the Mississippi Department of Archives and History, which has made them available on microfilm— by the late 1770s, Judith was answering similar cries for help by corresponding with people all over New England. In 1782, moving into the world of publication, she wrote a catechism for children and printed it privately, expecting correctly that she would be charged with arrogance and heresy, if not worse, but accepting this as a small price to pay for spreading a faith based on God's boundless love.

On the Unitarian side, Margaret Fuller (1810–1850) helped validate the rank and file's yearnings for mystical insights and spirituality at a time when the clerical leadership was embracing empirical tendencies. Ignoring the customary restrictions on a woman's proper place, she pulled up a seat for herself in the circle of young Bostonian intellectuals that included Unitarians James Freeman Clarke, William Henry Channing, Theodore Parker, George Ripley, and Ralph Waldo Emerson. In this company of Transcendentalists, ordained men who challenged the adequacy of church leaders and biblical texts to decide what constituted higher truth, Fuller had ideal conditions in which to develop her view that such truth was revealed to one's soul, without mediation, by an indwelling God. In 1840, Fuller founded *The Dial*, the major Transcendentalist periodical, and served as its editor for the next several years.

Most religiously liberal women in Fuller's day were much too restrained by social custom to flaunt their religious perspectives as she did, but screened from the public eye, they too were wrestling with traditional doctrine. The intensity of this revisionist undercurrent is palpable in the letters of Sarah Alden Bradford Ripley (1793–1867), another unusually bright Boston native. Raised by parents who worshiped at First Church, where William Ellery Channing, the senior Henry Ware, and other influential clergy presided, she grew up a child of enlightenment Unitarianism, for which she had to answer to both the orthodox censors and her own doubts. On the one hand, her legacy of abiding trust in a beneficent deity, belief in human perfectibility, insistence on self-improvement, openness to a rational reading of scripture, and the insights of science was assailed by traditional Christians as a facile faith of convenience and comfort. On the other, her time and location in antebellum New England, her prodigious reading, family connections, and marriage to Unitarian minister Samuel Ripley—half brother of Mary Moody Emerson, Ralph Waldo's aunt—placed her squarely at the center of Unitarian controversy, where the harsh tone abraded her spirit while the frames of reference excluded her. Comfortable Harvard professors and well-heeled clergymen, who presumed that their lives were the norm and thus proof of their point, asserted that God's great affection was apparent in people's bright, happy lives and that suffering and discord—distant and abstract impediments—were only incidental to the greater scheme of divine benevolence.

After years of being exhaustively trained in the life of parish squabbles, demands from a growing family, and trying to make ends meet by housing a boarding school under her, the pastor's wife could only conclude that the learned scholars were wrong. From where she stood, the generous God they described was nowhere in sight, and she was ready to look for him somewhere else. She was weary of hearing young clergy talk as if they had outdistanced their embalmed colleagues by strutting on theological treadmills as if they were going somewhere. Persuaded by her own reading of Plato and German philosophy, she moved from the confident faith of her youth to a skepticism that undercut the keystones of Christian tradition and what her own husband continued to preach. In her darkest moments, logic told her that human life had no higher utility than to propagate and bury corpses to fertilize the "dirty planet" on which people crawled from birth to death. Humans flattered themselves in thinking that, just for existing, God would reward them by taking them to some exalted place and giving them permanent residence. By the time she emerged from the Unitarian fray as a widow of fifty-two, the best Ripley could claim in the way of an honest religious belief was an "earnest desire" and "yearning for the peace that flowed from a consciousness of union" with God here and now (Undated letter to Mary Moody Emerson).

Ripley was not the only Unitarian woman to lose her girlhood religion to unresolved doubts, vague intimations, and reason. A far greater number, however, remained as attached as the Universalists to their inherited Christian moorings, and few abandoned their expectation of some greater life after death. In the Unitarian Church of the Messiah in St. Louis, for instance, Rev. William G. Eliot earned a large, appreciative following during the mid-nineteenth century by preaching a Christian message based on the gospel stories of Jesus' life and the promise of immortality. None was more grateful than Sally Smith (1828–1905), a young congregant who from 1847 to 1856 took notes during church services and expanded on them in her diary afterward. Smith's ability to reconstruct the sermons and how they affected her—a skill enhanced by her weekday job as the pastor's amanuensis, where Eliot composed his sermons aloud—captured with rare immediacy how the folks in the pews received what they heard. Orphaned while in her teens and still haunted by memories of her parents' slow deaths in Vermont, where she had grown up, she was "lost in a wilderness of woe" when she first went to Eliot's church with an aunt and uncle who gave her a home in St. Louis. Expecting little when she walked in, she left with a lighter heart, she wrote later, for almost as if he were reading her thoughts, he had given her the "happy belief" that all humankind "would meet in the world above, never more to be parted" (Diary, November 12, 1851).

In truth it would have been hard for the minister *not* to have known what young Smith was thinking. Even before the cholera epidemic, fire, and floods of 1849 claimed one of every ten residents in St. Louis, it had

been rare to find anyone in the city, then famous for dirt and disease, who had not in recent memory stood at the graveside of kin of close acquaintance. Eliot's message of immortality eased his congregants' hearts without losing its efficacy by exceeding the limits of what their reason could tolerate. His promise of life everlasting convinced them precisely because he did not camouflage its mystery by dressing it up in theories and fabrications. "Mr. Eliot could not tell what kind of bodies we would have, and did not think it necessary," Smith noted approvingly. "There would be but little pleasure to me, in thinking of the future life, if I thought it was not to be shared by my father and mother and all I love so well," but there was no need for a blueprint so long as she knew they would all be together (Diary, April 8, 1849).

Not all Unitarian women left church as satisfied as Sally Smith, for pastors like William Eliot had become the exception by the time she first heard him at the Church of the Messiah. Few Unitarian clergy still taught, as he did, a reverence for Jesus that placed the Nazarene above other humans, if lower than God, and used the gospel stories to anchor their message. In parishes where liberal sermons had morphed into lectures on fine theological points, many women who could not take flight with their faith, as Sarah Bradford Ripley did, chose instead to take up their pens and vent their displeasure. In New England, where Eliot's colleagues rushed to keep up with the latest fashions in preaching, women like Ellen Tucker Emerson had to live with the consequences without seeing any improvement during their lifetimes. When she was fifteen and in boarding school in western Massachusetts, this oldest daughter of Lidian Jackson and Ralph Waldo Emerson started protesting the "frightful fare" being served up as liberal religion. The preaching was "mostly doctrinal" and abstract and not at all what the laity wanted, she sulked in a letter addressed to her mother in April 1854. She was trying as hard as she could, she said, "to gain something by going to church," but the lectures were so long and convoluted, her brain got all tangled up, making her so uncomfortable she could hardly sit still. With the situation no better thirty years later, when a humanistic approach to God was the fashion in Unitarianism, Ellen assured a close friend that not only she, but "most of the people" she talked to, allowed that their spirits were starved, and the worst of it was the clergy thought they knew better. Glib "ministers of the modern kind" had pulled up the strong Christian roots that fortified Unitarians of the old school. They had turned the good food to thin gruel by teaching that Jesus "was only a man"—"valuable to the human race, exactly as Washington was, as a moral example"—and this did "not satisfy hungry souls" (Letter to Clara Dabney, July 28, 1881).

Although theological fashions had changed more

than once by the late 1800s—first as Charles Darwin's theory, which liberals embraced fearlessly, made sermons on science the vogue; and then as the study of social groups inspired the clergy to preach sociology—liberal sisters, accounting for most of the turnout on Sundays, still left church dissatisfied. Their discomfort devolved on the point that preachers were now so caught up in numbers and social theories that they could no longer address their listeners as humans, much less as women. Some like Kate Stevens Bingham of Portland, Oregon, were more mystified than aggravated by what they heard from liberal pulpits. When during the 1890s Bingham's minister used up his sermon time reading statistics and expert opinions about the consequences of drink, she heard little that seemed to relate to her life, though she lived with an alcoholic husband and knew intoxicants' ravages all too well.

Though many like Bingham did not complain out of deep-rooted loyalties to their pastors, the clergy's failure to speak the communicants' language produced a rumbling among liberal women from coast to coast well into the twentieth century. In 1919, poet T. S. Eliot's sister, Margaret Dawes Eliot (1871–1956), who had worked as a nurse, complained of the problem in Boston, where her own aching soul longed for someone to give her the comfort she tried to give others personally and professionally. The liberal church leadership there, she wrote to her cousin Thomas Lamb Eliot—who was himself a Unitarian pastor in Portland, Oregon—were so inclined to think in terms of the masses, they seemed to forget that groups were made up of individuals with individual needs. This problem of focus was more than a matter of not knowing how to communicate. By speaking in generalities and the language of textbooks, liberal preachers were taking the easy way out like the comfortable scholars who chose to ignore such difficult lives as Sarah Ripley's a century earlier. These clergy were still preaching liberal religion 100 years later as if it allowed them—and even obliged them—to sanitize life before they acknowledged it.

Not unique to New England, the feeling that liberal religion had lost its vital center was also expressed by lifelong members like Ruth Irish Preston (1859–1949) of Davenport, Iowa. Preston, who still remembered the helpful sermons and feeling of close community at the Unitarian church when she joined in the later nineteenth century, felt only the weight of lifeless preaching and low morale by the 1920s. The messages and their delivery were so soporific, she groused in her diary, she would have slept through them had she not been so uncomfortable sitting so long on hard pews. She managed to joke that the regular preacher drawled his syllables out to such lengths that had she been younger, she could have jumped rope over each of them while he reached for the next. Nor did Rev. Charles Lyttle, a his-

tory scholar from Meadville Theological School in Chicago, escape Preston's jabbing pen after coming to speak on the subject "Tonic for Tired Radicals." Preston doubted, she wrote in another entry, that she was a radical as he defined it, but she was sure she was tired after hearing the man drone on, showing no more involvement than those in the pews who were praying for rapid closure. Yet this irrepressible humor could not mask the grief that came through in Preston's admissions that there was no comfort in going to church anymore and, putting her pen aside, closed the book on her hopes for the liberal religious movement. Preston did not live to see the desperately needed revitalization. For that, the laity had to wait forty years until women entered the pulpits and fostered a new understanding of ordination and liberal ministry.

Stepping Up to the Pulpits

If the church's indifference to women was plain from the self-absorbed discourse and preaching, it also was evident from the assumption that females would be content to remain the drones who wanted no greater challenge or influence in the church. This impression was frequently reinforced by women who, bowed under the custom's weight, meekly deferred to the regnant sex and even defended the way things were done on the supposition that they were the better for it. Others, who realized the implications their chosen religion had for their sex but only complained of its failings privately, had little, if any, effect on the status quo. But there was a smaller number, beginning with Judith Sargent Murray (1751–1820), who quarreled openly with the double standard that shortchanged their sex and protested loudly enough about being a disadvantaged class in the church that they managed to get their brothers' attention if not the prompt action they wanted.

These outspoken women's demands touched the powers' most sensitive nerve when they staked their claim to ordination and settlement as parish ministers. The publishing feminist Judith Sargent Murray had laid a good deal of the groundwork for this assault on the male preserve by chiding the "haughty sex" for perpetuating an institutional narrowness that contradicted the democratic mandate of Universalist thought. A loveless first marriage had made her an expert on this repugnant behavior. The man to whom she had bound herself—as the best choice she had—at the age of eighteen was less than her equal but treated her as his subordinate and smugly cited St. Paul as justification. Murray's resolve to redeem her sex by deflating the fiction of male supremacy led her to rewrite the story of the first family in Paradise. In disputing that Eve was the cause of humankind's fall from grace, she aimed to demolish an argument some liberal churchmen still used to keep women shackled and silent (Murray, "On the Equality of the Sexes").

Adding her amen to Murray's critique, Mary Ashton Rice Livermore (1820–1905), another vigorous woman of letters, repeated the "natural right" and "common humanity" arguments that were the stock-in-trade of her antebellum feminist cohort. But being a Universalist minister's wife, as Murray had been, and a codirector of the midwestern arm of the Sanitary Commission—whose purpose was getting essential supplies and medical help to the wounded during the Civil War—Livermore had become convinced that there were also good practical reasons for opening more doors to women. Much of the nation's work, she said, was "badly done, or not done at all" because female talent was not being utilized; and nowhere was this more apparent than in the pulpits where liberal religion was preached (Livermore).

By the late 1850s, when Livermore started to edit a Universalist paper, *The Dial*, and to publish her advocacy of free speech in the church and beyond, the claim to this right had progressed well beyond mere polemics. Taking their lead from the evangelicals, liberal churchwomen had started appearing as part-time or licensed preachers two decades before. The first on record was Mary Ann Church of Merrickville, Upper Canada, who in 1838 was her sex's sole representative on a list of over 400 Universalist preachers in North America. Thirty years later, seven women were listed as spreading the message, a number that seemed even greater to those who felt threatened by such a bold breech of convention.

By the end of the war, two more Universalist women had been ordained to the ministry with their denomination's official endorsement, although for this they had needed extraordinary determination and very thick skins. The intrepid Olympia Brown (1835–1926)—whom Unitarian Universalists claim as the first woman to have cleared the hurdles when credentialed in 1863 by the Saint Lawrence Association of Universalists in Malone, New York—just barely surmounted the barriers put up by people who should have known better. Dr. Ebenezer Fisher, for one, the president of Canton Theological School in Malone, where Brown had prepared herself, scorned the idea of her putting this schooling to practical use and, unable to stop her, attended the ordination under protest. Nor was it just men who scowled at the graduate. Fisher's wife, whose attitude presaged a backlash from women that female clergy still face, refused to attend the service at all. She predicted darkly that Brown's foolishness would have others storming the schools the next term and, after that, moving into the field and deflating the price of preaching (Brown, *An Autobiography*). The alarm proved exaggerated, although it was only a matter of months before a second woman, who had not even been to a seminary,

petitioned to be ordained. This was Augusta Chapin (1829–1905), who, from the time she received the Universalist message at age seventeen, never doubted that she had been called to proclaim its good news and began proselytizing in Michigan. Chapin's aptitude as a preacher and the dearth of qualified men persuaded the state's Universalists to admit her to clerical fellowship in July 1836. But it was another three years before the next woman, Phebe Ann Hanaford (1829–1921), was ordained by the Universalists in Hingham, Massachusetts.

It took even longer, until 1871, for the first two Unitarian women to charge the clergy's male bastion. Some had needed the chance afforded during the Civil War to test their executive skills on male turf and realize that when it came to administration and leadership, they were more than a match for the men, who often took credit for what women did. When peace was restored, they carried this realization back to their churches, where women had not just been orchestrating social events to raise funds for new buildings but had been writing the hymns and prayers, providing the music for services, staffing the nurseries, teaching young Sunday scholars, and visiting with the sick and needy. In short, they now understood that they had not only been running the churches but doing the work of parish ministers without the title or salary. As the Unitarian Mary H. Graves (1839–1908) explained the process that led to her ordination a few months after Celia Burleigh, any self-respecting, devoted church sister who realized that she had been doing the job, and doing it well without a minister's wife assisting behind the scenes, would sooner or later want her work called by its rightful name and be properly compensated.

The professional status to which Graves's generation aspired was brought within reach by the wish for westward and rural expansion after the Civil War. Once the leadership realized how few ordained brothers were willing to give up the comforts of well-established parishes to do the hard work of starting new churches for frontier pay that would not feed their families, the simple arithmetic spoke for itself: Women had to be in the equation. When calls went out for all able workers, both the Unitarian and Universalist groups had females come forward, but hardly enough to squeeze out the men, as the doomsayers feared. Elizabeth Bruce, who took over her husband's ministry in rural Massachusetts after he died in 1874, complained the next year that out of the 700 or more Universalist clergy, there were just 10 women, counting herself, who had not been deterred by the church's prejudice. The Unitarian sisters were an even smaller minority. Still, the audacity of these exceptions so magnified the threat that the watchmen warned of a massive invasion and stepped up their efforts to stop it.

The ensuing debate over whether women, however

accomplished, should be ordained clergy raised questions, as well, about how committed the liberal establishment was to dismantling orthodox thought that thwarted the claims of conscience and human equality. By the mid-nineteenth century, most liberal clergy were practicing Joseph Buckminster's method of reading scripture as cultural texts that were best interpreted through the historians' and archaeologists' insights. This made it awkward for them, at best, to draw on St. Paul's explanation of Genesis 3 to support the contention that females were breaking God's law by speaking from pulpits. The best they could do on the basis of scripture was argue that biblical history furnished no precedent for women's being ordained, that Jesus had chosen no women to be his apostles, and this was sufficient grounds for not giving this role to them now.

Unable to block the invasion of women by citing a doctrine embodied in scripture, obstructionists tried to build barriers from what they claimed was sound reason based on the popular wisdom that God—whether One-in-One or One-in-Three—had created the sexes with different make-ups and separate domains that suited their attributes. While they did not believe it was "wicked," the Boston-based *Universalist* told its readers repeatedly during the early 1870s that they did think that it was "unwise" for a woman to venture into the ministry, an intrusion that carried her "out of the sphere . . . prescribed for her" by a nature abounding in sentiment and intuition and unencumbered by intellect. Veteran clergymen swaggered as they spoke of the rigors of preaching, the brutality of church politics, and the other ordeals "incident to all public positions" but indubitably "most bitter in the pastoral career." They predicted that women's frail constitution—her "greater delicacy and sensitiveness"—would never be able to "bear the buffets and frowns."

It was not uncommon that those who defended the women's call to ministry exploited the same premises, averring that women's distinctive traits would steady, not topple, a shaky vocation that desperately needed more balance. In the words of Cordelia Throop Cole—the Iowa Unitarian Association's secretary in 1880 who delivered the "Charge to Ordination" when Mary A. Safford (1851–1927) became the state's first liberal pastor—a sister need only have confidence in her "own simple sling," and her "slender woman's arm would reach its target." Her womanly way of doing the work would obviate the need, said Cole, to wear a "man's armour" or carry his heavy equipment (*Women's Standard*, December 17, 1908, 1–2).

On the other hand, when Iowa's clergywomen spoke for themselves, they were likelier to use the language of radicals who eschewed the separatist constructs as fictions that lured individuals into unhealthy compartments. This badly "mistaken psychology" had created a class of dysfunctional "hard-hearted men and hysterical women" and needed to be replaced by the facts, said Eleanor Gordon, a longtime colleague of Safford's, who pastored throughout the state and derided such stereotypes when writing for Iowa's suffrage paper, the *Woman's Standard*, in 1904. Depicting women as vines that needed the bracing of strong, manly oaks, she added, might "be all very well in poetry"; but her cohort's unparalleled record of starting new churches and rescuing others was proof that when summoned by duty, "the ever womanly" rolled up her sleeves and showed the world how "a man's work" and more should be done. Gordon's group would have liked to free the debate from the prism of gender entirely since what was at stake, as she said, was neither a man's nor a woman's work but in essence a human ministry. Their detractors, however, made gender the unyielding issue.

This was nowhere more evident than in the talk about women's weakness for marriage and how they would bolt from the ministry once their domestic yearnings were roused, leaving their parishes in the lurch after wasting everyone's time and emotional energy. This argument, while only partly warranted, worked an injustice on all women who had it thrown back at them when they tried to enter the seminaries. In reality, half of the women who sought ordination during the late nineteenth century realized beforehand that matrimony in any traditional sense would be incompatible with the demands of a parish, and rather than risk the consequences, they never tested this premise. The other half, however, did marry and then rarely used their credentials again, giving the critics enough ammunition to spray the entire group. Unitarian and Universalist sisters who got past the obstacles did so only by marrying clergy amenable to partnered ministries, by starting their own congregations from scratch, or by taking churches whose trustees were willing to have them because they seemed better than nothing—and were pleasantly surprised when they realized they had a lot more than they bargained for.

While many women who married were dwarfed by their husbands' ministries, and others worked out their destinies largely unnoticed in small, rural churches that faded away, a group that emerged in the heartlands made such a spectacle of themselves it was hard to forget there were less conspicuous sisters who also were changing the picture. In the Iowa Conference, a flagship for liberal expansion on the frontier, Unitarians Safford and Gordon built up a network of almost a dozen women who virtually took command of parish development during the late nineteenth century. The membership figures, financial reports, and personal tributes in archives leave no doubt of these women's fitness for teamwork and ministry. As outsiders by dint of their sex and religion and favorite targets for heretic-hunting Trinitarian neighbors, they understood the importance of making the church a safe home for parishioners scorned and ostracized as blights on the Christian community. To help their parishioners see themselves as a family, they filled their sermons and liturgy with the popular domestic images, adjusting them to represent better balanced relationships. They deleted *obey* from the old wedding vows and in general made the language more gender inclusive and less patriarchal. During the week, too, they gave "the church home" a more literal meaning than ever before by doing what lay preacher Caroline Dall (1822–1912) considered essential for their success. Dall, who held the academic and bureaucratic approaches responsible for the ministry's being "nowhere so narrow as in its human sympathies," cautioned her sisters against the preoccupation with "pulpit graces" and neglect of the "household of faith" that diminished their brothers' sacred calling (Dall, 223–236).

Although this model of shepherding congregations served women well for some twenty-five years and gave many good reason to think the momentum would carry them into the twentieth century, their growth stopped abruptly and their numbers plummeted after the century turned. The surplus of churches in small towns and the people's migrations to cities certainly had a part in this, as did the Social Gospel's penetration of mainline Protestantism during the 1890s. In these years, Universalist and Unitarian clergy were seeing young families defect to "more respectable" churches where they could hear liberal preaching without being tagged as unchristian or radical. But these currents, which hurt almost all liberal pastors, as well as a lot of conservatives, were only a part of the undertow that washed out the sisterhood's base. The women also had been feeling the impact of a rising concern by America's institutional leadership that the country was facing a crisis of effeminacy, losing its muscularity, and growing weaker. After trading the fiery Calvinist rhetoric for a gentler scripture that seemed soft and spineless beside their competition's "exacting masculine pages," liberal clergymen were particularly prone to this form of anxiety. They feared their clerical brotherhood had acquired a pantywaist reputation that kept men from coming to sit in the pews or entering the pulpits. Repairing the damage would have to begin with stemming the female influence.

To this end, denominational placement officers quietly took ordained women's names off referral lists or sent them to feeble churches in the last stage of terminal illness. Virility squadrons installed stronger locks to protect educational bastions from further intrusions by females. And some of the top brass—most notably Samuel A. Eliot, the American Unitarian Association's chief officer—attempted to steer women into corrals where they could be trained to be parish assistants, a work they had already mastered in the school of routine experience. As

the uprooted sisters predicted, this tactic did nothing but hasten an exodus from volunteer church work by self-possessed women who eyed the social reform crusades and secular service professions as more rewarding and genuinely ministerial. To judge from the record of women's official presence in parish ministry, the years from the turn of the century to the 1970s were deathly still. In truth, the female response to a ministerial calling during these decades was not so much silent as camouflaged by the old need for women with larger visions to enter men's sphere under cover and through the side doors. Through lay speaking, fund-raising, writing, social philanthropy, crusading for temperance, political suffrage, economic reforms, and world peace, Unitarian Universalist women performed a diverse ministry that was only belatedly given its name.

Typical was the vocational shift made by ordained minister Ada Tonkin, who in 1925 became the first fully credentialed woman installed in a liberal pulpit in Canada, Victoria's Universalists having brought her in as a last resort. When Tonkin arrived, she found the church already showing the signs of rigor mortis. After a year and a half of trying to raise the dead, she helped lay it to rest and found a more promising way to interpret God's call. This was penal reform, a witness with notable precedent in the nineteenth century, when Dorothea Dix was led by her conscience—one quickened in early adulthood by Boston Unitarian Joseph Tuckerman's ministry to the city's unfortunates—to advocate for better treatment of prisoners and the mentally ill. Dix, whose Unitarian ties remained strong all her life, concentrated on changing the way institutions were run. On the other hand, Tonkin, who became the director of the Women's Protective Division of the Vancouver Police Force in 1929, focused on the prevention of crime and rehabilitation. For both Tonkin and Dix, the punitive mind that made jails living hells was close kin to the brutal imagination that saw humanity as corrupt and condemned to burn, and opposing the first was a form of promoting the second.

For liberal women who felt called to higher service outside the home, the most common alternatives to the church's ordained ministry have been—by choice or default—in the field of education. Long seen as compatible with women's sphere, this field has not only been friendlier, but for females whose liberal theology promises human perfectability, education has been a tenet of faith and a motive to teach and create better schools in the religious and secular settings. At the same time, it was also for years a sore spot for those whose faith had been bruised by hearing churchmen who valorized learning reinforce sexist ideals that effectively put advanced study beyond women's reach. The religious impulse behind this vocational choice was captured by Margaret Fuller, who wished to be self-supporting and free to put her talents to use. With few other options, Fuller became an educator to reach her personal goals. In 1837, after working in Unitarian A. Bronson Alcott's school in Boston, where the teachers had freedom to try out progressive theories of education, Fuller became the head of the Green Street School in Providence, Rhode Island. There, she revealed in her journal, with the older girls as her special charge, she aimed to make these emerging women conscious of their potential by appealing "not to their weakness but to their strength." "I told them of my happiness," she wrote of this mutually fruitful time, and explained to the girls that she had tried to give them "the loftiest motives" to live full lives by making "every other end subordinate to that of spiritual growth" (Spring 1837).

Liberal Sisterhoods' Larger Ministries

Like many orthodox Christian women, those in the liberal religious traditions understood early that making a usable history—like doing ministry, lay or ordained—was a group enterprise that empowered not only the group but each individual who extended herself to share her strength with her sisters. It was liberal women's collective visions that gave birth to churches, expanded their purpose, and raised the money required to realize their dreams. These achievements were all the more impressive given the fact that laywomen, just like the sisters who sought ordination, had to contend with brothers who tried to co-opt or derail their initiatives out of a deep-rooted fear of female autonomy.

The first to build muscle by forming a group were the Universalist women, who in 1869 created the Women's Centenary Aid Association (WCAA, 1869–1871). This vigorous corps went through various reincarnations—as the Women's Centenary Association (WCA, 1871–1905), the Women's National Missionary Association (WNMA, 1905–1939), and the Association of Universalist Women (AUW, 1939–1963)—before consolidating with its Unitarian counterpart as the Unitarian Universalist Women's Federation (UUWF) in 1963. Conceived in anticipation of the 1870 milestone, the completion of the denomination's first century in America, the Women's Centenary Aid Association's organizers' aim was to form a body of women "for special work" independent of the national Convention, where Universalist men controlled the coffers and the agenda and refused to have women sitting with them on the board. To achieve self-sufficiency, planners solicited workers and funds nationwide and stunned the most confident canvassers when they netted some $35,000 and 13,000 members, enough to put faith into action on women's own terms.

By the end of its first decade, President Caroline A. Soule was able to say that all of the goals set forth by

the founders—to subsidize pauperized parishes; to foster Sunday Schools; to help worthy students, especially females, prepare themselves for the ministry; to relieve the needs of disabled preachers, ministers' wives, and orphans; to distribute denominational literature; and to practice what Universalists preached through mission projects at home and abroad—had been achieved in large measure. Not the least of the organization's feats was fending off the barrage of attacks from the "zealous defenders of man's prerogative," who felt the women's independence threatened the General Conference's status. The brothers accused them of being too proud of themselves and weak in church loyalties, but the pointed fingers just strengthened the sisters' resolve to retain what was rightfully theirs. They would never relinquish their name, their money, or charter, Soule assured the Convention trustees when she heard that they were about to make such a demand.

Quick as they were to dig in their heels when their right to exist was questioned, the Universalist sisters were just as firm in resisting rigid provincial perspectives that would have diminished their purpose. Eager to clasp the hands of more women, they took steps to soften their demarcations, in 1882 rubbing out the boundaries set by their charter so as to bring in their sisters from Canada's British-owned provinces. In acknowledgment, too, that America's borders extended south and west of New England, during the early twentieth century, they turned their attention to South Carolina, financing preaching circuits that led to the organization of twenty liberal congregations, whose outreach helped soften the negative feelings toward northerners and religious iconoclasts. Overseas, Universalist women started a sewing school in Korea and two missionary homes in Japan. By the end of the twentieth century, though, the most beloved jewel on the crown of accomplishments was the Clara Barton Camp for Diabetic Girls. Established in North Oxford, Massachusetts, in 1921, this camp, on the land where Barton once lived, was named to honor the Universalist woman whose ministry was to create the Red Cross and advance the profession of nursing.

That the Unitarian women were also ready to get past divisive distinctions was evident in 1889, when they launched a national movement to unite on the broadest possible basis. The name they proposed—the Alliance of Unitarian and Other Liberal Christian Women—was to make room for Jews as theologically unitarian and, under the second clause, for a generous range of liberal Protestants. When midwestern women expressed their reluctance to carry so broad a banner, the easterners put their philosophy squarely before them: If anything was to be learned from their liberal brothers, who were slower to work together and "sore with bruises" from trying to pound their definitions of freedom in worship into each other, it was that the sisters ought not to repeat their mistakes. It was "too much . . . to claim all the mental clearness and courage" for themselves. "That we *all may be one*" was their aim, and to make that possible, said the East Coast's leaders, "*we* shall forget theology in our living faith and burning love." Most of the ordained sisters had already made this their operative principle. Eliza Tupper Wilkes (1844–1917), who was credentialed in 1871 by the Universalists and later served Unitarian churches in the Upper Great Plains, winced when a Unitarian bureaucrat took her to task for not preaching what he considered legitimate liberal religion.

The racial divide was harder for liberal religion's reformers to cross, an incongruity often obscured—to many within as well as outside the fold—by some of its members' high visibility in crusading for human justice. In the nineteenth century, Universalists and Unitarians crowded the front lines opposing slavery, maintaining the Underground Railroad, and running mission schools for freed slaves. A hundred years later, the liberal religious body was quick to ally itself with the civil rights movement and its systemic reforms. Yet this still overwhelmingly white middle-class faith community of the twentieth century was just a few generations away from liberals who not only welcomed the theory of evolution but used Charles Darwin's teachings to bolster their claim to racial superiority but endorsed policies proposed to protect "pure white blood" in the twentieth century. When Unitarian Universalists rushed to support Martin Luther King, Jr.'s demonstrations, it had not been sixty years since Unitarian money had paid to print tracts promoting white supremacy and spreading fears about race suicide. It was not surprising that they were still struggling to cleanse themselves of the bigotry and move beyond the abolitionists' well-intended paternalism.

If denial kept many religious liberals from overcoming this problem by parsing it—by admitting how much education and class had to do with whether one builds walls or bridges—the record of women's experiences shows that others acknowledged their prejudices and, by facing them honestly, helped the next generations achieve more authentic relationships. Celia Parker Woolley (1848–1918), a daughter of New England abolitionists, rejected not only the blatant injustices blacks had to bear but also the indirect damage inflicted when whites treated them as less educable inferiors. The more she saw of middle-class blacks like the lecturer Fannie Barrier Williams (1855–1944), the more convinced she was that if given the same advantages, people of color could make the same progress as any other group. After a decade writing columns for *Unity*, the weekly paper pitched to the Unitarians' radical wing, Woolley was ready to challenge her cohort of privileged ladies when she became president of the Chicago Woman's Club in

the late 1890s. Willing to sacrifice harmony and to risk the loss of good friends, she confronted the club sisters with their hypocrisy in retaining a motto that stated, "Nothing that is human is alien to us," then barring women from membership on the basis of race or religion. At the end of a bitter fight, the bylaws were changed, and Woolley's friend Williams became the first woman of color ever to sign the club's roster. Woolley went on to become a Unitarian minister, receiving her ordination in 1896 and serving two churches briefly before deciding to leave the privileged parishes for a ministry devoted to rubbing out lines that segregated the races. In 1904 she and her husband, a dentist, moved from their home in an upscale Caucasian neighborhood into a house on the edge of Chicago's South Side, just over the line that divided the city's black and white populations. There she started the Frederick Douglass Center, envisioning it as a modified social settlement where "the best people of both races," to use Woolley's words, could get acquainted as equals, discuss their differences, and discover their common concerns. Having found her real ministry at the Center, Woolley devoted the rest of her days to fostering better relationships between the races, frequently drawing harsh criticism from labor groups and black journalists, who scoffed at her interracial forums, genteel teas, and sedate Sunday afternoon worship services. These did nothing for those most in need, they said, dismissing as inconsequential the Center's aim of building a climate free of paternalistic dynamics. Nor did her death in 1918 put an end to the criticism. Historians would continue to question the depth and sincerity of her motives, noting how willing she was to assure those who shrieked at the idea of racial mixing—and threatened to close down the Center one way or another—that her aim was to bring the races together only in "non-social ways." But if statements like these made Woolley sound wobbly, she stood by her vision of building a climate where the black and white guests were willing to pool their resources because they trusted each other. Because she did, the Center became the birthplace of the Urban League and the National Association for the Advancement of Colored People. Within the limits she set for herself, Woolley accomplished her mission, offering up her life in the service of what she believed, and this was a time when few others, lay or ordained, were willing or able to go as far.

Liberal clergy like Caroline Bartlett Crane (1858–1935), whose rousing Social Gospel sermons during the 1890s packed the hall at All Souls Unitarian Church in Kalamazoo, Michigan, was awed and humbled by Woolley's ability to give her private as well as her public life to the cause of racial justice. Professionally, Crane did her utmost to practice the liberal message she preached. She made a point of including the city's black residents in her ministry's outreach. She took pains to see that any who came to worship were cordially welcomed and given good seats near the front. She provided an all-black cultural club with rooms in the church until they were able to find a permanent meeting place in the members' own churches. In 1905, after hearing about the Douglass Center, Crane thought about forming an interracial partnership for her city and as a first step invited black and white leaders to a luncheon in her home. When, as expected, the public was scandalized by this event, Crane welcomed the chance to declare publicly in defense that she would not hesitate ever to meet and break bread with respectable people in the interest of any good cause like racial justice. Yet internal resistance—her deeply lodged doubts that the races were really equal and a visceral fear of racial mixing—kept Crane from going much farther than making such statements, endorsing blacks' self-help initiatives, and entertaining a handful of "fine or gifted negroes" in her home. The awkward truth was, she confessed to a friend late in life, she had felt it was only fair that all people should " 'have their place in the sun'—education and opportunity to develop their individual gifts," but this feeling was always "uncomfortably mixed" with the fear that she "might be helping along the wrong sort of thing if one looked at larger and more fundamental issues" (Letter to an unidentified friend, April 18, 1927).

Difficult as it was in Crane's day and up to the time of merger for the Unitarian Universalists to admit to the problems that paralyzed their faith in matters of race, they eventually learned that in failing to do so the movement was shamefully compromised. This message caught liberals off guard when delivered during the 1960s, as hundreds of the denomination's men and women were demonstrating for black civil rights in the South, some even giving their lives for the cause. In 1965, not long after James Reeb, a minister from Massachusetts, was fatally beaten in Selma, Alabama, and quickly enshrined as a martyr, Viola Gregg Liuzzo, a Unitarian Universalist from Detroit, Michigan, joined the protest in Selma and met the same fate. But for all its vaunted activism, the liberal movement remained overwhelmingly white, and there were so few liberal clergy of color, they counted how many they were on their fingers. Inevitably, cries of racism started to fill church boardrooms and engulf the proceedings at General Assemblies. The rest of the decade and part of the next saw the movement turn on itself as it waged a bitter internecine war whose lines were drawn not along racial lines but over the issue of how to respond to the charges. The wounds were allowed to fester for almost two decades until the 1990s, when Unitarian Universalist women, sensitized by the demeaning effect of sexism's glass walls and ceilings, challenged the liberal body to take a frank look at its racist structures and work to remove them, not cover up or indulge their selective memories. Two past presidents of the Unitarian Universalist Women's Federation played a major role in the framing and passage of the denomination's Anti-Racism Resolution in 1997 and its implementation. Under the banner "Journey toward Wholeness," these women and others worked to create a raft of self-studies, youth and adult education curricula, workshops, publications, and videos to raise the denomination's consciousness and help it evolve to be fully inclusive and worthy of its name.

Religiously liberal women's pursuit of an equal political voice was provoked by the same fundamental tensions surrounding race. To many, no cause made it more imperative that they lock arms with each other and women of other faiths, if not necessarily women of other races. The Gordon sisters of New Orleans—Kate (1861–1932) and Jean Margaret (1865–1931)—were Unitarians, active social reformers, and ardent suffragists but were also opposed to black women having the vote. In a desperate effort to keep franchise issues under the states' control, and the ballot box in the hands of white people, they campaigned against the Nineteenth Amendment's ratification in Tennessee, where the victory was sealed anyway. There were also a number of otherwise forward-thinking women in northern states who came out as "antis," if only because of their fears of upsetting the social order and tampering with the roles they believed God had fashioned to fit the sexes' different natures. Despite the existence of this substantial minority opposing the vote, the liberal religious community earned the reputation for breeding suffragists by supplying a disproportionate number of the pro-franchise leadership. As one of the leaders, Unitarian Julia Ward Howe observed, it was hardly surprising that fighting for suffrage felt like a sacred duty when one's religion was based on the same democratic beliefs as one's claim to the full rights of citizenship. In Howe's case, this insight was sharpened by lessons learned from a difficult marriage to a man who raged against women's involvement in public affairs and disparaged her causes. For others like Mary Safford and Eleanor Gordon, who chose not to marry at all so as to be free to have full-time careers in the ministry, and even for those like Lucy Stone, who were blessed with unconventional, egalitarian marriages, it was knowing the struggle and satisfactions in gaining domestic autonomy that spurred them to fight for their sex's political rights. In 1868, Howe and Stone established the New England Woman's Suffrage Association and two years later launched *The Woman's Journal*, which served as the major organ of the women's movement for forty years.

In the Midwest, the feminist forces were also galvanized by religious liberals, especially after the sister clergy controlled a broad network of pulpits. Not surprisingly, soon after Ida Hultin (1858–1938), a vigorous franchise crusader, was called in 1886 to be minister to the Des Moines Unitarians, a room in her church was turned into an office from which the Great Plains' major suffrage paper *The Woman's Standard* was launched. In 1913, when Iowa's suffrage movement seemed mortally wounded, Mary Safford, by now a veteran minister who for almost thirty-five years had been breathing new life into seemingly hopeless churches, took up the challenge. Reviving the troops, she led the campaign to a triumph that almost miraculously put an end to a forty-year stretch of bitter defeats.

In Canada, too, Dr. Emily Stowe, whose struggle to enter the medical field had perfected her grasp of sexist dynamics, used subtler tactics to rouse and organize feminist indignation. In 1879, after joining Toronto's Unitarian church, where women had equal rights on paper but not a prayer of holding an office, Stowe used the women's literary society to disguise her efforts to drum up enough support for public dissent. Ten years later, she had the constituency to declare her aim unequivocally by establishing the Dominion Women's Enfranchisement Association. As its president, a position she held until her death in 1903, Stowe recruited American suffrage leaders like coreligionists Julia Ward Howe and Susan B. Anthony to encourage the sisters to keep the faith north of the border. Iceland's attention to women's rights issues was also focused by liberal religionists, most notably through the tireless work of Margaret Benedictsson, one of the Winnipeg Unitarian congregation's founding members. In 1898, with her husband Sigfus, Benedictsson started *Freyja*, a radical monthly whose thrust raised awareness of gender-based problems that called for reform. A decade later, she founded the Icelandic Women's Suffrage Association, a group that provided the Manitoba suffrage movement with major support. Ironically, while the crusades for suffrage extended these sisters' access to platforms from which to proclaim their liberal evangel, the triumph that made the Nineteenth Amendment the law of the land in 1920 marked the end of their era of visible ministry.

It was not until the human rights movements erupted almost fifty years later that the liberal churchwomen's hushed discontent with their marginal roles recovered its voice. The heightened awareness that something was wrong and the realization of what it was came not from the denominational merger of 1961 but from an eye-opener outside the institution: the 1963 publication of Betty Friedan's *The Feminine Mystique*. Women like Marjorie Leaming, whose 1967 ordination and settlement proved to be harbingers of her sex's return to the parish ministry, found in Friedan's analysis of women's paralyzing malaise the insight and courage to challenge the problem that stood between women and their calling. Revitalized, UU feminists laid the groundwork for change by placing a series of resolutions before the Uni-

tarian Universalist Association's (UUA) General Assemblies in 1964, 1970, 1973, and 1977. These bills of intent called for parity in the treatment of applicants to the liberals' theological schools; recruitment of all able candidates for the ministry and equality in the salaries paid; the elimination of sexist assumptions and language by all UUA personnel; and the creation of a Women and Religion Committee to assist in the implementation of these objectives.

If the passage of this agenda had any effect in the first ten years, it was only to nudge the issue onto the edge of the movement's conscience. Its failure to build the momentum to demonstrate any significant progress was documented in 1974 by a study made under the auspices of the Unitarian Universalist Women's Federation. The findings showed that of some 750 credentialed UU clergy, fewer than 40 were women, only 5 had pulpits, and these few were working for such meager salaries that, even serving more than one church, they were earning substandard incomes. Women were running into fierce prejudice when they applied to divinity schools, requested financial support, or interviewed for available settlements. By 1979, however, with the muttered abuses aired openly and the leadership now more attentive, the number of women being ordained had caught up with and outstripped the men by a hair's breadth. By the end of the twentieth century, females had pulled ahead three to one in divinity schools, and in active ministerial service, women were better than even with men.

Denominational leaders and women themselves may take pride in statistics like these, but few would pretend that they tell the whole story or that full equality has been achieved. They acknowledge that ordained women more frequently than their male counterparts serve in associate, part-time "extension," interim, and nonparish placements, or in ministries of religious education. They are well aware, too, that those who are solo or senior pastors are more often settled in smaller churches, though this may be to their advantage and a matter of choice. In the 1990s, addressing lingering prejudices, UUA personnel implemented affirmative action workshops to move congregations beyond categorical thinking when searching for new leadership. In a further show of concern, the Association's top brass undertook "a sexism audit," a partial self-study described as a first step toward rooting out dubious practices in their own operations at their headquarters in Boston. The question of how well these measures have translated policy into fair practice continues to be a matter of debate.

Like the numbers, moreover, no list of remedial steps or corporate directives can suggest the influence women have had in the evolution of liberal religious practice since the 1970s, particularly in its forms of worship, sense of identity, and understandings of ordained ministry's manifold expressions. It cannot convey the sisters' success in moving the fold toward a gender-inclusive and nonhierarchical language that better embodies the essence of liberal theology. Nor does it describe how women have given the pulpits more power to reach the pews by admitting as sacred texts the intuitive revelations and personal stories that resonate at the grassroots. Thanks to a series of publications put out by the Women's Federation, the authority and absorption of female perspectives, which have their own range of inflections, have grown significantly since the 1970s; and liberal religion—which never was monolithic—has come to be even more pluralistic, more willing to make a place for Christian, humanistic, and earth-centered spirituality, Jewish and Buddhist affinities, and the exploration of feminist theology. Shirley Ranck's curriculum *Cakes for the Queen of Heaven* (1989)—which continues to make a significant impact on women throughout North America and beyond—and Elizabeth Fisher's *Rise Up and Call Her Name: A Woman-Honoring Journey in Global Earth-Based Spiritualities* (1993)—have raised awareness of women's rich stories and cultural diversity. At the same time, with its book of essays, *Finding Our Way* (1992), the Women's Federation put the denomination on notice that women would no longer keep the whispered secrets and cover the festering wounds left on them, their families, and their faith community by ministers who abused their power through improper sexual conduct. To prepare for prophetic essays like these, the Federation had already published two volumes of *Transforming Thought* (1988 and 1989), in which clergywomen, sister scholars, and educators articulated alternatives to their male counterparts' abstract and sexist constructions of Unitarian Universalist principles. Down-to-earth and accessible, these revisionist treatments of liberal religion's distinctive elements put the lie to the myth that a living faith and its tenets can ever be disembodied.

Far extending the reach of these publications, an ever-expanding stream of books released by Beacon Press—which the Unitarians founded in 1854 and continued to own until passing it on to the UUA at merger—has brought readers cutting-edge titles in women's spirituality, feminist theology, and women in liberal and other religious traditions. Mary Daly's *Beyond God the Father*, released in 1972, was only the first "to rock the patriarchal firmament." Aroused by voices like these, Unitarian Universalist women have prodded their movement to look within itself and address, along with its sexist mind-set, its history of racist, ageist, and classist attitudes. Indeed, to judge from the strength of its voices, the female contingent has been ordained to keep its movement of vast potential from growing too comfortable with its past, too smug in its present con-

trition and gains, and too confident of its salvation anytime soon.

SOURCES: For a denominational overview, see David Robinson's *The Unitarians and the Universalists* (1985) and Phillip Hewett's *Unitarians in Canada* (1978). Each of the two volumes published as *The Larger Hope* (1979, 1985)—Russell Miller's history of Universalism's first 200 years—has an excellent chapter devoted to Universalist women. Records pertaining to Unitarian, Universalist, and Unitarian Universalist women clergy are housed at Andover-Harvard Library at Harvard Divinity School; Meadville Lombard Theological School Library in Chicago; the Flora Lamson Hewlett Library and Starr King School for the Ministry, both affiliated with the Graduate Theological Union at the University of California in Berkeley; and the Schlesinger Library of Radcliffe College at Harvard. The manuscripts of the Judith Sargent Murray Papers, consisting of twenty letter books, are held by the Mississippi Department of Archives and History in Jackson, where they have been put on microfilm for use on site and out of state. Murray's essay "On the Equality of the Sexes" appeared in *Massachusetts Magazine* (March and April 1790). Caroline H. Dall, *The College, the Market, and the Court* was published in 1868. Margaret Fuller's journal writings were published in two volumes as *Memoirs of Margaret Fuller Ossoli* (1852–1853); and her *Women in the Nineteenth Century* was published in 1845. For the definitive study of Sarah Alden Ripley, see Joan W. Goodwin's *The Remarkable Mrs. Ripley* (1999). The unpublished diaries of Sarah Smith Flagg reside in the Library Archives at the University of Illinois in Edwardsville. Ellen Tucker Emerson's correspondence has been edited by Edith E. W. Gregg and published in two volumes as *The Letters of Ellen Tucker Emerson* (1982). Margaret Dawes Eliot's letter is housed with the Eliot Family Papers at the Reed College Library Archives in Portland, Oregon. The diaries of Ruth Irish Preston can be read in the Archives of the Davenport, Iowa, Unitarian Church. Mary Livermore's autobiography *The Story of My Life* was published in 1897. Olympia Brown's unfinished autobiography, completed and edited by Gwendolyn Brown Willis, was published as *An Autobiography* in *The Journal of the Unitarian Historical Society* 4 (1963). Brown's speeches and writings were edited by Dana Greene and published as *Suffrage and Religious Principle* in 1988. For an in-depth account of religiously liberal women's emergence as ordained Unitarian clergy, grassroots successes, institutional struggles, and secular ministries, see Cynthia Grant Tucker's *Prophetic Sisterhood* (1990). Cordelia Throop Cole's "Charge" at Mary Safford's ordination was published in *Unity* 5 (1880). Meadville Lombard Theological School has the largest collection of Celia Parker Woolley's papers. "The Frederick Douglass Center," published in *Unity* 81 (1918) following Woolley's death, is an admiring retrospective of her purpose and programs, while Fannie Barrier Williams's "The Frederick Douglass Center" in *Southern Workman* 35 (1906) is an announcement of the Center's birth and promise from the perspective of Woolley's African American collaborator. Records of the Midwest's attitude toward the formation of a National Alliance of Unitarian and Other Liberal Christian Women—including the letter written by an unidentified East Coast member on January 2, 1889, explaining the rationale for the organization's name—are at Meadville Lombard Theological School. The Caroline Bartlett Crane Papers are in the Regional History Archives of Western Michigan University Archives in Kalamazoo, Michigan. Books bearing the Beacon Press imprint include such titles as *Diving Deep and Surfacing,* Carol Christ's study of women's autobiographies and spiritual quests; Starhawk's *Dreaming the Dark* on women's empowerment through ritual; Tucker's *Prophetic Sisterhood*; Sandy Boucher's *Turning the Wheel,* a study of feminism and Buddhist practice; and Paula Gunn Allen's *Grandmothers of the Light,* a collection of Goddess stories from Native American civilizations.

Evangelical Protestantism

WOMEN IN PENTECOSTALISM
Edith Blumhofer

THE STORY OF women and American Pentecostalism is at once more complex and more predictable than a cursory look at history or statistics suggests. A (very) short list of female Pentecostal preachers comes readily to mind, headed by Aimee Semple McPherson, the controversial evangelist who died in 1944. While some Pentecostal women have had prominent roles, others have understood their faith to limit their public voice. Specific expectations about women's behavior and participation differ by region, ethnicity, and denomination. Deeply rooted assumptions about gender and family interact with notions of liberty in the Spirit and muddle understandings of women in ministry. To make sense of a complicated story, it is necessary to examine ideas about gender relationships in early American Pentecostalism before moving on to assess how this religious movement has shaped—and been shaped by—understandings of women in relationship to men. As Pentecostals wrestle over statements about ministering women, one New Testament passage provides a consistent subtext: "I permit no woman to teach or to have authority over a man; she is to remain silent" (1 Timothy 2:12, New Revised Standard Version [NRSV]). Pentecostals have pushed hard at boundaries, but in the end most defer in one way or another to these words. Other Encyclopedia essays review in depth the experiences of women in African American, Latino, and charismatic groups. This essay focuses predominantly on Euro-American Pentecostal denominations whose histories illuminate at once the variety and the sameness of Pentecostalism's place for women.

Early Ethos

A convenient and conventional starting place is Azusa Street in Los Angeles in 1906. There Pentecostals transformed an abandoned frame building that had once been a Methodist church into a simple mission that remains the most compelling symbol of the fervor that launched the global Pentecostal movement. The name of the mission, Apostolic Faith, conveyed one primary feature of early Pentecostalism: Adherents saw themselves in continuity with the Christianity practiced in the apostolic era. The apostles spoke in tongues at the moment of baptism with the Holy Spirit (Acts 2), and so too did Pentecostals. St. Paul wrote of spiritual "utterance" gifts (1 Corinthians 12:7–11). Pentecostals expected to exercise those gifts—tongues, prophecy, interpretation of tongues. For women, this restorationist drive held promise and peril. The same writer who as-

Florence Crawford, the feisty Holiness woman with whom early pilgrims to Azusa Street Faith Mission in Los Angeles were forced to reckon, followed a "call" to the northwest and settled in Portland, Oregon. Her self-aggrandizement and overbearing claims to spiritual authority irreparably breached her marriage. *Courtesy of the Flower Pentecostal Heritage Center.*

was prayer, Bible reading, or singing. . . . Those baptized in the Holy Ghost lived in this atmosphere as naturally as fish live in water. Hence, there was almost no teasing or joking, no relating of amusing anecdotes. There was little of ordinary visiting. . . . We were looking for Jesus only, and we found Him! (Goss, 192–193)

Reports of Pentecostal meetings at the Azusa Street mission set the ideal for some. They intimated chaotic moments, but participants insisted that divine order prevailed. "The testimony meetings which precede the preaching often continue for two hours or more and people are standing waiting to testify all the time," wrote one of the leaders. "As soon as it is announced that the altar is open for seekers for pardon, sanctification, the baptism with the Holy Ghost and healing of the body, the people rise and flock to the altar."

What kind of preaching is it that brings them? Why, the simple declaring of the Word of God. There is such power in the preaching of the Word in the Spirit that people are shaken on the benches. . . . Many fall prostrate under the power of God, and often come out speaking in tongues. Sometimes the power falls on people and they are wrought upon by the Spirit during testimony or preaching and receive Bible experiences. . . . It is while under the power of the Spirit you see the hands raised and hear the speaking in tongues. While one sings a song learned from heaven with a shining face, the tears will be trickling down other faces. Many receive the Spirit through the laying on of hands. ("Bible Pentecost," *The Apostolic Faith* [November 1906]: 1)

Animated by such beliefs, male and female Pentecostals reveled in religious experiences that assured them of God's presence, power, and unlimited favor. They coveted unconventional intensity manifested in emotional fervor. They believed the Spirit lived within them, and that meant that anything was possible. Their religious culture valued exhortation, testimony to religious experiences (like conversion, healing, physical and spiritual protection, answered prayer), song, and other forms of lay participation.

In such a setting, women easily gained visibility. Like men, women might exercise any spiritual gift. They tes-

serted male and female oneness in Christ (Galatians 3: 28) enjoined women's silence in the church (1 Timothy 2:12). Recovering dimensions of apostolic experience did not, in itself, assure clarity about woman's place.

The conviction that Pentecostalism represented a divine restoration of apostolic Christianity was linked to the certainty that history was about to culminate in the return of Christ. Preoccupation with the second coming energized Pentecostals to pursue their own holiness and the world's conversion. At first they expected that the gift of tongues would bridge language barriers and accelerate the agonizingly slow task of global evangelism. But with or without miraculous speech, they eagerly set out to spread the word: Christ was coming soon, and the Apostolic Faith restored was nothing less than Christ's equipping the church for his return. It presaged a brief worldwide evangelistic opportunity that would usher in the end of time, and this required the energetic participation of women and men (*Anderson; Blumhofer, Restoring the Faith; Wacker*).

Early Pentecostal services were not "typical" Protestant gatherings. Spontaneous worship and impromptu preaching broke out wherever Pentecostals gathered— at train depots, in one another's homes, or on street corners. "Wherever we happened to meet," Ethel Goss reminisced,

whether in each other's home or elsewhere, and whether there was a minister present or not, there

WOMEN IN PENTECOSTALISM ᴖ 395

tified to religious experience, exhorted, and preached. And women were among the first to leave Los Angeles to herald the Pentecostal message (often simply stated as "Pentecost has come!") elsewhere. Within a year, Pentecostal women as well as men had circled the globe. In the United States, at the Azusa Street Apostolic Faith Mission, two white women, Florence Crawford and Clara Lum, among others, shared speaking and editorial responsibilities with William J. Seymour, the African American preacher generally regarded as the leader. Women organized urban missions or identified missions they had already established with Pentecostalism. The right to do so seemed clearly authenticated by the immediate working of the Holy Spirit within them. In a context that celebrated spiritual gifts and personal testimony, women and men, boys and girls spoke, sang, and shouted without regard to age or gender.

Certainty about the imminence of the end encouraged women's public voice. Citing Joel 2 as quoted by St. Peter in Acts 2, Pentecostals noted the ancient promise that in the last days sons and daughters would prophesy and handmaidens would be empowered by the Holy Spirit. Referencing one of Jesus' parables, Pentecostals affirmed women as "eleventh-hour laborers." This enabled Pentecostals to support public roles for women in general without dealing in detail with troublesome issues in church history. In the "eleventh hour," just before the dawning of the new age, old rules no longer applied: The urgency of the moment and the coming new age justified women's expanded place in gospel work.

In the larger evangelical world that most Pentecostals had inhabited before embracing a more radical Pentecostal stance, women's prodigious activities fueled evangelistic, educational, publishing, and benevolent enterprises. The relentless expansion of woman's sphere had prompted some acknowledged male leaders to move cautiously toward affirming woman's public voice in religious meetings. Baptist A. J. Gordon, friend of evangelist D. L. Moody and pastor of Boston's Clarendon Street Baptist Church, authored an important article affirming ministering women (Gordon, 910–921). Often cited, Gordon's views valued woman's speech in "mixed assemblies" but fell short of addressing fundamental issues of gender and authority. Gordon's colleague Frederick L. Chapell included women in his study of appropriate "eleventh-hour laborers" (Chapell, 59–65). Bible training schools like Moody's in Chicago, Gordon's in Boston, or Albert Simpson's in New York prepared women for various forms of public Christian service (Brereton). In the same cities, older denominations reinvigorated the role of the deaconess. Salvation Army lassies became familiar figures in urban slums. Frances Willard and the Women's Christian Temperance Union

and a host of similar societies offered women leadership opportunities in religiously based endeavors at home and abroad. The Holiness movement, too, produced scores of female evangelists, missionaries, Bible teachers, and editors.

Nurtured in such environments or attuned to new possibilities, then, some early Pentecostals simply embraced Pentecostal teaching and continued what they had already been doing. Among the most visible of these was Emma C. Ladd, wife of the popular Republican chief justice of the Iowa Supreme Court. A deeply religious woman, Ladd took her turn with other socially prominent Des Moines Protestant women to lead services at a rescue mission in a poor section of town. In 1907 she accepted Pentecostal teaching and turned the crowded mission premises into a powerhouse of Pentecostalism. Her social standing assured press coverage of the protracted, highly charged services over which she presided. In June 1907, the first page of Des Moines papers published a complaint against her: "Mrs. Scott M. Ladd Will Be Arrested. She disturbs neighbors with her queer 'mission' " ("Wife of Judge Ladd Is to Be Arrested," The Des Moines Capital, 18 June 1907). Although she avoided arrest by leaving town until the complainant withdrew his objections, reporters remained interested, and Judge Ladd promised to "get to the bottom of the matter." When reporters and ministers visited her mission, they found Ladd curiously inactive amid the hubbub, yet clearly in her element: "Two hundred people stifled together in the low-ceilinged mission room. The heat was intolerable. Shouts deafened the religionists. Cries excited the people. Five persons lay at length on the floor and beat themselves and uttered gibberish. Smiling serenely, the wife of State Supreme Judge Ladd sat back and watched the proceedings" (9). She soon bowed to pressure from her husband and turned the leadership over to others, but she remained the mission's benefactor and most ardent supporter (Blumhofer, "Emma Cromer Ladd: Iowa's Pentecostal Pioneer," Assemblies of God Heritage, 18.3–4 [Fall–Winter 1998–1999]: 21–24, 46, 48–50).

Carrie Judd Montgomery also brought an established ministry in Oakland, California, into the Pentecostal movement. Wealthy, educated, and reared an Episcopalian, Montgomery joined the Christian and Missionary Alliance (non-Pentecostal) after experiencing a healing. She avidly supported the Salvation Army but ultimately threw in her lot with the Pentecostals among whom she gained considerable renown. Her businessman husband George could be referenced as leader, but his wife overshadowed him in every aspect of ministry— a church, a monthly magazine, Triumphs of Faith, and the "Home of Peace" (Montgomery, "Under His Wings": The Story of My Life). Open to "tired Missionaries and

Christian workers" for rest, it also welcomed "the sick to come and wait upon God for Divine Healing and Spiritual blessing" (Montgomery, "Home of Peace," *Triumphs of Faith*, 35 [January 1915]: 24).

The reading of scripture that justified this apparent minimizing of a gender gap based in Pentecostal understandings of the Holy Spirit and the end times also encouraged them to rationalize and limit woman's sphere. Lest any women be too bold, the *Apostolic Faith* (Los Angeles) pointed the way. Contrasting Pentecost with earlier Jewish custom, the paper acknowledged women's "anointing" with and by the Holy Spirit: "All the women received the . . . oil of the Holy Ghost and were able to preach the same as men . . . so they both have come together and work in the Gospel." But a stern reminder followed: "No woman that has the Spirit of Jesus wants to usurp authority over the man," the unsigned article thundered. "The more God uses you in the Spirit, the more humbled and meek and tender you are" (William Seymour, ed. "Who May Prophesy?" *The Apostolic Faith* [January 1908]: 2).

It was one thing if the community understood that the Holy Spirit chose to do something, but quite another if people ventured to act on their own. One of the earliest Pentecostal writers on women's role in the church agreed that women might prophesy and manifest other "utterance gifts" listed in the New Testament. But, the author, Houston attorney Warren Fay Carothers, reasoned that in a truly Pentecostal meeting, being used by the Holy Spirit to speak in tongues, interpret tongues, or prophesy involved no use of human intellect. Men, women, or children functioned simply as empty channels through whom the Spirit chose to flow. If intellect intruded, then only men could have the floor, for the place to "test woman's call" was not at the anointing but in the scriptures that forbade women to instruct men. "Man is especially made in the image and likeness of God," Carothers avowed, "and is therefore by right the sovereign of all creation. It is man's prerogative to rule in all things." To Carothers's mind, the divine distinction between male and female was most faithfully evident in "the chivalrous Southland" and nothing was "more heavenly than the sincere observance of this distinction" (Carothers, 43–48).

Further, though women preached, evangelized, and conducted missions, their missions were not churches in the usual sense. Questions of administering the sacraments, of credentialing, or of connectionalism did not apply. Rather, evangelism held center stage. So Millicent and Ethel, wives of southern Pentecostal evangelist, Howard Goss, gained repute as evangelists, but Howard—likable, handsome but less gifted as a public speaker—provided an affirming male presence. Howard could be counted upon to defer to his wife's "leading,"

and all the while his endorsement—presumed or verbal—legitimated her public ministry (Goss). With regard to preaching men, Howard maintained: "A preacher whose wife did not carry the burden for souls, who was not interested enough herself to pray, fast, consecrate, take the burden of the altar work, live the same kind of life her husband lived, was soon out of the work and on the sidelines" (189).

Ellen Hebden, an English immigrant whose name is closely associated with the beginnings of Pentecostalism in Ontario, operated similarly. Her husband James exercised nominal leadership at their mission on Toronto's Queen Street, but people everywhere recognized Ellen as the person in charge. She wielded cultural authority that assured her place. She did not replace James; rather, she overshadowed him by her adept use of spiritual gifts. "The Lord," she boasted, "gave me twenty-two languages one night in a public meeting; and hundreds of verses of poetry have been given by the Spirit, also the interpretation of many. . . . I have been able to write all the languages that God has spoken through me, and many marvelous sketches [oil paintings that she claimed the Spirit interpreted] have been drawn" (Hebden, *"How Pentecost Came,"* 3). No one marveled at her gifts more than she. Writing in the third person she exulted: "At times she is apparently in Spirit as John was at Patmos and then has apparently joined in the worship in heaven, but has also given many messages as from the Spirit of God to the people" (Hebden, "Pentecostal Work," 2).

Within limits, then, women gained public visibility as evangelists, missionaries, and personal workers. They countered objections by referencing the Spirit's endument. Their religious world stressed lay initiative, and they gained more visibility among Pentecostals than in many other settings. But this belied a fundamental social and cultural traditionalism with regard to gender relationships. And early Pentecostals either did not engage the issue or simply ignored larger questions that agitated in denominations where women pursued access to religious leadership.

As initial fervor gave way to institutionalization, Pentecostals found it advisable to address questions of authority and order. As the radically millenarian movement settled in for the long haul, issues that had languished in the heat of revival occasionally emerged. If it was not "the eleventh hour," what should women's roles be? If preaching was not always strictly prophetic utterance, might women preach? How might woman's public leadership impact her assent to male headship in the marriage relationship? What priorities should govern Pentecostal family relationships? Pentecostal ambiguity about woman's freedom and her submission prompted vascillation between daughters speaking their visions and women keeping silence. How might the tension be resolved?

Marriage and Family

Although the breathless activity of early Pentecostals left little time for reflection on gender relationships, early Pentecostal periodicals reveal significant pressures introduced by a common emphasis on yieldedness to the Spirit. There were Pentecostal men who apparently paid their wives little attention. They deemed the "call to serve" to have more important eternal consequences than mundane matters like supporting a family. Even those who professed eagerness for time with families regarded absence as part of the cross they were called to embrace gladly. The researcher readily notes that many women—especially the spouses of evangelists, missionaries, and pastors—have gone down in history without first names. Some were never referred to at all. The marital status of male leaders is not always evident. Other wives, known simply as "sister" or dubbed "wife," had no apparent personal identity but rather existed to serve their husbands, bear them children, and eke out a meager existence. They often led difficult lives under trying circumstances.

From public records—though not from her husband's prolific pen—the researcher can discover the name of Bessie Mae Durham (first wife of prominent Chicago Pentecostal preacher William Durham) and glean a sense of her dismal life. Bessie Mae died in 1908 at age twenty-seven after giving birth to her third child. The family knew no privacy, lived from hand to mouth, and Bessie Mae, the mother of two toddlers, kept her husband's Chicago mission open whenever he felt "led" or "called" to go on the road and evangelize elsewhere. As a newlywed in 1906, she spent her entire first pregnancy on the road, sharing uncertain living conditions in many homes as William moved about from Chicago to Boston, then on to California, preaching. The baby, born in Minnesota, came "home" to a curtained-off area in the Chicago mission. Bessie Mae did not preach, and William Durham's many writings mention neither her nor their children by name. The Pentecostal movement consumed his energy, shaped his identity, but left no time for any semblance of family life (Blumhofer, "William Durham," *Portraits of a Generation,* 123–142). The Pentecostal map of life, while staunchly traditional in terms of defined relationships, often flaunted customary family values in the name of a higher calling.

Another evangelist, the peripatetic Frank Bartleman, left his long-suffering wife and young children while he followed "divine leadings" to preach abroad. He traveled "by faith," moving about as funds (generally meager free-will offerings) permitted, and in 1910 had only $11 to leave with his wife when he embarked for a trip around the world. Responsible for their children, with neither home nor job, she supported the family by menial labor and infrequent offerings for the uncertain duration (Bartleman, *How Pentecost Came,* 142; Bartleman, *Around the World by Faith,* 6–7). The ubiquitous Pentecostal evangelist Daniel Awrey spent much of his life on the road, a valued presence at any camp meeting or convention in the United States or abroad. It seemed irrelevant to him or to his appreciative public that he had a wife and six children eking out a meager existence in rural Tennessee (Glenn Gohr, "Telling the Lord's Secrets," *Assemblies of God Heritage* [Winter 2000–2001]: 22–28; Daniel Awrey, "Life Sketches," *The Latter Rain Evangel* [March 1910]: 19; and Daniel Awrey, "Telling the Lord's Secrets," *The Latter Rain Evangel* [November 1909]: 2). When he took them along—as he did in 1910—their circumstances were even more problematic than at home. He settled them in a rented house in Shanghai—strangers, not part of a missionary community—and a week later claimed a divine leading to sail alone for several months in the states (Bartleman, *Around the World by Faith,* 75–76). Driven by "the call," such Pentecostals affirmed a hierarchical model of family relationships but often left women and children to fend for themselves. Under a guise of traditionalism, then, long-suffering Pentecostal wives learned to manage on their own, although they apparently affirmed the husband's headship.

The tendency among early Pentecostals to neglect family for ministry became so acute that by 1907 *The Apostolic Faith* (Los Angeles) began commenting on marital and family obligations. Citing cases in which wives had left husbands "claiming that the Lord has called her to do mission work, and to leave the little children at home to fare the best they can," Azusa Street Mission leader William Seymour urged women and men to responsible action. Women who insisted "God means for them to hate their children and husband, and go off and try to save somebody else's home, or the heathen, when their own home needs to be saved" violated clear biblical teaching. So did men—"precious husbands," Seymour called them—whose enthusiasm for evangelism excused them from family obligations. Such people assumed mistakenly, the paper bristled, "that the Lord does not want them to be bothered with their families" ("Bible Teaching on Marriage and Divorce," *The Apostolic Faith* [January 1907]: 3).

This inclination to impulsive action and reckless abandonment to the slightest inkling of divine prompting directly influenced attitudes toward women. While women used it occasionally to justify leaving their families, it more often induced men to forge out in new endeavors. Though teaching on the subject of family was not always direct, and though the emphasis on the Holy Spirit promised enthusiastic moments that validated women's gifts, Pentecostals struggled from the outset with tension between divine promptings and traditional obligations. And from the beginning, leaders everywhere found it necessary to rein in enthusiasts of both sexes. Even a casual look at the sources suggests, however, that most often the women bore the brunt of neglect. Men like Frank Crawford—whose wife Florence followed her ministry calling while neglecting her marriage vows—were exceptions, not the rule. Noted for urging continence in marriage, Crawford reportedly banished from her Portland workers' training home any would-be workers who married ("Camp Meeting," *Time*, August 19, 1935: 35). Despite certain expanded opportunities for women in the gathered community of saints, Pentecostal men tended to expect women to respect male headship, support men's public roles, and tolerate unsettledness, penury, and loneliness. And Pentecostal women generally did not demur. They bore children, earned meager support, and kept families together, all the while deferring to the husband as head. Married men had little apparent difficulty going where they chose, with or without resources to take along, much less leave with their families. And Pentecostal piety—they called it "faith"—justified their leaving their women and children indefinitely, often penniless, to survive by their own faith. The assuring words of the gospel song "God will take care of you" had ominous import on a person. Only rarely—as in the case of Martin L. Ryan, an Oregon preacher and editor who led a band of Pentecostal missionaries to Japan—did wives opt out. In 1910 Ryan's wife successfully sued him for divorce on the grounds of harsh treatment and neglect. In 1907 the family had accompanied Ryan to Japan where Ryan had first neglected his family and then sent them home with the vague assurance that God would provide for their needs ("Alleged Crank in Limelight," *The Daily Oregon Statesman* [January 7, 1911]: 1, 6; "Divorce Granted," *The Daily Oregon Statesman* [March 18, 1911]: 5). Such circumstances did not necessarily favor the aggrieved spouse. Among Pentecostals Ryan's apparent dedication to the cause was as likely to work in his favor as against him.

The same might be said of Florence Crawford, the feisty Holiness woman with whom early pilgrims to Azusa Street were forced to reckon. Crawford followed a "call" to the Northwest and settled in Portland, Oregon. She parted from her building contractor husband of sixteen years, though no divorce papers were served. Her self-aggrandizement and overbearing claims to spiritual authority irreparably breached her marriage. Her husband played no part in her lifelong efforts under the banner of the Apostolic faith in Portland, Oregon, and did not embrace her faith until after her death. Noted for her stern preaching against divorce and remarriage, Crawford hardly modeled marital bliss, but she cast herself as the wronged party on spiritual

grounds, and her constituency did not question her stance. A writer for *Time* magazine commented in 1935: "She advocates celibacy, recommends contence among married folk, was chagrined when her two children married. Stern, dowdy in dress, 'Mother' Crawford lavishes affection only on her kennel of Pomeranian dogs" (*Time* [August 19, 1935]: 35).

Christine Gibson, founder of Zion Bible Institute in Providence (later Barrington), Rhode Island, believed the Holy Spirit prompted her to err in the opposite direction. Gibson married a divorced Pentecostal preacher (whose alienated spouse was living) after painstakingly documenting God's dealings with her that made the marriage "right" in a religious setting that overwhelmingly thought it "wrong." Her action deeply divided Pentecostals in the Northeast, but the roster of the Pentecostal stalwarts who supported her was also impressive. In a day when many in the broader culture frowned on divorce and remarriage, Gibson's behavior seemed to justify suspicions that Pentecostals were prone to scandalous behavior (Wilson, *Obedience of Faith*).

While Crawford's and Gibson's publics were regional, Pentecostal evangelist Aimee Semple McPherson fascinated a national audience. Born Aimee Elizabeth Kennedy in Ingersoll, Ontario, Canada, in 1890, she married Irish-born Pentecostal evangelist Robert Semple in 1908 and went with him to Hong Kong in 1910. Their missionary dreams were cut short by Semple's death ten weeks after their arrival, and his widow sailed for home. In 1912, she married a young divorcé, Harold McPherson. They made their home in Providence, and the future seemed promising until Aimee rediscovered her call to preach. Restless in the traditional domestic sphere, Aimee left Harold to rededicate her life to evangelism. Her emotional struggle over leaving was tempered by her confusion over whether she had sinned by marrying a divorced man. Harold soon joined her on the road and over the next few years made halfhearted attempts to help his wife's efforts. Gifted and capable, she needed him more as business manager than as partner on her platform. Harold's request for ministry credentials with the Assemblies of God was denied because of his divorce (Aimee as yet held no credentials with any organization), and in 1918, he and Aimee finally parted ways. They divorced amicably in 1921. Aimee did not contest Harold's charge of desertion. In the meantime, she countered occasional criticism of woman's preaching by inviting audiences to "hear from the Holy Ghost": "Some of you say you don't like to hear a woman preach. Neither do I. I prefer to hear from the Holy Ghost." McPherson's adoring public apparently agreed that her enormous evangelistic successes were a mark of God's favor and had little trouble with her marital status or her gender. In their eyes, Harold had wronged her. Her mysterious six-week disappearance in 1926 generated numerous rumors of sexual intrigue, but she roundly denied all and none was proven. The response to her third marriage in 1931 to David Hutton, a vaudeville singer twelve years her junior, finally revealed some limits to the license her public would grant. While the marriage did not last long (on their wedding day Hutton was sued for breach of promise)—and in spite of McPherson's acknowledgment that she had acted imprudently—her following divided, and she spent the rest of her life in a severely limited, though still influential, sphere (Blumhofer, *Aimee Semple McPherson*). With the notable exception of the commissary she devised to feed Los Angeles' hungry during the depression, her work in the last decade of her life (1934–1944) was primarily directed toward the constituency she had already built.

Tensions between divine calling and family obligation were not the only gender-related issues that faced early Pentecostals. Recurrent advocacy of marital purity—abstinence from sex within marriage—and of spiritual marriage—recognizing spiritual affinity for a partner other than one's spouse—persisted for decades. Fascination with holiness often pointed the devout toward an ascetic path. Convictions about the imminent end of the world or the priority of evangelism encouraged some to heed literally New Testament suggestions that one could better face end-time troubles without children or spouse.

From the outset, sexual innuendo pursued Pentecostals. San Antonio newspapers reported in 1907 that Charles Parham, the Kansas Pentecostal preacher who first declared (1901) speaking in tongues the "uniform initial evidence" of baptism by the Holy Spirit, had been arrested for sodomy. The roster of male pastors and evangelists whose extramarital affairs occasioned their sudden disappearance from prominence includes some of the most ardent early leaders, like Levi Lupton, a Quaker-turned-Pentecostal editor, Bible school proprietor, and evangelist from Alliance, Ohio, and R. L. Erickson, pastor of Chicago's Stone Church. Later, no Pentecostal preacher denounced sexual sins more robustly than Jimmy Swaggart. In 1989—a few years after sexual escapades and financial misconduct had demolished fellow-Pentecostal Jim Bakker's PTL (Praise the Lord/People That Love)—Swaggart's penchant for prostitutes brought down his multimillion-dollar television empire. As had others before them, people who revel in the Spirit occasionally rationalize their own (though generally not others') freedom from conventional morality. Over the years Pentecostals have countered that the physicality of their worship opened them to unfair criticism. Promiscuous laying on of hands, emotional prayer with arms intertwined, or physical movement in worship seemed to outsiders at best suggestive and at worst scandalous. Also troubling were marriages contracted in response to prophetic direction, a recurrent problem on the movement's margins.

Ministry

Early Pentecostal understandings of ordination help clarify the ambiguous status of women in ministry. The movement's reliance on lay efforts as well as the preponderance of female adherents assured women's busyness. But what about ordination? During the 1990s, annual reports from the National Council of Churches cited Pentecostals, particularly the Assemblies of God, for openness toward female ordination. A historical overview helps explain why this has not translated into equal opportunities for leadership for Pentecostal women. Since the emergence of Pentecostalism, there have been ordained Pentecostal women. But that simple statement begs the question of ordination's meaning.

Pentecostals view ordination differently than do many other Protestants. Ordination does not presuppose office, and Pentecostals authorize several kinds of ministry besides that of Word and sacrament. They issue Christian worker's licenses, sometimes called credentials, to legitimate an individual's calling or training for a specific task like youth or women's ministries. Many Pentecostal women have engaged in evangelism and home or foreign missions, often with ministerial licenses that stipulate their appropriate activity sphere. Some early Pentecostal women had been recognized as evangelists during their years of affiliation with healing evangelist John Alexander Dowie's Christian Catholic Church. Such setting apart entailed the fulfillment of specific obligations as well as submission to male authority. At times, then, Pentecostals simply recognized as Christian workers women whom others had already set apart or commissioned for evangelistic work. Teacher and evangelist Lilian Yeomans, for example, had been credentialed by R. C. Horner's Holiness Movement Church, a small Canadian denomination. Her credentials from that non-Pentecostal group helped legitimate her early Pentecostal efforts and made it unnecessary for Pentecostals to decide whether or not to ordain her. Other women, then, came into the Pentecostal movement with ministry gifts acknowledged by a form of credentials. But Dowie, for one, had not permitted them to be pastors. He strongly encouraged women to marry and come under a husband's ministry authority. Ministry partnerships did not jeopardize male headship in the home.

The case of one former resident of Dowie's Zion City, Illinois, Marie Burgess, illustrates how Pentecostals might use the word *ordination*. Burgess opened a small Pentecostal mission in Manhattan's Times Square in 1907. A few years later she married an Irish immigrant evangelist, Robert Brown. They affiliated with the Assemblies of God in 1916. Marie Brown's application for credentials with the Assemblies of God listed five ordinations. In her milieu, ordination connoted the laying on of hands of a supportive community in an act of commissioning a new form of service. So, for example, when Brown left Illinois for a short mission stint in Wisconsin, she was "ordained." When she went to Manhattan, she was ordained again, and once in Manhattan and married to Robert Brown, she was ordained again. Ordination entailed no necessary relationship to a specific group or constituency, no espousal of creed, no real accountability. The right to administer the sacraments of the church (especially the Lord's Supper), if it followed, was assumed rather than granted.

Regional and ethnic differences are also apparent. The story of Pentecostalism among Italian immigrants, for example, centered in 1907 in Chicago among disaffected former members of First Italian Presbyterian Church. In this group, gender relationships followed the patterns typical among Italian Protestants. Women wore head coverings and left church business to their husbands, though female voices in testimony and song were welcomed in male-led gatherings. As Pentecostal testimonies spread through extended Italian families in other parts of the country, this pattern did not change. Early Scandinavian Pentecostals, too, tended to opt for conservative models of credentialed congregational leadership. Many of this small constituency had been reared in Swedish Baptist congregations where male leadership was the norm, and they brought their gender assumptions with them into Pentecostalism. German Pentecostals did the same. Those who argue that Pentecostal experience is inherently supportive of ministering women would do well to consider ethnic Pentecostal stories. In these contexts, gender relationships affirmed ethnic patterns that were not easily erased by religious experience.

Women who persisted invited the same harassment that male Pentecostal evangelists sometimes encountered. Howard Goss recalled a Sunday in an Ozark mountain church:

> While my wife was preaching an evangelistic sermon under a heavy anointing, some disturbers threw a few stones and fired several shots through the windows of the church. One round passed directly before Ethel's face, but she was so absorbed in the message God was giving out through her, that she noticed nothing wrong until the audience automatically bowed over and completely disappeared among the seats. (Goss, 158–159)

This muddled record of women's ministry activities in Pentecostalism's formative years must not obscure woman's extensive cultural authority. By speaking in tongues—and even more by interpreting tongues—

women delivered God's word where they could not preach or serve communion. By writing text for religious songs, women helped mold popular understanding of the meaning of religious experience. By editing many Pentecostal papers—Anna Reiff was the longtime editor of the nationally circulated *Latter Rain Evangel*, Carrie Judd Montgomery produced *Triumphs of Faith*, Elizabeth Sexton issued *The Bridegroom's Messenger*, Harriet Duncan and Elizabeth Baker edited *Trust*, Cora MacIlvary published *El Bethel*—women helped select and mold the public face and record of Pentecostalism. By teaching in—or running their own—Bible schools, other women trained future Pentecostal leaders. Among the better-known such endeavors was a small Bible school in Rochester, New York, conducted by five sisters, the daughters of Methodist pastor James Duncan. Throughout his life, Duncan was an amiable nonassertive male presence in his daughters' efforts. In 1907 the sisters joined the Pentecostal movement. Called Elim, their Bible school featured female and male instructors (under the direction of the sisters), and the student body included an impressive list of emerging Pentecostal males of influence, among them Ralph M. Riggs who in 1953 would become general superintendent of the Assemblies of God. The sisters ostensibly objected to female pastors, but they themselves manifested the creativity that contributed to the rapid growth of Pentecostalism. As the father's nonintervention satisfied the need for male covering, they effectively functioned as pastors of their mission. When their father died and they decided to exchange their storefront for a modest tabernacle, they prayed for a male pastor. When no satisfactory male presented himself, the sisters announced that they had received a divine command to invoke the Holy Spirit as pastor. The women then pastored the tabernacle until they agreed on a male pastor who would conform to their expectations. Meanwhile, a male board of deacons presided at communion. The implication for Elim students seemed clear: Local congregations needed male leaders for all but prophetic functions, but invoking the Spirit legitimized temporary female leadership. Outside the local church, however, these women taught, edited, and evangelized. In so doing, they simply adapted long-established women's spheres. With careful rationalizations, independent Pentecostal women found ways to serve as they pleased.

A handful of early white Pentecostal women exercised such a degree of caring influence within the larger constituency that they were named "mother." In general, these were women who had charismatic gifts but also expanded the domestic sphere to include their Pentecostal networks. Mother Mary Moise operated a home for Christian workers in St. Louis. Mother Arthur facilitated Charles Parham's early Pentecostal efforts. Mother Flower—Alice Reynolds Flower, the wife of a longtime

Assemblies of God administrator—touched thousands beyond her immediate family through her teaching, writings, counsel, and spiritual authority. Mother Crawford was a controversial pioneer of Pentecostalism in the Northwest. Tens of thousands knew Minnie Kennedy, the biological mother of evangelist Aimee Semple McPherson, as Mother Kennedy. Young single women missionaries nurtured at Carrie Judd Montgomery's Home of Peace knew her as "Mother Montgomery." Such "mothers" were exceptions rather than the rule. In Euro-Pentecostalism, "mothers" tended to belong to the first generation, and the title is no longer in general use.

The early Pentecostal custom of calling everyone "brother" and "sister," recognizing the community of believers as a new family, also languished after the first generation. Even as some early Pentecostals seemed inclined to devalue the nuclear family, the constituency faithfully stressed relationships in the family of God. The use of *brother* and *sister* also manifested a democratic impulse in Pentecostalism. Leaders—male or female, national or local—were addressed alike. The early adherents (in sharp contrast to later generations) eschewed titles like "reverend" or "doctor" to distinguish themselves from "dead denominational churches," and so designations for men and women were the same regardless of role, education, or marital status.

In sum, in their eagerness to restore elements of New Testament Christianity, some Pentecostals advocated sexual abstinence expressed either in singleness or in "marital purity." At the same time, others denounced such views and endorsed the traditional family. At times, this was more an embracing of traditional sexual arrangements than a celebration of the husband-wife and parent-child relationships. Still others valued close family ties even in the throes of otherworldly religious excitement. A suspicion of woman as temptress lurked in the wings, finding expression in occasional tracts and sermons as well as in stern guidelines for female modesty. Historian Robert Mapes Anderson has observed that as Pentecostals became more affluent, dress and entertainment taboos typically yielded to embracing what was once forbidden. Nowhere is this more apparent than in changing Pentecostal attitudes toward women's adornments.

Pentecostal Denominations

For a variety of reasons, the fluid and mobile world of Pentecostals gave way to the structured environment of denominations. After 1906 small regional groups that existed before the spread of Pentecostalism added Pentecostal doctrine to their statements of faith. They identified with the movement and became its first fledgling denominations. The roles of women in the Church of God in Christ or the Pentecostal Holiness Church generally followed patterns established before the groups were Pentecostal. Women evangelized, pioneered missions and Sunday Schools, and went abroad as missionaries but seldom assumed formal pastoral office. Public perceptions of women in leadership in fact focused more on evangelists than on pastors. But the majority of Pentecostals at first explicitly resisted formal associations. They networked in camp meetings, subscribed to an ever-changing array of papers published by men and women "as the Lord provided," and rode the rails to religious camps and conventions. Railroads offered discounts to ordained male preachers. In a milieu devoted to "living by faith," few received salaries, and rail discounts enabled mobility. Women workers were instructed to "trust the Lord for full fare."

The Assemblies of God

The largest Euro-Pentecostal denomination is the Assemblies of God. Formed in 1914 to "conserve" the revival by introducing standards of accountability, coordinating missionary support, and creating educational opportunities, this denomination mobilized Pentecostals from different regional, ethnic, and religious backgrounds into a national constituency.

The 1914 organizing council of the Assemblies of God hinted at limitations ahead with the statement that Galatians 3:28 ("In Christ there is neither male nor female") did not apply to ministry. Rather, the text indicated that "in the matter of salvation, the lines of sex are blotted out." Citing 1 Timothy 2:12, it affirmed that women were to be subject to men while acknowledging their role as "helpers in the Gospel." The Assemblies of God granted women licenses to evangelize but denied them ordination as pastors. And although the first foreign missions board included Susan Easton, an experienced missionary to India under the Woman's Missionary Union, Easton is the only woman in Assemblies of God history to have so served, and her tenure lasted barely one year.

In 1920, the Assemblies of God did act to license women as assistant pastors. But this was more a response to a specific need than the resolution of an issue. In this instance, the denomination responded to men who wanted to leave their wives in charge when they evangelized elsewhere. It regularized the status quo rather than creating new options for women. Assemblies of God opposition to women's ordination as pastors was reiterated regularly until 1935, when, meeting in San Francisco, delegates to the denomination's biennial meeting—apparently with little discussion—voted to grant women ordination as elders, the denomination's term for pastors. The 1935 resolution merits a close look. First, vocal opponents charged that it would not have passed, had the denominational meeting been accessible to more delegates. Many Pentecostal pastors felt the depression keenly (and were unaware that the issue would surface) and had been unable to travel to California. Second, the resolution perpetuated old reservations, asserting "a difference between the ministry of men and of women in the church." To qualify for ordination as pastors, women were required to be "matured and not less than 25 years of age" and to have a developed and generally acceptable "ministry of the Word." Similar wording was not deemed necessary for men, about whom such characteristics might apparently be assumed. In addition, women could "administer the ordinances of the church when such acts [were] necessary," presumably in the absence of a qualified male.

Suspicions about woman's moral influence had deepened in the 1920s as flappers came to symbolize the "new woman" of the post–World War I era. Denunciations of the new woman were as much part of the era as the fads that inspired them. "The prevailing flapper and child Prodigy Evangelism prove the effeminacy of our present ministry," bristled independent Pentecostal evangelist Frank Bartleman with a thinly veiled reference to Aimee Semple McPherson and her convert Uldine Utley. "Effeminate men follow a female ministry too largely through a spirit of fleshly attraction to the opposite sex" (Bartleman, "Flapper Evangelism"). "Next to every good woman is a deep chasm," warned the Assemblies of God teacher Peter C. Nelson, founder of Southwestern Bible Institute in Enid, Oklahoma, "and alas, many have already fallen into it."

During the same years, a gradual process of institutional, emotional, and spiritual segregation effectively directed women's energies into supportive roles. In the Assemblies of God as in other Pentecostal denominations, an auxiliary women's organization marshaled the talents of the denomination's women into traditionally acceptable spheres. Several women evangelists (notably Zelma Argue [1900–1980] and Hattie Hammond [1907–1994]) gained national followings in the Assemblies of God between the world wars, but they functioned as evangelists in settings usually controlled by male leaders, an arrangement with which many Pentecostals had been comfortable.

Despite—or perhaps because of—public rhetoric affirming female submission and the hierarchical side of Christianity, Assemblies of God women generally seemed contented and fulfilled in service. As missionaries, editors, teachers, and evangelists and occasionally as pastors, they implemented their calls in ways women had for decades. Women enjoyed extensive cultural authority, then, and much grassroots Pentecostal activity depended on their prodigious efforts. But institutional segregation and public pronouncements usually channeled women's aspirations into particular endeavors. It is true that after 1935 the sphere for Assemblies of God

women was potentially somewhat broader than the sphere for other Pentecostal women. But additional burdens placed on women seeking ordination as Assemblies of God pastors made it apparent that the ethic of domesticity thrived among Assemblies of God women as well as men. And ordination failed to translate into equal access to positions of authority in church leadership. After 1935, the denomination could effectively evade the issue, claiming that it had been resolved and that women were to blame if they did not pursue pastorates. In fact, there had been no recorded discussion, and the issues that historically discouraged women's ordination had not been addressed.

The Pentecostal Church of God

In contrast to the Assemblies of God, the much smaller Pentecostal Church of God (with headquarters in Joplin, Missouri, from 1951) never admitted reservations about female pastors. Ida Tribbett, the first woman this group authorized as an evangelist, received her credentials at the Pentecostal Church of God's organizational meeting in Chicago in December 1919. "Our sister has a good, straight, clean and sane message," one of her male colleagues promised. Known for her willingness to pray for the sick, Tribbett offered an impressive sampling of results she attributed to simple faith: "In this ministry God has opened the eyes of the blind, unstopped deaf ears, healed the broken bones, lengthened shortened limbs, healed tuberculosis, epilepsy, cancers, in fact all manner of disease. Just as He said He would, praise His name."

The Pentecostal Church of God tackled as well the controversial matter of credentialing divorced and remarried people. Insisting that "innocent parties" had the right to remarry, adherents of this small Pentecostal denomination until late in the twentieth century (when the Church of God and the Pentecostal Holiness Church relaxed their rules) were the only Pentecostals to credential divorced and remarried individuals.

Despite this apparent openness toward women, a 1966 denominational list of representative leaders past and present includes sixty-one names, but just three women, one a pastor's wife. The other two, Ferne Isabel Bruce and Hazel Kleintop, spent their adult lives as missionary evangelists and, for a brief period, as copastors. They extended their influence in the church by writing Sunday School quarterlies and children's papers and organizing youth work. Photos suggest that the Pentecostal Church of God—like most Pentecostal denominations—harbored misgivings about women's sexuality, urged female modesty, and frowned on bobbed hair and makeup as part of a larger determination to assure sexual purity among the faithful (Martin; Moon). Pentecostal Church of God women are far more likely to be evangelists than pastors, and (in specific deference to 1 Timothy 2:12) all executive positions at the district and national levels are reserved for men.

The International Church of the Foursquare Gospel

Gender perceptions in Aimee Semple McPherson's International Church of the Foursquare Gospel offer a third slightly nuanced Pentecostal denominational perspective. As the best-known female Pentecostal preacher, McPherson was assumed to favor equality between the sexes and ordination for women. A closer look at what she modeled suggests that her views were more complex. McPherson had no scruples about using sexuality to her advantage. She came to regard gender not as an encumbrance but as a gift. A background in the Salvation Army made her comfortable with preaching women, but she saw herself as an evangelist rather than as a pastor and always manifested a preference (real or imagined) for traditional arrangements in the home and church. In Angelus Temple, the church she built in Los Angeles, McPherson permitted only male elders, at least one of whom always sat with her on the platform. Elders presided with her over the communion table and assisted her at baptisms. The Foursquare Church commissioned female evangelists and their training school, the Lighthouse of Foursquare Evangelism, featured female and male teachers, none more respected than devotional author Lilian Yeomans, M.D. (whose Assemblies of God evangelist's credentials were jeopardized by her association with McPherson). Since McPherson's death in 1944, national denominational offices have been held exclusively by men, but ordained female pastors, married or single, may serve in the International Church of the Foursquare Gospel (Blumhofer, *Aimee Semple McPherson*).

The denomination boasts no consensus. In 1998 a committee issued an emphatic endorsement of female ministry, justifying this with an appeal to a long list of women in the Bible as well as to pragmatic evidence. Buried within the report are the usual Pentecostal cautions in the customary code language: "There are cultural issues associated with being a woman in ministry. Our commitment to the authority of Scripture and quality biblical interpretation requires that we attempt to define what is cultural and what is biblical. Women, like men, must be diligent to study the Scriptures and understand God's calling on their lives." The Foursquare statement favors freeing women to exercise their gifts. The committee recognized, however, that at least three biblically based positions on women's ministry flourished within the denomination. Foursquare complementarians consider that males and females differ in function, with males given priority in leadership. Egalitarians

stress equality and copartnership. Those who hold to male headship maintain that this is a necessary "redemptive means" to recover the partnership lost when Eve and Adam fell. The Foursquare committee acknowledged no difficulty with 1 Timothy 2:12. In their minds, its proscription on female teaching is not absolute ("Women in Ordained Leadership Ministry," 8, 11).

McPherson's particular blend of performance, preaching, and feminine appeal contributed to her notoriety among Pentecostals and the suspicions they harbored about her. Simmering beneath the surface in the prolific criticism she endured within the movement before 1926 were economic, theological, and gender issues as well as envy of her success. After 1926, explicit sexual innuendo circulated both within and outside Pentecostalism, nourished by the boastings of the likes of actor Milton Berle and Canadian journalist Gordon Sinclair. After her death, as part of a bid for recognition by the larger evangelical community, the Foursquare Church took a clear step back from its founder and her legacy of feminine leadership beyond the local church.

Open Bible Standard Churches

The Open Bible Standard Churches trace their origins to tensions in the International Church of the Foursquare Gospel during the 1930s. This small Pentecostal denomination with headquarters in Des Moines, Iowa, has had a tradition of female evangelists, and a few single women have undertaken pastoral responsibilities for small congregations that could not support a male pastor. Otherwise, women are barred from executive leadership (Mitchell, 47–48).

The Church of God (Cleveland)

Even before identifying itself with the Pentecostal movement in 1907, the Church of God (Cleveland, Tennessee) was indebted to the labors of women. As evangelists, church founders, missionaries, editors, and educators, women have been indispensable to the expanding international efforts of this Pentecostal denomination. In general meetings, gender matters first surfaced when some delegates to the denomination's Second General Assembly (1907) worried aloud about the preponderance of females in the handful of affiliated churches scattered among the mountains of eastern Tennessee and western North Carolina. Pointing out the women honored in the New Testament record, the Church of God Assembly responded by affirming women's public activities. In 1908, the Third General Assembly authorized female deacons, but the 1909 Assembly decided against ordaining women. As the Church of God became more centralized and specified ordination as a prerequisite for office, this 1909 decision effectively curtailed women's opportunities. With the creation of a male Body of Elders in 1916, Church of God women lost the right to vote in General Assemblies. A 1913 decision excluded them from participation in church business and government and denied women the right to perform marriages, although the denomination's dominant early personality, Ambrose Jessup Tomlinson, encouraged women to continue to find public ways to support their male pastors' efforts.

As is the case in the Assemblies of God, then, Church of God board members, college presidents, and national administrators have been men. This reflects, in part, the replacing of pragmatic with institutional ideals. The creation of a national office prompted statements of requirements for local leadership. Before this centralization, women had served as state and local superintendents. After it, such roles were restricted to ordained clergy. This situation evidences how Pentecostals deal (or do not deal) with 1 Timothy 2:12. The large measure of participatory freedom women often enjoy in Pentecostal settings often remains bounded by this passage in ways that few outsiders recognize.

Church of God activist Alda Harrison demonstrates how women have nonetheless wielded wide influence. The founder of the denomination's youth organization and the editor (unsalaried) of its youth publication *The Lighted Pathway*, Harrison tirelessly lobbied denominational headquarters for a consolidated youth program. She and other women provided curricula for youth, but when the denomination formed its Youth Literature Board in 1944, it appointed five men to oversee the production of youth materials.

The same Alda Harrison urged the Church of God to organize its women for effective service. The denomination opted for a women's ministries model devised by a pastor's wife, Mrs. S. J. Wood, of Electra, Texas, who in 1929 mobilized the women of her husband's congregation as the Ladies' Willing Worker Band. Incorporated into the general church program in 1938, an Office of Ladies' Ministries encouraged women in traditional female roles as wives and mothers while galvanizing their resources to promote church programs.

Numerous Church of God (Cleveland) women expedited their denomination's missionary efforts. For a time, this group counted among its missionaries a redoubtable personality, Lillian Trasher (1887–1961). The founder and matron of a large orphanage in Assiout, Egypt, Trasher later joined the Assemblies of God. Affectionately known in the United States as the "Nile Mother," Trasher over the years reared and educated thousands of up-and-coming Egyptian professionals. Lucy Leatherman, another irrepressible early Pentecostal with roots in Azusa Street, also threw in her lot with the Church of God, serving as its missionary in South America. With their going and giving, such women con-

tributed immeasurably to establishing Pentecostal foreign missions.

Not surprisingly, over the years women constitute a decreasing percentage of pulpit ministers and are largely absent from administrative leadership, although they have found ways to wield cultural influence. Like adherents of other Euro-American Pentecostal denominations, Church of God members have often responded to feminism by identifying with its opponents. Thus Pentecostal women's agendas, both secular and religious, tend to prompt endorsements of traditional forms of gender relationships that stand in sharpest contrast to the perceived values of the feminist movement (Crews, 92–97; Dirksen, 165–196; Roebuck).

The United Pentecostal Church

During World War I, a serious disagreement over the Godhead permanently split the Pentecostal movement. While most Euro-Pentecostals are Trinitarians, a significant minority of Pentecostals prefer to stress the Oneness of God. They are often called Oneness (or, because they emphasize the power of the name of Jesus, "Jesus Only") Pentecostals. United Pentecostals, members of the largest white Oneness denomination, have a long history of being more conservative than other Pentecostals on matters of female dress and "outward adornment." In their ranks, men hold most leadership positions and their "Ladies' Ministries" focuses on supporting women in their roles as wives and mothers. While women serve in education and missions, when authority looms as an issue, men come to the fore.

Conclusion

At the end of the twentieth century, social realities challenged all Pentecostal denominations to reassert their views on gender and family. Euro-Pentecostal denominations tend to endorse the traditional views represented by James Dobson's Focus on the Family or Elisabeth Eliot's many writings on female submission. Relationships between husband and wife or parents and children, then, value woman's place in the home. At the same time, social realities have forced Pentecostals to come to terms with women's work outside the home, divorce and remarriage, and single parenting. Pentecostals actively reject abortion and homosexuality. Feminism prompted a distinct backlash, and the successful quest for women's access to ordination in traditional denominations affirmed some Pentecostals in the view that women's right to religious office rested squarely on liberal—and thus on wrong—theology.

As a popular religious movement, Pentecostalism has a vibrant independent sector. Some of its adherents never join denominations; others express disaffection by setting out on their own. And though preaching remains important in defining leaders and providing access to power, other options abound. Women who sense discrimination can find ample activities in extradenominational activities if they opt not to break denominational ties. Television, radio, the World Wide Web, glossy magazines like *Charisma*, or an ever-expanding conference circuit afford entrepreneurial women the chance to wield influence while at the same time espousing traditional views on home and family.

The pastorate, not the pulpit, has historically been the obstacle for Pentecostal women seeking full ministry recognition. In Pentecostal denominations the pastorate signals full ordination, which, in turn, opens the door to administrative leadership. If Assemblies of God women in fact wanted this, one might assume—since the denomination has permitted female pastors since 1935—they would have it. But the Assemblies of God circumstance reminds one how large cultural impediments loom. College presidencies, district superintendencies, the general and executive presbyteries, and national elective office remain the purview of men. And in theory, at least, a woman might be pastor in a congregation that denies women the right to serve communion or serve as deacon or elder.

Pentecostal women gathered in denominational congregations have not as a group enthusiastically embraced the notion of female pastors. Resistance from other women, from congregations, and from entrenched leaders has worked to shape the possibilities for those women whose denominations permit them to pursue a calling to pastoral leadership. If local congregations of the International Church of the Foursquare Gospel seem to present a different face, the denomination's hierarchy does not. And the (Cleveland) Church of God's long resistance to female ordination has not evoked denomination-wide protest. Declining numbers of women in all areas of credentialed Pentecostal ministry became most evident from World War II on. Pentecostal constituencies see larger issues of gender at stake and would rather affirm traditional relationships than experiment with or seem to endorse the new.

Beyond the pastorate, though, Pentecostal denominations depend on the commitment of women. Prodigious female efforts have helped propel Pentecostal denominations around the world, but—when they address the matter at all—Pentecostal denominations still wrestle with the gender issues early Pentecostals identified at the movement's outset. And so, within a framework molded by traditional social commitments, Pentecostalism values women's speech within boundaries. Women and men occasionally test the boundaries, but most Pentecostal denominations celebrate the sphere they allot women without disrupting male institutional control. For the most part, women do not merely acquiesce:

They thrive. And as they have historically, they find expanding opportunities to wield culture authority or to push the boundaries while rationalizing ways to convince the constituency that they are not defying woman's sphere. But whatever the momentum those on the cutting edge achieve, they are sure to meet deeply embedded resistance grounded more or less in the literal sense of 1 Timothy 2:12. For Pentecostals, that remains the single Pauline passage that theologically compromises women's rights to religious leadership roles. Cultural objections remain relevant and may be validated by appeal to 1 Timothy 2:12.

Nonetheless, women swarm to Pentecostal services. Some find the setting compelling, with its openness to emotional and verbal expression. Women leaders have often been active in healing ministries, especially public and private prayer for the recovery of the sick. They have tended as well to expound the "deeper life" with its stress on cultivating intimate relationship with Christ through spiritual disciplines like protracted prayer ("waiting on God"). In New York City, Robert Brown gained a reputation for his stern sermons. His wife Marie followed Brown's uncompromising words with tender reminders of God's loving call. Their congregation liked to say that Robert exposed their wounds, but Marie "poured on the healing oil." Thousands have found women's evangelistic appeals compelling, and other women identify readily with women's evangelistic preaching—often storytelling punctuated with self-revealing commentary.

SOURCES: For an overview of early Anglo Pentecostalism, see Robert Mapes Anderson, *Vision of the Disinherited* (1979); Edith L. Blumhofer, *Restoring the Faith* (1993); and Grant A. Wacker, *Heaven Below* (2001). *Portraits of a Generation* (2002), edited by James Goff and Grant Wacker, offers biographical studies of influential Pentecostal women and men. Social scientist Elaine Lawless has done several regional studies of female Pentecostals focusing especially on southern Indiana. Historical studies focusing on particular Pentecostal denominations offer insights about women's roles, especially Mickey Crews, *The Church of God* (1990); Carolyn Dirksen, "Let Your Women Keep Silence," in *The Promise and the Power*, ed. Donald N. Bowdle (1980); Larry Martin, *In the Beginning* (1994); Robert Bryant Mitchell, *Heritage and Horizons* (1982); and the pamphlet "Women in Ordained Leadership Ministry in the International Church of the Foursquare Gospel" (1998). The best-known female Pentecostal evangelist, Aimee Semple McPherson, has received recent scholarly attention. See Daniel Epstein, *Sister Aimee* (1993), and Edith L. Blumhofer, *Aimee Semple McPherson: Everybody's Sister* (1993). Wayne Warner's *Kathryn Kuhlman* (1993) details the life of another woman evangelist. David Edwin Harrell's *All Things Are Possible* (1976) ably weaves women's contributions into the story of the post–World War II salvation-healing revival. Several dissertations address aspects of women's roles in particular Pentecostal settings—for example, David Roebuck, "Limiting Liberty: The

Church of God and Women Ministers" (Ph.D. diss., Vanderbilt University, 1997). The best archival collection is the Flower Pentecostal Heritage Center (FPHC) in Springfield, Missouri. Its Web site at http://www.agheritage.org/ offers an introduction to the holdings. Its quarterly publication, *Assemblies of God Heritage*, includes articles about women in Pentecostalism. Pentecostalism's early publications allow the researcher to glimpse the hopes that fueled the movement. Some are available on the FPHC Web site; more can be purchased from FPHC on CD-ROM. The *Apostolic Faith* (Los Angeles), the *Latter Rain Evangel*, *The Promise*, *Triumphs of Faith*, and *The Bridal Call* are typical of dozens of similar occasional publications that helped transform a popular movement into an ongoing American religious presence. Women edited some of these and contributed generously to all of them. Pentecostals have diligently produced pamphlets and books brimming with testimonies and exhortations. Few were more prolific than Frank Bartleman, whose undated pamphlet "Flapper Evangelism, Fashion's Fools Headed for Hell" and *How Pentecost Came to Los Angeles* (1925) and *Around the World by Faith* (n.d.) are cited in the text. Carrie Judd Montgomery's autobiographical *"Under His Wings": The Story of My Life* (1936); Ethel Goss's, *Winds of God* (1977), and Aimee Semple McPherson's *This Is That* (1919) offer accounts of Anglo American Pentecostalism's formative years through women's eyes.

Also see the following references: A. J. Gordon, "The Ministry of Women," *Missionary Review of the World* (December 1894); Ellen Hebden, "How Pentecost Came," *The Promise* (May 1907); Ellen Hebden, "Pentecostal Work," *The Promise* (October 1909); A. L. Worth, *Pentecostal Messenger* (April 15, 1933): 4; Frederick L. Chapell, *Eleventh-Hour Laborers* (1898); Virginia Lieson Brereton, *Training God's Army* (1990); Warren Fay Carothers, *Church Government* (1909); Mary Campbell Wilson, *The Obedience of Faith* (1993); and Elmer Louis Moon, *The Pentecostal Church* (1996).

WOMEN IN THE SALVATION ARMY
Diane Winston

Hallelujah Lasses

FROM THE START, the Salvation Army's full-scale deployment of women as preachers and pastors was singular among nineteenth-century Protestant groups. While women in some revivalist sects initially held such roles, they usually lost the right once early enthusiasms hardened into denominational lines. Those denominations that did ordain women had few churches that would accept them since conventional feminine activities, such as teaching children, visiting the poor, and tending the sick, were considered more appropriate for a woman's religious calling.

But equality between the sexes was built into the Army, mirroring the relationship between its founders, William and Catherine Booth. The Booths were British evangelicals whose spiritual sensibilities leaned to lively praise services focused on saving souls. The Salvation Army began in London in 1865 as the Christian Mission, a religious outreach to the unchurched masses. William and Catherine, an ardent proponent of women's right to preach, delivered the gospel message to poor and working-class people wherever they were found. In 1878, when Booth changed the name of his organization to the Salvation Army, he was already called "The General," and his new "army" rapidly adopted a military look and language. Its newspaper was the *War Cry*, ministers were "officers," and members were "soldiers."

At first, the Army's female shock troops, dubbed "Hallelujah lasses" by detractors, provided musical accompaniment for male evangelists. But when William saw the lasses' success at attracting crowds, he encouraged them to preach. In 1880, when the Booths bade farewell to the first official Army invasion of America, the landing party was made up of one man and seven women. The man, George Scott Railton, was a protégé of the Booths and an early supporter of women's equality. Writing to Catherine Booth from the United States, he noted, "Those English may stick to their men as hard as they like, but I am certain it is the women who are going to burst up the world, especially the American women" (Watson, 61).

Women Warriors

William Booth allegedly said, "Some of my best men are women," and nowhere was that more true than in the United States. Many of the Army's earliest American recruits were women, and its initial leadership, from 1886 to 1934, included three exemplary females. Feminine mettle was displayed from the outset. After landing in New York and staging a succession of headline-grabbing events (from appearing at a notorious concert saloon to challenging City Hall's restrictions on outdoor preaching), Railton left his female deputies. Traveling west, he stationed women leaders in New Jersey and Philadelphia. There, he also commissioned the first native-born American officer, Jennie Dickinson.

Philadelphia also was home to the Shirley family, English Salvationists who, with William Booth's blessing, had started the American mission in advance of the official landing party. When Eliza Shirley, a teenage officer, asked the General if she could set up a corps (the Army equivalent of a church) in the American city where her parents were emigrating, the General reluctantly agreed. But when the Shirleys sent back press reports of their success (following several setbacks including an incident of physical persecution), Booth decided to send Railton and the seven lasses to launch a full-scale mission. Arriving in Philadelphia, Railton joined forces with the Shirleys and made their adopted home the site of the Army's first national headquarters.

Commander Evangeline Booth and other members of the Salvation Army at their National Congress c. 1905. Evangeline Booth comfortably wielded command and, unlike Maud Booth or Emma Booth-Tucker, did not share power with a husband. A supporter of women's suffrage, Evangeline extolled new opportunities for women while also advocating traditional notions of female moral and religious superiority. *Courtesy of the Library of Congress.*

During its early years in the United States, the Army grew steadily despite frequent changes in leadership. The movement's enthusiasm and vitality attracted curious-seekers to its street services and revivals. Once drawn in, many were soon snared. As the *War Cry*, the Army's weekly newspaper, reported, "Sister A. Hartelius sees no reason why the devil's children should have the monopoly of dancing and singing on the way to hell, while we who are on the way to heaven are expected to be silent and still" (*American War Cry*, April 3, 1886, 1). Yet the obvious excitement, evidenced in lively meetings and rollicking street corner services, also attracted criticism. Many members of the media and the ministerial elite condemned the Army's brass bands, women preachers, and militarylike marching as vulgar, sensationalistic, and distinctly unchristian.

Likewise, critics charged that female Salvationists had sacrificed their respectability. According to allegations, women became hysterical at Army services and were compromised by living in coed barracks. Some even claimed that Army officers seduced female recruits. Not surprisingly, women who joined the movement were characterized as low class and coarse, and when daughters of the middle and upper classes enlisted, their families often mourned them. Accordingly, when Maud Booth, daughter of a respectable English clergyman, came to take command of the American Army with her husband Ballington, the young woman faced several significant hurdles.

Months before the Ballington Booths arrived in New York, the Army's new headquarters, the local press reported the story of their romance, informing readers all about the gang of religious zealots who had estranged a father from his child. Maud Charlesworth's escapades with the Salvation Army, and the consequences for parents of impressionable daughters, were duly noted by New York's opinion makers:

The real moral of this story is that parents who do not wish their children to become officers in the Salvation Army had better forbid attending meetings in the first instance. The part the Army assigns to women has extraordinary attraction in these times. They can in every way be the rivals of men, they can take an absolute equal part in the establishment and building up of the new organization. By the side of such experiences as this career opens to them, the ordinary routine of home must appear intolerably dull. (*New York Times*, March 11, 1883, 5)

Maud Booth's story exemplified the attraction that the Army held for young, middle- and upper-class women. Raised in London in the last quarter of the nineteenth century, Booth surely was aware of popular currents in religion, philanthropy, and gender that ranged from debates about the new woman to social work initiated by pioneer reformers such as Octavia Hill. While the Charlesworths had taught their children the importance of religion, Booth deemed their practice of Anglicanism remote and, worse, lacking opportunities for female service. Thus, the Salvation Army's appeal was twofold: It provided a way to channel spiritual commitments into meaningful work, and it treated women as autonomous human beings who could lead and command. The very act of joining represented a form of the rebellion popular among youthful idealists of any era. By becoming a Salvationist, a young person like Maud Charlesworth could live out her parents' values—even as the vibrant and exuberant expression of those values shocked the older generation.

When Maud Charlesworth attended a Salvationist "Holiness service" for Christians seeking to deepen their faith, she decided that her former religious practice had been lifeless. Over her parents' objections, she attended Army meetings, and although she was forbidden to participate in any Army activity except visiting the poor, she disregarded these strictures. Befriended by the Booths' daughters, Charlesworth was welcomed into the family, and when Ballington proposed to her she accepted (though she acceded to her father's request to postpone the wedding until her twenty-first birthday). In the interim, she moved into the Booth household and worked at the Women's Training Home where she instructed future Army officers in an intensive course of general education, religious instruction, and practical guidance on how to organize and run a corps.

The opportunity to be a religious leader made the Army attractive to privileged women like Maud Charlesworth. For those who were not content to be just a "friendly visitor" to the poor, yet were more spiritually inclined than a settlement house worker might be, the Army held appeal. It was one of the few purely religious endeavors that welcomed women as equals to men (although women did not rise in the administrative ranks

as easily as their male counterparts did). Army women also could assume more traditional roles, serving as slum sisters, living among and tending to the poor, or working as rescue workers, assisting "fallen women" and unwed mothers seeking to reform.

In general, the well-to-do women who joined the Army were the daughters of professional men from large towns and cities. Most had strong religious feelings untapped by the churches they attended. Alice Terrell, a New Yorker of "Puritan-Knickerbocker" descent, discovered the Army when it took over the downtown church that her congregation had abandoned. "Little Alice" became a soldier in 1882 and served with corps in New York, New Jersey, and Pennsylvania. The Swift sisters of Poughkeepsie encountered the Army during their European tour. Both enlisted: Suzie became the first female editor of an Army publication, and Elizabeth married Samuel Brengle, one of the Army's foremost writers on spirituality. Emma Van Norden, daughter of a wealthy New York banker, wrote for the *War Cry* under the byline TAO (trust and obedience). And Carrie Judd Montgomery, a bestselling author of books on faith healing, became a Salvationist when she and her millionaire husband became convinced that Army missions were the most effective way to reach the unchurched.

Most of these women had successful Army careers. Some were promoted to ensure the visibility of respectable women; others moved upward because their education and background prepared them for leadership. Such women, when confronted by hostile characterizations in the media, ardently defended themselves. Aware of popular prejudices toward the lassies, Salvationists countered them with depictions of their own. Thus even if the *New York Times* declared "whoever joins the Salvation Army from the nature of the case bids good-bye to respectability as much as if he went on the stage of a variety show" (*New York Times*, February 2, 1892, 4), the example of Maud Booth suggested otherwise. Booth's words and deeds, her Army persona, challenged the notion that becoming a Salvationist meant an end to a woman's good name. Even as she forcefully defended women's abilities and rights, Booth never compromised her "refined" and "angelic" demeanor. While serving as a role model for young women seeking lives of holy service, she also inspired trust among hundreds of auxiliaries, the Army's wealthy beneficiaries, whom she addressed in parlor meetings and public forums.

Early in her tenure, Maud Booth began a weekly *War Cry* column to provide women officers with both spiritual solicitude and practical advice. These columns, often written as letters from the Army "Mother" to "her girls," offered encouragement to young women who had defied social convention by joining the Army and then struggled, often alone, to start up corps in unfamiliar towns. Between the late 1880s and the mid 1890s, the

War Cry also ran many articles, letters, and columns that addressed the Army's deployment of women. Did Salvationist activities—such as selling newspapers in saloons, preaching outdoors, and serving as religious leaders—undermine a woman's natural modesty and render her unwomanly? Such activities, at odds with traditional norms of female behavior, antagonized critics as well as created anxiety for some of the women expected to perform them. Writing to her officers, Booth argued that the desire to save sinners and the determination to "crucify" self by disregarding "taste, worldly opinion, and natural obligation" bestowed the "power to rise above" one's circumstances.

> Do you think that God's women warriors should think that it looks unwomanly to do this or that, such as selling "*War Crys*" in the saloons? This is the heaviest cross I have to bear. Often I think that the idea of a young girl going in a crowd of rough men to sell papers goes against our nature; don't you think so? Must salvation destroy a woman's sensitive nature?
>
> I do not think for a moment that God wants his women to be anything else but modest but I cannot see that they in any way endanger their modesty by entering a saloon as God's messenger. That would be Christ's mission were He on earth today. Nor do I think that salvation must destroy a woman's sensitive nature. Jesus Christ's sensitive nature was not destroyed. (*American War Cry*, September 24, 1887, 8)

On the other hand, Booth fully understood the opportunities that the Army offered women. Salvationists believed that God gave each woman "talents, capacities, abilities" to use properly. "Therefore in opening the way for women to talk and sing and pray for God and souls, in public and otherwise, the Army does not give them any privilege, but merely puts them in the way of exercising their rights." Moreover, the Army respected females' autonomy, noting "every woman has the right to be the proprietor of her person, her time, her powers, and all else that belongs to her" (*American War Cry*, July 5, 1890, 3). Yet alongside Booth's spirited defense of women's rights was an understanding of gender differences endemic to the era. Even as she sought to vindicate women's equality in all spheres, Booth upheld certain distinctions such as feminine modesty and masculine chivalry. Anticipating critics of women's rights, she argued that women's tender nature guaranteed they would not seek mastery over the opposite sex.

Still, Booth was not always consistent. She believed that to succeed Salvationist women needed to commingle some masculine qualities along with their feminine nature. The result was the "Woman Warrior." The woman warrior wed gentleness and loving kindness to courage, strength, and action. While some scholars have suggested that religious groups like the Army used religion to instill middle-class notions of respectability among the poor and working class, Booth's pronouncements on women warriors indicate otherwise. She did not always hold herself or her female followers to conventional standards; rather, a spiritual mission often conflicted with society's notions of ladylike behavior. "I presume all officers have had the good sense to discard gloves altogether in this hot weather," she wrote in a column. "I have always looked upon this as one of the emancipations the Salvation Army has brought to women. The opinion of the world on what is ladylike dressing does not enter into Salvation Army dressing" (*American War Cry*, August 4, 1894, 9).

Yet not all Salvationist women were ready to abandon the notions of respectability implicit in the image of the lady. Aware of the popular belief that most Army women had been saved from the dregs of society, and thus represented a degraded version of the sex, some officers sought to clarify their actual social status. According to one Army wife, all the women warriors she knew had been saved since childhood and raised in "refined" settings. Noted another:

> To those of our readers or critics who have "with the larger majority" always held that the ranks of the Salvation Army are altogether made up and recruited from the riff-raff and bob-taildom of society, we say, "Hold it a bit!" Perhaps they will be surprised to find that Major Chatterton and a great many others have been gathered in, not from the slums or the haunts of shame, or the purlieus of iniquity but from the ranks of upper tendom [the wealthiest class] and aristocracy. (*American War Cry*, July 8, 1893, 4)

More typically, however, women warriors hailed from modest backgrounds. Actual profiles as well as the stories in Salvationist periodicals indicate that many grew up in small towns. Watching an Army parade from the window and catching a whiff of wider possibilities, a sheltered young woman might seek escape. In fictional accounts, these unworldly females often realized the emptiness of their lives when confronted by the Salvationist alternative. Tension rose when the protagonist's attachment to material goods (especially clothes) and social conventions (particularly women's roles) conflicted with her desire for a service-filled, God-centered life. In some stories, the heroine dies before she is saved and, with her last breath, regrets her ill-spent years.

Real-life stories often were less dramatic. Recruits were the daughters of farmers or small businessmen; they had been baptized in a church, usually Methodist or Episcopal, but had either fallen away or found their religious practice unfulfilling. Although the 1880s and 1890s were a time of expanding opportunities for women, these late teens and young adults were not part of the tide. Few careers were open to them unless they left home. But absent the press of financial need, many lacked the impetus to strike out on their own. Opting instead to follow the social and domestic rounds of their mothers and grandmothers, some wondered if this were all life had to offer.

The Army provided a solution. Attending a Salvationist meeting, a young woman found radiant faces testifying to a vital faith. If she decided to join the Army and her family disowned her, she had little time to grieve. An officer was expected to move to a city with few resources, quickly build a corps, and make it self-sufficient. Within a few months, she would be sent somewhere else. Writing about her own "eventful life," Capt. A. Y. Dixon began, "[M]y birth occurred in Western Pennsylvania where also I was reared—a farmer's daughter." Dixon said she was willful and selfish until, at age eighteen, she lost both her husband and mother. Seeking forgiveness for past sins, Dixon found salvation and joined the Army. She served corps in her home state, in Connecticut, and in Massachusetts, where she was attacked and imprisoned. Sentenced for the crime of marching in the streets, Dixon spent sixty days in a state workhouse toiling at "arduous" labor and surviving in "loathsome" conditions (*American War Cry*, February 22, 1890, 1, 2). Nevertheless, she stayed true to her mission, evangelizing her fellow prisoners.

Like Dixon, many women who joined the Army were young, idealistic, and mobile. When Minnie Myers first saw the Army in her hometown of Alpena, Michigan, she disliked them, "but underneath it all I loved them because their lives were so pure." (*American War Cry*, October 4, 1890, 10). She became a soldier and was sent to Detroit, where she was beaten and horsewhipped by persecutors. May Harris grew up in the Connecticut hills, the daughter of a Danbury furrier. Although her father was not religious, he took the family to an Army meeting, where Harris was converted. After enlisting, she was stationed in a small town where an angry mob burned down the corps' building and threatened to throw her into the fire, too.

Lassies such as A. Y. Dixon, Minnie Myers, and May Harris met Maud Booth's expectations for women warriors. Unlike their more privileged Salvationist sisters who held administrative and editorial positions, these women did frontline work that often sparked local resistance. While officers serving in New York slum posts were rarely attacked after the early 1880s, lassies in small towns and cities experienced physical violence throughout the decade. Such attacks indicate that female Salvationists were not considered respectable women in many communities. That men felt no compunction about horsewhipping or jailing them suggests the lassies' role as public religious figures placed them beyond the pale of acceptable gender behavior.

Back at Army headquarters, Booth attempted to stretch behavioral bounds for male as well as female Salvationists. Notwithstanding the masculine bias inherent in the Army's militant rhetoric, as well as a policy of promotion favoring male officers, Booth began alternating the "Women's Warrior Column" with articles for Salvationist men. Just as she offered practical advice on topics such as leadership and public speaking for women officers, she instructed men on mastering the basic domestic arts. "Why should men be obligated to depend on women for so many things as if they were still small children? Why should they make and keep a house in upside down, untidy condition because they have not a woman's ability to keep it clean and tidy? You have the notion that it is not manly to do anything or to know anything about such matters." Booth admitted there was some self-interest involved.

> Is not the lack of common sense one of the reasons some of my bright, useful women warriors are persuaded to give up a single career three or four years before they ought to think of such a thing, by men who are not nearly so concerned about finding a good capable co-captain as to get someone to do their cooking, washing, etc. (*American War Cry*, September 22, 1894, 8)

While it is impossible to know whether Booth was more interested in preserving the independence of her women warriors or in engendering self-sufficiency among the men, it is possible to speculate that she was trying to build independent, self-reliant officers of both sexes. The Army was unusual for expanding women's options, but few of its leaders—Maud Booth was an exception—realized that assuming new roles required both sexes to develop new skills.

As the first modern religious movement to treat women as equals, the Army offered a compelling, if sometimes contradictory, vision of gender. Praised by women's advocates, the Army was called "the best field at this time for comparing the services of men and women in the regeneration of humanity" by the Rev. Anna Howard Shaw (*The Chautauquan*, 494). But it is equally true that Salvationist women frequently performed tasks associated with the domestic sphere, and in some ways, slum sisters, those who lived among the poor, were the apotheosis of "true womanhood." These selfless women modeled Christian virtues by "mothering," that is, by nursing, cleaning, cooking, and tending children. Their adherence to social norms may explain why their ministrations received more media attention than the exploits of women warriors who, despite the hard work of pioneering corps, received most coverage when jailed or beaten.

To the public, slum angels were conflated with the "true woman," while woman warriors were representative of the new woman—desexed and aggressive. This was never Booth's intention, but at a time when women's roles and behavior were increasingly debated, the notion of women warriors may have been too unsettling for mass appeal. After internal Army politics led to the resignation of Maud and Ballington Booth in 1895, there were no more columns for women warriors. Maud's female successors, sisters-in-law Emma Booth-Tucker and Evangeline Booth, were more conventional. They accepted both the Army's stated goal of equality for women as well as the limitations imposed on it by contemporary society.

Slum Angels

Building the Kingdom of God was second nature to Emma Moss Booth, the fourth child born to William and Catherine Booth. The qualities that so impressed her American contemporaries, a serious intellect commingled with a maternal heart, were evident from childhood. Emma's intensity compensated for a reserved and withdrawing nature that, according to her intimates, resulted from an avid dislike of public attention. Though skilled at handling crowds and a renowned orator, Emma, unlike her brother Ballington or her sister Evangeline, did not enjoy the limelight.

In 1887, Emma married widower Frederick St. George Lautour Tucker, the Salvationist officer who "invaded" India. The couple wed in a large hall where 5,000 spectators contributed a total of $25,000 for the privilege of watching the ceremony. Tucker, following the custom of the men who married into the Booth family, adopted a hyphenated surname. Instead of going on a honeymoon, the newlyweds sailed to India to resume missionary work, but Emma Booth-Tucker fared poorly in the hot climate. She returned home so ill that her doctors expected her to die. When she did recover, "Fritz" (as she called her husband) moved back to London, and the two served jointly as the Army's foreign secretaries.

When the Ballington Booths resigned in 1896, William Booth asked the Booth-Tuckers to take over the American command. (The Ballington Booths went on to start the Volunteers of America.) Emma Booth-Tucker's steady intelligence reminded William of his wife who had died six years earlier. But compared with her sister-in-law Maud, Booth-Tucker projected a subdued style of female leadership. When addressing female Salvationists, she focused less on their public roles and responsibilities than on the difficulties of balancing work and family. During her six years in the United States,

she not only shared command with her husband but also experienced six pregnancies. Constantly in the public eye, she traveled as much as, and often independently of, Frederick. But wherever she was and whatever she did, Booth-Tucker projected a "mother's heart"—a nurturing image resonant with the cult of domesticity. In fact, she came to represent the epitome of the "womanly woman" whose implicit moral authority guaranteed her place on the public stage.

In her attempt to balance work and family, Booth-Tucker resembled a late-twentieth-century career woman. She led a national movement, traveled extensively, and cared for seven children. Press coverage of her speaking engagements placed her all around the nation—leading revivals and visiting the growing network of Salvationist social service programs. In "A Peep in My Diary," a *War Cry* story by Brigadier Alice Lewis, Booth-Tucker is depicted juggling interviews, speaking engagements, and correspondence while visiting the sick, leading worship services, and coordinating volunteers. Reporters from the secular press focused on her dedication to her family. Methodically overseeing even the smallest details, she cut her children's hair, sewed their clothes, and regularly led them in Bible study.

The Booth-Tuckers continued the Ballington Booths' crusade to make the Army more respectable. Among their strategies was expanding social services. Slum work, for example, spread from New York to other large cities. By 1895, there were posts in Philadelphia, Boston, Chicago, Brooklyn, Buffalo, and St. Louis. The work proved popular with the media. Women reporters, in particular, fell sway to the slum workers' mystique, portraying them as "slum angels" toiling selflessly amidst urban squalor. Such accounts often began with the journalist disguising herself in a plain frock and patched apron so she, too, could pass unnoticed in the city's bleakest streets. In an article for the *New York World*, Julia Hayes Percy began her night of revelation ("revelations of such misery, depravity, and degradation that, having been gazed upon, life can never be quite the same afterward") by sharing tea and plum cake at the Army's Brooklyn barracks. Percy and the slum sisters took a ferry to Manhattan where the reporter, overwhelmed by the "vile stench," breathlessly compared the "dirt and garbage" with the Salvationists' abode of warmth and cleanliness (*American War Cry*, March 1, 1890, 1).

Throughout the 1890s, many newspapers, magazines, and journals published accounts of the Army's slum work, citing the dedication of its workers in the domestic mission field. But the outreach never expanded to the degree that the Army's other social services, such as rescue work and industrial homes, did. Weekly notices in the *War Cry* advertised for "good, devoted girls" willing "to sacrifice everything and go and live among the poor," but few answered the call. Slum work was among the most grueling of the Army's activities, and women attracted by the Salvationists' promise of gender equality found few opportunities for public ministry and leadership in the tenements. Those who chose slum work were primarily single women whose simplicity and deep faith made toil and privation possible.

Just as the slum sisters saw themselves bringing God's love to the "poor creatures" whom they tended in the slums, they felt equally impassioned to save the more hardened sinners whom they encountered in dives, brothels, and dance halls. One *War Cry* article saluted ten cadets who visited 1,025 saloons in one week. The reporter described the range of reactions elicited by the lassies, including a dousing of warm liquor and cold beer. More often, articles recounted the life-changing experiences that Salvationists spurred among the denizens of demimonde. An 1892 piece described a typical night. The group started out at a dance hall where patrons wept when the women "dealt earnestly and tenderly with them about their souls and salvation." Next, they visited a brothel where lewd songs, violent brawls, and pervasive profanity approximated Salvationist notions of hell. But no sooner did the lassies begin a hymn than they were surrounded by listeners who, falling to their knees, joined in "Room for Jesus" (*American War Cry*, February 20, 1892, 10).

Of far greater scope than the work in the slums were the Army's efforts to rescue fallen women. Salvationist outreach to prostitutes and unwed mothers began in 1884 with the opening of a "rescue home" in London. Soon after, the Army announced plans for a similar home in New York, and Morris Cottage, an Army haven for "fallen women," opened in 1886. Before long the *War Cry* reported that Morris Cottage had attracted enough residents to warrant expansion. Salvationists stressed the work's familial dimensions. The door of the rescue home was always open, and residents were free to leave if and when they wanted. *War Cry* narratives, whether fictional or depicting "real life," usually presented "fallen women" as innocent victims, "more sinned against than sinning." In fact, the ministry was deemed so important that the Army opened a training garrison in upper Manhattan just to prepare female officers for rescue work.

Upon assuming command, the Booth-Tuckers tripled the number of rescue homes in six years. Emma also oversaw the founding of a women's industrial home where residents, graduates of the rescue homes, learned skills such as bookbinding, fancy needlework, and expert dressmaking. Maud had placed reformed prostitutes as servants in Christian homes, but Emma saw a need for other options. Fallen women from the middle and upper classes looked down on domestic service, and their best hope lay in finding work they enjoyed.

Building on the familiar Victorian construction of sisterhood, women taking care of each other and defining a sphere they could control, Salvationists used the rhetoric of home to define optimal social relationships. To explain why an Army rescue home succeeded when other attempts failed, an unnamed philanthropist, who turned over the operation of his rescue home to the Army, explained that "the tone of that place was uplifted from one of patronage to sisterliness. Our matron and her assistants were good and pious women, but had looked on the inmates as beings apart. They were 'fallen women' that was the conscious spirit. The Army sisters came and all that changed. Nothing more was heard of 'fallen women'; it was sister to sister" (*American War Cry*, June 11, 1920, 8).

In October 1903, Emma was killed in a train wreck while traveling from the Army's farm colony in Colorado to meet her husband in Chicago. The *War Cry* eulogized her as "the incarnation of true womanhood." The secular press agreed.

> She never talked women's rights. She took them. She was accustomed to the respect, the admiration, and obedience of the men she met, and she seems to have been as little given to theorizing about the political or social relations of men and women as she was over the training of children. With a temperament emphatically masterful and militant, she did the things, says Ensign Carr, "that other women talk about." (*New York Tribune*, November 11, 1903, sec. 2, 4)

Emma both built on and disregarded Maud Booth's ideas about gender. By embodying the womanly woman, one who saw her work in the world as a form of enlarged moral housekeeping, Emma provided a safe vision of Salvationist womanhood that bridged the Victorian and Progressive Eras. Moreover, her privacy, piety, and devotion to family reinforced the image of respectability that Maud and other female officers sought to project. Not surprisingly, during Emma's tenure the public image of the rank-and-file lassie improved as Army women gained a new respectability alongside a deep admiration for their work.

The Sallies

In 1904, when Frederick Booth-Tucker returned to England, William Booth sent his daughter Evangeline to command the American Army. Evangeline Cory Booth was actually named Eva after the heroine of *Uncle Tom's Cabin*. But she adopted the name "Evangeline" in later life when temperance and women's rights crusader Frances Willard suggested it sounded more distinguished for a leader. Evangeline Booth comfortably wielded command, and unlike Maud Booth or Emma

Booth-Tucker, she did not share power with a husband. A supporter of women's suffrage, Booth extolled new opportunities for women while also advocating traditional notions of female moral and religious superiority. In the pamphlet *Woman*, she acknowledged the spread of the women's movement worldwide and celebrated the possibilities it offered, including the right to choose a fulfilling career over a feckless marriage. But Booth urged her female readers not to abandon their most precious legacy: fostering and safeguarding religious faith.

In many ways, Booth enacted masculine behavior while espousing feminine ideals. Like many of her contemporaries, including Frances Willard and Jane Addams, she paid homage to women's traditional home-making role while casting it in a broader context: "We women have made many homes in the world. But we have now the task of changing the world into a home" (*Woman*, 16). Likewise, despite the equality of ministerial opportunity offered to Salvationist lassies, the Army still upheld Victorian notions of womanhood. Twenty years earlier Maud Booth evoked the image of women warriors as militant fighters who nevertheless, like Jesus, retained their modesty. But Evangeline promoted a softer model for her female troops. Although she supported suffrage and women's rights, she maintained the home-centered language of mothers and sisters when describing the role of female Salvationists.

Booth's reputation grew as she involved the Army in the issues of the day. Her vocal support for Prohibition, a movement whose grassroots popularity did not preclude political controversy, was criticized by some as religious meddling in politics. However, her swift responses to emergencies and disasters, including the 1906 San Francisco earthquake, raised the Army's status in Americans' eyes: Salvationists were on the scene when and where they were needed. Booth also was an excellent steward. When she arrived in New York, Army property was valued at $1.5 million; when she left, thirty years later, that figure had risen to $48 million plus a capital account of an additional $35 million.

In the midst of the Progressive Era, an action-oriented age, the Salvation Army was known first and foremost as an action-oriented religion. Its popular image had changed from a vulgar, ragtag religious mission to a respected provider of social services. Several factors predating Evangeline Booth's tenure expedited this transformation, including the astute public relations as well as the administrative and financial accomplishments of the Booth-Tuckers. But Booth's contributions were also significant. Even as she continued the Army's institutionalization by overseeing the acquisition of property, the systematization of fund-raising, and the creation of a strong, centralized bureaucracy, Booth gave the Army a human face—her own. Through public performances and a steady barrage of coverage in Army publications and the secular press, she came to symbolize the movement she led.

The greatest change in the Army's image occurred after General John Pershing granted it permission to provide social and welfare work to American troops during World War I. Booth quickly decided that American overseas forces needed a little "mothering." No more than 250 Salvationists actually served in France (and only a minority of these were women), but the accolades they received far outstripped their numbers. Setting up "huts" near the soldiers' camps, Salvation Army lassies—nicknamed Sallies—sewed clothes, banked paychecks, and prayed with men going off to fight. Having selected lassies of impeccable virtue, Booth's plan, to bring a bit of home to the front, won the doughboys' hearts. Through their letters and testimonials, the soldiers' praise of the Sallies catapulted the Army into the front ranks of American social service providers. As one soldier wrote, "These good women create an atmosphere that reminds us of home, and out of the millions of men over there not one ever dreams of offering the slightest sign of disrespect or lack of consideration to these wonderful women" (*American War Cry*, June 15, 1918, 4).

The Sallies, always ready to serve the troops, darned socks, mended uniforms, and fried thousands of crullers each day. As soon as the women mastered cooking under wartime conditions, there were always hot drinks and baked goods available. Whenever possible they even delivered coffee and doughnuts to the front. At night, they used a box for a pulpit and held religious meetings. Their services were simple, mostly made up of gospel songs and short talks. These religious meetings started small, but the crowd grew as men joined in the singing of the old, familiar tunes. By the evening's end, several often raised their hands for prayer, some even converted. Salvationists found it easy to share their faith on the battlefield; faced with death on a daily basis, many soldiers were eager to hear what they had to say.

The zeal for service that inspired Sallies to persist under enemy fire was expressed in their diaries as a placid acceptance of danger and discomfort. The monumental difficulties attendant upon everyday life at the battlefront were recounted in matter-of-fact tones. It rained incessantly, the mud was knee-deep, and living conditions ranged from stark to primitive. The bitter cold often forced the women to sleep in their clothes. Not surprisingly, opportunities to bathe were infrequent. Then, there was the horror of the war itself: the constant shelling and bombing, the ever-present gas masks, the dead and mutilated bodies. Through it all, the Sallies persevered with dignity and quiet determination. Gazing at the graves of the soldiers she had known, Margaret

Sheldon, one of the first Sallies to arrive at the front, vowed "to live better and be braver in the struggle of life" (Margaret Sheldon diary).

After the war, the Army never again worried about its survival. Its coffers were kept full by a grateful public. And by the 1930s, Evangeline Booth's secular talents were as admired as her spiritual gifts. Praising her financial acumen in a *New York Times* profile, writer S. J. Woolf noted "the peculiar quality about her is the strange combination of hard-headed business ability coupled with a poetic sense of the beautiful, and a mystic love of music" (*New York Times*, March 20, 1930, 1). Woolf was also struck by the commander's histrionics. She seemed more like a stage character than the leader of a large organization. In fact, her self-conscious theatricality contributed to the reification of the Army's image from a youthful fighting force to an old-timey band of do-gooders. As the Army's living symbol, Booth's air of high drama appeared increasingly out of sync with the times. And when she was elected general of the International Army, many of her officers bid her farewell with fulsome testimonials, ticker tape parades—and not a little relief. After her thirty-year reign, there was a quiet desire for the organization to move on. In 1939, when her stint in the High Command ended, Booth returned to the States and lived quietly in retirement. When she died in 1950, the secular press scarcely noticed her passing.

The Salvationist Legacy

After Evangeline Booth, no unmarried woman ever again headed the American Army. And while wives subsequently shared the top command with their husbands, none enjoyed the degree of power and popularity that marked the tenure of both Maud Booth and Emma Booth-Tucker. At the lower levels of Army hierarchy, single women increasingly found themselves directing "women's work," outreach to women, children, and families, while married women followed the husband's postings regardless of their own gifts and talents. For an organization that initially raised the bar for female participation and equality, the Army—by the start of the twenty-first century—had fallen behind many of its sister Protestant denominations.

In seeking to advance their careers, Army women today point to the movement's historic legacy and cite the Founding Mothers, Catherine Booth and her daughters. Nevertheless, the Army's rootedness in a historical moment, the late Victorian era, and its concomitant understandings of gender and religion, has normalized a set of assumptions increasingly antithetical to the contemporary world. At the outset, fired by millennial hopes, the Army offered a revolutionary view of gender,

pushing the era's notions of women's roles to the limit. When the movement became as interested in its own continuity as in the Second Coming, it adopted language that explained the deployment of women in socially acceptable ways. Accordingly, subversive lassies and woman warriors gave way to slum angels and Sallies. Still, even as the latter hallowed notions of home and family among World War I troops, the Army continued to push the limits of female behavior by stationing young women at the battles' front lines.

The experience of women in the Salvation Army illustrates the both/and quality of change. Without question, the Salvationist example expanded possibilities for women's religious leadership. After the Army appeared on American soil, the number of female clergy steadily rose from a handful to the hundreds. And while the Army's model of female autonomy and independence initially sparked criticism and even persecution, the changing nature of gender roles at the end of the nineteenth century soon enabled the rest of the country to catch up with the Salvationist example. Why the nation continued to move on while the Army, more or less, marched in place is an intriguing question with no simple answer. From the insidiousness of institutional sexism to the misogyny of key Christian teachings, familiar answers only go so far. In an organization in which some of the best men are women, there remains the promise that men and women, one day, will be truly equal.

SOURCES: The Salvation Army Archives, housed at the Army's American headquarters in Alexandria, Virginia, is the most comprehensive source for the American papers of Evangeline Booth and Emma Booth-Tucker. Some of Maud Ballington Booth's papers are there, too; others are located at the Special Collections Department, University of Iowa Libraries (Iowa City), and at the Volunteers of America headquarters in Alexandria, Virginia. Papers for all three women also can be found at the International Headquarters of the Salvation Army in London. The American archives have a full collection of the *War Crys* publications as well as papers and diaries of Army officers, such as Margaret Sheldon. Evangeline Booth was a prolific author, and among her works are *Love Is All* (1908), *Toward a Better World* (1928), and *Woman* (1930). There are also several biographies of Evangeline Booth including Philip W. Wilson's *General Evangeline Booth of the Salvation Army* (1948). Among the biographies of other key Salvationists are Bernard Watson's *Soldier Saint* (1970), the story of George Railton, and Susan Welty's *Look Up and Hope! The Motto of the Volunteer Prison League: The Life of Maud Ballington Booth* (1961). More general works about the Booths and Army women include Andrew Mark Eason's *Women in God's Army: Gender and Equality in the Early Salvation Army* (2002), Edward H. McKinley's *Marching to Glory: The History of the Salvation Army in the United States, 1880–1992* (1995), Lillian Taiz's *Hallelujah Lads and Lasses: Remaking the Salvation Army in America, 1880–1930* (2001), and Diane Winston's *Red Hot and Righteous: The Urban Religion of the Salvation Army* (1999).

REVIVALISM
Priscilla Pope-Levison

MORE THAN A century and a half ago, revivalism was described as "the grand absorbing theme and aim of the American religious world" (Colton, 59). Similar sentiments continue concerning its contemporary import. The roots of revivalism in North America can be traced to the mid-eighteenth century when Theodore Frelinghuysen (1691–1748), a German-born Calvinist minister in New Jersey, initiated a preaching campaign the climax of which was a call for individuals to repent from their sin and to be converted to faith in Jesus Christ. Through subsequent generations, the core of revivalism has remained remarkably similar, consisting of a series of decision-centered religious services whose purpose is to produce conversions in individuals en masse. The central actor in these services is a charismatic figure who is at once speaker, dramatist, and worship leader. Music, drama, prayers, and personal testimonies are used to heighten the emotionally charged atmosphere that characterizes revivalism. These elements were utilized quite effectively, for instance, by Aimee Semple McPherson in the early decades of the twentieth century.

> When, at the close of her sermon, she asked the sinners to come forward and be saved, her voice was low, compassionate, and tender; the lights were dimmed; the music mournful and pleading. Then, as the slow, sad, solemn procession started down the aisles, she would suddenly shout, "Ushers, jump to it! Turn on the lights and clear the one-way street for Jesus!" As the lights blazed on and the organ boomed, the meeting would suddenly start to bounce and jump. (McWilliams, 51)

Some historians differentiate between *revival* and *revivalism*. *Revivalism* is thought to reflect a programmed script with a predictable purpose, while the term *revival* exhibits a more spontaneous, unexpected character. In their view, revival is best understood simply as an increased interest in religious matters that results in an upsurge in conversions. Other historians contend that this distinction between revivalism and revival is difficult to maintain consistently across the diversity of denominations, geographical areas, and historical epochs. These scholars tend to use *revival* and *revivalism* interchangeably. Another word related to revivalism, *awakening*, refers to a larger phenomenon of sustained religious interest over a length of time, breadth of geography, and depth of cultural impact.

While historians may differ on nomenclature, they are certain that revivalism was primarily within the domain of male religious leaders. Chronicling revivalism in North America routinely begins with figures such as Jonathan Edwards (1703–1758) and George Whitefield (1714–1770), central characters in the First Great Awakening, and continues through each generation from Charles Finney (1792–1875), Dwight Moody (1837–1899), and Billy Sunday (1862–1935) to Billy Graham (1918–   ). The omission of women from these surveys and studies obscures the foundational and frequent role women have played in revivalism, particularly since the early nineteenth century.

Although the sheer number of American women revivalists of the last two centuries prohibits a person-by-person introduction, individual portraits meld into a composite picture when their shared characteristics are considered. Most came from relatively poor socioeconomic backgrounds. These women tended to emerge from rural areas where their family subsisted on farming or manual labor. The economic straits of their families often compelled them to leave school early and forego an education—an element of their childhood they would later lament.

The early years of Maria Woodworth-Etter (1844–1924), an early Pentecostal revivalist, exemplifies this scenario. Her autobiography begins with the death of her father, leaving her mother with eight children to feed and clothe. Maria and her older sisters were forced to end their formal education in order to help provide for their family.

> My oldest sisters and myself had to leave home and work by the week. We had not only ourselves to clothe, but also to provide for our brothers and sisters at home. . . . I wanted to go to school where I could learn, for I longed for an education; and I often cried myself to sleep over this matter. I would have my books in the kitchen, where I could read a verse and commit it to memory, then read another, and so on, thus improving every opportunity while at my work. (Woodworth, 16–17)

These difficulties were compounded for African American women by racial prejudice. The formal education of Amanda Berry Smith (1837–1915), a former slave, washerwoman, and Methodist Holiness revivalist, was fragmentary since it took place around the edges of the white children.

> There were a great many farmers' daughters, large girls, and boys, in the winter time, so that the school would be full, so that after coming two and

Maria Woodworth-Etter (1844–1924), an early Pentecostal evangelist, traveled across the country preaching to thousands of people. At one meeting in Oakland, California, she spent over a thousand dollars of her own money to put up a tent that accommodated 8,000 people. *Courtesy of the Flower Pentecostal Heritage Center.*

a half miles, many a day I would get but one lesson, and that would be while the other scholars were taking down their dinner kettles and putting their wraps on. All the white children had to have their full lessons, and if time was left the colored children had a chance. I received in all about three months' schooling. (Smith, *An Autobiography*, 27)

At times, the disparity between their meager education and the elevated role of a revivalist led to unconventional experiences. Maria Woodworth-Etter solved the disparity by a vision that rendered education redundant, one in which the Bible literally became an open book to her.

I told him [Jesus] I wanted to study the Bible; that I did not understand it well enough. Then there appeared upon the wall a large open Bible, and the verses stood out in raised letters. The glory of God shone around and upon the book. I looked, and I could understand it all. . . . I saw more in that vision than I could have learned in years of hard study. (Woodworth, 37)

There were exceptions, of course. Harriet Livermore (1788–1868), an itinerant revivalist, was born into an

elite New England family with an impressive political and military lineage. Livermore attended boarding schools in New England from age eight until her late teen years. Her superior education and familial connections helped propel her revivalistic work to national attention. Through the late 1820s and mid-1830s, she preached in churches in many New England towns as well as four times before the U.S. Congress. Despite her affluent background, Livermore spent her last years in poverty and died alone in a Philadelphia alms house after her popularity and resources had dwindled in the 1840s.

Jennie Fowler Willing (1834–1916), a Methodist Holiness revivalist, was also well educated, although, unlike Livermore, Willing was self-educated. She was unable to attend school after age nine due to intense periods of pain, the result of a fall into a well when she was a toddler. Her fervent desire to learn prompted her to develop a method of self-education. She set aside fifteen minutes a day for study; if for any reason she skipped a day, the fifteen minutes were doubled the next day. In that daily period, she taught herself a range of subjects, including five languages. The success of her method was confirmed by Illinois Wesleyan University who hired her in 1874 as professor of English language and literature.

Livermore and Willing proved to be the exceptions rather than the rule. More often than not, women revivalists consciously rued their lack of education and attempted to validate their roles through a claim to the Holy Spirit, revelations or visions, and inspired abilities. Such characteristics are also evident in the denominations from which the revivalists emerged.

The denominations most represented by women revivalists were those that valued the heart over the head and the witness of the Holy Spirit over education, such as Methodists, Free Will Baptists, Christian Connection, and in the twentieth century, various Pentecostal denominations that emphasize the palpable presence and activity of the Holy Spirit. In a more Spirit-centered atmosphere, women were able to overcome the "man-fearing spirit"—a reference to their prior timidity about preaching in public—and to follow the Spirit's call into revivalistic work. In a Spirit-centered atmosphere, innovations were more likely to be encouraged, such as laymen and laywomen praying aloud, exhorting, and preaching.

Although few women revivalists actually affiliated with the Quakers, this religious group that promoted the

Holy Spirit's promptings and the public ministry of women provided resources, role models, and sanction for women revivalists. The Quakers were a source of encouragement to revivalists Harriet Livermore, who attended Quaker meetings for a while after her conversion, and Amanda Berry Smith, who was serving in a Quaker household when she was converted. Along with their religious beliefs, the unadorned, dark attire of Quaker women provided a model of clothing that revivalists, such as Sojourner Truth, Livermore, and Smith, adopted. They believed that Quaker clothing conformed most closely to scriptural injunctions and set them apart from worldly fashion.

Two Spirit-centered movements that generated a large number of women revivalists were the Holiness movement in the mid- to late nineteenth century and the Pentecostal movement in the early twentieth century. The Holiness movement gave priority to a person's public testimony to the work of the Spirit in one's life, especially with regard to sanctification, a second blessing subsequent to conversion that resulted in an individual's entire consecration to God. The sanctification experience, then, became the litmus test for men and women speaking in a public gathering. Many women revivalists who claimed sanctification were associated with the Holiness movement, including Sojourner Truth, Phoebe Palmer, Mary Lee Cagle, Amanda Berry Smith, Jennie Fowler Willing, and Alma White. Several decades later, the Pentecostal movement gave priority to the life-transforming event following conversion known as the baptism in the Holy Spirit, an event confirmed by supernatural signs, such as speaking in tongues. As with the Holiness movement, Pentecostals recognized the power of the Holy Spirit as that which licensed men and women to preach. The Pentecostal movement embraced women revivalists, such as Maria Woodworth-Etter, Aimee Semple McPherson, Ida B. Robinson, and Kathryn Kuhlman.

Moving beyond the woman's sphere of home and family to engage in revivalistic work was not easy, and many women faced difficult family issues and relationships. For some women the issue was the care of their children while they traveled to preach at revival meetings. Often family members would care for the children. Still, the separation of mother and child was difficult, as Alma White (1862–1946), a former Methodist Holiness preacher who founded the Pillar of Fire denomination, discovered when she left her two-year-old son who was recovering from a long, serious illness in the care of her mother. "To leave him in care of others was almost like taking a mother's heart from her body, but the Lord had spoken and it would have been perilous to disobey. It was no more than He required of others, and why should I have any controversy" (White, 48).

Others interpreted the tragic death of their children

as evidence of God's call to revivalistic work. Although Maria Woodworth-Etter at first protested the call due to her young son Willie, his death freed her from that responsibility. In her autobiography, she wrote, " 'O Lord! I can not take Willie with me, nor can I leave him behind.' Then the Lord saw fit to take him out of the way; so he laid his hand on my darling little boy, and in a few days took him home to heaven" (Woodworth, 31). In all Woodworth-Etter lost five of six children at a young age. Similarly, Amanda Berry Smith lost four of five children. When Smith finally began revivalistic work in earnest, after putting it off for many years due to family constraints, her only surviving child was an adolescent.

Some women revivalists also had to contend with antagonistic husbands. In this regard, the marriages of Amanda Berry Smith and Maria Woodworth-Etter exemplify the difficulties at home that plagued many. Smith suffered through two unhappy marriages that were complicated by poverty and infant mortality. She married her second husband, James Smith, in large part because he expressed falsely, in order to win her affections, a desire to become an ordained minister. She had hoped to be a minister's wife and through that position to be active in ministry. The conflicts between them kept them separated throughout most of their married life. When her husband died, Smith became a full-time revivalist.

As with Smith, Woodworth-Etter also had hoped to marry an "earnest Christian" with whom she could do mission work. Unfortunately, her first husband, Philo Woodworth, proved to be a trial. A business manager of sorts for her revivals, he threatened to damage his wife's reputation by his mercenary business enterprises during her meetings. As the *Weekly Courier* (Wabash, Indiana, August 21, 1885), reported, "Sunday morning he was dispensing cigars and plugging watermelons for the million, and the nickels, dimes and quarters flowed into his till in a steady stream, while the wife was laboring with care-burdered sinners." Eventually Maria sued her husband for divorce on the grounds of repeated adultery.

Alma White preached her first sermon in her husband's pulpit, and they even shared the revival platform for several years, alternating the preaching and the encouragement of awakened sinners at the altar. However, when Alma became the more popular preacher, their marriage and revivalistic partnership began to dissolve, cutting short several revivals. Following their marital separation, they were never reconciled. Alma's legacy was not nullified by this; sons Arthur and Ray embraced their mother's work and became leaders in the denomination she founded, the Pillar of Fire.

Although many women revivalists experienced discord in their marriage, some marriages actually benefitted the work of revivalism. Phoebe and Walter Palmer, for example, were a well-known revivalistic partnership. Phoebe (1807–1874), a Methodist Holiness revivalist, was active for twenty years on her own, while Walter stayed home to keep up his medical practice and manage their household. Later they joined forces for an extended revival tour of Great Britain.

Still others embarked on revivalistic work to carry on their husband's work after his death. Mary Lee Cagle (1864–1955), a Church of the Nazarene revivalist, had felt the call to preach in her childhood, but it was at her evangelist husband's deathbed that she resolved to put on his mantle and preach the gospel. She held revival meetings and started churches primarily in Texas and Arkansas for the denomination her husband had founded, the New Testament Church of Christ, which later merged with the Church of the Nazarene.

Similarly, Helen "Ma" Sunday (1868–1957), wife of Billy Sunday, began her own career as a revivalist after Billy's death. Prior to his death, Helen had been intimately involved in Billy's revival work behind the scenes. Her primary responsibility was to manage the campaigns, which involved choosing the site where a large, temporary structure would be built, overseeing the publicity and the finances, supervising the staff, which numbered as high as twenty-six, and meeting with the committee of churches in each city. In an interview before Billy's 1917 campaign in New York City, which many consider his high point, Helen explained the different roles that she and Billy brought to their ministry.

> You know, we have thought of coming [to New York] many times before this, but I never would consent until I was sure everything would be done properly. It wasn't enough to have a committee of one hundred. It wasn't enough to have the influential men in New York give us their money or even their sympathy. They had to be willing to work. I knew what it meant to tackle New York. Mr. Sunday didn't. He is always so wrapped up in the campaign of the moment that he can't make any plans for the future. I'm the one that has to look ahead. (Dorsett, 106–107)

At Billy's deathbed in 1935, Helen begged God for direction for what to do with the rest of her life. When requests came for her to speak at memorial services for her husband, she interpreted them as a call from God to continue Billy's ministry. For the next twenty-two years, she preached at Bible Conferences and one-day revival meetings. She also accepted invitations to preach during the meetings of younger revivalists, such as Billy Graham.

In order to take advantage of every conceivable venue, revivalists often adopted an itinerant lifestyle.

The strenuous demands prior to more modern, comfortable modes of transportation were exacerbated for women due to the potential for sexual assault and vulnerability to robbery. Added to the uncertain vicissitudes of itinerancy was the financial insecurity that pressured revivalists throughout their journeys. As a result, they were compelled to raise funds by selling their memoirs and other books, accepting voluntary offerings, and depending on the generosity of friends, family, and churches. They were forced as well to resort to other more creative methods. Harriet Livermore recalled how she pawned silver spoons to underwrite her work.

> Since I have traveled and appointed meetings in the name of the Lord I have often carried an empty purse. And by this means twice I have been obliged to travel on foot till my feet were badly festered, and my whole frame entirely exhausted. I have, or rather once had, three large silver spoons and six small ones, formerly the property of my deceased mother.... These spoons have been of service to me, since I have been exposed to the open world, a selfish unfeeling theater of gain, in affording me present relief in any sudden exigency, by pawning them to some wealthy, trusty Christian for the money I needed. (Livermore, 63–64)

In the earliest days, male and female revivalists preached in churches and public halls. At the beginning of the nineteenth century, another venue was developed, the camp meeting. Participants in these outdoor meetings would literally camp nearby in order to attend the daily and nightly services that lasted anywhere from several days to several weeks. At these camp meetings, where the openness and freedom of the great outdoors replaced the strictures of church structures, the emotional side of revivalism rose to its height. Fervent preaching at all hours of the day and night, spirited singing of hymns and gospel tunes, and impassioned exhorting of awakened sinners evoked various physical responses in the participants, such as groaning, crying out, falling down as if dead, jerking, barking, and snapping teeth.

In the less reserved atmosphere of a camp meeting, where religious experience was more valued than church order, women found opportunity to preach. Even children could find a platform for speaking at camp meetings. At a camp meeting near Terre Haute, Indiana, in 1848, a girl about eight years old was converted.

> Within about an hour after her conversion, while many seekers were at the alter [sic] ... the same little girl came on the stand, her face all lighted up with joy, and in her childish way, meekly asked

the question, "Wouldn't you let me talk to the people?" She was at once lifted and stood on a chair, when she delivered an exhortation in connection with her personal experience, so clear and impressive, that it sent a thrill throughout the large assembly. It was believed then by the most intelligent men and woman present that the child was directly inspired. As a result of her talk more than fifty souls were there and then so convicted of sin that they came rushing to the alter [*sic*], to find peace and pardon in believing. Among the many who were brought to Christ through the child's speech was her aged grandfather. (Smith, *Indiana Methodism*, 156–157)

As the crowds gathering for revival meetings increased, a larger space beyond the capacity of many churches was needed that could be transported by the revivalist. Among the first to use a large tent for revival meetings, as early as 1842, were the Millerites, a group who believed that the world was soon going to end and Jesus would return to take Christian believers out of this world. They encouraged women to preach as evidence of the coming apocalypse. By the last decades of the nineteenth century, a few women revivalists, such as Maria Woodworth-Etter, traveled with their own tent. In order to hold the increasingly large crowds that attended her 1890 Oakland, California, meetings, Woodworth-Etter spent $1,325 for a tent spacious enough to accommodate 8,000 people.

A generation later, Aimee Semple McPherson (1890–1944), who founded an independent Pentecostal denomination, the International Church of the Foursquare Gospel, began her revivalism work in a 40 × 80 foot tent. She recalled the first time she pitched this tent in vivid detail.

Knowing little of the winds and power of the elements which have to be taken into consideration when picking out a location for a tent meeting, we, in our ignorance, selected a fine, high hill, on the bluff of the bay where those who came to meeting could enjoy the breeze and the water. The series of meetings was almost over when one forenoon the last wind storm came, and in spite of all our efforts, down went the big tent with many tears in its rotten old seams which we had worked for hours to sew up, just a short time ago. (McPherson, 87)

McPherson's sense of commitment to her revivalistic work was matched by her spirit of resourcefulness; she and a little boy managed to ready the tent for the evening revival.

Another venue for revivalism was generated with the advent of the automobile, which was simultaneously a mode of transportation and a platform for communication. Roman Catholic author and lecturer Martha Moore Avery (1851–1925) and her coworker David Goldstein traveled together in the summers throughout New England in their customized Model-T autovan and held meetings for the Catholic Truth Guild, an organization they founded in 1915 to promote Catholicism and patriotism. Their autovan made the visual connection between things Catholic and things American. Quotes from George Washington and Archbishop William O'Connell decorated either side of the car, a miniature star-spangled banner was attached to the hood, a large, lighted crucifix adorned the sounding board, and the van itself was painted in the papal colors of yellow and white. The sounding board folded out at a forty-five-degree angle from the front of the car. When the seats were stacked on top of another, they formed a table and a lectern for the speaker to use. Avery and Goldstein admitted that the van was designed to call attention to itself and thus to draw a crowd.

Similarly, Aimee Semple McPherson's gospel car publicized its purpose by sporting several phrases in letters of gold, such as "Where will you spend eternity?"; "Judgment day is coming"; and "Get Right with God." "Sometimes when we leave the car on some errand, we find on returning that a crowd has gathered about the faithful car which is holding its own street meeting and preaching all by itself; and who can say with what results for eternity?" (McPherson, 127).

When radio and television broadcasting began, women revivalists quickly availed themselves of these venues as well. McPherson claimed to be the first woman ever to preach a sermon over the radio. On February 6, 1924, only eighteen months after the nation's first broadcast station began, she went on the air. Although nervous about her debut, she claimed to have talked "somehow as I had seldom talked before. The room with its electrical apparatus was forgotten, and all I could think of was the sailor boys, mothers' boys on the ships at sea, the sick in the homes where receivers had been installed, and I prayed and preached and prayed again and did most everything but take up the collection" (403). Several years later in 1924, a radio station was installed in her Angelus Temple. At 7:00 A.M., the station broadcast *The Sunshine Hour*, which McPherson performed live when she was in Los Angeles.

One of the most popular religious radio programs of the twentieth century, *Heart-to-Heart*, began in northwest Pennsylvania in 1948, hosted by Kathryn Kuhlman (1907–1976), an independent Pentecostal revivalist. Kuhlman's radio style was folksy and conversational, as is evident in her opening line, "Hello there, and have you been waiting for me?" The demand for her program was so persistent that the Kathryn Kuhlman Foundation continued to rebroadcast taped radio programs for six years after her death. Kuhlman also branched out into television broadcasting. She hosted a television series in the 1970s titled *I Believe in Miracles*, a half-hour program that featured a short meditation by Kuhlman as well as an interview conducted by her of a person who had been healed at one of her services.

In addition to the women who preached, women also participated in revivals often behind the scenes. Women promoted and prolonged revivals through their influence within the family. Particularly in an age such as the nineteenth century, when women were custodians of religion in the domestic sphere, women oftentimes held sway over children, husbands, and other relatives. The compelling force of this influence is nowhere more apparent than in the conversion of Theodore Dwight Weld, the well-known abolitionist. Weld's aunt

> resorted to a pious deception to entice her young kinsman to a revival meeting at the Utica Presbyterian Church. She convinced him to attend a morning service on the pretense that Finney would not be preaching until later in the day. Once in the church and in the presence of the despised preacher, the young man realized that he had been caught in a female trap. . . . When he attempted a second escape, the pious but wily aunt whispered in his ear, "You'll break my heart if you go!" (Ryan, 95–96)

Along with preaching, women participated in revivalism in other ways. Exhorters had the recognized role of encouraging sinners to repent with fervent pleas and words of encouragement. As early as the 1740s, women exhorters were speaking in public in the churches following the (male) minister's sermon; as such, they were among the first women in North America to speak in public. One woman, Bathsheba Kingsley, boldly moved beyond the church building and frequently helped herself to her husband's or a neighbor's horse and rode to nearby towns in order to exhort further afield. She justified her action on the grounds that God who, through "immediate revelations from heaven" (Brekus, 23), had called her to this work. In 1741 and again in 1743, Kingsley's enthusiastic behavior was examined by a tribunal of ministers that included Jonathan Edwards. Although she was not excommunicated, she was compelled to cease her itinerant exhorting.

Many revivalists, such as Harriet Livermore, Sojourner Truth, Amanda Berry Smith, and Ida B. Robinson, sang as well as preached. Livermore

> sang plaintive songs about sinners praying for mercy, she moved her audiences to tears, and when she encouraged them to join her in such

rousing folk tunes as "Shout Old Satan's Kingdom Down," she made them jump to their feet in excitement. Since no revival meeting was complete without a round of exuberant singing, Livermore used hymns as well as sermons to kindle the fires of revival. (Brekus, 199–200)

Women also composed hymns that were used in revivalism. The most renowned female composer of gospel hymns was Fanny Crosby (1820–1915). Although she became blind from a doctor's misuse of poultices when only a few weeks old, Crosby was a teacher, poet, composer, speaker at Young Men's Christian Association (YMCA) meetings, and a tireless worker in New York City's missions. She composed more than 8,000 gospel hymns, including "Rescue the Perishing," "Pass me not, O gentle Savior," and "Jesus, keep me near the Cross," which were favorites of revivalist Dwight L. Moody and his song leader Ira Sankey.

In her own words, Crosby traced her love for writing hymns to her affinity for poetic expression.

> Very early in life I began to write bits of verse. From my eighth year I can remember little poetic pictures forming themselves in my mind. When I gathered flowers and caught their fragrance I wanted to say something poetic about them. . . . As I wandered down by the brook with my grandmother, listening to the rippling of the waters, I felt something in my soul that I wanted to say about the rivulet and the river.

When she wrote down these poetic verses, she testified, "Such songs have power to quiet/The restless pulse of care,/And come like the benediction/That follows after prayer" (Jackson, 61–62).

Toiling alongside preachers, exhorters, and singers were altar workers whose task was to bring awakened sinners through to professed conversion. For many converts, it was at the altar that conversion happened. Aimee Semple McPherson's own career in revivalism began in this way. Looking back after years of revivalistic work, McPherson would still recall the rigor required in her first experience as an altar worker.

> Never have I worked harder at the altar services in our own meetings than at that camp meeting. We stayed as late as twelve and sometimes two in the morning, praying for seekers and were up again to early morning meeting. He [God] was restoring my soul, He was leading me out to green pastures. I had come to this camp meeting to see God, and Oh, how He did reveal himself to me!" (McPherson, 83)

An integral component of revivalism preceding, sustaining, and following a revival meeting was female prayer meetings. Before a revival, women prayed together for an awakened interest in religion in their community. During the meeting, women's prayer groups convened regularly to pray for its success and to encourage newly awakened persons in the way of salvation. Afterward, women met to pray together for a continuation of the impact from the meeting.

One of the most significant prayer meetings that women initiated and presided over was the Tuesday Meeting for the Promotion of Holiness, a weekly gathering for prayer that undergirded the Holiness revival of the nineteenth century. This New York City meeting, organized by Sarah Lankford, began as a women's prayer meeting in 1835. Several years later, Lankford's sister, Phoebe Palmer, took over the leadership, and the Tuesday meeting began to attract influential clergymen and laymen as well as women. By mid-century, the Tuesday meeting provided a pattern for home prayer meetings throughout the country.

Women's prayer meetings were at the heart of the so-called Laymen's Revival of 1857–1858 that swept across the United States. The designation of this revival as a laymen's revival is unfortunate since women gathered for prayer meetings with the same numbers and fervor as did men. Elizabeth Finney, the second wife of revivalist Charles G. Finney, began women's prayer meetings in Boston in December 1857, three months prior to the start of businessmen's prayer meetings there. According to Charles Finney, the Boston revival was

characterized far above all precedent by the individual activity and labour of the female members of the churches. If the business men have had their daily meetings, so have the women; if the men have visited and conversed with individuals, so have the women. . . . In Boston, I have seen the vestries crowded to suffocation with ladies' prayers meetings. (Long, 70)

Like their male counterparts, women revivalists espoused a traditional message of repentance as the antidote to original sin and new birth in Jesus Christ as the answer to the devil's wiles. The revival message built to a climax at which point sinners were pressed to repent of their sins and be born again. While this core message of salvation in Jesus Christ did not waver from male to female revivalists, women revivalists also preached against the prejudice toward women speaking in public. At least once in the course of a revival meeting that extended beyond a few days, they would preach a sermon in defense of women preaching.

The biblical defense in these sermons was populated by prominent women of the Bible: Deborah, Miriam, Huldah, Anna, Esther, the four prophesying daughters of Philip the evangelist, Mary who first proclaimed the risen Lord, Phoebe, Priscilla, the women in Acts 1 who prayed alongside the disciples, and the Samaritan woman in John 4 who testified about Jesus to her people were cited. The defense also appealed to specific scriptures that supported women's preaching, including Galatians 3:28 (". . . there is neither male nor female") and Philippians 4:3 ("Help those women which labored with me in the gospel"), though by far the dominant text in this regard was Peter's sermon at Pentecost in Acts 2:16: "This is what was spoken through the prophet Joel: 'In the last days it will be, God declares, that I will pour out my Spirit upon all flesh, and your sons and your daughters shall prophesy.' " These words required no sophisticated interpretation. Its meaning was obvious to women revivalists.

Women revivalists also dared to tread among those biblical texts that would seem to have undercut their activities, particularly 1 Timothy 2:12 ("I permit no woman to teach or to have authority over a man; she is to keep silent") and 1 Corinthians 14:34 ("Let your women keep silence in the churches"). They tended to understand the injunction of 1 Timothy 2 as applicable to family relationships rather than church ordinances since Paul was addressing everyday affairs of life in the larger context of the passage. Their interpretation maintained that while man is head of the woman in the home, he is not in the church.

On the conundrum of 1 Corinthians 14, they argued, first, that those who opposed their preaching were selectively applying the injunction to be silent to the act of preaching but not to praying and singing. If praying and singing broke silence, why not preaching? Their opponents, in other words, should either ban all female vocalization or permit all. Second, they contended that Paul's command was not to be universalized. Paul was addressing the Corinthian church that was in a specific, unique state of confusion in which everyone was offering simultaneously a psalm, an interpretation, or a prophecy. Such an injunction, addressed to a concrete situation in the early church, did not apply to the revivalism preaching of later generations. With these interpretations of biblical texts, women strove to persuade their hearers of the right, indeed the biblical mandate, of women to preach in public.

After a series of successful revival meetings in an area, some gathered their converts into churches. Among the most successful church planters was Maria Woodworth-Etter who established many churches in the Midwest for the denomination—Church of God (Winebrenner)—in the 1880s and 1890s, until her conflicted relationship with that denomination forced her to relinquish her ordination. She then founded several nondenominational Pentecostal churches, including one in Indianapolis that she served until her death.

Some women revivalists went further by gathering the churches they had established into new denominations in order to resolve the conflict that their gender or their success created with their denominational colleagues. For example, criticism from Colorado Methodists over her Holiness preaching prompted Alma White to establish a new denomination in 1901. In 1918, she was consecrated as the first bishop in her denomination, the Pillar of Fire. Ida B. Robinson (1891–1946) was a pastor in Philadelphia with the United Holy Church of America. In the mid-1920s, she felt called by the Holy Spirit to come out and begin a new denomination in order to provide more leadership opportunities for women. She testified that God said to her, "Come out on Mount Sinai" and "I will use you to loose the women." Robinson founded the Mount Sinai Holy Church of America in 1924, and at its inception, all of the denomination's officers were women. Due to Robinson's successful revivalistic work, the new denomination soon claimed churches in many states along the East Coast.

Women revivalists also established schools to solidify the faith and biblical knowledge of the new converts and to train them in various skills that accompanied revivalism work. Aimee Semple McPherson founded a school in Los Angeles, Lighthouse of International Foursquare Evangelism (LIFE), that offered courses in "fishing [a reference to evangelism taken from Jesus' words to the disciples—'I will make you fishers of men'], altar work, singing, music, street meetings, hospital visitation, prison work and preaching" (Blumhofer, 254–255).

The concomitant concern to preserve the younger generation from too much worldly influence prompted Alma White to concentrate on building schools rather than church buildings. Under her leadership, the Pillar of Fire denomination founded close to two dozen schools from New Jersey to California. Ida B. Robinson's denomination, the Mount Sinai Holy Church of America, founded a school in Philadelphia in order to teach a variety of essential subjects, including the fundamentals of the denomination's faith and order.

While women revivalists could lay claim to conversions numbering in the tens of thousands, increasing church attendance and filling the classrooms of their schools, they could also point to protégées, a subsequent generation of women revivalists whom they had served as midwives. Harriet Livermore considered as her spiritual daughter Sarah Righter Major (1808–1884), the first woman preacher for the Church of the Brethren, since Major was converted and encouraged to preach through Livermore's ministry. Although Aimee Semple McPherson was not converted by Maria Woodworth-Etter, McPherson respected the elder revivalist as a mentor and joyfully anticipated their meeting. "For years I have been longing to meet Sister Etter, and have been talking about it more in recent months. I have longed to hear her preach and be at her meetings. Tomorrow Mrs. Etter's tabernacle will be open and I will have the desire of my heart. Glory!" (McPherson, 145). In turn, Uldine Utley (1912–1995), a child evangelist in the 1920s, was converted through the preaching of McPherson and immediately launched her own revivalistic work.

Women in each generation have entered the arena of revivalism despite resistance from family as well as foes. Their courage and fortitude have enabled them to make the most of every conceivable venue from church sanctuaries and camp meetings to tents and television. They have participated through sermon and song, prayer and persuasion. Despite all this, they have disappeared, for the most part, into relative obscurity, while the lives and ministries of their male counterparts have been preserved for posterity in textbooks, monographs, and devotional materials. Nevertheless, these women celebrate that their reward comes from their faithfulness to their call. In the words of Annie May Fisher, a revivalist in the Church of the Nazarene who was converted under the ministry of Mary Lee Cagle:

I have craved no greater joy than to be permitted to stand at last before the throne of God among the most of my precious sisters who have told the sorrowing of our risen Lord and there lay our trophies at His feet and hear Him commend us for being faithful to our call. (Fisher, "Woman's Right to Preach," 32, self-published)

SOURCES: Cited autobiographies of women revivalists include Amanda Smith, *An Autobiography: The Story of the Lord's Dealings with Mrs. Amanda Smith, the Colored Evangelist* (1921); Mary Lee Cagle, *Life and Work of Mary Lee Cagle: An Autobiography* (1928); Maria B. Woodworth, *The Life and Experience of Maria B. Woodworth* (1885); Alma White's *Truth Is Stranger Than Fiction* (1913); and Aimee Semple McPherson's *This Is That* (1919). Cited secondary sources include Calvin Colton, *History and Character of American Revivals of Religion* (1832); Carey McWilliams, "Sunlight in My Soul," in *The Aspirin Age*, ed. Isabel Leighton (1949); Lyle Dorsett, *Billy Sunday and the Redemption of Urban America* (1991); Catherine Brekus, *Strangers & Pilgrims: Female Preaching in America, 1740–1845* (1998); Samuel Livermore, *Harriet Livermore, the Pilgrim Stranger* (1884); John L. Smith, *Indiana Methodism, a Series of Sketches and Incidents* (1892); Mary Ryan, *Cradle of the Middle Class: The Family in Oneida County, New York, 1790–1865* (1981); S. Trevena Jackson, *Fanny Crosby's Story of Ninety-four Years* (1915); Kathryn Teresa Long, *The Revival of*

1857–58: Interpreting an American Religious Awakening (1998); and Edith Blumhofer, *Aimee Semple McPherson: Everybody's Sister* (1993). Additional important works include Martha Blauvelt, "Women and Revivalism," in *Women and Religion in America*, vol. 1, *The Nineteenth Century: A Documentary History*, ed. Rosemary Radford Ruether and Rosemary Skinner Keller (1981), 1–45; Nancy Hardesty, *Your Daughters Shall Prophesy: Revivalism and Feminism in the Age of Finney* (1991); Jeannette Hassey, *No Time for Silence: Evangelical Women in Public Ministry around the Turn of the Century* (1986); and Leonard Sweet, *The Minister's Wife: Her Role in Nineteenth-Century American Evangelicalism* (1983).

HOLINESS MOVEMENTS
Nancy A. Hardesty

HOLINESS REFERS TO the Christian doctrine and experience of "sanctification" (becoming holy or righteous), attaining "Christian perfection," or "perfect love." It also came to be referred to as "baptism with the Holy Spirit."

The notion is based primarily on Jesus' injunction in Matthew 5:48 (New Revised Standard Version [NRSV])—"Be perfect, therefore, as your heavenly Father is perfect"—and Leviticus 19:2—"You shall be holy, for I the LORD your God am holy." The slogan for many participants was "HOLINESS UNTO THE LORD," found in numerous places in Hebrew Scriptures (see Exodus 28:36, 39:30; Zechariah 14:20). In the King James Version of the Bible, the phrase is usually printed in capital letters.

Women played a variety of critical roles in two distinct North American strands: Wesleyan and Keswick Holiness. Women defined these American theologies, preached, and taught them. Holiness compelled women to testify to their experience and gave them the inner strength to do so. Subsequent generations of Holiness women preached this doctrine and founded denominations. Many taught a doctrine of healing and founded healing homes. Many were empowered to work in a variety of social reforms. Subsequent to the Azusa Street Revival in Los Angeles, California, which began in the spring of 1906, many Holiness women and men spoke in tongues and moved into Pentecostalism.

Wesleyan Holiness

The American Wesleyan Holiness movement was defined and fostered by the two Worrall sisters of New York City: Sarah Lankford (Palmer) (1806–1896) and Phoebe Palmer (1807–1874). Their father Henry was an English Methodist, their mother Dorothea Wade an American. Both sisters experienced Christian conversion at early ages. Sarah married an architect, and Phoebe a physician, Walter C. Palmer (1804–1896). Both sisters sought the experience of sanctification. Sarah found it first on May 21, 1835. She had been attending two prayer meetings (at Allen Street and Mulberry Street Methodist churches), so she invited both to meet together at the home the Lankfords shared with the Palmers. It became the famed "Tuesday Meeting for the Promotion of Holiness," which survived for more than sixty years and spawned similar meetings around the world. Phoebe experienced sanctification on July 26, 1837. Until 1839 the Tuesday Meeting was for women only, but that December Phoebe L. Upham wanted to bring her husband along: Thomas Upham, Congregational clergyman and professor at Bowdoin College. From then on men and women, lay and clergy, from across the United States and around the world visited the Tuesday Meeting.

John Wesley (1703–1791), the founder of the Methodist Church, had published *A Plain Account of Christian Perfection* (1766, 1777). While Martin Luther (1483–1546) had emphasized "justification by faith," he declared that one is always *simul justus et peccator*, simultaneously justified and yet sinful. One is never perfect. Wesley, however, had studied the theology of the Eastern or Orthodox church, which teaches that human beings certainly do sin and require God's forgiveness but still retain the possibility of perfection, or divinization (*theosis*). Wesley preferred to speak of the goal as "perfect love," being able to "love the Lord your God with all your heart, and with all your soul, and with all your mind ... [and] your neighbor as your self" (Matthew 22:37, 39; see Leviticus 19:18; Deuteronomy 6:5). For most people, Wesley thought this would be a lifelong process. However, some of Wesley's colleagues claimed to have attained such a state, and he eventually conceded that they possibly had.

The notion of holiness was first transmitted to American women through such works as the *Life of Hester Ann Rogers* (1756–1794), and *The Life of Mrs. [Mary Bosanquet] Fletcher* (1739–1815), as well as stories about the lives of women preachers and workers who followed Wesley, for example, Grace Murray (1715–1800) and Sarah Mallett (Boyce) (1765–after 1843) (see Stevens).

As Phoebe Palmer reflected on her experience and Methodist teaching in these classics, she formulated her own theology, published in *The Way of Holiness* (1843), *Entire Devotion to God: A Present to My Christian Friend* (1845), and *Faith and Its Effects* (1848). She also edited *The Guide to Holiness* from 1866 until her death. Her husband and sister continued to publish it until their deaths. Wesley had taught that sanctification was generally a long process, but then Christians of his period also saw salvation as something to be sought over time, something to wait for. American revivalist Charles Fin-

ney (1792–1874) declared, "Religion is something to *do*, not something to *wait for*" (Finney, 207). He urged people to make a decision *now*. So when a Presbyterian asked Phoebe Palmer, "Whether there is not a *shorter way?*" to attain Holiness, she decided there was.

Palmer taught that one had only to "lay one's all upon the altar." Then since Christ is the altar and "the altar sanctifies the gift" (see Exodus 29:37; Matthew 23: 19; Romans 12:1–2), one can simply trust the word of God that one is holy. Wesley taught that one would receive assurance from the Holy Spirit, but Palmer said one need not look for any particular feeling or emotion. Since according to Palmer's reading, God had promised Holiness in scripture, it would be done.

"Dr. and Mrs. Phoebe Palmer," as they were often called, spread this message through evangelistic meetings in the United States and Canada. During the Civil War, they spent four years in the "Old World" (1859–1863)—preaching in the British Isles—which resulted in their 1870 book *Four Years in the Old World*. When a religious paper in England criticized Mrs. Palmer for speaking in public, her rights were defended by a local Methodist minister's wife, Catherine Mumford Booth (1829–1890) in a pamphlet titled *Female Ministry*. Catherine and her husband William eventually left the Methodists and founded a Holiness denomination, the Salvation Army.

In 1866 the Palmers spoke at First Methodist Church, Evanston, Illinois. One of those who sought and found Holiness was Frances Willard (1839–1898). That year she was raising money among women to build (Barbara) Heck Hall at Garrett Theological Seminary, in part by selling a special centennial edition of Abel Stevens's *The Women of Methodism*. Unfortunately Willard admitted later that she lost the experience because she did not comply with the final step in Palmer's shorter way: testifying publicly to the experience (Garrison, 73, 75).

Colleagues of the Palmers in New York City included Martha Jane Foster (1819–1890) and John Inskip (1816–1884), also ardent advocates of Holiness. The Methodists already held a series of camp meetings along the eastern seaboard. At the urging of Mrs. Harriet Drake, who volunteered to pay half the expenses for a Holiness camp meeting, Inskip and a group of pastors formed the National Camp Meeting Association for the Promotion of Holiness in 1866. The first national camp meeting was July 17–26, 1867, in Vineland, New Jersey. Meetings were held from Old Orchard Beach, Maine, to Augusta, Georgia, to Round Lake, Illinois. In 1880 Mrs. Osie M. Fitzgerald (b. 1813) founded the Women's Union National Holiness Camp Meeting and rented Mount Tabor campgrounds in New Jersey, where women's camp meetings continued for years.

One of the featured singers and speakers was Amanda Berry Smith (1837–1915). Born in slavery, she found Holiness one Sunday in Pastor John Inskip's Methodist church. At the same time God freed her from her fear of whites. But, as she says in her *Autobiography* (1893), "some people don't get enough of the blessing to take prejudice out of them, even after they are sanctified" (226).

Keswick Holiness

Although the term *Keswick* comes from a meeting site in England, American Quaker Hannah Whitall Smith (1832–1911) was instrumental in defining this form of Holiness, which is also sometimes referred to as Reformed Holiness or "the higher Christian life." Smith and her husband Robert Pearsall Smith (1827–1899) were Philadelphia birthright Quakers. As a young mother in New Jersey, where Robert was managing one of her family's glassworks, Hannah became involved in a Methodist prayer group, and there in 1867 she found Holiness. Robert already had experienced it at a Methodist camp meeting. He began to publish a Holiness paper. To assist the effort, she wrote a series of articles that eventually became *A Christian's Secret to a Happy Life* (1875, enlarged in 1889), a Holiness classic still readily available today not only in bookstores but on religious book racks in pharmacies and convenience stores (at least in the South).

They teamed up with Mary Morse Adams (1818–1904) and William Boardman (1810–1886), Congregational minister and author of *The Higher Christian Life* (1839). In 1873 Robert accompanied the Boardmans to England for the Broadlands Convention. In 1874 Hannah went along to attend the Oxford Union Meeting for the Promotion of Scriptural Holiness. The men were allowed to preach in evening services, while the women more often gave very popular afternoon "Bible readings," in which they would read through a text, pausing between phrases to explain and illustrate.

The Smiths were supposed to be the featured speakers at the first Keswick Convention in 1875, but when Robert was accused of an indiscretion, they returned to the States. Robert never recovered his faith or his public ministry, but Hannah's spirituality deepened. After the tragic death of their eldest son, she moved the family permanently to England. Their eldest daughter Alys married philosopher Bertrand Russell. Daughter Mary left the father of her two daughters to live in Italy with famed art critic Bernard Berenson. Son Logan Pearsall Smith became an arbiter of the English language and dedicated books to his longtime male companion. Hannah ended up rearing her granddaughters Rachel or "Ray," who married into the Strachey family and was active in the British suffrage movement, and Margaret, student of Anna Freud and one of England's first psychoanalysts.

Wesleyan Holiness initially stressed purity and cleansing from sin. Phoebe Palmer wrote a hymn titled "The Cleansing Wave":

Oh, now I see the cleansing wave.
  The fountain deep and wide;
Jesus, my Lord, mighty to save,
  Points to His wounded side.

Chorus:

The cleansing stream, I see, I see,
  I plunge and oh, it cleanseth me.
Oh, praise the Lord! It cleanseth me,
  It cleanseth me—yes, cleanseth me.

The music was written by daughter Phoebe Palmer Knapp (1839–1908), more famous for collaborating with Fanny Crosby on "Blessed Assurance." Hannah Whitall Smith and Mary Boardman tended to speak of "entire

consecration" and to expect an "enduement with power" that would enable one to live a holy life.

The First American Keswick conference was held in 1913 in Princeton, then moved to Keswick, New Jersey, where it remains to this day. Keswick piety was more readily accepted by fundamentalist Christian groups that emerged after 1920, especially those from Baptist and Presbyterian contexts. Wesleyan Holiness had some very direct influences on the Pentecostal movement that emerged in the Azusa Street Revival in Los Angeles in 1906.

Holiness Empowered Women

On numerous occasions Phoebe Palmer proclaimed, "HOLINESS is POWER!" Theologian Susie Stanley in *Holy Boldness: Women Preachers' Autobiographies and the Sanctified Self* argues that the experience of Holiness enabled many women to transcend the limiting social constructs of their day. They drew strength from the examples of French mystic Madame Guyon and Wesleyan foremothers Rogers and Bosanquet. The spiritual experience itself gave their lives new meaning. The mandate to testify to their experience motivated them to speak out despite the social strictures of their day. Stanley analyzes thirty-four American Holiness women who wrote autobiographies to record and advance their ministries as preachers, healers, and social reformers. Her list is far from exhaustive.

Preachers and Denominational Leaders

We have already spoken of Phoebe Palmer's impact on Catherine Booth and the formation of the Salvation Army. Within the Army, women have been able to attain all ranks of leadership, with spouses usually holding the same rank. In 1887 son Ballington Booth (1857–1940) and his wife Maud Charlesworth Booth (1865–1948) were sent to lead the Army in the United States. In 1896 the couple resigned to form the Volunteers of America, which they structured more democratically. So Emma Moss Booth-Tucker (1860–1903) and her husband Frederick St. George Booth-Tucker (1853–1929) took over as commanders of the American Salvation Army until 1904. Daughter Evangeline Booth (1865–1950) served as commander of the Canadian Salvation Army from 1896 to 1904, as U.S. commander from 1904 to 1935, and finally as international general from 1934 to 1939.

Holiness teaching spread across the South largely through the preaching of ministers of the Methodist Episcopal Church, South, and the Wesleyan Methodist Church. However, in northern Alabama and southern Tennessee, Holiness was preached by Mary Lee Wasson Harris Cagle (1864–1955) and her circle of friends. Mary

Lee Wasson was converted in an Alabama Methodist revival at age fifteen. At twenty she met Holiness revivalist Robert Lee Harris (1861–1894), and in 1891 they married. Having had a call to ministry early in life, she thought being a minister's wife would suffice. Together they formed the New Testament Church of Christ. When her husband died, she realized that God was calling her to keep the fledgling movement afloat. On December 14, 1899, she was ordained in the group's home church at Milan, Tennessee. Also ordained was Elliot J. Doboe Sheeks (1872–1946), a native of Kentucky, raised in the Cumberland Presbyterian Church. Sanctified in a Holiness revival, she married businessman Edwin H. Sheeks and became a Methodist. When she felt the call to preach, her supportive husband bought her a tent in which to hold revivals. Eventually their base was a church in Memphis. Donie Mitchum generally pastored the Milan church, while Cagle and Sheeks toured as evangelists and church planters. She too was married to a supportive businessman. Mary Lee expanded the church to Texas, where she met Henry Clay Cagle (b. 1874), a native of Newnan, Georgia. Both saved and sanctified in her meetings, he married her on August 8, 1900. Their marriage lasted fifty years. Together they pastored a number of churches. Eventually the Cagles rejected Pentecostalism and merged the New Testament Church of Christ with the Church of the Nazarene. In 1905 Fannie McDowell Hunter (c. 1860–?) published *Women Preachers*, containing the stories of seven women in the New Testament Church of Christ: Cagle, Sheeks, Mitchum, Annie May Fisher, Lillian Polle, Fannie Suddarth, and herself, as well as that of Johnny Hill Jernigan, later ordained by the Pilgrim Holiness Church.

Rebecca Laird included Cagle in her *Ordained Women in the Church of the Nazarene: The First Generation* (1993). Another southern woman who became an elder in the Church of the Nazarene was Frances Rye McClurken (1865–1966), whose husband J. O. McClurken formed the Pentecostal Mission, a loose association of Holiness groups in middle Tennessee. Originally Cumberland Presbyterians, the McClurkens, married in 1882, found Holiness while ministering in California. They returned to Tennessee to preach Holiness. Frances and many in the Pentecostal Mission favored merging with the Nazarenes, but McClurken himself, while encouraging his wife to preach, opposed the Nazarenes' commitment to women's ministry, so the merger was not consummated until after his death in 1914. Frances settled in Nashville, where she played an active part in the work of Trevecca Nazarene College, originally founded by the McClurkens as a Bible school to train missionaries (Laird, 122–130).

The Church of the Nazarene originated with the southern California work of Phineas Bresee (1838–?),

originally an upstate New York Methodist who pastored the First Methodist Church of Los Angeles until his Holiness views caused controversy. One of the early Nazarene leaders was Lucy Pierce Knott (1856–1940), a native of Kentucky. She was licensed to preach in 1899 and ordained by Bresee in 1903 at the Mateo Street Mission (later the Compton Avenue Church). Later she and her son J. Proctor Knott shared pastoral leadership at the Hollywood church of the Nazarene (Laird, 43–50).

The Holiness movement gave birth to a variety of new churches and denominations. While resistance to slavery was primarily responsible for the founding of the Free Methodist Church in 1844 and the Wesleyan Methodist Church in 1860, both emphasized Holiness. Wesleyan leader B. T. Roberts argued fervently for *Ordaining Women* (1891).

When Daniel S. Warner (1842–1925) founded the Church of God Reformation (Anderson, Indiana) in 1880, women white and black were active as preachers. For example, Iowan Mary Cole (1853–after 1914) was converted in 1871 and sanctified shortly thereafter. In 1875 she felt called to preach but resisted for seven years. While suffering as "a hopeless invalid," she read the Holiness works of Wesley, the Fletchers, Rogers, and Palmer. After being healed, she joined her brother Jeremiah in holding evangelistic meetings. Fearless in the face of a mob, some said she was Jessie James in drag. Twice she was egged while preaching, once with frozen eggs! She titled her 1914 autobiography *Trials and Triumphs of Faith*. The Church of God (Anderson) tradition continues today with such women ministers as Susie Stanley, author of *Holy Boldness* (2002), and Cheryl Sanders, *Saints in Exile* (1996). The small Pillar of Fire denomination was founded by Alma White (1862–1945), who declared herself the first woman bishop. Susie Stanley chronicled her life in *Feminist Pillar of Fire: The Life of Alma White* (1993).

Divine Healing

Initially the Wesleyan Holiness movement remained within the Methodist Episcopal Church. Leaders of the National Camp Meeting Association, and its corollary, the National Holiness Association, were generally male clergy, loyal to their respective denominations. In the 1880s Holiness became very popular in the Methodist Episcopal Church, South. Increasingly, however, those ministers and laypeople who advocated Holiness found themselves in tension with their churches. Some Holiness people did say uncharitable things about others: referring to certain Christians as "dead" and their churches as "iceboxes." Denominational leaders responded by calling Holiness proponents fanatics and troublemakers. Some who preached Holiness were disciplined by demotion to poorer and less-desirable churches. Others were forced out of their churches entirely. In 1894 the Methodist Episcopal Church, South, declared that Holiness "evangelists" could not enter a territory without express permission from the local pastor and the bishop.

Some Holiness people began to preach three ideas that the established denominations found disturbing: restoration of the New Testament church, divine healing, and the premillennial second coming of Jesus. Most Protestants in the nineteenth century were postmillennialists, feeling that it was the duty of Christians to achieve a just and peaceful earth for Christ to come and reign over. This fueled such reform movements as abolition, woman's rights, and temperance. Holiness people (and later Pentecostals and Fundamentalists) adopted dispensational premillennialism, including the any-moment Rapture, a theological system invented by John Nelson Darby (1800–1882), founder in England of the Plymouth Brethren. Darby made seven trips to the United States to publicize his views, which were welcomed by evangelist D. L. Moody and codified for many in the notes of the Scofield Reference Bible (1909). The National Camp Meeting Association eventually prohibited speakers from mentioning either healing or premillennialism, considering both far too divisive.

While many Christians have practiced different forms of divine healing, many of those who advocated it in the late nineteenth century professed one or another form of Holiness. Advocates were sure that "Jesus Christ is the same, yesterday and today and forever" (Hebrews 13:8). Jesus worked miracles of healing, the disciples worked miracles of healing, healings have occurred down through the centuries in the church, and therefore Christians today should expect miracles of healing. James 5:14–16 gives the instructions: "Are any among you sick? They should call for the elders of the church and have them pray over them, anointing them with oil in the name of the Lord. The prayer of faith shall save the sick, and the Lord will raise them up." They also selectively noted the declaration in Mark 16:18c: "[T]hey will lay their hands on the sick and they will recover."

The movement seems to have begun in the Northeast with Methodist layman Ethan Otis Allen (1813–1902), grandson of the Revolutionary War hero. Healed of consumption, or tuberculosis, through the prayers of his Methodist class leader in 1846, he began to pray for the healing of others. Newspaper stories in 1877 led Sarah Freeman Mix (1832–1884), an African American woman (sometimes mistakenly referred to as Elizabeth Mix) in Wolcottville (now Torrington), Connecticut, to summon Allen to pray for her neighbor. In the course of the evening, he turned to Mrs. Mix and suggested that she needed healing prayer as well. She was instantly

healed of tuberculosis. The disease was epidemic in the late 1800s; black communities were particularly hard hit. Sarah and Edward Mix had lost seven children and numerous relatives to lung problems. Allen also sensed that Sarah had the gift of healing and encouraged her ministry. She began to pray for her family, friends, relatives, and as her fame spread, strangers. Together the Mixes published a paper titled *Victory through Faith*. Mrs. Mix collected *Faith Cures and Answers to Prayer Healing by Faith* (1882), and after her death in 1884, Edward Mix published *The Life of Mrs. Edward Mix, Written by Herself in 1880* (see the 2002 reprint edition of both with introduction by Rosemary Gooden).

Mrs. Mix's memory has been preserved mostly through the writings of her most famous patient, Carrie Judd (1858–1946) of Buffalo, New York. An Episcopalian, Judd had fallen on an icy stone sidewalk in 1877 and injured her back. The chronic pain rendered her a total invalid. One day a family member saw a story about Mrs. Edward Mix in the newspaper. Carrie asked her sister to write. Mrs. Mix replied, assuring Judd that she would be the object of prayer in the Mix home the next Wednesday afternoon, February 26, 1879. She instructed Judd to cease taking any medicines and to gather those who could support her in prayer at the given time. Mix told Judd to "*act faith* . . . get right out of bed and begin to walk by faith" (Judd, 18). With family and friends praying downstairs, and alone with just her nurse, Judd prayed and then sat up in bed, stood up, and walked to a chair. From that time on she was healed.

Judd first told her story in *The Prayer of Faith* (1880), accompanied by a letter of verification from her pastor and by a short biblical and theological defense of divine healing. She soon began publishing a periodical, *Triumphs of Faith*, and opened Faith Rest Cottage in Buffalo, where those seeking healing could come to rest, learn more about the teaching, and be prayed with and for by those of faith. When Judd married George Montgomery (1851–1930) in 1890, she moved to Oakland, California, where she founded another healing home. When healing advocate A. B. Simpson (1843–1919) formed the Christian and Missionary Alliance (C&MA) denomination in 1898, Judd Montgomery was a national officer. After Carrie and George Montgomery became involved in Pentecostalism, Carrie continued to work within the Alliance, even though Simpson kept the C&MA within the Holiness orbit.

First to publicize the notion of divine healing widely was Charles Cullis (1833–1892), an Episcopal physician in Boston, who had been sanctified at Phoebe Palmer's Tuesday Meeting in 1862. Frustrated in his practice, he began in 1864 by opening a home for "Indigent and Incurable Consumptives," a form of hospice. After studying scripture references to healing, Cullis in January 1870 asked Lucy Drake (Osborn) (1844–?), whom he had diagnosed as having a fatal brain tumor, if he could anoint her and pray for her. Reluctantly but with little to lose, Drake agreed and was healed. She published her autobiography *Heavenly Pearls Set in a Life: A Record of Experiences and Labors in America, India and Australia* in 1893. Cullis became aware of European antecedents—particularly the work of Dorothea Trudel (1813–1862) in Mannedorf, Switzerland. He published Trudel's *Prayer of Faith* in 1872. Charles and Lucretia Cullis, along with William and Mary Boardman, visited a number of European advocates in 1873. Boardman published *Faith Work under Dr. Cullis* in 1874 and *The Great Physician* in 1881 (British title: *The Lord That Healeth Thee*).

Jennie Smith (1842–?), the "Railroad Evangelist," was healed on April 23, 1878. She suffered from an agonizing leg ailment that required that she keep her leg encased in a heavy wooden box. From her home in Ohio, she traveled to various Holiness conventions. Since she was required to lie on a cot, she traveled in the baggage car and thus had the opportunity to share her faith with the many railroad workers who assisted her. When she first heard divine healing discussed, she accepted the premise but felt it too presumptuous to ask for herself. Eventually after a partially successful surgery in Philadelphia, she felt led to gather a group of believers around her bed. One pastor tried to talk her out of it. About 9 P.M. he left. When the group returned to prayer, she was enabled to get up and walk around without assistance or pain. She continued to travel to Holiness meetings, though now in regular coaches. Both before and after her healing, she supported herself with a series of books including *Valley of Baca: A Record of Suffering and Triumph* (1878) and *From Baca to Beulah* (1880).

Holiness periodicals and some journals devoted more specifically to healing were filled with stories of healings, the vast majority of them by women. As with the experience of sanctification, so too in the case of healing, it was vital that one testify publicly to the experience. Most understood healing as "in the atonement," a part of Jesus Christ's atoning work. They quoted Matthew 8: 17 where the gospel writer uses Isaiah 53:4 to say that Jesus "took our infirmities, and bare our sicknesses." Even though she herself remained blind, hymn writer Fanny Crosby (1820–1915) built on Palmer's imagery to write this healing hymn:

There is healing in the fountain.
  Come, behold the crimson tide,
Flowing down from Calvary's mountain,
  Where the Prince of Glory died.

Chorus:

Oh, the fountain! Blessed healing fountain!
  I am glad 'tis flowing free.
Oh, the fountain! Precious, cleansing fountain!
  Praise the Lord, it cleanseth me.

Women often opened "faith homes," meaning that they relied on God by faith to meet the institution's financial needs. Most of these women had themselves been dramatically healed. Knowing the struggles firsthand, they invited the sick to come to their home, to learn the biblical and theological bases for divine healing, to be encouraged and supported by prayer, to find strength and courage to pray the prayer of faith for themselves, to be anointed with oil, and to have hands laid on them for healing. The experiences of Holiness and healing gave the women who presided over these homes faith and personal self-confidence to pray for the sick and to lay hands on them without assistance from male clergy.

Mrs. Sarah Mix invited people into her home. In 1882 the Boardmans, along with Mrs. Elizabeth Baxter (1837–1926), Charlotte Murray, and Elizabeth Sisson (1843–1934), a native of New London, Connecticut, opened Bethshan in London. Mary Shoemaker (c. 1846–1916), a friend of Allen's, ran Shiloh Faith Home in Springfield, Massachusetts, from 1893 until her death. Carrie Judd first opened Faith Rest Cottage in Buffalo. After her marriage to George Montgomery, she opened the Home of Peace in Oakland, California, in 1893. Mrs. Elizabeth V. Baker (c. 1849–1915) and her four sisters (Mary E. Work, Nellie A. Fell, Susan A. Duncan, and Harriet "Hattie" M. Duncan) opened Elim Faith Home in 1895 in Rochester, New York. Other women who operated healing homes included Dora Griffin Dudley of Grand Rapids, Michigan; Mary H. Mossman (c. 1826–after 1909) of Ocean Grove, New Jersey; and Sara M. C. Musgrove (1839–1933) of Troy, New York.

Many women evangelists included divine healing as a special emphasis in their meetings. One was South Carolinian Mattie E. Perry. Born in 1858, she began by assisting evangelists at camp meetings. Sometimes she traveled with her father or brother, both Methodist ministers. Eventually she traveled on her own, always stressing divine healing. Many testified to being healed in her meetings. Her autobiography, *Christ and Answered Prayer*, was published in 1939.

Another was evangelist Maria (she pronounced it "Ma-rye-a") Woodworth-Etter (1844–1924). Initially a preacher of salvation and sanctification, she eventually began to lay hands on people for healing within the context of her public meetings. She was also noted for going into hour-long trances in the midst of preaching.

She published three editions of her autobiography: *The Life, Work and Experiences of Maria Beulah Woodworth* (1894), *Signs and Wonders* (1916), and *Acts of the Holy Ghost, or the Life, Work and Experience of Mrs. M. B. Woodworth-Etter, Evangelist* (1922). When she settled down to pastor a local church in Indianapolis, she passed the mantle to Aimee Semple McPherson (1890–1944), who visited her in 1918.

Social Reforms

Holiness also empowered many women to engage in a variety of social reforms. Phoebe Palmer worked at the Five Points Mission, an outreach to the poor of New York City. She gave Antoinette Brown Blackwell (1825–1921) her initial tour of the facility and the neighborhood. In 1853 Brown became the first woman in the United States to be formally ordained as a minister. Mattie Perry worked with the poor in the mill villages of Spartanburg, South Carolina. Joanna Moore (1832–?) traveled extensively in the Mississippi Delta, trying to encourage and uplift recently freed slaves.

Many Holiness women were temperance advocates. Frances Willard became president of the Woman's Christian Temperance Union (WCTU) and the World's Woman's Christian Temperance Union. Hannah Whitall Smith was the WCTU's superintendent of evangelism before she moved to England, where she continued her involvement with the WCTU. It was she who introduced Willard to British WCTU president Lady Isabel Somerset. Both Willard and Smith worked diligently for woman's suffrage as well.

Holiness women were active in education. Elizabeth Baker and her sisters in Rochester, New York, founded not only the Elim healing home but also the Elim Bible training school. Mattie Perry founded Elhanan, an orphanage and school for needy children, in Marion, North Carolina.

Women of the Holiness movements opened homes with a variety of ministries in addition to healing. Many welcomed missionaries and other Christian workers who needed rest and refreshing. In 1866 in Belton, Texas, Mrs. Martha McWhirter had an experience in which she spoke in tongues and heard God speaking back to her, telling her to establish the "Woman's Commonwealth," a celibate community for women who wished to leave their abusive husbands. White Holiness missionary Joanna Moore opened a home for elderly black women in New Orleans.

Holiness women also reached out to the homeless and destitute. The women at Elim offered a dormitory for homeless and derelict men and served them free meals. Emma M. Whittemore established a home for former prostitutes, and Martha A. Lee ("Mother Lee") (b. 1842) reached out to shelter young women who became pregnant out of wedlock (in the late nineteenth century many were cast out of their families and drifted into prostitution to support themselves and their child).

The Twentieth Century

With the advent of Pentecostalism in 1906, many Holiness groups, especially in the South, became Pentecostal. Some Holiness denominations such as the Church of the Nazarene and the Church of God (Anderson, Indiana) continued to ordain women, but as these denominations reached out for wider cultural acceptance in the first half of the century, they often neglected and even discouraged women's ministry. With the advent of biblical feminism in the 1960s, however, they began to recover their historical memory of these early women leaders, and this gave rise to a new generation of ordained women. Susie Stanley has pulled many of them together in gatherings of an organization known as Wesleyan/Holiness Women Clergy.

Other Holiness denominations such as the Christian and Missionary Alliance, under the influence of fundamentalism, have flatly rejected women's ordination despite having had significant numbers of women pastors and evangelists in the early 1900s.

SOURCES: Helpful sources include Rosemary Gooden's lengthy introduction to *Faith Cures and Answers to Prayer Healing by Faith* (2002); Nancy A. Hardesty, *Women Called to Witness: Evangelical Feminism in the Nineteenth Century* (1984, 1999) *Faith Cure: Divine Healing in the Holiness and Pentecostal Movements,* (2003); Rebecca Laird, *Ordained Women in the Church of the Nazarene: The First Generation* (1993); Jean Miller Schmidt, *Grace Sufficient: A History of Women in American Methodism, 1760–1939* (1999); and Susie Cunningham Stanley, *Holy Boldness: Women Preachers' Autobiographies and the Sanctified Self* (2002) and *Feminist Pillar of Fire: The Life of Alma White* (1993). Additional sources: Abel Stevens, *The Women of Methodism* (1866); Charles Finney, *Lectures on Revivals of Religion* (1835); Stephen Olin Garrison, *Forty Witnesses* (1888); and Carrie Judd, *Prayer of Faith* (1880).

THE SANCTIFIED CHURCH(ES)
Cheryl Townsend Gilkes

WITHIN AFRICAN AMERICAN Protestantism, the term *Sanctified Church* distinguishes a family of denominations, networks of congregations, and congregations that have their roots in the Holiness, Pentecostal, and Apostolic church movements in the United States. Racial oppression and changes in its institutional arrangements over time provide important turning points in the historical outline of the African American experience in the United States. New religious formations, for instance, the beginning of the African Methodist Episcopal (AME) Church in 1787 and the founding of the Progressive National Baptist Convention in 1961, also mark dramatic historical turning points. Although religion is often analyzed and evaluated in terms of its responses to racial oppression, the religious history of African Americans is a history of social, cultural, and moral agency—a proactive dimension of communal life that not only muted and subverted the impact of racial oppression but also shaped major streams of religion and popular culture in the United States. An area of diverse expressions of women's religious leadership, the Sanctified Church is one such aspect of African American religious history.

The term *Sanctified Church* is indigenous to the African American religious experience. Although there is some history of conflict between the Sanctified Church and larger older Baptist and Methodist denominations,

the phrase "Sanctified Church" is not a pejorative term. Instead, it acknowledges continuities with the larger Afro-Protestant mainstream in prayer, preaching, testimony, and music traditions and in some doctrinal beliefs, such as believers' baptism by immersion.

Emerging during the late nineteenth and early twentieth centuries, these denominations all emphasize some aspect of sanctification and share ritual practices emphasizing the work of the Holy Ghost (or Holy Spirit) through such activities as "shouting," the "holy dance," speaking in tongues, healing, and other spiritual gifts. While both Holiness and Pentecostal denominations emphasize religious experiences with sanctification, Pentecostal denominations usually highlight speaking in tongues in statements of doctrine and discipline. Pentecostal denominations, some of which began as nineteenth-century Holiness churches, usually trace their origins to the Azusa Street Revival, which ran from

Some denominations were organized by women such as Bishop Ida Robinson, who founded the Mount Sinai Holy Church in 1924 in Philadelphia. The Church of God in Christ, a Pentecostal denomination which is the largest of the Sanctified Churches, does not routinely ordain women to be pastors, elders, or bishops, but women are central to the history, growth, and sustenance of the denomination as church founders and administrators. *Courtesy of Mt. Sinai Church, Philadelphia, Pennsylvania.*

1906 to 1913 in Los Angeles, California. The largest African American Pentecostal denomination, the Church of God in Christ, began in 1897 as a Holiness denomination.

Novelist and anthropologist Zora Neale Hurston (1895–1961) pointed to the Sanctified Church as a song-making movement and cultural protest that preserved aspects of African American worship considered primitive and unseemly by an emerging black middle class. Usually classified as sects and cults, because of the marginal appearance of their storefront churches in northern urban ghettos, the roots of these denominations and their annual convocations are usually in the South.

Sanctified Church congregations tend to be around 90 percent female. Regardless of specific denominational rules concerning the ordination of women, all these denominations are dependent on elaborate and prominent women's organizations to provide significant professional, lay, and clerical leadership in the churches, particularly in the area of education. Some denominations, while not officially ordaining women to the offices of elder, pastor, or bishop, can point to a significant history of women founding and having charge of congregations. Women "speakers" conduct revivals and church services in a manner indistinguishable from that of men "preachers." Some denominations (for instance, the Mount Calvary Holy Church, the Mount Sinai Holy Church of America, and the House of God Which Is the Church of the Living God, Pillar and Ground of the Truth, Inc.) ordain women. Some denominations were organized by women, such as Bishop Ida Robinson (1891–1946), who founded the Mount Sinai Holy Church in 1924 in Philadelphia. The Church of God in Christ, a Pentecostal denomination that is the largest of the Sanctified Churches, does not routinely ordain women to be pastors, elders, or bishops, but women are central to the history, growth, and sustenance of the denomination as church founders and administrators. As missionaries, evangelists, national evangelists, supervisors, and church mothers, the women of the Church of God in Christ not only maintain a national network of women's organizations under the aegis of a powerful Women's Convention, but these women also preach revivals, carry out assignments on behalf of bishops, educate clergy and laity, and pastor churches in the absence of male elders. Organization of a prominent, somewhat autonomous, powerful women's convention or department is a characteristic feature of these churches. Some observers of black Holiness and Pentecostal denominations have pointed to the roles of women as a prominent, if not defining, feature of these churches. Women from these churches, in their interactions across congregations and denominations, help to underscore the emphasis on the person of the Holy Ghost (Spirit) that is prominent among African Amer-ican Christians, regardless of their various denominational doctrines.

Holiness and Pentecostal churches were formed during the last half of the nineteenth and throughout the twentieth centuries within movements that for brief moments were uncharacteristically interracial. Consequently black people were a part of every single stream of the movements that gave rise to those churches, which in 1990 ranged in size from the largest, the Church of God in Christ, with at least 4.5 million members, to some smaller church networks with less than 10,000 members and less than fifteen churches.

Some black Holiness and Pentecostal churches started as interracial churches from which white members withdrew to establish segregated bodies: For example, white clergy in the Church of God in Christ eventually formed the Assemblies of God, and white members of the Pentecostal Assemblies of the World withdrew to form the Pentecostal Church Inc. The term *Sanctified Church* also encompassed black congregations within interracial but predominantly white Holiness and Pentecostal denominations, such as the Church of God (Cleveland, Tennessee) and Church of God (Anderson, Indiana), where African Americans fellowshipped fully with their white brothers and sisters and where they also maintained specialized fellowships and camp meetings for African Americans.

The Sanctified Church is an extended family of black churches that shaped two significant movements in American Protestantism, the Holiness and Pentecostal movements. Although these movements, especially Pentecostalism, are described largely in terms of white institutional histories and male leaders, the Holiness and Pentecostal movements are among the most significant religious settings for women's religious history. Both movements emphasize sanctification and the work of the Holy Spirit in the process.

The Sanctified Church is a social location, a cultural constituency, a historically connected and contested component of the Black Church, a response to social change, and a response to racism. The Sanctified Church is also a specialized area of Christian spirituality. While any Christian will argue that sanctification is an important component of Christian doctrine and history, in other words, that all Christian churches should be sanctified, the phrase *Sanctified Church* is a term indigenous to the Black Church, and African Americans use it to denote more than 100 church bodies of various sizes and organizational complexities. Several of these denominations produced exceptionally large congregations called megachurches and, at the end of the twentieth century and into the twenty-first, influenced the growth and style of a wide variety of white churches, especially Holiness, Pentecostal, and Charismatic. Because of the traditional emphases on pastors and bishops when telling the histories of churches, there is a tendency to understate or erase the importance of women, even in those smaller denominations where they do serve as pastors and bishops. However, the national cultural impacts of these churches are often the result of women's activities.

Women and the Sanctified Church

Religion in the United States is predominantly female and African American religion even more so. Women exercise varying degrees of leadership depending on the specific denomination. Some of these churches and denominations ordain women to all of the ranks of ministry; some do not. Some, like Mount Sinai Holy Church of America, Alpha and Omega Pentecostal Church of America, and Church of the Living God, the Pillar and Ground of the Truth, Inc. (Lewis Dominion), were founded by women. All these churches depend on women's activities and organizations for their survival. In most, women are revered as founders and organizers of congregations and denominations, even those that do not ordain women to serve in every office. In some of these church groups, in addition to their roles as founders and pioneers, women also occupy the offices of presiding bishop, elder, and pastor alongside of the traditional female roles of evangelist, missionary, prayer band leader, church mother, and teacher. Of course these roles vary from church to church, but in addition to traditional and nontraditional leadership roles, women do all the essential work of the church, particularly education and fund-raising.

The Sanctified Church is one of the most significant vehicles for women's voices, and the reach of these churches' women extends throughout the Black Church and the entire organizational life of African Americans in the United States. Evangelists and women elders from Holiness and Pentecostal churches are often called upon to be the preachers and guest speakers for Women's Day and Missionary services in Baptist and Methodist churches. Those women who are singing evangelists, for instance, Mother Willie Mae Ford Smith, Madame Emily Bram, and Pastor Shirley Caesar, conduct revivals not only in the Sanctified Church but also in Baptist and Methodist churches. Through these women's networks and their cross-denominational interaction in local communities, the influence of the Sanctified Church is extended beyond the boundaries of congregation and denomination. Women's networks foster the kinship that exists among these churches in spite of their doctrinal differences.

Women who feel a call to lead in the Black Church have often found a better reception in the Sanctified Church. Not only do some Holiness and Pentecostal denominations ordain women fully to all aspects of ministry, but the churches who do not often provide formal structures for women's leadership and authority. Strong and somewhat autonomous women's departments with highly visible national and regional leaders sometimes empower women in ways that give them more authority outside their congregations than they may exercise in their local settings. In the Church of God in Christ, for instance, women who are national evangelists have had to preach revival successfully in seven states in order to achieve that status. Some of the early leaders in the Church of God in Christ, for instance, Mother Lizzie Woods Roberson (1860–1945), the first head of the Women's Department, started in other denominations. Mother Roberson was originally Baptist. In addition to the national convocation of the denomination, the women of the Church of God in Christ meet in their own separate convention where their history, roles, and purposes as women are openly and specifically discussed.

Black women across denominational lines share an emphasis on the Holy Spirit in the expression of their Christianity. Holiness and Pentecostal churches explicitly underscore the operation of the Holy Spirit in the life of the believer as the most salient aspects of their doctrine. However, the traditions of women's emphasis on the Holy Spirit in black churches antedates and parallels the birth of the Holiness and Pentecostal movements. Black women's voices were heard at the very origins of the Holiness movement and were woven throughout the Methodist roots of Holiness. Jarena Lee (1783–?), Julia Foote (1823–1901), Rebecca Cox Jackson (1795–1871), and others were preaching women in the nineteenth century who emphasized sanctification and the operation of the Holy Spirit. Florence Spearing Randolph (1866–1951), an African Methodist Episcopal Zion elder whose preaching spanned the nineteenth and twentieth centuries, also emphasized sanctification in her preaching. Amanda Berry Smith (1837–1915), a Holiness preacher, and Zilpha Elaw (c. 1790–c. 1850) exerted tremendous influence on both black and white people in the camp meetings that gave rise to the Holiness movement. All of these women were at some point in their lives affiliated with the AME or the African Methodist Episcopal Zion (AMEZ) Churches. Foote and Randolph were ordained AMEZ elders, and Jarena Lee was licensed within the AME Church.

Not only were black women inextricably linked to the interracial origins of the Holiness movement, but their role in the origins of Pentecostalism is even more prominent. One problem with Pentecostal history is the tendency for white historians to marginalize the role of black people. However, all Pentecostal historians agree on the pivotal importance of the 1906 Azusa Street Revival in California as the wellspring of twentieth-century Pentecostalism. The leader of the revival, William Seymour (1870–1922), first preached the doctrine of speaking in tongues at a Holiness church pastored by a black woman, Rev. Neely Terry. In the controversy that followed, some of her members left with Seymour and eventually founded the Azusa Street Mission. The Azusa Street Revival lasted three years and drew national and international attention; some of that attention was precisely because of the interracial and intercultural reality of those meetings. Classically Pentecostal denominations and congregations in the United States and throughout the world usually trace their origins to the Azusa Street Revival. Women were prominent throughout the revival, and the Pentecostal movement established itself early as a significant vehicle for black and white women's voices. Because the emphasis on the Holy Spirit in the Black Church predated the Holiness and Pentecostal movements and because the role of the Holy Spirit in worship was a well-defended aspect of Afro-Christian worship, Holiness and Pentecostal religion, although a source of intense debate and conflict at times, did not create the formidable divisions within the black community that came to exist among whites. The mobility of women across denominational boundaries undoubtably served to modify the impact of conflicts.

An additional source of "kinship" between the Sanctified Church and the rest of the Black Church can be found in the roles women played in the education of church leadership, congregations, and the black community at large. Many adherents to Holiness and Pentecostal doctrine were African Americans who believed fervently in the primacy of the Holy Spirit in their worship. They rejected the attempts of well-meaning Baptists, Methodists, and Presbyterians to dampen the ardor of black worship at the end of slavery. These same believers, however, agreed fervently with their more formal brothers and sisters about the importance of education. Thus women educators within the churches and in the segregated school systems of the North and South were able to carve out an admirable role for themselves that was respected by the entire community. Black women members of Holiness and Pentecostal churches were active in the clubs and sororities that shaped a liberationist infrastructure in the black community. Thus women served as unifying dynamic in the face of the religious, political, and social conflicts that often divided prominent men such as Booker T. Washington and W. E. B. Du Bois. When Mary McLeod Bethune utilized her influence to have black women invited to lunch at the White House, Pentecostal women from the Church of God in Christ were included. One of the founders of the sorority Delta Sigma Theta, Pauline Oberdorfer Minor, was a part of the Holiness movement. Women's adherence to a "religion of the Spirit" helped to make the Sanctified Church a vehicle for cultural revitalization among black people.

The Sanctified Church as a Cultural Revitalization Movement

The first scholarly usage of the term *Sanctified Church* was probably in Zora Neale Hurston's 1928 essay "The Sanctified Church." During her travels in the South to collect folklore, she described the way itinerant men and women—evangelists and missionaries—traveled through the camps of migrant workers, competing with the "juke joints" where blues, dancing, and other forms of secular entertainment were available. In her essay, Hurston pointed out that the Sanctified Church and its membership ("the Saints") offered a cultural revitalization to the Black Church that preserved a musical tradition and provided continuities with the African religious background and its impact on black Protestantism. She also noted that the only place where people continued to sing spirituals in a manner faithful to the folk traditions, which included shouting, clapping, and dancing, was in the Sanctified Church. Her argument that the leaders in these churches had their antecedents in African religious traditions has been borne out by Lamin Sanneh's scholarship on African independent churches and Joseph Murphy's more nuanced explorations of African spirituality in a global context.

Musical scholars argue that the Sanctified Church also revitalized the overall Black Church by providing a nurturing space for the emergence of gospel music—a cultural development that has been global in its consequences. Although the formal origins of gospel music rest with the copyrighted work of Thomas A. Dorsey, who was Baptist, the preservation of the oral traditions of African American church music and the expansion of the musical repertoire with the improvisation of praise songs that were continuous with the traditions of the spirituals took place in the Sanctified Church. Women gospel singers such as Mother Willie Mae Ford Smith, Shirley Caesar, Mahalia Jackson, Clara Ward, and Edna Gallmon Cooke carried these traditions forward into black religious popular culture. Mother Willie Mae Ford Smith (1904–1994), a Baptist who became Apostolic, actively taught the new singing traditions as a revivalist in black churches and through the National Convention of Gospel Choirs and Choruses, a significant vehicle of religious interaction across denominational lines. As members of the Sanctified Church preserved a deep spiritual tradition within the black experience, they also constantly reseeded and revitalized the more sedate Protestant settings in the Black Church.

The Sanctified Church as Social Location

When African Americans meet for the first time, an important part of the initial conversation involves ascertaining social locations and intersecting personal histories. In spite of differences of class, education, and geographic origins, discussion of religion often provides an opportunity for the initial search for common ground. Even if they are not current members of churches, religion still works as a way of discussing people, places, and events they may know. When such conversations occur and the question "What church do you attend?" arises, the answer "the Sanctified Church" may elicit one of several reactions. The conversation may continue by asking about others they may or may not know, or the interrogator may then respond, "Which one?" In response a member of the Sanctified Church will share the specific denomination of which he or she is a member, and an excited conversation about the complexity of this religious world, the richness of religious experience, the particulars of distinguishing beliefs and doctrines, or all of these dimensions may follow.

The conversation may also explore their experiences growing up in their respective churches. Sometimes such conversations highlight the ways that the Sanctified Church influenced the identity and socialization of the nonmember: memories of storefront churches whose lively music could be heard as one walked home from Baptist, Methodist, and other denominational services. Sometimes members of other churches, usually teenagers, would sit in the back of these churches. As outsiders, their memories were dominated by ladies in white uniforms, music accompanied by tambourines, guitars, and drums, and circles of believers helping a shouting member to express herself safely. Conversations about the Sanctified Church among black insiders and outsiders elicit shared memories of mandatory speeches by children at Christmas and Easter, special days that began with Sunday School, proceeded through long morning services, punctuated by dinners—usually chicken but sometimes turkey. Dinner would be followed by an afternoon program and the early evening youth group meeting. The search for common ground would also generate memories of night services (to serve the men and women who worked in household service who could not attend during the regular time) and memories of special annual days that demonstrated continuity between the Sanctified Church and the rest of the African American Christian family.

An important dimension of the shared culture of these churches revolved around the strong women and men in their families who belonged to these churches and about churches and church members who pushed children to achieve as much as possible and, if they failed in their strivings, taught them how to recover and redeem their failures and get back on the path. Thus it is not surprising that during the late twentieth century, as a consequence of the civil rights movement, there was tremendous geographic and social mobility among young people from the Sanctified Church. They be-

came important agents in the revitalization of black Methodist, Baptist, and other denominational churches, a phenomenon that sociologists C. Eric Lincoln and Lawrence Mamiya have identified as "neo-Pentecostalism."

The Sanctified Church became a social location where doctrinal and biblical meanings and interpretations were contested and renegotiated. The proper response to the self-designation "Sanctified Church" is: "Which one?" African Americans use the phrase "the Sanctified Church" to indicate predominantly black Holiness, Pentecostal, Apostolic, and Deliverance congregations and denominations; the phrase can sometimes include Spiritual, Independent, and Community churches—especially when it is used as a stylistic rather than a narrowly doctrinal label. When the designation is stylistic, it refers to the experiential and ritual dimensions of the church; the worship style is more ecstatic, emphasizing manifestations of the "Holy Ghost" (Holy Spirit) such as loud demonstrative words of praise, overt gestures of praise such as clapping and raising one's hands, speaking in tongues, the holy dance, prophesying, and anointing with oil for blessing and healing. Much of this praise activity is collectively referred to as "shouting" among African Americans. Prior to the late twentieth century, these churches usually had a monopoly on the styles of music that featured drums, tambourines, guitars, and a variety of other instruments in addition to pianos and organs. The gospel music of the Sanctified Church was often more energetic and faster than that in Baptist and Methodist congregations. Indeed, historians of gospel music identify the Sanctified Church as the most nurturing matrix of the new movement, although prominent founders of gospel music, such as Thomas A. Dorsey, Sallie Martin, Willie Mae Ford Smith, and Mahalia Jackson, were Baptist; eventually "Mother" Smith, as she was called, joined a Pentecostal congregation in the Church of God Apostolic precisely because of Baptist attitudes against women's preaching.

The term *Sanctified Church* often refers to the storefront churches of northern cities that were dismissed by historians and social scientists as "sects and cults." The storefront image also carried with it an image of poverty and disadvantage and therefore an assumed irrelevance. The realities beneath these images are often far more complex. Urban storefront churches have been the most open and welcoming to the poor and dispossessed, especially during the great migration of the early twentieth century when southern migrants were often in search of churches that reflected their folk cultures and when these churches, as relatively new denominations, were seeking to exploit northern migration as an opportunity for growth in terms of absolute numbers and the extent of their national networks. Women missionaries and evangelists traveled to northern urban centers for the express purpose of organizing churches; they set up tents in vacant lots and preached revivals until they had enough interested members to start or "dig out" a congregation. Representatives in the form of teams of women and men from these same church networks also traveled to migrant work camps throughout the South, offering worship services in tents and clearings. Such activities provided a connection that would prove fruitful for workers' families when they migrated to the North.

During the late twentieth century, especially during and after the recessions of the 1970s that intensified poverty and social isolation in black urban ghettos, women pastors in urban storefronts often served as the front line of needed services to the most impoverished and distressed in black neighborhoods. Either denominationally or stylistically or both, these churches qualified for the designation "Sanctified Church."

Sanctified Church as Religiocultural Constituency

Black Holiness, Pentecostal, and Apostolic churches are bodies of believers who emerged from controversies over church culture and ritual in the late nineteenth and early twentieth centuries in the United States. The cultural controversies within black churches erupted during and after slavery when Christian missionaries, both black and white—Baptist, Methodist, Presbyterian, and Congregational—traveled to the South in order to convert the slaves and freed people. Enslaved Christians had been self–catechizing since 1820, pursuing a style of Christianity that depended heavily on an oral tradition of spirituals they themselves had created, a selection of English hymns, a liberationist view of the Bible, and an ecstatic worship tradition that emphasized the operation of the Holy Ghost (Holy Spirit) in the process of conversion to and perseverance in the Christian life. Slaves believed that worship could not take place without the presence of the Holy Ghost made visible through the actions of the worshippers. Furthermore, the Spirit often arrived on the wings of a song. These songs often involved the ring shout, an act of worship where the entire congregation moved together in a counterclockwise ring while singing and using their hands and feet to generate complex African-style rhythms. This unique combination of elements, what W. E. B. Du Bois called "the preacher, the music, and the frenzy," elicited controversy among the educated northern missionaries who sought to teach literacy and decorum. Newly freed slaves often defended their traditions, informing missionaries that the silence they were teaching flew in the face of Jesus' own warnings that if the worshippers were to "hold their peace" that "the rocks would cry out" (Litwack, 462).

Bishop Daniel Payne of the African Methodist Episcopal (AME) Church traveled throughout the South seeking to eliminate what he called the freed people's "fist and heel religion." Pastors often informed him that if the Spirit was not present in worship that the people would go where the Spirit could be found.

An additional pressure on the churches came in the form of literacy. Churches seeking to improve their status and uplift members of the community began to insist on higher education on the part of clergy. Literacy also implied hymnals and musical notation, restricting severely the pool of choir members. In some Baptist, Methodist, Presbyterian, and Congregational churches, the mainstream denominations most engaged in missionary work and education, spirituals were seen as relics of slavery and simply were not sung. In other places, the spirituals were presented in an arranged form for choirs and soloists, displacing the oral tradition. A woman born around 1890 explained to this author why she and her two siblings, third-generation African Methodists, joined three different denominations of the Sanctified Church (Church of God in Christ; Church of God [Anderson, Indiana]; and the House of God, which is the Church of the Living God, the Pillar and Ground of the Truth, Inc.). She stated simply that "the people did not want to sing the songs the right way any more or pray the prayers." As a religiocultural constituency, the Sanctified Church provided a vehicle for those committed to the old-time religion to defend their folk-rural and folk-urban traditions of worship.

While defending their folk-rural, Spirit-filled traditions, freed people did not reject education and literacy. Their piety centered around the Bible and many insisted that they wanted "to learn to read that Blessed Book before I die" (Litwack, 471). Their strategies to acquire literacy are legendary; missionaries who taught children during the day found themselves besieged by adults at night who offered to pay for their services at night schools with produce and labor. In terms of religiocultural controversies, literate black Christians, who emphasized the operation of the Holy Ghost (Holy Spirit) in their worship, found ways to defend their practices biblically. They appealed primarily to the worship instructions embedded in the Psalms where worshippers were instructed to praise God with dancing, shouting, drums, stringed instruments, and songs. One of the most important church founders was Charles Harrison Mason (1866–1961) of the Church of God in Christ. Although currently the largest Pentecostal denomination, the Church of God in Christ began as a Holiness church in 1897. After a controversy erupted over the doctrine preached at Azusa Street, Mason was instrumental in reorganizing the church as Pentecostal. Mason left behind a series of essays that exhorted "the saints" to dance, not in a worldly way but in a way consistent with the instructions found in the Bible (Ross, Patterson, and Atkins). Such creative biblical interpretation not only defended the folk traditions of religious life, but it also contributed to tremendous doctrinal controversies and, consequently, an extraordinary diversity within the Sanctified Church. The 100-plus organized church bodies that exist today are a consequence of this creative conflict.

The Sanctified Church(es) as Doctrinal Constituencies

The controversies over culture and ritual also facilitated controversies over church doctrine. An additional inspiration for doctrinal discussion and debate came from white churches and church leaders for whom issues of doctrine weighed more heavily than issues of ritual and experience. Because of hostile attitudes toward Holiness and Pentecostal doctrines and the labeling of churches as "holy rollers" by the mainstream culture, especially among Baptists, Holiness and Pentecostal leaders argued doctrine as a strategy to uplift the status of their churches. Black Holiness and Pentecostal churches suffered the approbrium of racist stereotypes as well. The extra pressure of racism required that defense of their worship style be particularly articulate.

For African Americans, doctrinal issues often connected with questions about racial-ethnic identity and gender roles, especially since the educators within black congregations and denominations were women. In some cases these churches and their leaders engaged in strategies to defend and uplift black women. William Christian (1856–1928), the founder of the Church of the Living God–Christian Workers for Fellowship, was jailed in the South for preaching against the sexual exploitation of black women by white men. The Women's Convention of the Church of God in Christ urged women to travel together in pairs in order to avoid sexual exploitation by men of any color. Many of the conventions and traditions concerning dress, although highly restrictive and conservative, represented well-meaning strategies to defend black women in a hostile world.

The importance of educated women to the development of church leadership and to education and missions confounded and complicated any arguments about women's subordination. The biblical foundations of the operation of the Holy Ghost or Holy Spirit rested in biblical texts such as Acts 2 (the description of the day of Pentecost) that also implied universal human equality. The creative and innovative biblical arguments around worship and spiritual doctrine also provided opportunities to highlight the diverse roles of women in the Bible, therefore reinforcing arguments supporting women's leadership. In the context of the Jim Crow South and a Jim Crow–affirming culture, these argu-

ments posed some problems. By World War I, white Pentecostals rejected racial egalitarianism at the same time that black Pentecostals affirmed that God is no "respecter of persons," and sometimes that meant women persons. Some of these controversies over doctrine, particularly those involving Pentecostal and Apostolic doctrines, were global in their reach.

Controversies over worship style preceded and led to biblically grounded controversies over doctrine. Black people in the United States participated in every denominational body, organization, and movement that emphasized life in the Spirit, the operation of the Holy Spirit, or some variety of sanctification, perfectionism, Holiness, or Spirit baptism. Such participation included Methodism, Shakers, and the Society of Friends. The nature and operation of the Holy Ghost in worship was one of the oldest sources of controversy among Christians generally. In the United States, debates over the Holy Spirit took place in a highly democratized religious context. The Holiness movement and, later, the Pentecostal movement were important vehicles for pursuing some of these doctrinal issues surrounding the Holy Ghost/Holy Spirit. The Methodists, Shakers (United Society of Believers in Christ's Second Appearing), and Quakers (Society of Friends) were three movements that emphasized the operation of the Holy Spirit within the experience of the believer. Various branches of Methodism, including the African Methodist connections, became part of the religious mainstream and, at the same time, significant religious roots for the Holiness movement. It is important to remember that Methodist churches are the foundation for the specific doctrinal conversation concerning sanctification.

Black women became leaders in these various movements. Amanda Berry Smith (1837–1915), an African Methodist Episcopalian, became a Holiness preacher traveling throughout the United States, England, India, and West Africa. Rebecca Cox Jackson (1795–1871), known primarily as an elder within the Shakers, also began her life in the African Methodist Episcopal Church. She preached among praying bands in the Holiness movement and the AME Church. Eventually, Jackson became a Shaker when the AME Church found her revelation on celibacy unacceptable. Sanctification was an important theme among black women preachers of the late nineteenth and early twentieth century, even if they were formally unaffiliated with the Holiness and Pentecostal movements. This affinity for sanctification among women made it possible for Holiness and Pentecostal women to have an impact on the larger community through the clubs of the National Association of Colored Women and the Woman's Christian Temperance movement. People like Ida B. Wells Barnett and Hallie Quinn Brown supported the work of Amanda Berry Smith. Pauline Oberdorfer Minor, one of the founders of the black women's sorority Delta Sigma Theta, was a leader in "the Apostolic Church of Philadelphia," probably the Apostolic Faith Churches of God.

Black people within white Holiness churches also emerged as leaders in Holiness denominations and ranked among the principal founders of the Pentecostal movement. It is quite possible that calling black Pentecostal and Holiness churches "the Sanctified Church" may have come from Church of God (Sanctified Church) and Original Church of God (or Sanctified Church). Both of these black Holiness denominations predated the formation of the Church of God in Christ and, unlike most other Holiness and Pentecostal bodies, practiced a congregational polity—a polity reflecting their Baptist roots. Both groups pride themselves as adherents to "original" tenets of Holiness—"Holiness through sanctification by the Holy Spirit."

Within overwhelmingly Baptist black communities, the controversies over sanctification were often publicly presented as conflicts among clergymen over appropriate levels of piety. Although those conflicts existed, churches were founded because both women and men felt the call to Holiness, callings sometimes experienced through dreams, visions, and dramatic life events. Once they were convinced of the rightness of Holiness, the importance of Holiness was often communicated from person to person in conversations as well as through revivals preached throughout their communities. In the case of C. P. Jones, one of the founders with C. H. Mason of the Church of God in Christ in 1897, his thinking about doctrine was sparked when a white Holiness minister simply asked him about his "theory of Holiness." A number of denominations practiced footwashing as an "ordinance" along with baptism by immersion and communion. Occasionally there are controversies over the proper practice of communion—leavened or unleavened bread, grape juice, wine, or water. The churches known as "Apostolic" were part of the controversy concerning the Trinitarian baptismal formula ("in the name of the Father, the Son, and the Holy Spirit") and a baptismal formula emphasizing Jesus only ("in the name of Jesus"). Some groups sidestep this controversy by baptizing using either doctrine or both. The dynamics of debate are such that there are always new and emerging syntheses arising out of old arguments.

Adherence to doctrines that emphasized the Spirit was also underscored by the development of an "Afro-Baptist faith" during slavery where encounters with Jesus in the Spirit ("travels") were a normative component of conversion. The visionary experiences that slaves narrated anticipated many of the contemporary practices associated with being "slain in the Spirit" in contemporary Pentecostal, Apostolic, Deliverance, and neo-Pentecostal churches. This is one reason why, in the context of the Black Church, it may be more appropriate to talk about the reclamation of tradition instead of the emergence of neo–Pentecostalism.

Vehicle for Women's Voices

Women represent a majority—in many cases, a large majority—of the memberships of black churches. As a result, they define the style and culture of the churches. Women are also largely responsible for the organizational integrity of African American churches—they raise the money to pay clergy salaries and church mortgages as well as to provide benevolence and scholarships. Women are the missionaries whose projects and efforts shape church calendars and forge and maintain alliances among networks of churches. In every area, music, ushering, social uplift, benevolence, hospitality, and proclamation (preaching and speaking), women make a serious and vital difference. Historically African American churchwomen have been working women, and their employment outside the home gives them an investment power in their churches that is distinct in women's religious history. Their investments have occurred in the most important formative moments of black churches. This is particularly true throughout the histories of the denominations and congregations that comprise the Sanctified Church. The Sanctified Church, as a result, is a religious phenomenon whose character and dynamics are the distinctive product of women's enterprise and spirituality.

SOURCES: Horace Clarence Boyer and Lloyd Yearwood, *How Sweet the Sound: The Golden Age of Gospel* (1995). Stanley M. Burgess, Gary B. McGee, and Patrick H. Alexander, *Dictionary of Pentecostal and Charismatic Movements* (1988). Shirley Caesar, *Shirley Caesar: The Lady, the Melody, and the Word—An Autobiography* (1998). Bettye Collier-Thomas, *Daughters of Thunder: Black Women Preachers and Their Sermons, 1850–1979* (1998). Jualyne E. Dodson and Cheryl Townsend Gilkes, "Something Within: Social Change and Collective Endurance in the Sacred World of Black Christian Women," in *Women and Religion in America*, vol. 3, *The Twentieth Century*, ed. Rosemary Radford Ruether and Rosemary Skinner Keller (1986), 80–128. W. E. B. Du Bois, "Of the Faith of the Fathers," in *The Souls of Black Folk* (1903, 1999), 119–129. Arthur Huff Fauset, *Black Gods of the Metropolis* (1944). Cheryl Townsend Gilkes, "The Role of Women in the Sanctified Church," *Journal of Religious Thought* 43.1 (1986): 24–41. Cheryl Townsend Gilkes, "The Roles of Church and Community Mothers: Ambivalent American Sexism or Fragmented African Familyhood?" *Journal of Feminist Studies in Religion* 2.2 (Fall 1986): 41–59. Cheryl Townsend Gilkes, "Together and in Harness: Women's Traditions in the Sanctified Church," *Signs: Journal of Women in Culture and Society* 10.4 (Summer 1985): 678–699. Zora Neale Hurston, *The Sanctified Church* (c. 1928, 1982). Clifton Johnson and A. P. Watson, eds., *God Struck Me*

Dead: Religious Conversion Experiences and Autobiographies of Ex-Slaves (1969). C. Eric Lincoln and Lawrence H. Mamiya, *The Black Church in the African American Experience* (1990). Leon F. Litwack, *Been in the Storm So Long: The Aftermath of Slavery* (1979). Joseph M. Murphy, *Working the Spirit: Ceremonies of the African Diaspora* (1994). Peter J. Paris, *The Spirituality of African Peoples: The Search for a Common Moral Discourse* (1995). Daniel A. Payne, *Recollections of Seventy Years: Bishop Daniel Alexander Payne* (1968). Wardell Payne, ed., *Directory of African American Religious Bodies: A Compendium by the Howard University School of Divinity* (1991). Albert J. Raboteau, *Slave Religion: The Invisible Institution in the Antebellum South* (1978). German R. Ross, J. O. Patterson, and Julia Mason Atkins, *History and Formative Years of the Church of God in Christ with Excerpts from the Life and Works of Its Founder—Bishop C. H. Mason* (1969). Cheryl Sanders, *Saints in Exile: The Holiness-Pentecostal Experience in African American Religion and Culture* (1996). Lamin Sanneh, *West African Christianity: The Religious Impact* (1983). Harold Dean Trulear, "Reshaping Black Pastoral Theology: The Vision of Bishop Ida B. Robinson," *Journal of Religious Thought* 46.1 (1989): 17–31. Carter G. Woodson, *The History of the Negro Church* (1921, 1972).

FUNDAMENTALISM
Margaret L. Bendroth

FUNDAMENTALISM IS EASY to describe but difficult to define with precision. It is often used as a blanket term for socially, religiously, or politically conservative movements, or it is used in reference to militant, anti-Western, antimodernist groups in developing sections of the world. This general usage is often confusing, but it does point toward some common roots of antimodern protest movements. In its broadest sense, fundamentalism is a militant reaction to twentieth-century secularism, coupled with an urge for separation from the world as a means of maintaining theological and behavioral purity. Fundamentalism is also a religion of the book, upholding an authoritative text as a clear guide to all matters of belief and conduct and divinely inspired without factual error.

In this sense, fundamentalism is inimical to feminism, with its agenda of personal freedom and political equality. And indeed, political and social antimodernist movements generally emphasize the necessity of women's role within the home as a primary line of defense against the spread of secular ideals.

This essay deals with fundamentalism in a more narrow sense, as a theological movement that arose within North American Protestant churches in the late nineteenth century. In many ways, this specific type of fundamentalism followed the general antifeminist pattern, upholding biblical precepts and a divinely ordained order in defense of a gendered hierarchy. At particular

issue were passages from the writings of St. Paul (1 Corinthians 11:3–16, 14:34–35 and 1 Timothy 2:9–15), prohibiting women from speaking in religious assemblies or from exercising authority over men.

But North American fundamentalism was also a popular movement. Although it shared some of the general characteristics of antimodern protest movements, it was also heavily influenced by the American revivalistic tradition. Revivalism emphasized emotional preaching and a democratic theology that placed all converts on an equal plane at the foot of the cross; especially in the early twentieth century, this egalitarianism tempered the antifeminist impulse within fundamentalism. Furthermore, in the marketplace of American religious faiths, where no one group enjoyed official status or state support, fundamentalist institutions required volunteer labor and support in order to survive. Thus, women, always the majority of Protestant church membership, were a constituency too important to be ignored or suppressed, even by church leaders who believed that the Bible forbade women to assume any positions of leadership. Not surprisingly perhaps, fundamentalist precepts about women's place did not always coincide with practice. Even those concerned about the authority of the Bible did not always agree on its application to particular circumstances. Attitudes toward women in the fundamentalist movement were therefore complex, often inconsistent, and tended to defy easy categorization.

The North American fundamentalist movement first began to emerge in the 1870s and 1880s within northern Protestant churches, primarily among Baptists and Presbyterians. It coalesced in reaction to the growing formalism of Gilded Age religion and also to emerging intellectual challenges to Christianity. Early fundamentalists (who did not yet use this term to refer to themselves) identified "modernism" with theological liberalism and especially the higher criticism, that is, efforts to apply scientific and historical methods to the study of the Old and New Testaments. Above all they insisted on the supernatural truth of Christianity, resisting all attempts to "explain away" biblical accounts of miracles or Christ's virgin birth. Leading biblical theologians at Princeton Seminary, Benjamin Warfield and Archibald A. Hodge, became leaders in the cause of scriptural authority. They argued that the Bible was not only infallible in all its teachings but completely inerrant in its textual form, that is, divinely inspired without any errors of fact.

Many, but not all, of these biblicist conservatives believed that the Second Coming of Christ was imminent. (The Princeton theologians were a major exception here.) This expectation was based on a system of biblical interpretation known as dispensational premillennial-

THE FULCRUM

Although the fundamentalist movement saw women in their domestic role as the moral bulwark against an evil world, as this cartoon from the *Sunday School Times* suggests, women played active roles in establishing Bible schools, organizing schools for "Christian workers," and even preaching. *Courtesy of Archives, Gordon-Conwell Theological Seminary.*

ism. Conceived by John Nelson Darby, leader of the conservative Plymouth Brethren churches in Great Britain, and disseminated by Cyrus Scofield's popular reference Bible, dispensational theology attempted to systematize all the complexities of biblical history into a single story line. This narrative divided God's work throughout human history into a set of distinct time periods, or dispensations. Each period, beginning with creation and the fall of humanity, was distinguished by a different set of divine ground rules, established by God in response to human disobedience. The last dispensations, relying heavily on interpretation of the book of Revelation, laid out the story of the future, in which human evil would multiply and Christ would return suddenly to initiate a thousand-year reign, or a millennial age, on earth.

From the start, women played an ambiguous role in the fundamentalist movement, for a combination of theological and cultural reasons. The story of women in Bible institutes is a good case in point. Women were highly visible and active in these schools, usually small

and locally based institutions that arose in response to the need for trained evangelists and missionaries. The Bible was the focus of the curriculum but was complemented with practical instruction in various methods of evangelism. In other words, Bible schools offered a version of a seminary education without the prerequisite of a college degree. In the late nineteenth and early twentieth centuries, women, who had only limited access to most colleges and seminaries, flocked to Bible schools. The curriculum was particularly attractive to women because it emphasized preparation for foreign missions, an area already established as "women's work" in Protestant culture.

But Bible schools were also attractive to young women because well-known leaders of this movement actively supported women's public "ministry." A. B. Simpson, founder of the Christian and Missionary Alliance, and also Nyack Bible Institute, listed "the ministry of women" as one of the five fundamental pillars of his new movement. A. J. Gordon (1836–1895), founder of the Boston Missionary Training School (later

Gordon College and Gordon-Conwell Theological Seminary), believed that women were meant to play a key role in the evangelization of the world, citing the text in Acts 2 that "your sons and daughters shall prophesy ... and on my servants and on my handmaidens I will pour out in those days of Spirit and they shall prophesy." He publically supported their right to preach in an influential article in *The Missionary Review of the World* on "The Ministry of Women" (1894). In its early years, Gordon's school graduated many women who became missionaries, traveling evangelists, or even pastors of churches in rural New England.

A. J. Gordon's wife Maria Hale Gordon (fl. 1888) also played an important role in the school's founding, serving as secretary and treasurer in its early years and eventually on the faculty as a Bible teacher. She also managed the young women students' living quarters. A self-effacing woman in private, Maria Gordon took on public speaking engagements and even political activism because she believed God was calling her to do so. She was head of the Boston chapter of the Woman's Christian Temperance Union and a frequent speaker at D. L. Moody's Northfield Conferences for Christian workers. In 1894 she spoke on "women evangelists," declaring that "in these 'last days' it would seem as if the master were saying to every woman, 'Behold, I have set before *you* an open door.' Doors which have long been shut through a misapprehension of Scriptural truth are now flung wide open, and ... [women] have full liberty to perform any ministry to which the Holy Ghost may call them; and the majority of Christian churches will bid them 'God speed' " (Gordon, 150). One of her associates described Gordon, probably aptly, as a woman who "knew what people ought to do and planned to see that they did it, but was surprisingly forgiving if they didn't" (Wood, 33–34).

Women also helped establish Bible schools. In 1873, the famous evangelist Dwight L. Moody urged one of his associates, Emma Dryer, to begin organizing a school for "Christian workers" in Chicago, based on the deaconess institute for women missionaries in Mildmay, England. In 1876 Dryer organized the Bible Work of Chicago to train women for various types of religious work, including home visitation and Bible distribution. Dryer's organization also provided a variety of resources for poor women, including sewing classes, mothers' meetings, Sunday School classes, and charity distribution. In 1886 Dryer began organizing a series of public meetings at the Moody Church in Chicago, featuring well-known dispensationalist teachers; she hoped that, with Moody's support, these efforts might lead to a full-fledged Bible institute to train women workers. Yet, as became clear in an address Moody gave that same year, calling for the training of "gap men" to bring the gospel to the world, women were not to be the school's primary focus. Moody, and the Bible institute he established in 1889, emphasized the importance of training men for Christian work.

Moody's decision illustrates an ambivalence about women's presence in Bible schools, and it reflects a growing concern among a wide variety of Protestants about the underrepresentation of men in religious institutions. Although women were a fairly consistent two-thirds majority of church members throughout the nineteenth century, concern about religious "feminization" began to intensify in the post–Civil War era. Protestant leaders worried that the overrepresentation of women would afix an image of Christianity as a weak, sentimental faith, not suitable for vigorous, red-blooded males. To correct this impression, and to move men to more active participation, they increasingly turned to special measures, including denominationally based "brotherhood" groups, as well as revivals featuring "men only" meetings.

Early fundamentalists readily adopted the aggressive language of masculine revivalism. Its confrontational style suited their dissatisfaction with religious formalism in churches and with what they perceived as a "feminized," accommodationist liberal theology taking over Protestant seminaries. Ex-baseball player Billy Sunday (1862–1935) was particularly famous for his boisterous platform style, characterized by physical displays that included jumping atop his pulpit, running vigorously after Satan, and occasionally smashing a chair to dramatize his hatred for the saloon. His famous temperance sermons—"Follow the Water Wagon" and "The Trail of the Serpent"—appealed to masculine solidarity and pride and usually ended with an appeal for repentant "trail-hitters," men who came forward to shake Sunday's hand as a symbol of their resolve to live a better life. Other fundamentalist pastors adopted this masculine persona, most notably Mark Mathews, the "pistol-packing parson" of Seattle, and Minneapolis Baptist William Bell Riley, whose preaching portfolio included a popular sermon on "She-Men, or How Some Become Sissies," depicting modernists as weak-kneed fops.

But women participated in citywide revivals as well, most often as members of a frontline revivalist's team of "personal workers." Sunday's own entourage included a number of well-known women. Grace Saxe and Florence McKinney were popular Bible teachers; Frances Miller, sometimes referred to as a "female Billy Sunday," held meetings for shop girls and secretaries. Sunday's wife Helen, popularly known as "Ma Sunday," helped manage his campaigns and maintained a popular newspaper advice column ("Ask Ma Sunday").

One of the best known of these female evangelists was Virginia Asher (1869–1937), a soprano soloist and "personal worker" with Sunday and with his predecessor J. Wilbur Chapman. Born in 1869 to Irish Catholic parents in Chicago, Asher underwent an evangelical conversion at D. L. Moody's church when she was eleven years old. There she eventually met William Asher, whom she married, and began training for Christian service work. The Ashers' only child died in infancy, and they spent their lives engaged in various types of urban evangelism. In her travels with Chapman and Sunday, Asher specialized in "women's work," including efforts among prostitutes as well as young working women, a group she considered especially prey to temptation. A statuesque, physically imposing woman with a mound of snowy white hair, Asher led Bible classes, canvased crime-ridden areas of cities for converts, and during mass meetings in the Chapman and Sunday crusades, stationed herself in the hallways outside of the revival sanctuary, ready to counsel sinners in distress. "If a man approaches her in a spirit of bravado or thinking to get some fun out of it," a newspaper reporter noted in 1909, "he soon finds that he has met a real woman, absolutely sincere, entirely convinced of the truth of her message and of the need for her hearer to receive and accept the Christ she follows. She is not to be turned away by any sophistries or argument, but keeps right at her hearer until he drops his eyes, usually tear-filled, and then she has him" ("Women's Share in Revivals," 16). Asher also became well known for her work among young women, especially the meetings she held at the Winona Lake Bible Conference in Indiana. There in 1922 she established the first Virginia Asher Businesswomen's Council, an organization directed toward the spiritual needs of young working women. Other local chapters formed in cities visited by the Sunday campaign. The organization's goal was "to promote a spirit of friendliness, helpfulness and responsibility for other girls among all business women of the city and to associate them in personal loyalty to Jesus Christ" (Sanders, 11). By 1938 Virginia Asher Businesswomen's Councils had formed in sixteen cities around the country.

By the 1920s, some female evangelists were becoming national celebrities. Catherine Booth, a leader in the Salvation Army, and Aimee Semple McPherson, a Pentecostal revivalist, received the most attention, and notoriety, but many other women followed Asher's path. Uldine Utley (1912–), for example, achieved fame while still a young girl. Born in Durant, Oklahoma, she lived a relatively restricted, impoverished life until a visit to a McPherson meeting convinced her that she was called to a similar career in evangelism. She began her preaching career in 1924 and by 1926 had arrived in New York. John Roach Straton, a nationally known fundamentalist leader and pastor of the Calvary Baptist Church, served as her patron and promoter, despite criticism that he was allowing a woman to preach, against biblical precept.

But even in its early stages, the fundamentalist move-ment's male leadership was ambivalent about women's participation. Although nearly all disliked Aimee Semple McPherson—as much for the emotionalism they associated with her revivals as for her gender—some condoned female evangelists as a permissible measure in the face of Christ's imminent return; female missionaries and evangelists were simply needed to help in world evangelization as the Second Coming drew near. They were clear, however, in their preference for men and allowed women to lead only as a stopgap measure made necessary because of masculine abdication of responsibility.

Dispensationalist theology also contributed to fundamentalist reluctance to encourage female leadership. The system was, on the whole, pessimistic about social change and assumed that in any given situation human disobedience would arise in opposition to God's commands. This meant, first of all, that dispensationalists had little interest in a morally optimistic cause like woman's suffrage, which predicted a widespread reversal of social ills once women achieved the franchise. Indeed, dispensationalist writers tended to see any form of feminine leadership as a sign of the growing disorder and disobedience that would characterize the End Times. In 1886, St. Louis Presbyterian James Brookes published an article in the dispensationalist press on "The Infidelity of Women," an immoderate diatribe against the female sex in general. "The prominence assigned to women," Brookes wrote, "amid the evils of the last days and the hastening of the crash of the present dispensation, is well worth serious attention. . . . [I]t has long been observed that when women lose conscience and faith, they surpass men not only in the indulgence of their grovelling appetites but in the atrocity of their deeds" (Brookes, 387).

Negative views of women also drew from dispensationalists' understanding of Genesis 1–3, especially the story of the first sin. They placed great emphasis on the fact that Eve was the first to disobey, then tempted her husband Adam to do likewise. Woman's original sin was insubordination, a failure to follow the rules set by God, and this tendency toward rebelliousness, dispensationalists believed, had characterized the female gender ever since. God's curse on Eve, in Genesis 3:14–19, in particular the admonition that she was to be ruled over by her husband, was not just a temporary punishment but a necessary restraint on all women for all time. Even Christ himself could not alter women's status. Although Christ had proclaimed a new gospel dispensation to replace the old rule of Hebrew law, dispensationalists believed that some of the original rules had to remain in place. In particular, the stigma of Eve's transgression was to last until the Second Coming; it was described by Elizabeth Needham, wife of evangelist George C. Needham, as a "moral disability" whose "humiliation will abide even upon the last woman to the end of the age" (Needham, 11).

This interpretation, and its implications for the role of women, placed dispensational theology directly at odds with the Holiness and Pentecostal movements. These two groups appeared around the same time as fundamentalism and are in many ways similar: All opposed religious formalism and modernist theology and urged their followers to live pure lives separated from sin. Holiness movements, however, most of which formed within the Methodist Church, emphasized the necessity of personal purity and followed John Wesley's belief in the possibility of moral perfection within a person's lifetime—a prospect fundamentalists rejected as unrealistic and theologically unsound. Holiness groups stressed the necessity of full consecration to God, often experienced as a powerful "second blessing" occurring some time after conversion from sin. Pentecostal groups added to this the necessity of speaking in tongues as evidence of the Holy Spirit's presence, based on the story of the first Pentecost in the biblical account in Acts 2. Fundamentalists, in contrast, did not believe that such miraculous, emotional events were necessarily signs of grace; dispensationalists in fact discounted their authenticity, since they argued that these spiritual gifts were only imparted by God for a particular dispensation, during the early days of the New Testament church.

The three movements also disagreed about the role of women. Holiness and Pentecostal teaching upheld the importance of Eve's original sin but did not see it as a permanent disability. They argued that the curse in Genesis 3:15, that Adam would rule over Eve, was lifted by Christ's death and resurrection, as were all the penalties of sin set in place in the Garden of Eden. Thus, Holiness and Pentecostal groups had no clear theological warrant for prohibiting women in leadership. In their early days especially, they readily employed women as evangelists and preachers. If a woman could demonstrate an authentic divine calling to preach, and the necessary spiritual gifts to fulfill it, she could be formally licensed for such a ministry. Although this openness to women's ministry did not last, especially as even these groups adopted more professional standards of ministerial preparation, in principle no one with a genuine calling by the Spirit to public ministry could be rejected.

By the 1920s, the loose coalition of theological conservatives began to take on the character of a unified movement and began referring to themselves as "fundamentalists." In 1910 northern Presbyterian conservatives compiled a list of five "fundamentals," a theological inventory that included nonnegotiable assent to (1) the inerrancy of the Bible, (2) the virgin birth, (3) the substitutionary atonement (the efficacy of Christ's death as an atonement for human sin), (4) the resurrection, and (5) the reality of miracles. Other lists, including the one drawn up by William Bell Riley and his World's Christian Fundamentals Association, included a statement on Christ's Second Coming. In 1920 Baptist editor Curtis Lee Laws was the first to refer to the movement as "fundamentalist," reflecting the importance of a twelve-volume multiauthored series of theological essays titled *The Fundamentals*, published and widely distributed between 1910 and 1915.

Fundamentalism was also increasingly identified with opposition to Darwinism, a system of thought that not only contradicted a literal reading of the creation story in Genesis 1 but appeared to deny God a meaningful role in creation and human beings a special status apart from the animal world. In 1925, the World's Christian Fundamentals Association hired William Jennings Bryan to prosecute John Scopes, a Tennessee schoolteacher who had broken a state law against the teaching of evolution. Clarence Darrow, a lawyer for the American Civil Liberties Union, defended Scopes. Bryan succeeded in winning his case, but in the media circus that surrounded the trial, his views on science and religion began to look ridiculous. In the eyes of the educated middle-class public, fundamentalism became increasingly synonymous with socially backward anti-intellectualism.

During the 1920s, fundamentalists also undertook battles for control of their denominations, with the fiercest fighting among northern Baptists and Presbyterians. Baptist fundamentalists largely failed in their efforts to hold the denomination to a more conservative standard; for a few years, however, matters looked brighter among the Presbyterians. In 1923 Princeton Seminary New Testament scholar J. Gresham Machen published *Christianity and Liberalism*, in which he argued that because liberalism denied key doctrines like the divinity of Christ, it was not really Christian. In 1925 Machen's fellow Presbyterian conservatives attempt to censure the New York presbytery for ordaining ministerial candidates who did not hold to the five fundamentals they had issued in 1910. The measure failed, and two years later the Presbyterian General Assembly passed a vote declaring that the five fundamentals were not valid indicators of orthodoxy. In 1929, Machen and his cobelligerents departed from Princeton and the Presbyterian denomination, establishing a smaller alternative base of operations in the Orthodox Presbyterian Church and Westminster Seminary, located outside Philadelphia.

Women did not play much of a role in these disputes. Although active in denominational organizations, especially in home and foreign missions, most churchwomen avoided theological confrontation for pragmatic reasons. They tended to view doctrinal debates as a peculiarly masculine affectation, a distraction from more important humanitarian or evangelistic concerns. As a leading Baptist laywoman later concluded, "Baptist women are not interested in theology. . . . They want more real religion" ("Editorial Comment," 5). Moreover, since very few women had systematic theological training, they were for all practical purposes barred access to denominational deliberations.

Churchwomen also had few incentives to side with fundamentalists. In 1929 Presbyterian conservatives opposed as "modernistic" a measure that would have allowed women to be ordained as ministers and elders in local congregations. Pittsburgh pastor Clarence Macartney argued against the measure because, as he put it, "many of the subtle and dangerous and seductive heresies and perversions and distortions of the gospel of Jesus Christ have sprung from the brain of woman. . . . From Eve down to Mrs. [Mary Baker] Eddy [founder of the Christian Science movement], women have played a sad part in the spread of anti-Christian doctrines" (Macartney, 8). Fundamentalists also criticized foreign missionary organizations, where women predominated, for not maintaining doctrinal standards. Few of the women's organizations even bothered to answer such charges, although in 1927 Lucy Waterbury Peabody formed a breakaway conservative missionary group, the Association of Baptists for Evangelism in the Orient.

Even so, by the end of the 1920s the fundamentalist movement was far less open to women in leadership than before. In 1930 a consortium of leaders from the Independent Fundamental Churches in America, which had included a number of female pastors when its parent organization formed in 1924, explicitly prohibited women from membership. Part of the reason for this was a growing suspicion that women were not natural allies of a religious cause such as fundamentalism. During the 1920s, an era in which young women began smoking in public and wearing "flapper-style" short skirts and bobbed hair, the old Victorian idea that all women were naturally more moral than all men began to look like a doubtful proposition. During the 1920s, at least from a fundamentalist perspective, men seemed far better champions of religion than women.

Growing restrictions on women also reflected the fact that the movement was institutionalizing. During the 1930s and 1940s, after most fundamentalist leaders had departed from mainline denominations, conservatives embarked on a vigorous effort to build an alternative subculture of churches, schools, and religious agencies. And indeed they largely succeeded in building a functioning network of "faith-based" foreign mission agencies, radio ministries, and Bible schools and colleges. Here, as always, women were present, and often in numbers that threatened to overshadow the smaller proportion of male recruits. Some institutions, wary of the perception that they were less than professional because of their high female enrollments, attempted to place quotas on women applicants. In 1930 Gordon College of Theology and Missions—once criticized as a "short-cut school"—began allowing only a third of its entering class to be female, an action that immediately reduced its lopsided gender ratio. Over the years, as Gordon grew from a small Bible school into a college and seminary, women played a smaller and smaller role. When the Gordon Divinity School formed in 1944, nearly all the students were men. In 1947 Gordon College's faculty attempted to restrict their A. B. degree to male students only; women students were to receive a bachelor's degree in religious education, since it was assumed they had no need for a broader liberal arts curriculum.

But in most cases, fundamentalist institutions relied on their female constituencies out of necessity. Overwhelming numbers of foreign missionary recruits were women, especially in the smaller, nondenominational, "faith-based" agencies that multiplied in the 1930s and 1940s. In 1929, when the China Inland Mission sent out a call for 200 new recruits, 70 percent of them turned out to be women, nearly all of them single. By the late 1940s, the General Association of Regular Baptists listed more female missionaries than clergymen. Radio ministries also included many women. In the 1930s, "Aunt Teresa" Worman was the popular host of a Know Your Bible (KYB) class for children on the Chicago-based Moody Bible Institute station (WMBI). Women also wrote inspirational missionary literature: Mary Geraldine Guinness Hudson had some twenty books published and coauthored with her husband an enduringly popular biography of her father-in-law, China Inland Mission founder Hudson Taylor. Fundamentalists also read devotional literature and fiction written by women like Ruth Stull and Grace Livingston Hill.

In contrast to earlier patterns of women's church work, fundamentalist organizations had few female auxiliaries, or indeed, separate women's groups of any kind. This was due in part to the small, enterpreneurial character of these new institutions; it also reflected the gradual decline of the Victorian ethos that assumed that because men and women were inherently different, they required separate organizations in order to work effectively.

The career of Elizabeth Evans (1899–1989) is a good illustration of women's changing role in mid-twentieth-century fundamentalist institutions. Her father Joseph Evans was a self-taught Baptist minister who moved his wife and nine children frequently, from Lynchburg, Virginia, to Des Moines, Iowa, and then to New York, where he began work with the Salvation Army. In 1912 he received an inheritance from his sister, and the family settled in Nyack, a New York City suburb. Evans's father continued his itinerant preaching career, as did her mother, Elizabeth Hicks Morrell Evans, who maintained a mission in downtown Nyack. As a young girl Elizabeth Evans had already decided upon a foreign missionary career and studied at A. B. Simpson's Missionary Training Institute in Nyack and then Wheaton College in Illinois to realize her goal. Intent on learning to live independently on the mission field, Evans took courses in physics, surveying, trigonometry, and commercial law, often as the only female in her classes.

Upon graduation in 1922, family circumstances required her to delay overseas missionary work; instead, Evans took a position at an orphanage in Rumney, New Hampshire, run by a small Pentecostal ministry known as the First Fruit Harvesters. Joel A. Wright had founded the group in 1897, and in 1929 his entrepreneurial son, J. Elwin Wright, took over the ministry and renamed it the New England Fellowship. Under this organizational rubric, Evans fashioned a multifaceted career as a traveling preacher and evangelist, conference organizer, bookstore manager, and author of religious education curricula. In 1937 she began a rural education ministry that included a full roster of summer Bible schools for children and regular religious instruction during the school year. Each year she recruited, trained, and devised curricula for scores of young women volunteers from local Christian colleges and some 21,000 children in northern New England. Evans also supplied each woman with a car and initiated them into the mysteries of automobile maintenance and winter driving through the often perilous back roads of Vermont and New Hampshire.

In many ways, she was the quintessential "woman in a man's world," often brusque and dauntingly efficient. Like many fundamentalist women of her generation in "full-time Christian service," she never married. Evans also never paused to justify her public role and refused to sentimentalize her status as a woman. Asked in later life if she had ever found her sex a hindrance, she laughingly declined the idea, commenting, "They needed everyone, you know." Yet when Wright and a group of influential supporters organized the National Association of Evangelicals (NAE) in 1942, Evans was not an official delegate but attended as secretary and took minutes on the proceedings. The NAE was "for the men," she explained to an interviewer some years later, "and some of us single girls were there to help them out" (Taped interview). Evans finally went to the foreign mission field in Taiwan in 1956, returning in 1977. She lived in semiretirement with her sister Katherine until her death in 1989.

Religious educator Henrietta Mears (1890–1963) was Evans's equal in creative energy. Born into a wealthy and influential Minnesota family—her brother Norman was a member of the St. Paul City Council—she began her career at age eighteen, teaching in the public schools and leading a Bible class for girls in William Bell Riley's First Baptist Church in Minneapolis. The class grew from 5 to 500 in a short time, and in the wake of that success, Mears moved to southern California in 1928 to become director of Christian education at the Hollywood Presbyterian Church. In 1933 she cofounded Gospel Light Publications, soon a major source of religious education curricula for fundamentalist churches. Mears was efficient as well as charismatic; Clarence Roddy, a homiletics professor at Fuller Seminary in Pasadena, once declared her the best preacher in southern California, even though Mears herself never sought ordination and would not have described her many speaking occasions as "preaching." Described as a "human dynamo," Mears grew the Sunday School program at Hollywood Presbyterian from a few hundred students to over 4,000 within three years of her arrival. She also presided over an immensely popular Bible study class for college students and became a beloved personal mentor for many future leaders, including evangelist Billy Graham as well as Bill Bright, the founder of Campus Crusade for Christ, and Richard Halverson, later chaplain of the U.S. Senate. This focus on male students was not accidental; Mears was clear that her first priority was training men as future leaders, not women, whom she deemed to be primarily "followers."

The careers of Elizabeth Evans and Henrietta Mears suggest some of the difficulties in pinning down "women's role" in the fundamentalist movement. Throughout the 1930s and 1940s, various standards of biblical application prevailed, depending on circumstances. The movement's unofficial position was that leadership positions were ideally "men's work," to be filled by women only by absolute necessity. As a consequence, women moved into a variety of roles that, at least technically, violated biblical precepts against female preaching. They also worked under the assumption that if a man did come forward with the requisite skills, he would automatically receive their job. Thus, though women encountered relatively few absolute barriers to participation in fundamentalist institutions, they did not always receive positive sanction for doing work that properly belonged to the other sex.

World War II was an important turning point for the fundamentalist movement. On the one hand, it began to lose its militantly separatist character; the formation of the National Association of Evangelicals in 1942 marked a new generation of "neoevangelical" leaders—Harold Ockenga, Carl F. H. Henry, Billy Graham, Charles Fuller—committed to broader cooperation within the conservative Protestant world and more purposeful engagement with the intellectual currents of American society. Yet on many social issues, including gender, neoevangelicals did not significantly depart from older fundamentalist patterns.

During this same time, attitudes toward women and

gender roles took a decidedly conservative turn. Popular speakers like John R. Rice insisted on the necessity of feminine submission in the home as well as in the church. (Rice is perhaps best known for a book excoriating *Bobbed Hair, Bossy Wives, and Women Preachers*, published in 1941.) During the 1950s, fundamentalist and neoevangelical writers increasingly referred to women's role in terms of a divinely ordained order of masculine dominance and feminine obedience. Bill Gothard, leader of a popular series on "Basic Youth Conflicts," argued that men were the primary leaders in God's "chain of command" and women spiritually secondary. Fundamentalist magazines praised women who chose to minister within their families instead of undertaking careers in church work. Although this new concern for ordered households reflected some of the cultural conservatism of the postwar era, the fundamentalist insistence on obedience to authority was far more stringent than any standards of behavior they had previously attempted to maintain. Although fundamentalists had always believed that women were to be submissive to men, they did not attempt to force this rule into practice, especially as fundamentalist institutions grew apace during the 1930s and 1940s. Some fundamentalist leaders during this time even admitted that they were unsure about how the Pauline texts on women applied to the modern age. But by the 1950s, these doubts had all but disappeared in the wider fundamentalist movement.

By the 1960s and 1970s fundamentalism was losing its organizational clarity. The importance of the neoevangelical thrust, as well as the emergence of new groups, including charismatics and the Jesus movement among the young, in many ways signaled the end of the old-style militant separatism that first characterized fundamentalism. The rise of the Moral Majority and leader Jerry Falwell's entrance into politics also suggest that religious conservatism was moving in some strikingly different directions. The multifaceted evangelical movement of the 1970s and 1980s drew from a variety of theological and cultural sources, including fundamentalism, but also white and black Pentecostalism, Wesleyan Holiness traditions, and conservative Calvinist and Lutheran denominations. Southern Baptists, who had tended to dismiss fundamentalism as a movement of northern Yankees, also became part of this coalition, as the South in general became more integrated into American national culture during this time. In many ways the fundamentalist label simply does not apply to religious movements after the 1960s; fundamentalism had played an important role in bringing the modern evangelical movement into being but certainly has not defined its political or theological agenda in recent years.

Still, it is possible to trace the influence of funda-

mentalism in the continuing resistance of modern evangelicals toward women in leadership roles. The tacit understanding that theological matters, and especially the defense of orthodox doctrine, are predominantly "men's work," is certainly a fundamentalist legacy that has hindered women from full engagement in evangelical outreach. The tendency to equate women's issues, including feminism, with theologically liberal notions also suggests the ongoing importance of the fundamentalist past.

Evangelical leadership has also remained predominantly male. Especially in comparison to liberal and mainline seminaries, evangelical schools have been slow to attract women students in large numbers or to place them in church positions. Some evangelical denominations, including Southern Baptists and conservative Presbyterian groups, still prohibit women's ordination. Various evangelical parachurch organizations have also arisen in explicit opposition to feminism. In the 1980s Beverly LaHaye led the Concerned Women for America, a conservative counterpart to the National Organization for Women. In 1989 the Council on Biblical Manhood and Womanhood issued a statement endorsing masculine leadership and feminine submission as the only godly model of marriage.

Suspicions toward feminism remain, though that movement's values have clearly shaped much current evangelical thought and practice. Studies about the rhetoric of submission, for example, find within it a subtext of female empowerment, as outwardly submissive wives learn to demand reciprocal concessions from their husbands. Even the Promise Keepers' movement, calling for men to take greater leadership in home and church, in a way endorses the feminist criticism of absent fathers and irresponsible husbands. Certainly the Promise Keepers movement reflects an older fundamentalist concern about religious "feminization" and the need for greater male representation in church work—yet within a world where the old fundamentalist dichotomies have less and less explanatory power.

Within the past several decades, North American religious conservatism has become a complex and rapidly changing phenomenon, drawing from a variety of social and theological sources. Although old-style fundamentalist separatism no longer defines the center of this movement, its legacy persists. And indeed, as evangelicals continue to debate women's right to ordination or the meaning of gender roles in marriage, the continuing strength of these controversies suggests the importance of women's long and complex role within American fundamentalism.

SOURCES: Janette Hassey's *No Time for Silence: Evangelical Women in Public Ministry around the Turn of the Century* (1986) provides an overview of women's activities in the early stages of fundamentalism. See also Maria Gordon, "Women as Evangelists," *Northfield Echoes* 1 (1894): 147–151, for a defense of women's right to preach, as well as "Women's Share in Revivals," *Boston Globe*, February 17, 1909, 16, and Lena S. Sanders, *The Council Torchbearer: A Tribute to Mrs. Virginia Asher* (1936), for a description of Virginia Asher's evangelistic career. A taped interview with Elizabeth Evans in the Billy Graham Center archives at Wheaton College (1985) also includes valuable information about women's work in fundamentalist institutions. Nathan R. Wood, *A School of Christ* (1953), also gives a good account of some gender dynamics within a fundamentalist Bible school. A good summary is found in Michael S. Hamilton, "Women, Public Ministry, and American Fundamentalism, 1920–1950," *Religion and American Culture* 3 (Summer 1993): 171–196. Betty DeBerg, *Ungodly Women: Gender and the First Wave of American Fundamentalism* (1990), and Margaret Bendroth, *Fundamentalism and Gender, 1875 to the Present* (1993), include overviews of controversial literature about women. For examples see James H. Brookes, "Infidelity among Women," *Truth; Or, Testimony for Christ* 12 (August 1886): 385–388; Elizabeth Needham, *Woman's Ministry* (1895); and Clarence Macartney, "Shall We Ordain Women as Ministers and Elders?" *Presbyterian*, November 7, 1929, 8.

AMERICA'S EVANGELICAL WOMEN: MORE THAN WIVES AND MOTHERS— REFORMERS, MINISTERS, AND LEADERS

Jane Harris

PERSONS OUTSIDE THE evangelical community may imagine the evangelical woman as a submissive wife and subservient church member. A brief history of women in the evangelical movement discredits that picture. *Evangelicalism* refers to the movement that grew out of a series of revivals that progressed through various Protestant denominations in Britain and North America in the eighteenth and early nineteenth centuries. The denominations influenced by the revivals lacked a common theology but developed a set of emphases, or hallmarks of evangelicalism. These distinctive characteristics included a stress on the individual's conversion to Christian faith, understood as a life-changing, personal, and emotional experience; a piety sustained through prayer and Bible study; an emphasis on the all-encompassing authority of the Bible; a missionary zeal for sharing the gospel; and a focus on Christ's sacrifice upon the cross as the sole means of salvation.

Evangelicalism emerged in a mix of Puritanism, revivalism, and Wesleyan theology and piety that affected women's religious experiences differently, depending on their region and their race. In New England, the legacy of Puritanism weighed heavily on women caught up in the first wave of evangelicalism in the mid-eighteenth century. By the end of the eighteenth century, John Wes-

ley's theology and Methodist piety introduced additional influences that became woven into American evangelicalism. Among Wesley's legacies to evangelicalism were an emphasis on lay leadership, an energetic style of preaching, and a vision for social change. White women in the South found in early-nineteenth-century evangelicalism solace and strength to sustain them in the midst of the isolation and hardships of life on the frontier. Black women, whether in the North or South, responded positively to this expression of Christianity. The vitality and emotion of a Christianity infused by the revival spirit perhaps resonated with the religions of the African peoples from whom they had been severed. In the eighteenth and nineteenth centuries, evangelicalism spread in the wake of revivals from North to South and from East to West, bringing into churches both black and white members by the tens of thousands. This movement in Protestant Christianity profoundly shaped the character of religious life until the turn of the twentieth century. At the beginning of the twenty-first century, evangelicalism forms a subculture that continues to contour the religious experiences and lives of millions of women.

Colonial Period (1607–1775)

Northern Puritanism

Puritan theology and its "strenuous and self-searching" piety (Hall, 128) influenced the theology and practices in the evangelical movement, which arose when Puritanism weakened. Puritan thought stressed God's sovereignty, human sinfulness, and the election by God of some persons for salvation and all others for condemnation. To overcome sin, proper Puritan conduct involved strict observance of the Sabbath, temperance in drinking, daily prayer and Bible study, and the realization of a work of grace in one's life. Either through self-interrogation or the fruits of their discipline, Puritans discerned their spiritual state of salvation or damnation. As early as the seventeenth century, Puritan dissenters, including Anne Hutchinson (1591–1643), challenged the clerical authorities on matters of theology. Among other ideas, they emphasized personal experience as a more appropriate indicator of a state of grace than an individual's behavior or good works. By the end of the eighteenth century, women counted as the largest percentage of church members, yet both females and males demonstrated an increasing disaffection from the church. Fewer residents of New England, by the mid-eighteenth century, practiced the strenuous Puritan piety or sought full church membership.

Puritan attitudes toward women alternated between associating them with a seductive or gullible Eve and portraying some as pious and virtuous members of

God's elect. In time, the prevailing image of Puritan womanhood glorified marriage and motherhood. Those women who did not believe that they were created to be wives and mothers and shirked their obligations to serve their husbands threatened the hierarchically ordered Puritan society. Consequences for unconventional women ranged from being the subjects of gossip to being excommunicated from the church and banished from their colony, as Anne Hutchinson was in 1638.

For the most part, Puritan women yielded positions of religious leadership to men. Even notable dissenters and religious leaders such as Hutchinson directed their greatest energies to their family. Both the ambivalence about women and the image of the good Puritan woman set the tone for women not only in the church in New England but also in the South and, later, in evangelical circles.

As revivals stirred, some Puritan clergy softened their preaching about women. For practical purposes, the religious leaders advocated literacy for women, in order that they could read the Bible. For theological reasons, Cotton Mather and other ministers declared that women and men were spiritual equals, which in effect meant that both were equally depraved sinners. In time, Mather argued that women were more spiritual than men, because they came so close to death during childbirth. Some Puritan clergy preached that marriage was a loving companionship and that the home was a place of nurture of godly human beings.

Throughout the colonial era, Puritan women formed bonds of sisterhood as they gathered in female-only associations to practice their piety and to encourage one another. Although little is known about the women's societies of seventeenth- and eighteenth-century Puritan New England, historians suspect that their activities were harmless enough not to disturb the religious authorities. The practice of networking among women has a lengthy history in American religious life, because the religious context permitted acceptable female friendships outside the family circle. Evangelicalism provided additional opportunity for women to meet for religious purposes, with the effect of providing personal encouragement, emotional support, and spiritual direction for participants.

Southern Frontier Religion

In the seventeenth and eighteenth centuries, colonial southerners lived in more isolated, lonely, and unstable circumstances than did New Englanders. On the whole, rural women in the colonial South faced many hardships. Southern women married earlier than New England women and bore more children. Early death for southern women was common, as was early widowhood for those who survived childbirth; southern women who married before age twenty typically had husbands who

were ten years older. The women of the South labored, whether as plantation mistresses, farm wives, or slaves in the fields and households. For those who participated in religious activities, the benefits of socializing were as important as any spiritual effects. One can assume, however, that religious life did offer solace and meaning in the midst of life on the South's isolated farms and plantations (Mathews, "The Religious Experience of Southern Women," 195).

Family formed the core of life for the women in the South. From the seventeenth through much of the nineteenth century, the church proved less significant for southern women than for Puritan women. Southern women participated less in the church because the frontier environment diminished the influences of the dominant Anglican Church on the scattered populations of Maryland, Virginia, the Carolinas, and Georgia. The home and family were the central religious institutions for southern women and men until the nineteenth century.

The ideal of southern womanhood resembled the image of the good Puritan woman. According to the South's clergy, women's greatest accomplishment was to marry and bear children. Male leadership was the norm in the religious sphere, as in all other areas of family life. In matters of church government and ritual, women stayed silently behind the scenes. By the eighteenth century, however, southern women began to hear sermons that proclaimed women's superior spiritual nature, equipping them to raise devout, moral offspring. Few white southern women left testimonies of their faith, for as many as 75 percent were illiterate in the seventeenth century and 50 percent in the eighteenth century. According to historian Alice Mathews, the writings of some elite southern women, such as Martha Laurens Ramsay (1759–1811), Betsy Foote Washington, and Eliza Lucas Pinckney (1722–1793), depicted a piety that included private devotions, the writing out of religious exercises, the development of personal prayers, and the keeping of a diary as a form of religious expression and spiritual introspection (Mathews, "The Religious Women," 198).

For black women in New England and the South, life and religion were decidedly different. Women slaves in the American colonies had participated in religious traditions where women were often priests and ritual leaders. For several decades after 1619 when the first slaves arrived in the colonies, black women and men were often excluded from church membership and prohibited from formal religious activity. Some slaveholders refused to introduce black people to Christianity for fear that conversion might require the slave owner to free the bondswomen and bondsmen. In 1641 in Massachusetts, the first black woman was baptized into full membership of a Puritan church. Where colonial Christians had any success in converting Africans, women were the

tradition. An emphasis on human depravity and divine sovereignty continued. If anything, the vivid portrayals of human sinfulness evoked even greater humiliation and anxiety than earlier. Both Puritan and evangelical piety stressed conversion, but evangelicalism marked the experience not as a process but as a singular moment that thereafter defined one's relationship with God.

The empowering conversion experience affected evangelical men and women differently, according to historian Susan Juster, who outlined an "Awakening" model of conversion, in which the individual, God, and the devil related in a psychological and spiritual triangle. After the 1740s, hearing a powerful sermon or reading a timely passage of scripture excited the conversion experience. Then, as the individual drew closer to God in the experience of grace, the devil threatened this intimacy. According to Juster, women employed vividly physical images to convey the closeness of their relationship with God and the fear of separation from God after their conversion. Newly converted men expressed concern for the spiritual conditions of other people, but women engaged in introspection. Some early evangelical women wrote that they were willing to leave family and friends behind if this would speed their reunion with Christ. One new convert declared that she "felt love to Christ" and thought that she "could freely leave all in this world to serve him" (Juster, 73).

Evangelical faith was not, however, monolithic, even at its origins. Two distinct streams formed, in part, because of their teachings about the assurance of salvation following the conversion experience. For evangelicals shaped by Puritan thought, conversion did not necessarily relieve the anxiety produced by the profound sense of sin. The age-old Puritan uncertainty about the state of one's soul lingered, for the Calvinist focus on the human impossibility of knowing the mind of an all-powerful God remained. Evangelical preachers of a Puritan bent stressed the cultivation of the fruits of the Spirit (love, joy, peace, patience, kindness, generosity, faithfulness, gentleness, and self-control) and religious activism as remedies for spiritual anxiety.

Female Societies offered converted women appropriate religious outlets for their activism. Historian Susan Hill Lindley relates the story of Sarah Osborn (1714–1796) of Newport, Rhode Island, who led a Female Society in her home from the 1740s until the 1790s. She provided spiritual counsel to young women. She also

most likely to respond positively to the Christian faith. Some scholars have speculated that black women endorsed Christianity in the hope that their conversions would benefit themselves and their families. During the seventeenth and eighteenth centuries, the majority of black women and men rejected the Christianity of their masters. The advent of religious revivals changed their orientation to Christianity. While Puritan and Anglican Christianity, which dominated much of colonial America's religious life, held minimal appeal, evangelical Christianity proved enormously popular in communities of African peoples, whether free or slave.

Early Evangelicalism

Northern Manifestation

Evangelicalism began in religious revival. In the late seventeenth century, as political disturbances and Indian threats disrupted New England life, some Puritans welcomed a renewal of religious fervor, in the form of local revivals. As a result of periodic outbreaks of intense religious activity, as the eighteenth century dawned, more men joined congregations, though not in sufficient numbers to become the majority. For seventy years, until the more sustained and widespread revivals of the First Great Awakening (1730–1760), the scattered revivals recharged some Puritans' religious commitments.

Neither the manner of delivery nor the theology that framed revival preaching departed entirely from Puritan taught African Americans to read when they came to her home each Sunday evening. In correspondence with a respected local minister, Osborn noted that her religious work did not compromise her roles in the home. She understood herself as following God in her leadership of the Female Society. Moreover, she explained that no male leaders were willing to accept the responsibilities that she shouldered.

Among other changes, the First Great Awakening of 1730–1760 increased the involvement of laywomen such as Sarah Osborn in the life of the church. By the 1770s, John Wesley's Methodism became another source of encouragement for female religious leadership. Wesley's theology proved more hopeful than Puritanism, for the convert received an assurance of salvation. Moreover, Wesley taught that the Holy Spirit entered the lives of women and men, empowering them to minister in the world. Wesley's encouragement of spirit-filled persons to pursue their God-given ministries proved crucial to the enlargement of evangelical women's roles in church life.

While neither Puritans nor Methodists dismissed women's obligations as wives and mothers, both strands of evangelical tradition opened more public roles. Claiming the authority of piety, rather than learning, the laity undertook clerical functions. Laymen preached. Although laywomen did not usually proclaim the gospel from a pulpit, they embraced other public religious roles. During revival meetings, women testified to the transforming experience of conversion. As they listened to the testimonies of others, women assessed the state of the soul of the witness. Converted women offered spiritual advice to those outside their families and even criticized the clergy. Small though those roles may seem, early evangelical women could move beyond home and hearth to express their own religious experiences and understandings. However, the family did continue to be a primary focus of their religious concerns. Bringing husbands and children into the Christian faith was an important activity for evangelical women.

When women were faithful to the ministries that God gave them, they proved effective witnesses of God's grace, and John Wesley took note and affirmed this spiritual independence of women. Wesley's theology, grounded in an Arminian emphasis on the freedom of humans to respond assuredly to the grace of God for salvation, freed women to act on the promptings of the Spirit in their lives. Moreover, he advocated the public ministries of women, although stopping short of endorsing their ordination. Women within the Wesleyan tradition led prayer and preaching services and brought converts to the faith. Without ordination, however, they were ineligible to govern in the Methodist Episcopal Church, after its organization in the United States in 1784. In the home, Wesleyan women witnessed and brought their husband and children to the faith, just as

Puritan evangelicals did. Outside the home Wesleyan women prayed, preached, and evangelized. The effectiveness of these women contributed, in part, to a later generation's pronouncement of the spiritual superiority of women.

SOUTHERN MANIFESTATION

In the South, early evangelical thought and practice, particularly in Methodist and Baptist expressions, shaped women's religious roles. Evangelicalism hallowed the domestic realm. Within the "family religion" encouraged by eighteenth-century southern clergy, males were to lead prayer in the home three times daily, conduct Scripture reading at dawn and dusk, and initiate family conversations about salvation (Mathews, *Religion in the Old South*, 98–99). Women were to follow their husband's religious leadership. By the turn of the nineteenth century, the home supplanted the church as the proper forum for nurturing children and preparing them for an adult conversion experience. According to historian Donald G. Mathews, by the early nineteenth century, an ideal of evangelical womanhood developed in the South with the woman now portrayed as the center of "family religion."

The conversion experience marked the beginning of southern evangelical women's independence, for their spiritual transformation was theirs alone. In many cases, as documented by Mathews, these women acted without the approval of their husband or extended family. For some newly converted women, the church offered their sole sense of worth, caring, and companionship. With the demands of household, farm or plantation, and family, women knew few places to call their own. Mathews argues that the church provided southern women with psychological and social space.

Psychological space opened from the moment of conversion. Moreover, women shared their experience in a public place, where men and women appreciatively heard them as they offered in their own voice the narrative of their spiritual transformation. One must remember the isolation of southern women, the lack of education and even literacy, and the ostensible religious subordination of women within their families to appreciate the degree to which the testifying of the newly converted woman changed her, perhaps as much as the conversion itself. Southern women, converted during the early-nineteenth-century revivals, discovered their own voices. Many evangelical women tapped reservoirs of strength and determination to defy their husbands or family as they shaped their lives according to the teachings and values of the renewed faith to which they committed themselves.

When southern women formed community among themselves, they met to pray, plan, educate, and serve. By the 1830s, women's missionary, education, and aid societies provided significant social outlets. Through the activities of these female associations, women developed leadership skills and enlarged their visions both of the world and their own lives. Among the ideas incubated within the female church societies was the necessity of education for women. Evangelical denominations founded academies and colleges for women in the South throughout the nineteenth century, thus beginning a debate about the purposes of women's education. Among the early southern institutions for women's higher education were Mary Baldwin in Virginia, Judson in Alabama, Agnes Scott in Georgia, Maryland Methodists' Goucher College, and Virginia Presbyterians' Randolph Macon College for Women. Most evangelicals no doubt perceived a college education as strengthening women in their responsibilities as mothers and church members, but educated women extended their roles beyond the family as teachers and organization leaders.

Even with the expansion of southern women's inner and outer lives by the evangelical movement, constraints limited their exercise of their voices and their spiritual gifts. The ideal of the evangelical woman was set against the image of the worldly southern lady. The southern "lady" usually occupied the higher social strata of society; evangelical women came from the middle and lower classes. The ideal evangelical woman, as portrayed from the pulpit and in religious periodicals, was everything that the southern lady was not—conscientiously maternal, mentally disciplined, and morally mature. Mathews describes the evangelical southern woman as called to be useful, by setting good examples and doing good works; "she was to be perpetually busy doing the Lord's work, but never completing it; she was to be intensely devoted to serving the servants, but never rewarded with gratitude; she was to be supreme in her sphere, but bounded by it" (Mathews, *Religion in the Old South*, 120).

When searching for an ideal evangelical woman, one might look at the preacher's wife. As southern revivalists settled down to pastor churches, they married. Some of these women never aspired to be anyone other than the wife of the man they married. Others identified marriage to a preacher as a calling in itself. Women who embraced their role as the pastor's wife often became the leaders of the women in the church. "Even when their advice to others seemed to indicate submissiveness, these women through their many activities—teaching, visiting, writing, organizing missionary societies—provided role models of independence and responsibility for younger women" (Mathews, *Religion in the Old South*, 239). Thus, within the limits set by evangelicalism, new possibilities emerged for women to act as autonomous individuals. Even in the early twenty-first century, perhaps the best-known evangelical woman is Ruth Bell Graham (1920–), wife of the preeminent

evangelical (and southern) preacher Billy Graham and a respected figure in her own right.

AFRICAN AMERICAN EVANGELICALS

Evangelicalism opened the doors of Christianity for thousands of black women and men to enter the faith. (By the twentieth century, 60 percent of African Americans who expressed a religious preference were Baptist.) White evangelicals often objected to the distinctive black evangelical tradition, with its gospel music, lively rituals, and caller-response style of preaching. In the case of some black women, evangelicalism turned their worlds upside down. While the majority of these women became involved in useful lay ministries, a few pioneered as preachers, including Jarena Lee (1783–?), Zilpha Elaw (1790–?), and Julia A. J. Foote (1823–1900), who were northerners affiliated with the Methodist tradition. Their remarkable stories have been preserved in spiritual autobiographies, from which we learn the struggles that these nineteenth-century women had in pursuing their calling. Had the three evangelists been willing to accept their conventional roles as wives and mothers and confined their responsibilities in the church to that of exhorter, which was open to women in the Methodist Church, their stories would not claim our attention. Exhortation involved teaching Sunday School classes, leading prayer meetings, and preaching at the discretion of a male clergy. Lee, Elaw, and Foote felt a greater claim upon them, following their experiences of conversion and sanctification, which John Wesley described as a freedom from sin, so that the believer felt completely identified with God in thought, word, and deed.

For this trio sanctification became the ground for their calling as evangelists. Lee preached to mixed audiences of men and women, blacks and whites. Despite the initial disapproval of the ecclesiastical authorities of the African Methodist Episcopal Church (AMEC), Jarena Lee traveled hundreds of miles a year, between 1820 and 1849 (when her activities can last be documented), and preached hundreds of sermons. Zilpha Elaw met Jarena Lee in 1839 while both were preaching in western Pennsylvania. Elaw was an itinerant preacher in the North, in the nation's slaveholding states, and eventually in England. From 1845 until her death in 1900, Julia A. J. Foote assumed a number of leadership roles in the AMEC. She began her ministry with home-based meetings, despite the objections of both her husband and her pastor. In 1845, at the age of twenty-two, Foote launched her itinerancy, which took her from her home in Binghamton, New York, as far west as Cincinnati. She participated in Holiness revivals in Ohio before becoming an African Methodist Episcopal Zion (AMEZ) missionary. The Holiness movement began in the United States in the 1840s to preserve John Wesley's teaching of entire sanctification and Christian perfection. The

Holiness tradition stressed two stages of conversion, the first involving salvation and the second resulting in full sanctification that led to Christian perfection from sin in this life. In 1894 Foote became the first woman ordained deacon in the AMEZ Church. Shortly before her death in 1900, she was the second woman ordained an elder in her church. These three women's lives attest to the power of the evangelical movement to liberate women to struggle against the obstacles to living and acting boldly, as they felt God empowered them to do.

Black women, whether engaged in public ministries such as Lee, Elaw, and Foote, or in leadership within their own congregations, were more likely than white evangelical women to receive recognition for their efforts. In her studies of churchwomen in Petersburg, Virginia, historian Suzanne Lebsock found that the most striking feature of the records left by men of the white churches was their persistent failure to acknowledge women's collective contributions to the life of their congregations. In the black churches, however, this was not the case. For example, the records of the Gillfield Baptist Church were full of references to the contributions from the Good Samaritan Sisters, the women of the Musical Society, and the Female Building Society. Lebsock suggested that the long experience of female breadwinning within the black community led to valuing and recording women's achievements (Lebsock, 225).

Nineteenth-Century Reform

Throughout the nineteenth century, evangelicalism dominated America's religious landscape. Evangelical spokeswomen, Catharine Beecher (1800–1878) and Harriet Beecher Stowe (1811–1896), in particular, encouraged the new view of women as the moral guardians of the home. In their work as churchwomen, educators, and writers, the Beecher sisters advanced the ideal of America's evangelical women as spiritual exemplars. These changes in the portrayal of American women took place in the context of a society undergoing industrialization, particularly in the Northeast and Middle Atlantic regions, where men and women increasingly acted within separate spheres. During this era, the "cult of domesticity" arose, which exalted women's devotion to family and household, as well as their purity and piety. In her home and with her children, the nineteenth-century woman's actions and decisions were final. Even in the twentieth century, much of this ideal of womanhood continued to define evangelical women's understanding of themselves.

Although the home was their primary sphere of activity, these women responded to the needs of their day. After the Revolution, the women of America's churches formed cent, mite, and sewing circles to raise monies for a variety of church projects. The cent and mite so-cieties promoted fund-raising for missions, often giving little girls "mite boxes" in which to save their pennies to support foreign missionaries. Women's organizations drew on a long history of female networking to launch an age of reform and women's activism. The reform movements of the antebellum period became arenas for leadership on the part of elite women. Between 1800 and 1837, privileged women started early female benevolence and reform societies in communities of the Northeast and Middle Atlantic states. They assisted the poor, promoted literacy, and contributed to the moral improvement of young men. Widows and orphans, who were bereft of male protection, received benevolence from the upper-class churchwomen of their communities. The elite women who organized and funded the early women's societies learned to protect and value other women and their children. In the process, they acquired powers denied prior to this period. For example, women's societies solicited money and organized Sunday Schools, orphanages, and asylums. The societies and their sponsored projects required female directors, who were granted legal powers, property rights, financial responsibilities, and managerial duties usually withheld from women.

By the 1830s, women organized themselves in peer groups of similar age, ethnicity, and social standing. The Maternal Associations, Daughters of Temperance, and Female Religious and Moral Societies, which were begun by black women, as well as upper-class white women, expressed the peculiar concerns of women as wives and mothers. Sexual behaviors, in particular, dominated the agendas of many female societies as they dealt with prostitution and sexual promiscuity.

The Female Societies occupied ambiguous ground as social institutions. Male leadership and formal structures defined public institutions. Although the women acted within the public realm, their organizations failed the definition as a public organization because of the absence of male supervision and the presence of informal patterns of association. Women created their societies when neighbors and kinswomen joined together for common projects and purposes. Thus, female networking remained socially acceptable, despite the enlarged social roles these networks offered their members.

The influence of the evangelical movement on women's organizations was evident when middle- and working-class women, having been converted during the revivals of the Second Great Awakening (1800–1830), entered the ranks of reforming women after 1830. They sought different objectives from those of the more privileged women of the early benevolence and reform societies, for the evangelical women wanted to transform human behavior and attitudes in a battle against sin in all areas of society. The Female Religious and Moral Societies of 1837 to 1860 attempted to eliminate prostitution, for example, by aggressively condemning immoral and unrepentant men. Social upheavals and economic dislocations gave rise to the temperance movement. Some temperance women attacked aristocratic privilege, which protected the upper class from the vagaries of the economy. They also aggressively challenged the purveyors and users of alcohol, which threatened the security of women and children. The Woman's Christian Temperance Union, under the dynamic leadership of Methodist Frances Willard, loomed large among nineteenth-century women's organizations.

Some reforming women addressed the issue of slavery as participants in the abolition movement. Social historian Nancy Isenberg has argued that the targets for women's moral outrage about slavery were the male slave owners, whose greed, lust, and selfishness perpetuated the evils of slavery. In addition to praying, writing, and speaking against slavery, antislavery women mounted educational campaigns. Isenberg wrote that abolitionists thought that they could reach the hearts and minds of American women and, through female sympathies for oppressed slave women, move the nation toward emancipation.

Other reform movements reached out to America's impoverished, urban populations. One of these efforts, the Sunday School Movement, began in New York City in 1802, when Joanna Bethune (1796–1849) and her mother Isabella Graham (1742–1814) adapted the ideas of British evangelicals to the American urban context. Another transatlantic movement, the deaconesses, involved some American evangelicals in the establishment of religious orders of single women committed to ministry among the sick, orphaned, and impoverished. From 1870 until 1900, several American denominations, in particular the Methodist Episcopal Church, started 100 deaconess houses. Most American evangelicals, however, spurned these religious sisterhoods, for they too closely resembled Catholic religious orders. Moreover, the evangelical idealization of marriage and motherhood left virtually no room for the encouragement of celibate, single, religious women's activism. Methodists, however, were the evangelicals most open to deaconesses, whom historian Mary Agnes Doughtery has called the agents of applied Christianity, which involved changing people's views and attitudes to win them to a new "religio-social faith" (Doughtery, in Thomas and Keller, *Women in New Worlds*, 203). By the late nineteenth century, training schools, such as the Methodists' New England Deaconess Home and Training School, Scarritt Bible and Training School, and Chicago Training School for City, Home, and Foreign Missions, provided American women with religious education in preparation for their ministries.

Higher education for American women grew, in significant measure, from the evangelical vision of Mary Lyon (1797–1849). She dreamed of Mount Holyoke Female Seminary, established in 1837 in South Hadley, Massachusetts, as a "school for Christ," where "the daughters of the church" would be educated and inspired with a missionary spirit to take the gospel and moral reform to the world. One finds an indication of Lyon's success when surveying the rosters of women missionaries and missionary society leaders who were indeed alumnae of Mount Holyoke. Moreover, Mount Holyoke became a prototype for other religiously oriented women's academies and colleges, which were established more slowly throughout the South, typically under the auspices of the Methodist and Baptist denominations, and later in the Midwest and West.

The missionary movement of the nineteenth and early twentieth centuries drew from the evangelizing impulses of churchwomen. Women who stayed home provided essential support in the form of prayer, fundraising, and recruiting. The women who remained in America eventually organized their efforts through female missionary societies, modeled on the earlier benevolence and reform societies. Although interdenominational missionary organizations developed in the early nineteenth century, the more typical pattern was for an individual denomination to house its own sending and support agencies. The female missionary society leaders, many of whose accomplishments have become obscured by history, often wielded significant power as they controlled tens of thousands of dollars dispensed to further world evangelization.

Women, both married and single, left the United States for mission fields such as Burma, India, China, Persia, Liberia, and Nigeria. The names and accomplishments of many of the thousands of missionary women are lost to us. From extant missionary correspondence, diaries, and reports, historians know that married women faced huge challenges as wives and mothers. Numbers of early missionary wives did not survive childbirth, or they suffered the effects of childbearing, which weakened their resistance to disease. America's first missionary wife, Ann Hasseltine Judson (1789–1826), died in Burma, after thirteen years of missionary service. One of her most important roles was to correspond with women in the United States, to whom she related details of her life and the lives of Burmese women. In this way, Judson and other missionary women educated America's women about the world, especially about other women's lives. For single missionary women, opportunities for service as physicians, educators, and evangelists opened overseas that would never have been available to them at home. They realized achievements and fulfillment that few would have experienced in America. The missionary enterprise of the nineteenth and early twentieth century benefited from women's commitments, both on the mission fields and in America, where they provided enormous energy and funding to extend Christianity around the globe.

Whether at home or abroad, women's emergence into the religious public sphere did not subvert the dominating ideal of women as wives and mothers. In the 1830s Phoebe Palmer (1807–1874) became a central figure in the interdenominational Holiness movement, which stressed Wesley's idea of a "second blessing" that followed conversion and produced entire sanctification or a holy life. The movement eventually generated new churches such as the Wesleyan Methodist Church (1843), the Free Methodist Church (1860), and the Church of God (1880s). Phoebe Palmer's Tuesday Meeting for the Promotion of Holiness was a catalyst for the larger Holiness movement. As men and women gathered weekly in her New York City home, she always emphasized the roles of wife and mother and encouraged the women who participated to seek a balance in their lives between domesticity and religion. Palmer not only taught and evangelized; she engaged in projects that served the needs of New York City's poor, imprisoned, and uneducated. One historian has argued that Palmer never moved from her benevolence and reform work to the women's movement, as some evangelical women did, because she "never shed a sense of uneasiness at neglecting domestic duties" (Loveland, 470). Palmer was more concerned with women's spiritual state than their earthly circumstances, which might well distinguish the perspective of many evangelical women activists. Large numbers of Methodist women failed to emulate her balance between ministry and domesticity, for the Methodist Church interpreted Palmer's work as unique.

By contrast with Phoebe Palmer, Anna Howard Shaw (1847–1919) followed her calling without including domesticity in the balancing of her life. Shaw was a Methodist woman called to ministry, medicine, and activism in the women's movement. She left frontier Michigan in 1876 to pursue theological studies at Boston University. The Methodist Protestant Church (a progressive off-shoot of the Methodist Episcopal Church that formed in the 1820s) ordained her in 1880 as a parish minister in East Dennis, Massachusetts. Finding the parish too limiting, Shaw completed a medical degree so that she might address the needs of women's bodies, as well as their souls, and worked for three years as a physician among women of Boston's slums. Shaw assumed the presidency of the National American Woman's Suffrage Association from 1904 to 1915, which she led with a vision of reform that integrated feminism, a faith in the ideals of democracy, and her Christian theology (Pallaver, 220).

Throughout the nineteenth century, American Protestants worked out their understanding of the roles of women. Evangelical denominations incorporated women in a variety of ways. Although John Wesley affirmed the ministries of women, American Methodists greatly debated their roles. Until 1880, the Methodist Episcopal Church licensed women to preach, but the General Conference of that year ceased the licensing, while continuing to recognize women's lay ministries. Local congregations provided avenues of service for Methodist deaconesses. Only in 1904, however, did Methodist women receive the rights to become official delegates within the church's governing bodies. The Holiness tradition, unlike the Methodism from which it sprang, remained open to women's ministries, believing that the Holy Spirit gifted and empowered them. Holiness evangelist, author, and temperance and suffragist leader Hannah Whitall Smith (1832–1911) found open doors in Holiness circles, where she preached in the United States and Britain, becoming known as "the angel of the churches" (Dieter, 2). In 1887, Christian and Missionary Alliance (C&MA) movement leader Albert B. Simpson taught that a person controlled by the Holy Spirit had no choice but to be a missionary and share the Christian gospel with others either at home or overseas. Thus, the newly established C&MA enthusiastically welcomed women's ministries in the cause of evangelizing the world.

Baptist women, by contrast, often faced limited options for their ministries. Southern Baptists refused from 1845 until 1918 even to allow women to serve as messengers (delegates) to the annual Southern Baptist Convention (SBC). Yet among Southern Baptists of the nineteenth and twentieth centuries, one of the best known and loved figures was Lottie Moon (1840–1912), the single woman missionary to China. Moon went to China in 1873 as an evangelist in Tengchow/Dengzhou and P'ingtu/Pingdu. She used creative approaches, including baking cookies, to overcome the Chinese people's fear of her. She adopted traditional Chinese dress and learned the language and culture as means of sharing her Faith. Throughout her years in China, Moon corresponded with SBC churches, encouraging fund-raising to support foreign missions and recruitment of additional missionaries. Even today, the annual SBC offering for foreign missions is named in honor of Moon. In 1912, China confronted both war and famine. Moon refused to eat when those around her were starving, so she distributed her food to her Chinese neighbors. By the end of 1912, Moon was so frail from starvation that another missionary escorted her back to the United States. On Christmas Eve 1912, Moon died on board ship in the harbor at Kobe, Japan. Her death and her life in China have made Moon a legend (some say even a saint) among Southern Baptists.

Despite the examples of Moon and other committed women, Southern Baptists were reluctant to embrace new roles for women. Southern churches in general lagged behind evangelicals elsewhere in responding to the social concerns that animated the benevolence and reform efforts of the nineteenth century. The missionary movement inspired southern evangelical participation, and the temperance movement garnered the attention and commitments of many. Most white evangelicals in the South, however, shunned such efforts as the abolition movement and, later, the suffrage movement.

While churches debated, individual, gifted women left indelible marks upon evangelicalism. Among some of the most influential women were hymn writers, such as Fanny Crosby (1820–1915; author of thousands of gospel song texts, such as "Blessed Assurance," "I Am Thine O Lord," and "Rescue the Perishing"), Charlotte Elliott (1789–1871; "Just as I Am, Without One Plea"), Frances Ridley Havergal (1836–1879; "I Gave My Life for Thee"), Cecil Frances Alexander (1818–1895; "Jesus Calls Us O'er the Tumult"). Historian Mark Noll has recently written about the importance of gospel hymns within evangelicalism, for they conveyed what Noll argues is the best of evangelical theology. Some of the most beloved hymns, still sung by millions of evangelicals, were penned by women of the nineteenth and early twentieth century. These hymn writers continue to leave their stamp upon the experiences of evangelical Christians. Their work as theologians and hymn writers has been woven into the very fabric of evangelicalism.

For many black evangelical women, music offered a significant way to proclaim the gospel and minister. In the twentieth century, singers such as Mother Willie Mae Smith (1904–1994) preached through their singing. Lucie E. Campbell (1885–1963) played a significant role in compiling several hymnbooks that remain standards among contemporary African American evangelicals. Other musically gifted women, such as Roberta Martin (1907–1969), participated in the National Convention of Gospel Choirs and Choruses, where she helped refine the genre of gospel music. Sallie Martin (1896–1988) established a publishing house, Martin and Morris Music Company, which disseminated gospel songs and enabled the national convention to survive and grow.

Historian Randall Balmer has argued that evangelical songs often idealized women. Songbooks written after 1840 contained hymns such as "Tell Mother I'll Be There," in which the text portrays women alternately praying and weeping for their children or waiting for their wayward, sometimes drunken son to come home. The evangelical paeans to motherhood annually reach a crescendo on Mother's Day, in a celebration of female goodness and piety. Balmer has suggested that while American Catholics have adored the Blessed Virgin Mary, American evangelicals have worshiped the image of the godly wife and mother (Balmer, 72–73).

Conflicts and Charismatic Leaders in the Twentieth Century

Extolling marriage and motherhood as the female ideal hearkened back to the Puritan roots of the tradition, even as the evangelical movement and the nation itself experienced profound social changes. Early decades of the twentieth century brought significant shifts in women's roles in the larger culture and in the evangelical churches. By the twentieth century, evangelicalism's dominance in America ended. The movement took on both broad and narrow meanings, as described by historian George Marsden. In its broad context, twentieth-century evangelicalism encompassed the hallmarks noted earlier. In a more narrow sense, evangelicalism has become a religious subculture wherein millions of Americans belong to Protestant denominations but also identify with the evangelical community. The network of institutions and organizations that sustain the evangelical subculture include publishing houses such as Eerdmans; Bible institutes such as Columbia Bible Institute; colleges such as Wheaton College; seminaries such as Fuller Theological Seminary; and voluntary groups such as the National Association of Evangelicals.

Fundamentalism entered evangelicalism in the 1890s and influenced evangelical life throughout the twentieth century. Marsden has defined fundamentalists as "militant evangelicals who battled against modernists' accommodations of the gospel message to modern intellectual and cultural trends" (Marsden, xii). The fundamentalist-modernist controversy of the first two decades of the twentieth century evoked a new mood among evangelicals, one of fear and negativism. The introduction of the literary-historical methods of biblical criticism and challenges to Christian theology brought by scientific theories of evolution polarized American Protestants, particularly in the Northern Baptist and Northern Presbyterian denominations. Modernists welcomed the new ideas, while fundamentalists identified them as threats to the very core of evangelical theology—the authority of the Bible, the atoning work of Christ, and the reality of the supernatural realm. The controversy subsided after the Scopes trial in Dayton, Tennessee, in 1926, after which the fundamentalists retreated to build a foundation that sustained later activism, when they returned to public visibility in the 1970s.

The turn of the twentieth century cast a new mood over American women. In the post–World War I era, Americans as a whole lost their optimism as the nation tried to make sense of life after the war. Simultaneously evangelicals tried to recover the vitality siphoned from the movement by the fundamentalist-modernist conflict. Activist evangelical women joined other American women in a retreat from the public sphere. One enticement for a return to domesticity may have been the offering of a new model for marriage, which stressed companionship and the appeal of family life.

Nevertheless, some evangelical women charted other paths. Aimee Semple McPherson (1890–1944) became one of America's most colorful evangelists. In 1921, she founded the ministry that became the International Church of the Foursquare Gospel, a Pentecostal denomination. She also pioneered in the use of radio, along with southern Californian Grace Fuller (1885–1966), who with her husband Charles produced the extremely popular *Old-Fashioned Revival Hour* from the mid-1930s through the 1940s.

During the early years of the twentieth century, black and white evangelical women encouraged great strides in Christian education. From the 1930s, two sisters, Mary (1910–1997) and Lois (1907–1998) LeBar, led the Christian Education Department at Wheaton College, where they trained hundreds of young women and men. In southern California, Henrietta Mears (1890–1963) became widely respected as a Bible teacher and mentor of future pastors. Among African American women, the role of educator was singularly significant. Some of the most outstanding African American evangelicals of the nineteenth and twentieth centuries were church-women who educated the black people of the South and the southern black migrant to America's urban areas. Among these legendary educators were Anna Julia Cooper (1858–1964), Juliette Derricotte (1897–1931), Lucy Craft Laney (1854–1933), Mary Church Terrell (1863–1954), Hallie Q. Brown (1845–1949), Charlotte Hawkins Brown (1883–1961), Nannie Helen Burroughs (1879–1961), Ida B. Wells Barnett (1862–1931), and Mary McLeod Bethune (1875–1955). The black educator was a leader in her community, and despite her subordination to the male church leaders, she wielded much influence within the churches.

In characterizing the era between 1920 and 1950, some scholars of evangelicalism have said that evangelicals of the period may aptly be called fundamentalists. Contrary to popular assumptions about women and fundamentalism, the middle years of the twentieth century were not a wasteland for evangelical/fundamentalist women. Two contrary forces collided during these decades. Fundamentalists purposefully identified the true faith with masculine values and liberalism with femininity, understood as weak and shallow. This portrayal perpetuated ambivalence about women. On the other hand, as the evangelical/fundamentalist movement of the era engaged in network building of agencies and organizations, women contributed the strength of their numbers and talents to the expansion of the movement. Historian Michael Hamilton has described women assuming public ministries such as teaching Sunday School, supporting missionary work overseas, doing visitation, working

with youth, and providing music leadership. An increasing number of Bible institutes trained the women whose public roles sustained the evangelical movement.

After 1940 neoevangelicalism separated from the older evangelical/fundamentalist movement. The male neoevangelical leaders, Billy Graham chief among them, affirmed the conservative theology of the older movement but added a more positive spirituality and an intellectual orientation not present in fundamentalism. What scholars today call evangelicalism is the expression of neoevangelicalism that has developed, in distinction from fundamentalism, over the last sixty years. The evangelical scholar Margaret Lamberts Bendroth (1954–   ) notes that neoevangelicals have had no influential female leaders. The absence of female leadership and the continued ambivalence about women have profoundly affected the course of the discussions among evangelicals, during the last decades of the twentieth century, about the propriety of women's ordination, for example.

The late twentieth century witnessed an increased diversity among evangelicals, which now include such ethnic European denominations as the Dutch Reformed and Christian Reformed Churches, along with Pentecostal and Holiness denominations, Baptists, Adventists, Brethren, Church of Christ, Church of God, Mennonites, and independent congregations. Most significantly, a sense of belonging to a community or subculture, as Randall Balmer described it, remains. Evangelical organizations at the turn of the twenty-first century range from the politically radical Sojourners Community in Washington, D.C., to the charismatic Women's Aglow Fellowship International. Black and white evangelicals, throughout the twentieth century, traveled separate paths. The white evangelical tendency to embrace the status quo immobilized them in the midst of the civil rights crises of mid-century. In the South, in particular, most white evangelicals shunned involvement in the call for justice raised by black clergy such as Martin Luther King, Jr. Many evangelical women did rally to respond to the influence of feminism. Some joined with evangelical scholar Mary Stewart Van Leeuwen in the organization Christians for Biblical Equality, where they worked for a biblically based egalitarian church and world. Other evangelicals, desiring order above all else, held fast to the traditional ideal of women as wives and mothers. Within the evangelical subculture, women live between the ideal of womanhood that celebrates the roles of devoted wife, nurturing mother, and committed church member and the reality of life in an age when the majority of women must work outside the home and all women face change, uncertainty, and choices.

SOURCES: For an understanding of the history of American evangelicalism, these works are essential: Randall Balmer,

Blessed Assurance: A History of Evangelicalism in America (1999); George Marsden, ed., *Evangelicalism and Modern America* (1984); and Mark A. Noll, *American Evangelical Christianity* (2001). Historian David D. Hall, in *World of Wonder, Days of Judgment* (1990), reconstructs religious life in colonial New England and sets the stage for Susan Juster's *Disorderly Women: Sexual Politics and Evangelicalism in Revolutionary New England* (1994), which portrays evangelicalism's early effects on women. Donald G. Mathews's, *Religion in the Old South* (1977), Alice E. Mathews's "The Religious Experience of Southern Women," in *Women and Religion in America*, ed. Rosemary Radford Ruether and Rosemary Skinner Keller, vol. 2 (1983), and Suzanne Lebsock's *The Free Women of Petersburg* (1984) provide histories of southern women's religious experiences. Comprehensive histories of women in American religion include Susan Hill Lindley, *"You Have Stept Out of Your Place": A History of Women and Religion in America* (1996); Ruth A. Tucker and Walter L. Liefled, *Daughters of the Church* (1987); and Rosemary Radford Ruether and Rosemary Skinner Keller, eds., *Women and Religion in America*, 3 vols. (1981–1986). The following works address particular women or issues: William L. Andrews, ed., *Sisters of the Spirit: Three Black Women's Autobiographies of the Nineteenth Century* (1986); Hilah E. Thomas and Rosemary Skinner Keller, eds., *Women in New Worlds* (1981); Nancy G. Isenberg, "Women's Organizations," in *Encyclopedia of American Social History*, vol. 3 (1993); Mary D. Pellauer, *Toward a Tradition of Feminist Theology* (1991); Anne C. Loveland, "Domesticity and Religion in the Antebellum Period: The Career of Phoebe Palmer," *The Historian* 39.3 (1977): 455–471; M. E. Dieter, "Hannah Whitall Smith: A Woman for All Seasons," *Holiness Digest* (Fall 1999); Michael S. Hamilton, "Women, Public Ministry, and American Fundamentalism, 1920–1950," *Religion and American Culture* 3 (1993): 171–196; and Margaret Lamberts Bendroth, "Fundamentalism and Femininity: Points of Encounter between Religious Conservative and Women, 1919–1935," *Church History* 61.2 (1992): 221–233.

THE CHARISMATIC MOVEMENT
R. Marie Griffith

THE CHARISMATIC MOVEMENT developed during the second half of the twentieth century as an impulse for spiritual renewal among mainline Protestants, Roman Catholics, and some Orthodox worshipers. At one time, the movement's name simply specified Christians who were drawn to a particular kind of intense religious experience and committed to bringing that experience back into their own home churches, in hopes of reviving the faith of those who were thought to be merely nominal Christians. Over time, however, the designation has become far more diffuse, as those calling themselves "charismatic" have increasingly abandoned their churches of origin for Pentecostal, fundamentalist, or independent evangelical churches. By the end of the twentieth century, participants in the movement would more often describe themselves as "spirit-filled" than as charismatic—or eschewing labels altogether, would simply call themselves Christians, a time-honored method for distinguishing between so-called true and false adherents of the tradition. Whatever the complexities of this terminology, the designation *charismatic movement* remains useful as a way of describing evangelical Christians who, like other evangelicals, rely heavily on the Bible in all things and hold a strict view of eternal salvation but who also practice an acutely embodied faith. In that sense, charismatics are evangelicals who incorporate dance, singing, vocalized prayer and prophesying, the laying on of hands, shouting, laughing, spiritual warfare (a form of aggressive shouting and pantomimed combat against demonic forces), and other physical and vocal manifestations into their corporate worship.

As with the Pentecostal movement that emerged some fifty years earlier, the charismatic movement is distinguished by a special interest in the spiritual "gifts" or "charisma" described in the New Testament, particularly the gifts of spirit baptism, glossolalia (speaking in tongues), healing, and prophesy. Also like the Pentecostal movement, the charismatic movement as a whole has taken a notably conservative position on gender roles, insisting on doctrinal adherence to the ideal of female submission to male headship. Early associated with the efforts of influential men—Oral Roberts, Demos Shakarian, and Dennis Bennett, most prominently—the movement has been fortified and sustained through the enthusiastic participation and leadership of women. If women have been more in evidence in charismatic pews than pulpits, notable women have yet made their mark as charismatic principals, from faith healer Kathryn Kuhlman to evangelists and authors such as Corrie ten Boom, Tammy Faye Bakker, Beverly LaHaye, Rita Bennett, Joyce Meyer, and Juanita Bynum.

While it is impossible to give a precise date of origin for this charismatic movement, most historians look to the 1950s and early 1960s as the time when charismatic beliefs and worship practices emerged into view on a large scale. It is worth noting that this method of dating the movement relies on a chronicle of male-led organizations and male pastors who pushed the gifts of healing and spirit baptism into the public eye. An account centered on women's participation, while still noting this period as a crucial signpost of the movement's expansion, would nonetheless highlight the broad participation of women in the healing revivals that took place across the country during the 1940s, not to mention the denominational crossings among Pentecostals, Methodists, Baptists, independents, Catholics, and others much earlier. Those traversings, and the networks they spawned, laid the foundation for the diverse ecumenical participation that has long characterized the charismatic movement, alternately pleasing and confounding ob-

Until her death in 1976, Kathryn Kuhlman was the most famous female evangelist associated with the charismatic movement. In the last decade of her life, she was widely regarded as the most sought after healing evangelist in the nation, exclusive of gender. *Courtesy of the Flower Pentecostal Center.*

servers with its theological variety. Like the spirit-oriented movements of prior eras, well known to have opened up roles and vocations for women largely unavailable in traditional institutions, the charismatic movement has held enormous appeal for the millions of women who have developed, nourished, and continuously reshaped it.

History of the Movement

Even as the healing revivals of such figures as William Branham and Oral Roberts attracted more women than men, early charismatic organizations were directed exclusively toward the latter, particularly businessmen. This emphasis was no accident. The Full Gospel Business Men's Fellowship International (FGBMFI) originated in 1952 under the guidance of Demos Shakarian and Roberts. Shakarian was perturbed by the clear predominance of women at revival meetings, who seemed

to outnumber men by a ratio of ten to one. His new organization shortly reached beyond its founding Pentecostal circles into the mainline Protestant churches, drawing from the large pool of successful middle-class men in attendance. The group's magazine, *Full Gospel Voice*, was launched in 1953, and by 1972 the organization had an annual operating budget of more than $1 million. Magazine issues were filled with positive tales of spiritual and financial growth, while photographs depicted well-attended meetings in grand hotel ballrooms and other extraecclesial spaces, hosting men at worship. The goal, as it had been for generations of Protestant male leaders in America, was to strengthen Christianity's attractions for the male populace by making it seem vigorous and respectable, that is, manly.

Those efforts reaped breathtaking results, according to those leading the way. Indeed, the Fellowship was a highly successful organizing force for the charismatic movement during the 1950s and 1960s, gathering men into the charismatic fold and funding many independent revivalists outside of ordinary church structures. Although racially monolithic—the early charismatic movement was composed almost exclusively of Anglo-Americans, though Shakarian's Armenian American heritage lent it some semblance of cultural variety—the group was denominationally diverse, providing an ecumenical venture far more successful than most other interchurch initiatives of the period. In what was, from one angle, a precursor to later groups such as the Promise Keepers, men gathered together to share their testimonies, lay hands on one another for healing, and induct newcomers into the mysteries of the spiritual gifts, all the while keeping a focus on the particular issues that faced them as men in American culture.

While the Fellowship continued to grow as an independent or parachurch organization, the charismatic movement also gained ground within denominations and local congregations. Roman Catholics experienced their own form of Pentecost as the movement swept through parishes across the country, particularly the Midwest. Vatican II (1962–1965), persuaded by Léon-Joseph Cardinal Suenens, officially recognized the importance of charismatic gifts and urged a renewed openness to them. In February 1967, a prayer group of faculty and students formed at Duquesne University (Pittsburgh), and later that same year similar groups formed at the University of Notre Dame, Michigan State University, and the University of Michigan. Such meetings, especially at Catholic institutions such as Notre Dame, spilled out into stadium assemblies that drew hundreds, and eventually thousands, of people into corporate worship. While the third annual gathering at Notre Dame, for instance, drew around 450 people from many states and Canadian provinces, the fifth meeting attracted nearly 5,000 people. By 1976, that number had reached 30,000, and organizers decided to promote regional events instead. While Catholic participation in the charismatic movement is difficult to measure, hundreds of thousands of Catholics have participated over time.

In the meantime, charismatic worship gained further ground in many Protestant congregations, particularly Episcopalian ones. One of the most famous and influential of the latter was Dennis Bennett's Episcopal church near Seattle, Washington. While formerly the rector of a wealthy parish in California, Bennett experienced Spirit baptism accompanied by speaking in tongues, an occurrence he related to his shocked parishioners on April 3, 1960. This event led to Bennett's resignation and reassignment to St. Luke's Church in the Seattle suburb of Ballard, Washington, where he became renowned for his leadership in the charismatic movement. Seattle also became an originating point for charismatic women's organizations, when four women from

the area organized a devotional group that would come to be known as Women's Aglow Fellowship International, or simply Aglow.

For telling the history of women in the charismatic movement, no event is more important than the formation of Aglow. For decades this group (the name comes from the verse in Romans 12:11, "Be aglow and burning with the Spirit") was the vital organizing force for bringing women into the charismatic movement. Like its early founders, most participants in the early decades were from mainline Protestant and Roman Catholic congregations (a number of these were connected to Dennis Bennett's church). They sought, then and later, to draw in women from all Christian denominations, as well as those who were outside the Christian fold, in order to bring them into a deeper experience and understanding of God's blessings. As an ecumenical or transdenominational venture, Aglow members have long deemphasized theological differences in favor of a "simple" gospel that they claim is the essence of the biblical tradition. They have promoted this simple gospel in monthly local prayer meetings, regional retreats, and annual national and international conferences. Through these various components, women have shared both their sufferings and their testimonies with each other, prayed and worshiped together, and fortified one another's faith in the Christian God.

Just as important, Aglow—later officially renamed Aglow International—has offered a space for women to occupy positions of leadership in women-only settings and to observe other women teaching, preaching, and evangelizing on a scale rarely, if ever, seen in their local churches. While promoting what would in most mainline settings be perceived as a conservative view of women and gender, these female leaders have served to establish women's authority in ways unthinkable within Pentecostal and charismatic culture prior to the formation of Aglow. Both in their sheer presence as women standing in pulpits and lecterns and in their subtle reconfigurations of male teachings on women's proper place in the public and private spheres, Aglow leaders have slowly but surely enhanced the roles available to women in the charismatic movement. Such power is not always used benignly, of course, and female no less than male leaders have sometimes abused their positions so as to dampen or even silence other women's voices of which they disapprove. Meanwhile, however, women not occupying positions of official leadership have found other religious means for asserting individual authority, through such practices as public prayer, prophesy, and scriptural interpretation. The potential impact of the confidence gained in such female-only settings, transferred back into local congregations, is vast.

Churches that house charismatic practitioners have not, however, been eager to accept women in the highest leadership positions or, often enough, even in intermediate ones. Like so many conservative denominational bodies, the highest achievable ministerial position often resides in the area of education, particularly children's education, which is still seen as women's work. Charismatic churches, in short, do not believe that women are authorized by scripture to serve as senior pastors. Whether this position can be credibly sustained over time, as growing numbers of women rise to wide fame in charismatic and evangelical culture as television and stadium evangelists, is questionable. Women such as Anne Graham Lotz, Jan Crouch, Joyce Meyer, and Juanita Bynum, like their predecessors Kathryn Kuhlman and Aimee Semple McPherson, draw enormous crowds of women (and no small numbers of men) to their circuit of TV shows and revival meetings. Their popularity has long rivaled and frequently exceeded that of many male evangelists. Whether conservative Christians will continue to maintain a theological distinction between the role of evangelist and that of church pastor, and whether most will perpetually insist on women's unfitness for the latter position, is an open question. Attitudes opposing women as teachers have already been dramatically transformed in the past half century, a shift that is due in no small part to the unrelenting efforts of individual women leaders and, even more, to broad-based organizations such as Aglow.

Other women's groups followed in Aglow's footsteps, most of them avoiding the older designation "charismatic" and seeking to bridge the theological rifts that were of such import to earlier generations of Pentecostals, fundamentalists, and evangelicals. With the rise of the men's group Promise Keepers in the early 1990s, increasing media attention was devoted to women's organizations such as Promise Reapers, Praise Keepers, and Women of Faith. In the early twenty-first century, the trend seems to be toward the merging of women's organizational efforts into enormous conferences such as Global Celebration for Women, held in the Houston Astrodome in September 2001, with over 30,000 women in attendance. (Of course, such efforts are often enough supported by male leaders or by larger reformist groups such as the conservative Institute on Religion and Democracy, which endorsed the Global Celebration.) Bringing together female leaders and participants from Pentecostal, fundamentalist, parachurch, and denominational groups, this gathering exemplifies what could well be termed the charismaticization of evangelical culture, with the experiential emphasis of the charismatic movement now permeating other sectors—including ones formerly hostile to such embodied applications—of American Christianity. As the example of Promise Keepers shows, men have surely played a vital role in this diffusion of charismatic practice into other religious arenas; yet as the Promise Keepers' short peak and rapid demise also suggest, women's presence has been steadier, more evident, and arguably more influential all along the way.

Charismatic Views of Women and Gender

For most of the charismatic movement's history, leaders have viewed women's status as a fairly straightforward issue: Wives are to be submissive to their husbands, and women more generally are to submit to pastors and other men in leadership positions. Much has been made of scriptural verses such as Ephesians 5:22 "Wives, submit to your husbands as to the Lord" (New International Version [NIV]), and charismatic women have been no less vocal than their male counterparts in thrusting this teaching to the center of Christian practice. Books such as Shirley Boone's *One Woman's Liberation* (1972), Marabel Morgan's bestseller *The Total Woman* (1973), and Beverly LaHaye's *I Am a Woman by God's Design* (1980) led the way in instructing women to surrender their will to that of their husbands, in order to receive greater happiness all around. As the charismatic Morgan's enormously popular book put it:

> God ordained man to be the head of the family, its president.... A Total Woman is not a slave. She graciously chooses to adapt to her husband's way, even though at times she may desperately not want to. He in turn will gratefully respond by trying to make it up to her and grant her desires. He may even want to spoil her with goodies. (82–83)

Using different methods to make this point, charismatic authors agreed for many years that the command of female submission was unambiguous and vital to everyday Christian life.

During the 1980s, however, a perceptible, if subtle, shift began to take place. The changing realities of women's lives, including their increasing presence in the white-collar workforce, have mixed with older ideals of proper gender roles to produce distinctive understandings of true Christian womanhood. Charismatic female authors, who were once virtually obliged to state that they were mothers and homemakers, began to acknowledge themselves and their readers as, most likely, career women. More and more women also began writing about domestic problems such as marital discontent, divorce, abuse, alcoholism, and drug addiction. Unlike most of the early charismatic literature of the 1960s and 1970s, written by women who assumed their audience to be mostly housewives with children, charismatic literature produced in the 1990s and beyond presumed little about its readers' domestic status except that their lives are probably full of heartache or at least confusion over their roles as Christian women. As increasing numbers of charismatic women became divorced, single mothers themselves, or acknowledged abusive or alcohol-drenched childhoods, the older idealism about domestic bliss was somewhat tempered.

Amid these social changes, the older ideal of the submissive, generally passive wife gradually began to give way to newer models of women warriors battling the forces of Satan—often in very vocal, even violent ways, as women pounded their fists in the air and screamed for Satan to leave them and their children alone—and helping one another surmount the ordinary obstacles of their lives. In gatherings of charismatic women at the turn of the twenty-first century, for instance, women are far more likely to be praised for being battle-strong and powerful, capable of bringing God's will to bear on a fallen world, than for being meek servants of their husbands. In all, changing ideals of Christian womanhood in charismatic culture have been intricately connected to changing social patterns in American marriage, family, and work patterns since the 1960s, and the variegation of such ideals reflects choice as well as uncertainty about dissolving gender-role boundaries.

Still, like the Pentecostal and broader evangelical movements in America, the charismatic movement reflects continued tension between the presence of prophesying daughters and the traditionalist readings of scripture that have persistently taught women and men that their roles are separate and unequal. Male ministers, especially, have often discussed issues of submission and authority in ways that emphasize men as protectors or "coverings" for women in both the home and church. Yet, with or without the benefits of ordination, women have perpetually risen up as preachers, evangelists, and even pastors, challenging the doctrine of female submission in both subtle and not so subtle ways. Theologically, moreover, particularly as more and more charismatic women have received university and seminary education, they have come to talk more vigorously about the "mutual submission" principle advocated in Ephesians 5:21 ("Submit to one another out of reverence for Christ") than the older, one-sided view of wifely or female submission. Yet this remains a contested ideal, as other women and men in the charismatic movement along with other evangelical and fundamentalist circles continue to insist upon a divine hierarchy that places man just under God in power, appointed to rule over woman.

Influential Women

The charismatic movement has always been fortified by the presence of women who have dedicated their lives to spreading the gospel of God's everyday, experiential presence in the lives of true believers. To use their own terminology, women have opened their hearts to the message of joy and peace that is at the core of the charismatic gospel. They have, moreover, earnestly sought to fill the lives of other women, men, and children with the joyousness that they believe only a close relationship with Jesus can bring. In some cases, this commitment has meant ministering to prisoners or other people living in relative isolation from the church and in dire need of human care. In others, living out the charismatic faith has meant starting or participating in support groups of other women who seek to be freed from their own emotional "strongholds" (a charismatic term for the psychological obstacles that they believe Satan uses to distance them from God and each other). While most of these women remain anonymous in the written histories, a few have achieved widespread fame within the charismatic movement. It should be noted that several of the women described here publicly avoided the use of the term *charismatic* for particular reasons; and yet they have not only worked closely with charismatic Christians but, more important, been a source of enormous influence and change in the charismatic movement over time.

Kathryn Kuhlman

Until her death in 1976, Kathryn Kuhlman (1907–1976) was the most famous female evangelist associated with the charismatic movement. In the last decade of her life, she was widely regarded as the most sought-after healing evangelist in the nation, exclusive of gender. Like Oral Roberts, Kuhlman emerged out of the healing revival of the post–World War II era, traveling vast distances to offer high-energy healing services in meeting halls and auditoriums across the country. Like the Pentecostal evangelists Maria B. Woodworth-Etter (1844–1924) and Aimee Semple McPherson (1890–1944), Kuhlman drew people from all walks of life to her famous services, including many who disavowed a woman's right to preach. Yet countless numbers were won over by her warmth for the afflicted and her unending insistence that God did and would perform miracles for those who believed. The sick, disabled, and terminally ill flocked to her meetings expecting to be healed, and countless numbers visited the stage and told praising audiences about the miracles they had received. As with any healing ministry, there were plenty of dubious critics who lambasted her claim that God healed through her; but no one doubted the powerful appeal she held for people of all kinds.

Kuhlman's ministry was headquartered in Pittsburgh, Pennsylvania, where she arrived in 1948 after a period of itinerant evangelism and a stint as the founding pastor of the Denver Revival Tabernacle in Colorado. For years she preached three times a week to several hundred people in Pittsburgh's grand Carnegie Music Hall. As her fame grew, her travel schedule became grueling;

she was invited to cities and towns in all parts of the country as well as overseas. During the 1960s she produced several bestselling books, including *I Believe in Miracles, God Can Do It Again,* and *Nothing Is Impossible with God.* That same decade she launched her highly successful television ministry, ultimately producing 500 programs of her thirty-minute show, *I Believe in Miracles.* A seemingly permanent fixture on religious radio, she also broadcast 4,000 radio shows, amid traveling far and wide to preside over her healing services and speak to groups such as the Full Gospel Business Men's Fellowship. While the media ventures all thrived, it was in person that her power was most profoundly felt, as scores of people fell to the floor, "slain in the spirit" (a Pentecostal/charismatic term for a kind of divinely induced trance) and claiming to have experienced some kind of miracle, healing or otherwise, in her presence. Her long white dresses, deep voice, and mysterious, almost eerie demeanor no doubt added to her appeal.

Like many of her female predecessors (and not a few of her male counterparts), Kuhlman was viciously attacked in the press as a swindler and a fraud. News reports gleefully recounted Kuhlman's lavish lifestyle, the lawsuits filed by disgruntled former employees, her supposed sexual liaisons and other hypocrisies, and poignant stories from people who had not been healed under her touch. Still, her fans never ceased to defend her, noting how much she had done not only for the sick but also for the poor, as she had never shied away from entering the most poverty-stricken neighborhoods and lending both her hands and her money for their restoration. Kuhlman was surely a complicated figure, as the controversies perpetually swirling around her suggest, and no credible account of her can fail to see the monomania to which she often enough fell prey. Yet she was a woman who achieved enormous power in a thoroughly male-dominated world, and people loved her for the kindness she seemed to show them. She intentionally reached across all denominations and made little of theological niceties beyond her overriding vision of God's miraculous, loving power. This broad ecumenicism that she practiced was a potent force in the development of the charismatic movement, and it is in those circles more than anywhere else that her memory is treasured.

CORRIE TEN BOOM

Born in Amsterdam, Holland, Cornelia Arnolda Johanna ten Boom (1892–1983) first gained fame in the United States less for her evangelistic career than for books such as *The Hiding Place* (1971), which was made into a popular film of the same name in 1975. In her own words, ten Boom recounted how, during the Nazi occupation of Holland, her family housed Jews in a secret room in order to save their lives. In 1944 the entire family was arrested by the Gestapo and sent to prison. Ten Boom herself was eventually transported to the notorious prison at Ravensbruck, Germany, where her sister died in 1945, just days before ten Boom was released. In 1945 ten Boom traveled to the United States before returning to Germany, where she commenced the itinerant preaching career that would continue for most of the rest of her life.

During the 1950s and 1960s, she traveled widely around the world, sometimes as part of the revival team of evangelist J. Edwin Orr and other times on her own. She preached in dozens of countries, including Australia, Bermuda, Borneo, Czechoslovakia, Formosa, Hong Kong, Hungary, India, Japan, Korea, New Zealand, Poland, Russia, South Africa, Uganda, the United States, and Vietnam. This grueling schedule took a toll on her health, and during the mid-1960s she took a year's rest in Uganda. Along the way, she employed various female traveling companions to assist with her schedule and keep her company. The first of these, Connie van Hoogstraten, stayed with ten Boom until 1967. The second, Ellen de Kroon, traveled with her until 1976, when she married the chaplain of Oral Roberts University. Pam Rosewell, her final travel companion, stayed with ten Boom for the rest of her life.

Through her writing, ten Boom was able to reach the vast numbers who were unable to attend one of her revivalistic meetings. Along with a newsletter that she regularly sent to her advocates, she wrote and published many books about her life, devotion to God, and prophecy. Her many works published in English, besides *The Hiding Place*, include: *A Prisoner—And Yet!* (1947), *Amazing Love* (1953), *Not Good If Detached* (1963), *Plenty for Everyone* (1967), *Common Sense Not Needed: Some Thoughts about an Unappreciated Work among Neglected People* (1968), *Marching Orders for the End Battle* (1970), *Tramp for the Lord* (1974), *Corrie ten Boom's Prison Letters* (1975), *In My Father's House: The Years before the Hiding Place* (1976), and *A Tramp Finds a Home* (1978).

Ever an ecumenical figure, supported by such world-famous evangelicals as Billy and Ruth Graham (whose production company, Worldwide Pictures, produced the film version of *The Hiding Place*), ten Boom was most closely associated with the charismatic movement. Seeking to heal rather than perpetuate divisions among Christians, she believed that this movement represented an outpouring of the Holy Spirit upon the times and that it would be a unifying force for all of Christendom. Many of her books were coauthored by famous charismatic leaders such as Jamie Buckingham (coauthor of *Tramp for the Lord*) and John and Elizabeth Sherrill (coauthors of *The Hiding Place*). She also worked closely with the charismatic leader Dave Wilkerson, founder of the ministry Teen Challenge. Her warm ecumenism gave credibility to the charismatic movement at a time when it was struggling for acceptance among mainstream Christians. She, perhaps more than any other leader of the time, brought credibility to the charismatic wing among evangelical circles that had previously dismissed it.

Ten Boom's near constant travel and speaking schedule were detriments to her health, and she took time off to recuperate on several occasions. In 1977 she purchased a home in southern California and moved permanently to the United States, a beloved icon of faith, courage, and reconciliation for Christians of many persuasions. She suffered a major stroke the next year, losing her speech and most of her mobility. She died on her ninety-first birthday, April 15, 1983.

Tammy Faye Bakker

Although many Christians would eventually disavow Tammy Faye Bakker (b. 1942), she was for many years the television queen of the charismatic movement and, indeed, of the broader American evangelical movement. Born in poverty in Minnesota, the eldest of eight children, she rose to fame as a young woman along with her then-husband Jim. Before Jim Bakker's 1988 arrest on charges of fraud and mismanagement (after an embarrassing liaison with *Playboy* model Jessica Hahn), the couple helped build the three largest Christian television networks in the world: CBN (Christian Broadcasting Network), with Pat Robertson; TBN (Trinity Broadcasting Network), with Paul and Jan Crouch; and PTL (Praise the Lord/People That Love), which Jim and Tammy Faye Bakker built themselves. The couple also built a Christian theme park in North Carolina, called Heritage USA. For a time that park was the third most visited resort in the entire United States; in its last year of existence, in fact, it had 6 million visitors. Tammy Faye has also recorded twenty-five albums and written three books: the bestselling *I Gotta Be Me* (1978), *Run to the Roar* (1980), and her autobiography *Tammy: Telling It My Way* (1996).

If Jim Bakker was the financial (mis)manager of the pair, Tammy Faye was the vibrant personality who propelled their successive television shows and surrounding networks to such lucrative heights. Famously made up (her gummy black eyelashes are legendary), she possessed the personal vibrancy to match her colorful clothes, bleached blonde hair, and permanently tanned skin. A laughingstock to many, Faye throve on her garish reputation and, à la Liberace, proudly reveled in her campy style, making it a centerpiece of her attraction. She sang, prayed, preached, and wept on her many TV broadcasts, and during the years of her ascendancy, she had far more loyal fans than mocking critics. Raised in the Assemblies of God, a Pentecostal denomination, she took easily to the looser, more ecumenical ways of the charismatic movement; and while her style made her controversial within it, she was beloved by Christians far and wide.

Faye's connections to the American gay community are interesting and worth noting, for she was long beloved by many gay men for her drag queen appearance. Far more important, she was the first and, for many years, the only charismatic leader to reach out to gay men dying of AIDS, preaching vehemently about the need for the churches to cease their condemnations and act lovingly as Jesus would toward this massive suffering. Most noncharismatics did not take seriously the depth of Bakker's convictions on this or any other issue, and many chortled when the Bakkers' ministry was effectively destroyed in the courts, followed shortly thereafter by the dissolution of their marriage. It was, nonetheless, she along with her husband who put the charismatic movement in people's living rooms as never before. Still insisting that she did no legal wrong, other than helping to overextend their empire and being forced to beg television viewers to bail them out financially, Bakker later married their former collaborator, Roe Messner, and moved with him to Palm Springs, California. There she has maintained an inspirational Web site, where she discusses the hard lessons she has learned about the rigidity, bigotry, and hypocrisy of the charismatic-evangelical world and dispenses her own philosophy of love and tolerance for all. A documentary about her life, *The Eyes of Tammy Faye*, was released in 2000 to wide acclaim.

Jan Crouch

Like Bakker, Jan Crouch got her early start on television working with her husband Paul. With the Bakkers, Jan and Paul started the TBN Network, over which they continued to reign into the early twenty-first century (they allegedly forced the Bakkers out of the network in the mid-1970s). Eventually the world's largest Christian television network, by 2003 TBN was reportedly carried on over 3,100 television stations, twenty-one satellites, the Internet, and thousands of cable systems in the United States and across the world. Openly charismatic, the Crouches have invited all the stars of the Pentecostal-charismatic world onto their set, and they have openly preached the charismatic gospel to millions of listeners. If Jan Crouch's Dolly Partonesque style has offended the taste of many Christian leaders, she has nonetheless occupied the queen's throne of popular charismatic culture ever since Tammy Faye Bakker was deposed.

Often the butt of criticism within the evangelical world for her supposed doctrinal errors and silly cornball humor, the reign of Crouch and her less colorful husband has been shaken but not toppled in the early twenty-first century amid charges of corruption. If their story echoes that of their onetime friends the Bakkers, so too has Crouch modeled her physical appearance upon that of Bakker, with the same love of heavy makeup, blonde bouffant hair, and glittering nails; indeed, she has gone so far as to have her breasts enlarged and to offer seminars on Christian liposuction, provided by her own cosmetic surgeon. Whatever charismatic Christians may think of such luxuries, Crouch has made it her mission to reach people at home with a gospel of Christianity as an everyday faith, one that shuns the dour puritanism of old in favor of an ecstatic embrace of experiential pleasures. Mixing this theology of fun with the apocalyptic edge that is characteristic of charismatic culture, Crouch provides listeners with enough biblical literalism to assure them of her seriousness, while yet exhibiting for them all the fullness that a spirit-filled life is said to offer.

Beverly LaHaye

Another woman who, while married to a famous man, has earned fame in her own right as a charismatic leader is Beverly LaHaye. The author of many bestselling books, LaHaye is also the founder and president of Concerned Women for America, the nation's largest right-wing public policy women's organization, which now has over 600,000 members who regularly advocate for school prayer and rally against abortion. LaHaye, the wife of author Tim LaHaye (most famous as the primary author of the apocalyptic *Left Behind* novel series), has also been a regular radio personality with her nationally syndicated daily show, *Beverly LaHaye Today* (formerly *Beverly LaHaye Live*, named Talk Show of the Year in 1993). She was especially powerful during the Ronald Reagan presidential administration: Voted Christian Woman of the Year in 1984 and Churchwoman of the Year in 1988, she also received a Religious Freedom Award in 1991. Some of LaHaye's most popular books have been *The Spirit-Controlled Woman* (1976, 1995), *Who But a Woman?* (1984), and *Who Will Save Our Children? 30 Strategies for Protecting Your Child from a Threatening World* (1991).

Though officially a Southern Baptist, LaHaye has become well known and loved in charismatic circles and has openly embraced charismatic believers. In fact, she and her husband have both received their warmest welcome among charismatic believers, to the point that they have been vociferously criticized by fundamentalist Christians who think their theology has softened and become unscriptural. Like Pat Robertson, the charismatic leader and founding president of the Christian Coalition, Beverly LaHaye represents the political side of the charismatic movement, appealing to charismatic Christians (and other conservative evangelicals) who believe that American law should be explicitly tied to Christian theology. The agenda advanced by LaHaye, self-styled as "profamily," is one that she supports by means of literalistic scriptural interpretation, and the issue of abortion is one on which charismatics have, in particular, taken her side.

Pairing LaHaye with the charismatic movement may seem a strange coupling, yet it highlights two points: first, the immense impact that some noncharismatic leaders, women and men, have made upon the charismatic movement, helping to bridge worlds that were once at odds; and second, the increasingly close ties between the charismatic movement and the conservative agenda of the New Christian Right. During the early years of the charismatic movement, its adherents held a diverse range of political opinions; and while most were antiabortion, they were not so easy to peg on other political issues. Countless charismatic worshipers supported Southern Baptist Democrat Jimmy Carter in the 1976 presidential election, and many continued to advocate for his policies throughout the years of his administration. By the early to middle years of the 1980s, however, "charismatic Christianity" had come to connote a far narrower range of political perspectives. With the rise of evangelical public policy groups such as Jerry Falwell's Moral Majority, James Dobson's Focus on the Family, Pat Robertson's Christian Coalition, and Beverly LaHaye's Concerned Women for America, most charismatics found their leaders and congregations, if not themselves, solidly in the right wing of political participation.

When Aglow meetings turned easily to talk of the latest Beverly LaHaye initiative, then, or when charismatic women leaders passed out Concerned Women for America newsletters or even petitions to sign on behalf of school prayer, this was no aberration. Leaders of Aglow and like organizations, though purportedly nonpolitical, could presume that most of their constituency agreed with the LaHaye agenda and voted solidly as conservative Republicans in every election. Older leaders of the charismatic movement, those who had been at the helm during the 1960s, openly lamented this politicization of charismatic Christianity and the transition to a solid right-wing agenda; but they were minority voices within the charismatic world. Conservative antifeminist women like LaHaye, along with her male counterparts, did more to shift the tides of the charismatic movement in this political direction than anyone else.

Rita Bennett

Another woman married to a famous man yet highly influential in her own right is Rita Bennett, the widow of Dennis Bennett, who died in 1991. A former elementary school teacher and social worker, Bennett and her husband founded the interdenominational Christian Renewal Association, a nonprofit charitable organization that she has run out of her home in Edmonds, Washington, for many years. She was an early speaker and organizer for Aglow and has been a public figure in the charismatic movement since the 1960s. Bennett has refrained, however, from seeking the spotlight as a charismatic spokeswoman and has focused her efforts on devotional and psychological writing rather than political activism or religious leadership. Since cowriting the million-copy bestseller *The Holy Spirit and You* with her husband, Bennett has authored eight books, including *How to Pray for Inner Healing: Making Peace with Your Inner Child* (1991) and *To Heaven & Back: True Stories of Those Who Have Made the Journey* (1997), while also writing poetry and songs.

Bennett's has been a quieter style of influence than that of Kuhlman, Bakker, or LaHaye, as she counsels people and leads private workshops on how to be what she calls "emotionally free." Her work embodies the older style of charismatic leadership, insistent upon the mystery of the Holy Spirit rather than on the cold facts of political programs. She also illustrates the more therapeutic side of the charismatic movement, as she mines the Bible along with other resources to help women and men cope with wounds in their lives that have not been resolved through counseling. No longer a major figure in the charismatic movement, Bennett has remained committed to upholding the memory of her husband and writing about what she believes to be the true and prophetic meaning of the movement for all people.

Joyce Meyer

As the influence of other charismatic women leaders has either shifted into the political arena or receded altogether, the ministry of Joyce Meyer (b. 1943) has risen to fill the void. Meyer's nationally syndicated show *Life in the Word* is broadcast daily on radio and television to thousands of listeners across the nation and the world. The Missouri-based teacher has written numerous books that range across such topics as depression, stress, abuse, weight loss, and emotional healing to spiritual warfare, biblical teachings, and treatises on "America's Christian heritage." As this diversity of subjects makes clear, Meyer has deftly combined the therapeutic emphasis of the charismatic movement with the apocalyptic, political focus of activist writers such as LaHaye, and the enormous acclaim given by Meyer in the religious community suggests that this has produced an effective combination indeed. Her books include *How to Succeed at Being Yourself: Finding the Confidence to Fulfill Your Destiny* (1999), *Be Healed in Jesus' Name* (2000), and *Knowing God Intimately: Being as Close to Him as You Want to Be* (2003).

Meyer's teachings belong to the side of the charismatic movement known as the Word of Faith, propounded by such figures as Oral Roberts, Kenneth Hagin, Kenneth Copeland, Marilyn Hickey, and Robert Tilton and linked to what is elsewhere known as "pros-

perity theology." This group and their likeminded followers teach that human beings have the power to construct their own destiny and reality simply through the "faith-filled" (or "fear-filled") words they utter. If one desires money, for instance, speaking the word for money is all that is needed to achieve wealth. By the same token, one can curse one's financial status—indeed, one's entire future—simply by speaking the wrong words or speaking evil of one's life. Meyer's teachings in this area are unambiguous, and the titles of many of her books, videos, and cassette series, such as *Ten Ways to Have Power with God*, are also indicative of this teaching.

Even as the Word of Faith instruction has come under increasing attack within the evangelical world, Meyer has achieved enormous fame as the best known female evangelist of the early twenty-first century. Like so many other popular charismatic female leaders, she adeptly alternates between speaking intimately as a woman to other women and speaking authoritatively as a divinely sent teacher to men and women alike. The most ardent admirers of her therapeutic books are undoubtedly women, but her providentialist, apocalyptic teachings on America's spiritual and moral decline, as well as her books on harnessing divine power, are aimed at reaching everyone. Her prim, ladylike style undoubtedly appeals to the scores of television viewers who are turned off by Jan Crouch's flashy ostentation, while her mix of humor and severity calls to mind a particular style dearly loved by conservative Christians.

Juanita Bynum

One of Meyer's most successful protégeés is Juanita Bynum, a former flight attendant who is now possibly the most prominent African American woman evangelist in the world. Raised in a black Pentecostal church in Chicago that is affiliated with the Church of God in Christ, Bynum is now well known as a "Prophetess" who preaches to large gatherings of women about the life issues they face. Like the other women discussed here, Bynum represents the ecumenical tone of the charismatic movement, for while she has been accused by strict Pentecostals of muting traditional doctrine, her broad-based teachings have made her a star in charismatic circles. She speaks of "those of us in the charismatic and Pentecostal movement" as if these are one, and her audience is thoroughly multiracial. Her message has been, however, one that is particularly directed to black women, who in turn can relate to many of the trials and sufferings she has endured in her own life. She began preaching soon after graduating from her denomination's boarding school, Saints Academy of the Church of God in Christ in Lexington, Mississippi.

Though for some years a preacher and an author, Bynum rose to national prominence during the 1990s as one of the women regularly featured as speakers at the "Woman Thou Art Loosed" national conferences directed by T. D. Jakes. Jakes, who pastors the multiracial 17,000-member Potter's House megachurch in Dallas, Texas, similarly grew up Pentecostal and has transitioned into a more ecumenical brand of charismatic Christianity. The platform he provided for Bynum— 52,000 women heard her speak at one 1998 conference in Atlanta—has propelled her into the high-energy world of auditorium and media evangelism, and she now heads the New York–based Morning Glory Ministries while keeping up a full speaking and writing schedule. The author of several books and sermon series, her most famous is *No More Sheets: The Truth about Sex* (1998), a guide for women to overcome sexual promiscuity, manipulation, and brokenness, based on her own story. Like Joyce Meyer, whom she credits as her mentor, Bynum combines a biblical emphasis with therapeutic teachings about finding joy amid suffering and learning to submit to higher authorities. In one of her favorite stories, Bynum's own submission to the harsh rebuke of a male pastor resulted in a rough marriage ending in divorce, a short bout with anorexia nervosa, living on government assistance, and other hardships. Rather than sounding bitter about her lot, Bynum describes all these difficulties as part of God's plan for breaking her spirit and making her more useful for religious service. She captured this story and her ultimate victory as a gospel preacher in her book *Don't Get Off the Train* (1997).

Bynum's fast-growing appeal for Christian women surely reflects the brutal candor with which she has delved into her own biography and the peace she offers to other women, especially those dealing with a difficult sexual history or a hurtful relationship. As a divorced woman unafraid to speak out on behalf of women's need to extract themselves from abusive men, she has undeniably made many charismatic leaders nervous. Her blunt words about married life—and her own delightedly single status—make her something of an anomaly in charismatic preaching circles. Yet she, like others, continues to insist on the theme of submission, in ways that closely enfold her within the charismatic world. For women who are hurting, Bynum's teachings have enormous appeal, and she is likely to remain one of the most successful American charismatic preachers for some time to come.

Women in the Charismatic World Today

As this listing of disparate women evangelists, authors, preachers, and prophetesses suggests, the charismatic movement has been anything but monolithic. Having once been a fairly limited, easily discernible movement among mainline Protestants and Roman Catholics searching for what they termed a "deeper experience of God" than that offered in their home congregations, the charismatic movement would later become extremely diffuse. It encompasses Christians from fundamentalist, Pentecostal, and evangelical backgrounds, all who would in earlier periods have shunned the charismatic label. While this confederation of multiple theological positions and scriptural interpretations has been a source of much contentiousness—charismatic leaders have relentlessly accused one another of heresy and hypocrisy—it has also made possible both missionary and political alliances that carry immense weight in domestic and world affairs. From the charismatic movement's most committed insiders to its staunchest critics, all agree that it has exercised profound and lasting changes upon the character of American Christianity and its global counterparts.

Many more women than those named here have played a vital role in these transformations. A more comprehensive list of female leaders and muses in the movement would have to go beyond those discussed in this essay to include, for instance, Myrtle D. Beall, Katie Fortune, Marilyn Hickey, Iverna Thompkins, Roxanna Brant, Daisy Osborn, Agnes Sanford, Ruth Carter Stapleton, Gloria Copeland, and Annette Capps. Many have risen through the ranks alongside the more famous ministries of their husbands; others, like Joyce Meyer, never fail to be pictured with their husbands even when the latter are relatively unknown. None of their vigorous efforts could have been sustained, however, without the far greater numbers of ordinary women who have purchased their books and tapes; donated funds to their ministries; and populated the pews, stadium and auditorium seats, and living rooms into which charismatic women evangelists have preached.

To a great extent, the leadership and service opportunities available for women in charismatic culture have not significantly changed since the charismatic movement first emerged into view. Certainly there are far more women in positions of influence and visibility than in the early days, in large part because of television and other media that have depended upon colorful personalities such as Tammy Faye Bakker and Jan Crouch to gain and retain an audience. But the women that one sees in those televised venues, like those who lead stadium revivals or speak about political issues on syndicated radio programs, are exceptions to the prohibitions on women's full and equal capacity for leadership that remain in effect in charismatic circles. As before, most charismatic women of influence are devotional writers and workshop leaders; those who preach are generally careful to call their work "evangelizing," "teaching," or "prophesying." Moreover, no woman described here, or anywhere else in charismatic circles, is allowed to pastor a church. Many, including relatively recent arrivals such as Juanita Bynum, relentlessly emphasize the theme of submission to authority; and while they couch this theme rather differently than did their male predecessors—and many of their current male counterparts—that motif of submissiveness has deep echoes for women in American culture. No charismatic woman listening to a lecture on submission is likely to overlook its profoundly gendered implications.

Women outside the fold may not thrill to the prospect of charismatic theology having such vociferous advocates among female believers, however old a story this kind of antifeminist advocacy turns out to be. Still, it is worth understanding the worldview that these women inhabit as their core identity. As we know from women's history, the potential for this kind of submissive ideology to be undercut by the very women who preach it is inestimable. Women of earlier eras who were active in Protestant mission movements, for instance, often adopted postures of meekness and docility even as they carved out new roles and prominent vocations for women within their own denominations. No informed observer of American evangelicalism thinks that women today are limited to the same status they occupied during the 1890s or 1950s, or even the 1970s.

Indeed, the rise in women's status that has been helped by the charismatic movement is at the core of some of the most forceful critiques of the movement itself. As a typical example, witness Robert Liichow, a former charismatic minister who now refers to the charismatic movement as "charismania" and, as an evangelical zealous to purge the wheat from the chaff, is one of its most public and vehement critics. Documenting what he views as women's ever present roles in Christian heresies, he sums up his attack on charismatic women:

> The historical fact remains that Pentecostalism's origin and spread in large part is due to the activity of women. The question is does God bless and use people who are in direct violation of His Word? If women are not divinely sanctioned to serve as elders and pastors, can true blessings flow from them in these areas of ministry? Much of the rampant error today in the Charismatic Movement can be directly traced back to the activity of the women cited in this section. (Liichow)

Liichow's attack corresponds almost perfectly with others long directed at religious movements in which women have been allowed to preach and teach.

All told, the status of women in the charismatic movement remains precarious and contested. The issue of female submission, which once appeared to be shifting ground toward "mutual submission" (at least among women), has returned with a vengeance at the turn of the twenty-first century. While the popularity of multi-ple female evangelists has never been higher, internal carpings about women's supposed heretical propensities are louder than ever. Nor are women in charismatic church pews charging the gates of seminaries or bursting into pulpits to demand their full and equal rights as daughters of Jesus. But the growing rates at which they are watching their Christian sisters preach on religious television, paying money to go to Christian conferences with an all-female slate of evangelists, and purchasing the prophetic teachings delivered to God's chosen women are signs of the time. The charismatic movement, whatever else its character, is a movement of ecstatic experience and joyous speech. As history shows, women's voices in these settings are not readily silenced, however much some male leaders may wish otherwise.

SOURCES: Fenton Bailey and Randy Barbato, *The Eyes of Tammy Faye*, Lions Gate Films (2000). R. Marie Griffith, *God's Daughters: Evangelical Women and the Power of Submission* (1997). Beverly LaHaye, *I Am a Woman by God's Design* (1980). Rev. Robert S. Liichow, "The Women of Neo-Pentecostalism," 1997, at http:www.discernment.org/womenof.htm. Meredith B. McGuire, *Pentecostal Catholics: Power, Charisma, and Order in a Religious Movement* (1982). Marabel Morgan, *The Total Woman* (1973). Mary Jo Neitz, *Charisma and Community: A Study of Religious Commitment within the Charismatic Renewal* (1987). Margaret Poloma, *The Charismatic Movement: Is There a New Pentecost?* (1982).

EURO-AMERICAN EVANGELICAL FEMINISM

Reta Halteman Finger and S. Sue Horner

EUROPEAN AMERICAN EVANGELICAL feminism emerged in the early 1970s in response to shifts within evangelicalism and the cultural impact of second wave feminism. Some within the separatist fundamentalist world desired to reengage with society by addressing the pressing issues of the day such as race, militarism, and poverty and to develop broader evangelical approaches to biblical interpretation. They saw these shifts as a reclamation of nineteenth-century evangelicalism and therefore began calling themselves "neoevangelicals." Such interaction with society entailed taking seriously or at least acknowledging the growing societal influence of the women's liberation movement.

The mixing of feminism and evangelicalism gave rise to four organizations. The Evangelical Women's Caucus (EWC) and Christian feminist magazine *Daughters of Sarah* both emerged in 1974. In 1975 EWC held its first national conference in Washington, D.C., and since that time has developed into a national organization that sponsors biennial conferences and publishes a news-

At this 1990 worship service, the Evangelical Women's Caucus split and once again, in recognition of the breadth of women (and some men) it attracted, changed its name to the Evangelical and Ecumenical Women's Caucus. The organization today retains that mix of ecumenism, evangelicalism/ biblicism, and feminist focus that is evident in national biennial conferences. *Courtesy of the Evangelical and Ecumenical Women's Caucus/ Pamela Quayle Hasegawa.*

letter, *Update. Daughters of Sarah* began formal publication in 1975, committed to an ecumenical, dialogical perspective. Initially organized as a collective/ consciousness-raising group, the magazine was based in Chicago and eventually relocated to Garrett-Evangelical Theological Seminary in Evanston before ceasing publication in 1996.

In 1987 two additional organizations formed in response to challenges raised by EWC, specifically EWC's affirming position on gay and lesbian civil rights and its broad ecumenical spirit. Christians for Biblical Equality (CBE) identified with evangelical feminism but desired to focus primarily on biblical rationales for gender equality and on marriage issues, including sexual abuse. CBE sees this focus as preserving the original mission of EWC.

The second organization, the Council on Biblical Manhood and Womanhood, identified itself as preserv-

ing traditional evangelical teaching on gender roles, or a complementarian position. This means that even though women and men are equally created in God's image, they also are created for distinct roles. Therefore, the Council on Biblical Manhood and Womanhood views an evangelical feminist position as a distortion of God's plan for humankind detailed in the Bible. In *Recovering Biblical Manhood & Womanhood: A Response to Evangelical Feminism* (1991), editors John Piper and Wayne Grudem make their case for biblical complementarity:

A controversy of major proportions has spread through the church. . . . Men and women simply are not sure what their roles should be. . . . But the vast majority of evangelicals have not endorsed the evangelical feminist position, sensing that it does not really reflect the pattern of biblical truth. . . .

[S]till the controversy shows signs of intensifying, not subsiding. Before the struggle ends, probably no Christian family and no evangelical church will remain untouched.

The issue of gender roles is still very much in debate within evangelicalism. The findings of a survey on gender roles conducted by Christianity Today International's research department was reported in the March 11, 2002, *Christianity Today.* Eighty-eight percent reported confusion on a biblical understanding of women's and men's roles. These organizations demonstrate two challenges that evangelical or biblical feminism brings to evangelicalism: concern about biblical authority and how to interpret scripture, and how to balance personal evangelism with engagement in social issues.

The history of evangelical feminism includes significant articles published in evangelical magazines. These early articles tried both to challenge women's secondary roles and also to take into account evangelical interpretations of Pauline concepts of headship. Current editor of the Evangelical and Ecumenical Women's Caucus's (EEWC) *Update* Letha Dawson Scanzoni wrote one of the earliest evangelical feminist articles for *Eternity* magazine in 1966. In the article, "Woman's Place: Silence or Service," Scanzoni identified the inconsistencies and often absurdities associated with teaching on women's submission. She pointed out that there were numerous examples within the church of women teaching and leading, as well as broadening employment opportunities for women. However, at this early point of feminist awareness she also made the disclaimer that "this article is not intended as an impassioned clamor for women's rights or female pastors!"

In 1968, Scanzoni wrote a second article for *Eternity* on marriage as "partnership." She discussed the "socially-constructed" nature of "masculine" and "feminine" characteristics, such as intuition, reason, and sensitivity. However, "partnership" still entailed a biblical image of headship, restated as "loving direction by a husband."

In December 1970 evangelist Billy Graham wrote "Jesus and the Liberated Woman" for *The Ladies' Home Journal.* Graham stated that boredom is "The Problem That Has No Name" (a reference to the language used by Betty Friedan in *The Feminine Mystique* [1963]). Graham called women's problem a spiritual problem—a failure to accept one's God-given duty. God's plan for men is that of husband, father, and protector; and for women, wife, motherhood, and homemaker. Graham said that Christ brought women new prestige, but Christ did not free women from the home.

In January 1971 Nancy Hardesty published "Women: Second-class Citizens?" in *Eternity* magazine. The same month Ruth A. Schmidt, then professor of Spanish literature at State University of New York, Albany, wrote "Second-Class Citizenship in the Kingdom of God" for *Christianity Today.* Schmidt began, "I'm tired of being considered a second-class citizen in the Kingdom of God. I'm not considered that by God, of course, but by men. . . . The church visible has in its life and ministry ignored to a frightening degree the truth of Galatians 3:28: 'There is no such thing as Jew and Greek, slave and freeman, male and female; for you are all one person in Christ Jesus.'" Schmidt acknowledged that the evangelical church was making some improvements in race relations but had little awareness of prejudice against women. She is an early example of how evangelical feminists attempted to address both the evangelical and feminist worlds as she was often asked to speak on the topic of Christianity and feminism in women's studies classes at the university.

By 1973 Scanzoni's tone had changed. In her 1973 article in *Christianity Today* on "The Feminist and the Bible," she sets out the compatibility of feminism and Christianity. She rehearses the historical legacy of the nineteenth-century women's rights movement, a "fervently religious" enterprise. She begins: "Many Christians dismiss the women's liberation movement as a kooky modern fad. . . . This image of women's lib is unfortunate; it misses the whole point of the movement and encourages the widespread suspicion that Christianity and feminism are incompatible." One year later, in 1974, the same year that EWC started, Scanzoni and Hardesty published their five-year project, *All We're Meant to Be: A Biblical Approach to Women's Liberation.* This volume became in many respects for evangelical women what *The Church and the Second Sex* (1972) by Mary Daly was for mainstream religious women.

The Evangelical Women's Caucus

The Evangelical Women's Caucus has a nearly thirty-year history starting as a task force at the 1974 meeting of Evangelicals for Social Action. EWC incorporated in 1978 and two years later in recognition of its international reach changed its name to the Evangelical Women's Caucus International. By 1990 the organization had split and, once again in recognition of the breadth of women (and some men) it attracted, changed its name to the Evangelical and Ecumenical Women's Caucus. The organization today retains that mix of ecumenism, evangelicalism/biblicism, and feminist focus that is evident in national biennial conferences, its newsletter *Update*, and its Web page (http:www.eewc.com/).

In Chicago on Thanksgiving weekend in 1973 some fifty evangelical leaders were invited to a workshop on evangelicals and social concerns. Nancy Hardesty, then assistant professor at Trinity College and doctoral student at the University of Chicago Divinity School, was one of six women in attendance. She had earlier written Ron Sider, chair of the planning committee, a letter outlining women's rights issues, including abortion and pornography. She also stated: "Christian organizations are going to have to clean up their own houses before they can speak to the world." Hardesty's agenda was straightforward: equal access for women to the ministry, seminaries, and denominational administration; revision of hiring, pay, and benefit practices; and the development of day care centers, vocational counseling and training, and family counseling.

At the meeting the participants agreed that evangelicals needed to repent of the sin of indifference and move into a "balanced biblical concern for both social restructuring and individual conversion." In order to get their message out to the broader evangelical world, they drafted the "Chicago Declaration," published in 1974. Hardesty contributed two sentences on gender equality for the ten-paragraph statement: "We acknowledge that we have encouraged men to prideful domination and women to irresponsible passivity. So we call both men and women to mutual submission and active discipleship."

Hardesty also joined a group of evangelical women connected to North Park Theological Seminary in Chicago who had formed a feminist Bible-study group. From their study, the group, led by Lucille Sider Dayton, Ron Sider's sister, decided to start a newsletter, *Daughters of Sarah*. They hoped this newsletter would develop a network of women and men interested in discussing Christian feminist issues. By the time of the second gathering of Evangelicals for Social Action on Thanksgiving weekend, 1974, the first issue of *Daughters of Sarah* was in the mail and included an article by Hardesty, a biblical exegesis of Genesis 1 and 2, "Woman: Helper or Companion?"

The second meeting of Evangelicals for Social Action had over 100 invited participants. The task force on women's issues presented twelve proposals for approval by the larger group. The proposals included developing regional conferences to build a grassroots movement; using *Daughters of Sarah* as a national clearinghouse for dissemination of Christian feminist materials; evaluating Sunday School curricula for sexist bias and publishing the results; promoting equal opportunity for women's education in evangelical colleges and seminaries; examining Christian bookstores for sexist materials; educating Evangelicals for Social Action on the use of nonsexist language; compiling a directory of evangelical feminists; and endorsing the Equal Rights Amendment. After approval by the group the task force agreed to form the Evangelical Women's Caucus and use the *Daughters of Sarah* mailing address.

EWC's first national conference was held in Washington, D.C., in the fall of 1975. Nearly 400 women and

a dozen men from thirty-six states and Canada attended. The theme was "Women in Transition: A Biblical Approach to Feminism." Speakers included English professor Virginia Ramey Mollenkott, Lucille Sider Dayton and Don Dayton, Nancy Hardesty, and Letha Scanzoni. Hardesty defined biblical feminism as "the commitment of those Christians who believe it is essential to have a personal relationship to God through Jesus Christ, who accept the Bible as God's inspired word, who have a deep concern for love and justice between the sexes, and who desire to find the whole counsel of God on this issue." Two resolutions easily passed: one, an affirmation of the Equal Rights Amendment and a second supporting the efforts of Roman Catholic sisters meeting that same weekend in Detroit to discuss ordination and the leadership issues in the Catholic Church.

In 1978 the largest conference EWC ever organized was held in Pasadena, California, cosponsored with Fuller Seminary. Nearly 1,000 women and some 50 men from thirty-five states and a number of other nations attended. Planner Roberta Hestenes, then chair of the Ministry Division at Fuller, asserted, "This conference indicates that biblical feminism has come of age." Controversial topics, such as homosexuality and inclusive God language, were not avoided, but the EWC conference planners did not want to reduce the topic of biblical feminism to a debate over homosexuality.

The topic of how engaged EWC should be on social issues was addressed in the December 1980 *Update* by founding coordinator Joyce Erickson. She acknowledged the diversity of opinions within EWC on issues like abortion, nuclear weapons, and homosexuality. However, she framed EWC's primary purpose as the promotion of a feminist interpretation of the Bible to the church and society. Nevertheless, EWC continued its support of the Equal Rights Amendment (ERA) and worked with the National Organization for Women on its campaign for the passage of the ERA from 1981 to 1982.

By the sixth EWC conference held at Wellesley College, Massachusetts, in 1984, the issue of homosexuality became the primary focus of the business meeting. Among other resolutions offered on political involvement such as protesting nuclear arms, racism, and pornography, the most problematic was the one that enjoined members to take "a firm stand to support with love homosexual persons in an attitude of justice which is against the oppression involved in sexism, racism, classism, heterosexism, or homophobia."

After an emotional discussion of the appropriateness of EWC taking stands on any controversial political issues, a decision was made to poll the membership by mail. The result was an evenly split organization. Forty-six percent of EWC members wanted to support only the Equal Rights Amendment resolution. Forty-eight percent wanted EWC to be politically active, both passing resolutions and working on a range of issues that affect women.

At the seventh EWC conference in Fresno, California, in 1986, the issue of resolutions came to a head, accompanied by broader concerns. These included the mission of EWC, the recognition of homosexual members (some 5 percent of the total membership), how to handle diversity and consensus, and concerns over the viability of the organization.

Three resolutions passed—on racism, on violence against women, and on civil rights for homosexual persons. Resolution three stated: "Whereas homosexual people are children of God, and because of the biblical mandate of Jesus Christ that we are all created equal in God's sight, and in recognition of the presence of the lesbian minority in the Evangelical Women's Caucus International, EWCI takes a firm stand in favor of civil rights protection for homosexual persons." Despite the two-to-one vote, a number of members were deeply distressed and felt they could no longer be members of EWC.

Christians for Biblical Equality

By the fall of 1986, Catherine Kroeger, fearful that women in conservative churches, as well as international women, would find EWC too extreme an organization, began developing an organization that focused solely on "biblical" feminism. Supported by Alvera Mickelson, retired journalism professor at Bethel College, and educator and author Gretchen Gabelein Hull, Kroeger made connections with a two-year-old British evangelical group called "Men, Women, and God," affiliated with theologian John Stott's London Institute for Contemporary Christianity. As chair of Evangelicals for Social Action, Ron Sider also supported this fledgling organization. Although he affirmed all people's civil rights, he was opposed to the practice of homosexuality. *Christianity Today* (October 3, 1986) reported, "We want to do everything we can to promote a biblical feminism that does not condone practicing homosexuality," Sider said. "At the same time, we have no interest in mounting negative campaigns against anyone."

By early spring of 1987 the Kroegers' Christian studies center in St. Paul began publication of *Priscilla Papers*, a magazine devoted to the equality and ministry of women based on a belief in the authority and inspiration of the Bible. In August 1987, Men, Women and God: Christians for Biblical Equality incorporated with a mission to "make known the biblical basis for freedom in Christ to those in evangelical and conservative churches."

Catherine Kroeger was named spokeswoman for the new organization, and the board of directors included a number of well-known authors and academics including clinical psychologist James Alsdurf, Denver Conservative Baptist Seminary professor James Beck, Evangelical Round Table board member Gretchen Gaebelein Hull, national president of the Reformed Presbyterian Women's Association Faith Martin, and Bethel College and Bethel Theological Seminary (Minnesota) professors, respectively, Alvera and Berkeley Mickelsen. In the faith statement of the new organization, reported in the fall 1987 issue of *Priscilla Papers*, two items are notable: first, belief in the Bible as "the final authority for faith and practice," and second, belief "in the family, celibate singleness, and heterosexual marriage as the patterns God designed for us."

In July 1989 CBE hosted its first national conference at Bethel College, St. Paul, Minnesota, attracting over 200 attendees. CBE continues to sponsor biennial conferences as well as topical conferences on marriage and abuse. *Priscilla Papers*, edited by Hull from 1988 to 2000, has developed into required reading for evangelical academics according to Fuller Seminary New Testament professor David Scholer. Currently, this scholarly-oriented magazine is edited by a former editor with *Christianity Today*, Carol Theissen. CBE also publishes *Mutuality*, a newsletter that contains personal stories and promotes an extensive book service.

Kroeger, currently president emerita, resigned in 1995 after overseeing the development of an organization that is in dialogue with evangelicalism and represents progressive evangelicalism. CBE's current president is Mimi Haddad. She manages an organization of seven full-time staff and one part-time staff; a membership of approximately 2,000; twenty-three grassroots chapters in thirteen states; four international chapters, two in Canada and one each in Norway and South Africa; and five international resource centers, two in Australia and one each in Germany, Austria, and Ireland. CBE continues to stay focused on its message of biblical equality and presents a positive, nondefensive posture. It remains dedicated to scholarship but also desires to "popularize" its message in order to reach the widest possible swath of evangelical Christians.

Daughters of Sarah

Daughters of Sarah began as a newsletter in 1974 and evolved into a bimonthly magazine and in the 1990s into a quarterly journal. In the late 1980s *Daughters of Sarah* was at its height with 6,800 subscribers. However, by 1993 the subscriber base had dropped to under 5,000, in no small part due to the loss of two significant editors, Reta Halteman Finger and Annette Bourland Huizenga, who had left to pursue doctoral work and ministry, respectively. Additionally, because of publishing challenges, internal changes in staff and board of directors, and decline in grassroots support, *Daughters of Sarah* ceased publication in 1996.

This loss to Christian feminist dialogue with an evangelical/biblical slant was replaced, in some respects, by Pat Gundry's "PHOEBE-L," an online discussion list on faith and feminism formed in 1996. In the fall of 2001 *Daughters of Sarah* illustrator, editorial committee member, and writer Kari Sandhass and editor Reta Finger published *The Wisdom of Daughters: Two Decades of the Voice of Christian Feminism*, a collection of selected articles and poetry as a tribute to all the women (and men) who had faithfully articulated Christian/biblical feminist issues over twenty-two years.

Evangelical Feminism and Biblical Interpretation

Talking about evangelical feminist biblical hermeneutics since second wave feminism began in the early 1970s is like shooting at a moving target. Evangelical hermeneutics itself has been undergoing constant change. Today one might speak of "core evangelicalism," which has most of its roots in Reformed or Calvinist traditions, and "penumbra evangelicalisms," which draw from other historical traditions with different emphases. Methodist, Holiness, charismatic, or Anabaptist theology and biblical interpretation would be included among the latter (see, for example, *Streams of Living Water: Celebrating the Great Traditions of Christian Faith* by Richard J. Foster [1998]).

This section will deal with the development of evangelical feminist biblical interpretation as it has evolved from a single movement in the 1970s and early 1980s to two broader streams since then. "Core" evangelical feminism is represented by the organization Christians for Biblical Equality, with its newsletter *Priscilla Papers*, while the Evangelical and Ecumenical Women's Caucus and the magazine *Daughters of Sarah* (*DOS*) stand (or stood) in the "penumbra," with one foot in the evangelical world and another closer to mainstream church traditions.

Leaders within these organizations had primarily come from conservative churches, some from fundamentalist backgrounds with severe repression of women's gifts. Although a selectively literal interpretation of scripture had for long been used to keep them "in their place," these women did not react by throwing out their Bibles. Rather, they opened them with renewed vigor and sought to reinterpret restrictive texts and search for liberating ones.

Early attempts at feminist biblical interpretation in the 1970s examined texts traditionally restricting women from church leadership, such as 1 Corinthians 11:3–16, 14:33–36, and 1 Timothy 2:9–15; or coleadership in the home, such as the household codes of Colossians 3:18–4:

1, Ephesians 5:21–6:9, and 1 Peter 3:1–6, which called for women to submit to their husbands. The meaning of the term *head* was explored and its traditional understanding as "authority" challenged (Snodgrass and Hardesty, 1–6).

1 Corinthians 14:33–36, with its command that women be silent in church, was now explained in terms of women interrupting worship by asking questions out of ignorance, or because women in their former pagan religions were used to whipping worshipers into a frenzy by repetitive babble and were repeating similar practices in Christian worship (Kroeger and Kroeger, 10–13).

Evangelical feminists responded favorably to Phyllis Trible's detailed egalitarian exegesis of Genesis 2–3 in *God and the Rhetoric of Sexuality* (1978). The name of the newsletter *Daughters of Sarah* called for a new approach to 1 Peter 3:6 where Sarah calls her husband "lord." Few evangelical women before this had been sent back to the original story of Abraham and Sarah in Genesis, where the context of "lord" simply means "husband" and where Sarah comes across as a strong-willed woman who tends to call the shots in her marriage relationship with Abraham (Hardesty and Scanzoni, "Why Sarah?" 1–2). But at that time no racial or class analysis critiqued Sarah for her treatment of her Egyptian slave Hagar. And although the Sarah texts were well exegeted, the more hermeneutical question of 1 Peter's selective use of scripture was not tackled.

Another method of empowerment for women was the search for strong, effective women in the Bible, such as Deborah, Esther, Miriam, or Huldah. Stories of Jesus' women disciples or other faithful women in the gospels were lifted up as role models in magazines like *The Other Side* or *Sojourners*. Leonard Swidler's early essay "Jesus Was a Feminist" and a later volume on *Biblical Affirmations of Woman* (1979) inspired many evangelical feminists to claim Jesus was on their side—and their opponents were the entrenched Pharisees. This, however, sometimes produced the unfortunate effects of pitting Jesus against the apostle Paul or exaggerating first-century Jewish patriarchy in order to highlight Jesus' pro-woman stance.

New Testament professor David Scholer, trained in hermeneutics, emerged as a strong advocate of evangelical feminism. Evidence of his interpretive principles can be seen in very early issues of *Daughters of Sarah*, especially on difficult texts like 1 Timothy 2:8–15, where women's authority to teach is called into question (May 1975). *All We're Meant to Be: Biblical Feminism for Today*, by Nancy Hardesty and Letha Scanzoni (1974), Paul Jewett's *MAN as Male and Female* (1975), and Virginia Mollenkott's *Women, Men, and the Bible* (1977) provided additional biblical support for the position of evangelical feminism. Willard Swartley's *Slavery, Sab-*

bath, War, and Women (1983) compared church attitudes on these four social issues over a long period of time, demonstrating inconsistencies in biblical interpretation and setting up helpful hermeneutical principles that supported women's full participation in church leadership. Aida Spencer's *Beyond the Curse: Women Called to Ministry* (1985) examined texts from both the Hebrew Bible and the New Testament to make the case for women's ministries.

In the mid-1970s, articles about female imagery for God in the Bible appeared, along with others questioning male-generic language. Virginia Mollenkott's *The Divine Feminine* (1983) and the publication of the *Inclusive Language Lectionary* (1983) pushed biblical feminists to grapple seriously with language as a justice issue. Both passionate and practical, Nancy Hardesty's *Inclusive Language in the Church* (1987) clarified the theological need for nonsexist language as well as raising critical issues of biblical translation.

By the 1980s, however, differences in methods of biblical interpretation were showing up among evangelical feminists, as well as the disagreements over some social issues discussed above. What did the term *evangelical* mean? If it included all those who held scripture as authoritative (though not necessarily inerrant) and generally had roots in conservative and some mainstream churches, the movement was quite inclusive. But if *evangelical* primarily meant those from Reformed or Baptist traditions, feminists from other backgrounds preferred to opt out. Many members of *Daughters of Sarah* and EWC, for example, hailed from a wide range of church backgrounds that included Pentecostal, Roman Catholic, Russian Orthodox, Methodist, Holiness, Anabaptist/Mennonite, Seventh-Day Adventist, Presbyterian, and other Protestant churches. Both organizations preferred the term *biblical feminism* or the broader *Christian feminism*.

A "Core Evangelical" Feminist Hermeneutic

When several chapters of EWC left to form Christians for Biblical Equality in 1987, it became increasingly clear that there were also differences of opinion about biblical hermeneutics. CBE sees itself as standing squarely within the evangelical world, with a view of scripture as divinely inspired and that ranges from "inerrant" to "infallible." A clear and distinct position is that egalitarianism is the will of God and that this is taught in scripture. Only the fall of humankind is responsible for the sinful patriarchy reflected in some scriptures, with certain laws attempting to relieve women of the worst effects of it. Readers must differentiate between *prescriptive* and *descriptive* statements. Many stories and other passages describe patriarchy and its harmful effects, and these can be used in a negative sense for our instruction. Prescriptive state-ments, those intended to be taught, affirm mutuality. Then, with the coming of Jesus in the New Testament, God's desire for total equality and mutuality between the sexes is clarified and established.

Much of CBE's biblical exegesis is directed toward challenging traditional evangelical positions. For example, Gilbert Bilizekian maintains a running dialogue throughout his book *Beyond Sex Roles* (1985) with James Hurley's *Man and Woman in Biblical Perspective* (1981). In *Equal to Serve: Women and Men in the Church and Home* (1987), Gretchen Gabelein Hull draws on her own experiences of sex discrimination and double messages in conservative churches as she argues for a biblical view of male-female equality. *Priscilla Papers,* CBE's biennial conferences, and recent books by Rebecca Merrill Groothuis, such as *Women Caught in the Conflict: The Culture War between Traditionalism and Feminism* (1994) and *Good News for Women: A Biblical Picture of Gender Equality* (1997), capture well the essential evangelical feminist position and its biblical hermeneutics.

In early 2002, InterVarsity Press published the 900-page *IVP Women's Bible Commentary*, edited by Catherine Kroeger and Mary Evans, which includes an essay on every book of the canonical Bible plus 100 short articles on various topics scattered throughout. With ninety contributors, its attitude toward scripture is both feminist and evangelical. It discusses every biblical text dealing with women, laws that affect women, or male attitudes toward women. Invariably, both women and scripture are viewed in a positive light. These interpreters understand the cultural backgrounds of the Bible to be patriarchal, but they see the texts as sympathetic toward women by mitigating the harshness of patriarchy. Rather than understanding the texts themselves to be androcentric and sometimes restrictive of women, every effort is made to protect the scriptures as both authoritative (perhaps infallible) and positive toward women.

For example, Numbers 5:11–31 discusses the procedure involved in Hebrew law when a husband suspects his wife of adultery but cannot prove it. He brings her to the priest, who makes the woman drink a potion of water and dust from the floor of the tabernacle. If she becomes ill, she is guilty; if not, she is innocent. But even if she is proved innocent, the husband is not held accountable for his jealousy or suspicions (verse 31).

A more mainstream feminist interpreter such as Katharine Doob Sakenfeld in the *Women's Bible Commentary* (1992), edited by Carol A. Newsom and Sharon H. Ringe notes that most of the wording of this law presumes that the woman is guilty (except for verse 14) and recognizes the indignity, helplessness, or even terror that such a law would mean for women with jealous husbands.

But Dorothy Irvin in the *IVP Commentary* stresses the law's humaneness. In Numbers 5:19, the priest addresses the woman about her behavior "while under her husband's authority," which Irvin sees as positive, since it limits the law to women who are at that time married to a husband, leaving out betrothed girls, concubines, or women divorced from their husbands. Even more important to Irvin is the limitation of the absolute authority of the husband. He cannot kill his wife for suspected adultery, or he will be convicted as a murderer. Rather, he must cool his anger by bringing an offering to the priest and going through the ritual in the presence of this authoritative third party.

Both of these commentators are carefully exegeting the same text. But the evangelical feminist interpretation is at the same time protective of the biblical text in a way the other is not. In her books, Groothuis would label the latter feminist hermeneutic "liberal."

Perhaps the most striking example of hermeneutical dissimilarity in the New Testament is the attitude taken toward the author of Luke-Acts. In the *IVP* volume, both Catherine Clark Kroeger (Luke) and Rosemary M. Dowsett (Acts) highlight the Lukan author as very positive toward women and their leadership. "No book of the Bible," says Kroeger, "is more dependent on the witness of women or more concerned with their welfare than the Gospel of Luke" (561).

Conversely, both the Newsom/Ringe commentary and *Searching the Scriptures: A Feminist Commentary* (1994) (edited by Elisabeth Schussler Fiorenza, challenge this rosy picture by noting that Luke tends to silence women and does not portray them as leaders. Turid Karlsen Seim in *Searching the Scriptures* (728–762) looks at both sides and concludes that Luke transmits a "double message" about women (761).

Although some interpreters in the *IVP* commentary recognize and comment on some of the critical and controversial issues in biblical interpretation, such as authorship, they prefer (with the possible exception of 2 Peter) the traditional attributions.

The New International Version and Inclusive Language

That evangelical feminism has had an effect on the evangelical church at large was made evident in 1997 by the furor raised when the International Bible Society (IBS) in conjunction with Zondervan Publishing Company made plans to publish in the United States an inclusive language edition of the New International Version (NIV) of the Bible, which is the translation favored by evangelicals. Members of the Religious Right, including *World* magazine (Olansky, 12–15) and James Dobsen's Focus on the Family organization, raised such an outcry about "unisex language" and "changing the Word of God" that plans were withdrawn.

The battle raged on throughout most of the year. Moderate evangelicals argued the case for using inclusive language, "because language keeps changing," against fundamentalists who held that patriarchy and male leadership is God's intention for human relationships and who maintained that changing masculine pronouns into plurals would distort the inerrant Word of God. Although this was a male-male fight (men appear to occupy most or all high administrative positions in evangelical publishing), the work of evangelical feminists in supporting the use of inclusive language lay behind the struggle. In 2002 an inclusive language edition called Today's New International Version (TNIV) was finally published in the United States, but the Southern Baptist denomination and the Council on Biblical Manhood and Womanhood actively lobby against it.

An Alternate Biblical Feminism

Because some Christian feminists either moved away from "core evangelicalism" or were never there in the first place, the Evangelical Women's Caucus and *Daughters of Sarah* magazine provided a broader theological and hermeneutical emphasis. The seeds of this can already be seen in *All We're Meant to Be* by Letha Scanzoni and Nancy Hardesty, first published in 1974. Although the methodology uses a literal approach, there is more openness to alternative interpretations of scripture. Later editions (1985, 1992) show an increasing departure from a more ideological evangelical commitment but nevertheless take the biblical writings seriously and draw conclusions from a close reading of the text. Hardesty and Scanzoni interact with mainstream feminist biblical scholarship, as well as portraying an increasing understanding of and openness to gay and lesbian issues.

When discussing Paul's theology, Fuller Seminary theologian Paul Jewett's 1975 *MAN as Male and Female* argued that Paul speaks sometimes as a sexist rabbi and sometimes as a liberated Christian. In a somewhat similar vein, Virginia Mollenkott in *Women and Men and the Bible* (1975) compared Paul's struggle over women's issues to some of the Davidic psalms, whose ethics we do not approve of either. Paul was inconsistent, as all humans are, she suggested, and the Bible faithfully records that inconsistency. For evangelicals, these were daring propositions at the time. Both Jewett and Mollenkott considered themselves evangelical, with a high view of scripture, but neither of these positions was accepted by "core" evangelical feminists—nor by various other Christian feminists either.

As *Daughters of Sarah* grew, the "evangelical" label stretched more broadly. Members became more comfortable calling themselves "Christian feminists" who deeply cared about and interacted with the Bible. Views evolved over the years as we (Finger was editor for fifteen years; Horner served on the editorial board) pondered, debated, rejected, and absorbed views of mainstream Christian feminists, as well as those of Jewish feminists. Three areas in particular show adjustments in "penumbra evangelical" feminist biblical hermeneutics.

First, although we had affirmed scriptural authority (though never inerrancy), we came to see that the biblical documents do not uniformly teach gender equality. Most or all were written by men in patriarchal cultures and reflect an androcentric, sometimes even misogynist, bias. For us, it was coming to terms with the human side of scripture and the sense that we did not need to protect it. Second, we challenged a common interpretive contrast often held by lay Christian feminists—that Jesus was pro-women and Paul was antiwomen. Rather, everything we know about Jesus is already secondhand; and Paul's letters, both those of disputed and undisputed authorship, must be understood as occasional and meant to address particular situations. A far more complex hermeneutic is needed here.

Third, the insights of Jewish feminists concerning the diversity of Judaism in the first century C.E. changed our original assumption that Jesus stood in stark contrast to a solidly patriarchal and repressive cultural background. Rather, Jesus was fully a Jew who drew on some of the more liberating elements already present in his religious culture.

A major part of the life work of the evangelical New Testament scholar David Scholer has been biblical hermeneutics, especially as it relates to gender issues. Both "core" and "penumbra" evangelical feminists owe much to his tireless efforts. Following are paraphrased the six guidelines for evangelical feminist hermeneutics that he developed for a workshop at the 1984 conference of the Evangelical Women's Caucus and that continue to be helpful:

1. One must accept the fact that our confession of scripture as God's word means that revelation is bound to and found in historical particularity. Yet those very particularities allow it to be free. Stories about specific events have more lasting ability to communicate than eternal but abstract truths.

2. Every text does not speak to every situation at all times and places. One must honestly confront issues of relativity, such as the command for women not to teach in 1 Timothy 2:8–15.

3. Scripture is pluriform, and one must use sound hermeneutical principles to decide which texts inform which other texts. For example, does Galatians 3:28 provide the window from which to view 1 Timothy 2, or is it the other way around?

4. The early church was larger and broader than the New Testament, and thus we must make room for the reconstruction of its history. This reconstruction can be used as a critical tool to assist in in-

terpreting scripture but should not replace it. (This guideline reflects an openness to Elisabeth Schussler Fiorenza's method of historical reconstruction but stops short of moving the locus of authority beyond written scripture to the reconstruction itself or to the present community of women-church.)

5. Though scripture is to be accepted as authoritative, it always requires interpretation. All interpretations are subjective and can be skewed by the historical, cultural, and personal limitations of the interpreter.

6. Thus evangelical feminist biblical hermeneutics can identify patriarchal and sexist texts and assumptions and understand them as limited texts and assumptions limited by cultural particularity, by canonical balance, and by particular authors' intentions of limitation. Such texts are not polemicized against, not excluded, but understood from a particular vantage point.

Evangelical feminism has had a broad reach. It has faithfully added to scholarship on the equality of women and men within Christianity. EEWC and *Daughters of Sarah* have worked to provide a forum for discussion of any and all social issues in relation to biblical and faith commitments. Perhaps this breadth led to the demise of *Daughters* and a membership that hovers around 300 for EEWC. But EEWC continues to see itself as a biblical, feminist, prophetic organization working to eliminate sexism in the church, building bridges between feminists and Christians, and enabling the development of full personhood expressed in actions by Christian women and men. CBE has thrived by its focus on biblical exegesis, involving both women and men in leadership and strong management. Regardless, all the organizations of evangelical feminism desire that women and men act responsibly and justly out of an informed ethical reflection, hoping for women and men to become all they are meant to be.

SOURCES: Evangelical and Ecumenical Women's Caucus and *Daughters of Sarah* papers are found in the Archives of Women in Theological Scholarship, Union Theological Seminary, New York, New York; Evangelicals for Social Action papers, Billy Graham Center Archives, Wheaton, Illinois. Publications of evangelical feminism include *Daughters of Sarah*, November 1974–Winter 1996; *Priscilla Papers*, 1987– ; *Update*, Summer 1977– . Significant writings include Letha Dawson Scanzoni and Nancy A. Hardesty, *All We're Meant to Be: A Biblical Approach to Women's Liberation* (1974); Letha Scanzoni and Virginia Ramey Mollenkott, *Is the Homosexual My Neighbor? Another Christian View* (1978); John Piper and Wayne Grudem, eds., *Recovering Biblical Manhood & Womanhood: A Response to Evangelical Feminism* (1991); Sandra Sue Geeting Horner,

"Becoming All We're Meant to Be: A Social History of the Contemporary Evangelical Feminist Movement: A Case Study of the Evangelical and Ecumenical Women's Caucus" (Ph.D. diss., Northwestern University, 2000); Reta Halteman Finger and Kari Sandhaas, eds., *The Wisdom of Daughters: Two Decades of the Voice of Christian Feminism* (2001); S. Sue Horner, "Trying to Be God in the World: The Story of the Evangelical Women's Caucus and the Crisis over Homosexuality," in *Gender, Ethnicity and Religion: Views from the Other Side*, ed. Rosemary Radford Ruether (2002). David Scholer's six hermeneutical principles and other hermeneutical analysis is from Reta Halteman Finger, "Scripture as Friend and Enemy: Feminist Biblical Hermeneutics," *Update: Newsletter of the Evangelical Women's Caucus* 11.4 (Winter 1987–1988): 1–4, 15. The inclusive language NIV debate was noted in news articles in consecutive 1997 issues of *Christianity Today* (June 16: 52–53, 55; July 14: 62–64; August 11: 58), followed by a debate, "Do Inclusive-Language Bibles Distort Scripture?" in the October 27 issue: "Yes," Wayne Grudem, 27–32; "No," Grant Osborne, 33–38. Additional Sources: Klyne Snodgrass and Nancy Hardesty, "Head: What Does It Mean?" *DOS* (July 1976); Catherine Kroeger and Richard Kroeger, "Strange Tongues or Plain Talk?" *DOS* (July/August 1986); Nancy Hardesty and Letha Scanzoni, "Why Sarah?" *DOS* (March 1975); Leonard Swidler, "Jesus Was a Feminist," *South East Asia Journal of Theology*, 13.1 (1971): 102–110; and Susan Olansky, "Femme Fatale: The Feminist Seduction of the Evangelical Church," *World* (March 29, 1997).

Hispanic Protestantism

&

U.S. LATINA *EVANGÉLICAS*
Elizabeth Conde-Frazier and
Loida I. Martell Otero

THIS ESSAY BRINGS to the fore the stories and contributions of an eclectic group of women who use a variety of self-referent terms (Protestants, *Protestantes*, *feministas*, *mujeristas*) but whom will be referred to here as U.S. Latina *evangélicas*. They come from different educational, ethnic, and cultural backgrounds. Notwithstanding this diversity, they share a common heritage: a history of proud and strong women who have been innovative *luchadoras* (fighters) in the name of the gospel. Their stories have largely remained in the arena of oral narrative, the primary source for this essay. They are presented here so that their legacy and struggles may be given a rightful place in the larger history of the Christian church.

Generic terms such as *U.S. Hispanic* and *Latina* hide the fact that many of these women come from various countries of origin. They are Mexican Americans, Puerto Ricans, Cubans, Dominicans, Central and South Americans, or the subsequent generations arising from these groups, who reside in the continental United States. The terms have now been adopted, however, to symbolize the common issues that they face on a daily basis (*en la vida cotidiana*). This cultural diversity is compounded by the historical fact that U.S. Latinas are the biological and cultural mix of Europeans who invaded the New World and the indigenous peoples they conquered so violently. African slaves that were imported also contributed to that mix. This process of miscegenation, or hybridization, came to be known as *mestizaje* or *mulatez*. This biological mixing inevitably brought about a particular religious mixing. Initially, the encounter of Iberian Catholicism (already a *mestizaje* of Christian, Semitic, and Islamic roots) with Amerindian beliefs produced a *mestizo* Catholicism in the New World. Later, this Catholicism encountered not only African religions but also North American Protestantism. Thus, a particular Protestant expression was created that never fully broke with its Catholic and indigenous moorings. It is a *mestizo* Protestantism.

Although figures vary, it has been estimated that approximately 20 percent of the U.S. Latina/o community is Protestant. Latinas tend to refer to themselves as either Protestants or *Protestantes* if they are born in the United States and are English-dominant. Spanish-dominant Latinas, or those whose country of origin is in Latin America or the Caribbean, tend to call themselves *evangélicas*. This latter term does not have the sociopolitical implications often associated with the En-

<blockquote>477</blockquote>

La Casa was a community center founded in 1946 by the First Presbyterian Church of San Gabriel, Los Angeles, under the leadership of Rev. César and Mrs. Angelita Rodríguez de Lizárraga. Her life and work as a pastor's wife exemplify how men are often the ones formally called to a particular ministry by a church but both (*wives* with their husbands) do the work. Angelita not only helped establish *La Casa*, she was also its first director, serving on a part-time basis. *Used by permission of David Lizárraga.*

glish term *evangelical*. Rather, the term emphasizes that they are a people of the gospel (*evangelio*).

Religion and spirituality play a dominant role for most U.S. Latinas/os. *La vida cotidiana* (daily life) is permeated by religious practices, beliefs, and values. These beliefs, like U.S. Latina culture, can be traced back to their *mestizo* origins (i.e., European, indigenous, and African roots). A particular aspect of this religiosity is its organic and incarnational character: Rather than being an abstract deity who is "up there" or beckoning from the future, God is the One who resides among us. The material world is permeated by the spiritual.

U.S. Latina/o Catholic theologians have pointed out that the most authentic expression of this religiosity is popular religion (i.e., popular Catholicism). Popular Protestantism differs somewhat from popular Catholicism. Unlike its Catholic counterpart, most expressions of popular Protestantism are not voices against an institutional, hierarchical church per se. Rather, they tend to be a protest against the domination of Eurocentric cultural expressions within ecclesial institutions (whether these be local congregations or denominational institutions). Popular Protestantism represents a resistance to the cultural hegemony of a European way of preaching, worshipping, and believing. Like popular Catholicism, popular Protestantism has been a voice of

protest over the marginalization of U.S. Latinas/os in the life of the church. U.S. Latina *evangélicas*, in particular, have been a force of resistance against the marginalization of women in the church and in the larger community.

Recently, a growing group of U.S. Latina *evangélicas* involved in theological reflection have begun to question the traditional assumptions of their past, while still affirming the scriptural and ecclesial roots from which they have risen. In an article titled "New Visions in Latin America: A Protestant View," Beatríz Melano Couch uses the term "radical evangelical" for a similar theological position.

They represent an effort to break with the theological dualism of conservative churches and to overcome "otherworldliness" by the analysis and immersion in the Latin American problematic. Their aim is to conscienticize the most conservative Protestant elements in order to produce a renewal of the churches; their point of departure is a rigorous biblical exegesis and they are moving toward a realistic understanding of the social, economic, political and cultural situation of Latin America. . . . They expose and denounce the structures of oppression and dependency and call for

Christian commitment to bring about needed changes. (Couch, 212–213)

Although her description refers to the particular context of Latin America, her words resonate with many of the women theologians emerging from the U.S. Latina *evangélica* world. Many of these women share a background that has its foundation in the life of the church. It is not surprising to find, therefore, that many have served in some leadership role in their churches, whether in ordained or lay ministries. They have a strong belief in the person and work of the Holy Spirit. The Spirit is not conceived as an impersonal force subsumed into the Father and the Son. The belief in the gifts of the Spirit has supported women's struggle to validate their ministries, often against the tide of institutional resistance and sexism. While sympathetic to liberation theologies, many of these U.S. Latina *evangélicas* are suspicious that social sciences and Marxism are held to be equally authoritative with scripture. Consistent with Protestant tradition, they continue to affirm that scripture is authoritative for faith and practice. They also affirm that it needs to be reread with the guidance of the Holy Spirit in order to rediscover God's Word of affirmation and liberation of all people, especially of the marginalized and oppressed. Together with liberation theologies, they critique the excessive privatism, individualism, and false spiritualization of the gospel that has traditionally been sustained by Protestant thought and belief. They believe that the gospel calls for a holistic salvation, that is, one that is concerned not only with the eschatological (i.e., God's promised future that is yet to come) but also with *la vida cotidiana* (in every dimension of daily life).

The hallmark of U.S. Latina *evangélicas* is a strong sense of mission. They seek to serve the church and communities in the name of the Savior professed and preached. However, that sense of service has been fulfilled at a price. They have survived and struggled within a social context of daunting challenges. As women who live and work in U.S. Latina communities, they know far too well that too many live in overwhelming poverty. Their communities have long dealt with issues of underemployment, poor health care, poor educational opportunities, cultural and linguistic discrimination, poor housing, and other related issues. People are made invisible, marginalized solely because of their Latina heritage. Black U.S. Latinas/os face an added burden of racism, both within and without their own communities. In light of such overwhelming conditions, U.S. Latina women have often been mainstays. They have been at the front lines of social battles that seek to improve their communities. They have always fought for the survival of their children, families, and *pueblo* (people). This is a sharp contrast to the stereotypical view, often propagated by the media, of Latina women as passive and submissive. History has witnessed to the fact that women have been *luchadoras* who have served as civil rights, community, religious, and political leaders, in the past and the present. U.S. Latina *evangélicas* have been creative and innovative in responding to the problems and challenges faced by their communities.

Interestingly enough, the very churches that have led U.S. Latinas to a vision of service have also been the institutions that have been stumbling blocks toward the realization of the ministries they sought to fulfill. A recent study by María Pérez y González has documented the cultural and theological barriers that many U.S. Latina *evangélicas* have overcome in order to carry out their ministries. It shows that U.S. Latina *evangélica* churches failed to provide for women in ministry in various ways. There is a lack of financial or family support and a lack of mentoring programs for those women who wish to be formally trained in theological programs. Scriptural evidence portraying women in leadership roles has been absent. This goes hand in hand with an insistent interpretation of scripture that seeks to circumscribe women's roles in the church and the home to traditional roles. Women who have been shaped by these traditional understandings about the family and society often present the most serious stumbling blocks to women in ministry. This barrier proves to be a serious one, considering that approximately 60 percent of members of U.S. Latina *evangélica* churches are women. Furthermore, it is precisely these women who carry out the teaching functions in their churches. Therefore, the influence they exert can pose an obstacle to women who seek to enter ministry. Indeed, they can exert a detrimental effect at all levels of *la vida cotidiana*.

The lack of support from local churches is only compounded by the fact that U.S. Latina *evangélica* churches are in themselves already marginalized from the centers of power and the economic resources of the larger church structures. In many denominations, churches are "colonized" realities: They are constantly struggling against the imposed theological and religious Eurocentric values of the dominant culture. Their voices are not heard. Their presence is not valued. U.S. Latina *evangélicas* are doubly marginalized: within their local churches and from the larger religious and denominational structures.

The history of U.S. Latina *evangélicas* cannot be fully appreciated outside this context of ostracism, discrimination, and marginalization in both social and ecclesial realms. Nevertheless, U.S. Latina *evangélica* women have risen above these barriers to respond to their calls to ministry. This is due, in great part, to the importance of prayer: listening to God's voice from within. *Evangélicas* consider the Holy Spirit an important source of authority for their daily faith and practice. Prayer allows them to discern the moving of the Spirit: that is, to discern how the Spirit is acting in their lives, in the lives of their communities, and in their own ongoing ministries. The Spirit is the One who grants the gifts necessary for effectively carrying out one's calling. The Holy Spirit is the midwife of their ministries. U.S. Latina *evangélicas* are clear that these gifts are not given to fulfill personal agendas but to serve the common good (1 Corinthians 12: 4–6, 11). In Ephesians 4: 12, gifts are distributed in order to equip those called to ministry to assist in building up the body (i.e., the community of faith). According to Markus Barth, the Greek term used for "equip" (*kartartismos*) can also be translated as "to set or heal broken bones." The body of Christ, indeed, the community, cannot flourish if its "bones" (the infrastructure that gives a community its sense of well-being) are "fractured." Gifts are for healing the brokenness of the community

A U.S. Latina *evangélica*'s sense of call is, therefore, centered on the authority of the Holy Spirit rather than on that of the church. Whenever there has been a conflict between the ecclesial structures and a woman's own sense of vocation, they have depended on discerning the Spirit's voice. It is not a privatistic or individualistic response. Discernment entails a process. This process has been learned through mentoring and community. It is a *discernimiento en conjunto* (discernment as a collaborative process) that includes dialogue, participation in spiritual retreats, attending seminars or courses (such as those offered in church-based *institutos*), and through fellowship where women reflect theologically with each other. Since this is how many have come to understand calls to ministry, this is also how they have been empowered to carry out ministries beyond the traditions and theology of the church. It is not surprising that many such ministries have been carried outside the church's supportive structures. However, rather than stifle *evangélicas*, this has resulted either in the development of innovative ministries or in the fulfillment of politically and socially unpalatable ministries.

Prayer imparts a sense of compassion and a deep love for those to whom U.S. Latina *evangélicas* minister. This sense of compassion informs and shapes their ministries. Prayer empowers them to respond to vocational calls, overcoming the social and ecclesial structural barriers faced on a daily basis. It allows U.S. Latinas to embrace the suffering that is present in their communities and to transform that pain into the creative work of social action and justice.

Pastoral Ministries

For as long as there have been U.S. Latina *evangélica* churches in the United States, there have been women in ministry. Concurrent with the dearth of material doc-

umenting the presence of the *evangélica* church, there has been little to virtually no documentation of *evangélicas*. Recent scholarship has sought to correct this. This lack does not minimize the importance and influence that the Latina *evangélica* church in the United States and *evangélica* women have had in the community. Women such as the Rev. Leoncia Rosado Rousseau and the Rev. Aimee García Cortese have played important roles in New York City. They have become important models for many women, and their ministries have had a greater impact than in the immediate geographical area they served.

Reverend Rosado was born in Toa Alta, Puerto Rico, on April 11, 1912. Her father lost the family farm and became very ill with tuberculosis. The family was separated and distributed among various relatives. She was sent to live with an uncle when she was seven years old and put to work scrubbing floors, cleaning, and doing the family laundry. The uncle was physically abusive to her, so she was taken from his home and returned to her mother who lived in a small storefront. At the age of eleven she started attending the Lutheran Church and shortly afterward began leading a procession of up to thirty children to Sunday School every Sunday.

She began her career in the late 1930s. She responded to a sense of call and became a missionary and evangelist by the age of twenty. In 1935, she moved to New York City where she preached on the street corners, visited the sick, and assisted in the general organization of the church. In spite of her myriad ministries, both in the United States and in Latin America, Mama Leo (as she was fondly called) was never considered a pastor until her husband passed away. Then, and with much trepidation, she took on the pastoral duties of the Damascus Christian Church. Her heart was moved by a deep sense of compassion for the people of New York, especially for those who lived at the fringes of society. At a time when working with substance abusers was considered a social and ecclesial taboo, Mama Leo established a grassroots program to combat drug abuse and provide a refuge for gangs, addicts, alcoholics, and ex-convicts. Initially the members of the church were opposed to working with these young people. However, because of the vision Reverend Rosado had of this work, her response was, "Yes, here! Because God mandates it of us. The church which closes its being and heart to the clamor of lost souls does not have a right to a place in the community. What do you think you are here for?" (Sánchez-Korrol, 59). This program preceded better-known programs like Teen Challenge, or secular-based programs such as Odyssey House. In spite of the controversy, she was able to underwrite it with church funds as the work expanded into the five boroughs of the city. Up to 300 of those rehabilitated through this program eventually entered the ministry. Many are still active in various youth programs today. For example, Way Out Ministries was modeled on Mama Leo's prophetic ministry begun decades ago.

The Rev. Aimee García Cortese was born in Bronx, New York, on May 26, 1929, growing up in the South Bronx. She preached her first sermon by the time she was fifteen years old. She looks back and credits women like Leoncia Rosado Rousseau and Elisa Alicéa (a lay member of a church in Ciales, Puerto Rico) with opening the way for other women in religious life. "Elisa (Alicéa) was also a tremendous role model in the sense of daring to be innovative. . . . Leo was somebody to learn from . . . she was one hundred years ahead of her time" (Sánchez-Korrol, 62). Like the *evangélicas* of her time, Aimee was named a "missionary evangelist" for the Spanish Assemblies of God. This was a position often reserved for women in Pentecostal churches that did not recognize the validity of ordained ministry for them. They were allowed to preach but not from the pulpit. Missionary evangelists were often called to carry out ministries in some of the most dangerous communities. While not initially embraced by the very churches that had sent these women, they eventually gained ecclesial support when the churches saw them bear fruit in the community. Much of this work entailed social services and outreach programs that served the poorest of the poor. This reality led many *evangélicas*, including García Cortese, to pioneer new areas of ministry.

García Cortese eventually became the associate minister of the Thessalonica Christian Church in the Bronx. She began doing volunteer work at the Bedford Hills Correctional Facility for women. When Paul Markstrom, the director of prison ministries of the Assemblies of God, found out, he opened the doors for her to be ordained. The Spanish Eastern District had denied her ordination, but Reverend Markstrom referred her to the New York district. "Through him, God opened the back door for me and I was ordained, bypassing the Spanish district." Aimee then became the first female chaplain to serve in the New York State Department of Corrections. In 1964, she was also ordained by the Wesleyan Methodist Church of Puerto Rico.

In 1981 she founded the Crossroads Tabernacle Church in the Bronx, which served as a model for other ministries. Along with more traditional programs such as Bible classes, the church provided youth and community programs, recreational programs, and support ministries for women, men, and families. The church also provided a rehabilitation program for substance abusers. Reverend García Cortese affirms that "the authority of the scriptures and the unction of the Holy Spirit is the only authority we have. Jesus gives us illumination and we have only to answer his call. We are not here to beat anyone or to prove anything to anyone. We are here to answer the call and the road of faithfulness to God will lead us beyond the authority of any man" (personal interview).

Many other women have served as innovative pastors in their communities. One of these was Ana María Falcon García, born on April 18, 1954. She is pastor of one of the largest churches of the Iglesia Cristiana Pentecostal, Inc., in the city of Willimantic, Connecticut. The church is involved in prison ministries and has a television program. They are known for the many services they provide the community such as providing food, help finding jobs and with translations, and networking with other service agencies. Falcon García is part of the Pastoral Care Committee at the local hospital and on the mayor's committee that deals with the problems of drug addiction in the community. She teaches in the Hispanic Program at Hartford Seminary. She was ordained in July 1990, becoming the second woman ordained by her denomination.

On May 27, 1987, Falcon García introduced and defended an amendment to the constitution of her denomination that would allow the ordination of women. She recounts that experience:

> I introduced new biblical understanding showing how women had been called to take roles of leadership that placed them in authority over men. I also showed how men and women were equal until the fall. To live redeemed lives means to live equally with one another. Neither the man nor the woman is to dominate the other. The amendment passed unanimously! Minerva Rivera was the first woman ordained after the amendment passed. She was ordained in Puerto Rico in June of 1990. She was a woman who had pastored for ten years under the title of missionary, the highest position allowed for a woman until the amendment passed. When I was ordained the next month it was she who poured the oil over me. (personal interview)

Julie Ramírez is pastor of one of the largest Assemblies of God congregations in Hartford, Connecticut. At a listening conference for women in ministry held at her church in the spring of 1997, Reverend Ramírez told her story.

> It was the Holy Spirit who called me and the only one to whom I was responsible for responding boldly to my call. I did not argue with the men. I simply carried out my ministry. Mine was a ministry that they did not want. It had no prestige and no money. Today I have a building that takes up half a city block with classrooms and rooms

for a retreat center as well as a worship center. All that is due to the Holy Spirit. The men who tried to humiliate me are now showcasing me. (personal interview)

Both these women were able to plant churches where men had failed earlier. Sent by their denominations with no funds, they encountered many problems. Their lives of prayer and sacrifice, a deep sense of call, a tremendous creativity, and gifts as entrepreneurs made their ministries models for others to follow.

Other women have made their marks serving in different capacities in their denominations, often working in the face of resistance by more traditional-minded people. Irma Violeta Cruz served as director of Educational Ministries for American Baptist Churches/USA for many years. Reverend Liliana Da Valle presently serves as area minister for the American Baptist Churches of Massachusetts. Although this essay deals primarily with Latina *evangélicas* residing on the mainland of the United States, there are two women residing on the island of Puerto Rico who should be mentioned for overcoming barriers. The Rev. Yamina Apolinaris was the first executive minister of the American Baptist Churches, Puerto Rico Convention, serving until 1998. Maribel Piña was the first female moderator for the Iglesia Evangélica Unida—the Puerto Rican branch of the United Church of Christ.

Many women have been forced to work outside the structures of their denominations. Unwilling to be hindered from fulfilling the vocations received from God, they started their own movements. Esmeralda Collazo of Framingham, Massachusetts, started El Movimiento del Dios Vivo (Movement of the Living God). She is a bivocational pastor. Her ministry involves outreach to children and single mothers. Among other programs, her church runs an after-school program called Mejores Días/ Better Days. The program offers homework tutoring, recreation, and snacks in a safe environment.

Grassroots Ministries

Women, under the title of *misionera* (missionary evangelist), have carried out grassroots ministries, working among traditionally underserved communities. However, it was not until the 1990s that many of them began to organize nonprofit organizations.

The Rev. Elizabeth D. Ríos is a certified minister of the Assemblies of God, with a master's degree in management. She is currently pursuing doctoral work in religious education at Fordham University. As chief administrative officer of the Latino Pastoral Action Center, she was called on to spearhead a program called Latinas in Ministry by the New York City Mission Society. This program was created in light of the previously cited

study by Pérez y González. In 1998, Ríos renamed the program the Center for Emerging Female Leadership (CEFL). Among other activities, the CEFL sponsors retreats, workshops, and conferences that seek to empower women in ministry. Ríos believes that women have unique styles of leadership and should not have to compromise them because of patriarchal structures. In order to encourage women, she developed a training program to teach women how to create nonprofit organizations.

This kind of program, which trains and gives technical assistance, has enabled women to create their own organizations. For example, the Rev. Olga Torres directs Angels Unaware, the only U.S. Latina agency in the state of New York that serves special needs children. Alexie Torres Fleming developed Youth Ministries for Peace and Justice, a program tailored to support young people who seek to have a voice in their communities and who are especially concerned about issues of peace and justice for the poor. One of the unique aspects of the Rev. Ana Villafañe's Way Out Ministries is that it uses the participants of its program to serve the community in many ways. Thus, former substance abusers who had been the bane of their communities now work in soup kitchens, providing human resources to those in need and working in church-related community programs.

The Rev. Brixeida Márquez is of Puerto Rican descent. She came to New York City in the early 1960s and owned her own taxi company when she sensed her calling to found the Free Forever Prison Ministries program in Bridgeport, Connecticut. This program reaches out to incarcerated persons all over the state of Connecticut and provides support for their families. She has expanded the program to include a facility that provides care for ex-convicts with AIDS. Along with her board members, she works with an extensive group of supporters and volunteers.

Before U.S. Latina *evangélicas* began to form their own organizations, they often carried out their ministries within the existing ecclesial structures. This often implied being under male, non-Latino leadership. U.S. Latina *evangélicas/os*, especially the women, were often disempowered. Still, they sought to be faithful to their sense of vocation. Ignacia Torres and Angelita Rodríguez de Lizárraga were two such women.

Ignacia Torres was born in the city of Campeche in the Yucatan peninsula. The Los Angeles Presbytery hired her as a social worker in 1947. Previously, she had worked in various social ministries under the pastorate of the Rev. Alejandro Trujillo, including the Azusa Home of Neighborly Service, La Casa de San Gabriel, and Cleland House. Her work was to assist the directors and board members of the centers.

La Casa was a community center founded in 1946 by the First Presbyterian Church of San Gabriel under the leadership of the Rev. César and Mrs. Angelita Rodríguez de Lizárraga. Angelita's life and work as a pastor's wife exemplify how men are often the ones formally called to a particular ministry by a church, but both (*wives* with their husbands) do the work. Angelita not only helped establish La Casa, she was also its first director, serving on a part-time basis. In an interview, she described her accomplishments while serving in that capacity. She organized local franchises of well-known groups affiliated with the Girl Scouts organization, a Mother's club, and a youth club. She then went on to found a well-baby clinic (an unheard of thing at the time) and an innovative toy loan program. She explained, "At first I did it as a minister's wife [without pay]. Later they paid me $75.00 per month" (Atkins-Vásquez, 168). Angelita also organized its board of directors to ensure that people from the community, including businesspeople, served as members alongside those representing local Anglo churches.

Theological Education

One of the most exciting areas in recent history for U.S. Latina *evangélica* women has been in theological education. There has been a steady increase of Latina women completing Ph.D. degrees in theology and serving their communities in academia. However, much work remains to be done. The Hispanic Theological Initiative (HTI), an organization that through myriad programs supports U.S. Latinas in theological education, reports that at present approximately sixteen Latinas have completed doctoral degrees in religion or theology. They found, however, that many still struggle with a continued sense of isolation, marginalization, and lack of support that hinder many of those who enter advanced degree programs. HTI was created to provide scholarships, mentoring programs, and training workshops to support these students. It has also sponsored Latinas in Theology—a group of doctoral Catholic and *evangélica* Latinas who come together to reflect theologically, as well as to network and support each other. Meanwhile, the number of U.S. Latina *evangélicas* who have successfully completed their doctoral studies has steadily increased.

The first U.S. Latina *evangélica* woman to complete a Ph.D. in theology was Daisy L. Machado. She is Cuban and the first U.S. Latina to be ordained in the Disciples of Christ Church in the United States. In 1996 she received her Ph.D. in Church History from the University of Chicago. She was the first director of the Hispanic Theological Initiative and one of the founding members of Latinas in Theology. She has worked extensively with U.S. Latina/o communities in the Northeast and in the Southwest, as both pastor and historian, and is currently on the faculty of Brite Divinity School in Fort Worth, Texas. She is a noted keynote speaker and preacher. She

is one of the coeditors of *A Reader in Latina Feminist Theology: Religion and Justice* (2002) and has published a number of other articles.

Elizabeth Conde-Frazier was the second U.S. Latina *evangélica* woman to obtain a doctoral degree. She completed her studies in practical theology and religious education, receiving her Ph.D. from Boston College in 1998. She is a second-generation Puerto Rican and an ordained minister with the American Baptist Churches/USA. She was the first director of the Orlando E. Costas Hispanic and Latin American Ministries Program at Andover Newton Theological School in Massachusetts. Presently, she is on the faculty at Claremont School of Theology in California. A highly regarded public speaker and preacher, she has published articles about the teaching ministry of healing in the U.S. Latina community, spirituality and its relationship to the body, and multicultural religious education.

Zaida Maldonado Pérez obtained her doctorate in the area of historical theology, specializing in early church studies, from Saint Louis University in 1999. She was the first island-born Puerto Rican to complete a Ph.D. in theology. A member of the United Church of Christ, Maldonado Pérez has taught at the Evangelical Seminary of Puerto Rico. She is a well-regarded preacher who has published a number of articles. A former director of the Hispanic Theological Initiative located at Princeton Theological Seminary in New Jersey, she is currently a faculty member of Asbury Theological Seminary in Orlando, Florida.

Teresa Chávez Sauceda graduated from Graduate Theological Union (Berkeley, California) with a Ph.D in social ethics. Esther Díaz Bolet, who completed her degree in Christian education, is currently teaching at Southwestern Baptist Theological Seminary in Fort Worth, Texas. Nora O. Lozano-Díaz completed her doctoral degree in systematic theology at Drew University (Madison, New Jersey) and remains part of the faculty of the Hispanic Baptist Theological School in San Antonio, Texas. Suzanne Segovia Hoeferkamp completed her degree in systematic theology from the Lutheran School of Theology in Chicago. Awilda González-Tejera graduated from Boston University with a degree in New Testament. Leticia Guardiola Saenz hopes to complete her degree in New Testament at Vanderbilt University. She served as director of the Orlando E. Costas Hispanic and Latin American Ministries program and is currently on the faculty of Drew University. Loida Martell Otero was the first Puerto Rican woman to practice veterinary medicine on the island. She left a growing practice in Puerto Rico to respond to God's call to ministry. She is currently a Ph.D. candidate in systematic theology at Fordham University and an ordained minister of the American Baptist Churches USA. A well-regarded preacher, she has published articles on *evangélica* theology and salvation. She also coedited *Teología en Conjunto: A Collaborative Hispanic Protestant Theology* (1997).

María E. Pérez y González is a sociologist and currently part of the faculty of Brooklyn College in the department of Puerto Rican Studies. She has been an active lay leader in the Evangelical Lutheran Church and has participated in various forums involving theological education. She has carried out important studies about U.S. Latina *evangélica* women. One of these studies, alluded to earlier, led to the formation of Latinas in Ministry in New York City. She is of Puerto Rican descent and obtained her degree in 1993 in sociology with concentrations in ethnic minority integration processes, demography, and mental health and Hispanics from Fordham University.

The story of U.S. Latina *evangélicas*, especially those who have exerted some ministry—ordained or lay—has been an integral part of the story of the success of the Protestant church in the Latino community. A (male) pastor once quipped that if all the women left his church, he would have to close his doors for good. Women have been the teachers, the preachers, the missionaries, the builders, the *luchadoras*, and the mainstays of their church communities. Many have struggled for the survival of their families and for the communities at large. They have often been at the front lines of social transformation: the nameless, unsung prophets who have stood on the ground of their faith and in the name of the God of that faith. In San Juan, Puerto Rico, there is a monument to such women called *La Rogativa* (the Prayer). It reminds the people of that Caribbean island that when the city was under siege, a group of women came out to pray for deliverance. Very soon after that prayer, the enemy's naval forces departed because the sailors had taken ill. The city was saved: not by the sword of the city's soldiers but by the spirit of prayer that these women exhibited. Tertullian considered martyrs the seeds upon which the church was built. It can be stated unequivocally that the U.S. Latina church—indeed, the church of the Americas—has been built upon the seeds of the prayers, tears, and struggles of Latina women, *evangélica* and Catholic alike.

SOURCES: Jane Atkins-Vásquez has recorded the history of women within the Hispanic church in southern California in *Hispanic Presbyterians in Southern California: One Hundred Years* (1988). The work includes some oral histories. Hedda Garza has made an excellent historical recounting of the struggles and spirit of Latina women in the United States in *Latinas: Hispanic Women in the United States* (1994). Beatríz Melano Couch's article "New Visions in Latin America: A Protestant View," in *The Emergent Gospel: Theology from the Underside of History*, ed. Sergio Tomes and Virginia Fabella (1978), presents a good background of *evangélica* belief in Latin America. It also provides a more ecumenically balanced view of the emergent theologies that seek liberation in Latin America. María E. Pérez y González does a thorough study of *evangélicas* involved in a diversity of ministries, discussing the issues, concerns, and needs specific to them and the role that theological education can play in their development in *Latinas in Ministry: A Pioneering Study on Women Ministers, Educators and Students of Theology* (1993). The historian Virginia Sánchez-Korrol takes seriously the call to ministry of three pioneer women, showing how their ministries influenced not only the church but also their communities at large in her seminal work "In Search of Unconventional Women": Histories of Puerto Rican Women in Religious Vocations before Mid-Century," *Oral History Review* 16 (Fall 1988): 47–63. Santiago Soto Fontánez documents the history of the Hispanic Northern Baptist Church in New York in a bilingual book titled *Misión a la Puerta/Mission at the Door* (1982). *Teología en Conjunto: A Collaborative Hispanic Protestant Theology* (1997), edited by José David Rodríguez and Loida I. Martell Otero, is one of the first works seeking to systematize *evangélica/o* theology. It includes articles by three *evangélica* theologians: Teresa Chávez Sauceda, Loida Martell Otero, and Elizabeth Conde-Frazier. Conde-Frazier's article, titled "Hispanic Protestant Spirituality," presents an understanding of the spirituality that empowers Latina *evangélicas* to radical ministry even beyond the authority structures and patriarchy of their churches. Thomas Weaver is the general editor of the three-volume *Handbook of Hispanic Cultures in the United States* (1994). In the *Anthropology* volume, Beatriz Morales discusses "Latino Religion, Ritual and Culture," providing statistics on the religious affiliations found among the Latino population, as well as discussing such religious beliefs as *curanderismo* (indigenous healing practices).

RACE AND GENDER IN LATINA EXPERIENCE
Teresa Chávez Sauceda

LATINA IDENTITY IN the United States is shaped in and through confrontation with sexism, racism and ethnocentrism, and classism. These social categories of gender, race, and class interact dynamically with each other, creating structures of social hierarchy, privilege, and marginalization. As social structures, they are fluid created through historical relationships, articulated through social and political institutions, and contested through social, political, and economic movements. They are interconnected, interacting in complex ways that make it impossible to treat them as isolated phenomena. Economic systems cannot be understood apart from the assignment of gender roles in the division of labor or the way racial divisions have restricted and exploited the participation of Latinas and other racialized groups. Racism cannot be understood merely as attitude or worldview apart from political and economic structures or gender division in social roles. Racism is embedded in, and perpetuated through, the systems and institutions of our society. This is also true for gender roles.

Latina scholars argue for the need to create new ways of doing theory, of analyzing and interpreting the world as they perceive it in a way that empowers Latinas in their struggle for social change, for a rational analysis that makes sense from the standpoint of women of color, using the categories of race, ethnicity, class, and gender as the analytical framework. This revisioning of history makes the invisible visible, giving voice to the experience of those who have been marginalized and silenced. It traces the interconnections and interactions between the categories of gender, race, and class, paying close attention not only to how these categories have been constructed and articulated through social institutions but to how oppressed groups have contested and redefined their meaning. Latina theorists have constructed a dialogue that crosses traditional academic lines, including the voices of poets, activists, and artists along with social scientists, philosophers, and theologians, to articulate the Latina experience in a way that empowers social change and redirects the trajectory of racial politics.

Race is a social construct, rooted in a history of conquest, expansion, genocide, enslavement, colonization, and economic exploitation. Race continues today to function to exclude those defined as "other" from the power to participate and to contribute in all spheres of life as self-determining moral agents. Race renders Latinas invisible and voiceless in the dominant culture.

Reading Our Own History

Developing a theoretical framework to interpret Latina experience is a process, a conversation that brings many voices from multiple disciplines to the table. It requires an examination of the history of Latinas and the Latina/o community that explores the factors that have contributed to the racialized identity of Latinas, recognizes the ways in which Latinas have resisted the homogenization of this racialized identity, and is cognizant of the interactions between race, ethnicity, class, and gender. The development of this history is itself a racial project, part of the empowerment of Latinas in naming and determining their own directions for the future.

As a social institution, the church has played a critical role in the historical processes of racialization. It has legitimized racism with theological rationales and promoted the goals of the racial state by sanctioning such racial projects as slavery and Manifest Destiny. At other times the church has been a voice of opposition and an agent for change, providing space for racialized groups to contest the structures of racism.

As Europe extended its reach across oceans and continents in the sixteenth and seventeenth centuries, the roots of racialization are found in the introduction of slavery, economic exploitation, and the extermination of indigenous peoples. The ideology of race developed to rationalize and sanction the actions of nation–states in subjecting whole continents. These activities presupposed a worldview in which Europeans saw themselves as a chosen people—privileged and entitled—distinguished from the "other" who was defined as heathen or barbarian, less than fully human.

In a prescientific world, the earliest rationalizations for this division of the human community were religious, as in the debate in Valladolid, Spain in 1550 between philosopher Ginés Sepulveda and Bartolomé de Las Casas, Dominican bishop in Chiapas, Mexico. Sepulveda articulated the prevailing view of the day, claiming that the indigenous people under Spanish colonial rule were inferior to their Spanish rulers in every way, much like children to adults or women to men. Las Casas, who spent his life living and working in the Americas, argued for the full humanity of the indigenous people. What was officially at stake was the question of the conversion of indigenous peoples to Catholicism, but their arguments would have much broader implications, as they provided the philosophical underpinnings of the racial state. The great European philosophers of the Enlightenment—Hegel, Kant, Hume, Locke—all expressed stridently racist views. Religious language would gradually be supplanted by scientific justifications. In the 1700s race begins to emerge as a biological construct with efforts to classify races or species of peoples, along with the emerging scientific classification of all living organisms.

In North America both religious and scientific justifications were employed to sanction the institution of slavery and the virtual removal of indigenous peoples from the colonized regions of what are now considered the eastern and southern United States. With expansion into the West and Southwest, the goals of the racial state were articulated politically through the doctrine of Manifest Destiny. Political, economic, and social power was consolidated in one racial group—white males of European heritage. Racial privilege was first encoded in law in the United States with passage of the Naturalization Law defining U.S. citizenship in 1790. It extended eligibility to free white immigrants only, excluding more people than it included. In a society also rigidly organized by gender, white women had privilege relative to women and men of color but little power relative to white males. Society was also highly organized by class. Only white males with property could vote, for example.

Rev. Santos Elizondo was a pastor and church planter in El Paso and Juarez, Texas, in the late 1800s. The Latina/o Protestant church created a public space where the private language of Spanish expressed identity as much as faith. *Courtesy of the Nazarene Archives.*

Women, in most instances, were not permitted to own property, have sole custody of their children, or vote. White women of wealth held privilege relative to white men and women of lower classes, but again, they held little power relative to their male peers.

Latinas and Latinos first entered the socioeconomic sphere of the United States through occupation and conquest, from the Florida peninsula, around the Gulf of Mexico, and across the western half of the continent. In the push to occupy and control the continent from East to West, the white-black racial hierarchy of the United States came into contact with new social groups. It became necessary to categorize and assign each group a place in the racial hierarchy. Spanish and Mexican colonists who had themselves displaced, enslaved, and exploited the indigenous populations across the Southwest found themselves redefined racially by a new occupying power.

In the Mexican territory north of the Rio Grande, Mexican colonial society in the seventeenth and eighteenth centuries was also highly stratified by race and class. Indigenous and *mestiza* women (having European and indigenous ancestry) occupied the lowest rungs of social life, European-born white male Spaniards occupied the highest. The influx of U.S. settlers in the Southwest had a direct impact on the social structures of race in the Mexican colonial culture. One example is found in marriage records kept by Roman Catholic priests in New Mexico in this era. These records carefully note the *calidad* (social status) of bride and groom. Early Spanish colonists made distinctions between Spaniard and Indian as well as between Spanish born and those born in the Americas to Spanish parents. From 1693 to 1759, there is little mention of race, social and economic class appearing to be the most significant factors. In the next two decades there is a shift. Race is identified in 78 percent of the records, with seven different categories identified: Español (Spanish), Negro (black), and Indio (Indian) and their various combinations. From 1780 to 1800, with the growth of the Anglo population from the United States in the region, there is further change as the polarization between white and Indian, Anglo and Mexican, increases. By 1800 the significant categories are white, Mexican, and Indian. The intermediate categories of race, so important in colonial Mexican society, began to disappear.

The status of Mexican women was also shaped by their class and color, with some distinctions from their male peers. In the early stages of U.S. occupation, when large numbers of white men moving west found few white women in the region, Mexican women made attractive wives, particularly if their Spanish ancestry showed in a lighter complexion and more European features. Marriages between Mexican men and Anglo women were much rarer and more likely to provoke scandal, particularly in white society. As racial lines became more rigid through the 1800s, lower-class *mestiza* women were increasingly denigrated as morally inferior and sexually promiscuous.

The reality was that as their social status was eroded by race, Mexican women found themselves more vulnerable to abuse and rape by white men. Class status continued to make a difference for the daughters of the *rancheros* (landholders), who were sought after as wives by white men who used their marital status to gain access to Mexican wealth and property. Contemporary descriptions of these relationships often emphasized the Caucasian/European ancestry of these daughters of the Mexican elite.

Throughout the West and Southwest the second half of the nineteenth century is marked by the struggle for group position. Race was defined legally, as in the 1848 Treaty of Guadalupe Hidalgo, which specified that Mexicans were a "white" population and accorded the political-legal status of "free white persons," in contrast to blacks and indigenous peoples living in the region who were denied the full rights of citizenship. Despite the legal protections of the treaty and, as in California, a state constitution that accorded the former Mexican citizens the same legal rights as free white persons, their actual status was much more ambiguous. The public racializing discourse institutionalized the privileged status of white men in opposition to Mexicans, Native Americans, and Asian immigrants. Color and class combined to deny the Mexicanos equal status in the eyes of the rapidly growing white population. A new racial hierarchy emerged out of the competition for social, economic, and political power.

For white immigrants moving from what was then the United States to the western territories, the Mexican residents they encountered were not perceived as white in the same way they saw themselves. The predominantly Protestant immigrants were deeply suspect of Mexican Catholicism and the ranching lifestyle of colonial Mexico, which seemed to require very little industry on the part of the *rancheros*. *Semicivilized* and *semibarbarian* were terms frequently applied to Mexicans. Working-class Mexicans were often classified or labeled as "Indian" in order to deny legal rights extended only to whites. Upper-class Mexicanas/os, with their claims to European ancestry, gained only grudging acceptance from white immigrants who could not dismiss them and their established socioeconomic and political power as easily as they could marginalize the more vulnerable *mestiza/o* and indigenous populations.

Throughout the western half of the continent, a new racial hierarchy was articulated and enforced through economic and political structures. In the first half of the nineteenth century the United States expanded its territory tenfold through invasion, occupation, conquest, annexation, and purchase. White U.S. settlers in Mexican territory justified the geographic displacement, economic exploitation, and political disenfranchisement of both the indigenous people and Mexican colonial settlers with religious zeal, claiming simply to be following God's injunction to occupy the land of promise, prosper economically, and fulfill their divine calling—their Manifest Destiny.

The California experience, where this transformation and displacement happened in the span of a few short years, is illustrative of the dynamics of racial politics. The rapid rate of change, with territorial annexation in 1848 and the gold rush in 1849 that brought white immigrants by the thousands almost overnight, brings the processes of racialization into sharp focus.

The Californios enjoyed an ambiguous status in the first years of statehood. California's state constitution codified racial status, conferring citizenship only to "free white persons." In contrast to blacks and indigenous people, Mexicans were defined as "white," based largely on their "mixed-blood ancestry." A number of the Californio elite were elected to the first state legislature, but the rapid influx of large numbers of Anglo voters into the state quickly rendered the Mexicans' political influence marginal. As the white population grew to majority status and political dominance in California, Mexicans became the specific target of racially discriminatory laws. One example is a law that was popularly known as the "Greaser Act" and targeted Mexican citizens. It made vagrancy a crime and permitted arrest and imprisonment or levied fines, which one could pay either in cash or through temporary labor.

In the occupation and conquest of Mexico's northern provinces, "Hispano" or Mexican identity coalesced in opposition to "Anglo" identity. Where social identity in Mexican colonial society was highly stratified by class and gender, as a racialized group, Mexican identity asserted itself across divisions of class and gender in opposition or resistance to the cultural hegemony of the dominant white society. Even in the most repressive periods of racism in the United States, there is evidence of oppositional culture asserting itself, sometimes almost covertly and sometimes at great cost. In the heavily oppressive environment of the Southwest in the 1800s, opposition can be found in places that are not explicitly political: Spanish-language newspapers, personal correspondence, autobiographical narratives, and nostalgic writing, including cookbooks that recorded traditions, customs, and social history along with recipes.

Toward the end of the nineteenth century, the rhetoric of Manifest Destiny would extend beyond the continent to sanction U.S. expansion. U.S. military occupation of Puerto Rico and Cuba in 1898 following the war with Spain, propelled by the ideology of Manifest Destiny, extended economic and political influence without incorporating the people or the territory directly into the commonweal of the United States. In the twentieth century, migration from Latin America contributed significantly to the growth of the Latina/o population in the United States. Immigrant groups have encountered the systemic racism of U.S. society with varying experiences. The degree to which Latina/o immigrant groups have been welcomed—or deterred—in their entry into the workforce and sociopolitical life in the United States has been influenced by a variety of factors, including the overall economic conditions, political perceptions about why they have come to the United States, and education and other resources they bring with them, as well as racial perceptions.

For example, Cuban exiles in the 1960s, whose presence in Miami supported official U.S. opposition to the Cuban government, encountered a far more open reception than Mexican farm laborers and domestic workers on the West Coast, Puerto Rican migrants in New York City in the same era, or the refugees of Central American civil conflicts in the 1970s. In the 1980s Cuban refugees met with a very different reception. A tight job market and a highly politicized anti-immigrant movement contributed to strong negative public sentiment, fueled by perceptions that the "Marielitos," many of whom came from a much lower socioeconomic status than their 1960s counterparts, were an undesirable addition to U.S. society. Nor is it coincidental that 40 percent of the Mariel refugees were mulatto or black, compared to 3 percent of the 1960s refugees.

New Directions in Racial Politics and the Role of the Church

Throughout the history of race in the United States, racial identity is constantly in flux as the dominant culture asserts pressure to control and racialized communities struggle to assert their own voices. In the decades following the civil rights movement of the 1960s, coalition building across ethnic lines emerged as a critical strategy as Latinas/os sought to build political power locally and on the national level. Through community building and political organizing Latinas/os oppose and contest existing class and racial hierarchies and continue to challenge the assumptions of a privileged white Eurocentric culture. At the same time, Latinas/os resist societal pressures to homogenize Latina/o identity—asserting the significance of retaining identity with their distinct national heritages is part of the resistance to the hegemony of the dominant culture. Latinas/os struggle to impact the direction of racial politics in the United States.

The church is one of the social institutions within the Latina/o community where this struggle to claim space and voice is taking place. Latinas' struggle to gain equity within the institutional church, to legitimize their own forms of religious expression within those institutional structures, and to contribute their own theological voice to the life of the larger church community is central to the struggle against racism.

The church came as an arm of the conquest in the Americas. In the conquest and colonization of North America, the Protestant ethos gave its sense of divine providence and its missionary zeal to the ideology of Manifest Destiny, literally equating Protestant Christianity with democracy, capitalism, and modern civilization. Claims for the cultural superiority of the West were directly attributed to the racial superiority of that people whose identity stemmed from their roots in the northern European Anglo-Saxon-Teutonic tradition. The political and economic success of the United States, they believed, verified their status as a "chosen people" of God. The survival and prosperity of their colonies and the success of their revolution against the power of Great Britain all revealed God's true intentions—a divinely ordained destiny confirmed by amazingly rapid growth in the decades following that conflict. Although the rhetoric of Manifest Destiny was contested by some on theological and biblical grounds, these arguments did little to dissuade the strong climate of cultural supremacy and its intimate association with Protestant religion.

The historical Latina/o Protestant church in the United States is a result of missionary efforts, an extension of the conquest and Manifest Destiny. The early missionaries were evangelists of Eurocentric culture as much as the gospel of Christian faith. They saw the first generation of Latina/o Protestants as converts rescued from both papalism and an inferior, backward culture. Yet in spite of ethnocentric biases and the church's identification with Eurocentric culture and the forces of conquest and exploitation, the development of Latina/o

Protestant churches also resulted in the creation of a space for cultural resistance and opportunity to build solidarity within predominantly white denominations to contest the structures of race in the United States.

The Latina/o Protestant church created a public space where the private language of Spanish expressed identity as much as faith. The local congregation became an arena for articulating an oppositional consciousness, for resisting the homogenization of the dominant culture. In the Roman Catholic Church, the expressions of popular religion similarly nurtured Latina/o identity as well as faith, despite strident efforts on the part of the institutional Church to reject and privatize expression of popular religiosity and faith. As Latina/o Catholics have gained voice within the Church, the practices of faith that are central to the Latina/o community have moved from the privacy of the home to the public sphere of the Church. In recent decades they have been further legitimized by scholarly study and theological reflection.

For the Latina/o community, the Church has provided space for cultural resistance—in the survival of popular religiosity among Latina/o Catholics and its struggle for acceptance by official Catholicism, in the survival of third- and fourth-generation Protestant churches that continue to worship in Spanish, and in a growing Pentecostal movement that articulates a spirituality that invokes a vision of social justice.

The strength of popular religion, handed on from generation to generation through the family, represents a continuing strand of the historical dissidence of indigenous people—a creative *mestizaje*, blending indigenous and Spanish religious practices in an expression of Christian faith. It also represents a space in which Latinas have been central to the process of preserving the cultural traditions and identity through the family. The role of popular religion as a liberating, empowering voice of the people comes to the fore in the United States, where it is also a vehicle for resisting racial homogenization and cultural hegemony.

The role of indigenous beliefs in the work of scholars such as Gloria Anzaldua, the growing acceptance of popular religiosity in the institutional church, and the development of a Latina/o theology in the United States make important contributions to resisting the dehumanizing effects of oppression and redirecting the trajectory of racial politics. *Mujerista* theology, articulated by Ada María Isasi-Díaz, has emphasized that empowering the moral agency of Latinas is central to the process of social change.

Racism and Interlocking Systems of Oppression

Patterns of racism and ethnocentrism are systemic and deeply embedded in the fabric of life in the United States. Despite decades of civil rights legislation and affirmative action programs, Latinas continue to be grossly underrepresented in higher education, in professional occupations, and at managerial levels of private industry and government. While the Latina/o community has made significant inroads in the political arena at the local level in communities like San Antonio and Miami, they continue to be largely ignored or excluded by the political agenda at the national level.

Latina group identity is itself a construct of racialization, a product of racial politics. Although racial categories are closely linked to perceived physical differences, race as a biological concept is nonsensical when viewed through the lens of Latina experience. Those who identify themselves as Latina today may trace their ancestors to the indigenous Amerindians of North and South America, to European, African, or Asian ancestors, or any combination of these. As a result of this diverse heritage, Latinas cover the spectrum of human possibilities in terms of color and other physical attributes normally employed to categorize people by race. On a personal or individual level, Latinas identify themselves primarily in ethnic terms, referring to their national heritage or origin. Language and culture, including religious expression, are critical to their sense of identity.

Yet the dominant society works to define Latinas as a unitary, homogenized racial group, and Latinas frequently describe the experience of discrimination and oppression in this society as racism. The tendency to ignore ethnic diversity and to homogenize Latina identity is itself perceived as an expression of racism, a refusal by the dominant culture to accept Latinas on their own terms, insisting on an assigned identity promulgated by a hegemonic, Eurocentric culture.

The growing sense of political unity among Latinas is, at least in part, a response to the dynamics of racial politics in the United States. The same factors that marginalize Latinas from full participation in the socioeconomic and political institutions of the dominant society have pushed Latinas to build coalitions around common goals.

In this process, Latinas redefine the racial agenda, as they not only insist on honoring differences of gender and class among themselves in the process of doing theory but also uphold the significance of differences of ethnicity, culture, and religion. In other words, Latinas respond to a racialized identity by employing that identity to challenge the negative political and economic consequences of racism and by articulating an alternative vision of society that asserts a different set of normative values for community—one that *includes* rather than *excludes* difference.

Identity is a survival issue for Latinas. The assumptions of cultural assimilation reflect the structures of power that render Latinas invisible in the cultural and racial hegemony of the dominant culture. Culture and ethnicity become resources for Latinas as they contest the structures of a racialized society. Language, customs, values, and worldview take on political significance in a cultural and political context that seeks to exclude difference.

In the experience of the Latina community, cultural assimilation does not erase color prejudice, and Latinas argue that the loss of culture and ethnic identity is too high a price to pay for social inclusion. The devaluing of the Spanish language and Latina/o cultures is directly connected to lower educational achievement and greater rates of poverty among Latinas, as it strips away the inherent cultural resources of a people to sustain themselves. The Church has played a critical role in the struggle to assert a self-defined Latina identity to the extent that it has provided public space where use of the Spanish language is celebrated and faith is articulated through culturally defined expressions.

Race and Gender

Gender difference may begin in the biological differences between men and women, but as a social construct, gender is articulated and contested through all aspects of women's and men's lives and relationships, reaching far beyond those aspects of life that might be directly tied to biological difference. While the reality of gender division may be universal, the experience of gender oppression is highly differentiated, shaped by historical location and factors such as race, ethnicity, class, and religion.

At the forming of the U.S. Constitution women could not vote, own property, or retain custody of their own children. While women of any color were denied the privileges and many of the protections of citizenship, African American women held no legitimate place in the United States except as property, and indigenous women were the object of governmental policies of planned removal and genocide. While many of the legal barriers to women's equality have been removed, women continue to earn, on average, less than their male counterparts in the same occupations. The glass ceiling is still a reality in most professional occupations. Disparities persist in politics and social policies. Women continue to be more at risk from domestic violence, more likely to be poor following a divorce, and more likely to be raising children as a single parent.

While there is some commonality in the way women are affected by sexism in society, Latina feminists argue that there is no universal woman's experience. Gender construction in the United States is nuanced by race and class, differentiating the experience of sexism and the construction of gender identity for Latinas from white

women and, to a lesser degree, from other women of color. Latinas confront racism within the white women's movement, and they confront sexism in the Latina/o community. Differences of education, class, heritage, and immigrant status add texture to the tapestry of Latina experience. The complexity of this fabric is intensified yet again when we include the perspectives and experience of lesbian, bisexual, and transgendered Latinas who not only struggle with gender oppression but must also confront the heterosexism of both the Latina/o community and the dominant society.

Race and Ethnicity

The connection between racism and ethnocentrism is rooted in the expectation of the dominant culture that Latinas sacrifice cultural distinctiveness and ethnic identity to achieve political voice and economic parity. The popular imagery of the melting pot may have implied that everyone was welcome to bring their own contribution to "flavor" the pot, but the reality has been that those who differed from the norm of Eurocentric culture in the United States were expected to disappear culturally—to have any distinctive contribution of their own evaporate as they become invisible in their cultural conformity. Underlying this expectation are deep-seated racial assumptions that associate color and difference with cultural inferiority.

For Latinas, the expectations and assumptions of cultural assimilation are inherently oppressive. The presumption that Latinas should give up every vestige of their own cultural heritage to obtain the rights and privileges of full participation in society denies any sense of worth in Latina/o cultures. Moreover, the myth of assimilation is that no matter how well Latinas adapt to the patterns of the dominant culture, regardless of educational and economic achievement, racism still impacts their lives—color still creates barriers. In the racial politics of the United States, the maintenance of distinctive cultural norms, values, and traditions, the persistence of ethnic identity in the face of tremendous social pressure operates as a strategy of resistance.

Cultural citizenship, articulating a political voice through identity with their ethnic heritage, is fundamental to the full participation of the Latina community in the United States as an authentic, viable, self-actuated voice. This link between race and ethnicity creates a tension that requires Latinas to become cultural critics—affirming the positive, constructive elements of their culture while critiquing the sexism and other destructive elements. It also requires astute political awareness and critique of the social, economic, and political pressures that drive cultural assimilation. The use of language is one area where the complex interaction of cultural and political power is readily apparent as Latinas struggle to retain the use of the Spanish language within their communities. Ethnocentric projects such as the English-only movement and voter-mandated suspension of bilingual education programs exemplify racial projects of the dominant culture whose explicit goal is to marginalize the voices of diversity in the Latina/o community.

While it is theoretically possible to be ethnocentric and not racist, or racist and not ethnocentric, in a racial state where everyone is categorized by race, ethnocentrism functions as a mechanism of the centers of power, articulating the *ideology* of the racial state. Ethnocentrism operates in the racial state to sanction, justify, and rationalize the existing racial hierarchy and perpetuate racial differentiation.

Race and Class

Racial and patriarchal norms are embedded in economic structures. Class analysis that takes into consideration the links between economic oppression and gender/racial/ethnic exploitation is critical to understanding that poverty is a creation of the economic system rather than the product of either moral failure or cultural inferiority—notions that reinforce both racism and sexism. In the economic arena, Latinas confront both gender and racial bias. Economic institutions and practices play a critical role in creating and sustaining racial/ethnic, gender, and class subordination and marginalization, maintaining the normative status of the dominant patriarchal Eurocentric culture.

A greater proportion of the Latina community lives below the poverty level in contrast to the dominant white population. Studies on the participation of Latinas in the workplace demonstrate the complex factors that impact employment and economic status. The economic vulnerability of Latinas, rooted in both racial and gender identity, is evident in that Latinas are more likely to work in marginal jobs with a combination of low wages, poor benefits, poor working conditions, and high turnover. Workforce participation is affected by such factors as education levels, stereotypic perceptions of employers, access to employment opportunities—including availability of public transportation—and other institutionalized patterns of racism and sexism.

A fuller understanding of the interaction of race and gender in the lives of Latinas in the economic arena must take into account the relationship between patriarchy and capitalism within Latina/o culture. The role of family and gender-role expectations impact on the participation of Latinas in the workforce. Familial support for educational and occupational success is critical to Latinas. While Latina/o cultures are historically patriarchal, feminist scholars argue that familial support, especially that of the mother, can partially overcome the barriers of sexism.

Family values may also mitigate sexism in gender roles in the face of economic pressures. For example, in her groundbreaking research, Patricia Zavella studied working-class Mexican and Chicano families in an agricultural community in California. She found that when gender bias in the workplace meant that women could get better-paying, more permanent employment in the canneries than their husbands, families with healthy relationships between husband and wife were more likely to demonstrate flexibility in adjusting responsibilities in the home, with fathers redefining their own sense of machismo from being dependent on providing the sole financial support for their family to include supporting their family in many ways, including caring for their children.

Race and Sociopolitical Status

Race and gender bias are not strictly functions of economic systems. Economic structures are not absolute barriers. A growing Latina middle class finds that racism continues to impact their lives in complex ways even while economic opportunities are more readily available. Latinas also find racial discrimination deeply embedded in the social patterns of society outside the economic sphere. They are often frustrated by attitudes of racial bias that continue to perceive them as aliens regardless of however many generations they may have lived in the United States. Racism and sexism undermine the status and erode the power of Latinas in very personal ways as well—professionals whose colleagues do not hear their ideas, professors whose students do not accept their critique, business owners who find it harder to get loans. Latinas in every profession share experiences like these despite their educational and economic achievements. And they struggle to retain their sense of ethnic identity and cultural ties regardless of economic status. While middle-class Latinas have a greater degree of economic stability, they continue to confront questions of self-definition and self-determination, balancing economic success with cultural survival.

These personal experiences are symptomatic of systemic racism and gender bias in our social and political institutions. The consequences of racism are still evident in employment patterns, but racism in the political arena also means that Latina voices are not included in the decision-making processes that determine social and economic policies that affect their lives, perpetuating patterns of exclusion and disempowerment. Latinas continue to struggle to make their voices heard in education, social welfare, health, and environmental policies.

In many respects, racial politics continue to be submerged, addressed indirectly or "in code" under the rubric of issues like urban poverty or welfare reform. Increasingly for Latinas, immigration had become the locus for racial tension. It is also one issue around which political unity among various Latina ethnic groups is strengthening.

The vocabulary of racial politics continues to change as the trajectory of racial politics is influenced by racialized groups themselves. Changing labels used in the federal census evidence the government's inability to institutionalize racial identity. Shifting racial/ethnic terms of identity "reflect the struggles through which racial minorities press their demands for recognition and equality and dramatize the state's uncertain efforts to manage and manipulate those demands" (Omi and Winant, 82). The greater the degree to which racialized groups participate in defining racial meanings and racial norms themselves, the more liberating the dynamics of racial politics becomes.

Despite the rich cultural diversity among Latinas themselves, the experience of racism is increasingly recognized as a common, even unifying experience. Thus, the history of race for Latinas is marked both by the imposition of racial attitudes and racial labels that ignore the diversity of Latina identity and by shifting self-perceptions that have created a self-affirming collective identity built on solidarity in their collective struggle against racism. Latina consciousness and participation in racial politics in the United States reflect a degree of acculturation and adaptation—a recognition of the racial structure of the United States—at the same time they confront the oppressive consequences of racism. Coalitions across ethnic lines reflect a pragmatic reality—greater numbers translate into greater political power. At the same time, such coalitions among Latinas are committed to honoring ethnic identity, redefining racial identity in ways that empower Latinas for full engagement and participation in the United States.

While Christianity has been used to sanction racism, the institutional church has also provided public space for Latinas to assert their identity and exercise their voice in community, thus contributing to the liberating processes of contesting and resisting racialization.

SOURCES: For the theory of race as a social construct, see Michael Omi and Howard Winant, *Racial Formation in the United States: From the 1960's to the 1980's* (1990). Critical sources in developing a methodology for doing racial history and analysis of Latina experience include Genaro Padilla, *My History, Not Yours: The Formation of Mexican American Autobiography* (1993); Tomas Almaguer, *Racial Faultlines: The Historical Origins of White Supremacy in California* (1994); Gloria Anzaldua, *Borderlands/La Frontera: The New Mestiza* (1987); and Ada María Isasi Díaz, *En la Lucha/In the Struggle: Elaborating a Mujerista Theology* (1993). Sources for the role of the church include David Maldonado, ed., *Protestantes/Protestants: Hispanic Christianity within Mainline Traditions* (1999), and the work of Isasi-Díaz and numerous other scholars of Roman Catholicism.

HISPANIC PENTECOSTAL WOMEN
Gastón Espinosa

LATINAS HAVE PLAYED a vital role in the origins and development of the Latino Pentecostal movement. They not only participated at the now-fabled Azusa Street Revival (1906–1909), but they also helped spread the Latino Pentecostal movement throughout the United States, Mexico, and Puerto Rico. The Latino Pentecostal movement has grown from just a handful of women and men in 1906 to more than 10 million people attending more than 150 Pentecostal denominations throughout the United States, Mexico, and Puerto Rico by the end of the twentieth-century.

Latinos/as began attending the Azusa Street Revival shortly after it opened on April 9, 1906. The Azusa Street newspaper reports that Abundio and Rosa López attended on May 29 and shortly thereafter conducted open-air evangelistic meetings in Los Angeles' Mexican Plaza District. In one of the few written testimonies by Mexicans then attending the revivals, the Lópezes stated:

We testify to the power of the Holy Spirit in forgiveness, sanctification, and the baptism with the Holy Ghost and fire. We give thanks to God for this wonderful gift which we have received from Him, according to the promise. Thanks be to God for the Spirit which brought us to the Azusa Street Mission, the Apostolic Faith, old-time religion. . . . I thank God also for the baptism of the Holy Ghost and fire which I received on the 5th of June, 1906. We cannot express the gratitude and thanksgiving which we feel moment by moment for what He has done for us, so we want to be used for the salvation and healing of both soul and body. I am a witness of His wonderful promise and marvelous miracles by the Holy Ghost. (*The Apostolic Faith,* October 1906)

The couple organized the first Latino Pentecostal ministry in the United States. Although the revival's founder and leader, William J. Seymour, ordained Abundio in 1909, Rosa's clerical status is less clear. What is certain is that she was one of the first Spanish-speaking Pentecostal evangelists in North America.

The Azusa Street Revival attracted not only Mexican immigrants like Rosa López but also Mexican Americans like Susie Villa Valdéz. After Villa Valdéz's conversion in 1906, this seamstress-turned-evangelist took the Pentecostal message to prostitutes, alcoholics, and immigrants living in the "slums" of Los Angeles and to the migrant farm labor camps of Riverside and San Bernardino. Villa Valdéz combined her evangelism, social work, and mu-

sical talents to reach out to the poor and marginalized in California for the rest of her life.

While there are no documents that prove Rosa López and Susie Villa Valdéz were ordained to the ministry, the evidence does indicate that they were actively engaged in evangelistic preaching, social work, and pastoral ministry to women and men. Given the limited role of women in public life in Mexican culture and society, it is not surprising that Latinas do not figure more prominently than they do in the early literature. The tension between the prophetic and priestly views on women in ministry at the Azusa Street Revival and in early Pentecostalism began to crystallize along theological and denominational lines after Latinos left the Mission to create their own Trinitarian and Oneness Pentecostal movements. Latino Oneness Pentecostals reject the doctrine of the Trinity and insist that a person must be baptized in Jesus' name only for salvation (Acts 2:38).

In general, the Trinitarian Latino Pentecostal movement has adopted a more prophetic attitude (openness to women preachers and leadership over men) toward women in ministry, while the Oneness movement has adopted a more priestly attitude (restricting the role of women to lay leadership over women and youth only). Still other denominations such as the Latin American Council of Christian Churches have taken a middle ground that allows for women to pastor, teach, and evangelize but not perform marriage rites, baptisms, communion, or funerals.

The Latino Oneness movement strictly prohibits the ordination and licensure of women to the ministry. In fact, women are prohibited from exercising any kind of spiritual authority over men in the church. This is quite remarkable given the fact that both Anglo-American and black Oneness Pentecostal denominations have a long history of credentialing women to the ordained ministry. Latina Oneness women in the Apostolic Assembly of the Faith in Christ Jesus, the largest such denomination, are also asked to wear a headcovering when they pray and to abstain from cutting their hair or wearing jewelry, cosmetics, and pants.

The present ban on women ministers in the Apostolic Assembly is complicated by the fact that Latinas served as deaconesses, evangelists, and church planters in the early Oneness movement. In Apostolic Assembly folklore, Romanita Carbajal de Valenzuela is known as the first person to take the Oneness message to Mexico. Little is known about her life except that she fled to Los Angeles from Villa Aldama, Chihuahua, Mexico, in the wake of the Mexican Revolution. After reportedly coming into contact with people who attended the Azusa Street Revival, she was converted to Pentecostalism around 1912. In November 1914 Valenzuela returned to Villa Aldama and converted twelve members of her family to Pentecostalism and planted the first Oneness church in Mexico. Shortly thereafter, she converted a Methodist pastor named Rubén Ortega to the Apostolic doctrine and placed him in charge of the congregation. After instructing Ortega in Pentecostal theology, she returned to Los Angeles, where she helped her husband or relative, Genaro Valenzuela, pastor the Spanish Apostolic Faith Mission on North Hill Street. After 1914 Carbajal de Valenzuela fades into obscurity.

Carbajal de Valenzuela was not the only woman to minister in ways now prohibited by the Apostolic Assembly. Nellie Rangel, the leading Apostolic Assembly historian, claims that in 1928 Nicolasa de García, Delores (Lolita) de Gonzáles, and María Apolinar Zapata all served as deaconesses, an office Apostolic women are now prohibited from holding.

Despite this early tradition, Apostolics and most other Oneness groups maintain that women should not be ordained to the ministry nor exercise spiritual authority over men. They base this position on their interpretation of the Bible, which they believe prohibits women from the ordained ministry and from exercising spiritual authority over men.

The ban on women in ministry was not called into question in a major way until the 1990s. Today, the greatest challenge comes from young acculturated second-, third-, and fourth-generation college and graduate students who have been influenced by the feminist and Chicano movements as well as the example of other denominations that ordain women. Unlike their parents or grandparents, most of their cultural reference points are from the United States, not Latin America.

Despite the categorical restriction banning women from the ordained ministry, Apostolic women evangelize and teach men on the mission field, in high school and college-age Sunday School classes, in marriage seminars, and when men attend Sunday School lessons and national women's society conventions.

Despite the prohibition on women in ministry, to conclude that women do not exercise power and influence in the Assembly would be wrong. Although the Ladies Auxiliary traces its roots back to the local churches in the 1930s, the first national organization was not organized until 1950. The Auxiliary has grown from 150 adult women in 1950 to over 12,000 in 1996. The organization encourages ethnic and spiritual unity, spiritual and moral growth, confraternity, family, and a sense of divine community.

The growing power and influence of the Ladies Auxiliary is evident in their being the main fund-raising organization in the Assembly. Their most important project is the annual Blue Flower Project (Flor Azul), which began in 1972–1973 as a fund-raiser for the foreign missions department. In 1996, Auxiliary president Georgina Mazón claimed that the project raised $420,000 for the department of foreign missions. For this reason and many others, Apostolic Assembly president Baldemar Rodríguez stated that the Auxiliary's contributions to the denomination "are indispensable." Summarizing the growing clout of women, one Apostolic woman proudly stated that "tamales have built our churches." Indeed, tamales have built more than just churches. The Auxiliary's fund-raising projects have also given women a voice that one woman prophetically stated will one day lead to women on the national board.

The Latino Trinitarian Pentecostal Movement

The major difference between Latino Oneness and Trinitarian Pentecostalism is that while they both admonish women to exercise their spiritual gifts, only the Trinitarian Pentecostal movement allows women to exercise a prophetic ministry to women *and* men. This position is justified by the famous passage in Joel 2 saying that in the last days of the world God would pour out God's spirit on all flesh and that their sons and daughters shall prophesy.

Making up approximately 80 to 90 percent of all Latino Pentecostals in the United States, the Latino Trinitarian Pentecostal movement has a long but checkered history of ordaining and credentialing women to the prophetic ministry. The practice of ordaining women in the Hispanic Districts of the Assemblies of God is an outgrowth of the larger Anglo-American Assemblies of God's position on women in ministry. The Assemblies of God has ordained women to the ministry since it was founded in Hot Springs, Arkansas, in 1914. The founder of the Hispanic Districts of the Assemblies of God, Henry C. Ball (1896–1989), adopted this prophetic view of women when he began his ministry to Mexicans in south Texas in 1915.

The Hispanic District's doctrinal beliefs are virtually identical to those of the larger General Council of the Assemblies of God. They teach that a person must be born again (John 3) to go to heaven and that speaking in tongues is the initial, physical evidence of the baptism with the Holy Spirit (1 Corinthians 12, 14). In contrast to the Apostolic Assembly, they are Trinitarian in theology and ordain women. They believe that Jesus Christ will return any day to set up his 1,000-year millennial kingdom on earth. Although they place a heavy emphasis on holy living, they do not have a strict dress code and do not require women to wear a head covering. In sharp contrast to virtually all Latino Oneness Pentecostal denominations, women are allowed to cut their hair and wear modest jewelry and cosmetics.

The first Assemblies of God evangelists to effectively minister among Latinos in the United States were Anglo-American. The most important woman was Alice E. Luce (1873–1955). A former British Episcopalian missionary to India, Luce converted to Pentecostalism in India and later felt called to evangelize Mexico. After H. C. Ball ordained her in 1915, she conducted evangelistic work in Monterrey, Mexico, and then later in Texas and California.

In 1918 Luce left Texas to pioneer the Assemblies of God work in Los Angeles. Like Abundio and Rosa López twelve years earlier, Luce rented a hall in the Mexican Plaza District and began conducting evangelistic services. Despite the difficulties she faced as an Anglo woman ministering in Mexican Los Angeles, she conducted open-air services and offered prayers for the sick. Luce had a tremendous impact on the formation of the Latino Assemblies of God. She not only established the precedent of women in prophetic ministry, but she and other evangelists such as Aimee Semple McPherson and Kathryn Kuhlman also inspired Latinas such as Nellie Bazán, Francisca Blaisdell, Chonita Morgan Howard, and countless others to enter the ministry.

Dionicia Feliciano was the first Latina on record to be ordained by the Assemblies of God. A Puerto Rican, she, along with her husband Solomon, was ordained an evangelist in San Jose, California, in July 1916. Dionicia pioneered the Assemblies of God work in California, Puerto Rico, and the Dominican Republic from 1913 to the 1940s. During her career, she inspired many women to become ministers.

One Mexican American Luce inspired was Manuelita (Nellie) Treviño Bazán (1895–1995). Nellie was one of the first Mexican American women to be ordained to the Pentecostal ministry in the United States. Ball ordained Nellie and her husband Demetrio in 1920. They served in Texas, New Mexico, and Colorado. She preached from the pulpit at least thirty times a year, conducted door-to-door evangelistic work, composed poetry, raised ten children, and wrote articles for *La Luz Apostólica* (the denomination's Spanish-language periodical) and her own autobiography. She also personally planted three churches during her seventy-five years in the ministry.

While Bazán was allowed to exercise her prophetic ministry on a regular basis in the Assemblies of God, she was also expected to submit to her husband's spiritual authority at home. As at the Azusa Street Revival, women's roles in the Hispanic Districts were paradoxical—women were exhorted to exercise their prophetic gifts and also submit to their husband's authority. Early Latino Pentecostals did not believe the point of the prophetic gifts was to erase gender distinctions; rather, they were to empower women for Christian service in the cataclysmic, end-time drama that lay ahead.

While Bazán ministered in Texas, Colorado, and New Mexico, Francisca D. Blaisdell (c. 1885–1941) conducted evangelistic work in Arizona and northern Mexico beginning in 1916. Around 1922 she organized the first Assemblies of God women's organization in North America, later called the Women's Missionary Council. A year later, she was ordained to the ministry by Juan Lugo and H. C. Ball. Blaisdell pastored churches in Douglas, Arizona, Agua Prieta, Sonora, Mexico (1932–1933, 1938–1939), and El Paso, Texas (1933–1935).

Like Blaisdell, Concepción (Chonita) Morgan Howard (1898–1983) was a Mexican immigrant. Unlike Bazán, her father was an Anglo and her mother was a

Mexican. Chonita was converted to Pentecostalism in 1913 in the small mining town of San Jose de las Playitas, Sonora, Mexico. Not long after her conversion and baptism with the Holy Spirit around 1913, she felt called to the ministry. She traveled the dusty evangelistic trail on horseback in southern Arizona and northern Mexico, preaching the Pentecostal message. She eventually traveled to California where she came under the influence of George and Carrie Judd Montgomery, two former Azusa Street participants. Under their influence, she began evangelistic work in California around 1915. Four years later, in 1919, she met and married a young Anglo Pentecostal preacher named Lloyd Howard, who was pastoring a small group of Mexicans in the border town of Pirtleville, Arizona. She copastored with her husband. In 1928, the Assemblies of God recognized her evangelistic talent and ordained her.

In addition to Morgan Howard's pastoral and evangelistic work, she served as the second president of the Women's Missionary Council (Concilio Misionero Femenil) from 1941 to 1962. From 1966 to 1968, she pastored Betel Asamblea de Dios in Douglas, Arizona. Morgan Howard conducted pioneer evangelistic work in California, Arizona, New Mexico, and northern Mexico, from 1915 to 1968. Her fifty-three-year pioneer ministry touched the lives of thousands of Latinas and helped establish the Assemblies of God work on both sides of the border. Despite the fact that most Latinas were ordained or credentialed as evangelists, women such as Morgan Howard did pastor their own churches.

The ministry of Latinas in the United States helped set the precedent for women in ministry in Mexico. Some of the first Mexican women credentialed to the Pentecostal ministry in Mexico were Srita Cruz Arenas, Catarina García, Juana Medellín, and Raquel Ruesga. They were all credentialed by the Assemblies of God in the 1920s.

Despite the fact that Latinas had been ordained since 1916, it was uncommon for a single woman to pastor her own church or even be ordained to the pastoral ministry. More often than not, women were licensed to preach rather than ordained and served as auxiliaries. Latinas who married Anglo pastors had a much better chance of being fully ordained than women married to Latino men. While the number of Latinas ordained between 1916 and 1970 was low, there has been a sharp increase since the early 1980s. The liberalizing tendency of a younger generation of Latino Assemblies of God leaders has helped shaped this trend.

Aimee García Cortese's (1929–   ) life and ministry in the Hispanic Districts of the Assemblies of God provides an excellent window into the struggle women have faced in the ministry. Born to Puerto Rican parents in New York City in 1929, Cortese was raised in a small

Spanish-speaking Pentecostal storefront church in the early 1940s and 1950s. Reacting against the legalism she saw in the church, she became involved with a Lutheran and then a Methodist Church before returning to the Assemblies of God in the late 1950s.

After graduating from the Spanish Eastern District of the Assemblies of God–sponsored Instituto Bíblico Hispano in New York City and Central Bible College in Springfield, Missouri, she sought ordination in that District in 1957. Her request for ordination was denied for no other reason than her gender. She later protested the decision in a letter in 1958 to J. Roswell Flower, the superintendent of the Assemblies of God. After a long, drawn-out struggle, she was finally ordained to the ministry by the District in 1962, but only after Anglo-American leaders in Springfield put pressure on the District.

Reflecting the gender bias still prevalent in the Hispanic Districts, after she was ordained she still found it difficult to find a job as a pastor. This prompted her to organize her own church, Crossroads Tabernacle, in 1982 in the South Bronx. Rather than remain bitter, she said she holds no grudges against the Spanish Eastern District. Perhaps this is because her ministry in the South Bronx has met with phenomenal success. Cortese's active ministry has touched the lives of thousands of people. Her church has grown from 37 people in 1982 to 1,500 in 1997, making it one of the largest predominantly Latino churches in New York State. The gender discrimination she faced in the Hispanic Districts is slowly abating, according to Cortese.

One of the major reasons why Latinas have been able to exercise a prophetic voice in the Hispanic Districts is education. Women have received formal ministerial and theological training in the Latino Pentecostal Bible schools since at least 1926, something Apostolic Assembly women have been (and still are) unable to receive in the United States. The percentage of Latinas attending Bible school has been very high historically. It is not insignificant that a woman founded the second Spanish-speaking Pentecostal Bible Institute in the United States. In 1926, Alice Luce founded Berean Bible Institute (later called the Latin American Bible Institute [LABI]) in San Diego, California. The first graduating class at Berean Bible Institute in 1928 consisted of three women: D. Adeline Sugg, Ursula Riggio, and María Grajeda. Women have always made up a significant portion of the graduating classes of the Latin District Bible schools. Theological training has been pivotal in opening up doors to ministry, theologizing, and writing articles for periodicals such as La Luz Apostólica and The Word.

While the majority of Mexican women who graduated from the Bible institutes in California, Texas, New York, and Puerto Rico did not go into the ordained ministry, many did choose to become actively involved in the national women's organization. The Women's Missionary Council (WMC) has grown from 1 woman in 1922 to over 44,600 Latinas in 1995, making it one of the largest Latina women's associations in the United States. The purpose of the Council was to encourage and propagate evangelistic and social work in the U.S.–Mexico borderlands.

Despite a guarded openness to prophetic women's voices in the Assemblies of God, many Latinas who really wanted complete autonomy and freedom prior to 1960 have ministered outside of the Assemblies of God. In the late 1930s and early 1940s, Reverend Leoncia Rosado Rousseau (1912–   ) helped found the Damascus Christian Church denomination in New York City. Born in Toa Alta, Puerto Rico, Leoncia was converted during an evangelistic crusade on the island in 1932. Under the tutelage of her pastor, Vicente Ortiz, she began evangelizing youth throughout the island. Prompted by a vision from God in 1935, she migrated to New York City, where she attended Francisco Olazábal's church in Spanish Harlem. After Olazábal's death, the Latin American Council of Christian Churches split into a number of councils or denominations. One of these was the Damascus Christian Church pastored by Rosado. Unlike more conventional denominations, the Damascus Christian Church also targeted drug addicts, prostitutes, alcoholics, and other social outcasts. In 1957, she pioneered one of the first Protestant church–sponsored drug-rehab programs in the United States through the Damascus Youth Crusade. Rosado's pioneer work among social outcasts in el barrio earned her the nickname "Mama Leo" by those with whom she worked. Her social work attracted the attention of New York State leaders like former Governor Nelson Rockefeller. At almost ninety years of age she was still pastoring in New York City. Rosado's innovative urban ministry, preaching skills, and mystical spiritual experiences have made "Mama Leo" well known throughout the Puerto Rican Pentecostal movement.

Like Mama Leo, Juanita García Peraza (d. 1970) founded an indigenous Latino Pentecostal denomination among Puerto Ricans in the 1940s. A former Roman Catholic, García Peraza was born and raised in Hatillo, Puerto Rico. From a wealthy family, she used her inheritance to open a successful department store in the city of Arecibo. Throughout the 1930s she battled gastroenteritis. She promised that if God would cure her, she would serve God for the rest of her life. She was reportedly healed of her illness around 1940 through the prayers of a missionary. In response to her healing, she began attending a Pentecostal church in Arecibo.

After she left the church in Arecibo, she believed God called her to form her own movement. In the early 1940s she founded the Mita Congregation Inc. in Arecibo. She and her followers began preaching the triple message of love, liberty, and unity. In 1949, Fela González had a divine revelation in which God stated that the Holy Spirit was to be called "Mita." Many of García Peraza's disciples came to believe that she was the incarnation of the Holy Spirit on earth and referred to her as Mita, or the "Goddess." After her death in 1970, the leadership of Congregation Mita passed to Teófilo Vargas Seín. Mita Congregation differs from other traditional forms of Pentecostalism not only in its theology but also in the operation of cooperatives and social service activities for its parishioners. In 1978, the University Hispano Americana posthumously awarded Juanita García Peraza an honorary doctorate for her exceptional religious and social work in Puerto Rico.

Throughout the 1930s, 1940s, and 1950s Latina Pentecostal evangelists like Aurora Chávez, Matilde and Julia Vargas, María Jimenez, and a small number of other Latinas served as pastors, evangelists, and teachers throughout the Latino Pentecostal movement. Some women like Chávez, who worked with the Concilio Peña de Horeb in the Southwest, and Matilde Vargas, who worked with the New York–based Assembly of Christian Churches, were talented evangelists. Reverend Chávez, who dressed in a cape like Aimee Semple McPherson, conducted evangelistic healing crusades throughout the Southwest during the 1950s.

Despite the difficulties that Pentecostal women such as García Cortese have faced, many Latino Pentecostal denominations have turned a new leaf in their attitudes toward women in the ministry. By 1997 the Spanish Eastern District, which once gave Cortese so many problems, then had the highest percentage and largest raw number of credentialed and ordained women in the Hispanic Districts. The total number of Latina clergywomen (ordained, licensed, certified, etc.) in the Assemblies of God has increased from 624 in 1990 to 741 in 1997. The number of Latinas fully ordained in the Assemblies of God has almost doubled, going from 80 women in 1990 to 141 women in 1997. At that time, the percentage of clergywomen in the Hispanic Districts (25.1 percent) was significantly higher than the average for Anglo-American Districts (15.8 percent) nationwide. The Assemblies of God now claims more Latina clergy than any other denomination in the United States, including the United Methodist church—which claims 90 to 100 Latina clergywomen. The Assembly of Christian Churches denomination based in New York City now allows women to play a greater role in ministry than ever before. In short, there tends to be a movement among Latino Pentecostal traditions toward affirming their early Pentecostal roots and allowing women to play a greater role in ministry—both lay and ordained.

Latinas have been attracted to the Pentecostal movement because it has allowed them to serve as evangelists, pastors, missionaries, Bible school teachers, authors, and church planters and because of its strong emphasis on community, moral standards, family, enthusiastic worship services, divine healing, and "a personal relationship with the living God." It also offers Latinas an opportunity to serve in their denominational church leadership (as many denominations are indigenous or Spanish-language) without having to assimilate, learn the English language, or attend college or seminary—something that most ordinary working-class women are simply unable to do or afford. These factors afford Pentecostal women a sense of hope, possibility, and opportunity that they find attractive and empowering.

SOURCES: For further information on Hispanic Pentecostal women, see Felipe Emmanuel Agredano Lozano, "The Apostolic Assembly at the Crossroads: The Politics of Gender" (paper presented at the Society for Pentecostal Studies, Wheaton, Ill., 1994); Apostolic Assembly Ladies Auxiliary, *Confederación Nacional de Sociedades Femeniles Dorcas Reglamentos* (By-Laws) (1994); Gastón Espinosa, " 'Your Daughters Shall Prophesy': A History of Women in Ministry in the Latino Pentecostal Movement in the United States," in *Women and Twentieth-Century Protestantism,* ed. Margaret Lamberts Bendroth and Virginia Lieson Brereton (2002); Loida Martell Otero, "Women Doing Theology: Una Perspectiva Evangélica," *Apuntes* (Fall 1994): 67–85; Mita Congregación, "Centenario del Natalicio de la Persona de Mita," *El Nueva Dia,* July 6, 1997; Maria Elizabeth Pérez y González, *Latinas in Ministry: A Pioneering Study on Women Ministers, Educators, and Students of Theology* (1993); and Virginia Sánchez-Korrol, "In Search of Unconventional Women: Histories of Puerto Rican Women in Religious Vocations before Mid-Century," in *Barrios and Borderlands: Cultures of Latinos and Latinas in the United States,* ed. Denis Lynn Daly Heyck (1994).

ASIAN PROTESTANTISM

ASIAN PACIFIC AMERICAN PROTESTANT WOMEN
Rita Nakashima Brock and Nami Kim

ASIAN PACIFIC AMERICAN women's history begins in the nineteenth century and is intricately linked with that of men, who started arriving in North America around 1763. Before the 1960s, those of Asian and Pacific Island ancestries commonly identified themselves by their country of origin or ethnicity. Asian Americans initially used this term to refer to themselves as a Pan-Asian American racial group as they developed movements for racial justice in the 1960s. In this same period, Asian American scholars turned the lens of racial oppression on Asian American history, for example, in studies of lynching, forced labor, illegal and unconstitutional imprisonment, and hate crimes. The word *oriental* came to be regarded as a racist term, imposed by European colonists to refer to Asians.

The first use of *Asian American* meant those of East and Southeast Asian ancestry predominantly, but as the term increasingly included those from South Asia and the Pacific Islands, the word *Pacific* was added. Asian Pacific American, commonly abbreviated APA, refers to immigrants and long-term permanent residents as far back as six generations. Though Russians and Middle Easterners are generally not regarded as Asians, Palestinian scholar Edward Said's concept of "orientalism" has become definitive in analyses of race.

The dominant society has related to Asian Pacific Americans as if they were foreign nationals. Depending on American foreign policy, Asian Pacific Americans could be regarded as friend or foe, even those who had been citizens of the United States for many generations. Before the late 1960s, stereotypes of Asian Americans were focused on the "Yellow Peril." For example, during World War II, American citizens of Japanese ancestry were illegally imprisoned; the subsequent cold war resulted in Americans of Chinese ancestry being regarded with suspicion. The murder of Chinese American Vincent Chin in Detroit in 1982 was based on the mistaken assumption that he was Japanese at a time when Japanese business threatened the American auto industry. His murder galvanized APA struggles for justice like no other incident in American history.

Throughout this time of shifting stereotypes, APA women have been regarded as objects of masculine colonial desire. They have been depicted as exotic, sexually sophisticated, submissive, suicidal, and preferring to love white men, captured in such images as "geisha," Suzy Wong, Madame Butterfly, and Miss Saigon.

In the 1970s new stereotypes emerged of the "model minority." Eventually, by the mid-1980s Asian Pacific

498

Americans had, in states such as California, been deemed de facto whites and excluded by the term *minority*. Asian Pacific Americans are most often absent or grouped with whites in statistics measuring minority social status, such as income, academic achievement, and occupation.

History

Large numbers of Asian men arrived in North America beginning in 1843 as forced laborers, merchants, or gold prospectors. Women were discouraged from leaving Asia—the one exception was girls for prostitution—since men with wives in America were less likely to send money home or return to Asia. Around 1860, small numbers of women and girls began to be transported as prostitutes or wives. From the mid-1870s, Christian missionary campaigns against prostitution and restrictive immigration laws decreased the number of Chinese prostitutes. In 1900 most Japanese females in the United States had been lured or brought by Japanese men as prostitutes. Between 1900 and 1920, the Japanese government and Japanese in the United States cooperated to reduce the sex trafficking of females.

From 1790 until 1952, a congressional law prohibited nonwhite persons from becoming naturalized citizens. Many Asian immigrants lived their entire lives in the United States without the possibility of citizenship. Asian immigration slowed in the early twentieth century with the passage of laws such as the Chinese Exclusion Act in 1882. By the mid-twentieth century, the majority were second- or third-generation Americans. Until 1968,

Asian American women were few in proportion to men: in 1900, there were twenty-six Chinese men to one woman, with similar Japanese ratios; in 1910, ten Korean men to one woman.

In the late nineteenth century, many Protestant churches sent missionaries to APA communities on the two American coasts. The oldest Asian American Protestant churches were founded by such mission efforts, as well as by Asian Christians who were converted in Asia and sent to North America as missionaries. During the late nineteenth and early twentieth century in Hawaii, Congregationalist missionaries formed churches among the native Hawaiians. Queen Liliuo'Kalani, the last Hawaiian monarch in the mid-nineteenth century and a member and choir director of Kawaiahao Church, tried to strengthen the Hawaiian constitution to restore power to her people but was overthrown by the American military, with cooperation from members of the Congregational church.

From 1907 to 1924, 45,000 Japanese and 1,000 Korean picture brides immigrated to Hawaii and California to marry men who worked on plantations and farms. Using the arranged marriage customs of Japan and Korea, men were matched with partners in Asia through the exchange of pictures. Sometimes these arranged husbands sold their wives into the sex trade. Congregationalist missionaries also formed churches in these communities.

Many Chinese American and Korean American Protestant women in the early twentieth century were internationalists. They promoted the independence of their respective "mother lands," China and Korea, from im-

Renee Tajima-Peña, a third-generation Japanese American married to a Mexican American, believes her work as a documentary filmmaker reflects her Protestant upbringing, though not always explicitly. Her Presbyterian family inspired her work for justice, especially racial and economic justice.
Photographer William Short and courtesy of Renee Tajima-Peña.

perial aggressions by Europe and Japan. Their efforts on behalf of Asian nationalist causes, however, did not undermine their struggle to promote women's issues in America. Three women's organizations in San Francisco are noteworthy during a time of skewed sex ratios and harsh immigrant life: The Korean Ladies' Organization, the Chinese Women's Jeleab (Self-Reliance) Association, and the Chinese YWCA (Young Women's Christian Association). The Korean Ladies' Organization, the first women's organization, was formed in 1908 to promote the Korean language, church activities, and solidarity among Koreans.

In 1913, the Jeleab Association was established by immigrant women and their American-born daughters. This association was inspired by the "1911 Chinese revolution and by the membership policies of the Chinese Native Sons of the Golden State, which excluded women" (Young, in Yilan, 242). The association's statement of purpose challenged the limited role of women and their lack of education and asserted the association's aspirations for women's rights in both countries. The association attracted many members. For instance, Clara G. Lee, daughter of Reverend Chan Hon Fun and Ow Muck Gay, was a founding member and one of the first Chinese women to register to vote. T. L. Lee, a Baptist minister's wife, taught the evening class for reading and writing Chinese with "plans to tackle English next" (245).

Like the Jeleab Association, the Chinese YWCA, founded in 1916, was active in promoting women's rights in their community in both countries, as well as in fund-raising for Chinese war relief. Jane Kwong Lee emigrated from China to pursue further education after attending a mission school for girls in Canton. Although a college graduate, Lee, like other educated Chinese American women, could not find an appropriate job except in Chinatown. Lee coordinated the YWCA from 1935 to 1944 and was a community activist. Lee shared the nationalist concern for China with other concerned Chinese Americans and was aware that women's rights were global. After observing a National YWCA conference, Lee emphasized that "China-born and American-born Chinese" should cooperate for mutual support and for China's national defense (432–451).

After 1946 many more Asian women arrived who were married to non-Asians. According to Alice Yun Chai,

[I]n the aftermath of World War II, the Korean War, and the Vietnam War, many Asian women entered this country as war brides. As a result of a series of laws, between 1946 and 1952, a large number of Asian war brides from China, the Philippines, Japan, and Korea came to this country as non-quota immigrants. Close to 70,000 Japanese war brides between 1947 and 1977 came to the United States, and 3,241 Filipinos arrived from the early 1950s to the late 1970s. Since the late 1960s, most Asian wives of non-Asian US servicemen today are predominantly Filipinos, Korean, Vietnamese, and Thai women. (Chai, "Coping," 58–59)

These women tend to take on the religious practices of their husbands, who are predominantly Christian.

The 1965 Immigration Act opened doors for a second wave of Asian Pacific immigration and citizenship, with an immigration rate equal to European countries. Since 1968 the majority of Asian immigrants have been women. This reflects the aftermath of war that resulted in large numbers of refugee women and children, a migration pattern of reunifying families as a priority of immigration policy, and the arrival of many more war brides. By 1990 two-thirds of Asian Pacific Americans were first-generation immigrants and refugees, and the population had doubled. At the end of the twentieth century, one-third of all legal immigrants were from Asia, over a quarter million annually.

Protestant Women

The majority of Asian immigrants since 1968 have declared themselves Christian, both Catholic and Protestant. This new group demonstrates the influence of early Christian missionary activity in Asia with regard to negative attitudes toward Asian religions. Immigrant APA churches are more likely to be theologically conservative, to evangelize aggressively, and to refrain from extensive interaction with other religious groups or the larger society. At the same time, first-generation churches tend to hold more strongly to traditional Asian social attitudes toward male dominance, family, and community. APA women have struggled with the male dominance of their ancestral traditions, as well as with the racism and sexism of the dominant American society and its forms of Christianity. For some women, Christianity acts as a liberating force against Buddhism because it is not associated with Asian cultural forms of male dominance and promises women salvation on equal footing with men.

Several Asian cultural values affect the self-understandings and meaning frameworks of APA Protestants. First, the individual is less important than the social unit because Asian education encourages thinking of the whole before the parts. The interdependence of human beings and the primacy of social relationships are assumed. Religious commitments indicate group membership. A sense of duty, not only to one's community and family but also to one's ancestors, is as important as personal faith or salvation. Hence, evangelism is highly valued to increase groups. Individual religious commitments are understood to be produced by transcendent powers to which the individual surrenders, a pattern common among shaman-based religions in Asia and among evangelicals. Finally, Western dualistic ideas are exclusive and dominated by either-or thinking, whereas Asian dualisms tend to be inclusive and interactive—opposites are fluid and interpenetrating. Ambiguity and paradox are inherent in life.

Christianity has functioned paradoxically in APA life. It has been a means of entry into the political and social norms of the dominant culture, at the same time churches have maintained ethnic enclaves and practices. Both these dimensions are evident in the lives of Protestant women.

APA Protestant women in the second half of the twentieth century represent a spectrum of life experiences within North America, ranging from laypeople involved in church work, community professionals, campus ministers, and scholars to clergy in local churches and ecclesial administration. Their work has included activism in the larger society and the church, ordained ministry, and academic leadership.

Doreen Der-McLeod, a social worker and an elder in the Presbyterian Church of Chinatown in San Francisco, has played multiple and significant roles in various social service agencies as well as numerous Presbytery and national church committees. Der-McLeod's great-grandfather immigrated to the United States in the late 1800s. She is, however, the first generation *born* in America due to the complex history of immigration law that did not allow Chinese men to bring their wives for generations. Her religious commitment is reflected in her social work. "God, as creator, calls us to be in relationship with not only God, but all of Creation. Therefore, we are called to be neighbors (not just to family, not just to the Chinese community, but all) and to be stewards of God's creation."

In December 2000, Der-McLeod became executive director at the Donaldina Cameron House, an organization started by the Presbyterian Church (USA) in San Francisco's Chinatown in the mid-1870s. As a teenager, Der-McLeod participated in Cameron House's youth program, which influenced her decision to join the church.

The youth program at Cameron House allowed me to experience a community of faith. It nurtured youth to grow mentally, physically, socially and spiritually (what was then known as the Four Square program). A major influence in my choice to be a social worker was the Christian Service Staff at Cameron House. These women were dedicated to helping, supporting and enabling immigrant women and children to adjust to life in this new country.

At Cameron House Der-McLeod planned to "provide leadership in meeting the needs of the Chinatown community in the 21st century and to promote youth to grow mentally, physically, socially and spiritually through our various youth programs." Cameron House also provides advocacy, counseling, and legal support for immigrant women and victims of domestic violence in the Chinese and Vietnamese communities.

Renee Tajima-Peña, a third-generation Japanese American, married to a Mexican American, believes her work as a documentary filmmaker reflects her Protestant upbringing, though not always explicitly. Her Presbyterian family inspired her work for justice, especially racial and economic justice. Tajima-Peña's paternal grandfather, Kengo Tajima, came to the United States because of religious persecution in Japan. He studied theology at Yale and the University of California at Berkeley. Before becoming a pastor of Japanese American churches in Los Angeles, he spent some time as a circuit-riding preacher in places like Provo Canyon, Utah, ministering to Asian railroad workers.

Tajima-Peña's family went to the Altadena First Presbyterian Church where her uncle, Donald Toriumi, was the pastor.

If I look back on my life, I can see how at each critical juncture—the decision to become a student activist, a media activist, marrying outside of my race, loving and sacrificing for my son, foregoing certain material rewards, trying to be a *mensch*, has been a function of Christian values I learned at home—the perception of injustice and inequality, and the responsibility of the individual to work collectively for social change.

Her 1989 Academy Award–nominated film *Who Killed Vincent Chin?* demonstrates Tajima-Peña's concern for racial justice. Her Sundance Film Festival award-winner *My America: or Honk If You Love Buddha* uses the theme of pilgrimage to compare changes in Asian America from her childhood in the 1960s to the early 1990s.

As Tajima-Peña notes,

I wanted to be a part of changing the world. For the first decade of my career I focused on racial justice. My films still look at issues of race, but with greater emphasis on economic inequality—I'm working on projects on the working poor and immigrant workers. . . . My primary venue is my people—Asian Americans—but I try to look at us through a broader lens and at social justice for all. Richard Pryor has said that justice should not be defined as "Just Us." For example, affirmative action in education may not be immediately beneficial for all Asian Americans, but diversity and equality in education has a greater use.

May Chun was also interested in justice as a United Methodist laywoman. Chun was the assistant superintendent of education and state librarian for Hawaii and president of the United Methodist Women in the Pacific and Southwest Annual Conference. While working as a librarian and administrator, Chun sought ways to respond to the needs of the homeless people in her native Hawaii. In 1984, Chun was named Conference Lay Woman of the Year for her many years of work for the church.

Dora A. Lee, a prominent physician in the mid-twentieth century, was a pioneer in establishing a grant fund for Asian and Native Americans while serving on the United Methodist Commission on Global Ministry of the Health and Welfare Division from 1970 to 1978. This was the first fund for Asian and Native American students in a health-related field in her denomination. Lee's maternal grandfather was a Chinese medicine practitioner who converted to Christianity in Hong Kong. Her mother was also a Christian. Her father, a second-generation Chinese American, was an interpreter for the U.S. government immigration service in Arizona in 1909 until the family moved back to San Francisco in 1920 and became active in the First Chinese Baptist church there. Lee's mother founded an interdenominational Chinese mothers' club in Oakland. Her sister taught Sunday School for sixty-six years. Though Lee became a Methodist, her spirit was ecumenical: "For 50 years I was Methodist; before [I was] Baptist. But it makes no difference for me. . . . I'm very grateful and blessed because of the heritage I received from my parents. What I do is to try to do what they did; help other people" (Chong).

Rebekah Keumha Kim's life reflects experiences of many young educated evangelical Christians. She grew up in a rural area of South Korea in the 1950s as the seventh of ten children and became the first Christian in her family while a college student. "From my childhood, I was nihilist. I felt emptiness. The underlying issue of my life was meaninglessness. Thus I searched all books. But I couldn't be satisfied. . . . I realized that true love and true freedom can be found only in Jesus Christ."

Although Kim received a Master of Divinity from Golden Gate Baptist Seminary in 1984, she had not sought ordination. "Personally, I'm not YET [sic] ordained, but maybe in the future. I didn't want to be the topic of controversy. I want to encourage all the younger women ministers to get ordained as soon as possible, the sooner the better." As she notes in 2000, "There are biblical passages that discriminate against women, but Jesus never discriminated against women. . . . Jesus was radically revolutionary especially on women's issues. . . . This world has a problem with women, but God and Jesus don't have a problem. The church and Christian world have biases against women."

Kim has served as Southern Baptist chaplain at Harvard United Ministry, representing the Harvard/Radcliffe Asian Baptist Student Koinonia, one branch of an organization she founded as the Asian Baptist Student Koinonia at the University of California at Berkeley in 1982. Kim played a crucial role in its rapid growth in the 1980s and 1990s, to Boston, New York, Los Angeles, and Seattle. In the 1990s evangelical APA college student groups were one of the fastest-growing areas of Asian American Protestantism.

Some APA women's activism has been focused on transformation of the church. Hope Omachi Kawashima, a third-generation Japanese American, was interned as a child with her family during World War II. Her grandparents came to the United States before 1900, later establishing a Japanese Methodist church in California. Kawashima worked as a music therapist for three years after her college graduation, then went to San Francisco Theological Seminary for a master's degree in sacred music and Christian education. The only Asian American delegate among twenty-five voting members on the Methodist Hymnal Revision Committee in 1985, Kawashima secured the inclusion of at least two hymns each from different Asian countries.

I wanted to include more Asian hymns, but [it was] hard to make room for new ones because people want to keep the old hymns. . . . The difficult part was the negative feelings people have about including too many Asian hymns. . . . I had to do a lot of talking to individuals in order to break down the negative feelings toward Asian hymns. (Chong)

A legacy of strong Pacific Island women persists in the United Church of Christ. In the 1980s Martha Dayag served with Hui Kahea Pono, a group in the Hawaii Conference dedicated to supporting Hawaiian sovereignty. When the denomination apologized in 1993 to the Hawaiian people for their participation in the overthrow of their government and offered reparations, Dayag served on the Apology Follow-Up Task Force. Julia Matsui Estrella, a Japanese Okinawan from Hawaii, was the first woman to direct the Pacific and Asian Center for Theology and Strategies in Berkeley, California, during the 1990s and has long been an activist on social justice issues for Asian women. She, along with Mary Tomita and Miya Okawara, founded their denominational Pacific Islander and Asian American Ministries organization.

C. Nozomi Ikuta, also United Church of Christ and

a third-generation Japanese American, is one of a few Asian American Protestant clergywomen who have worked at the national level in a mainline Protestant church. Ikuta's maternal great-grandmother was a member of the Kumamoto Band, Congregational converts in Japan who helped establish Doshisha University in Kyoto, Japan. Her mother attended Doshisha and obtained Congregational funds after World War II to travel to Cleveland to continue her education. Ikuta describes her experience of growing up in an all-white church: "Many of [the members] were ignorant about the reality of people of color (many felt that telling me that they didn't think of me as being Japanese was a compliment)." As a student at Harvard Divinity School, Ikuta was introduced to the Pacific and Asian Center for Theology and Strategies in Berkeley. Through them, she became involved in the Pacific and Asian American Ministries of the United Church of Christ.

Ikuta in the 1990s served the Division of the American Missionary Association of the United Church Board for Homeland Ministries.

My work exposed me to social justice movements led by people of color, including the effort to free Puerto Rican political prisoners. Meeting these prisoners and their supporters was powerfully moving for me—they were so committed to their ideals. I learned new meanings to Jesus' call to the cross, which I had understood in much more domesticated or metaphorical terms as a modern, North American Christian. They helped me understand crucifixion and discipleship as much more contemporary demands.

In 2000, Ikuta began work in Cleveland as the minister and team leader for Covenantal Relations and as executive associate to the general minister and president of the United Church of Christ.

Naomi Southard, an ordained United Methodist, has been active in both national administrative work and local churches of her denomination since the late 1970s. Granddaughter of Japanese immigrants, Southard grew up Buddhist and attended the first Buddhist church in the United States. She became a Christian during college and pursued her Master of Divinity at Harvard Divinity School. After serving a Japanese American church in California, she moved to New York in 1982 as the Methodist's associate general secretary for the General Commission on Christian Unity and Interreligious Concerns. Later, in California, Southard served as the executive director of the National Federation of Asian American United Methodists. She left the Federation in the early 1990s to pursue a doctorate at the Graduate Theological Union at Berkeley.

Theological education has also seen women's leadership. Stacy D. Kitahata is a member of the Evangelical Lutheran Church in America and, until 2001, was dean of community at the Lutheran School of Theology at Chicago. She was one of the few APA women, and the youngest executive staff person, to work with her denomination from its formation in 1988, as a member of the staff of the Division for Global Mission for nine years. She was also the first APA woman to hold a cabinet-level position in a Lutheran seminary. Kitahata, a third-generation Japanese American laywoman, provided pastoral care courses and coordinated spiritual formation while facilitating community activities at the seminary. Although she did not expect to spend her life working in the church, she believes it is important work. "I, as an Asian American in a predominantly white institution, can make a unique difference. . . . I define my role as someone who is breaking stereotypes, offering fresh alternative approaches to teaching, learning, collaborating, theologizing, planning, etc." Other leaders in Protestant institutions in the 1990s include Katie Choy-Wong, Chinese American and dean of admissions at American Baptist Seminary of the West in the Bay Area, and Mary Paik, Korean American and vice president and dean for student life at McCormick Theological Seminary in Chicago.

Among major changes in APA women's lives in the late twentieth century has been the emergence of women scholars in higher education and seminaries. The first generation began completing theological doctorates in the 1980s, and a number rose to positions of leadership in the academy.

Alice Yun Chai, a Korean Methodist academician, is an activist in various movements for social change within and outside the church. Chai has taught cross-cultural courses in the Women's Studies Program at the University of Hawaii. As the only Asian female member of the California-Pacific United Methodist Annual Conference Commission on the Status and Role of Women from 1980 to 1988, Chai coordinated outreach and educational programs and the Bilingual Domestic and Legal Hotline for Korean immigrant women and Korean women married to American military personnel. "My urgent task as an Asian American feminist church woman has been to raise consciousness and to influence the church in challenging various contradictions as the church performs a complex series of functions which historically have upheld the interconnected hierarchies of domination and exploitation" (Chai, "The Struggle of Asian and Asian American Women").

Sociologist Jung Ha Kim started in a Buddhist family in South Korea and attended Zen Buddhist/Shinto temples when her family moved to Tokyo, Japan. Since immigration to the United States, Kim has been affiliated with many Protestant Christian churches, including an African American Baptist church in downtown Atlanta in the 1990s. Reflecting upon how she became religious, Kim recalls, "Externally, experiences of constant (im)migration and resettlement helped me to reflect upon the larger meaning of ultimate concern. I've been blessed with many people, especially women, who inspired me to live a 'faithful life,' regardless."

While teaching at Georgia State University, Kim works as a board member and community consultant at the Center for Pan Asian Community Services Inc. in Atlanta. She is also a member of the Governor's Educational Committee.

> Just as praxis and theory can be seen as two sides of the same coin, work in the academic context and in the community cannot be separated. Playing many roles, such as translating, mediating, teaching, negotiating, and learning, I see myself as a person committed to making concrete and meaningful connections between the two.

Theologian Rita Nakashima Brock was born in the mid-twentieth century in Fukuoka, Japan, and is coauthor of this essay. Brock was raised in the United States from the age of six by her Japanese mother, a war bride, and her white stepfather, a soldier in the American military. Her upbringing in Protestantism shaped her commitments both to freethinking and to justice. Her early experiences of anti-Japanese racism in the United States and of the civil rights and antiwar movements at Chapman College inspired her to be an activist. In college, she abandoned a premed major, became a member of the Christian Church (Disciples of Christ), and was inspired to pursue a doctorate in feminist theology, which combined her activism with her religious sensibilities. After eighteen years teaching, she was an administrator at the Radcliffe Institute at Harvard University from 1997 to 2001.

Kwok Pui-Lan, professor of theology and spirituality at Episcopal Divinity School and an Asian feminist theologian, has been a prolific writer, covering issues that range from multiculturalism, biblical interpretation, and spirituality to postcolonial theory. Born and raised in Hong Kong, Kwok came for doctoral study in 1984 to the Harvard Divinity School. Since then, Kwok has been involved in various community activities along with her academic commitment. She also became an American citizen. She has been chair of the board of the Boston Asian Task Force against Domestic Violence. Kwok's involvement with this organization is in accordance with her own conviction that "religious commitment should not only be to the church, but also to the transformation of the world." Her conviction grew out of her earlier experience in many Asian countries witnessing various responses of churches to women's situations, deepening her understanding of Christian faith.

Influenced by her parents who practiced Chinese folk religion, Kwok has emphasized religion not so much as a belief system but as practices, not only in her teaching but also in her involvement with the Ecumenical Association of Third World Theologians.

> I was influenced by Chinese religious pluralistic sensibilities and spirituality. I began to have multiple understandings of religion. . . . My understanding of Christianity also comes from a different background which emphasizes cultural and religious practices. I do not see religious practices as separate from everyday experiences. This is what I introduce to my students—to see your whole life as spiritual practices.

Like many APA theologians, Lai Ling Elizabeth Ngan, associate professor in Hebrew Bible at George W. Truett Theological Seminary, Baylor University, did not aspire to a teaching career at a seminary. She switched to ministry while she was finishing her master's thesis in pharmacology. For Ngan, the choice of career was a "gradual unfolding." Raised in a devout Buddhist family, Ngan went to a Catholic girls school, then attended Baptist church at the age of fifteen and was baptized at seventeen, two weeks before coming to the United States from Hong Kong.

> I have chosen to be a Baptist because of some key historical teachings in the Baptist tradition, such as the priesthood of believers, competency of the soul, autonomy of the local church, religious freedom and freedom of conscience. On the scheme of Christendom, I think I am quite conservative, but open and accepting of others in their beliefs and religious traditions (or the lack of them). In this aspect, I think I may not be like many Baptists and would be considered rather liberal, but there are at least fifty-two types of Baptist, and we pride ourselves in agreeing to disagree.

Gale Yee, a third-generation Chinese American, is the oldest of twelve children and grew up in a predominantly African American and Puerto Rican neighborhood in Chicago. Having had a very zealous mother who converted to Roman Catholicism from Buddhism, Yee was also active in the Catholic Church. "While working at Loyola University, I was able to ask some questions of theology professors. . . . When I finally asked one professor whether my grandmother, who was Buddhist, would go to hell or not after she died, the professor suggested that I should study theology at Loyola." Yee eventually became professor of Hebrew Scripture and the director of the Feminist Liberation

Theologies Program at Episcopal Divinity School in Cambridge, Massachusetts, in 1998.

Yee has served on various committees in the academy and in ecumenical associations. She was involved with the Pacific and North American Asian Women in Theology and Ministry (PANAAWTM), mentoring younger women. The undergirding and guiding principle of her life is the belief in social justice that has a theological and biblical grounding in the message of Jesus. Yee became Episcopalian in 2001.

Nami Kim, coauthor of this essay, was born and raised in South Korea. She came to the United States in 1993 and pursued graduate study in theology at the Harvard Divinity School. Formerly a Methodist, she became a member of the United Church of Christ. Her research examined the problems and possibilities of the homogenizing category of "Asian women."

Among the theological issues that emerge in these women's and others' work are concerns for justice, women's rights, the meaning of marginality and cross-cultural identity, culturally sensitive interpretation, and the interrelationships of individuals with families and communities. In challenging the Protestant paradigm that privileges faith or belief over life practices, Asian Pacific American theologians examine the many complex dimensions of Christianity for their sisters in North America, not as a goal to be achieved but as an ongoing lifelong activity.

SOURCES: Material for the numerous profiles that appear throughout this essay was obtained through face-to-face, phone, and email interviews conducted in fall 2000 by Nami Kim, unless otherwise noted. In addition, see the following: Elizabeth Young, "The Most Unique Club in America: A Club of Chinese Women," *San Francisco Chronicle*, February 8, 1914, 5, quoted in Liu Yilan's "The Purpose of the Chinese Women's Jeleab Association," in *Unbound Voices*, ed. Judy Yung (1999), 242; Alice Yun Chai, "Coping with the Oppressions of Gender, Class and Race: Asian Immigrant Women [China, Japan, Korea, the Philippines]," *Engage/Social Action* 11.4 (April 1983): 58–59; Dr. Key Ray Chong, interviewer, "Asian American United Methodists," in *The General Commission on Archives and History: The United Methodist Church* (1992); and Alice Yun Chai, "The Struggle of Asian and Asian American Women toward a Total Liberation," in *Spirituality and Social Responsibility*, ed. Rosemary S. Keller (1993), 249–263.